S0-AFK-920

THE GLAMOUR MAGAZINE AFTER FIVE COOKBOOK

BY

BEVERLY PEPPER

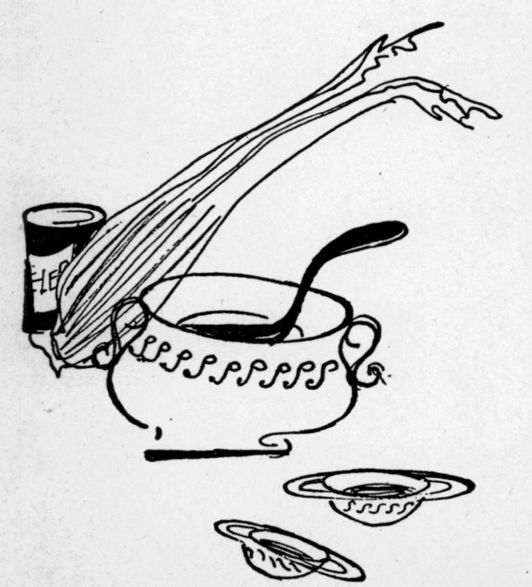

1952

DOUBLEDAY & COMPANY, INC., GARDEN CITY, N.Y.

LIBRARY OF CONGRESS CATALOG CARD NUMBER: 52-11006

Printed in the United States at
The Country Life Press, Garden City, N.Y.
First Edition

INTRODUCTION

This book was originally planned, when it first appeared in magazine form, as a chart to aid the working girl who comes home, tired and spent, from her office only to face the insurmountable problem of preparing an original meal for her husband or companion. That was why it was called *After Five Cooking*.

But this same problem involving menu planning, recipes, marketing, cooking time required, and food waste faces thousands of other American women too, for where it was possible, once upon a time, to spend hours planning meals, marketing, then cooking, today we simply cannot repeat this pattern and live. Either we are working at jobs outside the home or we have other interests. The result for many is that the home, which is the primary goal of us all, suffers—as does our companionship with good foods.

So here is a solution—a cookbook which is *not a cookbook* —not in the ordinary sense, but a declaration of independence from kitchen slavery, a declaration of love for good eating. Taken broadly, perhaps it is also a frank admission of a change in the American way of life.

In this book the original *After Five Cooking* menus are now linked up for your convenience—recipes and once-a-week shopping lists for two people for the whole year, with Sunday dinners for four, plus the addition of twenty-four gangfests and gourmet dinners. All told, there are more than 300 different menus with 1000 dishes taken from travels in Europe and America to enliven your daily fare.

No weekday meal takes more than an hour's time—many less than half that. There is a basic plan to eliminate all waste, this controlled by the shopping list, with specific leftover dishes designated by asterisks, to save you cooking time and costs.

You will utilize every possible short cut, take frozen, canned, and prepared foods, and serve them each with a difference. Wines, herbs, and spices, used subtly as they should be, will soon become effortless and convenient as salt and pepper. The shopping lists given are based on the immediate week's requirements, planned on the assumption you'll always keep on hand a good supply of the staples listed below:

flour	olive oil	bouillon cubes, chicken and beef
milk	wine vinegar	bay leaves
butter	tarragon vinegar	whole black peppers for grinding
eggs	rice	grated Parmesan cheese
sugar	chili sauce	cooking wines, red, white (sweet, dry)
salt	dry bread crumbs	cooking sherry
pepper	onions	mixed dried herbs
paprika	garlic	dried herbs, every kind
cayenne	ketchup	
dry mustard	bread	
prepared mustard	Worcestershire sauce	
powdered spices, every kind	Tabasco sauce	
salad oil		

Other staples are listed on a required-for-this-month basis and can be bought as needed.

Prepare your own French dressing once a week. Three parts oil, one part wine or tarragon vinegar, salt, freshly ground pepper to taste, a crushed garlic clove if you like—then vary as suggested in the recipes. If you don't have a pepper mill, buy one. You'll feel amply repaid.

Keep plenty of bouillon cubes on hand. One cube, chicken or beef as specified, to a cup of water is standard strength for use in all recipes. For fresher flavor and economy, grate your own Parmesan cheese, store in a jar. Ready-buttered bread crumbs save a great deal of time. Mix one cupful of dry crumbs thoroughly with a quarter cup of melted butter, store tightly covered in the refrigerator.

Since you will make only one major trip to the market each week, good refrigeration and correct storage are important. Roasts and whole poultry should be removed at once from wrappings, lightly covered with wax paper, kept very cold. Cut and chopped meats should be rewrapped tightly in wax paper and stored in the meat tray. Giblets, liver, and kidneys, wrapped, may be kept frozen in the freezing compartment until needed. They should be completely defrosted before use. If your refrigerator does not have adequate meat storage space, or the freezer section cannot accommodate a week's supply of frozen foods, buy what you need en route home, or, if necessary, substitute canned foods.

If you do not already own a good crisper, buy one big enough to accommodate an occasional bunch of broccoli, asparagus, or carrots as well as the celery and greens. All salad materials and parsley should be washed and drained before storing. Watercress should be especially carefully picked over and then stored either in the crisper or in water in a covered bowl. Mint will keep nicely just standing in water like a bunch of flowers on the refrigerator shelf.

To semi-thaw frozen foods for the evening meal, place below the freezer before leaving in the morning. To defrost completely, place on a lower shelf. When a recipe calls for a half box of frozen food, or when only two portions of whipped potatoes are required, divide the block by chopping with an ice pick. Keep the rest rewrapped and solidly frozen until needed.

The recipes in this book have been tested. If you find you're taking longer to prepare a meal than the allotted time, check on the kitchen arrangement. Are the herbs and condiments on the shelf before you? Knives sharp? Have you enough working surface? If you've too small a space for a permanent table, use one on wheels. Read your recipe thoroughly, laying out all the necessary ingredients before starting; extra steps in one meal add up, in one year, to useless miles of trotting.

Good cooking, like good driving, calls for courage and plain common sense. Courage comes after the first fling.

So deck your table with flowers, or maybe just leaves with candlelight. Sit down with a smile and a happy heart. It's your victory—enjoy it. Remember, however you slice, bake, or casserole it—it's food, it's fun, and like life at times, it can be truly out of this world!

B. P.

CONTENTS

MARCH

APRIL

MAY

SEPTEMBER

OCTOBER

NOVEMBER

DECEMBER

PARTY MENUS

JANUARY

Recheck your basic staples—and now have you

powdered sugar
brown sugar
curry powder
salt
cinnamon
cloves
caraway seeds
thyme
sage
nutmeg
lemons
whole cloves
chili powder
soy sauce
almonds
horseradish
walnuts
garlic
ginger
honey

SHOPPING LIST

MEAT

4 loin pork chops double-thick
½ chicken (broiler, cut in pieces)
3 shoulder lamb chops
½ lb. bacon
1 lb. chopped chuck steak

FROZEN FOODS

2 boxes string beans
1 box spinach
1 box asparagus cuts
1 box Brussels sprouts
2 boxes corn kernels
1 box strawberries
1 box rhubarb
1 box peas
1 box cooked shrimps

FRESH FRUITS AND VEGETABLES

2 bananas
1 head lettuce
2 tomatoes
1 bunch chives
2 Idaho potatoes
1 small ripe pineapple
1 bunch watercress
2 oranges
1 bunch parsley
2 pears

SUNDRIES

1 small can apricots
1 #1 can potatoes
1 6-oz. can boned chicken
1 can cranberry sauce
1 box raisins
1 box ladyfingers
1 small jar Bar-le-Duc currant jam
1 small jar pitted olives, green or black
2 small cans tomato juice
¼ lb. Cheddar cheese
½ pt. sour cream
1 3-oz. pkg. cream cheese
2 cans consommé
1 can cream of celery soup

TIME 1 HR. SERVES 4

SUNDAY

Egg Drop Consommé
Pork Chops w. Bananas
Buttered String Beans
Corn Kernels
Sugared Pineapple
Coffee

EGG DROP CONSOMMÉ: 2 cans. Drop in 1 beaten egg after soup comes to simmer. Stir rapidly until egg shreds, about 2 min.

PORK CHOPS W. BANANAS: 4 large loin, double-thick pork chops. Trim excess fat. Rub with 1 tsp. salt, 1/8 tsp. pepper, and 1/4 tsp. dry mustard. Brown well both sides in hot greased pan, then add 1/4 c. sherry. Cover. Cook over low heat until nearly tender (30 min.), then add 2 sliced bananas and 1/2 c. sour cream. Continue cooking gently until bananas are soft, about 15 min.

CORN KERNELS: 2 boxes. Prepare as directed. Add 2 tbs. melted butter mixed with 2 dashes Tabasco, salt and pepper to taste.

TIME 25 MIN. SERVES 2

MONDAY

Orange-Tomato Bouillon
Chicken Curry w. Rice
Cranberry Sauce
Green Salad
Spiced Raisins
Coffee

ORANGE-TOMATO BOUILLON: Add 1 c. tomato juice, 1/4 c. orange juice to 1 c. bouillon. Serve piping hot.

CHICKEN CURRY W. RICE: Heat 2 tbs. butter, add 2 bay leaves, 2 tbs. curry powder, dash cayenne pepper, 2/3 tsp. brown sugar, and 2 minced onions. Cook until onions are soft, about 5 min. Add 1 6-oz. can chicken diced and dusted with 1 tbs. flour. Stir in 1 c. boiling water, salt and pepper to taste. Simmer 10 min. Serve with 1 1/2 c. prepared precooked rice.

SPICED RAISINS: Cook 1 c. raisins in 1 c. water 10 min. Add 1 tbs. cornstarch mixed with 1 1/2 tbs. water. Stir until thickened. Add 1/8 tsp. cinnamon, 1/8 tsp. cloves, 1/2 c. brown sugar. Heat until sugar melts. Serve warm with cream.

TUESDAY

TIME 40 MIN. SERVES 2

Asparagus Bouillon
Apricot Beef Loaf
Green Peas
Caraway Potatoes
Strawberries & Cream
Coffee

ASPARAGUS BOUILLON: Dissolve 2 bouillon cubes in 1½ c. boiling water. Add ¼ box asparagus cuts. Boil 5 min. (Cook rest of asparagus for tomorrow.)

APRICOT BEEF LOAF: To 1 lb. chopped beef add ½ c. chopped drained, canned apricots, ½ c. soft bread crumbs, 1½ tsp. salt, ¼ tsp. pepper, 1 finely minced onion, and 1 egg. Mix well. Shape into loaf. Bake in hot oven (450°) 30 min.

GREEN PEAS: 1 box. Add leaf of lettuce, pinch thyme. Cook as directed.

CARAWAY POTATOES: 1 can. Boil. Roll in 2 tbs. melted butter. Sprinkle with caraway seeds.

WEDNESDAY

TIME 25 MIN. SERVES 2

Cream of Celery Soup
Shrimps & Olives
Rice
**Asparagus Salad*
**Rhubarb & Strawberry Compote*
Coffee

SHRIMPS & OLIVES: 1 box shrimps, defrosted. Sauté 1 sliced garlic clove in ⅓ c. butter. Add shrimps, ½ c. chopped olives (black or green), salt to taste. Heat 10 min., jiggling pan now and then. Serve over rice.

RICE: Prepare 3 c. precooked rice as directed on pkg. Reserve 1 c. for Friday.

ASPARAGUS SALAD: Arrange asparagus with sliced tomato on lettuce. Garnish with crumbled bacon. Serve with French dressing.

RHUBARB & STRAWBERRY COMPOTE: 1 box rhubarb. Prepare as directed. Reserve half and chill for breakfast. Add leftover strawberries to remainder. Serve warm or cold.

THURSDAY

TIME 55 MIN. SERVES 2

Chicken Italian style
Spinach w. Chives
Stuffed Idaho Potatoes
Pears w. Cream Cheese & Bar-le-Duc
Coffee

CHICKEN ITALIAN STYLE: ½ broiler cut in pieces. Rub well with salt, pepper, and paprika. Place in shallow casserole. Brush with 3 tbs. oil, add 1 minced garlic clove, dash sage, 1 tbs. minced parsley, ⅓ c. white wine. Cover. Bake in moderate oven (375°) 30 min. Baste well, bake uncovered until tender, well browned, 15 min. more.

SPINACH W. CHIVES: 1 box. Prepare as directed, adding 2 tbs. chopped chives, squeeze of lemon.

STUFFED BAKED IDAHO POTATOES: 2. Brush with salad oil. Bake until tender, about 45 min. Cut slit in each, insert stick of Cheddar. Replace in oven until cheese melts, about 10 min.

FRIDAY

TIME 30 MIN. SERVES 2

Tomato Juice
French Lamb Chops
Brussels Sprouts
**Rice Salad*
Orange Charlotte
Coffee

TOMATO JUICE: Serve with lemon quarters and freshly ground black pepper.

FRENCH LAMB CHOPS: 3 shoulder chops. Sprinkle salt and pepper. Sear quickly in hot pan. Add 1 tbs. butter. Sauté until brown. Add ½ c. white wine, ½ tsp. chopped parsley. Simmer 5 min.

BRUSSELS SPROUTS: 1 box. Prepare as directed. Add 1 tbs. cream, dash nutmeg.

RICE SALAD: Mix 1 c. cooked rice with 1 tsp. curry powder. Toss with chopped watercress, lettuce, and ¼ cup French dressing.

ORANGE CHARLOTTE: Mix 2 beaten egg yolks, 2 tbs. sugar, grated rind and juice ½ orange and ½ lemon in top of double boiler. Stir over hot water until thick. Cool slightly. Fold in 2 egg whites beaten stiff with 2 tbs. sugar. Pour into glasses lined with ladyfingers. Chill.

SHOPPING LIST

MEAT

3 lbs. boneless ham butt precooked
4 ¼″ slices beef liver, ¾ lb.
1 small flank steak, about 1½ lbs.

FROZEN FOODS

1 box Lima beans
3 boxes peas
1 box corn kernels
1 box asparagus

FRESH FRUITS AND VEGETABLES

6 sweet potatoes
1 head Boston lettuce
1 head iceberg lettuce
2 cucumbers
1 bunch chives
1 lb. tomatoes
1 bunch scallions
1 ripe avocado
1 bunch celery
1 bunch parsley
1 head escarole
2 green peppers
2 seedless oranges
1 finochio (fennel, opt.)
fruit for Thursday

SUNDRIES

8 oz. thin spaghetti
1 small can rolled anchovies
1 small can pimiento
1 small can apricots
¼ lb. American cheese
1 pkg. vanilla ice cream mix
¼ lb. Roquefort
½ pt. sour cream
½ pt. heavy cream
10-oz. can minced clams
¼ lb. Gorgonzola cheese
1 #1 tall can potatoes
1 small can pears, home-style
1 small can shredded coconut
1 can condensed cream of asparagus soup
1 can condensed black bean soup
3 cans consommé
1 can condensed green pea soup

PICK UP ON YOUR WAY HOME

THUR.—French bread

SUNDAY

TIME 2 HRS. SERVES 4

Cucumber Consommé
Baked Ham
Whipped Sweet Potatoes
Buttered Peas
Tossed Green Salad
Avocado Ice Cream
Coffee

CUCUMBER CONSOMMÉ: Prepare 2 cans consommé as directed. Add diced half cucumber, peeled, 2 tbs. sherry. Simmer 5 min.

BAKED HAM: 3 lbs., ready-cooked, boneless. Score fat. Dot with whole cloves. Make paste of 1 tbs. apricot juice, ½ c. brown sugar. Coat ham. (Save apricots for Wednesday.) Bake in hot oven (425°) 45 min. Baste with apricot juice.

WHIPPED SWEET POTATOES: Peel 6 boiled sweet potatoes. Whip with a little milk, lots of butter, 1 tbs. sherry.

AVOCADO ICE CREAM: Prepare vanilla ice cream mix as directed. After first freezing and beating stir in 1 avocado pressed through strainer. Complete freezing.

MONDAY

TIME 25 MIN. SERVES 2

Black Bean & Asparagus Soup
Beef Liver & Herbs
Buttered Lima Beans
Escarole Salad
Assorted Cheeses
Crackers
Coffee

BLACK BEAN & ASPARAGUS SOUP: Heat 1 can undiluted black bean with 1 can undiluted asparagus, 1 soup can milk. Add ½ c. liquid from Lima beans. Do not boil. Beat with egg beater. Add 1 tbs. cream before serving.

BEEF LIVER W. HERBS: 4 ¼″ slices. Dip in milk, dust with seasoned flour. Sauté in 1 tbs. butter. Meanwhile, melt 2 tbs. butter, add ½ tsp. each thyme, minced parsley, chopped chives, 1 minced garlic clove, juice ½ lemon, salt and pepper to taste. Blend well. Serve hot over liver.

BUTTERED LIMA BEANS: 1 box. Prepare as directed. Reserve liquid for soup.

ESCAROLE SALAD: Escarole, French dressing with extra dash onion juice.

TUESDAY

TIME 25 MIN. SERVES 2

Broiled Flank Steak
**Sautéed Cucumbers*
Potatoes in Wine
Boston Lettuce Salad
Home-Style Canned Pears w. Whipped Cream
Coffee

BROILED FLANK STEAK: Rub with salt, pepper. Brush with 2 tbs. ketchup, sprinkle with 1 slivered clove of garlic, 4 crushed whole cloves. Dot with butter. Place on preheated broiler rack, broil directly under high flame about 15 min., without turning. Allow edges to burn slightly. Carve on bias, slicing meat about ¼″ thick. Save any left over.

SAUTÉED CUCUMBERS: 1½. Peel. Cut into sticks. Dip in beaten egg, flour. Sauté in 2 tbs. salad oil until brown.

POTATOES IN WINE: Boil 1 can potatoes. Drain. Dress with 1 tbs. white wine mixed with 1 tbs. melted butter.

WEDNESDAY

TIME 25 MIN. SERVES 2

Green Pea Bouillon
**Apricot-Ham Turnovers*
Corn Kernel Chili
Sour Cream Celery
Coffee w. Twist of Lemon Peel

GREEN PEA BOUILLON: To 2 bouillon cubes add 1½ c. boiling water, 1 can undiluted pea soup, liquid from celery.

APRICOT-HAM TURNOVER: Use leftover ham and apricots. Sandwich apricots between 2 thin ham slices per person. Toothpick together. Sprinkle lightly with brown sugar. Fry in 2 tbs. butter, basting often.

CORN KERNEL CHILI: Prepare 1 box corn kernels as directed. Add ¼ tsp. chili powder and 1 tbs. minced onion simmered soft in 1½ tbs. butter.

SOUR CREAM CELERY: Dice 4 stalks celery and boil in just enough salted water to cover for 10 min. Drain off liquid, save for soup. Add salt and pepper to taste, 1½ tbs. butter. Simmer 3 min. Serve topped with 2 tbs. sour cream.

TIME 25 MIN. SERVES 2

THURSDAY

Spaghetti, Clam Sauce
Buttered Asparagus
Antipasto Salad
Cheese Bread
Fresh Fruit
Coffee

SPAGHETTI, CLAM SAUCE: Heat ½ c. butter. Add 1 can minced clams, 1 cup chopped scallions, 4 finely minced cloves of garlic, salt and pepper to taste. Pour sauce over (8 oz.) hot, drained spaghetti. Cover with grated Parmesan cheese.

ANTIPASTO SALAD: Arrange tomatoes, sliced celery hearts (reserve outside stalks for Friday), pimiento, anchovy, green pepper, etc., with lettuce. (For a real coup try the Italian markets for finochio [fennel].)

CHEESE BREAD: Blend 1½ tbs. Gorgonzola cheese with 4 tbs. butter. Slit French bread in deep diagonals, but not through. Spread each section and outer crust with cheese blend. Bake in hot oven (450°) 5 min.

TIME 25 MIN. SERVES 2

FRIDAY

Egg Drop Soup
**Chinese Leftovers w. Peas and Rice*
Oranges w. Coconut
Chinese Tea

EGG DROP SOUP: Dilute 1 can consommé with ½ soup can water. Bring to boil over high heat. Pour in 1 beaten egg, stirring rapidly until egg shreds, about 2 min.

CHINESE LEFTOVERS W. PEAS AND RICE: Cut all week's leftover meats into 1″ pieces, brown in 3 tsp. salad oil. Stir in 2 c. diced celery and 1 diced green pepper. Sauté 5 min. Add 1 box peas and any leftover vegetables, diced, except potatoes. Add ¾ c. bouillon. Simmer 10 min. Thicken with 1 tbs. cornstarch blended with ⅓ c. water, 2 tsp. soy sauce. Serve with 1½ c. prepared precooked rice.

ORANGES W. COCONUT: Peel and slice 2 chilled seedless oranges. Sprinkle with brown sugar and shredded coconut.

SHOPPING LIST

MEAT

4-lb. eye round beef roast
½ lb. pork sausage (link)
½ chicken, broiler

FROZEN FOODS

2 boxes chopped spinach
1 box asparagus cuts
1 box Lima beans
1 box potato puffs
1 box broccoli
1 box string beans
1 box fillet of sole

FRESH FRUITS AND VEGETABLES

1 head lettuce
2 tomatoes
1 head chicory
1 green pepper
1 bunch watercress
1 bunch scallions
4 Idaho potatoes
6 ripe kumquats

SUNDRIES

1 can baked apples
½ pt. sour cream
½ pt. light cream
½ pt. heavy cream
1 16-oz. can salmon
1 #1 can mixed vegetables
1 #2 can potatoes
¼ lb. Roquefort cheese
1 small can apricots
1 small can spiced peaches
1 small can shoestring beets
1 small can sliced apples
1 pkg. maple junket
1 small can tomato juice
1 4-oz. can sliced mushrooms
1 can cream of celery soup

PICK UP ON YOUR WAY HOME

FOR SUN.—1 pt. chocolate-chip ice cream

TIME 2 HRS. SERVES 4

SUNDAY

Roast Beef
Stuffed Baked Potatoes
Spinach w. Sour Cream
Green Salad
Ice-Cream-Filled Baked Apples
Coffee

ROAST BEEF: 4 lbs. eye round. Prepare as usual, or pierce beef in 4 or 5 places and insert slivers of garlic deep down. Add 1 c. red wine to baste. (Cook 25 min. to pound for rare at 325°, 40 min. for well done.) Reserve at least 1½ c. meat for Thursday.

STUFFED BAKED POTATOES: 4 Idaho. Bake (allow at least 55 min. at 325°). Halve. Scoop out potato, add ½ c. minced scallions, ⅓ c. milk or cream, salt and pepper to taste. Replace in jackets. Top each half with 1 tbs. butter. Return to oven for 15 min. Serve sprinkled with paprika.

SPINACH W. SOUR CREAM: 2 boxes. Cook as directed. Drain, stir in 3 tbs. sour cream.

TIME 25 MIN. SERVES 2

MONDAY

Salmon Casserole
Asparagus & Watercress Salad
Buttered String Beans
Kumquats
Coffee

SALMON CASSEROLE: Drain liquor from salmon, reserving ⅓ c. Remove skin and bones. Place in center of greased baking dish. Sprinkle with black pepper, top with ½ onion and ½ green pepper sliced paper-thin. Add the ⅓ c. salmon liquor. Slice ½ can potatoes, arrange around fish. Dot with butter. Pour ⅓ c. sour cream over salmon. Sprinkle with paprika. Bake in hot oven (425°) 20 min.

ASPARAGUS & WATERCRESS SALAD: Combine cut asparagus (½ box, semi-thawed), 1 finely chopped onion. Toss with lettuce and watercress. Add 2 tbs. crumbled Roquefort cheese to ¼ c. French dressing.

KUMQUATS: Wash fully ripe kumquats. Eat with peel.

TUESDAY

TIME 45 MIN. SERVES 2

Tomato Juice
Toad in the Hole
Buttered Broccoli
Porcupine Apples
Coffee

TOAD IN THE HOLE: Arrange ½ lb. pork sausages in shallow baking pan. Bake in hot oven (425°) until lightly browned, about 10 min. Mix and sift 1 cup flour with ½ tsp. salt. Stir in 2 eggs, then 1 c. milk. Beat well with rotary beater. Pour off half of sausage fat. Return to oven. When sizzling again, pour on the batter. Bake about 30 min. until puffed up and browned.

PORCUPINE APPLES: Cover mounds of canned sliced apples with whipped cream. Pierce all over with blanched, halved almonds.

WEDNESDAY

TIME 40 MIN. SERVES 2

Chicken & Cheese Melt
Potato Puffs
Beet & Horseradish Salad
Sherried Maple Junket
Coffee

CHICKEN & CHEESE MELT: ½ broiler, cut in pieces. Rub with salt and pepper. Place on broiling pan skin side down. Dot with butter. Sprinkle with garlic salt. Broil. When brown, turn, brush with 2 tbs. melted butter, sprinkle with 2 tbs. Roquefort. Broil until cheese has melted and chicken is tender.

BEET & HORSERADISH SALAD: Toss small can shoestring beets with ½ c. sliced celery and ¼ c. French dressing mixed with 2 tbs. horseradish, 1 tbs. minced onion, 1 tbs. sugar.

SHERRIED MAPLE JUNKET: Prepare 2 servings maple junket as directed, using ½ c. milk and ½ c. light cream. Add 1 tbs. sherry just before pouring into glasses.

THURSDAY

TIME 25 MIN. SERVES 2

Chicken Bouillon
**Beef, Strogonoff-style*
Tossed Salad
Apricots w. Shredded Walnuts
Coffee

CHICKEN BOUILLON: To 2½ cups chicken bouillon add 1 bay leaf, 1 minced onion. Simmer 5 min.

BEEF, STROGONOFF-STYLE: Cut Sunday's leftover meat into 1″ cubes. Sauté 1½ sliced onions until brown in 2 tbs. butter. Add 1 can sliced mushrooms, drained, and more butter if necessary. Flour beef lightly, add to sizzling mushrooms. Add leftover vegetables of week, including Monday's ½ can potatoes, diced. Cook about 10 min. Stir in ½ c. sour cream, salt and coarse pepper to taste. Cook 1 min.

APRICOTS W. SHREDDED WALNUTS: 1 can apricots, chilled. Serve sprinkled with shredded walnuts.

FRIDAY

TIME 40 MIN. SERVES 2

Curried Cream of Celery Soup
Fillet of Sole Sauté
Baked Lima Beans
Tomato Salad
Spiced Peaches
Coffee

CURRIED CREAM OF CELERY SOUP: 1 can. Prepare as directed. Add ¼ tsp. curry powder. Top with dash paprika.

FILLET OF SOLE SAUTÉ: 1 box, defrosted. Dust with flour. Brush with beaten egg and roll in bread crumbs. Fry in ¼ c. hot salad oil until brown. Mix 2 tbs. lemon juice with 2 tbs. chopped watercress, pour over fillets.

BAKED LIMA BEANS: 1 box. Prepare as directed. Drain. Place in buttered baking dish with ½ cup light cream, ½ tsp. salt. Cover. Bake in hot oven (425°) 20 min. Serve sprinkled with crumbled bacon.

TOMATO SALAD: Peel tomatoes after dipping in boiling water. Slice thickly. Sprinkle with salt and pepper. Serve with French dressing.

SHOPPING LIST

MEAT

4 lbs. loin of pork for roast
1 sirloin steak, small and thick
1 beef kidney, about 1 lb.
2 slices veal cutlet, pounded thin

FROZEN FOODS

1 box French-fried potatoes
1 box broccoli
1 box succotash
1 pkg. fillet of sole
1 box whipped potatoes

FRESH FRUITS AND VEGETABLES

1 bunch radishes
1 head lettuce
4 tomatoes
1 green pepper
1 small cucumber
1 head escarole
1 bunch parsley
1 orange
2 tangerines
1 small pineapple
1 small bunch carrots
2 lbs. potatoes
¼ lb. green grapes
2 ripe persimmons

SUNDRIES

1 #2 can freestone peaches
8 oz. thin spaghetti
1 small can anchovies
1 box ready-to-bake hard rolls
½ pt. sour cream
1 #2 can diced beets
6 almond macaroons (preferably stale)
½ pt. heavy cream
½ pt. light cream
1 small can apricot nectar
1 large can grated cheese
1 12-oz. can apple juice
1 #2 can apple sauce
1 can cream of celery soup
1 can cream of chicken soup
1 can tomato soup
1 can consommé
1 can green pea soup

SUNDAY

TIME 3 HRS. SERVES 4

Apple-glazed Roast Pork
Orange-Butter Beets
Mashed Potatoes
Radish & Lettuce Salad
Peaches in Wine
Coffee

APPLE-GLAZED ROAST PORK: 4 lbs. loin. Rub with sherry, salt and pepper, dash sage and thyme. Place in roasting pan with ½ c. white wine, ½ c. apple juice, 1 sliced onion, 1 bay leaf. Roast 2 hrs. in moderate oven (350°), basting frequently; then coat with ½ c. apple sauce, sprinkle with 2 tbs. brown sugar. Roast 45 min. longer.

ORANGE-BUTTER BEETS: 1 can. Heat. Drain. Add ½ tsp. grated orange rind to 2 tbs. melted butter; serve over beets.

RADISH & LETTUCE SALAD: Slice radishes, chunk lettuce. Dress with ¼ c. mayonnaise mixed with ¼ c. French dressing.

PEACHES IN WINE: 1 can. Drain; soak peaches in 1 c. dry white wine 1 hr. before serving.

MONDAY

TIME 25 MIN. SERVES 2

Spaghetti, Green Sauce
Lettuce, Tomato & Anchovy Salad
Garlic Rolls
Tangerines on Pineapple
Coffee

SPAGHETTI, GREEN SAUCE: Brown 4 minced garlic cloves in ½ c. salad oil. Add 1 c. chopped parsley. Simmer 5 min. Season with black pepper. Serve over boiled spaghetti (8 oz.) with lots of grated cheese.

LETTUCE, TOMATO & ANCHOVY SALAD: Break lettuce, quarter tomatoes, garnish with anchovies. Serve with ½ c. sour cream mixed with 2 tbs. lemon juice, salt and pepper to taste.

GARLIC ROLLS: 1 box ready-to-bake. Mash 1 clove garlic in 1 tbs. butter. Brush rolls. Bake as directed.

TANGERINES ON PINEAPPLE: Peel 2 tangerines, press open gently. Slit segments with sharp knife, remove seeds. Arrange on fresh pineapple slices. Sugar lightly.

TUESDAY

TIME 25 MIN. SERVES 2

Broiled Sirloin Steak
French-Fried Potatoes
Buttered Carrots
French Salad
Apple Macaroon
Coffee

BROILED SIRLOIN STEAK: Broil sirloin your favorite method. But well done, medium, or rare, do not butter steak until you are ready to serve.

BUTTERED CARROTS: 4. Scrape, slice thin. Boil in ½ c. water 10 min. Drain. Dress with melted butter, dash of ginger.

FRENCH SALAD: Arrange chilled escarole leaves as individual servings. Sprinkle with paprika. Add 2 minced cloves of garlic to ¼ c. French dressing.

APPLE MACAROON: Heat 1 c. apple sauce. Stir in 6 crumbled macaroons, 2 drops almond flavoring. Pour into dessert glasses. Chill. Serve with cream.

WEDNESDAY

TIME 25 MIN. SERVES 2

Curried Green Pea Soup
Beef Kidney & Rice
Broccoli Amandine
Sliced Persimmons w. Cream
Coffee

CURRIED GREEN PEA SOUP: Prepare 1 can pea soup as directed, add ¼ tsp. curry powder. Serve with dash paprika.

BEEF KIDNEY & RICE: Dip kidney into boiled salted water. Slice very thin, discarding white centers and tubes. Brown quickly in 2 tbs. butter. Sprinkle with 2 tbs. sherry, ½ tsp. salt, ⅛ tsp. pepper. Add 1 c. heavy cream, ½ tsp. horseradish. Simmer gently 10 min. Serve on 1½ c. prepared precooked rice.

BROCCOLI AMANDINE: Prepare 1 box broccoli as directed. Blanch 2 tbs. almonds. (Cover with boiling water, cool, slip off skins.) Chop. Brown in 1 tsp. butter, sprinkle over broccoli.

TIME 35 MIN. SERVES 2

THURSDAY

Chicken Celery Soup
Veal, Scaloppini-style
Succotash
**Pineapple Grape Cup*
Coffee

CHICKEN CELERY SOUP: Combine 1 can cream of chicken and 1 can cream of celery soup. Add 1 soup can milk. Heat gently. Serve with lemon quarters.

VEAL, SCALOPPINI-STYLE: Dust 2 slices veal cutlet with seasoned flour, brown in 2 tbs. salad oil. Add 1 minced green pepper, 1 small sliced onion; sauté until soft, about 5 min. Add 1 can undiluted tomato soup. Sprinkle with 3 tbs. grated cheese. Cover. Heat until cheese melts.

SUCCOTASH: 1 box. Prepare as directed. Add ½ tsp. paprika and 1 tbs. butter.

PINEAPPLE GRAPE CUP: Mix diced fresh pineapple with seeded green grapes. Pour on ½ c. apricot nectar mixed with 2 tbs. honey.

TIME 30 MIN. SERVES 2

FRIDAY

Clear Consommé
Fillet of Sole Amandine
Whipped Potatoes
Vegetable Salad
Cucumber Dressing
Caramel Custard
Coffee

FILLET OF SOLE AMANDINE: 1 box sole, defrosted. Dust fillets lightly with seasoned flour. Sauté in ¼ c. butter. Serve sprinkled with ¼ c. chopped blanched almonds lightly browned in 1 tbs. butter. Garnish with lemon quarters.

VEGETABLE SALAD: Arrange any leftover vegetables with sliced tomatoes on lettuce. Add ¼ c. grated cucumber, ¼ tsp. prepared mustard to ½ c. French dressing. Serve separately.

CARAMEL CUSTARD: Heat ¼ c. sugar until lightly browned. Pour into 2 custard cups. Beat 1 egg, add 1 c. milk, ¼ c. sugar, ¼ tsp. vanilla. Mix well. Pour over caramel. Set cups in pan of hot water and bake in moderate oven (375°) 20 min.

FEBRUARY

Recheck your basic staples—and now have you

whole cloves
honey
thinly sliced white bread
lemons
brown sugar
cinnamon
basil
powdered sugar
capers
nuts
rosemary or tarragon
nutmeg
thyme
soy sauce
biscuit mix
orange marmalade
brandy
rum
horseradish
chutney
maple syrup

SHOPPING LIST

MEAT

3½ lbs. boneless pre-cooked ham, butt end
¾ lb. chopped beef, chuck
2 veal chops
½ lb. bacon

FROZEN FOODS

1 box wax beans
2 boxes asparagus
1 box French-fried potatoes
1 box corn on the cob
1 box haddock fillets
1 box peas

FRESH FRUITS AND VEGETABLES

3 Idaho potatoes
1 bunch parsley
1 banana
1 tomato
1 bunch celery
3 seedless oranges
1 small green pepper
1 large head lettuce
1 bunch radishes
1 small cucumber

SUNDRIES

1 box ginger snaps
¼ lb. Roquefort cheese
¼ lb. sliced American cheese
1 #1 can sweet potatoes
1 4-oz. can mushrooms
1 box dessert shells
1 small box raisins
½ pt. heavy cream
1 small can shredded coconut
1 box ladyfingers
1 small can applesauce
1 small can potatoes
1 8-oz. can peach halves
1 can cream of mushroom soup
1 can condensed cream of asparagus soup
1 can condensed pea soup
1 can chicken broth
1 can condensed consommé
1 can condensed tomato soup
2 cans condensed vegetable soup

PICK UP ON YOUR WAY HOME

FOR SUN.—1 pt. orange ice

SUNDAY

TIME 1 HR. SERVES 4

Vegetable Soup w. Crumbled Ginger Snaps
Baked Honey Ham
Roquefort Asparagus
Stuffed Baked Potato Halves
Orange Shells
Coffee

BAKED HONEY HAM: 3½ lbs. precooked boneless. Score fat, dot with cloves, cover with ½ c. honey. Bake 45 min. in moderate oven (375°). Baste with ½ c. orange juice.

ROQUEFORT ASPARAGUS: 2 boxes. Cook as directed. Heat 5 tbs. butter, 2 tbs. vinegar, 3½ tbs. Roquefort cheese. Stir until cheese melts. Serve over asparagus.

STUFFED BAKED POTATO HALVES: 3 Idaho. Bake about 50 min. Cut in two lengthwise. Scoop out, mash with 3 tbs. butter, salt, paprika, ¼ c. milk, and ½ c. condensed pea soup. Refill shells. Bake 10 min.

ORANGE SHELLS: Fill sponge shells with whipped cream. Top with orange ice.

MONDAY

TIME 30 MIN. SERVES 2

Stuffed Hamburgers
Buttered Wax Beans
Orange & Onion Salad
Bread & Butter Pudding
Coffee

STUFFED HAMBURGERS: ¾ lb. chopped beef. Mix in ½ tsp. salt, ⅛ tsp. pepper, and 1 finely minced garlic clove. Make 4 thin patties. Sandwich 1 slice American cheese between each 2 patties. Curl slice of bacon around edge. Broil both sides under low flame until well browned and cooked through.

ORANGE & ONION SALAD: Slice thinly 1 onion, 1 seedless orange. Add 1½ c. shredded lettuce, toss with ¼ c. French dressing.

BREAD & BUTTER PUDDING: Line small baking dish with 2 thin slices buttered bread. Sprinkle with 2 tbs. raisins, 1 tsp. grated lemon rind. Beat 2 eggs, stir in 2 tbs. sugar, 1½ c. milk. Pour over bread. Set dish in pan of hot water. Bake in moderate oven (375°) 20 min.

TIME 20 MIN. SERVES 2

TUESDAY

**Chicken-Pea Soup*
Spanish Omelet
French-Fried Potatoes
Sherried Ambrosia
Coffee

CHICKEN-PEA SOUP: Mix 1 can chicken broth, ½ can leftover pea soup, ¾ soup can water, salt and white pepper to taste, 1 tbs. sherry. Simmer few min.

SPANISH OMELET: Dice 1 peeled tomato, 1 small green pepper, ½ onion, 1 stalk celery. Add 1 tbs. minced parsley, ½ can mushrooms with 2 tbs. liquid, ¼ tsp. salt, dash pepper. Chop together. Simmer 10 min. Add 1 tbs. butter. Beat 4 eggs with ½ tsp. salt, dash pepper until frothy. Heat 2 tbs. butter in frying pan, pour in eggs. Cook over medium heat until brown underneath. Add vegetables, fold. Continue cooking until center is just set.

SHERRIED AMBROSIA: Slice 1 peeled orange, 1 banana. Sprinkle with 1 tbs. sherry, ¼ c. shredded coconut.

TIME 30 MIN. SERVES 2

WEDNESDAY

**Ham Baked in Milk*
Green Peas
Buttered Sweet Potatoes
Charlotte Russe
Coffee

HAM BAKED IN MILK: 1 slice, 1″ thick. Mix 1 tsp. dry mustard, 4 tbs. brown sugar. Spread over ham. Place in baking dish with just enough milk to cover. Bake 25 min. in moderate oven (375°).

GREEN PEAS: 1 box. Prepare as directed. Dress with 2 slices crumbled bacon, 1 tbs. butter.

BUTTERED SWEET POTATOES: 1 can. Drain. Brush with melted butter. Sprinkle with 1 tsp. cinnamon mixed with 1 tsp. powdered sugar. Bake 12 min.

CHARLOTTE RUSSE: Line glasses with ladyfingers. Fill with sweetened whipped cream.

THURSDAY

TIME 40 MIN. SERVES 2

**Cream of Mushroom Soup*
Veal Casserole
Lettuce & Onion Salad
Broiled Peach Halves
Coffee

CREAM OF MUSHROOM SOUP: 1 can. Prepare as directed. Add the ½ can leftover mushrooms and liquid.

VEAL CASSEROLE: Rub 2 veal chops with 2 tsp. paprika, 1 tsp. flour, ½ tsp. salt, ⅛ tsp. pepper. Brown 1 garlic clove in 2 tbs. butter. Add chops, brown on both sides. Add ½ tsp. rosemary, 1 bay leaf, ¼ c. water, 1 small can potatoes, drained. Cover, cook over moderate heat about 30 min. Add ¼ c. white wine last 5 min.

LETTUCE & ONION SALAD: Shred lettuce. Cut 1 onion into thin shavings. Arrange in bowl in alternate layers, sprinkling French dressing on each layer.

BROILED PEACH HALVES: Drain 1 small can peach halves. Dot with butter, brown sugar. Broil. Serve with cream.

FRIDAY

TIME 25 MIN. SERVES 2

Asparagus Consommé
Poached Fillet of Haddock
Corn on the Cob
Radish & Cucumber Salad
**Applesauce w. Ginger Snaps*
Coffee

ASPARAGUS CONSOMMÉ: Combine 1 can each asparagus soup and consommé. Add ½ soup can water. Simmer.

POACHED FILLET OF HADDOCK: 1 box, defrosted. Heat in frying pan 1 can condensed tomato soup, ¼ tsp. salt, 1 bay leaf, 1 small minced onion, white pepper to taste. Add fillets, simmer 7 min., turn. Simmer until done. Add ½ tbs. butter. Serve on toast that has been sprinkled with grated cheese.

RADISH & CUCUMBER SALAD: Wash, slice 6 radishes. Sprinkle with salt, let stand 10 min. Pare and slice thinly 1 cucumber. Mix with radishes. Serve on lettuce leaf with French dressing.

SHOPPING LIST

MEAT

2 or 3 veal chops
1 lb. bacon
5 lbs. mussels
2 slices beef liver, ¼″ thick

FROZEN FOODS

1 box French-fried potatoes
1 box asparagus
1 box peas
1 box cod fillets
1 box whipped potatoes

FRESH FRUITS AND VEGETABLES

1 head iceberg lettuce
1 head escarole
2 tomatoes
1 bunch celery
1 orange
2 bananas
1 bunch endive
3 potatoes
1 lb. McIntosh apples
1 small bunch carrots
1 cucumber
2 white onions
1 bunch parsley

SUNDRIES

1 small can anchovy fillets
1 3-oz. can tomato juice
1 small can pears
¼ lb. Cheddar cheese, sliced
1 4-oz. can pimiento
2 boxes ready-to-bake rolls
8 oz. thin spaghetti
1 can fig pudding
½ pt. light cream
½ pt. heavy cream
2 oz. peanut brittle
1 pkg. instant vanilla dessert
2 small cans apple juice
1 can cream of celery soup
1 can condensed pea soup
1 can consommé
1 can condensed tomato soup

PICK UP ON YOUR WAY HOME

THUR.—2 Biscuits Tortoni; French bread

SUNDAY

TIME 25 MIN. SERVES 2

Moules Marinière
Vegetable Salad w. Anchovies
Hot Rolls
Fig Pudding w. Cream
Coffee

MOULES MARINIÈRE: Scrub 5 lbs. mussels well under cold running water. Discard open ones. Place in large pot. Add ¾ c. water, 3 c. white wine, 1 tbs. butter, ½ c. chopped parsley, 1 clove garlic, 1 tbs. lemon juice, dash cayenne. Cover, cook over medium heat until all the mussels are opened, about 12 min. Serve immediately in shells on soup plate, juice and all. Dunk rolls in juice.

VEGETABLE SALAD W. ANCHOVIES: Combine lettuce, chunked, 3 sliced boiled potatoes, 2 sliced onions, ⅓ c. small stuffed olives, 1 can anchovy fillets. Garnish with sliced hard-cooked eggs, 1 tsp. capers, 1 tsp. minced parsley. Add French dressing at the table.

MONDAY

TIME 30 MIN. SERVES 2

Tomato Juice
Breaded Veal Chops
Asparagus
Sherried Carrots
Stuffed Nutted Pears
Coffee

BREADED VEAL CHOPS: Rub with salt and pepper. Dip in beaten egg, then in bread crumbs. Sauté in 2 tbs. butter 25 min. Turn often.

ASPARAGUS: 1 box. Prepare as directed. Put aside 2 or 3 spears for tomorrow. Heat 2 tbs. butter until light brown. Add 1 tsp. lemon juice; salt, pepper to taste. Serve over asparagus.

SHERRIED CARROTS: Scrape 4 carrots, slice thin. Cook covered in ½ c. salted water 10 min. Remove cover, add 1 tbs. butter, boil rapidly 5 min. Add 1 tbs. sherry.

STUFFED NUTTED PEARS: 1 can pear halves. Stuff cavities with whipped cream, dust with nut crumbs, pour on 1 tbs. pear juice. Reserve rest of juice.

TIME 45 MIN. SERVES 2

TUESDAY

**Pea Soup w. Asparagus Tips*
Cheese & Eggs Italian
French-Fried Potatoes
Escarole & Pimiento Salad
Apple Betty
Coffee

CHEESE & EGGS ITALIAN: In cup-size casseroles (or one small heat-proof serving dish) place 4 tbs. olive oil (¾ cup if using one dish). Heat. Drop in each casserole 2 unbeaten eggs, salt and white pepper to taste, pinch rosemary or tarragon, 1 tbs. ketchup, 3 dashes Tabasco, 2 thin slices Cheddar. Cover. Cook over very low heat until done. Just before serving, pour off extra oil and sprinkle with 2 slices crumbled bacon.

APPLE BETTY: Mix 1 c. thinly sliced peeled apples with ⅓ c. buttered bread crumbs, ⅓ c. sugar, ½ tsp. cinnamon. Pour on leftover pear juice. Bake in greased dish in moderate oven (375°) 40 min. Serve with cream.

TIME 30 MIN. SERVES 2

WEDNESDAY

Consommé w. Celery
Spanish Liver & Bacon
Peas & Onions
Orange-Banana Cream
Coffee

CONSOMMÉ W. CELERY: 1 can. Prepare as directed. Add any leftover vegetables, diced. Garnish with slivers of celery.

SPANISH LIVER & BACON: 2 slices, ¼″ thick. Cut into strips 2″ wide. Sprinkle with juice 1 lemon, salt, pepper. Roll. Wrap each with ½ strip bacon. Arrange in shallow baking dish. Cover with 1 can condensed tomato soup. Bake 20 min. in moderately hot oven (425°).

PEAS & ONIONS: To 1 box peas, add 2 white onions, minced, ½ tsp. salt, ⅛ tsp. pepper, ½ tsp. thyme, then cook as directed.

ORANGE-BANANA CREAM: Mash 2 bananas smooth, gradually stir in ⅓ c. orange juice, then 1 tbs. cream. Pour into 2 dessert glasses. Chill.

THURSDAY

TIME 25 MIN. SERVES 2

Hot Apple Juice
Spaghetti & Egg Cheese
Cucumber & Tomato Salad
Garlic Bread
Biscuit Tortoni
Black Coffee

SPAGHETTI & EGG CHEESE: Boil 8 oz. spaghetti. Fry 8 slices bacon until rich brown, drain well on paper. Drop 2 eggs in large serving bowl, beat until frothy. Add ½ c. grated cheese, mix well, then stir in 3 tbs. melted butter and drained bacon, crumbled. Add hot, drained spaghetti, toss well at the table. Serve with additional grated cheese.

GARLIC BREAD: French or Italian style. Mash 1 minced garlic clove with 4 tbs. butter. Slice bread almost through in a series of diagonals. Spread each section with garlic butter. Heat in hot oven (425°) 5 min. Save 2 slices.

FRIDAY

TIME 50 MIN. SERVES 2

**Cream of Celery Soup*
Cheese-Stuffed Fillets
Whipped Potatoes
Endive, French Dressing
Peanut Brittle Pudding
Coffee

CREAM OF CELERY SOUP: 1 can. Prepare as directed. Garnish with cubed leftover garlic bread.

CHEESE-STUFFED FILLETS: 1 box cod, semi-thawed. Slit in half lengthwise, then cut crosswise. Dip the four pieces in beaten egg. Make into 2 sandwiches with 2 slices Cheddar, secure with toothpicks, sprinkle with salt, pepper, 1 tbs. flour. Sauté in 3 tbs. butter 25 min., turning once.

PEANUT BRITTLE PUDDING: Prepare ½ pkg. instant vanilla dessert. Crush 2 oz. peanut brittle, fold lightly into pudding. Pour into serving glasses. Top with whipped cream.

SHOPPING LIST

MEAT & FISH

2 veal cutlets, ¾ lb., pounded thin
½ lb. bacon
½ lb. chopped beef (opt.)
1½ lbs. scallops
6 chicken livers

FROZEN FOODS

2 boxes cut green beans
1 box peas
1 box asparagus
1 box Brussels sprouts
1 box French-fried potatoes
1 box raspberries

FRESH FRUITS AND VEGETABLES

2 heads lettuce
1 bunch watercress
1 bunch celery
3 green peppers
6 tomatoes
2 pears
1 bunch parsley
1 ripe pineapple

SUNDRIES

½ lb. sharp Cheddar cheese
1 ginger ale or beer
1 7-oz. flat can red salmon
1 tube ready-to-bake biscuits
1 4-oz. can mushrooms
1 small can pitted black cherries
1 small pkg. Chinese tea
1 12-oz. can vegetable juice
½ pt. heavy cream
1 8-oz. can carrots
1 small can sliced apples
1 pkg. instant tapioca
1 small jar marrons
1 small jar green olives
2 oz. Gorgonzola cheese
2 small cans potatoes
1 small shredded coconut
1 8-oz. can wax beans
1 can tomato soup
1 can clam broth
1 can vegetable soup
2 cans consommé

PICK UP ON YOUR WAY HOME

TUES.—2 slices poundcake; Parker House rolls
THUR.—½ lb. boiled ham (opt.)

SUNDAY

TIME 25 MIN. SERVES 4

Watercress Consommé
Chinese Scallops & Vegetables
Rice
Shredded Pineapple
Chinese Tea

WATERCRESS CONSOMMÉ: 2 cans consommé. Prepare as directed. Add ½ stalk finely diced celery, salt and pepper to taste. Bring to boil. Add 1 beaten egg, stirring rapidly until egg separates. Add 1 c. chopped watercress. Serve immediately.

CHINESE SCALLOPS & VEGETABLES: 1½ lbs. Cook 2 boxes cut green beans as directed. Dust scallops with seasoned flour. Sauté until brown in 6 tbs. oil. Add ½ c. bouillon, 6 quartered tomatoes, beans, and 3 tbs. soy sauce mixed with ⅓ c. cold water. Cook, stir until thickened. Serve over 3 c. prepared pre-cooked rice.

SHREDDED PINEAPPLE: Peel ripe pineapple. Shred downward with fork, discarding core. Sugar to taste.

MONDAY

TIME 25 MIN. SERVES 2

Vegetable Juice
Veal w. Olives
Parsley Potatoes
Wax Bean Salad
Raspberry Shortcake
Coffee

VEAL W. OLIVES: 2 cutlets pounded thin. Sprinkle with salt, pepper. Sauté quickly in butter. Add ⅓ c. white wine, 8 green olives cut into strips. Cover. Heat 10 min.

PARSLEY POTATOES: 1 can. Heat. Drain. Roll in 2 tbs. melted butter, then in 1 tbs. minced parsley.

WAX BEAN SALAD: Drain 1 small can wax beans (chilled). Toss with shredded lettuce. Season. Serve with French dressing.

RASPBERRY SHORTCAKE: Make 2 shortcakes with 1 c. biscuit mix and 6 tbs. heavy cream. Prepare as directed. Heat 1 box raspberries. Split and butter shortcakes. Fill and top, buttered sides up, with warm raspberries. Serve with cream.

TIME 40 MIN. SERVES 2

TUESDAY

Stuffed Peppers
Brussels Sprouts
Bay Leaf Carrots
Toasted Rolls
Coconut Bars
Coffee

STUFFED PEPPERS: Combine 1½ c. prepared precooked rice, 1 tbs. melted butter, 1 tbs. minced onion, 1 c. grated cheese (or ½ lb. seared chopped meat and 1 tbs. cheese). Mix well. Cut 3 green peppers in half lengthwise. Remove fibers. Boil 1 min. Dry. Stuff with rice mixture. Sprinkle with 2 tbs. buttered bread crumbs. Bake in moderate oven (375°) 20 min.

BAY LEAF CARROTS: 1 can. Heat with 1 bay leaf. Add 1 tbs. butter, salt and white pepper to taste.

COCONUT BARS: Cut 2 slices poundcake into strips 1½″ wide. Coat with butter and honey. Roll in shredded coconut. Heat in oven 5 min. Serve warm.

TIME 25 MIN. SERVES 2

WEDNESDAY

Vegetable Soup
Chicken Livers en Brochette
Sherried Mushrooms
French-Fried Potatoes
Lettuce w. Gorgonzola Dressing
Flaming Cherries
Coffee

CHICKEN LIVERS EN BROCHETTE: Wash 6 chicken livers in cold water mixed with juice 1 lemon. Dry. Cut uncooked bacon into squares. Arrange liver and bacon alternately on skewers. Roll in highly seasoned melted butter. Place in baking dish, bake in hot oven (425°) 8 min., or until bacon is crisp. Serve on toast rubbed lightly with garlic, with sherried mushrooms.

SHERRIED MUSHROOMS: 1 can. Drain. Sauté in 1 tbs. butter, add 1 tbs. sherry.

GORGONZOLA DRESSING: Add 1 tbs. Gorgonzola cheese to ¼ c. French Dressing. Pour over lettuce chunks, toss well.

FLAMING CHERRIES: Simmer 1 small can black cherries 5 min. before serving, then add 3 tbs. warmed brandy. Set aflame.

THURSDAY

TIME 30 MIN. SERVES 2

Welsh Rarebit on Toast
Buttered Asparagus
Browned Potatoes
Apple Tapioca
Coffee

WELSH RAREBIT ON TOAST: Melt 2 tbs. butter in top of double boiler. Add 1 tsp. Worcestershire sauce, ½ tsp. salt, ½ tsp. paprika, ¼ tsp. prepared mustard, ½ lb. Cheddar cheese, grated or sliced thin. Stir until cheese melts. Gradually add ½ c. beer or ginger ale, 1 slightly beaten egg. (½ lb. ham diced and sautéed lightly in butter may be added too.) Cook until thick. Serve on toast.

BROWNED POTATOES: 1 can. Drain. Coat with melted butter, salt, pepper, paprika. Bake in moderate oven (375°) about 25 min., turning occasionally to brown on all sides.

APPLE TAPIOCA: Heat 1 can sliced apples. Place in baking dish. Cover with prepared (½ pkg.) instant tapioca. Top with 1 egg white beaten stiff with 2 tbs. sugar. Bake 20 min.

FRIDAY

TIME 35 MIN. SERVES 2

Tomato & Clam Broth
Salmon Loaf
Rice
Peas w. Parsley
Orange Buttered Biscuits
Pears w. Marrons au Rhum
Tea

TOMATO & CLAM BROTH: Combine 1 can tomato soup, 1 can clam broth. Season with salt, cayenne.

SALMON LOAF: 1 can red salmon. Discard skin and bones. Mash with ⅓ c. minced celery, ½ tsp. salt, ⅛ tsp. pepper, ½ c. milk, ⅓ c. dry bread crumbs, 1 tbs. butter, pinch of tarragon. Add 1 beaten egg. Place in small buttered pan coated with bread crumbs. Bake in hot oven (450°) 20 min. Serve with 1½ c. prepared precooked rice.

ORANGE BUTTERED BISCUITS: 1 box ready-to-bake biscuits. Insert 1 tsp. butter, ½ tsp. marmalade in each. Bake as directed.

PEARS W. MARRONS AU RHUM: Add 1 tbs. rum to marrons. Serve over sliced chilled pears.

SHOPPING LIST

MEAT

4–6 shoulder lamb chops
2 veal cutlets
1 rack spareribs, about 1½ lbs.

FROZEN FOODS

2 boxes broccoli
1 box peas
1 box green beans
1 box Lima beans
1 box string beans
1 box cod fillets
1 box fillet of sole

FRESH FRUITS AND VEGETABLES

1 head romaine
1 head escarole
1 bunch watercress
1 lb. tomatoes
1 head iceberg lettuce
1 grapefruit
1 pt. strawberries
2 limes
1 persimmon
1 avocado
2 seedless oranges

SUNDRIES

1 small can crushed pineapple
1 small pkg. potato chips
1 8-oz. can potatoes
1 small can pimiento
½ pt. sour cream
1 small jar tartar sauce
1 pkg. pitted dates
1 #2 can diced carrots
½ pt. heavy cream
1 small can apricot nectar
1 small coffee cake or brioche
1 can vegetable soup
1 can black bean soup
1 can tomato soup
1 can pepper pot soup
1 can clam chowder

PICK UP ON YOUR WAY HOME

FOR SUN.—1½ pts. vanilla ice cream

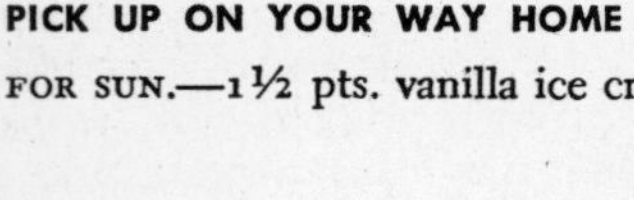

SUNDAY

TIME 35 MIN. SERVES 4

Vegetable-Onion Soup
Lamb Chops Pineapple
Broccoli
Caramel Carrots
Coupe Arabian
Coffee

VEGETABLE-ONION SOUP: 1 can vegetable. Add 1 chopped onion, 2 c. bouillon. Simmer 10 min. Serve with grated cheese.

LAMB CHOPS PINEAPPLE: 4–6 shoulder. Rub with salt, pepper. Broil on one side, turn, spread with drained crushed pineapple, sprinkle with brown sugar, dot with butter, brown.

BROCCOLI: 2 boxes. Prepare as directed. Add buttered bread crumbs seasoned with salt, paprika, 1 tsp. grated lemon rind.

CARAMEL CARROTS: Heat 1 can carrots. Drain. Add 2 tbs. butter, salt and pepper, 2 tbs. brown sugar. Caramelize over low flame.

COUPE ARABIAN: Soak ½ c. chopped pitted dates in ¼ c. brandy. Serve over vanilla ice cream. Top with whipped cream.

MONDAY

TIME 25 MIN. SERVES 2

Codfish w. Horseradish
Potato Chips
Green Beans Sauté
Lettuce & Tomato Salad
Strawberries in Red Wine
Coffee

CODFISH W. HORSERADISH: 1 box, semi-thawed. Cut in 3 pieces. Dip in bread crumbs, beaten egg, then again in crumbs. Fry in 3 tbs. butter. (Save one piece for Wednesday.) Heat 1 tbs. butter in top of double boiler, blend in 1 tbs. flour, slowly add ½ c. milk. Stir until smooth, then add 3 tbs. sour cream, 1 tbs. capers, and 2 tbs. horseradish. Serve over fillets.

GREEN BEANS SAUTÉ: 1 box. Prepare as directed. Drain. Brown half garlic clove in 2 tbs. salad oil, add 2 tbs. butter, 1 tsp. lemon juice, beans, salt and pepper to taste. Heat 5 min.

STRAWBERRIES IN RED WINE: Add 2 tbs. sugar, ½ tsp. grated orange rind, ⅓ c. red wine to 1 c. sliced strawberries. Chill.

TIME 25 MIN. SERVES 2

TUESDAY

Black Bean & Tomato Soup
Veal Squares
Rice w. Peas
Orange & Persimmon Salad
Coffee

BLACK BEAN & TOMATO SOUP: Combine 1 can tomato, 1 can black bean. Add 1½ soup cans milk, salt and pepper to taste. Mix with egg beater. Heat to simmer. Add 1 tbs. cream just before serving. Reserve some for tomorrow.

VEAL SQUARES: Cut 2 veal cutlets into 2″ squares. Season with salt, pepper, 1 tsp. paprika. Dip in beaten egg, then bread crumbs. Brown in 2 tbs. bacon fat.

RICE W. PEAS: Add 1 box semi-thawed peas to 1⅓ c. dry precooked rice. Then cook rice as directed for "extra tender." Salt, pepper to taste. Save ½ c. for tomorrow. Serve topped with veal.

ORANGE & PERSIMMON SALAD: Arrange thin slices orange and persimmon on watercress. Serve with ½ c. French dressing mixed with 1 tbs. chutney.

TIME 25 MIN. SERVES 2

WEDNESDAY

**Beef Bouillon Mélange*
**Fish & Vegetable Omelet*
Mixed Greens
Broiled Grapefruit w. Maple Syrup
Coffee

BEEF BOUILLON MÉLANGE: Combine leftover soup with 1 c. beef bouillon.

FISH & VEGETABLE OMELET: Cut leftover cod fillet into small pieces. Add 1 tbs. grated onion, 1 finely chopped garlic clove, 1 tsp. parsley, and the ½ cup rice and peas left over from yesterday. Add 4 eggs beaten until frothy with dash nutmeg, ½ tsp. salt, ⅛ tsp. pepper. Fry in 2 tbs. butter. Heat 1 sliced tomato in 1 tbs. butter. When bottom of omelet is brown, place tomato slices on one side and fold over. Cook until inside of omelet is firm.

MIXED GREENS: Toss romaine, iceberg lettuce, escarole with ¼ c. French dressing. Garnish with sliced pimiento.

THURSDAY

TIME 35 MIN. SERVES 2

Pepper Pot Soup
Broiled Spareribs w. Honey
Mustard String Beans
Parsley Potatoes
Croûte aux Fruits w. Rum
Coffee

BROILED SPARERIBS W. HONEY: Rub 1 rack spareribs with garlic, then salt and pepper. Spread both sides with honey. Sprinkle with tsp. basil. Broil meaty side up. Turn once. Add dots of butter. Cook until very brown. Turn again. Sprinkle with 2 tbs. lemon juice, more dots of butter, 3 tbs. red wine. Cook until edges are burnt.

MUSTARD STRING BEANS: 1 box. Prepare as directed. Drain. Stir in 1 tsp. prepared mustard.

CROÛTE AUX FRUITS W. RUM: Add 1 diced seedless orange, ½ c. apricot nectar to 1 can fruits for salad. Heat. Add broken pieces of coffee cake and 1 tbs. rum. Serve hot.

FRIDAY

TIME 35 MIN. SERVES 2

Clam Chowder
Stuffed Fillet of Sole
Green Salad w. Garlic Toast Squares
Whipped Avocado
Coffee

CLAM CHOWDER: 1 can. Prepare as directed. Diced vegetables and meat leftovers may be added.

STUFFED FILLET OF SOLE: 1 box, defrosted. Brush fillets with oil. Spread generously with tartar sauce, roll, secure with toothpicks. Dip in bread crumbs. Sauté in 4 tbs. butter until golden brown. Serve with lemon quarters.

GREEN SALAD W. GARLIC TOAST SQUARES: Toast 2 slices bread, rub with garlic, cut into ½″ squares. Toss greens in French dressing, garnish with toast squares.

WHIPPED AVOCADO: Cut avocado in half. Scoop out pulp. Mash. Add 2 tbs. powdered sugar, 2 tbs. lime juice. Refill shells.

MARCH

Recheck your basic staples—and now have you

molasses
corn meal
ginger
cinnamon
toothpicks
basil
tarragon
almonds
lemons
nutmeg
thin-sliced white bread
curry powder
orange marmalade
powdered sugar
crème de menthe
brown sugar
coarse salt
marjoram
whole cloves

SHOPPING LIST

MEAT

3 lbs. beef round
¾ lb. chopped chuck steak (opt.)
½ flank steak, cut lengthwise, tenderized
½ lb. bacon

FROZEN FOODS

1 box chopped spinach
1 box peas
1 box Brussels sprouts
1 box Lima beans
1 box codfish fillets

FRESH FRUITS AND VEGETABLES

9 small new potatoes
1 bunch celery
2 heads lettuce
1 orange
1 grapefruit
1 bunch parsley
1 bunch watercress
3 green peppers
2 bananas
1 bunch carrots
2 tomatoes
2 or 3 pears

SUNDRIES

1 #2 can grapefruit juice
1 small can tomato purée
½ pt. sour cream
½ pt. heavy cream
1 small can beets
8 oz. macaroni
½ lb. sharp cheese
1 box gingerbread mix
1 #1 can potatoes
1 jar maraschino cherries
1 pkg. vanilla pudding
1 small can potatoes
1 8-oz. can crushed pineapple
1 #1 can tomato juice
1 tube ready-to-bake biscuits
2 boxes ready-to-bake rolls
1 small jar stuffed olives
1 can mock turtle soup
1 can clam broth
1 can condensed cream of mushroom soup
1 can condensed tomato soup

PICK UP ON YOUR WAY HOME

FOR SUN.—1 pt. vanilla ice cream

SUNDAY

TIME 3 HRS. 15 MIN. SERVES 4

Grapefruit Juice
Pot Roast w. Vegetables
Hot Rolls for Dunking
Tossed Green Salad
Indian Pudding w. Ice Cream
Coffee

POT ROAST W. VEGETABLES: 3 lbs. round. Cut slits in meat, push stuffed olives deep down, as many as you wish. Dust meat with seasoned flour. Brown on all sides in own fat. Add 1 c. tomato juice. Cover, simmer 2½ hrs., then add 2 c. sliced, scraped carrots, 9 new potatoes, peeled, 3 sliced onions, 1 c. diced celery. Cook another ½ hr.

INDIAN PUDDING W. ICE CREAM: Slowly stir 4 tbs. yellow corn meal, ¼ tsp. salt into 1½ c. scalded milk in top of double boiler. Cook, stir until thick, about 20 min. Add 2 tbs. butter, 2 tbs. sugar, 3 tbs. molasses, ¼ tsp. ginger, ½ tsp. cinnamon. Pour into casserole, then add 1½ c. cold milk. Bake in slow oven (300°) 3 hrs. Serve warm with scoop of ice cream.

MONDAY

TIME 45 MIN. SERVES 2

Mock Turtle Soup
Nut Loaf
Buttered Beets
Sliced Pears w. Sour Cream
Coffee

MOCK TURTLE SOUP: Heat 1 can mock turtle soup. Add 2 tbs. sherry. Serve with cheese and crackers.

NUT LOAF: Heat 1 #1 can potatoes. Drain. Mash. Add salt, pepper to taste. Chop 1 large celery stalk, boil 5 min. in 1 cup water; drain, saving liquid for Thursday. Combine celery and potatoes with ½ c. chopped nuts, 1½ tbs. butter, 1 beaten egg, ½ tsp. salt, ½ tsp. paprika, 2 tbs. minced onion. (Potatoes may be replaced with ¾ lb. seasoned chopped meat.) Turn into greased pan, bake in hot oven (425°) 30 min. Heat 1 can tomato soup for sauce.

SLICED PEARS W. SOUR CREAM: Blend 1 tbs. top milk with 2 tbs. powdered sugar, ½ c. sour cream. Pour over sliced pears (unpeeled). Sprinkle with grated nutmeg.

TUESDAY

TIME 40 MIN. SERVES 2

Flank Steak Rolls
Spinach w. Cheese
Buttered Peas
Watercress w. Slivered Almonds, French Dressing
Grapefruit Maraschino
Coffee

FLANK STEAK ROLLS: ½ small tenderized flank steak. Rub with salt, pepper, garlic. Cut into 4 strips, place 1 strip bacon on each, roll, toothpick together. Sprinkle with flour, brown on all sides quickly in 1 tbs. butter. Pour on 1 small can tomato purée; add ½ tsp. salt, ⅛ tsp. pepper, ½ chopped onion, pinch of basil. Cover, simmer about 30 min., until tender.

SPINACH W. CHEESE: Drain 1 box defrosted spinach. Mix 2 tbs. butter, 1 tsp. flour, ½ tsp. salt, dash cayenne, 4 tbs. sour cream. Bring to boil. Stir in 3 tbs. grated cheese, ¼ tsp. dry mustard and the spinach. Simmer 5 min.

WATERCRESS W. SLIVERED ALMONDS: Sprinkle ½ bunch watercress with juice ½ lemon. Add ¼ cup slivered almonds. Serve with French dressing.

GRAPEFRUIT MARASCHINO: Halve. Core. Add 1 tbs. maraschino syrup to each half.

WEDNESDAY

TIME 45 MIN. SERVES 2

Macaroni & Cheese
Brussels Sprouts
Hearts of Lettuce Salad
Bananas w. Pineapple
Coffee

MACARONI AND CHEESE: To boiled, drained macaroni (4 oz.), add 1 tsp. grated onion, ½ c. milk, 1 can undiluted cream of mushroom soup, salt and pepper to taste. Alternate layers of macaroni mixture in greased baking dish with layers of grated or cubed sharp cheese (½ lb.). Bake in moderate oven (375°) 30 min.

BANANAS W. PINEAPPLE: Mix 2 sliced bananas, ¼ c. maraschino cherries, ¼ c. crushed pineapple. Top with whipped cream. Save remaining pineapple for Friday.

TIME 45 MIN. SERVES 2

THURSDAY

*Roast Stuffed Peppers
Buttered Lima Beans
Sliced Tomato Salad
Hot Gingerbread w. Orange Sauce
Coffee

ROAST STUFFED PEPPERS: 3 green peppers. Prepare 1½ c. precooked rice, substituting Monday's celery liquid for part of the water. Cut peppers in half lengthwise, remove inner fibers, plunge into boiling water 1 min. Remove, dry, stuff with 1½ c. leftover pot roast, diced or finely shredded, mixed with the prepared rice, ½ minced onion, 1 beaten egg, ½ tsp. salt, ⅛ tsp. pepper. Top with 2 tbs. buttered bread crumbs. Bake in moderate oven (350°) 30 min.

HOT GINGERBREAD W. ORANGE SAUCE: Prepare 1 pkg. gingerbread mix as directed. For sauce, prepare ½ pkg. vanilla pudding. Add ⅓ c. more milk and ½ tsp. grated orange rind. Save ½ gingerbread for tomorrow.

TIME 25 MIN. SERVES 2

FRIDAY

Clam Broth
*Cod Lyonnaise w. Vegetables
Lettuce, Olive Dressing
Southern Biscuits
*Pineapple Gingerbread Squares
Coffee

COD LYONNAISE W. VEGETABLES: Cut 1 box semi-thawed cod into chunks, roll in flour. Sauté in 2 tbs. butter with 1 small can potatoes, drained and sliced. Add leftover vegetables (if none, use #1 can potatoes) cooking until thoroughly heated. Sprinkle with juice ½ lemon.

OLIVE DRESSING: To ½ c. mayonnaise, add 1 tbs. chopped olives, ¼ tsp. parsley.

SOUTHERN BISCUITS: 1 tube. Tuck pinch grated lemon or orange peel into each ready-to-bake biscuit. Bake as directed.

PINEAPPLE GINGERBREAD SQUARES: Cut leftover gingerbread into squares. Cover with pineapple. Top with whipped cream.

SHOPPING LIST

MEAT

2 lbs. short ribs of beef cut in 4 pieces
2 thin slices beef liver, ¾ lb.
2 slices veal cutlet, pounded thin
1 pair sweetbreads
½ broiling chicken, cut up

FROZEN FOODS

2 boxes peas
1 box asparagus
1 box chopped spinach
1 box raspberries

FRESH FRUITS AND VEGETABLES

4 bananas
4 sweet potatoes
1 bunch parsley
¼ lb. endive
4 seedless oranges
1 small head cabbage
1 head iceberg lettuce
1 small bunch carrots
1 small cucumber
1 apple
2 pears

SUNDRIES

1 small box dates
1 small can tomato paste
1 4-oz. can mushrooms
½ pt. sour cream
½ pt. heavy cream
¼ lb. Cheddar cheese, sliced thin
1 small can tuna fish flakes
1 can baked apples
1 small can beets
1 small jar Bar-le-Duc jam
1 small pkg. cream cheese
2 dessert shells
1 small jar peanut butter
1 can applesauce
2 small cans apple juice
1 12-oz. can vegetable juice
1 box ready-to-bake rolls
2 cans black bean soup
1 can pea soup, condensed
1 can cream of mushroom soup
1 can chicken broth
1 can tomato soup

PICK UP ON YOUR WAY HOME

TUES.—corn bread

TIME 2 HRS. SERVES 4

SUNDAY

Black Bean Soup
Braised Short Ribs
Green Peas
Guatemalan Sweet Potatoes
Stuffed Baked Apples
Coffee

BRAISED SHORT RIBS: 4 pieces, about 2 lbs. Roll in flour. Place in pot. Cover. Brown in hot oven (450°) about 30 min., then sprinkle with salt and pepper, spread with ¼ c. ketchup, add 2 sliced onions, ¾ c. boiling water. Reduce heat to moderate (350°), bake covered 1½ hrs.

GUATEMALAN SWEET POTATOES: Boil 4 sweet potatoes. Peel. Mash with 2 bananas. Season with ⅓ tsp. salt, dash nutmeg. Add 2 tbs. milk, then 1 egg beaten until frothy, more milk if necessary. Place in greased baking dish. Bake 20 min.

STUFFED BAKED APPLES: 1 can. Fill centers with sliced dates. Heat. Serve warm with cream.

TIME 25 MIN. SERVES 2

MONDAY

Apple Juice
Liver w. Orange & Rice
Cole Slaw
Hot Rolls
Raspberries w. Sour Cream
Coffee

LIVER W. ORANGE & RICE: Dust 2 thin slices beef liver lightly with mixture of 3 tbs. flour, 1 tsp. dry mustard, ½ tsp. salt, ⅛ tsp. pepper. Brown in 2 tbs. butter. Stir in 1 small minced onion, then 4 tbs. white wine, 1 tsp. mixed dried herbs. Simmer over very low heat. Brown 1 sliced orange in 1 tbs. salad oil. Drain. Sprinkle with ½ tsp. sugar. Serve liver and sauce over 1½ c. prepared precooked rice. Top with browned orange.

COLE SLAW: Shred ½ cabbage. Mix with 1 chopped apple, ½ chopped onion. Combine 2 tbs. lemon juice, ½ c. whipped cream, 1 tsp. dry mustard, sugar to taste. Mix well with cabbage.

TUESDAY

TIME 35 MIN. SERVES 2

Sweetbreads w. Pea Purée
Buttered Beets
Corn Bread
Orange & Endive Salad
Apple Charlotte
Coffee

SWEETBREADS W. PEA PURÉE: Dip 1 pair sweetbreads in boiling water. Remove skin and waste. Sauté in 1 tbs. butter until golden brown. Stir in 1 tsp. flour, 3 tbs. sherry, 1 can mushrooms with liquid, salt and pepper to taste. Simmer 12 min. Serve over heated undiluted pea soup.

ORANGE & ENDIVE SALAD: Peel and slice seedless orange. Toss with endive and 1 tsp. dried mint. Serve with French dressing.

APPLE CHARLOTTE: Line small baking dish with thin slices bread dipped in ¼ c. melted butter, reserving 1 piece for top. Fill with 1 can apple sauce mixed with 1 tbs. lemon juice. Top with bread sprinkled with 2 tbs. sugar. Bake in moderate oven (425°) 30 min.

WEDNESDAY

TIME 35 MIN. SERVES 2

Tomato & Mushroom Soup
Chicken & Onions
**Hot Buttered Cabbage*
Grated Carrot Salad
Pears w. Cream Cheese & Bar-le-Duc
Coffee

TOMATO & MUSHROOM SOUP: Combine ½ can mushroom, ½ can tomato (reserve remainder for Friday), 1 soup can milk. Beat smooth. Simmer.

CHICKEN & ONIONS: ½ broiler, cut up. Rub with garlic, salt, pepper, brush with salad oil. Broil skin side up until brown. Slice 2 large onions, sauté in 1½ tbs. butter in large frying pan. Stir in 1½ tbs. flour, then ½ tsp. salt, ⅛ tsp. white pepper, ½ tsp. chopped parsley, 1 tsp. lemon juice. Add browned chicken, cook over low heat until tender, about 20 min.

HOT BUTTERED CABBAGE: Slice ½ cabbage. Boil, covered, in very little salted water until just tender. Add salt and pepper to taste, 1 tbs. butter.

TIME 30 MIN. SERVES 2

THURSDAY

Sherried Vegetable Juice
Veal, Spinach & Cheese
Asparagus w. Butter Sauce
Orange Shortcake
Coffee

SHERRIED VEGETABLE JUICE: Add 1 tbs. sherry to each glass chilled.

VEAL, SPINACH & CHEESE: 2 veal cutlets, pounded very thin. Brown quickly in 1 tbs. butter. Add 2 tbs. tomato paste, ½ c. bouillon, 1 bay leaf, salt, pepper. Simmer 10 min. Prepare 1 box spinach as directed. Drain. Stir in 2 tbs. sour cream. Place on heatproof platter, cover with veal and sauce, top with 2 slices Cheddar. Broil until cheese melts.

ASPARAGUS W. BUTTER SAUCE: 1 box. Prepare as directed. Dress with 2 tbs. melted butter mixed with 2 dashes Tabasco, 1 tsp. tarragon vinegar, 1 tsp. chopped parsley.

ORANGE SHORTCAKE: Fill 2 dessert shells with orange segments. Boil ⅓ c. sugar, ⅓ c. orange juice 1 min. Add 1 tsp. grated orange rind. Pour over all.

TIME 25 MIN. SERVES 2

FRIDAY

**Chicken-Wednesday Soup*
Tuna Fish Curry
Rice
Lettuce w. Cucumber Dressing
Macaroon Bananas
Coffee

CHICKEN-WEDNESDAY SOUP: Heat 1 can chicken broth, ½ can each mushroom soup, tomato soup, water.

TUNA FISH CURRY: In top of double boiler blend 2 tbs. flour, 4 tbs. melted butter with 1 tsp. curry powder. Add 1 c. milk. Cook, stirring until thick and smooth. Add ¼ c. sherry, pinch of sugar, 1 tbs. minced parsley, 1 can tuna, flaked, salt and pepper to taste. Cover. Cook 20 min. Serve with 1½ cups prepared precooked rice.

CUCUMBER DRESSING: To ½ c. French dressing add ¼ c. grated cucumber, ½ tsp. prepared mustard.

MACAROON BANANAS: Mix 2 tbs. peanut butter, ⅓ c. sugar, 2 tbs. lemon juice. Spread over 2 sliced, peeled bananas in greased pan. Bake in moderate oven (375°) 20 min.

SHOPPING LIST

MEAT

3½ lbs. precooked boneless ham, butt end
1¼ lbs. ground lamb
5 frankfurters
1¼ lbs. porterhouse steak, 1½″ thick
½ lb. bacon

FROZEN FOODS

2 boxes peas
1 box corn
1 box sliced peaches
1 box string beans
1 box French-fried potatoes
1 box fillet of sole
1 box whipped potatoes

FRESH FRUITS AND VEGETABLES

2 heads lettuce
1 bunch parsley
4 Idaho potatoes
1 bunch chicory
1 bunch celery
1 bunch watercress
1 bunch chives
1 small eggplant
4 tomatoes
1 green pepper

SUNDRIES

1 pkg. fruit gelatin
1 8-oz. can pineapple chunks
1 small bottle chocolate sprinkles
¼ lb. Roquefort cheese
1 #1 can potatoes
1 small jar marrons in syrup
½ pt. heavy cream
1 small pkg. oatmeal cookies
1 4-oz. can sliced mushrooms
½ pt. sour cream
1 8-oz. can fruit cocktail
sweet and sour pickles
1 can vegetable soup

PICK UP ON YOUR WAY HOME

FOR SUN.—1½ pts. vanilla ice cream
MON.—2 or 3 chocolate cupcakes
THUR.—1 pt. strawberries
1 box spongecake shells

TIME 1 HR. SERVES 4

SUNDAY

Orange Marmalade Baked Ham
Peas w. Mustard Butter
Baked Potatoes
Mixed Greens
Marrons Glacés
Coffee

ORANGE MARMALADE BAKED HAM: 3½ lbs. precooked, boneless. Score fat, dot with cloves, spread with ½ c. orange marmalade. Bake in moderate oven (375°) 45 min. Baste with orange juice.

PEAS W. MUSTARD BUTTER: 2 boxes. Cook as directed. Serve with 2 tbs. melted butter mixed with 1½ tsp. prepared mustard, salt and pepper to taste.

BAKED POTATOES: 4 Idaho. Rub with butter. Bake at least 50 min. at 375°. Serve halved, add pat of butter, grated cheese.

MIXED GREENS: Mix chicory with watercress. Toss with French dressing.

MARRONS GLACÉS: Pour 2 tbs. marrons with syrup over each serving of vanilla ice cream.

TIME 30 MIN. SERVES 2

MONDAY

Broiled Lamb Patties
Whole Kernel Corn w. Dried Herbs
Lettuce & Chicory Salad
Devil's Food Mounds
Coffee

BROILED LAMB PATTIES: Combine 1¼ lbs. ground lamb with 2 tbs. grated onion, 1 tsp. salt, ⅛ tsp. pepper, 1 tbs. Worcestershire sauce. Mold into 8 patties. Dot with butter, broil. Save 2 patties for Wednesday.

WHOLE KERNEL CORN W. DRIED HERBS: 1 box. Prepare as directed. Add 1 tbs. melted butter mixed with 1 tsp. mixed dried herbs.

DEVIL'S FOOD MOUNDS: Smother plain chocolate cupcakes with whipped cream and chocolate sprinkles.

FOR TOMORROW: Prepare ½ box fruit gelatin as directed. Add pineapple chunks.

TUESDAY

TIME 50 MIN. SERVES 2

Bouillon w. Celery Curls
**Ham-Filled Eggplant*
Buttered String Beans
Pineapple Gelatin
Coffee

BOUILLON W. CELERY CURLS: Simmer 2 c. bouillon. Serve garnished with celery curls.

HAM-FILLED EGGPLANT: Cut eggplant in half lengthwise. Scoop out meat, dice, add 1 minced onion, 1 chopped green pepper, 2 diced tomatoes, ¼ c. boiling water. Cook rapidly until tender, about 10 min. Drain, mash, add 1 tbs. butter, ½ tsp. salt, ⅛ tsp. pepper, 1 c. diced leftover ham. Fill shells with mixture. Place in greased baking dish, top with buttered crumbs. Bake in hot oven (450°) 40 min., or until shell is tender.

WEDNESDAY

TIME 25 MIN. SERVES 2

Fruit Cocktail
**Stuffed Frankfurters*
Hashed Brown Potatoes
Lettuce & Tomato Salad
Oatmeal Cookies
Coffee

STUFFED FRANKFURTERS: 5. Mash 2½ tbs. Roquefort cheese with leftover lamb patties. Split frankfurters open lengthwise. Fill with mixture, bind with strips of bacon. Broil until bacon is crisp, frankfurters piping hot.

HASHED BROWN POTATOES: 1 can. Dice and season. Heat 2 tbs. oil in frying pan, add potatoes, press down with spatula, packing tightly. Fry slowly without stirring. When brown underneath, fold over omelet-style and serve.

LETTUCE & TOMATO SALAD: Lettuce and tomatoes on individual plates. Serve with French dressing.

TIME 25 MIN. SERVES 2

THURSDAY

Mock Onion Soup
Broiled Porterhouse
French-Fried Potatoes
Sweet & Sour Pickles
Strawberry Shortcake
Coffee

MOCK ONION SOUP: Add 3 finely chopped onions, 1 tsp. parsley to 2 c. bouillon. Simmer until onions are soft. Add salt, pepper to taste. Serve with floats of toast rubbed with garlic and heavily sprinkled with grated cheese.

BROILED PORTERHOUSE: 1½ lbs., 1½″ thick. Preheat broiler, grease, rub with garlic if liked. For rare, allow 12 to 15 min., turning occasionally; for well done, 25–30 min. Salt, pepper both sides, spread with butter when done.

FRENCH-FRIED POTATOES: 1 box. Prepare as directed.

STRAWBERRY SHORTCAKE: Wash and hull strawberries, slice, sprinkle with powdered sugar. Pile in dessert shells, top with whipped cream.

TIME 45 MIN. SERVES 2

FRIDAY

Vegetable Soup w. Sour Cream
Fillet of Sole w. Mushrooms
Whipped Potatoes
Scalloped Peaches
Coffee

VEGETABE SOUP W. SOUR CREAM: 1 can vegetable soup. Prepare as directed. Serve piping hot with blobs of cold sour cream.

FILLET OF SOLE W. MUSHROOMS: 1 box, defrosted. Dust with flour, season, dip in beaten egg, then in bread crumbs. Fry in 3 tbs. butter until brown. Simmer ¼ c. chopped chives, 1 finely chopped onion in 3 tbs. oil. Add 1 4-oz. can sliced mushrooms, well drained, 1 tbs. butter, 1 tsp. minced parsley, 1 tsp. tarragon, 1 tbs. lemon juice. Serve over fish.

SCALLOPED PEACHES: Mix 1 box defrosted peaches with ½ c. dry bread crumbs, ¼ tsp. cinnamon, 2 tbs. melted butter. Bake covered 25 min. Uncover. Bake 15 min. more.

SHOPPING LIST

MEAT

4 lbs. roasting chicken
3 shoulder lamb chops
3 veal chops
½ lb. bacon

FROZEN FOODS

2 boxes broccoli
1 box Brussels sprouts
1 box chopped spinach
1 box potato puffs
1 pkg. corn on the cob
1 small box peas

FRESH FRUITS AND VEGETABLES

1 head escarole
1 pear
1 head lettuce
1 banana
1 Bermuda onion
1 bunch watercress
1 small bunch chives
2 limes
1 small cucumber
1 bunch parsley
1 grapefruit
2 apples
1 lb. tomatoes
1 green pepper

SUNDRIES

1 pt. sour cream
1 #1 can greengage plums
1 small can pimiento
1 small can vegetable juice
¼ lb. Camembert cheese
½ lb. green noodles
1 #1 can pickled beets
¼ lb. Cheddar cheese
1 pkg. poultry stuffing
1 small box cornflakes
1 can condensed cream of mushroom soup
2 cans condensed tomato soup
1 can pepper pot soup
1 can condensed pea soup

PICK UP ON YOUR WAY HOME

FOR SUN.—1 pt. lemon ice
TUES.—1 6-oz. can boned chicken if needed
FRI.—2 salmon steaks
½ pt. light cream

TIME 2 HRS. SERVES 4

SUNDAY

Tomato-Pea Soup
Roast Chicken
Broccoli, Horseradish Sauce
Bacon-Stuffed Potatoes
Tossed Salad
Lemon Ice w. Crème de Menthe
Coffee

TOMATO-PEA SOUP: 1 can tomato soup, 1 can pea soup. Combine. Add 1½ soup cans milk. Simmer. Add 1 tbs. cream just before serving.

ROAST CHICKEN: 1 4-lb. chicken. Stuff with prepared poultry stuffing. Brush with melted bacon fat. Roast 1 hr. in moderate oven (350°), then add 1½ c. sherry, roast 45 min. more. Baste often.

BROCCOLI W. HORSERADISH SAUCE: 2 boxes. Prepare as directed. Heat 1 c. sour cream, ½ tsp. prepared horseradish, ½ tsp. prepared mustard, salt and pepper to taste. Serve over broccoli.

BACON-STUFFED POTATOES: 4 Idaho. Rub with butter, bake 55 min. at 350°. Split open, tuck in 1 slice crumbled bacon, pat of butter. Sprinkle with paprika.

TIME 20 MIN. SERVES 2

MONDAY

Cinnamon Lamb Chops
Buttered Brussels Sprouts
Spanish Salad
Mixed Fruit in Lime Juice
Coffee

CINNAMON LAMB CHOPS: 3 shoulder. Rub with ½ tsp. cinnamon, ¾ tsp. salt, ⅛ tsp. pepper. Dip in 1 beaten egg, cornflake crumbs, again into egg, again into crumbs. Sauté in 3 tbs. butter about 20 min., until tender.

BUTTERED BRUSSELS SPROUTS: 1 box. Cook as directed. (Save liquid for tomorrow.) Dress with 2 tbs. melted butter, sprinkle with grated cheese.

SPANISH SALAD: Cover 1 sliced Bermuda onion with French dressing. Let stand 15 min. Toss with watercress, sliced pimiento, slices of cucumber.

MIXED FRUIT IN LIME JUICE: Peel and slice 1 pear, 1 banana. Sweeten juice 2 limes to taste, pour over fruit.

TUESDAY

TIME 20 MIN. SERVES 2

**Vegetable Cocktail*
**Chicken à la King w. Rice*
Broiled Tomatoes
Camembert Cheese & Crackers
Coffee

VEGETABLE COCKTAIL: To 1 can vegetable juice add Brussels sprout liquor to taste and lots of coarse black pepper. Serve with lemon quarters.

CHICKEN À LA KING W. RICE: To 1 can cream of mushroom soup add 1 box defrosted peas, dash paprika, pinch sage, ½ minced green pepper, 1 sliced pimiento, 1½ c. diced leftover chicken (or 1 small can). Simmer 5 min. Add ¼ c. sherry. Serve over 1½ c. prepared precooked rice.

BROILED TOMATOES: 2. Slice. Place in greased pan. Dot with butter, 1 finely minced garlic clove. Sprinkle with salt and pepper. Broil under low heat. Do not turn.

WEDNESDAY

TIME 30 MIN. SERVES 2

Veal Chops Paprika
Buttered Green Noodles
Iceberg Lettuce, Egg Dressing
Broiled Grapefruit
Coffee

VEAL CHOPS PAPRIKA: 3 chops. Rub with ¾ tsp. salt, ⅛ tsp. pepper, 1 tsp. paprika. Brown in bacon fat with 1 chopped onion. Stir in 1 can undiluted tomato soup, 3 tbs. sour cream. Cover, simmer about 20 min. Serve with prepared green noodles, buttered and sprinkled with 2 slices crumbled bacon.

EGG DRESSING: To ½ c. mayonnaise add 1 minced hard-cooked egg, 1 tbs. minced onion.

BROILED GRAPEFRUIT: 2 halves. Core, loosen segments. Dot each with ½ tbs. butter, sprinkle with 2 tbs. brown sugar. Broil 15 min. under low heat. Add 1 tbs. sherry to each.

TIME 30 MIN. SERVES 2 **THURSDAY**

Pepper Pot Soup
Cheese & Spinach Patties
Corn on the Cob
Tossed Salad, Sour Cream Dressing
Greengage Plums
Coffee

CHEESE & SPINACH PATTIES: Heat 2 tbs. butter, add ¼ c. flour, blend well. Add ¼ tsp. salt, ¼ tsp. paprika, ½ c. milk. Stir over medium heat until thick. Add 1 slightly beaten egg yolk, ¼ c. cubed Cheddar cheese, ½ box chopped spinach completely thawed and thoroughly drained. Heat, stir until cheese melts. Cool. Flour hands, shape mixture into 6 patties. Sauté in 2 tbs. butter. Garnish with crisp bacon.

CORN ON THE COB: 1 box completely thawed. Cook as directed. Serve with coarse salt and melted butter.

SOUR CREAM DRESSING: Add 2 tbs. sour cream, 1 tbs. lemon juice, 1 tbs. chopped chives to ¼ cup French dressing. Toss with greens.

TIME 20 MIN. SERVES 2 **FRIDAY**

Broiled Salmon w. Herbs
Spiced Beets
Potato Puffs
Pan-Fried Apples
Coffee

BROILED SALMON W. HERBS: 2 salmon steaks. Mix together 1 tbs. grated onion, 3 tbs. melted butter, juice of 1 lemon, ½ tsp. salt, ⅛ tsp. pepper, ¼ tsp. marjoram, 1 tbs. minced parsley, 1 tbs. chopped watercress or chives. Place fish on rack under broiler. Pour on half the mixture. Broil 5 min. Turn, cover with remaining sauce, continue broiling until done. Garnish with watercress.

SPICED BEETS: Place 1 can pickled beets in saucepan. Add 5 whole cloves. Heat. Drain, serve with pat of butter.

PAN-FRIED APPLES: Slice 2 unpeeled apples ¼″ thick. Fry slowly in 2 tbs. butter 5–10 min. Sprinkle with sugar. Serve with cream.

APRIL

Recheck your basic staples—and now have you

marjoram
thyme
brown sugar
sage
lemons
vanilla
caraway seeds
powdered sugar
crackers
cinnamon
celery seeds
capers
nutmeg
biscuit mix
salted crackers
instant coffee
coarse salt
whole cloves

SHOPPING LIST

MEAT

2 lbs. chuck steak cut in 1" pieces
6 lamb kidneys

FROZEN FOODS

1 can orange juice
1 box peaches
1 box broccoli
1 box cut green beans
1 box haddock fillet

FRESH FRUITS AND VEGETABLES

1 bunch carrots
1 bunch celery
2 heads lettuce
1 cucumber
2 tomatoes
4 potatoes
1 small pineapple
1 bunch parsley
½ lb. grapes

SUNDRIES

1 #2 can tomato juice
½ pt. sour cream
1 #1 can potatoes
½ lb. noodles
1 pkg. poultry stuffing
1 small pkg. shelled pistachio nuts
1 12-oz. can vegetable juice
1 small jar tartar sauce
1 small jar ripe pitted olives
1 small can shredded coconut
1 small can pimiento
1 4-oz. can sliced mushrooms
1 pkg. cornflakes
1 pkg. custard flavor dessert
1 small can Kadota figs
2 slices poundcake
1 container ready-whipped cream
1 pkg. vanilla dessert
1 pkg. piecrust mix
1 portion Roquefort cheese
1 #1 can carrots
1 pkg. quick oats
1 can condensed cream of mushroom soup
1 can cream of asparagus soup
1 can chicken broth
1 can condensed tomato soup
1 can pea soup

PICK UP ON YOUR WAY HOME

WED.—2-lb. broiler (whole)
THUR.—½ lb. ground veal

SUNDAY

TIME 3 HRS. SERVES 4

Hot Tomato Juice
Beef Stew w. Vegetables
Green Salad
Floating Island
Coffee

HOT TOMATO JUICE: Add 1 tbs. frozen orange juice to 1 can tomato juice. Season with salt, cayenne. Simmer. Serve hot.

BEEF STEW W. VEGETABLES: 2 lbs. chuck steak in 1″ pieces. Dust with 1 tbs. flour. Brown quickly on all sides in 1 tbs. fat in heavy saucepan. Add 2 c. boiling water, 1 bay leaf, 3 chopped onions, 1 tbs. minced parsley, ¼ tsp. dried marjoram, ¼ tsp. dry mustard, 1 tsp. salt, ¼ tsp. pepper, 1 tbs. Worcestershire. Cover. Simmer 2 hrs., then add 6 carrots, sliced, 4 stalks celery, sliced, 6 small onions, 4 quartered potatoes, peeled. Cover. Simmer about ½ hr., until vegetables are done.

FLOATING ISLAND: Prepare 1 pkg. custard dessert as directed. Chill in serving bowl. Garnish with mounds of whipped cream.

MONDAY

TIME 30 MIN. SERVES 2

Pea Soup
Mustard Kidneys on Rice
Carrots Caruso
Lettuce w. Roquefort Dressing
Kadota Figs
Coffee

PEA SOUP: 1 can. Prepare as directed. When simmering, whip in 1 beaten egg yolk. Remove from heat. Stir in 1 tbs. butter.

MUSTARD KIDNEYS ON RICE: 6 lamb. Dip in boiling water. Slice thin, discarding cores and tubes. Sauté quickly in 2 tbs. butter. Remove. Add another tbs. butter to pan, put in 1 crushed garlic clove, ½ can drained sliced mushrooms. Lower heat. Stir in 1 tbs. flour, then 1 c. bouillon. Bring to boil. Stir in 3 tbs. red wine, 2 tbs. sour cream mixed with 1 tbs. dry mustard. Add kidneys. Simmer 15 min. Serve over 1½ c. prepared precooked rice.

CARROTS CARUSO: 1 can. Drain, add ½ tsp. thyme, ¼ c. cream. Heat.

TIME 25 MIN. SERVES 2

TUESDAY

**Leftover Stew w. Sour Cream*
Buttered Noodles
Shredded Lettuce & Tomato Salad
Quick Peach Upside Down Cake
Coffee

LEFTOVER STEW W. SOUR CREAM: Add leftover mushrooms (with liquid) to leftover stew. Stir in 3 tbs. sour cream, ¼ c. sherry. Simmer 10 min. Serve over buttered noodles (4 oz.) prepared as directed on package.

SHREDDED LETTUCE & TOMATO SALAD: Toss shredded lettuce, sliced tomatoes, and 1 tbs. finely chopped pistachio nuts with ¼ c. French dressing.

QUICK PEACH UPSIDE DOWN CAKE: Melt 1 tbs. butter in shallow baking pan. Sprinkle with ¼ c. brown sugar. Pour in 1 box defrosted peaches. Cover with 2 slices poundcake. Bake in hot oven (450°) about 15 min. Serve warm, fruit side up, with whipped cream.

TIME 55 MIN. SERVES 2

WEDNESDAY

Vegetable Juice
Roast Stuffed Broiler
Mushroom Sauce
Broccoli w. Grapes
Coffee Cream Pie
Coffee

ROAST STUFFED BROILER: Stuff 2-lb. broiler with prepared stuffing, ¼ tsp. sage. Brush with melted butter, sprinkle with salt, pepper. Bake in moderately hot oven (425°) 35–40 min., turning and basting occasionally with additional melted butter. Heat undiluted cream of mushroom soup and serve as gravy.

BROCCOLI W. GRAPES: 1 box. Cook as directed. Drain. Garnish with ½ c. halved seeded grapes heated in 2 tbs. butter.

COFFEE CREAM PIE: Prepare baked pie shell with piecrust mix. Add 1 tbs. instant coffee and 2 tbs. sugar to 1 pkg. vanilla pudding. Prepare as directed. Cool slightly. Fill baked pie shell. Chill. Garnish with whipped cream.

THURSDAY

TIME 20 MIN. SERVES 2

Asparagus & Chicken Soup
Veal Patties w. Tomato Sauce
Green Bean Salad
Sliced Fresh Pineapple
Coffee

ASPARAGUS & CHICKEN SOUP: Combine 1 can chicken broth with 1 can asparagus soup. Add ½ c. water, salt, pepper to taste, and slivers of leftover chicken, if any.

VEAL PATTIES W. TOMATO SAUCE: Combine ½ lb. ground veal with ⅓ c. quick-cooking oats, ½ tsp. salt, ⅛ tsp. pepper, ½ tsp. Worcestershire, 1 beaten egg. Shape into small patties. Sauté until well browned in 2 tbs. butter. Serve with 1 can heated condensed tomato soup.

GREEN BEAN SALAD: Prepare ½ box green beans as directed. Drain. Mix 1 tbs. lemon juice, 1 tbs. minced onion, ¼ c. chopped celery, strips of pimiento with ¼ c. French dressing. Pour over hot green beans, garnish with lettuce.

FRIDAY

TIME 25 MIN. SERVES 2

Baked Cornflake Fish
Parsley Potatoes
Cucumber Salad, Olive Dressing
**Pineapple in Whipped Cream*
Coffee

BAKED CORNFLAKE FISH: 1 box fillets, defrosted. Brush with mayonnaise. Sprinkle with salt and pepper. Dip in crushed cornflakes. Place in buttered baking dish, dot with butter. Bake in very hot oven (500°) 10–15 min., until well browned. Serve with tartar sauce.

PARSLEY POTATOES: Boil 1 can potatoes. Drain. Season. Roll in melted butter, then in minced parsley.

CUCUMBER SALAD, OLIVE DRESSING: Chop 8 ripe olives, add to ¼ c. French dressing. Serve over 1 thinly sliced chilled cucumber. Garnish with paprika.

PINEAPPLE IN WHIPPED CREAM: Chunk leftover pineapple, sprinkle with shredded coconut, and smother with whipped cream.

SHOPPING LIST

MEAT

½ lb. chipped beef
2 or 3 veal chops
6 chicken livers
2 shoulder lamb chops
2 small round steaks

FROZEN FOODS

1 box mixed vegetables
1 box chopped spinach
1 box cut green beans
1 box peas
1 box raspberries
1 box whipped potatoes

FRESH FRUITS AND VEGETABLES

1 lb. rhubarb
1½ lbs. asparagus
2 heads lettuce
2 grapefruit
1 green pepper
2 tomatoes
6 or 7 new potatoes
2 pears
1 bunch parsley
1 orange
1 apple

SUNDRIES

1 small can crab meat flakes
1 small pkg. ground almonds
1 4-oz. can sliced mushrooms
8 oz. thin spaghetti
1 sponge layer
1 pkg. vanilla junket
2 portions Roquefort cheese
1 can vegetable juice
1 can cream of chicken soup
1 can condensed tomato soup

PICK UP ON YOUR WAY HOME

FOR SUN.—1 pt. brick ice cream
MON.—assorted cookies
WED.—1 pt. strawberries
FRI.—½ lb. cod fillet
½ pt. heavy cream

SUNDAY

TIME 30 MIN. SERVES 4

Broiled Grapefruit
Chipped Beef
Jacket Potatoes
Fresh Asparagus Salad
Baked Alaska
Coffee

BROILED GRAPEFRUIT: 4 halves. Core, loosen segments, pour 1 tbs. sherry over each half. Sprinkle with 2 tbs. brown sugar, dot with butter. Broil under low heat about 15 min.

CHIPPED BEEF: ½-lb. pkg. Shred meat. Brown in ¼ c. butter. Season with pepper. Stir in 3 tbs. flour. Brown flour, then add 1½ c. milk gradually and bring to boil slowly, stirring constantly. Serve on toast, sprinkle with ¼ c. ground almonds.

BAKED ALASKA: Beat 3 egg whites until stiff, folding in 3 tbs. sugar, 1 tsp. vanilla, dash salt. Place ice cream on sponge layer trimmed to leave 1″ border. Completely cover with egg whites. Bake in hot oven (450°) about 5 min., until light brown.

MONDAY

TIME 40 MIN. SERVES 2

Veal Chops in Wine w. Mushrooms
Caraway Vegetables
Stewed Rhubarb & Cookies
Tea

VEAL CHOPS IN WINE W. MUSHROOMS: 2 or 3 chops. Dip in seasoned flour. Sauté until brown in 2 tbs. butter. Remove chops to casserole. Stir ½ c. white wine into drippings. Simmer until thickened, adding 1 tsp. flour if necessary. Pour over chops. Cover with 1 can sliced mushrooms, drained, dot with butter. Cover. Bake about 20 min. in hot oven (450°), until chops are tender.

CARAWAY VEGETABLES: Prepare 1 box mixed vegetables as directed. Drain. Add salt, pepper to taste, 1 tbs. butter. Stir in 1 tbs. caraway seeds.

STEWED RHUBARB: Trim and wash 1 lb. rhubarb, cut in 1″ pieces. Place in top of double boiler, stir in ½ c. sugar. Cook, covered, over boiling water about 30 min., until soft. Chill.

TIME 35 MIN. SERVES 2

TUESDAY

California Vegetable Cocktail
Spaghetti w. Chicken Liver Sauce
**Mixed Vegetable Salad*
Pears w. Roquefort Cheese
Coffee

CALIFORNIA VEGETABLE COCKTAIL: Mix 1 c. vegetable juice with ½ c. orange juice. Serve very cold.

CHICKEN LIVER SAUCE: Brown 6 chicken livers in 4 tbs. butter over high heat. Remove livers, chop. Add 2 minced garlic cloves, 1 large sliced onion, pinch dry mustard, 1 tbs. flour, ½ tsp. salt, ⅛ tsp. pepper. Stir in ½ c. beef bouillon, 1 tbs. mixed herbs, the chopped livers. Simmer until onion is soft, about 20 min. Serve over boiled, drained spaghetti (8 oz.).

MIXED VEGETABLE SALAD: Combine ¼ box chopped spinach, semi-thawed, with leftover mixed vegetables. Mix well with ¼ c. tart French dressing. Serve on lettuce, garnish with hard-cooked egg, yolk and white chopped separately.

TIME 40 MIN. SERVES 2

WEDNESDAY

Cream of Chicken Soup
Hot Salted Pan Steaks
**Spinach & Onions*
Tossed Green Salad
Strawberries Romanoff
Coffee

CREAM OF CHICKEN SOUP: 1 can. Prepare as directed. Garnish with chopped green pepper.

HOT SALTED PAN STEAKS: 2 round. Brush with tarragon vinegar. Sear in dry hot salted pan (½ tsp. salt). Add 1 tbs. butter. Cook until tender.

SPINACH & ONIONS: ¾ box spinach. Add 1 small sliced onion, 1 tbs. red wine. Cook as directed.

TOSSED GREEN SALAD: Serve garnished with grated cheese.

STRAWBERRIES ROMANOFF: Wash and hull 1 pt. strawberries. Sprinkle with 2 tbs. powdered sugar mixed with 1 tsp. grated orange rind. Pour on ½ c. red wine. Chill.

THURSDAY

TIME 45 MIN. SERVES 2

Lamb Chops in the Bag
Apple Mashed Potatoes
**Buttered Green Beans*
Lettuce & Tomato Salad
**Vanilla Junket w. Rhubarb*
Coffee

LAMB CHOPS IN THE BAG: 2 shoulder chops. Season with salt, pepper, few grains cayenne. Brown quickly over high heat. Chop 2 hard-cooked eggs, add 2 tbs. melted butter, ½ tsp. chopped parsley, 1 pinch dried thyme, ¼ tsp. salt, ⅛ tsp. pepper, 2 crumbled crackers, ½ tsp. grated onion. Place each chop on a large round of paper, greased on both sides. Pile egg mixture on chops, dot with butter. Fold paper over, twist ends closed. Bake in shallow dish in a hot oven (425°) 25 min.

APPLE MASHED POTATOES: Prepare ½ box whipped potatoes as directed. Beat in 1 grated apple, peeled and cored, pinch of cinnamon, a little extra milk to make smooth and creamy, salt and pepper to taste.

FRIDAY

TIME 30 MIN. SERVES 2

French Fish Potpourri
Peas & Cheese
Sherried Raspberry Squares
Coffee

FRENCH FISH POTPOURRI: Combine 1 can condensed tomato soup with 1½ c. beef bouillon. Bring to simmer. Add ½ lb. cod fillet, chunked, 1 small can crab meat flakes, ½ tsp. salt, ¼ tsp. pepper, few grains cayenne. Simmer about 10 min. Add ½ c. sherry. Serve over dry toast rubbed with garlic.

PEAS & CHEESE: Cook 1 box peas. Drain, sprinkle with 2 tbs. grated cheese. Add ¼ c. *warmed* French dressing, serve on lettuce leaves.

SHERRIED RASPBERRY SQUARES: Cut ½ box frozen raspberries into squares. Spoon 1 tbs. sherry over each. Top with whipped cream. Serve rest for breakfast.

SHOPPING LIST

MEAT

4 tenderloin steaks
2 veal cutlets
¾ lb. chopped chuck steak

FROZEN FOODS

1 box peas
1 box potato puffs
3 boxes French-fried potatoes
1 pkg. cooked shrimps
1 box haddock fillets

FRESH FRUITS AND VEGETABLES

1 bunch watercress
2 limes
4 tart apples
2 heads lettuce
8 tomatoes
1 bunch carrots
2 green peppers
1 Bermuda onion
1 bunch celery
½ lb. grapes

SUNDRIES

1 small can minced oysters
1 lb. can chili con carne
1 small can anchovy fillets
1 8-oz. can grapefruit segments
1 small can potatoes
½ pt. sour cream
1 small can apricots
1 box salted crackers
2 or 3 portions Camembert
1 jar mint jelly
6 ladyfingers
1 can carrots
1 can condensed cream of celery soup
1 can condensed tomato soup

PICK UP ON YOUR WAY HOME

FOR SUN.—1½ pts. lemon sherbet
WED.—2 hamburger buns
THUR.—1 lb. asparagus
½ pt. heavy cream
FRI.—4 bran muffins

SUNDAY

TIME 25 MIN. SERVES 4

Cuban Shrimp Cocktail
Sliced Steaks
Raw Vegetable Salad
French-Fried Potatoes
Lemon Sherbet
Coffee

CUBAN SHRIMP COCKTAIL: 1 pkg. defrosted shrimps. Arrange on lettuce in serving glasses. For sauce, cover with 1 c. mayonnaise mixed with ½ c. sour cream, 1 tbs. minced watercress, ¼ tsp. salt, ⅛ tsp. pepper, freshly squeezed lime juice to taste.

SLICED STEAKS: 4 tenderloins. Rub with salt, pepper, ½ tsp. dry mustard. Broil. Butter when done. (Remove tail ends and set aside for Tuesday.) Serve sliced.

RAW VEGETABLE SALAD: Cut 4 carrots into matchsticks, toss with 4 stalks celery, diced, 2 green peppers, diced, 3 sliced tomatoes, 1 sliced Bermuda onion, ½ box defrosted peas, 1 head lettuce, chunked, and ½ c. French dressing. Garnish with anchovy fillets.

MONDAY

TIME 35 MIN. SERVES 2

Chili Con Carne
Rice
Lettuce & Tomato Salad
Mocha Pudding
Coffee

CHILI CON CARNE: 1 can. Heat. Serve over 1½ c. prepared precooked rice.

MOCHA PUDDING: Cream 3 tbs. butter, beat in ½ c. brown sugar, ¼ tsp. vanilla, then 2 egg yolks, and 1 tsp. instant coffee dissolved in ⅓ c. cold water. Pour into dessert glasses lined with ladyfingers. Chill.

TIME 25 MIN. SERVES 2

TUESDAY

Canned Grapefruit
**Smothered Steak*
**Peas & Potato Salad*
Camembert Cheese & Crackers
Coffee

SMOTHERED STEAK: Slice leftover steak ends into 1" pieces. Cook 2 large sliced onions in 2 tbs. butter until soft. Dust meat with seasoned flour, place under onions. Cook, uncovered, 5 min. Combine 1 tbs. prepared mustard, ½ tsp. celery seed, ½ can condensed tomato soup, 1 tbs. sherry. Add to steak and onions. Simmer 10 min.

PEAS & POTATO SALAD: Prepare ½ box leftover peas as directed. Boil 1 small can potatoes. Dice. Mix potatoes and peas, pour on ½ c. French dressing. Let stand until steak is ready, then drain and garnish with mayonnaise.

TIME 15 MIN. SERVES 2

WEDNESDAY

Hamburgers w. Celery Sauce
Minted Carrots
Potato Puffs
Apple Pan Dowdy
Milk

HAMBURGERS W. CELERY SAUCE: ¾ lb. chopped beef. Shape into 4 patties. Pan-broil in hot skillet. Heat 1 can condensed cream of celery soup, add salt, pepper to taste, dash Tabasco sauce. Serve hamburgers on toasted buns, cover with celery sauce.

MINTED CARROTS: 1 can. Drain. Add 1 tbs. mint jelly, 1 tbs. butter. Heat.

APPLE PAN DOWDY: Peel and slice 4 tart apples into buttered shallow baking dish. Sprinkle with ½ c. sugar, ½ tsp. cinnamon, dot with 2 tbs. butter. Cover with biscuit dough (1 c. biscuit mix, ⅓ c. milk) rolled thin. Bake 20 min. in moderate oven (350°). Break crust into apples. Bake 10 min. more. Serve hot with cream sweetened and dusted with nutmeg.

THURSDAY

TIME 25 MIN. SERVES 2

**Tomato Bouillon*
Veal w. Oyster Sauce
Fresh Asparagus
Spanish Salad
Chilled Grapes
Coffee

TOMATO BOUILLON: Heat ½ can tomato soup with ½ c. bouillon and 1 crushed bay leaf. Top each serving with 1 tbs. sour cream.

VEAL W. OYSTER SAUCE: Heat 2 tbs. butter, blend in 1 tbs. flour, then add 1 c. milk, stirring over medium heat until smooth and creamy. Add ½ can minced oysters, juice and all. (Use rest of oysters for breakfast, with scrambled eggs.) Cut 2 veal cutlets into 2″ squares. Dip in beaten egg, then bread crumbs. Brown in 2 tbs. butter. Serve on toast, covered with oyster sauce.

SPANISH SALAD: Toss ½ head lettuce, chunked, 1 quartered tomato, 1 thinly sliced onion, 1 tbs. capers with ¼ c. French dressing. Garnish with carrot sticks.

FRIDAY

TIME 20 MIN. SERVES 2

Broiled Haddock,
Mustard Sauce
Broiled Tomatoes
French-Fried Potatoes
Hot Bran Muffins
Apricot Rum Whip
Coffee

BROILED HADDOCK W. MUSTARD SAUCE: 1 box fillets, defrosted. Brush with melted butter. Sprinkle with seasoned flour. Broil. Heat 2 tbs. butter, stir in 1 tbs. flour, add ¾ c. milk, stir over medium heat until thickened, then stir in 1 beaten egg yolk, 1 tbs. prepared mustard, salt and pepper to taste. Serve over fish.

BROILED TOMATOES: Halve 2 tomatoes. Sprinkle with ¼ c. buttered bread crumbs mixed with 1 finely minced garlic clove. Broil 10 min.

APRICOT RUM WHIP: Drain 1 small can apricots. Press through sieve. Add 1 tsp. rum. Fold into 1 stiffly beaten egg white, then into ¼ c. whipped cream. Chill.

SHOPPING LIST

MEAT

2 lbs. round steak cut into 2" chunks
¾ lb. chicken livers
2 shoulder lamb
2 pork steaks chops

FROZEN FOODS

1 box peas
1 box potato puffs
1 box Brussels sprouts
1 box chopped spinach
1 box strawberries
1 pkg. corn on the cob
1 box cauliflower
1 box fillet of sole

FRESH FRUITS AND VEGETABLES

2 heads lettuce
1 bunch parsley
1 lb. tomatoes
2 pears
1 bunch celery
1 green pepper
4 Idaho potatoes

SUNDRIES

1 small bag potato chips
½ pt. sour cream
2 boxes ready-to-bake poppy-seed rolls
½ lb. American cheese
1 #2 can pineapple juice
1 small can apple-sauce
1 can beets
1 can baba au rhum
1 small can wax beans
1 #2 can tomato juice
1 can baked apples
1 small jar mint jelly
1 #1 can clam juice
1 can black bean soup
1 can condensed cream of mush-room soup

PICK UP ON YOUR WAY HOME

TUES.—½ pt. vanilla ice cream
½ lb. chopped beef if no meat left over
WED.—coffee cake

SUNDAY

TIME 3 HRS. SERVES 4

Frozen Tomato Cocktail
Beef Paprika
Stuffed Baked Potatoes
Buttered Cauliflower w. Peas
Poppy-Seed Rolls
Baba au Rhum
Coffee

FROZEN TOMATO COCKTAIL: Combine 2 c. tomato juice, 2 tsp. lemon juice, ½ tsp. sugar, ½ tsp. salt, ¼ c. minced onion, ¼ c. minced celery. Chill 1 hr. Strain. Add 1 tsp. minced parsley. Freeze quickly, stirring frequently. Serve in sherbet glasses.

BEEF PAPRIKA: 2 lbs. round steak in 2″ chunks. Sauté 1 minced garlic clove and 6 large sliced onions in ¼ c. butter. Add meat, brown well, then add 1 tsp. salt, ¼ tsp. pepper, 1 tbs. paprika, then 2½ c. water. Simmer 2 hrs., until tender. Add 3 tbs. cornstarch mixed with 2 tbs. water. Stir until thick. (Save ¾ c. gravy for Tuesday.)

STUFFED BAKED POTATOES: 4 Idaho. Bake. Halve. Scoop out, whip with ¼ c. butter, ½ c. sour cream, salt and pepper to taste, 2 tbs. grated cheese. Fill shells. Reheat.

MONDAY

TIME 25 MIN. SERVES 2

Chicken-Liver Eggs
Sweet-Sour Beets
Tossed Greens
Baked Apples w. Honey & Almonds
Coffee

CHICKEN-LIVER EGGS: Sauté 2 tbs. minced onion in 2 tbs. butter. Add ¾ lb. chicken livers, diced. Cook 5 min. Combine 4 eggs, 4 tbs. top milk, 1 tsp. thyme, ½ tsp. salt, dash pepper. Beat well with a fork, pour over livers and cook slowly. When bottom is firm, place under broiler to brown top. Serve with toast triangles. Garnish with parsley.

SWEET-SOUR BEETS: Drain 1 can beets. Reserve liquid. Heat 2½ tbs. butter, stir in 1 tbs. cornstarch, 1 tbs. sugar, ⅓ c. beet liquid. Stir until thick, add salt, pepper, beets, 1½ tbs. vinegar.

BAKED APPLE W. HONEY & ALMONDS: 1 can baked apples. Fill each with 1 tbs. honey, 1 tbs. slivered blanched almonds. Dot with butter. Bake in hot oven (450°) 20 min.

TIME 40 MIN. SERVES 2 **TUESDAY**

Black Bean Soup
**Beef Roll w. Cheese Sauce*
Spinach w. Lemon
Lettuce & Tomatoes
Pineappled Ice Cream
Coffee

BEEF ROLL W. CHEESE SAUCE: Combine 1 c. diced leftover meat, or ½ lb. browned chopped meat, with ¾ c. leftover gravy, 3 tbs. minced onion, ½ minced green pepper, salt and pepper to taste. Blend 1 c. biscuit mix with ⅓ c. milk. Flatten dough into square about ⅓″ thick, cover with meat mixture and roll. Bake in hot oven (425°) 30 min. For sauce, heat ¼ lb. diced American cheese, 2½ tbs. butter, 1 tsp. Worcestershire, ¼ c. milk, stirring until smooth.

SPINACH W. LEMON: 1 box. Prepare as directed. Save ½ c. for Thursday. Serve with lemon quarters.

PINEAPPLED ICE CREAM: Pour 2 tbs. pineapple juice over each serving ice cream.

TIME 30 MIN. SERVES 2 **WEDNESDAY**

**Minted Pineapple Juice*
Lamb Chops in Mushroom Sauce
Potato Puffs
Parmesan Brussels Sprouts
Coffee Cake
Coffee

MINTED PINEAPPLE JUICE: Dissolve 1 tsp. mint jelly in leftover pineapple juice. (Shake in shaker or use rotary beater.) Serve chilled.

LAMB CHOPS IN MUSHROOM SAUCE: 2 shoulder. Brown quickly in 1 tbs. butter. Season with salt, pepper, cover with 1 can cream of mushroom soup diluted with ¼ c. water. Simmer about 20 min. Add 2 tbs. sherry just before serving.

PARMESAN BRUSSELS SPROUTS: 1 box. Cook as directed. Dress with 2 tbs. melted butter, ⅛ tsp. nutmeg, sprinkling grated Parmesan cheese.

THURSDAY

TIME 30 MIN. SERVES 2

**Spinach & Tomato Soup*
Broiled Pork Steaks
Corn on the Cob
Celery & Onion Salad
Frosty Strawberries
Coffee

SPINACH & TOMATO SOUP: Heat ¼ c. diced fresh tomato in 1 tbs. butter. Add ½ c. leftover spinach, 2 c. bouillon. Simmer slowly 8 min., add salt, pepper to taste. Serve with fingers of buttered toast sprinkled with grated cheese and browned under broiler.

BROILED PORK STEAKS: 2. Rub with salt, pepper. Dot with butter, broil under high heat. Turn, spread with apple sauce. Lower heat, broil until done.

CELERY & ONION SALAD: Mix together 2 or 3 diced celery stalks, 1 sliced sweet onion, lettuce chunks. Toss with ¼ c. French dressing. Sprinkle with 1 tbs. sherry.

FROSTY STRAWBERRIES: 1 box, semi-thawed. Serve with sour cream. Use any left over for breakfast.

FRIDAY

TIME 45 MIN. SERVES 2

Hot Clam Juice
Almond Buttered Fish Fillets
Wax Beans
Potato Chips
Baked Pears
Coffee

ALMOND BUTTERED FISH FILLETS: 1 box, semi-thawed. Season with salt. Cook slowly in 2 tbs. butter. Turn, sprinkle with 2 tbs. chopped blanched almonds. Cover. Continue cooking until done. Serve with lemon wedges and parsley.

POTATO CHIPS: 1 small pkg. Sprinkle with coarse salt. Heat in moderate oven (375°) about 10 min.

BAKED PEARS: Peel, halve, and core 2 pears. Pierce with cloves. Place in casserole, add ¼ c. sugar, ½ c. water. Cover. Bake in moderate oven (375°) 40 min.

MAY

Recheck your basic staples—and now have you

whole cloves
thyme
lemons
honey
biscuit mix
cinnamon sticks
baking powder
nutmeg
tarragon
cinnamon
basil
marjoram
dry white wine
caraway seeds
mixed nuts
walnuts
almonds
brown sugar
curry powder
powdered sugar
powdered ginger

SHOPPING LIST

MEAT

3 lbs. round beef
2 shoulder lamb chops
2 large slices beef liver, ½″ thick
¾ lb. chopped chuck steak

FROZEN FOODS

1 box Ford Hook Lima beans
1 box string beans
1 box corn kernels
1 box French-fried potatoes

FRESH FRUITS AND VEGETABLES

⅛ lb. mushrooms
1 bunch parsley
1 lb. tomatoes
6 carrots
1 bunch scallions
1 bunch radishes
1 bunch celery
2 parsnips
4 leeks
2 white turnips
2 seedless oranges
3 cucumbers
1 head lettuce
2 cantaloupes

SUNDRIES

1 small can grape juice
1 box cloverleaf rolls
1 #1 can new potatoes
1-lb. can sliced apples
½ pt. sour cream
1 can condensed tomato soup
1 small jar mint jelly
1 small can plums
1 small can apricots
1 small jar ripe olives
1 pkg. pie crust mix
1 #2 can black cherries
1 small jar blackberry jam

PICK UP ON YOUR WAY HOME

FOR SUN.—1 pt. vanilla ice cream; French bread
THUR.—2 hamburger buns; ½ pt. heavy cream
FRI.—2 salmon steaks

TIME 5½ HRS. SERVES 4 **SUNDAY**

Cantaloupe
Pot au Feu
Raw Mushroom Salad
French Bread
Vanilla Ice Cream, Black Cherries au Rhum
Coffee

POT AU FEU: 3 lbs. round beef. Place in deep saucepan. Cover with cold water. Add 2 tsp. salt, ¼ tsp. pepper. Bring to boil. Skim. Add 6 scraped carrots, 2 parsnips, halved, 2 white turnips, halved, 4 stalks celery, halved, 2 whole onions stuck with 4 cloves each, 3 leeks cut in pieces, 1 tsp. thyme, 1 tsp. parsley, 2 bay leaves. Bring to boil again. Lower heat. Simmer 4½–5 hrs. Add more salt and pepper if necessary. Arrange vegetables around meat. Strain stock and serve as soup over dry toast rubbed with garlic.

RAW MUSHROOM SALAD: Wash 1 c. fresh mushrooms, slice thin, mix with 1 c. coarsely chopped parsley, ½ c. chopped leeks, 2 minced garlic cloves, ½ c. French dressing. Serve on lettuce.

BLACK CHERRIES AU RHUM: 1 can cherries (reserve ½ c.). Serve hot over ice cream, adding 1 tbs. heated rum to each portion.

TIME 35 MIN. SERVES 2 **MONDAY**

Grape Juice
Lamb Chops in Mint Sauce
Succotash
Individual Spring Salads
Hot Cloverleaf Rolls
Plum & Apricot Pie
Coffee

LAMB CHOPS IN MINT SAUCE: 2 shoulder. Rub with salt and pepper. Brown quickly on both sides, then lower heat. Add ¼ c. mint jelly, ¼ tsp. dry mustard, juice half a lemon, dash Worcestershire sauce. Cook uncovered 25 min., turn occasionally.

SUCCOTASH: ½ box Lima beans, ½ box corn kernels. Prepare as directed, mix, salt and pepper to taste, add 2 tbs. butter.

INDIVIDUAL SPRING SALADS: Toss broken lettuce, radish slices, tomatoes with ¼ c. French dressing. Garnish with ripe olives.

PLUM & APRICOT PIE: Mix 1 small can plums, ½ small can apricots in small deep dish, stir in 2 tsp. cornstarch mixed with 1 tbs. lemon juice. Cover with prepared piecrust (½ pkg.). Bake in hot oven (425°) 20 min.

TUESDAY

TIME 25 MIN. SERVES 2

Tomato-Egg Drop Soup
Chinese Liver w. Cucumbers
Rice
Chilled Honey Oranges
Tea

TOMATO-EGG DROP SOUP: Combine 1 can condensed tomato soup with 1 c. bouillon. Bring to boil. Add 1 beaten egg, stirring rapidly until egg shreds. Simmer 5 min.

CHINESE LIVER W. CUCUMBERS: 2 slices, ½″ thick. Cut into strips ½″ wide. Blend 2 tsp. cornstarch, 1 tsp. salt, ⅛ tsp. pepper, 3 tbs. salad oil. Add liver, stir until well coated. Fry in 2 tbs. salad oil, stirring constantly until brown. Add peeled cucumbers sliced into thin 3″ strips, ½ c. bouillon. Cover. Cook 5 min. Serve over 1½ c. prepared precooked rice. Garnish with thinly sliced scallions.

CHILLED HONEY ORANGES: Peel and segment 2 seedless oranges. Dip each segment in honey. Chill in ice tray.

WEDNESDAY

TIME 20 MIN. SERVES 2

**Beef au Gratin*
**Lima Beans w. Celery*
**Corn Kernel Salad*
**Cherries & Apricots*
Coffee

BEEF AU GRATIN: Sauté 2 sliced onions in 2 tbs. butter until soft. Blend in 1 tbs. flour, then add 1 c. leftover stock (or bouillon), 1 tbs. vinegar, salt and pepper to taste, and 1½ c. diced leftover beef. Simmer 5 min. Place in heatproof dish, sprinkle with 2 tbs. grated cheese mixed with 2 tbs. buttered bread crumbs. Brown under broiler.

LIMA BEANS W. CELERY: Dice 2 large celery stalks, boil in 1 c. salted water 10 min. Add ½ box Lima beans, cook 15 min. Drain, add salt and pepper to taste, 1 tbs. butter, 2 tbs. cream.

CORN KERNEL SALAD: Cook ½ box corn kernels as directed. Drain. Mix with 1 c. shredded lettuce, stir in ¼ tsp. mustard mixed with juice 1 lemon. Toss with ¼ c. French dressing.

TIME 30 MIN. SERVES 2

THURSDAY

Hamburgers in Red Wine
French-Fried Potatoes
Whipped Cream Cakes w. Blackberry Sauce
Coffee

HAMBURGERS IN RED WINE: Shape ¾ lb. chopped chuck into 4 patties. Heat ½ c. red wine with 4 cloves, ½ tsp. dry mustard, 1 cinnamon stick, pinch black pepper. Simmer 5 min. Pan-broil patties to taste, season with salt and pepper. Strain and add the spiced wine. Simmer 3 min. Serve on bun halves, pour on wine sauce. Garnish with sliced tomatoes and thinly sliced onion.

WHIPPED CREAM CAKES W. BLACKBERRY SAUCE: Stir 2 tbs. sugar into ⅔ c. whipped cream. Add ½ tsp. vanilla, 1 egg beaten foamy. Fold in ⅓ c. flour sifted with 1 tsp. baking powder, pinch salt. Bake in greased muffin pans 20 min. in moderate oven (375°). For sauce, heat ½ c. blackberry jam, add 2 tbs. lemon juice.

TIME 40 MIN. SERVES 2

FRIDAY

Salmon Steak Casserole
Sliced Cucumber
Apple Cobbler w. Cream
Coffee

SALMON STEAK CASSEROLE: Sauté 2 salmon steaks in 2 tbs. salad oil 4 min. on each side. Remove. Add 1 small can potatoes, drained. Brown lightly. Arrange salmon, potatoes, and 1 box defrosted string beans in buttered shallow casserole. Add salt and pepper to taste, 1 tsp. dried tarragon, 1 tbs. lemon juice, 1 c. sour cream. Bake covered in hot oven (425°) 25 min.

SLICED CUCUMBER: Slice thin, add ¼ c. French dressing. Chill. Drain. Serve with mayonnaise.

APPLE COBBLER W. CREAM: Heat 1 can sliced apples with dash nutmeg, 1 tbs. butter until boiling. Pour into baking dish. Stir 3 tbs. cream into ½ c. biscuit mix. Spoon over hot apples. Bake 15 min.

SHOPPING LIST

MEAT

1 large broiler cut in pieces
½ lb. bacon
4 loin or 2 shoulder lamb chops
1 frankfurter
2 or 3 thin slices beef liver
1 lb. round steak

FROZEN FOODS

1 box corn on the cob
1 box string beans
1 box spinach
1 box asparagus
3 boxes peas
2 boxes potato puffs
1 box raspberries

FRESH FRUITS AND VEGETABLES

1 head lettuce
1 bunch radishes
10 tomatoes
1 bunch celery
12 mushrooms
1 bunch scallions
1 avocado
1 head romaine
2 seedless oranges
1 bunch parsley
2 grapefruit
1 bunch watercress

SUNDRIES

1 small can tomato paste
½ lb. sliced Swiss cheese
1 small can sweet potatoes
1 small can baked apples
1 small can pimiento
1 4-oz. can sliced mushrooms
1 #1 can potatoes
1 box ready-to-bake rolls
½ pt. heavy cream
¼ lb. salted almonds
1 8-oz. can carrots
1 6-oz. can crab meat
1 pkg. vanilla junket
4 sponge dessert shells
1 jar chocolate sauce
1 small can freestone peaches
1 can pea soup
1 can condensed cream of celery soup

PICK UP ON YOUR WAY HOME

FOR SUN.—1 pt. vanilla ice cream
TUES.—1 6-oz. can chicken, if needed
THUR.—1 pt. strawberries

TIME 1 HR. SERVES 4

SUNDAY

Chicken w. Tomatoes
Potato Puffs
Buttered Peas
Avocado & Grapefruit Salad
Luxuro Cakes
Coffee

CHICKEN W. TOMATOES: 1 large broiler in 4 pieces. Shake in paper bag with 1 tsp. salt, ⅛ tsp. pepper, ⅔ c. flour. Brown slowly in ½ c. butter. Add 12 sliced mushrooms, 6 peeled, quartered tomatoes, ½ c. chopped scallions, ½ c. sherry. Simmer covered until tender, about 35 min. Serve sprinkled with 1 tbs. minced parsley.

AVOCADO & GRAPEFRUIT SALAD: Alternate grapefruit segments, wedges of avocado, and strips of pimiento on leaves of romaine. Serve with French dressing.

LUXURO CAKES: Fill 4 sponge shells with vanilla ice cream. Top with chocolate sauce and salted almonds.

TIME 25 MIN. SERVES 2

MONDAY

Lamb Chops w. Mushroom & Carrot Sauce
Hot Rolls
Wilted Lettuce
Raspberries in Red Wine
Coffee

LAMB CHOPS W. MUSHROOM & CARROT SAUCE: 2 loin or shoulder chops. Circle each with bacon strip. Rub with salt and pepper. Broil. Heat 2 tbs. butter, add ½ minced garlic clove, 1 sliced onion. Cook until soft. Add 1 can carrots and 1 can sliced mushrooms (with liquid). Cover. Simmer 5 min., then add 1 tsp. tomato paste, 2 tbs. red wine. Cook 5 min. longer. Serve over chops.

WILTED LETTUCE: ½ head. Separate leaves. Fry 3 slices bacon, remove and drain. Stir 5 tbs. vinegar, 3 tbs. water, 1½ tsp. sugar, ½ tsp. salt, dash pepper into hot bacon fat. Pour over lettuce. Garnish with crumbled bacon. Serve immediately.

RASPBERRIES IN RED WINE: ¾ box raspberries, defrosted. Pour on ¼ c. red wine.

TUESDAY

TIME 30 MIN. SERVES 2

Pea Soup w. Frankfurters
**Chicken, String Bean & Bacon Salad*
Corn on the Cob
**Vanilla Junket w. Raspberries*
Coffee

PEA SOUP W. FRANKFURTERS: Prepare 1 can as directed. Add 1 sliced frankfurter. Simmer.

CHICKEN, STRING BEAN & BACON SALAD: Prepare 1 box string beans as directed. Drain and chill. Reserve ½ c. for Thursday. Fry 3 slices bacon until crisp. Add 2 tbs. bacon fat, 2 tbs. ketchup, pinch of sugar to ¼ c. French dressing. Toss beans, 1 c. diced chicken (leftover or canned), 2 sliced tomatoes, and ½ head chunked lettuce with dressing. Garnish with sliced radishes, ¼ lb. Swiss cheese cut in strips, and the crumbled bacon.

CORN ON THE COB: 1 pkg., defrosted. Prepare as directed. Use sugar instead of salt in the water.

VANILLA JUNKET W. RASPBERRIES: Prepare 2 servings junket as directed. Serve with leftover ¼ box raspberries, defrosted.

WEDNESDAY

TIME 25 MIN. SERVES 2

Sautéed Liver
Panned Spinach
Sweet Potatoes
Orange & Watercress Salad
Baked Apples
Coffee

SAUTÉED LIVER: 2 or 3 thin slices. Dust with seasoned flour. Add 1 tbs. butter to frying pan. Brown a split garlic clove, remove, then sauté liver gently until browned. Stir in 2 tbs. vinegar.

PANNED SPINACH: 1 box, semi-thawed. Break into pieces, add 1 finely diced onion, ¼ tsp. salt, dash cayenne. Sauté in 2 tbs. bacon fat 15 min. Drain well.

SWEET POTATOES: 1 small can. Drain, slice, brown in 1 tbs. butter.

ORANGE & WATERCRESS SALAD: Peel 2 seedless oranges, slice thin with sharp knife. Serve on watercress with French dressing.

BAKED APPLES: 1 can. Fill apples with sweetened whipped cream, dust with cinnamon.

TIME 45 MIN. SERVES 2 **THURSDAY**

Celery-Smothered Steak & Potatoes
Basil Tomatoes & Vegetables
Lemon Strawberries
Coffee

CELERY-SMOTHERED STEAK & POTATOES: Sprinkle 1 lb. round steak with salt, pepper. Brown quickly on both sides. Remove. Add 2 tbs. butter to pan, then 1 can potatoes, sliced. Brown on one side. Turn over, add steak. Cook 15 min. Cover with condensed celery soup. Cook until steak is tender, about 25 min. Garnish with ½ c. celery slivers.

BASIL TOMATOES & VEGETABLES: Add ½ tsp. basil to 3 tbs. French dressing. Pour on 2 sliced tomatoes and any leftover green vegetable. Chill covered until serving time. Add more salt and pepper if necessary.

LEMON STRAWBERRIES: Wash and hull 1 pt. strawberries. Sprinkle with 2 tbs. lemon juice sweetened to taste, pinch grated lemon peel.

TIME 30 MIN. SERVES 2 **FRIDAY**

Creamed Crab Meat w. Asparagus on French Toast
Tossed Green Salad
Freestone Peaches w. Sherry
Coffee

CREAMED CRAB MEAT W. ASPARAGUS: Prepare 1 box asparagus and 1 box peas as directed. Keep hot. Dip 3 slices bread into 1 beaten egg mixed with ½ c. milk. Sauté golden brown in 1 tbs. butter. Keep warm. Heat 3 tbs. butter, blend in 3 tbs. flour, then slowly add 2 c. milk, stirring until smooth. Add 1 6-oz. can crab meat, 1 tbs. lemon juice, salt and pepper to taste. Heat. Arrange asparagus on 3 halves French toast per serving, surround with peas, and pour creamed crab meat over all. Garnish with pimiento.

FREESTONE PEACHES W. SHERRY: Drain juice from 1 small can peaches. Mix 2 tbs. sherry with ¼ c. juice. Pour over peaches. Chill.

SHOPPING LIST

MEAT

- 2¾ lbs. round steak
- ¾ lb. chopped chuck steak
- ½ lb. boiled ham, in 2 slices
- 2 or 3 veal chops

FROZEN FOODS

- 2 boxes peas
- 1 box scallops
- 1 box potato puffs
- 1 box peaches
- 1 box Lima beans
- 1 pkg. waffles

FRESH FRUITS AND VEGETABLES

- 1 large bunch celery
- 2 green peppers
- 1 small escarole
- 1 cucumber
- 2 lbs. tomatoes
- 1 bunch scallions
- 1 bunch parsley
- 1 lime
- 1 bunch chives
- 1 bunch watercress
- 1 pt. blueberries
- 1 small pineapple
- 2 iceberg lettuce
- 1 seedless orange
- 8 or 9 new potatoes

SUNDRIES

- 2 small pkg. cream cheese
- ¼ lb. Roquefort cheese
- 2 small sponge layers
- 1 #1 can tomatoes
- 1 4-oz. can sliced mushrooms
- ½ pt. sour cream
- 1 #1 can grapefruit juice
- 1 jar borsch
- 1 box noodles
- ½ pt. heavy cream
- 1 jar stuffed olives
- 2 #1 cans potatoes
- 1 tube ready-to-bake biscuits
- 1 small can beets
- 1 small can apricot nectar
- 1 can baked apples
- 2 cans madrilene
- 1 can condensed cream of mushroom soup

PICK UP ON YOUR WAY HOME

FRI.—½ pt. light cream

TIME 3¼ HRS. SERVES 4 **SUNDAY**

Jellied Madrilene
Swiss Steak
New Potatoes
Piquant Peas
Stuffed Celery
Peach Layer Cake
Coffee

SWISS STEAK: 2¾ lbs. round steak. Trim edges. Rub both sides with lots of salt and pepper, pound flour into steak. Brown in 3 tbs. butter over high heat. Add 1 large sliced onion, 1½ lbs. tomatoes, sliced, ½ c. water, 1 c. red wine, 3 bay leaves, ¼ tsp. basil, ¼ tsp. marjoram. Cover. Simmer 3 hrs.

PIQUANT PEAS: Prepare 2 boxes as directed. Reheat 1 min. with ¼ c. white wine, 2 tbs. vinegar, 1 minced scallion, pinch parsley, salt and pepper to taste.

STUFFED CELERY: 5 or 6 stalks. Stuff with a mixture of 1 pkg. cream cheese, 4 tbs. Roquefort, and 2 tbs. minced almonds.

PEACH LAYER CAKE: Spread 1 box defrosted peaches on 2 sponge layers. Put together. Top with whipped cream.

TIME 35 MIN. SERVES 2 **MONDAY**

New Orleans Meat Balls on Garlic Noodles
Breath of Spring Salad
Chunked Pineapple w. Sour Cream, Nutmeg
Coffee

NEW ORLEANS MEAT BALLS: To ¾ lb. chopped steak add ½ tsp. salt. Roll into balls, flatten, place a stuffed olive in each. Roll again. Place in pan with ¼ c. melted butter, stir in 1 thinly sliced onion, 1 chopped green pepper. Cover, simmer 5 min. Add 1 can tomatoes, drained, ½ can mushrooms, drained, 1 bay leaf, pinch parsley, thyme, ½ tsp. salt, pepper, 1 sliced garlic clove. Cook covered 25 min. Serve over garlic noodles.

GARLIC NOODLES: Cook 4 oz. noodles as directed. Add 3 split garlic cloves to water. Stir occasionally.

BREATH OF SPRING SALAD: Toss chopped watercress, diced celery, diced cucumber, diced tomato, iceberg lettuce in ¼ c. French dressing made with lemon juice instead of vinegar.

TUESDAY

TIME 25 MIN. SERVES 2

Chilled Grapefruit Juice
**Ragout of Beef*
Caraway Lima Beans
Beet Salad
Apples Marguerite
Coffee

RAGOUT OF BEEF: Cut 1½ c. leftover meat in 1″ squares. Heat 2 tbs. butter, add meat, 2 tbs. sherry, ½ can leftover mushrooms with liquid, 3 tbs. sour cream, 1 tbs. leftover gravy, if any, and ½ c. bouillon. Bring to boil. Add ¼ tsp. thyme. Thicken with 1 tbs. flour. Stir until smooth, add salt and pepper to taste. Simmer 15 min. Add 2 tbs. red wine. Serve garnished with parsley.

CARAWAY LIMA BEANS: 1 box. Prepare as directed. Add 2 tbs. butter, sprinkle with 1 tsp. caraway seeds.

BEET SALAD: Toss ½ can beets, drained, with ¼ c. minced celery, 1 tbs. nut crumbs, ¼ c. French dressing. Serve on lettuce.

APPLES MARGUERITE: Pour apricot nectar over baked apples. Surround with "petals" of blanched split almonds.

WEDNESDAY

TIME 25 MIN. SERVES 2

Chilled Borsch
Ham Slices w. Stuffed Lettuce
Blueberry Waffles
Iced Coffee

CHILLED BORSCH: 1 small jar. Serve cold with hot boiled potatoes (1 small can).

STUFFED LETTUCE: Blend together 1 pkg. cream cheese, 4 tbs. Roquefort. Add 1 minced green pepper, 1 small minced tomato, 1 small minced onion, 1 tbs. milk, ¼ tsp. salt, dash pepper, then leftover beets, drained, and Limas, if any. Hollow out 1 head lettuce. Stuff. Chill. Serve in wedges on plate with ham slices.

BLUEBERRY WAFFLES: Toast 1 pkg. frozen waffles as directed. Butter generously, pile with ½ pt. sugared blueberries. Serve with lemon wedges.

TIME 40 MIN. SERVES 2

THURSDAY

Veal Chops in Mushroom Sauce
Potato Puffs
Tomato & Chive Salad
Pineapple w. Honey & Lime
Coffee

VEAL CHOPS IN MUSHROOM SAUCE: Rub 2 or 3 chops with ½ tsp. salt, ⅛ tsp. pepper, ¾ tsp. dry mustard. Dip in bread crumbs, in beaten egg, again in crumbs. Brown 1 garlic clove in butter. Remove. Sauté chops on both sides until brown. Add ½ cup dry white wine, ½ can condensed mushroom soup. Cover. Cook over low heat about 30 min., until chops are done.

TOMATO & CHIVE SALAD: Toss 2 quartered tomatoes, 1 tbs. chopped chives, shredded lettuce in ¼ c. French dressing.

PINEAPPLE W. HONEY & LIME: Mix ¼ c. honey with 2 tbs. lime juice. Pour over sliced fresh pineapple.

TIME 50 MIN. SERVES 2

FRIDAY

**Scallops en Casserole*
Escarole & Orange Salad
Hot Biscuits
Blueberries & Cream
Coffee

SCALLOPS EN CASSEROLE: 1 box scallops, defrosted. Cook 1 large onion, sliced, 1 green pepper, sliced, in 2 tbs. butter until soft. Stir in ½ can leftover condensed mushroom soup, 1 c. canned tomatoes, drained, 1 pinch dried basil. Arrange scallops in baking dish, pour on sauce, surround with 1 small can potatoes, diced. Sprinkle with buttered bread crumbs. Bake covered 30 min. in moderate oven (375°). Remove cover, bake 10 min. longer.

ESCAROLE & ORANGE SALAD: Pour ¼ c. French dressing over 1 orange, peeled and cut in sections. Chill. Combine with escarole. Garnish with thin green pepper strips.

SHOPPING LIST

MEAT

- 4 lbs. shoulder of lamb, bone removed, leave untied
- ½ lb. bacon
- 1 beef kidney
- 2 large loin pork chops
- 2 slices smoked salmon

FROZEN FOODS

- 1 box Lima beans

FRESH FRUITS AND VEGETABLES

- 1 bunch mint
- 2 lbs. asparagus
- 1 tomato
- 1 bunch radishes
- 1 lime
- 1 bunch watercress
- 1 lb. rhubarb
- 4 Idaho potatoes
- 1 bunch scallions
- 1 banana
- 1 head Boston lettuce
- 1 head escarole
- 3 green peppers
- 1 small honeydew melon

SUNDRIES

- ½ pt. sour cream
- 1 small can pimiento
- 1 small can tomato juice
- 1 #1 can sweet potatoes
- 1 small can pineapple chunks
- 1 #1 can potatoes
- 1 small box dried apricots
- 1 4-oz. can sliced mushrooms
- ½ pt. heavy cream
- 1 small can applesauce
- 1 tube ready-to-bake biscuits
- 1 small can carrots
- 1 pkg. stuffing
- 1 can condensed pea soup
- 1 small pkg. pitted dates
- 1 small can sliced peaches
- 1 small pkg. raisins

PICK UP ON YOUR WAY HOME

FOR SUN.—tiny rolls for 4
TUES.—2 sponge dessert shells
WED.—1 loaf French bread
FRI.—2 small mackerel

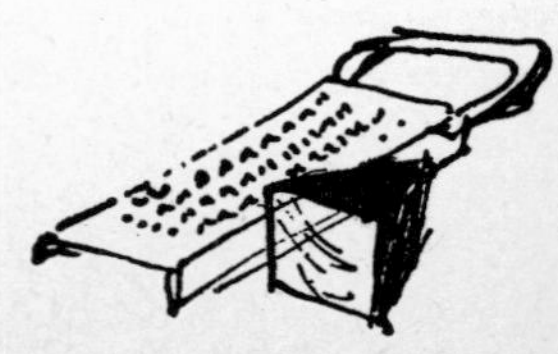

TIME 3 HRS. SERVES 4 **SUNDAY**

Stuffed Lamb
Fresh Asparagus
Baked Potatoes
Tiny Hot Rolls
Rhubarb Compote
Coffee

STUFFED LAMB: 4 lbs. shoulder, boned. Prepare stuffing of 1½ c. soft bread crumbs, ¼ c. butter, ½ tsp. salt, ⅛ tsp. pepper, ⅓ c. finely chopped dried apricots, 1 tbs. honey. Rub meat with salt and pepper. Tuck stuffing into pocket, roll and tie. Rub with butter. Roast in moderate oven (325°) 2½ hrs.

BAKED POTATOES: 4 Idaho. Rub with bacon fat. Bake until done, about 55 min., at 325°. Serve popped open, insert pat of butter, dust with paprika.

RHUBARB COMPOTE: Mix 1 c. brown sugar, 3 c. diced rhubarb, ½ c. sliced pitted dates. Stir in 1 sliced banana. Bake in covered casserole 1¼ hrs. Serve warm with cream.

TIME 30 MIN. SERVES 2 **MONDAY**

Kidney & Mushrooms w. Rice
Radish & Green Pepper Salad
Spiced Apple Snow
Coffee

KIDNEY & MUSHROOMS W. RICE: Dip 1 beef kidney in boiling water. Slice thin, discarding core and tubes. Sauté in 2 tbs. butter over high heat. Add 3 finely chopped scallions, 1 4-oz. can mushrooms, drained, sauté another 5 min. Blend in 2 tbs. flour, then stir in 1 c. bouillon, ½ c. red wine. Simmer 20 min. Serve over 1½ c. prepared precooked rice.

RADISH & GREEN PEPPER SALAD: Toss broken lettuce, sliced radishes, sliced green pepper with ¼ c. French dressing.

SPICED APPLE SNOW: Beat 2 tbs. powdered sugar into 1 stiffly beaten egg white. Fold in ⅔ c. applesauce and ⅛ tsp. nutmeg. Chill. Top with whipped cream dusted lightly with nutmeg.

TUESDAY

TIME 30 MIN. SERVES 2

**Curried Lamb Pie*
Escarole Salad
Peach Dreams
Iced Coffee

CURRIED LAMB PIE: Dice 1½ c. leftover lamb. Heat 1 tbs. butter, blend in 1 tbs. flour, ¾ tsp. curry powder. Add ½ c. bouillon, stirring until smooth and thickened. Add 1 small can carrots with liquid, 1 small chopped onion, ¼ c. raisins (opt.), and the lamb. Simmer 10 min. Pour into casserole, cover with split ready-to-bake biscuits, bake in hot oven (425°) about 20 min.

ESCAROLE SALAD: Break escarole in pieces. Sprinkle with 1 tbs. lemon juice. Serve with mayonnaise.

PEACH DREAMS: Drain juice from 1 small can sliced peaches. Arrange in sponge dessert shells. Dust with ½ tsp. cinnamon mixed with 1 tsp. powdered sugar. Add 1 tbs. sherry, 1 tbs. chopped pecans to ¼ c. juice, pour over peaches. Chill. Serve with whipped cream.

WEDNESDAY

TIME 50 MIN. SERVES 2

Melon w. Powdered Ginger
Smoked Salmon Salad
Hot French Bread
**Date Crumbles*
Coffee

SMOKED SALMON SALAD: Mix 2 slices smoked salmon, diced, with 1 (#1) can potatoes, drained and diced, chopped white of 1 hard-cooked egg, salt and pepper to taste, ¼ c. mayonnaise, 1 tbs. lemon juice. Serve on lettuce and watercress. Sprinkle with sieved hard-cooked egg yolk.

DATE CRUMBLES: To 1 well-beaten egg add ½ c. sugar, 1 tsp. baking powder, pinch salt, 2 tsp. flour, ½ c. chopped walnuts, ½ c. chopped dates. Spread on well-greased pan. Bake in slow oven (300°) 45 min. Crumble. Mix with ½ c. whipped cream. Pile in glasses.

TIME 35 MIN. SERVES 2

THURSDAY

Wine Cooler
Hawaiian Pork Chops
Sweet Potatoes
Smothered Green Peppers & Onions
Coffee

WINE COOLER: Mix ½ c. lemon juice with 1 c. dry white wine, sweeten to taste. Pour over ice cubes, garnish with mint leaves.

HAWAIIAN PORK CHOPS: 2 loin. Sprinkle with salt and pepper. Brown quickly on both sides, add juice from 1 small can chunked pineapple. Simmer 10 min. Place in baking dish, top with pineapple, surround with 1 can sweet potatoes. Pour on drippings, bake in hot oven (425°) until tender, about 25 min.

SMOTHERED GREEN PEPPERS & ONIONS: Heat 2 tbs. bacon fat, add 2 sliced green peppers, 1 sliced onion, ¼ tsp. salt, ⅛ tsp. pepper. Simmer covered until tender, about 10 min.

TIME 40 MIN. SERVES 2

FRIDAY

Chilled Pea Soup w. Sherry
Spanish Mackerel
Buttered Lima Beans
Shredded Lettuce, Sour Cream
Minted Melon Balls
Iced Tea

CHILLED PEA SOUP W. SHERRY: 1 can. Beat in 1 soup can cold milk. Add 3 tbs. sherry. Chill.

SPANISH MACKEREL: 2 small mackerel. Sprinkle with salt and pepper inside and out. Mix ½ c. packaged stuffing with 3 tbs. tomato juice, 1 small tomato, minced, ½ tsp. basil. Stuff fish lightly. Wrap 1 strip bacon around each. Place in greased dish, bake in hot oven (450°) about 25 min., until fish flakes. Baste with 2 tbs. lemon juice mixed with 2 tbs. tomato juice. 5 min. before fish is done, add ¼ c. white wine.

SHREDDED LETTUCE W. SOUR CREAM: Toss 1½ c. shredded lettuce with ¼ c. sour cream, 2 tbs. lemon juice. Garnish with minced scallions and chopped pimiento.

MINTED MELON BALLS: Sprinkle with 2 tbs. lime juice mixed with 1 tbs. powdered sugar. Garnish with sugared mint.

JUNE

Recheck your basic staples—and now have you

crème de cacao
grenadine syrup
onion salt
celery salt
caraway seeds
capers
walnuts
lemons
powdered ginger
thyme
basil
sage
marjoram
tarragon
honey
brown sugar
saffron

—Have you

toothpicks
cheesecloth
wax paper

SHOPPING LIST

MEAT

3½ lbs. chicken pieces
1 pair sweetbreads
¼ lb. bacon
¼ lb. boiled ham
¾ lb. veal cutlet in 2 slices pounded thin

FROZEN FOODS

1 box potato puffs
1 box chopped spinach
1 box string beans
1 box whipped potatoes

FRESH FRUITS AND VEGETABLES

4 large sweet red peppers
7 tomatoes
1 bunch celery
3 seedless oranges
1 sweet onion
1 bunch radishes
1 head iceberg lettuce
4 Idaho potatoes
1 bunch watercress
1 bunch chives
1 pt. blueberries
1 small avocado
1 head Boston lettuce
2 green peppers
1 grapefruit
4 peaches
1 cantaloupe

SUNDRIES

1 3-oz. cream cheese
1 pkg. piecrust mix
1 box chocolate pudding
1 small bar sweet chocolate
1 box cinnamon rolls
1 qt. can vegetable juice
1 small can tomato paste
1 small can pimiento
½ pt. sour cream
½ pt. heavy cream
½ lb. American cheese
2 slices poundcake
3 oz. bleu cheese
4 oz. noodles
1 small jar pitted olives
1 jar infant custard
1 small can asparagus tips
1 can condensed ox-tail soup
1 can condensed cream of celery soup

PICK UP ON YOUR WAY HOME

FOR SUN.—1 ice cream roll
MON.—½ apple pie
TUES.—rye bread; 2 or 3 ears corn
WED.—1 pt. strawberries
THURS.—Russian black bread
FRI.—1 lb. codfish steaks; ½ pt. heavy cream

SUNDAY

TIME 1½ HRS. SERVES 4

Iced Vegetable Juice
Rio Grande Chicken
Baked Potatoes
Avocado Fruit Salad
Cinnamon Rolls
Chocolate Baked Alaska
Iced Coffee

RIO GRANDE CHICKEN: 3½ lbs., cut up. Brown quickly in 3 tbs. salad oil. Sprinkle with 1 tsp. salt, ¼ tsp. pepper, ¼ tsp. marjoram, ¼ tsp. thyme. Add 2 sliced onions, 2 chopped garlic cloves. Cover, cook very slowly 1 hr. Add 4 large sweet red peppers cut in strips, 4 medium tomatoes, diced, ¼ tsp. basil, cook 15 min. Garnish with 2 peeled sliced oranges. (Reserve ¾ c. chicken for Tuesday.)

AVOCADO FRUIT SALAD: 1 c. cantaloupe balls, 1 sliced avocado, 1 chopped sweet onion, ½ c. French dressing. Serve on lettuce.

CHOCOLATE BAKED ALASKA: At serving time place frozen ice cream roll on baking sheet. Brush top with 1 tbs. brandy. Cover completely with 2 egg whites stiffly beaten with 2 tbs. sugar. Brown in hot oven (450°) 3 min.

MONDAY

TIME 30 MIN. SERVES 2

Texas Sweetbreads on Spinach
Potato Puffs
Lettuce, Watercress & Radish Salad
Apple Pie & American Cheese
Coffee

TEXAS SWEETBREADS ON SPINACH: Dip 1 pair sweetbreads into boiling water. Remove skin and waste, split in half lengthwise, dust with flour. Sauté quickly in 2 tbs. butter, add 1 tbs. sherry. Remove sweetbreads. Stir in 1 tbs. flour, ½ tsp. tomato paste, ¼ tsp. tarragon, 1 c. chicken bouillon. Bring to boil, stirring constantly. Add salt and pepper to taste. Return sweetbreads. Cover, cook over moderate heat 10 min. Serve on 1 box prepared chopped spinach mixed with 2 tbs. sour cream.

LETTUCE, WATERCRESS & RADISH SALAD: Toss lettuce, sliced radishes, watercress in garlic-rubbed bowl with ¼ c. French dressing.

APPLE PIE & AMERICAN CHEESE: Warm pie in oven before serving.

TIME 40 MIN. SERVES 2

TUESDAY

**Chilled Vegetable Juice w. Sour Cream*
**Chicken & Ham Salad*
Hot Corn on the Cob
Sliced Rye Bread
Blueberry Frost
Iced Coffee

CHILLED VEGETABLE JUICE W. SOUR CREAM: Beat 1 c. chilled vegetable juice with ½ c. sour cream, salt and pepper to taste. Serve in bowls. Sprinkle with chives.

CHICKEN & HAM SALAD: Mix ½ c. diced boiled ham, ¾ c. diced chicken, 3 oz. crumbled bleu cheese with ¼ tsp. celery salt and ½ cup French dressing. Chill 15 min. Drain well. Serve tossed with torn Boston lettuce. Garnish with 1 sliced hard-cooked egg. Serve with ¼ c. mayonnaise mixed with 1 tsp. finely chopped pimiento, 1 tsp. minced chives, 2 tbs. chili sauce, 2 tbs. tarragon vinegar, 1 tbs. heavy cream.

BLUEBERRY FROST: Crush 1½ c. blueberries, add ½ c. sugar, pinch salt. Fold in ½ c. whipped cream. Freeze at least 30 min. Garnish with grated lemon peel. Serve on sliced pound-cake.

TIME 35 MIN. SERVES 2

WEDNESDAY

Radishes & Celery Hearts
Wiener Schnitzel
Spanish String Beans
Strawberries w. Whipped Custard
Coffee

WIENER SCHNITZEL: ¾ lb. veal cutlet in 2 slices, pounded thin. Dip in flour, then in beaten egg mixed with ½ tsp. salt, ⅛ tsp. pepper, 2 tbs. water, then in bread crumbs. Sauté in 3 tbs. butter until golden brown on both sides. Garnish with 2 slices lemon, 8 pitted olives, 1 finely chopped hard-cooked egg.

SPANISH STRING BEANS: 1 box. Cook as directed. Drain, then add 2 tbs. oil, ¼ tsp. sage. Heat until beans have absorbed oil, then add pulp of 1 large tomato, salt and pepper to taste.

STRAWBERRIES W. WHIPPED CUSTARD: Beat into 1 jar infant custard ½ c. whipped cream, 1 tsp. grated lemon rind. Chill. Serve over 1½ c. washed, hulled strawberries.

THURSDAY

TIME 30 MIN. SERVES 2

Oxtail Noodles
Asparagus Tip Salad
Russian Black Bread
**Filled Grapefruit Halves*
Coffee

OXTAIL NOODLES: Cook 2 diced onions with 2 diced green peppers in 1½ tbs. butter until tender. Add 1 can condensed oxtail soup with ¾ c. milk. Add 1 c. cubed American cheese. Stir until melted. Slowly add 3 well-beaten egg yolks, ¼ tsp. salt, a few grains cayenne. Stir until thickened, serve on (4 oz.) boiled noodles.

ASPARAGUS TIP SALAD: Arrange 1 small can drained asparagus tips on mixed salad greens. Add any leftover corn from cob and 1 onion cut into thin shavings. Dress with French dressing. Garnish with 1 slice crumbled bacon.

FILLED GRAPEFRUIT HALVES: 2 grapefruit halves. Core, remove seeds, loosen sections. Fill with sugared blueberries and/or any leftover strawberry custard.

FRIDAY

TIME 45 MIN. SERVES 2

Chilled Cream of Celery Soup
Parmesan Cod Steaks
Whipped Potatoes
Tossed Green Salad
Chocolate-Chip Pie
Coffee

CHILLED CREAM OF CELERY SOUP: 1 can. Beat in 1 soup can cold milk, salt, pepper, and paprika to taste. Serve in chilled cups. Top with spoonfuls of mashed cream cheese.

PARMESAN COD STEAKS: 1 lb. codfish steaks. Dust with seasoned flour. Dip in 1 beaten egg, then in mixture of ½ c. bread crumbs, ¼ c. grated cheese. Sauté in 2 tbs. butter until brown. Cut 2 tomatoes in thick slices. Season with salt, pepper, basil, 1 minced garlic clove. Dot with butter, broil 5 min. Serve with cod and lemon quarters.

CHOCOLATE-CHIP PIE: Bake 1 8″ pie shell, using mix as directed. Fill with cooled chocolate pudding made with 1½ c. milk. Before serving sprinkle with ½ c. finely chopped nuts, spread with whipped cream, top with ¼ c. chocolate slivers.

SHOPPING LIST

MEAT

5 small pork fillets, about 3 lbs.
¼ lb. bacon
¾ lb. round of beef 1" thick
⅛ lb. boiled ham, sliced thin
¾ lb. veal cutlet, pounded thin

FROZEN FOODS

1 box French-style string beans
1 box French-fried potatoes
1 box Lima beans
1 box whipped potatoes

FRESH FRUITS AND VEGETABLES

1 small bunch parsley
1 bunch chives
1 bunch watercress
1 bunch dill
4 Idaho potatoes
1 bunch celery
1 apple
1 green pepper
1 banana
1 small basket raspberries
1 head Boston lettuce
1 head iceberg lettuce
1 head romaine
fruit for dessert

SUNDRIES

1 pt. sour cream
½ pt. heavy cream
1 small can tomato sauce
1 small can pimiento
1 tube ready-to-bake biscuits
3 oz. cream cheese
3 plain cupcakes
1 small jar pitted olives
1 small jar chopped sweet pickles
1 small jar anchovy fillets
¼ lb. Swiss cheese, sliced thin
1 pkg. vanilla tapioca pudding
1 small pkg. potato chips
8 oz. thin spaghetti
1 pkg. Italian bread sticks
1 small can apricot nectar
2 cans condensed tomato soup
1 can condensed pea soup
1 can Vichyssoise
1 can madrilene
1 can chicken gumbo soup

PICK UP ON YOUR WAY HOME

FOR SUN.—1½ pts. vanilla ice cream
FRI.—2 1½"-thick codfish steaks

SUNDAY

TIME 1½ HRS. SERVES 4

Chilled Tomato Soup
Cossack Pork
Baked Potatoes
Green Salad Bowl
Apricot Sundaes
Coffee

CHILLED TOMATO SOUP: 2 cans. Prepare as directed, with milk. Serve cold garnished with 2 tsp. finely chopped dill.

COSSACK PORK: 5 fillets. Heat 3 tbs. bacon fat in braising pan. Dust fillets with salt, pepper. Brown on all sides, add 2 sliced onions, 1 bay leaf, ¼ tsp. thyme, ¼ tsp. basil. Cook covered ¾ hr. Remove. Reserve 1 small fillet for Tuesday. Cut in thick slices. Reshape in pan, placing between each slice a purée made of 1 can condensed pea soup heated with 1 diced onion, salt and pepper to taste, and 1 chopped lettuce heart. Cover with 1½ c. sour cream mixed with 1 tbs. flour, 3 tbs. sherry. Cook covered 15 min., sprinkle with ½ c. bread crumbs. Broil until golden brown.

APRICOT SUNDAES: Pour 2 tbs. apricot nectar over each serving vanilla ice cream.

MONDAY

TIME 35 MIN. SERVES 2

Beef Ragout
Buttered Beans
Whipped Potatoes
Honey Cream
Lemon-Peel Coffee

BEEF RAGOUT: ¾ lb. beef cut in 1" pieces. Brown quickly in 1 tbs. salad oil. Add ¾ c. white wine, ½ tsp. salt, ¼ tsp. pepper, ¼ tsp. thyme, ¼ tsp. basil, ¼ tsp. sage. Simmer 20 min., add 3 tbs. tomato sauce, 1 crushed garlic clove, 1 chopped pimiento, 2 tbs. red wine. Cover. Cook 10 min.

BUTTERED BEANS: 1 box French-style string beans. Prepare as directed. Reserve half for tomorrow.

HONEY CREAM: Beat ¼ c. honey with 1 egg yolk. Stir in double boiler until thickened. Cool slightly. Mix with 1 stiffly beaten egg white, then 2 tbs. whipped cream. Serve chilled.

LEMON-PEEL COFFEE: Serve hot black coffee in glasses with small twist of lemon peel. Sweeten to taste.

TIME 25 MIN. SERVES 2 **TUESDAY**

Cold Vichyssoise
**Summertime Pork Salad*
Hot Biscuits
Raspberry Cupcakes
Coffee

COLD VICHYSSOISE: 1 can, chilled. Prepare as directed. Serve in cold bowls. Garnish with 1 tbs. chopped chives.

SUMMERTIME PORK SALAD: Combine 1 c. diced leftover pork, ½ box leftover cooked string beans, 1 diced unpeeled apple, ½ c. diced celery, 1 diced green pepper, 2 tbs. chopped sweet pickles, 1 onion sliced paper-thin, ½ c. mayonnaise, ½ tsp. salt, ¼ tsp. pepper. Serve on lettuce.

RASPBERRY CUPCAKES: 3. Mash 2 tbs. raspberries with ½ pkg. cream cheese, 2 tbs. sugar. Frost cakes. Garnish with raspberries.

TIME 25 MIN. SERVES 2 **WEDNESDAY**

Chicken Gumbo
Spaghetti w. Black Olive Sauce
Italian Bread Sticks
**Banana-Berries*
Coffee

CHICKEN GUMBO: 1 can. Prepare as directed. Serve with grated cheese.

BLACK OLIVE SAUCE: Sauté 1½ c. chopped onions in 2 tbs. fat. Add 2 chopped garlic cloves, 1 small jar pitted black olives, 3 slices bacon cut into bits, 3 chopped anchovy fillets, 2 tbs. chopped parsley. Cook 4 min. Place boiled, drained spaghetti (6 oz.) in serving dish with 1 tbs. salad oil. Mix well, cover with sauce. Serve with grated Parmesan cheese.

BANANA-BERRIES: Mash 1 banana, stir in 1 tbs. lemon juice, then 3 tbs. cream. Beat creamy, add 1 tbs. sugar. Serve as sauce over chilled raspberries.

THURSDAY

TIME 30 MIN. SERVES 2

Jellied Madrilene
Ham & Veal Swiss
French-Fried Potatoes
Romaine & Watercress Salad
Fruit Basket
Coffee

JELLIED MADRILENE: 1 can. Prepare as directed. Serve with lemon slices.

HAM & VEAL SWISS: Rub ¾ lb. pounded veal slices with salt and pepper. Place 1 slice boiled ham on each piece, then 1 slice Swiss cheese. Roll and secure with toothpicks. Roll in 1 beaten egg mixed with 2 tbs. water, then dip in flour. Fry in 2 tbs. butter over medium heat until golden brown on all sides.

ROMAINE & WATERCRESS SALAD: Rub bowl with cut garlic clove, alternate layers broken romaine, chopped watercress. Add chopped fresh parsley, serve with French dressing.

FOR TOMORROW: Prepare ½ pkg. vanilla tapioca pudding.

FRIDAY

TIME 20 MIN. SERVES 2

Italian Codfish
Buttered Lima Beans
Potato Chips
Caramel Tapioca
Coffee

ITALIAN CODFISH: 2 1½″-thick steaks. Tie in cheesecloth. Put in boiling water with ½ tsp. salt, 1 tbs. vinegar, simmer 10 min. For sauce, chop 1 garlic clove with 3 sprigs parsley, 1 anchovy, 1 tbs. capers, 2 pitted olives, yolk of 1 hard-cooked egg, 1 tbs. soft white bread crumbs soaked in vinegar. Mix into smooth paste, then add ⅓ c. oil, 1 tbs. at a time, salt, pepper, and additional vinegar to taste.

POTATO CHIPS: 1 small pkg. Sprinkle with salt, warm in oven.

CARAMEL TAPIOCA: Melt 1 tbs. butter in saucepan, add ¼ c. brown sugar, stir until syrupy. Pour over tapioca prepared yesterday. Serve with or without cream.

SHOPPING LIST

MEAT

3 lbs. veal knuckle sawed in 2″-thick slices
3 cube steaks ¼″ thick
6 slices Canadian bacon

FROZEN FOODS

1 box peas
1 box green beans
1 box French-fried potatoes
1 box rhubarb

FRESH FRUITS AND VEGETABLES

1 bunch celery
1 bunch parsley
7 carrots
1 sweet onion
1 small eggplant
1 banana
2 tomatoes
1 iceberg lettuce
1 head chicory
½ lb. white grapes
1 bunch watercress
1 small acorn squash
1½ lbs. broccoli
2 large peaches
1 small cantaloupe
6 tiny new potatoes

SUNDRIES

1 #1 can tomato purée
2 or 3 portions Camembert
1 small box raisins
1 4-oz. can pimiento
1 4-oz. can sliced mushrooms
1 #1 tall can new potatoes
1 can tuna-fish flakes
1 small can pears
1 small jar apricot jam
1 small bar sweet chocolate
1 box ready-to-bake rolls
2 small cans apple juice
1 small can diced beets
1 small can corn kernels
1 small jar mint jelly
4 ladyfingers
12 oz. thin spaghetti
½ pt. yogurt or sour cream
1 can condensed cream of mushroom soup
1 can condensed consommé

PICK UP ON YOUR WAY HOME

MON.—black bread
WED.—½ pt. tutti-frutti ice cream
THUR.—½ pt. heavy cream
FRI.—4 mackerel fillets, skin left on

SUNDAY

TIME 2 HRS. SERVES 4

Veal Osso Bucco
Spaghetti
Mixed Green Salad
Cantaloupe Halves w. Sherry
Coffee

VEAL OSSO BUCCO: 3 lbs. veal knuckle in 2″-thick slices. Rub meat with 1 tsp. salt, ¼ tsp. pepper. Brown well in 3 tbs. oil, add 2 large sliced onions, 2 small chopped celery stalks, 1 chopped carrot. Cook until onions are soft and carrots brown, then add 1 bay leaf, 1 minced garlic clove, ¼ tsp. thyme, ¼ tsp. basil, 2 small strips lemon peel, 1 #1 can tomato purée, ½ c. white wine. Bring to boil gradually, then add 6 whole carrots. Cover, simmer 1½ hrs., stirring occasionally. 5 min. before serving add salt and pepper to taste, sprinkle with 1 tsp. grated lemon peel, 1 tsp. chopped parsley. (Reserve about 1 c. meat for tomorrow.) Serve with (8 oz.) boiled spaghetti and grated cheese.

CANTALOUPE HALVES W. SHERRY: Pour 1 tbs. sherry into each chilled melon half.

MONDAY

TIME 55 MIN. SERVES 2

Jellied Consommé
**Mediterranean Pilaff*
Yogurt
Aubergine Salad
White Grapes
Camembert & Black Bread
Coffee

MEDITERRANEAN PILAFF: Prepare 3 c. precooked rice as directed, adding 3 tbs. raisins, ¼ tsp. saffron. Use strong bouillon instead of water. Fry 1 large sliced onion with 1 sliced banana in 2 tbs. oil. Add 1 minced garlic clove, 2 diced tomatoes, 1 4-oz. can pimiento, drained and diced, and 1 c. shredded leftover veal. Cook 5 min. Add cooked rice, heat and stir 5 min. Serve with bowl of cold yogurt or sour cream.

AUBERGINE SALAD: Peel 1 small eggplant, cut in ½″ pieces, cook in double boiler 45 min. Press through coarse sieve, add 1 finely minced garlic clove, ¼ tsp. salt, ⅛ tsp. pepper, 2 tsp. olive oil, 2 tsp. lemon juice, 1 tbs. chopped parsley. Chill quickly. Serve in lettuce cups.

TIME 30 MIN. SERVES 2

TUESDAY

Mushroom-Tuna Casserole
**Chicory & Grape Salad*
Hard Rolls
Meringue Pears, Chocolate Sauce
Iced Coffee

MUSHROOM-TUNA CASSEROLE: Heat 1 can condensed cream of mushroom soup with 1 4-oz. can sliced mushrooms, drained, 1 tbs. butter, 1 #1 can potatoes, drained, 1/8 tsp. pepper, 1/2 tsp. marjoram, 1 tbs. sherry. Stir in 1 can tuna fish. Turn into shallow buttered casserole. Sprinkle 2 tbs. grated cheese, 2 tbs. buttered bread crumbs. Bake in hot oven (425°) 20 min.

CHICORY & GRAPE SALAD: Toss lettuce, watercress, and chicory with 1/2 c. sliced white grapes, 1/4 cup French dressing.

MERINGUE PEARS W. CHOCOLATE SAUCE: To juice from 1 small can pears add 1 tbs. apricot jam, 2 tbs. sherry. Boil 5 min. Add 1 oz. sweet chocolate, stir over low heat until smooth. Beat 1 egg white stiff with 3 tbs. sugar, pinch salt. Spread over pears, brown in oven 5 min. Serve with sauce.

TIME 50 MIN. SERVES 2

WEDNESDAY

Canadian Bacon w. Acorn Squash and Broccoli
**Grilled Cheese Rolls*
Tossed Salad
Tutti Frutti Peaches
Coffee

ACORN SQUASH: 1 small. Halve, remove seeds. Place in each half 1 tsp. honey, 1 tsp. butter, 1/2 tsp. salt. Bake in hot oven (400°) 45 min. Serve filled with 1/2 box cooked, buttered peas.

BROCCOLI: 1 1/2 lbs. Remove tough leaves, trim lower stalks. Cook covered, standing upright in 2″ boiling water, about 20 min. For sauce, heat 1/2 c. mayonnaise mixed with 2 tsp. lemon juice, 1/4 tsp. salt, 1 tbs. milk.

GRILLED CHEESE ROLLS: 2 leftover hard rolls split in two. Dip split sides in milk, then in grated Parmesan cheese. Dot with butter, broil until brown.

TUTTI-FRUTTI PEACHES: Mash 1/2 pt. tutti-frutti ice cream with fork, add 1 tbs. sherry. Serve over 2 sliced, chilled peaches.

THURSDAY

TIME 35 MIN. SERVES 2

Iced Apple Juice
Virginia Cube Steaks
French-Fried Potatoes
Hot Buttered Green Beans
Beet & Celery Salad
Scalloped Rhubarb
Coffee

VIRGINIA CUBE STEAKS: 3 cube steaks ¼" thick. Rub with seasoned flour. Heat 1 tbs. butter and 1 tbs. oil in frying pan. When very hot, brown steaks quickly, 45 seconds for both sides. Serve immediately on toast with sliced Bermuda onion.

BEET & CELERY SALAD: Drain 1 small can diced beets. Toss with ½ c. diced celery, 1 finely sliced onion, sprinkle with lemon juice. Serve on lettuce with mayonnaise mixed smooth with a little cream.

SCALLOPED RHUBARB: 1 box rhubarb, defrosted. Arrange in baking dish in alternate layers with ½ c. buttered crumbs mixed with ¼ c. sugar. Dot with 1 tbs. butter, bake in hot oven (450°) 30 min. Serve warm with cream.

FRIDAY

TIME 30 MIN. SERVES 2

Mexican Mackerel
Jacket-Boiled Potatoes
**Corn Salad*
Melon Russe
Iced Tea

MEXICAN MACKEREL: 4 fillets, skin left on. Rub with cut lemon, brush with 1 tbs. melted butter, place in baking dish, skin side up. Cover with wax paper, bake in moderate oven (350°) 20 min. Mix ½ c. mayonnaise with 1 tbs. tarragon vinegar, 2 tsp. dry mustard, pinch cayenne, 2 tbs. cream, salt to taste. Pour over fillets, brown under broiler.

CORN SALAD: Marinate 1 small can drained corn kernels in 2 tbs. oil, 1 tbs. vinegar, ¼ tsp. salt, dash pepper, ¼ tsp. paprika, ¼ tsp. dry mustard 15 min. Mix in any leftover vegetables, diced. Serve drained on chicory.

MELON RUSSE: Line each serving glass with 4 ladyfingers. Fill each with 3 tbs. diced cantaloupe, 1 tbs. mint jelly. Top with whipped cream.

SHOPPING LIST

MEAT

3 lbs. loin of veal roast
½ lb. beef liver, ¼″ thick
4 strips salt pork
½ lb. boiled ham
1¼ lbs. rib steak, 1″ thick
¼ lb. bacon

FROZEN FOODS

3 boxes peas
1 box French-fried potatoes

FRESH FRUITS AND VEGETABLES

1 small honeydew melon
8 tiny new potatoes
1 bunch radishes
2 oranges
1 small bunch watercress
1 small cantaloupe
½ lb. seedless grapes
4 Idaho potatoes
1 head romaine
8 tomatoes
1 small cucumber
1 small bunch celery
1 head escarole
1 small avocado
2 artichokes
1 large leek
1 pt. blueberries

SUNDRIES

1 pt. heavy cream
½ pt. sour cream
1 can tuna fish flakes
1 small can anchovies
3 chocolate cupcakes
1 box ready-to-bake rolls
1-lb. can kidney beans
1 4-oz. can pimiento
1 small bottle grenadine syrup
¼ lb. macaroni
⅛ lb. sliced Cheddar cheese
1 tube ready-to-bake biscuits
1 can condensed tomato soup
1 can condensed cream of celery soup
2 oz. peanut brittle

PICK UP ON YOUR WAY HOME

THUR.—1 pt. lemon sherbet cookies
FRI.—1 doz. oysters

SUNDAY

TIME 3¾ HRS. SERVES 4

Veal in Pork Blanket
Buttered Peas w. Onions
Baked Idaho Potatoes
Watercress & Escarole Salad
Cackoo Melon
Coffee

VEAL IN PORK BLANKET: 3 lbs. loin roast. Place in deep casserole, cover with white cooking wine, add 1 split garlic clove, 1 tsp. salt, ½ tsp. pepper. Cover, let stand 3 or more hours, turning often. Discard half the wine, remove roast to roasting pan, cover with strips salt pork. Roast uncovered in moderate oven (325°) 40 min. to pound. Baste often. Save 2 thick slices.

BUTTERED PEAS W. ONIONS: Prepare 2 boxes peas as directed. Add 1 sliced onion cooked in 1 tbs. butter until soft.

CACKOO MELON: 1 small honeydew. Remove top, scoop out seeds. Pour in 3 tbs. crème de cacao. Replace top. Chill at least 3 hours. Slice into 4 rings. (Save top and bottom slices for Wednesday.) Fill with 2 c. whipped cream flavored with 1 tbs. crème de cacao.

MONDAY

TIME 25 MIN. SERVES 2

Hungarian Liver
Caraway Potatoes
Garden Salad
Oranges & Grapes in Grenadine
Coffee

HUNGARIAN LIVER: ½ lb. beef liver cut ¼″ thick. Dust with ½ tsp. salt, ¼ tsp. pepper, 1 tbs. flour. Brown quickly on both sides in 2 tbs. butter. Add 2 sliced onions, ½ c. bouillon, cook slowly 10 min. Remove liver to warm platter. Add ½ c. sour cream, dash cayenne, ¼ tsp. paprika, ¼ tsp. Worcestershire sauce to onions. Cook 1 min. Serve over liver.

CARAWAY POTATOES: 8 tiny new. Wash. Boil until tender. Serve peeled, buttered, sprinkled with caraway seeds.

GARDEN SALAD: 6 sliced radishes, 2 quartered tomatoes, ½ cucumber, sliced. Serve on escarole, French dressing.

ORANGES & GRAPES IN GRENADINE: Chill segments 2 oranges, ½ c. washed grapes, 2 tbs. grenadine.

TIME 20 MIN. SERVES 2 **TUESDAY**

Tomato Soup
**Anchovy Veal*
Avocado Salad
Hot Ginger Rolls
Chocolate Crème Cakes
Coffee

TOMATO SOUP: 1 can. Prepare as directed. Add sour cream.

ANCHOVY VEAL: 2 slices leftover. Mash together 4 anchovy fillets, 1 tsp. capers. Mix with 3 tbs. mayonnaise, 1 tbs. lemon juice. Spread over veal slices. Serve cold with lemon wedges.

AVOCADO SALAD: Arrange 1 sliced, peeled avocado, 2 slices diced crisp bacon, ½ c. diced celery on romaine. French dressing.

HOT GINGER ROLLS: 1 box ready-to-bake. Mix ½ tsp. powdered ginger with 1 tbs. butter. Spread on rolls, bake as directed.

CHOCOLATE CRÈME CAKES: 3 chocolate cupcakes. Split ¾ way down center, fill with vanilla-flavored whipped cream, sprinkle with chopped walnuts.

TIME 45 MIN. SERVES 2 **WEDNESDAY**

**Chilled Melon Cup*
Sautéed Ham w. Kidney Beans
Artichokes Vinaigrette
Coffee

SAUTÉED HAM W. KIDNEY BEANS: Cut ½ lb. boiled ham in long strips, sauté in 2 tbs. butter with 2 chopped onions. Add 1 can kidney beans, 2 chopped tomatoes, 1 minced garlic clove, ¼ tsp. salt, ¼ tsp. pepper, 1 tsp. chopped parsley. Mix. Cook 15 min. Serve very hot on 1½ c. prepared precooked rice. (Prepare extra ½ c. rice for tomorrow.)

ARTICHOKES VINAIGRETTE: 2. Remove outer leaves. Trim bases. Place upright in 2″ boiling water. Cook covered 35 min. Drain, cool. Mix ½ tsp. salt, ¼ tsp. pepper, pinch each sugar, mustard, onion salt, ¼ tsp. Worcestershire, 1 minced garlic clove, 1 minced onion, 3 tbs. olive oil, 1 tbs. lemon juice, 1 tbs. tarragon vinegar, 1 chopped hard-cooked egg. Serve with artichokes.

THURSDAY

TIME 30 MIN. SERVES 2

Steak au Poivre
French-Fried Potatoes
Colony Salad
Lemon Sherbet
Cookies
Iced Coffee

STEAK AU POIVRE: 1–1¼ lbs. rib steak, 1″ thick. Preheat broiler, broil 3 min. on one side. Turn, dot with 1 tbs. butter, sprinkle thickly (about 1 tsp.) with coarsely ground fresh black pepper. Complete broiling 15 min. for rare, 25 min. for well done.

COLONY SALAD: Slice 1 small can pimiento, drained, add 2 tbs. chopped chives, 2 large sliced tomatoes, 1 tbs. chopped parsley, ½ c. cooked rice. Sprinkle with garlicky French dressing. Serve on escarole.

LEMON SHERBET: 1 pt. Sprinkle with crushed peanut brittle.

ICED COFFEE: Make double-strength black coffee. Sweeten to taste while still hot. Pour over ice cubes. Top with whipped cream.

FRIDAY

TIME 30 MIN. SERVES 2

Shipwreck Oysters
Leek & Tomato Salad
Hot Buttered Biscuits
Cantaloupe w. Blueberries
Coffee

SHIPWRECK OYSTERS: Break ¼ lb. macaroni into 1½″ pieces. Boil uncovered in 1½ qts. salted water until just tender. Heat 1 can condensed cream of celery soup. Season with ½ tsp. prepared mustard, ⅛ tsp. pepper. Add 2 tbs. minced celery, ½ box peas, defrosted, and 12 drained oysters. Cook until oysters begin to curl around edges. Place drained macaroni in shallow greased casserole, cover with oyster mixture. Top with ⅛ lb. sliced Cheddar. Bake in hot oven (450°) 15 min.

LEEK & TOMATO SALAD: Cut 1 raw leek into thin shavings. Arrange with 2 sliced tomatoes on romaine. French dressing.

CANTALOUPE W. BLUEBERRIES: Slice 2 1½″-thick rings from cantaloupe, remove rind. Fill with blueberries, top with whipped cream.

JULY

Recheck your basic staples—and now have you

caraway seeds
horseradish
lemons
walnuts or pecans
powdered sugar
crème de menthe
capers
basil
rosemary
brown sugar
curry powder
cinnamon
nutmeg
honey
saffron
sage
thyme
brandy
soy sauce

SHOPPING LIST

MEAT

1 large broiler, quartered
¾ lb. ground beef
6 lamb kidneys
2 veal cutlets, pounded thin

FROZEN FOODS

2 boxes peas
1 box asparagus
1 box cod fillets
1 box French-fried potatoes

FRESH FRUITS AND VEGETABLES

2 lbs. white turnips
1 head romaine
1 head escarole
1 head iceberg lettuce
1 small head cabbage
1 apple
3 solid peaches
2 cucumbers
3 ripe bananas
2 tomatoes
1 small honeydew melon
1 bunch celery
4 green peppers
1 bunch parsley
8 tiny new potatoes
5 carrots
1 pt. raspberries
1 small box red currants

SUNDRIES

⅛ lb. Gorgonzola cheese
1 small box salted crackers
½ pt. sour cream
1 small can cream-style corn
1 4-oz. can sliced mushrooms
½ pt. heavy cream
1 pkg. Italian bread sticks
1 small jar anchovy paste
8-oz. pkg. macaroni
1 small can tomato sauce
1 small jar anchovies
1 small can tomatoes
1 small can pimiento
2 ladyfingers
1 can chicken broth

PICK UP ON YOUR WAY HOME

WED.—½ pt. vanilla ice cream
FRI.—black bread

TIME 1½ HRS. SERVES 4 **SUNDAY**

Paprika Chicken
Buttered Rice w. Peas
Caraway Turnips
Tossed Romaine & Escarole
Raspberries, Red Currant Sauce

PAPRIKA CHICKEN: 1 large broiler, quartered. Sprinkle with 1 tbs. paprika, salt, pepper. Sauté 5 sliced onions in 3 tbs. butter until golden. Add chicken, cook 10 min. Beat 1 egg yolk into ¾ c. sour cream, add ½ tsp. salt, ¼ tsp. pepper, spread over chicken. Simmer covered until tender, about 1 hr.

CARAWAY TURNIPS: 2 lbs. Scrub, pare, dice. Boil in small amount salted water 15 min. Drain, mash with 3 tbs. butter, salt and pepper to taste, ½ tsp. caraway seeds.

RASPBERRIES W. RED CURRANT SAUCE: Boil 1 c. red currants, ¾ c. sugar 15 min. Strain, chill. Serve over fresh raspberries.

TIME 55 MIN. SERVES 2 **MONDAY**

Deviled Meat Loaf
Tomatoes in Corn
Cabbage & Apple Salad
Banana Snow
Coffee

DEVILED MEAT LOAF: Mix ¾ lb. ground beef, ½ c. soft bread crumbs, 1 egg, 2 tbs. chopped green pepper, ½ tsp. dry mustard, 1½ tsp. Worcestershire sauce, 1 tsp. horseradish, ¾ tsp. salt, ¼ tsp. pepper. Shape into loaf, spread with 2 tbs. ketchup, bake in moderate oven (350°) 45 min.

TOMATOES IN CORN: Slice 2 tomatoes in half, broil 10 min. Heat 1 small can cream-style corn with ½ can sliced mushrooms, salt, pepper, dash Tabasco. Serve over tomatoes.

CABBAGE & APPLE SALAD: Mix 1½ c. chopped cabbage, 1 chopped unpeeled apple, 2 tbs. mayonnaise, 2 tbs. cream, juice ½ lemon, ½ tsp. sugar, paprika. Serve in cabbage leaves.

BANANA SNOW: Beat 1 egg white stiff, add 1 tbs. sugar, beat in 2 mashed bananas with 1 tsp. lemon juice. Sprinkle with nut crumbs.

TUESDAY

TIME 30 MIN. SERVES 2

Cold Chicken Soup
Ukrainian Kidneys
Boiled Potatoes
Carrot & Celery Salad
Honeydew de Menthe
Iced Tea

COLD CHICKEN SOUP: Heat 1 can chicken broth to boiling, stir into 2 egg yolks mixed with ¼ tsp. salt, dash cayenne. Add ½ c. cream. Chill. Serve garnished with toasted croutons.

UKRAINIAN KIDNEYS: Split 6 lamb kidneys, discard core, white tubes. Slice thin, dust with 1 tbs. flour. Brown in 1 tbs. butter. Add 2 tbs. bouillon, 1 chopped onion, ¼ tsp. salt, ⅛ tsp. pepper, cook 5 min. Add 1 diced peeled cucumber, cook 10 min. more. Before serving stir in 3 tbs. sour cream.

CARROT & CELERY SALAD: Toss ½ c. chopped celery, ½ c. shredded carrot with broken escarole in ¼ c. French dressing. Garnish with sliced banana.

HONEYDEW DE MENTHE: Dissolve 2 tbs. powdered sugar in ¼ c. crème de menthe. Pour over 3 honeydew wedges. Reserve 1 for tomorrow.

WEDNESDAY

TIME 35 MIN. SERVES 2

Ponte Vecchio Veal
Asparagus, Egg Sauce
Mixed Green Salad
Italian Bread Sticks
**Fruit Parfait*
Coffee

PONTE VECCHIO VEAL: 2 cutlets pounded thin. Spread with 2 tbs. anchovy paste mixed with 6 chopped capers, ⅛ tsp. basil, 1 tbs. white wine. Roll, secure with toothpicks. Roll in flour, then in 1 beaten egg mixed with ½ tsp. salt, ⅛ tsp. pepper, 2 tbs. hot water, and again in flour. Fry in 3 tbs. hot oil until golden brown.

ASPARAGUS W. EGG SAUCE: Prepare 1 box asparagus as directed; mash yolk 1 hard-cooked egg with ½ tsp. prepared mustard and 1 tbs. mayonnaise. Serve over well-drained asparagus.

FRUIT PARFAIT: Alternate spoonfuls honeydew, vanilla ice cream in parfait glasses. Top with whipped cream, dot mint jelly.

TIME 35 MIN. SERVES 2

THURSDAY

Deep-Sea Macaroni
**Peas w. Mushrooms*
Raw Vegetable Salad
Gorgonzola Cheese & Crackers
Viennese Coffee

DEEP-SEA MACARONI: Boil 6 oz. unbroken macaroni. Sauté 1 chopped onion in 2 tbs. olive oil and 1 tbs. butter. Add 1 can tomato sauce, salt, pepper, ¼ tsp. basil, bring to boil, add 1 tbs. chopped parsley and 6 mashed anchovies. Mix thoroughly. Pour over drained macaroni. Sprinkle with 3 tbs. melted butter, 4 tbs. Parmesan cheese.

RAW VEGETABLE SALAD: Cut 2 carrots, 2 stalks celery, 1 green pepper into thin strips, slice 1 small white onion paper-thin. Marinate in ¼ cup French dressing 15 min. Toss with shredded lettuce, pinch basil.

VIENNESE COFFEE: To each cup double-strength hot black coffee add sugar to taste. Top with 1 tbs. whipped cream.

TIME 35 MIN. SERVES 2

FRIDAY

Beachcomber Cod
French-Fried Potatoes
Cucumber & Celery Salad
Black Bread
Baked Stuffed Peaches
Iced Coffee

BEACHCOMBER COD: Boil 1 box cod 5 min. Drain. (Reserve 2 tbs. fish for Sunday.) Sauté 1 large sliced onion, 2 sliced green peppers, in ¼ c. olive oil until soft. Add 1 small can tomatoes, ½ tsp. salt, ¼ tsp. pepper, cook 10 min. Cut fish into pieces, place half in buttered casserole, add layer tomato mixture, then remaining fish, top with tomato mixture. Bake in moderate oven (350°) 25 min.

BAKED STUFFED PEACHES: 3 large. Halve. Remove pit and a little pulp. Mix pulp with 2 crumbled ladyfingers, 8 chopped almonds, ½ tsp. sugar, ¼ tsp. grated lemon rind. Stuff peach halves. Pour on ½ c. white wine. Sprinkle with 1 tbs. sugar, dot with 1 tbs. butter, bake 30 min. Serve warm.

SHOPPING LIST

MEAT

3 lbs. lamb cut from leg (1 piece)
¼ lb. bacon
⅛ lb. boiled ham
¾ lb. ground veal

FROZEN FOODS

1 box haddock
1 box peas
1 box pineapple

FRESH FRUITS AND VEGETABLES

1 white onion
2 heads iceberg lettuce
6 tomatoes
1 bunch celery
1 large bunch radishes
1 green pepper
2 oranges
2 bananas
1 small eggplant
1 carrot
1 bunch chives
3 peaches
1 leek
1 cucumber
1 bunch parsley
8 or 9 new potatoes
2 small zucchini

SUNDRIES

1 small jar anchovy fillets
1 large jar stuffed olives
⅛ lb. bleu cheese
1 #2 can sliced apples
2 sponge dessert shells
1 small can peas
1 pkg. Parker House rolls
1 can crab meat
1 tube ready-to-bake biscuits
1 can chicken fricassee (not boned)
2 #1 can potatoes
1 small jar currant jelly
1 pkg. gingerbread mix
1½ pts. light cream
1 small box currants
1 4-oz. can sliced mushrooms
2 English muffins
1 small can tomato sauce
¼ lb. cottage cheese
1 can clam chowder
2 cans asparagus soup
1 small can pimiento

PICK UP ON YOUR WAY HOME

TUES.—2 or 3 ears corn
WED.—½ angel food cake
THUR.—½ pt. heavy cream
FRI.—½ pt. vanilla ice cream

TIME 1¾ HRS. SERVES 4

SUNDAY

Iced Asparagus Soup
Lamb Casserole
**Spanish Salad*
Crème Brûlée
Coffee

LAMB CASSEROLE: 3-lb. piece from leg. Insert 3 sliced garlic cloves, sprinkle with salt, pepper, ¼ tsp. rosemary. Brown lightly on all sides in 2 tbs. oil. Add 8 or 9 small new potatoes, peeled, 4 quartered tomatoes, 1 small eggplant, peeled and diced. Simmer covered 1½ hrs.

SPANISH SALAD: Mix 2 tbs. leftover codfish, 6 anchovies, 8 olives, 1 thinly sliced white onion, 2 pimiento slices, broken lettuce. Toss with ½ c. French dressing. Garnish with 2 sliced hard-cooked eggs.

CRÈME BRÛLÉE: Scald 2 c. cream with 2 tbs. brown sugar, stir into 4 beaten egg yolks. Cook over hot water, stirring until thickened. Chill in custard cups. Top each with 1 tbs. brown sugar. Caramelize under low heat. Serve cold.

TIME 30 MIN. SERVES 2

MONDAY

Crab-Stuffed Zucchini
Parker House Rolls
Lettuce Wedges, Bleu Cheese Dressing
Spiced Fruit
Iced Tea

CRAB-STUFFED ZUCCHINI: Halve 2 small zucchini lengthwise. Boil in salted water 10 min., until just tender. Drain, scoop out seeds. Sauté 1 small chopped onion in 1 tbs. butter 5 min. Blend in 1 tsp. curry powder, 1 tbs. flour. Stir in ½ c. light cream. Add 1 can crab meat, salt and pepper to taste. Fill zucchini halves. Top with buttered bread crumbs, bake in moderate oven (375°) 20 min.

BLEU CHEESE DRESSING: 3 tbs. salad oil, 1 tbs. vinegar, 1 tbs. bleu cheese, ½ tsp. salt, ⅛ tsp. white pepper. Beat well.

SPICED FRUIT: Line serving dishes with long slices 2 bananas dipped in orange juice. Fill with ½ can sliced apples mixed with 1 diced orange. Dust with cinnamon and nutmeg, top with currant jelly.

TUESDAY

TIME 25 MIN. SERVES 2

Clam Chowder
Salted Crackers
**Lamb w. Cold Greens*
Corn on the Cob
**Hot Apple Sponge*
Iced Coffee

CLAM CHOWDER: 1 can. Prepare as directed. Add a dash or two of Tabasco.

LAMB W. COLD GREENS: Mix 1 c. diced leftover lamb with ½ c. diced peeled cucumber, 1 small can peas, drained, ½ c. sliced radishes, 1 diced green pepper, ¼ c. French dressing. Chill 20 min. Just before serving combine with 1 c. shredded lettuce, garnish with 2 slices crumbled bacon.

HOT APPLE SPONGE: Cook leftover ½ can sliced apples with 1 tbs. butter, 2 tbs. sugar, ½ tsp. grated lemon rind, 1 tbs. currants, ½ tsp. cinnamon 10 min. Serve hot on sponge dessert shells.

WEDNESDAY

TIME 25 MIN. SERVES 2

Lemon Chicken Fricassee
Ham-Stripped Peas
Hot Biscuits
Lettuce w. Tomatoes and Chives
Angel Food Cake w. Frozen Pineapple
Coffee

LEMON CHICKEN FRICASSEE: 1 can chicken fricassee, bone in. Drain. Brown chicken in 2 tbs. butter, remove to heatproof dish. Stir into pan 1 tbs. sherry, 1 tbs. white wine, ½ tsp. grated lemon rind, ½ tsp. grated orange rind, 1 tbs. lemon juice, ⅛ tsp. salt, dash pepper, ½ c. cream. Surround chicken with 1 #1 can potatoes, sliced. Pour on sauce. Top with 1 tbs. grated Parmesan cheese, 4 paper-thin lemon slices. Dot with butter, broil under low heat until well browned.

HAM-STRIPPED PEAS: Cut ⅛ lb. boiled ham into very fine strips. Sauté in 1 tbs. butter 5 min. Add to ½ box peas prepared as directed on box.

LETTUCE W. TOMATOES AND CHIVES: Arrange 2 sliced tomatoes on lettuce. Sprinkle with minced chives. Serve with French dressing.

TIME 35 MIN. SERVES 2

THURSDAY

Veal Patties on Toasted English Muffins
Scrambled Eggs
**Tomato Sauce*
Mixed Relish
**Cuban Peaches*
Iced Tea

VEAL PATTIES ON TOASTED ENGLISH MUFFINS: To ¾ lb. ground veal add 1 egg yolk, ½ tsp. salt, ¼ tsp. pepper, ½ tsp. paprika, ½ chopped onion, 1 minced garlic clove, 1 4-oz. can sliced mushrooms, drained and minced, 1 tbs. sherry. Shape into 4 patties, dust with flour, sauté in 2 tbs. butter. Serve on split toasted English muffins surrounded by scrambled eggs. Cover with 1 small can tomato sauce simmered 5 min. with ½ box leftover peas, 1 tsp. sherry.

MIXED RELISH: Arrange celery, olives, radishes, and carrot sticks on crushed ice.

CUBAN PEACHES: Chop 3 peeled, pitted peaches with leftover pineapple chunks. Stir in 2 tbs. honey. Top with whipped cream.

TIME 35 MIN. SERVES 2

FRIDAY

Haddock Bouillabaisse
Cottage Cheese & Cucumber Salad
Hot Gingerbread w. Ice Cream
Black Coffee

HADDOCK BOUILLABAISSE: 1 box. Cook 2 thickly sliced onions, 1 sliced leek, 2 split garlic cloves in 2 tbs. oil 8 min. Add 3 c. water, ¾ tsp. salt, ¼ tsp. pepper, pinch cayenne, ½ tsp. saffron, 1 bay leaf, ½ tsp. mixed dried herbs. Bring to boil. Add 1 #1 can potatoes, drained and sliced, the haddock cut in squares, ¼ c. red wine. Simmer 20 min. Add 1 tbs. chopped parsley, serve over dry toast rubbed with garlic.

COTTAGE CHEESE & CUCUMBER SALAD: Cut 1 large peeled cucumber into 1″-thick slices. Remove centers, dice. Crisp shells in iced water, drain dry. Mix ½ c. cottage cheese, 1 tbs. chopped chives, 1 tbs. mayonnaise, and diced cucumber. Stuff into shells. Garnish with paprika, serve on lettuce.

SHOPPING LIST

MEAT

1½ lbs. ground beef
1 lb. veal cutlets ½″ thick
½ lb. beef liver ½″ thick
2 shoulder lamb chops
¼ lb. boiled ham
2 small sausages
¼ lb. bacon

FROZEN FOODS

1 box Ford Hook Lima beans
1 box potato puffs
1 box asparagus
1 box whipped potatoes
1 can grapefruit juice

FRESH FRUITS AND VEGETABLES

1 bunch parsley
1 head iceberg lettuce
1 cucumber
½ lb. mushrooms
1 small eggplant
2 red bananas for Thur.
1 pt. blueberries
1 small cauliflower
1 bunch scallions
1 large honeydew melon
1 small cantaloupe
4–6 ears corn
1 avocado
1 tomato
1 bunch mint
1 head chicory
1 bunch celery
4 green peppers
3 lemons
2 apples
1 orange
1 bunch chives
1 sweet red pepper

SUNDRIES

6 frankfurter rolls
1 small can tomato sauce
1 box cookies
½ pt. heavy cream
1 small bottle ginger ale
½ pt. sour cream
1 small can corn kernels
1 small can potatoes
1 small can tomatoes
2 wedges Camembert cheese
1 small can tomato paste
2 sponge dessert shells
1 can condensed consommé
1 can madrilene
1 can condensed cream of mushroom soup

PICK UP ON YOUR WAY HOME

THUR.—2 English muffins
1 pkg. washed spinach
FRI.—1 lb. mackerel, split
French bread

TIME 30 MIN. SERVES 4 **SUNDAY**

Garden Barbecue
Corn on the Cob
Mixed Vegetable Salad Bowl
Fruit-Filled Melon
Coffee

GARDEN BARBECUE: Combine 1½ lbs. ground beef, 1 chopped garlic clove, 3 tbs. chopped onion, 1 tsp. salt, ¼ tsp. pepper, ¾ tsp. sage, dash Tabasco, 1 tbs. chopped parsley. Shape into 5″ rolls. Brown over hot coals or broil. Roll in chopped parsley. Serve on frankfurter rolls.

MIXED VEGETABLE SALAD BOWL: Mix 1 diced tomato, 1 sliced cucumber, 1 c. slivered celery, 1½ c. cauliflower pieces, 1 green pepper cut into rings. Serve on lettuce with French dressing.

FRUIT-FILLED MELON: Halve 1 large honeydew. Scoop out fruit and dice. Decorate 1 shell with mint leaves, fill with diced melon mixed with 1 c. cantaloupe balls, 1 c. blueberries. Serve cold with sprinkling of ginger ale.

TIME 40 MIN. SERVES 2 **MONDAY**

Jellied Consommé
Parmesan Breaded Veal Cutlets
**Cauliflower w. Mushrooms*
Potato Puffs
Cookies
**Crushed Fruit Frost*

PARMESAN BREADED VEAL CUTLETS: 1 lb., ½″ thick. Cut in serving pieces. Roll in flour, dip in slightly beaten egg, then in fine bread crumbs. Set aside for 10 min., then sauté slowly in fat 15 min. Turn, sprinkle 1 tsp. Parmesan cheese on each slice, sauté 12 min. more. Serve with 1 can heated tomato sauce.

CAULIFLOWER W. MUSHROOMS: Break into flowerets. Cook covered 10 min. in ½ c. boiling salted water. Drain. Top with buttered bread crumbs and 1 c. sliced fresh mushrooms browned in 2 tbs. butter.

CRUSHED FRUIT FROST: Boil ½ c. sugar, ½ c. water 5 min. Chill. Add juice 3 lemons, 1½ c. water. Crush 4 tbs. leftover cantaloupe, 2 mint leaves, place in glasses. Fill with crushed ice, pour on lemonade. Garnish with mint leaves, cantaloupe balls.

TUESDAY

TIME 40 MIN. SERVES 2

Square Liver
Lima Beans & Celery
Green Salad
Blueberry Shortcake
Coffee

SQUARE LIVER: ½ lb. beef or calf liver cut in 1″ squares. Brown quickly in 2 tbs. butter. Remove and keep warm. Add 2 finely sliced large onions to pan, cook until golden. Add 1 tbs. flour, 2 tsp. tomato paste, 1 c. red wine, 1 tsp. vinegar, 1 tbs. water, 1 bay leaf, ¼ tsp. thyme, 1 garlic clove, ½ tsp. salt, ¼ tsp. pepper, dash cayenne. Cook 5 min. Add liver. Simmer 6 min.

LIMA BEANS & CELERY: 1 box. Cook as directed, adding ½ c. thinly sliced celery. Drain, add ¼ c. cream, salt, pepper, 1 tsp. butter. Heat thoroughly.

BLUEBERRY SHORTCAKE: Crush ½ c. blueberries with 2 tbs. powdered sugar. Fill 2 dessert shells. Top with whipped cream and garnish with ½ c. whole blueberries.

WEDNESDAY

TIME 40 MIN. SERVES 2

Cold Madrilene
**Corn-Stuffed Peppers*
Asparagus w. Mushroom Sauce
Avocado, Orange & Onion Salad
Coffee

CORN-STUFFED PEPPERS: Cut tops off 3 large green peppers, remove seeds and fibers, drop in boiling salted water for 5 min. Drain. Prepare ½ c. precooked rice, add 1 small can drained corn kernels or 1 c. leftover corn scraped from cob, 2 tbs. chili sauce, any finely chopped leftover meats, ¼ c. bread crumbs, 3 tbs. melted butter, ½ tsp. salt, ¼ tsp. pepper. Stuff peppers. Top each with small piece bacon. Place upright in greased dish, bake in moderately hot oven (400°) 25 min.

ASPARAGUS W. MUSHROOM SAUCE: 1 box. Prepare as directed. Serve on 2 slices toast, pour on 1 can heated condensed cream of mushroom soup.

AVOCADO, ORANGE & ONION SALAD: Marinate 1 peeled, diced avocado with 1 diced orange and ½ thinly sliced onion 30 min. Serve on lettuce with French dressing.

TIME 40 MIN. SERVES 2

THURSDAY

Grapefruit Juice
Andalusian Lamb
Spinach Salad
Toasted Split Muffins
Sliced Red Bananas & Cream
Coffee

ANDALUSIAN LAMB: Sprinkle 2 shoulder chops with salt and pepper. Brown in 1 tbs. bacon fat, 1 tbs. oil, remove to casserole. Sauté ¼ lb. diced boiled ham, 1 small can potatoes, drained and sliced, 1 sliced onion in pan drippings 5 min. Add 1 small can tomatoes, cook 5 min. more, add ½ tsp. salt, ½ tsp. freshly ground black pepper. Pour over chops. Bake covered in hot oven (425°) 25 min. Garnish with 2 link sausages cut in small pieces and fried to rich brown.

SPINACH SALAD: Rinse 1 pkg. washed spinach. Cook covered over low heat 5 min. Drain. Dry over low heat, toss with 1 sliced sweet red pepper, 1 tbs. minced onion, ¼ c. French dressing. Serve on lettuce. Garnish with crumbled crisp bacon.

TIME 35 MIN. SERVES 2

FRIDAY

Baked Split Mackerel
Whipped Potatoes
Sautéed Sliced Eggplant
Parisian Salad
French Bread
Camembert w. Apples
Iced Coffee

BAKED SPLIT MACKEREL: 1 lb. split. Place open (skin side down) on greased shallow dish. Brush with 3 tbs. melted butter mixed with ½ tsp. salt, ¼ tsp. pepper, ½ tsp. paprika. Bake in hot oven (450°) 25 min. For sauce, heat 1 tbs. butter, blend in 1 tbs. flour, stir in 1 c. warm sour cream, 2 tbs. horseradish, 1 tsp. vinegar, ½ tsp. salt, 1 tsp. chopped chives. Simmer 5 min.

SAUTÉED SLICED EGGPLANT: Cut unpeeled eggplant in ½" slices. Boil 5 min. Drain, sauté in hot oil until soft and light brown. Drain on paper, sprinkle salt, pepper, garnish with parsley.

PARISIAN SALAD: Wash and slice almost to the tip ½ c. raw, unpeeled mushrooms. Mix with ½ c. chopped fresh parsley, ¼ c. chopped scallions, ¼ c. garlicky French dressing. Serve on chicory.

SHOPPING LIST

MEAT

3 lbs. top round steak
1½-lb. broiler, quartered
¼ lb. bacon
1 beef kidney

FROZEN FOODS

1 box French-style string beans
1 box whipped potatoes
1 can pineapple juice

FRESH FRUITS AND VEGETABLES

7 tomatoes
1 head chicory
1 large bunch celery
1 apple
1 grapefruit
1 orange
1 bunch watercress
2 pears
2 green peppers
2 apricots
3 new potatoes
1 small bunch dandelion greens
1 small bunch scallions
2 plums
1 iceberg lettuce
1 cucumber
1 bunch parsley
1 lime
2 large peaches
½ casaba melon
1 pt. blackberries

SUNDRIES

1 8-oz. can sliced mushrooms
1 small jar pitted greet olives
1 small can tomato paste
1 #2 can potatoes
1 tall tin chocolate wafers
1 pt. heavy cream
1 box ready-to-bake rolls
1 portion Roquefort cheese
1 large can California sardines
1 #1 can diced carrots
1 small can pimiento
1 #1 can potatoes
1 box blueberry muffins
1 small can tomatoes
1 small spongecake
1 can shrimps
1 pkg. lemon junket
1 small jar stem ginger
1 can condensed pea soup

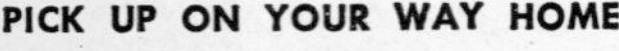

PICK UP ON YOUR WAY HOME

FRI.—1 lb. fillet of sole
1 bunch watercress

TIME 3½ HRS. SERVES 4 **SUNDAY**

French Beef Daube
Summer Salad Bowls
Hot Rolls
Chocolate Icebox Cake
Coffee

FRENCH BEEF DAUBE: 3 lbs. top round steak. Discard fat, cut in small chunks. Brown quickly, a few at a time, in 3 tbs. butter. Remove. Stir in 3 tbs. flour, add 1 8-oz. can sliced mushrooms, 1 small jar pitted green olives, 1 tsp. tomato paste, 1 c. bouillon. Stir, bring to boil. Add ½ c. white wine, 1 bay leaf, the beef, 1 #2 can potatoes, drained. Cover, simmer 1½ hrs. Set aside 1½ c. meat for tomorrow. Add 1 tbs. brandy. Serve topped with 3 thinly sliced tomatoes and 3 tbs. grated cheese.

SUMMER SALAD BOWLS: Toss pulled chicory, 1 c. chopped celery, 1 shredded unpeeled apple, 1 c. grapefruit sections with ½ c. French dressing. Individual bowls.

CHOCOLATE ICEBOX CAKE: Prepare as directed on wafer tin.

TIME 25 MIN. SERVES 2 **MONDAY**

Chilled Pea Soup
**Roquefort Steak & Potatoes*
Watercress Shrimp Salad
Blackberry Flummery
Cold Milk

CHILLED PEA SOUP: 1 can. Beat in 1 soup can cold milk, dash cayenne. Serve ice-cold with paprika.

ROQUEFORT STEAK & POTATOES: Mix 3 tbs. Roquefort cheese, 1 tbs. melted butter with 2 tbs. milk, 1 tsp. Worcestershire. Add juice 1 lemon, ¼ tsp. salt, ⅛ tsp. pepper, dash Tabasco, 1 tbs. minced onion. Place leftover daube in shallow casserole. Add 3 boiled potatoes, sliced. Cover with cheese mixture, place under broiler until cheese melts and beef is thoroughly heated.

WATERCRESS SHRIMP SALAD: Mix chopped watercress with 4 chopped shrimp (save remainder for tomorrow), 1 diced green pepper, juice 1 lemon. Serve with mayonnaise.

BLACKBERRY FLUMMERY: Cook 1 c. blackberries in 1 c. water 5 min. Add ½ c. sugar mixed with 2 tbs. cornstarch, dash salt. Stir, boil 5 min. Add 1 tsp. lemon juice. Serve with sugar and cream.

TUESDAY

TIME 20 MIN. SERVES 2

**Sea-Food Cocktail*
Sardines Basque
Whipped Potatoes
Lemon Junket
Iced Tea

SEA-FOOD COCKTAIL: Arrange leftover shrimps in lettuce-lined glasses. Cover with 3 tbs. mayonnaise mixed with 1 tbs. chili sauce, 2 dashes Tabasco, pepper to taste.

SARDINES BASQUE: 1 large can. Sauté ½ #1 can carrots, drained, 2 large thinly sliced onions, ½ box defrosted French-style string beans in 3 tbs. butter, cook slowly 5 min. Add 2 diced tomatoes, 2 diced pimientos, cook 3 min. Remove to shallow serving casserole. Add drained sardines to pan, cook 1 min. each side. Place on hot vegetables, sprinkle with 1 tbs. grated Parmesan and pan drippings. Brown under broiler.

LEMON JUNKET: Prepare 2 portions as directed. Garnish with whipped cream and leftover blackberries.

WEDNESDAY

TIME 1 HR. SERVES 2

**Chicken Casserole*
St. Laurent Salad
Blueberry Muffins
Jellied Peaches
Coffee

CHICKEN CASSEROLE: 1 small broiler, quartered. Brown in 1 tbs. butter. Rub with cut lemon, salt, pepper, ¼ tsp. sage, 1 tsp. grated lemon rind. Pour 1 can potatoes into casserole, add ½ can carrots, ½ box defrosted string beans. Place chicken on top, cover, bake in moderate oven (400°) 50 min.

ST. LAURENT SALAD: Arrange chopped dandelion greens with thinly sliced scallions on tomato slices with lettuce. Garnish with chopped hard-cooked egg. Serve with French dressing.

JELLIED PEACHES: Dip 2 large peaches in boiling water to loosen skin. Peel. Coat with ½ c. melted, cooled currant jelly. Chill.

TIME 35 MIN. SERVES 2

THURSDAY

Bayou Kidney Stew
Orange & Pimiento Salad
Fruit Wine Cooler
Spongecake
Coffee

BAYOU KIDNEY STEW: Cut 1 beef kidney into ¾″ slices, discarding core. Dust with flour, salt, pepper. Fry 2 slices bacon, diced, until crisp, add kidneys and brown. Add 1 sliced onion, 1 sliced green pepper, 3 sliced green olives, 1 minced garlic clove, 1 tbs. chopped parsley, 1 bay leaf, ⅛ tsp. thyme, 1 small can tomatoes, ½ tsp. salt, ¼ tsp. pepper. Cover, simmer 25 min. Serve with toast triangles or whipped potatoes.

ORANGE & PIMIENTO SALAD: Rub 1 slice toast with cut garlic clove, place in bottom of salad bowl, cover with lettuce leaves. Add 1 sliced, peeled orange, 2 sliced pimientos. Serve with ½ c. French dressing mixed with 1 minced hard-cooked egg.

FRUIT WINE COOLER: Cut 2 pears, 2 apricots, 2 plums into pieces. Place in bottom of tall glasses, fill with ice cubes, pour in white wine. Drink wine with meal, eat fruit with spongecake as dessert.

TIME 35 MIN. SERVES 2

FRIDAY

Iced Pineapple Juice
Indo-Chinese Sole
Rice
Soya Watercress
Casaba Melon w. Lime Wedges
Coffee

INDO-CHINESE SOLE: 1 lb. fillets. Sauté in ¼ c. oil 10 min. Brown 2 crushed garlic cloves in 1 tbs. butter 6 seconds. Discard garlic. Add ¼ c. vinegar, ⅓ c. sugar, 1 tsp. soy sauce, ⅛ tsp. pepper. Add 1 tbs. cornstarch mixed with ½ c. cold water. Bring to boil. Add ¼ c. finely sliced peeled cucumber, 1 sliced onion, 1 tbs. diced stem ginger, peel of 1 lemon cut in fine slivers. Cook 5 min. Pour over fish. Garnish with parsley. Serve with 1½ c. prepared precooked rice.

SOYA WATERCRESS: Boil (1 bunch) washed watercress 8 min. in small amount of water. Drain well. Chop, mix with 1 tsp. soy sauce. Serve cold.

AUGUST

Recheck your basic staples—and now have you

chili powder
orange marmalade
basil
honey
celery salt
nutmeg
lemons
soy sauce
almonds
powdered sugar
cinnamon
caraway seeds
corn meal
celery seed
rum (light)
crème de menthe (opt.)
grenadine syrup

—Have you

toothpicks
long skewers
aluminum foil

SHOPPING LIST

MEAT

- about 1¾ lbs. boneless shoulder of lamb, cut in 12 1½" cubes
- 1 lb. ground beef chuck
- ½ lb. bacon
- 2 2-oz. slices boiled ham
- ½ lb. veal cutlet

FROZEN FOODS

- 1 box peas
- 1 box string beans
- 1 box strawberries
- 1 box potato puffs
- 1 box scallops

FRESH FRUITS AND VEGETABLES

- 12 small white onions
- 1 box blueberries
- 3 seedless oranges
- 7 or 8 ears corn
- ½ watermelon
- 6 green peppers
- 1 small cantaloupe
- 1 bunch celery
- 2 or 3 carrots
- 6 tomatoes
- 1 lb. Lima beans
- 1 bunch endive
- 2 peaches
- 1 cucumber

SUNDRIES

- 8 frankfurter rolls (optional)
- 1 small jar stuffed olives
- 1 12-oz. can vegetable juice
- 1 8-oz. pkg. thin spaghetti
- 1 6-oz. can crab meat flakes
- ½ pt. heavy cream
- 1 small can tomato sauce
- ½ lb. Cheddar cheese
- 1 tube ready-to-bake biscuits
- 1 4-oz. can sliced mushrooms
- 1 #2 can tomato juice
- 1 can condensed vegetable soup

PICK UP ON YOUR WAY HOME

MON.—1 pt. vanilla ice cream
TUES.—½ green apple pie
black bread
FRI.—2 slices plain cake, rye bread

SUNDAY

TIME 35 MIN. SERVES 4

Shish Kabob
Buttered Rice or Split Frankfurter Rolls
Corn on the Cob
Watermelon
Iced Tea

SHISH KABOB: About 1¾ lbs. lamb cut into 12 1½″ cubes. Cover cubes with French dressing. Chill at least 6 hrs., preferably overnight. Peel 12 small white onions, quarter 4 firm tomatoes, 4 green peppers; arrange with lamb cubes on 4 skewers at least 18″ long. Brush with French dressing. Broil, turning frequently, brushing with more dressing, until well done, about 20 min. Serve with buttered rice or slip off skewers into 2 scooped-out frankfurter rolls if outdoors.

CORN: 7 or 8 fresh ears. Boil in water sweetened with 1 tbs. sugar. Cook until iust tender, about 6 min. Save any left over for Tuesday.

MONDAY

TIME 40 MIN. SERVES 2

Barbecued Meat Loaves
Fresh Lima Beans & Celery
Green Salad Bowl
Orange Parfait
Black Coffee

BARBECUED MEAT LOAF: 1 lb. ground beef. Add 2 slices minced bacon, 2 tbs. dry bread crumbs, 1 tbs. minced onion, 1 tsp. salt, dash pepper, 2 tbs. milk. Form into 2 loaves, place in greased baking dish. Mix ⅓ c. ketchup, 2 tbs. vinegar, ¼ tsp. Worcestershire sauce, ½ tsp. chili powder, 1 tbs. minced onion. Spread over loaves. Bake 25 min. in moderate oven (375°). Baste. Bake 10 min. longer.

FRESH LIMA BEANS & CELERY: Shell 1 lb. Lima beans. Cook covered until tender in ¼ c. salted water. Boil 1 c. thinly sliced celery in ¼ c. salted water 5 min. Add 1 tbs. butter, drained Lima beans, 3 tbs. cream.

ORANGE PARFAIT: Mix 1 c. diced orange segments with 2 tbs. marmalade. Alternate with vanilla ice cream in tall glasses.

TIME 40 MIN. SERVES 2

TUESDAY

Vegetable-Tomato Soup
**Cold Meat Loaf*
Hercules Salad
**Corn Casserole*
Russian Black Bread
New Green Apple Pie
Coffee

VEGETABLE-TOMATO SOUP: 1 can vegetable. Dilute with 1 soup can tomato juice instead of water.

HERCULES SALAD: Combine 1 c. diced Cheddar, ½ c. diced celery, 8 stuffed olives, 1 crushed garlic clove, ½ c. French dressing. Chill 15 min. Remove garlic. Mix with chunked lettuce, 2 quartered tomatoes. Serve with thinly sliced leftover meat loaf.

CORN CASSEROLE: Beat 1 egg; add ½ c. milk, ½ tsp. salt, dash pepper, ½ tsp. grated onion. Stir in 1 c. corn cut from cob. Pour into small buttered casserole. Bake in moderate oven (350°) 35 min., or until just set.

TIME 30 MIN. SERVES 2

WEDNESDAY

Cantaloupe w. Fresh-Ground Black Pepper
Veal-Ham Florentine
Hot Biscuits
Green Bean-Carrot Salad
Blueberries & Cream
Iced Coffee Supreme

VEAL-HAM FLORENTINE: ½ lb. veal cutlet cut in 2 slices and 2 (2-oz.) slices boiled ham. Sprinkle ¼ tsp. basil on each slice of veal, top with ham. Secure with toothpicks. Dust "sandwiches" lightly with flour. Sauté in 3 tbs. butter about 6 min., turning twice. Add ½ c. white wine ½ min. before removing from heat.

GREEN BEAN-CARROT SALAD: ½ box green beans. Cook. Drain well. Mix with ¼ c. French dressing, chill 15 min. Add 1 small sliced onion, ½ c. thinly sliced raw carrot. Serve on lettuce.

ICED COFFEE SUPREME: Double-strength black coffee. Sweeten to taste while hot, pour over ice, top with whipped cream.

THURSDAY

TIME 45 MIN. SERVES 2

Chilled Vegetable Juice
Spaghetti w. Crab Meat Sauce
French Peas
Cucumber Sticks
Cold Glazed Peaches
Black Coffee

CRAB MEAT SAUCE: Brown ½ c. chopped onion, 2 garlic cloves, ½ tsp. minced parsley, ½ tsp. chopped celery in 3 tbs. oil. Add 2 sliced tomatoes, ½ c. tomato sauce, ¼ c. water, salt and pepper, ¼ tsp. paprika. Simmer 30 min. Add 1 can crab meat flakes, ¼ c. sherry, simmer 5 min. Serve over hot spaghetti (8 oz.) mixed with 3 tbs. grated cheese.

FRENCH PEAS: 1 box. Add 2 minced lettuce leaves, 2 diced onions, 2 tbs. chopped parsley, ¼ tsp. pepper. Cook in bouillon instead of water.

CUCUMBER STICKS: Peel, cut 1 cucumber in narrow sticks 3″ long. Crisp in ice water. Drain. Add ¼ c. peppery French dressing.

COLD GLAZED PEACHES: Halve 2 ripe peaches. Heat ¼ c. honey. Coat peaches. Chill in ice tray.

FRIDAY

TIME 40 MIN. SERVES 2

**Sea Island Scallops*
Potato Puffs
Rye Bread
Orange & Endive Salad
Sherried Strawberries
Coffee

SEA ISLAND SCALLOPS: 1 box defrosted. Place in ¾ c. cold water, bring to boil. Drain, reserve liquid. Cook 1 minced onion in 2 tbs. butter until soft. Add 1 4-oz. can sliced mushrooms (drained), ½ box defrosted leftover green beans. Sauté 3 min. Sprinkle 1½ tbs. flour over all, blend well. Stir in ⅔ c. liquid from scallops. Stir in ⅓ c. milk, scallops, 1 tsp. salt, ⅛ tsp. pepper. Simmer 20 min.

ORANGE & ENDIVE SALAD: Peel 2 seedless oranges, segment, arrange on endive. Serve with French dressing.

SHERRIED STRAWBERRIES: Pour ½ c. sherry over ½ box defrosted strawberries. Serve on sliced plain cake.

SHOPPING LIST

MEAT

3½-lb. fryer cut in serving pieces
¾ lb. ground beef
¾ lb. veal cutlet 1½" thick
6 lamb kidneys
½ lb. bacon
¾ lb. raw ham

FROZEN FOODS

1 box crushed pineapple
1 box Lima beans
1 box boysenberries
1 box broccoli
1 box Brussels sprouts
1 pkg. haddock fillets
1 box whipped potatoes

FRESH FRUITS AND VEGETABLES

2 ripe avocados
1 head lettuce
2 small cantaloupe
1 romaine
1 bunch mint
½ lb. white grapes
3 peaches
1 bunch celery
1 green pepper
1 small cucumber
2 bananas
1 small bunch chives
4 apricots
¼ lb. black cherries
1 bunch watercress
4 tomatoes
3 lbs. peas

SUNDRIES

1 pt. sour cream
4 jars infant puréed sweet potatoes
½ pt. heavy cream
2 tubes ready-to-bake biscuits
8-oz. pkg. noodles
1 small can apple juice
1 #1 can potatoes
1 can condensed cream of celery soup
2 cans consommé

PICK UP ON YOUR WAY HOME

FOR SUN.—1 pt. vanilla ice cream
WED.—small poundcake
THUR.—rye bread
petit fours

SUNDAY

TIME 50 MIN. SERVES 4

Jellied Consommé w. Lemon
Carpetbagger Fried Chicken
Hot Biscuits
Avocado Sweet Potatoes
Minted Peas
Cantaloupe à la Mode
Coffee

JELLIED CONSOMMÉ W. LEMON: 2 cans. Prepare as directed. Serve with lemon wedges.

CARPETBAGGER FRIED CHICKEN: 3½-lb. fryer cut in pieces. The night before place chicken in shallow dish, spread over it mixture of 1 c. sour cream, 1 tbs. lemon juice, 1 tsp. Worcestershire sauce, 1 tsp. celery salt, ½ tsp. paprika, 2 cloves minced garlic, 1 tsp. pepper, 1 tsp. salt. Cover. Chill overnight. Drain well. Coat with flour. Fry slowly in 1″ hot fat about 45 min.

AVOCADO SWEET POTATOES: Heat 4 jars infant puréed sweet potato, add 2 mashed avocados, 1 tbs. butter, salt, pepper, dash nutmeg, ½ can crushed pineapple. Reheat.

MINTED PEAS: Shell. Add dash salt, pepper, sugar, sprig mint, 1 c. water. Simmer covered 8–15 min.

MONDAY

TIME 45 MIN. SERVES 2

Egg Drop Soup
Cantonese Noodles
Watercress, Romaine, White Grape Salad
**Pineapple Banana Split*
Iced Tea

EGG DROP SOUP: Add 1 slightly beaten egg to 2 c. boiling bouillon, stir rapidly about 2 min., until egg shreds.

CANTONESE NOODLES: Fry ¾ lb. ground beef, 1 c. chopped onion, 1 c. chopped celery, 4 quartered tomatoes, ½ chopped green pepper in 2 tbs. oil until onions are soft. Add 2½ tsp. soy sauce, ½ tsp. salt, ⅛ tsp. pepper. Bring to boil, simmer 30 min. Serve over boiled noodles. Sprinkle with 1 tbs. chopped almonds.

PINEAPPLE BANANA SPLIT: Split 2 peeled bananas lengthwise, put together with crushed pineapple. Top with whipped cream, dust with nutmeg.

TIME 55 MIN. SERVES 2

TUESDAY

Iced Apple Juice
Veal Steak
Lima Beans
Lettuce & Cucumbers w. Sour Cream and Chives
Frosted Boysenberries
Cold Milk

VEAL STEAK: ¾ lb. veal cutlet cut 1½″ thick. Dip meat in 1 slightly beaten egg, then bread crumbs, salt, pepper. Dip into egg again, then into bread crumbs. Brown on each side in 2 tbs. hot fat. Add 1 can condensed cream of celery soup, 1 small chopped onion. Cover tightly and simmer 45 min., or until tender.

LIMA BEANS: 1 box. Prepare as directed. Serve buttered, dusted with paprika. (Save ½ cup for Friday.)

FROSTED BOYSENBERRIES: ½ box. Serve semi-frozen with powdered sugar and cream.

TIME 20 MIN. SERVES 2

WEDNESDAY

Kidneys en Brochette
Buttered Rice
Broiled Peaches
Broccoli Parmesan
Poundcake
Coffee

KIDNEYS EN BROCHETTE: 6 lamb kidneys. Dip into boiling water. Remove white membranes. Split lengthwise. Cut 2 thick slices bacon into 6 squares each. Alternate bacon squares and kidney halves on 2 skewers. Salt and pepper. Broil under moderate heat about 5 min.

BUTTERED RICE: Add 1½ tbs. butter to 1½ c. prepared precooked rice.

BROILED PEACHES: Peel and halve 1 or 2 ripe peaches. Brush with melted butter, sprinkle with sugar, dust with cinnamon. Broil beside kidneys.

BROCCOLI PARMESAN: 1 box. Prepare as directed. Dress with 1 tbs. melted butter mixed with 2 tbs. grated Parmesan cheese.

THURSDAY

TIME 45 MIN. SERVES 2

Indiana Ham w. Celery
Danish Brussels Sprouts on Crisp Lettuce
Rye Bread
Fresh Fruit with Petit Fours
Coffee

INDIANA HAM W. CELERY: ¾ lb. raw ham. Dice, place in saucepan with 2 c. diced celery, 1 c. cold water. Simmer 10 min., drain. Heat 2 tbs. butter, add 2 tbs. flour, blend well, then 1 c. milk, salt, pepper, ¼ tsp. basil, ⅛ tsp. dry mustard. Stir over medium heat. Place 1 small can potatoes, drained, and the ham and celery in buttered shallow casserole. Cover with sauce. Sprinkle with bread crumbs. Bake in moderate oven (375°) 25 min.

DANISH BRUSSELS SPROUTS: 1 box. Prepare as directed. Dress with 2 tbs. melted butter mixed with ½ tsp. caraway seeds. Serve at last minute on crisp lettuce leaves.

FRESH FRUIT: Chill washed apricots, ripe peaches, black cherries. Serve whole.

FRIDAY

TIME 25 MIN. SERVES 2

Old-Fashioned Fish Fry
Whipped Potatoes
Vegetable Salad
**Boysenberry Sponge*
Iced Coffee

OLD-FASHIONED FISH FRY: 1 pkg. fillets, semi-thawed. Salt and pepper. Dip in slightly beaten egg, then in flour. Dip in egg again, then in corn meal. Fry fish in heavy frying pan in ¼ c. butter. Brown quickly on both sides, reduce heat and finish cooking.

VEGETABLE SALAD: Lettuce, ½ green pepper, sliced, Tuesday's Lima beans, and any other leftover vegetables, with French dressing.

BOYSENBERRY SPONGE: Mix ¾ c. diced poundcake with ½ box thawed boysenberries, crushed and sweetened. Top with whipped cream.

SHOPPING LIST

MEAT

2¼ lbs. sirloin steak, 1" thick
1 pair sweetbreads
6 oz. sliced boiled ham
1 lb. boneless shoulder of veal

FROZEN FOODS

1 box peas
1 box cod fillets

FRESH FRUITS AND VEGETABLES

6 or 8 medium new potatoes
7 juicy peaches
1 small bunch radishes
1 pt. blackberries
3 heads lettuce
1 bunch celery
2 tomatoes
2 pears
2 green peppers
1 cucumber
1 small honeydew
1 small bunch watercress
1 small summer squash
1 bunch scallions
3 carrots
1 orange

SUNDRIES

⅛ lb. Roquefort cheese
⅛ lb. bleu cheese
1 pkg. pilot crackers
1 small can diced beets
1 can tuna fish flakes
1 4-oz. can sliced mushrooms
1 tube ready-to-bake biscuits
½ pt. light cream
1 box ready-to-bake poppy-seed rolls
1 can clam chowder
1 can condensed cream of mushroom soup
1 can madrilene
1 can condensed pea soup

PICK UP ON YOUR WAY HOME

MON.—blueberry muffins
WED.—1 small pumpernickel
THUR.—⅛ lb. ladyfingers

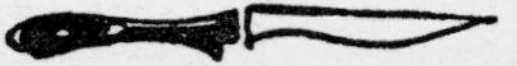

SUNDAY

TIME 30 MIN. SERVES 4

Steak Fingers
Prospector Potatoes
Lettuce, Bleu Cheese Dressing
Chilled Peaches in Wine
Iced Tea

STEAK FINGERS: 2¼ lbs. 1″-thick sirloin. Broil medium or rare. Slice into fingers, lay on fingers of toast. Arrange on each plate spoke-wise around small cup sauce for dunking. Sauce: 1 c. chili sauce, ¾ c. tomato sauce, ¼ c. Worcestershire, 1 tbs. horseradish, dash Tabasco, sprinkling celery seed.

PROSPECTOR POTATOES: 6 or 8 medium-sized new potatoes. Scrub with stiff brush—do not pare. Cut into ½″ cubes. Add to 2 tbs. hot fat in skillet. Cover, cook over medium heat until done, 10–15 min. Stir often.

CHILLED PEACHES IN WINE: Peel, slice 4 ripe peaches, pour on ½ c. white wine, chill.

MONDAY

TIME 35 MIN. SERVES 2

Clam Chowder w. Pilot Crackers
**Galapagos Salad*
Onion Carrots
Blueberry Muffins
Sharp Honeydew
Black Coffee

GALAPAGOS SALAD: Shred lettuce heart, mix with ¼ box peas (semi-thawed), ½ c. diced celery, 4 sliced radishes, 1 can tuna flakes. Add ½ c. French dressing, let stand 20 min. Line serving bowl with lettuce leaves. Drain mixture, adding any left-over steak or potatoes cut in matchsticks, and pile in center. Garnish with sliced hard-cooked egg. Serve with mayonnaise.

ONION CARROTS: 3 carrots, scraped. Dice 1 small onion, cook in 2 tbs. butter until soft. Add thinly sliced carrots, 1 tsp. salt, ⅛ tsp. pepper, 2 tbs. water. Cover, cook until tender, about 10 min.

SHARP HONEYDEW: Slice 1″ rings from melon, remove rind. Fill centers with crumbled Roquefort, shower with lemon juice.

TIME 30 MIN. SERVES 2

TUESDAY

Sweetbreads w. Rice Provençal
Sliced Tomato & Cucumber Salad
Blackberry & Apple Compote
Coffee

SWEETBREADS: 1 pair. Dip in boiling water, remove skin and waste. Sauté quickly in 2 tbs. butter, remove. Stir in 1 tbs. flour, 1 tsp. salt, ⅛ tsp. pepper. Blend well, add 1 can mushrooms with liquid, 3 tbs. sherry, ½ c. chicken bouillon. Bring to boil, stirring constantly. Return sweetbreads to pan, add 2 tbs. red wine, 1 bay leaf. Cover, cook over moderate heat 12 min.

RICE: Heat 1 can undiluted pea soup, pour over 1½ c. prepared precooked rice. Top with sweetbreads and sauce.

BLACKBERRY & APPLE COMPOTE: Wash 1 c. blackberries, add 1 green apple peeled and sliced, ¼ c. sugar, ¼ c. water. Bring to boil. Cover, simmer until apple is tender, about 5 min. Chill.

TIME 40 MIN. SERVES 2

WEDNESDAY

Cold Ham w. Baked Vegetables
Thinly Sliced Pumpernickel
Pear & Date Salad, Cream Dressing
Iced Coffee

BAKED VEGETABLES: Place ¾ can drained diced beets in greased baking dish. Combine 1 tbs. flour, 2 tbs. sugar, ¼ c. orange juice, 1 tsp. salt, pour over beets. Dot with butter, bake in hot oven (400°) 35 min. Peel one small summer squash cut in ½″ slices. Arrange in shallow baking dish, sprinkle with ½ tbs. flour, ½ tsp. salt, ⅛ tsp. pepper, then add ¾ c. hot milk. Top with 2 tbs. bread crumbs mixed with ¼ c. grated cheese. Bake 30 min. Serve with 6 oz. boiled ham slices garnished with sliced green pepper, radishes, scallions.

PEAR & DATE SALAD: Arrange peeled sliced pears with sliced dates on shredded lettuce and watercress. Serve with ⅓ c. mayonnaise blended with 3 tbs. cream.

THURSDAY

TIME 35 MIN. SERVES 2

Jellied Madrilene
**Veal Casserole*
Hot Biscuits
Crisp Green Salad
Peach Ladyfingers
Coffee

MADRILENE: 1 can. Chill. Serve topped with a little softened cream cheese sprinkled with chopped chives.

VEAL CASSEROLE: 1 lb. boneless shoulder veal cut in 1½" pieces. Dredge with seasoned flour, dip in 1 slightly beaten egg, then in bread crumbs. Brown in 2 tbs. butter. Arrange in low casserole. Sprinkle with 1 tsp. salt, ⅛ tsp. pepper. Add yesterday's beets, any leftover squash, ½ green pepper, diced. Pour on 1 can condensed cream of mushroom soup. Cover. Bake in moderate oven (375°) about 45 min., until veal is tender.

HOT BISCUITS: 1 tube. Bake topped with a sprinkling of grated lemon peel.

PEACH LADYFINGERS: Wash 2 large ripe peaches, slice thinly. Bring 1 c. water, ¼ c. sugar or honey to boil. Add 2 cloves, peaches. Simmer covered 8 min. Serve hot or cold over split ladyfingers.

FRIDAY

TIME 45 MIN. SERVES 2

Fish in Foil
Corn on the Cob
**Buttered Peas*
Poppy-Seed Rolls
**Mixed Fruit in Wine*
Iced Tea

FISH IN FOIL: 1 box cod fillets, defrosted. Lay each portion on sheet of aluminum foil. Top with 2 slices green pepper, 1 slice onion, salt, pepper, 1 tsp. minced parsley. Dot with butter. Wrap compactly, folding edges under. Cook each package about 25 min. under broiler or on outdoor grill over hot coals. Turn occasionally. Serve in the wrapping.

MIXED FRUIT IN WINE: Peel and dice 1 ripe peach, combine with leftover blackberries, diced leftover honeydew, 2 tbs. powdered sugar, ¼ c. white wine. Chill.

SHOPPING LIST

MEAT

3 lbs. beef, top round
½ lb. bacon
2 1½"-thick boned and rolled loin lamb chops
⅛ lb. salami

FROZEN FOODS

2 boxes succotash
1 can pineapple juice
1 box potato puffs
1 box green peas
1 box asparagus
1 pkg. boiled shrimps
1 box haddock fillets

FRESH FRUITS AND VEGETABLES

2 Bermuda onions
1 small bunch radishes
2 iceberg lettuce
4 tomatoes
1 small bunch parsley
1 small bunch mint
1 small bunch chives
1 large bunch celery
1 ripe pineapple
1 green pepper
2 large mushrooms
1 endive
8 ripe peaches
2 pears

SUNDRIES

1 small jar stuffed olives
½ pt. sour cream
2 cans tomatoes (1 #1 and 1 #2)
1 8-oz. pkg. thin spaghetti
1 4-oz. can sliced mushrooms
1 jar infant puréed prunes
1 pkg. potato chips
½ pt. heavy cream
½ pt. light cream
1 6-oz. can boned chicken
1 box sponge layers
1 pkg. corn bread mix
1 small jar pimiento
1 small can sardines
1 box ready-to-bake rolls
1 12-oz. can V-8 juice
1 can French-fried onions
1 can Vichyssoise soup

PICK UP ON YOUR WAY HOME

TUES.—3 hamburger buns
¾ lb. round steak, if needed
WED.—spumoni
FRI.—½ pt. heavy cream

SUNDAY

TIME 3½ HRS. SERVES 4

Cuban Roast w. Hot Cornbread
Sliced Bermuda Onions
Succotash
Mixed Green Salad w. Tomatoes
Fresh Peach Layer Cake
Iced Coffee

CUBAN ROAST: 3 lbs. top round. With sharp knife cut deep slits on each side of roast. Push in small stuffed olives. Brown 3 strips fat bacon in deep saucepan, drain, reserve to garnish succotash. Brown roast on all sides in bacon fat. Sprinkle with 1½ tsp. salt, ¼ tsp. pepper. Add 1 sliced onion, cook 5 min., then add 1 #2 can tomatoes, cook 10 min. Add 1 c. rum, simmer covered 3 hrs. Serve with thinly sliced Bermuda onions.

MIXED GREEN SALAD: Toss 3 quartered tomatoes, chunks iceberg lettuce, cut romaine, escarole with French dressing.

FRESH PEACH LAYER CAKE: Peel and slice 8 juicy peaches, sprinkle with 1 tbs. lemon juice, ½ c. powdered sugar. Chill. Spread between 2 sponge layers, top with whipped cream.

MONDAY

TIME 35 MIN. SERVES 2

Vichyssoise w. Chives
Shrimp & Asparagus Salad
Hot Rolls
Pineapple in Wine
Coffee

SHRIMP & ASPARAGUS SALAD: Prepare 1 box asparagus, add 1 box defrosted cooked shrimps mixed with ¼ c. chopped celery, 1 tsp. minced parsley. Pour on ½ c. French dressing, chill 15 min. Drain. Arrange on shredded lettuce, garnish with 1 sliced hard-cooked egg. Serve with ½ c. mayonnaise mixed with 2 tbs. chopped chives, 2 tbs. lemon juice.

PINEAPPLE IN WINE: Dice fresh pineapple, pour on ½ c. white wine. Chill.

TIME 50 MIN. SERVES 2

TUESDAY

**Hawaiian Mint Cocktail*
**Beef Barbecue on Buns*
Potato Chips
Shoestring Salad
Grenadine Pears
Coffee

HAWAIIAN MINT COCKTAIL: Put 1 tbs. slivered leftover pineapple into each tall glass, add crushed ice, another 2 tbs. pineapple slivers. Fill with diluted frozen pineapple juice. Top with mint.

BEEF BARBECUE ON BUNS: 1½ c. leftover roast, diced, or ¾ lb. diced round steak. Arrange meat in shallow baking dish. Pour on ¼ c. Worcestershire mixed with ½ c. ketchup. Bake in moderate oven (350°) 45 min. Serve on hot split buns.

SHOESTRING SALAD: Cut 3 carrots, 2 stalks celery, 1 green pepper into shoestrings. Pour on ¼ c. French dressing and chill. Toss with shredded lettuce, sprinkle with basil.

GRENADINE PEARS: Peel, slice 2 ripe pears. Simmer 15 min. in ¼ c. water, ¼ c. grenadine. Serve chilled with cream.

TIME 30 MIN. SERVES 2

WEDNESDAY

Antipasto
Chicken Tetrazzini
Garlic Rolls
Spumoni
Coffee

ANTIPASTO: Arrange on each plate 2 lettuce leaves, ½ pimiento, 2 stalks celery, 3 or 4 sardines, radishes, olives, 2 slices salami, lemon wedges. Serve with oil and vinegar on the side.

CHICKEN TETRAZZINI: Sauté 1 chopped green pepper, 1 chopped onion in 3 tbs. butter until lightly browned. Add 1 #1 can tomatoes (save juice), 1 4-oz. can sliced mushrooms (save juice), 1 6-oz. can diced boned chicken. Alternate layers of boiled broken spaghetti (4 oz.) and chicken mixture in greased casserole. Pour on 1 c. mixed tomato and mushroom juices, 2 tbs. sherry. Sprinkle with grated Parmesan cheese. Bake in moderate oven (375°) 35 min.

GARLIC ROLLS: Add 1 clove garlic, crushed, to ¼ c. melted butter. Let stand 15 min. Brush on ready-to-bake rolls.

THURSDAY

TIME 30 MIN. SERVES 2

Chilled Vegetable Juice
Horseradish Chips
Lamb Chop Grill
Potato Puffs
**Orange-Pineapple au Rhum*
Coffee

HORSERADISH CHIPS: Heat leftover potato chips 10 min. in moderate oven (350°). Cool, spread with 1 tbs. butter mixed with 1 tbs. horseradish.

LAMB CHOP GRILL: 2 1½"-thick boned, rolled loin lamb chops. Wrap slice bacon around each, broil under moderate heat about 25 min. Turn frequently. About 5 min. before chops are done salt, pepper, dot with butter; place thick slice tomato, large mushroom cap on each. Salt, pepper, baste with drippings, sprinkle lightly with basil.

ORANGE-PINEAPPLE AU RHUM: Mix ½ c. diced leftover pineapple, ½ c. diced orange segments, 1 tbs. powdered sugar, 1 tsp. lemon juice, 2 tbs. rum. Chill.

FRIDAY

TIME 25 MIN. SERVES 2

Mediterranean Buttered Fish
French-Fried Onions
Celery-Seed Peas
Watercress & Endive Salad
Lemon-Prune Cream
Iced Coffee

MEDITERRANEAN BUTTERED FISH: 1 box semi-thawed fillets. Add 2 tbs. chopped parsley, 2 tbs. minced green pepper, 1 tsp. grated onion to 1 slightly beaten egg. Salt, pepper, dip in flour, in egg mixture, then in bread crumbs. Fry in 2 tbs. butter. Pour on 1 tbs. lemon juice mixed with 2 tbs. browned butter.

CELERY-SEED PEAS: 1 box. Prepare as directed. Dress with 2 tsp. melted butter mixed with 1½ tsp. celery seed.

LEMON-PRUNE CREAM: Mix 1 jar infant puréed prunes, 1 egg white, 1 tbs. lemon juice, 2 tbs. sugar, ⅛ tsp. grated lemon rind. Beat with rotary beater until mixture holds shape, about 5 min. Pour in glasses, chill. Top with whipped cream, sprinkle with ½ tsp. grated lemon rind, 1 tsp. sugar.

SEPTEMBER

Recheck your basic staples—and now have you

almonds
basil
lemons
sage
thyme
brown sugar
dried mint
dried parsley
cream of tartar
vanilla extract
marjoram
coarse salt
soy sauce
horseradish
crackers
whole cloves
powdered cloves
jam or orange marmalade
powdered ginger
powdered sugar
nutmeg
rum
sliced bread
curry powder
walnuts or pecans
celery seed

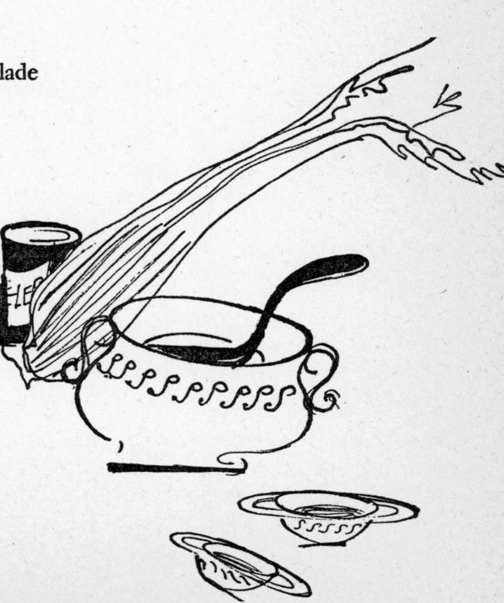

SHOPPING LIST

MEAT

1¾ lbs. flank steak, pounded thin
¾ lb. pork steak ¾″ thick
6 pork sausages
1 lb. lamb shoulder cut in 2″ cubes

FROZEN FOODS

2 boxes broccoli
2 boxes French-fried potatoes
1 box asparagus cuts
1 box Lima beans
1 box mixed vegetables
1 can orange juice

FRESH FRUITS AND VEGETABLES

6 small potatoes
1 head iceberg lettuce
½ Cranshaw melon
2 seedless oranges
½ lb. seedless grapes
3 green apples
1 lb. ripe red plums
4 tomatoes
1 bunch parsley
1 bunch celery
1 green pepper
1 bunch chives
1 small cucumber
1 bunch watercress

SUNDRIES

1 small can pimiento
1 small jar pitted olives
1 small jar minced pickles
1 8-oz. pkg. thin spaghetti
1 box Parker House rolls
½ pt. heavy cream
1 #1 can tomatoes
1 #1 can potatoes
½ pt. sour cream
1 box ready-to-bake poppy-seed rolls
⅛ lb. Roquefort cheese
1 box cloverleaf rolls
1 8-oz. can carrots
1 can onion soup
1 can condensed consommé

PICK UP ON YOUR WAY HOME

WED.—1 loaf French bread
THUR.—½ pt. light cream
FRI.—1 2-lb. mackerel

TIME 2½ HRS. SERVES 4 **SUNDAY**

California Beefsteak
Broccoli w. Almonds
French-Fried Potatoes
Mixed Salad
Cranshaw Melon
Coffee

CALIFORNIA BEEFSTEAK: 1¾ lbs. flank steak, pounded thin. Rub with 2 tsp. salt, 2 crushed cloves garlic. Place in shallow pan, sprinkle with 1 tbs. grated orange rind. Cover with 1 c. orange juice. Let stand 2 hrs. Drain. Brush with salad oil and broil under high heat about 15 min. Do not turn. Serve in ¼″ diagonal slices.

BROCCOLI W. ALMONDS: 2 boxes. Cook and drain. Add ¼ c. blanched almonds, ¼ tsp. salt to ¼ c. melted butter. Pour over hot broccoli.

MIXED SALAD: Combine 3 sliced tomatoes, 1 small can sliced pimientos, ½ c. pitted olives, ½ c. chopped celery, 2 tbs. chopped chives, ¼ tsp. basil with ½ c. oil, 2 tbs. lemon juice, 1 tbs. chopped parsley. Serve on lettuce.

TIME 30 MIN. SERVES 2 **MONDAY**

Consommé
Sweet & Sour Pork
Rice
Buttered Asparagus
Oranges & Frosted Grapes
Tea

SWEET & SOUR PORK: ¾ lb. pork steak cut in 1½″ x ¾″ oblongs. Dust with salt and pepper. Coat with flour, dip in 1 well-beaten egg. Fry in 1″ salad oil 15 min. Heat 2 cloves garlic in 1 tbs. oil. Remove. Add ¼ c. vinegar, ¼ c. water, ⅓ c. sugar, 1 tsp. soy sauce, and ⅛ tsp. pepper, then add 1½ tsp. cornstarch blended with 2 tbs. cold water. Stir over moderate heat until boiling. Add the pork, drained on paper, and ¼ c. minced drained pickles. Stir 1 min., serve on 1½ c. prepared pre-cooked rice.

ORANGES & FROSTED GRAPES: Dip small bunches of seedless grapes in slightly beaten egg white. When almost dry dip in powdered sugar. Arrange on circles of orange segments. Chill.

TUESDAY

TIME 35 MIN. SERVES 2

Onion Soup
Spaghetti con Olio
Mixed Vegetables
Cloverleaf Rolls
Zabaglione
Coffee

SPAGHETTI CON OLIO: 8 oz. Cook in 2 qts. fast-boiling salted water 8 min. Drain well. Brown 4 chopped garlic cloves with 2 tbs. minced parsley in 4 tbs. olive oil. Add spaghetti, 1 tsp. salt, ⅛ tsp. pepper. Mix well. Cook over low heat about 15 min., continually separating spaghetti with a fork. Drain off excess oil. Toss with 1 c. grated Parmesan cheese, serve very hot.

ZABAGLIONE: Mix 3 egg yolks with 3 tbs. sugar in top of double boiler, slowly beat in ¼ c. sherry. Place over hot water, beat with rotary beater until like soft whipped cream, about 5 min. Serve at once in individual glasses. Keep egg whites covered tightly in refrigerator for next Sunday.

WEDNESDAY

TIME 35 MIN. SERVES 2

Spanish Sausages
Roquefort Salad
French Bread
Steamed Date-Nut Roll
w. Whipped Cream
Coffee

SPANISH SAUSAGES: 6. Place in well-buttered casserole. Bake in moderate oven (350°) 10 min. Remove from oven, pour off all but 1 tbs. fat. Stir in 1 tbs. flour, then ½ c. white wine. Simmer over low heat until done, about 20 min. Meanwhile cook 1 box Lima beans. Drain. Heat 2 tbs. oil in saucepan, add beans and ¼ tsp. sage. Cook 5 min. Add 1 c. canned tomatoes, salt and pepper to taste. Cook another 5 min. Mix 2 tbs. cream with sausages; serve on toast surrounded by beans and tomatoes.

ROQUEFORT SALAD: Iceberg lettuce, watercress, and 2 tbs. crumbled Roquefort. Toss with French dressing.

TOMORROW'S LAMB: Cut 1 lb. shoulder in 2″ pieces, marinate overnight in ¾ c. French dressing mixed with 1 tbs. dry mustard, 2 tbs. ketchup, 1 tbs. Worcestershire sauce, 2 tbs. vinegar.

TIME 50 MIN. SERVES 2

THURSDAY

Quick Lamb Stew
Parker House Rolls
Shredded Lettuce & Green Pepper Salad
Apple Crumb
Coffee

QUICK LAMB STEW: 1 lb. lamb shoulder in 2″ cubes, marinated overnight. Drain. Roll in flour. Brown quickly in 2 tbs. fat. Add 1 c. boiling water, 1 tbs. marinade, 1 bay leaf, ¼ tsp. thyme, ¼ tsp. basil, ¼ tsp. parsley, ½ tsp. salt, ¼ tsp. pepper. Add 1 small can potatoes, drained, 3 stalks celery, diced, 3 sliced onions. Cover. Simmer 30 min. Add 1 can carrots, drained, ¼ c. red wine. Simmer 10 min.

APPLE CRUMB: Peel and core 3 green apples, slice thin. Arrange in small baking dish. Top with crumb mixture of ¼ c. flour, ⅓ c. brown sugar, and 2 tbs. butter. Bake in hot oven (425°) 35 min. Serve warm with cream.

TIME 35 MIN. SERVES 2

FRIDAY

Paprika Mackerel
Jacket Potatoes
Tomato & Cucumber Salad
Poppy-Seed Rolls
Stewed Plums
Coffee

PAPRIKA MACKEREL: 1 2-lb. mackerel. Cook 1 chopped onion in 1 tbs. butter until soft. Place in buttered shallow casserole. Add mackerel. Season with ½ tsp. salt and 1 tbs. paprika. Cover with ½ c. sour cream. Bake in hot oven (425°) 25 min. Mix 1 egg yolk with 1 tsp. melted butter, 2 tbs. lemon juice. Serve over fish.

JACKET POTATOES: 6 small potatoes. Scrub, do not peel. Boil in salted water until tender, about 20 min.

TOMATO & CUCUMBER SALAD: Slice thinly 1 small unpeeled cucumber, arrange on lettuce. Garnish with 1 tomato cut in wedges. Sprinkle with ½ tsp. dried mint, 2 tbs. lemon juice.

STEWED PLUMS: Wipe waxy bloom from 1 lb. plums. Add 1 c. water and ¾ c. sugar. Simmer gently, covered, 15 min. Serve warm or cold with cream.

SHOPPING LIST

MEAT

1 lb. sirloin steak about ½″ thick
¾ lb. veal cutlet sliced thin
2 2-lb. broilers cut up
½ lb. bacon

FROZEN FOODS

2 boxes peas
1 box asparagus
1 box fillet of sole
1 box whipped potatoes

FRESH FRUITS AND VEGETABLES

4 Idaho potatoes
1 large cucumber
2 tomatoes
1 Boston lettuce
1 ripe pear
2 oranges
6 peaches
1 cantaloupe
1 pt. blueberries
1 iceberg lettuce
10 white onions
1 endive

SUNDRIES

1 #1 can potatoes
½ pt. sour cream
2 4-oz. cans sliced mushrooms
1 8-oz. pkg. noodles
1 small can carrots
¼ lb. Cheddar cheese
1 small can tomato purée
½ pt. heavy cream
1 small can beets
1 small can apricot nectar
1 pkg. semi-sweet chocolate bits
1 12-oz. can tomato juice
1 small can crab meat
4 oz. water chestnuts (opt.)
1 can consommé

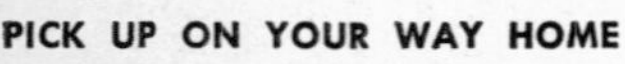

PICK UP ON YOUR WAY HOME

FOR SUN.—1 pt. ice cream
TUES.—½ lb. ground pork
THUR.—small loaf sliced whole-wheat bread

TIME 2½ HRS. SERVES 4 **SUNDAY**

Chicken in Wine
Buttered Peas
Baked Potatoes
Meringue Ring Glacé w. Fruit
Coffee

CHICKEN IN WINE: 2 2-lb. broilers cut in serving pieces. Rub with salt, pepper. Roll in flour. Brown all sides quickly in butter. Add 10 small white onions and 3 slices bacon, diced. Cover, cook 15 min. Drain fat. Add 1 4-oz. can sliced mushrooms, ¾ c. red wine, ½ bay leaf, ½ tsp. minced parsley, ¼ tsp. thyme, ¼ tsp. marjoram, and more salt and pepper if necessary. Cook 15 min. more.

MERINGUE RING GLACÉ W. FRUIT: Beat 4 egg whites with ¼ tsp. cream of tartar, gradually beat in ⅔ c. sugar, 2 tbs. at a time, ½ tsp. vanilla. Spoon to form circle on baking sheet covered with brown paper. Bake 1½ hrs. in very slow oven (250°). Cool. Serve filled with ice cream. Top with 1½ c. sliced peaches, cantaloupe balls, and blueberries mixed together.

TIME 35 MIN. SERVES 2 **MONDAY**

Steak-in-Salt
Cucumbers in Sour Cream Sauce
Whipped Potatoes
Green Salad
Apricot Cup
Coffee

STEAK-IN-SALT: 1 lb. sirloin about ½″ thick. Mix 1 c. coarse salt with water to give a nice "mud-pie" consistency. Spread firmly and evenly on one side. Broil 1″ away from hot broiler, salt side up. Cook until slightly brown. Remove, coat other side, broil until paste is barely hard, about 4 min. Remove salt. Season with pepper, dot with butter.

CUCUMBERS IN SOUR CREAM SAUCE: 1 cucumber. Peel, slice thin. Heat 1 tbs. butter, blend in 1 tbs. flour, then ½ c. bouillon. Stir until smooth. Add 3 tbs. sour cream, 1 tbs. lemon juice, 1 minced garlic clove, salt, pepper, cucumber. Simmer 10 min.

APRICOT CUP: Add 1 peeled sliced pear to leftover blueberries and cantaloupe balls, arrange in glasses. Cover with apricot nectar. Chill.

TUESDAY

TIME 30 MIN. SERVES 2

Egg Drop Soup
Chinese Fried Meat Balls
Noodles
Buttered Asparagus
Orange Mounds
Tea

EGG DROP SOUP: Bring 1 can consommé, diluted, or 2 c. bouillon to simmer. Drop in 1 beaten egg, stir constantly until egg shreds, about 2 min.

CHINESE FRIED MEAT BALLS: ½ lb. ground pork. Mix with ½ can sliced, drained mushrooms, 4 oz. chopped water chestnuts (opt.), ½ can crab meat flakes, 1 tsp. salt, ⅛ tsp. pepper, ⅛ tsp. sugar. Roll into nut-sized balls. Dust with cornstarch, dip in beaten egg, fry 15 min. in deep hot oil. Drain on paper. Serve on (4 oz.) prepared noodles with soy sauce at hand.

ORANGE MOUNDS: Dice 2 peeled chilled oranges, mound in serving dishes, cover with whipped cream, sprinkle with little grated lemon peel.

WEDNESDAY

TIME 35 MIN. SERVES 2

**Crab Meat Cocktail*
Baked Veal Cutlet
Buttered Carrots
Tomatoes & Mushrooms
Cheddar Cheese Slices, Crackers
Coffee

CRAB MEAT COCKTAIL: Arrange leftover crab meat on lettuce. Combine 2 tbs. chili sauce, ½ tsp. horseradish, ⅓ tsp. salt, pinch of cayenne, 1½ tbs. vinegar, 3 tbs. oil, 1½ tsp. minced chives, ½ tsp. dry mustard. Pour over crab meat.

BAKED VEAL CUTLET: ¾ lb. cutlet, sliced thin. Dust with salt, pepper, ⅛ tsp. sugar. Dip in bread crumbs, beaten egg, again in crumbs. Place in well-greased baking dish. Dot with 1 tbs. butter. Bake in hot oven (450°) 25 min.

TOMATOES & MUSHROOMS: Drain ½ can leftover mushrooms, sauté in 1 tbs. butter with 1 sliced garlic clove, 2 sliced tomatoes. Add ½ tsp. salt, ⅛ tsp. pepper, sprinkle minced parsley.

TIME 35 MIN. SERVES 2

THURSDAY

Tomato Juice
Risotto Milanese
Scrambled Eggs
Boston Lettuce Salad
Whole-Wheat Bread
Chocolate Custard
Coffee

RISOTTO MILANESE: Heat 2 tbs. butter, add 1 chopped onion, 1 c. raw rice, stir over medium heat 5 min. Add 2 c. boiling bouillon, 2 tbs. white wine, 2 tbs. tomato purée, pinch saffron, 1 tsp. salt, 1/8 tsp. pepper. Mix. Cook very slowly, tightly covered, 20 min. Top with 3 tbs. grated cheese, 1 tbs. melted butter.

CHOCOLATE CUSTARD: Heat 1 c. milk, add 1/2 c. semi-sweet chocolate bits. Bring to boil, stirring constantly. Pour over 3 slightly beaten egg yolks, stirring well. Strain into dessert glasses. Chill.

TIME 35 MIN. SERVES 2

FRIDAY

Spanish Sole au Gratin
Buttered Beets
Potato Layers
Endive w. Russian Dressing
Baked Peaches w. Sour Cream
Coffee

SPANISH SOLE AU GRATIN: 1 box sole, defrosted. Season with 1/2 tsp. salt, 1/8 tsp. pepper, 1 tsp. lemon juice. Place in low casserole, cover with 1 small chopped onion, 1 tbs. minced parsley, 1 c. white wine, then with buttered bread crumbs. Bake in hot oven (425°) 20–25 min.

POTATO LAYERS: 1 can potatoes. Slice 1/4″ thick. Place in layers in small frying pan with 3/4″ oil. Season each layer. Cover. Cook over high heat 25 min., drain off oil. Serve upside down, garnish with parsley.

RUSSIAN DRESSING: Mix 1 tbs. chili sauce, 2 tbs. mayonnaise.

BAKED PEACHES W. SOUR CREAM: Halve 3 washed peaches. Place in shallow baking dish with a little water. Dot each half with 1 tsp. butter, sprinkle with 1 tbs. brown sugar. Bake in hot oven (425°) 25 min. Serve with sour cream.

SHOPPING LIST

MEAT

2½ lbs. chuck or round steak
2 lamb kidneys
2 pork sausages
¼ lb. boiled ham
¾ lb. pork steak
1½–2 lb. broiler, split
½ lb. bacon

FROZEN FOODS

1 box peas
1 box asparagus cuts
1 box French-fried potatoes
1 box spinach
1 box broccoli

FRESH FRUITS AND VEGETABLES

1 bunch celery
2 lbs. tomatoes
1 bunch parsley
4 Idaho potatoes
1 head escarole
1 bunch chives (or scallions)
1 head lettuce
1 bunch watercress

SUNDRIES

1 qt. vegetable juice
1 small can pimiento
1 4-oz. can sliced mushrooms
1 small can minced clams
½ pt. heavy cream
⅛ lb. Cheddar cheese
8 small ladyfingers
1 small jar ripe olives
1 jar chocolate frosting
1 #2 can applesauce
1 pkg. gingerbread mix
1 #1 can potatoes
1 8-oz. can sweet potatoes
1 tube ready-to-bake biscuits
1 pkg. piecrust mix
1 small can sliced pineapple
1 can cream of mushroom soup
1 can condensed tomato soup

PICK UP ON YOUR WAY HOME

FOR SUN.—1½ pts. butter pecan ice cream
FRI.—2 or 3 ears corn
1 small whole cod, about 2½ lbs.
½ pt. heavy cream

TIME 2½ HRS. SERVES 4

SUNDAY

Hot Vegetable Juice
Crisp Crackers
Beef Pot Roast w. Celery
Stuffed Baked Potatoes
Sherry Pecan Ice Cream
Coffee

HOT VEGETABLE JUICE: Garnish with thin lemon slices, chopped watercress.

BEEF POT ROAST W. CELERY: 2½ lbs. chuck or round steak. Brown on all sides over high heat in melted beef fat. Add 1 lb. tomatoes, quartered, 1 c. red wine, 3 sliced garlic cloves, 1 tbs. chopped parsley, 6 or 7 bruised whole cloves, 1 tbs. salt, ¼ tsp. pepper. Bring to boil. Lower heat. Simmer 2 hrs. Add 2 c. sliced celery 10 min. before serving.

STUFFED BAKED POTATOES: 4 Idaho. Scrub, brush with oil. Bake in hot oven (425°) until done, about 45 min. Cut slit in each, insert stick of Cheddar. Replace in oven until cheese melts.

SHERRY PECAN ICE CREAM: Pour 1 tbs. sherry over each portion of butter pecan.

TIME 25 MIN. SERVES 2

MONDAY

Baked Flamingo Hash w. Eggs
Escarole Salad
Hot Biscuits
Charlotte Russe
Coffee

BAKED FLAMINGO HASH W. EGGS: Brown well 2 sliced sausages. Sauté ¼ lb. boiled ham cut in small squares in 2 tbs. butter with 1 small onion, chopped. When onion begins to brown, add ½ box peas, ½ box asparagus cuts, 1 box French-fried potatoes cut in 1″ pieces, 1 sliced pimiento. Mix well, fry 7 min. Add browned sausages, mix, turn into shallow buttered casserole. Break 2 eggs into hollows made with back of spoon. Bake in hot oven (425°) until eggs set, about 10 min.

ESCAROLE SALAD: Arrange escarole leaves on chilled plates, add French dressing with extra dash of onion juice.

CHARLOTTE RUSSE: Place 1 tbs. jam or orange marmalade in each serving dish, arrange 4 ladyfingers around sides, fill with sweetened whipped cream.

TUESDAY

TIME 40 MIN. SERVES 2

**Hot Bouillon Cups*
**Steak & Kidney Pie*
**Asparagus Salad w. Crumbled Bacon*
Coffee w. Lemon Peel

HOT BOUILLON CUPS: Add enough bouillon to leftover vegetable juice to make 1½ c. Serve piping hot.

STEAK & KIDNEY PIE: Dip 2 lamb kidneys into boiling salted water. Slice thin, discarding white centers and tubes. Sauté with 1 small diced onion and 1 4-oz. can sliced mushrooms, drained, in 2 tbs. butter until onions soften. Add leftover peas, diced leftover pot roast and gravy. Thicken with 1 tbs. flour, transfer to baking dish. Cover with prepared piecrust mix, press crust down well over edge. Slash top in a few places to allow steam to escape. Brush with white of egg, then a little milk. Bake in hot oven (450°) 25 min. Serve with horseradish.

WEDNESDAY

TIME 40 MIN. SERVES 2

Cream of Mushroom Soup
Intoxicated Pork
Spinach w. Chives
Whipped Potatoes
Sliced Tomatoes
Hot Gingerbread w. Spiced Applesauce
Tea

INTOXICATED PORK: ¾ lb. pork steak. Rub well with salt, pepper. Brown in 1½ tbs. oil with 2 garlic cloves, 1 tsp. dried parsley. Add 1½ c. red wine (chianti is the endorsed intoxicator). Simmer 30 min. Arrange on hot dish, pour on sauce, surround with ½ box fluffy whipped potatoes.

SPINACH W. CHIVES: 1 box. Prepare as directed, adding 2 tbs. chopped chives, squeeze of lemon.

HOT GINGERBREAD W. SPICED APPLESAUCE: Mix ½ pkg. gingerbread mix with ½ c. water. Pour in greased, lined loaf pan. Bake in moderate oven (350°) 20 min. (Reserve half for tomorrow. When cool, frost with prepared chocolate frosting.) Serve hot with 1 c. applesauce spiced with ⅛ tsp. ground clove.

TIME 40 MIN. SERVES 2 **THURSDAY**

Florentine Chicken
Broiled Pineapple
Glazed Sweet Potatoes
Mixed Vegetable Salad
Chocolate Gingercake
Coffee

FLORENTINE CHICKEN: 1½–2-lb. broiler, split. Mix 2 tbs. oil or melted butter, 1 tsp. salt, ⅛ tsp. pepper, 1 tsp. powdered ginger. Brush over chicken, place on oiled broiler, skin side down. Sprinkle with 1 tsp. chopped onion, ½ tsp. dried parsley. Broil under low heat until light brown. Turn, brush with sauce again, sprinkle with 1 tbs. chopped onion, ½ tsp. dried parsley. Continue broiling until chicken is tender, about 25 min.

GLAZED SWEET POTATOES: 1 can sweet potatoes. Drain. Sprinkle with salt, sugar. Place under broiler with 4 drained pineapple slices after turning chicken. Dot with butter.

MIXED VEGETABLE SALAD: Broken lettuce, ripe olives, and any leftover vegetables with French dressing.

CHOCOLATE GINGERCAKE: Prepared yesterday. Slice thin.

TIME 40 MIN. SERVES 2 **FRIDAY**

Tomato-Clam Soup
Baked Cod
Buttered Broccoli
Corn on the Cob
**Apple Cream*
Coffee

TOMATO-CLAM SOUP: Combine 1 can minced clams with 1 can condensed tomato soup, 1 tsp. lemon juice. Warm. Add ½ c. milk or cream, salt, pepper. Simmer 3 min. Do *not* boil.

BAKED COD: 1 whole cod. Lay fish in buttered casserole on 2 sliced onions. Add salt, pepper, ½ tsp. grated lemon peel. Cover with 3 slices fat bacon. Bake in hot oven (450°) about 30 min. Garnish with watercress.

BUTTERED BROCCOLI: 1 box. Prepare as directed. Dress with ¼ c. grated Parmesan cheese, 2 tbs. melted butter.

APPLE CREAM: Whip ½ c. cream, beating in ¼ c. powdered sugar, 1 tbs. sherry. Fold in ½ c. applesauce. Chill. Dust with nutmeg.

SHOPPING LIST

MEAT

- 2½ lbs. rack of lamb, bones cracked
- 4 ¼″ slices beef liver
- 2 thick loin pork chops

FROZEN FOODS

- 1 box peas
- 1 box whole strawberries
- 1 box spinach
- 2 boxes green beans
- 1 pkg. raw scallops

FRESH FRUITS AND VEGETABLES

- 2 sweet red peppers
- 3 oranges
- 1 head lettuce
- 1 head chicory
- 1 bunch watercress
- 1 bunch parsley
- 1 carrot
- 1 endive
- 2 tomatoes
- 3 bananas
- 1 apple
- 6 or 7 potatoes
- fresh fruit for dessert

SUNDRIES

- 1 large can pears
- 1 small can tomatoes
- 1 small jar pickle relish
- 1 small can grated coconut
- 1 8-oz. can sweet potatoes
- 1 #2 can chicken fricassee, boneless
- 1 tube ready-to-bake biscuits
- 1 #1 can shrimp
- 1 small can carrots
- 1 small can potatoes
- 1 can condensed pepper pot soup
- 1 can condensed cream of asparagus soup

PICK UP ON YOUR WAY HOME

THUR.—½ pt. heavy cream

TIME 1½ HRS. SERVES 4

SUNDAY

Runaway Lamb Racks w. Sweet Red Peppers
Buttered String Beans
Parsley Potatoes
Pears au Rhum
Coffee

RUNAWAY LAMB RACKS: 2½ lbs. rack of lamb, bones cracked. Place in shallow casserole with 1 tsp. salt, ¼ tsp. pepper, 1 bay leaf, 1 tsp. butter. Brown in hot oven (450°) 15 min. Turn twice. Reduce heat to moderate (350°). Add 1 c. white wine. Bake 40 min., basting occasionally. Add 2 sliced sweet red peppers sautéed in 1 tbs. butter with 1 clove garlic, 1 tsp. chopped parsley. Cook 10 min.

BUTTERED STRING BEANS: 2 boxes. Prepare as directed. Dress with 2 tbs. butter.

PARSLEY POTATOES: Scrub 6 or 7 potatoes. Boil in salted water until tender, about 30 min. Skin, roll in 2 tbs. melted butter, sprinkle with minced parsley.

PEARS AU RHUM: 1 large can. Mix ½ c. syrup, ½ c. rum. Fill pear centers with whipped cream. Pour rum syrup around pears.

TIME 25 MIN. SERVES 2

MONDAY

Beef Liver Sauté on Fried Bread
Creamed Peas
Browned Orange Slices
Mixed Green Salad
Coffee

BEEF LIVER SAUTÉ ON FRIED BREAD: 4 slices ¼″. Sauté in mixture of 2 tbs. oil, 2 tbs. butter with 1 tsp. chopped parsley. Sprinkle with salt, pepper, remove, keep warm. Fry 2 slices bread in oil-butter mixture. Serve liver on fried bread, garnish with browned orange slices.

CREAMED PEAS: ½ box, semi-thawed. Sprinkle with 2 tsp. flour, add 1 tbs. butter, 1 bay leaf, ⅓ c. milk. Bring to boil, stir, simmer until peas are tender, about 10 min.

BROWNED ORANGE SLICES: Cut 1 unpeeled orange in ½″ slices, brown both sides quickly in 1 tbs. oil. Sprinkle with ½ tsp. sugar.

TUESDAY

TIME 35 MIN. SERVES 2

*Shrimp & *Lamb Curry*
Rice
**Green Bean Salad*
Frozen Strawberry Slices
Coffee

SHRIMP & LAMB CURRY: 1 can shrimp, at least 1 c. leftover lamb, diced. Fry ½ onion, sliced, ½ carrot, sliced, in 1 tbs. butter until soft. Add 2 tbs. curry powder, heat 1 min. Stir in 1 tbs. flour, ½ c. canned tomatoes, ¾ c. bouillon. Add ½ c. chopped apple, ¼ tsp. pickle relish, simmer 8 min. Add shrimps, drained, and lamb, cook 10 min. Heap on dish, surround with 1½ c. prepared precooked rice. Garnish with parsley, chutney, coconut.

GREEN BEAN SALAD: Combine lettuce, chicory, and Sunday's leftover beans with French dressing.

FROZEN STRAWBERRY SLICES: ½ box frozen. Cut in thin slices, sprinkle with juice ½ lemon, nut crumbs.

WEDNESDAY

TIME 45 MIN. SERVES 2

Pepper Pot Soup
Onion Pork Chops
Sweet Potatoes
Mustard Tomatoes
Endive Salad
Caramel Bananas
Coffee

ONION PORK CHOPS: 2 thick loin chops. Boil 2 large sliced onions until soft, about 10 min. Drain, mash with 1 tsp. butter. Stir in 1 tbs. flour, ¼ tsp. salt, ⅛ tsp. pepper, pinch sage, 1 beaten egg. Sprinkle chops with salt, pepper. Place in baking dish, cover with onion mixture, surround with 1 can drained sweet potatoes brushed with melted butter. Bake in moderate oven (375°) until tender, about 30 min. Baste. Top with melted butter.

MUSTARD TOMATOES: 2. Halve, salt and pepper. Spread with 1 tbs. prepared mustard mixed with 1 tbs. mayonnaise. Bake 25 min. in buttered baking dish.

CARAMEL BANANAS: Boil 3 tbs. sugar, 3 tbs. water until golden brown. Place 3 split, peeled bananas in buttered frying pan, spoon on sauce. Cook very slowly 15 min. Serve hot.

TIME 30 MIN. SERVES 2 **THURSDAY**

**Chicken Pot Pie*
Carrots w. Celery Seed
Watercress, Lemon Mayonnaise
**Strawberry Snow*
Coffee

CHICKEN POT PIE: 1 can chicken fricassee. Mix with ½ box defrosted leftover peas, ¼ tsp. paprika. Heat to simmer. Turn into small baking dish, cover with split ready-to-bake biscuits. Bake in hot oven (450°) 15 min. Bake rest of biscuits, split, toast for breakfast.

CARROTS W. CELERY SEED: 1 can carrots. Heat. Drain, season, add ½ tsp. celery seed, 1 tsp. butter.

LEMON MAYONNAISE: Mix 1 tbs. grated lemon peel, ¼ c. mayonnaise.

STRAWBERRY SNOW: Mash ½ box defrosted leftover strawberries, drain slightly. Beat with 1 egg white until stiff, fold in ½ c. whipped cream. Chill.

TIME 30 MIN. SERVES 2 **FRIDAY**

Cream of Asparagus Soup
Camillo Scallops
Chili Spinach
Broiled Potatoes
Tossed Salad
Fresh Fruit
Coffee

CAMILLO SCALLOPS: 1 pkg., defrosted. Dip in seasoned beaten egg, then bread crumbs. Place in buttered pan, dot with butter. Broil 10 min., turning once. Heat 2 tbs. olive oil, 1 tbs. melted butter, add 1 tsp. chopped onion, ½ minced garlic clove, 1 tsp. chopped parsley. Sauté 5 min. Serve over scallops.

CHILI SPINACH: 1 box. Slightly undercook. Drain, mix with 1 tbs. chili sauce.

BROILED POTATOES: 1 can. Cut in thick slices. Sprinkle with salt, brush with melted butter. Broil beside scallops.

OCTOBER

Recheck your basic staples—and now have you

thyme
basil
curry powder
walnuts
lemons
cinnamon
orange marmalade
almonds
chutney
plain gelatin
whole cloves
brown sugar
dry white wine
capers
soy sauce
ginger
almond flavoring
powdered clove
rum
poultry seasoning
nutmeg
maple syrup

—And have you

toothpicks

SHOPPING LIST

MEAT

2½ lbs. top round beef cut in small squares
2 veal cutlets, about ¾ lb., pounded thin
1½-lb. chicken, broiler

FROZEN FOODS

1 box Lima beans
1 box string beans
1 box fillet of sole
1 box chopped spinach
1 box peas and carrots

FRESH FRUITS AND VEGETABLES

12 small white onions
8 carrots
2 Idaho potatoes
1 bunch celery
½ lb. Tokay grapes
3 tomatoes
2 green peppers
1 head lettuce
1 small cucumber
1 bunch parsley
1 endive
2 apples
1 banana
2 oranges

SUNDRIES

4-oz. can sliced mushrooms
1 small can tomato paste
1 lb. chocolate-covered peppermints
⅛ lb. Roquefort cheese
1 8-oz. can tomatoes
1 small can figs
1 small can apple-sauce
1 8-oz. can diced beets
1 small jar anchovy paste
1 tube ready-to-bake biscuits
1 pt. sour cream
½ pt. heavy cream
1 small Camembert cheese
½-lb. pkg. wide lasagne noodles
1 pkg. Italian bread sticks
¼ lb. Swiss cheese
1 small can potatoes
1 can condensed tomato soup
1 can condensed cream of mushroom soup
2 cans cream of celery soup

PICK UP ON YOUR WAY HOME

FOR SUN.—French bread; 1 small angel food cake
THUR.—sliced rye bread

SUNDAY

TIME 2¼ HRS. SERVES 4

Cream of Celery Soup
Huguenot Stew
Lettuce Hearts, Roquefort Dressing
Hot Buttered French Bread
Chocolate-Peppermint Angel Food
Coffee

HUGUENOT STEW: 2½ lbs. top round beef. Cut in squares, dredge with flour, brown in 2 tbs. butter over high heat. Add ¼ c. sherry, 12 small white onions, 1 4-oz. can mushrooms, 1 tbs. tomato paste, 1¼ c. red wine, ½ tsp. salt, ¼ tsp. pepper, 1 bay leaf, pinch thyme, pinch basil, 8 small whole carrots, scraped. Simmer covered until tender, about 2 hrs.

CHOCOLATE-PEPPERMINT SAUCE: Stir 20 chocolate peppermints with 2 tbs. butter in double boiler until melted. Pour hot over wedges of angel food.

MONDAY

TIME 40 MIN. SERVES 2

Cheese Lasagne
Buttered Spinach
Beet & Cucumber Salad, Anchovy Dressing
Italian Bread Sticks
Applesauce w. Figs
Coffee

CHEESE LASAGNE: Boil 4 oz. wide lasagne noodles until tender, drain. Mix 1 can condensed mushroom soup with ¼ lb. cottage cheese, ¼ tsp. curry powder. Alternate layers of noodles, ¼ lb. sliced Swiss cheese, and soup mixture in buttered casserole. Top with ¼ c. buttered bread crumbs mixed with 2 tbs. grated Parmesan cheese. Bake in moderate oven (375°) 25 min.

BUTTERED SPINACH: ½ box, chopped. Prepare as directed. Dress with 2 tbs. butter.

BEET & CUCUMBER SALAD: Mix 1 can drained diced beets, 1 small peeled cucumber, minced, chunks of lettuce with ¼ c. French dressing mixed with 1 tsp. anchovy paste.

APPLESAUCE W. FIGS: Drain 1 can figs cut in strips, heat with 1 tsp. lemon juice, 1 c. applesauce, ¼ c. fig syrup. Serve with whipped cream.

TIME 45 MIN. SERVES 2 **TUESDAY**

**Lumberjack Beef*
String Beans
Baked Potatoes
Tokay Fruit Cup
Coffee

LUMBERJACK BEEF: Dice leftover beef, dust with flour. Brown in 1 tbs. butter. Add 1 minced garlic clove, 1 sliced onion, 1 diced green pepper, ½ tsp. dried thyme, 1 bay leaf, 1 can condensed tomato soup, 1 box string beans. Cook covered 20 min. Pour over baked potatoes, split in half lengthwise.

BAKED POTATOES: 2 Idaho. Rub with salad oil. Bake in hot oven (425°), about 45 min.

TOKAY FRUIT CUP: Combine ½ c. halved, seeded Tokay grapes, 1 sliced banana, ¼ c. walnuts. Pour on ½ c. orange juice sweetened with honey to taste.

TIME 30 MIN. SERVES 2 **WEDNESDAY**

**Veal Florentine*
Lima Beans & Tomatoes
Crisp Celery Stalks
Cinnamon Apple Slices w. Sour Cream
Coffee

VEAL FLORENTINE: 2 cutlets pounded thin. Rub with salt, pepper. Dip in flour, in beaten egg yolk, then in bread crumbs. Sauté in 2 tbs. butter 5 min. on one side. Turn. Add ½ box leftover chopped spinach, defrosted. Cover, cook 10 min.

LIMA BEANS & TOMATOES: Sauté 1 small chopped onion, 1 tbs. chopped green pepper in 1 tbs. butter 5 min. Add 1 can drained tomatoes, ¼ tsp. grated lemon rind, salt and pepper to taste, 1 box Lima beans. Cook until beans are tender, about 12 min. Save any left over for Friday.

CINNAMON APPLE SLICES W. SOUR CREAM: Cut 2 unpeeled apples in ½″ slices. Spread with 2 tbs. sugar, 1 tsp. cinnamon, dot with butter. Broil under moderate heat until soft, about 10 min.

THURSDAY

TIME 45 MIN. SERVES 2

Chicken w. Almonds
Parsley Potatoes
Buttered Peas & Carrots
**Marmalade Whip*
Coffee

CHICKEN W. ALMONDS: 1½-lb. broiler, split. Rub with ½ lemon. Roll in 3 tbs. melted butter. Season with salt, pepper, pinch thyme. Broil under low heat, skin side down first. Turn several times, baste with more melted butter, until done, about 35 min. In large frying pan combine ½ c. sour cream, ½ c. crushed blanched almonds, 1 tsp. flour, ½ c. bouillon, salt and pepper to taste. Stir until boiling. Add broiled chicken, 1 bay leaf. Cover, cook 5 min. Serve on toasted rye bread.

MARMALADE WHIP: Mix 1 tbs. lemon juice with 2 tbs. orange marmalade, stir into ½ c. whipped cream. Fold in 1 c. small pulled pieces angel food cake. Chill in serving glasses. Top with whipped cream, dab of marmalade.

FRIDAY

TIME 25 MIN. SERVES 2

Fillet of Sole Creole w.
**Vegetables*
Hot Buttered Biscuits
Endive & Lettuce w.
Chutney Dressing
Camembert & Crackers
Black Coffee

FILLET OF SOLE CREOLE W. VEGETABLES: 1 box sole, defrosted. Dust fillets with seasoned flour, sauté in 3 tbs. butter. Cook 3 sliced tomatoes in 2 tbs. melted fat with 1 chopped garlic clove 3 min. Place sole on tomatoes. Cover with ½ box spinach, semi-thawed, mixed with ½ c. sour cream, ½ tsp. salt, ¼ tsp. pepper, juice ½ lemon, 1 tbs. grated cheese, and any leftover vegetables. Sprinkle with 3 tbs. buttered bread crumbs mixed with 3 tbs. grated cheese. Broil under low heat until sauce bubbles, cheese crumbs brown.

ENDIVE & LETTUCE W. CHUTNEY DRESSING: Toss endive strips with chunks of lettuce. Add 1 tbs. chutney to ¼ c. French dressing.

SHOPPING LIST

MEAT

3 lbs. ready-cooked boneless ham
5 lamb kidneys
3 minute steaks
½ lb. bacon

FROZEN FOODS

1 box asparagus
2 boxes broccoli (or 1 large bunch fresh)
1 box peas
1 box spinach

FRESH FRUITS AND VEGETABLES

2 oranges
1 bunch parsley
1 Boston lettuce
1 chicory
1 iceberg lettuce
3 oranges
4 large firm tomatoes
4 sweet potatoes
6 white onions
1 green pepper
1 bunch celery

SUNDRIES

1 small jar currant jelly
12 ladyfingers
2 4-oz. cans sliced mushrooms
1 small can tomato paste
1 small pkg. noodles
1 small can boned chicken
1 small can pimiento
1 #1 tall can bamboo shoots (or bean sprouts)
1 small jar spiced peaches
1 box instant vanilla dessert
1 pt. heavy cream
1 #2 can crushed pineapple
1 small pkg. cream cheese
1 small jar guava jelly
1 small can pears
1 can French-fried onions
¼ lb. candied ginger
2 cans pea soup
1 box butterthins
1 can cream of asparagus soup

PICK UP ON YOUR WAY HOME

TUES.—½ pt. oysters
2 English muffins
FRI.—6 large scallops
½ pt. heavy cream

SUNDAY

TIME 3½ HRS. SERVES 4

Split Pea Soup
Harvest Ham
Buttered Broccoli
Baked Sweet Potatoes
Tossed Salad
Pineapple Icebox Cake
Coffee

HARVEST HAM: 3 lbs. ready-cooked boneless ham. Score fat, dot with whole cloves. Mix 4 tbs. currant jelly, 1 tsp. grated orange rind, 2 tbs. brown sugar, 3 tbs. sherry, pinch cayenne. Spread over ham. Bake in hot oven (425°) about 45 min. Baste with ½ c. orange juice mixed with 2 tbs. lemon juice.

PINEAPPLE ICEBOX CAKE: Soak 2 tbs. granulated gelatin in ½ c. cold water for 5 min. Stir over low heat with ½ c. sugar, 1 can crushed pineapple, ¼ tsp. salt, 1 tbs. lemon juice until sugar dissolves. Chill. When mixture begins to thicken fold in 2 c. whipped cream. Line mold with ladyfingers. Pour in pineapple mixture, place any leftover ladyfingers on top. Chill until firm, about 3 hrs. Turn out on serving dish, decorate with whipped cream.

MONDAY

TIME 30 MIN. SERVES 2

Cream of Asparagus Soup
Kidney Stew w. Rice
Broiled Tomatoes
Spiced Peaches
Coffee

CREAM OF ASPARAGUS SOUP: 1 can. Prepare as directed. Garnish with crumbled bacon.

KIDNEY STEW W. RICE: 5 lamb kidneys. Skin, split, remove core and tubes. Brown quickly in 1 tbs. butter. Remove. Blend in 2 tsp. flour. Add 1 4-oz. can mushrooms, 6 halved white onions, ½ tsp. tomato paste, ½ c. white wine, ½ c. bouillon. Stir until boiling, simmer 10 min. Add kidneys, ½ tsp. salt, ¼ tsp. pepper, ¼ c. chopped parsley. Simmer 10 min. Serve on 1½ c. prepared precooked rice.

BROILED TOMATOES: 2. Slice 1″ thick. Arrange in shallow pan. Salt and pepper to taste. Dot with butter. Broil about 8 min. Sprinkle with basil.

TIME 40 MIN. SERVES 2

TUESDAY

**Ham & Oyster Scallop w. Peas*
Toasted English Muffins
Chicory Salad
Cream Cheese, Guava Jelly & Butterthins
Coffee

HAM & OYSTER SCALLOP W. PEAS: Heat 2 tbs. butter, blend in 2 tbs. flour, add ½ c. milk, ½ c. white wine, stirring until smooth and thick. Add 1 c. diced leftover ham, ½ pt. drained fresh oysters, ½ box defrosted peas, salt and pepper to taste. Pour into shallow buttered casserole, sprinkle with buttered bread crumbs. Bake in moderately hot oven (425°) 25 min. Serve on split English muffins, toasted and buttered.

CHICORY SALAD: Toss chicory, green pepper rings, sliced pimiento, sprinkling of capers with ¼ c. French dressing.

TIME 35 MIN. SERVES 2

WEDNESDAY

Mirabeau Minute Steak
French-Fried Onions
Asparagus w. Lemon Butter
Lettuce Heart Salad, Russian Dressing
Orange Soufflé
Coffee

MIRABEAU MINUTE STEAK: 3 minute steaks. Rub with cut onion, salt, pepper. Spread with ¼ tsp. anchovy paste. Cook in very hot greased pan 1 min. Turn often.

ASPARAGUS W. LEMON BUTTER: 1 box. Prepare as directed. Dress with 2 tbs. melted butter mixed with 2 tbs. lemon juice, salt and pepper to taste, dash Tabasco.

ORANGE SOUFFLÉ: Mix 4 tbs. flour, 1 tbs. sugar in saucepan, blend in ½ c. orange juice, 1 tbs. lemon juice. Stir over low heat until smooth and thick. Beat in 2 egg yolks, 1 at a time, then stir in 1 tbs. orange marmalade, fold in 2 egg whites beaten stiff with ¼ tsp. salt, 3 tbs. sugar. Turn into thickly buttered, then sugared, small deep casserole. Bake in moderately hot oven (400°) 25 min. Sprinkle lightly with sugar and serve immediately.

THURSDAY

TIME 25 MIN. SERVES 2

Oriental Hodgepodge
Soya Spinach
Toast Triangles
Olives
Celery
Ginger Pears
Tea

ORIENTAL HODGEPODGE: Boil 4 oz. noodles 8 min. Cut 1 can boneless chicken into chunks, sauté in 1 tbs. oil 1 min. Add 1 4-oz. can sliced mushrooms (drain, save liquid), 1 can bamboo shoots (or well-drained bean sprouts), heat. Stir in 1 tbs. cornstarch mixed with mushroom liquid, 1 tsp. soy sauce. Cook 5 min. Rinse noodles under cold water, drain well. Fry in 1 tbs. oil 1½ min., turning frequently. Serve topped with chicken mixture. Garnish with 1 finely sliced onion.

SOYA SPINACH: 1 box. Undercook, drain well. Mix with 1 tbs. soy sauce. Serve cold.

GINGER PEARS: 1 small can. Slice pears, add 1 tbs. slivered candied ginger. Serve chilled, with or without cream.

FRIDAY

TIME 35 MIN. SERVES 2

Scallop Kabobs
**Buttered Peas*
Rice
**Vegetable Salad*
Almond Cream
Coffee

SCALLOP KABOBS: 6 scallops. Poach in salted boiling water with 2 tbs. lemon juice, 1 bay leaf, 1 sliced onion 5 min. Drain. Flour lightly, brush with beaten egg, dip in bread crumbs. Alternate on skewers with bacon squares, tomato quarters, roll in 2 tbs. melted butter. Broil 10 min., turning occasionally. Serve over 1½ c. precooked rice prepared with pinch saffron, 2 bay leaves.

VEGETABLE SALAD: Marinate any leftover spinach and asparagus, diced, in ¼ c. French dressing 15 min. Drain, toss with lettuce leaves, serve with mayonnaise.

ALMOND CREAM: Prepare ½ pkg. instant vanilla dessert, add drop almond flavoring, 2 tbs. slivered blanched almonds. Chill. Top with whipped cream.

SHOPPING LIST

MEAT

5½–6 lbs. shoulder of lamb
3 large Italian sausages or large garlic frankfurters, about ¾ lb.
1 pork tenderloin, about 1 lb.

FROZEN FOODS

1 box corn kernels
2 boxes asparagus
1 box string beans

FRESH FRUITS AND VEGETABLES

2 bunches celery
1 apple
2 green peppers
1 orange
4 tomatoes
1 bunch chives
1 Boston lettuce
1 iceberg lettuce
½ lb. cranberries
1 bunch carrots
1 banana
1 bunch radishes
5 or 6 yams
fresh fruit for dessert
1 bunch watercress

SUNDRIES

1 12-oz. can pineapple juice
2 boxes Parker House rolls
1 #1 can tomato juice
1 4-oz. can sliced mushrooms
1 small can pimiento
1 small date and nut cake
1 pt. heavy cream
1 #2 can plums
1 8-oz. can beets
1 8-oz. can carrots
1 box ready-to-bake rolls
¼ lb. Gorgonzola cheese
2 #1 cans potatoes
1 bar sweet chocolate
1 jar infant puréed apricots with applesauce
2 slices poundcake
1 pkg. piecrust mix
1 can oxtail soup
2 cans consommé
1 can cream of mushroom soup

PICK UP ON YOUR WAY HOME

FOR SUN.—1 pt. vanilla ice cream
WED.—pumpernickel bread
FRI.—2 salmon steaks, about ¾ lb.
1 pt. butter pecan ice cream

SUNDAY

TIME 3¼ HRS. SERVES 2

Sherried Consommé
Hawaiian Roast Lamb
Candied Yams Flambé
Buttered Asparagus
Radishes & Olives
Parker House Rolls
Stewed Plums à la Mode
Coffee

HAWAIIAN ROAST LAMB: 5½–6 lbs. shoulder. Wipe meat. Rub with cut garlic, then lemon juice, dust with salt, pepper, pinch dried thyme. Roast in slow oven (325°) 30–35 min. per pound. Baste with 1½ c. pineapple juice. Thicken gravy with 2 tbs. flour, add pinch ginger, 1 tbs. brown sugar.

CANDIED YAMS FLAMBÉ: 5 or 6. Boil 10 min. Peel. Slice lengthwise ½″ thick. Arrange 1 layer in shallow buttered casserole. Mix ½ c. brown sugar, ½ tsp. grated orange rind, ¼ tsp. cinnamon, ¼ tsp. powdered clove. Alternate yams and sugar mixture. Dot with butter, pour on ¼ c. rum. Bake 35 min. To serve, pour on 3 tbs. heated rum, set aflame.

MONDAY

TIME 50 MIN. SERVES 2

Oxtail Soup
Italian Sausage Casserole
Boston Lettuce Salad
Apricot Strudel
Coffee

ITALIAN SAUSAGE CASSEROLE: Slice 1 large onion, arrange in shallow buttered casserole. Add 1 sliced green pepper, 2 quartered tomatoes, 1 box semi-thawed corn kernels. Sprinkle with ½ tsp. salt, ⅛ tsp. pepper, pinch basil. Top with 3 large Italian sausages (or large garlic frankfurters). Bake in moderately hot oven (425°) 45 min.

APRICOT STRUDEL: Mix 1 jar infant puréed apricots with applesauce, 3 tbs. chopped nuts, 1 tbs. lemon juice, ½ tsp. lemon rind, ½ tsp. brown sugar. Spread on plain cake slices, top with whipped cream.

TIME 45 MIN. SERVES 2

TUESDAY

Tomato Juice
**Lamb Puppies on Carrots*
Garlic Rolls
Mixed Vegetable Salad
Date & Nut Cake
Coffee

LAMB PUPPIES ON CARROTS: 4 large slices leftover lamb, ¼″ thick. Heat 1 tbs. butter, add 1 small chopped onion, 1 stalk celery, chopped, ½ 4-oz. can sliced mushrooms, drained. Sauté 12 min. Stir in ½ c. soft bread crumbs, ¼ tsp. salt, ½ tsp. poultry seasoning. Spread on 2 lamb slices. Top with other slices, sandwich-style, fasten with toothpicks. Place 1 can drained carrots in shallow casserole, lay lamb sandwiches on top. Add 1 c. bouillon. Bake in moderate oven (375°) 25 min.

MIXED VEGETABLE SALAD: To ¼ c. French dressing add 1 tsp. minced onion, 1 stalk chopped celery, ½ chopped green pepper, 1 pimiento cut in strips, ½ can drained sliced mushrooms, diced leftover asparagus, if any. Serve on lettuce.

TIME 45 MIN. SERVES 2

WEDNESDAY

New Brunswick Casserole
Mixed Green Salad
Cheese w. Pumpernickel Bread
Fruit Bowl
Coffee

NEW BRUNSWICK CASSEROLE: Hard-cook 4 eggs. Heat 2 tbs. butter, blend in 2 tbs. flour, 1 small minced onion, 1 minced garlic clove, 3 tbs. minced parsley, then 2 c. milk. Stir over low heat until smooth and thick. Add salt and pepper to taste, ¼ tsp. nutmeg, dash cayenne. In buttered casserole alternate layers of sliced hard-cooked egg, potatoes (1 can, drained and sliced), string beans (1 box, defrosted), and sauce, sprinkling each layer with buttered bread crumbs mixed with 1 tsp. minced chives. Top with buttered crumbs. Bake in moderately hot oven (425°) 35 min.

MIXED GREEN SALAD: Watercress, iceberg lettuce, Boston lettuce, and paper-thin onion rings with French dressing.

THURSDAY

TIME 45 MIN. SERVES 2

Cream of Mushroom Soup
Raw Carrot Strips
Apple Pork Tenderloin
Celery à Dente
Buttered Beets
Cranberry & Banana Pie
Coffee

APPLE PORK TENDERLOIN: 1 tenderloin. Dust with seasoned flour. Brown over high heat in 2 tbs. butter. Top with 1 thickly sliced apple. Add 1 tbs. sherry, ½ c. cream. Cover, simmer 30 min.

CELERY À DENTE: Boil 2 c. thinly sliced outer stalks in 1 c. water 10 min. Drain. Salt, pepper to taste, ½ tsp. nutmeg.

CRANBERRY & BANANA PIE: Prepare ½ pkg. pastry mix as directed. Line 8″ pie plate, pierce all over with fork. Bake in hot oven (425°) 15 min. Cook 1 c. cranberries with ½ c. sugar, ¼ c. water, covered, until skins burst, about 5 min. Drain, reserve juice. Pour mixture into baked shell, top with 1 sliced banana. Pour on juice, bake 15 min. Serve hot with cream.

FRIDAY

TIME 40 MIN. SERVES 2

Baked Salmon Hollandaise
Lyonnaise Potatoes
Broiled Tomatoes
**Celery Hearts & Mayonnaise*
Chocolate Pecan Ice Cream
Coffee

BAKED SALMON HOLLANDAISE: 2 steaks, about ¾ lb. Dust with salt, pepper. Place in flat casserole. Pour on 2 tbs. melted butter. Broil 3 min. Add ½ c. red wine, 1 sliced onion, 1 garlic clove, ¼ tsp. thyme, ¼ c. water. Cover with wax paper. Bake in moderately hot oven (425°) 12–15 min., until done. In double boiler mix 3 tbs. cream, 2 egg yolks, 3 tbs. fish liquid. Stir over hot water until thickened. Add 3 tbs. butter a little at a time, juice ½ lemon. Serve over fish.

LYONNAISE POTATOES: 1 can. Drain. Slice. Mix with 1 sliced onion, fry in 2 tbs. butter about 15 min., hashing with knife.

CHOCOLATE PECAN ICE CREAM: Mix ¼ c. coarsely grated chocolate into 1 pt. butter pecan ice cream.

SHOPPING LIST

MEAT

2 racks spareribs, about 4 lbs.
¾ lb. veal cutlet cut in 1″ squares
1 small duckling, split
½ lb. beef liver sliced thin
2 chicken livers

FROZEN FOODS

2 boxes corn on the cob
1 box French-fried potatoes
1 box potato puffs
1 box broccoli
1 box succotash
1 box cut asparagus

FRESH FRUITS AND VEGETABLES

1 cucumber
1 onion
5 oranges
3 apples
1 lemon
2 bananas
2 heads lettuce
1 small eggplant
½ lb. mixed green and purple grapes
1 bunch celery
1 grapefruit
1 green pepper
1 tomato

SUNDRIES

1 #1 can tomatoes
4 oz. candied ginger
1 #1 can tomato juice
½ pt. sour cream
1 box fruit gelatin
1 box Graham crackers
1 box poppy-seed rolls
½ pt. heavy cream
1 8-oz. can diced carrots
1 box pilot crackers
1 small can tomato paste
1 small jar olives
1 #1 tall can potatoes
1 jar currant jelly
1 4-oz. can sliced mushrooms
1 small jar pimiento
1 small can pineapple slices
1 can turtle soup
1 can tomato soup
1 can condensed pea soup
2 cans pepper pot soup

PICK UP ON YOUR WAY HOME

FOR SUN.—1½ pts. vanilla ice cream
WED.—½ pumpkin pie
FRI.—1 lb. codfish cut in 2″ pieces

SUNDAY

TIME 1 HR. 25 MIN. SERVES 4

Pepper Pot Soup
Barbecued Spareribs
Corn on the Cob
Onion & Cucumber Salad
Poppy-Seed Rolls
Orange & Apple Ginger Glacé
Coffee

BARBECUED SPARERIBS: 2 racks, about 4 lbs., cracked. Heat 1 c. vinegar with 2 tbs. butter, ½ tsp. black pepper, dash cayenne, 1 tsp. salt, 1 small can tomatoes, ½ tsp. Worcestershire. Mix well. Brush both sides of ribs with sauce. Place in large roasting pan. Pour on remaining sauce. Bake in moderately hot oven (425°) about 50 min. Baste frequently.

ONION & CUCUMBER SALAD: Peel 1 cucumber, 1 onion, slice thin. Marinate in ½ c. vinegar mixed with ½ c. water, 1 tsp. salt, 1 tsp. sugar. Drain, serve on lettuce with French dressing.

ORANGE & APPLE GINGER GLACÉ: Arrange slices of 2 unpeeled oranges and 2 apples on serving dish. Sprinkle with 1 tsp. powdered ginger. Pile vanilla ice cream in center, garnish with chopped candied ginger.

MONDAY

TIME 30 MIN. SERVES 2

Hot Spiced Tomato Juice
Cyclops Veal
French-Fried Potatoes
Sliced Bananas, Chopped Nuts & Cream
Coffee

HOT SPICED TOMATO JUICE: Season with salt, pepper, dash powdered clove, 1 tsp. lemon juice. Serve piping hot.

CYCLOPS VEAL: ¾ lb. veal cutlet cut in 1″ squares. Roll in seasoned flour. Sauté 1 large sliced onion in 2 tbs. butter until soft. Add veal, 2 tsp. paprika, 1 c. milk, stir constantly until thickened. Cover, simmer 30 min. Prepare 1 box asparagus cuts as directed. Drain, add to veal. Transfer to shallow casserole. Break an egg on top. Sprinkle with 2 tbs. grated Parmesan cheese mixed with 1 tbs. buttered bread crumbs. Place under broiler until egg sets.

TIME 35 MIN. SERVES 2

TUESDAY

Braised Liver on Toast
Succotash
Celery in Sour Cream
Broiled Grapefruit
Coffee

BRAISED LIVER ON TOAST: ½ lb. beef liver sliced thin. Dip in 1 c. boiling bouillon, then dust with seasoned flour. Brown in 2 tbs. butter, add the bouillon, simmer covered 20 min. Remove liver, keep warm. Add to liquid 1 tbs. lemon juice, 1 tsp. mixed dried herbs, 1 crushed garlic clove. Boil rapidly 5 min. to reduce. Serve on toast.

SUCCOTASH: 1 box. Prepare as directed. Serve with melted butter seasoned with 3 or 4 dashes Tabasco.

CELERY IN SOUR CREAM: Mix 1½ c. crisp celery cut in ¼″ slices with ½ c. seasoned sour cream. Serve sprinkled with paprika.

BROILED GRAPEFRUIT: Halve grapefruit, loosen sections, remove core. Add 1 tbs. maple syrup mixed with 1 tbs. sherry to each half. Dot with butter. Broil under very low heat 15 min.

TIME 1 HR. SERVES 2

WEDNESDAY

Mock Turtle Soup
Broiled Duckling in Orange Sauce
Hot Potato Puffs
Buttered Broccoli
Tossed Green Salad
Green & Purple Grapes
Pumpkin Pie
Coffee

MOCK TURTLE SOUP: 1 can. Combine with 1 can condensed pea soup, ¼ c. sherry. Simmer.

BROILED DUCKLING IN ORANGE SAUCE: 1 duckling, split. Rub with lemon juice, then with bacon drippings, dust with salt, pepper. Broil 20 min., turning frequently. Heat 2 tbs. butter in large frying pan, blend in 1 tsp. flour, stir in ½ c. orange juice, 1 tsp. grated orange rind, ½ tsp. salt, ⅛ tsp. pepper, ¼ cup dry white wine, 1 tbs. currant jelly. Simmer 5 min. Add duck. Simmer covered until duck is done, about 30–35 min.

FOR TOMORROW: Prepare 1 pkg. fruit gelatin.

THURSDAY

TIME 35 MIN. SERVES 2

**Chicken Liver & Duck Pilaff*
Spanish Salad
Graham-Cracker Gelatin
Coffee

CHICKEN LIVER & DUCK PILAFF: Sauté 2 diced chicken livers in 2 tbs. butter 5 min. with ½ c. chopped olives, 1 small diced eggplant, 1 4-oz. can drained, sliced mushrooms. Add any leftover duckling, minced, salt and pepper to taste, 2 tbs. sherry. Simmer 10 min. Serve over 3 cups precooked rice, prepared with ⅛ tsp. pepper, pinch saffron.

SPANISH SALAD: Toss thinly sliced onion, pimiento, green pepper, unpeeled apple, broken lettuce with French dressing. Serve in garlic-rubbed bowl.

GRAHAM-CRACKER GELATIN: Into each sherbet glass, crumble 2 Graham crackers. Dice gelatin and add. Top with whipped cream. Sprinkle with more Graham-cracker crumbs mixed with a little grated lemon peel.

FRIDAY

TIME 35 MIN. SERVES 2

Cream of Tomato Soup
Pilot Crackers
Cod Provençal
O'Brien Potatoes
Orange & Pineapple Slices
Coffee

COD PROVENÇAL: 1 lb. cut in 2″ pieces. Fry in 2 tbs. very hot oil 5 min. Drain on paper. Brown 1 can carrots, drained, 1 chopped garlic clove, 1 chopped onion in 2 tbs. butter. Add 1 diced tomato, 1 c. white wine, 1 jigger brandy (opt.), 1 tsp. tomato paste, ⅛ tsp. paprika, ½ c. water. Add cod. Simmer 15 min.

O'BRIEN POTATOES: 1 can. Chop. Place half in small casserole, sprinkle with 1 tbs. minced onion, 1 tbs. minced green pepper, 2 tbs. grated cheese, salt, pepper, dots of butter. Repeat. Bake 25 min. in moderate oven (375°).

ORANGE & PINEAPPLE SLICES: Split 1 small can pineapple slices with sharp knife. Alternate in bowl with very thin orange slices. Pour on pineapple syrup mixed with ¼ c. orange juice. Chill.

NOVEMBER

Recheck your basic staples—and now have you

rosemary
honey
whole cloves
biscuit mix
basil
mace
nutmeg
Madeira wine
strong sherry
saffron
corn meal
chili powder
powdered sugar
lemons
thyme
confectioners' sugar
sage
ginger
tarragon
brown sugar
horseradish
sliced bread
orange marmalade
soy sauce
curry powder

SHOPPING LIST

MEAT

3½ lbs. smoked beef tongue
½ lb. chopped beef chuck
¼ lb. bacon

FROZEN FOODS

1 box French-style string beans
1 box sliced peaches

FRESH FRUITS AND VEGETABLES

3 tomatoes
2 green peppers
1 lb. zucchini
1 pineapple
2 bananas
1 head chicory
1 bunch celery
1 head lettuce
10 small potatoes
1 Boston lettuce
2 large Idaho potatoes

SUNDRIES

1 small jar pitted olives
1 #2 can creamed-style corn
1 can French-fried onions
1 pkg. Italian bread sticks
1 small can green-gage plums
1 small can sweet potatoes
1 6-oz. can boned chicken
2 #1 cans tomatoes
1 #1 can okra (opt.)
1 box muffins
1 box mixed cookies
1 12-oz. can vegetable juice
1 small can fruits for salad
assorted cheeses for dessert
1 small can tomato paste
¼ lb. rattrap cheese
1 small can cherries
1 slice poundcake
1 4-oz. can sliced mushrooms
1 can pea soup
1 can black bean soup
1 can condensed oxtail soup

PICK UP ON YOUR WAY HOME

FOR SUN.—1½ pts. vanilla ice cream
TUES.—1 bunch broccoli
½ pt. heavy cream
WED.—1 pkg. washed spinach
THUR.—¾ lb. potato salad
FRI.—¾ lb. halibut steak

TIME 3 HRS. SERVES 4

SUNDAY

HOME-STYLE CORN SOUP: Dice 2 strips bacon. Fry. Add 1 minced onion, ½ green pepper, chopped. Cook 5 min. Add 1 #2 can creamed-style corn, 2 c. bouillon, 1 tbs. cornstarch mixed with 2 tbs. water. Simmer 10 min. Add 1 c. milk, salt and pepper to taste. Serve piping hot, do not boil.

Home-Style Corn Soup
Tongue Casserole
Boston Lettuce Salad
Pineapple Slices w. Ice Cream
Cookies
Coffee

TONGUE CASSEROLE: 3½ lbs. smoked beef tongue. Scrub well. Cover with boiling water, simmer 1½ hrs. Drain, reserving 1 c. liquid. Skin, remove root ends. Melt 3 tbs. butter in large saucepan. Brown tongue on all sides. Add 3 sliced tomatoes, 3 sliced onions, 10 pitted olives, ¼ tsp. rosemary, ½ tsp. parsley, 1 bay leaf, 6 peppercorns, 8–10 small scrubbed potatoes, and the 1 c. liquid. Simmer 1 hr.

TIME 20 MIN. SERVES 2

MONDAY

TROPICAL HAMBURGERS: ¾ lb. chopped chuck steak. Combine with 1 minced onion, ½ garlic clove, minced, 1 mashed banana, ½ tsp. salt, ¼ tsp. pepper. Shape into patties. Dust with flour, sauté in 2 tbs. very hot oil. Don't overcook—best rare.

Tropical Hamburgers
French-Fried Onions
Zucchini Sauté
Chicory & Lettuce Salad
Italian Bread Sticks
Greengage Plums
Coffee

ZUCCHINI SAUTÉ: 1 lb. Scrub well. Cut in ¼″ slices. Sauté 1 tsp. chopped onion, 1 tbs. chopped green pepper in 4 tsp. olive oil until soft. Add zucchini. Cook, turning often, until tender and brown. Season with salt and pepper to taste, pinch sugar.

TUESDAY

TIME 30 MIN. SERVES 2

Pea Soup
**Virginia Tongue w. Sweet Potatoes*
Buttered Broccoli
Peach Cobbler
Coffee

VIRGINIA TONGUE W. SWEET POTATOES: Slice leftover tongue. Arrange in shallow pan. Spread with honey, dot with whole cloves. Place 1 small can sweet potatoes, drained, around tongue, brush with melted butter. Bake in moderately hot oven (400°) 20 min.

BUTTERED BROCOLLI: Wash, discard outer leaves, hard stock. Cut in even lengths. Arrange flat in skillet. Sprinkle with ½ tsp. salt. Pour on 1 c. boiling water. Cover tightly, cook over low heat 15 min. or until tender. Dress with 2 tbs. butter.

PEACH COBBLER: Heat 1 box peaches, stir in 1 tbs. cornstarch mixed with 2 tbs. water. Bring to boil. Add 1 tbs. butter, ⅛ tsp. cinnamon, pour into small casserole. Stir ⅓ c. cream into 1 c. biscuit mix, spoon onto peaches. Bake in moderately hot oven (400°) about 20 min. Serve with cream.

WEDNESDAY

TIME 30 MIN. SERVES 2

Hot Vegetable Juice
Bayou Chicken & Rice
Spinach Salad
Hot Muffins
Fruit Compote
Coffee

BAYOU CHICKEN & RICE: Mix 1 can chicken, diced, with 1½ c. prepared precooked rice. Heat 2 tbs. butter, add 1 large onion, minced, 1 chopped garlic clove, 1 chopped green pepper, 1 cup canned tomato, 1 cup sliced okra (opt.), 1 c. sliced celery. Cook 5 min. Add chicken, rice, 2 dashes Tabasco, ½ tsp. basil, pinch mace, ½ tsp. salt, ⅛ tsp. pepper. Turn into low buttered casserole. Top with 2 tbs. bread crumbs mixed with 1 tbs. grated cheese. Bake in moderate oven (375°) 20 min.

SPINACH SALAD: 1 pkg. "washed" spinach. Rinse. Drain. Cook uncovered 8 min. Drain, chop, drain again. Serve on lettuce with French dressing. Garnish with sliced hard-cooked egg.

FRUIT COMPOTE: Add 1 sliced banana to 1 small can chilled fruits for salad.

TIME 1 HR. SERVES 2

THURSDAY

Black Bean Soup
Rattrap Soufflé w. String Beans
Potato Salad
Cherry Plops
Coffee

BLACK BEAN SOUP: 1 can. Prepare as directed. Garnish with 2 slices crumbled crisp bacon.

RATTRAP SOUFFLÉ W. STRING BEANS: Heat 1 tbs. butter, blend in 1½ tbs. flour. Add ½ c. milk, ½ tsp. salt, ¼ tsp. pepper, ¼ tsp. basil, stirring over low heat until thickened. Stir in ¾ c. coarsely grated rattrap cheese, 1 small can tomato paste, 2 well-beaten egg yolks, ½ box French-style string beans, defrosted. Remove from heat. Fold in 2 egg whites, stiffly beaten. Pour into casserole, bake in moderate oven (350°) 45 min.

CHERRY PLOPS: 1 small can cherries. Drain juice, add 2 tbs. sugar mixed with 1 tsp. cornstarch. Heat until thickened. Fill dessert glasses with diced poundcake. Add sauce. Top with cherries.

TIME 1 HR. SERVES 2

FRIDAY

**Halibut Casserole*
Baked Oxtail Potatoes
**Green Beans & Mushrooms*
Hot Rolls
Assorted Cheese & Crackers
Coffee

HALIBUT CASSEROLE: ¾ lb. halibut steak. Rub with salt, pepper. Place in buttered baking dish. Brush with oil, cover with 1 small can tomatoes, drained, ½ onion, thinly sliced, and any leftover cooked vegetables. Dot with butter, bake 20 min. in moderate oven (425°). Add ¼ c. heavy cream. Bake 10 min.

BAKED OXTAIL POTATOES: 2 large. Rub with oil. Bake in moderate oven (425°) until done, about 50 min. Halve lengthwise. Scoop out, beat in ½ can condensed oxtail soup, salt and pepper to taste, paprika, 1 tsp. butter, 1 tbs. grated cheese. Fill shells, reheat in oven 10 min.

GREEN BEANS & MUSHROOMS: ½ box leftover beans. Prepare as directed. Mix with 1 4-oz. can sliced mushrooms, drained and sautéed in 1 tbs. butter.

SHOPPING LIST

MEAT

1½ lbs. veal cutlet
¾ lb. ground round steak
2 large cube steaks, about ½ lb., pounded thin
2 thick shoulder lamb chops
½ lb. bacon

FROZEN FOODS

2 boxes peas
1 box asparagus
1 box strawberries
1 box boiled shrimp (or 1 large can)
1 box whipped potatoes

FRESH FRUITS AND VEGETABLES

1 small head cauliflower
1 bunch watercress
3 green peppers
2 tomatoes
1 bunch chives
1 banana
2 heads lettuce
1 bunch radishes
1 cucumber
1 bunch celery
1 small pineapple
1 pear
1 apple
1 endive
1 orange
6 white onions

SUNDRIES

1 qt. cranberry juice
1 small can tomato purée
2 #1 cans tomatoes
1 small jar chopped olives
1 box Parker House rolls
1 4-oz. can sliced mushrooms
⅛ lb. bleu cheese
1 small jar deviled chicken
1 small can potatoes
2 sponge layers
1 #2 can corned beef hash
1 tube ready-to-bake biscuits
1 small can mixed vegetables
1 pkg. baking chocolate
1 can tomato soup

PICK UP ON YOUR WAY HOME

FOR SUN.—1 ice cream roll
WED.—½ pt. heavy cream

TIME 40 MIN. SERVES 4 **SUNDAY**

Chilled Cranberry Juice
Roman Madeira Veal
Risotto
Buttered Peas
Endive & Watercress Salad
Ice Cream Roll
Coffee

ROMAN MADEIRA VEAL: 1½ lbs. veal cutlet cut in 1" squares. Dust with ½ cup flour mixed with 1 tsp. salt, ½ tsp. white pepper, dash cayenne, ¼ tsp. dry mustard, ½ tsp. sugar, ⅛ tsp. nutmeg. Brown quickly in ⅓ c. oil over high heat, stirring lightly until slightly crisp on all sides. Add ½ c. Madeira wine (or strong sherry). Cook uncovered over medium heat 10 min.

RISOTTO: Melt 2 tbs. butter in saucepan. Add 1 chopped onion and 1½ c. dry rice. Stir over medium heat 5 min. Add 3 cups boiling bouillon, 3 tbs. white wine, 3 tbs. tomato purée, a good pinch saffron, ½ tsp. salt, ¼ tsp. pepper. Mix well. Cook tightly covered over very low heat 20 min.

TIME 45 MIN. SERVES 2 **MONDAY**

Tomato Bouillon
Tamale Pie
Sliced Onion, Radish & Cucumber Salad
Parker House Rolls
Pineapple Matchsticks
Coffee

TOMATO BOUILLON: Mix 1 can tomato soup with 1 c. bouillon.

TAMALE PIE: Stir ¾ c. corn meal into 2 c. boiling water, add ½ tsp. salt. Cook over low heat 12 min., stirring occasionally. Brown 1 garlic clove in 1 tbs. salad oil, add 1 chopped onion, cook until soft, about 5 min. Stir in ¾ lb. ground round steak, 1 chopped green pepper. Cook 5 min., then add 1 #1 can tomatoes, ½ c. chopped olives, ½ tsp. salt, 2 tbs. chili powder, ½ tsp. dried basil, ¼ tsp. pepper. Spread half corn meal in low casserole, add meat mixture, cover with remaining corn meal. Bake in moderate oven (375°) 25 min.

PINEAPPLE MATCHSTICKS: ½ small pineapple. Peel, cut into matchsticks. Sprinkle with 1 tbs. powdered sugar, 1 tbs. lemon juice. Top with whipped cream.

TUESDAY

TIME 45 MIN. SERVES 2

Stuffed Beef Rolls
Whipped Potatoes
Steamed Onions
**Diced Fresh Fruit w. Bleu Cheese*
Coffee

STUFFED BEEF ROLLS: 2 cube steaks, pounded thin. Rub with salt, pepper, thyme. Brown on both sides in 1 tbs. butter. Mix 1 chopped onion, 1 minced clove garlic, 1 tbs. chopped celery, 2 slices bacon, diced, 2 whole cloves. Pile on steaks. Roll up, tie. Bake with ½ chopped green pepper, 1 chopped onion, ½ c. bouillon, ½ c. red wine, covered, in moderately hot oven (425°) 35 min.

STEAMED ONIONS: Heat 3 tbs. butter, add 6 white onions sliced ¼" thick, ¼ tsp. sugar, ½ tsp. salt, ⅛ tsp. pepper, 2 tbs. boiling water. Cover. Simmer 15 min. Turn once.

DICED FRESH FRUIT W. BLEU CHEESE: Mix diced leftover pineapple, unpeeled pear, unpeeled apple, 2 tbs. crumbled bleu cheese.

WEDNESDAY

TIME 50 MIN. SERVES 2

Radishes and Butter
Poulet Lamb Chops w. New Potatoes
Mustard Cauliflower
Green Salad
Sherried Strawberries
Coffee

POULET LAMB CHOPS W. NEW POTATOES: 2 shoulder chops 1" thick. Brown quickly on all sides. Place in buttered casserole, spread with 2 tbs. deviled chicken. Add 1 4-oz. can mushrooms, drained, 1 small can potatoes, drained. Bake in moderate oven (375°), until tender, about 35 min. Add 3 tbs. chicken bouillon to juices.

MUSTARD CAULIFLOWER: Cut in pieces. Cook covered in ½ c. salted water over low heat until tender, about 15 min. For sauce, heat 1 tbs. butter, blend in 1 tbs. flour, 1 tbs. prepared mustard. Add ½ c. milk, stirring until thickened, salt and pepper to taste, 1 tsp. lemon juice.

SHERRIED STRAWBERRIES: Mix ½ box strawberries, defrosted, with 1 tbs. sherry. Top with whipped cream sprinkled with grated orange peel.

TIME 35 MIN. SERVES 2

THURSDAY

Corned Beef Hasherole
Asparagus Salad
**Berry-Banana Crush*
Coffee

CORNED BEEF HASHEROLE: 1 #2 can. Cut 3 bacon slices in squares. Sauté. Remove. Add 2 sliced onions, cook until tender, about 5 min. Add corned beef hash, 1 #1 can tomatoes, drained, ¼ tsp. salt, ⅛ tsp. pepper, 1 tsp. dried parsley, bacon. Transfer to greased casserole. Sprinkle with grated cheese. Bake in moderate oven (375°) 15 min. Make 2 depressions side by side. Drop in 2 eggs. Season with salt, few drops Tabasco. Continue baking until eggs set, about 15 min.

ASPARAGUS SALAD: ½ box. Cook, drain. Chill. Serve on lettuce with mayonnaise and chopped chives.

BERRY-BANANA CRUSH: Crush leftover strawberries. Combine with 1 sliced banana. Serve with cream.

TIME 35 MIN. SERVES 2

FRIDAY

**Shrimp Jambalaya*
Rice
**Vegetable Salad*
Hot Biscuits
Chocolate Whipped Cream Cake
Coffee

SHRIMP JAMBALAYA: 1 pkg. frozen boiled, or 1 large can, drained. Sauté lightly in 2 tbs. salad oil, add 2 chopped tomatoes, 1 diced green pepper, 1 diced onion, ¼ tsp. paprika, 1 crushed garlic clove, 1 bay leaf, ½ box leftover asparagus diced. Simmer 20 min. Stir in 1 tsp. cornstarch mixed with 1 tbs. water, salt and pepper to taste. Serve on 1½ c. prepared precooked rice.

VEGETABLE SALAD: Marinate 1 small can mixed vegetables, drained, in ¼ c. French dressing 15 min. Add dash Tabasco, sprinkling of chives. Serve on lettuce.

CHOCOLATE WHIPPED CREAM CAKE: Melt 2 squares unsweetened chocolate in top of double boiler. Remove from boiling water. Stir in ¾ c. confectioners' sugar, 2 tbs. hot water. Beat in 1 egg, then 1 tbs. butter. Put 2 sponge layers together with whipped cream. Top with chocolate frosting.

SHOPPING LIST

MEAT

2 lbs. eye round beef
½ lb. pork steak
2 frankfurters
½ lb. beef liver
1 large turkey drumstick, leg bone and tendons removed
1 turkey liver and/or heart
¼ lb. bacon

FROZEN FOODS

1 pkg. corn on the cob
1 box peas
1 box succotash
1 box fillets of flounder

FRESH FRUITS AND VEGETABLES

1½ lbs. tomatoes
1 large bunch carrots, about 9
1 bunch watercress
1 bunch chives
2 oranges
3 heads lettuce
1 green pepper
2 apples
1 small cabbage
1 endive
1 bunch Emperor grapes
4 sweet potatoes

SUNDRIES

½ lb. thin spaghetti
½ pt. sour cream
1 small can tomato paste
1 box ready-to-bake rolls
1 #1 tall can grapefruit sections
1 can tuna fish flakes
1 4-oz. can sliced mushrooms
1 tube ready-to-bake biscuits
1 pkg. prepared poultry stuffing
½ pt. light cream
1 small can oysters
1 can cranberry jelly
1 can baked beans
1 small Edam cheese
1 small can beets
1 pkg. chocolate junket
1 can cream of asparagus soup
2 cans condensed cream of mushroom soup
1 can condensed beef soup
1 can condensed oxtail soup

PICK UP ON YOUR WAY HOME

FOR SUN.—biscuit tortoni for 4
FOR THUR.—1 small mince pie

TIME 2 HRS. SERVES 4

SUNDAY

Meat Mongole Soup
Italian Beef Roast w. Carrots
Spaghetti
Lettuce w. Sour Cream
Biscuit Tortoni
Coffee

MEAT MONGOLE SOUP: Combine 1 can beef soup, 1 can oxtail, 2 cans water. Simmer.

ITALIAN BEEF ROAST W. CARROTS: 2 lbs. eye round. Brown on all sides in 3 tbs. butter. Add 6 thinly sliced onions, 1 lb. tomatoes, quartered, 1 c. red wine, 1 tsp. salt, ¼ tsp. pepper. Cover. Cook over low heat 2 hrs., adding 8 or 9 whole scraped carrots after first hour. Serve with boiled spaghetti (8 oz.), tossed lightly with 2 tbs. melted butter and ½ c. grated Parmesan cheese. (Reserve at least 1 cup meat for Tuesday.)

LETTUCE W. SOUR CREAM: Toss broken lettuce with ½ c. sour cream. Sprinkle with chopped chives, salt, pepper.

TIME 45 MIN. SERVES 2

MONDAY

Mock Cassoulet
Mixed Green Salad
Apple Slices & Edam Cheese
Coffee

MOCK CASSOULET: ½ lb. pork steak, 2 frankfurters, 3 slices bacon. Cut all into 1″ pieces. Brown in 1 tbs. butter. Remove meat. Add 2 sliced onions, 1 c. boiling bouillon. Cook until onions are tender, about 15 min. Replace meat, add 1 can baked beans, salt and pepper to taste, 1 bay leaf. If necessary, add more bouillon to moisten. Turn into shallow casserole, bake in hot oven (425°) 20 min.

MIXED GREEN SALAD: Toss broken lettuce, watercress, and sliced endive with ¼ c. French dressing. Add few thin slices onion, serve in individual bowls rubbed with garlic.

TUESDAY

TIME 30 MIN. SERVES 2

**Beef Pie à la Strogonoff*
Buttered Beets
Onion & Tomato Salad
Hot Buttered Rum Grapefruit
Coffee

BEEF PIE À LA STROGONOFF: At least 1 c. leftover beef cut in 1″ squares. Heat 1 tbs. butter, add 1 tbs. flour, stir over low heat until lightly browned. Add 1 c. bouillon, stir until smooth and thickened. Add 1 tsp. tomato paste, ¼ c. sour cream, beef, any leftover vegetables, 1 tbs. grated onion, ½ tsp. salt, ¼ tsp. pepper. Simmer 10 min. Remove to casserole. Cover with split ready-to-bake biscuits. Bake in hot oven (450°) 15 min. Bake rest of biscuits at same time for tomorrow.

ONION & TOMATO SALAD: Toss lettuce, sliced tomatoes, paper-thin onion slices with French dressing.

HOT BUTTERED RUM GRAPEFRUIT: Boil ½ c. sugar, ¼ c. grapefruit syrup 5 min. Add 2 tbs. butter, 2 tbs. rum. Stir until butter melts. Serve over drained canned grapefruit.

WEDNESDAY

TIME 25 MIN. SERVES 2

Tuna-Mushroom Casserole
Corn on the Cob
Apple Cabbage
Toasted Split Biscuits
Chocolate Junket
Cookies
Coffee

TUNA-MUSHROOM CASSEROLE: Sauté 1 4-oz. can sliced mushrooms, drained, 1 minced green pepper, 1 minced onion in 2 tbs. butter. Add 1 can condensed cream of mushroom soup, 1 tsp. Worcestershire sauce, ⅛ tsp. dried tarragon, 1 can flaked tuna fish, salt, pepper. Simmer 8 min. Coat bottom of shallow buttered casserole with ¼ c. dry bread crumbs. Pour in mixture. Top with buttered bread crumbs. Bake in hot oven (450°) 10 min.

APPLE CABBAGE: Mix 2 c. coarsely grated cabbage with 1 chopped apple (peeled and cored) in saucepan. Add ½ c. boiling water. Cook tightly covered 10 min. Drain. Add 1 tsp. butter, ¼ tsp. paprika, ¼ c. sour cream, salt and pepper to taste. Cook 5 min.

TIME 2 HRS. SERVES 2

THANKSGIVING

Oyster-Stuffed Drumstick
Giblet Sauce
Candied Sweet Potatoes
Buttered Peas
Cranberry Jelly
Tossed Green Salad
Hot Mince Pie
Coffee

OYSTER-STUFFED DRUMSTICK: 1 large drumstick, leg bone and tendons removed. Mix 1½ c. prepared stuffing with ½ c. oyster liquor and 1 small can chopped oysters, drained. Fill drumstick, fasten with toothpicks. Rub with bacon drippings, bake in moderate oven (350°) about 1½ hrs., until tender.

GIBLET SAUCE: Simmer 1 liver and/or heart 30 min. Remove. Chop fine. Combine with 1 can condensed mushroom soup, ½ c. giblet broth, 2 tbs. drippings from turkey. Heat, stir until smooth. Season to taste.

CANDIED SWEET POTATOES: 4. Boil 20 min. Drain, peel, slice. Arrange in shallow dish. Add ½ c. brown sugar, ¼ c. melted butter, salt and pepper to taste, ¼ c. water, 2 tsp. sherry, pinch mace. Bake in moderate oven (350°) 45 min.

TIME 20 MIN. SERVES 2

FRIDAY

Cream of Asparagus Soup
Flounder Meunière
**Orange & Onion Slaw*
Succotash
Chilled Emperor Grapes
Coffee

FLOUNDER MEUNIÈRE: 1 box fillets, defrosted. Spread with ¼ c. seasoned sour cream. Let stand 5 min. Dip in flour. Brown lightly on both sides in 2 tbs. butter. Remove, keep hot. Stir in 1 tbs. more butter, 1 tsp. finely chopped parsley, 1 tbs. lemon juice. Simmer 5 min. Pour over fillets. Garnish with lemon quarters, parsley.

ORANGE & ONION SLAW: Mix ½ onion sliced paper-thin, ½ c. orange segments, 1 c. finely shredded cabbage. Stir in ¼ c. mayonnaise mixed with 1 tsp. lemon juice.

SHOPPING LIST

MEAT

- 2 racks spareribs, about 4 lbs.
- ¾ lb. lean chopped beef
- 2 or 3 shoulder pork chops
- ¾ lb. lamb steak, ¼″ thick, cut in 2″ squares
- ½ lb. beef liver
- ½ lb. bacon

FROZEN FOODS

- 2 boxes string beans
- 1 box French-fried potatoes
- 1 box potato puffs
- 1 box asparagus
- 1 grapefruit juice

FRESH FRUITS AND VEGETABLES

- 4 green apples
- 4 large sweet potatoes
- 1 green pepper
- 1 carrot
- 1 bunch chives
- 2 grapefruit
- 2 heads lettuce
- 2 cucumbers
- 2 tomatoes
- 2 bananas
- 1 bunch celery

SUNDRIES

- 1 qt. apple juice
- 1 small box prunes
- ½ pt. light cream
- 1 small jar relish
- 1 small can potatoes
- 1 box muffins
- 1 small can bean sprouts
- 1 4-oz. can sliced mushrooms
- 1 6-oz. can crab meat flakes
- 1 French bread
- ¼ lb. candied ginger
- 1 #2 can crushed pineapple
- 1 pkg. Chinese almond cakes
- 1 small can pears
- 1 small box Graham crackers
- 1 pkg. instant vanilla dessert
- 1 can tomato soup
- 2 cans onion soup
- 1 can condensed chicken noodle soup

PICK UP ON YOUR WAY HOME

FRI.—½ pt. heavy cream

SUNDAY

TIME 1 HR. 10 MIN. SERVES 4

Onion Soup
Fruited Spareribs
Baked Sweet Potatoes
String Beans w. Horseradish
Tossed Green Salad
Grapefruit
Coffee

ONION SOUP: 2 cans. Add 2 tbs. sherry, 1 large sliced onion. Simmer until onion is tender, about 15 min. Toast 4 slices French bread, sprinkle with grated Parmesan cheese, brown lightly under broiler. Float in soup.

FRUITED SPARERIBS: 2 racks. Brush with lemon juice. Rub with salt, pepper. Place in buttered roasting pan with 1 c. apple juice. Cover with 8 pitted prunes, 4 green apples, sliced thick. Dot with butter, bake in hot oven (450°) 45 min. Baste, adding more apple juice if necessary.

STRING BEANS W. HORSERADISH: 2 boxes. Prepare as directed. (Reserve ½ c. for Tuesday.) Serve with ¼ c. horseradish mixed with ¼ c. cream, 1 tbs. chopped chives.

GRAPEFRUIT: 2. Boil ½ c. grapefruit juice, ¼ c. sugar 5 min. Add ¼ c. white wine. Fill each grapefruit with syrup.

MONDAY

TIME 35 MIN. SERVES 2

Norwegian Meat Balls
Baked Cucumbers
French-Fried Potatoes
Sliced Tomatoes w. Relish
Spiced Islands
Coffee

NORWEGIAN MEAT BALLS: ¾ lb. chopped lean beef. Add 1 chopped onion, ½ c. milk, ½ tsp. sage, ½ tsp. ginger, ½ tsp. salt, ⅛ tsp. pepper. Mix well, let stand 20 min. Squeeze out milk, shape into cakes, fry in 2 tbs. butter.

BAKED CUCUMBERS: Peel 2 cucumbers. Dice. Melt 2 tbs. butter in shallow casserole. Add cucumbers, salt, pepper. Cover. Bake in a hot oven (425°) 20 min.

SPICED ISLANDS: Trim 2 bread slices, sauté in 1 tbs. butter, 1 tbs. cinnamon, 1 tsp. nutmeg. Remove. Spread with orange marmalade. Broil until bubbling. Serve hot with cream.

TUESDAY

TIME 45 MIN. SERVES 2

**Apple Juice*
Nebraska Pork Pie
**String Bean Salad*
Hot Muffins
Hawaiian Baked Bananas
Coffee

NEBRASKA PORK PIE: Trim excess fat from 2 or 3 shoulder pork chops. Sauté with 1 small can potatoes, sliced, in 1 tbs. butter over high heat. Place 3 slices bacon in casserole, add sautéed potatoes, 1 thinly sliced onion, top with chops, add 1 c. bouillon. Sprinkle with 2 tbs. bread crumbs mixed with 1 tbs. grated Parmesan cheese. Dot with slivers of fat cut from pork chops. Bake in moderate oven (375°) 35 min.

STRING BEAN SALAD: Marinate leftover string beans with 1 tsp. minced onion in ¼ c. French dressing 15 min. Serve on lettuce.

HAWAIIAN BAKED BANANAS: 2 washed. Cut lengthwise slit in each. Break pulp with fork, adding 1 tsp. minced candied ginger to each one. Place in buttered baking dish. Cover with ½ can crushed pineapple. Bake in moderate oven (375°) 30 min.

WEDNESDAY

TIME 30 MIN. SERVES 2

Clear Bouillon w. Celery
**Chinese Lamb*
Rice
Almond Cakes
Tea

CLEAR BOUILLON W. CELERY: Simmer 2 c. chicken bouillon 5 min. Add ½ c. thinly sliced celery, serve immediately.

CHINESE LAMB: ¾ lb. lamb steak cut in 2″ squares. Brown quickly in 3 tbs. oil. Add 1 tsp. soy sauce. Drain 1 cup bean sprouts, 1 4-oz. can sliced mushrooms, add to meat. Mix in leftover ½ can crushed pineapple, 1 thinly sliced onion, 2 tbs. soy sauce, ⅛ tsp. powdered ginger, 1 c. bouillon, ½ tsp. salt, ¼ tsp. pepper. Cook 15 min. over medium heat. Add 2 tbs. cornstarch mixed with 2 tbs. white wine, 1 tbs. water. Stir until thickened. Serve on 1½ c. prepared precooked rice.

TIME 35 MIN. SERVES 2 **THURSDAY**

Chicken Velvet Soup
Mock Terrapin
Buttered Asparagus
Pears in Orange Sauce
Coffee

CHICKEN VELVET SOUP: Heat 1 can chicken noodle soup with 1 soup can milk. Add pinch cayenne, ¼ tsp. salt, pinch curry powder. Mix 1 well-beaten egg yolk with 1 tbs. soup. Beat into hot soup just before serving.

MOCK TERRAPIN: ½ lb. beef liver. Rub with ½ tsp. salt, dash cayenne. Sauté in 2 tbs. butter over high heat. Remove, cut in 1″ pieces, dust lightly with flour, return to pan. Add 1 tbs. dry mustard mixed with ¾ c. water, simmer 5 min. Add 1 finely chopped hard-cooked egg, 2 tbs. sherry, pinch dry basil. Simmer 5 min. Serve on buttered toast, garnish with crisp bacon.

PEARS IN ORANGE SAUCE: Drain 1 small can pears. Mix 1 tbs. orange marmalade, 2 tbs. pear syrup. Pour over pears. Chill.

TIME 30 MIN. SERVES 2 **FRIDAY**

Tomato Soup
Craburgers
Potato Puffs
Carrot & Green Pepper Salad
Graham-Cracker Pie
Coffee

CRABURGERS: Mix 1 6-oz. can crab meat flakes with 1 egg yolk, 1 tsp. Worcestershire, 3 tbs. bread crumbs, 2 tbs. cream, salt, pepper, pinch cayenne, ¼ tsp. mustard. Shape into patties. Place in greased shallow dish, sprinkle with 2 tbs. grated Parmesan cheese, dot with butter, bake in moderately hot oven (375°) 15 min.

CARROT & GREEN PEPPER SALAD: Cut 1 crisp scraped carrot into matchsticks, add ½ green pepper cut in strips. Toss lightly in 2 tbs. French dressing. Serve on lettuce.

GRAHAM-CRACKER PIE: Roll 8 Graham crackers into fine crumbs. Mix with 2 tbs. sugar, 2 tbs. soft butter. Press evenly to line 8″ pie plate. Bake 8 min. Prepare instant vanilla dessert with 1½ c. milk. Fill pie shell. Chill. Top with whipped cream, sprinkle with 1 tbs. Graham crumbs.

DECEMBER

Recheck your basic staples—and now have you

orange marmalade
lemons
cinnamon
powdered clove
brandy
nutmeg
capers
whole cloves
thyme
curry powder
almonds
mixed herbs
sage
powdered sugar
vanilla extract
cornflakes
caraway seeds
walnuts or pecans
basil
chili powder
maple syrup
horseradish
rum
instant coffee
cognac or rum

SHOPPING LIST

MEAT

5½ lbs. pork loin
¾ lb. round steak cut on bias in 1" strips
⅛ lb. bacon
5 frankfurters
1 2-oz. slice boiled ham
½ lb. beef liver sliced ¼" thick

FROZEN FOODS

1 box peas
1 box green beans
1 box French-fried potatoes
1 box whipped potatoes

FRESH FRUITS AND VEGETABLES

1 head cauliflower
4 Idaho potatoes
1 head lettuce
1 head escarole
3 green peppers
fresh fruit for Monday
1 tomato
1 bunch chives
1 banana
1 bunch parsley
1 apple
1 bunch celery
6 small new potatoes

SUNDRIES

1 small jar cherry jam
1 #2 can Bing cherries
2 4-oz. cans sliced mushrooms
1 small can tomato sauce
1 small can apple slices
1 #1 can potatoes
1 #1 can tomatoes
1 small can fruit cocktail
1 small jar dill pickles
½ pt. heavy cream
1 small pkg. raisins
1 small jar stuffed olives
2 portions Gruyère cheese
1 small can pears
1 small can chocolate syrup
2 slices plain cake
1 can green pea soup
1 can tomato soup

PICK UP ON YOUR WAY HOME

WED.—½ pt. heavy cream
FRI.—1 lb. halibut steak ½" thick
4 Parker House rolls
1 bunch watercress

SUNDAY

TIME 4¼ HRS. SERVES 4

Roast Loin of Pork w. Spiced Fruit Sauce
Baked Idaho Potatoes
Peas & Cauliflower
Tossed Green Salad
Brandied Bing Cherries
Coffee

ROAST LOIN OF PORK W. SPICED FRUIT SAUCE: 5½ lbs. Rub with salt, pepper, 1 cut garlic clove. Roast uncovered in slow oven (325°) 4 hrs. Pour off fat, leaving 3 tbs. drippings. Pour in 2 c. boiling water, 2 tbs. orange marmalade, 2 tbs. cherry jam, grated rind and juice 1 lemon, ½ tsp. cinnamon, ¼ tsp. powdered clove, ¼ c. sherry. Bring to boil, serve with pork. (Save 1½ c. meat for Tuesday.)

PEAS & CAULIFLOWER: Cut 1 head cauliflower into flowerets. Boil in salted water to cover 8 min. Drain. Cook 1 box peas as directed. Drain. Mix with cauliflower, 2 tbs. melted butter.

BRANDIED BING CHERRIES: Chill 1 can cherries. Add 1 tbs. brandy to each serving. Garnish with whipped cream.

MONDAY

TIME 40 MIN. SERVES 2

Green Pea Soup
Strasbourg Casserole
Egg Salad Vinaigrette
Fresh Fruit w. Gruyère Cheese
Coffee

STRASBOURG CASSEROLE: Rub shallow casserole with cut garlic clove, then bacon grease. Put in 5 frankfurters, halved lengthwise, cover with 1 can potatoes, sliced, 1 can sliced mushroms. Add ½ tsp. salt, ¼ tsp. pepper, ⅛ tsp. nutmeg, 1 bay leaf, 1 diced green pepper, 1 #1 can tomatoes, drained. Sprinkle with buttered bread crumbs. Bake in moderate oven (375°) 35 min.

EGG SALAD VINAIGRETTE: Add ½ tsp. chopped chives, ½ tsp. dry mustard to ¼ c. French dressing. Pour over 1 sliced hard-cooked egg arranged on lettuce. Garnish with ½ tsp. capers.

FOR TOMORROW: Beat ¼ c. chocolate syrup into 1 c. whipped cream. Spread between 2 slices plain cake. Cover top and sides. Chill overnight.

TIME 30 MIN. SERVES 2

TUESDAY

Tomato Soup w. Herbs
**Curried Pork, Almond & Raisin Rice*
Escarole Salad
Chocolate Refrigerator Cake
Coffee

TOMATO SOUP W. HERBS: 1 can. Prepare as directed. Add 1 tsp. mixed herbs.

CURRIED PORK: Cut leftover pork in small sticks. Sauté 1 chopped onion, 1 bay leaf, 1 chopped garlic clove, ⅛ tsp. thyme in 3 tbs. butter. Mix 1½ tbs. flour with 1 tbs. curry powder, stir into onion mixture. Add 1½ c. bouillon, stirring until smooth and thickened, 1 diced tomato, 1 chopped unpeeled apple, 1 chopped banana, 1 tbs. white wine. Simmer 5 min. Add pork, cook 10 min.

ALMOND & RAISIN RICE: Prepare 1½ c. precooked rice as directed, adding ¼ c. raisins and substituting bouillon for water. Stir in 1 tbs. butter, ¼ c. chopped blanched almonds.

FOR TOMORROW: Marinate ¾ lb. sliced round steak in 1 c. vinegar, 1 c. water, 1 sliced onion, 1 bay leaf, 3 cloves, 1 tsp. salt.

TIME 40 MIN. SERVES 2

WEDNESDAY

Grenada Steak
Parsley Potatoes
Green Beans
Celery Hearts
Stewed Apple Slices w. Spiced Cream
Coffee

GRENADA STEAK: Drain marinated round steak, let stand 15 min. Brown quickly in 1 tbs. oil. Add ½ c. marinade, 1 sliced onion, 1 small green pepper, diced, 1 small can tomato sauce, ¼ tsp. sage, salt, pepper to taste. Cover, simmer 20 min.

PARSLEY POTATOES: 6 new potatoes. Scrub. Boil until tender, 20 min. Peel. Roll in 2 tbs. melted butter, 1 tsp. chopped parsley.

STEWED APPLE SLICES W. SPICED WHIPPED CREAM: 1 can apple slices. Add 1½ tbs. powdered sugar, ¼ tsp. each nutmeg, cinnamon, clove, pinch salt, and ½ tsp. vanilla to 1 c. whipped cream. Beat until blended. Serve over cold apple slices.

THURSDAY

TIME 45 MIN. SERVES 2

Beef Liver w. Ham & Celery
Whipped Potatoes
Mixed Greens w. Olive Dressing
Baked Pear Halves
Coffee

BEEF LIVER W. HAM & CELERY: ½ lb. ½″ thick. Dice, roll in seasoned flour. Brown quickly in 2 tbs. bacon drippings. Remove, keep warm. Add 2 onions sliced paper-thin, 1 diced green pepper, 1 c. sliced celery, 1 can sliced mushrooms, 2 oz. sliced boiled ham, diced, 1 minced garlic clove, 1 bay leaf, pinch dried thyme, ½ tsp. salt, ¼ tsp. pepper, ¼ c. dry white wine. Cover. Cook 15 min. Add liver, 1 tbs. sherry. Heat 5 min.

OLIVE DRESSING: Add 2 tbs. chopped stuffed olives to ¼ c. French dressing.

BAKED PEAR HALVES: 1 small can pear halves. Drain syrup, mix with 1 tbs. butter, 1 tbs. lemon juice, 1 tbs. sugar. Simmer 5 min. Arrange pears in shallow casserole. Pour on syrup. Bake in moderate oven (350°) 30 min.

FRIDAY

TIME 25 MIN. SERVES 2

Fruit Cup
Halibut Steak w. Hot Tartar Sauce
French-Fried Potatoes
Parker House Rolls
Watercress Salad
Lemon Cream
Coffee

HALIBUT STEAK: 1 lb., ½″ thick. Dip in salted milk, then crushed cornflakes. Place in greased baking pan over 1 thinly sliced onion, 2 slices bacon. Dot with 1 tbs. butter, bake in hot oven (500°), about 10 min. Garnish with lemon slices.

HOT TARTAR SAUCE: Combine ½ c. mayonnaise, 1 tsp. grated onion, 1 tbs. butter. Cook over low heat 5 min. Add 1 tsp. vinegar, 1 tbs. chopped dill pickles, 1 tbs. chopped olives, 1 tsp. minced parsley.

LEMON CREAM: Mix 1 egg yolk, ⅓ c. sugar, 2 tbs. lemon juice, ½ tsp. lemon rind in top of double boiler. Stir over hot water until smooth and thick. Cool slightly. Fold in 1 stiffly beaten egg white, then ½ c. whipped cream. Chill.

SHOPPING LIST

MEAT

3 lbs. veal from leg, cut in 1″ cubes
¼ lb. boiled ham, sliced thin
4 loin or shoulder pork chops
¼ lb. bacon

FROZEN FOODS

1 box peas
1 box cut green beans
1 box corn kernels
1 pkg. boiled shrimp
1 box peaches

FRESH FRUITS AND VEGETABLES

1 pkg. washed spinach
7 firm tomatoes
1 green pepper
1 bunch celery
1 head lettuce
1 chicory
1 small eggplant
½ Santa Claus melon
1 orange
4 or 5 small new potatoes
1 small green cabbage
3 carrots
1 apple
1 pear
1 banana
1 bunch parsley
1 bunch scallions
1 small bunch grapes
1 avocado

SUNDRIES

8 oz. egg noodles
¼ lb. Swiss cheese, sliced thin
1 box ready-to-bake poppy-seed rolls
1 #1 can potatoes
2 or 3 slices plain cake
1 #2 can tomato juice
2 4-oz. cans sliced mushrooms
1 #1 can tomatoes
1 small can shredded coconut
½ pt. heavy cream
1 small jar pickle relish
1 can French-fried onions
1 can cream of asparagus soup
1 can condensed consommé
1 can condensed cream of mushroom soup

PICK UP ON YOUR WAY HOME

FOR SUN.—1 small loaf rye bread
TUES.—½ pt. vanilla ice cream
3 or 4 chocolate cupcakes
WED.—½ mince pie
¾ lb. potato salad
THUR.—1 small broiler cut in pieces
½ pt. heavy cream
FRI.—4 Parker House rolls

SUNDAY

TIME 5½ HRS. SERVES 4

Cream of Asparagus Soup
Hungarian Goulash w. Noodles
Wilted Spinach
Sliced Celery & Tomatoes
Hot Rye Bread
Santa Claus Melon w. Lemon Wedges
Black Coffee

HUNGARIAN GOULASH W. NOODLES: 3 lbs. veal from leg. Start this very early in the day. Cut veal in 1″ cubes, discard fat. Dust veal with paprika. Sauté 3 sliced onions in 3 tbs. oil 5 min. Add veal. Stir 10 min. over high heat. Add 1 can undiluted consommé. Cover. Simmer 2 hrs. Set aside until 1 hr. before serving. Then add ⅓ c. caraway seeds, 1 tsp. salt, ¼ tsp. pepper. Simmer 45 min. Reserve 1½ c. veal for Monday. Serve remainder over (8 oz.) buttered boiled noodles.

WILTED SPINACH: 1 cellophane package. Rinse. Dry thoroughly in towel. Chop coarsely, add 1 finely chopped onion. Fry 3 slices diced bacon until crisp. Add 3 tbs. vinegar, ¼ tsp. salt, ⅛ tsp. pepper, ¼ tsp. dry mustard. Heat, pour over spinach.

MONDAY

TIME 35 MIN. SERVES 2

Tomato Juice
**Scalloped Veal Casserole*
Cabbage Wedges, Parsley Butter
Peach Upside-Down Cake
Coffee

SCALLOPED VEAL CASSEROLE: Cut leftover veal in ½″ pieces. Add 1 can undiluted cream of mushroom soup, ⅛ tsp. pepper, 1 green pepper, diced. Put ¾ box defrosted peas in shallow casserole. Top with veal mixture, 1 can potatoes, sliced. Brush with butter. Bake in hot oven (425°) 30 min.

CABBAGE WEDGES, PARSLEY BUTTER: ½ small cabbage. Cut in 3 wedges. Cook in boiling salted water to cover 10 min. Drain. Add 2 tbs. melted butter mixed with 2 tsp. minced parsley.

TIME 50 MIN. SERVES 2

TUESDAY

**Consommé w. Green Peas*
Relish Pork Chops
French-Fried Onions
Corn Kernels
Garlic Salad Bowl
Ice Cream Cupcakes

CONSOMMÉ W. GREEN PEAS: Add ¼ box leftover peas, ¼ tsp. ground black pepper to 1 can condensed consommé. Dilute with ½ soup can water.

RELISH PORK CHOPS: 4 loin or shoulder chops. Rub with salt, pepper, roll in flour. Brown quickly in 1 tbs. butter. Add 2 tsp. Worcestershire sauce, 2 sliced onions, ½ c. bouillon. Cover, simmer 40 min. Drain. Spread each with 1 tbs. pickle relish, 1 tbs. "gravy." Broil 5 min.

GARLIC SALAD BOWL: Rub bowl with cut garlic clove. Toss broken lettuce and chicory with ¼ c. French dressing.

ICE CREAM CUPCAKES: Scoop out chocolate cupcakes. Fill with vanilla ice cream. Replace cake top, cover with whipped cream, sprinkle with shredded coconut.

TIME 45 MIN. SERVES 2

WEDNESDAY

Ham & Eggplant Casserole
Hot Potato Salad
Poppy-Seed Rolls
Mince Pie
Coffee

HAM & EGGPLANT CASSEROLE: Peel 1 small eggplant, cut in ¼″ slices, sprinkle with salt, let stand 10 min. Dry well. Sauté in 3 tbs. butter until soft. Place in shallow casserole alternate layers of eggplant, 3 sliced tomatoes sprinkled lightly with salt, pepper, and basil, ¼ lb. thinly sliced Swiss cheese, ¼ lb. thinly sliced boiled ham. Sprinkle with ¼ c. grated Parmesan cheese. Bake in moderate oven (375°) 20 min.

HOT POTATO SALAD: Heat 1 tbs. olive oil, 1 tbs. vinegar. Add ¾ lb. prepared potato salad. Heat thoroughly. Taste, season.

THURSDAY

TIME 45 MIN. SERVES 2

Chicken Provençal
Carrots
Jacket Potatoes
**Cole Slaw*
Fiesta Fruit Compote
Coffee

CHICKEN PROVENÇAL: 1 small broiler cut in pieces. Brown well in 2 tbs. butter. Add 2 tbs. sherry, 1 stalk diced celery, 1 4-oz. can drained, sliced mushrooms, cook 2 min. Add 1 tsp. flour, 1 c. bouillon, blend well, bring to boil. Lower heat, add 1 bay leaf, ¼ tsp. sage, 1 tsp. salt, ¼ tsp. pepper, 1 c. sliced carrot. Cover, cook 25 min.

COLE SLAW: Shred leftover ½ cabbage, about 2 c. Dress with ½ c. heavy cream sharpened with 2 tbs. vinegar, dash cayenne, salt and pepper to taste.

FIESTA FRUIT COMPOTE: Peel, halve, core 1 pear, 1 apple. Combine with ½ c. sugar, ⅓ c. water, ¼ c. orange juice, 1 tbs. lemon juice, 1 tbs. grated orange rind, 1 diced banana, ¼ c. halved seeded grapes. Cover. Simmer 25 min. Chill.

FRIDAY

TIME 30 MIN. SERVES 2

Shrimp & Rice
New Orleans Bean Salad
Parker House Rolls
Avocado w. Sherry
Coffee

SHRIMP & RICE: 1 pkg. shrimps, semi-thawed. Sauté 1 minced onion in 1 tbs. butter 5 min. Add ¼ c. chopped parsley, ¼ c. chopped scallions. Stir over medium heat, then add shrimps, 1 #1 can tomatoes, 1 4-oz. can sliced mushrooms, 2 or 3 dashes Tabasco, ½ tsp. salt, ¼ tsp. pepper, ¼ tsp. celery salt, ¾ c. raw Carolina rice, 1 c. boiling bouillon. Cover tightly. Cook over low heat 20 min.

NEW ORLEANS BEAN SALAD: 1 box defrosted green beans. Cook 1 thinly sliced onion in 1 tbs. butter 5 min. Add beans, ¼ c. highly seasoned French dressing. Cover. Cook 8 min. Pour over chunked lettuce.

AVOCADO W. SHERRY: Halve ripe avocado. Remove pit. Pour 1 tbs. sherry into each half.

SHOPPING LIST

MEAT

3 lbs. round steak ¾″ thick
1 small beef or 5 lamb kidneys
¾ lb. ham steak ½″ thick

FROZEN FOODS

2 boxes asparagus
2 boxes squash
1 box strawberries
1 box succotash
1 box peas and carrots
1 box cauliflower

FRESH FRUITS AND VEGETABLES

1 head lettuce
1 romaine
1 grapefruit
1 bunch parsley
1 small cucumber
1 bunch endive
1 small yellow squash
1 orange
1 bunch chives
2 bananas
¼ lb. grapes
2 pears

SUNDRIES

1 #2 can tomato juice
1 small can diced beets
1 small can pimiento
1 small can tomato paste
1 small jar stuffed olives
2 #1 cans new potatoes
1 tube ready-to-bake biscuits
1 4-oz. can sliced mushrooms
8-oz. pkg. spaghetti
1 12-oz. can vegetable juice
4 spongecake shells
2 portions Camembert cheese
½ pt. heavy cream
1 small jar anchovy paste
1 small bar sweet chocolate
1 can condensed cream of chicken soup
1 can cream of celery soup
1 can consommé
1 can condensed pepper pot soup

PICK UP ON YOUR WAY HOME

FOR SUN.—ice cream pie
THUR.—½ pt. vanilla ice cream
FRI.—2 salmon steaks
4 hard rolls

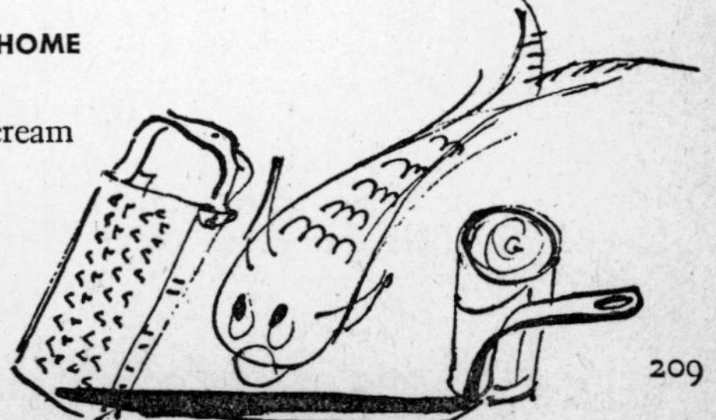

SUNDAY

TIME 2¼ HRS. SERVES 4

Pounded Round Steak
Baked Asparagus
Winter Squash
Chiffonade Salad
Ice Cream Pie w. Hot Maple Syrup
Coffee

POUNDED ROUND STEAK: 3 lbs. ¾″ thick. Mix ¼ c. flour with 2 tsp. salt, ¼ tsp. pepper, ¼ tsp. powdered thyme. Pound and work into steak. Cut in 6 portions. Brown quickly in 2 tbs. oil. Place in roasting pan with 2 c. tomato juice, 1 can sliced mushrooms, 4 sliced onions, and pan drippings. Cover, bake in moderate oven (350°) 2 hrs. (Save 2 portions for Tuesday.)

BAKED ASPARAGUS: 2 boxes, semi-thawed. Arrange in buttered shallow casserole. Cover with 1 can condensed cream of chicken soup mixed with ½ c. milk. Top with 1 tbs. bread crumbs mixed with 1 tbs. grated cheese. Bake 35 min.

CHIFFONADE SALAD: Add 1 chopped hard-cooked egg, 1 tsp. parsley, 1 tsp. minced onion, dash paprika to ¾ c. French dressing. Serve over lettuce hearts.

MONDAY

TIME 25 MIN. SERVES 2

Vegetable Juice
Kidneys w. Rice
Peas & Carrots
Grapefruit aux Fraises
Coffee

KIDNEYS W. RICE: 1 small beef or 5 lamb kidneys. Dip in boiling water. Remove. Slice thin, discarding white centers and tubes. Sauté quickly in 2 tbs. butter, stirring constantly. Add 1½ bouillon cubes dissolved in ½ c. boiling water, 2 tbs. vinegar. Cover, simmer gently 10 min. Meanwhile brown 2 thinly sliced onions in 2 tbs. salad oil. Drain, add to kidneys. Stir in 1 tsp. sugar, 1 tsp. flour mixed with 3 tbs. sherry, cook until slightly thickened. Salt, pepper to taste. Serve on 1½ c. prepared precooked rice.

GRAPEFRUIT AUX FRAISES: Cut in half. Remove fruit, dice, mix with ¼ box strawberries, defrosted, 1 tbs. sugar. Remove all membrane from grapefruit shells, fill with fruit.

TIME 40 MIN. SERVES 2

TUESDAY

Cream of Celery Soup
**Mexican Beef w. Olives*
Yellow Squash in Cream
Pears w. Camembert
Coffee

CREAM OF CELERY SOUP: 1 can. Prepare as directed. Garnish with paper-thin slivers of crisp celery.

MEXICAN BEEF W. OLIVES: Leftover round steak, about 1½ c. Cut in ½″ cubes. Sauté 3 thinly sliced onions in 2 tbs. oil 5 min. Stir in 1 tbs. chili powder, add meat, 1 small can tomato paste, 1 c. boiling bouillon, 1 small can potatoes. Season with salt, pepper, dash cayenne. Cover, simmer 25 min. Add ½ c. sliced stuffed olives. Cook 10 min.

YELLOW SQUASH IN CREAM: Scrub, dice. Cook covered in ½ c. salted water until tender, about 10 min. Drain if necessary. Add salt and pepper to taste, 1 tbs. butter, then 2 tbs. cream.

PEARS W. CAMEMBERT: Scrub pears. Chill. Serve Camembert at room temperature.

TIME 25 MIN. SERVES 2

WEDNESDAY

Consommé w. Minced Parsley
Barbecued Ham Steak
Succotash
Mixed Greens
**Strawberry Shortcake*
Coffee

BARBECUED HAM STEAK: ¾ lb. ½″ thick. Prepare barbecue sauce of 2 tbs. butter, ¼ c. ketchup, 2 tbs. oil, 1 tbs. vinegar, 1 tsp. chili powder, juice 1 lemon, 1 tsp. Worcestershire sauce, 1 tsp. drained horseradish, 1 tsp. prepared mustard, salt and pepper to taste. Boil 2 min. Brush one side of steak with sauce. Broil under high heat 5 min. Reduce heat to moderate. Turn, brush other side, broil until deep brown.

STRAWBERRY SHORTCAKE: Pile ¾ box defrosted strawberries in sponge dessert shells. Top with whipped cream.

THURSDAY

TIME 35 MIN. SERVES 2

Pepper-Pot Spaghetti
Beet & Cauliflower Salad w. Anchovy Dressing
Hot Biscuits
Rum Cream Cakes
Coffee

PEPPER-POT SPAGHETTI: Heat 1 can condensed pepper pot soup, add ¼ c. grated cheese, 1 tbs. minced onion, 2 dashes Tabasco, salt, pepper. Simmer 10 min. Add 3 tbs. sherry. Serve over (6 oz.) boiled, drained spaghetti.

BEET & CAULIFLOWER SALAD W. ANCHOVY DRESSING: Cook 1 box cauliflower. Chill. Arrange on lettuce with ½ can drained diced beets, ¾ small cucumber, peeled and diced. Dress with ¼ c. French dressing mixed with 1 tsp. anchovy paste.

RUM CREAM CAKES: Pour 2 tbs. rum into 2 sponge dessert shells. Fill with ½ pt. vanilla ice cream mixed quickly with ¼ c. sliced seeded grapes.

FRIDAY

TIME 25 MIN. SERVES 2

**Piquant Beet Cocktail*
**Salmon Steaks w. Cucumber Sauce*
Paprika Potatoes
Endive Salad
Hard Rolls
Sliced Bananas w. Grated Chocolate
Coffee

PIQUANT BEET COCKTAIL: Combine 2 tsp. sugar, 1 tsp. cornstarch, ¼ tsp. salt, 1 tsp. grated lemon rind, 1 tsp. orange rind, 1 tbs. orange juice, 1 tbs. butter, liquid from beets. Stir, bring to boil. Add ½ can beets. Simmer 5 min. Serve on lettuce leaves.

SALMON STEAKS W. CUCUMBER SAUCE: 2 steaks. Rub with salt, pepper, brush with oil. Broil 6 min. on each side. Sauce: Mix 1 tbs. vinegar, 1 tsp. lemon juice, ½ tsp. grated onion, salt and pepper to taste, 2 dashes Tabasco, 2 tbs. melted butter, 2 tbs. grated peeled cucumber, 1 tbs. chopped chives.

PAPRIKA POTATOES: 1 can. Heat. Drain. Roll in melted butter. Dust with paprika.

SLICED BANANAS W. GRATED CHOCOLATE: Pour cream over sliced bananas. Cover thickly with coarsely grated sweet chocolate.

SHOPPING LIST

MEAT

½ lb. chopped beef
¾ lb. veal cutlet sliced very thin
3 pork sausages
half turkey, about 4½ lbs.

FROZEN FOODS

1 box Brussels sprouts
2 boxes broccoli
1 pkg. corn on the cob
1 box asparagus tips
1 box chopped spinach

FRESH FRUITS AND VEGETABLES

2 tomatoes
1 bunch celery
2 seedless oranges
1 small chicory
1 Bermuda onion
1 bunch parsley
1 bunch watercress
2 heads iceberg lettuce
5 or 6 sweet potatoes

SUNDRIES

1 pkg. poultry stuffing
1 pt. sour cream
1 8-oz. can grapefruit
⅛ lb. Cheddar cheese
1 #1 can potatoes
1 small pkg. green noodles
1 can cranberry sauce
1 4-oz. can chopped mushrooms
1 4-oz. can sliced mushrooms
1 tube ready-to-bake biscuits
1 small pkg. pitted dates
1 small can wax beans
½ pt. heavy cream
1 jar prepared chocolate frosting
1 #2 can crushed pineapple
3 slices poundcake
1 1-lb. can plum pudding
½ pt. light cream
1 pkg. piecrust mix
1 small can pimiento
1 #2 can sliced apples
2 cans consommé madrilene
1 can vegetable soup

PICK UP ON YOUR WAY HOME

FOR SUN. OR XMAS—8 crescent rolls
WED.—1 small can boned turkey if needed
1 small can cranberry sauce, if none left over
FRI.—½ pt. oysters

SUNDAY or CHRISTMAS DAY TIME 2 HRS. SERVES 4

Spiced Madrilene
Roast Half Turkey
Mushroom Stuffing
Cranberry Sauce
Baked Sweet Potatoes
Buttered Broccoli
Crescent Rolls
Green Salad
Plum Pudding w. Egg Nog Sauce
Coffee

SPICED MADRILENE: 2 cans. Add 5 cloves. Simmer 5 min. Add thin lemon slices.

ROAST HALF TURKEY: 4½–5 lbs. Place skin side up on rack in open roasting pan, rub with 2 tbs. flour creamed with 2 tbs. butter. Roast in moderate oven (350°), 25 min. per pound. After 1 hr. remove, stuff with 3 c. packaged stuffing prepared as directed, adding 1 can chopped mushrooms, extra tbs. melted butter. Replace skin side down. Finish roasting in cheesecloth dipped in bacon drippings.

EGG NOG SAUCE: Beat 2 egg yolks until frothy, stir in 1 c. sifted powdered sugar. Beat in ¼ c. brandy or sherry, then fold in 2 c. whipped cream.

MONDAY TIME 45 MIN. SERVES 2

Sausage-Potato Bake
Crushed Pineapple
Asparagus Tips
Celery & Tomatoes
Mocha Cake
Coffee

SAUSAGE-POTATO BAKE: Simmer 5 pork sausages in bouillon 10 min. Slice in ¼″-thick rounds. Arrange layer of sliced potatoes (1 can) in greased baking dish. Sprinkle with ½ tsp. flour, ¼ tsp. salt, ⅛ tsp. pepper. Add half the sausage, cover with remaining sliced potatoes, ½ tsp. flour, salt, pepper, sausage. Add ¾ c. milk, sprinkle with 2 tbs. grated cheese. Dot with butter, bake in moderate oven (375°) 30 min. Serve with ½ can cold crushed pineapple.

CELERY & TOMATOES: Mix 1 c. sliced celery, 2 tomatoes, diced. Sprinkle ¼ tsp. basil, 1 tbs. oil, 1 tbs. vinegar, salt, pepper.

MOCHA CAKE: Stir 1 tsp. instant coffee, ½ tsp. water. Mix with ¼ c. prepared chocolate frosting. Spread on 2 poundcake slices.

TIME 40 MIN. SERVES 2 **TUESDAY**

Kummel Casserole
Brussels Sprouts
Watercress w. Mustard Mayonnaise
Caramel Grapefruit
Coffee

KUMMEL CASSEROLE: Sauté 2 large sliced onions with ½ lb. chopped beef in 2 tbs. butter. Beat 2 eggs with 1 c. sour cream, ½ tsp. salt, ¼ tsp. pepper, ½ tsp. caraway seeds. Place 3 or 4 slices white bread in bottom of shallow casserole. Cover with meat and onions, pour on sauce. Bake in moderate oven (375°) 20 min.

MUSTARD MAYONNAISE: Mix 1 tbs. prepared mustard with ¼ c. mayonnaise.

CARAMEL GRAPEFRUIT: Pour 1 small can grapefruit into small shallow baking dish. Sprinkle with ¼ c. brown sugar mixed with 2 tbs. flour. Dot with 1 tbs. butter, bake in moderate oven (350°) 10 min. Top with 1 slice poundcake cut in two. Bake another 10 min. Serve upside down with whipped cream.

TIME 20 MIN. SERVES 2 **WEDNESDAY**

**Turkey Newburg on Toast*
Corn on the Cob
Lettuce & Onion Salad
**Crushed Pineapple w. Cranberry Cubes*
Coffee

TURKEY NEWBURG ON TOAST: Leftover turkey, at least 1 c. (or 1 small can boned turkey), cut into slivers. Melt 2 tbs. butter in top of double boiler over hot water. Stir in ½ c. milk, ¼ c. heavy cream. Heat. Stir in 2 beaten egg yolks, ¼ tsp. salt, ¼ tsp. paprika. When smooth and thickened, stir in turkey. Heat. Just before serving stir in ¼ c. sherry.

LETTUCE & ONION SALAD: Cut 1 Bermuda onion into thin shavings. Alternate in bowl with layers shredded lettuce. Sprinkle French dressing on each layer.

CRUSHED PINEAPPLE W. CRANBERRY CUBES: Cut leftover cranberry sauce into small cubes, mix with ½ can crushed pineapple. Serve in sherbet glasses.

THURSDAY

TIME 40 MIN. SERVES 2

Veal w. Green Noodles
Wax Bean & Pimiento Salad
Deep-Dish Apple Pie w. Cheese
Coffee

VEAL W. GREEN NOODLES: ¾ lb. cutlet, sliced very thin. Dust with flour, brown in 1 tbs. butter over high heat. Remove to shallow casserole. Add 1 4-oz. can sliced mushrooms, with liquid, to pan, simmer 5 min. Add ½ tsp. salt, ¼ tsp. pepper, pour over veal. Cover with ½ c. sour cream, bake in hot oven (450°) 15 min. Just before serving add 2 tbs. cognac or rum. Serve with (4 oz.) boiled, buttered green noodles.

WAX BEAN & PIMIENTO SALAD: 1 can wax beans. Drain, chill. Toss with shredded lettuce, strips of pimiento, ¼ c. French dressing.

DEEP-DISH APPLE PIE W. CHEESE: Pour 1 can sliced apples into small deep baking dish. Add 1 tbs. butter, ¼ tsp. cinnamon. Cover with prepared piecrust. Bake in hot oven (450°), 25 min. Serve warm with slices of Cheddar cheese.

FRIDAY

TIME 35 MIN. SERVES 2

Vegetable Soup
Oyster Pot Pie
Buttered Spinach
Tossed Green Salad
Orange Arabian
Coffee

OYSTER POT PIE: Sauté 1 c. sliced onions in 3 tbs. butter 5 min. Stir in 2 tbs. flour, blend well. Gradually add oyster liquid, ½ c. milk, stir until smooth. Add 1 tsp. chopped parsley, ½ pt. oysters, salt and pepper to taste. Simmer 3 min. Pour into buttered baking dish, cover with split ready-to-bake biscuits, sprinkle with paprika. Bake in hot oven (450°) 15 min.

ORANGE ARABIAN: Peel, dice 2 seedless oranges. Mix with 2 tbs. slivered blanched almonds, ½ c. sliced dates. Sprinkle with 2 tbs. powdered sugar.

PARTY MENUS

THANKSGIVING

CHRISTMAS

GOURMET

GANGFEST

These Gangfest Menus are planned with the accent on lighthearted gaiety for the hostess as well as her guests. At least one famous regional dish is featured in each menu, so the scene may be set accordingly. All are easy to prepare; all are fun to eat.

You'll find two quick and delectable versions of Pizza pie, one Neapolitan and one Provençal; a famous Italian dunking sauce called Bagna Cauda that gets hotter and hotter as it bubbles in the chafing dish; a traditional Irish Colcannon of cabbage, mashed potatoes, and bacon to be served on one huge platter in the middle of the table and eaten therefrom by each guest with his own spoon, to the tune of considerable merriment.

Then there's a "surprise" fry called Fritto Misto, melting Cheese Blintzes that can be prepared ahead of time, and a superb Alsatian Cheese Dunk just made for beer and the "Schnitzlebank" song.

Gourmet, Christmas, and Thanksgiving Menus strike a more decorous note, delectable fare combining the traditional with the different. You'll find Lobster Thermidor, Beef Bourguignonne, Oysters Rockefeller, Crêpes Suzette, Profiterolles Chantilly, and many other celebrated dishes. Don't be afraid to try them; you've already prepared several for weekday meals and they're very much easier than you'd think!

SERVES AT LEAST 8

THANKSGIVING

Shrimp & Avocado Cocktail
Chutney Sauce
Pilgrim Turkey
Oyster Dressing
Cranberry Sauce
Buttered Corn on the Cob
Asparagus & Watercress Salad
Toasted Almonds
Pumpkin Pie
Coffee

SHRIMP & AVOCADO COCKTAIL: Arrange 2 c. cold boiled shrimps and 2 peeled sliced avocados in 8 cocktail glasses. Cover with 1 c. mayonnaise mixed with 4 tbs. chopped drained chutney, 1 tbs. lemon juice, 1 tsp. curry powder, 3 tbs. chili sauce, 1 tsp. grated lemon rind.

PILGRIM TURKEY: 10 lbs. Sauté 1 lb. ground pork 10 min. in 2 tbs. bacon drippings. Add 1 large minced onion and 2 large grated raw sweet potatoes. Cook slowly another 10 min. Stir in 2 doz. quartered oysters, ¼ tsp. sage, ¼ tsp. marjoram, 2 tsp. salt, ½ tsp. black pepper, 1 tbs. chopped parsley, 4 c. soft bread crumbs. Remove from heat. Moisten with ⅔ c. sherry. Rub turkey inside and out with salt and pepper. Stuff lightly. Truss. Place breast side up on rack in open shallow roasting pan. Rub with 3 tbs. flour creamed with 4 tbs. butter, 1 tsp. paprika. Roast in moderately slow oven (325°) 25 min. per pound. Baste with bacon drippings.

ASPARAGUS & WATERCRESS SALAD: See January, Week 3, Monday. Increase amounts accordingly.

PUMPKIN PIE: Line 2 8″ pie pans with pastry, using mix as directed. To 2 c. cooked, strained (or canned) pumpkin add 1 c. brown sugar, 1 tbs. molasses, ½ tsp. salt, ¼ tsp. cloves, 1 tsp. cinnamon, ½ tsp. ginger, 2 slightly beaten eggs, 2 c. milk, and ¼ c. cream. Mix well. Pour into unbaked shells. Bake in moderately hot oven (425°) about 35 min., until knife inserted in center comes out clean.

CHRISTMAS

SERVES AT LEAST 4

Roast Goose
Prune Stuffing
Apple Sauce
Hot Biscuits
Guatemalan Sweet Potatoes
Buttered Broccoli
Romaine & Watercress Salad
Strawberry Cheesecake
Coffee

ROAST GOOSE: 10 lbs. Start day before Christmas. Wash bird inside and out. Rub with lemon, then with salt and pepper. Chill overnight. Prepare stuffing.

PRUNE STUFFING: Soak 1 lb. prunes 4 hrs. Add 1 thinly sliced lemon and equal parts water and red wine to cover. Simmer until tender. Heat ¼ c. butter in skillet, add ½ lb. chopped pork, ¼ c. grated onion, 12 finely chopped green olives. Stir over medium heat until pork is cooked but not browned, about 10 min. Add 1 tsp. salt, ¼ tsp. pepper, dash nutmeg, ⅛ tsp. thyme, ⅛ tsp. mace. Cool slightly. Add 2 beaten eggs. Drain cooked prunes, saving liquid, chop coarsely, add to mixture. Chill overnight. 2 hours before roasting stuff bird with prune mixture, sew up opening. Prick deeply into fat around legs and wings. Truss. Roast in moderately slow oven (325°) 25 min. to pound. Pour off fat. Make gravy with remaining drippings mixed with saved prune liquid. Salt and pepper to taste.

GUATEMALAN SWEET POTATOES: See March, Week 2, Sunday. Increase amounts accordingly.

ROMAINE & WATERCRESS SALAD: See June, Week 2, Thursday. Increase amounts accordingly.

STRAWBERRY CHEESECAKE: Mix 1½ c. fine Graham-cracker crumbs with 3 tbs. confectioners' sugar, 6 tbs. melted butter. Press firmly on bottom and sides of buttered 9″ spring-form pan. Chill thoroughly. Mix 1 lb. cream cheese with grated rind and juice 1 lemon, ½ tsp. salt, ½ c. sugar. Add 4 egg yolks, 1 at a time, beating vigorously after each. Stir in ½ c. cream. Fold in 4 stiffly beaten egg whites. Pour into lined pan. Bake in moderate oven (350°) until just firm, about 1 hr. Turn off heat, cool in oven if possible. Chill several hours. Before serving spread with 1 box drained, defrosted strawberries.

TIME 3 HRS. SERVES 4

GOURMET MENU I

Clam Bisque
Roast Pheasant
Mushrooms
White Onions
Wild Rice Stuffing
Buttered Asparagus
Brandied Cherry Bavaroise
Coffee

ROAST PHEASANT: 1 large. Singe, clean with damp cloth. Dry. Fill with wild rice stuffing. Truss. Bake uncovered in buttered casserole in hot oven (425°) 15 min. to brown. Cover breast with 3 strips fat bacon. Add 16 small white onions, 16 whole peeled mushrooms, ½ c. Madeira wine. Cover. Bake in slow oven (325°) 1½ hrs.

WILD RICE STUFFING: Wash ¾ c. wild rice thoroughly. Add to 1½ qts. boiling salted water. Boil rapidly, uncovered, until rice is tender, about 25–35 min. Heat 1 tbs. butter, add 1 large onion, chopped, ¼ lb. sausage meat. Sauté 10 min., stirring constantly. Add drained boiled rice, ½ tsp. salt, ¼ tsp. sage. Mix well.

BRANDIED CHERRY BAVAROISE: Soak 1 tbs. gelatin in ¼ c. water 5 min. Beat 2 egg yolks with ¼ c. sugar, pinch salt in top of double boiler. Stir in gradually 1 c. scalded milk. Place over boiling water. Stir constantly until thickened, about 5 min. Remove from heat. Stir in gelatin, 1 tbs. kirsch. Cool. When just beginning to set, whip until fluffy, then fold in 1 c. pitted brandied cherries, drained, and 1 c. heavy cream, whipped. Pour into 1-qt. mold that has been rinsed with cold water. Chill until set, at least 2 hrs. Unmold and garnish with sweetened whipped cream.

GOURMET MENU II

TIME 2 HRS. SERVES 4

Cream of Watercress Soup
Lobster Thermidor
Orange Buttered Biscuits
Matchstick Potatoes
Spring Salad Bowls
Mousse au Chocolat
Coffee

CREAM OF WATERCRESS SOUP: Soften 3 tbs. minced onion in 2 tbs. butter. Blend in 1 tbs. flour. Add 3 c. milk, 1 c. canned consommé, stirring until thickened. Add ½ tsp. salt, ⅛ tsp. pepper, 1½ c. finely chopped watercress, 2 chopped, peeled tomatoes. Whip in 1 beaten egg yolk. Remove from heat. Serve with dots of butter, dash nutmeg.

LOBSTER THERMIDOR: 2 2-lb. lobsters split, vein removed. Season with salt and pepper. Place in shallow pan. Broil slowly, basting often with melted butter. Remove meat from shells, dice. Place in top of double boiler with 4 tbs. melted butter. Add 2 tbs. sherry, dash nutmeg, paprika, then 3 egg yolks blended with 1½ c. cream. Stir over hot water until thick and smooth. Return to shells. Sprinkle with buttered bread crumbs. Brown under broiler. Serve with lemon wedges.

ORANGE BUTTERED BISCUITS: See February, Week 3, Friday. Increase amounts accordingly.

SPRING SALAD BOWLS: See May, Week 3, Monday. Increase amounts accordingly.

MOUSSE AU CHOCOLAT: Melt ¼ lb. semi-sweet chocolate in 2 tbs. milk over hot water. Remove from heat. Stir in 2 egg yolks, 1 at a time, and 1 tsp. rum. Fold in 3 stiffly beaten egg whites. Pour into dessert glasses. Chill. Serve with whipped cream.

TIME 2 HRS. SERVES 4

GOURMET MENU III

Crab Meat Chips
Roast Guinea Hen
Château Potatoes
Buttered Broccoli
Romaine Salad
Zabaglione
Coffee

CRAB MEAT CHIPS: 1 small can crab meat flakes. Mash well. Mix with 1 tbs. mayonnaise blended with 1 tbs. chili sauce, dash Tabasco. Spread on large crisp potato chips. Serve on chicory lettuce.

ROAST GUINEA HEN: 2, 2 lbs. each.
Clean, wipe with damp cloth. Fill each with 1 peeled, quartered apple, 1 small onion, a bit of parsley, 1 bay leaf. Sew up opening. Rub with butter. Roast uncovered, breast side down, in moderate oven (350°), basting frequently. When brown, about 30 min., turn and bake 45 min. longer. Serve with pan drippings mixed with 2 tbs. currant jelly, 1 tbs. applesauce, 1 tbs. sherry.

CHÂTEAU POTATOES: 1 lb. tiny new. Scrape. Bring to boil. Drain, dry. Heat 3 tbs. oil in shallow baking pan. Add potatoes, stirring to coat with oil. Bake, shaking occasionally, until brown and crusty, about 1 hr. at 350°. Salt. Serve with chopped parsley.

ZABAGLIONE: See September, Week 1, Tuesday. Increase amounts accordingly.

GOURMET MENU IV

TIME 1¼ HRS. SERVES 4

Piperade
Broiled Soft-Shell Crabs Maître d'Hôtel
Chicken Salad
Black Pumpernickel
White Bordeaux
Fresh Figs
Coffee

PIPERADE: Sauté 1 lb. sliced yellow onions in 2 tbs. bacon fat 5 min. Add 1 small can pimiento cut in strips, 1 lb. tomatoes, chopped, ½ tsp. salt, ¼ tsp. pepper, ¼ tsp. marjoram. Cook covered until of purée consistency, about 1 hr. Stir in 6 beaten eggs and cook, stirring until eggs "scramble." Serve with 8 strips crisp bacon.

BROILED SOFT-SHELL CRABS: 8. Clean, discarding spongy substance, wash, wipe. Dip in flour, then in oil. Preheat broiler. Broil under high heat 10 min., turning once. Serve on toast with Maître d'Hôtel Butter and lemon wedges.

MAÎTRE D'HÔTEL BUTTER: Blend together ¼ c. butter, 2 tbs. lemon juice, ¼ tsp. salt, dash cayenne, 1 tbs. minced parsley.

CHICKEN SALAD: Mix 1 c. diced chicken (canned or fresh) with 3 tbs. French dressing and 1 small chopped onion. Chill 30 min. Mix in ¼ c. diced celery, 3 strips bacon, crumbled, and 1 small head shredded lettuce. Serve garnished with 1 peeled, thinly sliced avocado.

TIME 1 HR. SERVES 4

GOURMENT MENU V

Quiche Lorraine
Veal en Papillote
Jacket Potatoes
Avocado & Lettuce Salad
Peaches in Hot Buttered Rum
Coffee

QUICHE LORRAINE: Prepare ½ pkg. pastry mix as directed. Line buttered 8″ pie plate. Cook 4 slices bacon until crisp. Beat 2 whole eggs and 2 egg yolks with ½ c. cream, 2 tbs. grated cheese, ½ tsp. salt, speck cayenne. Add crumbled bacon, ¼ lb. diced, lean boiled ham. Pour into pie plate. Bake in moderate oven (375°) 45 min.

VEAL EN PAPILLOTE: Sauté 4 veal chops in 2 tbs. butter. Season with salt and paprika. Keep warm. Cook 1 finely chopped onion in 1 tbs. butter until soft. Stir in ¼ lb. finely chopped, peeled mushrooms, ½ tsp. finely chopped parsley, ¼ tsp. powdered thyme, salt and pepper. Cook 5 min. Add 2 tbs. tomato purée, 2 tbs. bread crumbs. Cook over low heat until mixture is almost dry. Then cut 4 heart-shaped pieces of well-oiled wax paper which, when folded over each chop, will leave a 2″ margin all around. On one side of each paper place 1 tbs. mushroom sauce, then a small slice of ham, then 1 chop, another slice of ham, another tbs. sauce. Fold and roll edges of paper to close tightly. Twist and fold under ends. Keep warm. 10 min. before serving, place in hot oven (450°) to brown and swell up paper.

AVOCADO & LETTUCE SALAD: Toss 2 peeled, thinly sliced avocados with 1 small shredded lettuce. Sprinkle with ½ tsp. dried basil, 1½ tbs. chopped chives. Serve with French dressing.

PEACHES IN HOT BUTTERED RUM: Heat 2 c. hard cider with 2 tbs. brown sugar, dash salt, and 2 tbs. butter. Remove from heat. Stir in 1 #2 can sliced peaches, drained, 4 oz. rum. Serve piping hot sprinkled with cinnamon.

GOURMET MENU VI

TIME 3½ HRS. SERVES 4

Asparagus Consommé
Aioli
Watercress Salad
Thick Slices Poppy-Seed Bread
Dry Sauterne
Riz aux Fraises Kirsch
Coffee

ASPARAGUS CONSOMMÉ: See February, Week 1, Friday. Increase amounts accordingly.

AIOLI: 4½ lbs. of any or all of the following: mackerel, haddock, whiting, perch, cut in 2″ pieces. Tie in cheesecloth. Immerse in boiling water. Add 1 tbs. tarragon vinegar, 1 clove, 6 sprigs fresh parsley, 1 sliced onion, 1 tsp. salt. Simmer gently 15 min. Boil 1 lb. scraped new potatoes, 12 whole scraped carrots until tender. Drain. Chill. For sauce, mash 3 garlic cloves with 2 egg yolks, add 1 c. olive oil, 1 tbs. at a time, beating constantly (or all together in electric blender) as for mayonnaise, until thick. Season with salt, pepper, 1 tsp. lemon juice. Arrange cold fish and vegetables on platter. Garnish with 4 quartered lemons. Serve with sauce.

RIZ AUX FRAISES KIRSCH: Slice 3 c. strawberries, add ½ c. sugar, ½ c. kirsch. Chill. Wash ½ c. rice. Scald 1½ c. milk in top of double boiler. Add rice, ¼ tsp. salt. Cook until tender, about 45 min. Remove from heat. Stir in 1 tbs. gelatin dissolved in ¼ c. water, then 1 tsp. lemon juice and 2 beaten eggs. Place pan in bowl of crushed ice to cool, stirring occasionally. Stir in half the strawberries and 1 c. whipped cream. Then fold in 1 stiffly beaten egg white. Turn into 1-qt. mold rinsed with cold water. Chill until firm, at least 2½ hrs. Unmold. Serve remaining strawberries as sauce.

TIME 1 HR. SERVES 4

GOURMET MENU VII

Cheese Omelet
Brains au Beurre Noir
French-Fried Potatoes
Sautéed Mushrooms
Green Salad
Hot Fruit Compote
Coffee

CHEESE OMELET: To 5 eggs add 1 tbs. cream, ½ tsp. salt, speck pepper. Beat just enough to blend yolks. Drop into hot skillet 1½ tbs. butter, tipping pan to make sure sides and bottom are greased. Pour in eggs. Stir quickly with fork until eggs begin to set. Lift sides and allow eggs to run under. Shake pan occasionally to loosen omelet. When bottom is nicely browned and top is consistency of thick cream, sprinkle with ⅓ c. Parmesan cheese. Fold over. Serve on warm platter. Sprinkle lightly with additional grated cheese. Garnish with watercress.

BRAINS AU BEURRE NOIR: 2 pairs calf brains. Wash thoroughly, remove membrane. Soak 30 min. in cold salted water. Drain. Cover with boiling water, add 1 tbs. vinegar, 1 tsp. salt. Simmer 20 min. Drain. Plunge into cold water to harden. Dry. Dip in seasoned flour. Sauté in 2 tbs. butter until brown. Remove and keep warm. Brown ½ c. butter in frying pan. Stir in juice 1 lemon. Sprinkle 2 tbs. capers over brains. Pour the browned butter over all.

HOT FRUIT COMPOTE: 1½ c. mixed dried fruits. Cook as directed on package. Add 1 tbs. rum. Serve hot with whipped cream.

GOURMET MENU VIII

TIME 2½ HRS. SERVES 4

Moules Marinière
Beef Bourguignonne
Noodles Gratinée
Chicory & Cucumber Salad
Hot Rolls
Crème Caramel
Coffee

MOULES MARINIÈRE: See February, Week 2, Sunday.

BEEF BOURGUIGNONNE: 2 lbs. top round cut in small pieces. Brown ¼ lb. diced salt pork in 1 tsp. lard. Remove. Sprinkle beef with 1 tsp. salt, ¼ tsp. pepper. Brown in remaining fat. Add 24 tiny white onions and 6 small carrots cut in 1″ pieces. Brown quickly. Pour off fat. Add 1 chopped shallot (or leek), 1 crushed garlic clove. Blend in 1½ tbs. flour. Stir in 1 c. red wine, 1 c. bouillon. Bring to boil. Add 1 bay leaf, 2 or 3 sprigs parsley, ¼ tsp. thyme. Cover. Simmer gently 2 hrs. Sauté ¼ lb. sliced fresh mushrooms in 2 tbs. butter, add the browned salt pork. Serve as garnish on beef.

NOODLES GRATINÉE: ½ lb. Boil, drain, stir in 2 tbs. butter. Turn into casserole. Sprinkle with ¼ c. Parmesan cheese, dot with butter, brown under broiler.

CHICORY & CUCUMBER SALAD: Pulled chicory, thinly sliced cucumber, sliced radishes with French dressing.

CRÈME CARAMEL: Beat 2 whole eggs with 3 egg yolks, 4 tbs. sugar, ⅛ tsp. salt, 1 tsp. vanilla extract. Stir in slowly 2 c. scalded milk. Line 4 custard cups with caramel (½ c. sugar stirred over low heat until brown and syrupy), pour in the egg mixture. Set in pan of hot water and bake in a moderate oven (375°) 20–25 min., until set. Chill. Serve turned out on individual plates.

TIME 1 HR. SERVES 4

GOURMET MENU IX

Frogs' Legs Provençale
Carolina Rice
Garlic Bread
Grilled Tomatoes
Orange & Endive Salad
Profiterolles Chantilly
Coffee

FROGS' LEGS PROVENÇALE: 2 lbs. Wash in cold water. Dry. Soak in 1 c. seasoned milk 15 min. Drain. Dredge with flour. Sauté in 2 tbs. butter and 1 tbs. oil until well browned. Season with salt and pepper. Add 2 finely chopped garlic cloves, 1 tbs. chopped parsley, 1 tsp. chopped chives, 1 tbs. butter. Cook another min. Serve garnished with lemon quarters.

CAROLINA RICE: See February, Week 2, Tuesday. Increase amounts accordingly.

GARLIC BREAD: See February, Week 2, Thursday.

ORANGE & ENDIVE SALAD: See March, Week 2, Tuesday. Increase amounts accordingly.

PROFITEROLLES CHANTILLY: Melt ⅓ c. butter in ½ c. milk over low heat. Add dash each salt and sugar, then ½ c. sifted flour, all at once, stirring constantly until mixture is smooth and will not cling to pan. Remove from heat and beat in 2 whole eggs, 1 at a time, beating completely smooth between each addition. Drop by teaspoonfuls on greased baking sheet, shaping like walnut. Bake in hot oven (425°) 10 min., reduce heat to moderate (350°) and bake 10 min. longer. Cool. Cut open and fill with sweetened whipped cream. For sauce, stir 2 squares baking chocolate in 6 tbs. water over low heat. Add ½ c. sugar, dash salt, stirring constantly until smooth and slightly thickened. Remove from heat, beat in 2 tbs. butter, ½ tsp. vanilla. Cool. Serve over profiterolles.

GOURMET MENU X

TIME 1 HR. SERVES 4

Tournedos Béarnaise
Matchstick Potatoes
Peas w. Crumbled Bacon
Avocado & Lettuce Salad
French Dressing
Crêpes Suzette
Coffee

TOURNEDOS BÉARNAISE: 4 3½" round fillets of beef, 2" thick. Sprinkle with salt and pepper. Sauté in 2 tbs. butter, 2 tbs. oil over high heat, 5 min. on each side. Place on toast rounds trimmed to size. Cover with Béarnaise Sauce.

BÉARNAISE SAUCE: Boil 1 c. dry white wine with 1 tbs. tarragon vinegar, 1 finely chopped shallot (or leek), ¼ tsp. powdered tarragon, 4 peppercorns until reduced to 1 tbs. Strain into bowl. Place bowl over hot, not boiling, water. Gradually add 2 beaten egg yolks, alternating with ⅓ c. softened butter, 1 tbs. at a time. Beat with rotary beater until consistency of mayonnaise, adding more butter if necessary.

CRÊPES SUZETTE: Beat 6 tbs. flour with 2 whole eggs, 2 egg yolks, 1 tbs. oil, 1½ c. milk until the consistency of light cream, adding more milk if necessary. Rub a hot small frying pan lightly with buttered paper. Cover bottom of pan with thin layer of batter. Cook about 1 min. on each side. Keep warm until ready to serve. For sauce, rub 4 lumps sugar on rind of 1 orange. Add to ½ c. orange juice and crush. Heat 3 tbs. butter in chafing dish, add juice and 2 tbs. curaçao or brandy. Add crêpes one at a time, folding in half, then in half again. Sprinkle with 4 tbs. curaçao and 4 tbs. brandy, or ½ c. any other good liqueur. Ignite at table, basting with the flaming sauce.

TIME 2 HRS. SERVES 4

GOURMET MENU XI

Hot Beef Soup
Oysters Rockefeller
Roast Chicken
Baked Potatoes
Purée of Watercress
String Bean Salad
Soufflé au Chocolat
Coffee

OYSTERS ROCKEFELLER: 12 on half shell. Mix 1 chopped green onion, 1 tbs. chopped celery, 2 minced garlic cloves, ½ c. finely chopped cooked spinach, 2 chopped tarragon leaves. Put through meat chopper, then mix in 1 tsp. bread crumbs, dash of Tabasco, ¼ tsp. salt, 1 tsp. melted butter. Remove oysters from shells, reserving liquor. Cook in ½ c. dry white wine for 2 min. Put 1 tsp. oyster liquor in bottom of each oyster shell. Add oyster. Cover with spinach mixture, sprinkle with bread crumbs. Dot with butter. Place under broiler until brown.

PURÉE OF WATERCRESS: 2 bunches. Wash, chop finely, cook covered 10 min. in ½ c. boiling water. Heat 1½ tbs. butter, blend in 1½ tbs. flour, add ½ c. cream, ½ tsp. salt, ⅛ tsp. pepper, stirring until smooth and thick. Add drained watercress. Serve garnished with 1 sieved hard-cooked egg.

SOUFFLÉ AU CHOCOLAT: Heat 2 tbs. butter, blend in 2 tbs. flour, add ¾ c. milk, stirring until thickened. Beat in 3 egg yolks, 1 at a time. Remove from heat. Melt 2 squares chocolate with ¼ c. sugar and 2 tbs. water in top of double boiler. Beat into egg mixture, then fold in 4 egg whites stiffly beaten with ¼ c. sugar, ¼ tsp. salt. Turn into thickly buttered, then sugared 1½-qt. casserole. Bake in moderately hot oven (400°) 25 min. Sprinkle lightly with powdered sugar. Serve immediately.

GOURMET MENU XII

TIME 1½ HRS. SERVES 4

Mock Turtle Soup
Paella
Hearts of Lettuce w. Cucumber & Pimiento
French Bread
Poires Flambées
Coffee

MOCK TURTLE SOUP: See October, Week 4, Wednesday. Increase amounts accordingly.

PAELLA: 1 frying chicken, cut up. Make broth with giblets, neck, back. Brown chicken pieces in 3 tbs. butter with 1 chopped onion, 1 minced garlic clove, add 1 #2 can tomatoes with juice, 1 bay leaf, ¼ tsp. thyme, 2 tsp. salt, ¼ tsp. pepper, 2 medium diced unpeeled zucchini. Add 1 c. white wine, 1 c. chicken broth. Simmer 30 min. Add 1 c. rice and 1 c. chicken broth. Simmer until rice is tender, about 30 min., then add 1 tsp. saffron dissolved in ½ c. broth. Pour evenly over rice. Cook 5 min. more. Cook 1 box peas as directed. Mix with 12 boiled, shelled shrimps. Arrange chicken and rice on large platter, stirring peas and shrimps lightly into rice mixture.

HEARTS OF LETTUCE W. CUCUMBER & PIMIENTO: Combine chunked lettuce heart with 1 peeled sliced cucumber and 2 canned pimientos cut in strips. French dressing with pimiento juice to taste.

POIRES FLAMBÉES: Peel 4 pears, leaving stems on. Place in casserole, add ½ c. sugar and 1½ c. water. Cover. Bake in moderate oven (375°) until tender (test with toothpick), about 30–45 min. Arrange hot pears on hot serving dish, pour a little syrup around them. Sprinkle each with 1 tbs. sugar, 2 tbs. brandy. Ignite at table.

SERVES 8

GANGFEST AMERICAN

Angels on Horseback
Barbecued Spareribs
Baked Yams
Sweet Pickle Relish
Chilled Hard Cider
Orange Grape Bowls
Coffee

ANGELS ON HORSEBACK: 2 doz. oysters, fresh or frozen. Season each with paprika, minced shallot, few drops lemon juice. Wrap in ½ slice bacon. Fasten with toothpick. Broil until bacon is crisp, turning once. Remove toothpicks. Serve hot on fried rounds of bread.

BARBECUED SPARERIBS: 4 lbs. Cut into individual ribs. Marinate a few hours in 2 c. soy sauce, 1 c. brown sugar, 1 tsp. lemon juice, ½ tsp. salt, ¼ tsp. ground black pepper. Bake in hot oven (425°) 1½ hrs., basting with marinade. Place under broiler to darken glaze 5 min. before serving. Serve dressed with paper "panties."

ORANGE GRAPE BOWLS: Segment 6 seedless oranges, removing all membrane. Cut 1 large ripe pineapple into fingers. Line individual bowls (or dessert glasses) with alternating orange and pineapple pieces. Fill the center with 1 lb. washed seeded white grapes. Pour on ½ c. grenadine. Chill at least 1 hr.

GANGFEST BOSTON

SERVES AT LEAST 8

Real Boston Baked Beans
Mustard Relish
French Salad
Brown Bread
Green Apples
Cheddar Cheese
Cold Beer and/or Coffee

BOSTON BAKED BEANS: Wash and pick over 4 c. pea beans. Soak overnight in 2 qts. cold water. In morning, drain, cover with fresh water, simmer over low heat until tender. (To test, place a few beans in spoon and blow on them; if done, the skins will break.) Drain. Place 1 quartered onion in bottom of bean pot or deep casserole. Cut ¾ lb. salt pork in thick slices, place 2 or 3 slices on top of onion. Pour half the drained beans on top. Place another 2 or 3 pork slices over them. Cover with rest of beans, then the salt pork. Mix together 1 tbs. salt, 4 tbs. brown sugar, 1 tsp. dry mustard, ½ c. molasses, 1 c. boiling water. Pour over beans. Add enough additional water to cover entirely. Cover and bake 6 to 8 hrs. in very slow (250°) oven. If beans seem dry during cooking, add a little more boiling water. Uncover during last hour of baking to brown top. *Quicker Method:* Good, too. To 2 16-oz. cans pork and beans add 4 tbs. brown sugar, ½ tsp. dry mustard. Cover completely with 8 bacon strips and 4 tbs. ketchup. Bake in moderate oven (375°) 30 min.

FRENCH SALAD: See January, Week 4, Tuesday. Increase amounts accordingly.

SERVES 8

GANGFEST DEEP SEA

Martinique Logs
Shrimp Dunk
Horns of Plenty
Fruit Wine Cooler
Chocolate Baked Alaska
Black Coffee

MARTINIQUE LOGS: Pick over and mash 1 6-oz. can crab meat flakes. Mix with 4 c. ground left-over cooked meat, or 1 lb. cooked chopped beef. Add juice 1 lime, 1 tsp. salt, ½ tsp. dry mustard, 2 dashes Angostura, pinch nutmeg, 3 or more dashes Tabasco sauce, 1 c. soft bread crumbs fried crisp in 3 tbs. olive oil. Cut thin slices off top of 16 frankfurter buns. Hollow out center. Brush with olive oil. Brown in hot oven (450°). Fill with mixture, sprinkle with ½ c. buttered bread crumbs mixed with ⅛ tsp. curry powder. Return to oven to heat and brown, about 10 min.

SHRIMP DUNK: Mix together 1 qt. sour cream, 1 pt. creamed cottage cheese, 1 tsp. salt, 1 tbs. lime juice, ½ c. finely chopped chives, dash cayenne. Chill well. Serve in bowl sprinkled with paprika. Surround with boiled shrimp, fresh celery, thinly sliced fresh brown bread.

HORNS OF PLENTY: Spread 24 thin slices cooked smoked tongue lightly with tarragon mustard. Roll into cornucopias. Secure with toothpick. Tuck in sprays of watercress.

FRUIT WINE COOLER: See July, Week 4, Thursday. Increase amounts accordingly.

CHOCOLATE BAKED ALASKA: See June, Week 4, Sunday. Increase amounts accordingly.

GANGFEST DIXIE

SERVES 8

Black-Eyed Peas
Corn Pones
Hercules Salad
Peçan Pie
Coffee

BLACK-EYED PEAS: Wash and pick over 4 c. black-eyed peas. Soak overnight in cold water. Cook in same water with 1½-lb. piece pork shoulder or bacon. Add 1 bay leaf, ¼ tsp. thyme, 1 tbs. chopped parsley, 4 whole cloves, 1 garlic clove, 1 doz. peppercorns, ¾ tsp. salt, 1 large quartered onion. Cover. Simmer until tender, about 2½ hrs. These peas should never be dry—add boiling water when needed.

CORN PONES: Mix 2 c. white corn meal with 1 tsp. salt, add 1½ c. boiling water, 1 tbs. melted shortening, ¼ c. milk. Shape into small cakes ¾″ thick. Bake on greased baking sheet in hot oven (450°) 15 min. Serve wrapped in napkin to keep hot. Eat with lots of butter.

HERCULES SALAD: See August, Week 1, Tuesday. Increase amounts accordingly.

PECAN PIE: Line 2 8″ pie shells with pastry, using mix as directed. Heat to boiling point 1½ c. brown sugar, ½ c. butter, 1 c. light corn syrup, ¼ tsp. salt. Stir gradually into 5 well-beaten eggs. Add 2 c. pecans, 1 tsp. vanilla. Pour hot mixture into unbaked shells. Bake in a moderate oven (375°) 35 min.

SERVES AT LEAST 8

GANGFEST UNITED NATIONS

Spread-Your-Owns and Finger Foods
Mixed Drinks
Marshmallow Prunes
Coffee

SPREAD-YOUR-OWNS:
Serve these flanked with thinly sliced, buttered pumpernickel and rye, crackers, celery, radishes, crisp lettuce leaves sprinkled with celery salt, potato chips:

BELGIAN MIX: Mix 1 c. cottage cheese, ½ c. deviled ham, 1 tbs. horseradish, ¼ c. sour cream, ½ tsp. salt, ¼ tsp. pepper, few grains cayenne, ¼ c. chopped watercress, 3 tbs. chopped chives, 1 tsp. grated onion, ½ tsp. anchovy paste. Chill.

ENGLISH OYSTERS: Add 1 tsp. butter to 1 pt. oysters and liquor. Heat over hot water 5 min. Drain. Chop fine with 1 tsp. grated onion, 1 tsp. minced parsley, 1 tsp. sherry, salt, pepper, dash cayenne, dash mace. Cream with 2 tbs. butter. Chill.

DUTCH DUNK: Mash 6 oz. bleu cheese, 6 oz. cream cheese, 4 strips crisp bacon, 2 tsp. minced onion, ½ c. cream.

PAIN DAUSÉE: Mix 3 grated large sweet onions, 2 tbs. chopped parsley, ¼ c. sour cream, 1 tbs. tarragon vinegar, coarsely ground black pepper and salt to taste. Serve with French bread.

FINGER FOODS:

BACON BLANKETS: Mix together ¼ c. tomato juice, 1 beaten egg, ¾ c. bread crumbs, ¼ tsp. salt, 1 tsp. lemon juice, dash pepper, 1 tsp. chopped parsley, 1 6½-oz. can crab meat flakes. Roll into finger-size 3″ lengths. Wrap each in ½ slice bacon. Secure with toothpick. Broil until crisp, turning frequently.

CUCUMBERS: Peel 3 cucumbers. Halve crosswise. Scoop out pulp. Fill with "Dutch-Dunk" (omitting cream). Chill several hours. Serve sliced thin on crackers with anchovy paste.

CHICKEN CANAPÉS: Spread 24 small triangles thinly sliced brown bread with butter, then chutney. Place on each a piece canned chicken. Top with buttered white bread. Serve cold, or dip in beaten egg and fry in butter until brown and serve hot.

PRUNES: Cover 18 large prunes with equal parts dry white wine and water. Add 3 tbs. sugar. Simmer until tender. Cool. Drain. Pit. Stuff with marshmallow halves. Heat to serve.

GANGFEST ALSATIAN

SERVES 8

Alsatian Cheesepot w. Raw Cauliflower
Carrot Sticks, Celery
Black Bread
Chicken & Ham Canapés
Black Beer
Taffy Apples
Coffee

ALSATIAN CHEESEPOT: Remove rind from 3 Camembert and 1 Liederkranz cheese. Heat ½ lb. butter, blend in 2 tbs. flour, add 1 c. milk, stirring until smooth and thick. Add ½ lb. cottage cheese, ¼ lb. Roquefort, 2 c. cream, the Camembert and Liederkranz. Heat, stirring constantly until smooth. Remove from heat. Add ½ c. chopped green olives, 1 tbs. chopped pimiento, ½ c. chopped chives, ½ tsp. salt, dash cayenne. Serve cold in large colorful bowl surrounded by raw cauliflower buds, raw carrot, celery, and cucumber sticks, black bread and crackers—all for dunking.

CHICKEN & HAM CANAPÉS: 1 12-oz. can boned chicken, 1 lb. thinly sliced ham. Chop chicken, mix with ½ c. chopped blanched almonds, moisten with mayonnaise, add salt and pepper to taste. Cut ham slices in half. Put spoonful of chicken mixture on each half. Roll. Secure with toothpicks. Chill.

TAFFY APPLES: 8 small sweet apples. Wash. Dry thoroughly. Remove stems. Stick each with a lollipop stick. Heat 2 c. sugar, 1 c. water, ⅔ c. light corn syrup, stirring until sugar is dissolved. Boil over high heat until a few drops of syrup will instantly become brittle when dropped in cup of cold water. Remove pan from heat and set in pan of cold water for a moment, stir in a few drops of red coloring, then place over hot water and dip apples. Place on buttered tin to harden.

SERVES 8

GANGFEST CENTRAL EUROPEAN

Beet Borsch
Cheese Blintzes
Sour Cream
Tart Orange Preserves
Canadian Bacon
Mixed Green Salad
Peach Crumb
Coffee

BEET BORSCH: 2 jars beet borsch or enough for 8. Serve hot or cold with sour cream at side. Try serving 1 hot boiled potato in each portion.

CHEESE BLINTZES: Mix 1 tsp. salt, ½ tsp. sugar with 2 c. sifted flour. Beat 2 egg yolks, add 3 c. milk. Stir into flour mixture. Add 1½ tbs. melted butter. Fold in 2 stiffly beaten egg whites. Butter small frying pan lightly. Pour in about 2 tbs. batter, just enough to cover bottom of pan. Cook on one side only until light brown. Remove. Repeat until batter is used up, about 32 blintzes. Mix 1 qt. cottage cheese with 2 egg yolks, 2 tbs. sugar, 2 tbs. soft butter. Place 2 level tbs. on browned side of each blintz. Fold 2 sides into cheese, flap over ends. Store in refrigerator. (All this can be done the morning of the Gangfest or even the day before.) When ready to serve, fry in lots of butter. Surround with crisp Canadian bacon, about 1½ lbs. Serve wtih bowls of sour cream and orange preserves.

MIXED GREEN SALAD: See November, Week 3, Monday. Increase amounts accordingly.

PEACH CRUMB: 2 #2 cans sliced peaches. Arrange drained fruit in large shallow baking dish. Slowly add ½ c. sugar to 4 well-beaten eggs. Beat well. Stir in 3 c. Graham-cracker crumbs, 4 tbs. melted butter, 1 tsp. cinnamon, pinch salt. Mix well. Pour over peaches. Bake in moderate oven (350°) 30 min. Serve warm with peach syrup heated with 1 tsp. grated lemon rind.

GANGFEST CHINESE

SERVES 8

Egg Drop Soup
Beef Chop Suey
Sweet & Sour Pork
Chinese Fried Meatballs
Rice
Oriental Melon
Jasmine Tea

EGG DROP SOUP: See January, Week 2, Friday. Increase amounts accordingly.

BEEF CHOP SUEY: Cut 1¾ lbs. round steak in ¼″ strips. Brown in 4 tbs. salad oil. Stir in ¾ c. minced onions, 2 c. diced celery, ¾ c. bouillon. Cover. Simmer 10 min. Thicken with 1 tbs. cornstarch blended with ⅓ c. water, add 1½ tbs. soy sauce, ⅛ tsp. pepper, ½ tsp. brown sugar, 1 c. Chinese bean sprouts. Stir until thoroughly heated.

SWEET & SOUR PORK: See September, Week 1, Monday. Increase amounts accordingly.

CHINESE FRIED MEATBALLS: See September, Week 2, Tuesday. Increase amounts accordingly.

ORIENTAL MELON: 2 cantaloupes. Cut off tops for covers. Stand upright, taking thin slice off bottom to level. Remove seeds, carefully scoop out meat. Dice. Add 1 c. sliced fresh pineapple, 6 diced bananas. Sprinkle with ½ c. powdered rock candy, 2 tbs. sugar, 6 tbs. kirsch. Fill melons, replace tops. Seal with strips of cloth spread with butter. Place on ice or in coldest part of refrigerator for 6 hrs. Serve with tops removed.

JASMINE TEA: A fancy orange pekoe tea delicately scented with petals of jasmine. Make in a warmed china teapot, using 6 tsp. tea to 6 c. freshly boiling water. Let stand in a warm place 3 min. Serve throughout the meal, preferably in small Chinese tea bowls and without cream or lemon. The measured tea leaves may be tied loosely in a cheesecloth bag—have two or three ready to speed the replenishing of the pot.

SERVES 8

GANGFEST IRISH

Irish Colcannon
Radish Bowl w. Cucumber Sticks
Celery Cuts & Carrot Shavings
Mixed Cheese Board
Gaelic Cherries
Pot of Tea

IRISH COLCANNON: Shred 1 large head cabbage. Cook tightly covered in ½ c. water until tender, about 20 min. Mash together with 12 large boiled, peeled potatoes. Beat in ½ c. butter, 3 tbs. grated onion, salt and pepper to taste. Add ¼ c. cream, more if needed, mashing and whipping until light. Serve very hot, piled high on heated platter. Make well in center for large lump of butter. Surround with about 30 half slices crisp bacon. Traditionally, everyone eats from the same platter, each person using his own spoon and helping himself. The table is "set" afterward for later courses.

GAELIC CHERRIES: Put 2 #2 cans black cherries in saucepan with 1 c. claret, 1 3″ stick cinnamon, 3 whole cloves, 1 tbs. sugar. Bring to simmer over low heat. Remove cherries. Simmer syrup until reduced to 1½ c. Stir in 3 tbs. red currant jelly. Strain. Chill cherries and sauce separately. Pour 3 tbs. syrup over each serving. Top with slightly sweetened whipped cream flavored with 1 tbs. brandy.

TEA: Make strong, full-flavored tea and serve the Old World way. Allow 2 tsp. tea or 2 tea bags to each measuring cup freshly boiling water. Let stand 5 min. Remove bags or strain tea into warmed serving pot. Keep warm. To serve, place cups, lump sugar, milk or cream, a jug or bottle of boiling hot water beside the teapot. The hostess then pours each cup to individual taste, sugar first, then milk, then double-strength tea, diluting with hot water according to the strength desired.

GANGFEST NEAPOLITAN

SERVES 8

Vegetable Hors d'Oeuvres
Neapolitan Pizza
Chianti
Mixed Green Salad
Italian Bread
Coffee Parfait
Petit Fours

VEGETABLE HORS D'OEUVRES: Heat ¼ c. butter, blend in ¼ c. flour, add 3 c. vegetable juice, stirring until thickened. Boil 5 min., stir in ¼ c. butter, 2 tbs. prepared mustard, ¼ c. lemon juice. Serve hot, surrounded by flowerets of raw cauliflower, carrot sticks, cucumber sticks, scallions, sliced dill pickles.

NEAPOLITAN PIZZA: Prepare piecrust (4 pkgs.) for 8 8″ pie plates. Prick all over, dot with butter. Bake in hot oven (425°) 2 min. Set aside. Chop together 1 2-oz. can anchovy fillets, ⅓ lb. Italian salami or boiled ham, ¼ c. pitted olives, 1 large onion, 5 peeled tomatoes. Mix with 1 mashed garlic clove, ½ lb. finely diced mozzarella or Münster cheese. Spread on 8 shells, dot each with 1 tbs. butter. Bake in moderate oven (375°) until crust is browned, about 20 min.

COFFEE PARFAIT: Boil 1½ c. sugar, ½ c. water, 1 tbs. instant coffee until syrup will spin thread from tip of spoon. Pour very slowly, whipping constantly, over 8 beaten egg yolks. Whip until cold. Fold in 2½ c. whipped cream. Freeze in mold packed in ice and salt, or in freezer trays, for at least 4 hrs.

SERVES 8

GANGFEST PROVENÇAL

Hot Pissaladière
Cocktail Frankfurters
Dry Red Wine
Dandelion Salad
Mixed Nut Meats
Fruit Bowl
Coffee

HOT PISSALADIÈRE: Cook 3½ lbs. sliced onion in ¼ c. olive oil over low heat, covered, until puréed, about 40 min. Cut 2 loaves of bread lengthwise into 8 1″-thick slices. Remove crusts. Brush one side lightly with olive oil. Brown lightly under broiler. Cover browned side with onion purée, dot with pitted black olives, and crisscross generously with anchovy fillets. Bake on well-oiled baking sheet in hot oven (425°) 10 min.

COCKTAIL FRANKFURTERS: 3 doz. tiny cocktail frankfurters. Broil. Pierce with gaily colored toothpicks and serve.

DANDELION SALAD: Dice ¼ lb. fat salt pork, fry until crisp, remove, drain on soft paper. Add 2 #2 cans tiny new potatoes, drained, cook 5 min. Parboil 2½ lbs. dandelion greens 3 min., drain and dry thoroughly over low heat. Mix with potatoes in wooden salad bowl, garnish with fried salt pork, serve with French dressing.

GANGFEST ITALIAN

SERVES 8

La Bagna Cauda
Lots of Italian Bread
Gamay Rosé Wine
Ice Cream Pie
Coffee

LA BAGNA CAUDA: This is the great regional sauce of Piemonte. Raw vegetables are dipped into the simmering sauce and eaten with the fingers.

SAUCE: Combine 1½ c. olive oil with 1½ c. melted butter. Add 16 well-pounded anchovy fillets and 10 crushed garlic cloves. Mix well. Add 5 diced hot red peppers or more if your palate can take it. Bring very, very slowly to a boil. Simmer 10 min. Then set chafing dish in the middle of the table, keep simmering. On each individual plate place any or all of the following washed and well-dried vegetables: 1 small, very tender artichoke, 2 or 3 crisp celery stalks, ½ split endive, 2 tomato quarters, ¼ head lettuce, 10 radishes, ¼ raw cauliflower, ¼ raw fennel, 2 spring onions. Serve about 3 long loaves of Italian bread and a good Gamay Rosé wine to cool off the palate between dips.

INDEX

m	≈ *Mann*	**man** [mæn]
n	≈ *Nase*	**nose** [noʊz]
ŋ	≈ *Ding*	**thing** [θɪŋ]
p	≈ *Park*	**happy** ['hæpɪ]
r	nicht gerollt, Zunge am Gaumen	**room** [ru:m]
s	≈ *lassen*	**see** [si:]
t	≈ *Tisch*	**tall** [tɔ:l]
z	≈ *Hase*	**is** [ɪz]
ʃ	≈ *Schuh*	**shop** [ʃɑ:p]
tʃ	≈ *tschüs(s)*	**cheap** [tʃi:p]
ʒ	≈ *Garage*	**vision** ['vɪʒn]
dʒ	≈ *Dschungel*	**just** [dʒʌst]
θ	≈ *Fluss*, aber mit der Zungenspitze hinten an den Schneidezähnen	**thanks** [θæŋks]
ð	≈ *Sonne*, aber mit der Zungenspitze hinten an den Schneidezähnen	**that** [ðæt]
v	≈ *wer*	**very** ['verɪ]
w	≈ [u:], Lippen gerundet	**water** ['wɔ:tər]

: bedeutet Längung des voranstehenden Vokals
' bedeutet Betonung der folgenden Silbe

Das *t* in der Mitte eines Wortes wird meist deutlich weicher gesprochen, mehr wie ein *d*: **tomato** [tə'meɪdoʊ].

Langenscheidt
Universal-Wörterbuch Amerikanisches Englisch

Englisch – Deutsch
Deutsch – Englisch

Völlige Neubearbeitung

Herausgegeben von der
Langenscheidt-Redaktion

Langenscheidt

Berlin · München · Wien · Zürich · New York

Bearbeiter: Benjamin R. Dorvel, Dr. Helen Galloway, Gudrun Pradier
Projektleitung: Heike Pleisteiner
Neue deutsche Rechtschreibung nach den gültigen amtlichen Regeln und DUDEN-Empfehlungen

Ergänzende Hinweise, für die wir jederzeit dankbar sind, bitten wir zu richten an:
Langenscheidt Verlag, Postfach 40 11 20, 80711 München
redaktion.wb@langenscheidt.de

Typografisches Konzept nach: KOCHAN & PARTNER GmbH, München
Satz: Claudia Wild, Stuttgart
Druck: Mercedes-Druck, Berlin
Bindung: Stein + Lehmann GmbH, Berlin
Printed in Germany
ISBN 978-3-468-18042-2

10012

Inhalt

Hinweise für die Benutzer

Alphabetische Reihenfolge

Die Stichwörter sind streng alphabetisch geordnet. Ausgenommen davon sind die englischen phrasal verbs, die ihrem jeweiligen Grundverb zugeordnet sind. So stehen beispielsweise *do away with, do up, do with* und *do without* direkt im Anschluss an das Verb *do*, jedoch vor dem nächsten Hauptstichwort *dock*, das ja alphabetisch korrekt zwischen *do away with* und *do up* eingeordnet werden müsste. Die Umlaute *ä, ö, ü* werden wie *a, o, u*, das *ß* wie *ss* behandelt. Dementsprechend steht z. B. *träumen* hinter *Traum* und vor *traumhaft*. Redensarten und feste Wendungen sind in der Regel unter dem ersten bedeutungstragenden Element der Wendung zu finden, *alles Gute!* und *schon gut!* findet man also unter *gut*.

Rechtschreibung

Die Schreibung der deutschen Wörter richtet sich nach den gültigen amtlichen Regeln und DUDEN-Empfehlungen der neuen deutschen Rechtschreibung, gültig seit dem 1.8.2006.

In diesem Wörterbuch wird der Bindestrich am Zeilenanfang wiederholt, wenn mit Bindestrich geschriebene Wörter getrennt werden.

Grammatische Hinweise

Angaben zu den Stammformen der unregelmäßigen englischen Verben, zu unregelmäßigen Pluralformen bei den Substantiven sowie zu den unregelmäßigen Steigerungen bei den Adjektiven stehen nach dem jeweiligen Stichwort in Spitzklammern:

swim ⟨swam, swum⟩ [swɪm, swæm, swʌm] **1** V/I schwimmen

child ⟨children⟩ [tʃaɪld, ˈtʃɪldrən] S Kind *n*

good [gʊd] **2** ADJ ⟨better, best⟩ gut; (*geeignet*) passend; (*ausgiebig*) gründlich; (*artig*) brav; (*höflich*) nett, lieb

Eine Liste der im Wörterbuch enthaltenen englischen unregelmäßigen Verben befindet sich außerdem im Anhang des Wörterbuchs auf den Seiten 542–544.

Nach Stichwörtern ist immer deren Wortart (z. B. ADJ, ADV, PRON) bzw. Genus (F, M, N) angegeben. Das Genus der Substantive steht auch nach den Übersetzungen (*m, f, n*):

candy bar S Schokoriegel *m*

awesome [ˈɒːsəm] ADJ *umg* super, geil

Handy N cell, cellphone

Bei Verben wird zwischen dem transitiven (mit direktem Objekt), intransitiven (ohne direktes Objekt), reflexiven (rückbezüglichen) Gebrauch

(V/T, V/I, V/R) sowie Hilfsverben (V/AUX) unterschieden. Diese Hinweise stehen jeweils nach dem Stichwort:

pitch [pɪtʃ] (...) **2** V/T (*Zelt*) aufschlagen; (*Ball*) werfen; (*neues Produkt*) anpreisen

vacation [veɪˈkeɪʃən] (...) **2** V/I Urlaub machen

must ⟨had to, had to⟩ [mʌst, hæd tə] **1** V/AUX müssen

Erläuternde Hinweise und Sachgebiete

Erläuternde Hinweise in kursiver Schrift und Sachgebiete erleichtern die Wahl der richtigen Übersetzung.

Bezeichnungen der sprachlichen oder stilistischen Ebene stehen bei Ausdrücken, die von der Standardsprache abweichen:

fig steht für figurativen Gebrauch,
pej für abwertenden Sprachgebrauch,
umg für umgangssprachlichen Gebrauch und
vulg für vulgär.

Zur Bedeutungsdifferenzierung dienen zugehörige Objekte oder Subjekte oder auch Angaben, die einen Bezug zum allgemeinen Verwendungskontext herstellen:

break up **1** V/I aufbrechen; (*Versammlung*) sich auflösen; (*Ehe*) in die Brüche gehen; (*Paar*) sich trennen

breakdown S Panne *f*; (*Maschine*) Störung *f*; (*Person, System etc*) Zusammenbruch *m*

Fachsprachliche Sachgebiete werden meist abgekürzt in verkleinerten Großbuchstaben angegeben:

dressing S GASTR Dressing *n*, Soße *f*; MED Verband *m*

Grammatikangaben in kursiver Schrift zeigen, wie ein Wort oder Ausdruck gebraucht wird:

inform [ɪnˈfɔːrm] V/T informieren (*of, about* über *+akk*)

Ebenfalls kursiv erscheinen umschreibende Entsprechungen für ein Stichwort oder eine Wendung, für die es keine direkte Übersetzung gibt:

BLT *abk* = bacon, lettuce and tomato sandwich; *mit Frühstücksspeck, Kopfsalat und Tomaten belegtes Sandwich*

Lexikografische Zeichen

~ Die Tilde (das Wiederholungszeichen) vertritt das Stichwort innerhalb des Artikels:

rush [rʌʃ] **1** S Eile *f*; (*auf Karten etc*) Ansturm *m* (*for* auf *+akk*); **be in a ~** es eilig haben; **there's no ~** es eilt nicht

; Der Strichpunkt trennt Übersetzungen, die sich in der Bedeutung unterscheiden:

Druck **1** M PHYS pressure; *fig* (*Belastung*) stress; **j-n unter ~ setzen** put sb under pressure **2** M TYPO (*Vorgang*) printing; (*Produkt, Schriftart*) print

, Das Komma verbindet ähnliche Übersetzungen:

clunker ['klʌŋkər] S *umg* (*Auto*) Klapperkiste *f*, Schrottkiste *f*

/ Der Schrägstrich zeigt alternative Bedeutungen in einer Struktur:

Ferien PL vacation *sg*; **~ haben/machen** be/go on vacation

cool [ku:l] **1** ADJ kühl, gelassen; *umg* (*toll*) cool, stark **2** V/T & V/I (ab)kühlen; **~ it** reg dich ab! **3** S **keep/lose one's ~** *umg* ruhig bleiben/durchdrehen

≈ Die Wellenlinie steht vor einer Synonymangabe in Schrägschrift bzw. gibt an, dass die Übersetzung nur eine ungefähre Entsprechung des Stichworts ist:

interstate ['ɪntərsteɪt] ADJ zwischenstaatlich; **~ (highway)** ≈ Bundesautobahn *f*

AAA [trɪpəl'eɪ] *abk* = American Automobile Association *amerikanischer Automobilklub;* ≈ ADAC *m*

→ Der Pfeil bedeutet *siehe* und verweist auf einen anderen Worteintrag.

1 **2** Arabische Zahlen in hellgrauen Kästchen gliedern Übersetzungen mit stark unterschiedlicher Bedeutung sowie Wortarten innerhalb eines Eintrags:

Steuer **1** N AUTO steering wheel **2** F tax

honor ['ɑːnər] **1** VT ehren; (*von Bank: Scheck*) einlösen; (*Vertrag*) einhalten **2** S Ehre *f*

Die Aussprache des Englischen

Die Aussprache der Stichwörter steht mit Betonungsangaben in eckigen Klammern meist direkt hinter dem blau gedruckten Stichwort. Wenn unterschiedliche Wortarten eines Stichworts unterschiedlich ausgesprochen werden, erscheint die Lautschrift an entsprechend anderer Stelle. Die Umschrift wird mit den Zeichen der *International Phonetic Association* wiedergegeben, vgl. die Erklärung der phonetischen Zeichen vorne im Buch.

record **1** ['rekɔːrd] S MUS (Schall)platte *f*; (*Bestleistung*) Rekord *m* (...) **2** ['rekɔːrd] ADJ Rekord- **3** [rɪ'kɔːrd] V/T aufzeichnen; (*auf CD, DVD etc*) aufnehmen (...)

Für Wortzusammensetzungen, wie z. B. *turn signal* (Beispiel unten), bei denen die Lautschrift von *turn* und *signal* im Wörterbuch enthalten ist, wird auf eine erneute Ausspracheangabe verzichtet:

turn signal S AUTO Blinker *m*

turn [tɜːrn] **1** S Drehung *f*; **make a left ~** nach links abbiegen (...) **3** V/I (...) (*Fahrer, Auto etc*) abbiegen (...); **~ left/right** links/rechts abbiegen

signal ['sɪgnl] **1** S Signal *n* **2** V/I (*in Auto*) blinken

Englisch – Deutsch

A

a, an [eɪ, ə, æn, ən] ART ein/eine/ein; **~ man** ein Mann; **~n apple** ein Apfel; **three times ~ week** dreimal pro Woche/in der Woche

AAA [trɪpəl'eɪ] *abk* = American Automobile Association *amerikanischer Automobilklub*; ≈ ADAC *m*

aback ADV **taken ~** erstaunt

abandon [ə'bændən] V/T (*Person*) verlassen; (*Hoffnung, Projekt*) aufgeben

abbey ['æbɪ] S Abtei *f*

abbreviation [əbri:vɪ'eɪʃən] S Abkürzung *f*

ABC *abk* = American Broadcasting Corporation *amerikanische Fernsehgesellschaft*

abdomen ['æbdəmən] S Unterleib *m*

ability [ə'bɪlətɪ] S Fähigkeit *f*

able ['eɪbl] ADJ fähig; **be ~ to do sth** etw tun können

aboard [ə'bɔ:rd] ADV & PRÄP an Bord *+gen*

abolish [ə'bɑ:lɪʃ] V/T abschaffen

abortion [ə'bɔ:rʃən] S Abtreibung *f*

about [ə'baʊt] **1** ADV (*räumlich*) herum, umher; (*nicht präzise*) ungefähr; (*Uhrzeit*) gegen; **be ~ to** im Begriff sein zu; **there's a bunch of people ~** es sind eine Menge Leute da **2** PRÄP (*betreffend*) über *+akk*; **there is nothing you can do ~ it** da kann man nichts machen

above [ə'bʌv] **1** ADV oben; **children aged 8 and ~** Kinder ab 8 Jahren; **on the floor ~** ein Stockwerk höher **2** PRÄP über; **~ all** vor allem **3** ADJ obig

abroad [ə'brɔ:d] ADV im Ausland; **go ~** ins Ausland gehen

absent ['æbsənt] ADJ abwesend **absent-minded** [æbsənt'maɪndəd] ADJ zerstreut

absolute ['æbsəlu:t] ADJ absolut; (*Unsinn etc*) vollkommen, total **absolutely** ADV absolut; vollkommen; **~!** genau!

absorb [əb'zɔ:rb] V/T absorbieren; *fig* (*Wissen*) in sich aufnehmen **absorbent** ADJ absorbierend; **~ cotton** Watte *f*

abundance [ə'bʌndəns] S Reichtum *m* (*of* an *+dat*)

abuse **1** [ə'bju:s] S (*mit Worten*) Beschimpfungen *pl*; (*sexuell*) Missbrauch *m* **2** [ə'bju:z]

VT missbrauchen **abusive** [ə'bjuːsɪv] ADJ beleidigend
AC 1 *abk* = alternating current; Wechselstrom *m* 2 *abk* = air conditioning; Klimaanlage *f*
a/c *abk* = account; Kto.
accelerate [ək'seləreɪt] VI (*Auto*) beschleunigen; (*Fahrer*) Gas geben
accent ['æksent] S Akzent *m*
accept [ək'sept] VT annehmen; akzeptieren; (*Verantwortung*) übernehmen **acceptable** ADJ annehmbar
access ['ækses] S Zugang *m*; IT Zugriff *m* **accessible** [æk'sesəbl] ADJ (leicht) zugänglich/erreichbar **accessory** [æk'sesərɪ] S Zubehörteil *n* **access road** S Zufahrtsstraße *f*
accident ['æksɪdənt] S Unfall *m*; **by ~** zufällig **accidental** [æksɪ'dentl] ADJ unbeabsichtigt; (*Treffen*) zufällig; (*Todesfall*) durch Unfall **accident-prone** ['æksɪdəntproʊn] ADJ vom Pech verfolgt
acclimate ['ækləmeɪt] VT **~ oneself** sich gewöhnen (*to* an +*akk*)
accommodate [ə'kɑːmədeɪt] VT unterbringen **accommodation(s)** [əkɑːmə'deɪʃən(z)] S (PL) Unterkunft *f*
accompany [ə'kʌmpənɪ] VT begleiten
accomplish [ə'kʌmplɪʃ] VT erreichen
accord [ə'kɔːrd] S **of one's own ~** freiwillig **according to** PRÄP nach, laut +*dat*
account [ə'kaʊnt] S (*Bank*) Konto *n*; (*Beschreibung*) Bericht *m*; **on ~ of** wegen; **take into ~** berücksichtigen, in Betracht ziehen **accountant** S Buchhalter(in) *m(f)* **account for** VT erklären; Rechenschaft ablegen für
accurate ['ækjʊrət] ADJ genau
accusation [ækjʊ'zeɪʃən] S Anklage *f*, Beschuldigung *f* **accuse** [ə'kjuːz] VT beschuldigen; JUR anklagen (*of* wegen *gen*)
accustomed [ə'kʌstəmd] ADJ gewohnt
ace [eɪs] 1 S (*Karten, Tennis*) Ass *n* 2 ADJ Star- 3 VT (*Tennis*) ein Ass servieren; (*Prüfung*) mit Glanz bestehen
ache [eɪk] 1 S Schmerz *m* 2 VI wehtun
achieve [ə'tʃiːv] VT erreichen **achievement** S Leistung *f*
acid ['æsɪd] 1 S Säure *f* 2 ADJ sauer
acknowledge [ək'nɑːlɪdʒ] VT anerkennen; (*Fehler*) zugeben; (*Eingang von Brief*) bestätigen **acknowledgement** S Anerkennung *f*; (*Brief*) Empfangsbestätigung *f*
acoustics [ə'kuːstɪks] S PL Akustik *f*
acquaintance [ə'kweɪntəns]

S Bekannte(r) *m/f(m)*
acquire [ə'kwaɪr] VT erwerben, sich aneignen
across [ə'krɑːs] 1 PRÄP über +*akk*; **he lives ~ the street** er wohnt auf der anderen Seite der Straße 2 ADV hinüber, herüber
act [ækt] 1 S (*Handlung*) Tat *f*; JUR Gesetz *n*; THEAT Akt *m* 2 VI handeln; sich verhalten; THEAT spielen; **~ as** (*Person*) fungieren als; (*Gegenstand*) dienen als 3 VT (*eine Rolle*) spielen **action** ['ækʃən] S (*von Film, Roman*) Handlung *f*; (*in Film*) Action *f*; MIL Kampf *m*; **take ~** etwas unternehmen; **put a plan into ~** einen Plan in die Tat umsetzen **activate** ['æktɪveɪt] VT aktivieren **active** ['æktɪv] ADJ aktiv; (*Kind*) lebhaft **activity** [æk'tɪvətɪ] S Aktivität *f*; (*Zeitvertreib*) Beschäftigung *f*; (*organisiert*) Veranstaltung *f* **actor** ['æktər] S Schauspieler(in) *m(f)* **actress** ['æktrəs] S Schauspielerin *f*
actual ['æktʃʊəl] ADJ wirklich **actually** ADV eigentlich; (*überrascht*) tatsächlich
acupuncture ['ækjʊpʌŋktʃər] S Akupunktur *f*
ad [æd] *abk* = advertisement
A.D. *abk* = Anno Domini; nach Christi, n. Chr.
adapt [ə'dæpt] 1 VI sich anpassen (*to +dat*) 2 VT anpassen (*to +dat*); (*neu schreiben*) bearbeiten (*for* für) **adapter** S ELEK Zwischenstecker *m*, Adapter *m*
add [æd] VT (*Zutat*) hinzufügen; (*Zahlen*) addieren **add up** 1 VI (*Sinn ergeben*) stimmen 2 VT (*Zahlen*) addieren
addicted [ə'dɪktəd] ADJ **~ to drugs** drogensüchtig
addition [ə'dɪʃən] S Zusatz *m*; (*zu Rechnung*) Aufschlag *m*; MATH Addition *f*; **in ~** außerdem, zusätzlich (*to* zu) **additional** ADJ zusätzlich, weiter
additive ['ædətɪv] S Zusatz *m*
address [ə'dres] 1 S Adresse *f* 2 VT (*Brief*) adressieren; (*Person*) anreden
adequate ['ædɪkwət] ADJ angemessen; ausreichend
adhesive [əd'hiːsɪv] S Klebstoff *m* **adhesive tape** S Klebstreifen *m*
adjacent [ə'dʒeɪsənt] ADJ benachbart
adjoining [ə'dʒɔɪnɪŋ] ADJ benachbart, Neben-
adjust [ə'dʒʌst] 1 VT einstellen; richtig stellen; (*Geschwindigkeit etc*) regulieren; (*Position*) verstellen 2 VI sich anpassen (*to +dat*) **adjustable** ADJ verstellbar
administration [ədmɪnə'streɪʃən] S Verwaltung *f*; POL Regierung *f*
admirable ['ædmərəbl] ADJ bewundernswert **admiration**

[ædmə'reɪʃən] S Bewunderung *f* **admire** [əd'maɪr] V/T bewundern
admission [əd'mɪʃən] S Zutritt *m*; (*an der Uni*) Zulassung *f*; (*in Museum etc*) Eintritt *m*
admission fee S Eintrittspreis *m* **admit** [əd'mɪt] V/T hereinlassen (*to* in *+akk*); (*an der Uni*) zulassen; (*Schuld, Fehler*) zugeben, gestehen; **be ~ted to the hospital** ins Krankenhaus eingeliefert werden
adolescent [ædə'lesnt] S Jugendliche(r) *m*/*f*(*m*)
adopt [ə'dɑːpt] V/T (*Kind*) adoptieren; (*Idee*) übernehmen
adoption [ə'dɑːpʃn] S (*von Kind*) Adoption *f*; (*von Plan etc*) Übernahme *f*
adorable [ə'dɔːrəbl] ADJ entzückend **adore** [ə'dɔːr] V/T anbeten; (*Person*) über alles lieben, vergöttern
adult [ə'dʌlt, 'ædʌlt] **1** ADJ erwachsen; (*Film etc*) für Erwachsene **2** S Erwachsene(r) *m*/*f*(*m*)
adultery [ə'dʌltərɪ] S Ehebruch *m*
advance [əd'væns] **1** S (*Geld*) Vorschuss *m*; (*in der Wissenschaft*) Fortschritt *m*; **in ~** im Voraus **2** V/I vorrücken **3** V/T (*Geld*) vorschießen **advance booking** S Reservierung *f*; THEAT Vorverkauf *m* **advanced** ADJ (*modern*) fortschrittlich; (*Kurs, Niveau*) für Fortgeschrittene
advantage [əd'væntɪdʒ] S Vorteil *m*; **take ~ of** ausnutzen; Nutzen ziehen aus
adventure [əd'ventʃər] S Abenteuer *n*
advertise ['ædvərtaɪz] **1** V/T werben für; (*in Zeitung*) inserieren; (*Stelle*) ausschreiben **2** V/I Reklame machen **advertisement** [ædvər'taɪzmənt] S Werbung *f*, Anzeige *f* **advertising** S Werbung *f*
advice [əd'vaɪs] S Rat(schlag) *m* **advisable** [əd'vaɪzəbl] ADJ ratsam **advise** [əd'vaɪz] V/T raten (*sb* j-m); **~ sb to do sth/not to do sth** j-m zuraten/abraten, etw zu tun
aerial ['erɪəl] **1** S Antenne *f* **2** ADJ Luft-
aerobics [e'roʊbɪks] S SG Aerobic *n*
affair [ə'fer] S Sache *f*, Angelegenheit *f*; (*Skandal*) Affäre *f*; (*Liebesaffäre*) Verhältnis *n*
affect [ə'fekt] V/T (ein)wirken auf *+akk*; (*Gesundheit, Organ*) angreifen; (*emotional*) berühren; (*gelten für*) betreffen; (*Gleichgültigkeit etc*) vortäuschen **affection** [ə'fekʃən] S Zuneigung *f* **affectionate** [ə'fekʃənət] ADJ liebevoll
afford [ə'fɔːrd] V/T sich leisten
affordable [ə'fɔːrdəbl] ADJ erschwinglich
Afghanistan [æf'gænɪstæn] S Afghanistan *n*
afraid [ə'freɪd] ADJ **be ~** Angst

haben (*of* vor *+dat*); **be ~ that** ... fürchten, dass ...; **I'm ~ I don't know** das weiß ich leider nicht

Africa ['æfrıkə] S Afrika *n* **African** 1 ADJ afrikanisch 2 S Afrikaner(in) *m(f)* **African American, Afro-American** ['æfroʊ-] S 1 ADJ afroamerikanisch 2 S Afroamerikaner(in) *m(f)*

after ['æftər] 1 PRÄP nach; **ten ~ five** zehn nach fünf; **be ~ sb/sth** hinter j-m/etw her sein; **~ all** schließlich 2 KONJ nachdem 3 ADV **soon ~** bald danach **afternoon** S Nachmittag *m*; **in the ~** nachmittags **after-shave (lotion)** S Rasierwasser *n* **afterward(s)** ['æftərwərd(z)] ADV nachher; danach

again [ə'gen] ADV wieder; noch einmal; **~ and ~** immer wieder

against [ə'genst] PRÄP gegen; **~ the law** gesetzwidrig, illegal

age [eıdʒ] 1 S Alter *n*; (*historisch*) Zeitalter *n*; **at the ~ of four** im Alter von vier (Jahren); **what ~ is she?** wie alt ist sie?; **under ~** minderjährig 2 V/I altern, alt werden **aged** 1 [eıdʒd] ADJ **~ thirty** dreißig Jahre alt; **a son ~ twenty** ein zwanzigjähriger Sohn 2 ['eıdʒəd] ADJ betagt **age limit** S Altersgrenze *f*

agency ['eıdʒənsı] S Agentur *f*

agenda [ə'dʒendə] S Tagesordnung *f*; Programm *n*

agent ['eıdʒənt] S WIRTSCH Vertreter(in) *m(f)*; (*von Schauspieler*) Agent(in) *m(f)*

aggression [ə'greʃn] S Aggression *f* **aggressive** [ə'gresıv] ADJ aggressiv

ago [ə'goʊ] ADV **two days ~** heute vor zwei Tagen; **not long ~** (erst) vor Kurzem

agony ['ægənı] S Qual *f*

agree [ə'gri:] 1 V/T (*Termin, Preis*) vereinbaren; **~ to do sth** sich bereit erklären, etw zu tun; **~ that ...** sich einig sein, dass ...; beschließen, dass ...; zugeben, dass ... 2 V/I übereinstimmen (*with* mit); (*einem Vorschlag etc*) zustimmen; (*Einigung erzielen*) sich einigen (*about, on* auf *+akk*); (*Essen*) **not ~ with sb** j-m nicht bekommen **agreement** S Übereinstimmung *f*; (*Vertrag*) Abkommen *n*, Vereinbarung *f*

agricultural [ægrı'kʌltʃərəl] ADJ landwirtschaftlich, Landwirtschafts- **agriculture** ['ægrıkʌltʃər] S Landwirtschaft *f*

ahead [ə'hed] ADV **be ~** führen, vorne liegen; **~ of** vor *+dat*

aid [eıd] 1 S Hilfe *f*; **in ~ of** zugunsten *+gen*; **with the ~ of** mithilfe *+gen* 2 V/T helfen *+dat*, unterstützen

Aids [eɪdz] *akr* = acquired immune deficiency syndrome; Aids *n*
aim [eɪm] **1** VT (*Waffe, Kamera*) richten (*at* auf *+akk*) **2** VI **~ at** (*mit Waffe*) zielen auf *+akk*; *fig* abzielen auf *+akk*; **~ to do sth** beabsichtigen, etw zu tun **3** S Ziel *n*
ain't [eɪnt] *umg kontr von* **am not, is not, are not, has not, have not**
air [er] **1** S Luft *f*; **in the open ~** im Freien **2** VT lüften **airbag** S AUTO Airbag *m* **air-conditioned** ADJ mit Klimaanlage **air conditioning** S Klimaanlage *f* **aircraft** S Flugzeug *n* **airfield** S Flugplatz *m* **air force** S Luftwaffe *f* **airline** S Fluggesellschaft *f* **airmail** S Luftpost *f*; **by ~** mit Luftpost **airplane** S Flugzeug *n* **air pollution** S Luftverschmutzung *f* **airport** S Flughafen *m* **airside** **1** S *Teil des Flughafens nach der Sicherheitskontrolle* **2** ADV **be located ~** (*Restaurant etc*) sich nach/hinter der Sicherheitskontrolle befinden **3** ADJ **~ restaurant** Restaurant nach/hinter der Sicherheitskontrolle **air-traffic controller** S Fluglotse *m*, Fluglotsin *f*
aisle [aɪl] S Gang *m*; (*in Kirche*) Seitenschiff *n*; **~ seat** Sitz *m* am Gang
AK *abk* = Alaska
AL *abk* = Alabama
alarm [ə'lɑːrm] **1** S Alarm *m*; (*Gerät*) Alarmanlage *f* **2** VT beunruhigen **alarm clock** S Wecker *m* **alarmed** ADJ alarmgesichert **alarming** ADJ beunruhigend
alcohol ['ælkəhɑːl] S Alkohol *m* **alcohol-free** ADJ alkoholfrei **alcoholic** [ælkə'hɑːlɪk] **1** ADJ (*Getränk*) alkoholisch **2** S Alkoholiker(in) *m(f)*
alert [ə'lɜːrt] **1** ADJ wachsam **2** S Alarm *m* **3** VT warnen (*to* vor *+dat*)
alien ['eɪlɪən] **1** S Ausländer(in) *m(f)*; (*aus dem Weltall*) Außerirdische(r) *m/f(m)* **2** ADJ fremd; ausländisch; (*aus dem Weltall*) außerirdisch
alike [ə'laɪk] ADJ & ADV gleich; ähnlich
alive [ə'laɪv] ADJ lebendig; **keep sth ~** etw am Leben erhalten
all [ɔːl] **1** ADJ (*mit pl*) alle; (*mit sg*) ganz; **~ the kids** alle Kinder; **~ the time** die ganze Zeit; **why me of ~ people?** warum ausgerechnet ich? **2** PRON alles; alle; **~ of** ganz; **~ of them came** sie kamen alle **3** S alles **4** ADV ganz; **~ along** von Anfang an; **~ at once** auf einmal
allegation [ælə'geɪʃən] S Behauptung *f* **alleged** [ə'ledʒd] ADJ angeblich
allergic [ə'lɜːrdʒɪk] ADJ allergisch (*to* gegen) **allergy**

['ælərdʒɪ] S Allergie *f*
alleviate [ə'li:vɪeɪt] VT (*Schmerzen*) lindern
alley ['ælɪ] S (enge) Gasse; Durchgang *m*; (*Bowling*) Bahn *f*
alliance [ə'laɪəns] S Bündnis *n*
alligator ['æləgeɪtər] S Alligator *m*
all-night ADJ (*Café, Kino*) die ganze Nacht geöffnet
allocate ['æləkeɪt] VT zuweisen, zuteilen (*to dat*)
allow [ə'laʊ] VT erlauben (*sb* j-m); bewilligen; (*Zeit*) einplanen **allow for** VT berücksichtigen; (*Kosten*) einkalkulieren **allowance** S (*vom Staat*) Beihilfe *f*; (*von Elternteil*) Unterhaltsgeld *n*
all right [ɔ:l'raɪt] **1** ADJ okay, in Ordnung; **I'm ~** mir geht's gut **2** ADV ganz gut **3** INT okay, alles klar
ally ['ælaɪ] S Verbündete(r) *m*/*f*(*m*); HIST Alliierte(r) *m*/*f*(*m*)
almond ['ɑ:mənd] S Mandel *f*
almost ['ɔ:lmoʊst] ADV fast
alone [ə'loʊn] ADJ & ADV allein
along [ə'lɑ:ŋ] **1** PRÄP entlang *+akk*; **~ the river** den Fluss entlang; am Fluss entlang **2** ADV weiter; **~ with** zusammen mit; **all ~** von Anfang an, die ganze Zeit **alongside** **1** PRÄP neben *+dat* **2** ADV nebenher
aloud [ə'laʊd] ADV laut
alphabet ['ælfəbet] S Alphabet *n*
already [ɔ:l'redɪ] ADV schon, bereits
also ['ɔ:lsoʊ] ADV auch
altar ['ɔ:ltər] S Altar *m*
alter ['ɔ:ltər] VT ändern **alteration** [ɔ:ltə'reɪʃən] S Änderung *f*
alternate **1** ['ɔ:ltərnət] ADJ abwechselnd **2** ['ɔ:ltərneɪt] VI abwechseln (*with* mit) **alternating current** S Wechselstrom *m* **alternative** [ɔ:l-'tɜ:rnətɪv] **1** ADJ Alternativ- **2** S Alternative *f*
although [ɔ:l'ðoʊ] KONJ obwohl
altitude ['æltɪtu:d] S Höhe *f*
altogether [ɔ:ltə'geðər] ADV insgesamt; ganz und gar
aluminum [ə'lu:mɪnəm] S Aluminium *n*
always ['ɔ:lweɪz] ADV immer
am [æm] *Präsens von* **be**; bin
a.m. *abk* = ante meridiem; vormittags, vorm.
amateur ['æmətʃʊr] **1** S Amateur(in) *m*(*f*) **2** ADJ Amateur-; (*Theater etc*) Laien-
amazed [ə'meɪzd] ADJ erstaunt (*at* über *+akk*) **amazing** ADJ erstaunlich
ambassador [æm'bæsədər] S Botschafter *m*
ambiguous [æm'bɪgjʊəs] ADJ zweideutig
ambition [æm'bɪʃən] S Ambition *f*, Ehrgeiz *m* **ambitious** [æm'bɪʃəs] ADJ ehrgeizig
ambulance ['æmbjʊləns] S

Krankenwagen *m*
America [ə'merıkə] S Amerika *n* **American** 1 ADJ amerikanisch 2 S Amerikaner(in) *m(f)*; **Native ~** Indianer(in) *m(f)*
amnesia [æm'ni:ʒə] S Gedächtnisverlust *m*
among [ə'mʌŋ] PRÄP unter +*dat*
amount [ə'maʊnt] 1 S Menge *f*; (*von Geld*) Betrag *m*; **a large/small ~ of ...** ziemlich viel/wenig ... 2 V/I **~ to** sich belaufen auf +*akk*
Amtrak® ['æmtræk] S *amerikanische Eisenbahngesellschaft*
amuse [ə'mju:z] V/T amüsieren; unterhalten **amusement** S (*Freude*) Vergnügen *n*; (*Zeitvertreib*) Unterhaltung *f* **amusement park** S Vergnügungspark *m* **amusing** ADJ amüsant
an [æn, ən] ART ein(e)
analysis [ə'næləsıs] S Analyse *f* **analyze** ['ænəlaız] V/T analysieren
ancestor ['ænsestər] S Vorfahr *m*
anchor ['æŋkər] 1 S Anker *m* 2 V/T verankern
anchovy ['æntʃoʊvı] S Sardelle *f*
ancient ['eınʃənt] ADJ alt; *umg* (*Person, Kleidung*) uralt
and [ænd, ənd] KONJ und
anemic [ə'ni:mık] ADJ blutarm
anesthetic [ænəs'θetık] S Narkose *f*; (*Substanz*) Narkosemittel *n*
angel ['eındʒəl] S Engel *m*; **~ food cake** *Art Biskuitkuchen*
anger ['æŋgər] 1 S Zorn *m* 2 V/T ärgern
angina [æn'dʒaınə] S Angina Pectoris *f*
angle ['æŋgl] S Winkel *m*; *fig* Standpunkt *m*
angry ['æŋgrı] ADJ verärgert; (*heftiger*) zornig; **be ~ with sb** auf j-n böse sein
animal ['ænəməl] S Tier *n*
animated ['ænəmeıtəd] ADJ lebhaft; **~ movie** Zeichentrickfilm *m*
aniseed ['ænısi:d] S Anis *m*
ankle ['æŋkl] S (Fuß)knöchel *m*
annex 1 S ['æneks] Anbau *m* 2 V/T [ə'neks] annektieren
anniversary [ænı'vɜ:rsərı] S Jahrestag *m*
announce [ə'naʊns] V/T bekannt geben; RADIO, TV ansagen **announcement** S Bekanntgabe *f*; (*offiziell*) Bekanntmachung *f*; RADIO, TV Ansage *f* **announcer** S RADIO, TV Ansager(in) *m(f)*
annoy [ə'nɔı] V/T ärgern **annoyed** ADJ ärgerlich; **be ~ with sb (about sth)** sich über j-n (über etw) ärgern **annoying** ADJ ärgerlich; (*Person*) lästig, nervig
annual ['ænjʊəl] 1 ADJ jährlich 2 S Jahrbuch *n*

anonymous [ə'nɑːnɪməs] ADJ anonym
anorexia [ænə'reksɪə] S Magersucht *f* **anorexic** ADJ magersüchtig
another [ə'nʌðər] ADJ & PRON ein(e) andere(r, s); (*zusätzlich*) noch eine(r, s); **let me put it ~ way** lass es mich anders sagen
answer ['ænsər] **1** S Antwort *f* (*to* auf *+akk*) **2** V/I antworten; (*am Telefon*) sich melden **3** V/T antworten *+dat*; (*Frage, Brief*) beantworten; (*Telefon*) gehen an *+akk*, abnehmen; (*Tür*) öffnen **answering machine** S Anrufbeantworter *m*
ant [ænt] S Ameise *f*
Antarctic [ænt'ɑːrktɪk] S Antarktis *f*
antenna ⟨antennae⟩ [æn'tenə, -teniː] S ZOOL Fühler *m*; RADIO Antenne *f*
antibiotic [æntɪbaɪ'ɑːtɪk] S Antibiotikum *n*
anticipate [æn'tɪsəpeɪt] V/T erwarten, rechnen mit **anticipation** [æntɪsə'peɪʃən] S Erwartung *f*
antifreeze ['æntɪfriːz] S Frostschutzmittel *n*
antique [æn'tiːk] **1** S Antiquität *f* **2** ADJ antik
antiseptic [æntɪ'septɪk] **1** S Antiseptikum *n* **2** ADJ antiseptisch
antlers ['æntlərz] S PL Geweih *n*
anxiety [æŋ'zaɪətɪ] S Sorge *f* (*about* um) **anxiety attack** S Panikattacke *f* **anxious** ['æŋkʃəs] ADJ besorgt (*about* um); ängstlich
any ['enɪ] **1** ADJ (*in Fragen: unübersetzt*) **do you have ~ money?** hast du/haben Sie Geld?; (*verneinend*) **I don't have ~ money** ich habe kein Geld; (*egal welche(r, s)*) **take ~ card** nimm/nehmen Sie irgendeine Karte **2** PRON (*in Frage*) **do you want ~?** (*im sg*) willst du/wollen Sie etwas (davon)?; (*im pl*) willst du/wollen Sie welche?; (*verneint*) **I don't have ~** ich habe keine/keinen/keins; (*egal welche(r, s)*) **you can take ~ of them** du kannst/Sie können jede(n, s) beliebige(n) nehmen **3** ADV (*in Frage*) **are there ~ more strawberries?** gibt es noch Erdbeeren?; **can't you work ~ faster?** kannst du/können Sie nicht schneller arbeiten?; (*verneint*) **not ~ longer** nicht mehr **anybody** PRON irgendjemand; jeder; (*in Frage*) jemand **anyhow** ADV → anyway **anyone** PRON irgendjemand; jeder; (*in Frage*) jemand **anyplace** ADV irgendwo; (*Richtung*) irgendwohin; (*an jedem Ort*) überall **anything** PRON (irgend)etwas; alles; **~ else?** sonst noch etwas?; **she didn't tell me ~** sie hat mir nichts gesagt **any-**

time ADV jederzeit **anyway, anyways** ADV **I didn't want to go there ~** ich wollte da sowieso nicht hingehen; **thanks ~** trotzdem danke; **~, as I was saying, …** jedenfalls, wie ich schon sagte, … **anywhere** ADV irgendwo; *(Richtung)* irgendwohin; *(an jedem Ort)* überall

AP *abk* = American plan; Vollpension *f*

apart [ə'pɑ:rt] ADV auseinander; **~ from** außer; **live ~** getrennt leben

apartment [ə'pɑ:rtmənt] S Wohnung *f* **apartment block** S Wohnblock *m* **apartment building** S Wohnhaus *n*

ape [eɪp] S (Menschen)affe *m*

apologize [ə'pɑ:lədʒaɪz] V/I sich entschuldigen **apology** S Entschuldigung *f*

apostrophe [ə'pɑ:strəfɪ] S Apostroph *m*

Appalachian Mountains [æpə'leɪʃn] S PL *Gebirgssystem im Osten Nordamerikas*

appalled [ə'pɒ:ld] ADJ entsetzt *(at* über *+akk)* **appalling** [ə'pɒ:lɪŋ] ADJ entsetzlich

apparent [ə'pærənt] ADJ offensichtlich *(to* für); *(dem Schein nach)* scheinbar **apparently** ADV anscheinend

appeal [ə'pi:l] **1** V/I *(dringend)* bitten *(for* um, *to +akk)*; JUR Berufung einlegen; **~ to sb** j-m zusagen **2** S Aufruf *m* *(to* an *+akk)*; JUR Berufung *f*; *(Anziehung)* Reiz *m* **appealing** ADJ ansprechend, attraktiv

appear [ə'pɪr] V/I erscheinen; THEAT auftreten; *(so aussehen, als ob)* scheinen **appearance** S Erscheinen *n*; THEAT Auftritt *m*; *(Äußeres)* Aussehen *n*; **at first ~** auf den ersten Blick

appendicitis [əpendə'saɪtəs] S Blinddarmentzündung *f* **appendix** [ə'pendɪks] S Blinddarm *m*; *(in Buch)* Anhang *m*

appetite ['æpətaɪt] S Appetit *m*; *fig* Verlangen *n* **appetizer** ['æpətaɪzər] S Vorspeise *f*

applause [ə'plɒ:z] S Beifall *m*, Applaus *m*

apple ['æpl] S Apfel *m* **applejack** ['æpldʒæk] S Apfelschnaps *m* **apple pie** S gedeckter Apfelkuchen *m* **apple sauce** S Apfelmus *n*

appliance [ə'plaɪəns] S Gerät *n* **applicable** ['æplɪkəbl] ADJ anwendbar; *(auf Formular)* zutreffend **applicant** ['æplɪkənt] S Bewerber(in) *m(f)* **application** [æplɪ'keɪʃən] S *(auf Reisepass etc)* Antrag *m* *(for* auf *+akk)*; *(um Stelle)* Bewerbung *f* *(for* um) **application form** S Anmeldeformular *n* **apply** [ə'plaɪ] **1** V/I zutreffen *(to* auf *+akk)*; *(um Stelle)* sich bewerben *(for* um) **2** V/T *(Salbe)* auftragen; *(in die Praxis umsetzen)* anwenden; *(Bremse)*

betätigen
appoint [əˈpɔɪnt] V/T ernennen **appointment** [əˈpɔɪntmənt] S Verabredung *f*; (*beim Arzt, Frisör*) Termin *m*
appreciate [əˈpriːʃɪeɪt] V/T zu schätzen wissen; (*verstehen*) einsehen **appreciation** [əpriːʃɪˈeɪʃən] S Anerkennung *f*, Würdigung *f*
approach [əˈproʊtʃ] **1** V/I sich nähern **2** V/T (*Ort*) sich nähern *+dat*; (*Person*) herantreten an *+akk*
appropriate [əˈproʊprɪət] ADJ passend; (*Verhalten*) angemessen; (*Bemerkung*) treffend **appropriately** ADV passend; treffend
approval [əˈpruːvəl] S Anerkennung *f*, Zustimmung *f* (*of* zu) **approve** [əˈpruːv] **1** V/T billigen **2** V/I **~ of sth/sb** etw billigen/von j-m etwas halten; **I don't ~** ich missbillige das
approx [əˈprɑːks] = approximately; ca. **approximate** [əˈprɑːksəmət] ADJ ungefähr **approximately** ADV ungefähr, circa
apricot [ˈæprɪkɑːt] S Aprikose *f*
April [ˈeɪprəl] S April *m*; → September
apron [ˈeɪprən] S Schürze *f*
aquarium [əˈkwerɪəm] S Aquarium *n*
Aquarius [əˈkwerɪəs] S ASTROL Wassermann *m*
AR *abk* = Arkansas
Arab [ˈærəb] S Araber(in) *m(f)* **Arabic** [ˈærəbɪk] **1** S (*Sprache*) Arabisch *n* **2** ADJ arabisch
arcade [ɑːrˈkeɪd] S Arkade *f*; (*mit Läden*) Einkaufspassage *f*; (*in Einkaufszentrum*) Spielhalle *f*
arch [ɑːrtʃ] S Bogen *m*
archbishop [ɑːrtʃˈbɪʃəp] S Erzbischof *m*
archeologist [ɑːrkɪˈɑːlədʒɪst] S Archäologe *m*, Archäologin *f*
architect [ˈɑːrkɪtekt] S Architekt(in) *m(f)* **architecture** [ˈɑːrkɪtektʃər] S Architektur *f*
archway [ˈɑːrtʃweɪ] S Torbogen *m*
Arctic [ˈɑːrktɪk] S Arktis *f*
are [ə, *stressed* ɑːr] *Präsens von* be
area [ˈerɪə] S (*Region*) Gebiet *n*, Gegend *f*; (*in Quadratmetern etc*) Fläche *f*; (*innerhalb eines Gebäudes*) Bereich *m*, Zone *f*; *fig* (*von Arbeit, Studium*) Bereich *m*; **the Boston ~** der Bostoner Raum **area code** S Vorwahl *f*
aren't [ɑːrnt] *kontr von* **are not**
argue [ˈɑːrgjuː] V/I streiten (*about, over* über *+akk*); **~ that ...** behaupten, dass ...; **~ for/against ...** sprechen für/gegen ... **argument** S Argument *n*; (*Auseinandersetzung*) Streit *m*; **have an ~** sich streiten
Aries [ˈeriːz] S SG ASTROL Widder *m*
arise <arose, arisen> [əˈraɪz, ə-

'roʊz, ə'rɪzn] VI sich ergeben, entstehen; (*Problem, Frage, Wind*) aufkommen

arm [ɑːrm] **1** S Arm *m*; (*von Pulli*) Ärmel *m*; (*von Stuhl*) Armlehne *f* **2** VT bewaffnen **armchair** ['ɑːrmtʃer] S Lehnstuhl *m* **armed** [ɑːrmd] ADJ bewaffnet **arm floats** S PL Schwimmflügel *pl* **armpit** ['ɑːrmpɪt] S Achselhöhle *f* **arms** [ɑːrmz] S PL Waffen *pl*

army ['ɑːrmɪ] S Armee *f*

aroma [ə'roʊmə] S Duft *m*, Aroma *n* **aromatherapy** [əroʊmə'θerəpɪ] S Aromatherapie *f*

arose [ə'roʊz] *prät von* **arise**

around [ə'raʊnd] **1** ADV herum, umher; (*präsent*) hier (irgendwo); (*annähernd*) ungefähr; (*mit Zeitangabe*) gegen; **all ~** rundherum; **I'll be ~ at 8** ich werde um acht Uhr da sein; **the other way ~** umgekehrt **2** PRÄP (*umschließend*) um ... (herum); (*innerhalb von Stadt etc*) in ... herum; **~ (about)** (*in etwa*) ungefähr; **~ the corner** um die Ecke; **she lives ~ here** sie wohnt hier in der Gegend

arr. *abk* = arrival, arrives; Ank.

arrange [ə'reɪndʒ] VT (an)ordnen; (*künstlerisch*) arrangieren; (*Ort, Zeit, Treffen*) vereinbaren, festsetzen; (*organisieren*) planen; **~ that ...** es so einrichten, dass ...; **we ~d to meet up at eight o'clock** wir haben uns für acht Uhr verabredet **arrangement** S Anordnung *f*; (*Abmachung*) Vereinbarung *f*, Plan *m*; **make ~s** Vorbereitungen treffen

arrest [ə'rest] **1** VT festnehmen **2** S Festnahme *f*

arrival [ə'raɪvəl] S Ankunft *f* **arrivals** S Ankunftshalle *f* **arrive** [ə'raɪv] VI ankommen (*at* bei, in *+dat*)

arrogant ['ærəgənt] ADJ arrogant

arrow ['æroʊ] S Pfeil *m*

art [ɑːrt] S Kunst *f*

artery ['ɑːrtərɪ] S Schlagader *f*, Arterie *f*

art gallery S Kunstgalerie *f*

arthritis [ɑːr'θraɪtəs] S Arthritis *f*

artichoke ['ɑːrtɪtʃoʊk] S Artischocke *f*

article ['ɑːrtɪkl] S Artikel *m*, Gegenstand *m*

artificial [ɑːrtɪ'fɪʃəl] ADJ künstlich, Kunst-

artist ['ɑːrtɪst] S Künstler(in) *m(f)* **artistic** [ɑːr'tɪstɪk] ADJ künstlerisch

as [æz, əz] **1** ADV wie; (*in der Rolle von*) als; **such ~ ...** wie etwa ...; **~ ... ~** so ... wie; **~ soon ~ he comes** sobald er kommt; **twice ~ much** zweimal so viel; **~ for ...** was ... betrifft **2** KONJ (*begründend*) da, weil; (*zeitlich*) als, während; **~ if, ~ though** als ob; **leave it**

~ it is lass es so (wie es ist)
asap ['eɪsæp] *akr* = as soon as possible; möglichst bald
ash [æʃ] S Asche *f*; (*Baum*) Esche *f*
ashamed [ə'ʃeɪmd] ADJ beschämt; **be ~ (of sb/sth)** sich (für j-n/etw) schämen
ashore [ə'ʃɔːr] ADV an Land
ashtray ['æʃtreɪ] S Aschenbecher *m*
Asia ['eɪʃə] S Asien *n* **Asian** 1 ADJ asiatisch 2 S Asiat(in) *m(f)*
aside [ə'saɪd] ADV beiseite, zur Seite; **~ from** außer
ask [æsk] V/T & V/I fragen; (*Frage*) stellen; (*Gefallen*) bitten um; **~ sb the way** j-n nach dem Weg fragen; **~ sb to do sth** j-n darum bitten, etw zu tun **ask for** V/T bitten um
asleep [ə'sliːp] ADJ & ADV **be ~** schlafen; **fall ~** einschlafen
asparagus [əs'pærəgəs] S Spargel *m*
ass [æs] S *a. fig* Esel *m*; *vulg* Arsch *m*
assassinate [ə'sæsəneɪt] V/T ermorden **assassination** [əsæsə'neɪʃn] S Ermordung *f*
assault [ə'sɔːlt] 1 S Angriff *m*; JUR Körperverletzung *f* 2 V/T überfallen, herfallen über *+akk*
assemble [ə'sembl] 1 V/T (*Einzelteile*) zusammensetzen 2 V/I sich versammeln **assembly** [ə'semblɪ] S Versammlung *f*
assess [ə'ses] V/T einschätzen
assessment S Einschätzung *f*
asset ['æset] S Vermögenswert *m*; *fig* Vorteil *m*; **~s** *pl* Vermögen *n*
assign [ə'saɪn] V/T zuweisen
assignment S Aufgabe *f*, Auftrag *m*
assist [ə'sɪst] V/T helfen *+dat*
assistance S Hilfe *f* **assistant** S Assistent(in) *m(f)*, Mitarbeiter(in) *m(f)*
associate [ə'soʊsɪeɪt] 1 V/T verbinden (*with* mit) 2 V/I **~ with sb** mit j-m verkehren **association** [əsoʊsɪ'eɪʃən] S Verband *m*, Vereinigung *f*
assorted [ə'sɔːrtəd] ADJ gemischt **assortment** S Auswahl *f* (*of* an *+dat*)
assume [ə'suːm] V/T annehmen (*that* … dass …); (*Amt, Verantwortung*) übernehmen
assure [ə'ʃʊr] V/T versichern *+dat*
asthma ['æsmə] S Asthma *n*
astonished [ə'stɑːnɪʃt] ADJ erstaunt (*at* über) **astonishing** ADJ erstaunlich **astonishment** S Erstaunen *n*
astounding [ə'staʊndɪŋ] ADJ erstaunlich
astray [ə'streɪ] ADV **go ~** (*Brief etc*) verloren gehen; (*Person*) vom Weg abkommen
astrology [ə'strɑːlədʒɪ] S Astrologie *f*
astronaut ['æstrənɒːt] S Astronaut(in) *m(f)*
astronomy [əs'trɑːnəmɪ] S

Astronomie *f*
asylum [əˈsaɪləm] S (*Heim*) Anstalt *f*; (*politisch*) Asyl *n* **asylum seeker** S Asylbewerber(in) *m(f)*
at [æt] PRÄP (*örtlich*) **~ the door** an der Tür; **~ home** zu Hause; **~ John's** bei John; **~ school** in der Schule; **~ the theater** im Theater; **~ lunch/work** beim Essen/bei der Arbeit; (*Richtung*) **point ~ sb** auf j-n zeigen; **he looked ~ me** er sah mich an; (*Zeit*) **~ 2 o'clock** um 2 Uhr; **~ Easter/Christmas** zu Ostern/Weihnachten; **~ the moment** im Moment; **~ (the age of) 16** im Alter von 16 Jahren, mit 16; (*Preis*) **~ $5 apiece** zu je 5 Dollar; (*Geschwindigkeit*) **~ 20 mph** mit 20 Meilen pro Stunde
ate [eɪt] *prät von* eat
athlete [ˈæθliːt] S Athlet(in) *m(f)*, Leichtathlet(in) *m(f)* **athletics** [æθˈletɪks] S SG Sport *m*
Atlantic [ətˈlæntɪk] S **the ~ (Ocean)** der Atlantik
ATM *abk* = automated teller machine; Geldautomat *m* **ATM card** S ≈ EC-Karte *f*
atmosphere [ˈætməsfɪr] S Atmosphäre *f*; Stimmung *f*
atom [ˈætəm] S Atom *n*
atom(ic) bomb [ˈætəm, əˈtɑːmɪk] S Atombombe *f*
attach [əˈtætʃ] V/T befestigen, anheften (*to* an *+dat*); **be ~ed to sb/sth** an j-m/etw hängen
attachment S IT Attachment *n*, Anhang *m*
attack [əˈtæk] **1** V/T & V/I angreifen **2** S Angriff *m* (*on* auf *+akk*); MED Anfall *m*
attempt [əˈtempt] **1** S Versuch *m* **2** V/T versuchen
attend [əˈtend] **1** V/T teilnehmen an *+dat*; (*Vorlesung, Schule*) besuchen **2** V/I anwesend sein **attendance** S Anwesenheit *f*
attention [əˈtenʃən] S Aufmerksamkeit *f*; **(your) ~ please** Achtung!; **pay ~ to sth** etw beachten; **pay ~ to sb** j-m aufmerksam zuhören
attic [ˈætɪk] S Dachboden *m*; (*bewohnt*) Mansarde *f*
attitude [ˈætɪtuːd] S Einstellung *f* (*to, towards* zu), Haltung *f*
attorney [əˈtɜːrnɪ] S Rechtsanwalt *m*, Rechtsanwältin *f*; **~ general** Justizminister(in) *m(f)*
attract [əˈtrækt] V/T anziehen; (*Aufmerksamkeit*) erregen; **be ~ed to** *od* **by sb** sich zu j-m hingezogen fühlen **attraction** [əˈtrækʃən] S Anziehungskraft *f*; (*für Touristen*) Attraktion *f* **attractive** ADJ attraktiv; reizvoll
ATV *abk* = all-terrain vehicle; Geländefahrzeug *n*
auction [ˈɒːkʃən] **1** S Versteigerung *f*, Auktion *f* **2** V/T versteigern
audience [ˈɒːdɪəns] S Publi-

kum *n*; RADIO Zuhörer *pl*; TV Zuschauer *pl*
audio ['ɒːdɪoʊ] ADJ Ton-
audio guide S Audioguide *m* (*elektronischer Museumsführer*)
audition [ɒː'dɪʃən] 1 S Probe *f* 2 V/I THEAT vorspielen, vorsingen
auditorium [ɒːdɪ'tɔːrɪəm] S Zuschauerraum *m*
August ['ɒːgəst] S August *m*; → September
aunt [ænt] S Tante *f*
au pair [oʊ'per] S Aupairmädchen *n*, Aupairjunge *m*
Australia [ɒː'streɪlɪə] S Australien *n* **Australian** 1 ADJ australisch 2 S Australier(in) *m(f)*
Austria ['ɒːstrɪə] S Österreich *n* **Austrian** 1 ADJ österreichisch 2 S Österreicher(in) *m(f)*
authentic [ɒː'θentɪk] ADJ echt; authentisch
author ['ɒːθər] S Autor(in) *m(f)*, Verfasser(in) *m(f)*
authority [ə'θɑːrətɪ] S Autorität *f*; **the authorities** *pl* die Behörden *pl* **authorize** ['ɒːθəraɪz] V/T genehmigen
auto ⟨-s *pl*⟩ ['ɒːtoʊ] S Auto *n*
autograph ['ɒːtəgræf] S Autogramm *n*
automatic [ɒːtə'mætɪk] 1 ADJ automatisch; **~ gear shift** Automatikschaltung *f* 2 S (*Auto*) Automatikwagen *m*
automobile ['ɒːtəmoʊbiːl] S Auto(mobil) *n*
autopsy ['ɒːtɑːpsɪ] S Autopsie *f*
autotrain ['ɒːtoʊtreɪn] S Autoreisezug *m*
autumn ['ɒːtəm] S Herbst *m*
auxiliary [ɒːg'zɪlɪərɪ] 1 ADJ Hilfs- 2 S Hilfskraft *f*
availability [əveɪlə'bɪlətɪ] S Lieferbarkeit *f*, Verfügbarkeit *f*
available [ə'veɪləbl] ADJ erhältlich; (*existent*) vorhanden; (*Produkt*) lieferbar; (*Person*) erreichbar; **be/make ~ to sb** j-m zur Verfügung stehen/stellen
avalanche ['ævəlɑːnʃ] S Lawine *f*
Ave *abk* = avenue
avenue ['ævənuː] S Allee *f*
average ['ævrɪdʒ] 1 S Durchschnitt *m*; **on ~** im Durchschnitt 2 ADJ durchschnittlich
avocado ⟨-s *pl*⟩ [ævə'kɑːdoʊ] S Avocado *f*
avoid [ə'vɔɪd] V/T vermeiden
avoidable ADJ vermeidbar
awake [ə'weɪk] 1 V/I ⟨awoke/awaked, awoken⟩ [ə'woʊk, ə'woʊkən] aufwachen 2 ADJ wach
award [ə'wɔːrd] 1 S Preis *m*, Auszeichnung *f* 2 V/T zuerkennen (*to sb* j-m); verleihen (*to sb* j-m)
aware [ə'wer] ADJ bewusst; **be ~ of sth** sich einer Sache *gen* bewusst sein; **I wasn't ~ that**

... es war mir nicht klar, dass ...

away [əˈweɪ] ADV weg; **look ~** wegsehen; **he's ~** er ist nicht da; (*auf Reise*) er ist verreist; SPORT **they're (playing) ~** sie spielen auswärts; **three miles ~** drei Meilen (von hier) entfernt

awesome [ˈɒːsəm] ADJ *umg* super, geil

awful [ˈɒːfʊl] ADJ schrecklich, furchtbar **awfully** ADV furchtbar

awkward [ˈɒːkwərd] ADJ (*Verhalten*) ungeschickt; (*Situation, Schweigen*) peinlich; (*nicht einfach*) schwierig

awning [ˈɒːnɪŋ] S Markise *f*

awoke [əˈwoʊk] *prät von* awake **awoken** [əˈwoʊkən] *pperf von* awake

ax [æks] S Axt *f*

axle [ˈæksl] S TECH Achse *f*

AZ *abk* = Arizona

B

B & B *abk* = bed and breakfast

babe [beɪb] S *umg* Schatz *m*

baby [ˈbeɪbɪ] S Baby *n*; (*von Tier*) Junge(s) *n*; *umg* Schatz *m*; **have a ~** ein Kind bekommen **baby carriage** S Kinderwagen *m* **baby food** S Babynahrung *f* **baby shower** S Party für die werdende Mutter

babysit *irr* V/I babysitten

babysitter S Babysitter(in) *m(f)*

bachelor [ˈbætʃələr] S Junggeselle *m*

back [bæk] **1** S Rücken *m*; (*Haus, Münze*) Rückseite *f*; (*Stuhl*) Rückenlehne *f*; (*Auto*) Rücksitz *m*; (*von Zug*) Ende *n*; SPORT Verteidiger(in) *m(f)*; **at the ~ of ..., in ~ of ...** (*innen*) hinten in ...; (*außen*) hinter ...; **~ to front** verkehrt herum **2** V/T unterstützen; (*Auto*) rückwärtsfahren **3** V/I rückwärtsgehen *od* rückwärtsfahren **4** ADJ Hinter-; **~ wheel** Hinterrad *n* **5** ADV zurück; **they're ~** sie sind wieder da **back down** V/I nachgeben **back up** **1** V/I (*Auto etc*) zurücksetzen **2** V/T unterstützen; IT sichern; (*Auto*) zurückfahren

backache S Rückenschmerzen *pl* **backbone** S Rückgrat *n* **backdoor** S Hintertür *f* **background** S Hintergrund *m* **backhand** S SPORT Rückhand *f* **backpack** S Rucksack *m* **backpacker** S Rucksacktourist(in) *m(f)* **backpacking** S Rucksacktourismus *m* **back seat** S Rücksitz *m* **backside** S *umg* Po *m* **back street** S Seitensträßchen *n* **backstroke** S Rückenschwimmen *n* **back-up** S Unterstützung *f*; **~ (copy)** IT Sicherungskopie *f* **backward** [ˈbækwərd] **1** ADJ (*Region*) rückständig; **~ movement** Rückwärtsbewegung *f* **2** ADV rückwärts **backwards** ADV rückwärts **backyard** S Garten *m* hinter dem Haus

bacon [ˈbeɪkən] S Frühstücksspeck *m*

bacteria [bækˈtɪrɪə] S PL Bakterien *pl*

bad ⟨worse, worst⟩ [bæd, wɜːrs, wɜːrst] ADJ schlecht, schlimm; (*Geruch*) übel; **I have a ~ back** mir tut der Rücken weh; **I'm ~ at math** ich bin schlecht in Mathe; **go ~** schlecht werden, verderben

badge [bædʒ] S Abzeichen *n*

badly [ˈbædlɪ] ADV schlecht; **~ wounded** schwer verwundet; **need sth ~** etw dringend brauchen **bad-tempered** [bædˈtempərd] ADJ schlecht gelaunt

bag [bæg] S Tüte *f*, Beutel *m*, Tasche *f*

bagel [ˈbeɪgl] S Bagel *m* (*ringförmiges Brotteiggebäck*)

baggage [ˈbægɪdʒ] S Gepäck *n* **baggage car** S Gepäckwagen *m* **baggage check** S Gepäckschein *m* **baggage (re)claim** S Gepäckrückgabe *f* **baggage room** S Gepäckaufbewahrung *f*

baggy [ˈbægɪ] ADJ (zu) weit; (*Hose, Anzug*) ausgebeult

Bahamas [bəˈhɑːməz] S PL **the ~** die Bahamas *pl*

bail [beɪl] S Kaution *f*

bait [beɪt] S Köder *m*

bake [beɪk] V/T & V/I backen **baked Alaska** S *Eiscreme auf einem Stück Kuchen, bedeckt mit Baiser und kurz überbacken* **baked beans** S PL *weiße Bohnen in Tomatensoße* **baked potato** ⟨-es *pl*⟩ S in der Schale gebackene Kartoffel, Ofenkartoffel *f* **baker** S Bäcker(in) *m(f)* **bakery** [ˈbeɪkərɪ] S Bäckerei *f* **baking powder** S Backpulver *n*

balance [ˈbæləns] **1** S Gleichgewicht *n* **2** V/T ausgleichen

balcony [ˈbælkənɪ] S Balkon *m*

bald [bɒːld] ADJ kahl; **be ~** eine Glatze haben; **~ eagle** weißköpfiger Adler (*Wappentier der USA*)

ball [bɒːl] S Ball *m*; **have a ~** *umg* sich prima amüsieren

ballet [bæˈleɪ] S Ballett *n* **ballet dancer** S Balletttänzer(in) *m(f)*

balloon [bəˈluːn] S Ballon *m*, Luftballon *m*

ballpark [ˈbɒːlpɑːrk] S Baseballstadion *n*; **~ figure** Richtzahl *f*, Näherungswert *m* **ballpoint (pen)** [ˈbɒːlpɔɪnt] S Kugelschreiber *m* **ballroom** [ˈbɒːlruːm] S Tanzsaal *m*

Baltic [ˈbɑːltɪk] ADJ **~ Sea** Ostsee *f*; **the ~ States** die balti-

schen Staaten; **the ~s** das Baltikum
bamboo [bæm'bu:] S Bambus *m*
ban [bæn] 1 S Verbot *n* 2 V/T verbieten
banana [bə'nænə] S Banane *f* **banana split** S Bananensplit *n*
band [bænd] S Gruppe *f*, Bande *f*; (*Rock*) Band *f*; (*aus Stoff, Gummi*) Band *n*
bandage ['bændɪdʒ] 1 S Verband *m*; (*elastisch*) Bandage *f* 2 V/T verbinden
Band-Aid® ['bændeɪd] S Heftpflaster *n*
bang [bæŋ] 1 S Knall *m*, Schlag *m* 2 V/T & V/I knallen; (*Tür*) zuschlagen, zuknallen
bangs [bæŋz] S PL (*von Frisur*) Pony *m*
banister(s) ['bænəstər(z)] S (PL) (Treppen)geländer *n*
bank [bæŋk] S FIN Bank *f*; (*Fluss*) Ufer *n* **bank account** S Bankkonto *n* **bank balance** S Kontostand *m* **bank code** S Bankleitzahl *f* **bankrupt** ['bæŋkrʌpt] V/T ruinieren; **go ~** Pleite gehen **bank statement** S Kontoauszug *m*
baptism ['bæptɪzəm] S Taufe *f* **baptize** [bæp'taɪz] V/T taufen
bar [bɑ:r] 1 S Bar *f*, Lokal *n*; (*Eisen*) Stange *f*; (*Schokolade*) Riegel *m*, Tafel *f*; (*Seife*) Stück *n*; (*Tresen*) Theke *f* 2 PRÄP außer
barbecue ['bɑ:rbəkju:] S (*Gerät*) Grill *m*; (*Feier*) Barbecue *n*, Grillfete *f*; **have a ~** grillen
barber shop ['bɑ:rbərʃɑ:p] S Friseurgeschäft *n* (*für Herren*)
bar code ['bɑ:rkoʊd] S Strichkode *m*
bare [ber] ADJ nackt **barefoot** ADJ & ADV barfuß **barely** ADV kaum
bargain ['bɑ:rgən] 1 S günstiges Angebot, Schnäppchen *n*; (*Handel*) Geschäft *n* 2 V/I (ver)handeln
bar hop ['bɑ:rhɑ:p] V/I **we're going ~ping** wir machen einen Kneipenbummel
bark [bɑ:rk] 1 S (*Baum*) Rinde *f*; (*Hund*) Bellen *n* 2 V/I bellen
barkeep(er) ['bɑ:rki:p(ər)] S Barbesitzer(in) *m(f)*; Barkeeper *m*, Barmann *m*, Barfrau *f*
barley ['bɑ:rlɪ] S Gerste *f*
barn [bɑ:rn] S Scheune *f*
barracks ['bærəks] S PL Kaserne *f*
barrel ['bærəl] S Fass *n*
barrier ['bærɪər] S (*Straße*) Absperrung *f*; (*Eisenbahnübergang*) Schranke *f*
bartender ['bɑ:rtendər] S Barkeeper(in) *m(f)*
base [beɪs] 1 S Basis *f*; (*Lampe, Säule*) Fuß *m*; MIL Stützpunkt *m*; (*Baseball*) Base *n*, Mal *n* 2 V/T gründen (*on* auf *+akk*); **be ~d on sth** auf etw *dat* basieren
baseball S Baseball *m* **base-**

ball cap S Baseballmütze *f* **basement** S Kellergeschoss *n*

bash [bæʃ] *umg* **1** S Schlag *m*; (*Feier*) Party *f* **2** V/T hauen

basic ['beɪsɪk] ADJ einfach; Grund-; (*Unterschied etc*) grundlegend; (*im Prinzip*) grundsätzlich **basically** ADV im Grunde **basics** S PL **the ~** das Wesentliche

basil ['bæzl, 'beɪzl] S Basilikum *n*

basin ['beɪsn] S (Wasch)becken *n*

basis ['beɪsɪs] S Basis *f*; **on a monthly ~** monatlich

basket ['bæskət] S Korb *m* **basketball** S Basketball *m*

bass [beɪs] **1** S MUS Bass *m*; ZOOL Barsch *m* **2** ADJ MUS Bass-

bassinet [bæsə'net] S Kindertragetasche *f*

bastard ['bæstərd] S *vulg* Arschloch *n*

bat [bæt] S **1** S ZOOL Fledermaus *f*; SPORT (*Baseball*) Schlagholz *n* **2** V/I (*in Baseball*) schlagen

bath [bæθ] **1** S Bad *n*; (*in Badezimmer*) Badewanne *f*; **take a ~** baden **2** V/T (*Kind etc*) baden **bathe** [beɪð] V/T & V/I (*Wunde etc*) baden **bath foam** S Badeschaum *m* **bathing suit** ['beɪðɪŋsu:t] S Badeanzug *m* **bathrobe** ['bæθroʊb] S Bademantel *m* **bathroom** S Bad(ezimmer) *n*; Toilette *f*; **go to the ~** auf die Toilette gehen **bath towel** S Badetuch *n* **bathtub** S Badewanne *f*

baton [bə'tɑ:n] S MUS Taktstock *m*; (*Polizei*) Schlagstock *m*

batter ['bætər] **1** S GASTR Teig *m*; SPORT (*Baseball*) Schlagmann *m* **2** V/T heftig schlagen

battery ['bætərɪ] S ELEK Batterie *f* **battery charger** S Ladegerät *n*

battle ['bætl] S Schlacht *f*; *fig* Kampf *m* (*for* um) **battlefield** S Schlachtfeld *n*

bay [beɪ] S (*am Meer*) Bucht *f* **bay leaf** S Lorbeerblatt *n*

bayou ['baɪu:] S *sumpfiger Flussarm, besonders in Louisiana und anderen Südstaaten*

BBQ *abk* = barbecue; Barbecue *n*

B.C. *abk* = before Christ; vor Christi Geburt, v. Chr.

be ⟨was/were, been⟩ [bi:, wʌz/wɜ:r, bi:n] **1** V/I sein; werden; (*Lage*) liegen, sein; **she's French** sie ist Französin; **he wants to ~ a doctor** er will Arzt werden; **I'm too hot** mir ist zu warm; **she's not well** ihr geht's nicht gut; **the book is 15 dollars** das Buch kostet 15 Dollar; **how much is that altogether?** was macht das zusammen?; **how long have you been here?** wie lange bist du/sind Sie schon da?; **have you ever been to Mexico?** warst du/waren Sie schon einmal in Mexiko?; **there is/are** es gibt, es ist/sind **2** V/AUX (*Passiv*) werden; **he was run over** er ist überfahren worden, er wurde überfahren; (*Verlaufsform*) **I was walking on the beach** ich ging am Strand spazieren; (*Infinitiv: Vorhaben, Zwang*) **the car is to ~ sold** das Auto soll verkauft werden

beach [biːtʃ] S Strand *m*

bead [biːd] S (*aus Holz, Glas*) Perle *f*; (*Wasser*) Tropfen *m*

beak [biːk] S Schnabel *m*

beam [biːm] **1** S Balken *m*; (*Licht*) Strahl *m* **2** V/I strahlen

bean [biːn] S Bohne *f* **bean curd** S Tofu *m*

bear [ber] **1** V/T ⟨bore, borne⟩ [bɔːr, bɔːrn] tragen; ertragen **2** S Bär *m* **bearable** ADJ erträglich

beard [bɪrd] S Bart *m*

beat [biːt] **1** V/T ⟨beat, beaten/beat⟩ [ˈbiːtn] schlagen; prügeln; **~ sb at tennis** j-n im Tennis schlagen; **~ it!** *umg* hau ab! **2** S (*von Herz, Trommel etc*) Schlag *m*; MUS Takt *m* **beat up** V/T zusammenschlagen **beaten** [ˈbiːtn] *pperf von* beat; **off the ~ track** abgelegen

beautiful [ˈbjuːtəfʊl] ADJ schön; herrlich **beauty** [ˈbjuːtɪ] S Schönheit *f* **beauty spot** S lohnendes Ausflugsziel

beaver [ˈbiːvər] S Biber *m*

became [bɪˈkeɪm] *prät von* **become**

because [bɪˈkɑːz] **1** ADV & KONJ weil **2** PRÄP **~ of** wegen *+gen od dat*

become ⟨became, become⟩ [bɪˈkʌm, bɪˈkeɪm] V/I werden

bed [bed] S Bett *n*; (*im Garten*) Beet *n* **bed and breakfast** S Übernachtung *f* mit Frühstück; Pension *f* **bedding** S Bettzeug *n* **bed linen** S Bettwäsche *f* **bedroom** S Schlafzimmer *n* **bedspread** S Tagesdecke *f* **bedtime** S Schlafenszeit *f*

bee [biː] S Biene *f*

beech [biːtʃ] S Buche *f*

beef [biːf] S Rindfleisch *n* **beefburger** S Hamburger *m* **beefsteak tomato** ⟨-es *pl*⟩ S Fleischtomate *f*

beehive [ˈbiːhaɪv] S Bienenstock *m*

been [biːn] *pperf von* **be**

beer [bɪr] S Bier *n*

beet [biːt] S Rote Beete

beetle [ˈbiːtl] S Käfer *m*

before [bɪˈfɔːr] **1** PRÄP vor; **the day ~ yesterday** vorgestern **2** KONJ bevor **3** ADV vorher; **have you been there ~?** waren Sie/warst du schon einmal dort?

beforehand ADV vorher

beg [beg] **1** V/T **~ sb to do sth** j-n inständig bitten, etw zu tun **2** V/I betteln (*for* um)

began [bɪˈgæn] *prät von* **begin** **beggar** [ˈbegər] S Bettler(in) *m(f)*
begin ⟨began, begun⟩ [bɪˈgɪn, bɪˈgæn, bɪˈgʌn] VT & VI anfangen, beginnen **beginner** S Anfänger(in) *m(f)* **beginning** S Anfang *m* **begun** [bɪˈgʌn] *pperf von* **begin**
behalf [bɪˈhæf] S **on ~ of, in ~ of** im Namen/Auftrag von; **on my ~** für mich
behave [bɪˈheɪv] VI sich benehmen **behavior** [bɪˈheɪvɪər] S Benehmen *n*
behind [bɪˈhaɪnd] **1** PRÄP hinter **2** ADV hinten **3** S *umg* Hinterteil *n*
beige [beɪʒ] ADJ beige
being [ˈbiːɪŋ] S (*Existenz*) Dasein *n*; (*Person*) Wesen *n*
belch [beltʃ] **1** S Rülpser *m* **2** VI rülpsen
Belgian [ˈbeldʒən] **1** ADJ belgisch **2** S Belgier(in) *m(f)* **Belgium** [ˈbeldʒəm] S Belgien *n*
belief [bɪˈliːf] S Glaube *m* (*in* an *+akk*), Überzeugung *f* **believe** [bɪˈliːv] VT glauben (*in* an *+akk*) **believe in** VI glauben an *+akk*
bell [bel] S (*Kirche*) Glocke *f*; (*Fahrrad, Tür*) Klingel *f* **bellboy, bellhop** S Page *m* **bell pepper** S Paprikaschote *f*, Paprika *m*
belly [ˈbelɪ] S Bauch *m* **belly button** S *umg* Bauchnabel *m*
belong [bɪˈlɑːŋ] VI gehören (*to sb* j-m); (*einem Klub etc*) angehören *+dat* **belongings** S PL Habe *f*
below [bɪˈloʊ] **1** PRÄP unter **2** ADV unten
belt [belt] S Gürtel *m*; (*in Auto*) Gurt *m* **beltway** S Umgehungsstraße *f*
bench [bentʃ] S Bank *f*
bend [bend] **1** S Biegung *f*; (*Straße*) Kurve *f* **2** VT ⟨bent, bent⟩ [bent] biegen; (*Kopf, Arm*) beugen **3** VI sich biegen; (*Person*) sich beugen **bend down** VI sich bücken
beneath [bɪˈniːθ] **1** PRÄP unter **2** ADV darunter
beneficial [benəˈfɪʃl] ADJ gut, nützlich (*to* für) **benefit** [ˈbenəfɪt] **1** S Vorteil *m*, Nutzen *m*; (*für Arbeitslosen etc*) Unterstützung *f*; **for your ~** deinetwegen **2** VT guttun *+dat* **3** VI Nutzen ziehen (*from* aus)
bent [bent] **1** *prät, pperf von* **bend** **2** ADJ krumm; *umg* korrupt
berry [ˈberɪ] S Beere *f*
beside [bɪˈsaɪd] PRÄP neben; **~ the sea** am Meer **besides** [bɪˈsaɪdz] **1** PRÄP außer **2** ADV außerdem
best [best] **1** ADJ beste(r, s); **the ~ thing (to do) would be to ...** das Beste wäre zu ... **2** S der/die/das Beste; **all the ~** alles Gute **3** ADV am besten
best man ⟨men⟩ S Trauzeuge *m*

bet ⟨bet/betted, bet/betted⟩ [bet, betɪd] **1** VT & VI wetten (*on* auf *+akk*); **you ~** *umg* und ob!; **I ~ he'll be late** er kommt mit Sicherheit zu spät **2** S Wette *f*

betray [bɪ'treɪ] VT verraten

better ['betər] ADJ & ADV besser; **get ~** (*nach Krankheit*) sich erholen, wieder gesund werden; (*in Fähigkeiten*) sich verbessern; **I'm much ~ today** es geht mir heute viel besser; **you'd ~ go** du solltest/Sie sollten lieber gehen

between [bɪ'twi:n] **1** PRÄP zwischen; unter **2** ADV (**in**) **~** dazwischen

beware [bɪ'wer] VT **~ of sth** sich vor etw *dat* hüten

beyond [bɪ'jɑ:nd] **1** PRÄP (*räumlich*) jenseits *+gen*; (*zeitlich*) über ... hinaus; (*von Verantwortung etc*) außerhalb *+gen* **2** ADV darüber hinaus

biased ['baɪəst] ADJ voreingenommen

bib [bɪb] S Latz *m*

Bible ['baɪbl] S Bibel *f*; **~ Belt** *die frommen Staaten des Südens der USA*

bicycle ['baɪsɪkl] S Fahrrad *n*

bid [bɪd] **1** VT ⟨bid, bid⟩ bieten **2** S Versuch *m*; (*bei Auktion*) Gebot *n*

big [bɪg] ADJ groß; **it's no ~ deal** *umg* (das) macht nichts, keine Sorge **big-headed** ADJ eingebildet

bike [baɪk] S Rad *n* **bike path, bikeway** S Radweg *m*

bikini [bɪ'ki:nɪ] S Bikini *m*

bilingual [baɪ'lɪŋgwəl] ADJ zweisprachig

bill [bɪl] S *Geld* Banknote *f*; Rechnung *f*; POL Gesetzentwurf *m*; ZOOL Schnabel *m* **billfold** ['bɪlfoʊld] S Brieftasche *f*

billion ['bɪlɪən] S Milliarde *f*

bin [bɪn] S Behälter *m*

bind ⟨bound, bound⟩ [baɪnd, baʊnd] VT binden; zusammenbinden; (*Wunde*) verbinden

binge [bɪndʒ] S *umg* Sauferei *f*

binoculars [bɪ'nɑ:kjələrz] S PL Fernglas *n*

biological [baɪə'lɑ:dʒɪkəl] ADJ biologisch **biology** [baɪ'ɑ:lədʒɪ] S Biologie *f*

birch [bɜ:rtʃ] S Birke *f*

bird [bɜ:rd] S Vogel *m*

birth [bɜ:rθ] S Geburt *f* **birth certificate** S Geburtsurkunde *f* **birthday** S Geburtstag *m*; **happy ~** herzlichen Glückwunsch zum Geburtstag **birthday card** S Geburtstagskarte *f* **birthday party** S Geburtstagsfeier *f* **birthplace** S Geburtsort *m*

biscuit ['bɪskɪt] S *Art weiches Brötchen*

bisexual [baɪ'sekʃʊəl] ADJ bisexuell

bishop ['bɪʃəp] S Bischof *m*

bit [bɪt] **1** *prät von* bite **2** S Stück(chen) *n*; IT Bit *n*; **a ~ (of ...)** ein bisschen ...; **a ~ tired**

etwas müde; **~ by ~** allmählich; **for a ~** ein Weilchen; **quite a ~** ganz schön viel
bitch [bɪtʃ] **1** S Hündin *f*; *pej* (*Frau*) Miststück *n*, Zicke *f*; **son of a ~** *vulg* Hurensohn *m*, Scheißkerl *m* **2** V/I meckern (*about* über *+akk*) **bitchy** ADJ gemein, zickig
bite [baɪt] **1** V/T & V/I ⟨bit, bitten⟩ [bɪt, 'bɪtn] beißen **2** S Biss *m*, Bissen *m*; (*von Insekt*) Stich *m*; **have a ~** eine Kleinigkeit essen **bitten** *pperf von* bite
bitter ['bɪtər] ADJ bitter
black [blæk] ADJ schwarz; **~ eye** blaues Auge **blackberry** S Brombeere *f* **blackbird** S (*in Europa*) Amsel *f* **black box** S FLUG Flugschreiber *m* **blackcurrant** S Schwarze Johannisbeere **blackmail** **1** S Erpressung *f* **2** V/T erpressen **blackout** S MED Ohnmacht *f*
bladder ['blædər] S Blase *f*
blade [bleɪd] S Klinge *f*; (*von Propeller*) Blatt *n*; (*von Gras*) Halm *m*
blame [bleɪm] **1** S Schuld *f* **2** V/T **~ sth on sb** j-m die Schuld an etw *dat* geben; **he is to ~** er ist daran schuld
bland [blænd] ADJ (*Geschmack*) fade
blank [blæŋk] ADJ leer, unbeschrieben; (*Blick*) ausdruckslos
blanket ['blæŋkət] S (Woll)decke *f*
blast [blæst] **1** S Windstoß *m*; (*Explosion*) Druckwelle *f* **2** V/T sprengen
blaze [bleɪz] **1** V/I lodern; (*Sonne*) brennen **2** S Brand *m*, Feuer *n*
bleach [bli:tʃ] **1** S Bleichmittel *n* **2** V/T bleichen **bleachers** S PL unüberdachte Stadiontribüne
bleed ⟨bled, bled⟩ [bli:d, bled] V/I bluten
bleeper ['bli:pər] S *umg* Piepser *m*
blend [blend] **1** S Mischung *f* **2** V/T mischen **3** V/I sich mischen **blender** S Mixer *m*
bless [bles] V/T segnen; **~ you!** Gesundheit! **blessing** S Segen *m*
blew [blu:] *prät von* **blow**
blind [blaɪnd] **1** ADJ blind; (*Ecke*) unübersichtlich **2** S Rollo *n* **3** V/T blenden **blind alley** S Sackgasse *f* **blind spot** S AUTO toter Winkel
blink [blɪŋk] V/I blinzeln; (*von Licht*) blinken **blinker** S AUTO Blinker *m*
bliss [blɪs] S Glückseligkeit *f*
blister ['blɪstər] S Blase *f*
blizzard ['blɪzərd] S Schneesturm *m*
block [blɑ:k] **1** S (*aus Holz, Stein, Eis*) Block *m*, Klotz *m*; (*Gebäude*) Häuserblock *m*; **two ~s from here** zwei Straßen weiter **2** V/T (*Straße*) blockieren; (*Abfluss*) verstopfen **blockage**

['blɑːkɪdʒ] S Verstopfung *f* **blockbuster** ['blɑːkbʌstər] S Knüller *m*; (*Film*) Kinohit *m* **block letters** S PL Blockschrift *f*

blog [blɑːg] S IT Blog *m od n*

blond(e) [blɑːnd] **1** ADJ blond **2** S Blondine *f*, blonder Typ

blood [blʌd] S Blut *n* **blood count** S Blutbild *n* **blood donor** S Blutspender(in) *m(f)* **blood poisoning** S Blutvergiftung *f* **blood pressure** S Blutdruck *m* **blood sample** S Blutprobe *f* **blood sausage** S ≈ Blutwurst *f* **blood type** S Blutgruppe *f* **bloody** ADJ (*Hände, Schlacht*) blutig

bloom [bluːm] **1** S Blüte *f* **2** V/I blühen

blossom ['blɑːsəm] **1** S Blüte *f* **2** V/I blühen

blouse [blaʊz] S Bluse *f*

blow [bloʊ] **1** S Schlag *m* **2** V/I & V/T ⟨blew, blown⟩ [bluː, bloʊn] (*Wind*) wehen, blasen; (*Trompete etc*) blasen; **~ one's nose** sich die Nase putzen **blow up** **1** V/I explodieren **2** V/T sprengen; (*Ballon etc*) aufblasen; FOTO vergrößern **blow-dry** V/T föhnen **blow job** S *vulg* **give sb a ~** j-m einen blasen **blown** [bloʊn] *pperf von* **blow**

BLT *abk* = bacon, lettuce and tomato sandwich *mit Frühstücksspeck, Kopfsalat und Tomaten belegtes Sandwich*

blue [bluː] ADJ blau; *umg* (*unglücklich*) trübsinnig, niedergeschlagen **blueberry** S Blaubeere *f* **blue cheese** S Blauschimmelkäse *m* **blues** S PL **have the ~** *umg* niedergeschlagen sein

blunt [blʌnt] ADJ (*Messer*) stumpf; *fig* unverblümt

blurred [blɜːrd] ADJ verschwommen, unklar

blush [blʌʃ] V/I erröten

board [bɔːrd] **1** S Brett *n*; (*Komitee*) Ausschuss *m*; (*in Firma*) Vorstand *m*; **~ and lodging** Unterkunft und Verpflegung; **on ~** an Bord **2** V/T (*Zug, Bus*) einsteigen in *+akk*; (*Schiff*) an Bord *+gen* gehen **board game** S Brettspiel *n* **boarding card**, **boarding pass** S Bordkarte *f*, Einsteigekarte *f* **boarding school** S Internat *n* **boardwalk** S Holzsteg *m*; (*am Strand*) (hölzerne) Uferpromenade

boast [boʊst] **1** V/I prahlen (*about* mit) **2** S Prahlerei *f*

boat [boʊt] S Boot *n*, Schiff *n*

bobby pin ['bɑːbɪpɪn] S Haarklammer *f*

bobcat ['bɑːbkæt] S Rotluchs *m*

bobsled ['bɑːbsled] S Bob *m*

body ['bɑːdɪ] S Körper *m*; (*toter Körper*) Leiche *f*; (*Auto*) Karosserie *f* **bodyguard** S Leibwächter *m*, Leibwache *f* **body piercing** S Piercing *n* **body-**

work S Karosserie *f*
boil [bɔıl] **1** VT & VI kochen **2** S MED Geschwür *n* **boiler** S Boiler *m* **boiling** ADJ kochend (heiß)
bold [boʊld] ADJ kühn, mutig; (*Farbe*) kräftig; (*Schrift*) fett
bomb [bɑ:m] **1** S Bombe *f*; **that's the ~!** das ist (ja) der Hammer! **2** VT bombardieren
bond [bɑ:nd] S Bindung *f*; FIN Anleihe *f*
bone [boʊn] S Knochen *m*; (*bei Fisch*) Gräte *f* **boner** S *umg* Schnitzer *m*; *vulg* (*Erektion*) Ständer *m*
bonfire ['bɑ:nfaır] S Feuer *n* (im Freien)
bonus ['boʊnəs] S Bonus *m*, Prämie *f*
boo [bu:] **1** VT auspfeifen **2** VI buhen **3** S Buhruf *m*
book [bʊk] **1** S Buch *n*; (*Briefmarken etc*) Heft *n* **2** VT bestellen; buchen; **fully ~ed (up)** ausgebucht; (*Vorstellung*) ausverkauft **book in** VT eintragen; **be booked in at a hotel** ein Zimmer in einem Hotel bestellt haben **bookcase** S Bücherregal *n* **booking** S Buchung *f* **booking office** S BAHN Fahrkartenschalter *m*; THEAT Vorverkaufsstelle *f* **booklet** S Broschüre *f* **bookmark** S *a.* IT Lesezeichen *n* **bookshelf** S Bücherbord *n*; **bookshelves** Bücherregal *n* **bookstore** S Buchhandlung *f*
boom [bu:m] **1** S Boom *m*; (*Geräusch*) Dröhnen *n* **2** VI boomen; *umg* florieren
boost [bu:st] **1** S Auftrieb *m* **2** VT (*Verkauf etc*) ankurbeln; (*Profit etc*) steigern **booster (shot)** S Wiederholungsimpfung *f*
boot [bu:t] **1** S Stiefel *m* **2** VT IT laden, booten
booth [bu:θ] S (*auf Markt*) Bude *f*; (*auf Messe*) Stand *m*
booze [bu:z] **1** S *umg* Alkohol *m* **2** VI *umg* saufen
border ['bɔ:rdər] S Grenze *f*; (*Ende, Kante*) Rand *m*
bore [bɔ:r] **1** *prät von* bear **2** VT (*Loch*) bohren; (*Person*) langweilen **3** S langweilige Sache **bored** ADJ **be ~** sich langweilen **boredom** S Langeweile *f* **boring** ADJ langweilig
born [bɔ:rn] ADJ **he was ~ in Los Angeles** er ist in Los Angeles geboren
borne [bɔ:rn] *pperf von* bear
borough ['bʌroʊ] S Bezirk *m*
borrow ['bɑ:roʊ] VT borgen
Bosnia and Herzegovina ['bɑ:znıə ən hɜ:rtsəgoʊ'vi:nə] S Bosnien-Herzegowina *n*
boss [bɑ:s] S Chef(in) *m(f)*, Boss *m*
both [boʊθ] **1** ADJ beide; **~ the books** beide Bücher **2** PRON beide; beides; **~ (of) the boys** die beiden Jungs; **I like ~ of them** ich mag sie (alle)

beide **3** ADV **~ X and Y** sowohl X als auch Y
bother ['bɑːðər] **1** V/T ärgern, belästigen; **it doesn't ~ me** das stört mich nicht; **I'm not ~ed** das ist mir egal **2** V/I sich kümmern (*about* um); **don't ~** (das ist) nicht nötig, lass es! **3** S Mühe *f*, Ärger *m*
bottle ['bɑːtl] **1** S Flasche *f* **2** V/T (in Flaschen) abfüllen **bottle opener** S Flaschenöffner *m*
bottom ['bɑːtəm] **1** S (*von Gefäß etc*) Boden *m*; (*von Gegenstand*) Unterseite *f*; *umg* (*von Person*) Po *m*; **at the ~ of the sea/table/page** auf dem Meeresgrund/am Tabellenende/unten auf der Seite **2** ADJ unterste(r, s); **be ~ of the class** Klassenletzte(r) sein
bought [bɒːt] *prät, pperf von* buy
bounce [baʊns] V/I (*Ball*) springen, aufprallen
bound [baʊnd] **1** *prät, pperf von* **bind 2** ADJ gebunden; verpflichtet; **it's ~ to happen** es muss so kommen; **be ~ for ...** auf dem Weg nach ... sein **boundary** ['baʊndərɪ] S Grenze *f*
bouquet [bʊ'keɪ] S (*Blumen*) Strauß *m*; (*Wein*) Blume *f*
bow 1 [boʊ] S Schleife *f*; (*Instrument, Waffe*) Bogen *m* **2** [baʊ] V/I sich verbeugen **3** [baʊ] S Verbeugung *f*; (*Schiff*) Bug *m*
bowels ['baʊəlz] S PL Darm *m*
bowl [boʊl] **1** S Schüssel *f*, Schale *f*; (*für Tier*) Napf *m*; (*zum Kegeln*) Kugel *f* **2** V/T (*Kugel*) rollen **bowling** ['boʊlɪŋ] S Kegeln *n*; Bowling *n* **bowling alley** S Kegelbahn *f*
bow tie [boʊ'taɪ] S Fliege *f*
box [bɑːks] S Schachtel *f*, Karton *m*, Kasten *m*; (*auf Formular*) Kästchen *n*; THEAT Loge *f* **boxing** S SPORT Boxen *n* **box office** S (*Kino, Theater*) Kasse *f*
boy [bɔɪ] S Junge *m* **boyfriend** ['bɔɪfrend] S (fester) Freund **boy scout** S Pfadfinder *m*
bra [brɑː] S BH *m*
bracelet ['breɪslət] S Armband *n*
braces ['breɪsəs] S PL (*für Zähne*) Spange *f*
bracket ['brækət] **1** S (*im Text*) Klammer *f*; TECH Träger *m* **2** V/T einklammern
brag [bræg] V/I angeben
braid [breɪd] **1** S Zopf *m*; Borte *f* **2** V/T flechten
brain [breɪn] S ANAT Gehirn *n*, Verstand *m*; **~s** *pl* (*Intelligenz*) Grips *m*
brake [breɪk] **1** S Bremse *f* **2** V/I bremsen **brake fluid** S Bremsflüssigkeit *f* **brake light** S Bremslicht *n* **brake pedal** S Bremspedal *n*
branch [bræntʃ] S Ast *m*, Zweig *m*; (*von Geschäft, Bank*

etc) Filiale *f*, Zweigstelle *f* **branch off** V/I abzweigen
brand [brænd] S WIRTSCH Marke *f*
brand-new [brænd'nu:] ADJ (funkel)nagelneu
brandy ['brændɪ] S Weinbrand *m*
brash [bræʃ] ADJ frech
brass [bræs] S Messing *n*
brave [breɪv] ADJ tapfer, mutig
Brazil [brə'zɪl] S Brasilien *n* **brazil nut** [brə'zɪlnʌt] S Paranuss *f*
bread [bred] S Brot *n* **breadcrumbs** S PL Brotkrumen *pl*; GASTR Paniermehl *n* **breaded** ADJ paniert
breadth [bredθ] S Breite *f*
break [breɪk] **1** S (*Knochen, Beziehung*) Bruch *m*; (*Unterbrechung*) Pause *f*; (*Reise*) Kurzurlaub *m*; **give me a ~** hör auf damit! **2** V/T <broke, broken> [broʊk, 'broʊkən] (*Knochen*) brechen; (*Stock, Porzellan*) zerbrechen; (*Gerät*) kaputt machen; (*Versprechen*) nicht halten; (*Schweigen*) brechen; (*Gesetz*) verletzen; (*Neuigkeit*) mitteilen (*to sb* j-m); **I broke my leg** ich habe mir das Bein gebrochen **3** V/I (auseinander)brechen; zerbrechen; (*Gerät, Spielzeug*) kaputtgehen; (*Tag*) anbrechen; (*Neuigkeit*) bekannt werden **break down** V/I eine Panne haben; (*Maschine*) versagen; (*Person*) zusammenbrechen **break in** V/I einbrechen **break into** V/T einbrechen in +*akk* **break off** V/I & V/T abbrechen **break out** V/I ausbrechen **break up** **1** V/I aufbrechen; (*Versammlung*) sich auflösen; (*Ehe*) in die Brüche gehen; (*Paar*) sich trennen **2** V/T aufbrechen; (*Ehe*) zerstören; (*Versammlung*) auflösen
breakdown S Panne *f*; (*Maschine*) Störung *f*; (*Person, System etc*) Zusammenbruch *m*
breakfast ['brekfəst] S Frühstück *n*; **have ~** frühstücken
break-in ['breɪkɪn] S Einbruch *m* **breakup** ['breɪkʌp] S (*Versammlung*) Auflösung *f*; (*Ehe*) Zerrüttung *f*
breast [brest] S Brust *f* **breastfeed** V/T stillen **breaststroke** S Brustschwimmen *n*
breath [breθ] S Atem *m* **breathalyze** ['breθəlaɪz] V/T (ins Röhrchen) blasen lassen **breathalyzer®** S Promillemesser *m* **breathe** [bri:ð] V/T & V/I atmen **breathless** ['breθləs] ADJ atemlos **breathtaking** ['breθteɪkɪŋ] ADJ atemberaubend
bred [bred] *prät, pperf von* breed **breed** [bri:d] **1** S Rasse *f* **2** V/I <bred, bred> [bred] sich vermehren **3** V/T züchten
breeze [bri:z] S Brise *f*
brew [bru:] V/T (*Bier*) brauen; (*Tee*) kochen **brewery** S

Brauerei *f*
bribe [braɪb] **1** S Bestechungsgeld *n* **2** V/T bestechen **bribery** ['braɪbərɪ] S Bestechung *f*
brick [brɪk] S Backstein *m*
bride [braɪd] S Braut *f* **bridegroom** S Bräutigam *m* **bridesmaid** S Brautjungfer *f*
bridge [brɪdʒ] S Brücke *f*; (*Karten*) Bridge *n*
brief [bri:f] **1** ADJ kurz **2** V/T instruieren (*on* über *+akk*) **briefcase** S Aktentasche *f* **briefs** S PL Slip *m*
bright [braɪt] ADJ hell; (*Farbe*) leuchtend; (*sonnig*) heiter; (*schlau*) intelligent; (*Idee*) glänzend **brighten up** V/I sich aufheitern; (*Person*) fröhlicher werden
brilliant ['brɪljənt] ADJ strahlend; (*Person*) brillant; (*Idee*) glänzend; *umg* **it was ~** es war genial
brim [brɪm] S Rand *m*
bring ⟨brought, brought⟩ [brɪŋ, brɒ:t] V/T bringen; mitbringen **bring back** V/T zurückbringen; (*Erinnerungen*) wecken **bring in** V/T hereinbringen; (*neues System etc*) einführen **bring out** V/T herausbringen **bring up** V/T (*Kind*) aufziehen; (*Frage*) zur Sprache bringen
Britain ['brɪtn] S Großbritannien *n* **British** ['brɪtɪʃ] **1** ADJ britisch **2** S **the ~** *pl* die Briten *pl*
broad [brɒ:d] ADJ breit; (*Akzent*) stark; **in ~ daylight** am helllichten Tag **broadband** ['brɒ:dbænd] IT **1** S Breitband *n* **2** ADJ Breitband- **broadcast** ['brɒ:dkæst] **1** S Sendung *f* **2** *irr v/t & v/i* senden; übertragen
broccoli ['brɑ:kəlɪ] S Brokkoli *pl*
brochure [broʊ'ʃʊr] S Prospekt *m*, Broschüre *f*
broil [brɔɪl] V/T (auf dem Rost) braten, grillen
broke [broʊk] **1** *prät von* break **2** ADJ *umg* pleite **broken** ['broʊkən] *pperf von* break
broker ['broʊkər] S Makler(in) *m(f)*
bronchitis [brɑ:ŋ'kaɪtəs] S Bronchitis *f*
brooch [broʊtʃ] S Brosche *f*
broom [bru:m] S Besen *m*
brothel ['brɑ:θl] S Bordell *n*
brother ['brʌðər] S Bruder *m* **brother-in-law** ⟨brothers-in-law⟩ S Schwager *m*
brought [brɒ:t] *prät, pperf von* bring
brow [braʊ] S (Augen)braue *f*; (*von Kopf*) Stirn *f*
brown [braʊn] ADJ braun **brown bread** S Mischbrot *n*, Vollkornbrot *n* **brownie** ['braʊnɪ] S GASTR Brownie *m* **brown paper** S Packpapier *n* **brown rice** S Naturreis *m*
browse [braʊz] V/I (*in Buch*)

blättern; (*in Laden*) herumschauen **browser** S IT Browser *m*
bruise [bru:z] **1** S blauer Fleck **2** V/T **~ one's arm** sich einen blauen Fleck (am Arm) holen
brush [brʌʃ] **1** S Bürste *f*, Handbesen *m*; (*zum Malen*) Pinsel *m* **2** V/T bürsten; fegen; **~ one's teeth** sich die Zähne putzen
Brussels sprouts [brʌslz'spraʊts] S PL Rosenkohl *m*, Kohlsprossen *pl*
brutality [bru:'tælɪtɪ] S Brutalität *f*
bubble ['bʌbl] S Blase *f* **bubble bath** S Schaumbad *n*; Badeschaum *m* **bubbly** ['bʌblɪ] **1** ADJ sprudelnd; (*Person*) quirlig **2** S *umg* Schampus *m*
buck [bʌk] S (*Geld*) Dollar *m*; (*Tier*) Bock *m*
bucket ['bʌkət] S Eimer *m*
buckle ['bʌkl] **1** S Schnalle *f* **2** V/I TECH sich verbiegen **3** V/T zuschnallen
buckskin ['bʌkskɪn] S Wildleder *n*
bud [bʌd] S Knospe *f*; → buddy
Buddhist ['bu:dɪst] **1** ADJ buddhistisch **2** S Buddhist(in) *m(f)*
buddy ['bʌdɪ] S *umg* Kumpel *m*
budget ['bʌdʒət] **1** S Budget *n* **2** ADJ preisgünstig
buffalo ⟨-es *pl*⟩ ['bʌfəloʊ] S Büffel *m* **buffalo wings** S PL gegrillte *od* frittierte Hähnchenflügel *pl*
buffet [bə'feɪ] S (kaltes) Büfett
bug [bʌg] **1** S IT Bug *m*, Programmfehler *m*; (*zum Abhören*) Wanze *f*; *Tier* Insekt *n*; *umg* (*Krankheit*) Infektion *f* **2** V/T *umg* nerven
buggy® ['bʌgɪ] S (*für Baby*) Buggy® *m*; Kinderwagen *m*
build ⟨built, built⟩ [bɪld, bɪlt] V/T bauen **building** S Gebäude *n* **building site** S Baustelle *f* **built** *prät, pperf von* build **built-in** ADJ (*Schrank etc*) Einbau-, eingebaut
bulb [bʌlb] S BOT (Blumen)zwiebel *f*; ELEK Glühbirne *f*
Bulgaria [bʌl'gerɪə] S Bulgarien *n* **Bulgarian** **1** ADJ bulgarisch **2** S (*Person*) Bulgare *m*, Bulgarin *f*; (*Sprache*) Bulgarisch *n*
bulimia [bə'lɪmɪə] S Bulimie *f*
bulky ['bʌlkɪ] ADJ sperrig; (*Person*) stämmig
bull [bʊl] S Stier *m* **bulldozer** ['bʊldoʊzər] S Planierraupe *f*
bullet ['bʊlɪt] S Kugel *f*
bulletin ['bʊlɪtɪn] S Bulletin *n*, Bekanntmachung *f* **bulletin board** S schwarzes Brett
bullshit ['bʊlʃɪt] S *umg* Scheiß *m*
bully ['bʊlɪ] S Tyrann *m*
bum [bʌm] S *umg* Penner *m*
bumblebee ['bʌmblbi:] S Hummel *f*

bump [bʌmp] **1** S *umg* Beule *f*; (*Straße*) Unebenheit *f*; (*Schlag*) Stoß *m* **2** V/T stoßen; **~ one's head** sich den Kopf anschlagen (*on* an *+dat*) **bump into** V/T stoßen gegen; *umg* (*treffen*) (zufällig) begegnen *+dat* **bumper** **1** S AUTO Stoßstange *f* **2** ADJ Riesen-; Rekord- **bumpy** ['bʌmpɪ] ADJ holp(e)rig
bun [bʌn] S (süßes) Brötchen
bunch [bʌntʃ] S (*Blumen*) Strauß *m*; *umg* (*Menschen*) Haufen *m*; **~ of keys** Schlüsselbund *m*
bundle ['bʌndl] S Bündel *n*
bunk [bʌŋk] S Koje *f* **bunk bed(s)** S (PL) Etagenbett *n*
bunny ['bʌnɪ] S Häschen *n*
buoy ['bu:ɪ] S Boje *f*
burden ['bɜ:rdn] S Last *f*
bureau ['bjʊroʊ] S Büro *n*; (*von Regierung*) Amt *n* **bureaucracy** [bjʊ'rɑ:krəsɪ] S Bürokratie *f*
burger ['bɜ:rgər] S Hamburger *m* **burger joint** S Hamburgerlokal *n*
burglar ['bɜ:rglər] S Einbrecher(in) *m(f)* **burglar alarm** S Alarmanlage *f* **burglarize** V/T einbrechen in *+akk* **burglary** S Einbruch *m*
burial ['berɪəl] S Beerdigung *f*
burn ⟨burnt/burned, burned⟩ [bɜ:rn, bɜ:rnt, bɜ:rnd] **1** V/T verbrennen; (*Essen*) anbrennen; **~ one's hand** sich die Hand verbrennen **2** V/I brennen **3** S Brandwunde *f*
burp [bɜ:rp] **1** V/I rülpsen **2** V/T (*Baby*) aufstoßen lassen
burst ⟨burst, burst⟩ [bɜ:rst] **1** V/T platzen lassen **2** V/I platzen; **~ into tears** in Tränen ausbrechen
bury ['berɪ] V/T begraben; beerdigen; (*Schatz*) vergraben
bus [bʌs] **1** S Bus *m* **2** V/T **~ tables** (*im Restaurant*) das Geschirr von den Tischen abräumen **busboy** S Hilfskellner *m* **bus driver** S Busfahrer(in) *m(f)* **busgirl** S Hilfskellnerin *f*
bush [bʊʃ] S Busch *m*
business ['bɪznəs] S Geschäft *n*, Unternehmen *n*; (*Angelegenheit*) Sache *f*; **I'm here on ~** ich bin geschäftlich hier; **it's none of your ~** das geht dich nichts an **business card** S Visitenkarte *f* **business class** S FLUG Businessclass *f* **business hours** S PL Geschäftsstunden *pl* **businessman** ⟨-men *pl*⟩ S Geschäftsmann *m* **businesswoman** ⟨-women *pl*⟩ S Geschäftsfrau *f*
bus service S Busverbindung *f* **bus shelter** S Wartehäuschen *n* **bus station** S Busbahnhof *m* **bus stop** S Bushaltestelle *f*
bust [bʌst] **1** S Büste *f* **2** ADJ kaputt; **go ~** Pleite gehen
busy ['bɪzɪ] ADJ beschäftigt; (*Straße, Platz*) belebt; *Telefon*

besetzt; **~ signal** Besetztzeichen *n*
but [bʌt, bət] **1** KONJ aber; nur; **not this ~ that** nicht dies, sondern das **2** PRÄP außer; **nothing ~ ...** nichts als ...; **the last/next house ~ one** das vorletzte/übernächste Haus
butcher ['bʊtʃər] S Metzger(in) *m(f)*
butt [bʌt] S *umg* Hintern *m*
butter ['bʌtər] S Butter *f* **butterfly** S Schmetterling *m*
buttocks ['bʌtəks] S PL Gesäß *n*
button ['bʌtn] **1** S Knopf *m*; Anstecker *m* **2** V/T zuknöpfen **buttonhole** S Knopfloch *n*
buy [baɪ] **1** S Kauf *m* **2** V/T ⟨bought, bought⟩ [bɒ:t] kaufen (*from* von) **buyer** S Käufer(in) *m(f)*
buzz [bʌz] **1** S Summen *n* **2** V/I summen **buzzer** ['bʌzər] S Summer *m*
by [baɪ] **1** PRÄP (*Verfasser*) von; (*Verkehrsmittel*) mit; (*in der Nähe von*) bei, an; (*anhand von*) durch; (*nicht später als*) bis; (*gemäß*) nach; **go ~ train/bus/car** mit dem Zug/Bus/Auto fahren; **send ~ mail** mit der Post® schicken; **~ arrangement** nach Vereinbarung; **a house ~ the river** ein Haus am *od* beim Fluss; **leave ~ the back door** durch die Hintertür rausgehen; **~ day/night** tags/nachts; **they'll be here ~ five** bis fünf Uhr müssten sie hier sein; **rise ~ 10%** um 10% steigen; **~ oneself** allein **2** ADV vorbei
bye-bye ['baɪbaɪ] INT *umg* Wiedersehen, tschüss
bypass S Umgehungsstraße *f*; MED Bypass *m* **byroad** S Nebenstraße *f* **bystander** S Zuschauer(in) *m(f)*
byte [baɪt] S Byte *n*

C [si:] *abk* = Celsius; C
c *abk* = circa; ca.
CA *abk* = California; Kalifornien *n*
cab [kæb] S Taxi *n*
cabbage ['kæbɪdʒ] S Kohl *m*
cabin ['kæbɪn] S SCHIFF Kajüte *f*; FLUG Passagierraum *m*; (*Holzhaus*) Hütte *f* **cabin crew** S Flugbegleitpersonal *n*
cabinet ['kæbɪnət] S Schrank *m*, Vitrine *f*; POL Kabinett *n*
cable ['keɪbl] S ELEK Kabel *n* **cable-car** S Seilbahn *f* **cable television**, **cablevision** S Kabelfernsehen *n*
cabstand ['kæbstænd] S Taxistand *m*
cactus ['kæktəs] S Kaktus *m*
Caesar salad [si:zər'sæləd] S *gemischter römischer Salat mit Croûtons*

café [kæ'feɪ] S Café *n* **cafeteria** [kæfə'tɪrɪə] S Cafeteria *f*
caffeine ['kæfi:n] S Koffein *n*
cage [keɪdʒ] S Käfig *m*
Cajun ['keɪdʒən] **1** S *französischstämmige(r) Bewohner(in) Louisianas* **2** ADJ GASTR scharf gewürzt
cake [keɪk] S Kuchen *m* **cake shop** S Konditorei *f*
calculate ['kælkjəleɪt] V/T berechnen; kalkulieren **calculator** ['kælkjəleɪtər] S Taschenrechner *m*
calendar ['kæləndər] S Kalender *m*
calf ⟨calves *pl*⟩ [kæf, kævz] S Kalb *n*; ANAT Wade *f*
California [kælɪ'fɔ:rnɪə] S Kalifornien *n*
call [kɒ:l] **1** V/T rufen; (*bezeichnen, Namen geben*) nennen; TEL anrufen; IT, FLUG aufrufen; **what's this ~ed?** wie heißt das? **2** V/I rufen (*for help* um Hilfe); (*besuchen*) vorbeikommen; (*Zug*) **~ at … in …** halten **3** S Ruf *m*; TEL Anruf *m*; IT, FLUG Aufruf *m*; **make a ~** telefonieren; **give sb a ~** j-n anrufen; **be on ~** Bereitschaftsdienst haben **call back** V/T & V/I zurückrufen **call for** V/T (*vom Bahnhof etc*) abholen; (*fordern*) verlangen **call off** V/T absagen **caller** S Besucher(in) *m(f)*; TEL Anrufer(in) *m(f)*
calm [kɑ:m] **1** S Stille *f*, Ruhe *f*; (*Meer*) Flaute *f* **2** V/T beruhigen **3** ADJ ruhig **calm down** V/I sich beruhigen
calorie ['kælərɪ] S Kalorie *f*
calves [kævz] *pl von* **calf**
camcorder ['kæmkɔ:rdər] S Camcorder *m*
came [keɪm] *prät von* **come**
camera ['kæmərə] S Fotoapparat *m*, Kamera *f* **camera phone** S Fotohandy *n*
camomile ['kæməmaɪl] S Kamille *f*
camouflage ['kæməflɑ:ʒ] S Tarnung *f*
camp [kæmp] **1** S Lager *n*, Zeltplatz *m* **2** V/I zelten, campen **3** ADJ *umg* theatralisch, tuntig
campaign [kæm'peɪn] **1** S Kampagne *f*; POL Wahlkampf *m* **2** V/I sich einsetzen (*for/against* für/gegen)
camper ['kæmpər] S (*Person*) Camper(in) *m(f)*; (*Fahrzeug*) Wohnmobil *n* **campground** ['kæmpgraʊnd] S Zeltplatz *m*, Campingplatz *m* **camping** S Zelten *n*, Camping *n* **campsite** ['kæmpsaɪt] S Zeltplatz *m*, Campingplatz *m*
campus ['kæmpəs] S Universitätsgelände *n*, Campus *m*
can ⟨could, been able⟩ [kæn, kʊd, bi:n'eɪbl] **1** V/AUX (*Fähigkeit*) können; (*Erlaubnis*) dürfen; **I ~not** *od* **~'t see** ich kann nichts sehen; **~ I go now?** darf ich jetzt gehen? **2** S Dose *f*;

(*für Wasser etc*) Kanne *f*

Canada ['kænədə] S Kanada *n* **Canadian** [kə'neɪdɪən] **1** ADJ kanadisch **2** S Kanadier(in) *m(f)*

cancel ['kænsəl] V/T (*pläne*) aufgeben; (*Treffen*) absagen; WIRTSCH (*Bestellung*) stornieren; IT löschen; FLUG streichen; **be ~ed** (*Zug, Bus, Vorstellung*) ausfallen **cancellation** [kænsə'leɪʃən] S Absage *f*; WIRTSCH Stornierung *f*; FLUG gestrichener Flug

cancer ['kænsər] S MED Krebs *m* **Cancer** S ASTROL Krebs *m*

candidate ['kændədeɪt] S Bewerber(in) *m(f)*; POL Kandidat(in) *m(f)*

candle ['kændl] S Kerze *f*

candy ['kændɪ] S Bonbon *n*, Süßigkeiten *pl* **candy bar** S Schokoriegel *m* **candy store** S Süßwarenladen *m*

canned [kænd] ADJ Dosen-

cannot ['kænɑːt, kə'nɑːt] *kontr von* **can not**

canoe [kə'nuː] S Kanu *n* **canoeing** S Kanufahren *n*

can opener ['kænoʊpnər] S Dosenöffner *m*

can't [kænt] *kontr von* **can not**

canvas ['kænvəs] S Segeltuch *n*, Zeltstoff *m*; (*zum Malen*) Leinwand *f*

canyon ['kænjən] S Felsenschlucht *f*

cap [kæp] S Mütze *f*; (*Flasche etc*) Verschluss *m*, Deckel *m*

capability [keɪpə'bɪlətɪ] S Fähigkeit *f* **capable** ['keɪpəbl] ADJ fähig; **be ~ of sth** zu etw fähig (*od* imstande) sein

capacity [kə'pæsətɪ] S Fassungsvermögen *n*; (*Können*) Fähigkeit *f*; (*Eigenschaft, Rolle*) Funktion *f*

cape [keɪp] S Cape *n*, Umhang *m*; GEO Kap *n*

caper ['keɪpər] S Kaper *f*

capital ['kæpətl] S FIN Kapital *n*; (*in Schrift*) Großbuchstabe *m*; **~ (city)** Hauptstadt *f* **capitalism** S Kapitalismus *m* **capital punishment** S die Todesstrafe

Capitol ['kæpɪtl] S **the ~** das Capitol (*Kongressgebäude in Washington, DC*); das Regierungsgebäude (*eines US-Bundesstaates*) **Capitol Hill** S *der amerikanische Kongress*

Capricorn ['kæprɪkɔːrn] S ASTROL Steinbock *m*

capsule ['kæpsəl] S Kapsel *f*

captain ['kæptən] S Kapitän *m*; (*Armee*) Hauptmann *m*

capture ['kæptʃər] **1** V/T (*Person*) fassen, gefangen nehmen; (*Stadt*) einnehmen; IT (*Daten*) erfassen **2** S Gefangennahme *f*; IT Erfassung *f*

car [kɑːr] S Auto *n*; BAHN Wagen *m*

carbohydrate [kɑːrbə'haɪdreɪt] S Kohle(n)hydrat *n* **carbon** ['kɑːrbən] S Kohlenstoff *m*

carburetor ['kɑːrbəreɪtər] S Vergaser *m*
card [kɑːrd] S Karte *f*; (*Material*) Pappe *f* **cardboard** S Pappe *f*; **~ box** Karton *m*; (*kleiner*) Pappschachtel *f*
cardigan ['kɑːrdɪgən] S Strickjacke *f*
cardphone ['kɑːrdfoʊn] S Kartentelefon *n*
care [ker] **1** S Sorge *f*, Sorgfalt *f*; (*von alten Menschen, Kranken*) Pflege *f*; **take ~** vorsichtig sein; (*beim Abschied*) mach's gut!; (*bei Adresse*) **~ of** bei; **take ~ of** sorgen für, sich kümmern um **2** V/I **I don't ~** es ist mir egal; **~ about sth** Wert auf etw *akk* legen; **he ~s about her** sie liegt ihm am Herzen **care for** V/T sorgen für, sich kümmern um; (*gernhaben*) mögen
career [kə'rɪr] S Karriere *f*, Laufbahn *f*
carefree ['kerfriː] ADJ sorgenfrei **careful**, **carefully** ADJ & ADV sorgfältig; (*nicht leichtsinnig*) vorsichtig **careless**, **carelessly** ADJ & ADV nachlässig; (*Fahrer*) leichtsinnig; (*Bemerkung*) unvorsichtig
cargo ⟨-(e)s Pl⟩ ['kɑːrgoʊ] S Ladung *f*
Caribbean [kærə'biːən] **1** S Karibik *f* **2** ADJ karibisch
caring ['kerɪŋ] ADJ mitfühlend; liebevoll, fürsorglich
carnival ['kɑːrnəvəl] S Volksfest *n*, Karneval *m*; Jahrmarkt *m*
carol ['kærəl] S Weihnachtslied *n*
carpenter ['kɑːrpəntər] S Zimmermann *m*
carpet ['kɑːrpət] S Teppich *m*
car phone S Autotelefon *n*
carpool S Fahrgemeinschaft *f*; (*Fahrzeuge*) Fuhrpark *m* **car rental**, **car rental company** S Autovermietung *f*
carriage ['kærɪdʒ] S (*mit Pferden*) Kutsche *f*
carrier ['kærɪər] S WIRTSCH Spediteur(in) *m(f)*
carrot ['kærət] S Karotte *f*
carry ['kærɪ] V/T tragen; (*Passagiere*) befördern; (*mit sich tragen*) bei sich haben **carry on** **1** V/I weitermachen **2** V/T fortführen; **~ working** weiter arbeiten **carry out** V/T ausführen, durchführen
cart [kɑːrt] S Wagen *m*, Karren *m*; (*im Supermarkt*) Einkaufswagen *m*
carton ['kɑːrtən] S (Papp)karton *m*; (*Zigaretten*) Stange *f*
cartoon [kɑːr'tuːn] S Cartoon *m od n*, Karikatur *f*; (*im Kino*) (Zeichen)trickfilm *m*
cartridge ['kɑːrtrɪdʒ] S (*Film*) Kassette *f*; (*Drucker, Stift*) Patrone *f*; (*Kopierer*) Kartusche *f*
carve [kɑːrv] V/T & V/I (*Holz*) schnitzen; (*Stein*) meißeln; (*Fleisch*) schneiden, tranchieren **carving** S (*Holz*) Schnitze-

rei *f*; (*Stein*) Skulptur *f*
car wash S Autowaschanlage *f*
case [keɪs] S Kiste *f*, Schachtel *f*; (*für Brille*) Etui *n*; JUR Fall *m*; **in ~** falls; **in that ~** in dem Fall; **in ~ of fire** bei Brand; **it's a ~ of ...** es handelt sich hier um ...
cash [kæʃ] **1** S Bargeld *n*; **in ~** bar; **~ on delivery** per Nachnahme **2** V/T (*Scheck*) einlösen
cash desk S Kasse *f*
cashier [kæ'ʃɪr] S Kassierer(in) *m(f)*
cash machine S Geldautomat *m*
casing ['keɪsɪŋ] S Gehäuse *n*
casino ⟨-s *pl*⟩ [kə'si:noʊ] S Kasino *n*
casserole ['kæsəroʊl] S Kasserolle *f*; (*Essen*) Schmortopf *m*
cassette [kæ'set] S Kassette *f*
cast ⟨cast, cast⟩ [kæst] **1** V/T werfen; THEAT, FILM besetzen; (*Rollen*) verteilen **2** S THEAT, FILM Besetzung *f*; MED Gipsverband *m*
castle ['kæsl] S Burg *f*
casual ['kæʒʊəl] ADJ (*Bemerkung*) beiläufig; (*Verhalten, Art*) (nach)lässig, zwanglos; (*Kleidung*) leger; (*Arbeit etc*) Gelegenheits-; (*Blick etc*) flüchtig
casually ADV (*etw sagen*) beiläufig; (*treffen*) zwanglos; (*gekleidet*) leger
casualty ['kæʒʊəltɪ] S Verletzte(r) *m/f(m)*; Tote(r) *m/f(m)*
cat [kæt] S Katze *f*, Kater *m*
catalog ['kætəlɑ:g] S Katalog *m*
cataract ['kætərækt] S Wasserfall *m*; MED grauer Star
catarrh [kə'tɑ:r] S Katarr(h) *m*
catastrophe [kə'tæstrəfɪ] S Katastrophe *f*
catch [kætʃ] **1** S Fang *m* **2** V/T ⟨caught, caught⟩ [kɒ:t] fangen; (*Dieb*) fassen; (*Zug, Bus*) nehmen; (*nicht verpassen*) erreichen; **~ a cold** sich erkälten; **~ fire** Feuer fangen; **I didn't ~ that** das habe ich nicht verstanden/gehört
catch up V/T & V/I **~ with sb** j-n einholen; **~ on sth** etw nachholen
category ['kætəgɔ:rɪ] S Kategorie *f*
cater ['keɪtər] V/I die Speisen und Getränke liefern (*for* für)
cater for V/T eingestellt sein auf *+akk*
catering S Versorgung *f* mit Speisen und Getränken, Gastronomie *f*
cathedral [kə'θi:drəl] S Kathedrale *f*, Dom *m*
Catholic ['kæθlɪk] **1** ADJ katholisch **2** S Katholik(in) *m(f)*
catsup ['kætsəp] S Ketschup *n od m*
cattle ['kætl] S PL Vieh *n*
caught [kɒ:t] *prät, pperf von* catch
cauliflower ['kɒ:lɪflaʊər] S Blumenkohl *m*
cause [kɒ:z] **1** S Ursache *f* (*of* für), Grund *m* (*for* zu); (*Angelegenheit, Ziel*) Sache *f*; **for a**

good ~ für wohltätige Zwecke **2** VT verursachen
causeway ['kɒːzweɪ] S Damm *m*
caution ['kɒːʃən] **1** S Vorsicht *f*; JUR, SPORT Verwarnung *f* **2** VT (ver)warnen **cautious** ['kɒːʃəs] ADJ vorsichtig
cave [keɪv] S Höhle *f*
cayenne (pepper) [kɪ'en] S Cayennepfeffer *m*
CCTV *abk* = closed circuit television; Videoüberwachungsanlage *f*
CD *abk* = Compact Disc; CD *f* **CD player** S CD-Spieler *m* **CD-ROM** *abk* = Compact Disc Read Only Memory; CD-ROM *f*
cease [siːs] **1** VI aufhören **2** VT beenden; **~ doing sth** aufhören, etw zu tun
ceiling ['siːlɪŋ] S Decke *f*
celebrate ['seləbreɪt] VT & VI feiern **celebration** [selə'breɪʃən] S Feier *f* **celebrity** [sɪ'lebrətɪ] S Berühmtheit *f*, Star *m*
celery ['selərɪ] S (Stangen)sellerie *m od f*
cell [sel] S Zelle *f*; Mobiltelefon *n*, Handy *n*
cellar ['selər] S Keller *m*
cello ⟨-s *pl*⟩ ['tʃeloʊ] S Cello *n*
cellphone ['selfoʊn], **cellular phone** ['seljələrfoʊn] S Mobiltelefon *n*, Handy *n*
cement [sɪ'ment] S Zement *m*
cemetery ['seməterɪ] S Friedhof *m*
cent [sent] S (*von Dollar, Euro etc*) Cent *m*
center ['sentər] S **1** S Mitte *f*; (*geografisch, von Stadt etc*) Zentrum *n* **2** VT zentrieren
centimeter ['sentɪmiːtər] S Zentimeter *m*
central ['sentrəl] ADJ zentral **Central America** S Mittelamerika *n* **central heating** S Zentralheizung *f* **centralize** VT zentralisieren **central locking** S AUTO Zentralverriegelung *f* **central station** S Hauptbahnhof *m*
century ['sentʃʊrɪ] S Jahrhundert *n*
ceramic [sɪ'ræmɪk] ADJ keramisch
cereal ['sɪrɪəl] S (*Weizen etc*) Getreide *n*; (*Cornflakes etc*) Frühstücksflocken *pl*
ceremony ['serəmoʊnɪ] S Feier *f*, Zeremonie *f*
certain ['sɜːrtən] ADJ sicher (*of +gen*); (*Zeitpunkt, Alter etc*) bestimmt **certainly** ADV sicher; bestimmt; **~!** aber sicher!; **~ not** ganz bestimmt nicht!
certificate [sər'tɪfɪkət] S Bescheinigung *f*; (*in Schule*) Zeugnis *n*
Cesarean [sɪ'zerɪən] ADJ **~ (section)** Kaiserschnitt *m*
chain [tʃeɪn] **1** S Kette *f* **2** VT **~ (up)** anketten
chair [tʃer] S Stuhl *m*; (*mit Polstern*) Sessel *m*; (*bei Versammlung*) Vorsitzende(r) *m/f(m)*

chairman ⟨-men *pl*⟩ S Vorsitzende(r) *m*/*f*(*m*) **chairperson** S Vorsitzende(r) *m*/*f*(*m*) **chairwoman** ⟨-women *pl*⟩ S Vorsitzende *f*

chalet [ʃæ'leɪ] S Berghütte *f*, Ferienhäuschen *n*

chalk [tʃɒ:k] S Kreide *f*

challenge ['tʃæləndʒ] **1** S Herausforderung *f* **2** V/T (*Person*) herausfordern; (*Aussage*) bestreiten

champagne [ʃæm'peɪn] S Champagner *m*

champion ['tʃæmpɪən] S SPORT Meister(in) *m*(*f*) **championship** S Meisterschaft *f*

chance [tʃæns] S (*etw Ungeplantes*) Zufall *m*; (*Aussicht*) Möglichkeit *f*; (*Chance*) Gelegenheit *f*; (*Wagnis*) Risiko *n*; **by ~** zufällig

change [tʃeɪndʒ] **1** V/T verändern; ändern; (*Geld, Reifen, Windel*) wechseln; (*wechseln gegen*) (um)tauschen; **~ one's clothes** sich umziehen; **~ trains** umsteigen; **~ gear** AUTO schalten **2** V/I sich ändern; sich verändern; (*andere Sachen anziehen*) sich umziehen **3** S Veränderung *f*, Änderung *f*; (*von Einkauf*) Wechselgeld *n*; (*Münzen*) Kleingeld *n*; **for a ~** zur Abwechslung; **can you give me ~ for $10?** können Sie mir auf 10 Dollar herausgeben? **change over** V/I sich umstellen (*to* auf *+akk*)

changing room S Umkleideraum *m*

channel ['tʃænl] S Kanal *m*; RADIO, TV Kanal *m*, Sender *m* **channeling island** S Verkehrsinsel *f* **channel-surfing** S Zappen *n*

chaos ['keɪɑ:s] S Chaos *n*

chaotic [keɪ'ɑ:tɪk] ADJ chaotisch

chapel ['tʃæpəl] S Kapelle *f*

chapter ['tʃæptər] S Kapitel *n*; (*von Verein etc*) Ortsgruppe *f*

character ['kærəktər] S Charakter *m*, Wesen *n*; (*Theaterstück, Roman*) Figur *f*; TYPO Zeichen *n* **characteristic** S typisches Merkmal

charbroil ['tʃɑ:rbrɔɪl] V/T auf dem Holzkohlengrill grillen

charcoal ['tʃɑ:rkoʊl] S Holzkohle *f*

charge [tʃɑ:rdʒ] **1** S (*Geld*) Gebühr *f*; JUR Anklage *f*; **free of ~** gratis, kostenlos; **be in ~ of** verantwortlich sein für **2** V/T (*Geld*) verlangen; JUR anklagen; (*Batterie*) laden; **I'd like to ~ it** ich möchte gerne mit Kreditkarte bezahlen

charity ['tʃærətɪ] S (*Institution*) wohltätige Organisation; **for ~** für wohltätige Zwecke

charley horse ['tʃɑ:rlɪhɔ:rs] S Muskelkater *m*

charm [tʃɑ:rm] **1** S Charme *m* **2** V/T bezaubern **charming** ADJ reizend, charmant

chart [tʃɑ:rt] S Diagramm *n*;

(*für Piloten, Segler*) Karte *f*
charter flight ['tʃɑːrtərflaɪt] S Charterflug *m*
chase [tʃeɪs] 1 V/T jagen, verfolgen 2 S Verfolgungsjagd *f*, Jagd *f*
chassis ['ʃæsɪ] S AUTO Fahrgestell *n*
chat [tʃæt] 1 V/I plaudern; IT chatten 2 S Plauderei *f* **chatroom** S IT Chatroom *m*
chauffeur ['ʃoʊfər] S Chauffeur(in) *m(f)*, Fahrer(in) *m(f)*
cheap [tʃiːp] ADJ billig; (*schlechte Qualität*) minderwertig
cheat [tʃiːt] V/T & V/I betrügen; (*in Schule, Spiel*) mogeln
check [tʃek] 1 V/T überprüfen (*for* auf *+akk*); TECH kontrollieren; (*mit Haken versehen*) abhaken; FLUG (*Gepäck*) einchecken; (*Mantel*) abgeben 2 S Kontrolle *f*; Scheck *m*; (*im Restaurant*) Rechnung *f*; (*auf Stoff*) Karo (-muster) *n*; **could I have the ~, please?** ich möchte bitte zahlen **check in** V/T & V/I FLUG einchecken; (*Hotel*) sich anmelden **check out** V/I sich abmelden, auschecken **check up** V/I nachprüfen **check book** S Scheckheft *n* **check card** S Scheckkarte *f*; Debitkarte *f*
checkers ['tʃekərz] S SG Damespiel *n*
check-in ['tʃekɪn] S (*Flughafen*) Check-in *m*; (*Hotel*) Anmeldung *f* **check-in desk** S Abfertigungsschalter *m* **checking account** S Scheckkonto *n* **checkout** S (*Supermarkt*) Kasse *f* **checkout time** S (*Hotel*) Abreise(zeit) *f* **checkpoint** S Kontrollpunkt *m*
checkroom S Garderobe *f*; Gepäckaufbewahrung *f*
checkup S MED (ärztliche) Untersuchung
cheek [tʃiːk] S Backe *f*, Wange *f*
cheer [tʃɪr] 1 S Beifallsruf *m*; **~s** (*beim Trinken*) prost! 2 V/T zujubeln *+dat* 3 V/I jubeln
cheer up 1 V/T aufmuntern 2 V/I fröhlicher werden
cheerful ['tʃɪrfʊl] ADJ fröhlich **cheerleader** S Cheerleader *m*, Einpeitscherin *f* (*bei Sportveranstaltungen*)
cheese [tʃiːz] S Käse *m*
cheesecake S Käsekuchen *m*
chef [ʃef] S Koch *m*, Küchenchef(in) *m(f)*
chemical ['kemɪkəl] 1 ADJ chemisch 2 S Chemikalie *f*
chemistry ['keməstrɪ] S Chemie *f*
cherry ['tʃerɪ] S Kirsche *f*
cherry tomato ⟨-es *pl*⟩ S Kirschtomate *f*
chess [tʃes] S Schach *n*
chest [tʃest] S Brust *f*; (*Behälter*) Kiste *f*; **~ of drawers** Kommode *f*
chestnut ['tʃesnʌt] S Kastanie *f*

chew [tʃuː] VT & VI kauen **chewing gum** S Kaugummi *m*

chick [tʃɪk] S Küken *n*; (*Person*) Mädchen *n*, (junge) Frau **chicken** S Huhn *n*; (*als Essen*) Hähnchen *n*; (*Angsthase*) Feigling *m* **chicken breast** S Hühnerbrust *f* **chickenpox** S Windpocken *pl* **chicken shit** S *umg* (*Feigling*) Hosenscheißer *m*; **be ~** Scheiße sein

chickpea S Kichererbse *f*

chief [tʃiːf] **1** S (*von Abteilung*) Leiter(in) *m(f)*; (*Boss*) Chef(in) *m(f)*; (*von Stamm*) Häuptling *m* **2** ADJ Haupt- **chiefly** ADV hauptsächlich

child ⟨children⟩ [tʃaɪld, 'tʃɪldrən] S Kind *n* **childhood** S Kindheit *f* **childish** ADJ kindisch **child lock** S Kindersicherung *f* **childproof** ADJ kindersicher **children** ['tʃɪldrən] *pl von* child **child seat** S Kindersitz *m*

chili ['tʃɪlɪ] S Pepperoni *pl*; (*Gewürz*) Chili *m* **chiliburger** S Hamburger *m* mit Chili con carne

chill [tʃɪl] **1** S Kühle *f*; MED Erkältung *f* **2** VT kühlen **3** ADJ *umg* (*Atmosphäre etc*) ungezwungen, lässig, locker **chill out** VI *umg* chillen, relaxen **chilled** ADJ gekühlt **chilly** ['tʃɪlɪ] ADJ kühl, frostig

chimney ['tʃɪmnɪ] S Schornstein *m*

chin [tʃɪn] S Kinn *n*

china ['tʃaɪnə] S Porzellan *n*

China ['tʃaɪnə] S China *n* **Chinese** [tʃaɪ'niːz] **1** ADJ chinesisch **2** S (*Person*) Chinese *m*, Chinesin *f*; (*Sprache*) Chinesisch *n*

chip [tʃɪp] **1** S (*Holz*) Splitter *m*; (*Beschädigung*) angeschlagene Stelle; IT Chip *m*; **~s** *pl* Kartoffelchips *pl* **2** VT anschlagen, beschädigen

chipmunk ['tʃɪpmʌŋk] S Streifenhörnchen *n*

chiropodist [kɪ'rɑːpədɪst] S Fußpfleger(in) *m(f)*

chives [tʃaɪvz] S PL Schnittlauch *m*

chlorine ['klɔːriːn] S Chlor *n*

chocolate ['tʃɑːklət] S Schokolade *f*; (*Konfekt*) Praline *f*; **a bar of ~, a ~ bar** eine Tafel Schokolade; **a box of ~s** eine Schachtel Pralinen **chocolate cake** S Schokoladenkuchen *m*

choice [tʃɔɪs] **1** S Wahl *f*, Auswahl *f* **2** ADJ auserlesen; (*Produkt*) Qualitäts-

choir ['kwaɪr] S Chor *m*

choke [tʃoʊk] **1** VI sich verschlucken; SPORT die Nerven verlieren **2** VT erdrosseln **3** S AUTO Choke *m*

cholesterol [kə'lestərɔːl] S Cholesterin *n*

choose ⟨chose, chosen⟩ [tʃuːz, tʃoʊz, 'tʃoʊzn] VT wählen; sich aussuchen; **there are**

three to ~ from es stehen drei zur Auswahl
chop [tʃɑ:p] 1 V/T (zer)hacken; klein schneiden 2 S (*Fleisch*) Kotelett *n* **chopsticks** S PL Essstäbchen *pl*
chorus ['kɔ:rəs] S Chor *m*; (*von Lied*) Refrain *m*
chose, chosen [tʃoʊz, 'tʃoʊzn] *prät, pperf von* choose
chowder ['tʃaʊdər] S *dicke Suppe mit Meeresfrüchten*
christen ['krɪsn] V/T taufen **christening** S Taufe *f* **Christian** ['krɪstʃən] 1 ADJ christlich 2 S Christ(in) *m(f)* **Christian name** S Vorname *m*
Christmas ['krɪsməs] S Weihnachten *pl* **Christmas card** S Weihnachtskarte *f* **Christmas Day** S der erste Weihnachtstag **Christmas Eve** S Heiligabend *m* **Christmas tree** S Weihnachtsbaum *m*
chronic ['krɑ:nɪk] ADJ MED chronisch
chuck [tʃʌk] V/T *umg* schmeißen; (*Job*) hinschmeißen
chunk [tʃʌŋk] S Klumpen *m*; (*Brot*) Brocken *m*; (*Fleisch*) Batzen *m*
church [tʃɜ:rtʃ] S Kirche *f* **churchyard** S Kirchhof *m*
chute [ʃu:t] S Rutsche *f*
CIA *abk* = Central Intelligence Agency; CIA *f*
cigar [sɪ'gɑ:r] S Zigarre *f* **cigarette** [sɪgə'ret] S Zigarette *f*
cinch [sɪntʃ] S **it's a ~** es ist ein Kinderspiel
cinema ['sɪnəmə] S **the ~** der Film, die Filmkunst
cinnamon ['sɪnəmən] S Zimt *m*
circle ['sɜ:rkl] 1 S Kreis *m* 2 V/I kreisen **circuit** ['sɜ:rkɪt] S Rundfahrt *f*; (*zu Fuß*) Rundgang *m*; (*für Rennen*) Rennstrecke *f*; ELEK Stromkreis *m* **circular** ['sɜ:rkjələr] 1 ADJ (kreis)rund, kreisförmig *f* 2 S Rundschreiben *n* **circulation** [sɜ:rkjə'leɪʃən] S Kreislauf *m*; (*Zeitung*) Auflage *f*
circumstances ['sɜ:rkəmstænsəz] S PL Umstände *pl*; (*finanziell*) Verhältnisse *pl*; **in/under the ~** unter den Umständen; **under no ~** auf keinen Fall
circus ['sɜ:rkəs] S Zirkus *m*
citizen ['sɪtɪzn] S Bürger(in) *m(f)*, Staatsangehörige(r) *m*/*f(m)* **citizenship** S Staatsangehörigkeit *f*
city ['sɪtɪ] S Stadt *f*, Großstadt *f* **city desk** S Lokalredaktion *f* **city hall** S Rathaus *n*
civil ['sɪvəl] ADJ Bürger-; staatsbürgerlich; (*nicht militärisch*) zivil **civilian** [sɪ'vɪljən] S Zivilist(in) *m(f)* **civilization** [sɪvəlaɪ'zeɪʃən] S Zivilisation *f*, Kultur *f* **civilized** ['sɪvəlaɪzd] ADJ zivilisiert, kultiviert **civil rights** S PL Bürgerrechte *pl* **civil servant** S (Staats)beamte(r) *m*, (Staats)beamtin *f* **civil**

war S Bürgerkrieg *m*; **the Civil War** der amerikanische Bürgerkrieg (*1861-1865*)

claim [kleɪm] **1** VT beanspruchen; (*Sozialhilfe etc*) beantragen; (*Schadenersatz etc*) fordern; (*aussagen*) behaupten (*that* dass) **2** S Forderung *f* (*for* für), Anspruch *m* (*to* auf +*akk*); **~ for damages** Schadenersatzforderung *f* **claimant** S Antragsteller(in) *m(f)*

clam [klæm] S Venusmuschel *f* **clambake** S Picknick *n* am Strand; große, laute Party **clam chowder** S *dicke Muschelsuppe (mit Sellerie, Zwiebeln etc)*

clap [klæp] VI (Beifall) klatschen

clarify ['klærəfaɪ] VT klären

clash [klæʃ] **1** VI zusammenstoßen (*with* mit); sich auseinandersetzen (*with* mit); *fig* (*Farben*) sich beißen **2** S Zusammenstoß *m*; (*Streit*) Auseinandersetzung *f*

class [klæs] **1** S Klasse *f* **2** VT einordnen, einstufen

classic ['klæsɪk] **1** ADJ (*Fehler, Beispiel*) klassisch **2** S Klassiker *m* **classical** ['klæsɪkəl] ADJ (*Musik, Ballett*) klassisch

classify ['klæsəfaɪ] VT klassifizieren; **classified advertisement** Kleinanzeige *f*

classroom ['klæsru:m] S Klassenzimmer *n*

classy ['klɑ:sɪ] ADJ *umg* nobel, exklusiv

clause [klɒ:z] S LING Satz *m*; JUR Klausel *f*

claw [klɒ:] S Kralle *f*

clay [kleɪ] S Lehm *m*; (*zum Töpfern*) Ton *m*

clean [kli:n] **1** ADJ sauber; (*drogenfrei*) clean **2** VT sauber machen; (*Teppich etc*) reinigen; (*Fenster, Schuhe, Gemüse*) putzen; (*Wunde*) säubern **clean up** **1** VT sauber machen **2** VI aufräumen **cleaner** S (*Person*) Putzmann *m*, Putzfrau *f*; (*Substanz*) Putzmittel *n*; (*Geschäft*) Reinigung *f* **cleanse** [klenz] VT reinigen; (*Wunde*) säubern **cleanser** S Reinigungsmittel *n*

clear [klɪr] **1** ADJ klar; deutlich; (*Gewissen*) rein; (*Straße etc*) frei; **be ~ about sth** sich über etw im Klaren sein **2** ADV **stand ~** zurücktreten **3** VT (*Straße, Zimmer*) räumen; (*Tisch*) abräumen; JUR freisprechen (*of* von) **4** VI (*Nebel*) sich verziehen; (*Wetter*) aufklaren **clear away** VT wegräumen; (*Geschirr*) abräumen **clear up** **1** VI aufräumen; (*Wetter*) sich aufklären **2** VT (*Zimmer*) aufräumen; (*Abfall*) wegräumen; (*Angelegenheit*) klären **clearance sale** S Räumungsverkauf *m* **clearing** S Lichtung *f* **clearly** ADV klar; (*sprechen etc*) deutlich; (*offensichtlich*) eindeutig

clergyman ⟨-men pl⟩

['klɜːrdʒɪmæn] S Geistliche(r) *m* **clergywoman** ⟨-women *pl*⟩ S Geistliche *f*
clerk [klɜːrk] S (*in Verwaltung etc*) Büroangestellte(r) *m/f(m)*; (*in Geschäft*) Verkäufer(in) *m(f)*
clever ['klevər] ADJ schlau, klug
cliché [kliː'ʃeɪ] S Klischee *n*
click [klɪk] **1** S Klicken *n*; IT Mausklick *m* **2** V/I klicken; **~ on sth** IT etw anklicken
client ['klaɪənt] S Kunde *m*, Kundin *f*; JUR Mandant(in) *m(f)*
cliff [klɪf] S Klippe *f*
climate ['klaɪmət] S Klima *n*
climax ['klaɪmæks] S Höhepunkt *m*
climb [klaɪm] **1** V/I klettern; (*Flugzeug*) steigen; (*Straße*) ansteigen **2** V/T (*Berg*) besteigen; (*Baum*) klettern auf +*akk* **3** S Aufstieg *m* **climbing** S Klettern *n*, Bergsteigen *n*
cling ⟨clung, clung⟩ [klɪŋ, klʌŋ] V/I sich klammern (*to* an +*akk*)
clinic ['klɪnɪk] S Klinik *f*
clip [klɪp] **1** S Klammer *f* **2** V/T anklemmen (*to* an +*akk*); (*Fingernägel*) schneiden
clock [klɑːk] S Uhr *f*; AUTO *umg* Tacho *m* **clockwise** ADV im Uhrzeigersinn
close **1** [kloʊs] ADJ nahe (*to* +*dat*); (*Freund*) eng; (*Ähnlichkeit*) groß; **~ to the beach** in der Nähe des Strandes **2** [kloʊs] ADV dicht; **he lives ~ by** er wohnt ganz in der Nähe **3** [kloʊz] V/T schließen; (*Straße*) sperren; (*Diskussion*) abschließen **4** [kloʊz] V/I schließen **5** [kloʊz] S Ende *n* **close down** **1** V/I schließen; (*Fabrik*) stillgelegt werden **2** V/T (*Geschäft*) schließen; (*Fabrik*) stilllegen **closed** [kloʊzd] ADJ (*Straße*) gesperrt; (*Geschäft*) geschlossen **closed circuit television** S Videoüberwachungsanlage *f* **closely** ['kloʊslɪ] ADV eng, nah; (*folgen*) dicht; (*beobachten*) genau
closet ['klɑːzət] S Schrank *m*
closing ['kloʊzɪŋ] ADJ **~ date** letzter Termin; Einsendeschluss *m*; **~ time** (*von Geschäft*) Ladenschluss *m*
closure ['kloʊʒər] S Schließung *f*; Abschluss *m*
clot [klɑːt] **1** S (**blood**) **~** Blutgerinnsel *n* **2** V/I gerinnen
cloth [klɑːθ] S (*Material*) Tuch *n*; (*zum Putzen*) Lappen *m*
clothes [kloʊz] S PL Kleider *pl*, Kleidung *f* **clothespin** S Wäscheklammer *f* **clothing** ['kloʊðɪŋ] S Kleidung *f*
cloud [klaʊd] S Wolke *f*
cloudy ADJ (*Himmel*) bewölkt; (*Flüssigkeit*) trüb
clove [kloʊv] S Gewürznelke *f*; **~ of garlic** Knoblauchzehe *f*
club [klʌb] S Knüppel *m*; (*Organisation*) Klub *m*, Verein *m*; (*zum Tanzen*) Disko *f*; (*Golf*) Golfschläger *m*; **~s** *pl* (*Karten*)

Kreuz *n* **club class** S FLUG Businessclass *f* **club sandwich** S *Sandwich aus drei Toastscheiben belegt mit Hähnchen- oder Truthahnfleisch, Frühstücksspeck oder Schinken, Salat, Tomaten und Mayonnaise*

clue [klu:] S Anhaltspunkt *m*, Hinweis *m*; **he hasn't got a ~** er hat keine Ahnung

clumsy ['klʌmzɪ] ADJ unbeholfen, ungeschickt

clung [klʌŋ] *prät, pperf von* cling

clunker ['klʌŋkər] S *umg* (*Auto*) Klapperkiste *f*, Schrottkiste *f*

clutch [klʌtʃ] S AUTO Kupplung *f*

cm *abk* = centimeter(s) cm

c/o *abk* = care of; bei

Co *abk* = company

CO *abk* = Colorado

coach [koʊtʃ] **1** S BAHN (Personen)wagen *m*; SPORT Trainer(in) *m(f)* **2** V/T Nachhilfeunterricht geben *+dat*; SPORT trainieren **coach (class)** S FLUG Economyclass *f*

coal [koʊl] S Kohle *f*

coast [koʊst] S Küste *f* **coastguard** S Küstenwache *f* **coastline** S Küste *f*

coat [koʊt] S Mantel *m*, Jacke *f*; (*bei Tier*) Fell *n*, Pelz *m*; (*Farbe*) Schicht *f* **coat check** S Garderobe *f* **coat hanger** S Kleiderbügel *m* **coating** S Überzug *m*, Schicht *f*

cobweb ['ka:bweb] S Spinnennetz *n*

cocaine [koʊ'keɪn] S Kokain *n*

cock [ka:k] S Hahn *m*; *vulg* (*Penis*) Schwanz *m* **cockpit** ['ka:kpɪt] S (*Flugzeug, Rennwagen*) Cockpit *n* **cockroach** ['ka:kroʊtʃ] S Kakerlake *f*

cocky ['ka:kɪ] ADJ großspurig, von sich selbst überzeugt

cocoa ['koʊkoʊ] S Kakao *m*

coconut ['koʊkənʌt] S Kokosnuss *f*

cod [ka:d] S Kabeljau *m*

COD *abk* = cash on delivery; per Nachnahme

code [koʊd] S Kode *m*

coffee ['ka:fɪ] S Kaffee *m* **coffee break** S Kaffeepause *f* **coffee maker** S Kaffeemaschine *f* **coffee pot** S Kaffeekanne *f* **coffee press** S Kaffeebereiter *m* **coffee shop** S Café *n* **coffee table** S Couchtisch *m*

coffin ['ka:fɪn] S Sarg *m*

coin [kɔɪn] S Münze *f*

coincide [koʊɪn'saɪd] V/I zusammenfallen (*with* mit) **coincidence** [koʊ'ɪnsɪdəns] S Zufall *m*

coke [koʊk] S Koks *m*; **Coke**® Cola *f*

cold [koʊld] **1** ADJ kalt; **I'm ~** mir ist kalt, ich friere **2** S Kälte *f*; (*Krankheit*) Erkältung *f*, Schnupfen *m*; **catch a ~** sich erkälten **cold cuts** S PL Auf-

schnitt *m*
coleslaw ['koʊlslɒ:] S Krautsalat *m*
collaboration [kəlæbə'reɪʃən] S Zusammenarbeit *f*, Mitarbeit *f*
collapse [kə'læps] 1 V/I zusammenbrechen; einstürzen 2 S Zusammenbruch *m*, Einsturz *m*
collar ['kɑ:lər] S Kragen *m*; (*Hund etc*) Halsband *n*
colleague ['kɑ:li:g] S Kollege *m*, Kollegin *f*
collect [kə'lekt] 1 V/T sammeln; abholen 2 V/I sich sammeln 3 ADV **call ~** ein R-Gespräch führen **collect call** S R-Gespräch *n* **collection** [kə'lekʃən] S Sammlung *f*; REL Kollekte *f*; (*Briefkasten*) Leerung *f*
college ['kɑ:lɪdʒ] S (*als Teil von Universität, mit Wohnbereich*) College *n*, Fachhochschule *f*, Berufsschule *f*; Universität *f*; **go to ~** studieren
collide [kə'laɪd] V/I zusammenstoßen **collision** [kə'lɪʒən] S Zusammenstoß *m*
colloquial [kə'loʊkwɪəl] ADJ umgangssprachlich
colony ['kɑ:lənɪ] S Kolonie *f*
color S ['kʌlər] 1 S Farbe *f*; Hautfarbe *f* 2 V/T anmalen; färben **color-blind** ADJ farbenblind **colored** ADJ farbig; gefärbt **colorful** ADJ bunt; (*Leben*) bewegt **coloring** S (*bei Lebensmitteln*) Farbstoff *m*; (*von Haut*) Gesichtsfarbe *f* **color photo(graph)** S Farbfoto *n*
column ['kɑ:ləm] S Säule *f*; (*in Text*) Spalte *f*
comb [koʊm] 1 S Kamm *m* 2 V/T kämmen; **~ one's hair** sich kämmen
combination [kɑ:mbɪ'neɪʃən] S Kombination *f*, Mischung *f* (*of* aus) **combine** [kəm'baɪn] V/T verbinden (*with* mit); kombinieren
come ⟨came, come⟩ [kʌm, keɪm, kʌm] V/I kommen; ankommen; (*auf Liste*) stehen; (*mit Adjektiv*) werden; **~ and see us** besuchen Sie uns mal; **coming!** ich komm ja schon!; **~ first/second** erster/zweiter werden; **how ~ …?** *umg* wie kommt es, dass …? **come across** V/T stoßen auf *+akk* **come around** V/I vorbeikommen; (*nach Ohnmacht*) wieder zu sich kommen **come back** V/I zurückkommen **come down** V/I herunterkommen; (*Regen, Schnee, Preise*) fallen **come from** V/T kommen von; **where do you ~?** wo kommen Sie her?; **I ~ Dallas** ich komme aus Dallas **come in** V/I hereinkommen; ankommen **come on** V/I vorankommen; **~!** komm!; (*in Eile*) beeil dich!; (*Mut zusprechend*) los! **come out** V/I herauskommen;

(*Foto*) was werden; (*als Homosexueller*) sich outen **come to** 1 VI (*nach Ohnmacht*) wieder zu sich kommen 2 VT (*Summe*) sich belaufen auf *+akk* **come up** VI hochkommen; (*Sonne, Mond*) aufgehen **come up to** VT zukommen auf *+akk*; (*Wasser*) reichen bis zu **come up with** VT (*Idee*) haben; (*Lösung, Antwort*) kommen auf *+akk*
comedian [kə'mi:dıən] S Komiker(in) *m(f)* **comedy** ['kɑ:mədı] S Komödie *f*, Comedy *f*
come-on S *umg* Anmache *f*
comfort ['kʌmfərt] 1 S Komfort *m*; (*Hilfe*) Trost *m* 2 VT trösten **comfortable** ['kʌmfərtəbl] ADJ bequem; (*Einkommen*) ausreichend; (*Leben, Temperatur*) angenehm **comforting** ADJ tröstlich
comic ['kɑ:mık] 1 S Comic(-heft) *n*; (*Person*) Komiker(in) *m(f)* 2 ADJ komisch
comma ['kɑ:mə] S Komma *n*
command [kə'mænd] 1 S Befehl *m*; (*Kontrolle*) Führung *f*; MIL Kommando *n* 2 VT befehlen *+dat*
commemorate [kə'meməreıt] VT gedenken *+gen*
comment ['kɑ:ment] 1 S Bemerkung *f*, Anmerkung *f*, Kommentar *m* (*on* zu) 2 VI sich äußern (*on* zu) **commentary** ['kɑ:mənterı] S Kommentar *m* (*on* zu); TV, SPORT Livereportage *f* **commentator** ['kɑ:mənteıtər] S Kommentator(in) *m(f)*; TV, SPORT Reporter(in) *m(f)*
commerce ['kɑ:mɜ:rs] S Handel *m* **commercial** [kə'mɜ:rʃəl] 1 ADJ kommerziell; kaufmännisch; **~ break** Werbepause *f* 2 S TV Werbespot *m*
commission [kə'mıʃən] 1 S Auftrag *m*; (*Gebühr*) Provision *f*; (*Komitee*) Kommission *f* 2 VT beauftragen
commit [kə'mıt] 1 VT begehen 2 V/R **~ oneself** sich verpflichten (*to* zu) **commitment** S Verpflichtung *f*; POL Engagement *n*
committee [kə'mıtı] S Ausschuss *m*, Komitee *n*
common ['kɑ:mən] ADJ allgemein, alltäglich; (*Interessen*) gemeinsam; (*weit verbreitet*) häufig; *pej* gewöhnlich, ordinär; **have sth in ~** etw gemein haben **commonly** ADV häufig, allgemein **common sense** S gesunder Menschenverstand
communal [kə'mju:nl] ADJ gemeinsam; Gemeinschafts-, Gemeinde-
communicate [kə'mju:nıkeıt] VI kommunizieren (*with* mit) **communication** [kəmju:nı'keıʃən] S Kommunikation *f*, Verständigung *f*
communion [kə'mju:njən] S **(Holy) Communion** heiliges

Abendmahl; (*bei Katholiken*) Kommunion *f*
communism ['kɑ:mjʊnɪzəm] S Kommunismus *m*
community [kə'mju:nətɪ] S Gemeinschaft *f* **community service** S JUR Sozialdienst *m*
commute [kə'mju:t] V/I pendeln **commuter** S Pendler(in) *m(f)*
compact 1 [kəm'pækt] ADJ kompakt 2 ['kɑ:mpækt] S (*Make-up*) Puderdose *f*; (*Auto*) ≈ Mittelklassewagen *m* **compact disc** S Compact Disc *f*, CD *f*
companion [kəm'pænɪən] S Begleiter(in) *m(f)* **company** ['kʌmpənɪ] S Gesellschaft *f*; WIRTSCH Firma *f*; **keep sb ~** j-m Gesellschaft leisten
comparatively [kəm'pærətɪvlɪ] ADV verhältnismäßig
compare [kəm'per] V/T vergleichen (*with, to* mit); **~d with** *od* **to** im Vergleich zu **comparison** [kəm'pærɪsn] S Vergleich *m*; **in ~ with** im Vergleich mit (*od* zu)
compartment [kəm'pɑ:rtmənt] S BAHN Abteil *n*; (*Schreibtisch etc*) Fach *n*
compass ['kʌmpəs] S Kompass *m*
compassion [kəm'pæʃən] S Mitgefühl *n*
compatible [kəm'pætəbl] ADJ vereinbar (*with* mit); IT kompatibel
compensate ['kɑ:mpenseɪt] V/T entschädigen (*for* für)
compensation [kɑ:mpen'seɪʃən] S Entschädigung *f*, Schadenersatz *m*; JUR Abfindung *f*
compete [kəm'pi:t] V/I konkurrieren (*for* um); SPORT kämpfen (*for* um); (*an Turnier etc*) teilnehmen (*in* an *+dat*)
competent ['kɑ:mpətənt] ADJ fähig; JUR zuständig
competition [kɑ:mpə'tɪʃən] S Wettbewerb *m*; WIRTSCH Konkurrenz *f* (*for* um) **competitive** [kəm'petətɪv] ADJ konkurrenzfähig **competitor** S WIRTSCH Konkurrent(in) *m(f)*; SPORT Teilnehmer(in) *m(f)*
complain [kəm'pleɪn] V/I klagen; sich beschweren (*about* über *+akk*) **complaint** S Klage *f*, Beschwerde *f*, Beanstandung *f*; MED Leiden *n*
complete [kəm'pli:t] 1 ADJ vollständig; (*beendet*) fertig; (*Reinfall*) total; (*Glück*) vollkommen 2 V/T vervollständigen; (*Formular*) ausfüllen **completely** ADV völlig
complex ['kɑ:mpleks] 1 ADJ kompliziert 2 S Komplex *m*
complexion [kəm'plekʃən] S Gesichtsfarbe *f*, Teint *m*
complicated ['kɑ:mplɪkeɪtəd] ADJ kompliziert **complication** S Komplikation *f*
compliment ['kɑ:mpləmənt] S Kompliment *n* **compli-**

mentary [kɑːmplə'mentərɪ] ADJ lobend; (*umsonst*) Gratis-
component [kəm'poʊnənt] S Bestandteil *m*
compose [kəm'poʊz] V/T komponieren **composed** ADJ gefasst; **be ~ of** bestehen aus
comprehend [kɑːmprɪ'hend] V/T begreifen, verstehen
comprehensive [kɑːmprɪ'hensɪv] ADJ umfassend
comprise [kəm'praɪz] V/T umfassen, bestehen aus
compromise ['kɑːmprəmaɪz] **1** S Kompromiss *m* **2** V/I einen Kompromiss schließen
compulsory [kəm'pʌlsərɪ] ADJ obligatorisch
computer [kəm'pjuːtər] S Computer *m* **computer-controlled** ADJ rechnergesteuert **computer game** S Computerspiel *n* **computer-literate** ADJ **be ~** mit dem Computer umgehen können **computing** S Informatik *f*
con [kɑːn] *umg* **1** S Schwindel *m* **2** V/T betrügen (*out of* um)
conceal [kən'siːl] V/T verbergen (*from* vor *+dat*)
conceive [kən'siːv] V/T sich vorstellen; (*Kind*) empfangen
concentrate ['kɑːnsəntreɪt] V/I sich konzentrieren (*on* auf *+akk*) **concentration** S Konzentration *f*
concept ['kɑːnsept] S Begriff *m*
concern [kən'sɜːrn] **1** S Angelegenheit *f*; (*Angst*) Sorge *f* **2** V/T angehen; betreffen; (*sich befassen mit*) handeln von; **those ~ed** die Betroffenen; **as far as I'm ~ed** was mich betrifft **concerned** ADJ besorgt **concerning** PRÄP bezüglich, hinsichtlich *+gen*
concert ['kɑːnsərt] S Konzert *n*; **~ hall** Konzertsaal *m*
concession [kən'seʃən] S Zugeständnis *n*; Konzession *f*
conclude [kən'kluːd] V/T beenden, (ab)schließen; (*logisch*) folgern (*from* aus); **~ that …** zu dem Schluss kommen, dass … **conclusion** [kən'kluːʒən] S Schluss *m*, Schlussfolgerung *f*
concrete ['kɑːŋkriːt] **1** S Beton *m* **2** ADJ konkret
concussion [kən'kʌʃən] S Gehirnerschütterung *f*
condition [kən'dɪʃən] S Zustand *m*; (*Voraussetzung*) Bedingung *f*; **on ~ that …** unter der Bedingung, dass …; **~s** *pl* Verhältnisse *pl* **conditioner** S Weichspüler *m*; (*Haar*) Pflegespülung *f*
condo ⟨-s *pl*⟩ ['kɑːndoʊ] S → condominium
condolences [kən'doʊlənsəz] S PL Beileid *n*
condom ['kɑːndəm] S Kondom *n*
condominium [kɑːndə'mɪnɪəm] S Eigentumswohnung *f*
conduct **1** ['kɑːndʌkt] S Ver-

halten *n* **2** [kən'dʌkt] VT führen, leiten; (*Orchester*) dirigieren **conductor** [kən'dʌktər] S MUS Dirigent(in) *m(f)*; Zugführer(in) *m(f)*

cone [koʊn] S Kegel *m*; (*Eis*) Waffeltüte *f*; (*Tanne*) (Tannen)-zapfen *m*

conference ['kɑːnfərəns] S Konferenz *f*

confess [kən'fes] VT & VI **~ that ...** gestehen, dass ... **confession** [kən'feʃən] S Geständnis *n*; REL Beichte *f*

confidence ['kɑːnfɪdəns] S Vertrauen *n* (*in* zu), Selbstvertrauen *n* **confident** ADJ (*optimistisch*) zuversichtlich (*that ...* dass ...), überzeugt (*of* von); (*selbstbewusst*) selbstsicher

confidential [kɑːnfɪ'denʃəl] ADJ vertraulich

confirm [kən'fɜːrm] VT bestätigen **confirmation** [kɑːnfər'meɪʃən] S Bestätigung *f*; REL Konfirmation *f*

confuse [kən'fjuːz] VT verwirren; verwechseln (*with* mit); (*mehrere Dinge*) durcheinanderbringen **confused** ADJ (*Person*) konfus, verwirrt; (*Situation, Gefühle*) verworren **confusing** ADJ verwirrend **confusion** [kən'fjuːʒən] S Verwirrung *f*; (*von zwei Dingen*) Verwechslung *f*; (*Durcheinander*) Chaos *n*

congestion [kən'dʒestʃən] S Stau *m*

congratulate [kən'grætʃʊleɪt] VT gratulieren (*on* zu) **congratulations** [kəngrætʃʊ'leɪʃənz] S PL Glückwünsche *pl*; **~!** gratuliere!, herzlichen Glückwunsch!

congregation [kɑːŋgrə'geɪʃən] S REL Gemeinde *f*

congress ['kɑːŋgres] S Kongress *m*; **Congress** der Kongress **congressman** ⟨-men *pl*⟩, **congresswoman** ⟨-women *pl*⟩ S Mitglied *n* des Repräsentantenhauses

connect [kə'nekt] **1** VT verbinden (*with, to* mit); ELEK, TECH anschließen (*to* an *+akk*) **2** VI (*Zug, Flugzeug*) Anschluss haben (*with* an *+akk*); **~ing flight** Anschlussflug *m* **connection** [kə'nekʃən] S Verbindung *f*, Zusammenhang *m*; (*Zug, Flugzeug, Elektrogerät*) Anschluss *m* (*with, to* an *+akk*); (*persönlicher Kontakt*) Beziehung *f*

conscience ['kɑːnʃəns] S Gewissen *n*

conscious ['kɑːnʃəs] ADJ bewusst; MED bei Bewusstsein

consecutive [kən'sekjʊtɪv] ADJ aufeinanderfolgend

consent [kən'sent] **1** S Zustimmung *f* **2** VI zustimmen (*to dat*)

consequence ['kɑːnsəkwəns] S Folge *f*, Konsequenz *f*

conservation [kɑːnsər'veɪʃən] S Erhaltung *f*; (*von Natur*)

Naturschutz *m*
conservative [kən'sɜːrvətɪv] ADJ konservativ
consider [kən'sɪdər] V/T nachdenken über, sich überlegen; (*Möglichkeiten etc*) in Betracht ziehen; (*einschätzen*) halten für; **he is ~ed (to be)** ... er gilt als ... **considerable** [kən'sɪdərəbl] ADJ beträchtlich **considerate** [kən'sɪdərət] ADJ aufmerksam, rücksichtsvoll **consideration** [kənsɪdə'reɪʃən] S (*gegenüber anderen*) Rücksicht *f*; (*Gedanke*) Überlegung *f*; **take sth into ~** etw in Betracht ziehen **considering** [kən'sɪdərɪŋ] **1** PRÄP in Anbetracht *+gen* **2** KONJ da
consist [kən'sɪst] V/I **~ of ...** bestehen aus
consistent [kən'sɪstənt] ADJ (*Handeln*) konsequent; (*Meinungen*) übereinstimmend; (*Argumentation*) folgerichtig; (*Leistung*) beständig
consolation [kɑːnsə'leɪʃən] S Trost *m*
consonant ['kɑːnsənənt] S Konsonant *m*
conspicuous [kən'spɪkjʊəs] ADJ auffällig, auffallend
conspiracy [kən'spɪrəsɪ] S Verschwörung *f*, Komplott *n*
constant ['kɑːnstənt] ADJ ständig, dauernd; (*Temperatur etc*) gleichbleibend **constantly** ADV dauernd
constituency [kən'stɪtʃʊənsɪ] S Wahlkreis *m*
constitution [kɑːnstɪ'tuːʃən] S Verfassung *f*; (*von Person*) Konstitution *f*
construct [kən'strʌkt] V/T bauen **construction** [kən'strʌkʃən] S Bau *m*, Bauweise *f*; **under ~** im Bau befindlich **construction site** S Baustelle *f*
consulate ['kɑːnsʊlət] S Konsulat *n*
consult [kən'sʌlt] V/T um Rat fragen; (*Arzt*) konsultieren; (*Wörterbuch etc*) nachschlagen in *+dat* **consultant** S Berater(in) *m(f)* **consultation** [kɑːnsəl'teɪʃən] S Beratung *f*; MED Konsultation *f*
consume [kən'suːm] V/T verbrauchen; (*essen, trinken*) konsumieren **consumer** S Verbraucher(in) *m(f)*
contact ['kɑːntækt] **1** S (*physisch*) Berührung *f*; (*Beziehung*) Kontakt *m*; (*Person*) Kontaktperson *f* **2** V/T sich in Verbindung setzen mit **contact lenses** S PL Kontaktlinsen *pl*
contagious [kən'teɪdʒəs] ADJ ansteckend
contain [kən'teɪn] V/T enthalten **container** S Behälter *m*, Container *m*
contaminate [kən'tæməneɪt] V/T verunreinigen; (*chemisch etc*) verseuchen **contamination** [kəntæmə'neɪʃən] S Verunreinigung *f*; (*durch Radioaktivität*) Verseuchung *f*

contemporary [kən'tempəreri] ADJ zeitgenössisch **contempt** [kən'tempt] S Verachtung *f* **content** [kən'tent] ADJ zufrieden **content(s)** ['ka:ntent(s)] S (PL) Inhalt *m* **contest** 1 ['ka:ntest] S (Wett)kampf *m* (*for* um), Wettbewerb *m* 2 [kən'test] V/T kämpfen um *+akk*; (*Behauptung etc*) bestreiten **contestant** [kən'testənt] S Teilnehmer(in) *m(f)* **context** ['ka:ntekst] S Zusammenhang *m* **continent** ['ka:ntənənt] S Kontinent *m*, Festland *n* **continental** [ka:ntə'nentl] ADJ kontinental; ~ **breakfast** *kleines Frühstück mit Brötchen und Marmelade, Kaffee oder Tee* **continually** [kən'tınjəwəlı] ADV dauernd; immer wieder **continue** [kən'tınju:] 1 V/I weitermachen (*with* mit); fortfahren (*with* mit); (*Reise*) weiterfahren; (*Zustand*) fortdauern, anhalten 2 V/T fortsetzen **continuous** [kən'tınjʊəs] ADJ ununterbrochen; ständig **contraceptive** [ka:ntrə'septıv] S Verhütungsmittel *n* **contract** ['ka:ntrækt] S Vertrag *m* **contradict** [ka:ntrə'dıkt] V/T widersprechen *+dat* **contrary** ['ka:ntrərı] 1 S Gegenteil *n*; **on the** ~ im Gegenteil 2 ADJ ~ **to** entgegen *+dat* **contrast** 1 ['ka:ntræst] S Kontrast *m*, Gegensatz *m*; **in** ~ **to** im Gegensatz zu 2 [kən'træst] V/T entgegensetzen **contribute** [kən'trıbju:t] V/T & V/I beitragen (*to* zu); (*Geld*) spenden (*to* für) **contribution** [ka:ntrı'bju:ʃən] S Beitrag *m* **control** [kən'troʊl] 1 V/T beherrschen; (*Gefühle*) im Griff haben; TECH steuern; ~ **oneself** sich beherrschen 2 S Kontrolle *f*; (*Gefühle*) Beherrschung *f*; TECH Steuerung *f*; **~s** *pl* (*Knöpfe, Hebel*) Bedienungselemente *pl*; (*Fahrzeug, Flugzeug*) Steuerung *f* **control panel** S Schalttafel *f* **controversial** [ka:ntrə'vɜ:rʃəl] ADJ umstritten **convenience** [kən'vi:njəns] S Annehmlichkeit *f*; **at your** ~ wann es Ihnen passt **convenience food** S Fertiggericht *n* **convenience store** S Tante-Emma-Laden *m* **convenient** ADJ günstig, passend **convent** ['ka:nvənt] S Kloster *n* **convention** [kən'venʃən] S Konvention *f*; (*Zusammenkunft*) Konferenz *f* **conventional** ADJ herkömmlich, konventionell **conversation** [ka:nvər'seıʃən] S Gespräch *n*, Unterhal-

tung *f*
conversion [kən'vɜːrʃən] S Umwandlung *f* (*into* in *+akk*); (*Gebäude*) Umbau *m* (*into* zu); (*Währung, Maß*) Umrechnung *f* **convert** [kən'vɜːrt] V/T umwandeln; (*Person*) bekehren; IT konvertieren; **~ into dollars** in Dollar umrechnen **convertible** S AUTO Kabrio *n*
conveyor belt [kən'veɪərbelt] S Förderband *n*, Fließband *n*
convict 1 [kən'vɪkt] V/T verurteilen (*of* wegen) 2 ['kaːnvɪkt] S Strafgefangene(r) *m/f(m)* **conviction** S JUR Verurteilung *f*; (*Glaube*) Überzeugung *f*
convince [kən'vɪns] V/T überzeugen (*of* von) **convincing** ADJ überzeugend
cook [kʊk] 1 V/T & V/I kochen 2 S Koch *m*, Köchin *f* **cookie** S Keks *m*; IT Cookie *n* **cooking** S Kochen *n*; (*Essen*) Küche *f*
cool [kuːl] 1 ADJ kühl, gelassen; *umg* (*toll*) cool, stark 2 V/T & V/I (ab)kühlen; **~ it** reg dich ab! 3 S **keep/lose one's ~** *umg* ruhig bleiben/durchdrehen **cool down** V/I abkühlen; (*Person*) sich beruhigen **cooler** S Kühlbox *f*
cooperate [koʊ'aːpəreɪt] V/I zusammenarbeiten, kooperieren **cooperation** [koʊaːpə'reɪʃən] S Zusammenarbeit *f*, Kooperation *f*
cop [kaːp] S *umg* (*Polizist*) Bulle *m*
cope [koʊp] V/I zurechtkommen, fertig werden (*with* mit)
copier ['kaːpɪər] S Kopierer *m*
copper ['kaːpər] S Kupfer *n*; *umg* (*Geld*) Kupfermünze *f*
copy ['kaːpɪ] 1 S Kopie *f*; (*von Buch etc*) Exemplar *n* 2 V/T kopieren; nachahmen **copyright** S Urheberrecht *n*
cord [kɔːrd] S Schnur *f*; (*Material*) Kordsamt *m* **cordless** ['kɔːrdləs] ADJ schnurlos
core [kɔːr] S Kern *m*; (*von Apfel*) Kerngehäuse *n*
cork [kɔːrk] S Kork *m*; (*für Flasche*) Korken *m* **corkscrew** ['kɔːrkskruː] S Korkenzieher *m*
corn [kɔːrn] S Mais *m*; (*am Fuß*) Hühnerauge *n*; **~ on the cob** (gekochter) Maiskolben **cornbread** S Maisbrot *n* **corn dog** S *mit Maismehl paniertes Bratwürstchen*
corner ['kɔːrnər] 1 S Ecke *f*; (*von Straße*) Kurve *f*; SPORT Eckstoß *m* 2 V/T in die Enge treiben
corporation [kɔːrpə'reɪʃən] S WIRTSCH Aktiengesellschaft *f*
corpse [kɔːrps] S Leiche *f*
corral [kə'ræl] S Korral *m*, Pferch *m*
correct [kə'rekt] 1 ADJ richtig; korrekt 2 V/T korrigieren, verbessern **correction** S Korrektur *f*
correspond [kaːrə'spaːnd] V/I entsprechen (*to dat*), überein-

stimmen **corresponding** ADJ entsprechend
corridor ['kɔːrədər] S (*Gebäude*) Flur *m*; (*Zug*) Gang *m*
corrupt [kə'rʌpt] ADJ korrupt
cosmetics [kɑːz'metɪks] S PL Kosmetika *pl* **cosmetic surgery** S Schönheitschirurgie *f*
cosmopolitan [kɑːzmə'pɑːlətən] ADJ international; weltoffen
cost ⟨cost, cost⟩ [kɑːst] **1** V/T kosten **2** S Kosten *pl*; **at all ~s, at any ~** um jeden Preis; **~ of living** Lebenshaltungskosten *pl* **costly** ADJ kostspielig
costume ['kɑːstuːm] S Kostüm *n*, Verkleidung *f*
cot [kɑːt] S Campingliege *f*
cottage ['kɑːtɪdʒ] S kleines Haus; Landhäuschen *n* **cottage cheese** S Hüttenkäse *m*
cotton ['kɑːtn] S Baumwolle *f*; Watte *f* **cotton candy** S Zuckerwatte *f*
couch [kaʊtʃ] S Couch *f*, Sofa *n*
cough [kɑːf] **1** V/I husten **2** S Husten *m* **cough drop** S Hustenbonbon *n*
could [kʊd] *prät von* can; konnte; *Konditional* könnte; **~ you come earlier?** könntest du/könnten Sie früher kommen? **couldn't** *kontr von* **could not**
council ['kaʊnsl] S POL Rat *m*; (*von Gemeinde*) Gemeinderat *m*; (*von Stadt*) Stadtrat *m*
counsel ['kaʊnsl] **1** S Anwalt *m*, Anwältin *f*, Rechtsanwalt *m*, Rechtsanwältin *f*; Rat (-schlag) *m*; Beratung *f* **2** V/T (*Person*) beraten **counselor** ['kaʊnslər] S Berater(in) *m(f)*; Anwalt *m*, Anwältin *f*
count [kaʊnt] **1** V/T & V/I zählen; mitrechnen **2** S Zählung *f* **count on** V/T sich verlassen auf *+akk*; (*erwarten*) rechnen mit
counter ['kaʊntər] S (*Geschäft*) Ladentisch *m*; (*Lokal*) Theke *f*; (*Bank, Post®*) Schalter *m* **counterclockwise** ADV entgegen dem Uhrzeigersinn
countless ['kaʊntləs] ADJ zahllos, unzählig
country ['kʌntrɪ] S Land *n*; **in the ~** auf dem Land(e) **countryman** S Landsmann *m* **country road** S Landstraße *f* **countryside** S Landschaft *f*; (*ländliche Gegend*) Land *n*
county ['kaʊntɪ] S Verwaltungsbezirk *m*
couple ['kʌpl] S Paar *n*; **a ~ of** ein paar
coupon ['kuːpɑːn] S Gutschein *m*
courage ['kɜːrɪdʒ] S Mut *m*
courier ['kʊrɪər] S (*Tourismus*) Reiseleiter(in) *m(f)*; (*Bote*) Kurier *m*
course [kɔːrs] S Kurs *m*; (*bei Sportwettbewerb*) Strecke *f*; SCHIFF, FLUG Kurs *m*; (*Teil einer*

Mahlzeit) Gang *m;* **of ~** natürlich
court [kɔːrt] S SPORT Platz *m;* JUR Gericht *n*
courtesy ['kɜːrtəsɪ] S Höflichkeit *f*
courthouse ['kɔːrthaʊs] S Gerichtsgebäude *n* **court order** S Gerichtsbeschluss *m* **courtroom** S Gerichtssaal *m* **courtyard** ['kɔːrtjɑːrd] S Hof *m*
cousin ['kʌzn] S Cousin *m,* Cousine *f*
cover ['kʌvər] **1** V/T bedecken (*in, with* mit); (*Strecke*) zurücklegen; (*Kosten*) decken **2** S (*für Bett*) Decke *f;* (*Kissen*) Bezug *m;* (*Behälter*) Deckel *m;* (*Buch*) Umschlag *m;* **(insurance) ~** Versicherungsschutz *m* **cover charge** S Kosten *pl* für ein Gedeck
cow [kaʊ] S Kuh *f*
coward ['kaʊərd] S Feigling *m* **cowardly** ADJ feig(e)
cowboy ['kaʊbɔɪ] S Cowboy *m* **cowgirl** S Cowgirl *n* **cowhand** S Cowboy *m,* Cowgirl *n*
coyote [kaɪ'oʊtɪ] S Kojote *m*
cozy ['koʊzɪ] ADJ gemütlich
CPU IT *abk* = central processing unit; Zentraleinheit *f*
crab [kræb] S Krabbe *f*
crabby ['kræbɪ] ADJ mürrisch, reizbar
crack [kræk] **1** S Riss *m;* (*in Glas*) Sprung *m;* (*Droge*) Crack *n* **2** V/I (*Tasse, Glas*) einen Sprung bekommen; (*Wand, Eis etc*) einen Riss bekommen **3** V/T (*Knochen*) anbrechen; (*Nuss, Kode*) knacken
cracker ['krækər] S (*Gebäck*) Kräcker *m*
crackle ['krækl] V/I knistern; (*Telefonleitung*) knacken
cradle ['kreɪdl] S Wiege *f*
craft [kræft] S Handwerk *n,* Kunsthandwerk *n* **craftsman** ‹-men *pl*› S Handwerker *m*
cram [kræm] V/T stopfen (*into* in *+akk*); **be ~med with ...** mit ... vollgestopft sein
cramp [kræmp] S Krampf *m*
cranberry ['krænberɪ] S Preiselbeere *f*
crane [kreɪn] S Kran *m;* (*Vogel*) Kranich *m*
cranky ['kræŋkɪ] ADJ schlecht gelaunt
crap [kræp] *vulg* **1** S Scheiße *f,* Mist *m* **2** ADJ beschissen, Scheiß- **crappy** ADJ *umg* beschissen
crash [kræʃ] **1** V/I einen Unfall haben; (*zwei Fahrzeuge*) zusammenstoßen; (*Flugzeug, Computer*) abstürzen; (*Wirtschaft*) zusammenbrechen; **~ into sth** gegen etw knallen **2** V/T einen Unfall haben mit **3** S (*Auto*) Unfall *m;* (*Zug*) Unglück *n;* (*Kollision*) Zusammenstoß *m;* FLUG, IT Absturz *m;* (*Geräusch*) Krachen *n* **crash barrier** S Leitplanke *f* **crash helmet** S Sturzhelm *m*

crate [kreɪt] S Kiste *f*; *(Bier)* Kasten *m*
craving ['kreɪvɪŋ] S starkes Verlangen, Bedürfnis *n*
crawl [krɒ:l] **1** V/I kriechen; *(Baby)* krabbeln **2** S *(Schwimmen)* Kraul *n*
crayfish ['kreɪfɪʃ] S Languste *f*
crayon ['kreɪɑ:n] S Buntstift *m*
crazy ['kreɪzɪ] ADJ verrückt *(about* nach)
cream [kri:m] **1** S *(von Milch)* Sahne *f*, Rahm *m*; *(kosmetisch)* Creme *f* **2** ADJ cremefarben **cream cheese** S Frischkäse *m* **creamer** S Kaffeeweißer *m* **creamy** ADJ sahnig
crease [kri:s] **1** S Falte *f* **2** V/T falten; *(Kleidung)* zerknittern
create [kri:'eɪt] V/T schaffen; *(Unsicherheit etc)* verursachen **creative** [kri:'eɪtɪv] ADJ kreativ **creature** ['kri:tʃər] S Geschöpf *n*
credit ['kredət] S FIN Kredit *m*; *(auf Konto)* Guthaben *n*; *(für Arbeit, Leistung)* Anerkennung *f*; **~s** *(von Film)* Abspann *m* **credit card** S Kreditkarte *f*
creep ⟨crept, crept/creeped⟩ [kri:p, krept, kri:pt] V/I kriechen **creeps** S **he gives me the ~** er ist mir nicht ganz geheuer **creepy** ['kri:pɪ] ADJ gruselig, unheimlich **crept** [krept] *prät, pperf von* creep
cress [kres] S Kresse *f*
crew [kru:] S Besatzung *f*, Mannschaft *f* **crew cut** S Bürstenhaarschnitt *m*
crib [krɪb] S Kinderbett *n*
cricket ['krɪkət] S *(Insekt)* Grille *f*
crime [kraɪm] S Verbrechen *n* **criminal** ['krɪmənl] **1** S Verbrecher(in) *m(f)* **2** ADJ kriminell, strafbar
crisis ⟨crises *pl*⟩ ['kraɪsɪs, -si:z] S Krise *f*
crisp [krɪsp] ADJ knusprig **crispbread** S Knäckebrot *n*
critic ['krɪtɪk] S Kritiker(in) *m(f)* **critical** ADJ kritisch **critically** ADV kritisch; **~ ill/injured** schwer krank/verletzt **criticism** ['krɪtəsɪzəm] S Kritik *f* **criticize** ['krɪtəsaɪz] V/T kritisieren
Croatia [kroʊ'eɪʃə] S Kroatien *n*
crocodile ['krɑ:kədaɪl] S Krokodil *n*
crop [krɑ:p] S Ernte *f* **crops** S PL Getreide *n*
cross [krɑ:s] **1** S Kreuz *n*; **mark sth with a ~** etw ankreuzen **2** V/T *(Straße)* überqueren; *(Beine)* übereinanderschlagen; **it ~ed my mind** es fiel mir ein; **~ one's fingers** die Daumen drücken **cross out** V/T durchstreichen **crossbar** S *(Fahrrad)* Stange *f*; SPORT Querlatte *f* **cross-country skiing** S Langlauf *m* **crossing** S (Straßen)kreuzung *f*; *(über Straße)* Fußgängerüber-

weg *m*; (*mit Schiff*) Überfahrt *f* **crossroads** S SG OD PL Straßenkreuzung *f* **crosswalk** S Fußgängerüberweg *m* **crossword (puzzle)** S Kreuzworträtsel *n*
crouch [kraʊtʃ] V/I hocken
crow [kroʊ] S Krähe *f*
crowd [kraʊd] **1** S Menge *f* **2** V/I sich drängen (*into* in +*akk*; *around* um) **crowded** ADJ überfüllt
crown [kraʊn] **1** S Krone *f* **2** V/T krönen
crucial ['kru:ʃəl] ADJ entscheidend
crude [kru:d] **1** ADJ primitiv; (*Sprache, Witz*) derb, ordinär **2** S **~ (oil)** Rohöl *n*
cruel ['kru:əl] ADJ grausam (*to* zu, gegen); gefühllos **cruelty** S Grausamkeit *f*
cruise [kru:z] **1** S Kreuzfahrt *f* **2** V/I (*Schiff*) kreuzen; (*Auto*) mit Reisegeschwindigkeit fahren **cruise liner** S Kreuzfahrtschiff *n*
crumb [krʌm] S Krume *f*
crumble ['krʌmbl] V/T & V/I zerbröckeln
crumple ['krʌmpl] V/T zerknittern
crunchy ['krʌntʃı] ADJ knusprig
crush [krʌʃ] **1** V/T zerdrücken; (*Finger*) quetschen; (*Gewürze*) zerstoßen **2** S **have a ~ on sb** in j-n verknallt sein
crust [krʌst] S Kruste *f* **crusty** ADJ knusprig
crutch [krʌtʃ] S Krücke *f*
cry [kraı] **1** V/I rufen; schreien; (*Tränen vergießen*) weinen **2** S Ruf *m*, Schrei *m*
CT *abk* = Connecticut
Cuba ['kju:bə] S Kuba *n*
cube [kju:b] S Würfel *m* **cubic** ['kju:bık] ADJ Kubik-
cubicle ['kju:bıkl] S Kabine *f*
cucumber ['kju:kʌmbər] S Salatgurke *f*
cuddle ['kʌdl] **1** V/T in den Arm nehmen; schmusen mit **2** V/I kuscheln **3** S Liebkosung *f*, Umarmung *f* **cuddly** ['kʌdlı] ADJ verschmust
cuff [kʌf] S Manschette *f*; (*von Hose*) Aufschlag *m* **cufflink** S Manschettenknopf *m*
cuisine [kwı'zi:n] S Kochkunst *f*, Küche *f*
cul-de-sac ['kʌldəsæk] S Sackgasse *f*
culprit ['kʌlprət] S Schuldige(r) *m/f(m)*; Übeltäter(in) *m(f)*
cult [kʌlt] S Kult *m*
cultivate ['kʌltəveıt] V/T AGR (*Land*) bebauen; (*Getreide*) anbauen
cultural ['kʌltʃərəl] ADJ kulturell, Kultur- **culture** S Kultur *f*
cunning ['kʌnıŋ] ADJ schlau; gerissen
cup [kʌp] S Tasse *f*; (*Trophäe*) Pokal *m* **cupboard** ['kʌbərd] S Schrank *m* **cupcake** S kleiner Napfkuchen
curb [kɜ:rb] S Randstein *m*

curd [kɜːrd] S ~ **cheese, ~s** ≈ Quark *m*
cure [kjʊr] **1** S Heilmittel *n* (*for* gegen); (*von Krankheit*) Heilung *f* **2** V/T heilen; GASTR pökeln; räuchern
curious ['kjʊrɪəs] ADJ neugierig
curl [kɜːrl] **1** S Locke *f* **2** V/I sich kräuseln **curly** ADJ lockig
currant ['kɜːrənt] S (*getrocknet*) Korinthe *f*; (*Rote, Schwarze*) Johannisbeere *f*
currency ['kɜːrənsɪ] S Währung *f*; **foreign ~** Devisen *pl*
current ['kɜːrənt] **1** S (*in Wasser*) Strömung *f*; (*elektrisch*) Strom *m* **2** ADJ aktuell, gegenwärtig; (*Ausdruck*) gängig **currently** ADV zur Zeit
curry ['kɜːrɪ] S Currygericht *n*
curse [kɜːrs] **1** V/I fluchen (*at* auf +*akk*) **2** S Fluch *m*
cursor ['kɜːrsər] S IT Cursor *m*
curtain ['kɜːrtn] S Vorhang *m*
curve [kɜːrv] S Kurve *f* **curved** ADJ gebogen
cushion ['kʊʃən] S Kissen *n*
cuss [kʌs] V/I fluchen
custard ['kʌstərd] S ≈ Vanillesoße *f*
custom ['kʌstəm] S Brauch *m*, Gewohnheit *f* **customary** ['kʌstəmerɪ] ADJ üblich **customer** S Kunde *m*, Kundin *f* **customer loyalty card** S Kundenkarte *f* **customer service** S Kundendienst *m* **custom-made** ADJ nach Maß, maßgefertigt
customs ['kʌstəmz] S PL Zoll *m* **customs officer** S Zollbeamte(r) *m*, Zollbeamtin *f*
cut [kʌt] **1** V/T ⟨cut, cut⟩ schneiden; (*Kuchen*) anschneiden; (*Ausgaben, Löhne*) kürzen; (*Preise*) heruntersetzen **2** S Schnitt *m*; (*Verletzung*) Schnittwunde *f*; (*von Gehalt, staatlicher Leistung*) Kürzung *f* (*in gen*); **price ~** Preissenkung *f* **cut down** V/T (*Baum*) fällen; **~ on sth** etwas einschränken **cut off** V/T abschneiden; (*Gas, Elektrizität*) abdrehen, abstellen; TEL **I was ~** ich wurde unterbrochen
cute [kjuːt] ADJ putzig, niedlich; clever
cutlet ['kʌtlət] S Kotelett *n*, Schnitzel *n*
cut-rate ['kʌtreɪt] ADJ verbilligt
cwt *abk* = hundredweight; ≈ Zentner, Ztr.
cybercafé ['saɪbərkæfeɪ] S Internetcafé *n*
cycle ['saɪkl] **1** S Fahrrad *n* **2** V/I Rad fahren **cycling** S Radfahren *n* **cyclist** ['saɪkləst] S Radfahrer(in) *m(f)*
cylinder ['sɪləndər] S Zylinder *m*
cynical ['sɪnɪkəl] ADJ zynisch
Cypriot ['sɪprɪət] **1** ADJ zypriotisch **2** S Zypriote *m*, Zypriotin *f* **Cyprus** ['saɪprəs] S Zypern *n*

Czech [tʃek] **1** ADJ tschechisch **2** S (*Person*) Tscheche *m*, Tschechin *f*; (*Sprache*) Tschechisch *n* **Czech Republic** [tʃek] S Tschechische Republik, Tschechien *n*

D

DA *abk* = District Attorney; ≈Staatsanwalt *m*, ≈Staatsanwältin *f*
dab [dæb] VT (*Wunde, Nase etc*) betupfen (*with* mit)
dad(dy) ['dæd(ı)] S Papa *m*, Vati *m*
daily ['deılı] **1** ADJ & ADV täglich **2** S Tageszeitung *f*
daiquiri ['dækərı] S Daiquiri *m* (*alkoholisches Mixgetränk aus Rum und Fruchtsäften*)
dairy ['derı] S Molkerei *f* **dairy products** S PL Milchprodukte *pl*
dam [dæm] **1** S Staudamm *m* **2** VT stauen
damage ['dæmıdʒ] **1** S Schaden *m*; **~s** *pl* JUR Schadenersatz *m* **2** VT beschädigen; (*Ruf, Gesundheit*) schädigen, schaden *+dat*
damn [dæm] **1** ADJ *umg* verdammt **2** VT verurteilen; **~ (it)!** verflucht! **3** S **he doesn't give a ~** es ist ihm völlig egal
damp [dæmp] **1** ADJ feucht **2** S Feuchtigkeit *f*
dance [dæns] **1** S Tanz *m*; Tanzveranstaltung *f* **2** V/I tanzen **dance floor** S Tanzfläche *f* **dancer** S Tänzer(in) *m(f)* **dancing** S Tanzen *n*
dandruff ['dændrəf] S Schuppen *pl*
Dane [deın] S Däne *m*, Dänin *f*
danger ['deındʒər] S Gefahr *f* **dangerous** ADJ gefährlich
Danish ['deınıʃ] **1** ADJ dänisch **2** S (*Sprache*) Dänisch *n*; **the ~** *pl* die Dänen **Danish (pastry)** ['deınıʃ, deınıʃ'peıstrı] S Plundergebäck *n*
dare [der] V/I **~ (to) do sth** es wagen, etw zu tun; **I didn't ~ ask** ich traute mich nicht, zu fragen; **how ~ you** was fällt dir ein! **daring** ADJ (*Person*) mutig; (*Film, Kleidung*) gewagt
dark [dɑːrk] **1** ADJ dunkel; (*Stimmung*) düster, trübe; (*Mächte*) finster; **~ chocolate** Bitterschokolade *f*; **~ green** dunkelgrün **2** S Dunkelheit *f* **dark glasses** S PL Sonnenbrille *f* **darkness** S Dunkelheit *n*
darling ['dɑːrlıŋ] S Schatz *m*, Liebling *m*
dash [dæʃ] **1** V/I stürzen, rennen **2** S (*in Text*) Gedankenstrich *m*; (*von Flüssigkeit*) Schuss *m* **dashboard** S Armaturenbrett *n*
data ['deıtə] S PL Daten *pl* **data bank, data base** S Da-

tenbank *f* **data processing** S Datenverarbeitung *f*

date [deɪt] **1** S Datum *n*; (*Treffen*) Termin *m*; (*geschäftlich*) Verabredung *f*; (*mit Freund/Freundin*) Date *n*; (*Frucht*) Dattel *f*; **what's today's ~?** der Wievielte ist heute?; **out of ~** *adj* veraltet; **up to ~** *adj* (*Nachricht*) aktuell; (*Mode*) zeitgemäß **2** V/T (*Brief*) datieren; (*in Beziehung*) gehen mit **datebook** S Terminkalender *m* **dated** ADJ altmodisch **date of birth** S Geburtsdatum *n*

daughter ['dɒːtər] S Tochter *f* **daughter-in-law** ⟨daughters-in-law⟩ S Schwiegertochter *f*

dawn [dɒːn] **1** S Morgendämmerung *f* **2** V/I dämmern; **it ~ed on me** mir ging ein Licht auf

day [deɪ] S Tag *m*; **one ~** eines Tages; **by ~** bei Tage; **~ after ~, ~ by ~** Tag für Tag; **the ~ after/before** am Tag danach/zuvor; **the ~ before yesterday** vorgestern; **the ~ after tomorrow** übermorgen; **these ~s** heutzutage; **in those ~s** damals **day-care center** S Kita *f* (*Kindertagesstätte*) **daydream** **1** S Tagtraum *m* **2** V/I (mit offenen Augen) träumen **daylight** S Tageslicht *n* **day nursery** S Kita *f* (*Kindertagesstätte*) **day trip** S Tagesausflug *m*

dazzle ['dæzl] V/T blenden

DC **1** *abk* = direct current; Gleichstrom *m* **2** *abk* = District of Columbia; *Gebiet der Bundeshauptstadt Washington*

DE *abk* = Delaware

dead [ded] **1** ADJ tot; (*Zeh etc*) abgestorben **2** ADV genau; *umg* total, völlig; **~ tired** todmüde; **~ slow** (*Verkehrsschild*) Schritt fahren **dead end** S Sackgasse *f* **deadline** S Termin *m*, Frist *f* **deadly** ADJ tödlich

deaf [def] ADJ taub **deafening** ADJ ohrenbetäubend

deal [diːl] **1** V/T & V/I ⟨dealt, dealt⟩ [delt] (*Spielkarten*) geben, austeilen **2** S Geschäft *n*; (*Vereinbarung*) Abmachung *f*; **it's a ~** abgemacht!; **a good/great ~ of** ziemlich/sehr viel **deal in** V/T handeln mit **deal with** V/T sich beschäftigen mit; (*Buch, Film: als Inhalt*) behandeln; (*mit Person, Problem*) fertig werden mit; (*eine Sache*) erledigen **dealer** S WIRTSCH Händler(in) *m(f)*; (*von Rauschgift*) Dealer(in) *m(f)* **dealt** [delt] *prät, pperf von* deal

dear [dɪr] **1** ADJ lieb, teuer; **Dear Sir or Madam** Sehr geehrte Damen und Herren; **Dear David** Lieber David **2** S Schatz *m*; (*Anrede*) mein Schatz, Liebling **dearly** ADV (*lieben*) (heiß und) innig; (*be-

zahlen) teuer
death [deθ] S Tod *m*; (*bei Unfall*) Todesopfer *n* **death certificate** S Totenschein *m* **death penalty** S Todesstrafe *f*
debatable [dɪ'beɪtəbl] ADJ fraglich; (*Frage*) strittig **debate** [dɪ'beɪt] **1** S Debatte *f* **2** V/T debattieren
debit ['debɪt] **1** S Soll *n* **2** V/T (*Konto*) belasten **debit card** S (*Geldkarte*) Debitkarte *f*
debris [də'bri:] S Trümmer *pl*
debt [det] S Schuld *f*; **be in ~** verschuldet sein
decade ['dekeɪd] S Jahrzehnt *n*
decaf ['di:kæf] S *umg* koffeinfreier Kaffee **decaffeinated** [di:'kæfəneɪtəd] ADJ koffeinfrei
decay [dɪ'keɪ] **1** S Verfall *m*, Verwesung *f*; (*Zahn*) Karies *f* **2** V/I verfallen; verwesen; (*Holz*) vermodern; (*Zahn*) faulen; (*Laub*) verrotten
deceased [dɪ'si:st] S **the ~** der/die Verstorbene
deceive [dɪ'si:v] V/T täuschen
December [dɪ'sembər] S Dezember *m*; → September
decent ['di:sənt] ADJ anständig; *umg* **are you ~?** hast du was an?
decide [dɪ'saɪd] **1** V/T entscheiden; beschließen **2** V/I sich entscheiden; **~ on sth** sich für etw entscheiden, sich zu etw entschließen
decimal ['desəməl] ADJ Dezimal-
decision [dɪ'sɪʒən] S Entscheidung *f* (*on* über *+akk*); (*von Komitee, Jury etc*) Beschluss *m*; **make a ~** eine Entscheidung treffen **decisive** [dɪ'saɪsɪv] ADJ entscheidend; (*Person*) entscheidungsfreudig
deck [dek] S SCHIFF Deck *n*; (*von Spielkarten*) Blatt *n* **deckchair** S Liegestuhl *m*
declaration [deklə'reɪʃən] S Erklärung *f*; **Declaration of Independence** Unabhängigkeitserklärung *f* **declare** [dɪ'kler] V/T erklären; (*selbstsicher*) behaupten (*that* dass); (*beim Zoll*) **do you have anything to ~?** haben Sie etwas zu verzollen?
decline [dɪ'klaɪn] **1** S Rückgang *m* **2** V/T (*Einladung, Angebot*) ablehnen **3** V/I sinken, abnehmen; (*Gesundheit*) sich verschlechtern
decorate ['dekəreɪt] V/T (aus)schmücken; (*mit Tapete*) tapezieren; (*mit Farbe*) anstreichen **decoration** [dekə'reɪʃən] S Schmuck *m*; (*Vorgang*) Schmücken *n*; (*mit Tapete*) Tapezieren *n*; (*mit Farbe*) Anstreichen *n*
decrease **1** ['di:kri:s] S Abnahme *f* **2** [di:'kri:s] V/I abnehmen
dedicate ['dedəkeɪt] V/T widmen (*to sb* j-m) **dedicated** ADJ (*Person*) engagiert

deduct [dɪ'dʌkt] VT abziehen (*from* von) **deduction** [dɪ'dʌkʃən] S (*Geld*) Abzug *m;* (*logisch*) (Schluss)folgerung *f*
deed [di:d] S Tat *f*
deep [di:p] ADJ tief **deep-freeze** S Tiefkühltruhe *f,* Gefrierschrank *m* **deep-fry** VT frittieren
deer [dɪr] S Reh *n;* (*größer*) Hirsch *m*
defeat [dɪ'fi:t] **1** S Niederlage *f* **2** VT besiegen
defect ['di:fekt] S Defekt *m,* Fehler *m*
defend [dɪ'fend] VT verteidigen **defendant** S JUR Angeklagte(r) *m/f(m)* **defender** S SPORT Verteidiger(in) *m(f)* **defense** [dɪ'fens] S Verteidigung *f*
define [dɪ'faɪn] VT definieren; (*Pflichten etc*) bestimmen **definite** ['defənət] ADJ (*Entscheidung, Antwort*) klar, eindeutig; (*gewiss*) sicher; **it's ~** es steht fest **definitely** ADV bestimmt
defrost [di:'frɒ:st] VT (*Kühlschrank*) abtauen; (*Essen*) auftauen
degree [dɪ'gri:] S Grad *m;* (*an Universität*) akademischer Grad; **to a certain ~** einigermaßen
dehydrated [di:haɪ'dreɪtəd] ADJ (*Lebensmittel*) getrocknet, Trocken-; (*Haut, Körper*) ausgetrocknet
de-ice [di:'aɪs] VT enteisen
delay [dɪ'leɪ] **1** VT verschieben, aufschieben; **be ~ed** (*Ereignis, Abfahrt*) sich verzögern; **the flight was ~ed** die Maschine hatte Verspätung **2** S Verzögerung *f;* (*von Zug*) Verspätung *f;* **without ~** unverzüglich **delayed** ADJ (*Zug*) verspätet
delete [dɪ'li:t] VT (aus)streichen; IT löschen **deletion** S Streichung *f;* IT Löschung *f*
deli ['delɪ] S *umg* Feinkostgeschäft *n*
deliberate [dɪ'lɪbərət] ADJ absichtlich **deliberately** ADV mit Absicht, extra
delicate ['delɪkət] ADJ fein; (*Farbe, Person*) zart; *a.* MED empfindlich; (*Situation, Sache*) heikel
delicatessen [delɪkə'tesn] S SG Feinkostgeschäft *n*
delicious [dɪ'lɪʃəs] ADJ köstlich, lecker
delight [dɪ'laɪt] S Freude *f* **delighted** ADJ sehr erfreut (*with* über *+akk*) **delightful** ADJ entzückend; herrlich
deliver [dɪ'lɪvər] VT liefern (*to sb* j-m); (*Brief, Paket*) zustellen; (*Rede*) halten; (*Baby*) entbinden **delivery** S Lieferung *f;* (*Brief, Paket*) Zustellung *f;* (*Baby*) Entbindung *f* **delivery van** S Lieferwagen *m*
deluxe [dɪ'lʌks] ADJ Luxus-
Dem **1** *abk* = Democrat; Demokrat(in) *m(f)* **2** *abk* = Democratic; demokratisch

demand [dɪˈmænd] **1** VT verlangen (*from* von); (*Zeit, Geduld*) erfordern **2** S Forderung *f*, Verlangen *n* (*for* nach); WIRTSCH (*nach Waren*) Nachfrage *f*; **on ~** auf Wunsch; **in ~** gefragt **demanding** ADJ anspruchsvoll

democracy [dɪˈmɑːkrəsɪ] S Demokratie *f* **democrat, Democrat** POL [ˈdeməkræt] S Demokrat(in) *m(f)* **democratic** ADJ demokratisch; **the Democratic Party** POL die Demokratische Partei

demolish [dɪˈmɑːlɪʃ] VT abreißen; *fig* zerstören

demonstrate [ˈdemənstreɪt] VT & VI demonstrieren, beweisen **demonstration** S Demonstration *f*

denial [dɪˈnaɪəl] S Leugnung *f*; (*offiziell*) Dementi *n*

denim [ˈdenɪm] S Jeansstoff *m* **denims** S PL Bluejeans *pl*

Denmark [ˈdenmɑːrk] S Dänemark *n*

dense [dens] ADJ dicht; *umg* (*dumm*) schwer von Begriff

dent [dent] **1** S Beule *f*, Delle *f* **2** VT einbeulen

dental [ˈdentl] ADJ Zahn-; **~ floss** Zahnseide *f*; **~ hygienist** Dentalhygieniker(in) *m(f)* **dentist** S Zahnarzt *m*, Zahnärztin *f* **dentures** [ˈdentʃərz] S PL Zahnprothese *f*, Gebiss *n*

Denver boot [denvərˈbuːt] S Parkkralle *f*

deny [dɪˈnaɪ] VT leugnen, bestreiten; (*Bitte*) ablehnen

deodorant [diːˈoʊdərənt] S Deo(dorant) *n*

depart [dɪˈpɑːrt] VI abreisen; (*Bus, Zug*) abfahren (*for* nach, *from* von); (*Flugzeug*) abfliegen (*for* nach, *from* von)

department [dɪˈpɑːrtmənt] S Abteilung *f*; (*an Universität*) Institut *n*; POL Ministerium *n* **department store** S Kaufhaus *n*

departure [dɪˈpɑːrtʃər] S (*von Mitarbeiter*) Weggang *m*; (*von Person*) Abreise *f* (*for* nach); (*Zug, Bus*) Abfahrt *f* (*for* nach); (*Flugzeug*) Abflug *m* (*for* nach) **departure lounge** S FLUG Abflughalle *f* **departure time** S Abfahrtzeit *f*; FLUG Abflugzeit *f*

depend [dɪˈpend] VI **it ~s** es kommt darauf an (*whether, if* ob) **depend on** VT abhängen von; (*Person*) sich verlassen auf +*akk*; (*Person, Gegend*) angewiesen sein auf +*akk* **dependent** ADJ abhängig (*on* von)

deport [dɪˈpɔːrt] VT ausweisen, abschieben

deposit [dɪˈpɑːzɪt] **1** S (*bei Kauf*) Anzahlung *f*; (*Wohnung*) Kaution *f*; (*Flasche*) Pfand *n*; (*auf Konto*) Einzahlung *f*; (*Metall*) Ablagerung *f* **2** VT abstellen, absetzen; (*auf Konto*) einzahlen; (*etw Wertvolles*) deponieren

depressed [dɪ'prest] ADJ niedergeschlagen, deprimiert **depressing** ADJ deprimierend **depression** [dɪ'preʃən] S Depression *f*; METEO Tief *n*
deprive [dɪ'praɪv] V/T **~ sb of sth** j-n einer Sache berauben **deprived** ADJ (sozial) benachteiligt
dept *abk* = department; Abt.
depth [depθ] S Tiefe *f*
deputy ['depjətɪ] **1** ADJ stellvertretend, Vize-; **~ sheriff** Hilfssheriff *m* **2** S Stellvertreter(in) *m(f)*; POL Abgeordnete(r) *m/f(m)*
derail [dɪ'reɪl] V/T entgleisen lassen
derby ['dɜ:rbɪ] S Pferderennen *n*; (*Hut*) Melone *f*
dermatitis [dɜ:rmə'taɪtɪs] S Hautentzündung *f*
descend [dɪ'send] V/T & V/I hinabsteigen, hinuntergehen; (*Person*) **~** *od* **be ~ed from** abstammen von **descendant** S Nachkomme *m* **descent** [dɪ'sent] S (*von Berg*) Abstieg *m*
describe [dɪ'skraɪb] V/T beschreiben **description** [dɪ'skrɪpʃən] S Beschreibung *f*
desert **1** ['dezərt] S Wüste *f* **2** [dɪ'zɜ:rt] V/T verlassen; im Stich lassen **deserted** ADJ verlassen; (*Straße etc*) menschenleer
deserve [dɪ'zɜ:rv] V/T verdienen
design [dɪ'zaɪn] **1** S (*Plan*) Entwurf *m*; (*Auto, Maschine*) Konstruktion *f*; (*Objekt*) Design *n*; (*Planung*) Gestaltung *f* **2** V/T entwerfen; (*Maschine etc*) konstruieren **designer** [dɪ'zaɪnər] S Designer(in) *m(f)*; TECH Konstrukteur(in) *m(f)*
desirable [dɪ'zaɪrəbl] S wünschenswert; (*Person*) begehrenswert **desire** [dɪ'zaɪr] **1** S Wunsch *m* (*for* nach); (*sexuell*) Begierde *f* (*for* nach) **2** V/T wünschen; verlangen
desk [desk] S Schreibtisch *m*; (*Hotel*) Empfang *m*; (*Flughafen*) Schalter *m*
despair [dɪ'sper] **1** S Verzweiflung *f* (*at* über *+akk*) **2** V/I verzweifeln (*of* an *+dat*)
desperate ['despərət] ADJ verzweifelt; (*Situation*) hoffnungslos; **be ~ for sth** etw dringend brauchen, unbedingt wollen **desperation** [despə'reɪʃən] S Verzweiflung *f*
despite [dɪ'spaɪt] PRÄP trotz *+gen*
dessert [dɪ'zɜ:rt] S Nachtisch *m* **dessert spoon** S Dessertlöffel *m*
destination [destɪ'neɪʃən] S (*von Person*) (Reise)ziel *n*; (*von Ware*) Bestimmungsort *m*
destroy [dɪ'strɔɪ] V/T zerstören; vernichten **destruction** [dɪ'strʌkʃən] S Zerstörung *f*, Vernichtung *f*
detach [dɪ'tætʃ] V/T abnehmen; (*Formular*) abtrennen;

(*Gurt, Lasche*) lösen (*from* von)
detail ['di:teɪl] S Einzelheit *f*, Detail *n*; **in ~** ausführlich **detailed** ADJ detailliert, ausführlich
detain [dɪ'teɪn] V/T aufhalten; (*Polizei*) in Haft nehmen
detective [dɪ'tektɪv] S Detektiv(in) *m(f)* **detective story** S Krimi *m*
detergent [dɪ'tɜ:rdʒənt] S Reinigungsmittel *n*; (*für Kleidung*) Waschmittel *n*
deteriorate [dɪ'tɪri:əreɪt] V/I sich verschlechtern
determination [dɪtɜ:rmə'neɪʃən] S Entschlossenheit *f* **determined** [dɪ'tɜ:rmɪnd] ADJ (fest) entschlossen
detour ['di:tʊr] S Umweg *m*; (*von Verkehr*) Umleitung *f*
deuce [du:s] S (*Tennis*) Einstand *m*
devastate ['devəsteɪt] V/T verwüsten **devastating** ADJ verheerend
develop [dɪ'veləp] **1** V/T entwickeln; (*Krankheit*) bekommen **2** V/I sich entwickeln **development** S Entwicklung *f*; (*von Land, Gebiet*) Erschließung *f*
device [dɪ'vaɪs] S Vorrichtung *f*, Gerät *n*
devil ['devl] S Teufel *m*; **~'s food cake** *Art Schokoladentorte*
devoted [dɪ'voʊtəd] ADJ liebend; (*Diener etc*) treu ergeben
devotion S Hingabe *f*
devour [dɪ'vaʊr] V/T verschlingen
dew [du:] S Tau *m*
diabetes [daɪə'bi:ti:z] S Diabetes *m*, Zuckerkrankheit *f* **diabetic** [daɪə'betɪk] **1** ADJ zuckerkrank; (*Nahrungsmittel*) für Diabetiker **2** S Diabetiker(in) *m(f)*
diagnosis ⟨diagnoses *pl*⟩ [daɪəg'noʊsɪs, -si:z] S Diagnose *f*
diagonal [daɪ'ægənl] ADJ diagonal
diagram ['daɪəgræm] S Diagramm *n*
dial [daɪl] **1** S Skala *f*; (*Uhr*) Zifferblatt *n* **2** V/T TEL wählen **dial code** S Vorwahl *f*
dialect ['daɪəlekt] S Dialekt *m*
dialog ['daɪəlɑ:g] S Dialog *m*
dial tone S Amtszeichen *n*
dialysis [daɪ'æləsɪs] S MED Dialyse *f*
diameter [daɪ'æmətər] S Durchmesser *m*
diamond ['daɪmənd] S Diamant *m*; **~s** *pl* (*Karten*) Karo *n*
diaper ['daɪpər] S Windel *f*
diarrhea [daɪə'ri:ə] S Durchfall *m*
diary ['daɪrɪ] S (Taschen)kalender *m*; (*für Erlebtes*) Tagebuch *n*
dice [daɪs] S PL Würfel *pl*
dictionary ['dɪkʃənrɪ] S Wörterbuch *n*
did [dɪd] *prät von* **do** **didn't** ['dɪdnt] *kontr von* **did not**

die [daɪ] VI sterben (*of* an *+dat*); (*Pflanze, Tier*) eingehen; (*Motor*) absterben; **be dying to do sth** darauf brennen, etw zu tun; **I'm dying for a drink** ich brauche unbedingt was zu trinken **die down** VI nachlassen **die out** VI aussterben

diesel ['di:zəl] S Diesel *m*

diet ['daɪət] **1** S Kost *f*; (*Abnehmen*) Diät *f* **2** VI eine Diät machen **3** ADJ ~ **Coke®** Cola light®

difference ['dɪfrəns] S Unterschied *m*; **it makes no ~ (to me)** es ist (mir) egal; **it makes a big ~** es macht viel aus **different** ADJ andere(r, s); (*mit pl*) verschieden; **be quite ~** ganz anders sein (*from, than* als); (*zwei Personen, Dinge*) völlig verschieden sein **differently** ['dɪfrəntlɪ] ADV anders (*from, than* als); unterschiedlich

difficult ['dɪfəkəlt] ADJ schwierig **difficulty** S Schwierigkeit *f*

dig ‹dug, dug› [dɪg, dʌg] VT & VI graben; *umg* (*mögen*) stehen auf

digest [daɪ'dʒest] VT verdauen **digestion** [dɪ'dʒestʃən] S Verdauung *f*

digit ['dɪdʒɪt] S Ziffer *f* **digital** ['dɪdʒɪtəl] ADJ digital **digital camera** S Digitalkamera *f* **digital television**, **digital TV** S Digitalfernsehen *n*

dignified ['dɪgnəfaɪd] ADJ würdevoll **dignity** ['dɪgnətɪ] S Würde *f*

dill pickle [dɪl'pɪkl] S saure Gurke (*mit Dill eingelegt*)

dilute [daɪ'lu:t] VT verdünnen

dim [dɪm] **1** ADJ (*Licht*) schwach; (*Umriss*) undeutlich; (*dumm*) schwer von Begriff **2** VT verdunkeln; AUTO abblenden; **~med headlights** *pl* Abblendlicht *n*

dime [daɪm] S Zehncentstück *n*

dimension [daɪ'menʃən] S Dimension *f*; **~s** *pl* Maße *pl*

diminish [dɪ'mɪnɪʃ] **1** VT verringern **2** VI sich verringern

dimmer ['dɪmər] S Dimmer *m*; AUTO Abblendschalter *m*

dine [daɪn] VI speisen **dine out** VI außer Haus essen **diner** S Gast *m*; BAHN Speisewagen *m*; Speiselokal *n* **dinette** [daɪ'net] S Essecke *f*

dinghy ['dɪŋɪ] S Ding(h)i *n*, Schlauchboot *n*

dining car ['daɪnɪŋka:r] S Speisewagen *m* **dining room** S Esszimmer *n*; (*in Hotel*) Speiseraum *m*

dinner ['dɪnər] S Abendessen *n*; (*mittags*) Mittagessen *n*; (*förmlich*) Diner *n*; **have ~** zu Abend/Mittag essen **dinner jacket** S Smoking *m* **dinnertime** S Essenszeit *f*

dip [dɪp] **1** VT tauchen (*in* in *+akk*) **2** S (*Weg*) Bodensenke

f; (*Soße*) Dip *m*
diploma [dəˈploʊmə] S Diplom *n*
diplomatic [dɪpləˈmætɪk] ADJ diplomatisch
dipstick [ˈdɪpstɪk] S Ölmessstab *m*
direct [dəˈrekt] **1** ADJ direkt; unmittelbar; ~ **debit** Einzugsermächtigung *f*; ~ **train** durchgehender Zug **2** V/T richten (*at, to* an *+akk*); (*Film*) die Regie führen bei; (*Verkehr*) regeln **direct current** S ELEK Gleichstrom *m* **direction** [dəˈrekʃən] S Richtung *f*; FILM Regie *f*; **in the ~ of ...** in Richtung ...; **~s** *pl* (*zu einem Ort*) Wegbeschreibung *f* **directly** [dəˈrektlɪ] ADV direkt; (*zeitlich*) sofort **director** [dəˈrektər] S Direktor(in) *m(f)*, Leiter(in) *m(f)*; (*Film*) Regisseur(in) *m(f)* **directory** [dəˈrektərɪ] S Adressbuch *n*; Telefonbuch *n*; ~ **assistance** TEL Auskunft *f*
dirt [dɜːrt] S Schmutz *m*, Dreck *m* **dirty** ADJ schmutzig
disability [dɪsəˈbɪlətɪ] S Behinderung *f* **disabled** [dɪsˈeɪbld] **1** ADJ behindert, Behinderten- **2** S PL **the ~** die Behinderten *pl*
disadvantage [dɪsədˈvæntɪdʒ] S Nachteil *m*; **at a ~** benachteiligt
disagree [dɪsəˈgriː] V/I anderer Meinung sein; (*zwei Menschen*) sich nicht einig sein; (*zwei Aussagen*) nicht übereinstimmen; (*Essen, Wetter*) ~ **with sb** j-m nicht bekommen **disagreeable** ADJ unangenehm; (*Person*) unsympathisch **disagreement** S Meinungsverschiedenheit *f*
disappear [dɪsəˈpɪr] V/I verschwinden
disappoint [dɪsəˈpɔɪnt] V/T enttäuschen **disappointing** ADJ enttäuschend **disappointment** S Enttäuschung *f*
disapprove [dɪsəˈpruːv] V/I missbilligen (*of akk*)
disaster [dɪˈzæstər] S Katastrophe *f* **disastrous** [dɪˈzæstrəs] ADJ katastrophal
disbelief [dɪsbəˈliːf] S Ungläubigkeit *f*
disc [dɪsk] S Scheibe *f*, CD *f*; → disk; ANAT Bandscheibe *f*
discharge **1** [ˈdɪstʃɑːrdʒ] S MED Ausfluss *m* **2** [dɪsˈtʃɑːrdʒ] V/T (*Patient*) entlassen; (*Gase, Giftstoffe*) ausstoßen; MED ausscheiden
discipline [ˈdɪsəplɪn] S Disziplin *f*
disco ⟨-s *pl*⟩ [ˈdɪskoʊ] S Disko *f*; Diskomusik *f*
discomfort [dɪsˈkʌmfərt] S leichte Schmerzen *pl*, Unbehagen *n*
disconnect [dɪskəˈnekt] V/T (*Strom, Gerät*) abstellen
discount [ˈdɪskaʊnt] S Rabatt *m*
discover [dɪˈskʌvər] V/T entde-

cken **discovery** S Entdeckung *f*
discreet [dɪ'skri:t] ADJ diskret
discriminate [dɪ'skrɪməneɪt] V/I unterscheiden; **~ against sb** j-n diskriminieren **discrimination** [dɪskrɪmə'neɪʃən] S Diskriminierung *f*
discuss [dɪ'skʌs] V/T diskutieren, besprechen **discussion** [dɪ'skʌʃən] S Diskussion *f*
disease [dɪ'zi:z] S Krankheit *f*
disembark [dɪsəm'bɑ:rk] V/I von Bord gehen
disgrace [dɪs'greɪs] S Schande *f* **disgraceful** ADJ skandalös
disguise [dɪs'gaɪz] **1** V/T verkleiden; (*Stimme*) verstellen **2** S Verkleidung *f*
disgust [dɪs'gʌst] **1** S Abscheu *m*, Ekel *m* **2** V/T anekeln, anwidern **disgusting** ADJ widerlich; ekelhaft
dish [dɪʃ] S Schüssel *f*; (*Essen*) Gericht *n*; **~es** *pl* Geschirr *n*; **do/wash the ~es** abwaschen **dishcloth** S (*Abwasch*) Spültuch *n*
dishonest [dɪs'ɑ:nəst] ADJ unehrlich
dish soap S Geschirrspülmittel *n* **dishtowel** S Geschirrtuch *n* **dishwasher** S Geschirrspülmaschine *f* **dishwashing liquid** S Geschirrspülmittel *n*
disinfect [dɪsən'fekt] V/T desinfizieren **disinfectant** S Desinfektionsmittel *n*
disk [dɪsk] S IT Diskette *f* **disk drive** S Diskettenlaufwerk *n*
dislike [dɪs'laɪk] **1** S Abneigung *f* **2** V/T nicht mögen; **~ doing sth** etw ungern tun
dislocate ['dɪsloʊkeɪt] V/T MED verrenken, ausrenken
dismantle [dɪs'mæntl] V/T auseinandernehmen; demontieren
dismiss [dɪs'mɪs] V/T entlassen
disobedient [dɪsə'bi:dɪənt] ADJ ungehorsam **disobey** [dɪsə'beɪ] V/T nicht gehorchen *+dat*
disorder [dɪs'ɔ:rdər] S Unordnung *f*; (*Demo*) Aufruhr *m*; MED Störung *f*, Leiden *n*
disorganized [dɪs'ɔ:rgənaɪzd] ADJ chaotisch
dispatch [dɪ'spætʃ] V/T abschicken, abfertigen
dispense [dɪ'spens] V/T verteilen **dispenser** S (*Gerät*) Spender *m*, Automat *m*
disperse [dɪ'spɜ:rs] V/I sich zerstreuen
display [dɪ'spleɪ] **1** S Ausstellung *f*, Show *f*; (*Schaufenster*) Auslage *f*; TECH Anzeige *f*, Display *n* **2** V/T zeigen; (*Ware*) ausstellen
disposable [dɪ'spoʊzəbl] ADJ Wegwerf- **disposal** [dɪ'spoʊzəl] S Loswerden *n*; (*Müll*) Beseitigung *f*; **be at sb's ~** j-m zur Verfügung stehen; **have at one's ~** verfügen über **dispose of** V/T loswer-

den; (*Müll*) beseitigen
dispute [dɪ'spju:t] **1** S Streit *m*, Auseinandersetzung *f* **2** V/T bestreiten
disqualification [dɪskwɑ:ləfə'keɪʃən] S Disqualifikation *f* **disqualify** [dɪs'kwɑ:ləfaɪ] V/T disqualifizieren
disregard [dɪsrɪ'gɑ:rd] V/T nicht beachten
disrupt [dɪs'rʌpt] V/T stören; unterbrechen
dissatisfied [dɪs'sætəsfaɪd] ADJ unzufrieden
dissolve [dɪ'zɑ:lv] **1** V/T auflösen **2** V/I sich auflösen
distance ['dɪstəns] S Entfernung *f*; **in the/from a ~** in/aus der Ferne **distant** ADJ fern; (*Verwandter*) entfernt; (*Person*) distanziert
distil [dɪ'stɪl] V/T destillieren **distillery** S Brennerei *f*
distinct [dɪ'stɪŋkt] ADJ verschieden; (*Merkmal etc*) klar, deutlich **distinction** S Unterschied *m*; (*in Prüfung*) Auszeichnung *f* **distinctive** ADJ unverkennbar **distinctly** ADV deutlich
distinguish [dɪ'stɪŋgwɪʃ] V/T unterscheiden (*sth from sth* etw von etw)
distract [dɪ'strækt] V/T ablenken **distraction** [dɪ'strækʃən] S Ablenkung *f*, Zerstreuung *f*
distress [dɪ'stres] **1** S Not *f*, Leiden *n*; (*mental*) Qual *f*; (*seelisch*) Kummer *m* **2** V/T mitnehmen, erschüttern
distribute [dɪ'strɪbju:t] V/T verteilen; WIRTSCH (*Ware*) vertreiben **distribution** [dɪstrɪ'bju:ʃən] S Verteilung *f*; WIRTSCH (*Ware*) Vertrieb *m* **distributor** S AUTO Verteiler *m*; WIRTSCH Händler(in) *m(f)*
district ['dɪstrɪkt] S Gegend *f*; (*Verwaltung*) Bezirk *m* **district attorney** S Staatsanwalt *m*, Staatsanwältin *f*
disturb [dɪ'stɜ:rb] V/T stören; beunruhigen **disturbing** ADJ beunruhigend
ditch [dɪtʃ] **1** S Graben *m* **2** V/T *umg* (*Person*) den Laufpass geben *+dat*; (*Plan*) verwerfen
dive ⟨dove *od* dived, dived⟩ [daɪv, doʊv, daɪvd] **1** V/I tauchen **2** S Kopfsprung *m*; FLUG Sturzflug *m*; *umg* zwielichtiges Lokal **diver** S Taucher(in) *m(f)*
diverse [daɪ'vɜ:rs] ADJ verschieden **diversion** [daɪ'vɜ:rʃən] S (*Aufmerksamkeit*) Ablenkung *f* **divert** [daɪ'vɜ:rt] V/T ablenken; (*Verkehr*) umleiten
divide [dɪ'vaɪd] **1** V/T teilen; aufteilen **2** V/I sich teilen **divided highway** S Schnellstraße *f*
divine [dɪ'vaɪn] ADJ göttlich
diving ['daɪvɪŋ] S (Sport)tauchen *n*; (*von Sprungbrett*) Springen *n*; SPORT Kunstspringen *n* **diving board** S Sprungbrett *n*

division [dɪ'vɪʒən] S Teilung *f*; MATH Division *f*; (*Organisation*) Abteilung *f*; SPORT Liga *f* **divorce** [dɪ'vɔːrs] **1** S Scheidung *f* **2** V/T sich scheiden lassen von **divorced** ADJ geschieden; **get ~** sich scheiden lassen **divorcee** [dɪvɔːr'siː] S Geschiedene(r) *m/f(m)*

dizzy ['dɪzɪ] ADJ schwindlig

DJ ['diːdʒeɪ] **1** *abk* = dinner jacket; Smoking *m* **2** *abk* = disc jockey; Diskjockey *m*, DJ *m*

do ⟨did, done⟩ [duː, dɪd, dʌn] **1** V/AUX (*verneinend*) **I don't know** ich weiß es nicht; (*in Fragen*) **does she swim?** schwimmt sie?; (*betonend*) **he does like talking** er redet sehr gern; (*Verb ersetzend*) **they drink more than we ~** sie trinken mehr als wir; **please don't!** bitte tun Sie/tu das nicht!; (*zur Bestätigung*) **you know him, don't you?** du kennst/Sie kennen ihn doch, oder? **2** V/T tun, machen; (*Zimmer*) sauber machen; (*an der Uni*) studieren; AUTO (*Geschwindigkeit*) fahren; (*Entfernung*) zurücklegen; **~ the dishes** abwaschen **3** V/I vorankommen; (*genug sein*) reichen; **~ well/badly** gut/schlecht vorankommen; (*in Prüfung*) gut/schlecht abschneiden; **how are you doing?** wie geht's denn so? **4** S ⟨-s *pl*⟩ Party *f* **do away with** V/T abschaffen **do up** V/T (*Mantel*) zumachen; (*Paket*) verschnüren; (*sanieren*) wiederherrichten **do with** V/T brauchen; **I could ~ a drink** ich könnte einen Drink gebrauchen **do without** V/T auskommen ohne

dock [dɑːk] S Dock *n*; JUR Anklagebank *f*

doctor ['dɑːktər] S Arzt *m*, Ärztin *f*; (*als Titel, akademisch*) Doktor *m*

document ['dɑːkjʊmənt] S Dokument *n* **documentary** [dɑːkjʊ'mentərɪ] S Dokumentarfilm *m* **documentation** [dɑːkjʊmen'teɪʃən] S Dokumentation *f*

dog [dɑːg] S Hund *m* **doggie bag** ['dɑːgɪbæg] S *Tüte oder Box, in der Essenreste aus dem Restaurant mit nach Hause genommen werden können*

do-it-yourself [duːɪtjər'self] **1** S Heimwerken *n*, Do-it-yourself *n* **2** ADJ Heimwerker-

doll [dɑːl] S Puppe *f*

dollar ['dɑːlər] S Dollar *m* **dollar store** S Billigladen *m*

dolphin ['dɑːlfɪn] S Delphin *m*

domain [doʊ'meɪn] S Domäne *f*; IT Domain *f*

dome [doʊm] S Kuppel *f*

domestic [də'mestɪk] ADJ häuslich; (*innerhalb des Landes*) Innen-, Binnen- **domestic flight** S Inlandsflug *m*

dominant ['dɑːmɪnənt] ADJ dominierend, vorherrschend **donate** [doʊ'neɪt] V/T spenden **donation** S Spende *f*
done [dʌn] **1** *pperf von* **do** **2** ADJ gar; **well ~** durchgebraten
donkey ['dɑːŋkɪ] S Esel *m*
donor ['doʊnər] S Spender(in) *m(f)*
don't [doʊnt] *kontr von* **do not**
donut ['doʊnʌt] S Donut *m* (*rundes Hefegebäck*)
door [dɔːr] S Tür *f* **doorbell** S Türklingel *f* **door handle** S Türklinke *f* **doorknob** S Türknauf *m* **doormat** S Fußabtreter *m*
dope [doʊp] S *umg* (*Rauschgift*) Stoff *m*; Trottel *m*
dormitory ['dɔːrmətɔːrɪ] S Schlafsaal *m*; Studentenwohnheim *n*
dosage ['doʊsɪdʒ] S Dosierung *f* **dose** [doʊs] **1** S Dosis *f* **2** V/T dosieren
dot [dɑːt] S Punkt *m*; **on the ~** auf die Minute genau
double ['dʌbl] **1** ADJ & ADV doppelt; **~ the quantity** die zweifache Menge, doppelt so viel **2** V/T verdoppeln **3** S Doppelgänger(in) *m(f)*; FILM Double *n* **double bed** S Doppelbett *n* **double-click** V/T IT doppelklicken **double glazing** S Doppelverglasung *f* **double room** S Doppelzimmer *n* **doubles** S PL SPORT Doppel *n*
doubt [daʊt] **1** S Zweifel *m*; **no ~** ohne Zweifel, zweifellos, wahrscheinlich; **have one's ~s** Bedenken haben **2** V/T bezweifeln; (*Aussage*) anzweifeln **doubtful** ADJ zweifelhaft, zweifelnd
douchebag ['duːʃbæg] S *umg pej* Trottel *m*, Depp *m*
dough [doʊ] S Teig *m*; *umg* (*Geld*) Knete *f* **doughnut** S Donut *m* (*rundes Hefegebäck*)
dove **1** [dʌv] S Taube *f* **2** [doʊv] *prät von* **dive**
down [daʊn] **1** S Daunen *pl*, Flaum *m* **2** ADV unten; nach unten, herunter; hinunter **3** PRÄP herunter; hinunter; **drive ~ the hill** den Berg hinunter fahren; **walk ~ the street** die Straße entlang gehen **4** V/T *umg* (*Getränk*) runterkippen **5** ADJ niedergeschlagen, deprimiert **downfall** S Sturz *m* **downhill** ADV bergab **download** ['daʊnloʊd] V/T downloaden, herunterladen **down payment** S Anzahlung *f*
downsize **1** V/T verkleinern **2** V/I sich verkleinern **downstairs** [daʊn'sterz] ADV unten; (*rennen etc*) nach unten **downstream** ADV flussabwärts **downtown** **1** ADV in der Innenstadt; (*gehen, fahren*) in die Innenstadt **2** ADJ in der Innenstadt; **~ Chicago** die Innenstadt von Chicago
downward(s) ['daʊnwərd(z)]

ADV & ADJ nach unten; *(Trend etc)* Abwärts-

doze [doʊz] **1** VI dösen **2** S Nickerchen *n* **doze off** VI einnicken

dozen ['dʌzn] S Dutzend *n*

draft [dræft] S Entwurf *m*; MIL Einberufung *f*; (Luft)zug *m*; **there's a ~** es zieht; **~ beer** Bier *n* vom Fass, Fassbier *n*; **on ~** *(Bier)* vom Fass **drafty** ADJ zugig

drag [dræg] **1** VT schleppen **2** S *umg* **be a ~** *(langweilig)* stinklangweilig sein; *(aufwändig)* ein ziemlicher Schlauch sein **drag on** VI sich in die Länge ziehen

dragon ['drægən] S Drache *m* **dragonfly** S Libelle *f*

drain [dreɪn] **1** S Abfluss *m* **2** VT *(Wasser, Öl)* ablassen; *(Gemüse)* abgießen; *(Land, Gebiet)* entwässern, trockenlegen **3** VI *(Wasser)* abfließen **drainpipe** S Abflussrohr *n*

drama ['drɑːmə] S Drama *n* **dramatic** [drə'mætɪk] ADJ dramatisch

drank [dræŋk] *prät von* **drink**

drapes [dreɪps] S PL Vorhänge *pl*

drastic ['dræstɪk] ADJ drastisch

draw ⟨drew, drawn⟩ [drɒː, druː, drɒːn] **1** VT ziehen; *(Menschen)* anlocken, anziehen; *(Bild)* zeichnen **2** VI SPORT unentschieden spielen **3** S SPORT Unentschieden *n*; *(von Stadt etc)* Attraktion *f*; *(Lotterie)* Ziehung *f* **draw out** VT herausziehen; *(Geld)* abheben **draw up** **1** VT entwerfen; *(Liste)* erstellen **2** VI *(Auto)* anhalten **drawback** S Nachteil *m*

drawer ['drɔːr] S Schublade *f*

drawing ['drɒːɪŋ] S Zeichnung *f*

drawn [drɒːn] *pperf von* **draw**

dread [dred] **1** S Furcht *f* (*of* vor *+dat*) **2** VT sich fürchten vor *+dat*

dream ⟨dreamed *od* dreamt, dreamed *od* dreamt⟩ [driːm, driːmd, dremt] **1** VT & VI träumen *(about* von) **2** S Traum *m* **dreamt** [dremt] *prät, pperf von* **dream**

dreary ['drɪrɪ] ADJ *(Stadt, Wetter)* trostlos; *(Buch)* langweilig

drench [drentʃ] VT durchnässen

dress [dres] **1** S Kleidung *f*; *(für Frau)* Kleid *n* **2** VT anziehen; MED verbinden; **get ~ed** sich anziehen **dress up** VI sich fein machen; *(Kostüm)* sich verkleiden *(as* als) **dressing** S GASTR Dressing *n*, Soße *f*; MED Verband *m* **dressing gown** S Bademantel *m* **dressing table** S Frisierkommode *f*

drew [druː] *prät von* **draw**

dried [draɪd] ADJ getrocknet; *(Milch, Blumen)* Trocken-; **~**

fruit Dörrobst *n* **drier** ['draɪər] S → dryer
drift [drɪft] **1** V/I treiben **2** S (*Schnee*) Verwehung *f*; *fig* Tendenz *f*; **if you get my ~** wenn Sie mich richtig verstehen
drill [drɪl] **1** S Bohrer *m* **2** V/T & V/I bohren
drink ⟨drank, drunk⟩ [drɪŋk, dræŋk, drʌŋk] **1** V/T & V/I trinken **2** S Getränk *n*; (*alkoholisch*) Drink *m* **drinking water** S Trinkwasser *n*
drip [drɪp] **1** S Tropfen *m* **2** V/I tropfen
drive ⟨drove, driven⟩ [draɪv, droʊv, 'drɪvn] **1** V/T (*Fahrzeug, Passagier*) fahren; (*Viehherde*) treiben; TECH antreiben; **~ sb crazy** j-n verrückt machen **2** V/I fahren **3** S Fahrt *f*; (*vor Haus*) Einfahrt *f*, Auffahrt *f*; IT Laufwerk *n* **drive away**, **drive off** **1** V/I wegfahren **2** V/T vertreiben **drive-in** ADJ Drive-in-; **~ movie theater** Autokino *n* **driven** ['drɪvn] *pperf von* **drive** **driver** ['draɪvər] S Fahrer(in) *m(f)*; IT Treiber *m*; **~'s license** Führerschein *m*; **~'s seat** Fahrersitz *m* **driving** ['draɪvɪŋ] S (Auto)fahren *n* **driving test** S Fahrprüfung *f*
drizzle ['drɪzl] **1** S Nieselregen *m* **2** V/I nieseln
drop [drɑːp] **1** S (*Flüssigkeit*) Tropfen *m*; (*Preis, Temperatur*) Rückgang *m* **2** V/T fallen lassen; **~ sb a few lines** j-m ein paar Zeilen schreiben **3** V/I herunterfallen; (*Zahlen, Temperatur*) sinken, zurückgehen **drop by**, **drop in** V/I vorbeikommen **drop out** V/I aussteigen; (*an Schule/Uni*) die Schule/das Studium abbrechen **dropout** S Aussteiger(in) *m(f)*
drove [droʊv] *prät von* **drive**
drown [draʊn] **1** V/I ertrinken **2** V/T ertränken
drowsy ['draʊzɪ] ADJ schläfrig
drug [drʌg] **1** S MED Medikament *n*, Arznei *f*; (*illegal*) Droge *f*, Rauschgift *n*; **be on ~s** drogensüchtig sein **2** V/T (mit Medikamenten) betäuben **drug addict** S Rauschgiftsüchtige(r) *m/f(m)* **drug dealer** S Drogenhändler(in) *m(f)* **druggist** S Drogist(in) *m(f)* **drugstore** S Drogerie *f*
drum [drʌm] S Trommel *f*; **~s** *pl* Schlagzeug *n*
drunk [drʌŋk] **1** *pperf von* **drink** **2** ADJ betrunken; **get ~** sich betrinken **3** S Betrunkene(r) *m/f(m)*; (*Alkoholiker*) Trinker(in) *m(f)* **drunk-driving** S Trunkenheit *f* am Steuer **drunken** ADJ betrunken, besoffen
dry [draɪ] **1** ADJ trocken **2** V/T trocknen; (*Geschirr, Hände*) abtrocknen **3** V/I trocknen, trocken werden **dry-clean** V/T chemisch reinigen **dry cleaner** S chemische Reinigung **dryer** S Trockner *m*;

(*für Haare*) Föhn *m*; (*über Kopf*) Trockenhaube *f*
DST *abk* = Daylight Saving Time; Sommerzeit *f*
dual ['du:əl] ADJ doppelt
dubbed [dʌbd] ADJ synchronisiert
dubious ['du:bɪəs] ADJ zweifelhaft
duck [dʌk] S Ente *f*
dude [du:d] S *umg* Typ *m*; **~ ranch** Gäste-Ranch *f* (*Ranch, die zahlende Feriengäste aufnimmt*)
due [du:] **1** ADJ (*Bezahlung*) fällig; (*Sorgfalt*) angemessen; **~ to** infolge *+gen*, wegen *+gen* **2** ADV **~ south etc** direkt nach Süden etc
dug [dʌg] *prät, pperf von* **dig**
dull [dʌl] ADJ (*Wetter*) trübe; (*Film, Leben*) langweilig
dumb [dʌm] ADJ stumm; *umg* (*dumm*) doof, blöde
dummy ['dʌmɪ] **1** S Attrappe *f*; (*in Geschäft*) Schaufensterpuppe *f*; *umg* (*Person*) Dummkopf *m* **2** ADJ unecht, Schein-
dump [dʌmp] **1** S Abfallhaufen *m*; *umg* (*Ort*) Kaff *n* **2** V/T abladen; *umg* **he ~ed her** er hat mit ihr Schluss gemacht
dumpling ['dʌmplɪŋ] S Kloß *m*, Knödel *m*
Dumpster® ['dʌmpster] S (Müll)container *m*
dung [dʌŋ] S Dung *m*, Mist *m*
duplex ['du:pleks] S zweistöckige Wohnung; Doppelhaushälfte *f*
duplicate **1** ['du:plɪkət] S Duplikat *n* **2** ['du:plɪkeɪt] V/T kopieren; wiederholen
duration [dʊ'reɪʃən] S Dauer *f*
during ['dʊrɪŋ] PRÄP während *+gen*
dusk [dʌsk] S Abenddämmerung *f*
dust [dʌst] **1** S Staub *m* **2** V/T abstauben **dusty** ADJ staubig
Dutch [dʌtʃ] **1** ADJ holländisch **2** S (*Sprache*) Holländisch *n*; **go ~** sich (im Restaurant) die Rechnung teilen **Dutchman** ⟨-men *pl*⟩ S Holländer *m* **Dutchwoman** ⟨-women *pl*⟩ S Holländerin *f*
duty ['du:tɪ] S Pflicht *f*; (*Arbeit*) Aufgabe *f*; (*auf Waren*) Zoll *m*; **on/off ~** im Dienst/nicht im Dienst; **be on ~** Dienst haben **duty-free** ADJ zollfrei
DVD S *abk* = digital versatile disk; DVD *f* **DVD player** S DVD-Player *m* **DVD recorder** S DVD-Rekorder *m*
dye [daɪ] **1** S Farbstoff *m* **2** V/T färben
dyslexic [dɪs'leksɪk] ADJ legasthenisch; **be ~** Legastheniker(in) sein

E

each [iːtʃ] **1** ADJ jeder/jede/jedes **2** PRON jeder/jede/jedes; **I'll have one of ~** ich nehme von jedem eins; **they ~ have a car** jeder von ihnen hat ein Auto; **~ other** einander, sich **3** ADV je; **they cost 10 dollars ~** sie kosten 10 Dollar das Stück

eager ['iːgər] ADJ eifrig; begierig; **be ~ to do sth** darauf brennen, etw zu tun

eagle ['iːgl] S Adler *m*

ear [ɪr] S Ohr *n* **earache** ['ɪreɪk] S Ohrenschmerzen *pl* **eardrum** S Trommelfell *n* **earlobe** ['ɪrloʊb] S Ohrläppchen *n*

early ['ɜːrlɪ] ADJ & ADV früh; **be 10 minutes ~** 10 Minuten zu früh kommen; **in ~ June/2010** Anfang Juni/2010; **~ retirement** vorzeitiger Ruhestand

earn [ɜːrn] V/T verdienen **earnings** ['ɜːrnɪŋz] S PL Verdienst *m*, Einkommen *n*

earring ['ɪrɪŋ] S Ohrring *m*

earth [ɜːrθ] S Erde *f*; **what on ~ ...?** was in aller Welt ...? **earthquake** S Erdbeben *n*

ease [iːz] **1** V/T (*Schmerz, Qual*) lindern **2** S Leichtigkeit *f*; **feel at ~** sich wohlfühlen **easily** ['iːzəlɪ] ADV leicht

east [iːst] **1** S Osten *m*; **to the ~ of** östlich von **2** ADV (*Bewegung, Richtung*) nach Osten **3** ADJ Ost- **eastbound** ADJ (in) Richtung Osten **East Coast** S Ostküste *f* (*der USA*)

Easter ['iːstər] S Ostern *n*; **at ~** zu Ostern **Easter egg** S Osterei *n*

eastern ['iːstərn] ADJ Ost-, östlich **Easterner** S Oststaatler(in) *m(f)*

Easter Sunday S Ostersonntag *m*

East Side S *der südöstliche Teil Manhattans* **eastward(s)** ['iːstwərd(z)] ADV nach Osten

easy ['iːzɪ] ADJ leicht; (*Aufgabe, Lösung*) einfach; (*Leben*) bequem; (*Art*) ungezwungen **easy-going** ADJ gelassen

eat ⟨ate, eaten⟩ [iːt, eɪt, 'iːtn] V/T essen; (*Tier*) fressen **eat out** V/I zum Essen ausgehen **eat up** V/T aufessen **eaten** ['iːtn] *pperf von* **eat** **eatery** ['iːtərɪ] S Speiselokal *n* **eating irons** PL *umg* Besteck *n*

eavesdrop ['iːvzdrɑːp] V/I (heimlich) lauschen

eccentric [ɪk'sentrɪk] ADJ exzentrisch

echo ['ekoʊ] **1** ⟨-es *pl*⟩ S Echo *n* **2** V/I widerhallen

ecological [iːkə'lɑːdʒɪkl] ADJ ökologisch **ecology** [ɪ'kɑːlədʒɪ] S Ökologie *f*

economic [iːkə'nɑːmɪk] ADJ

wirtschaftlich, Wirtschafts- **economical** ADJ wirtschaftlich; (*Mensch*) sparsam **economics** S SG OD PL Wirtschaftswissenschaft *f* **economize** [ɪ'kɑːnəmaɪz] V/I sparen (*on* an *+dat*) **economy** [ɪ'kɑːnəmɪ] S (*von Land*) Wirtschaft *f*; (*beim Ausgeben*) Sparsamkeit *f* **economy class** S FLUG Economyclass *f*

ecstasy ['ekstəsɪ] S Ekstase *f*; (*Droge*) Ecstasy *f*

eczema ['eksəmə] S Ekzem *n*

edge [edʒ] S Rand *m*; (*Messer*) Schneide *f*; **on ~** nervös

edible ['edəbl] ADJ essbar

edit ['edɪt] V/T (*Zeitung*) herausgeben; (*Text*) redigieren; (*Film*) schneiden; IT editieren **edition** [ɪ'dɪʃn] S Ausgabe *f* **editor** S Redakteur(in) *m(f)*; (*von Buch*) Herausgeber(in) *m(f)*

EDT *abk* = Eastern Daylight Time; Sommerzeit *f* der östlichen Zeitzone

educate ['edʒəkeɪt] V/T (*Kind*) erziehen; (*an Schule, Uni*) ausbilden; (*Öffentlichkeit*) aufklären **educated** ADJ gebildet **education** [edʒə'keɪʃən] S Erziehung *f*; (*Studium etc*) Ausbildung *f*; (*als Studienfach*) Pädagogik *f*; (*Schulsystem*) Schulwesen *n*; (*Wissen*) Bildung *f* **educational** ADJ pädagogisch

effect [ɪ'fekt] S Wirkung *f* (*on* auf *+akk*) **effective** ADJ wirksam, effektiv

efficiency [ɪ'fɪʃənsɪ] S Leistungsfähigkeit *f*; (*Methode*) Wirksamkeit *f* **efficient** ADJ TECH leistungsfähig; (*Methode*) wirksam, effizient

effort ['efərt] S Anstrengung *f*; (*Bemühung*) Versuch *m*; **make an ~** sich anstrengen

e.g. *abk* = exempli gratia (for example); z. B.

egg [eg] S Ei *n* **egg beater** S Schneebesen *m* **eggcup** S Eierbecher *m* **eggplant** S Aubergine *f* **eggshell** S Eierschale *f*

ego ⟨-s *pl*⟩ ['iːgoʊ] S Ich *n*; (*Selbstvertrauen*) Selbstbewusstsein *n*

Egypt ['iːdʒɪpt] S Ägypten *n*

eight [eɪt] **1** NUM acht; **at the age of ~** im Alter von acht Jahren; **it's ~ (o'clock)** es ist acht Uhr **2** S (*Buslinie etc*) Acht *f*; (*Ruderboot*) Achter *m* **eighteen** [eɪ'tiːn] **1** NUM achtzehn **2** S Achtzehn *f*; → eight **eighteenth** ADJ achtzehnte(r, s); → eighth **eighth** [eɪtθ] **1** ADJ achte(r, s); **the ~ of June** der achte Juni **2** S Achtel *n*; **eightieth** ['eɪtɪəθ] ADJ achtzigste(r, s); → eighth **eighty** ['eɪtɪ] **1** NUM achtzig **2** S Achtzig *f*; **be in one's eighties** in den Achtzigern sein; → eight

either ['iːðər, 'aɪðər] **1** KONJ **~ ... or** entweder ... oder **2** PRON **~ of the two** eine(r, s)

von beiden **3** ADJ **on ~ side** auf beiden Seiten **4** ADV **I won't go ~** ich gehe auch nicht
elastic [ɪˈlæstɪk] ADJ elastisch
elbow [ˈelboʊ] S Ellbogen *m*
elder [ˈeldər] **1** ADJ (*von zweien/beiden*) älter **2** S Ältere(r) *m/f(m)* **elderly** **1** ADJ ältere(r, s) **2** S **the ~** *pl* die älteren Leute *pl* **eldest** [ˈeldɪst] ADJ älteste(r, s)
elect [ɪˈlekt] V/T wählen **election** [ɪˈlekʃən] S Wahl *f* **election campaign** S Wahlkampf *m*
electric [ɪˈlektrɪk] ADJ elektrisch; (*Auto, Motor, Rasierer*) Elektro-; **~ shock** Stromschlag *m* **electrical** ADJ elektrisch; **~ goods/appliances** *pl* Elektrogeräte *pl* **electrician** [ɪlekˈtrɪʃən] S Elektriker(in) *m(f)* **electricity** [ɪlekˈtrɪsətɪ] S Elektrizität *f* **electronic** [ɪlekˈtrɑːnɪk] ADJ elektronisch
elegant [ˈelɪgənt] ADJ elegant
element [ˈeləmənt] S Element *n* **elementary** [eləˈmentərɪ] ADJ einfach; grundlegend; **~ school** Grundschule *f*
elephant [ˈelɪfənt] S Elefant *m*
elevator [ˈeləveɪtər] S Fahrstuhl *m*
eleven [ɪˈlevn] **1** NUM elf **2** S (*Team, Bus etc*) Elf *f* → eight
eleventh [ɪˈlevnθ] **1** ADJ elfte(r, s) **2** S Elftel *n* → eighth
eliminate [ɪˈlɪməneɪt] V/T ausschließen (*from* aus), ausschalten; (*Problem*) beseitigen
elk [elk] S Wapitihirsch *m*; Elch *m*
else [els] ADV **anybody/anything ~** (*zusätzlich*) sonst (noch) jemand/etwas; (*anders*) ein anderer/etwas anderes; **somebody ~** jemand anders; **everyone ~** alle anderen; **or ~** sonst; (*als Drohung*) sonst passiert was! **elsewhere** ADV anderswo, woanders; (*Richtung*) woandershin
e-mail [ˈiːmeɪl] **1** V/I & V/T mailen (*sth to sb* j-m etw) **2** S E-Mail *f* **e-mail address** S E-Mail-Adresse *f*
embarrassed [ɪmˈbærəst] ADJ verlegen **embarrassing** ADJ peinlich
embassy [ˈembəsɪ] S Botschaft *f*
embrace [ɪmˈbreɪs] **1** V/T umarmen **2** S Umarmung *f*
emerge [ɪˈmɜːrdʒ] V/I auftauchen
emergency [ɪˈmɜːrdʒənsɪ] **1** S Notfall *m* **2** ADJ Not-; **~ brake** AUTO Handbremse *f*; **~ room** Unfallstation *f*
emigrate [ˈeməgreɪt] V/I auswandern
emotion [ɪˈmoʊʃən] S Emotion *f*, Gefühl *n* **emotional** ADJ (*Person*) emotional; (*Moment, Szene*) ergreifend
emphasis [ˈemfəsɪs] S Beto-

nung *f* **emphasize** ['emfəsaɪz] VT betonen
empire ['empaɪr] S Reich *n*
employ [ɪm'plɔɪ] VT beschäftigen; *(neue Mitarbeiter)* anstellen; *(Methode, Taktik)* anwenden **employee** [emplɔɪ'iː] S Angestellte(r) *m/f(m)* **employer** S Arbeitgeber(in) *m(f)* **employment** S Beschäftigung *f*; *(Arbeitsstelle)* Stellung *f*
empty ['emptɪ] **1** ADJ leer **2** VT leeren; ausleeren
enable [ɪ'neɪbl] VT **~ sb to do sth** es j-m ermöglichen, etw zu tun
enclose [ɪn'kloʊz] VT einschließen; *(einem Brief)* beilegen *(in, with dat)*
encounter [ɪn'kaʊntər] **1** S Begegnung *f* **2** VT *(Person etc)* begegnen *+dat*; *(Schwierigkeiten)* stoßen auf *+akk*
encourage [ɪn'kɜːrɪdʒ] VT ermutigen **encouragement** S Ermutigung *f*
encyclopedia [ɪnsaɪklə'piːdɪə] S Lexikon *n*, Enzyklopädie *f*
end [end] **1** S Ende *n*, Schluss *m*; *(Absicht)* Zweck *m*; **at the ~ of May** Ende Mai; **at the ~ of the day** im Endeffekt, letztendlich; **in the ~** schließlich; **come to an ~** zu Ende gehen **2** VT beenden **3** VI enden **end up** VI enden **ending** ['endɪŋ] S *(Story)* Ausgang *m*, Schluss *m*; *(Wort)* Endung *f*
endless ['endləs] ADJ endlos; *(Möglichkeiten)* unendlich
enemy ['enəmɪ] **1** S Feind(in) *m(f)* **2** ADJ feindlich
energetic [enər'dʒetɪk] ADJ energiegeladen; *(tatkräftig)* aktiv **energy** ['enərdʒɪ] S Energie *f*
enforce [ɪn'fɔːrs] VT durchsetzen; erzwingen
engaged [ɪn'geɪdʒd] ADJ verlobt; **get ~** sich verloben *(to mit)* **engagement** S Verlobung *f*
engine ['endʒən] S AUTO Motor *m*; BAHN Lokomotive *f*; **~ trouble** AUTO Defekt *m* am Motor **engineer** [endʒə'nɪr] S Ingenieur(in) *m(f)*; BAHN Lokomotivführer(in) *m(f)* **engineering** [endʒə'nɪrɪŋ] S Technik *f*; Maschinenbau *m*; *(Studienfach)* Ingenieurwesen *n*
England ['ɪŋglənd] S England *n* **English** ['ɪŋglɪʃ] **1** ADJ englisch **2** S *(Sprache)* Englisch *n*; **in ~** auf Englisch; **translate into ~** ins Englische übersetzen **Englishman** ⟨-men *pl*⟩ S Engländer *m* **English muffin** [ɪŋglɪʃ'mʌfɪn] S *Art Hefeteigbrötchen* **Englishwoman** ⟨-women *pl*⟩ S Engländerin *f*
engraving [ɪn'greɪvɪŋ] S Stich *m*
enjoy [ɪn'dʒɔɪ] VT genießen; **I ~ reading** ich lese gern; **he ~s teasing her** es macht ihm Spaß, sie aufzuziehen; **did**

you ~ the movie? hat dir der Film gefallen? **enjoyable** ADJ angenehm; (*Film, Buch*) unterhaltsam **enjoyment** S Vergnügen *n*; Freude *f* (*of* an +*dat*)

enlarge [ɪn'lɑːrdʒ] V/T vergrößern; (*Wissen*) erweitern

enormous, **enormously** [ɪ'nɔːrməs, -lɪ] ADJ & ADV riesig, ungeheuer

enough [ɪ'nʌf] **1** ADJ genug; **that's ~** das reicht!; Schluss damit!; **I've had ~** das hat mir gereicht; (*beim Essen*) ich bin satt **2** ADV genug, genügend

enroll [ɪn'roʊl] V/I sich einschreiben; (*für Kurs, an Schule*) sich anmelden

en suite [ɑːn'swiːt] ADJ & S **room with ~ (bathroom)** Zimmer *n* mit eigenem Bad

ensure [ɪn'ʃʊr] V/T sicherstellen

ENT *abk* = ear, nose and throat; HNO

enter ['entər] **1** V/T eintreten in +*akk*, betreten; einfahren in +*akk*; (*in Land*) einreisen in +*akk*; (*in Liste*) eintragen; IT eingeben; (*an Rennen, bei Wettbewerb*) teilnehmen an +*dat* **2** V/I (*zu j-m*) hereinkommen; (*irgendwohin*) hineingehen

enterprise ['entərpraɪz] S WIRTSCH Unternehmen *n*

entertain [entər'teɪn] V/T (*Gäste*) bewirten; (*Kinder, Gäste*) unterhalten **entertaining** ADJ unterhaltsam **entertainment** S Unterhaltung *f*

enthusiasm [ɪn'θuːzɪæzəm] S Begeisterung *f* **enthusiastic** [ɪnθuːzɪ'æstɪk] ADJ begeistert (*about* von)

entire, **entirely** [ɪn'taɪr, -lɪ] ADJ & ADV ganz

entrance ['entrəns] S Eingang *m*, Einfahrt *f*; (*Vorgang*) Eintritt *m*; THEAT Auftritt *m*

entree ['ɑːntreɪ] S GASTR Hauptgericht *n*

entry ['entrɪ] S Eingang *m*; (*Vorgang*) Eintritt *m*; (*mit Fahrzeug*) Einfahrt *f*; (*in Land*) Einreise *f*; (*Zugangserlaubnis*) Zutritt *m*; **'no ~'** „Eintritt verboten"; (*für Fahrzeuge*) „Einfahrt verboten" **entry phone** S Türsprechanlage *f*

envelope ['envəloʊp] S (Brief)umschlag *m*

envious ['envɪəs] ADJ neidisch

environment [ɪn'vaɪrənmənt] S Umgebung *f*; (*Ökologie*) Umwelt *f* **environmental** [ɪnvaɪrən'mentl] ADJ Umwelt- **environmentalist** S Umweltschützer(in) *m(f)*

envy ['envɪ] **1** S Neid *m* (*of* auf +*akk*) **2** V/T beneiden (*sb sth* j-n um etw)

epilepsy ['epɪlepsɪ] S Epilepsie *f* **epileptic** [epɪ'leptɪk] ADJ epileptisch

episode ['epɪsoʊd] S Episode *f*; TV Folge *f*

equal ['iːkwəl] **1** ADJ gleich (*to +dat*) **2** V/T gleichen; (*qualitätsmäßig*) gleichkommen *+dat* **equality** [ɪ'kwɑːlətɪ] S Gleichheit *f*; (*von Frauen etc*) Gleichberechtigung *f* **equally** ADV gleich; (*einschränkend*) andererseits

equip [ɪ'kwɪp] V/T ausrüsten; (*Küche*) ausstatten **equipment** S Ausrüstung *f*; (*für Küche etc*) Ausstattung *f*; **electrical ~** Elektrogeräte *pl*

equivalent [ɪ'kwɪvələnt] **1** ADJ gleichwertig (*to dat*); (*Menge etc*) entsprechend (*to dat*) **2** S Äquivalent *n*; (*Betrag*) gleiche Menge; (*Geld*) Gegenwert *m*

ER *abk* = emergency room; Unfallstation *f*

era ['ɪrə] S Ära *f*, Zeitalter *n*

erase [ɪ'reɪz] V/T ausradieren; (*Band, Datei*) löschen **eraser** S Radiergummi *m*

erect [ɪ'rekt] **1** ADJ aufrecht **2** V/T (*Gebäude, Denkmal*) errichten; (*Zelt*) aufstellen **erection** S Errichtung *f*; ANAT Erektion *f*

erotic [ɪ'rɑːtɪk] ADJ erotisch

erratic [ɪ'rætɪk] ADJ (*Verhalten*) unberechenbar; (*Busverkehr*) unregelmäßig; (*Leistung*) unbeständig

error ['erər] S Fehler *m*

escalator ['eskəleɪtər] S Rolltreppe *f*

escape [ɪ'skeɪp] **1** S Flucht *f*; (*aus Gefängnis*) Ausbruch *m* **2** V/I (*bei Verfolgung*) entkommen (*from dat*); (*aus Gefängnis*) ausbrechen (*from dat*); (*Gas*) ausströmen; (*Wasser*) auslaufen

escort **1** ['eskɔːrt] S (*Person*) Begleiter(in) *m(f)*; (*zur Bewachung*) Eskorte *f* **2** [ɪ'skɔːrt] V/T begleiten

especially [ɪ'speʃəlɪ] ADV besonders

essential [ɪ'senʃəl] **1** ADJ unentbehrlich, unverzichtbar; (*Teil von etwas*) wesentlich **2** S **the ~s** *pl* das Wesentliche **essentially** ADV im Wesentlichen

EST *abk* = Eastern Standard Time; Normalzeit *f* für die östliche Zeitzone

establish [ɪ'stæblɪʃ] V/T (*Firma*) gründen; (*neue Methode*) einführen; (*Beziehungen*) aufnehmen; (*Fakten, Unschuld*) nachweisen; **~ that ...** feststellen, dass ... **establishment** S Institution *f*; (*Firma*) Unternehmen *n*

estate [ɪ'steɪt] S Gut *n*; (*Landgut*) Landsitz *m*

estimate **1** ['estəmət] S Schätzung *f*; WIRTSCH Kostenvoranschlag *m* **2** ['estəmeɪt] V/T schätzen

Estonia [e'stoʊnɪə] S Estland *n* **Estonian** [e'stoʊnɪən] **1** ADJ estnisch **2** S (*Person*) Este *m*, Estin *f*; (*Sprache*) Estnisch *n*

ETA *abk* = estimated time of arrival; voraussichtliche An-

kunftszeit
eternal, eternally [ɪ'tɜ:rnl, -nəlɪ] ADJ & ADV ewig **eternity** S Ewigkeit *f*
ethical ['eθɪkəl] ADJ ethisch
ethnic ['eθnɪk] ADJ ethnisch; (*Kleidung, Essen*) landesüblich
euro ⟨-s *pl*⟩ ['jʊroʊ] S FIN Euro *m* **Europe** ['jʊrəp] S Europa *n* **European** [jʊrə'pi:ən] **1** ADJ europäisch **2** S Europäer(in) *m(f)*
evacuate [ɪ'vækjʊeɪt] V/T (*Platz, Ort*) räumen; (*Menschen*) evakuieren
evaluate [ɪ'væljʊeɪt] V/T auswerten
even ['i:vən] **1** ADJ (*Fläche*) eben; (*Verteilung, Atem*) gleichmäßig; (*Temperatur, Entfernung, Menge*) gleich; (*Zahl*) gerade **2** ADV sogar; **~ if** selbst wenn, wenn auch; **~ though** obwohl; **not ~** nicht einmal; **~ better** noch besser
evening ['i:vnɪŋ] S Abend *m*; **in the ~** abends, am Abend; **this ~** heute Abend **evening dress** S Abendkleidung *f*; (*von Frauen*) Abendkleid *n*
evenly ['i:vənlɪ] ADV gleichmäßig
event [ɪ'vent] S Ereignis *n*; (*organisiert*) Veranstaltung *f*; SPORT Disziplin *f*; **in the ~ of** im Falle *+gen*
eventually [ɪ'ventʃʊəlɪ] ADV am Ende; schließlich
ever ['evər] ADV je(mals); **don't ~ do that again** tu das ja nie wieder; **have you ~ been to Canada?** bist du schon einmal in Kanada gewesen?; **for ~** (für) immer
every ['evrɪ] ADJ jeder/jede/jedes; **~ other day** jeden zweiten Tag; **~ five days** alle fünf Tage **everybody** PRON jeder, alle *pl* **everyone** PRON jeder, alle *pl* **everything** PRON alles **everywhere** ADV überall; (*Richtung*) überallhin
evidence ['evɪdəns] S Beweise *pl*; (*einzelner*) Beweis *m*; (*von Zeuge*) Aussage *f*
evil ['i:vl] **1** ADJ böse **2** S Böse(s) *n*
evolve [ɪ'vɑ:lv] V/I sich entwickeln
ex- [eks] PRÄF Ex-, ehemalig
exact [ɪg'zækt] ADJ genau **exactly** ADV genau; **not ~ fast** nicht gerade schnell
exaggerate [ɪg'zædʒəreɪt] V/T & V/I übertreiben **exaggeration** S Übertreibung *f*
exam [ɪg'zæm] S Prüfung *f* **examination** [ɪgzæmə'neɪʃən] S MED Untersuchung *f*; (*Schule*) Prüfung *f*; (*Universität*) Examen *n* **examine** [ɪg'zæmən] V/T untersuchen (*for* auf *+akk*); (*Gepäck*) kontrollieren; (*Schule*) prüfen
example [ɪg'zæmpl] S Beispiel *n* (*of* für); **for ~** zum Beispiel
exceed [ɪk'si:d] V/T überschrei-

ten, übertreffen
excellent, excellently ['eksələnt, -lı] ADJ & ADV ausgezeichnet
except [ık'sept] **1** PRÄP außer +*dat*; **~ for** abgesehen von **2** V/T ausnehmen **exception** [ık'sepʃən] S Ausnahme *f* **exceptional** [ık'sepʃənl] ADJ außergewöhnlich
excess [ek'ses] S Übermaß *n* (*of* an +*dat*) **excess baggage** S Übergepäck *n*
exchange [ıks'tʃeındʒ] **1** S Austausch *m* (*for* gegen); Umtausch *m* (*for* gegen); FIN Wechsel *m* **2** V/T austauschen; (*Waren*) tauschen; (*Gekauftes*) umtauschen (*for* gegen); (*Geld*) wechseln **exchange rate** S Wechselkurs *m*
excited [ık'saıtəd] ADJ aufgeregt **exciting** ADJ aufregend; spannend
exclamation point [ekskləˈmeıʃənpɔınt] S Ausrufezeichen *n*
exclude [ıks'klu:d] V/T ausschließen **exclusive** [ıks'klu:sıv] ADJ (*Hotel etc*) exklusiv; (*Rechte auf Buch etc*) ausschließlich **exclusively** ADV ausschließlich
excursion [ıks'kɜ:rʃən] S Ausflug *m*
excuse **1** [ıks'kju:z] V/T entschuldigen; **~ me** Entschuldigung! **2** [ıks'kju:s] S Entschuldigung *f*, Ausrede *f*
execution [eksı'kju:ʃən] S (*von Plan, Aufgabe*) Ausführung *f*; (*Strafe*) Hinrichtung *f* **executive** [ıg'zekjʊtıv] S leitender Angestellter, leitende Angestellte
exercise ['eksərsaız] S (*Schule, Sport*) Übung *f*; (*körperlich*) Bewegung *f*; **get more ~** mehr Sport treiben
exhaust [ıg'zɒ:st] S Abgase *pl*; AUTO **~ (pipe)** Auspuff *m* **exhausted** ADJ erschöpft **exhausting** ADJ anstrengend
exhibit [ıg'zıbıt] S Ausstellungsstück *n* **exhibition** [eksə'bıʃən] S Ausstellung *f*
exist [ıg'zıst] V/I existieren; (*überleben*) leben (*on* von) **existence** S Existenz *f*; **come into ~** entstehen **existing** ADJ bestehend
exit ['eksət, 'egzət] S Ausgang *m*; (*für Fahrzeuge*) Ausfahrt *f*
exotic [ıg'zɑ:tık] ADJ exotisch
expand [ıks'pænd] **1** V/T ausdehnen, erweitern **2** V/I sich ausdehnen **expansion** [ıks'pænʃən] S Expansion *f*, Erweiterung *f*
expect [ık'spekt] **1** V/T erwarten; (*vermuten*) annehmen **2** V/I **she's ~ing** sie bekommt ein Kind
expense [ık'spens] S Kosten *pl*; (*einzeln*) Ausgabe *f*; **(business) ~s** *pl* Spesen *pl* **expensive** ADJ teuer
experience [ık'spırıəns] **1** S

Erfahrung *f*; Erlebnis *n* **2** V/T erfahren, erleben; (*Schlimmes*) durchmachen **experienced** ADJ erfahren
experiment [ɪk'sperɪmənt] **1** S Versuch *m*, Experiment *n* **2** V/I experimentieren
expert ['ekspɜ:rt] **1** S Experte *m*, Expertin *f*; Fachmann *m*, Fachfrau *f*; JUR Sachverständige(r) *m/f(m)* **2** ADJ fachmännisch, Fach-
expiration date [ekspɪ'reɪʃəndeɪt] S Verfallsdatum *n* **expire** [ɪk'spaɪr] V/I (*Pass, Vertrag*) ablaufen
explain [ɪk'spleɪn] V/T erklären (*sth to sb* j-m etw) **explanation** [eksplə'neɪʃən] S Erklärung *f*
explode [ɪk'sploʊd] V/I explodieren
exploit [ɪk'splɔɪt] V/T ausbeuten
explore [ɪk'splɔ:r] V/T erforschen
explosion [ɪk'sploʊʒən] S Explosion *f* **explosive** [ɪk'sploʊsɪv] **1** ADJ explosiv **2** S Sprengstoff *m*
export **1** ['ekspɔ:rt] S Export *m* **2** [ek'spɔ:rt] V/T & V/I exportieren **3** ['ekspɔ:rt] ADJ Export-
expose [ɪk'spoʊz] V/T (*Gefahren etc*) aussetzen (*to dat*); (*sichtbar machen*) freilegen; (*Dieb, Lügner*) entlarven
express [ɪk'spres] **1** ADJ (*Bus, Zug*) Express-, Schnell- **2** S BAHN Schnellzug *m* **3** V/T ausdrücken **4** V/R ~ **oneself** sich ausdrücken **expression** [ɪk'spreʃən] S (*sprachlicher*) Ausdruck *m*; (*im Gesicht*) Gesichtsausdruck *m* **expressway** S Schnellstraße *f*
extend [ɪk'stend] V/T (*Arme*) ausstrecken; (*Vertrag, Visum*) verlängern; (*Gebäude*) vergrößern, ausbauen; (*Geschäft*) erweitern **extension** [ɪk'stenʃən] S (*Vertrag, Visum*) Verlängerung *f*; TEL Anschluss *m* **extensive** [ɪk'stensɪv] ADJ (*Wissen*) umfangreich; (*Gebrauch*) häufig **extent** [ɪk'stent] S (*Kabel, Netz etc*) Länge *f*; (*Gegend, Gebäude*) Ausdehnung *f*; (*Grad, Ausmaß*) Umfang *m*, Ausmaß *n*; **to a certain/large ~** in gewissem/hohem Maße
exterior [ek'stɪrɪər] S Äußere(s) *n*
external [ek'stɜ:rnl] ADJ äußere(r, s), Außen-
extinct [ɪk'stɪŋkt] ADJ (*Arten*) ausgestorben
extinguish [ɪk'stɪŋgwɪʃ] V/T löschen **extinguisher** S Löschgerät *n*
extra ['ekstrə] **1** ADJ zusätzlich; ~ **charge** Zuschlag *m* **2** ADV besonders; ~ **large** (*Kleidung*) übergroß **3** S PL **~s** zusätzliche Kosten *pl*; (*bei Film*) Statisten *pl*; (*bei Auto etc*) Extras *pl*

extract 1 [ɪk'strækt] V/T herausziehen (*from* aus); (*Zahn*) ziehen 2 ['ekstrækt] S (*Buch*) Auszug *m*
extraordinary [ɪk'strɔːrdənerɪ] ADJ außerordentlich; (*merkwürdig*) ungewöhnlich; (*Leistung*) erstaunlich
extreme [ɪk'striːm] 1 ADJ äußerste(r, s); (*Ansichten, Maßnahmen*) extrem 2 S Extrem *n* **extremely** ADV äußerst, höchst
eye [aɪ] 1 S Auge *n*; **keep an ~ on sb/sth** auf j-n/etw aufpassen 2 V/T mustern **eyebrow** S Augenbraue *f* **eyelash** S Wimper *f* **eyelid** S Augenlid *n* **eyeshadow** S Lidschatten *m* **eyesight** S Sehkraft *f* **eye witness** S Augenzeuge *m*, Augenzeugin *f*

F

F *abk* = Fahrenheit
fabric ['fæbrɪk] S Stoff *m*
fabulous ['fæbjʊləs] ADJ sagenhaft
façade [fə'sɑːd] S Fassade *f*
face [feɪs] 1 S Gesicht *n*; (*Uhr*) Zifferblatt *n*; (*Berg*) Wand *f*; **be ~ to ~** (*Menschen*) einander gegenüberstehen 2 V/T & V/I (*Person*) gegenüberstehen *+dat*; (*am Tisch*) gegenübersitzen *+dat*; **~ north** (*Zimmer*) nach Norden gehen; **be ~d with sth** mit etw konfrontiert sein
facility [fə'sɪlətɪ] S Einrichtung *f*; Möglichkeit *f*
fact [fækt] S Tatsache *f*; **as a matter of ~, in ~** eigentlich, tatsächlich
factor ['fæktər] S Faktor *m*
factory ['fæktərɪ] S Fabrik *f*
factual ['fæktʃʊəl] ADJ sachlich
faculty ['fækəltɪ] S Fähigkeit *f*; (*an Universität*) Fakultät *f*; Lehrkörper *m*
fade [feɪd] V/I verblassen
fag [fæg], **faggot** ['fægət] S *umg pej* Schwule(r) *m*
fail [feɪl] 1 V/T (*Prüfung*) nicht bestehen 2 V/I versagen; (*Plan, Ehe*) scheitern; (*Schüler*) durchfallen; (*Sehkraft*) nachlassen **failure** ['feɪljər] S (*Person*) Versager(in) *m(f)*; (*Geschehen*) Versagen *n*; (*Maschine*) Ausfall *m*; (*Plan, Ehe*) Scheitern *n*
faint [feɪnt] 1 ADJ schwach; (*Geräusch*) leise 2 V/I ohnmächtig werden (*with* vor *+dat*)
fair [fer] 1 ADJ (*Haare*) (dunkel)blond; (*Haut*) hell; (*Behandlung*) gerecht, fair; (*Qualität*) ganz ordentlich; (*Wetter*) schön; **a ~ number/amount of** ziemlich viele/viel 2 ADV **play ~** fair spielen; *fig* fair sein; **~ enough** in Ordnung! 3 S

Jahrmarkt *m*; WIRTSCH Messe *f* **fair-haired** ADJ (dunkel)-blond **fairly** ADV (*behandeln*) fair; (*verstärkend*) ziemlich

fairy ['ferɪ] S Fee *f* **fairy tale** S Märchen *n*

faith [feɪθ] S Vertrauen *n* (*in sb* zu j-m); REL Glaube *m* **faithful, faithfully** ADJ & ADV treu

fake [feɪk] **1** S Fälschung *f* **2** ADJ vorgetäuscht **3** V/T fälschen

fall [fɒːl] **1** V/I ⟨fell, fallen⟩ [fel, 'fɒːlən] fallen; (*aus größerer Höhe; schwer*) stürzen; **~ ill** krank werden; **~ asleep** einschlafen; **~ in love** sich verlieben **2** S Fall *m*; (*Unfall*; *von Regierung*) Sturz *m*; (*Abnahme*) Sinken *n* (*in +gen*); (*Jahreszeit*) Herbst *m* **fall apart** V/I auseinanderfallen **fall down** V/I (*Person*) hinfallen **fall off** V/I herunterfallen; **fall out** V/I herausfallen; sich streiten **fall over** V/I hinfallen **fall through** V/I (*Plan etc*) ins Wasser fallen **fallen** ['fɒːlən] *pperf von* fall

false [fɒːls] ADJ falsch; (*Gebiss etc*) künstlich **false alarm** S blinder Alarm

fame [feɪm] S Ruhm *m*

familiar [fə'mɪljər] ADJ vertraut, bekannt

family ['fæməlɪ] S Familie *f*; (*alle Verwandten*) Verwandtschaft *f* **family doctor** S Allgemeinarzt *m*, Allgemeinärztin *f* **family name** S Familienname *m*, Nachname *m* **family practitioner** [fæməlɪpræk'tɪʃnər] S Allgemeinarzt *m*, Allgemeinärztin *f*

famous ['feɪməs] ADJ berühmt

fan [fæn] S Fächer *m*; ELEK Ventilator *m*; (*begeisterter Anhänger*) Fan *m*

fancy ['fænsɪ] ADJ (*Design, Stil*) kunstvoll; (*Geschmack*) ausgefallen

fan heater ['fænhiːtər] S Heizlüfter *m*

fanny ['fænɪ] S *umg* Po *m*; **~ pack** Gürteltasche *f*

fantastic [fæn'tæstɪk] ADJ fantastisch **fantasy** ['fæntəsɪ] S Fantasie *f*

far ⟨further *od* farther, furthest *od* farthest⟩ [fɑːr, 'fɜːrðər, 'fɜːrðəst] **1** ADJ weit; **the ~ end of the room** das andere Ende des Zimmers; **the Far East** der Ferne Osten **2** ADV weit; **~ better** viel besser; **as ~ as ...** bis zum *od* zur ...; (*mit Ortsnamen*) bis nach ...; **as ~ as I'm concerned** was mich betrifft, von mir aus; **so ~** soweit, bisher

fare [fer] S Fahrpreis *m*

farm [fɑːrm] S Bauernhof *m*, Farm *f* **farmer** S Bauer *m*, Bäuerin *f*, Landwirt(in) *m(f)* **farmhouse** S Bauernhaus *n* **farming** S Landwirtschaft *f* **farmland** S Ackerland *n*

fart [fɑːrt] **1** S *umg* Furz *m* **2**

VI umg furzen
farther ['fɑːrðər] ADJ & ADV *Komparativ von* far; → further **farthest** ['fɑːrðəst] ADJ & ADV *Superlativ von* far; → furthest
fascinating ['fæsɪneɪtɪŋ] ADJ faszinierend
fashion ['fæʃən] S (*Kleidung*) Mode *f*; (*Stil*) Art (und Weise) *f*; **be in ~** (in) Mode sein **fashionable** ADJ modisch
fast [fæst] 1 ADJ schnell; **be ~** (*Uhr*) vorgehen 2 ADV schnell; fest 3 S Fasten *n* 4 VI fasten
fasten ['fæsn] VT befestigen (*to* an *+dat*); (*Knopf, Kleid*) zumachen; **~ your seatbelts** bitte anschnallen
fast food S Fast Food *n* **fast forward** S Schnellvorlauf *m* **fast lane** S Überholspur *f*
fat [fæt] 1 ADJ dick; (*Fleisch*) fett 2 S Fett *n*
fatal ['feɪtl] ADJ tödlich
fate [feɪt] S Schicksal *n*
father ['fɑːðər] 1 S Vater *m*; (*Priester*) Pfarrer *m* 2 VT (*Kind*) zeugen **father-in-law** ⟨fathers-in-law⟩ S Schwiegervater *m*
fatigue [fə'tiːg] S Ermüdung *f*
fattening ['fætnɪŋ] ADJ **be ~** dick machen **fatty** ['fætɪ] ADJ (*Essen*) fettig
faucet ['fɒːsət] S Wasserhahn *m* **faucet water** S Leitungswasser *n*
fault [fɒːlt] S Fehler *m*; TECH Defekt *m*; ELEK Störung *f*; (*persönlich*) Schuld *f*; **it's your ~** du bist daran schuld **faulty** ADJ fehlerhaft; TECH defekt
fava bean ['fɑːvəbiːn] S Saubohne *f*
favor ['feɪvər] 1 S Gunst *f*; Gefallen *m*; **in ~ of** für 2 VT (*bevorzugen*) vorziehen **favorite** ['feɪvərət] 1 S Liebling *m*, Favorit(in) *m(f)* 2 ADJ Lieblings-
fax [fæks] 1 VT faxen 2 S Fax *n*
FBI *abk* = Federal Bureau of Investigation; FBI *n*
fear [fɪr] 1 S Angst *f* (*of* vor *+dat*) 2 VT befürchten
feast [fiːst] S Festessen *n*
feather ['feðər] S Feder *f*
feature ['fiːtʃər] 1 S (Gesichts)zug *m*; (*typisches*) Merkmal *n*; (*von Auto etc*) Ausstattungsmerkmal *n*; (*in Zeitung, Film*) Feature *n* 2 VT bringen, (als Besonderheit) zeigen
February ['febjʊərɪ, 'febrʊərɪ] S Februar *m*; → September
fed [fed] 1 *prät, pperf von* feed 2 S *umg* FBI-Agent(in) *m(f)*
federal ['fedərəl] ADJ Bundes-
fed up [fed'ʌp] ADJ **be ~ with sth** etw satthaben
fee [fiː] S Gebühr *f*; (*Arzt, Rechtsanwalt*) Honorar *n*
feed ⟨fed, fed⟩ [fiːd, fed] 1 VT (*Baby, Tier*) füttern; (*Familie: sorgen für*) ernähren 2 S (*für Baby*) Mahlzeit *f*; (*für Tiere*) Futter *n*; IT (*Papierzufuhr*) Zufuhr *f*

feel ⟨felt, felt⟩ [fi:l, felt] **1** VT fühlen; (*Schmerz*) empfinden; (*denken*) meinen **2** VI sich fühlen; **I ~ cold** mir ist kalt; **do you ~ like a walk?** hast du Lust, spazieren zu gehen? **feeling** S Gefühl *n*
feet [fi:t] *pl von* **foot**
fell [fel] **1** *prät von* **fall** **2** VT (*Baum*) fällen
fellow ['feloʊ] **1** S Fellow *m* (*Mitglied eines Colleges, einer wissenschaftlichen Gesellschaft etc*) **2** PRÄF **~ citizen** Mitbürger(in) *m(f)*; **~ traveler** Mitreisende(r) *m/f(m)*
felony ['felənı] S Verbrechen *n*
felt [felt] **1** *prät, pperf von* **feel** **2** S Filz *m*
female ['fi:meıl] **1** S (*von Tieren*) Weibchen *n* **2** ADJ weiblich; **~ doctor** Ärztin *f* **feminine** ['femənın] ADJ weiblich
fence [fens] S Zaun *m*
fender ['fendər] S AUTO Kotflügel *m* **fender bender** S *umg* AUTO *Verkehrsunfall mit Blechschaden*
ferris wheel ['ferıswi:l] S Riesenrad *n*
ferry ['ferı] **1** S Fähre *f* **2** VT übersetzen
festival ['festəvəl] S REL Fest *n*; KUNST, MUS Festspiele *pl*, Festival *n* **festivities** [fe'stıvətız] S PL Feierlichkeiten *pl*
fetch [fetʃ] VT holen; (*von Schule, Bahnhof etc*) abholen; (*Geld*) einbringen
fetus ['fi:təs] S Fötus *m*
fever ['fi:vər] S Fieber *n*
few [fju:] ADJ & PRON *pl* wenige *pl*; **a ~** *pl* ein paar
fiancé [fı'ɑ̃:nseı] S Verlobte(r) *m* **fiancée** S Verlobte *f*
fiber ['faıbər] S Faser *f*, Faserstoff *m*
fiction ['fıkʃən] S Prosaliteratur *f* **fictional** ADJ erfunden
fiddle ['fıdl] **1** S Geige *f*; (*Trick, Schwindelei*) Betrug *m* **2** VT (*Konten, Ergebnisse*) frisieren **fiddle with** VT herumfummeln an +*dat*
fidget ['fıdʒət] VI zappeln
field [fi:ld] S Feld *n*, Wiese *f*; *fig* (Arbeits)gebiet *n*
fierce [fırs] ADJ heftig; (*Tier, Aussehen*) wild; (*Kritik*) scharf
fifteen [fıf'ti:n] **1** NUM fünfzehn **2** S Fünfzehn *f*; → **eight** **fifteenth** ADJ fünfzehnte(r, s); → **eighth** **fifth** [fıfθ] **1** ADJ fünfte(r, s) **2** S Fünftel *n*; → **eighth** **fiftieth** ['fıftııəθ] ADJ fünfzigste(r, s); → **eighth** **fifty** ['fıftı] **1** NUM fünfzig **2** S Fünfzig *f*; → **eight, eighty**
fig [fıg] S Feige *f*
fight [faıt] **1** ⟨fought, fought⟩ [fɒ:t] VI kämpfen (*with, against* gegen; *for, over* um) **2** VT (*Person*) kämpfen mit; *fig* (*Krankheit, Feuer*) bekämpfen **3** S Kampf *m*; Schlägerei *f*; Streit *m* **fight off** VT abwehren
figure ['fıgjər] **1** S (*Person*)

Gestalt *f*; (*von Person*) Figur *f*; (*einzelne*) Zahl *f*, Ziffer *f*; (*Summe*) Betrag *m*; **a four-figure sum** eine vierstellige Summe **2** VT *denken* glauben **3** VI (*auftauchen, vorkommen*) erscheinen **figure out** VT herausbekommen; **I can't figure him out** ich werde aus ihm nicht schlau

file [faɪl] **1** S (*Werkzeug*) Feile *f*; (*Dokument*) Akte *f*; IT Datei *f*; (*für Dokumente*) Aktenordner *m* **2** VT (*Metall, Fingernägel*) feilen; (*Dokumente*) ablegen (*under* unter)

fill [fɪl] VT füllen; (*Zahn*) plombieren; (*Stelle, Posten*) besetzen **fill in** VT (*Loch*) auffüllen; (*aufklären*) informieren (*on* über) **fill out** VT (*Formular*) ausfüllen **fill up** VI AUTO volltanken

fillet [fɪ'leɪ] S Filet *n*

filling ['fɪlɪŋ] S GASTR Füllung *f*; (*Zahn*) Plombe *f*

film [fɪlm] **1** S Film *m* **2** VT filmen

filter ['fɪltər] **1** S Filter *m* **2** VT filtern

filthy ['fɪlθɪ] ADJ dreckig **final** ['faɪnl] **1** ADJ letzte(r, s); (*Stadium, Runde*) End-; (*Entscheidung, Version*) endgültig **2** S SPORT Endspiel *n*; (*bei Wettbewerb*) Finale *n* **finally** ADV zuletzt; schließlich, endlich

finance ['faɪnæns] **1** S Finanzwesen *n*; **~s** *pl* Finanzen *pl* **2** VT finanzieren **financial** [faɪ'nænʃəl] ADJ finanziell; Finanz-

find ⟨found, found⟩ [faɪnd, faʊnd] VT finden; **she ~s it difficult** es fällt ihr schwer **find out** VT herausfinden

fine [faɪn] **1** ADJ (*Linie*) dünn, fein; (*Essen, Wein*) gut; (*hervorragend*) herrlich; (*Wetter*) schön; **I'm ~** es geht mir gut; **that's ~** das ist OK **2** ADV gut **3** S JUR Geldstrafe *f* **4** VT JUR mit einer Geldstrafe belegen

finger ['fɪŋgər] **1** S Finger *m* **2** VT herumfingern an *+dat*

fingerprint S Fingerabdruck *m*

finish ['fɪnɪʃ] **1** S Ende *n*; SPORT Finish *n*; (*Linie*) Ziel *n* **2** VT beenden; (*Buch etc*) zu Ende lesen; (*Essen*) aufessen; (*Getränk*) austrinken **3** VI zu Ende gehen; enden; (*Person: mit etw*) fertig sein; aufhören; **~ first** SPORT als erster durchs Ziel gehen

Finland ['fɪnlənd] S Finnland *n* **Finn** S Finne *m*, Finnin *f*

Finnish **1** ADJ finnisch **2** S (*Sprache*) Finnisch *n*

fir [fɜːr] S Tanne *f*

fire [faɪr] **1** S Feuer *n*; Brand *m*; **set ~ to sth** etw in Brand stecken; **be on ~** brennen **2** VT (*Schüsse, Raketen*) abfeuern; *umg* (*entlassen*) feuern **3** VI AUTO (*Motor*) zünden; **~ at sb** auf j-n schießen **fire alarm**

S Feuermelder *m* **fire department** S Feuerwehr *f* **fire engine** S Feuerwehrauto *n* **fire escape** S Feuerleiter *f* **fire extinguisher** S Feuerlöscher *m* **firefighter** S Feuerwehrmann *m*, Feuerwehrfrau *f* **fireplace** S (offener) Kamin **fire station** S Feuerwache *f* **fire truck** S Feuerwehrauto *n* **fireworks** S PL Feuerwerk *n*

firm [fɜːrm] **1** ADJ fest **2** S Firma *f*

first [fɜːrst] **1** ADJ erste(r, s) **2** ADV zuerst; erstens; (*ankommen, fertig sein*) als erste(r); (*sich ereignen*) zum ersten Mal; **~ of all** zuallererst **3** S (*Person*) Erste(r) *m/f(m)*; **at ~** zuerst, anfangs **first aid** S erste Hilfe **first-class** **1** ADJ erstklassig; (*Abteil, Fahrkarte*) erster Klasse **2** ADV (*reisen*) erster Klasse **first floor** S Erdgeschoss *n* **first lady** S Frau *f* des Präsidenten **firstly** ADV erstens **first name** S Vorname *m*

fish [fɪʃ] **1** S Fisch *m* **2** V/I fischen; angeln **fishing** ['fɪʃɪŋ] S Fischen *n*; Angeln *n* **fishing line** S Angelschnur *f* **fishing pole** S Angelrute *f* **fish stick** S Fischstäbchen *n* **fish tank** S Aquarium *n* **fishy** ['fɪʃɪ] ADJ *umg* (*verdächtig*) faul

fist [fɪst] S Faust *f*

fit [fɪt] **1** ADJ MED gesund; SPORT in Form, fit; **keep ~** sich in Form halten **2** V/T passen *+dat*; (*montieren*) anbringen (*to* an *+dat*); (*in Auto, Gerät etc*) einbauen (*in* in *+akk*) **3** V/I passen; (*in Lücke*) hineinpassen **4** S (*Kleidungsstück*) Sitz *m*; MED Anfall *m* **fit in** **1** V/T (*terminlich*) unterbringen **2** V/I (*in Lücke*) hineinpassen; **he doesn't ~ (here)** er passt nicht hierher; **~ with sb's plans** sich mit j-s Plänen vereinbaren lassen **fitness** S MED Gesundheit *f*; SPORT Fitness *f* **fitted carpet** S Teppichboden *m* **fitting** ADJ passend

five [faɪv] **1** NUM fünf **2** S Fünf *f*; → **eight**

fix [fɪks] V/T befestigen (*to* an *+dat*); (*Termin*) festsetzen; (*Ort, Zeit*) ausmachen; (*Kaputtes*) reparieren; (*Essen*) zubereiten **fixed** ADJ (*Zeit, Betrag*) fest (-gesetzt); (*Position*) unveränderlich; (*Wahlen, Spiel*) manipuliert **fixings** S PL GASTR Beilagen *pl* **fixture** ['fɪkstʃər] S **~s (and fittings)** *pl* Ausstattung *f*

fizzy ['fɪzɪ] ADJ sprudelnd

FL *abk* = Florida

flabby ['flæbɪ] ADJ wabbelig

flag [flæg] S Fahne *f*

flake [fleɪk] S Flocke *f*

flame [fleɪm] S Flamme *f*

flan [flæn] S Obstkuchen *m*

flap [flæp] **1** S Klappe *f* **2** V/T (*Flügel*) schlagen mit **3** V/I flattern

flash [flæʃ] **1** S Blitz *m;* FOTO Blitzlicht *n;* **in a ~** im Nu **2** V/T **~ one's (head)lights** die Lichthupe betätigen **3** V/I aufblinken; *(heller)* aufblitzen **flashback** S Rückblende *f* **flashlight** S Taschenlampe *f* **flashy** ADJ grell, schrill; *pej* protzig

flat [flæt] **1** ADJ flach; eben; *(Getränk)* abgestanden; *(Reifen)* platt; *(Batterie)* leer; *(Weigerung)* glatt **2** S AUTO Reifenpanne *f* **flat screen** S IT Flachbildschirm *m* **flatten** V/T platt machen, einebnen

flatter ['flætər] V/T schmeicheln *+dat* **flattering** ADJ schmeichelhaft

flatware ['flætwer] S Besteck *n*

flavor ['fleıvər] **1** S Geschmack *m* **2** V/T Geschmack geben *+dat,* würzen **flavoring** S Aroma *n*

flawless ['flɒ:ləs] ADJ fehlerlos; *(Aussehen)* makellos

fled [fled] *prät, pperf von* flee

flee ⟨fled, fled⟩ [fli:, fled] V/I fliehen

fleet [fli:t] S Flotte *f*

flesh [fleʃ] S Fleisch *n*

flew [flu:] *prät von* fly

flexibility [fleksə'bılətı] S Biegsamkeit *f; fig* Flexibilität *f* **flexible** ['fleksəbl] ADJ biegsam; *(Person)* flexibel **flexitime, flextime** S gleitende Arbeitszeit, Gleitzeit *f*

flick [flık] S *umg* Film *m*

flicker ['flıkər] V/I flackern; TV flimmern

flight [flaıt] S Flug *m; (vor Polizei etc)* Flucht *f;* **~ of stairs** Treppe *f* **flight attendant** S Flugbegleiter(in) *m(f)*

fling [flıŋ] **1** V/T ⟨flung, flung⟩ [flʌŋ] schleudern **2** S Affäre *f;* **have a ~ (with sb)** eine Affäre (mit j-m) haben

flip [flıp] V/T schnippen **flip out** V/I *umg* ausflippen, verrückt werden

flipper ['flıpər] S Flosse *f*

flip side S Kehrseite *f*

flirt [flɜ:rt] V/I flirten

float [floʊt] V/I schwimmen; schweben

flock [flɑ:k] S *(Schafe; Gemeinde)* Herde *f; (Vögel)* Schwarm *m; (Leute)* Schar *f*

flood [flʌd] **1** S Hochwasser *n,* Überschwemmung *f; fig* Flut *f* **2** V/T überschwemmen **floodlight** S Flutlicht *n* **floodlit** ADJ angestrahlt

floor [flɔ:r] S Fußboden *m; (Geschoss)* Stock *m;* **first ~** Erdgeschoss *n;* **second ~** erster Stock

flop [flɑ:p] **1** S *umg* Reinfall *m,* Flop *m* **2** V/I misslingen, floppen

florist (shop) ['flɔ:rəst(ʃɑ:p)] S Blumengeschäft *n,* Blumenladen *m*

flour [flaʊr] S Mehl *n*

flourish ['flərıʃ] V/I gedeihen;

(*Geschäft*) gut laufen; (*boomen*) florieren
flow [floʊ] **1** S Fluss *m* **2** V/I fließen
flower ['flaʊər] **1** S Blume *f* **2** V/I blühen
flown [floʊn] *pperf von* **fly**
flu [flu:] S *umg* Grippe *f*
fluent ['flu:ənt] ADJ (*Sprache*) fließend; **be ~ in German** fließend Deutsch sprechen
fluid ['flu:ɪd] **1** S Flüssigkeit *f* **2** ADJ flüssig
flung [flʌŋ] *prät, pperf von* **fling**
flunk [flʌŋk] V/T *umg* (*Prüfung*) nicht bestehen, durchfallen bei
flush [flʌʃ] **1** S (*Toilette*) Wasserspülung *f*; (*auf Wangen*) Röte *f* **2** V/I (*Toilette*) spülen
flute [flu:t] S Flöte *f*
fly [flaɪ] **1** V/T & V/I ⟨flew, flown⟩ [flu:, floʊn] fliegen; **how time flies** wie die Zeit vergeht! **2** S (*Insekt*) Fliege *f*; (*an Hosen*) Hosenschlitz *m*
foam [foʊm] **1** S Schaum *m* **2** V/I schäumen
focus ['foʊkəs] **1** S Brennpunkt *m*; **in/out of ~** (*Foto*) scharf/unscharf **2** V/T (*Kamera*) scharf stellen **3** V/I sich konzentrieren (*on* auf *+akk*)
fog [fɑ:g] S Nebel *m* **foggy** ADJ neblig **fog light** S AUTO Nebelscheinwerfer *m*
foil [fɔɪl] S Folie *f*
fold [foʊld] **1** V/T falten **2** V/I *umg* (*Firma, Geschäft*) eingehen; (*beim Kartenspiel*) aussteigen **3** S Falte *f* **folder** S Aktenmappe *f*, Broschüre *f*; IT Ordner *m* **folding** ADJ zusammenklappbar; (*Fahrrad, Stuhl*) Klapp-
folk [foʊk] **1** S Leute *pl*; MUS Folk *m* **2** ADJ Volks-
follow ['fɑ:loʊ] **1** V/T folgen *+dat*; verfolgen; (*verstehen*) folgen können *+dat*; (*Nachrichten*) verfolgen **2** V/I folgen; (*Ergebnis*) sich ergeben (*from* aus) **follower** S Anhänger(in) *m(f)* **following** **1** ADJ folgend; **the ~ day** am (darauf)folgenden Tag **2** PRÄP nach
fond [fɑ:nd] ADJ **be ~ of** gernhaben, lieb haben **fondly** ADV liebevoll **fondness** S Vorliebe *f*, Zuneigung *f*
font [fɑ:nt] S Taufbecken *n*; TYPO Schriftart *f*
food [fu:d] S Essen *n*; Lebensmittel *pl*; (*für Tiere*) Futter *n* **food poisoning** S Lebensmittelvergiftung *f* **food processor** S Küchenmaschine *f*
fool [fu:l] **1** S Idiot *m*, Narr *m*; **make a ~ of oneself** sich blamieren **2** V/T (*täuschen*) hereinlegen **3** V/I **~ around** herumalbern; (*ohne viel zu tun*) herumtrödeln **foolish** ADJ dumm
foot [fʊt] **1** S ⟨feet⟩ [fi:t] Fuß *m*; (*Maßeinheit*) Fuß *m* (*30,48 cm*); **on ~** zu Fuß **2** V/T (*Rechnung*) bezahlen **football** S

Football *m* **footbridge** S Fußgängerbrücke *f* **footpath** S Fußweg *m* **footprint** S Fußabdruck *m* **footwear** S Schuhwerk *n*

for [fɔ:r] **1** PRÄP für; **what ~?** wozu?; **what's ~ lunch?** was gibt es zum Mittagessen?; (*wegen*) **famous ~** bekannt für, berühmt wegen; (*mit Zeitangabe*) **we talked ~ two hours** wir redeten zwei Stunden lang; (*bis jetzt*) **we have been talking ~ two hours** wir reden seit zwei Stunden; (*Entfernung*) **~ miles** meilenweit; **as ~ ...** was ... betrifft **2** KONJ denn

forbade [fər'bæd] *prät von* **forbid forbid** ⟨forbade, forbidden⟩ [fər'bɪd, fər'bæd, fər'bɪdn] V/T verbieten

force [fɔ:rs] **1** S Kraft *f*; Gewalt *m*; **come into ~** in Kraft treten; **the Forces** *pl* die Streitkräfte *pl* **2** V/T zwingen

forearm ['fɔ:rɑ:rm] S Unterarm *m*

forecast ['fɔ:rkæst] **1** V/T voraussagen; (*Wetter*) vorhersagen **2** S Vorhersage *f*

forefinger ['fɔ:rfɪŋgər] S Zeigefinger *m*

foreground ['fɔ:rgraʊnd] S Vordergrund *m*

forehead ['fɔ:rhed, 'fɑ:rɪd] S Stirn *f*

foreign ['fɑ:rən] ADJ ausländisch **foreigner** S Ausländer(in) *m(f)* **foreign exchange** S Devisen *pl* **foreign language** S Fremdsprache *f* **foreign minister** S Außenminister(in) *m(f)*

forest ['fɑ:rəst] S Wald *m*

forever [fə'revər] ADV für immer

forgave [fər'geɪv] *prät von* forgive

forgery ['fɔ:rdʒərɪ] S Fälschung *f*

forget ⟨forgot, forgotten⟩ [fər'get, fər'gɑ:t, fər'gɑ:tn] V/T & V/I vergessen **forgetful** ADJ vergesslich **forget-me-not** S Vergissmeinnicht *n*

forgive ⟨forgave, forgiven⟩ [fər'gɪv, fər'geɪv, fər'gɪvn] *irr* V/T verzeihen

forgot [fər'gɑ:t] *prät von* **forget forgotten** [fər'gɑ:tn] *pperf von* **forget**

fork [fɔ:rk] **1** S Gabel *f*; (*Straße*) Gabelung *f* **2** V/I (*Straße*) sich gabeln

form [fɔ:rm] **1** S Form *f*; (*Dokument*) Formular *n* **2** V/T bilden

formal ['fɔ:rməl] ADJ förmlich; formell **formality** [fɔ:r'mælətɪ] S Formalität *f*

format ['fɔ:rmæt] **1** S Format *n* **2** V/T IT formatieren

former ['fɔ:rmər] ADJ frühere(r, s); (*bei Erwähnung von zweien*) erstere(r, s) **formerly** ADV früher

forth [fɔ:rθ] ADV **and so ~** und so weiter **forthcoming**

['fɔːrθ'kʌmɪŋ] ADJ kommend, bevorstehend **fortieth** ['fɔːrtɪəθ] ADJ vierzigste(r, s); → eighth
fortunate ['fɔːrtʃənət] ADJ glücklich; **I was ~** ich hatte Glück **fortunately** ADV zum Glück **fortune** ['fɔːrtʃən] S (*Geld*) Vermögen *n*; **good ~** Glück *n*
forty ['fɔːrtɪ] **1** NUM vierzig **2** S Vierzig *f*; → eight, eighty
forward ['fɔːrwərd] **1** ADV vorwärts **2** ADJ dreist; direkt **3** S SPORT Stürmer(in) *m(f)* **4** V/T (*Post*) nachsenden; IT weiterleiten **forwards** ADV vorwärts
foster child ['fɑːstərtʃaɪld] S Pflegekind *n* **foster parents** ['fɑːstərperənts] S PL Pflegeeltern *pl*
fought [fɒːt] *prät, pperf von* fight
foul [faʊl] **1** ADJ (*Wetter*) schlecht; (*Geruch*) übel **2** S SPORT Foul *n*
found [faʊnd] **1** *prät, pperf von* find **2** V/T (*Firma etc*) gründen **foundations** [faʊn'deɪʃənz] S PL Fundament *n*
fountain ['faʊntən] S Springbrunnen *m* **fountain pen** S Füller *m*
four [fɔːr] **1** NUM vier **2** S Vier *f*; → eight **fourteen** [fɔːr'tiːn] **1** NUM vierzehn **2** S Vierzehn *f*; → eight **fourteenth** ADJ vierzehnte(r, s); → eighth **fourth** [fɔːrθ] ADJ vierte(r, s); → eighth **four-wheel drive** S Allradantrieb *m*; (*Auto*) Geländewagen *m*
fox [fɑːks] S Fuchs *m*
fraction ['frækʃən] S MATH Bruch *m*; (*kleiner Teil*) Bruchteil *m* **fracture** ['fræktʃər] **1** S MED Bruch *m* **2** V/T brechen
fragile ['frædʒəl] ADJ zerbrechlich
fragment ['frægmənt] S Bruchstück *n*
fragrance ['freɪgrəns] S Duft *m*
frame [freɪm] **1** S Rahmen *m*; (*Brille*) Gestell *n*; **~ of mind** Verfassung *f* **2** V/T einrahmen **framework** S Rahmen *m*, Struktur *f*
France [fræns] S Frankreich *n*
frank [fræŋk] ADJ offen
frankfurter ['fræŋkfɜːrtər] S (Frankfurter) Würstchen *n*
frankly ['fræŋklɪ] ADV offen gesagt
frantic ['fræntɪk] ADJ (*Aktivität*) hektisch; (*Anstrengungen*) verzweifelt
fraternity [frə'tɜːrnətɪ] S Verbindung *f*, Studentenverbindung *f*
fraud [frɒːd] S Betrug *m*; (*Person*) Schwindler(in) *m(f)*
freak [friːk] **1** S Anomalie *f*; (*Tier, Person*) Missgeburt *f*; *umg* (*Computerbegeisterter etc*) Fan *m*, Freak *m* **2** ADJ (*Unfall, Wetter*) außergewöhnlich, selt-

sam **freak out** VI *umg* ausflippen
freckle ['frekl] S Sommersprosse *f*
free [fri:] **1** ADJ & ADV frei; gratis, kostenlos; **for ~** umsonst **2** VT befreien **freebie** ['fri:bɪ] S *umg* Werbegeschenk *n* **freedom** ['fri:dəm] S Freiheit *f* **freelance** ['fri:lɑ:ns] **1** ADJ freiberuflich tätig; freischaffend **2** S Freiberufler(in) *m(f)* **free-range** ['fri:reɪndʒ] ADJ (*Hühner*) frei laufend; (*Ei*) Freiland- **freeway** ['fri:weɪ] S (gebührenfreie) Autobahn
freeze ⟨froze, frozen⟩ [fri:z, froʊz, 'froʊzn] **1** VI (*Person*) frieren; (*See*) zufrieren; (*Wasser*) gefrieren **2** VT einfrieren **freezer** S Tiefkühltruhe *f*; (*in Kühlschrank*) Gefrierfach *n* **freezing** ADJ eiskalt
freight [freɪt] S Fracht *f*, Frachtgebühr *f* **freight train** S Güterzug *m*
French [frentʃ] **1** ADJ französisch **2** S (*Sprache*) Französisch *n* **French bread** S Baguette *f* **French dressing** S Vinaigrette *f* **French fries** S PL Pommes frites *pl* **French kiss** S Zungenkuss *m* **Frenchman** ⟨-men *pl*⟩ S Franzose *m* **French toast** S *in Ei und Milch getunktes gebratenes Brot* **Frenchwoman** ⟨-women *pl*⟩ S Französin *f*
frequency ['fri:kwənsɪ] S Häufigkeit *f*; PHYS Frequenz *f* **frequent** ADJ häufig **frequently** ADV häufig
fresh [freʃ] ADJ frisch; (*Anfang, Laken*) neu **freshen** VI **~ (up)** (*Person*) sich frisch machen **freshman** ⟨-men *pl*⟩ S (*Universität, Highschool*) *Student(in) im ersten Jahr* **freshwater fish** S Süßwasserfisch *m*
Fri *abk* = Friday; Fr **Friday** ['fraɪdeɪ] S Freitag *m*; → Tuesday
fridge [frɪdʒ] S Kühlschrank *m*
fried [fraɪd] ADJ gebraten; **~ egg** Spiegelei *n*
friend [frend] S Freund(in) *m(f)*; (*weniger eng*) Bekannte(r) *m/f(m)*; **make ~s with sb** sich mit j-m anfreunden **friendly** ADJ freundlich **friendship** ['frendʃɪp] S Freundschaft *f*
fries [fraɪz] S PL Pommes *pl*
fright [fraɪt] S Schrecken *m* **frighten** VT erschrecken; **be ~ed** Angst haben **frightening** ADJ beängstigend
frog [frɑ:g] S Frosch *m*
from [frɑ:m] PRÄP von; (*örtlich*) aus; (*mit Zeitangabe*) ab; **where does she come ~?** woher kommt sie?; **it's ten miles ~ here** es ist zehn Meilen von hier (entfernt)
front [frʌnt] **1** S Vorderseite *f*, Fassade *f*; (*Krieg, Luftmassen*) Front *f*; (*am Meer*) Promenade *f*; **in ~, at the ~** vorne; **in ~ of** vor **2** ADJ vordere(r, s), Vor-

der-; (*ganz vorne*) vorderste(r, s); **~ desk** Rezeption *f*, Empfang *m*; **~ door** Haustür *f*; **~ page** Titelseite *f*
frontier [frʌn'tɪr] S Grenze *f*
front-wheel drive S AUTO Frontantrieb *m*
frost [frɑ:st] S Frost *m*; Reif *m* **frosting** S Zuckerguss *m*
froth [frɑ:θ] S Schaum *m*
frown [fraʊn] V/I die Stirn runzeln
froze [froʊz] *prät von* **freeze** **frozen** ['froʊzn] **1** *pperf von* **freeze** **2** ADJ (*Lebensmittel*) tiefgekühlt, Tiefkühl-
fruit [fru:t] S Obst *n*; (*einzelne*) Frucht *f*
frustrated ['frʌstreɪtəd] ADJ frustriert **frustration** [frʌs'treɪʃən] S Frustration *f*, Frust *m*
fry [fraɪ] V/T braten **frying pan** S Bratpfanne *f*
fuck [fʌk] V/T *vulg* ficken; **~ off** verpiss dich!; **~ sth up** etw versauen; **~ around** herumalbern; **~ with sb** sich mit j-m anlegen **fucking** ADJ *vulg* Scheiß-
fuel [fju:əl] S Kraftstoff *m*, Brennstoff *m* **fuel gauge** S Benzinuhr *f*
fulfill [fʊl'fɪl] V/T erfüllen
full [fʊl] ADJ voll; (*nach Essen*) satt; (*Mitglied, Beschäftigung*) Voll(zeit)-; (*komplett*) vollständig; **~ of ...** voller ... *gen* **full moon** S Vollmond *m* **full-time** ADJ **~ job** Ganztagsarbeit *f* **fully** ADV völlig; (*gesund werden*) voll und ganz; (*diskutieren*) ausführlich
fumes [fju:mz] S PL Dämpfe *pl*; (*Auto etc*) Abgase *pl*
fun [fʌn] S Spaß *m*; **for ~** zum Spaß; **it's ~** es macht Spaß; **make ~ of** sich lustig machen über *+akk*
function ['fʌŋkʃən] **1** S Funktion *f*; (*große Party*) Feier *f*; (*offiziell*) Empfang *m* **2** V/I funktionieren
fund [fʌnd] S Fonds *m*; **~s** *pl* Geldmittel *pl*
fundamental [fʌndə'mentl] ADJ grundlegend **fundamentally** ADV im Grunde
funding ['fʌndɪŋ] S finanzielle Unterstützung
funeral ['fju:nərəl] S Beerdigung *f* **funeral director** S Beerdigungsunternehmer(in) *m(f)*; Leichenbestatter(in) *m(f)*
funeral home, **funeral parlor** S Beerdigungsinstitut *n*
fungus <fungi *od* funguses *pl*> ['fʌŋgəs, 'fʌŋgaɪ] S Pilz *m*
funnel ['fʌnl] S Trichter *m*; (*von Schiff*) Schornstein *m*
funny ['fʌnɪ] ADJ (*witzig*) komisch, lustig; (*merkwürdig*) seltsam
fur [fɜ:r] S Pelz *m*; (*Tier a.*) Fell *n*
furious ['fjʊrɪəs] ADJ wütend (*with sb* auf j-n)

furnished ['fɜːrnəʃd] ADJ möbliert **furniture** ['fɜːrnətʃər] S Möbel *pl*; **piece of ~** Möbelstück *n*
further ['fɜːrðər] *Komparativ von* far **1** ADJ weitere(r, s); **until ~ notice** bis auf weiteres **2** ADV weiter **furthest** ['fɜːrðəst] *Superlativ von* far **1** ADJ am weitesten entfernt **2** ADV am weitesten
fury ['fjʊrɪ] S Wut *f*
fuss [fʌs] S Theater *n* **fussy** ADJ schwierig, kompliziert; pingelig
future ['fjuːtʃər] **1** ADJ künftig **2** S Zukunft *f*
fuze [fjuːz] **1** S ELEK Sicherung *f* **2** V/I ELEK durchbrennen

G

GA *abk* = Georgia
gadget ['gædʒət] S Vorrichtung *f*, Gerät *n*
gain [geɪn] **1** V/T (*Zeit, Unterstützung*) gewinnen; (*Vorteil, Respekt*) sich verschaffen; (*Wissen*) erwerben; (*Gewicht*) zunehmen **2** V/I (*besser werden*) gewinnen (*in* an *+dat*); (*Uhr*) vorgehen **3** S Gewinn *m* (*in* an *+dat*)
gal [gæl] S *umg* → girl
gale [geɪl] S Sturm *m*
gallery ['gælərɪ] S Galerie *f*, Museum *n*
gallon ['gælən] S Gallone *f* (*3,79 l*)
gallop ['gæləp] **1** S Galopp *m* **2** V/I galoppieren
gallstone ['gɒːlstoʊn] S Gallenstein *m*
gamble ['gæmbl] **1** V/I um Geld spielen, wetten **2** S **it's a ~** es ist riskant **gambling** S Glücksspiel *n*
game [geɪm] S Spiel *n*; (*Tiere*) Wild *n*
gang [gæŋ] S (*Kriminelle*) Bande *f*; (*Jugendliche*) Gang *f*, Clique *f*
gangster ['gæŋstər] S Gangster *m*
gangway ['gæŋweɪ] S (*Schiff*) Gangway *f*
gap [gæp] S Lücke *f*; (*zeitlich*) Pause *f*; (*altersmäßig, Geschmack*) Unterschied *m*
garage ['gærɑːʒ] S Garage *f*, (Auto)werkstatt *f*
garbage ['gɑːrbɪdʒ] S Müll *m*; *umg* (*Unsinn*) Quatsch *m* **garbage can** S Mülleimer *m*; (*draußen*) Mülltonne *f* **garbage disposal** S Müllschlucker *m* **garbage truck** S Müllwagen *m*
garbanzo [gɑːr'bɑːnzoʊ] S Kichererbse *f*
garden ['gɑːrdn] S Garten *m* **gardener** S Gärtner(in) *m(f)* **gardening** S Gartenarbeit *f*
garlic ['gɑːrlɪk] S Knoblauch

m
gas [gæs] S Gas *n*; Benzin *n*; MED Blähungen *pl*; **step on the ~** Gas geben; **have ~** Blähungen haben **gas cylinder** S Gasflasche *f*
gasket ['gæskət] S Dichtung *f*
gasoline ['gæsəli:n] S Benzin *n*
gasp [gæsp] V/I keuchen; nach Luft schnappen
gas pedal S Gaspedal *n* **gas pump** S Zapfsäule *f* **gas station** S Tankstelle *f* **gas tank** S Benzintank *m*
gastric ['gæstrɪk] ADJ Magen-
gate [geɪt] S Tor *n*; (*Sperre*) Schranke *f*; FLUG Gate *n*, Flugsteig *m* **gateway** S Tor *n*
gather ['gæðər] 1 V/T sammeln; **~ speed** beschleunigen 2 V/I sich versammeln; (*Folgerungen ziehen*) schließen (*from* aus) **gathering** S Versammlung *f*
gauge [geɪdʒ] S Meßgerät *n*
gave [geɪv] *prät von* **give**
gay [geɪ] ADJ schwul
gaze [geɪz] 1 S Blick *m* 2 V/I starren
gear [gɪr] S AUTO Gang *m*, Ausrüstung *f*; (*Kleidung*) Klamotten *pl*; **change ~** schalten **gearbox** S Getriebe *n* **gear shift** S Gangschaltung *f*; Schalthebel *m*
geese [gi:s] *pl von* **goose**
gel [dʒel] S Gel *n*
gem [dʒem] S Edelstein *m*; *fig* Juwel *n*
Gemini ['dʒemɪni:] S SG ASTROL Zwillinge *pl*
gender ['dʒendər] S Geschlecht *n*
gene [dʒi:n] S Gen *n*
general ['dʒenərəl] ADJ allgemein; **~ delivery** postlagernd; **~ election** Parlamentswahlen *pl*; **~ knowledge** Allgemeinbildung *f*; **~ store** Gemischtwarenhandlung *f* **generally** ['dʒenrəlɪ] ADV im Allgemeinen
generation [dʒenə'reɪʃən] S Generation *f*
generosity [dʒenə'rɑ:sətɪ] S Großzügigkeit *f* **generous** ['dʒenərəs] ADJ großzügig; (*Menge*) reichlich
genetic [dʒə'netɪk] ADJ genetisch, Gen- **genetically modified** [dʒənetɪklɪ'mɑ:dəfaɪd] ADJ gentechnisch verändert, genmanipuliert; → GM
genitals ['dʒenətlz] S PL Geschlechtsteile *pl*
genius ['dʒi:njəs] S Genie *n*
gentle ['dʒentl] ADJ sanft; zart **gentleman** ⟨-men *pl*⟩ S Herr *m*; Gentleman *m*
genuine ['dʒenjʊɪn] ADJ echt
geography [dʒɪ'ɑ:grəfɪ] S Geografie *f*; (*Schulfach*) Erdkunde *f*
germ [dʒɜ:rm] S Keim *m*; MED Bazillus *m*
German ['dʒɜ:rmən] 1 ADJ deutsch; **she's ~** sie ist Deut-

sche **2** S (*Person*) Deutsche(r) *m/f(m)*; (*Sprache*) Deutsch *n*; **in ~** auf Deutsch **Germany** ['dʒɜːrmənɪ] S Deutschland *n*
gesture ['dʒestʃər] S Geste *f*
get ⟨got, got *od* gotten⟩ [get, gaːt, 'gaːtn] **1** V/T bekommen, kriegen; **~ a cold/flu** sich erkälten/eine Grippe bekommen; (*gegen Geld*) kaufen; (*in Geschäft*) sich besorgen; (*Haustier*) sich anschaffen; **~ sb sth** j-m etw besorgen; (*herbringen*) j-m etw holen; **where did you ~ that (from)?** woher hast du/haben Sie das?; **~ a taxi** ein Taxi nehmen; (*überreden*) **~ sb to do sth** j-n dazu bringen, etw zu tun; (*zustande bringen*) **~ sth to work** etw zum Laufen bringen; **~ sth done** (*selbst*) etw machen; (*andere*) etw machen lassen; (*zum Ziel bringen*) **this isn't ~ting us anywhere** so kommen wir nicht weiter; (*verstehen*) **don't ~ me wrong** versteh mich nicht falsch! **2** V/I werden; **~ dressed** sich anziehen; **I'll ~ ready** ich mache mich fertig; **~ lost** sich verirren; (*ankommen*) **we got to Seattle at 5** wir kamen um 5 in Seattle an **get across** V/T **1** V/I über etw *akk* kommen **2** V/T klarmachen **get along** V/I (*mit Situation*) zurechtkommen; (*mit Leuten*) gut auskommen (*with* mit) **get at** V/T (*erreichen*) herankommen an *+akk*; **what are you getting at?** worauf wollen Sie hinaus?, was meinst du damit? **get away** V/I (*von Party etc*) wegkommen; (*Verbrecher*) entkommen (*from dat*); **he got away with it** er kam ungeschoren davon **get back** **1** V/I zurückkommen; TEL **~ to sb** j-n zurückrufen; **~ at sb** es j-m heimzahlen **2** V/T zurückbekommen **get by** V/I auskommen (*on* mit) **get down** **1** V/I heruntersteigen; **~ to business** zur Sache kommen **2** V/T aufschreiben; **it gets me down** *umg* es macht mich fertig **get in** V/I heimkommen; (*in Auto*) einsteigen **get into** V/T (*Auto*) einsteigen in *+akk*; (*Wut, Panik*) geraten in *+akk*; **~ trouble** in Schwierigkeiten kommen; **~ sth** anfangen, sich für etw zu begeistern **get off** **1** V/I (*aus Zug*) aussteigen (aus); (*von Pferd*) absteigen (von) **2** V/T (*Aufkleber*) los-/abbekommen; (*Kleidungsstück*) ausziehen **get on** V/I vorankommen; (*sich gut verstehen*) auskommen (*with* mit); (*in Zug*) einsteigen (in *+akk*); (*auf Pferd*) aufsteigen (auf *+akk*) **get out** **1** V/I herauskommen; (*aus Fahrzeug*) aussteigen **~!** raus! **2** V/T (*Taschentuch etc*) herausholen; (*Fleck, Nagel*) herausbekommen **get over** V/I (*Enttäuschung etc*) hinwegkommen über *+akk*; (*Krankheit*) sich

erholen von; (*Verlust*) sich abfinden mit **get through** VI durchkommen **get up** VI aufstehen **get-together** S Treffen *n*
ghetto ⟨-es *pl*⟩ ['getoʊ] S Ghetto *n*
ghost [goʊst] S Gespenst *n*; Geist *m*
giant ['dʒaɪənt] **1** S Riese *m* **2** ADJ riesig
gift [gɪft] S Geschenk *n*; (*Talent*) Begabung *f* **gifted** ADJ begabt **giftwrap** VT als Geschenk verpacken
gigantic [dʒaɪ'gæntɪk] ADJ riesig
giggle ['gɪgl] **1** VI kichern **2** S Gekicher *n*
gimmick ['gɪmɪk] S (*für/in Werbung*) Gag *m*
ginger ['dʒɪndʒər] **1** S Ingwer *m* **2** ADJ (*Haare*) kupferrot; (*Katze*) rötlichgelb **ginger beer** S Ingwerlimonade *f* **gingerbread** S Lebkuchen *m* (*mit Ingwergeschmack*)
giraffe [dʒə'ræf] S Giraffe *f*
girl [gɜ:rl] S Mädchen *n* **girlfriend** S (feste) Freundin **girl scout** S Pfadfinderin *f*
gist [dʒɪst] S **get the ~ (of it)** das Wesentliche verstehen
give ⟨gave, given⟩ [gɪv, geɪv, 'gɪvn] **1** VT geben; schenken (*to sb* j-m); (*Namen*) angeben; (*Rede*) halten; (*Blut, Geld*) spenden **2** VI (*Geländer*) nachgeben **give away** VT verschenken; (*Geheimnis*) verraten **give back** VT zurückgeben **give in** VI aufgeben **give up** VT & VI aufgeben **give way** VI (*Brücke, Geländer*) nachgeben; (*im Straßenverkehr*) die Vorfahrt beachten **given** ['gɪvn] *pperf von* **give**
glad [glæd] ADJ froh (*about* über); **I was ~ (to hear) that ...** es hat mich gefreut, dass ... **gladly** ADV gerne
glance [glæns] **1** S Blick *m* **2** VI einen Blick werfen (*at* auf +*akk*)
gland [glænd] S Drüse *f*
glare [gler] **1** S grelles Licht; stechender Blick **2** VI **~ at sb** j-n böse anstarren
glass [glæs] S Glas *n*; **~es** *pl* Brille *f*
glide [glaɪd] VI gleiten; (*Flugzeug, Vogel a.*) schweben
glimpse [glɪmps] S flüchtiger Blick
glitch [glɪtʃ] S kleiner Defekt; Panne *f*
glitter ['glɪtər] VI glitzern; (*Augen*) funkeln
global ['gloʊbəl] ADJ global, Welt-; **~ warming** die Erwärmung der Erdatmosphäre **globe** [gloʊb] S Kugel *f*, Erdball *m*; Globus *m*
gloomy ['glu:mɪ] ADJ düster
glorious ['glɔ:rɪəs] ADJ (*Sieg*) ruhmreich; (*Wetter, Tag*) herrlich **glory** ['glɔ:rɪ] S Herrlichkeit *f*

glove [glʌv] S Handschuh *m* **glove compartment** S Handschuhfach *n*
glow [gloʊ] V/I glühen
glucose ['glu:koʊz] S Traubenzucker *m*
glue [glu:] **1** S Klebstoff *m* **2** V/T kleben
GM *abk* = genetically modified; Gen-; **~ foods** *pl* gentechnisch veränderte Lebensmittel *pl*
go [goʊ] **1** V/I ⟨went, gone⟩ [went, ga:n] gehen; (*in Fahrzeug; reisen*) fahren; (*Flugzeug*) fliegen; (*Straße*) führen (*to* nach); (*Zug, Bus*) (ab)fahren; (*Zeit*) vergehen; (*Uhr, Gerät*) gehen, funktionieren; (*Maschine*) laufen; (*Farbe, Stil*) passen (*with* zu); (*Schmerz*) nachlassen; **I have to ~ to the doctor/to Detroit** ich muss zum Arzt/nach Detroit; **~ shopping** einkaufen gehen; **~ for a walk** spazieren gehen; **has he gone yet?** ist er schon weg?; **get sth ~ing** etw in Gang setzen; **keep ~ing** weitermachen; (*Maschine*) weiterlaufen; **how's the job ~ing?** was macht der Job?; **~ deaf** taub werden; **pizza to ~** Pizza zum Mitnehmen **2** V/AUX **be ~ing to do sth** etw tun werden; **I was ~ing to do it** ich wollte es tun **3** S ⟨-es *pl*⟩ Versuch *m*; **it's my ~** ich bin dran; **in one ~** auf einen Schlag; (*austrinken*) in einem Zug **go ahead** V/I vorausgehen; (*beginnen*) anfangen **go away** V/I weggehen; verreisen **go back** V/I (*Person*) zurückgehen **go by** **1** V/I vorbeigehen; (*Fahrzeug*) vorbeifahren; (*Jahre, Zeit*) vergehen **2** V/T (*urteilen*) gehen nach **go down** V/I (*Sonne, Schiff*) untergehen; (*Temperaturen*) zurückgehen; (*Preise*) sinken; **~ well/badly** gut/schlecht ankommen **go in** V/I hineingehen **go into** V/T (*eintreten*) hineingehen in *+akk*; (*Auto bei Zusammenstoß*) fahren gegen, hineinfahren in *+akk*; **~ teaching/politics/the army** Lehrer werden/in die Politik gehen/zum Militär gehen **go off** V/I (*Person*) weggehen; (*in Fahrzeug*) wegfahren; (*Lichter*) ausgehen; (*Alarm*) losgehen **go on** V/I (*Diskussion*) weitergehen; (*Licht*) angehen; **~ with** *od* **doing sth** etw weitermachen **go out** V/I (*Person*) hinausgehen; (*Licht, Feuer; Person: abends*) ausgehen; **~ for a meal** essen gehen **go up** V/I (*Temperatur, Preise*) steigen; (*Aufzug*) hochfahren **go without** V/T verzichten auf *+akk*; (*Essen, Schlaf*) auskommen ohne
goal [goʊl] S (*Absicht*) Ziel *n*; SPORT Tor *n* **goalkeeper** S Torwart *m* **goalpost** S Torpfosten *m*
goat [goʊt] S Ziege *f*
god [ga:d] S Gott *m*; **thank**

God Gott sei Dank **goddaughter** S Patentochter *f* **godfather** S Pate *m* **godmother** S Patin *f* **godson** S Patensohn *m*

goggles ['gɑ:glz] S PL Schutzbrille *f*; Skibrille *f*; Taucherbrille *f*

going ['goʊɪŋ] ADJ (*Preis, Gehalt*) üblich **goings-on** S PL Vorgänge *pl*

gold [goʊld] S Gold *n* **gold(en)** ADJ golden

golf [gɑ:lf] S Golf *n* **golf club** S Golfschläger *m*; Golfklub *m*

golf course S Golfplatz *m*

gone [gɑ:n] *pperf von* **go**; **he's ~** er ist weg **gonna** ['gənə] *umg kontr von* **going to**

good [gʊd] **1** S Wohl *n*; (*moralisch*) Gute(s) *n*; **it's no ~** (*doing sth*) es hat keinen Sinn *od* Zweck; (*Sache, Gerät*) es taugt nichts; **for ~** für immer **2** ADJ ⟨better, best⟩ gut; (*geeignet*) passend; (*ausgiebig*) gründlich; (*artig*) brav; (*höflich*) nett, lieb; **be ~ / no ~ at sport** gut/schlecht in Sport sein; **this just isn't ~ enough** so geht das nicht; **~ morning/evening** guten Morgen/Abend; **~ night** gute Nacht; **have a ~ time** sich gut amüsieren **goodbye** [gʊd'baɪ] INT auf Wiedersehen **Good Friday** S Karfreitag *m* **good-looking** ADJ gut aussehend

goods [gʊdz] S PL Waren *pl*, Güter *pl*

goose ⟨geese⟩ [gu:s, gi:s] S Gans *f* **goose bumps** S Gänsehaut *f*

gorge [gɔ:rdʒ] S Schlucht *f*

gorgeous ['gɔ:rdʒəs] ADJ wunderschön; **he's ~** er sieht toll aus

gossip ['gɑ:səp] **1** S Klatsch *m*; (*Person*) Klatschtante *f* **2** V/I klatschen, tratschen

got [gɑ:t] *prät, pperf von* **get** **gotta** ['gɑ:tə] *umg kontr von* **got to** **gotten** ['gɑ:tn] *pperf von* **get**

govern ['gʌvərn] V/T regieren; (*Provinz*) verwalten **government** S Regierung *f* **governor** S Gouverneur(in) *m(f)*

GP *abk* = General Practitioner; Allgemeinarzt *m*, Allgemeinärztin *f*

GPS S *abk* = global positioning system; GPS *n*; *umg* Navi *n*

grab [græb] V/T packen; (*Person*) schnappen

graceful ['greɪsfʊl] ADJ anmutig

grade [greɪd] S Niveau *n*; (*von Waren*) Güteklasse *f*; (*Schule*) Note *f*; (*Jahrgangsstufe*) Klasse *f* **grade crossing** S Bahnübergang *m* **grade school** S Grundschule *f*

gradient ['greɪdɪənt] S (*aufwärts*) Steigung *f*; (*abwärts*) Gefälle *n*

gradual, **gradually** ['grædʒʊəl, -lɪ] ADJ & ADV allmählich

graduate **1** ['grædʒʊət] S Absolvent(in) *m(f)* **2** ['grædʒʊeɪt] VI *(von Universität)* einen akademischen Grad erwerben *(from* an *+dat)*; *(von Schule)* die Abschlussprüfung bestehen *(from* an *+dat)* **graduation** [grædʒʊ'eɪʃn] S *(an Universität, Schule)* Abschlussfeier *f (mit feierlicher Überreichung der Zeugnisse)*

grain [greɪn] S Getreide *n*; *(von Getreide)* Korn *n*

gram [græm] S Gramm *n*

grammar ['græmər] S Grammatik *f*

grand [grænd] **1** ADJ *pej* großartig; prachtvoll **2** S *umg 1000 Dollar* **Grand Canyon** [grænd'kænjən] S Grand Canyon *m (Durchbruchstal des Colorado in Arizona)* **grand(d)ad** S *umg* Opa *m* **granddaughter** S Enkelin *f* **grandfather** S Großvater *m* **grandma** S *umg* Oma *f* **grandmother** S Großmutter *f* **grandpa** S *umg* Opa *m* **grandparents** S PL Großeltern *pl* **grandson** S Enkel *m* **grandstand** S SPORT Tribüne *f*

grant [grænt] **1** VT gewähren *(sb sth* j-m etw); **take sb/sth for ~ed** j-n/etw als selbstverständlich hinnehmen **2** S Subvention *f*, finanzielle Unterstützung; *(für Studium)* Stipendium *n*

grape [greɪp] S Weintraube *f*

grapefruit S Grapefruit *f*

graph [græf] S Diagramm *n*

grasp [græsp] VT ergreifen; *(verstehen)* begreifen

grass [græs] S Gras *n*; Rasen *m*

grasshopper S Heuschrecke *f*

grate [greɪt] **1** S Feuerrost *m* **2** VI kratzen **3** VT *(Käse)* reiben

grateful, **gratefully** ['greɪtfʊl, -fəlɪ] ADJ & ADV dankbar **gratitude** ['grætɪtu:d] S Dankbarkeit *f*

gratuity [grə'tu:ətɪ] S Gratifikation *f*

grave [greɪv] **1** S Grab *n* **2** ADJ ernst; *(Fehler)* schwer

gravel ['grævəl] S Kies *m*

graveyard ['greɪvjɑ:rd] S Friedhof *m*

gravy ['greɪvɪ] S Bratensoße *f*

gray [greɪ] ADJ grau **gray-haired** ADJ grauhaarig

graze [greɪz] **1** VI *(Kühe etc)* grasen **2** VT streifen; MED abschürfen **3** S MED Abschürfung *f*

grease [gri:s] **1** S *(Braten, Kochen)* Fett *n*; *(Maschine)* Schmiere *f* **2** VT einfetten; TECH schmieren **greasy** ADJ fettig; *(Hände, Werkzeug)* schmierig; *umg (Person)* schleimig

great [greɪt] ADJ groß; *umg* großartig, super; **a ~ deal of** viel **Great Britain** [greɪt'brɪtn] S Großbritannien *n*

great-grandfather S Urgroßvater *m* **great-grandmother** S Urgroßmutter *f*
Great Lakes S PL **the ~** die Großen Seen *pl* **greatly** ADV sehr; **~ disappointed** zutiefst enttäuscht
Greece [gri:s] S Griechenland *n*
greed [gri:d] S Gier *f* (*for* nach); Gefräßigkeit *f* **greedy** ADJ gierig; gefräßig
Greek [gri:k] **1** ADJ griechisch **2** S (*Person*) Grieche *m*, Griechin *f*; (*Sprache*) Griechisch *n*
green [gri:n] **1** ADJ grün **2** S Grün *n*; (*in Dorfmitte*) Dorfwiese *f*; **~s** *pl* grünes Gemüse **greenback** S *umg* Dollar(-schein) *m* **green bean** S grüne Bohne **green card** S Arbeitserlaubnis *f* **greenhouse** S Gewächshaus *n*; **~ effect** Treibhauseffekt *m* **green pepper** S grüner Paprika **green salad** S grüner Salat
greet [gri:t] VT grüßen **greeting** S Gruß *m*
grew [gru:] *prät von* grow
grid [grɪd] S Gitter *n* **gridlock** S Verkehrsinfarkt *m*
grief [gri:f] S Kummer *m*; (*über Verlust*) Trauer *f* **grieve** [gri:v] VI trauern (*for* um)
grill [grɪl] **1** S (*Gerät*) Grill *m* **2** VT grillen
grim [grɪm] ADJ (*Gesicht, Lachen*) grimmig; (*Lage, Aussichten*) trostlos
grimy ['graɪmɪ] ADJ dreckig, schmuddelig
grin [grɪn] **1** S Grinsen *n* **2** VI grinsen
grind ⟨ground, ground⟩ [graɪnd, graʊnd] VT mahlen; (*Messer*) schleifen; (*Fleisch*) durchdrehen
grip [grɪp] **1** S Griff *m*; **get a ~** nimm dich zusammen!; **get to ~s with sth** etw in den Griff bekommen **2** VT packen
grit [grɪt] S Splitt *m*; (*im Auge*) Staub *m*; **~s** *pl* Grütze *f*
grizzly (bear) ['grɪzlɪ(ber)] S Grizzly(bär) *m*
groan [groʊn] VI stöhnen (*with* vor *+dat*)
grocer ['groʊsər] S Lebensmittelhändler(in) *m(f)* **groceries** S PL Lebensmittel *pl*
groom [gru:m] **1** S Bräutigam *m* **2** VT **well ~ed** gepflegt
gross [groʊs] ADJ (*beleidigend*) derb; (*Fahrlässigkeit*) grob; (*widerlich*) ekelhaft; WIRTSCH brutto
ground [graʊnd] **1** *prät, pperf von* **grind** **2** S Boden *m*, Erde *f*; SPORT Platz *m*; **~s** *pl* (*um Haus herum*) (Garten)anlagen *pl*; (*für Verhalten, Tat*) Gründe *pl*; (*von Kaffee*) Satz *m* **3** VT erden **ground meat** S Hackfleisch *n*
group [gru:p] S Gruppe *f*
grow ⟨grew, grown⟩ [groʊ, gru:, groʊn] **1** VI wachsen;

(*Anzahl, Sorgen, Interesse*) zunehmen (*in* an); (*Zustand erreichen*) werden; ~ **into** ... sich entwickeln zu ... **2** VI/T (*Pflanzen*) ziehen; (*kommerziell*) anbauen **grow up** VI aufwachsen; erwachsen werden
growl [graʊl] VI knurren
grown [groʊn] *pperf von* grow
grown-up **1** [groʊn'ʌp] ADJ erwachsen **2** ['groʊnʌp] S Erwachsene(r) *m/f(m)* **growth** [groʊθ] S Wachstum *n;* (*von Menge, Interesse*) Zunahme *f;* MED Wucherung *f*
grudge [grʌdʒ] S Abneigung *f* (*against* gegen)
gruesome ['gru:səm] ADJ grausig
grumble ['grʌmbl] VI murren (*about* über *+akk*)
grumpy ['grʌmpɪ] ADJ *umg* mürrisch, grantig
grunt [grʌnt] VI grunzen
G-string ['dʒi:strɪŋ] S String *m,* Stringtanga *m*
guarantee [gærən'ti:] **1** S Garantie *f* (*of* für) **2** VI/T garantieren
guard [gɑ:rd] **1** S Wache *f;* Wächter(in) *m(f);* (*in Gefängnis*) Wärter(in) *m(f)* **2** VI/T bewachen **guardian** ['gɑ:rdɪən] S Vormund *m*
guess [ges] **1** S Vermutung *f;* (*von Betrag, Zahl*) Schätzung *f* **2** VI/T & VI raten; (*Betrag, Menge*) schätzen; ~ **what!** stell dir vor!; **I ~ you're right** da hast du wohl recht; **I ~ so** ich glaube schon
guest [gest] S Gast *m;* **be my ~** nur zu! **guest-house** S Pension *f* **guest room** S Gästezimmer *n*
guidance ['gaɪdəns] S Leitung *f;* (*Hilfe*) Rat *m;* (*für Karriere*) Beratung *f* **guide** [gaɪd] **1** S (*Person*) Führer(in) *m(f);* (*auf Reise*) Reiseleiter(in) *m(f);* (*Buch*) Reiseführer *m* **2** VI/T führen **guidebook** S Reiseführer *m* **guided tour** S Führung *f* (*of* durch) **guidelines** S PL Richtlinien *pl*
guilt [gɪlt] S Schuld *f* **guilty** ADJ schuldig (*of gen*); (*Blick*) schuldbewusst
guitar [gɪ'tɑ:r] S Gitarre *f*
gulf [gʌlf] S Golf *m*
gull [gʌl] S Möwe *f*
gulp [gʌlp] **1** S (kräftiger) Schluck **2** VI/T schlucken
gum [gʌm] S (*meist pl*) Zahnfleisch *n;* (*zum Kauen*) Kaugummi *m*
gun [gʌn] S Schusswaffe *f,* Gewehr *n,* Pistole *f* **gunfire** S Schüsse *pl*
gurney ['gɜ:rnɪ] S (fahrbare) Krankentrage
gush [gʌʃ] VI (heraus)strömen (*from* aus)
gut [gʌt] S Darm *m;* **~s** *pl* (*in Bauch*) Eingeweide *pl;* (*Mut*) Mumm *m*
gutter ['gʌtər] S Dachrinne *f;* Rinnstein *m,* Gosse *f*

guy [gaɪ] S̲ *(Mann)* Typ *m*, Kerl *m*; **~s** *pl* Leute *pl*
gym [dʒɪm] S̲ Turnhalle *f*, Fitnesscenter *n* **gymnasium** [dʒɪm'neɪzɪəm] S̲ Turnhalle *f*
gymnastics [dʒɪm'næstɪks] S̲ S̲G̲ Turnen *n*
gynecologist [gaɪnə'kɑːlədʒɪst] S̲ Frauenarzt *m*, Frauenärztin *f*, Gynäkologe *m*, Gynäkologin *f*

H

habit ['hæbət] S̲ Gewohnheit *f*
had [hæd] *prät, pperf von* **have**
haddock ['hædək] S̲ Schellfisch *m*
hadn't ['hædnt] *kontr von* **had not**
hail [heɪl] **1** S̲ Hagel *m* **2** V̲/̲I̲ hageln **3** V̲/̲T̲ **~ a cab** ein Taxi herbeirufen **hailstone** S̲ Hagelkorn *n* **hailstorm** S̲ Hagelschauer *m*
hair [her] S̲ Haar *n*, Haare *pl*; **get one's ~ cut** sich die Haare schneiden lassen **hairbrush** S̲ Haarbürste *f* **hair conditioner** S̲ Haarspülung *f* **haircut** S̲ Haarschnitt *m* **haircutter** S̲ Friseur *m*, Friseurin *f* **hairdo** ⟨-s *pl*⟩ S̲ Frisur *f* **hairdresser** S̲ Friseurin *f*, Friseur *m* **hairdryer** S̲ Haartrockner *m*, Fön® *m*; Trockenhaube *f* **hair spray** S̲ Haarspray *n* **hair style** S̲ Frisur *f* **hairy** A̲D̲J̲ haarig, behaart
hake [heɪk] S̲ Seehecht *m*
half [hæf] **1** S̲ ⟨halves *pl*⟩ Hälfte *f*; SPORT Halbzeit *f*; **cut in ~** halbieren **2** A̲D̲J̲ halb; **three and a ~ pounds** dreieinhalb Pfund; **~ an hour** eine halbe Stunde **3** A̲D̲V̲ halb, zur Hälfte; **~ asleep** fast eingeschlafen **half-hour** S̲ halbe Stunde **half price** S̲ **(at) ~** zum halben Preis **half-time** S̲ Halbzeit *f* **halfway** A̲D̲V̲ auf halbem Wege
halibut ['hæləbət] S̲ Heilbutt *m*
hall [hɒːl] S̲ Halle *f*; *(für Publikum)* Saal *m*; *(Eingangsbereich)* Flur *m*; *(größer)* Diele *f*
halt [hɒːlt] **1** S̲ Pause *f*, Halt *m*; **come to a ~** zum Stillstand kommen **2** V̲/̲T̲ ̲&̲ ̲V̲/̲I̲ anhalten
halve [hæv] V̲/̲T̲ halbieren
ham [hæm] S̲ Schinken *m*
hamburger ['hæmbɜːrgər] S̲ GASTR Hamburger *m*
hammer ['hæmər] **1** S̲ Hammer *m* **2** V̲/̲T̲ ̲&̲ ̲V̲/̲I̲ hämmern
hammock ['hæmək] S̲ Hängematte *f*
hamper ['hæmpər] **1** V̲/̲T̲ behindern **2** S̲ Geschenkkorb *m*, Picknickkorb *m*
hand [hænd] **1** S̲ Hand *f*; *(Uhr)* Zeiger *m*; *(Kartenspiel)* Blatt *n*; **~s off!** Finger weg!;

on the one ~ ..., on the other ~ ... einerseits ..., andererseits ...; **give sb a ~** j-m helfen (*with* bei); **get out of ~** außer Kontrolle geraten **2** VT (*weitergeben*) reichen (*to sb* j-m) **hand down** VT (*Tradition, Brauch*) überliefern; (*Erbstück*) vererben **hand in** VT einreichen; abgeben **hand out** VT verteilen **hand over** VT übergeben
handbag S Handtasche *f*
handbill S Flugblatt *n*
handbook S Handbuch *n*
handcuffs S PL Handschellen *pl*
handicap ['hændıkæp] **1** S Behinderung *f*, Handikap *n* **2** VT benachteiligen **handicapped** ADJ behindert
handicraft ['hændıkræft] S Kunsthandwerk *n*
handkerchief ['hæŋkərtʃıf] S Taschentuch *n*
handle ['hændl] **1** S Griff *m*; (*an Tür*) Klinke *f*; (*an Tasse*) Henkel *m*; (*zum Kurbeln*) Kurbel *f* **2** VT (*mit den Händen*) anfassen; (*Angelegenheit*) sich befassen mit; (*mit Leuten, Maschine*) umgehen mit; (*Problem*) fertig werden mit **handlebars** S PL Lenkstange *f*
hand luggage ['hændlʌgıdʒ] S Handgepäck *n* **handmade** ADJ handgefertigt; **be ~** Handarbeit sein **handset** S Hörer *m* **hands-free phone** S Freisprechanlage *f* **handshake** S Händedruck *m*
handsome ['hænsəm] ADJ (*Mann*) gut aussehend
handwriting ['hændraıtıŋ] S Handschrift *f* **handy** ['hændı] ADJ (*nützlich*) praktisch
hang ⟨hung, hung⟩ [hæŋ, hʌŋ] **1** VT (auf)hängen; (*bei Bedeutung „erhängen“*: ⟨hanged, hanged⟩) hängen **2** VI hängen; **~ tough** dranbleiben, nicht nachgeben; **~ loose** locker bleiben **3** S **he's got the ~ of it** er hat den Dreh raus **hang around** VI sich herumtreiben, rumhängen **hang on** VI sich festhalten (*to* an *+dat*); *umg* warten; **~ to sth** etw behalten **hang out** VI heraushängen; *umg* rumhängen **hang up** **1** VI TEL auflegen **2** VT aufhängen
hanger ['hæŋər] S Kleiderbügel *m* **hang-gliding** ['hæŋglaıdıŋ] S Drachenfliegen *n* **hangover** ['hæŋoʊvər] S (*durch Alkohol*) Kater *m*
hankie ['hæŋkı] S *umg* Taschentuch *n*
happen ['hæpən] VI geschehen; passieren; **I just ~ed to be in the neighborhood** ich kam zufällig vorbei
happily ['hæpəlı] ADV fröhlich, glücklich; (*zum Glück*) glücklicherweise **happiness** ['hæpınəs] S Glück *n* **happy** ['hæpı] ADJ glücklich; (*zufrieden*) **~ with sth** mit etw zufrie-

den; (*gerne bereit*) **be ~ to do sth** etw gerne tun; **Happy Christmas** fröhliche Weihnachten!; **Happy New Year** ein glückliches Neues Jahr!; **Happy Birthday** herzlichen Glückwunsch zum Geburtstag!

harassment [həˈræsmənt] S Belästigung *f*; (*am Arbeitsplatz*) Mobbing *n*

harbor [ˈhɑːrbər] S Hafen *m*

hard [hɑːrd] **1** ADJ hart; (*Frage, Aufgabe*) schwer, schwierig; (*Person*) hart(herzig); **don't be ~ on him** sei nicht zu streng zu ihm **2** ADV (*arbeiten*) schwer; (*laufen*) schnell; (*regnen, schneien*) stark; **try ~/~er** sich große/mehr Mühe geben **hardback** S gebundene Ausgabe **hard-boiled** ADJ (*Ei*) hart gekocht **hard copy** S IT Ausdruck *m* **hard disk**, **hard drive** S IT Festplatte *f* **harden** **1** V/T härten **2** V/I hart werden **hardly** [ˈhɑːrdlɪ] ADV kaum; **~ ever** fast nie **hardship** [ˈhɑːrdʃɪp] S Not *f* **hardware** S IT Hardware *f*; Haushalts- und Eisenwaren *pl* **hard-working** ADJ fleißig, tüchtig

hare [her] S Hase *m*

harm [hɑːrm] **1** S Schaden *m*; (*am Körper*) Verletzung *f*; **it wouldn't do any ~** es würde nicht schaden **2** V/T schaden +*dat*; (*Person, Tier*) verletzen **harmful** ADJ schädlich **harmless** ADJ harmlos

harsh [hɑːrʃ] ADJ (*Klima, Stimme*) rau; (*Licht, Töne*) grell; (*Kritik*) hart, streng

harvest [ˈhɑːrvəst] **1** S Ernte *f*, Erntezeit *f* **2** V/T ernten

has [hæz] *Präsens von* **have**

hash [hæʃ] S GASTR Haschee *n*; *umg* Haschisch *n*; **make a ~ of sth** etw vermasseln **hash browns** S PL ≈ Kartoffelpuffer/Rösti mit Zwiebeln *pl*

hasn't [ˈhæznt] *kontr von* **has not**

hassle [ˈhæsl] **1** S Ärger *m*; (*Trubel*) Theater *n* **2** V/T bedrängen

haste [heɪst] S Eile *f* **hastily**, **hasty** ADV & ADJ hastig; vorschnell

hat [hæt] S Hut *m*

hatch [hætʃ] S SCHIFF Luke *f*; (*Küche*) Durchreiche *f* **hatchback** [ˈhætʃbæk] S Wagen *m* mit Hecktür

hate [heɪt] **1** V/T hassen **2** S Hass *m*

haul [hɒːl] **1** V/T ziehen, schleppen **2** S (*Fang; von Dieben etc*) Beute *f* **haulage** [ˈhɒːlɪdʒ] S Transport *m*, Spedition *f*

haunted [ˈhɒːntəd] ADJ **a ~ house** ein Haus, in dem es spukt

have ⟨had, had⟩ [hæv, hæd] **1** V/T haben; **~ you got a light?** hast du/haben Sie Feuer?; **~ a baby** ein Kind bekommen; (*essen/trinken*) **what are you having?** was möchtest du/möchten Sie (essen/trinken)?; ~ **lunch/dinner** zu Mittag/Abend essen; ~ **a party** eine Party geben; ~ **sth done** etw machen lassen; **they had a good time** sie haben sich gut amüsiert **2** V/AUX (*zur Bildung des Perfekt*) haben/sein; **he has/he's seen it** er hat es gesehen; **she has/she's come** sie ist gekommen; ~ **(got) to do sth** etw tun müssen; (*in Frageanhängseln*) **you've been there, ~n't you?** du bist/Sie sind mal dort gewesen, nicht wahr? **have on** V/T (*Kleidung*) anhaben

Hawaii [hə'waii:] S Hawaii *n*

hawk [hɒ:k] **1** S Habicht *m* **2** V/I ~ **(a loogie)** sich räuspern (und ausspucken)

hay [heɪ] S Heu *n* **hay fever** S Heuschnupfen *m*

hazard ['hæzərd] S Gefahr *f*, Risiko *n* **hazardous** ADJ gefährlich **hazard warning lights** S PL Warnblinkanlage *f*

haze [heɪz] S Dunst *m*

hazelnut ['heɪzlnʌt] S Haselnuss *f*

hazy ['heɪzɪ] ADJ dunstig; (*Erinnerung*) verschwommen

he [hi:] PRON er

head [hed] **1** S Kopf *m*; (*von Abteilung etc*) Leiter(in) *m(f)*; ~ **of state** Staatsoberhaupt *n*; (*Münze*) **~s or tails?** Kopf oder Zahl?; *vulg* **give sb ~** j-m einen blasen **2** ADJ (*oberste(r, s)*) Ober- **3** V/T anführen; (*Organisation etc*) leiten **head for** V/T zusteuern auf *+akk* **headache** ['hedeɪk] S Kopfschmerzen *pl*, Kopfweh *n* **headfirst** ADJ kopfüber **heading** S Überschrift *f* **headlamp, headlight** S Scheinwerfer *m* **headline** S Schlagzeile *f* **headphones** S PL Kopfhörer *m* **headquarters** S PL (*von Firma etc*) Zentrale *f* **headrest** S Kopfstütze *f* **headscarf** ⟨-scarves *pl*⟩ S Kopftuch *n*

heal [hi:l] V/T & V/I heilen

health [helθ] S Gesundheit *f*; **good/bad for one's ~** gesund/ungesund; ~ **and beauty** Wellness *f* **health center** S Ärztezentrum *n* **health club** S Fitnesscenter *n* **health food** S Reformkost *f*; ~ **store** Bioladen *m* **health insurance** S Krankenversicherung *f* **healthy** ADJ gesund

heap [hi:p] **1** S Haufen *m* **2** V/T & V/I häufen

hear ⟨heard, heard⟩ [hɪr, hɜ:rd] V/T & V/I hören; ~ **about sth** von etw erfahren **hearing** S Gehör *n*; JUR Verhandlung *f* **hearing aid** S Hörgerät *n*

heart [hɑ:rt] S Herz *n*; **learn by ~** auswendig lernen; **~s** *pl* (*Karten*) Herz *n* **heart attack** S Herzanfall *m* **heartbeat** S Herzschlag *m* **heartbreak-**

ing ADJ herzzerreißend **heartbroken** ADJ todunglücklich, untröstlich **heartburn** S Sodbrennen *n* **heart failure** S Herzversagen *n* **hearty** ['hɑ:rtɪ] ADJ (*Mahl, Appetit*) herzhaft; (*Empfang*) herzlich

heat [hi:t] **1** S Hitze *f*; (*allgemein a.*) Wärme *f*; (*ansteigende etc*) Temperatur *f*; SPORT Vorlauf *m* **2** V/T heizen **heat up** **1** V/I warm werden **2** V/T aufwärmen **heated** ADJ beheizt; *fig* hitzig **heater** S Heizofen *m*; AUTO Heizung *f* **heating** ['hi:tɪŋ] S Heizung *f*

heaven ['hevn] S Himmel *m* **heavenly** ADJ himmlisch

heavily ['hevəlɪ] ADV (*regnen etc*) stark **heavy** ['hevɪ] ADJ schwer; (*Regen, Verkehr, Raucher etc*) stark

Hebrew ['hi:bru:] **1** ADJ hebräisch **2** S (*Sprache*) Hebräisch *n*

hectic ['hektɪk] ADJ hektisch

he'd [hi:d] *kontr von* **he had; he would**

hedge [hedʒ] S Hecke *f*

heel [hi:l] S ANAT Ferse *f*; (*von Schuh*) Absatz *m*

height [haɪt] S Höhe *f*; (*von Mensch*) Größe *f*

heir [er] S Erbe *m* **heiress** ['erəs] S Erbin *f*

held [held] *prät, pperf von* **hold**

helicopter ['heləkɑ:ptər] S Hubschrauber *m* **heliport** ['heləpɔ:rt] S Hubschrauberlandeplatz *m*

hell [hel] **1** S Hölle *f*; **go to ~** scher dich zum Teufel; **that's a ~ of a lot of money** das ist verdammt viel Geld **2** INT verdammt

he'll [hi:l] *kontr von* **he will; he shall**

hello [he'loʊ] INT hallo

helmet ['helmət] S Helm *m*

help [help] **1** S Hilfe *f* **2** V/T & V/I helfen *+dat* (*with* bei); **can I ~?** kann ich (Ihnen) behilflich sein?; **I couldn't ~ but laugh** ich musste einfach lachen; **I can't ~ it** ich kann nichts dafür; **~ yourself** bedienen Sie sich **helpful** ADJ (*Person*) hilfsbereit; (*Sache, Tipp etc*) nützlich **helping** S Portion *f* **helpless** ADJ hilflos

hem [hem] S Saum *m*

hemophiliac [hi:mə'fɪlɪæk] S Bluter *m* **hemorrhage** ['hemərɪdʒ] S Blutung *f* **hemorrhoids** ['hemərɔɪdz] S PL Hämorrhoiden *pl*

hen [hen] S Henne *f*

hepatitis [hepə'taɪtəs] S Hepatitis *f*

her [hɜ:r] **1** ADJ ihr; **she's hurt ~ leg** sie hat sich das Bein verletzt **2** PRON (*direktes Objekt*) sie; (*indirektes Objekt*) ihr; **it's ~** sie ist's

herb [ɜ:rb] S Kraut *n*

herd [hɜ:rd] S Herde *f*

here [hɪr] ADV hier; hierher;

come ~ komm her
hereditary [hə'redəterı] ADJ erblich **heritage** ['herətıdʒ] S Erbe *n*
hernia ['hɜːrnıə] S Leistenbruch *m*, Eingeweidebruch *m*
hero ⟨-es *pl*⟩ ['hıroʊ] S Held *m*
heroin ['heroʊın] S Heroin *n*
heroine ['heroʊın] S Heldin *f*
herring ['herıŋ] S Hering *m*
hers [hɜːrz] PRON ihre(r, s); **this is ~** das gehört ihr; **a friend of ~** ein Freund von ihr **herself** [hɜːr'self] PRON sich; (*verstärkend*) **she did it ~** sie hat es selbst gemacht; **(all) by ~** allein
he's [hiːz] *kontr von* **he is; he has**
hesitate ['hezəteıt] VI zögern; **don't ~ to ask** fragen Sie ruhig **hesitation** S Zögern *n*
heterosexual [hetərə'sekʃʊəl] ADJ heterosexuell
hi [haı] INT hi, hallo
HI *abk* = Hawaii
hiccup ['hıkʌp] S Schluckauf *m*
hickey ['hıkı] S *umg* Knutschfleck *m*
hick town S *umg* Nest *n*, Kaff *n*
hid [hıd] *prät von* **hide hidden** ['hıdn] *pperf von* **hide hide** [haıd] **1** ⟨hid, hidden⟩ [hıd, 'hıdn] VT verstecken (*from* vor +*dat*); (*Gefühle*) verbergen; (*von Baum etc*) verdecken **2** VI sich verstecken (*from* vor +*dat*) **hiding** ['haıdıŋ] S Tracht *f* Prügel; (*Versteck*) **be in ~** sich versteckt halten **hiding place** S Versteck *n*
high [haı] **1** ADJ hoch; (*Wind*) stark; (*nach Drogenkonsum*) high **2** ADV hoch **3** S METEO Hoch *n* **high beam** S AUTO Fernlicht *n* **highchair** S Hochstuhl *m* **higher education** S Hochschulbildung *f* **high heels** S PL Stöckelschuhe *pl* **high jump** S Hochsprung *m* **highlight** **1** S (*im Haar*) Strähnchen *n*; *fig* Höhepunkt *m* **2** VT (*mit Leuchtstift*) hervorheben **highlighter** S Textmarker *m* **highly** ADJ hoch, sehr; **I think ~ of him** ich habe eine hohe Meinung von ihm **high school** S Highschool *f*, ≈ Oberschule *f* (*für 15 bis 18-Jährige*) **high-speed** ADJ Schnell- **high tech** **1** ADJ Hightech- **2** S Hightech *n* **high tide** S Flut *f* **highway** S ≈ Autobahn *f*
hijack ['haıdʒæk] VT entführen, hijacken
hike [haık] **1** VI wandern **2** S Wanderung *f* **hiker** S Wanderer *m*, Wanderin *f* **hiking** S Wandern *n*
hilarious [hı'lerıəs] ADJ zum Schreien komisch
hill [hıl] S Hügel *m*; (*höher*) Berg *m* **hilly** ADJ hügelig
him [hım] PRON (*direktes Objekt*)

ihn; (*indirektes Objekt*) ihm; **it's ~** er ist's **himself** [hɪm'self] PRON sich; (*verstärkend*) **he did it ~** er hat es selbst gemacht; **(all) by ~** allein

Hindu ['hɪndu:] 1 ADJ hinduistisch 2 S Hindu *m*

hinge [hɪndʒ] S Scharnier *n*; (*an Türstock*) Angel *f*

hint [hɪnt] 1 S Wink *m*, Andeutung *f* 2 V/I andeuten (*at akk*)

hip [hɪp] S Hüfte *f*

hire [haɪr] V/T (*Arbeitnehmer*) anstellen

his [hɪz] 1 ADJ sein; **he's hurt ~ leg** er hat sich das Bein verletzt 2 PRON seine(r, s); **it's ~** es gehört ihm; **a friend of ~** ein Freund von ihm

historic [hɪ'stɑ:rɪk] ADJ (*Ereignis*) historisch **historical** ADJ (*Monument etc*) historisch; (*Studien etc*) geschichtlich **history** ['hɪstərɪ] S Geschichte *f*

hit [hɪt] 1 S Schlag *m*; (*mit Gewehr etc*) Treffer *m*; (*Film, CD etc*) Hit *m* 2 ⟨hit, hit⟩ *v/t* schlagen; (*Ziel etc*) treffen; **the car ~ a tree** das Auto fuhr gegen einen Baum; **~ one's head on sth** sich den Kopf an etw *dat* stoßen **hit (up)on** V/T stoßen auf *+akk* **hit-and-run** ADJ **~ accident** Unfall *m* mit Fahrerflucht

hitchhike ['hɪtʃhaɪk] V/I trampen

HIV *abk* = human immunodeficiency virus; HIV *n*

hive [haɪv] S Bienenstock *m*

hoarse [hɔ:rs] ADJ heiser

hoax [hoʊks] S Streich *m*, Jux *m*; blinder Alarm

hobby ['hɑ:bɪ] S Hobby *n*

hobo ⟨-es *pl*⟩ ['hoʊboʊ] S Penner(in) *m(f)*

hockey ['hɑ:kɪ] S Eishockey *n*

hold [hoʊld] 1 ⟨held, held⟩ [held] V/T halten; (*Paket etc*) enthalten; (*Platz bieten für*) fassen; (*Amt*) innehaben; (*Treffen*) abhalten; (*Person*) gefangen halten; **~ one's breath** den Atem anhalten; **~ the line** TEL bleiben Sie am Apparat 2 V/I halten; (*Wetter*) sich halten 3 S (*fester Griff/Tritt*) Halt *m*; (*von Schiff etc*) Laderaum *m* **hold on** V/I sich festhalten; TEL dranbleiben; **~ to sth** etw festhalten **hold out** 1 V/T ausstrecken; (*Hand etc*) hinhalten 2 V/I durchhalten **hold up** V/T hochhalten; (*Dach etc*) stützen; (*j-n, Verkehr*) aufhalten **holder** S (*von Pass, Weltrekord*) Inhaber(in) *m(f)* **holdup** S (*im Straßenverkehr*) Stau *m*; (*Raub*) Überfall *m*

hole [hoʊl] S Loch *n*; (*von Fuchs etc*) Bau *m* **hole puncher** S Locher *m*

holiday ['hɑ:lədaɪ] S Feiertag *m*

Holland ['hɑ:lənd] S Holland *n*

hollow ['hɑ:loʊ] 1 ADJ hohl; (*Worte*) leer 2 S Vertiefung *f*

holly ['hɑ:lı] S Stechpalme *f*
holy ['hoʊlı] ADJ heilig
home [hoʊm] **1** S Zuhause *n*, Heimat *f*; (*Institution*) Heim *n*; **at ~** zu Hause; **make oneself at ~** es sich bequem machen; **away from ~** verreist **2** ADV **go ~** nach Hause gehen/fahren **home address** S Heimatadresse *f* **homecoming** S *Zusammenkunft ehemaliger Studenten und Studentinnen einer Hochschule* **home country** S Heimatland *n* **home game** S SPORT Heimspiel *n* **homeless** ADJ obdachlos **homely** ADJ häuslich; (*Person*) unscheinbar **home-made** ADJ selbst gemacht **homemaker** S Hausfrau *f*
homeopathic [hoʊmıoʊ'pæθık] ADJ homöopathisch
home page ['hoʊmpeıdʒ] S IT Homepage *f* **home run** S (*Baseball*) *Lauf über alle 4 Male* **homesick** ADJ **be ~** Heimweh haben **homework** S Hausaufgaben *pl*
homicide ['hɑ:məsaıd] S Totschlag *m*
homosexual [hoʊmə'sekʃʊəl] ADJ homosexuell
honest ['ɑ:nəst] ADJ ehrlich **honesty** S Ehrlichkeit *f*
honey ['hʌnı] S Honig *m*; *umg* (*Anrede*) Liebling **honeydew melon** S Honigmelone *f* **honeymoon** S Flitterwochen *pl*
honk [hɑ:ŋk] **1** S Hupen *n* **2** V/I (*Auto*) hupen; (*Gans*) schreien **3** V/T **~ the horn** auf die Hupe drücken
honor ['ɑ:nər] **1** V/T ehren; (*von Bank: Scheck*) einlösen; (*Vertrag*) einhalten **2** S Ehre *f* **honorable** ADJ ehrenhaft **honorary** ['ɑ:nərerı] ADJ (*Mitglied etc*) Ehren-, ehrenamtlich
hooch [hu:tʃ] S *umg schwarz gebrannter Schnaps*
hood [hʊd] S Kapuze *f*; AUTO Verdeck *n*; Kühlerhaube *f*
hoof <hooves *pl*> [hu:f, hu:vz] S Huf *m*
hook [hʊk] S Haken *m* **hooked** ADJ besessen (*on* von); (*von Drogen*) abhängig sein (*on* von) **hooker** S *umg* Nutte *f*
hoot [hu:t] V/I AUTO hupen
hop [hɑ:p] **1** V/I hüpfen **2** S BOT Hopfen *m*
hope [hoʊp] **1** V/I & V/T hoffen (*for* auf +*akk*); **I ~ so/~ not** hoffentlich/hoffentlich nicht **2** S Hoffnung *f* **hopeful** ADJ hoffnungsvoll **hopefully** ADV hoffnungsvoll; (*wie ich hoffe*) hoffentlich **hopeless** ADJ hoffnungslos; miserabel
horizon [hə'raızn] S Horizont *m* **horizontal** [hɑ:rə'zɑ:ntl] ADJ horizontal
hormone ['hɔ:rmoʊn] S Hormon *n*
horn [hɔ:rn] S Horn *n*; AUTO

Hupe *f*
hornet ['hɔːrnət] S Hornisse *f*
horny ['hɔːrnɪ] ADJ *umg* geil
horoscope ['hɔːrəskoʊp] S Horoskop *n*
horrible, horribly ['hɔːrəbl] ADJ & ADV schrecklich **horrid** ['hɔːrəd] ADJ & ADV abscheulich **horrify** ['hɔːrəfaɪ] V/T entsetzen **horror** ['hɔːrər] S Entsetzen *n*
hors d'oeuvre [ɔːr'dɜːrv] S Vorspeise *f*
horse [hɔːrs] S Pferd *n* **horsepower** S Pferdestärke *f*, PS *n* **horse racing** S Pferderennen *n* **horseradish** S Meerrettich *m* **horse riding** S Reiten *n* **horseshoe** S Hufeisen *n*
hose [hoʊz] S Schlauch *m*
hospitable [hɑːs'pɪtəbl] ADJ gastfreundlich
hospital ['hɑːspɪtl] S Krankenhaus *n*
hospitality [hɑːspə'tælətɪ] S Gastfreundschaft *f*
host [hoʊst] **1** S Gastgeber *m*; TV Moderator(in) *m(f)*, Talkmaster(in) *m(f)* **2** V/T (*Party*) geben; TV moderieren
hostage ['hɑːstɪdʒ] S Geisel *f*
hostel ['hɑːstəl] S Wohnheim *n*; Jugendherberge *f*
hostile ['hɑːstl] ADJ feindlich **hostility** [hɑːs'tɪlətɪ] S Feindseligkeit *f*
hot [hɑːt] ADJ heiß; (*Getränk etc*) warm; (*stark gewürzt*) scharf; **I'm (feeling) ~** mir ist heiß **hot dog** S Hotdog *n*
hotel [hoʊ'tel] S Hotel *n* **hotel room** S Hotelzimmer *n*
hothouse S Treibhaus *n* **hot-water bottle** S Wärmflasche *f*
hour [aʊr] S Stunde *f*; **wait for ~s** stundenlang warten; **~s** *pl* (*von Läden etc*) Geschäftszeiten *pl* **hourly** ADJ stündlich
house **1** ⟨houses *pl*⟩ [haʊs, 'haʊzəz] S Haus *n*; **at my ~** bei mir (zu Hause); **to my ~** zu mir (nach Hause); **on the ~** auf Kosten des Hauses; **the House of Representatives** Repräsentantenhaus *n* (*Unterhaus des US-Kongresses*) **2** [haʊz] V/T unterbringen **household** S Haushalt *m* **housekeeping** S Haushaltung *f* **house-warming (party)** S Einzugsparty *f* **housewife** ⟨-wives *pl*⟩ S Hausfrau *f* **house wine** S Hauswein *m* **housework** S Hausarbeit *f* **housing** ['haʊzɪŋ] S Wohnungen *pl*; Wohnungsbau *m* **housing development** S Wohnsiedlung *f*
hover ['hʌvər] V/I schweben
how [haʊ] ADV wie; **~ many** wie viele; **~ much** wie viel; **~ are you?** wie geht es Ihnen?; **~ are things?** wie geht's?; **~'s work?** was macht die Arbeit?; **~ about ...?** wie wäre es mit ...? **howdy** ['haʊdɪ] INT *umg* Tag **however** [haʊ-

'evər] **1** KONJ jedoch, aber **2** ADV wie ... auch
howl [haʊl] V/I heulen
HQ *abk* = headquarters
hubcap ['hʌbkæp] S Radkappe *f*
Hudson River [hʌdsən'rɪvər] S *Fluss im Staat New York*
hug [hʌg] **1** V/T umarmen **2** S Umarmung *f*
huge [hju:dʒ] ADJ riesig
hum [hʌm] V/I & V/T summen
human ['hju:mən] **1** ADJ menschlich; **~ rights** *pl* Menschenrechte *pl* **2** S **~ (being)** Mensch *m* **humanity** [hju:'mænətɪ] S Menschheit *f*; (*Einstellung*) Menschlichkeit *f*
humble ['hʌmbl] ADJ demütig; bescheiden
humid ['hju:mɪd] ADJ feucht **humidity** [hju:'mɪdətɪ] S (Luft)feuchtigkeit *f*
humiliate [hju:'mɪlɪeɪt] V/T demütigen **humiliation** [hju:mɪlɪ'eɪʃn] S Erniedrigung *f*, Demütigung *f*
hummingbird ['hʌmɪŋbɜ:rd] S Kolibri *m*
humor ['hju:mər] S Humor *m*; **sense of ~** Sinn *m* für Humor **humorous** ['hju:mərəs] ADJ humorvoll; (*Geschichte*) lustig, witzig
hump [hʌmp] S Buckel *m*
hundred ['hʌndrəd] NUM **one ~, a ~** (ein)hundert; **a ~ (and) one** hundert(und)eins **hundredth** **1** ADJ hundertste(r, s) **2** S Hundertstel *n* **hundredweight** S Zentner *m* (*45,359 kg*)
hung [hʌŋ] *prät, pperf von* hang
Hungarian [hʌŋ'gerɪən] **1** ADJ ungarisch **2** S (*Person*) Ungar(in) *m(f)*; (*Sprache*) Ungarisch *n* **Hungary** ['hʌŋgərɪ] S Ungarn *n*
hunger ['hʌŋgər] S Hunger *m* **hungry** ['hʌŋgrɪ] ADJ hungrig; **be ~** Hunger haben
hunk [hʌŋk] S *umg* gut gebauter Mann
hunt [hʌnt] **1** S Jagd *f*; (*nach Arbeit, Wohnung*) Suche *f* (*for* nach) **2** V/T & V/I jagen; (*Arbeit etc*) suchen (*for* nach) **hunting** S Jagen *n*, Jagd *f*
hurdle ['hɜ:rdl] S *a. fig* Hürde *f*
hurl [hɜ:rl] V/T schleudern
hurricane ['hərəkeɪn] S Orkan *m*
hurry ['hɜ:rɪ] **1** S Eile *f*; **be in a ~** es eilig haben **2** V/I sich beeilen; **~ (up)** mach schnell! **3** V/T antreiben
hurt ⟨hurt, hurt⟩ [hɜ:rt] **1** V/T wehtun +*dat*; (*j-n, j-s Gefühle*) verletzen; **I've ~ my arm** ich habe mir am Arm wehgetan **2** V/I wehtun; **my arm ~s** mir tut der Arm weh
husband ['hʌzbənd] S Ehemann *m*
husky ['hʌskɪ] **1** ADJ rau **2** S Schlittenhund *m*

hut [hʌt] S Hütte *f*
hydroelectric [haɪdroʊɪ'lektrɪk] ADJ **~ power plant** Wasserkraftwerk *n*
hydrogen ['haɪdrədʒən] S Wasserstoff *m*
hygiene ['haɪdʒi:n] S Hygiene *f* **hygienic** [haɪ'dʒi:nɪk] ADJ hygienisch
hymn [hɪm] S Kirchenlied *n*
hyphen ['haɪfən] S Bindestrich *m*
hypnotize ['hɪpnətaɪz] V/T hypnotisieren
hypocrisy [hɪ'pɑ:krəsɪ] S Heuchelei *f* **hypocrite** ['hɪpəkrɪt] S Heuchler(in) *m(f)*
hypodermic [haɪpə'dɜ:rmɪk] ADJ & S **~ (needle)** Spritze *f*
hypothetical [haɪpə'θetɪkəl] ADJ hypothetisch
hysteria [hɪ'stɪrɪə] S Hysterie *f* **hysterical** [hɪ'sterɪkəl] ADJ hysterisch; (*äußerst lustig*) zum Totlachen

I

I [aɪ] **1** PRON ich **2** *abk* = Interstate
IA *abk* = Iowa
ice [aɪs] **1** S Eis *n* **2** V/T (*Kuchen*) glasieren **iceberg** S Eisberg *m* **icebox** S Kühlschrank *m* **icecold** ADJ eiskalt **ice cream** S Eis *n* **ice-cream parlor** S Eiscafé *n* **ice cube** S Eiswürfel *m* **iced** ADJ eisgekühlt; (*Kaffee etc*) Eis-; (*Kuchen*) glasiert **ice hockey** S Eishockey *n* **ice rink** S Kunsteisbahn *f* **ice skating** S Schlittschuhlaufen *n*
icon ['aɪkɑ:n] S Ikone *f*; IT Icon *n*, Programmsymbol *n*
ICU *abk* = intensive care unit
icy ['aɪsɪ] ADJ vereist; eisig
I'd [aɪd] *kontr von* **I would; I had**
ID **1** *abk* = identification; Ausweis *m* **2** *abk* = Idaho
idea [aɪ'di:ə] S Idee *f*; **(I've) no ~** (ich habe) keine Ahnung
ideal [aɪ'di:əl] **1** S Ideal *n* **2** ADJ ideal **ideally** ADV ideal; idealerweise
identical [aɪ'dentɪkəl] ADJ identisch; **~ twins** eineiige Zwillinge
identify [aɪ'dentəfaɪ] V/T identifizieren **identity** [aɪ'dentətɪ] S Identität *f* **identity card** S Personalausweis *m*
idiot ['ɪdɪət] S Idiot(in) *m(f)*
idle ['aɪdl] ADJ untätig; (*Person*) faul; (*Drohung*) leer
idol ['aɪdl] S Idol *n* **idolize** ['aɪdəlaɪz] V/T vergöttern
idyllic [ɪ'dɪlɪk] ADJ idyllisch
i.e. *abk* = id est; d. h.
if [ɪf] KONJ wenn, falls; (*in Fragen*) ob; **~ so** wenn ja
ignition [ɪg'nɪʃən] S Zündung *f* **ignition key** S AUTO Zünd-

schlüssel *m*
ignorance ['ɪgnərəns] S Unwissenheit *f* **ignorant** ADJ unwissend **ignore** [ɪg'nɔːr] V/T ignorieren, nicht beachten
IL *abk* = Illinois
I'll [aɪl] *kontr von* **I will; I shall**
ill [ɪl] ADJ krank
illegal [ɪ'liːgəl] ADJ illegal
illegitimate [ɪlɪ'dʒɪtəmət] ADJ unzulässig; (*Kind*) unehelich
illiterate [ɪ'lɪtərət] ADJ **be ~** Analphabet(in) sein
illness ['ɪlnəs] S Krankheit *f*
illuminate [ɪ'luːmɪneɪt] V/T beleuchten
illusion [ɪ'luːʒən] S Illusion *f*; **be under the ~ that ...** sich einbilden, dass ...
illustrate ['ɪləstreɪt] V/T illustrieren **illustration** S Abbildung *f*, Bild *n*
I'm [aɪm] *kontr von* **I am**
image ['ɪmɪdʒ] S Bild *n*, Image *n* **imagination** [ɪmædʒə'neɪʃən] S Fantasie *f*, Einbildung *f* **imaginative** [ɪ'mædʒənətɪv] ADJ fantasievoll **imagine** [ɪ'mædʒən] V/T sich vorstellen, sich einbilden
imitate ['ɪməteɪt] V/T nachahmen, nachmachen **imitation** [ɪmə'teɪʃən] **1** S Nachahmung *f* **2** ADJ imitiert, Kunst-
immaculate [ɪ'mækjʊlət] ADJ tadellos; makellos
immature [ɪmə'tʃʊr] ADJ unreif
immediate [ɪ'miːdɪət] ADJ unmittelbar; sofortig; (*Antwort*) umgehend **immediately** ADV sofort
immense, **immensely** [ɪ'mens, -lɪ] ADJ & ADV riesig, enorm
immigrant ['ɪməgrənt] S Einwanderer *m*, Einwanderin *f* **immigration** [ɪmə'greɪʃən] S Einwanderung *f*; (*am Flughafen etc*) Einwanderungskontrolle *f*
immobilizer [ɪ'moʊbɪlaɪzər] S AUTO Wegfahrsperre *f*
immoral [ɪ'mɔːrəl] ADJ unmoralisch
immortal [ɪ'mɔːrtl] ADJ unsterblich
immune [ɪ'mjuːn] ADJ MED immun (*from, to* gegen)
impact ['ɪmpækt] S Aufprall *m*; (*von Beschluss etc*) Auswirkung *f* (*on* auf *+akk*)
impatience [ɪm'peɪʃəns] S Ungeduld *f* **impatient**, **impatiently** ADJ & ADV ungeduldig
impede [ɪm'piːd] V/T behindern
imperfect [ɪm'pɜːrfɪkt] ADJ unvollkommen; (*Ware etc*) fehlerhaft
implant ['ɪmplænt] S MED Implantat *n*
implausible [ɪm'plɔːzəbl] ADJ unglaubwürdig
implement **1** ['ɪmpləmənt] S Werkzeug *n*, Gerät *n* **2** ['ɪmpləment] V/T durchführen

implication [ɪmplɪ'keɪʃən] S Folge *f*, Auswirkung *f*, Schlussfolgerung *f* **imply** [ɪm'plaɪ] V/T (*anspielen auf*) andeuten; bedeuten; **are you ~ing that ...** wollen Sie damit sagen, dass ...

impolite [ɪmpə'laɪt] ADJ unhöflich

import 1 [ɪm'pɔ:rt] V/T einführen, importieren 2 ['ɪmpɔ:rt] S Einfuhr *f*, Import *m*

importance [ɪm'pɔ:rtəns] S Bedeutung *f* **important** ADJ wichtig (*to sb* für j-n); bedeutend, einflussreich

impose [ɪm'poʊz] V/T (*Bedingungen etc*) auferlegen (*on dat*); (*Strafe, Sanktionen*) verhängen (*on* gegen) **imposing** [ɪm'poʊzɪŋ] ADJ eindrucksvoll, imposant

impossible [ɪm'pɑ:səbl] ADJ unmöglich

impotent ['ɪmpətənt] ADJ (*sexuell*) impotent

impractical [ɪm'præktɪkəl] ADJ unpraktisch; (*Plan*) undurchführbar

impress [ɪm'pres] V/T beeindrucken **impression** [ɪm'preʃən] S Eindruck *m* **impressive** ADJ eindrucksvoll

imprison [ɪm'prɪzn] V/T inhaftieren **imprisonment** S Inhaftierung *f*

improper [ɪm'prɑ:pər] ADJ (*Benehmen*) unanständig; (*Gebrauch*) unsachgemäß

improve [ɪm'pru:v] 1 V/T verbessern 2 V/I sich verbessern, besser werden; (*Patient, Schüler*) Fortschritte machen **improvement** S Verbesserung *f* (*in +gen; on* gegenüber), Verschönerung *f*

improvise ['ɪmprəvaɪz] V/T & V/I improvisieren

impulse ['ɪmpʌls] S Impuls *m*

in [ɪn] 1 PRÄP in *+dat*; (*Richtung, Bewegung*) in *+akk*; (*im Falle von*) bei; **~ the army** beim Militär; **~ itself** an sich; (*zeitlich*) **~ the morning** am Morgen; **at three ~ the afternoon** um drei Uhr nachmittags; **~ 2007** (im Jahre) 2007; **~ July** im Juli; **~ writing** schriftlich; **~ German** auf Deutsch; **one ~ ten** einer von zehn, jeder zehnte; **~ all** insgesamt 2 ADV (*gehen*) hinein; (*kommen*) herein; **be ~** zu Hause sein; (*in Mode*) in sein, modisch sein; **sb is ~ for sth** j-m steht etw bevor; j-d kann sich auf etw *akk* gefasst machen 3 *abk* = inch

IN *abk* = Indiana

inability [ɪnə'bɪlətɪ] S Unfähigkeit *f*

inaccessible [ɪnæk'sesəbl] ADJ *a. fig* unzugänglich

inaccurate [ɪn'ækjʊrət] ADJ ungenau

inadequate [ɪn'ædɪkwət] ADJ unzulänglich

inappropriate [ɪnə'proʊprɪət] ADJ unpassend; (*Kleidung* *etc*) ungeeignet; (*Bemerkung*) unangebracht

INC [ɪŋk] *abk* = Incorporated; AG, Aktiengesellschaft *f*

incapable [ɪn'keɪpəbl] ADJ unfähig (*of* zu); **be ~ of doing sth** nicht imstande sein, etw zu tun

incentive [ɪn'sentɪv] S Anreiz *m*

incessantly [ɪn'sesəntlɪ] ADV unaufhörlich

incest ['ɪnsest] S Inzest *m*

inch [ɪntʃ] S Zoll *m* (*2,54 cm*)

incident ['ɪnsɪdənt] S Vorfall *m*; (*unangenehm*) Zwischenfall *m* **incidentally** [ɪnsɪ'dentlɪ] ADV nebenbei bemerkt, übrigens

inclination [ɪnklɪ'neɪʃən] S Neigung *f*

include [ɪn'klu:d] V/T einschließen; (*in Liste, Gruppe*) aufnehmen **including** PRÄP einschließlich (*+gen*); **not ~ service** Bedienung nicht inbegriffen **inclusive** [ɪn'klu:sɪv] ADJ einschließlich (*of +gen*); Pauschal-

income ['ɪnkʌm] S Einkommen *n*; (*aus Geschäften*) Einkünfte *pl* **income tax** S Einkommensteuer *f*; (*auf Löhne, Gehälter*) Lohnsteuer *f*

incompatible [ɪnkəm'pætəbl] ADJ unvereinbar; (*Personen*) unverträglich; IT nicht kompatibel

incompetent [ɪn'kɑ:mpətənt] ADJ unfähig

incomplete [ɪnkəm'pli:t] ADJ unvollständig

incomprehensible [ɪnkɑ:mprɪ'hensəbl] ADJ unverständlich

inconsiderate [ɪnkən'sɪdərət] ADJ rücksichtslos

inconsistent [ɪnkən'sɪstənt] ADJ inkonsequent; (*Aussagen, Verhalten*) widersprüchlich; (*Arbeitsleistung*) unbeständig

inconvenience [ɪnkən'vi:nɪəns] S Unannehmlichkeit *f*; (*organisatorischer Art*) Umstände *pl* **inconvenient** ADJ ungünstig, unbequem

incorporate [ɪn'kɔ:rpəreɪt] V/T aufnehmen (*into* in *+akk*); (*beinhalten*) enthalten

incorrect [ɪnkə'rekt] ADJ falsch; (*nicht passend, unangebracht*) inkorrekt

increase **1** ['ɪnkri:s] S Zunahme *f* (*in* an *+dat*); (*von Menge, Tempo*) Erhöhung *f* (*in +gen*) **2** [ɪn'kri:s] V/T (*Preise, Tempo etc*) erhöhen; (*Wohlstand*) vermehren; (*Zahl*) vergrößern **3** [ɪn'kri:s] V/I zunehmen (*in* an *+dat*); (*Preise*) steigen; (*an Größe*) größer werden; (*an Zahl*) sich vermehren **increasingly** [ɪn'kri:sɪŋlɪ] ADV zunehmend

incredible, incredibly [ɪn'kredəbl] ADJ & ADV unglaublich; (*sehr gut*) fantastisch

incubator ['ɪnkjʊbeɪtər] S Brutkasten *m*

incurable [ɪnˈkjʊrəbl] ADJ unheilbar
indecent [ɪnˈdiːsnt] ADJ unanständig
indecisive [ɪndɪˈsaɪsɪv] ADJ (*Person*) unentschlossen; (*Ergebnis*) nicht entscheidend
indeed [ɪnˈdiːd] ADV tatsächlich; (*als Antwort*) allerdings; **very hot ~** wirklich sehr heiß
indefinitely [ɪnˈdefənətlɪ] ADV endlos; (*verschieben*) auf unbestimmte Zeit
independence [ɪndɪˈpendəns] S Unabhängigkeit *f* **independent** [ɪndɪˈpendənt] ADJ unabhängig (*of* von); (*Person*) selbstständig
index [ˈɪndeks] S Index *m*, Verzeichnis *n* **index finger** S Zeigefinger *m*
India [ˈɪndɪə] S Indien *n* **Indian** [ˈɪndɪən] **1** ADJ indisch; indianisch **2** S Inder(in) *m(f)*; *pej* Indianer(in) *m(f)*
indicate [ˈɪndɪkeɪt] V/T zeigen; (*Gerät*) anzeigen; hinweisen auf *+akk* **indication** [ɪndɪˈkeɪʃn] S Anzeichen *n* (*of* für)
indifferent [ɪnˈdɪfrənt] ADJ gleichgültig (*to, towards* gegenüber); mittelmäßig
indigestion [ɪndɪˈdʒestʃən] S Verdauungsstörung *f*
indignity [ɪnˈdɪgnətɪ] S Demütigung *f*
indirect, indirectly [ɪndɪˈrekt] ADJ & ADV indirekt
indispensable [ɪndɪˈspensəbl] ADJ unentbehrlich
individual [ɪndɪˈvɪdʒʊəl] **1** S Einzelne(r) *m/f(m)* **2** ADJ einzeln; eigen, individuell **individually** ADV einzeln
indoor [ˈɪndɔːr] ADJ (*Schuhe*) Haus-; (*Pflanzen etc*) Zimmer-; SPORT Hallen- **indoor climbing center, indoor climbing gym** S Kletterhalle *f* **indoors** [ɪnˈdɔːrz] ADV drinnen, im Haus
indulge [ɪnˈdʌldʒ] V/I **~ in sth** sich etw gönnen **indulgence** S Nachsicht *f*; (*unmäßig*) (übermäßiger) Genuss; Luxus *m*
industrial [ɪnˈdʌstrɪəl] ADJ Industrie-, industriell **industry** [ˈɪndəstrɪ] S Industrie *f*
inedible [ɪnˈedɪbl] ADJ nicht essbar, ungenießbar
ineffective [ɪnɪˈfektɪv] ADJ unwirksam, wirkungslos **inefficient** [ɪnɪˈfɪʃənt] ADJ unwirksam; (*Gebrauch, Maschine*) unwirtschaftlich; (*Methode etc*) unrationell
inequality [ɪnɪˈkwɑːlətɪ] S Ungleichheit *f*
inevitable [ɪnˈevɪtəbl] ADJ unvermeidlich **inevitably** ADV zwangsläufig
inexpensive [ɪnɪkˈspensɪv] ADJ preisgünstig
inexperienced [ɪnɪkˈspɪrɪənst] ADJ unerfahren
inexplicable [ɪnɪkˈsplɪkəbl] ADJ unerklärlich
infamous [ˈɪnfəməs] ADJ (*Per-*

son) berüchtigt *(for* wegen); *(Tat)* niederträchtig **infant** [ˈɪnfənt] S Säugling *m;* *(Kind)* Kleinkind *n* **infatuated** [ɪnˈfætʃʊeɪtəd] ADJ vernarrt *od* verknallt *(with* in *+akk)* **infect** [ɪnˈfekt] V/T *(Person)* anstecken; *(Wunde)* infizieren **infection** [ɪnˈfekʃən] S Infektion *f* **infectious** [ɪnˈfekʃəs] ADJ ansteckend **inferior** [ɪnˈfɪrɪər] ADJ *(Qualität)* minderwertig; *(Rangfolge)* untergeordnet **inferiority** [ɪnfɪrɪˈɑːrətɪ] S Minderwertigkeit *f* **infertile** [ɪnˈfɜːrtəl] ADJ unfruchtbar **inflammation** [ɪnfləˈmeɪʃən] S MED Entzündung *f* **inflatable** [ɪnˈfleɪtəbl] ADJ aufblasbar **inflate** [ɪnˈfleɪt] V/T aufpumpen; aufblasen; *(Preise)* hochtreiben **inflation** [ɪnˈfleɪʃən] S Inflation *f* **in-flight** [ˈɪnflaɪt] ADJ *(Verpflegung, Magazin)* Bord- **influence** [ˈɪnflʊəns] **1** S Einfluss *m (on* auf *+akk)* **2** V/T beeinflussen **influential** [ɪnflʊˈenʃəl] ADJ einflussreich **inform** [ɪnˈfɔːrm] V/T informieren *(of, about* über *+akk)*; **keep sb ~ed** j-n auf dem Laufenden halten **informal** [ɪnˈfɔːrməl] ADJ zwanglos, ungezwungen **information** [ɪnfərˈmeɪʃən] S Auskunft *f,* Informationen *pl* **information desk** S Auskunftsschalter *m* **information technology** S Informationstechnik *f;* Informationstechnologie *f* **informative** [ɪnˈfɔːrmətɪv] ADJ aufschlussreich **infra-red** [ɪnfrəˈred] ADJ infrarot **infrastructure** [ˈɪnfrəstrʌktʃər] S Infrastruktur *f* **infuriating** [ɪnˈfjʊrɪeɪtɪŋ] ADJ äußerst ärgerlich **ingenious** [ɪnˈdʒiːnɪəs] ADJ *(Person)* erfinderisch; *(Vorrichtung, Gerät)* raffiniert; *(Idee)* genial **ingredient** [ɪnˈgriːdɪənt] S GASTR Zutat *f* **inhabit** [ɪnˈhæbɪt] V/T bewohnen **inhabitant** S Einwohner(in) *m(f)* **inhale** [ɪnˈheɪl] V/T einatmen; *(Zigaretten)* MED inhalieren **inhaler** S Inhalationsgerät *n* **inherit** [ɪnˈherɪt] V/T erben **inheritance** S Erbe *n* **inhuman** [ɪnˈhjuːmən] ADJ unmenschlich **initial** [ɪˈnɪʃəl] **1** ADJ anfänglich **2** V/T mit Initialen unterschreiben **initially** ADV anfangs **initials** S PL Initialen *pl* **initiative** [ɪˈnɪʃətɪv] S Initiative *f* **inject** [ɪnˈdʒekt] V/T *(Arzneimittel, Droge etc)* einspritzen; **~ sb with sth** j-m etw (ein)spritzen

injure ['ɪndʒər] VT verletzen; **~ one's leg** sich das Bein verletzen **injury** ['ɪndʒərɪ] S Verletzung *f*
injustice [ɪn'dʒʌstɪs] S Ungerechtigkeit *f*
ink [ɪŋk] S Tinte *f* **ink-jet printer** S Tintenstrahldrucker *m*
inland ['ɪnlænd] **1** ADJ Binnen- **2** ADV landeinwärts
in-laws ['ɪnlɔːz] S PL *umg* Schwiegereltern *pl*
inline skates ['ɪnlaɪnskeɪts] S PL Inlineskates *pl*, Inliner *pl*
inmate ['ɪnmeɪt] S Insasse *m*
inn [ɪn] S Gasthaus *n*
inner ['ɪnər] ADJ innere(r, s); **~ city** Innenstadt *f*
innocence ['ɪnəsəns] S Unschuld *f* **innocent** ADJ unschuldig
innovation [ɪnə'veɪʃən] S Neuerung *f*
inoculation [ɪnɑːkjʊ'leɪʃən] S Impfung *f*
in-patient ['ɪnpeɪʃənt] S stationärer Patient, stationäre Patientin
input ['ɪnpʊt] S (*von Person*) Beitrag *m*; IT Eingabe *f*
inquire [ɪn'kwaɪr] VI sich erkundigen (*about* nach) **inquiry** [ɪn'kwaɪrɪ] S Anfrage *f*, Erkundigung *f* (*about* über *+akk*); (*von Kommission*) Untersuchung *f*; **'Inquiries'** „Auskunft"
insane [ɪn'seɪn] ADJ wahnsinnig; MED geisteskrank **insanity** [ɪn'sænətɪ] S Wahnsinn *m*
inscription [ɪn'skrɪpʃən] S Inschrift *f*
insect ['ɪnsekt] S Insekt *n*
insecure [ɪnsɪ'kjʊr] ADJ (*Person, Job*) unsicher; (*Regal etc*) instabil
insensitive [ɪn'sensətɪv] ADJ unempfindlich (*to* gegen); gefühllos
inseparable [ɪn'sepərəbl] ADJ unzertrennlich
insert **1** [ɪn'sɜːrt] VT einfügen; (*Münze*) einwerfen; (*Karte etc*) hineinstecken **2** ['ɪnsɜːrt] S (*Zeitung*) Beilage *f*
inside **1** [ɪn'saɪd, 'ɪnsaɪd] S **the ~** das Innere; die Innenseite; **from the ~** von innen **2** ['ɪnsaɪd] ADJ innere(r, s), Innen- **3** [ɪn'saɪd] ADV (*Ort*) innen; (*Richtung*) hinein; **go ~** hineingehen **4** [ɪn'saɪd, 'ɪnsaɪd] PRÄP (*Ort*) in *+dat*; (*Richtung*) in *+akk* ... hinein; (*zeitlich*) innerhalb *+gen* **inside out** ADV verkehrt herum; (*kennen*) in- und auswendig
insight ['ɪnsaɪt] S Einblick *m* (*into* in *+akk*)
insist [ɪn'sɪst] VI darauf bestehen; **~ on sth** auf etw *dat* bestehen **insistent** ADJ hartnäckig
insomnia [ɪn'sɑːmnɪə] S Schlaflosigkeit *f*
inspect [ɪn'spekt] VT prüfen, kontrollieren **inspection** S

Prüfung *f;* (*Eintrittskarten etc*) Kontrolle *f* **inspector** S (*bei Polizei*) Inspektor(in) *m(f)*; (*höherer Rang*) Kommissar(in) *m(f)*

inspiration [ınspı'reıʃən] S Inspiration *f* **inspire** [ın'spaır] V/T (*Respekt*) einflößen (*in dat*); (*j-n*) inspirieren

install [ın'stɒ:l] V/T (*Software*) installieren

installment [ın'stɒ:lmənt] S Rate *f*; (*von Geschichte*) Folge *f* **installment plan** S Ratenkauf *m*; **on the ~** auf Raten

instance ['ınstəns] S Fall *m*, Beispiel *n* (*of* für); **for ~** zum Beispiel

instant ['ınstənt] **1** S Augenblick *m* **2** ADJ sofortig **instant coffee** S löslicher Kaffee **instantly** ADV sofort

instead [ın'sted] ADV stattdessen **instead of** PRÄP (an)statt *+gen*

instinct ['ınstıŋkt] S Instinkt *m* **instinctive**, **instinctively** [ın'stıŋktıv, -lı] ADJ & ADV instinktiv

institute ['ınstıtu:t] S Institut *n* **institution** [ınstı'tu:ʃən] S Institution *f*, Einrichtung *f*; (*als Gebäude, Heim*) Anstalt *f*

instruct [ın'strʌkt] V/T anweisen **instruction** [ın'strʌkʃən] S (*bei Kursen*) Unterricht *m*; (*von Vorgesetztem*) Anweisung *f*; **~s for use** Gebrauchsanweisung *f* **instructor** S Lehrer(in) *m(f)*; Dozent(in) *m(f)*

instrument ['ınstrəmənt] S Instrument *n*

insufficient [ınsə'fıʃənt] ADJ ungenügend

insulate ['ınsəleıt] V/T ELEK isolieren; *fig* **~ sb from sth** j-n vor etw schützen **insulation** [ınsə'leıʃən] S Isolierung *f*

insulin ['ınsələn] S Insulin *n*

insult **1** ['ınsʌlt] S Beleidigung *f* **2** [ın'sʌlt] V/T beleidigen **insulting** [ın'sʌltıŋ] ADJ beleidigend

insurance [ın'ʃʊrəns] S Versicherung *f* **insure** [ın'ʃʊr] V/T versichern (*against* gegen)

integrate ['ıntəgreıt] V/T integrieren (*into* in *+akk*)

intellect ['ıntəlekt] S Intellekt *m* **intellectual** [ıntə'lektʃʊəl] ADJ intellektuell; (*Interessen etc*) geistig

intelligence [ın'telıdʒəns] S Intelligenz *f* **intelligent** ADJ intelligent

intend [ın'tend] V/T beabsichtigen; **~ to do sth** vorhaben, etw zu tun

intense [ın'tens] ADJ intensiv; (*Druck*) enorm; (*Konkurrenz*) heftig **intensity** S Intensität *f* **intensive** ADJ intensiv **intensive care unit** S Intensivstation *f*

intention [ın'tenʃən] S Absicht *f* **intentional**, **intentionally** ADJ & ADV absichtlich

interact [ıntər'ækt] V/I aufeinander einwirken **interactive** ADJ interaktiv

interchange ['ɪntərtʃeɪndʒ] S Autobahnkreuz *n* **interchangeable** [ɪntər'tʃeɪndʒəbl] ADJ austauschbar

intercom ['ɪntərkɑːm] S (Gegen)sprechanlage *f*

intercourse ['ɪntərkɔːrs] S Geschlechtsverkehr *m*

interest ['ɪntrest] **1** S Interesse *n*; FIN *(für angelegtes Geld)* Zinsen *pl*; WIRTSCH Anteil *m*; **be of ~** von Interesse sein *(to* für) **2** V/T interessieren **interested** ADJ interessiert *(in* an *+dat)*; **be ~ in** sich interessieren für; **are you ~ in coming?** hast du Lust, mitzukommen? **interesting** ADJ interessant **interest rate** S Zinssatz *m*

interface ['ɪntərfeɪs] S IT Schnittstelle *f*

interfere [ɪntər'fɪr] V/I sich einmischen *(with, in* in *+akk)* **interference** S Einmischung *f*; TV, RADIO Störung *f*

interior [ɪn'tɪrɪər] **1** ADJ Innen- **2** S Innere(s) *n*; Innenraum *m*; *(Haus, Auto)* Innenausstattung *f*

intermediate [ɪntər'miːdɪət] ADJ Zwischen-

intermission [ɪntər'mɪʃən] S Pause *f*

intern ['ɪntɜːrn] S Assistenzarzt *m*, Assistenzärztin *f*; Praktikant(in) *m(f)*

internal [ɪn'tɜːrnl] ADJ innere(r, s); *(Flug)* Inlands-; **~ revenue** Finanzamt *n* **internally** ADV innen; *(im Körper)* innerlich

international [ɪntər'næʃnəl] ADJ international; **~ match** Länderspiel *n*; **~ flight** Auslandsflug *m*

Internet ['ɪntərnet] S IT Internet *n* **Internet access** S Internetzugang *m* **Internet banking** S Onlinebanking *n* **Internet café** S Internetcafé *n* **Internet connection** S Internetanschluss *m* **Internet provider** S Internetprovider *m*

interpret [ɪn'tɜːrprət] V/I & V/T dolmetschen; *(auslegen)* interpretieren **interpretation** [ɪntɜːrprə'teɪʃən] S Interpretation *f* **interpreter** [ɪn'tɜːrprətər] S Dolmetscher(in) *m(f)*

interrogate [ɪn'terəgeɪt] V/T verhören **interrogation** [ɪnterə'geɪʃən] S Verhör *n*

interrupt [ɪntə'rʌpt] V/T unterbrechen **interruption** [ɪntə'rʌpʃən] S Unterbrechung *f*

intersection ['ɪntərsekʃən] S *(von Straßen)* Kreuzung *f*

interstate ['ɪntərsteɪt] ADJ zwischenstaatlich; **~ (highway)** ≈ Bundesautobahn *f*

interval ['ɪntərvəl] S *(räumlich, zeitlich)* Abstand *m*

intervene [ɪntər'viːn] V/I eingreifen *(in* in)

interview ['ɪntərvjuː] **1** S Interview *n*; *(bei Bewerbung)* Vor-

stellungsgespräch *n* **2** VT interviewen; (*Bewerber*) ein Vorstellungsgespräch führen mit
intestine [ɪnˈtestɪn] S Darm *m*; **~s** *pl* Eingeweide *pl*
intimate [ˈɪntəmət] ADJ (*Freunde*) vertraut, eng; (*Atmosphäre*) gemütlich; (*sexuell*) intim
intimidate [ɪnˈtɪmədeɪt] VT einschüchtern **intimidation** S Einschüchterung *f*
into [ˈɪntʊ] PRÄP in *+akk*; (*krachen*) gegen; **translate ~ German** ins Deutsche übersetzen; **be ~ sth** *umg* auf etw *akk* stehen
intolerant [ɪnˈtɑːlərənt] ADJ intolerant
intoxicated [ɪnˈtɑːksɪkeɪtəd] ADJ betrunken; *fig* berauscht
intricate [ˈɪntrɪkət] ADJ kompliziert
intrigue [ɪnˈtriːg] VT faszinieren
introduce [ɪntrəˈduːs] VT (*Person*) vorstellen (*to sb* j-m); (*etw Neues*) einführen (*to* in *+akk*)
introduction [ɪntrəˈdʌkʃən] S *Einführung f* (*to* in *+akk*); (*in Buch*) Einleitung *f* (*to* zu); (*von Person*) Vorstellung *f*
invade [ɪnˈveɪd] VT einfallen in *+akk*
invalid **1** [ˈɪnvəlɪd] S Kranke(r) *m/f(m)*; (*durch Unfall etc*) Invalide *m* **2** [ɪnˈvælɪd] ADJ ungültig
invaluable [ɪnˈvæljəbl] ADJ äußerst wertvoll, unschätzbar
invasion [ɪnˈveɪʒən] S Invasion *f* (*of* in *+akk*)
invent [ɪnˈvent] VT erfinden **invention** [ɪnˈvenʃən] S Erfindung *f* **inventor** S Erfinder(in) *m(f)*
invest [ɪnˈvest] VT & VI investieren (*in* in *+akk*)
investigate [ɪnˈvestɪgeɪt] VT untersuchen **investigation** [ɪnvestɪˈgeɪʃən] S Untersuchung *f* (*into +gen*)
investment [ɪnˈvestmənt] S Investition *f*
invigorating [ɪnˈvɪgəreɪtɪŋ] ADJ erfrischend, belebend; (*Gebräu*) stärkend
invisible [ɪnˈvɪzəbl] ADJ unsichtbar
invitation [ɪnvɪˈteɪʃən] S Einladung *f* **invite** [ɪnˈvaɪt] VT einladen
invoice [ˈɪnvɔɪs] S Rechnung *f*
involuntary [ɪnˈvɑːlənterɪ] ADJ unbeabsichtigt
involve [ɪnˈvɑːlv] VT verwickeln (*in sth* in etw *akk*); (*viel Arbeit etc*) zur Folge haben; **be ~d in sth** an etw *dat* beteiligt sein
inward(s) [ˈɪnwərd(z)] ADV nach innen **inwardly** [ˈɪnwərdlɪ] ADV innerlich
IOU [aɪoʊˈjuː] *abk* = I owe you; Schuldschein *m*
IQ *abk* = intelligence quotient; IQ *m*
Iran [ɪˈræn] S der Iran

Iraq [ɪ'ræk] S der Irak
Ireland ['aɪərlənd] S Irland *n*
Irish ['aɪrɪʃ] **1** ADJ irisch; **~ coffee** Irish Coffee *m* (*Kaffee mit einem Schuss Whiskey und Schlagsahne*) **2** S (*Sprache*) Irisch *n*; **the ~** *pl* die Iren *pl*
Irishman ⟨-men *pl*⟩ S Ire *m*
Irishwoman ⟨-women *pl*⟩ S Irin *f*
iron ['aɪərn] **1** S Eisen *n*; (*zum Bügeln*) Bügeleisen *n* **2** ADJ eisern **3** V/T bügeln
ironic(al) [aɪ'rɑːnək(əl)] ADJ ironisch
ironing board S Bügelbrett *n*
irony ['aɪrənɪ] S Ironie *f*
irrational [ɪ'ræʃənl] ADJ irrational
irregular [ɪ'regjʊlər] ADJ unregelmäßig
irrelevant [ɪ'reləvənt] ADJ belanglos, irrelevant
irresistible [ɪrɪ'zɪstəbl] ADJ unwiderstehlich
irresponsible [ɪrɪ'spɑːnsəbl] ADJ verantwortungslos
irritable ['ɪrɪtəbl] ADJ reizbar
irritate ['ɪrɪteɪt] V/T ärgern; (*bewusst*) reizen **irritation** [ɪrɪ'teɪʃən] S Ärger *m*; MED Reizung *f*
IRS *abk* = Internal Revenue Service; Finanzamt *n*
is [ɪz] *Präsens von* **be**; ist
Islam ['ɪzlæm] S Islam *m* **Islamic** [ɪz'læmɪk] ADJ islamisch
island ['aɪlənd] S Insel *f*
isn't ['ɪznt] *kontr von* **is not**
isolate ['aɪsəleɪt] V/T isolieren **isolated** ADJ (*Haus*) abgelegen **isolation** [aɪsə'leɪʃən] S Isolierung *f*
Israel ['ɪzreɪl] S Israel *n* **Israeli** [ɪz'reɪlɪ] **1** ADJ israelisch **2** S Israeli *m od f*
issue ['ɪʃuː] **1** S (*Angelegenheit*) Frage *f*; (*ungeklärtes*) Problem *n*; (*für Diskussion*) Thema *n*; (*Zeitung etc*) Ausgabe *f* **2** V/T ausgeben; (*Pass etc*) ausstellen; (*Aufträge*) erteilen; (*Buch*) herausgeben
it [ɪt] PRON (*als Subjekt*) er/sie/es; (*als direktes Objekt*) ihn/sie/es; (*als indirektes Objekt*) ihm/ihr/ihm; **the worst thing about ~** das Schlimmste daran; **who is ~? ~'s me/~'s him** wer ist da? ich bin's/er ist's; **that's ~** ja genau!; **~'s Charlie here** (*am Telefon*) hier spricht Charlie
IT *abk* = information technology; IT *f*
Italian [ɪ'tæljən] **1** ADJ italienisch **2** S Italiener(in) *m(f)*; (*Sprache*) Italienisch *n*
italic [ɪ'tælɪk] **1** ADJ kursiv **2** S PL **in ~s** kursiv
Italy ['ɪtəlɪ] S Italien *n*
itch [ɪtʃ] **1** S Juckreiz *m*; **I have an ~** mich juckt es **2** V/I jucken; **he is ~ing to ...** es juckt ihn, zu ... **itchy** ADJ juckend
it'd ['ɪtd] *kontr von* **it would; it had**

item [ˈaɪtəm] S Gegenstand *m*; (*in Katalog*) Artikel *m*; (*auf Liste*) Posten *m*; (*der Tagesordnung*) Punkt *m*; (*in Nachrichten*) Bericht *m*; TV (*Radio*) Meldung *f*
itinerary [aɪˈtɪnərərɪ] S Reiseroute *f*
it'll [ˈɪtl] *kontr von* **it will; it shall**
its [ɪts] PRON sein; (*weibliche Form*) ihr
it's [ɪts] *kontr von* **it is; it has**
itself [ɪtˈself] PRON sich; (*verstärkend*) **the house ~** das Haus selbst *od* an sich; **by ~** allein; **the door closes by ~** die Tür schließt sich von selbst
I've [aɪv] *kontr von* **I have**
ivy [ˈaɪvɪ] S Efeu *m* **Ivy League** [aɪvɪˈliːg] S *eine Gruppe von Elitehochschulen an der Ostküste der USA*

J

jab [dʒæb] V/T (*mit Ellbogen*) stoßen; (*Nadel, Messer*) stechen (*into* in *+akk*)
jack [dʒæk] S AUTO Wagenheber *m*; (*Karten*) Bube *m* **jack up** V/T (*Auto etc*) aufbocken
jackass S *umg pej* Depp *m*, Trottel *m*
jacket [ˈdʒækɪt] S Jacke *f*; (*von Anzug*) Jackett *n*; (*von Buch*) Schutzumschlag *m*
jack-knife ⟨jack-knives *pl*⟩ [ˈdʒæknaɪf] **1** S Klappmesser *n* **2** V/I (*LKW etc*) sich quer stellen
jacuzzi® [dʒəˈkuːzɪ] S Whirlpool® *m*
jail [dʒeɪl] **1** S Gefängnis *n* **2** V/T einsperren
jalapeño ⟨-s *pl*⟩ [hɑːləˈpeɪnjoʊ] S Peperoni *f*
jam [dʒæm] **1** S Konfitüre *f*, Marmelade *f*; (*Verkehr; Drucker*) Stau *m*; *umg* (*Dilemma*) Patsche *f* **2** V/T (*Straße*) verstopfen; **be ~med** (*Schublade etc*) klemmen; **~ on the brakes** eine Vollbremsung machen
jambalaya [dʒʌmbəˈlaɪə] S GASTR *stark gewürztes Reisgericht mit Fleisch, Gemüse und Meeresfrüchten*
jam-packed ADJ proppenvoll
janitor [ˈdʒænətər] S Hausmeister(in) *m(f)*
January [ˈdʒænjʊərɪ] S Januar *m*
Japan [dʒəˈpæn] S Japan *n* **Japanese** [dʒæpəˈniːz] **1** ADJ japanisch **2** S Japaner(in) *m(f)*; (*Sprache*) Japanisch *n*
jar [dʒɑːr] S Glas *n*
jaw [dʒɒː] S Kiefer *m*
jaywalk [ˈdʒeɪwɒːk] V/I die Straße vorschriftswidrig überqueren
jazz [dʒæz] S Jazz *m*
jealous [ˈdʒeləs] ADJ eifersüchtig (*of* auf *+akk*) **jealousy**

S Eifersucht *f*
jeans [dʒi:nz] S PL Jeans *pl*
Jell-O® ['dʒeloʊ] S Götterspeise *f*
jelly ['dʒelɪ] S Gelee *n*; Marmelade *f* **jelly bean** S Geleebonbon *n* **jellyfish** S Qualle *f* **jelly roll** S Biskuitrolle *f*
jeopardize ['dʒepərdaɪz] V/T gefährden
jerk [dʒɜ:rk] **1** S Ruck *m*; *umg pej* (*Blödmann*) Penner *m* **2** V/T ruckartig bewegen **3** V/I (*Seil*) rucken; (*Muskeln*) zucken
jet [dʒet] S (*Wasser*) Strahl *m*; (*Öffnung*) Düse *f*; (*Flugzeug*) Düsenflugzeug *n* **jetlag** S Jetlag *m* (*Müdigkeit nach langem Flug*)
Jew [dʒu:] S Jude *m*, Jüdin *f*
jewel ['dʒu:əl] S Edelstein *m*; *fig* Juwel *n* **jeweler** S Juwelier(in) *m(f)* **jewelry** S Schmuck *m*
Jewish ['dʒu:ɪʃ] ADJ jüdisch; **she's ~** sie ist Jüdin
jigsaw (puzzle) ['dʒɪgsɒ:(pʌzl)] S Puzzle *n*
jittery ['dʒɪtərɪ] ADJ *umg* ganz nervös
job [dʒɑ:b] S Arbeit *f*, Aufgabe *f*; (*bei Firma*) Stellung *f*, Job *m*; **what's your ~?** was machen Sie beruflich? **jobless** ADJ arbeitslos
jock [dʒɑ:k] S *umg, oft pej* Sportler *m*
jockey ['dʒɑ:kɪ] S Jockey *m*
jog [dʒɑ:g] **1** V/T (*Person*) anstoßen **2** V/I (*als Sport*) joggen
jogging S Jogging *n*; **go ~** joggen gehen
john [dʒɑ:n] S *umg* Klo *n*
John Hancock [dʒɑ:n'hænkɑ:k] S *umg* Friedrich Wilhelm (*Unterschrift*)
join [dʒɔɪn] **1** V/T verbinden (*to* mit); (*Klub etc*) beitreten *+dat*; **~ sb** sich j-m anschließen; (*an Tisch*) sich zu j-m setzen **2** V/I sich vereinigen; (*Flüsse*) zusammenfließen **join in** V/I & V/T mitmachen (*sth* bei etw)
joint [dʒɔɪnt] **1** S (*Knochen*) Gelenk *n*; (*Rohr*) Verbindungsstelle *f*; (*Fleisch*) Braten *m*; (*Marihuana*) Joint *m* **2** ADJ gemeinsam **joint account** S Gemeinschaftskonto *n* **jointly** ADV gemeinsam
joke [dʒoʊk] **1** S Witz *m*; Streich *m*; **for a ~** zum Spaß; **it's no ~** das ist nicht zum Lachen **2** V/I Witze machen; **you must be joking** das ist ja wohl nicht dein Ernst!
jot down [dʒɑ:t'daʊn] V/T sich notieren
journal ['dʒɜ:rnl] S (*persönliche Aufzeichnungen*) Tagebuch *n*; (*Fach-, wissenschaftliche*) Zeitschrift *f* **journalism** S Journalismus *m* **journalist** S Journalist(in) *m(f)*
journey ['dʒɜ:rnɪ] S Reise *f*; (*im Auto, Zug*) Fahrt *f*
joy [dʒɔɪ] S Freude *f* (*at* über *+akk*) **joystick** S IT Joystick

m; FLUG Steuerknüppel *m*
Jr *abk* = Junior; Junior *m*
judge [dʒʌdʒ] **1** S Richter(in) *m(f)*; SPORT Punktrichter(in) *m(f)* **2** V/T beurteilen (*by* nach) **3** V/I urteilen (*by* nach) **judg(e)ment** S JUR Urteil *n*; (*Meinung*) Ansicht *f*; **an error of ~** Fehleinschätzung *f*
juggle ['dʒʌgl] V/I jonglieren (*with* mit)
juice [dʒu:s] S Saft *m* **juicy** ADJ saftig
July [dʒu:'laɪ] S Juli *m*; → September
jumble ['dʒʌmbl] **1** S Durcheinander *n* **2** V/T **~ (up)** durcheinanderwerfen; (*Fakten*) durcheinanderbringen
jump [dʒʌmp] **1** V/I springen; (*ängstlich*) zusammenzucken; **~ to conclusions** voreilige Schlüsse ziehen **2** V/T überspringen; **~ the lights** bei Rot über die Kreuzung fahren **3** S Sprung *m*; (*für Pferde*) Hindernis *n* **jumper** S Trägerkleid *n*; (*Person, Pferd*) Springer(in) *m(f)* **jumper cable** S AUTO Starthilfekabel *n*
junction ['dʒʌŋkʃən] S (*von Straßen*) Kreuzung *f*; BAHN Knotenpunkt *m*
June [dʒu:n] S Juni *m*; → September
jungle ['dʒʌŋgl] S Dschungel *m*
junior ['dʒu:njər] **1** ADJ jünger; (*Stellung*) untergeordnet (*to sb* j-m) **2** S (*Universität, Highschool*) Student(in) im dritten Jahr **junior high (school)** S ≈ Mittelschule *f*
junk [dʒʌŋk] S Plunder *m* **junk food** S Junkfood *n* (*Nahrungsmittel mit geringem Nährwert*) **junkie** S *umg* Junkie *m*, Fixer(in) *m(f)*; *fig* (*Fan*) Freak *m* **junk mail** S Reklame *f*; IT Junkmail *f* **junkyard** S Schrottplatz *m*
jury ['dʒʊrɪ] S Geschworene *pl*; (*Wettkampf etc*) Jury *f*
just [dʒʌst] **1** ADJ gerecht **2** ADV (*soeben*) gerade; (*exakt*) genau; **~ as nice** genauso nett; (*nur knapp*) **~ in time** gerade noch rechtzeitig; (*unmittelbar*) **~ before/after ...** gleich vor/nach ...; (*in geringer Entfernung*) **~ around the corner** gleich um die Ecke; (*ein wenig*) **~ over an hour** etwas mehr als eine Stunde; (*nur*) **~ the two of us** nur wir beide; **~ a moment** Moment mal; (*absolut*) **it was ~ fantastic** es war einfach klasse; **~ about** so etwa; (*eingrenzend*) mehr oder weniger; **~ about ready** fast fertig
justice ['dʒʌstɪs] S Gerechtigkeit *f* **justify** ['dʒʌstɪfaɪ] V/T rechtfertigen
juvenile ['dʒu:vənaɪl] S **1** ADJ Jugend-, jugendlich **2** S Jugendliche(r) *m/f(m)*

K

k *abk* = thousand; **15k** 15 000
kangaroo [kæŋgəˈruː] S Känguru *n*
kayaking [ˈkaɪækɪŋ] S Kajakfahren *n*
KB *abk* = kilobyte; KB
keel [kiːl] S SCHIFF Kiel *m* **keel over** V/I (*Boot*) kentern; (*Person*) umkippen
keen [kiːn] ADJ begeistert (*on* von); (*fleißig*) eifrig; (*Verstand*) scharf; (*Interesse etc*) stark; **be ~ on sb** von j-m angetan sein; **she's ~ on riding** sie reitet gern; **be ~ to do sth** darauf erpicht sein, etw zu tun
keep ⟨kept, kept⟩ [kiːp, kept] **1** V/T behalten; (*Geheimnis*) für sich behalten; (*Regeln etc*) einhalten; (*Versprechen*) halten; (*Tagebuch etc*) führen; (*Tiere*) halten; (*Familie etc*) unterhalten, versorgen; (*Sache*) aufbewahren; **~ sb waiting** j-n warten lassen; **~ sb from doing sth** j-n davon abhalten, etw zu tun; **~ sth clean/secret** etw sauber/geheim halten; **'~ clear'** „(bitte) frei halten"; **~ this to yourself** behalten Sie das für sich **2** V/I (*Lebensmittel*) sich halten; (*mit Adjektiv*) bleiben; **~ quiet** sei ruhig!; **~ doing sth** etw immer wieder tun; **~ at it** mach weiter so!; **it ~s happening** es passiert immer wieder **keep back** **1** V/I zurückbleiben **2** V/T zurückhalten; (*Informationen*) verschweigen (*from sb* j-m) **keep off** V/T (*Person, Tier*) fernhalten; **'~ the grass'** „Betreten des Rasens verboten" **keep on** **1** V/I weitermachen; (*walking*) weitergehen; (*driving*) weiterfahren; **~ doing sth** etw immer wieder tun **2** V/T (*Mantel etc*) anbehalten **keep out** **1** V/T nicht hereinlassen **2** V/I draußen bleiben; **~** (*auf Schild*) Eintritt verboten **keep to** V/T (*Straße*) bleiben auf *+dat*; (*Plan*) sich halten an *+akk* **keep up** **1** V/I Schritt halten (*with* mit) **2** V/T aufrechterhalten; (*Geschwindigkeit*) halten; **keep it up!** *umg* weiter so!
keepsake [ˈkiːpseɪk] S Andenken *n*
kennel [ˈkenl] S Hundehütte *f*; Hundepension *f*
kept [kept] *prät, pperf von* **keep**
kerosene [ˈkerəsiːn] S Petroleum *n*
ketchup [ˈketʃʌp] S Ketchup *n od m*
kettle [ˈketl] S Kessel *m*
key [kiː] **1** S Schlüssel *m*; (*von Tastatur*) Taste *f*; MUS Tonart *f*; (*Landkarte etc*) Zeichenerklärung *f* **2** V/T **~ (in)** IT eingeben **3** ADJ entscheidend **key-**

board S (*Computer*) Tastatur *f* **keyhole** S Schlüsselloch *n* **keypad** S IT Nummernblock *m* **keyring** S Schlüsselring *m*

kick [kɪk] **1** S Tritt *m*; SPORT Stoß *m* **2** V/T & V/I treten **kick out** V/T *umg* rausschmeißen (*of* aus) **kick-off** S SPORT Anstoß *m*

kid [kɪd] **1** S Kind *n* **2** V/T (*necken*) auf den Arm nehmen **3** V/I Witze machen; **you're ~ding** das ist doch nicht dein Ernst!; **no ~ding** aber echt!

kidnap ['kɪdnæp] V/T entführen **kidnapper** S Entführer(in) *m(f)*

kidney ['kɪdnɪ] S Niere *f* **kidney bean** S rote Bohne, Kidneybohne *f*

kill [kɪl] V/T töten; (*mit Absicht*) umbringen; (*Unkraut*) vernichten **killer** **1** S Mörder(in) *m(f)* **2** ADJ *umg* toll

kilo ⟨-s *pl*⟩ ['ki:loʊ] S Kilo *n* **kilobyte** ['kɪləbaɪt] S Kilobyte *n* **kilogram** ['kɪləgræm] S Kilogramm *n* **kilometer** [kɪ'lɑ:mətər] S Kilometer *m*; **~s per hour** Stundenkilometer *pl*

kind [kaɪnd] **1** ADJ nett, freundlich (*to* zu) **2** S Art *f*; (*Käse etc*) Sorte *f*; **what ~ of ...?** was für ein(e) ...?; **this ~ of ...** so ein(e) ...; **~ of** (*+adj*) *umg* irgendwie

kindergarten ['kɪndərgɑ:rtn] S Kindergarten *m*

kindly ['kaɪndlɪ] **1** ADJ nett, freundlich **2** ADV liebenswürdigerweise

king [kɪŋ] S König *m* **kingdom** S Königreich *n* **king-size(d)** ADJ im Großformat; (*Bett*) extra groß

kiss [kɪs] **1** S Kuss *m* **2** V/T küssen

kit [kɪt] S Ausrüstung *f*; *umg* Sachen *pl*; (*zum Zusammenbauen*) Bausatz *m*

kitchen ['kɪtʃən] S Küche *f* **kitchenware** S Küchengeschirr *n*

kite [kaɪt] S Drachen *m*

kitten ['kɪtn] S Kätzchen *n*

kiwi ['ki:wi:] S (*Frucht*) Kiwi *f*

klutz [klʌts] S *umg* Tollpatsch *m*

km *abk* = kilometers; km

knack [næk] S Dreh *m*, Trick *m*; **get/have got the ~** den Dreh herauskriegen/heraushaben

knee [ni:] S Knie *n* **kneecap** S Kniescheibe *f* **kneel** ⟨knelt *od* kneeled, knelt *od* kneeled⟩ [ni:l, nelt, ni:ld] V/I knien; (*niederknien*) sich hinknien **knelt** [nelt] *prät, pperf von* **kneel**

knew [nu:] *prät von* **know**

knife ⟨knives *pl*⟩ [naɪf, naɪvz] S Messer *n*

knit [nɪt] V/T & V/I stricken

knob [nɑ:b] S (*an Tür*) Knauf *m*; (*an Radio etc*) Knopf *m*

knock [nɑ:k] **1** V/T schlagen; (*versehentlich*) stoßen; **~ one's**

head sich den Kopf anschlagen **2** V/I klopfen (*on, at* an +*akk*) **3** S Schlag *m*; (*an Tür etc*) Klopfen *n*; **there was a ~ (at the door)** es hat geklopft **knock down** V/T (*Gegenstand*) umstoßen; (*Person*) niederschlagen; (*mit Auto etc*) anfahren; (*Gebäude*) abreißen **knock out** V/T bewusstlos schlagen; (*Boxer*) k.o. schlagen

knot [nɑːt] S Knoten *m*

know ⟨knew, known⟩ [noʊ, nuː, noʊn] V/T & V/I wissen; (*Ort etc*) kennen; (*j-n/etw*) erkennen; (*Sprache*) können; **I'll let you ~** ich sage dir Bescheid; **I ~ some German** ich kann etwas Deutsch; **get to ~ sb** j-n kennenlernen; **be ~n as** bekannt sein als **know of** V/T kennen; **not that I ~** nicht dass ich wüsste **know-how** S Kenntnis *f*, Know-how *n* **know-it-all** S *umg* Klugscheißer *m* **knowledge** [ˈnɑːlɪdʒ] S Wissen *n*; (*eines Faches*) Kenntnisse *pl*; **to (the best of) my ~** meines Wissens **known** [noʊn] *pperf von* **know**

knuckle [ˈnʌkl] S (Finger)knöchel *m*; GASTR Hachse *f*

kook [kuːk] S *umg* Verrückte(r) *m/f(m)*

kph *abk* = kilometers per hour; km/h

KS *abk* = Kansas

KY *abk* = Kentucky

L

LA **1** *abk* = Los Angeles **2** *abk* = Louisianna

lab [læb] S *umg* Labor *n*

label [ˈleɪbl] **1** S Etikett *n*; (*an Tasche etc*) Anhänger *m*; (*klebend*) Aufkleber *m*; (*Plattenfirma*) Label *n* **2** V/T etikettieren; *pej* abstempeln

labor [ˈleɪbər] S Arbeit *f*; MED Wehen *pl*; **be in ~** Wehen haben

laboratory [ˈlæbrətɔːrɪ] S Labor *n*

Labor Day S Tag *m* der Arbeit (*1. Montag im September*) **laborer** S Arbeiter(in) *m(f)* **labor union** S Gewerkschaft *f*

lace [leɪs] **1** S (*Stoff*) Spitze *f*; (*Schuh*) Schnürsenkel *m* **2** V/T **~ (up)** zuschnüren

lack [læk] **1** V/T & V/I **be ~ing** fehlen; **we ~ the time** uns fehlt die Zeit **2** S Mangel *m* (*of* an +*dat*)

ladder [ˈlædər] S Leiter *f*; (*in Strumpfhose*) Laufmasche *f*

laden [ˈleɪdn] ADJ beladen (*with* mit)

ladies' room [ˈleɪdɪzruːm] S Damentoilette *f* **lady** [ˈleɪdɪ] S Dame *f* **ladybug** S Marienkäfer *m*

lag [læg] V/I **~ (behind)** zurück-

liegen
lager ['lɑ:gər] S helles Bier
laid [leɪd] *prät, pperf von* **lay**; **get ~** *umg (Sex haben)* flachgelegt werden; **get ~ off** *(Job)* entlassen werden **laid-back** ADJ *umg* cool, gelassen
lain [leɪn] *pperf von* **lie**
lake [leɪk] S See *m*
lamb [læm] S Lamm *n*; Lammfleisch *n* **lamb chop** S Lammkotelett *n*
lame [leɪm] ADJ lahm; *(Ausrede)* faul; *(Argument)* schwach
lamp [læmp] S Lampe *f*;
land [lænd] **1** S Land *n* **2** V/I *(Person)* an Land gehen; FLUG landen **landing** S Landung *f*; *(auf Treppe)* Treppenabsatz *m* **landlady** S Hauswirtin *f*, Vermieterin *f* **landlord** S Hauswirt *m*, Vermieter *m* **landowner** S Grundbesitzer(in) *m(f)* **landscape** S Landschaft *f* **landslide** S GEO Erdrutsch *m*
lane [leɪn] S enge Landstraße, Weg *m*; *(in Stadt)* Gasse *f*; *(Autobahn etc)* Spur *f*; SPORT Bahn *f*; **get in ~** *(als Autofahrer)* sich einordnen
language ['læŋgwɪdʒ] S Sprache *f*
lantern ['læntərn] S Laterne *f*
lap [læp] S Schoß *m*; *(bei Rennen)* Runde *f* **laptop** ['læptɑ:p] S Laptop *m*
large [lɑ:rdʒ] ADJ groß; **by and ~** im Großen und Ganzen
largely ADV zum größten Teil
large-scale ADJ groß angelegt, Groß-
laser ['leɪzər] S Laser *m*
lash out [læʃ'aʊt] V/I um sich schlagen; *(Geld ausgeben)* sich in Unkosten stürzen *(on* mit)
lasso ⟨-s, -es *pl*⟩ ['læsoʊ] S Lasso *n*
last [læst] **1** ADJ letzte(r, s); **the ~ but one** der/die/das vorletzte; **~ night** gestern Abend **2** ADV zuletzt; das letzte Mal; **at ~** endlich **3** S *(Person)* Letzte(r) *m/f(m)*; *(Sache)* Letzte(s) *n* **4** V/I dauern; *(Person)* durchhalten; *(Nahrung)* sich halten; *(Geld, Vorräte)* ausreichen **lasting** ADJ dauerhaft; *(Eindrücke)* nachhaltig **lastly** ADV schließlich **last name** S Nachname *m*
late [leɪt] **1** ADJ spät; zu spät; *(Zug)* verspätet; *(Ehemann etc)* verstorben; **be ~** zu spät kommen; *(Flugzeug etc)* Verspätung haben **2** ADV spät; *(ankommen)* zu spät **late availability flight** S Last-Minute-Flug *m* **lately** ADV in letzter Zeit **later** ['leɪtər] ADJ & ADV später; **see you ~** bis später **latest** ['leɪtəst] **1** ADJ späteste(r, s); *(Nachrichten)* neueste(r, s) **2** S **the ~** das Neueste; **at the ~** spätestens
Latin ['lætɪn] **1** S Latein *n* **2** ADJ lateinisch **Latina** [læ'ti:nə] S Amerikanerin *f* latein-

amerikanischer Abstammung **Latin America** [lætɪnəˈmerɪkə] S Lateinamerika *n* **Latin-American** **1** ADJ lateinamerikanisch **2** S Lateinamerikaner(in) *m(f)* **Latino** ⟨-s *pl*⟩ [læˈtiːnoʊ] S Amerikaner *m* lateinamerikanischer Abstammung

latter [ˈlætər] ADJ (*von zweien*) letztere(r, s); (*Teil, Jahre*) letzte(r, s), später

Latvia [ˈlætvɪə] S Lettland *n*

Latvian [ˈlætvɪən] **1** ADJ lettisch **2** S (*Person*) Lette *m*, Lettin *f*; (*Sprache*) Lettisch *n*

laugh [læf] **1** S Lachen *n* **2** V/I lachen (*at, about* über *+akk*); **~ at sb** sich über j-n lustig machen **laughter** [ˈlæftər] S Gelächter *n*

launch [lɒːntʃ] **1** S (*Schiff*) Stapellauf *m*; (*Rakete*) Abschuss *m*; (*Produkt*) Markteinführung *f*; (*Festivität*) Eröffnungsfeier *f* **2** V/T (*Schiff*) vom Stapel lassen; (*Rakete*) abschießen; (*Produkt*) einführen; (*Projekt*) in Gang setzen

laundromat [ˈlɒːndrəmæt] S Waschsalon *m* **laundry** [ˈlɒːndrɪ] S (*Betrieb*) Wäscherei *f*; (*schmutzige Kleidung*) Wäsche *f*

lavatory [ˈlævətɔːrɪ] S Toilette *f*

lavender [ˈlævɪndər] S Lavendel *m*

lavish [ˈlævɪʃ] ADJ verschwenderisch; (*Ausstattung*) üppig; (*Geschenk*) großzügig

law [lɒː] S Gesetz *n*; (*Rechtssystem*) Recht *n*; (*Studienfach*) Jura; (*von Sportart*) Regel *f*; **against the ~** gesetzwidrig **law-abiding** ADJ gesetzestreu **law court** S Gerichtshof *m* **law firm** S Anwaltskanzlei *f* **lawful** ADJ rechtmäßig

lawn [lɒːn] S Rasen *m* **lawn-mower** S Rasenmäher *m*

law school S juristische Fakultät **lawsuit** [ˈlɒːsuːt] S Prozess *m* **lawyer** [ˈlɒːjər] S Rechtsanwalt *m*, Rechtsanwältin *f*

laxative [ˈlæksətɪv] S Abführmittel *n*

lay [leɪ] **1** *prät von* **lie** **2** ⟨laid, laid⟩ [leɪd] V/T legen; *vulg* poppen, bumsen; (*Ei*) legen **3** ADJ Laien- **lay down** V/T hinlegen **lay on** V/T (*Essen, Gastfreundschaft*) anbieten; (*organisieren*) veranstalten, bereitstellen

layer [ˈleɪər] S Schicht *f*

layout [ˈleɪaʊt] S Gestaltung *f*; (*von Buch etc*) Layout *n*

laziness [ˈleɪzɪnəs] S Faulheit *f*

lazy [ˈleɪzɪ] ADJ faul; (*Tag, Zeit*) gemütlich

lb *abk* = pound; Pfd.

lead **1** [led] S Blei *n* **2** ⟨led, led⟩ [liːd, led] *v/t & v/i* führen; leiten; **~ the way** vorangehen **3** [liːd] S Führung *f*, Vorsprung *m* (*over* vor *+dat*); THEAT Hauptrolle *f*; ELEK Lei-

tung *f* **lead astray** VT irreführen **lead to** VT hinführen nach; führen zu
leaded ['ledəd] ADJ verbleit
leader ['li:dər] S Führer(in) *m(f)*, Vorsitzende(r) *m/f(m)*, Leiter(in) *m(f)*; SPORT der/die Erste; Tabellenführer *m* **leadership** ['li:dərʃɪp] S Führung *f*
lead-free [led'fri:] ADJ bleifrei
leading ['li:dɪŋ] ADJ führend, wichtig
leaf ⟨leaves *pl*⟩ [li:f, li:vz] S Blatt *n* **leaflet** ['li:flət] S Prospekt *m*, Flugblatt *n*, Merkblatt *n*
league [li:g] S Bund *m*; SPORT Liga *f*
leak [li:k] **1** S undichte Stelle; Leck *n* **2** VI undicht sein; auslaufen **leaky** ADJ undicht
lean [li:n] **1** ADJ mager **2** VI sich neigen; **~ against sth** sich an etw *akk* lehnen; **~ on sth** sich auf etw *akk* stützen **3** VT lehnen (*on, against* an *+akk*) **lean back** VI sich zurücklehnen **lean toward(s)** VT tendieren zu
leap [li:p] **1** S Sprung *m* **2** ⟨leapt *od* leaped, leapt *od* leaped⟩ [lept, li:pt] *v/i* springen **leap year** S Schaltjahr *n*
learn [lɜ:rn] VT & VI lernen; erfahren; **~ (how) to swim** schwimmen lernen **learner** S Anfänger(in) *m(f)*
lease [li:s] **1** S Pacht *f*, Pachtvertrag *m*; Miete *f*, Mietvertrag *m* **2** VT pachten; mieten
lease out VT vermieten
leash [li:ʃ] S Leine *f*
least [li:st] **1** ADJ wenigste(r, s); (*Sorge etc*) geringste(r, s) **2** ADV am wenigsten; **~ expensive** billigste(r, s) **3** S **the ~** das Mindeste; **not in the ~** nicht im geringsten; **at ~** wenigstens; (*mit Zahl*) mindestens
leather ['leðər] **1** S Leder *n* **2** ADJ ledern, Leder-
leave [li:v] **1** S Urlaub *m*; **on ~** auf Urlaub **2** ⟨left, left⟩ [left] *v/t* (*Ort, Person*) verlassen; (*Nachricht, Narbe etc*) hinterlassen; (*nach Tod*) hinterlassen (*to sb* j-m); (*anvertrauen*) überlassen (*to sb* j-m); **be left** übrig bleiben; **~ me alone** lass mich in Ruhe! **3** VI (weg)gehen, (weg)fahren; (*bei Reise*) abreisen; (*Bus, Zug*) abfahren (*for* nach) **leave behind** VT zurücklassen; (*Narbe*) hinterlassen **leave out** VT auslassen; (*Person*) ausschließen (*of* von)
leaves [li:vz] *pl von* **leaf**
lecture ['lektʃər] S Vortrag *m*; (*an Universität*) Vorlesung *f*; **give a ~** einen Vortrag/eine Vorlesung halten
led [led] *prät, pperf von* **lead**
LED *abk* = light-emitting diode; Leuchtdiode *f*
leek [li:k] S Lauch *m*
left [left] **1** *prät, pperf von* **leave** **2** ADJ linke(r, s) **3** ADV links; (*Bewegung, Richtung*)

nach links **4** S linke Seite; **the Left** POL die Linke; **on/to the ~** links (*of* von) **left-hand** ADJ linke(r, s); **~ bend** Linkskurve *f* **left-handed** ADJ linkshändig

leftovers S PL Reste *pl*

left-wing ADJ POL linksgerichtet; Links-

leg [leg] S Bein *n*; (*von Fleisch*) Keule *f*

legacy ['legəsı] S Erbe *n*, Erbschaft *f*

legal ['li:gəl] ADJ Rechts-, rechtlich; (*erlaubt*) legal; (*Obergrenze, Alter*) gesetzlich **legalize** V/T legalisieren **legally** ADV legal

legible ['ledʒəbl] ADJ leserlich

legislation [ledʒıs'leıʃn] S Gesetze *pl*

legitimate [lı'dʒıtəmət] ADJ rechtmäßig, legitim

leg room ['legrʊm] S Beinfreiheit *f*

leisure ['li:ʒər] **1** S Freizeit *f* **2** ADJ Freizeit-; **~ time** Freizeit *f* **leisurely** ['li:ʒərlı] ADJ gemächlich

lemon ['lemən] S Zitrone *f* **lemonade** [lemə'neıd] S Limonade *f*

lend ⟨lent, lent⟩ [lend, lent] V/T leihen

length [leŋθ] S Länge *f*; **4 meters in ~** 4 Meter lang; **what ~ is it?** wie lange ist es? **lengthy** ADJ sehr lange; (*Behandlung*) langwierig

lens [lenz] S Linse *f*; FOTO Objektiv *n*

lent [lent] *prät, pperf von* **lend**

Lent [lent] S Fastenzeit *f*

lentil ['lentl] S BOT Linse *f*

Leo ⟨-s *pl*⟩ ['li:oʊ] S ASTROL Löwe *m*

lept [lept] *prät, pperf von* **leap**

lesbian ['lezbıən] **1** ADJ lesbisch **2** S Lesbe *f*

less [les] ADJ & ADV & S weniger; **~ and ~** immer weniger; (*vorkommen*) immer seltener **lessen** ['lesn] **1** V/I abnehmen, nachlassen **2** V/T verringern; (*Schmerzen*) lindern

lesson ['lesn] S (*in Schule*) Stunde *f*; (*in Lehrbuch*) Lektion *f*; *fig* Lehre *f*; REL Lesung *f*; **~s start at 9** der Unterricht beginnt um 9

let ⟨let, let⟩ [let] V/T lassen; **~ sb have sth** j-m etw geben; **~'s go** gehen wir; **~ go (of sth)** (etw) loslassen **let down** V/T herunterlassen; im Stich lassen, enttäuschen **let in** V/T hereinlassen **let out** V/T hinauslassen; (*Schrei*) ausstoßen

lethal ['li:θəl] ADJ tödlich

let's *kontr von* **let us**

letter ['letər] S Buchstabe *m*; (*Postsendung*) Brief *m*; (*offiziell*) Schreiben *n*

lettuce ['letəs] S Kopfsalat *m*

leukemia [lu:'ki:mıə] S Leukämie *f*

level ['levl] **1** ADJ (*horizontal*) waagerecht; (*Boden*) eben;

(*Läufer etc*) auf selber Höhe **2** ADV (*laufen etc*) auf gleicher Höhe, gleich auf; **draw ~** (*in Rennen*) gleichziehen (*with* mit); (*Football etc*) ausgleichen **3** S Höhe *f*; (*Standard*) Niveau *n* **4** V/T (*Boden*) einebnen

lever ['levər] S Hebel *m*; *fig* Druckmittel *n*

liability [laɪə'bɪlətɪ] S Haftung *f*; (*Problem*) Belastung *f*; (*Pflicht; finanziell: Schuld*) Verpflichtung *f* **liable** ['laɪəbl] ADJ **be ~ for sth** für etw haften

liar ['laɪər] S Lügner(in) *m(f)*

liberal ['lɪbərəl] ADJ (*Portion etc*) großzügig; (*tolerant; a. politisch*) liberal

liberate ['lɪbəreɪt] V/T befreien

liberty ['lɪbərtɪ] S Freiheit *f*

Libra ['li:brə] S ASTROL Waage *f*

library ['laɪbrerɪ] S Bibliothek *f*; Bücherei *f*

license ['laɪsəns] **1** S Genehmigung *f*; WIRTSCH Lizenz *f*; (*Fahrerlaubnis*) Führerschein *m* **2** V/T genehmigen **licensed** ADJ (*Restaurant etc*) mit Schankerlaubnis **license number** S AUTO Kennzeichen *n* **license plate** S AUTO Nummernschild *n* **licensing hours** S PL Ausschankzeiten *pl*

lick [lɪk] **1** V/T lecken **2** S Lecken *n*

licorice ['lɪkərɪs] S Lakritze *f*

lid [lɪd] S Deckel *m*; (*am Auge*) Lid *n*

lie [laɪ] **1** S Lüge *f* **2** V/I lügen; **~ to sb** j-n belügen **3** ⟨lay, lain⟩ [leɪ, leɪn] *v/i* (*an Ort, Stelle*) liegen; (*auf Liege*) sich legen; (*Schnee*) liegen bleiben **lie down** V/I sich hinlegen

life ⟨lives *pl*⟩ [laɪf, laɪvz] S Leben *n*; **get ~** lebenslänglich bekommen **lifeboat** S Rettungsboot *n* **lifeguard** S Bademeister(in) *m(f)*, Rettungsschwimmer(in) *m(f)* **life insurance** S Lebensversicherung *f* **life jacket** S Schwimmweste *f* **lifeless** ADJ leblos **life preserver** S Rettungsring *m*; Schwimmweste *f* **life-saving** ADJ lebensrettend **life-size(d)** ADJ in Lebensgröße **lifestyle** S Lebensstil *m* **lifetime** S Lebenszeit *f*

lift [lɪft] V/T (hoch)heben; (*Verbot*) aufheben **lift up** V/T hochheben

ligament ['lɪgəmənt] S Band *n*

light [laɪt] **1** ⟨lit *od* lighted, lit *od* lighted⟩ [lɪt, 'laɪtəd] V/T beleuchten; (*Feuer*) anzünden **2** S Licht *n*; Lampe *f*; **~s** *pl* AUTO Beleuchtung *f*; (*Straßenverkehr*) Ampel *f*; **in (the) ~ of** angesichts *+gen* **3** ADJ hell; (*nicht schwer*) leicht; (*Strafe*) milde **light up** **1** V/T beleuchten; (*Zigarette*) anzünden **2** V/I (*Lichter, Augen etc*) aufleuchten **light bulb** S Glühbirne *f* **lighten** ['laɪtn] **1** V/I hell wer-

den **2** VT erhellen; (*Last*) leichter machen; *fig* erleichtern **lighter** ['laɪtər] S Feuerzeug *n* **light-hearted** ADJ unbeschwert **lighthouse** S Leuchtturm *m* **lighting** S Beleuchtung *f* **lightly** ADV leicht
lightning ['laɪtnɪŋ] S Blitz *m*
likable ['laɪkəbl] ADJ sympathisch **like** [laɪk] **1** VT mögen, gernhaben; **he ~s swimming** er schwimmt gern; **would you ~ ...?** hättest du/hätten Sie gern ...?; **I'd ~ to go home** ich möchte nach Hause (gehen); **I don't ~ the movie** der Film gefällt mir nicht **2** PRÄP wie; **what's it ~?** wie ist es?; **he looks ~ you** er sieht dir/Ihnen ähnlich; **~ that/this** so **likeable** ['laɪkəbl] ADJ sympathisch
likely ['laɪklɪ] ADJ wahrscheinlich
like-minded [laɪk'maɪndəd] ADJ gleich gesinnt **likewise** ['laɪkwaɪz] ADV ebenfalls
liking ['laɪkɪŋ] S (*zu Person*) Zuneigung *f*, Vorliebe *f* (*for* für)
lilac ['laɪlək] **1** S Flieder *m* **2** ADJ fliederfarben
lima bean ['laɪməbi:n] S Limabohne *f*
limb [lɪm] S Glied *n*
lime [laɪm] S (*Baum*) Linde *f*; (*Frucht*) Limone *f*; (*Substanz*) Kalk *m* **limelight** S *fig* Rampenlicht *n*
limit ['lɪmət] **1** S Grenze *f*; (*Schadstoffe*) Grenzwert *m*; **be over the ~** (*Geschwindigkeit*) das Tempolimit überschreiten; (*wegen Alkoholkonsums*) fahruntüchtig sein **2** VT beschränken (*to* auf *+akk*); (*Ausgaben*) einschränken **limitation** [lɪmə'teɪʃən] S Beschränkung *f*; Einschränkung *f* **limited** ADJ begrenzt
limo ⟨-s *pl*⟩ ['lɪmoʊ] S große Limousine
limp [lɪmp] **1** VI hinken **2** ADJ schlaff
line [laɪn] **1** S Linie *f*; (*von Text*) Zeile *f*; (*im Gesicht*) Falte *f*; (*von Menschen etc*) Reihe *f*; (*von Wartenden*) Schlange *f*; BAHN Bahnlinie *f*; TEL Leitung *f*; (*von Artikeln*) Kollektion *f*; **hold the ~** bleiben Sie am Apparat; **stand in ~** Schlange stehen **2** VT (*Kleidung*) füttern; (*Straßen*) säumen **line up** VI sich aufstellen; (*in Warteschlange*) sich anstellen
linen ['lɪnən] S Leinen *n*; (*Betttücher etc*) Wäsche *f*
liner ['laɪnər] S Überseedampfer *m*, Passagierschiff *n*
lingerie [lɑ:ndʒə'reɪ] S Damenunterwäsche *f*
link [lɪŋk] **1** S Verbindung *f*; (*von Kette*) Glied *n*; (*zu Person*) Beziehung *f* (*with* zu); (*zwischen Ereignissen*) Zusammenhang *m* **2** VT verbinden
lion ['laɪən] S Löwe *m*
lip [lɪp] S Lippe *f* **lipstick** S

Lippenstift *m*
liqueur [lɪ'kjʊr] S Likör *m*
liquid ['lɪkwəd] **1** S Flüssigkeit *f* **2** ADJ flüssig
liquor ['lɪkər] S Spirituosen *pl*
list [lɪst] **1** S Liste *f* **2** V/T auflisten, aufzählen
listen ['lɪsn] V/I zuhören **listen to** V/T (*j-m*) zuhören *+dat*; (*Radio*) hören; (*Rat*) hören auf
listener S Zuhörer(in) *m(f)*; (*Radio*) Hörer(in) *m(f)*
lit [lɪt] *prät, pperf von* **light**
liter ['liːtər] S Liter *m*
literally ['lɪtərəlɪ] ADV (*übersetzen etc*) wörtlich; (*zur Betonung*) wirklich, geradezu
literary ['lɪtərerɪ] ADJ literarisch; (*Kritiker, Zeitschrift etc*) Literatur- **literature** ['lɪtərətʃər] S Literatur *f*; (*Broschüren*) Informationsmaterial *n*
Lithuania [lɪθjʊ'eɪnɪə] S Litauen *n* **Lithuanian** [lɪθjʊ'eɪnɪən] **1** ADJ litauisch **2** S (*Person*) Litauer *m*, Litauerin *f*; (*Sprache*) Litauisch *n*
litter ['lɪtər] **1** S Abfälle *pl*; (*von Tieren*) Wurf *m* **2** V/T **be ~ed with** übersät sein mit **litter basket** S Abfallkorb *m*
little ['lɪtl] **1** ADJ ⟨smaller, smallest⟩ klein; (*mengenmäßig*) wenig; **a ~ while ago** vor kurzer Zeit **2** ADV & S ⟨fewer, fewest⟩ wenig; **a ~** ein bisschen, ein wenig; **for as ~ as $5** ab nur 5 Dollar; **~ by ~** nach und nach **little finger** S kleiner Finger
live **1** [laɪv] ADJ lebendig; ELEK geladen, unter Strom; TV live **2** [lɪv] V/I leben; (*am Leben bleiben*) überleben; (*in Ort, in Haus*) wohnen **3** V/T (*ein Leben*) führen **live on** **1** V/I weiterleben **2** V/T **~ sth** von etw leben; sich von etw ernähren **live up to** V/T (*seinem Ruf*) gerecht werden *+dat*; (*Erwartungen*) entsprechen *+dat* **live with** V/T (*Eltern*) wohnen bei; (*Partner*) zusammenleben mit; (*Schwierigkeiten*) sich abfinden mit **lively** ['laɪvlɪ] ADJ lebhaft
liver ['lɪvər] S Leber *f*
lives [laɪvz] *pl von* **life** **livestock** ['laɪvstɑːk] S Vieh *n*
living ['lɪvɪŋ] **1** S Lebensunterhalt *m*; **what do you do for a ~?** was machen Sie beruflich? **2** ADJ lebend **living room** S Wohnzimmer *n*
lizard ['lɪzərd] S ZOOL Eidechse *f*
load [loʊd] **1** S Last *f*; (*von LKW etc*) Ladung *f*; TECH *fig* Belastung *f*; **~s of, a ~ of** *umg* massenhaft **2** V/T (*Fahrzeug etc*) beladen; IT laden; (*Film in Kamera*) einlegen
loaf ⟨loaves *pl*⟩ [loʊf, loʊvz] S **a ~ of bread** ein (Laib) Brot
loan [loʊn] **1** S Leihgabe *f*; FIN Darlehen *n*; **on ~** geliehen **2** V/T leihen (*to sb* j-m)
loaves [loʊvz] *pl von* **loaf**
lobby ['lɑːbɪ] S Vorhalle *f*; POL

Lobby *f*
lobster ['lɑ:bstər] S Hummer *m*
local ['loʊkəl] **1** ADJ (*Verkehr, Zeit etc*) Orts-; (*Radio, Zeitung*) Lokal-; (*Behörden*) Kommunal-; (*Betäubung*) örtlich; **~ call** TEL Ortsgespräch *n*; **~ train** Nahverkehrszug *m* **2** S **the ~s** *pl* die Ortsansässigen *pl* **locally** ADV örtlich, am Ort
locate [loʊ'keɪt] V/T (*Lage*) ausfindig machen; (*an einem Ort*) errichten; **be ~d** sich befinden (*in, at* in +*dat*) **location** [loʊ'keɪʃən] S (*Position*) Lage *f*; FILM Drehort *m*
lock [lɑ:k] **1** S Schloss *n*; SCHIFF Schleuse *f*; (*von Haar*) Locke *f* **2** V/T (*Tür etc*) abschließen **3** V/I (*Tür etc*) sich abschließen lassen; (*Räder*) blockieren **lock in** V/T einschließen, einsperren **lock out** V/T aussperren **lock up** V/T (*Haus etc*) abschließen; (*Person*) einsperren **locker** ['lɑ:kər] S Schließfach *n* **locker room** S Umkleideraum *m* **locksmith** ['lɑ:ksmɪθ] S Schlosser(in) *m(f)*
locust ['loʊkəst] S Heuschrecke *f*
lodge [lɑ:dʒ] V/I in Untermiete wohnen (*with* bei) **lodger** S Untermieter(in) *m(f)* **lodging** S Unterkunft *f*
loft [lɑ:ft] S Dachboden *m*
log [lɑ:g] S Klotz *m*; SCHIFF Log *n* **log in** V/I IT sich einloggen **log off** V/I IT sich ausloggen **log on** V/I IT sich einloggen **log out** V/I IT sich ausloggen **log cabin** S Blockhaus *n*
logic ['lɑ:dʒɪk] S Logik *f* **logical** ADJ logisch
loin [lɔɪn] S Lende *f*
loiter ['lɔɪtər] V/I sich herumtreiben
loneliness ['loʊnlɪnəs] S Einsamkeit *f* **lonely** ['loʊnlɪ], **lonesome** ['loʊnsəm] ADJ einsam
long [lɑ:ŋ] **1** ADJ lang; (*Entfernung*) weit; **it's a ~ way** es ist weit (*to* nach); **for a ~ time** lange **2** ADV lange; **not for ~** nicht lange; **~ ago** vor langer Zeit; **before ~** bald; **all day ~** den ganzen Tag; **no ~er** nicht mehr; **as ~ as** solange **3** V/I sich sehnen (*for* nach); (*auf Rückkehr etc*) sehnsüchtig warten (*for* auf) **long-distance call** S Ferngespräch *n* **long-haul flight** S Langstreckenflug *m* **longing** S Sehnsucht *f* (*for* nach) **long jump** S Weitsprung *m* **long-range** ADJ Langstrecken-, Fern- **long-term** ADJ langfristig; (*Parkplatz etc*) Langzeit-
look [lʊk] **1** S Blick *m*; **~(s)** (*pl*) Aussehen *n*; **I'll have a ~** ich schau mal nach; **have a ~ at sth** sich etw ansehen; **can I have a ~?** darf ich mal sehen? **2** V/I schauen, gucken; (*kon-*

trollierend) nachsehen; (*gut, schlecht etc*) aussehen; **(I'm) just ~ing** ich schaue nur; **it ~s like rain** es sieht nach Regen aus **3** VT **~ what you've done** sieh dir mal an, was du da angestellt hast; (*aussehen*) **he ~s his age** man sieht ihm sein Alter an; **~ one's best** sehr vorteilhaft aussehen **look after** VT sorgen für; (*Kind etc*) aufpassen auf *+akk* **look at** VT ansehen, anschauen **look back** VI sich umsehen; *fig* zurückblicken **look down on** VT *fig* herabsehen auf *+akk* **look for** VT suchen **look forward to** VT sich freuen auf *+akk* **look into** VT (*Verbrechen etc*) untersuchen **look out** VI hinaussehen (*of the window* zum Fenster); Ausschau halten (*for* nach); **~!** Vorsicht! **look up** **1** VI aufsehen **2** VT (*Wort*) nachschlagen

loop [lu:p] S Schleife *f*

loose [lu:s] ADJ locker; (*Knopf*) lose **loosen** VT lockern, flexibilisieren; (*Knoten*) lösen

lord [lɔ:rd] S (*Herrscher*) Herr *m*; **the Lord (God)** Gott der Herr

lose ⟨lost, lost⟩ [lu:z, lɑ:st] **1** VT verlieren; **~ weight** abnehmen **2** VI verlieren; (*Uhr*) nachgehen **loser** S Verlierer(in) *m(f)* **loss** [lɑ:s] S Verlust *m* **lost** [lɑ:st] **1** *prät, pperf von* lose; **we're ~** wir haben uns verlaufen **2** ADJ verloren **lost-and-found** S Fundbüro *n*

lot [lɑ:t] S *umg* Menge *f*; Haufen *m*; **a ~** viel(e); **a ~ of money** viel Geld; **~s of people** viele Leute; **the (whole) ~** alles; **(parking) ~** Parkplatz *m*

lotion ['loʊʃən] S Lotion *f*

lottery ['lɑ:tərɪ] S Lotterie *f*

loud [laʊd] ADJ laut; (*Farbe*) schreiend **loudspeaker** S Lautsprecher *m*; (*von Stereoanlage*) Box *f*

lounge [laʊndʒ] **1** S (*im Hotel*) Aufenthaltsraum *m*; (*Flughafen*) Warteraum *m* **2** VI sich herumlümmeln; **~ in the sun** sich sonnen

lousy ['laʊzɪ] ADJ *umg* lausig

lovable ['lʌvəbl] ADJ liebenswert **love** [lʌv] **1** S Liebe *f* (*of* zu); SPORT null; **be in ~** verliebt sein (*with sb* in j-n); **fall in ~** sich verlieben (*with sb* in j-n); **make ~** (*sexuell*) sich lieben; **make ~ to** (*od* **with**) **sb** mit j-m schlafen; **give her my ~** grüße sie von mir; **~, Tom** liebe Grüße, Tom **2** VT lieben; (*Tätigkeit etc*) sehr gerne mögen; **~ to do sth** etw für sein Leben gerne tun; **I'd ~ a cup of coffee** ich hätte liebend gern eine Tasse Kaffee **love affair** S (Liebes)verhältnis *n*

lovely ['lʌvlɪ] ADJ schön, wunderschön; (*voller Charme*) reizend **lover** ['lʌvər] S Liebhaber(in) *m(f)* **loving** ADJ liebevoll

low [loʊ] **1** ADJ niedrig; (*Stimme, Ausschnitt etc*) tief; (*Qualität*) schlecht; (*Stimme, Musik*) leise; (*psychisch*) niedergeschlagen; **we're ~ on gas** wir haben kaum noch Benzin **2** S METEO Tief *n* **low-calorie** ADJ kalorienarm **low-emission** ADJ schadstoffarm **lower** ['loʊər] **1** ADJ niedriger; (*Stockwerk etc*) untere(r, s) **2** V/T herunterlassen; (*Augen, Preise*) senken; (*Druck*) verringern **low-fat** ADJ fettarm **low tide** [loʊ'taɪd] S Ebbe *f*

loyal ['lɔɪəl] ADJ treu **loyalty** S Treue *f*

luck [lʌk] S Glück *n*; **bad ~** Pech *n* **luckily** ADV glücklicherweise, zum Glück **lucky** ADJ (*Zahl, Tag etc*) Glücks-; **be ~** Glück haben

luggage ['lʌgɪdʒ] S Gepäck *n* **luggage compartment** S Gepäckraum *m* **luggage rack** S BAHN Gepäckablage *f*; AUTO Gepäckträger *m*

lukewarm ['lu:kwɔ:rm] ADJ lauwarm

lumber ['lʌmbər] S Bau-, Nutzholz *n* **lumberjack** ['lʌmbərdʒæk] S Holzfäller *m*

luminous ['lu:mənəs] ADJ leuchtend

lump [lʌmp] S Klumpen *m*; MED Schwellung *f*; (*in Brust*) Knoten *m*; (*Zucker*) Stück *n* **lump sum** S Pauschalsumme *f*

lunatic ['lu:nətɪk] **1** ADJ wahnsinnig **2** S Wahnsinnige(r) *m/f(m)*

lunch [lʌntʃ] S Mittagessen *n*; **have ~** zu Mittag essen **lunch break**, **lunch hour** S Mittagspause *f* **lunchtime** S Mittagszeit *f*

lung [lʌŋ] S Lunge *f*

lust [lʌst] S (sinnliche) Begierde (*for* nach)

Luxembourg ['lʌksəmbɜ:rg] S Luxemburg *n*; **from ~** luxemburgisch; **he's from ~** er ist Luxemburger **Luxembourger** S Luxemburger(in) *m(f)* **Luxembourgian** ADJ luxemburgisch

luxurious [ləkˈʃʊriəs] ADJ luxuriös, Luxus- **luxury** ['lʌkʃəri] S Luxus *m*

lynx [lɪŋks] S Luchs *m*

lyrics ['lɪrɪks] S PL Liedtext *m*

M

m *abk* = meter; m

M *abk* = medium; (*Größe*) M

ma [mɑ:] S *umg* Mama *f*

MA *abk* = Massachusetts

ma'am [mæm] S *höfliche Anrede für eine Frau, meist nicht*

übersetzt
machine [məˈʃiːn] S Maschine *f* **machinery** [məˈʃiːnərɪ] S Maschinen *pl*; *fig* Apparat *m*
mackerel [ˈmækrəl] S Makrele *f*
mad [mæd] ADJ wahnsinnig, verrückt; (*Hund*) tollwütig; (*verärgert*) wütend, sauer (*at* auf *+akk*); *umg* **~ about** verrückt nach
madam [ˈmædəm] S gnädige Frau
made [meɪd] *prät, pperf von* make
madly [ˈmædlɪ] ADV wie verrückt; (*total, extrem*) wahnsinnig **madman** ‹-men *pl*› S Verrückte(r) *m* **madness** [ˈmædnəs] S Wahnsinn *m*
magazine [ˈmægəziːn] S Zeitschrift *f*
magic [ˈmædʒɪk] **1** S Magie *f*, Zauberei *f*; *fig* Zauber *m* **2** ADJ Zauber-; (*Kräfte*) magisch **magician** [məˈdʒɪʃən] S Zauberer *m*, Zaub(r)erin *f*
magnet [ˈmægnət] S Magnet *m* **magnetic** [mægˈnetɪk] ADJ magnetisch
magnificent, magnificently [mægˈnɪfəsənt, -lɪ] ADJ & ADV herrlich, großartig
magnify [ˈmægnəfaɪ] V/T vergrößern **magnifying glass** S Vergrößerungsglas *n*, Lupe *f*
maid [meɪd] S Dienstmädchen *n* **maiden name** S Mädchenname *m*
mail [meɪl] **1** S Post *f*; (*Internet*) Mail *f* **2** V/T (*als Post*) aufgeben; (*versenden*) mit der Post® schicken (*to* an *+akk*) **mailbox** S Briefkasten *m*; IT Mailbox *f* **mailing list** S Adressenliste *f* **mailman** ‹-men *pl*› S Briefträger *m* **mail order firm** S Versandhaus *n*
main [meɪn] **1** ADJ Haupt- **2** S (*Rohr*) Hauptleitung *f* **mainland** S Festland *n* **mainly** ADV hauptsächlich **main road** S Hauptverkehrsstraße *f* **main street** S Hauptstraße *f*
maintain [meɪnˈteɪn] V/T (*Beziehung etc*) aufrechterhalten; (*Maschine, Straße*) instand halten; (*Flugzeug etc*) warten **maintenance** [ˈmeɪntənəns] S Instandhaltung *f*; TECH Wartung *f*
majestic [məˈdʒestɪk] ADJ majestätisch
major [ˈmeɪdʒər] **1** ADJ größer, groß; Haupt-; (*Stadt etc*) bedeutend, wichtig; MUS **A ~** A-Dur *n* **2** V/I **~ in sth** etw als Hauptfach studieren **3** S (*an der Uni*) Hauptfach *n* **majority** [məˈdʒɑːrətɪ] S Mehrheit *f* **major league** S SPORT oberste Spielklasse
make [meɪk] **1** S Marke *f* **2** ‹made, made› [meɪd] *v/t* machen; (*Produkt*) herstellen; (*Kleid*) nähen; (*Suppe etc*) zube-

reiten; (*Kuchen etc*) backen; (*Tee etc*) kochen; (*Rede*) halten; (*Geld*) verdienen; (*Entscheidung*) treffen; **it's made of gold** es ist aus Gold; **~ sb do sth** j-n dazu bringen, etw zu tun; (*mit Gewalt, Druck*) j-n zwingen, etw zu tun **make for** V/T zusteuern auf +*akk* **make of** V/T (*denken über*) halten von **make off** V/I sich davonmachen (*with* mit) **make out** 1 V/T (*Scheck*) ausstellen; (*Liste*) aufstellen; (*begreifen*) verstehen; (*sehen*) ausmachen 2 V/I *umg* knutschen **make up** 1 V/T (*Team etc*) bilden; (*Gesicht*) schminken; (*Geschichte*) erfinden; **~ one's mind** sich entscheiden; **make (it) up with sb** sich mit j-m aussöhnen 2 V/I sich versöhnen **make up for** V/T ausgleichen; (*Zeit*) aufholen **make-believe** ADJ Fantasie- **makeover** S gründliche Veränderung, Verschönerung *f* **makeshift** ADJ behelfsmäßig **make-up** S Make-up *n*, Schminke *f*

Malaysia [mə'leɪʒə] S Malaysia *n*

male [meɪl] 1 S Mann *m*; (*Tier*) Männchen *n* 2 ADJ männlich; **~ nurse** Krankenpfleger *m*

malfunction [mæl'fʌŋkʃən] 1 V/I nicht richtig funktionieren 2 S Defekt *m*

malicious [mə'lɪʃəs] ADJ boshaft; (*Beschädigung*) mutwillig

malignant [mə'lɪgnənt] ADJ bösartig

mall [mɒːl] S Einkaufszentrum *n*

malt [mɒːlt] S Malz *n*

Malta ['mɒːltə] S Malta *n* **Maltese** [mɒːl'tiːz] 1 ADJ maltesisch 2 S (*Person*) Malteser(in) *m(f)*; (*Sprache*) Maltesisch *n*

malt liquor S *starkes Bier*

mammal ['mæməl] S Säugetier *n*

man ⟨men⟩ [mæn, men] 1 S Mann *m*; (*Menschheit*) der Mensch, die Menschen *pl*; (*Schach etc*) Figur *f* 2 V/T besetzen

manage ['mænɪdʒ] 1 V/I zurechtkommen, es schaffen; **~ without sth** ohne etw auskommen, auf etw verzichten können 2 V/T (*Geschäft etc*) leiten; (*Sportler etc*) managen; (*Problem etc*) fertig werden mit; (*Arbeit etc*) schaffen **management** S Leitung *f*; (*Unternehmen*) Direktion *f*; (*Studienfach*) Management *n*, Betriebswirtschaft *f* **manager** S Geschäftsführer(in) *m(f)*; Abteilungsleiter(in) *m(f)*; Filialleiter(in) *m(f)*; (*von Sportler etc*) Manager(in) *m(f)*

maneuver [mə'nuːvər] 1 S Manöver *n* 2 V/T & V/I manövrieren

mango ⟨-es *pl*⟩ ['mæŋgoʊ] S Mango *f*

maniac ['meɪnɪæk] S Wahnsinnige(r) m/f(m); (*Fan*) Fanatiker(in) m(f)
manicure ['mænəkjʊr] S Maniküre f
manipulate [mə'nɪpjəleɪt] V/T manipulieren
mankind [mæn'kaɪnd] S Menschheit f **man-made** [mæn'meɪd] ADJ (*Produkt*) künstlich
manner ['mænər] S Art f; **~s** pl Manieren pl
mansion ['mænʃən] S Villa f, Herrenhaus n
manslaughter ['mænslɔːtər] S Totschlag m
manual ['mænjʊl] **1** ADJ manuell, Hand- **2** S Handbuch n
manufacture [mænjʊ'fæktʃər] **1** V/T herstellen **2** S Herstellung f **manufacturer** S Hersteller m
manure [mə'nʊr] S Dung m; (*a. künstlich hergestellter*) Dünger m
many ⟨more, most⟩ ['menɪ, mɔːr, moʊst] ADJ & PRON viele; **~ times** oft
map [mæp] S Landkarte f; (*von Stadt*) Stadtplan m
maple ['meɪpl] S Ahorn m **maple syrup** [meɪpl'sɪrəp] S Ahornsyrup m
marathon ['merəθɑːn] S Marathon m
marble ['mɑːrbl] S Marmor m; (*Glaskugel*) Murmel f
march [mɑːrtʃ] **1** V/I marschieren **2** S Marsch m; (*Protest*) Demonstration f
March [mɑːrtʃ] S März m; → September
mare [mer] S Stute f
margarine ['mɑːrdʒərən] S Margarine f
margarita [mɑːrgə'riːtə] S Margarita m (*Tequila mit Zitronensaft*)
margin ['mɑːrdʒən] S Rand m; (*finanziell etc*) Spielraum m; WIRTSCH Gewinnspanne f
marijuana [mærə'wɑːnə] S Marihuana n
marinated ['mærəneɪtəd] ADJ GASTR mariniert
marine [mə'riːn] ADJ Meeres-
marital ['mærətl] ADJ ehelich; **~ status** Familienstand m
marjoram ['mɑːrdʒərəm] S Majoran m
mark [mɑːrk] **1** S (*Schmutz etc*) Fleck m; (*Symbol etc*) Zeichen n **2** V/T (*anzeigen*) markieren; (*Schularbeit*) benoten, korrigieren; (*dreckig machen*) Flecken machen auf +akk **marker** S (*in Buch*) Lesezeichen n; (*Leuchtstift*) Marker m
market ['mɑːrkət] **1** S Markt m **2** V/T WIRTSCH (*Produkt*) auf den Markt bringen; (*Waren*) vertreiben **marketing** S Marketing n **market place** S Marktplatz m
marquee [mɑːr'kiː] S großes Zelt
marriage ['mærɪdʒ] S Ehe f;

(*Ereignis*) Heirat *f* (*to* mit) **married** ['mæri:d] ADJ verheiratet **marry** ['mærı] 1 V/T heiraten; (*Ehepaar*) trauen 2 V/I **~/get married** heiraten
marsh [mɑ:rʃ] S Marsch *f*, Sumpf *m*
marshal ['mɑ:rʃəl] S (*bei Veranstaltung*) Ordner *m*; Bezirkspolizeichef *m*; Vollzugsbeamte(r) *m*, Vollzugsbeamtin *f*; MIL Marschall *m*
marshmallow ['mɑ:rʃmeloʊ] S Marshmallow *n* (*Süßigkeit*)
marvel ['mɑ:rvəl] 1 S Wunder *n* 2 V/I staunen (*at* über *+akk*) **marvelous** ['mɑ:rvələs] ADJ wunderbar
mascara [mæ'skærə] S Wimperntusche *f*
mascot ['mæskɑ:t] S Maskottchen *n*
masculine ['mæskjələn] ADJ männlich
mashed [mæʃt] ADJ **~ potatoes** *pl* Kartoffelbrei *m*, Kartoffelpüree *n*
mask [mæsk] 1 S Maske *f* 2 V/T (*Gefühle*) verbergen
mass [mæs] S Masse *f*; (*von Menschen*) Menge *f*; REL Messe *f*; **~es of** massenhaft
massacre ['mæsəkər] S Blutbad *n*
massage [mə'sɑ:ʒ] 1 S Massage *f* 2 V/T massieren
massive ['mæsıv] ADJ (*Zunahme etc*) gewaltig; (*Mauer etc*) riesig
mass media [mæs'mi:dıə] S PL Massenmedien *pl*
master ['mæstər] 1 S Herr *m*; (*Handwerker*; *fig*) Meister *m* 2 V/T meistern; (*Sprache etc*) beherrschen **masterpiece** S Meisterwerk *n*
masturbate ['mæstərbeıt] V/I masturbieren
mat [mæt] S Matte *f*; (*für Tisch*) Untersetzer *m*
match [mætʃ] 1 S Streichholz *n*; SPORT Wettkampf *m*; (*Ballspiele*) Spiel *n*; (*Tennis*) Match *n* 2 V/T (*Farben etc*) passen zu; (*j-m*) gleichkommen *+dat* 3 V/I zusammenpassen **matchbox** S Streichholzschachtel *f* **matching** ADJ (*eine Sache*) passend; (*mehrere Sachen*) zusammenpassend
mate [meıt] 1 S (*Tier*) Weibchen *n*, Männchen *n* 2 V/I sich paaren
material [mə'tırıəl] S Material *n*; (*Tuch*; *fig: für Buch*) Stoff *m* **materialistic** [mətırıə'lıstık] ADJ materialistisch **materialize** [mə'tırıəlaız] V/I zustande kommen; (*Hoffnungen*) wahr werden
maternal [mə'tɜ:rnəl] ADJ mütterlich **maternity** [mə'tɜ:rnətı] ADJ **~ dress** Umstandskleid *n*; **~ leave** Elternzeit *f* (der Mutter); **~ ward** Entbindungsstation *f*
math [mæθ] S *umg* Mathe *f*
mathematical [mæθə'mæt-

ıkəl] ADJ mathematisch **mathematics** [mæθə'mætıks] S SG Mathematik *f*

matter ['mætər] **1** S (*Stoff*) Materie *f*; Sache *f*, Angelegenheit *f*; **a ~ of taste** eine Frage des Geschmacks; **no ~ how/what** egal wie/was; **what's the ~?** was ist los?; **as a ~ of fact** eigentlich **2** V/I darauf ankommen, wichtig sein; **it doesn't ~** es macht nichts

matter-of-fact ADJ sachlich, nüchtern

mattress ['mætrəs] S Matratze *f*

mature [mə'tʃʊr] **1** ADJ reif **2** V/I reif werden **maturity** [mə'tʃʊrətı] S Reife *f*

maximum ['mæksəməm] **1** ADJ Höchst-, höchste(r, s) **2** S Maximum *n*

may ⟨might⟩ [meı, maıt] V/AUX (*möglich sein*) können; (*die Erlaubnis haben*) dürfen; **we ~ as well go** wir können ruhig gehen

May [meı] S Mai *m*; → September

maybe ['meıbi:] ADV vielleicht

mayo ['meıoʊ] *umg*, **mayonnaise** [meıə'neız] S Mayo *f*, Mayonnaise *f*, Majonäse *f*

mayor ['meıər] S Bürgermeister *m*

maze [meız] S Irrgarten *m*; *fig* Wirrwarr *m*

MB *abk* = megabyte; MB *n*

MC *abk* = Master of Ceremonies; Showmaster *m*

me [mi:] PRON (*direktes Objekt*) mich; (*indirektes Objekt*) mir; **it's ~** ich bin's

ME *abk* = Maine

meadow ['medoʊ] S Wiese *f*

meal [mi:l] S Essen *n*, Mahlzeit *f*; **go out for a ~** essen gehen **meal time** S Essenszeit *f*

mean [mi:n] **1** V/T ⟨meant, meant⟩ [ment] bedeuten; (*der Meinung/Überzeugung sein*) meinen; (*beabsichtigen*) vorhaben; **I ~ it** ich meine das ernst; **what do you ~ (by that)?** was willst du damit sagen?; **~ to do sth** etw tun wollen; **it was ~t for you** es war für dich bestimmt (*od* gedacht); **it was ~t to be a joke** es sollte ein Witz sein **2** V/I **he ~s well** er meint es gut **3** ADJ (*boshaft*) gemein (*to* zu) **meaning** ['mi:nıŋ] S Bedeutung *f*; (*des Lebens, von Gedicht etc*) Sinn *m* **meaningful** ADJ sinnvoll **meaningless** ADJ ohne Sinn

means ⟨means *pl*⟩ [mi:nz] S Mittel *n*; (*finanziell*) Mittel *pl*; **by ~ of** durch, mittels; **by all ~** selbstverständlich; **by no ~** keineswegs; **~ of transportation** Beförderungsmittel *n*

meant [ment] *prät, pperf von* mean

meantime ['mi:ntaım] ADV **in the ~** inzwischen **meanwhile** ['mi:nwaıl] ADV inzwischen

measles ['mi:zlz] S SG Masern *pl*; **German ~** Röteln *pl* **measure** ['meʒər] **1** V/T & V/I messen **2** S (*Maßeinheit, Messlatte etc*) Maß *n*; (*Initiative, Schritt*) Maßnahme *f* **measurement** S (*Höhe, Breite etc*) Maß *n*
meat [mi:t] S Fleisch *n* **meatball** S Fleischbällchen *n* **meatloaf** S Hackbraten *m*
mechanic [mə'kænɪk] S Mechaniker(in) *m(f)* **mechanical** ADJ mechanisch **mechanism** ['mekənɪzəm] S Mechanismus *m*
medal ['medl] S Medaille *f*; Orden *m*
media ['mi:dɪə] S PL Medien *pl*
median strip ['mi:dɪənstrɪp] S Mittelstreifen *m*
Medicaid ['medɪkeɪd] S *staatliches Gesundheitsfürsorgeprogramm für Bedürftige*
medical ['medɪkəl] **1** ADJ medizinisch, Medizin-; (*Behandlung etc*) ärztlich **2** S Untersuchung *f* **Medicare** ['medɪker] S Krankenkasse *f* für ältere Leute **medication** [medɪ'keɪʃən] S Medikamente *pl*; **be on ~** Medikamente nehmen **medicinal** [mə'dɪsənl] ADJ Heil- **medicine** ['medəsən] S Arznei *f*; (*Wissenschaft*) Medizin *f*
mediocre [mi:dɪ'oʊkər] ADJ mittelmäßig
medium ['mi:dɪəm] **1** ADJ (*Qualität, Größe*) mittlere(r, s); (*Steak*) halbdurch; **~ (dry)** (*Wein*) halbtrocken; **~ sized** mittelgroß **2** S ⟨media⟩ Medium *n*, Mittel *n*
meet ⟨met, met⟩ [mi:t, met] **1** V/T treffen; (*Verabredung*) sich treffen mit; (*Schwierigkeiten*) stoßen auf +*akk*; (*zum ersten Mal*) kennenlernen; (*Anforderungen*) gerecht werden +*dat*; (*Termin*) einhalten; **pleased to ~ you** sehr angenehm!; **~ sb at the station** j-n vom Bahnhof abholen **2** V/I sich treffen; sich kennenlernen; **we've met (before)** wir kennen uns schon **meet up** V/T sich treffen (*with* mit) **meet with** V/T (*Gruppe*) zusammenkommen mit; (*Schwierigkeiten etc*) stoßen auf +*akk* **meeting** S Treffen *n*; (*geschäftlich*) Besprechung *f*; (*von Komitee etc*) Sitzung *f*; (*offiziell*) Versammlung *f* **meeting point** S Treffpunkt *m*
megabyte ['megəbaɪt] S Megabyte *n*
melody ['melədɪ] S Melodie *f*
melon ['melən] S Melone *f*
melt [melt] V/T & V/I schmelzen
member ['membər] S Mitglied *n*; (*von Stamm etc*) Angehörige(r) *m/f(m)*; **Member of Congress** Kongressabgeordnete(r) *m/f(m)* **membership** S Mitgliedschaft *f*
memo ⟨-s *pl*⟩ ['memoʊ] S Mit-

teilung *f*, Memo *n*
memorable ['memərəbl] ADJ unvergesslich **memorial** [mə'mɔːrɪəl] S Denkmal *n* (*to* für) **Memorial Day** S ≈ Volkstrauertag *m* (*letzter Montag im Mai*) **memorize** ['meməraɪz] V/T sich einprägen, auswendig lernen **memory** ['memərɪ] S Gedächtnis *n*; IT Speicher *m*; (*an Ereignis*) Erinnerung *f*
men [men] *pl von* man
mend [mend] **1** V/T reparieren; (*Kleidung*) flicken **2** S **be on the ~** auf dem Wege der Besserung sein
menopause ['menəpɒːz] S Wechseljahre *pl*
men's room S Herrentoilette *f*
mental ['mentl] ADJ geistig **mentality** [men'tælətɪ] S Mentalität *f* **mentally** ['mentəlɪ] ADV geistig, geistes-
mention ['menʃən] **1** S Erwähnung *f* **2** V/T erwähnen (*to sb* j-m gegenüber); **don't ~ it** bitte sehr, gern geschehen
menu ['menjuː] S Speisekarte *f*; IT Menü *n*
merchandise ['mɜːrtʃəndaɪs] S Handelsware *f*
mercifully ['mɜːrsəflɪ] ADV glücklicherweise **mercy** ['mɜːrsɪ] S Gnade *f*
merely ['mɪrlɪ] ADV bloß, lediglich
merge [mɜːrdʒ] V/I verschmelzen; AUTO sich einfädeln; WIRTSCH fusionieren
meringue [mə'ræŋ] S Baiser *n*
merit ['merət] S Verdienst *n*; (*von Sache, Angelegenheit*) Vorzug *m*
merry ['merɪ] ADJ fröhlich; **Merry Christmas** Fröhliche Weihnachten! **merry-go--round** S Karussell *n*
mess [mes] S Unordnung *f*, Durcheinander *n*; (*schmutzig*) Schweinerei *f*; (*Ärger*) Schwierigkeiten *pl*; **in a ~** (*ungeordnet*) durcheinander; (*nicht sauber*) unordentlich; *fig* (*Person*) in der Klemme; **make a ~ of sth** etw verpfuschen **mess around** V/I herummurksen (*with* an *+dat*); (*mit Worten*) herumalbern; (*untätig*) herumgammeln **mess up** V/T verpfuschen; in Unordnung bringen; schmutzig machen
message ['mesɪdʒ] S Mitteilung *f*, Nachricht *f*; **can I give him a ~?** kann ich ihm etwas ausrichten?; **please leave a ~** (*auf Anrufbeantworter*) bitte hinterlassen Sie eine Nachricht
messenger ['mesəndʒər] S Bote *m*
messy ['mesɪ] ADJ unordentlich; (*Situation*) verfahren
met [met] *prät, pperf von* **meet**
metal ['metl] S Metall *n* **metallic** [mə'tælɪk] ADJ metallisch

meter ['miːtər] S Zähler *m*; (*für Autos*) Parkuhr *f*; Meter *m od n* **meter maid** S Politesse *f*
method ['meθəd] S Methode *f*
metric ['metrɪk] ADJ metrisch; **~ system** Dezimalsystem *n*
Mexico ['meksəkoʊ] S Mexiko *n*
MI *abk* = Michigan
mice [maɪs] *pl von* **mouse**
microchip ['maɪkrətʃɪp] S IT Mikrochip *m* **microphone** S Mikrofon *n* **microscope** S Mikroskop *n* **microwave (oven)** S Mikrowelle(nherd) *f(m)*
mid [mɪd] ADJ **in ~ January** Mitte Januar; **he's in his ~ forties** er ist Mitte vierzig **midday** [mɪd'deɪ] S Mittag *m*; **at ~** mittags **middle** ['mɪdl] **1** S Mitte *f*; **in the ~ of** mitten in *+dat*; **be in the ~ of doing sth** gerade dabei sein, etw zu tun **2** ADJ mittlere(r, s), Mittel- **middle-aged** ADJ mittleren Alters **Middle America** S die amerikanische Mittelschicht; der Mittlere Westen **middle-class** ADJ mittelständisch; (*Familie, Wohnbezirk*) bürgerlich **Middle East** S **the ~** der Nahe Osten **middle finger** S Mittelfinger *m* **middle name** S zweiter Vorname **midnight** ['mɪdnaɪt] S Mitternacht *f* **midst** [mɪdst] S **in the ~ of** mitten in *+dat* **midsummer** ['mɪdsʌmər] S Hochsommer *m* **midway** [mɪd'weɪ] ADV auf halbem Wege **midweek** [mɪd'wiːk] ADJ & ADV in der Mitte der Woche **Midwest** [mɪd'west] S **the ~** der Mittlere Westen **midwife** ⟨-wives *pl*⟩ ['mɪdwaɪf] S Hebamme *f*
might [maɪt] **1** *prät von* **may**; (*Möglichkeit*) könnte; dürfte; (*Annahme*) würde **2** S Macht *f*, Kraft *f*
migraine ['maɪgreɪn] S Migräne *f*
migrant ['maɪgrənt] S Zugvogel *m*; **~ worker** Gastarbeiter(in) *m(f)* **migrate** [maɪ'greɪt] V/I abwandern; (*Vögel*) nach Süden ziehen
mike [maɪk] S *umg* Mikro *n*
mild [maɪld] ADJ mild; (*Person*) sanft
mile [maɪl] S Meile *f* (= *1,609 km*); **for ~s (and ~s)** ≈ kilometerweit; **~s per hour** Meilen pro Stunde **mileage** ['maɪlɪdʒ] S Meilen *pl*, Meilenzahl *f*
militant ['mɪlətənt] ADJ militant
military ['mɪləterɪ] ADJ Militär-, militärisch
milk [mɪlk] **1** S Milch *f* **2** V/T melken **milk chocolate** S Milchschokolade *f* **milk shake** S Milkshake *m*, Milchmixgetränk *n*
mill [mɪl] S Mühle *f*; (*Werk*) Fa-

brik *f*

milligram ['mɪlɪgræm] S Milligramm *n* **milliliter** S Milliliter *m* **millimeter** S Millimeter *m*

million ['mɪljən] S Million *f* **millionaire** [mɪljə'ner] S Millionär(in) *m(f)*

mimic ['mɪmɪk] 1 S Imitator(in) *m(f)* 2 V/T & V/I nachahmen

mince [mɪns] V/T (zer)hacken **mincemeat** ['mɪnsmiːt] S *süße Gebäckfüllung aus Rosinen, Äpfeln, Zucker, Gewürzen und Talg*

mind [maɪnd] 1 S Verstand *m*; (*a. Person*) Geist *m*; **he's out of his ~** er ist nicht bei Verstand; **keep sth in ~** etw im Auge behalten; **I've got a lot on my ~** mich beschäftigt so vieles im Moment; **change one's ~** es sich anders überlegen 2 V/T (*Baby etc*) aufpassen auf *+akk*; (*nicht mögen*) etwas haben gegen; **~ you, ...** allerdings ...; **I wouldn't ~ ...** ich hätte nichts gegen ...; **'~ the step'** „Vorsicht Stufe!" 3 V/I etwas dagegen haben; **do you ~ if I ...** macht es Ihnen etwas aus, wenn ich ...; **I don't ~** es ist mir egal, meinetwegen; **never ~** macht nichts

mine [maɪn] 1 PRON meine(r, s); **this is ~** das gehört mir; **a friend of ~** ein Freund von mir 2 S Bergwerk *n*; MIL Mine *f* **miner** S Bergarbeiter(in) *m(f)*

mineral ['mɪnərəl] S Mineral *n* **mineral water** S Mineralwasser *n*

minibus ['mɪnɪbʌs] S Kleinbus *m*

minimal ['mɪnəml] ADJ minimal **minimize** ['mɪnəmaɪz] V/T auf ein Minimum reduzieren, (ver)mindern **minimum** ['mɪnəməm] 1 S Minimum *n* 2 ADJ Mindest-

mining ['maɪnɪŋ] S Bergbau *m*

miniskirt S Minirock *m*

minister ['mɪnəstər] S REL Pastor(in) *m(f)*, Pfarrer(in) *m(f)*

minor ['maɪnər] 1 ADJ kleiner; (*Rolle etc*) unbedeutend; (*Eingriff, Delikt*) harmlos; MUS **A ~** a-Moll *n* 2 S (*junge Person*) Minderjährige(r) *m/f(m)*; (*an der Uni*) Nebenfach *n* **minority** [maɪ'nɑːrətɪ] S Minderheit *f*

mint [mɪnt] S Minze *f*; (*Süßigkeit*) Pfefferminz(bonbon) *n*

minus ['maɪnəs] PRÄP minus; ohne

minute 1 [maɪ'nuːt] ADJ winzig 2 ['mɪnət] S Minute *f*; **just a ~** Moment mal!; **any ~** jeden Augenblick

miracle ['mɪrəkl] S Wunder *n* **miraculous** [mə'rækjələs] ADJ unglaublich

mirror ['mɪrər] S Spiegel *m*

misbehave [mɪsbɪ'heɪv] V/I sich schlecht benehmen

miscalculation [mɪskælkjə'leɪʃən] S Fehlkalkulation *f*;

(*von Lage etc*) Fehleinschätzung *f*
miscarriage ['mɪskærɪdʒ] S MED Fehlgeburt *f*
miscellaneous [mɪsə'leɪnɪəs] ADJ verschieden
mischief ['mɪstʃəf] S Unfug *m*
mischievous [mɪs'tʃiːvəs] ADJ (*Person*) schelmisch; durchtrieben; (*Lächeln*) verschmitzt
miserable ['mɪzərəbl] ADJ (*Person*) todunglücklich; (*Bedingungen, Leben*) elend; (*Bezahlung, Wetter*) miserabel
miserly ['maɪzərlɪ] ADJ geizig
misery ['mɪzərɪ] S Elend *n*; (*Leid*) Qualen *pl*
misfortune [mɪs'fɔːrtʃən] S Pech *n*
misguided [mɪs'gaɪdəd] ADJ irrig; (*Optimismus*) unangebracht
misinform [mɪsən'fɔːrm] V/T falsch informieren
misinterpret [mɪsən'tɜːrprət] V/T falsch auslegen
misjudge [mɪs'dʒʌdʒ] V/T falsch beurteilen
mislay [mɪs'leɪ] *irr* V/T verlegen
misleading [mɪs'liːdɪŋ] ADJ irreführend
misprint ['mɪsprɪnt] S Druckfehler *m*
miss [mɪs] **1** V/T (*Ziel*) verfehlen; (*Ereignis*) nicht mitbekommen; (*Veranstaltung*) verpassen; (*Chance*) versäumen; (*Freunde etc*) vermissen **2** V/I nicht treffen; (*mit Gewehr etc*) danebenschießen; (*Ball, Schuss etc*) danebengehen **miss out** **1** V/T auslassen **2** V/I **~ on sth** etw verpassen
Miss [mɪs] S Fräulein *n*
missile ['mɪsəl] S Geschoss *n*; (*Angriffswaffe*) Rakete *f*
missing ['mɪsɪŋ] ADJ (*Person*) vermisst; (*Sache*) fehlend; **be/go ~** vermisst werden, fehlen
mission ['mɪʃən] S POL, MIL, REL Auftrag *m*, Mission *f*
Mississippi River [mɪsɪsɪpɪ'rɪvər] S *größter Strom Nordamerikas*
mist [mɪst] S (feiner) Nebel, Dunst *m* **mist up** V/I sich beschlagen
mistake [mɪ'steɪk] **1** S Fehler *m*; **by ~** aus Versehen **2** ⟨mistook, mistaken⟩ *irr v/t* falsch verstehen; (*etw mit etw, j-n mit j-m*) verwechseln (*for* mit)
mistaken ADJ (*Annahme, Ansicht etc*) falsch; **be ~** sich irren, falschliegen
mistletoe ['mɪsltoʊ] S Mistel *f*
mistreat [mɪs'triːt] V/T schlecht behandeln
mistress ['mɪstrəs] S Geliebte *f*
mistrust [mɪs'trʌst] **1** S Misstrauen *n* (*of* gegen) **2** V/T misstrauen *+dat*
misty ['mɪstɪ] ADJ neblig; dunstig
misunderstand ⟨misunderstood, misunderstood⟩ [mɪs-

ʌndər'stænd, mɪsʌndər'stʊd] *irr* V/T & V/I falsch verstehen **misunderstanding** S Missverständnis *n*; (*kleinerer Streit*) Differenz *f*
mitten ['mɪtn] S Fausthandschuh *m*
mix [mɪks] **1** S Mischung *f* **2** V/T mischen; vermischen (*with* mit); (*Drinks etc*) mixen **3** V/I (*Flüssigkeiten*) sich vermischen lassen **mix up** V/T zusammenmischen; (*irrtümlicherweise*) verwechseln (*with* mit) **mixed** ADJ gemischt **mixture** ['mɪkstʃər] S Mischung *f*; MED Saft *m* **mix-up** S Durcheinander *n*; Missverständnis *n*
ml *abk* = milliliter; ml
mm *abk* = millimeter; mm
MN *abk* = Minnesota
MO *abk* = Missouri
moan [moʊn] **1** S Stöhnen *n*; (*Beschwerde*) Gejammer *n* **2** V/I stöhnen; (*klagen*) jammern, meckern (*about* über *+akk*)
mobile ['moʊbaɪl] ADJ beweglich; (*auf Rädern*) fahrbar **mobility** [moʊ'bɪlətɪ] S Beweglichkeit *f*
mock [mɑːk] **1** V/T verspotten **2** ADJ Schein-
mode [moʊd] S Art *f*; IT Modus *m*
model ['mɑːdl] **1** S Modell *n*; (*positives Beispiel*) Vorbild *n*; (*Mode*) Model *n* **2** ADJ (*Eisenbahn*) Modell-; (*vorbildlich*) Muster- **3** V/T (*Figur aus Ton etc*) formen
modem ['moʊdem] S Modem *n*
moderate **1** ['mɑːdərət] ADJ mäßig; (*Ansichten, Politik*) gemäßigt; (*Einkommen, Erfolg*) mittelmäßig **2** ['mɑːdərət] S POL Gemäßigte(r) *m/f(m)* **3** ['mɑːdəreɪt] V/T mäßigen
modern ['mɑːdərn] ADJ modern, neu **modernize** ['mɑːdərnaɪz] V/T modernisieren
modest ['mɑːdəst] ADJ bescheiden **modesty** S Bescheidenheit *f*
modify ['mɑːdəfaɪ] V/T abändern
moist [mɔɪst] ADJ feucht **moisten** ['mɔɪsn] V/T befeuchten **moisture** ['mɔɪstʃər] S Feuchtigkeit *f* **moisturizer** ['mɔɪstʃəraɪzər] S Feuchtigkeitscreme *f*
molasses [mə'læsəz] S SG Melasse *f*
mold [moʊld] **1** S Form *f*; (*auf Essen*) Schimmel *m* **2** V/T formen **moldy** ADJ schimmelig
mole [moʊl] S (*auf Haut*) Leberfleck *m*; (*Tier*) Maulwurf *m*
molecule ['mɑːləkjuːl] S Molekül *n*
molest [mə'lest] V/T (sexuell) belästigen
mom [mɑːm] S Mutti *f*
moment ['moʊmənt] S Moment *m*, Augenblick *m*; **just a ~** Moment mal!; **at** (*od* **for**) **the ~** im Augenblick; **in a ~**

gleich
momentous [moʊ'mentəs] ADJ bedeutsam
momma ['mɑːmə] S Mama *f*
monastery ['mɑːnəsterɪ] S (*für Mönche*) Kloster *n*
Monday ['mʌndeɪ] S Montag *m*; → Tuesday
money ['mʌnɪ] S Geld *n*
monitor ['mɑːnətər] **1** S (*Bildschirm*) Monitor *m* **2** V/T (*Fortschritte*) überwachen
monk [mʌŋk] S Mönch *m*
monkey ['mʌŋkɪ] S Affe *m*
monster ['mɑːnstər] **1** S (*Tier, Sache*) Ungeheuer *n*, Monster *n* **2** ADJ Riesen- **monstrosity** [mɑːn'strɑːsətɪ] S Monstrosität *f*; (*Sache*) Ungetüm *n*
month [mʌnθ] S Monat *m* **monthly** **1** ADJ monatlich; Monats- **2** ADV monatlich **3** S Monats(zeit)schrift *f*
monument ['mɑːnjəmənt] S Denkmal *n* (*to* für) **monumental** [mɑːnjə'mentl] ADJ gewaltig
mood [muːd] S (*von Person*) Laune *f*; Stimmung *f*; **be in the ~ for sth** zu etw aufgelegt sein **moody** ADJ launisch
moon [muːn] S Mond *m* **moonlight** **1** S Mondlicht *n* **2** V/I schwarzarbeiten **moonlit** ADJ mondhell **moonshine** S Mondschein *m*; *umg illegal gebrannter Alkohol*
moor [mʊr] V/T & V/I festmachen
moose [muːs] S Elch *m*
mop [mɑːp] S Mopp *m* **mop up** V/T aufwischen
moral ['mɔːrəl] **1** ADJ moralisch; (*Werte*) sittlich **2** S Moral *f*; **~s** *pl* Moral *f*
morale [mə'ræl] S Stimmung *f*, Moral *f*
more [mɔːr] ADJ & PRON & ADV mehr; (*zusätzlich*) noch; **some ~ tea?** noch etwas Tee?; **are there any ~?** gibt es noch welche?; **I don't go there any ~** ich gehe nicht mehr hin; (*Komparativ*) **~ important** wichtiger; **~ and ~** immer mehr **moreover** ADV außerdem
morgue [mɔːrg] S Leichenschauhaus *n*
morning ['mɔːrnɪŋ] **1** S Morgen *m*; **in the ~** am Morgen, morgens; (*tags darauf*) morgen früh; **this ~** heute morgen **2** ADJ Morgen-; Früh-; (*Spaziergang etc*) morgendlich **morning-after pill** S die Pille danach
moron ['mɔːrɑːn] S Idiot(in) *m(f)*
morphine ['mɔːrfiːn] S Morphium *n*
mortal ['mɔːrtl] **1** ADJ sterblich; (*Wunde*) tödlich **2** S Sterbliche(r) *m/f(m)*
mortgage ['mɔːrgɪdʒ] **1** S Hypothek *f* **2** V/T mit einer Hypothek belasten
mortician [mɔːr'tɪʃən] S Leichenbestatter(in) *m(f)* **mortu-**

ary ['mɔːrtʃʊerɪ] S Leichenhalle *f*
Moslem ['mɑːzləm] ADJ & S → Muslim
mosque [mɑːsk] S Moschee *f*
mosquito ⟨-es *pl*⟩ [mə'skiːtoʊ] S (Stech)mücke *f*; (*in Tropen*) Moskito *m*
moss [mɑːs] S Moos *n*
most [moʊst] **1** ADJ meiste *pl*, die meisten **2** ADV (*mit Verben*) am meisten; (*mit Adjektiven*) ...ste; (*mit Adverbien*) am ...sten; (*sehr*) äußerst, höchst; **the ~ beautiful** der/die/das schönste **3** S das meiste, der größte Teil; (*Leute*) die meisten; **~ of the money** das meiste Geld; **five at the ~** höchstens fünf; **make the ~ of sth** etw voll ausnützen **mostly** ADV (*zeitlich*) meistens; (*in erster Linie*) hauptsächlich; (*überwiegend*) größtenteils
motel [moʊ'tel] S Motel *n*
moth [mɑːθ] S Nachtfalter *m*; (*in Wolle*) Motte *f*
mother ['mʌðər] **1** S Mutter *f* **2** V/T bemuttern **mother-in-law** ⟨mothers-in-law⟩ S Schwiegermutter *f* **mother-to-be** ⟨mothers-to-be⟩ S werdende Mutter
motion ['moʊʃən] S Bewegung *f*; (*in Sitzung etc*) Antrag *m* **motion picture** S Film *m*
motivate ['moʊtəveɪt] V/T motivieren
motor ['moʊtər] **1** S Motor *m* **2** ADJ Motor- **motorboat** S Motorboot *n* **motorcycle** S Motorrad *n* **motorist** ['moʊtərɪst] S Autofahrer(in) *m(f)*
motor vehicle S Kraftfahrzeug *n*
mount [maʊnt] **1** V/T (*auf Pferd*) steigen auf +*akk*; (*Ausstellung etc*) organisieren; (*Gemälde*) mit einem Passepartout versehen **2** V/I (*auf Pferd*) steigen **3** S Passepartout *n*
mountain ['maʊntən] S Berg *m* **mountaineer** [maʊntə'nɪr] S Bergsteiger(in) *m(f)*
mountaineering S Bergsteigen *n* **mountainside** S Berghang *m*
mourn [mɔːrn] **1** V/T betrauern **2** V/I trauern (*for* um)
mouse ⟨mice⟩ [maʊs, maɪs] S *a.* IT Maus *f* **mouse pad** S Mauspad *n*
mousse [muːs] S GASTR Creme *f*; (*für Haare*) Schaumfestiger *m*
moustache [mə'stæʃ, 'mʌstæʃ] S Schnurrbart *m*
mouth [maʊθ] S Mund *m*; (*Tier*) Maul *n*; (*Höhle*) Eingang *m*; (*Flasche*) Öffnung *f*; (*Fluss*) Mündung *f* **mouthful** S (*Getränk*) Schluck *m*; (*Essen*) Bissen *m* **mouthwash** S Mundwasser *n*
move [muːv] **1** S Bewegung *f*; (*Brettspiel*) Zug *m*; (*Maßnahme, Aktion*) Schritt *m*; (*in neue Wohnung etc*) Umzug *m*; **make a ~**

(*aufbrechen*) sich auf den Weg machen; **make a ~ on sb** j-n anmachen; **get a ~ on (with sth)** sich (mit etw) beeilen **2** VT bewegen; (*Gegenstand, Möbel*) rücken; (*Auto*) wegfahren; (*Waren*) befördern; (*Menschen*) transportieren; (*an andere Dienststelle etc*) versetzen; (*emotional*) bewegen, rühren; **~ house** umziehen **3** VI sich bewegen; (*Personen*) gehen; (*Fahrzeug*) fahren; (*in andere Stadt*) umziehen **move around** VI sich bewegen; (*reisen*) unterwegs sein **move away** VI weggehen; (*von einem Ort*) wegziehen **move in** VI (*in Haus*) einziehen **move on** VI weitergehen; (*Fahrzeug etc*) weiterfahren **move out** VI ausziehen **movement** S Bewegung *f*

movie ['mu:vɪ] S Film *m*; **the ~s** das Kino **movie theater** S Kino *n*

moving ['mu:vɪŋ] ADJ (*Film etc*) ergreifend, berührend

mow ⟨mowed, mown *od* mowed⟩ [moʊ, moʊd, moʊn] VT mähen **mower** S Rasenmäher *m* **mown** [moʊn] *pperf von* mow

mph *abk* = miles per hour; Meilen pro Stunde

MP3 player [empi:'θri:pleɪər] S MP3-Player *m*

Mr. ['mɪstər] S (*schriftliche Anrede*) Herr

Mrs. ['mɪsəz] S (*schriftliche Anrede*) Frau

Ms. [mɪz] S (*schriftliche Anrede für verheiratete oder ledige Frau*) Frau

MS *abk* = Mississippi

Mt *abk* = Mount; Berg *m*

MT *abk* = Montana

much ⟨more, most⟩ [mʌtʃ, mɔ:r, moʊst] **1** ADJ viel **2** ADV viel; sehr; **I don't like it ~** ich mag es nicht besonders; **thank you very ~** danke sehr **3** S viel; **he's not ~ of a cook** er ist kein großer Koch

mucus ['mju:kəs] S Schleim *m*

mud [mʌd] S Schlamm *m*

muddle ['mʌdl] **1** S Durcheinander *n* **2** VT **~ (up)** durcheinanderbringen

muddy ['mʌdɪ] ADJ schlammig; (*Schuhe etc*) schmutzig

muffin ['mʌfən] S Muffin *m*

muffler ['mʌflər] S Schalldämpfer *m*

mug [mʌg] **1** S (*große Tasse*) Becher *m*; *umg* (*Gesicht*) Visage *f* **2** VT (*Person*) überfallen **mugging** S Raubüberfall *m*

mule [mju:l] S Maulesel *m*

multicolored [mʌltɪ'kʌlərd] ADJ bunt **multicultural** ADJ multikulturell **multi-grade** ADJ (*Öl*) Mehrbereichs- **multilingual** [mʌltɪ'lɪŋwəl] ADJ mehrsprachig

multiple ['mʌltɪpl] **1** S Vielfache(s) *n* **2** ADJ mehrfach; (*mit Substantiv im pl*) mehrere

multiplex ['mʌltıpleks] ADJ & S ~ **(cinema)** Multiplexkino *n*
multiply ['mʌltıplaı] **1** V/T multiplizieren (*by* mit) **2** V/I sich vermehren
multipurpose [mʌltı'pɜ:rpəs] ADJ Mehrzweck-
mumble ['mʌmbl] V/T & V/I murmeln
munch [mʌntʃ] V/T & V/I mampfen
Munich ['mju:nık] S München *n*
municipal [mjʊ'nısəpəl] ADJ städtisch
murder ['mɜ:rdər] **1** S Mord *m* **2** V/T ermorden **murderer** S Mörder(in) *m(f)*
murmur ['mɜ:rmər] V/T & V/I murmeln
muscle ['mʌsl] S Muskel *m* **muscular** ['mʌskjələr] ADJ muskulös; (*Schmerzen, Krampf etc*) Muskel-
museum [mju:'zi:əm] S Museum *n*
mushroom ['mʌʃru:m] S (essbarer) Pilz; Champignon *m*
mushy ['mʌʃı] ADJ breiig
music ['mju:zık] S Musik *f* **musical** **1** ADJ Musik-; (*Stimme, Klang*) melodisch; (*Person*) musikalisch **2** S Musical *n* **musician** [mju:'zıʃən] S Musiker(in) *m(f)*
Muslim ['mʊzləm] **1** ADJ moslemisch **2** S Moslem *m*, Muslime *f*
mussel ['mʌsl] S Miesmuschel *f*
must ⟨had to, had to⟩ [mʌst, hæd tə] **1** V/AUX müssen; (*bei Verneinung*) dürfen; (*bei hoher Wahrscheinlichkeit*) **he ~ be there by now** er ist inzwischen bestimmt schon da; (*bei Vermutung*) **I ~'ve lost it** ich habe es wohl verloren **2** S Muss *n*
mustache [mə'stæʃ, 'mʌstæʃ] S Schnurrbart *m*
mustard ['mʌstərd] S Senf *m*
mustn't ['mʌsnt] *kontr von* **must not**
mute [mju:t] ADJ stumm
mutter ['mʌtər] V/T & V/I murmeln
mutton ['mʌtn] S Hammelfleisch *n*
mutual ['mju:tʃʊəl] ADJ gegenseitig
my [maı] ADJ mein; **I've hurt ~ leg** ich habe mir das Bein verletzt **myself** [maı'self] PRON *akk* mich; *dat* mir; (*verstärkend*) **I did it ~** ich habe es selbst gemacht; **(all) by ~** allein
mysterious [mı'stırıəs] ADJ geheimnisvoll, mysteriös; (*unerklärlich*) rätselhaft **mystery** ['mıstərı] S Geheimnis *n*; (*unerklärlich*) Rätsel *n*
myth [mıθ] S Mythos *m*; *fig* Märchen *n*

N

nail [neɪl] **1** S Nagel *m* **2** V/T nageln (*to* an) **nail clippers** S PL Nagelknipser *m* **nail file** S Nagelfeile *f* **nail polish** S Nagellack *m*
naive [naɪ'iːv] ADJ naiv
naked ['neɪkəd] ADJ nackt
name [neɪm] **1** S Name *m*; **his ~ is** … er heißt …; **what's your ~?** wie heißen Sie? **2** V/T nennen (*after* nach); benennen; (*für Posten*) ernennen (*as* als/zu); **a boy ~d** … ein Junge namens … **namely** ADV nämlich
nanny ['nænɪ] S Kindermädchen *n*
nap [næp] S **take a ~** ein Nickerchen machen
napkin ['næpkən] S Serviette *f*
narcotic [nɑːr'kɑːtɪk] **1** S Betäubungsmittel *n*; Rauschgift *n* **2** ADJ betäubend
narrow ['næroʊ] **1** ADJ eng, schmal; (*Sieg etc*) knapp **2** V/I sich verengen **narrow down** V/T einschränken (*to sth* auf etw *akk*) **narrow-minded** ADJ engstirnig
NASA ['næsə] *akr* = National Aeronautics and Space Administration; NASA *f* (*US Raumfahrtbehörde*)
nasty ['næstɪ] ADJ ekelhaft; (*Person*) fies; (*Bemerkung*) gehässig; (*Unfall, Wunde etc*) schlimm
nation ['neɪʃən] S Nation *f*
national ['næʃənl] **1** ADJ national; **~ anthem** Nationalhymne *f*; **National Guard** Nationalgarde *f* **2** S Staatsbürger(in) *m(f)* **nationality** [næʃə'nælətɪ] S Staatsangehörigkeit *f*, Nationalität *f* **nationwide** ADJ & ADV landesweit
native ['neɪtɪv] **1** ADJ einheimisch; (*Charakterzug*) angeboren, natürlich; **Native American** Indianer(in) *m(f)*; **~ country** Heimatland *n*; **~ language** Muttersprache *f*; **~ speaker** Muttersprachler(in) *m(f)* **2** S Einheimische(r) *m/f(m)*, Eingeborene(r) *m/f(m)*
NATO ['neɪtoʊ] *akr* = North Atlantic Treaty Organization; Nato *f*
natural ['nætʃrəl] ADJ natürlich; Natur-; (*als Charakterzug*) angeboren; **~ resources** *pl* Bodenschätze *pl* **naturally** ADV natürlich; von Natur aus **nature** ['neɪtʃər] S Natur *f*; (*Wesen, Charakter*) Art *f* **nature reserve** S Naturschutzgebiet *n*
naughty ['nɔːtɪ] ADJ (*Kind*) ungezogen; frech
nausea ['nɒːzɪə] S Übelkeit *f*

navel ['neɪvəl] S Nabel *m*
navigate ['nævəgeɪt] VI navigieren; (*im Auto*) lotsen, dirigieren **navigation** [nævə'geɪʃən] S Navigation *f* **navigation system** S Navigationssystem *n*
navy ['neɪvɪ] S Marine *f*
NBC *abk* = National Broadcasting Company *US Fernsehgesellschaft*
NC *abk* = North Carolina
ND *abk* = North Dakota
NE *abk* = Nebraska
near [nɪr] **1** ADJ nahe; knapp **2** ADV nahe, in der Nähe **3** PRÄP ~ **(to)** (*dicht neben*) nahe an *+dat*; in der Nähe *+gen* **nearby** [nɪr'baɪ] **1** ADJ nahe gelegen **2** ADV in der Nähe **nearly** ADV fast
neat [ni:t] ADJ ordentlich; (*Arbeit, Schrift*) sauber; *umg* prima, cool
necessarily [nesə'serəlɪ] ADV notwendigerweise; **not ~** nicht unbedingt **necessary** ['nesəserɪ] ADJ notwendig, nötig; **it's ~ to ...** man muss ... **necessity** [nə'sesətɪ] S Notwendigkeit *f*
neck [nek] S Hals *m*; (*Größenangabe*) Halsweite *f* **necklace** ['nekləs] S Halskette *f* **necktie** S Krawatte *f*
nectarine ['nektəri:n] S Nektarine *f*
née [neɪ] ADJ geborene
need [ni:d] **1** S Bedürfnis *n* (*for* für); (*Erfordernis*) Notwendigkeit *f*; (*Armut*) Not *f*; **be in ~ of sth** etw brauchen; **if ~(s) be** wenn nötig **2** VT brauchen; müssen
needle ['ni:dl] S Nadel *f*
needless, needlessly ['ni:dləs, -lɪ] ADJ & ADV unnötig; **needless to say** selbstverständlich
negative ['negətɪv] **1** S LING Verneinung *f*; FOTO Negativ *n* **2** ADJ negativ; (*Antwort*) verneinend
neglect [nɪ'glekt] **1** S Vernachlässigung *f* **2** VT vernachlässigen **negligence** ['neglədʒəns] S Nachlässigkeit *f*
negotiate [nɪ'goʊʃɪeɪt] VI verhandeln **negotiation** [nɪgoʊʃɪ'eɪʃən] S Verhandlung *f*
neighbor ['neɪbər] S Nachbar(in) *m(f)* **neighborhood** S Nachbarschaft *f* **neighboring** ADJ benachbart
neither ['ni:ðər, 'naɪðər] **1** ADJ & PRON keine(r, s) von beiden; **~ of us** keiner von uns beiden **2** ADV **~ ... nor ...** weder ... noch ... **3** KONJ **I'm not going** - **~ am I** ich gehe nicht - ich auch nicht
nephew ['nefju:] S Neffe *m*
nerd [nɜ:rd] S *umg* Schwachkopf *m*; Freak *m*
nerve [nɜ:rv] S Nerv *m*; Frechheit *f*; **he gets on my ~s** er geht mir auf die Nerven **nerve-racking** ADJ nerven-

aufreibend **nervous** ['nɜːrvəs] ADJ ängstlich; nervös
nest [nest] **1** S Nest *n* **2** V/I nisten
net [net] **1** S Netz *n*; **the Net** das Internet **2** ADJ (*Preis, Gewicht*) Netto-
Netherlands ['neðərləndz] S PL **the ~** die Niederlande *pl*
network ['netwɜːrk] S Netz *n*; TV, RADIO Sendenetz *n*; IT Netzwerk *n* **networking** S Networking *n* (*das Knüpfen und Pflegen von Kontakten, die dem beruflichen Fortkommen dienen*)
neutral ['nuːtrəl] **1** ADJ neutral **2** S (*bei Gangschaltung*) Leerlauf *m*
never ['nevər] ADV nie(mals); **~ before** noch nie; **~ mind** macht nichts! **never-ending** ADJ endlos **nevertheless** [nevərðə'les] ADV trotzdem
new [nuː] ADJ neu **New England** [nuː'ɪŋglənd] S Neuengland *n* **newly** ['nuːlɪ] ADV neu **newly-weds** S PL Frischvermählte *pl*
news [nuːz] S SG Nachricht *f*; RADIO, TV Nachrichten *pl*; **have you heard the ~?** hast du das Neueste gehört? **newspaper** ['nuːzpeɪpər] S Zeitung *f* **newsstand** S Zeitungskiosk *m*, Zeitungsstand *m*
New Year ['nuːjɪr] S das neue Jahr; **Happy ~** (ein) frohes Neues Jahr!; (*Trinkspruch*) Prosit Neujahr!; **~'s Day** Neujahr *n*, Neujahrstag *m*; **~'s Eve** Silvesterabend *m*
New Zealand [nuː'ziːlənd] S Neuseeland *n*
next [nekst] **1** ADJ nächste(r, s); **the week after ~** übernächste Woche; **you're ~** du bist jetzt dran **2** ADV als Nächstes; dann, darauf; **~ to** neben *+dat*; **~ to last** vorletzte(r, s); **~ door** nebenan
NFL *abk* = National Football League *US Football-Nationalliga*
NH *abk* = New Hampshire
Niagara Falls [naɪægrə'fɔːlz] S PL Niagarafälle *pl*
nibble ['nɪbl] V/T knabbern an *+dat*
nice [naɪs] ADJ nett, sympathisch; (*von Essen*) gut; (*Wetter*) schön; **have a ~ day** schönen Tag noch! **nicely** ADV nett; gut
nickel ['nɪkl] S CHEM Nickel *n*; (*Münze*) Nickel *m*
nickname ['nɪkneɪm] S Spitzname *m*
nicotine ['nɪkətiːn] S Nikotin *n*
niece [niːs] S Nichte *f*
night [naɪt] S Nacht *f*; (*vor dem Schlafengehen*) Abend *m*; **good ~** gute Nacht!; **at** (*od* **by**) **~** nachts **nightclub** S Nachtklub *m* **nightdress** S Nachthemd *n* **nightie** ['naɪtɪ]

S *umg* Nachthemd *n* **night life** ['naɪtlaɪf] S Nachtleben *n* **nightly** ADV jeden Abend; jede Nacht **nightmare** ['naɪtmer] S Albtraum *m* **nighttime** S Nacht *f*; **at ~** nachts

nine [naɪn] **1** NUM neun **2** S (*a. Buslinie etc*) Neun *f*; → eight **nineteen** [naɪn'tiːn] **1** NUM neunzehn **2** S (*a. Buslinie etc*) Neunzehn *f*; → eight **nineteenth** ADJ neunzehnte(r, s); → eighth **ninetieth** ['naɪntɪəθ] ADJ neunzigste(r, s); → eighth **ninety** ['naɪntɪ] **1** NUM neunzig **2** S Neunzig *f*; → eight, eighty **ninth** [naɪnθ] **1** ADJ neunte(r, s) **2** S Neuntel *n*; → eighth

nipple ['nɪpl] S Brustwarze *f*

nitrogen ['naɪtrədʒən] S Stickstoff *m*

NJ *abk* = New Jersey

NM *abk* = New Mexico

no [noʊ] **1** ADV nein; (*nach Komparativ*) nicht **2** ADJ kein; **in ~ time** im Nu; **~ way** *umg* keinesfalls; **~ smoking** Rauchen verboten **3** S ⟨-es *pl*⟩ Nein *n*

nobody ['noʊbədɪ] **1** PRON niemand; keiner; **~ else** sonst niemand, kein anderer **2** S Niemand *m*

nod [nɑːd] V/I & V/T nicken **nod off** V/I einnicken

no-fault ['noufɒːlt] S AUTO Vollkaskoversicherung *f*

noise [nɔɪz] S Lärm *m*; Geräusch *n* **noisy** ADJ laut; (*Menge etc*) lärmend

non- [nɑːn] PRÄF Nicht-; (*mit adj*) nicht-, un- **non-alcoholic** ADJ alkoholfrei

none [nʌn] PRON keine(r, s); **~ of it is any use** nichts davon ist brauchbar **nonetheless** [nʌnðə'les] ADV nichtsdestoweniger

non-fiction S Sachbücher *pl*

nonsense ['nɑːnsens] S Unsinn *m*

non-smoker [nɑːn'smoʊkər] S Nichtraucher(in) *m(f)* **non-smoking** ADJ Nichtraucher-

nonstop **1** ADJ (*Zug*) durchgehend; (*Flug*) Nonstop- **2** ADV (*reden*) ununterbrochen; (*fliegen*) ohne Zwischenlandung

noodles ['nuːdlz] S PL Nudeln *pl*

noon [nuːn] S Mittag *m*; **at ~** um 12 Uhr mittags

no one ['noʊwʌn] PRON niemand; keiner; **~ else** sonst niemand, kein anderer

nope [noʊp] ADV *umg* nee, nein

nor [nɔːr] KONJ **neither ... ~ ...** weder ... noch ...; **I don't smoke, ~ does he** ich rauche nicht, er auch nicht

normal ['nɔːrməl] ADJ normal **normally** ADV normalerweise

north [nɔːrθ] **1** S Norden *m*; **to the ~ of** nördlich von **2**

ADV (*Richtung*) nach Norden **3** ADJ Nord- **North America** S Nordamerika *n* **northbound** ADJ (in) Richtung Norden **northeast** **1** S Nordosten *m*; **to the ~ of** nordöstlich von **2** ADV (*Richtung*) nach Nordosten **3** ADJ Nordost- **northern** ['nɔːrðərn] ADJ nördlich, Nord- **northward(s)** ADV nach Norden **northwest** **1** S Nordwesten *m*; **to the ~ of** nordwestlich von **2** ADV (*Richtung*) nach Nordwesten **3** ADJ Nordwest-

Norway ['nɔːrweɪ] S Norwegen *n* **Norwegian** [nɔːr'wiːdʒən] **1** ADJ norwegisch **2** S (*Person*) Norweger(in) *m(f)*; (*Sprache*) Norwegisch *n*

nose [noʊz] S Nase *f* **nosebleed** S Nasenbluten *n* **nosey** ['noʊzɪ] → nosy

nostril ['nɑːstrəl] S Nasenloch *n*

nosy ['noʊzɪ] ADJ neugierig

not [nɑːt] ADV nicht; **~ one of them** kein einziger von ihnen; **~ at all** überhaupt nicht, keineswegs; (*Antwort auf Dank*) gern geschehen

note [noʊt] **1** S Notiz *f*; (*kurzer Brief*) paar Zeilen *pl*; (*in Buch etc*) Anmerkung *f*; MUS (*Notenzeichen*) Note *f*; (*konkret*) Ton *m*; **make a ~ of sth** sich etw notieren; **~s** *pl* Aufzeichnungen *pl* **2** V/T (*wahrnehmen*) bemerken (*that* dass); (*niederschreiben*) notieren **notebook** S Notizbuch *n*; IT Notebook *n* **notepad** S Notizblock *m* **notepaper** S Briefpapier *n*

nothing ['nʌθɪŋ] S nichts; **~ but ...** lauter ...; **for ~** umsonst

notice ['noʊtəs] **1** S Bekanntmachung *f*; (*auf schwarzem Brett etc*) Anschlag *m*; (*Aufmerksamkeit*) Beachtung *f*; (*Vorinformation*) Ankündigung *f*; (*von Arbeitsplatz, Wohnung*) Kündigung *f*; **on short ~** kurzfristig; **until further ~** bis auf weiteres; **hand in one's ~** kündigen; **take (no) ~ of (sth)** etw (nicht) beachten **2** V/T bemerken **noticeable** ['noʊtəsəbl] ADJ erkennbar; sichtbar

notify ['noʊtɪfaɪ] V/T benachrichtigen (*of* von)

notorious [noʊ'tɔːrɪəs] ADJ berüchtigt

noun [naʊn] S Substantiv *n*

novel ['nɑːvəl] **1** S Roman *m* **2** ADJ neuartig **novelty** S Neuheit *f*

November [noʊ'vembər] S November *m*; → September

novice ['nɑːvəs] S Neuling *m*

now [naʊ] ADV jetzt; (*einleitend*) also; **just ~** gerade; **by ~** inzwischen; **from ~ on** ab jetzt; **~ and again** (*od* **then**) ab und zu **nowadays** ADV heutzutage

nowhere ['noʊwer] ADV nirgends; **we're getting ~** wir

kommen nicht weiter; **~ near** noch lange nicht
nozzle ['nɑ:zl] S Düse *f*
nuclear ['nu:klɪər] ADJ (*Energie*) Kern-
nude [nu:d] **1** ADJ nackt **2** S (*Person*) Nackte(r) *m/f(m)*; (*Gemälde*) Akt *m* **nudist** S Nudist(in) *m(f)*, FKK-Anhänger(in) *m(f)*
nuisance ['nu:sns] S Ärgernis *n*; (*Person*) Plage *f*
nuke [nu:k] V/T *umg* in der Mikrowelle backen/erhitzen
numb [nʌm] **1** ADJ taub, gefühllos **2** V/T betäuben
number ['nʌmbər] **1** S Nummer *f*; MATH Zahl *f*; (*Menge*) (An)zahl *f*; **in large ~s** in großen Mengen; **a ~ of times** mehrmals **2** V/T nummerieren; (*dazugehören*) zählen (*among* zu)
numeral ['nu:mərəl] S Ziffer *f*
numerous ['nu:mərəs] ADJ zahlreich
nun [nʌn] S Nonne *f*
nurse [nɜ:rs] **1** S Krankenschwester *f*; (*Mann*) Krankenpfleger *m* **2** V/T (*Patient*) pflegen; (*Baby*) stillen **nursery** ['nɜ:rsərɪ] S Kindergarten *m*; Kinderzimmer *n*; (*für Pflanzen*) Gärtnerei *f*; (*für Bäume*) Baumschule *f* **nursery school** S Kindergarten *m*; **~ teacher** Kindergärtner(in) *m(f)*, Erzieher(in) *m(f)* **nursing** S (*Beruf*) Krankenpflege *f*; **~ home** Privatklinik *f*
nut [nʌt] S Nuss *f*; TECH (*für Schraube*) Mutter *f*; *umg* Spinner(in) *m(f)*
nutmeg ['nʌtmeg] S Muskat *m*, Muskatnuss *f*
nutrition [nu:'trɪʃən] S Ernährung *f* **nutritious** [nu:'trɪʃəs] ADJ nahrhaft
nuts [nʌts] *umg* **1** ADJ verrückt **2** S PL (*Hoden*) Eier *pl* **nutty** ['nʌtɪ] ADJ *umg* verrückt
NV *abk* = Nevada
NY *abk* = New York
NYC *abk* = New York City
nylon® ['naɪlɑ:n] **1** S Nylon® *n* **2** ADJ Nylon-

O

O [oʊ] S TEL Null *f*
oak [oʊk] **1** S Eiche *f* **2** ADJ Eichen-
oar [ɔ:r] S Ruder *n*
oasis ⟨oases *pl*⟩ [oʊ'eɪsɪs, -si:z] S Oase *f*
oath [oʊθ] S Eid *m*
oatmeal ['oʊtmi:l] S GASTR Haferflocken *pl* **oats** [oʊts] S PL Hafer *m*
obedience [oʊ'bi:dɪəns] S Gehorsam *m* **obedient** [oʊ'bi:dɪənt] ADJ gehorsam **obey** [oʊ'beɪ] V/T & V/I gehorchen +*dat*

object **1** ['ɑːbdʒekt] S Gegenstand *m*; Objekt *n*; (*von Verhandlungen etc*) Ziel *n* **2** [əb'dʒekt] V/I dagegen sein; Einwände erheben (*to* gegen); (*moralisch*) Anstoß nehmen (*to* an *+dat*) **objection** [əb'dʒekʃən] S Einwand *m* **objective** [əb'dʒektɪv] **1** S Ziel *n* **2** ADJ objektiv

obligation [ɑːblɪ'geɪʃən] S Pflicht *f*, Verpflichtung *f* **obligatory** [ə'blɪgətɔːrɪ] ADJ obligatorisch **oblige** [ə'blaɪdʒ] V/T **he felt ~d to accept the offer** er fühlte sich verpflichtet, das Angebot anzunehmen

obscene [əb'siːn] ADJ obszön

observation [ɑːbzər'veɪʃən] S Beobachtung *f*; (*Kommentar*) Bemerkung *f* **observe** [əb'zɜːrv] V/T (*wahrnehmen*) bemerken; beobachten; (*Regeln, Bräuche*) einhalten

obsessed [əb'sest] ADJ besessen (*with an idea etc* von einem Gedanken etc) **obsession** [əb'seʃn] S Manie *f*

obstacle ['ɑːbstəkl] S Hindernis *n* (*to* für)

obstinate ['ɑːbstənət] ADJ hartnäckig

obstruct [əb'strʌkt] V/T versperren; (*Rohr*) verstopfen; (*Entwicklung*) behindern, aufhalten **obstruction** [əb'strʌkʃən] S Blockierung *f*; (*von Rohr*) Verstopfung *f*; (*Gegenstand*) Hindernis *n*

obtain [əb'teɪn] V/T erhalten

obtainable ADJ erhältlich

obvious, **obviously** ['ɑːbvɪəs, -lɪ] ADJ & ADV offensichtlich

occasion [ə'keɪʒən] S Gelegenheit *f*; (*speziell*) (großes) Ereignis, Anlass *m* **occasional**, **occasionally** ADJ & ADV gelegentlich

occupant ['ɑːkjəpənt] S Bewohner(in) *m(f)*; (*von Fahrzeug*) Insasse *m*, Insassin *f* **occupation** [ɑːkjə'peɪʃən] S Beruf *m*; (*Tätigkeit*) Beschäftigung *f*; (*von Land etc*) Besetzung *f* **occupied** ADJ (*Land, Sitzplatz, Toilette*) besetzt; (*Person*) beschäftigt **occupy** ['ɑːkjəpaɪ] V/T (*Land etc*) besetzen; (*Zeit*) beanspruchen; (*Person*) beschäftigen

occur [ə'kɜːr] V/I vorkommen; **~ to sb** j-m einfallen

ocean ['oʊʃən] S Ozean *m*; (*allgemein*) das Meer

o'clock [ə'klɑːk] ADV **at 10 ~** um 10 Uhr

October [ɑːk'toʊbər] S Oktober *m*; → September

octopus ['ɑːktəpəs] S Krake *f*, Tintenfisch *m*

OD *abk* = overdose **1** S Überdosis *f* **2** V/I eine Überdosis Drogen nehmen

odd [ɑːd] ADJ sonderbar; (*Zahl*) ungerade; (*Schuh etc*) einzeln; **be the ~ one out** nicht dazugehören **odds** S PL Chancen *pl*

odometer [oʊ'dɑ:mətər] S AUTO Meilenzähler *m*
odor ['oʊdər] S Geruch *m*
of [ɑ:v, əv] PRÄP GEN von; (*Material*) aus; **the name ~ the hotel** der Name des Hotels; **the works ~ Shakespeare** Shakespeares Werke; **the fourth ~ June** der vierte Juni; (*zur Mengenangabe*) **a glass ~ water** ein Glas Wasser; (*bei Zeitangaben*) **it's five ~ three** es ist fünf vor drei; (*zur Nennung der Ursache*) **die ~ cancer** an Krebs sterben
off [ɑ:f] **1** ADV weg, fort; (*bei Urlaub*) frei; (*Gerät, Licht etc*) aus(geschaltet); (*bei Entfernung*) entfernt; (*Milch*) sauer; **I'll be ~ now** ich gehe jetzt; **the concert is ~** das Konzert fällt aus; **I got 10% ~** ich habe 10% Nachlass bekommen **2** PRÄP (*Richtungsangabe*) von; **get ~ the bus** aus dem Bus aussteigen; **he's ~ work/school** er hat frei/schulfrei; **take $20 ~ the price** den Preis um 20 Dollar herabsetzen
offend [ə'fend] V/T kränken **offender** S Straffällige(r) *m/f(m)* **offense** [ə'fens] S (*Verbrechen*) Straftat *f*; Vergehen *n*; (*von Gefühl*) Kränkung *f*; **cause/take ~** Anstoß erregen/nehmen; **no ~!** nichts für ungut! **offensive** [ə'fensɪv] **1** ADJ anstößig; beleidigend; (*Geruch*) übel, abstoßend; MIL, SPORT Offensiv- **2** S MIL Offensive *f*
offer ['ɑ:fər] **1** S Angebot *n* **2** V/T anbieten (*to sb* j-m); (*Geld, Chance etc*) bieten
office ['ɑ:fəs] S Büro *n*; (*Stellung*) Amt *n*; (*von Arzt, Anwalt*) Praxis *f* **office block** S Bürogebäude *n* **office hours** S PL Dienstzeit *f*; Geschäftszeiten *pl* **officer** ['ɑ:fəsər] S MIL Offizier(in) *m(f)*; Polizeibeamte(r) *m*, Polizeibeamtin *f* **office worker** ['ɑ:fəswɜ:rkər] S Büroangestellte(r) *m/f(m)* **official** [ə'fɪʃəl] **1** ADJ offiziell; (*Bericht*) amtlich **2** S Beamte(r) *m*, Beamtin *f*, Repräsentant(in) *m(f)*
off-line ADJ IT offline **off-peak** ADJ außerhalb der Stoßzeiten; (*Tarif, Fahrkarte*) verbilligt **off-ramp** S (Autobahn)-ausfahrt *f* **off-season** ADJ außerhalb der Saison **offside** [ɑ:f'saɪd] S SPORT Abseits *n*
often ['ɑ:fən] ADV oft; **every so ~** von Zeit zu Zeit
OH *abk* = Ohio
oil [ɔɪl] **1** S Öl *n* **2** V/T ölen **oil spill** S Ölteppich *m* **oil tanker** S Öltanker *m*; (*Fahrzeug*) Tankwagen *m* **oily** ADJ ölig; (*Haut, Haare*) fettig
ointment ['ɔɪntmənt] S Salbe *f*
OJ *abk* = orange juice; O-Saft *m*
OK, **okay** [oʊ'keɪ] ADJ *umg* okay, in Ordnung

old [oʊld] ADJ alt **old age** S Alter *n* **old-fashioned** ADJ altmodisch **old folks' home** S *umg* Altersheim *n*
olive ['ɑːləv] S Olive *f* **olive oil** S Olivenöl *n*
Olympic Games [oʊlɪmpɪk-'geɪmz] S PL Olympische Spiele *pl*
omelette ['ɑːmlət] S Omelett *n*
omit [oʊ'mɪt] V/T auslassen
on [ɑːn] 1 PRÄP (*Position*) auf *+dat*; (*mit Bewegung, Richtung*) auf *+akk*; (*bei Wand etc, Tag, Datum*) an *+dat*; (*mit Bewegung*) an *+akk*; **I haven't got it ~ me** ich habe es nicht bei mir; **~ TV** im Fernsehen; **~ the right** rechts; **~ the train/bus** im Zug/Bus; **~ Sunday** am Sonntag; **~ Sundays** sonntags 2 ADJ & ADV TV, ELEK an; **I've got nothing ~ for tonight** (*nichts geplant*) ich habe heute Abend nichts vor; **I've got nothing ~** (*keine Kleider an*) ich habe nichts an
once [wʌns] 1 ADV einmal; **at ~** sofort; (*zur gleichen Zeit*) gleichzeitig; **~ more** noch einmal; **for ~** ausnahmsweise (einmal); **~ in a while** ab und zu mal 2 KONJ wenn … einmal; **~ you've gotten used to it** sobald Sie sich daran gewöhnt haben
oncoming ['ɑːnkʌmɪŋ] ADJ entgegenkommend; **~ traffic** Gegenverkehr *m*
one [wʌn] 1 NUM eins 2 ADJ ein, eine, ein; (*nur diese(r, s) eine*) einzige(r, s); **~ day** eines Tages 3 PRON eine(r, s); (*die Leute im Allgemeinen*) man; **the ~ who/that …** der(jenige), der/die(jenige), die/das(jenige), das …; **this ~, that ~** dieser/diese/dieses; **the blue ~** der/die/das Blaue; **which ~?** welcher/welche/welches?; **~ another** einander **oneself** PRON sich **one-way street** S Einbahnstraße *f* **one-way ticket** S einfache Fahrkarte
onion ['ʌnjən] S Zwiebel *f*
on-line ['ɑːnlaɪn] ADJ IT online
only ['oʊnlɪ] 1 ADV nur; erst; **~ just arrived** gerade erst angekommen 2 ADJ einzige(r, s); **~ child** Einzelkind *n*
on-ramp S (Autobahn)auffahrt *f*
onto ['ɑːntʊ] PRÄP auf *+akk*; (*bei senkrechter Fläche*) an *+akk*
onward(s) ['ɑːnwərd(z)] ADV voran, vorwärts; **from today ~** von heute an, ab heute
open ['oʊpən] 1 ADJ offen, geöffnet; **in the ~ air** im Freien; **~ to the public** für die Öffentlichkeit zugänglich 2 V/T öffnen, aufmachen; (*Konferenz, Konto etc*) eröffnen 3 V/I (*Tür, Fenster etc*) aufgehen, sich öffnen; (*Geschäft, Bank etc*) öffnen, aufmachen; (*beginnen*) anfangen (*with* mit) **opening**

S Öffnung *f*; (*offiziell*) Eröffnung *f*; **~ hours** (*od* **times**) *pl* Öffnungszeiten *pl* **openly** ADV offen **open-minded** ADJ aufgeschlossen
operate ['ɑ:pəreɪt] **1** V/T (*Maschine etc*) bedienen; (*Bremse etc*) betätigen **2** V/I (*Maschine*) laufen; (*Bus etc*) verkehren (*between* zwischen); **~ (on sb)** MED (j-n) operieren **operating room** S Operationssaal *m* **operation** [ɑ:pə'reɪʃən] S (*von Maschine etc*) Bedienung *f*; MED Operation *f* (*on* an *+dat*); (*Aktion*) Unternehmen *n*; **in ~** (*Maschine, Gerät*) in Betrieb; **have an ~** operiert werden (*for* wegen)
opinion [ə'pɪnjən] S Meinung *f* (*on* zu); **in my ~** meiner Meinung nach
opponent [ə'poʊnənt] S Gegner(in) *m(f)*
opportunity [ɑ:pər'tu:nətɪ] S Gelegenheit *f*
oppose [ə'poʊz] V/T sich widersetzen *+dat*; (*Idee etc*) ablehnen **opposed** ADJ **be ~ to sth** gegen etw sein; **as ~ to** im Gegensatz zu **opposing** ADJ (*Mannschaft*) gegnerisch; (*Standpunkt*) entgegengesetzt **opposite** ['ɑ:pəzɪt] **1** ADJ (*Haus*) gegenüberliegend; (*Richtung*) entgegengesetzt **2** ADV gegenüber **3** PRÄP gegenüber *+dat* **4** S Gegenteil *n* **opposition** [ɑ:pə'zɪʃən] S Widerstand *m* (*to* gegen); POL Opposition *f*
optician [ɑ:p'tɪʃən] S Optiker(in) *m(f)*
optimistic [ɑ:ptə'mɪstɪk] ADJ optimistisch
option ['ɑ:pʃən] S Möglichkeit *f*, Wahl *f*; WIRTSCH Option *f* **optional** ADJ freiwillig
or [ɔ:r] KONJ oder; (*ansonsten*) sonst
OR **1** *abk* = Oregon **2** *abk* = operating room; Operationssaal *m*
oral ['ɔ:rəl] **1** ADJ mündlich; oral **2** S (*Prüfung*) Mündliche(s) *n* **oral surgeon** S Kieferchirurg(in) *m(f)*
orange ['ɔ:rəndʒ] **1** S Orange *f* **2** ADJ orangefarben **orange juice** S Orangensaft *m*
orbit ['ɔ:rbət] **1** S Umlaufbahn *f* **2** V/T umkreisen
orchard ['ɔ:rtʃərd] S Obstgarten *m*
orchestra ['ɔ:rkəstrə] S Orchester *n*; THEAT Parkett *n*
ordeal [ɔ:r'di:l] S Tortur *f*; (*psychische*) Qual *f*
order ['ɔ:rdər] **1** S Reihenfolge *f*; (*System*) Ordnung *f*; (*Anweisung*) Befehl *m*; (*Aussehen*) Zustand *m*; (*von Ware, im Restaurant*) Bestellung *f*; **out of ~** (*von Gerät etc*) außer Betrieb; (*unschicklich*) nicht angebracht; **in ~** (*Gegenstände*) richtig geordnet; (*funktionierend*) in Ordnung; **in ~ to do sth** um

etw zu tun **2** VT (*Papiere etc*) ordnen; (*als Vorgesetzter etc*) befehlen; (*Essen, Waren*) bestellen
ordinary ['ɔːrdəneri] ADJ gewöhnlich, normal
organ ['ɔːrgən] S MUS Orgel *f*; ANAT Organ *n*
organic [ɔːr'gænɪk] ADJ organisch; (*Anbau, Gemüse etc*) Bio-, Öko-; **~ food** Biokost *f*
organization [ɔːrgənaɪ'zeɪʃən] S Organisation *f*; (*Anordnung*) Ordnung *f* **organize** ['ɔːrgənaɪz] VT organisieren **organizer** S Organisator(in) *m(f)*; (elektronisches) Notizbuch
orgasm ['ɔːrgæzəm] S Orgasmus *m*
origin ['ɑːrədʒən] S Ursprung *m*; (*von Person*) Herkunft *f* **original** [ə'rɪdʒənl] **1** ADJ ursprünglich; (*Gemälde*) original; (*Idee*) originell **2** S Original *n* **originally** ADV ursprünglich
orphan ['ɔːrfən] S Waise *f*, Waisenkind *n* **orphanage** ['ɔːrfənɪdʒ] S Waisenhaus *n*
orthodox ['ɔːrθədɑːks] ADJ orthodox
orthopedic [ɔːrθə'piːdɪk] ADJ orthopädisch
other ['ʌðər] ADJ & PRON andere(r, s); **any ~ questions?** sonst noch Fragen?; **the ~ day** neulich; **every ~ day** jeden zweiten Tag; **someone/something or ~** irgendjemand/irgendetwas **otherwise** ['ʌðərwaɪz] ADV sonst; (*von der Art her*) anders
ought [ɒːt] V/AUX (*Verpflichtung*) sollte; (*Wahrscheinlichkeit*) dürfte; (*stärker*) müsste
ounce [aʊns] S Unze *f* (*28,35 g*)
our [aʊr] ADJ unser **ours** PRON unsere(r, s); **this is ~** das gehört uns; **a friend of ~** ein Freund von uns **ourselves** PRON uns; (*verstärkend*) **we did it ~** wir haben es selbst gemacht; **(all) by ~** allein
out [aʊt] **1** ADV hinaus/heraus; draußen; (*Person*) nicht zu Hause; (*Licht, Feuer*) aus; (*ohnmächtig*) bewusstlos; (*Buch*) herausgekommen; (*Ergebnisse*) bekannt gegeben **2** VT *umg* outen **outage** ['aʊtɪdʒ] S Stromausfall *m* **outboard motor** [aʊtbɔːrd'moʊtər] S Außenbordmotor *m* **outbreak** ['aʊtbreɪk] S Ausbruch *m* **outcome** ['aʊtkʌm] S Ergebnis *n* **outcry** ['aʊtkraɪ] S Protestwelle *f* (*against* gegen)
outdoor ['aʊtdɔːr] ADJ Außen-; SPORT im Freien; **~ swimming pool** Freibad *n* **outdoors** [aʊt'dɔːrz] ADV draußen, im Freien
outer ['aʊtər] ADJ äußere(r, s) **outer space** S Weltraum *m*
outfit ['aʊtfɪt] S Ausrüstung *f*; Kleidung *f* **outgoing** ['aʊtgoʊɪŋ] ADJ kontaktfreudig

outlet ['aʊtlet] S Auslass *m*, Abfluss *m*; Steckdose *f*; (*Geschäft*) Verkaufsstelle *f* **outline** ['aʊtlaɪn] S Umriss *m*; (*kurze Zusammenfassung*) Abriss *m* **outlook** ['aʊtlʊk] S Aussicht(en) *f* (*pl*); (*Haltung*) Einstellung *f* (*on* zu) **outnumber** [aʊt'nʌmbər] V/T zahlenmäßig überlegen sein *+dat*; **~ed** zahlenmäßig unterlegen

out of ['aʊtəv] PRÄP aus; (*Positionsangabe*) außerhalb *+gen*; **~ danger** außer Gefahr; **we are ~ bread** wir haben kein Brot mehr **out-of-date** ADJ veraltet **out-of-the-way** ADJ abgelegen

outpatient ['aʊtpeɪʃənt] S ambulanter Patient, ambulante Patientin **output** ['aʊtpʊt] S Produktion *f*; (*von Maschine*) Leistung *f*; IT Ausgabe *f*

outrage ['aʊtreɪdʒ] S (*über Beschluss etc*) Empörung *f* (*at* über); Schandtat *f*, Verbrechen *n*; Skandal *m* **outrageous** [aʊt'reɪdʒəs] ADJ unerhört; (*Auftreten etc*) unmöglich, schrill

outright ['aʊtraɪt] **1** ADV sofort **2** ADJ total; (*Ablehnung, Leugnen*) völlig; (*Sieger*) unbestritten **outside** **1** [aʊt'saɪd, 'aʊtsaɪd] S Außenseite *f*; **on the ~** außen **2** ['aʊtsaɪd] ADJ äußere(r, s), Außen-; (*Chance*) sehr gering **3** [aʊt'saɪd] ADV außen; **go ~** nach draußen gehen **4** [aʊt'saɪd, 'aʊtsaɪd] PRÄP außerhalb *+gen* **outsider** S Außenseiter(in) *m(f)* **outskirts** ['aʊtskɜːrts] S PL (*von Stadt*) Stadtrand *m* **outstanding** [aʊt'stændɪŋ] ADJ hervorragend; (*Schulden etc*) ausstehend **outward** ['aʊtwərd] **1** ADJ äußere(r, s); **~ journey** Hinfahrt *f* **2** ADV nach außen **outwards** ADV nach außen

oval ['oʊvəl] ADJ oval **Oval Office** S *Büro des Präsidenten im Weißen Haus*

ovary ['oʊvərɪ] S Eierstock *m*

oven ['ʌvn] S Backofen *m* **ovenproof** ADJ feuerfest

over ['oʊvər] **1** PRÄP (*Position*) über *+dat*; (*Bewegung*) über *+akk*; **from all ~ Maryland** aus ganz Maryland; **~ $20** mehr als 20 Dollar; **~ the phone/radio** am Telefon/im Radio; **~ the summer** während des Sommers **2** ADV (*Richtung*) hinüber/herüber; (*Veranstaltung, Sommer etc*) vorbei; (*Spiel, Kampf*) zu Ende; (*Beziehung*) aus; (*als Rest*) übrig; **~ there/in Europe** da drüben/drüben in Europa; **~ and ~ again** immer wieder; **start (all) ~ again** noch einmal von vorn anfangen; **children of 8 and ~** Kinder ab 8 Jahren **overall** ['oʊvərɒːl] **1** ADJ (*Lage etc*) allgemein; (*Länge etc*) Gesamt- **2** ADV insgesamt **overalls** S PL Overall *m* **over-**

board ['oʊvərbɔ:rd] ADV über Bord **overbooked** [oʊvər'bʊkt] ADJ überbucht **overcharge** [oʊvər'tʃɑ:rdʒ] V/T zu viel verlangen von **overcooked** [oʊvər'kʊkt] ADJ verkocht; (*Fleisch*) zu lange gebraten **overcrowded** [oʊvər'kraʊdəd] ADJ überfüllt **overdone** [oʊvər'dʌn] ADJ übertrieben; (*Essen*) zu lange gekocht; (*Fleisch*) zu lange gebraten **overdose** ['oʊvərdoʊs] S Überdosis *f* **overdraft** ['oʊvərdræft] S Kontoüberziehung *f* **overdrawn** [oʊvər'drɒ:n] ADJ überzogen **overdue** [oʊvər'du:] ADJ überfällig **over-easy** [oʊvər'i:zɪ] ADJ (*Spiegelei*) auf beiden Seiten leicht gebraten **overestimate** [oʊvər'estəmeɪt] V/T überschätzen **overflow** [oʊvər'floʊ] V/I überlaufen **overhead** **1** ['oʊvərhed] ADJ Hoch-, Ober-; ~ **locker** FLUG Gepäckfach *n* **2** [oʊvər'hed] ADV oben **overhear** [oʊvər'hɪr] *irr* V/T zufällig mit anhören **overheat** [oʊvər'hi:t] V/I (*Maschine, Motor*) heiß laufen **overjoyed** [oʊvər'dʒɔɪd] ADJ überglücklich (*at* über) **overland** **1** ['oʊvərlænd] ADJ Überland- **2** [oʊvər'lænd] ADV (*reisen*) über Land **overlap** [oʊvər'læp] V/I (*Termine etc*) sich überschneiden; (*Gegenstände*) sich teilweise decken **overload** [oʊvər'loʊd] V/T überladen **overlook** [oʊvər'lʊk] V/T überblicken; (*nicht bemerken*) übersehen; (*wohlwollend*) hinwegsehen über *+akk* **overnight** **1** ['oʊvərnaɪt] ADJ (*Zug etc*) Nacht-; ~ **bag** Reisetasche *f*; ~ **stay** Übernachtung *f* **2** [oʊvər'naɪt] ADV über Nacht **overpass** ['oʊvərpæs] S Überführung *f* **overseas** **1** ['oʊvərsi:z] ADJ Übersee-; ausländisch; *umg* Auslands- **2** [oʊvər'si:z] ADV (*reisen*) nach Übersee; (*leben, arbeiten*) in Übersee **oversleep** [oʊvər'sli:p] *irr* V/I verschlafen **overtake** [oʊvər'teɪk] *irr* V/T & V/I überholen **overtime** ['oʊvərtaɪm] S Überstunden *pl*; SPORT Verlängerung *f* **overturn** [oʊvər'tɜ:rn] V/T & V/I umkippen **overweight** [oʊvər'weɪt] ADJ **be** ~ Übergewicht haben **over-well** [oʊvər'wel] ADJ (*Spiegelei*) auf beiden Seiten durchgebraten **overwhelming** [oʊvər'welmɪŋ] ADJ überwältigend **overworked** [oʊvər'wɜ:rkt] ADJ überarbeitet

owe [oʊ] V/T schulden; verdanken; **how much do I ~ you?** was bin ich dir/Ihnen schuldig?

owing to PRÄP wegen *+gen*

owl [aʊl] S Eule *f*

own [oʊn] **1** V/T besitzen **2** ADJ eigen; **on one's ~** allein

owner S Besitzer(in) *m(f)*; (*von Firma etc*) Inhaber(in) *m(f)*

ownership S Besitz *m*
oxygen ['ɑ:ksədʒən] S Sauerstoff *m*
oyster ['ɔıstər] S Auster *f*
oz *abk* = ounces; Unzen *pl*
ozone ['oʊzoʊn] S Ozon *n*

P

p *abk* = page; S.
pa [pɑ:] S *umg* Papa *f*
PA 1 *abk* = Pennsylvania 2 *abk* = public address system; Lautsprecheranlage *f*
pace [peıs] S (*Geschwindigkeit*) Tempo *n*; (*mit Fuß*) Schritt *m*
pacemaker S MED Schrittmacher *m*
Pacific [pə'sıfık] S **the ~ (Ocean)** der Pazifik
pacifier ['pæsəfaır] S Schnuller *m*
pack [pæk] 1 S (*Zigaretten*) Schachtel *f*; (*Gang*) Bande *f*; (*zum Tragen*) Rucksack *m* 2 V/T *umg* tragen, dabeihaben; (*Tasche etc*) packen; (*Kleidung etc*) einpacken 3 V/I packen
package ['pækıdʒ] S Paket *n* **package tour** S Pauschalreise *f* **packaging** S Verpackung *f* **packet** S Päckchen *n*; Briefchen *n*
pad [pæd] S Schreibblock *m*; (*von Kleidungsstück*) Polster *n*
padding S Polsterung *f*
paddle ['pædl] 1 S Paddel *n*; Tischtennisschläger *m* 2 V/I paddeln
padlock ['pædlɑ:k] S Vorhängeschloss *n*
page [peıdʒ] S (*Buch*) Seite *f*
pager ['peıdʒər] S Piepser *m*
paid [peıd] 1 *prät, pperf von* pay 2 ADJ bezahlt
pail [peıl] S Eimer *m*
pain [peın] S Schmerz *m*; **be in ~** Schmerzen haben; **she's a (real) ~ (in the neck)** sie nervt
painful ADJ schmerzhaft
painkiller S schmerzstillendes Mittel
paint [peınt] 1 S Farbe *f* 2 V/T anstreichen; (*Bild*) malen
paintbrush S Pinsel *m*
painter S Maler(in) *m(f)*
painting S Bild *n*, Gemälde *n*
pair [per] S Paar *n*; **a ~ of shoes** ein Paar Schuhe; **a ~ of pants** eine Hose
pajamas [pə'dʒɑ:məz] S PL Schlafanzug *m*
Pakistan [pækı'stæn] S Pakistan *n*
pal [pæl] S *umg* Kumpel *m*
palace ['pæləs] S Palast *m*
pale [peıl] ADJ (*Gesicht*) blass, bleich; (*Farbe*) hell
palm [pɑ:m] S Handfläche *f*; Palme *f* **palmtop (computer)** S Palmtop(computer) *m*
pamper ['pæmpər] V/T verhätscheln
pan [pæn] S (*zum Kochen*) Topf

m; (*zum Braten*) Pfanne *f* **pancake** ['pænkeɪk] S Pfannkuchen *m*
panda ['pændə] S Panda *m*
pandemic [pæn'demɪk] S Pandemie *f*
panel ['pænl] S (*aus Holz*) Tafel *f*; (*in Diskussion*) Diskussionsteilnehmer *pl*; (*in Jury*) Jurymitglieder *pl*
panic ['pænɪk] **1** S Panik *f* **2** V/I in Panik geraten
panties ['pænti:z] S PL (Damen)slip *m* **pants** [pænts] S PL Hose *f* **pantyhose** ['pæntɪhoʊz] S PL Strumpfhose *f* **pantyliner** S Slipeinlage *f*
paper ['peɪpər] **1** S Papier *n*; Zeitung *f*; (*Prüfung*) Klausur *f*; (*Vortrag*) Referat *n*; **~s** *pl* (*Ausweis*) Papiere *pl*; **~ cup** Pappbecher *m* **2** V/T tapezieren **paperback** S Taschenbuch *n* **paper clip** S Büroklammer *f* **paperwork** S Schreibarbeit *f*
parachute ['pærəʃu:t] **1** S Fallschirm *m* **2** V/I abspringen
parade [pə'reɪd] **1** S (*bei Fest*) Umzug *m*; MIL Parade *f* **2** V/I vorbeimarschieren
paradise ['pærədaɪs] S Paradies *n*
paragliding ['pærəglaɪdɪŋ] S Gleitschirmfliegen *n*
paragraph ['pærəgræf] S Absatz *m*
parallel ['pærəlel] **1** ADJ parallel **2** S MATH *fig* Parallele *f*
paralyze ['pærəlaɪz] V/T lähmen; *fig* lahmlegen
paranoid ['pærənɔɪd] ADJ paranoid
parcel ['pɑ:rsl] S Paket *n*
pardon ['pɑ:rdn] S JUR Begnadigung *f*; **~ me/I beg your ~** verzeih/verzeihen Sie bitte; (*Einwand*) aber ich bitte dich/Sie; **I beg your ~?/~ me?** wie bitte?
parent ['perənt] S Elternteil *m*; **~s** *pl* Eltern *pl*; **~s-in-law** *pl* Schwiegereltern *pl* **parental** [pə'rentl] ADJ elterlich, Eltern-
parish ['pærɪʃ] S Gemeinde *f*
park [pɑ:rk] **1** S Park *m* **2** V/T & V/I parken **parking** S Parken *n*; **'no ~'** „Parken verboten" **parking lights** S PL Standlicht *n* **parking lot** S Parkplatz *m* **parking meter** S Parkuhr *f* **parking space**, **parking spot** S Parkplatz *m* **parking ticket** S Strafzettel *m*
parrot ['pærət] S Papagei *m*
parsley ['pɑ:rslɪ] S Petersilie *f*
part [pɑ:rt] **1** S Teil *m*; (*Maschine etc*) Teil *n*; THEAT Rolle *f*; (*Haar*) Scheitel *m*; **take ~** teilnehmen (*in* an *+dat*) **2** ADJ Teil- **3** V/T trennen; (*Haar*) scheiteln **4** V/I (*Personen*) sich trennen **partial** ['pɑ:rʃəl] ADJ teilweise, Teil-
participant [pɑ:r'tɪsəpənt] S Teilnehmer(in) *m(f)* **participate** [pɑ:r'tɪsəpeɪt] V/I teil-

nehmen (*in* an *+dat*)
particular [pər'tıkjələr] **1** ADJ (*speziell*) bestimmt; (*exakt*) genau; (*pingelig*) eigen; **in ~** insbesondere **2** S **~s** *pl* (*Details*) Einzelheiten *pl*; (*von Person*) Personalien *pl* **particularly** ADV besonders
parting ['pɑːrtıŋ] S Abschied *m*
partly ['pɑːrtlı] ADV teilweise
partner ['pɑːrtnər] S Partner(in) *m(f)* **partnership** S Partnerschaft *f*
partridge ['pɑːrtrıdʒ] S Rebhuhn *n*
part-time ['pɑːrttaım] **1** ADJ Teilzeit- **2** ADV **work ~** Teilzeit arbeiten
party ['pɑːrtı] **1** S Party *f*; POL, JUR Partei *f*; (*von Wanderern etc*) Gruppe *f* **2** V/I feiern
pass [pæs] **1** V/T vorbeigehen an *+dat*; vorbeifahren an *+dat*; reichen; (*Zeit*) verbringen; (*Prüfung*) bestehen; (*Gesetz*) verabschieden; (*Ball*) abspielen **2** V/I vorbeigehen; vorbeifahren; (*Zeit*) vergehen; (*bei Prüfung*) bestehen; (*beim Kartenspiel*) passen **3** S (*Dokument*) Ausweis *m*; SPORT Pass *m*; **make a ~ at sb** Annäherungsversuche bei j-m machen **pass away** V/I (*sterben*) verscheiden **pass by** **1** V/I vorbeigehen; vorbeifahren **2** V/T vorbeigehen an *+dat*; vorbeifahren an *+dat* **pass on** V/T weitergeben (*to* an *+akk*); (*Krankheit*) übertragen (*to* auf *+akk*) **pass out** V/I ohnmächtig werden; *umg* schnell einschlafen
passage ['pæsıdʒ] S (*zwischen Zimmern*) Gang *m*; (*in Buch etc*) Passage *f* **passageway** S Durchgang *m*
passenger ['pæsəndʒər] S Passagier(in) *m(f)*; (*Bus, Zug etc*) Fahrgast *m*; (*Zug*) Reisende(r) *m/f(m)*; (*in Auto*) Mitfahrer(in) *m(f)*
passer-by ⟨passers-by *pl*⟩ [pæsər'baı] S Passant(in) *m(f)*
passion ['pæʃən] S Leidenschaft *f* **passionate** ['pæʃənət] ADJ leidenschaftlich **passion fruit** S Passionsfrucht *f*
passive ['pæsıv] **1** ADJ passiv **2** S LING Passiv *n*
passport ['pæspɔːrt] S (Reise)pass *m* **passport control** S Passkontrolle *f*
password ['pæswɜːrd] S IT Passwort *n*
past [pæst] **1** S Vergangenheit *f* **2** ADV vorbei; **it's five ~** es ist fünf nach **3** ADJ vergangen; ehemalig **4** PRÄP (*Richtung*) an ... vorbei; (*Position*) hinter; (*zeitlich*) nach; **half ~ 10** halb 11
pasta ['pæstə] S Nudeln *pl*
paste [peıst] **1** V/T kleben; IT einfügen **2** S Kleister *m*
pastime ['pæstaım] S Zeitvertreib *m*
pastry ['peıstrı] S Teig *m*; (*Gebäck*) Stückchen *n*

patch [pætʃ] **1** S (*Stelle*) Fleck *m*; (*auf Kleidung etc*) Flicken *m* **2** V/T flicken
pâté [pæ'teɪ] S Pastete *f*
paternal [pə'tɜ:rnl] ADJ väterlich; väterlicherseits **paternity leave** [pə'tɜ:rnətɪli:v] S Elternzeit *f* (des Vaters) **paternity test** S Vaterschaftstest *m*
path [pæθ] S *a.* IT Pfad *m*; *a. fig* Weg *m*
pathetic [pə'θetɪk] ADJ kläglich, erbärmlich
patience ['peɪʃəns] S Geduld *f* **patient** **1** ADJ geduldig **2** S Patient(in) *m(f)*
patio ['pætɪoʊ] S Terrasse *f*
patriotic [peɪtrɪ'ɑ:tɪk] ADJ patriotisch
patrol car [pə'troʊlkɑ:r] S Streifenwagen *m* **patrolman** ⟨-men *pl*⟩ S Streifenpolizist *m*
patron ['peɪtrən] S (*Sponsor*) Förderer *m*, Förderin *f*; (*in Geschäft*) Kunde *m*, Kundin *f*
patronize ['peɪtrənaɪz] V/T von oben herab behandeln
pattern ['pætərn] S Muster *n*
pause [pɒ:z] **1** S Pause *f* **2** V/I (*beim Sprechen etc*) innehalten
pavement ['peɪvmənt] S Straßenpflaster *n*, Straßenbelag *m*
pay ⟨paid, paid⟩ [peɪ, peɪd] **1** V/T bezahlen; zahlen; **~ sb a visit** j-n besuchen **2** V/I zahlen; sich bezahlt machen; **~ for sth** etw bezahlen **3** S Bezahlung *f*, Lohn *m* **pay in** V/T (*auf Konto*) einzahlen **payable** ADJ zahlbar; (*Rückzahlung*) fällig
payee [peɪ'i:] S Zahlungsempfänger(in) *m(f)* **payment** S Bezahlung *f*; (*Geldbetrag*) Zahlung *f* **pay phone** S Münzfernsprecher *m*
PC **1** *abk* = personal computer; PC *m* **2** *abk* = politically correct; politisch korrekt
PD *abk* = Police Department; Polizeidirektion *f*
PDA *abk* = personal digital assistant; PDA *m*
PDF, **pdf** *abk* = portable document format; PDF *n*; **~ file** PDF-Datei *f*
pea [pi:] S Erbse *f*
peace [pi:s] S Frieden *m* **peaceful** ADJ friedlich
peach [pi:tʃ] S Pfirsich *m*
peacock ['pi:kɑ:k] S Pfau *m*
peak [pi:k] S (*Berg*) Gipfel *m*; *fig* Höhepunkt *m* **peak period** S Stoßzeit *f*, Hochsaison *f*
peanut ['pi:nʌt] S Erdnuss *f* **peanut butter** S Erdnussbutter *f*
pear [per] S Birne *f*
pearl [pɜ:rl] S Perle *f*
pebble ['pebl] S Kiesel *m*
pecan [pɪ'kæn] S Pekannuss *f*
peculiar [pɪ'kju:ljər] ADJ seltsam; eigentümlich **peculiarity** [pɪkjʊlɪ'ærətɪ] S Besonderheit *f*, Eigenartigkeit *f*
pedal ['pedl] S Pedal *n*
pedestrian [pə'destrɪən] S Fußgänger(in) *m(f)* **pedestri-**

an mall S Fußgängerzone *f*
pediatrician [pi:dɪə'trɪʃən] S Kinderarzt *m*, Kinderärztin *f*
pee [pi:] V/I *umg* pinkeln
peel [pi:l] **1** S Schale *f* **2** V/T schälen **3** V/I (*Farbe etc*) abblättern; (*Haut etc*) sich schälen
peer [pɪr] **1** S Gleichaltrige(r) *m/f(m)* **2** V/I starren
peg [peg] S (*für Kleider etc*) Haken *m*; (*für Zelt*) Hering *m*
pelvis ['pelvɪs] S Becken *n*
pen [pen] S Kuli *m*, Kugelschreiber *m*; Füller *m*
penalize ['pi:nəlaɪz] V/T bestrafen **penalty** ['penltɪ] S Strafe *f*; (*Eishockey*) Strafschuss *m*; (*Fußball*) Elfmeter *m*
pencil ['pensl] S Bleistift *m* **pencil sharpener** S (Bleistift)spitzer *m*
penetrate ['penətreɪt] V/T durchdringen; eindringen in *+akk*
penguin ['peŋgwɪn] S Pinguin *m*
peninsula [pə'nɪnsələ] S Halbinsel *f*
penis ['pi:nəs] S Penis *m*
penitentiary [penə'tenʃərɪ] S Strafvollzugsanstalt *f*
penknife ⟨penknives *pl*⟩ ['pennaɪf, 'pennaɪvz] S Taschenmesser *n*
penny ['penɪ] S Centstück *n*
pen pal S Brieffreund(in) *m(f)*
pension ['penʃən] S Rente *f*; (*von Beamten*) Pension *f* **pensioner** S Rentner(in) *m(f)*
pension plan S Rentenversicherung *f*
Pentagon ['pentəgɑ:n] S **the ~** das Pentagon (*Verteidigungsministerium der USA*)
Pentecost ['pentəkɒ:st] S Pfingsten *n*
penthouse ⟨penthouses *pl*⟩ ['penthaʊs, 'penthaʊzəz] S Dachterrassenwohnung *f*, Penthouse *n*
penultimate [pɪ'nʌltəmət] ADJ vorletzte(r, s)
people ['pi:pl] S PL (*Personen*) Leute *pl*, Volk *n*; (*Einwohner*) Bevölkerung *f*
pepper ['pepər] S Pfeffer *m*; (*Gemüse*) Paprika *m* **peppermint** S Pfefferminz *n*
per [pɜ:r] PRÄP pro; **~cent** Prozent *n* **percentage** [pər'sentɪdʒ] S Prozentsatz *m*
percussion [pɜ:r'kʌʃən] S MUS Schlagzeug *n*
perfect **1** ['pɜ:rfɪkt] ADJ perfekt; (*Stille etc*) völlig **2** [pər'fekt] V/T vervollkommnen **perfectly** ['pɜ:rfɪktlɪ] ADV perfekt; (*absolut*) völlig
perform [pər'fɔ:rm] **1** V/T (*Aufgabe*) ausführen; (*Theaterstück*) aufführen; MED (*Operation*) durchführen **2** V/I THEAT auftreten **performance** S (*in Theater etc*) Vorstellung *f*; (*bei Arbeit, von Motor etc*) Leistung *f*
perfume ['pɜ:rfju:m] S Duft

m; (*Kosmetik*) Parfüm *n* **perhaps** [pər'hæps] ADV vielleicht **period** ['pɪrɪəd] S (*Zeitspanne*) Zeit *f*, Zeitraum *m*; (*historisch*) Zeitalter *n*; (*Schule*) Stunde *f*; MED Periode *f*; (*Satzzeichen*) Punkt *m* **periodical** [pɪrɪ'ɑ:dɪkəl] S Zeitschrift *f* **perjury** ['pɜ:rdʒərɪ] S Meineid *m* **perm** [pɜ:rm] S Dauerwelle *f* **permanent, permanently** ['pɜ:rmənənt, -lɪ] ADJ & ADV ständig **permission** [pər'mɪʃən] S Erlaubnis *f* **permit** 1 ['pɜ:rmɪt] S Genehmigung *f* 2 [pər'mɪt] V/T erlauben, zulassen **persecute** ['pɜ:rsɪkju:t] V/T verfolgen **persist** [pər'sɪst] V/I (*überzeugungsmäßig*) bleiben (*in* bei); (*Regen etc*) andauern **persistent** ADJ beharrlich **person** ['pɜ:rsn] S Mensch *m*; Person *f*; **in ~** persönlich **personal** ADJ persönlich; privat **personality** [pɜ:rsə'nælətɪ] S Persönlichkeit *f* **personal organizer** S Organizer *m* **personnel** [pɜ:rsə'nel] S Personal *n* **perspective** [pər'spektɪv] S Perspektive *f* **persuade** [pər'sweɪd] V/T überreden; (*völlig umstimmen*) überzeugen **persuasive** [pər'sweɪsɪv] ADJ überzeugend

perverse [pər'vɜ:rs] ADJ eigensinnig; abwegig **pervert** 1 ['pɜ:rvɜ:rt] S Perverse(r) *m/f(m)* 2 [pər'vɜ:rt] V/T (*moralisch*) verderben **perverted** ADJ pervers **pessimistic** [pesə'mɪstɪk] ADJ pessimistisch **pest** [pest] S (*Insekt*) Schädling *m*; *fig* Nervensäge *f*; (*Sache*) Plage *f* **pesticide** ['pestəsaɪd] S Schädlingsbekämpfungsmittel *n* **pet** [pet] S (*Tier*) Haustier *n*; (*Person*) Liebling *m* **petition** [pə'tɪʃən] S Petition *f* **pharmacy** ['fɑ:rməsɪ] S Apotheke *f*; (*Wissenschaft*) Pharmazie *f* **phase** [feɪz] S Phase *f* **PhD** *abk* = Doctor of Philosophy; Dr. phil; (*schriftliche Arbeit*) Doktorarbeit *f* **phenomenon** ⟨phenomena⟩ [fɪ'nɑ:mənɑ:n, fɪ'nɑ:mənə] S Phänomen *n* **Philippines** ['fɪlɪpi:nz] S PL Philippinen *pl* **philosophical** [fɪlə'sɑ:fɪkəl] ADJ philosophisch **philosophy** [fɪ'lɑ:səfɪ] S Philosophie *f* **phone** [foʊn] S Telefon *n* **phone booth** S Telefonzelle *f* **phonecall** S Telefonanruf *m* **phonecard** S Telefonkarte *f* **phone number** S Telefonnummer *f* **photo** ⟨-s *pl*⟩ ['foʊtoʊ] S Foto *n* **photo booth** S Fotoauto-

mat *m* **photocopier** ['foʊtəkɑ:pɪər] S Kopiergerät *n* **photocopy** ['foʊtəkɑ:pɪ] **1** S Fotokopie *f* **2** V/T fotokopieren
photograph ['foʊtəgræf] **1** S Fotografie *f*, Aufnahme *f* **2** V/T fotografieren **photographer** [fə'tɑ:grəfər] S Fotograf(in) *m(f)* **photography** [fə'tɑ:grəfɪ] S Fotografie *f*
phrase [freɪz] S Redewendung *f*, Ausdruck *m* **phrase book** S Sprachführer *m*
physical ['fɪzɪkəl] **1** ADJ körperlich, physisch **2** S ärztliche Untersuchung **physically** ['fɪzɪklɪ] ADV körperlich, physisch; ~ **handicapped** körperbehindert **physician** [fɪ'zɪʃən] S Arzt *m*, Ärztin *f*
physics ['fɪzɪks] S SG Physik *f*
physiotherapy [fɪzɪoʊ'θerəpɪ] S Physiotherapie *f*
physique [fɪ'zi:k] S Körperbau *m*
piano ‹-s *pl*› ['pɪænoʊ] S Klavier *n*
pick [pɪk] V/T pflücken; (*einzelne Dinge, Personen*) auswählen; (*Team etc*) aufstellen **pick out** V/T auswählen **pick up** V/T (*vom Boden etc*) aufheben; (*Personen, Paket*) abholen; (*Frau etc*) *umg* aufreißen; (*Neues*) lernen
pickle ['pɪkl] **1** S saure Gurke; (*eingelegtes Gemüse*) (Mixed) Pickles *pl* **2** V/T einlegen
pickpocket ['pɪkpɑ:kɪt] S Taschendieb(in) *m(f)*
picnic ['pɪknɪk] S Picknick *n*
picture ['pɪktʃər] **1** S Bild *n* **2** V/T (*gedanklich*) sich vorstellen
picturesque [pɪktʃə'resk] ADJ malerisch
pie [paɪ] S (*mit Fleisch*) Pastete *f*; (*mit Obst*) Kuchen *m*
piece [pi:s] S Stück *n*, Teil *n*; (*Schach*) Figur *f*; (*Damespiel*) Stein *m*; **a ~ of cake** ein Stück Kuchen; *fig* ein Kinderspiel
pier [pɪr] S Pier *m*
pierce [pɪrs] V/T durchstechen, durchbohren; (*Kälte, Geräusch*) durchdringen **pierced** ADJ (*Körperteil*) gepierct
pig [pɪg] S Schwein *n*
pigeon ['pɪdʒən] S Taube *f*
pigheaded [pɪg'hedəd] ADJ dickköpfig **pigtail** ['pɪgteɪl] S Zopf *m*
pile [paɪl] S Haufen *m*; Stapel *m* **pile up** V/I sich anhäufen **pile-up** ['paɪlʌp] S AUTO Massenkarambolage *f*
pill [pɪl] S Tablette *f*; **the ~** die (Antibaby)pille; **be on the ~** die Pille nehmen
pillar ['pɪlər] S Pfeiler *m*
pillow ['pɪloʊ] S (Kopf)kissen *n* **pillowcase** S (Kopf)kissenbezug *m*
pilot ['paɪlət] S FLUG Pilot(in) *m(f)*
pimple ['pɪmpl] S Pickel *m*
pin [pɪn] **1** S Nadel *f*; (*zum Heften*) Stecknadel *f*; TECH Stift *m* **2** V/T (*mit Stecknadel*) heften

(*to* an *+akk*)
PIN [pın] *akr* = personal identification number; **~ (number)** PIN *f*, Geheimzahl *f*
pinch [pıntʃ] **1** S (*Salz*) Prise *f* **2** V/T zwicken **3** V/I (*Schuh*) drücken
pine [paın] S Kiefer *f*
pineapple ['paınæpl] S Ananas *f*
pink [pıŋk] ADJ rosa
pint [paınt] S Pint *n* (*0,473l*)
pipe [paıp] S (*zum Rauchen*) Pfeife *f*; (*für Flüssigkeit, Gas*) Rohrleitung *f*
pirate ['paırət] S Pirat(in) *m(f)*
pirated copy ['paırətəd ka:pı] S Raubkopie *f*
Pisces ['paısi:z] S SG ASTROL Fische *pl*; **she's a ~** sie ist Fisch
piss [pıs] **1** V/I *vulg* pissen **2** S *vulg* Pisse *f* **piss off** V/T *vulg* ankotzen **pissed (off)** ADJ *umg* (*total verärgert*) stocksauer
pistachio ⟨-s *pl*⟩ [pı'stæʃıoʊ] S Pistazie *f*
piste [pi:st] S (*Ski*) Piste *f*
pistol ['pıstl] S Pistole *f*
pit [pıt] S Grube *f*; (*Kohlengrube*) Zeche *f*; **be the ~s** *umg* grottenschlecht sein
pitch [pıtʃ] **1** S MUS (*von Instrument*) Tonlage *f*; (*von Stimme*) Stimmlage *f* **2** V/T (*Zelt*) aufschlagen; (*Ball*) werfen; (*neues Produkt*) anpreisen
pitch-black ADJ pechschwarz
pitcher ['pıtʃər] S Krug *m*; (*Baseball*) Werfer(in) *m(f)*
pitiful ['pıtıfəl] ADJ jämmerlich
pity ['pıtı] **1** S Mitleid *n*; **what a ~** wie schade **2** V/T Mitleid haben mit
pizza ['pi:tsə] S Pizza *f* **pizza parlor** ['pi:tsəpa:rlər] S Pizzeria *f*
pj's *abk* = pajamas; Pyjama *m*
place [pleıs] **1** S Stelle *f*; (*Stadt etc*) Ort *m*; (*Wohnstätte*) Haus *n*; (*Sitzplatz*) Platz *m*; **~ of birth** Geburtsort *m*; **at my ~** bei mir; **in third ~** auf dem dritten Platz; **in ~ of** anstelle von; **in the first ~** erstens; (*ohne Aufschub*) gleich; (*sowieso*) überhaupt **2** V/T stellen, setzen; legen; (*Annonce*) setzen (*in* in *+akk*); WIRTSCH (*Bestellung*) aufgeben
plaice [pleıs] S Scholle *f*
plain [pleın] **1** ADJ klar, deutlich; (*schlicht*) einfach; (*Person*) unattraktiv; (*Joghurt*) Natur- **2** S Ebene *f* **plainly** ADV offen; (*schlicht*) einfach; (*offensichtlich*) eindeutig
plan [plæn] **1** S Plan *m*; Konzept *n* **2** V/T planen; **~ to do sth, ~ on doing sth** vorhaben, etw zu tun **3** V/I planen
plane [pleın] S Flugzeug *n*
planet ['plænət] S Planet *m*
plank [plæŋk] S Brett *n*
plant [plænt] **1** S Pflanze *f*; (*Fabrik*) Werk *n* **2** V/T pflanzen
plantation [plæn'teıʃən] S Plantage *f*

plaque [plæk] S Gedenktafel *f*; (*Zähne*) Zahnbelag *m*
plaster ['plæstər] S (*an Wand*) Verputz *m*
plastic ['plæstɪk] 1 S Kunststoff *m* 2 ADJ Plastik- **plastic bag** S Plastiktüte *f* **plastic surgery** S plastische Chirurgie **plastic wrap** S Frischhaltefolie *f*
plate [pleɪt] S Teller *m*; (*aus Stein, Metall etc*) Platte *f*; (*Gedenktafel etc*) Schild *n*
platform ['plætfɔːrm] S BAHN Bahnsteig *m*
platinum ['plætnəm] S Platin *n*
play [pleɪ] 1 S Spiel *n*; THEAT (Theater)stück *n* 2 V/T spielen; spielen gegen; **~ hooky** (*Schule*) schwänzen 3 V/I spielen; **I'm just ~ing** nichts für ungut **play back** V/T abspielen **play down** V/T herunterspielen **player** S Spieler(in) *m(f)*; *umg* Aufreißer(typ) *m* **playful** ADJ (*Person*) verspielt; (*Bemerkung*) scherzhaft **playground** S Spielplatz *m* **playing card** S Spielkarte *f* **playing field** S Sportplatz *m* **playmate** S Spielkamerad(in) *m(f)*
plea [pliː] S Bitte *f* (*for* um)
plead [pliːd] V/I dringend bitten (*with sb* j-n); JUR **~ guilty** sich schuldig bekennen
pleasant, pleasantly ['pleznt, -lɪ] ADJ & ADV angenehm
please [pliːz] 1 ADV bitte 2 V/T gefallen *+dat*; **~ yourself** wie du willst/Sie wollen
pleased ADJ zufrieden; erfreut; **~ to meet you** freut mich, angenehm
pleasure ['pleʒər] S Vergnügen *n*, Freude *f*; **(it's) my ~** gern geschehen
pledge [pledʒ] 1 S Versprechen *n* 2 V/T versprechen
plenty ['plentɪ] S **~ of** eine Menge, viel(e); **be ~** genug sein, reichen
plot [plɑːt] 1 S Handlung *f*; (*Verschwörung*) Komplott *n*; (*Grundbesitz*) Stück *n* Land, Grundstück *n* 2 V/I ein Komplott schmieden
plow [plaʊ] 1 S Pflug *m* 2 V/T & V/I AGR pflügen
pluck [plʌk] V/T (*Augenbrauen etc*) zupfen; (*Hühnchen*) rupfen **pluck up** V/T **~ (one's) courage** Mut aufbringen
plug [plʌg] 1 S (*für Abfluss*) Stöpsel *m*; ELEK Stecker *m*; AUTO (Zünd)kerze *f*; *umg* Schleichwerbung *f* 2 V/T *umg* Reklame machen für **plug in** V/T anschließen
plum [plʌm] 1 S Pflaume *f* 2 ADJ *umg* Super-
plumber ['plʌmər] S Klempner(in) *m(f)*
plump [plʌmp] ADJ rundlich
plunge [plʌndʒ] 1 V/T (*Messer etc*) stoßen; (*in Wasser*) tauchen

2 VI stürzen; (*in Wasser*) tauchen
plural ['plʊrəl] S Plural *m*
plus [plʌs] **1** PRÄP plus; und **2** ADJ Plus-; **20 ~** mehr als 20 **3** S *fig* Plus *n*
p.m. *abk* = post meridiem **at 3 ~** um 3 Uhr nachmittags
pneumonia [nu:'moʊnɪə] S Lungenentzündung *f*
poached [poʊtʃt] ADJ (*Ei*) pochiert, verloren
PO Box *abk* = post office box; Postfach *n*
pocket ['pɑ:kɪt] **1** S Tasche *f* **2** VT einstecken **pocketbook** S Brieftasche *f* **pocket calculator** S Taschenrechner *m*
podcast ['pɑ:dkæst] S IT Podcast *m*
poem ['poʊəm] S Gedicht *n* **poet** ['poʊət] S Dichter(in) *m(f)* **poetic** [poʊ'etɪk] ADJ poetisch **poetry** ['poʊətrɪ] S Dichtung *f*, Gedichte *pl*
point [pɔɪnt] **1** S Punkt *m*, Stelle *f*, Spitze *f*; (*zeitlich*) Zeitpunkt *m*; (*Sinn*) Zweck *m*; (*in Diskussion etc*) Argument *n*; (*statt Komma*) Dezimalstelle *f*; **~ of view** Standpunkt *m*; **three ~ two** drei Komma zwei; **at some ~** irgendwann (mal); **get to the ~** zur Sache kommen **2** VT (*Gewehr etc*) richten (*at* auf *+akk*) **3** VI zeigen (*at, to* auf *+akk*) **point out** VT aufzeigen; hinweisen auf *+akk*
pointed ADJ spitz; (*Frage*) gezielt **pointer** S Zeiger *m*; (*Tipp*) Hinweis *m* **pointless** ADJ sinnlos
poison ['pɔɪzn] **1** S Gift *n* **2** VT vergiften **poisonous** ADJ giftig
poke [poʊk] VT stoßen, stupsen; (*Kopf etc*) stecken
Poland ['poʊlənd] S Polen *n*
polar ['poʊlər] ADJ Polar-, polar; **~ bear** Eisbär *m*
pole [poʊl] S Stange *f*; GEO, ELEK Pol *m*
Pole [poʊl] S Pole *m*, Polin *f*
polecat S Stinktier *n*
pole vault S Stabhochsprung *m*
police [pə'li:s] S Polizei *f* **policeman** <-men *pl*> S Polizist *m* **police officer** S Polizeibeamte(r) *m*, Polizeibeamtin *f* **police station** S (Polizei)wache *f* **policewoman** <-women *pl*> S Polizistin *f*
policy ['pɑ:ləsɪ] S Politik *f*; (*Prinzip*) Grundsatz *m*; (Versicherungs)police *f*
polish ['pɑ:lɪʃ] **1** S (*für Möbel*) Politur *f*; (*für Fußböden*) Wachs *n*; (*für Schuhe*) Creme *f*, Glanz *m*; *fig* Schliff *m* **2** VT polieren; (*Schuhe*) putzen; *fig* den letzten Schliff geben *+dat*
Polish ['poʊlɪʃ] **1** ADJ polnisch **2** S Polnisch *n*
polite [pə'laɪt] ADJ höflich **politeness** S Höflichkeit *f*
political, **politically** [pə'lɪtɪ-

kəl, -ɪ] ADJ & ADV politisch **politician** [pɑːlə'tɪʃən] S Politiker(in) *m(f)* **politics** ['pɑːlətɪks] S SG OD PL Politik *f*
poll [poʊl] S Wahl *f*, Umfrage *f*
pollen ['pɑːlən] S Pollen *m*, Blütenstaub *m* **pollen count** S Pollenflug *m*
pollute [pə'luːt] V/T verschmutzen **pollution** [pə'luːʃən] S Verschmutzung *f*
pond [pɑːnd] S Teich *m*
pony ['poʊnɪ] S Pony *n* **ponytail** S Pferdeschwanz *m*
pool [puːl] 1 S Schwimmbad *n*, Swimmingpool *m*; (*Spiel*) Poolbillard *n* 2 V/T (*Geld etc*) zusammenlegen
poor [pʊr] 1 ADJ arm; (*Qualität*) schlecht 2 S PL **the ~** die Armen *pl* **poorly** ADV schlecht
pop [pɑːp] 1 S (*Musik*) Pop *m*; (*Geräusch*) Knall *m*; Papa *m* 2 V/T stecken; (*Luftballon*) platzen lassen 3 V/I (*Luftballon*) platzen; (*Korken*) knallen; **~ in** (*Person*) vorbeischauen
Pope [poʊp] S Papst *m*
poppa ['pɑːpə] S Papa *m*
poppy ['pɑːpɪ] S Mohn *m*
Popsicle® ['pɑːpsɪkl] S Eis *n* am Stiel
popular ['pɑːpjələr] ADJ beliebt (*with* bei); (*Meinungen, Ansichten*) weit verbreitet
population [pɑːpjə'leɪʃən] S Bevölkerung *f*; (*von Stadt etc*) Einwohner *pl*
porcelain ['pɔːrsələn] S Porzellan *n*
porch [pɔːrtʃ] S Vorbau *m*; Veranda *f*
porcupine ['pɔːrkjəpaɪn] S Stachelschwein *n*
pork [pɔːrk] S Schweinefleisch *n* **pork chop** S Schweinekotelett *n*
porn [pɔːrn] S Porno *m* **pornographic** [pɔːrnə'græfɪk] ADJ pornografisch **pornography** [pɔːr'nɑːgrəfɪ] S Pornografie *f*
port [pɔːrt] S Hafen *m*; SCHIFF Backbord *n*; (*Wein*) Portwein *m*; IT Anschluss *m*
portable ['pɔːrtəbl] ADJ tragbar; (*Radio*) Koffer-
portal ['pɔːrtl] S IT Portal *n*
porter ['pɔːrtər] S (*für Gepäck*) Gepäckträger *m*
porthole ['pɔːrthoʊl] S Bullauge *n*
portion ['pɔːrʃən] S Teil *m*; (*Essen*) Portion *f*
portrait ['pɔːrtrət] S Porträt *n*
Portugal ['pɔːrtʃəgəl] S Portugal *n* **Portuguese** [pɔːrtʃə'giːs] 1 ADJ portugiesisch 2 S Portugiese *m*, Portugiesin *f*; (*Sprache*) Portugiesisch *n*
pose [poʊz] 1 S Haltung *f* 2 V/I posieren 3 V/T (*Problem etc*) darstellen
position [pə'zɪʃən] 1 S Stellung *f*, Position *f*, Lage *f*; (*Job*) Stelle *f*; (*Überzeugung*) Standpunkt *m* 2 V/T aufstellen; IT (*Cursor*) positionieren

positive ['pɑːzətɪv] ADJ positiv; (*überzeugt*) sicher
possess [pə'zes] V/T besitzen
possession [pə'zeʃən] S **~(s** *pl*) Besitz *m*
possibility [pɑːsə'bɪlətɪ] S Möglichkeit *f* **possible** ['pɑːsəbl] ADJ möglich; **as soon as ~** so bald wie möglich **possibly** ADV vielleicht
possum ['pɑːsəm] S Opossum *n*, Beutelratte *f*
post [poʊst] **1** S (*aus Holz, Metall*) Pfosten *m*; (*Job*) Stelle *f* **2** V/T **keep sb ~ed** j-n auf dem Laufenden halten **postage** ['poʊstɪdʒ] S Porto *n* **postal** ADJ Post- **postcard** S Postkarte *f*
poster ['poʊstər] S Plakat *n*, Poster *n*
postmark ['poʊstmɑːrk] S Poststempel *m*
post office ['poʊstɑːfəs] S Post® *f*
postpone [poʊst'poʊn] V/T verschieben (*till* auf *+akk*)
posture ['pɑːstʃər] S Haltung *f*
pot [pɑːt] **1** S Topf *m*; (*für Tee, Kaffee*) Kanne *f*; *umg* Marihuana *n* **2** V/T (*Pflanze*) eintopfen
potato ⟨-es *pl*⟩ [pə'teɪtoʊ] S Kartoffel *f* **potato chip** S Kartoffelchip *m*
potential [pə'tenʃəl] **1** ADJ potenziell **2** S Potenzial *n* **potentially** ADV potenziell
pottery ['pɑːtərɪ] S Töpferwaren *pl*
potty ['pɑːtɪ] S Töpfchen *n*
poultry ['poʊltrɪ] S Geflügel *n*
pound [paʊnd] S (*Gewichtseinheit*) Pfund *n* (*0,454 kg*); (*für Tiere*) Tierheim *n*; (*für Autos*) *Abstellplatz/Verwahrstelle für abgeschleppte Autos*
pour [pɔːr] V/T gießen; eingießen; (*Zucker, Mehl etc*) schütten
pouring ADJ (*Regen*) strömend
poverty ['pɑːvərtɪ] S Armut *f*
powder ['paʊdər] S Pulver *n*, Puder *m* **powdered sugar** [paʊdərd'ʃʊgər] S Puderzucker *m* **powder room** S Damentoilette *f*
power ['paʊər] **1** S Macht *f*; (*Veranlagung*) Fähigkeit *f*; (*Kraft*) Stärke *f*; ELEK Strom *m* **2** V/T betreiben, antreiben
powerful ADJ mächtig; stark; (*Argument*) durchschlagend
powerless ADJ machtlos
power outage S Stromausfall *m* **power station** S Kraftwerk *n* **power steering** S Servolenkung *f*
PR *abk* = public relations
practical, **practically** ['præktɪkəl, -ɪ] ADJ & ADV praktisch **practice** ['præktəs] **1** S Übung *f*, Gewohnheit *f*; (*von Arzt, Anwalt*) Praxis *f*; **put sth into ~** etw in die Praxis umsetzen **2** V/T üben; (*Beruf*) ausüben **3** V/I üben; (*Arzt, Anwalt*) praktizieren

prairie ['preri] S Prärie *f* **prairie dog** S Präriehund *m*
praise [preiz] **1** S Lob *n* **2** V/T loben
prawn [prɒ:n] S Garnele *f*, Krabbe *f*
pray [prei] V/I beten **prayer** [prer] S Gebet *n*
pre- [pri:] PRÄF vor-, prä-
preach [pri:tʃ] V/I predigen
precaution [prɪ'kɒ:ʃən] S Vorsichtsmaßnahme *f*
precede [prɪ'si:d] V/T vorausgehen *+dat* **preceding** [prɪ'si:dɪŋ] ADJ vorhergehend
precinct ['pri:sɪŋkt] S (*Verwaltung*) Bezirk *m*
precious ['preʃəs] ADJ kostbar; Edel-
precise, **precisely** [prɪ'saɪs, -lɪ] ADJ & ADV genau
predecessor ['pri:dəsesər] S Vorgänger(in) *m(f)*
predict [prɪ'dɪkt] V/T voraussagen **predictable** ADJ vorhersehbar; (*Person*) berechenbar
predominantly [prɪ'dɑ:mənəntlɪ] ADV überwiegend
preface ['prefɪs] S Vorwort *n*
prefer [prɪ'fɜ:r] V/T vorziehen (*to dat*), lieber mögen (*to* als); **~ to do sth** etw lieber tun **preferably** ['prefərəblɪ] ADV vorzugsweise, am liebsten **preference** ['prefərəns] S Vorliebe *f*
prefix ['pri:fɪks] S TEL Vorwahl *f*
pregnancy ['pregnənsɪ] S Schwangerschaft *f* **pregnant** ['pregnənt] ADJ schwanger; **twelve weeks/two months ~** in der dreizehnten Woche/im dritten Monat schwanger
prejudice ['predʒədɪs] S Vorurteil *n* **prejudiced** ADJ (*Person*) voreingenommen
preliminary [prɪ'lɪmənerɪ] ADJ vorbereitend; (*Ergebnisse*) vorläufig; (*Bemerkungen*) einleitend
premature [pri:mə'tʃʊər] ADJ vorzeitig; voreilig
premises ['preməsəz] S PL Räumlichkeiten *pl*; (*von Fabrik, Schule*) Gelände *n*
premium-rate ['pri:mɪəmreɪt] ADJ TEL zum Höchsttarif
preoccupied [pri:'ɑ:kjəpaɪd] ADJ beschäftigt; gedankenverloren
prepaid [pri:'peɪd] ADJ vorausbezahlt
preparation [prepə'reɪʃən] S Vorbereitung *f* **prepare** [prɪ'per] **1** V/T vorbereiten (*for* auf *+akk*); (*Essen*) zubereiten; **be ~d to do sth** bereit sein, etw zu tun **2** V/I sich vorbereiten (*for* auf *+akk*)
prerequisite [pri:'rekwɪzɪt] S Voraussetzung *f*
prescribe [prɪ'skraɪb] V/T vorschreiben; MED verschreiben
prescription [prɪ'skrɪpʃən] S Rezept *n*
presence ['prezns] S Gegenwart *f*; Anwesenheit *f* **present**

1 ['preznt] ADJ anwesend (*at* bei); gegenwärtig **2** ['preznt] S Gegenwart *f*; (*zum Geburtstag etc*) Geschenk *n*; **at ~** zurzeit **3** [prɪ'zent] V/T TV, RADIO präsentieren; (*Problem*) darstellen; (*Bericht*) vorlegen **present-day** ADJ heutig **presently** ADV bald; zurzeit

preservative [prɪ'zɜːrvətɪv] S Konservierungsmittel *n* **preserve** [prɪ'zɜːrv] V/T erhalten; (*Nahrungsmittel*) einmachen, konservieren

president ['prezədənt] S Präsident(in) *m(f)* **presidential** [prezə'denʃəl] ADJ Präsidenten-; (*Wahl*) Präsidentschafts-

Presidents' Day S *Feiertag am dritten Montag im Februar*

press [pres] **1** S Presse *f* **2** V/T & V/I drücken

pressure ['preʃər] S Druck *m* **pressurize** ['preʃəraɪz] V/T unter Druck setzen

presumably [prɪ'zuːməblɪ] ADV vermutlich **presume** [prɪ'zuːm] V/T & V/I annehmen

pretend [prɪ'tend] **1** V/T **~ that** so tun als ob; **~ to do sth** vorgeben, etw zu tun **2** V/I **she's ~ing** sie tut nur so

pretty ['prɪtɪ] **1** ADJ hübsch **2** ADV ziemlich

prevent [prɪ'vent] V/T verhindern; **~ sb from doing sth** j-n daran hindern, etw zu tun

preview ['priːvjuː] S FILM Voraufführung *f*; (*Trailer*) Vorschau *f*

previous, previously ['priːvɪəs, -lɪ] ADJ & ADV früher

prey [preɪ] S Beute *f*

price [praɪs] **1** S Preis *m* **2** V/T **it's ~d at $10** es ist mit 10 Dollar ausgezeichnet **priceless** ADJ unbezahlbar **price list** S Preisliste *f* **price tag** S Preisschild *n*

prick [prɪk] **1** S Stich *m*; *vulg* (*Penis*) Schwanz *m*; *vulg* (*Person*) Arsch *m* **2** V/T stechen in *+akk* **prickly** ['prɪklɪ] ADJ stachelig

pride [praɪd] S Stolz *m*, Hochmut *m*

priest [priːst] S Priester *m*

primarily [praɪ'merəlɪ] ADV vorwiegend **primary** ['praɪmərɪ] ADJ Haupt-; Grund-

prime [praɪm] **1** ADJ Haupt-; (*Qualität*) erstklassig **2** S **in one's ~** in den besten Jahren **prime time** S TV Hauptsendezeit *f*

primitive ['prɪmətɪv] ADJ primitiv

prince [prɪns] S Prinz *m*; (*als Herrscher*) Fürst *m* **princess** ['prɪnses] S Prinzessin *f*; Fürstin *f*

principal ['prɪnsəpl] **1** ADJ Haupt-, wichtigste(r, s) **2** S (*Schule*) Rektor(in) *m(f)*

principle ['prɪnsəpl] S Prinzip *n*; **on ~** aus Prinzip

print [prɪnt] **1** S Druck *m*; FOTO Abzug *m*; (*von Füßen,*

Fingern) Abdruck *m*; **out of ~** vergriffen **2** VT drucken; (*Foto*) abziehen **print out** VT IT ausdrucken **printed matter** S Drucksache *f* **printer** S Drucker *m* **printout** S IT Ausdruck *m*
prior ['praır] ADJ früher
priority [praı'ɑ:rətı] S Priorität *f*
prison ['prızn] S Gefängnis *n* **prisoner** S Gefangene(r) *m/f(m)*
privacy ['praıvəsı] S Privatleben *n* **private** ['praıvət] **1** ADJ privat; vertraulich **2** S **in ~** privat **privately** ADV privat; vertraulich **privatize** ['praıvətaız] VT privatisieren
privilege ['prıvəlıdʒ] S Privileg *n* **privileged** ADJ privilegiert
prize [praız] S Preis *m* **prizewinner** S Gewinner(in) *m(f)*
pro ⟨-s *pl*⟩ [proʊ] S Profi *m*; **the ~s and cons** *pl* das Für und Wider
pro- [proʊ] PRÄF pro-
probability [prɑ:bə'bılətı] S Wahrscheinlichkeit *f* **probable**, **probably** ['prɑ:bəbl, 'prɑ:bəblı] ADJ & ADV wahrscheinlich
probation [proʊ'beıʃən] S Probezeit *f*; JUR Bewährung *f*
problem ['prɑ:bləm] S Problem *n*
procedure [prə'si:dʒər] S Verfahren *n* **proceed** [proʊ'si:d] **1** VI fortfahren; (*in Angriff nehmen*) vorgehen **2** VT **~ to do sth** anfangen, etw zu tun **proceedings** S PL JUR Verfahren *n* **proceeds** ['proʊsi:ds] S PL Erlös *m*
process ['prɑ:ses] **1** S Prozess *m*, Vorgang *m*; Verfahren *n* **2** VT bearbeiten; verarbeiten; (*Film*) entwickeln
procession [prə'seʃən] S Umzug *m*
processor ['prɑ:sesər] S IT Prozessor *m*; GASTR Küchenmaschine *f*
produce **1** ['proʊdu:s] S AGR Produkte *pl*, Erzeugnisse *pl* **2** [prə'du:s] VT herstellen, produzieren; (*Agrarprodukt*) erzeugen; (*Film etc*) produzieren; (*als Ursache*) hervorrufen **producer** S Hersteller(in) *m(f)*; (*von Film etc*) Produzent(in) *m(f)*
product ['prɑ:dʌkt] S Produkt *n*, Erzeugnis *n* **production** [prə'dʌkʃən] S Produktion *f*; THEAT Inszenierung *f* **productive** [prə'dʌktıv] ADJ produktiv; ertragreich
profession [prə'feʃən] S Beruf *m* **professional** [prə'feʃənl] **1** S Profi *m* **2** ADJ beruflich; fachlich, Berufs-
professor [prə'fesər] S Professor(in) *m(f)*; Dozent(in) *m(f)*
profile ['proʊfaıl] S Profil *n*
profit ['prɑ:fıt] **1** S Gewinn *m* **2** VI profitieren (*by, from* von) **profitable** ADJ rentabel

profound [prə'faʊnd] ADJ tief; tiefgründig, profund **program** ['proʊgræm] **1** S Programm *n*; TV, RADIO Sendung *f* **2** V/T programmieren **programmer** S Programmierer(in) *m(f)* **programming** S IT Programmieren *n*
progress **1** ['prɑ:gres] S Fortschritt *m* **2** [prə'gres] V/I (*Arbeit, Krankheit etc*) fortschreiten; (*besser werden*) Fortschritte machen **progressive** [prə'gresɪv] ADJ fortschrittlich **progressively** [prə'gresɪvlɪ] ADV zunehmend
prohibit [proʊ'hɪbɪt] V/T verbieten
project ['prɑ:dʒekt] S Projekt *n*
prolong [prə'lɑ:ŋ] V/T verlängern
prom [prɑ:m] S (*Tanzveranstaltung*) *Ball für die Schüler und Studenten von Highschools oder Colleges*
prominent ['prɑ:mənənt] ADJ prominent; (*Eigenschaft etc*) auffallend
promise ['prɑ:məs] **1** S Versprechen *n* **2** V/T & V/I versprechen **promising** ADJ vielversprechend
promote [prə'moʊt] V/T befördern; fördern; WIRTSCH werben für **promotion** [prə'moʊʃən] S Beförderung *f*; WIRTSCH Werbung *f* (*of* für)
prompt [prɑ:mpt] ADJ prompt; pünktlich
prone [proʊn] ADJ **be ~ to sth** zu etw neigen
pronounce [prə'naʊns] V/T (*Wort*) aussprechen **pronunciation** [prənʌnsɪ'eɪʃən] S Aussprache *f*
proof [pru:f] S Beweis *m*; (*von Whisky etc*) Alkoholgehalt *m*
prop [prɑ:p] **1** S Stütze *f*; THEAT Requisit *n* **2** V/T **~ sth against sth** etw gegen etw lehnen **prop up** V/T stützen; *fig* unterstützen
proper ['prɑ:pər] ADJ richtig; anständig
property ['prɑ:pərtɪ] S Eigentum *n*; (*charakterisierend*) Eigenschaft *f*
proportion [prə'pɔ:rʃən] S Verhältnis *n*; (*Menge von etw*) Teil *m*; **~s** *pl* Proportionen *pl*
proposal [prə'poʊzl] S Vorschlag *m* **propose** [prə'poʊz] **1** V/T vorschlagen **2** V/I einen Heiratsantrag machen (*to sb* j-m)
proprietor [prə'praɪətər] S Besitzer(in) *m(f)*; (*Hotel etc*) Inhaber(in) *m(f)*
prosecute ['prɑ:sɪkju:t] V/T verfolgen (*for* wegen) **prosecution** [prɑ:sɪ'kju:ʃən] S strafrechtliche Verfolgung; Anklage *f* **prosecutor** ['prɑ:sɪkju:tər] S Ankläger(in) *m(f)*
prospect ['prɑ:spekt] S Aussicht *f*
prosperity [prɑ:'sperətɪ] S

Wohlstand *m* **prosperous** ADJ wohlhabend; (*Geschäft*) gut gehend
prostitute ['prɑːstətuːt] S Prostituierte(r) *m/f(m)*
protect [prə'tekt] V/T schützen (*from, against* vor *+dat*, gegen) **protection** [prə'tekʃən] S Schutz *m* (*from, against* vor *+dat*, gegen) **protective** ADJ beschützend; Schutz-
protein ['proʊtiːn] S Protein *n*, Eiweiß *n*
protest **1** ['proʊtest] S Protest *m*, Protestkundgebung *f* **2** [prə'test] V/I protestieren (*against* gegen); demonstrieren
Protestant ['prɑːtəstənt] **1** ADJ protestantisch **2** S Protestant(in) *m(f)*
proud, proudly [praʊd, -lɪ] ADJ & ADV stolz (*of* auf *+akk*)
prove [pruːv] V/T beweisen; sich erweisen als
proverb ['prɑːvɜːrb] S Sprichwort *n*
provide [prə'vaɪd] V/T zur Verfügung stellen; (*Getränke etc*) sorgen für; (*Person*) versorgen (*with* mit) **provide for** V/T (*Familie*) sorgen für **provided** KONJ ~ **(that)** vorausgesetzt, dass **provider** S IT Provider *m*
provision [prə'vɪʒən] S Bestimmung *f*; **~s** *pl* (*Verpflegung*) Proviant *m*
provoke [prə'voʊk] V/T provozieren; hervorrufen
prudent ['pruːdənt] ADJ klug; umsichtig
prudish ['pruːdɪʃ] ADJ prüde
prune [pruːn] **1** S Backpflaume *f* **2** V/T (*Baum etc*) zurechtstutzen
PS *abk* = postscript; PS *n*
pseudonym ['suːdənɪm] S Pseudonym *n*
psychiatric [saɪkɪ'ætrɪk] ADJ psychiatrisch; (*Krankheit*) psychisch **psychiatrist** [saɪ'kaɪətrɪst] S Psychiater(in) *m(f)* **psychiatry** [saɪ'kaɪətrɪ] S Psychiatrie *f*
psychic ['saɪkɪk] ADJ übersinnlich
psycho ['saɪkoʊ] S *umg* Psycho *m*, Verrückte(r) *m/f(m)*
psychoanalysis [saɪkoʊə'næləsɪs] S Psychoanalyse *f*
psychological [saɪkə'lɑːdʒɪkəl] ADJ psychologisch **psychology** [saɪ'kɑːlədʒɪ] S Psychologie *f* **psychopath** ['saɪkoʊpæθ] S Psychopath(in) *m(f)*
puberty ['pjuːbərtɪ] S Pubertät *f*
public ['pʌblɪk] **1** S **the (general)** ~ die (breite) Öffentlichkeit **2** ADJ öffentlich; (*staatlich*) Staats- *f*; ~ **holiday** gesetzlicher Feiertag; ~ **school** staatliche Schule; ~ **transportation** öffentliche Verkehrsmittel *pl*
publication [pʌblɪ'keɪʃən] S Veröffentlichung *f* **publicity** [pʌb'lɪsətɪ] S Publicity *f*; (*für Produkt*) Werbung *f* **publish**

['pʌblɪʃ] V/T veröffentlichen **publisher** S Verleger(in) *m(f)*; (*Firma*) Verlag *m*

pudding ['pʊdɪŋ] S Nachtisch *m*

puddle ['pʌdl] S Pfütze *f*

puff [pʌf] V/I schnaufen **puff paste** ['pʌfpeɪst] S Blätterteig *m*

puke [pju:k] *umg* **1** V/I & V/T kotzen **2** S Kotze *f*

pull [pʊl] **1** S Ziehen *n*; **give sth a ~** an etw *dat* ziehen **2** V/T ziehen; (*Seil etc*) ziehen an +*dat*; **~ a muscle** sich einen Muskel zerren; **~ sb's leg** j-n auf den Arm nehmen **3** V/I ziehen **pull down** V/T herunterziehen; (*Haus*) abreißen **pull in** V/I hineinfahren; (*Bus, Auto*) anhalten **pull on** V/T (*Kleidung*) anziehen **pull out** **1** V/I (*Auto etc*) ausscheren; (*Zug*) abfahren; (*sich zurückziehen*) aussteigen (*of* aus) **2** V/T herausziehen; (*Zahn*) ziehen; (*Truppen*) abziehen **pull up** **1** V/T (*Rollo, Hose etc*) hochziehen; (*Stuhl*) heranziehen **2** V/I anhalten **pullover** ['pʊloʊvər] S Pullover *m*

pulp [pʌlp] S Brei *m*; (*von Frucht*) Fruchtfleisch *n*

pulse [pʌls] S Puls *m*

pump [pʌmp] S Pumpe *f*; (*Tankstelle*) Zapfsäule *f* **pump up** V/T (*Reifen etc*) aufpumpen

pumpkin ['pʌmpkɪn] S Kürbis *m*

punch [pʌntʃ] **1** S (Faust)-schlag *m*; (*kaltes Getränk*) Bowle *f* **2** V/T schlagen; (*Papier, Fahrkarte*) lochen

punctual, punctually ['pʌŋktʃʊəl, -ɪ] ADJ & ADV pünktlich

punctuation [pʌŋktʃʊ'eɪʃən] S Interpunktion *f*

punish ['pʌnɪʃ] V/T bestrafen **punishment** S Strafe *f*, Bestrafung *f*

puppet ['pʌpət] S Marionette *f*

puppy ['pʌpɪ] S junger Hund

purchase ['pɜ:rtʃəs] **1** S Kauf *m* **2** V/T kaufen

pure [pjʊr] ADJ rein; sauber, pur **purely** ['pjʊrlɪ] ADV rein

purify ['pjʊrəfaɪ] V/T reinigen

purple ['pɜ:rpl] ADJ violett

purpose ['pɜ:rpəs] S Zweck *m*, Absicht *f*; **on ~** absichtlich

purse [pɜ:rs] S Handtasche *f*

pursue [pər'su:] V/T verfolgen; (*Hobby etc*) nachgehen +*dat*

pus [pʌs] S Eiter *m*

push [pʊʃ] **1** S Stoß *m* **2** V/T stoßen; (*Wagen etc*) schieben; (*Druckknopf, Tür*) drücken; (*Drogen*) dealen **3** V/I (*in Menge*) drängeln **push on** V/I (*mit Tätigkeit*) weitermachen **pusher** S (*Drogen*) Dealer(in) *m(f)*

pushy ADJ *umg* aufdringlich, penetrant

put ⟨put, put⟩ [pʊt] V/T tun; (*aufrecht*) stellen; (*flach*) legen; (*in Tasche etc*) stecken; (*mit Worten*) ausdrücken; (*schrift-*

lich) schreiben; **~ money into one's account** Geld auf sein Konto einzahlen **put away** VT wegräumen **put back** VT zurücklegen; *(Uhr)* zurückstellen **put down** VT *(Notizen etc)* aufschreiben; *(Aufstand)* niederschlagen; **put the phone down** (den Hörer) auflegen; **put one's name down for sth** sich für etw eintragen **put off** VT *(Termin, Treffen)* verschieben; **put sb off doing sth** j-n davon abbringen, etw zu tun **put on** VT *(Licht etc)* anmachen; *(Kleidung)* anziehen; *(Brille)* aufsetzen; *(Make-up, CD)* auflegen; **~ weight** zunehmen **put out** VT *(Hand)* ausstrecken; *(Licht, Zigarette)* ausmachen **put up** VT *(Hand)* hochheben; *(Bild)* aufhängen; *(Zelt)* aufstellen; *(Gebäude)* errichten; *(Preis)* erhöhen; *(Person)* unterbringen; **~ with** sich abfinden mit

puzzle ['pʌzl] **1** S Rätsel *n*, Geduldsspiel *n*; **(jigsaw) ~** Puzzle *n* **2** VT vor ein Rätsel stellen **puzzling** ADJ rätselhaft

pyramid ['pɪrəmɪd] S Pyramide *f*

quack [kwæk] VI quaken

quaint [kweɪnt] ADJ kurios; *(Dorf etc)* malerisch

qualification [kwɑːləfə'keɪʃən] S Qualifikation *f*; *(von Schule, Uni)* Abschluss *m* **qualified** ['kwɑːləfaɪd] ADJ qualifiziert **qualify** ['kwɑːləfaɪ] **1** VT *(Äußerung etc)* einschränken; **be qualified to do sth** berechtigt sein, etw zu tun **2** VI *(beruflich)* seine Ausbildung abschließen; *(Wettbewerb)* sich qualifizieren

quality ['kwɑːlətɪ] S Qualität *f*; *(von Person)* Eigenschaft *f*

quantity ['kwɑːntətɪ] S Menge *f*, Quantität *f*

quarantine ['kwɑːrəntiːn] S Quarantäne *f*

quarrel ['kwɑːrəl] **1** S Streit *m* **2** VI sich streiten

quarter ['kwɔːrtər] **1** S Viertel *n*, Vierteljahr *n*; Vierteldollar *m*; **a ~ of an hour** eine Viertelstunde **2** VT vierteln

quay [kiː] S Kai *m*

queen [kwiːn] S Königin *f*; *(Karten, Schach)* Dame *f*

queer [kwɪr] **1** ADJ *pej* schwul **2** S *pej* Schwule(r) *m*

quench [kwentʃ] VT *(Durst)* löschen

question ['kwestʃən] **1** S Frage *f* **2** V/T befragen; verhören; (*Behauptung etc*) bezweifeln **questionable** ADJ zweifelhaft; fragwürdig **question mark** S Fragezeichen *n* **questionnaire** [kwestʃə'ner] S Fragebogen *m*

quick [kwık] ADJ schnell; (*Blick etc*) kurz **quickly** ADV schnell

quiet ['kwaıət] **1** ADJ leise; still, ruhig; **keep ~ about sth** über etw *akk* nichts sagen **2** S Stille *f*, Ruhe *f* **quietly** ADV leise; ruhig

quilt [kwılt] S (Stepp)decke *f*

quit ⟨quit, quit⟩ [kwıt] **1** V/T verlassen; (*Job*) aufgeben **2** V/I aufhören; (*Arbeitsstelle*) kündigen

quite [kwaıt] ADV ziemlich; ganz, völlig; **~ a few** ziemlich viele

quiver ['kwıvər] V/I zittern

quiz [kwız] S Quiz *n*

quota ['kwoʊtə] S Anteil *m*; WIRTSCH, POL Quote *f*

quotation [kwoʊ'teıʃən] S Zitat *n*; (*preislich*) Kostenvoranschlag *m* **quotation marks** S PL Anführungszeichen *pl*

quote [kwoʊt] **1** V/T zitieren; (*Preis*) nennen **2** S Zitat *n*; (*preislich*) Kostenvoranschlag *m*

R

rabbi ['ræbaı] S Rabbiner *m*

rabbit ['ræbıt] S Kaninchen *n*

rabies ['reıbi:z] S SG Tollwut *f*

raccoon [ræ'ku:n] S Waschbär *m*

race [reıs] **1** S Rennen *n*; (*Menschen*) Rasse *f* **2** V/T um die Wette laufen/fahren **3** V/I rennen **racetrack** S Rennbahn *f*

racial ['reıʃəl] ADJ Rassen-

racing ['reısıŋ] S **(horse) ~** Pferderennen *n*

racism ['reısızəm] S Rassismus *m* **racist** **1** S Rassist(in) *m(f)* **2** ADJ rassistisch

rack [ræk] **1** S Ständer *m*, Gestell *n* **2** V/T **~ one's brains** sich den Kopf zerbrechen

racket ['rækət] S SPORT Schläger *m*; (*Lärm*) Krach *m*

radar ['reıdɑ:r] S Radar *n od m*

radiation [reıdı'eıʃən] S Strahlung *f*

radiator ['reıdıeıtər] S Heizkörper *m*; AUTO Kühler *m*

radical ['rædıkəl] ADJ radikal

radio ⟨-s *pl*⟩ ['reıdıoʊ] S Rundfunk *m*, Radio *n* **radioactivity** [reıdıoʊæk'tıvətı] S Radioaktivität *f* **radiotherapy** [reıdıoʊ'θerəpı] S Strahlenbehandlung *f*

radish ['rædɪʃ] S Radieschen *n*
radius ['reɪdɪəs] S Radius *m*; Umkreis *m*
raffle ['ræfl] S Tombola *f*
raft [ræft] S Floß *n*
rag [ræg] S Lumpen *m*, Lappen *m*
rage [reɪdʒ] **1** S Wut *f* **2** V/I toben; (*Krankheit*) wüten
raid [reɪd] **1** S Überfall *m* (*on* auf *+akk*); (*von Polizei*) Razzia *f* (*on* gegen) **2** V/T überfallen; (*Polizei*) eine Razzia machen in *+dat*
rail [reɪl] S Geländer *n*; (*auf Schiff*) Reling *f*; BAHN Schiene *f* **railing** S Geländer *n*; **~s** *pl* Zaun *m* **railroad** S Eisenbahn *f* **railroad station** S Bahnhof *m*
rain [reɪn] **1** S Regen *m* **2** V/I regnen **rainbow** ['reɪnboʊ] S Regenbogen *m* **raincheck** S **can I take a ~?** darf ich später darauf zurückkommen? **raincoat** S Regenmantel *m* **rainforest** S Regenwald *m* **rainy** ADJ regnerisch
raise [reɪz] **1** S Gehalts-/Lohnerhöhung *f* **2** V/T hochheben; (*Preis, Gehalt*) erhöhen; (*Kinder*) großziehen; (*Vieh*) züchten; (*Geld*) aufbringen; (*Einspruch*) erheben; **~ one's voice** laut werden
raisin ['reɪzən] S Rosine *f*
rally ['rælɪ] S POL Kundgebung *f*; AUTO Rallye *f*
RAM [ræm] *akr* = random access memory; RAM *m*
ramble ['ræmbl] **1** S Wanderung *f* **2** V/I wandern; (*Überflüssiges*) schwafeln
ramp [ræmp] S Rampe *f*
ran [ræn] *prät von* run
ranch [ræntʃ] S Ranch *f*
rancher ['ræntʃər] S Rancher(in) *m(f)*
rancid ['rænsəd] ADJ ranzig
random ['rændəm] **1** ADJ willkürlich **2** S **at ~** willkürlich; ziellos
rang [ræŋ] *prät von* ring
range [reɪndʒ] **1** S Auswahl *f* (*of* an *+dat*); WIRTSCH Sortiment *n* (*of* an *+dat*); (*Teleskop*) Reichweite *f*; (*Berge*) Kette *f*; **in this price ~** in dieser Preisklasse **2** V/I **~ from ... to ...** liegen zwischen ... und ...
rank [ræŋk] **1** S Rang *m*; Stand *m* **2** V/T einstufen **3** V/I **~ among** zählen zu
ransom ['rænsəm] S Lösegeld *n*
rape [reɪp] **1** S Vergewaltigung *f* **2** V/T vergewaltigen
rapid, rapidly ['ræpəd, -lɪ] ADJ & ADV schnell **rapid transit system** S öffentliches Nahverkehrssystem
rapist ['reɪpɪst] S Vergewaltiger *m*
rappel [rə'pel] V/I sich abseilen
rare [rer] ADJ selten, rar; vortrefflich; (*Steak*) blutig **rarely** ADV selten

rash [ræʃ] **1** ADJ unbesonnen **2** S MED (Haut)ausschlag *m*

raspberry ['ræzbərɪ] S Himbeere *f*

rat [ræt] S Ratte *f*

rate [reɪt] **1** S Rate *f*; (*Geschwindigkeit*) Tempo *n*; FIN Kurs *m*; (*von Zinsen etc*) Satz *m*; **at any ~** auf jeden Fall **2** V/T einschätzen (*as* als)

rather ['ræðər] ADV lieber; ziemlich; **I'd ~ not** lieber nicht; **or ~** vielmehr

ratio ⟨-s *pl*⟩ ['reɪʃɪoʊ] S Verhältnis *n*

rational ['ræʃənl] ADJ rational

rattle ['rætl] **1** S Rassel *f* **2** V/T klimpern mit; (*j-n*) durcheinanderbringen, verunsichern **3** V/I (*Fenster*) klappern; (*Gläser etc*) klirren **rattlesnake** S Klapperschlange *f*

rave [reɪv] V/I (*im Fieber etc*) fantasieren; (*Person*) toben; schwärmen (*about* von) **raving** ['reɪvɪŋ] ADJ **~ idiot** Vollidiot *m*

raw [rɒː] ADJ roh; (*Haut*) wund; (*Klima*) rau

ray [reɪ] S (*Licht*) Strahl *m*

razor ['reɪzər] S Rasierapparat *m* **razor blade** S Rasierklinge *f*

RC *abk* = Roman Catholic; römisch-katholisch

Rd *abk* = road; Str.

reach [riːtʃ] **1** S **within/out of (sb's) ~** in/außer (j-s) Reichweite; **within easy ~ of** nicht weit von **2** V/T erreichen; (*Ausdehnung*) reichen bis zu **3** V/I greifen (*for* nach) **reach out** V/I die Hand ausstrecken; **~ for** greifen nach

react [riː'ækt] V/I reagieren (*to* auf +*akk*) **reaction** [riː'ækʃən] S Reaktion *f* (*to* auf +*akk*)

read ⟨read, read⟩ [riːd, red] **1** V/T lesen; (*Zähler etc*) ablesen; **~ sth to sb** j-m etw vorlesen **2** V/I lesen; **~ to sb** j-m vorlesen **read out** V/T vorlesen **readable** ADJ (*Buch*) lesenswert; (*Schrift*) lesbar **reader** S Leser(in) *m(f)*

readily ['redəlɪ] ADV bereitwillig; leicht

reading ['riːdɪŋ] S Lesen *n*; (*Messgerät*) Zählerstand *m* **reading glasses** S PL Lesebrille *f* **reading matter** S Lektüre *f*

readjust [riːə'dʒʌst] **1** V/T (*Uhr, Gerät*) neu einstellen **2** V/I sich wieder anpassen (*to* an +*akk*)

ready ['redɪ] ADJ fertig, bereit; **are you ~ to go?** bist du so weit?; **get (oneself) ~** sich fertig machen **ready-made** ADJ Fertig-; (*Kleidung*) Konfektions-

real [riːl] **1** ADJ wirklich; eigentlich, echt; (*Genie*) richtig **2** ADV *umg* echt **real estate** S Immobilien *pl* **real estate agent** S Immobilienmakler(in) *m(f)* **realistic, realistically** [riːə'lɪstɪk, -lɪ] ADJ & ADV realistisch **reality** [ri:'ælətɪ] S Wirklichkeit *f* **realize** ['ri:əlaɪz] VT begreifen; (*Plan*) realisieren **really** ['ri:lɪ] ADV wirklich

realtor ['ri:ltər] S Grundstücksmakler(in) *m(f)*

reappear [ri:ə'pɪr] VI wieder erscheinen

rear [rɪr] **1** ADJ hintere(r, s), Hinter-; AUTO Heck- **2** S hinterer Teil; **at the ~ of** hinter *+dat*; (*innen*) hinten in *+dat* **rear light** S AUTO Rücklicht *n*

rearrange [ri:ə'reɪndʒ] VT umstellen; (*Konferenz etc*) verlegen (*for* auf *+akk*)

rearview mirror [rɪrvju:-'mɪrər] S Rückspiegel *m* **rear window** S AUTO Heckscheibe *f*

reason ['ri:zn] **1** S Grund *m* (*for* für); Verstand *m*, Vernunft *f* **2** VI **~ with sb** mit j-m vernünftig reden **reasonable** ADJ vernünftig; (*Angebot*) akzeptabel; (*Chance*) reell; (*Essen*) ganz gut **reasonably** ADV vernünftig; (*in hohem Maße*) ziemlich

reassure [ri:ə'ʃʊr] VT beruhigen; versichern

rebel **1** ['rebl] S Rebell(in) *m(f)* **2** [rɪ'bel] VI rebellieren **rebellion** [rɪ'belɪən] S Aufstand *m*

reboot [ri:'bu:t] VT & VI IT rebooten

rebuild [ri:'bɪld] *irr* VT wieder aufbauen

recall [rɪ'kɒ:l] VT sich erinnern an *+akk*; (*Produkt etc*) zurückrufen

receipt [rɪ'si:t] S Quittung *f*; (*von Waren etc*) Empfang *m* **receive** [rɪ'si:v] VT erhalten, bekommen; (*Leute*) empfangen **receiver** S TEL Hörer *m*; RADIO Empfänger *m*

recent ['ri:snt] ADJ vor Kurzem stattgefunden; (*Foto*) neueste(r, s); (*aktuell*) neu; **in ~ years** in den letzten Jahren **recently** ADV vor Kurzem; in letzter Zeit

reception [rɪ'sepʃən] S Empfang *m* **receptionist** S (*Hotel*) Empfangschef *m*, Empfangsdame *f*; (*Firma*) Empfangsdame *f*; MED Sprechstundenhilfe *f*

recess ['ri:ses] S (*Wand*) Nische *f*; (*Schule*) Pause *f*

recharge [ri:'tʃɑ:rdʒ] VT (*Batterie*) aufladen **rechargeable** [ri:'tʃɑ:rdʒəbl] ADJ wiederaufladbar

recipe ['resəpɪ] S Rezept *n* (*for* für)

recipient [rɪ'sɪpɪənt] S Empfänger(in) *m(f)*

recite [rɪ'saɪt] VT vortragen

reckless ['rekləs] ADJ leichtsinnig; rücksichtslos

reckon ['rekən] **1** VT schätzen; (*annehmen*) glauben **2** VI **~ with** rechnen mit

reclaim [rɪ'kleɪm] VT (*Gepäck*) abholen; (*Steuern etc*) zurückverlangen

recline [rɪ'klaɪn] VI sich zurücklehnen **reclining seat** S Liegesitz *m*

recognition [rekəg'nɪʃən] S Anerkennung *f* **recognize** ['rekəgnaɪz] VT erkennen; anerkennen

recommend [rekə'mend] VT empfehlen **recommendation** [rekəmen'deɪʃən] S Empfehlung *f*

reconfirm [ri:kən'fɜ:rm] VT (*Flug etc*) rückbestätigen

reconsider [ri:kən'sɪdər] VT noch einmal überdenken

reconstruct [ri:kən'strʌkt] VT wieder aufbauen; rekonstruieren

record **1** ['rekɔ:rd] S MUS (Schall)platte *f*; (*Bestleistung*) Rekord *m*; **keep a ~ of** Buch führen über *+akk* **2** ['rekɔ:rd] ADJ Rekord- **3** [rɪ'kɔ:rd] VT aufzeichnen; (*auf CD, DVD etc*) aufnehmen; **~ed message** Ansage *f* **recording** [rɪ'kɔ:rdɪŋ] S Aufnahme *f*

recover [rɪ'kʌvər] **1** VT zurückbekommen; (*Appetit, Kraft*) wiedergewinnen **2** VI sich erholen

recreation [rekrɪ'eɪʃən] S Erholung *f* **recreational** ADJ Freizeit-; **~ vehicle** Wohnmobil *n*

recruit [rɪ'kru:t] **1** S MIL Rekrut(in) *m(f)*; (*Verein etc*) neues Mitglied **2** VT MIL rekrutieren; (*Mitglieder*) anwerben; (*Mitarbeiter*) einstellen

rectangle ['rektæŋgl] S Rechteck *n* **rectangular** [rek'tæŋgjələr] ADJ rechteckig

recyclable [ri:'saɪkləbl] ADJ recycelbar, wiederverwertbar **recycle** [ri:'saɪkl] VT recyceln, wiederverwerten **recycling** S Recycling *n*, Wiederverwertung *f*

red [red] **1** ADJ rot **2** S **in the ~** in den roten Zahlen; **run a ~** bei Rot über die Ampel fahren

red cabbage S Rotkohl *m*

redcurrant S (Rote) Johannisbeere

redeem [rɪ'di:m] VT WIRTSCH einlösen

red-handed [red'hændəd] ADJ **catch sb ~** j-n auf frischer Tat ertappen **redhead** S Rothaarige(r) *m/f(m)*

redial [ri:'daɪl] VT & VI nochmals wählen

redirect [ri:də'rekt] VT umleiten; nachsenden

red light [red'laɪt] S (*Ampel*) rotes Licht; **run a ~** bei Rot über die Ampel fahren **red meat** S *Rind-, Lamm-, Rehfleisch*

redo [ri:'du:] *irr* VT nochmals machen

reduce [rɪ'du:s] VT reduzieren (*to* auf *+akk*, *by* um) **reduction** [rɪ'dʌkʃən] S Reduzie-

rung *f*, Ermäßigung *f*
reef [ri:f] S Riff *n*
reel [ri:l] S Spule *f*; (*an Angel*) Rolle *f*
ref [ref] S *umg* Schiri *m*
refer [rɪ'fɜ:r] 1 V/T **~ sb to sb/sth** j-n an j-n/etw verweisen; **~ sth to sb** etw an j-n weiterleiten 2 V/I **~ to** sich beziehen auf *+akk*; (*Buch*) nachschlagen in *+dat*
referee [refə'ri:] S Schiedsrichter(in) *m(f)*; (*Boxen*) Ringrichter *m*
reference ['refrəns] S Anspielung *f* (*to* auf *+akk*); (*Bewerbung*) Referenz *f*; (*Buch*) Verweis *m*; (*auf Dokument*) Aktenzeichen *n*; **with ~ to** mit Bezug auf *+akk* **reference book** S Nachschlagewerk *n*
refill 1 [ri:'fɪl] V/T nachfüllen 2 ['ri:fɪl] S Ersatzmine *f*; **would you like a ~?** darf ich nachschenken?
refine [rɪ'faɪn] V/T (*Zucker, Salz etc*) raffinieren; (*Qualität, Technik*) verfeinern **refined** ADJ (*kultiviert*) fein
reflect [rɪ'flekt] 1 V/T reflektieren; *fig* widerspiegeln 2 V/I nachdenken (*on* über *+akk*) **reflection** [rɪ'flekʃən] S Spiegelbild *n*; (*gedanklich*) Überlegung *f*
reflex ['ri:fleks] S Reflex *m*
reform [rɪ'fɔ:rm] 1 S Reform *f* 2 V/T reformieren; (*Person*) bessern
refrain [rɪ'freɪn] V/I **~ from doing sth** es unterlassen, etw zu tun
refresh [rɪ'freʃ] V/T erfrischen **refreshments** S PL Erfrischungen *pl*
refrigerator [rɪ'frɪdʒəreɪtər] S Kühlschrank *m*
refuel [ri:'fjʊəl] V/T & V/I auftanken
refugee [refjʊ'dʒi:] S Flüchtling *m*
refund 1 ['ri:fʌnd] S Rückerstattung *f* 2 [rɪ'fʌnd] V/T zurückerstatten
refusal [rɪ'fju:zəl] S Weigerung *f* **refuse** 1 ['refju:s] S Müll *m*, Abfall *m* 2 [rɪ'fju:z] V/T ablehnen; verweigern; **~ to do sth** sich weigern, etw zu tun 3 [rɪ'fju:z] V/I sich weigern
regain [rɪ'geɪn] V/T wiedergewinnen, wiedererlangen
regard [rɪ'gɑ:rd] 1 S **with ~ to** in Bezug auf *+akk*; **in this ~** in dieser Hinsicht; **~s** (*Brief*) mit freundlichen Grüßen; **give my ~s to …** viele Grüße an … *+akk* 2 V/T betrachten; **as ~s …** was … betrifft **regarding** PRÄP bezüglich *+gen* **regardless** ADJ **~ of** ohne Rücksicht auf *+akk*
regime [reɪ'ʒi:m] S POL Regime *n*
region ['ri:dʒən] S Region *f*, Gebiet *n* **regional** ADJ regional

register ['redʒəstər] **1** S Register *n* **2** VT registrieren lassen; (*Fahrzeug etc*) anmelden **3** VI (*für Kurs, in Hotel*) sich anmelden; (*an Universität*) sich einschreiben **registered** ADJ eingetragen; (*Brief*) eingeschrieben **registration** [redʒə'streɪʃən] S (*für Kurs*) Anmeldung *f*; (*an Universität*) Einschreibung *f*; AUTO Kraftfahrzeugbrief *m*

regret [rɪ'gret] **1** S Bedauern *n* **2** VT bedauern **regrettable** ADJ bedauerlich

regular ['regjələr] **1** ADJ regelmäßig; (*Größe*) normal **2** S Stammkunde *m*; Stammkundin *f*; (*in Gaststätte*) Stammgast *m*; (*Benzin*) Normalbenzin *n* **regularly** ADV regelmäßig

regulate ['regjəleɪt] VT regulieren; regeln **regulation** [regjə'leɪʃən] S Vorschrift *f*

rehearsal [rɪ'hɜːrsəl] S Probe *f* **rehearse** VT & VI proben

reimburse [riːɪm'bɜːrs] VT entschädigen; (*Kosten, Auslagen*) zurückerstatten

reindeer ['reɪndɪr] S Rentier *n*

reinforce [riːɪn'fɔːrs] VT verstärken

reject **1** ['riːdʒekt] S WIRTSCH Ausschussartikel *m* **2** [rɪ'dʒekt] VT ablehnen; *umg* **get ~ed** einen Korb kriegen **rejection** [rɪ'dʒekʃən] S Ablehnung *f*

relapse [rɪ'læps] S Rückfall *m*

relate [rɪ'leɪt] **1** VT (*Geschichte*) erzählen; (*Sache etc*) in Verbindung bringen (*to* mit) **2** VI **~ to** sich beziehen auf *+akk* **related** ADJ verwandt (*to* mit) **relation** [rɪ'leɪʃən] S Verwandte(r) *m/f(m)*; (*Verbindung*) Beziehung *f* **relationship** S Beziehung *f*, Verhältnis *n* **relative** ['relətɪv] **1** S Verwandte(r) *m/f(m)* **2** ADJ relativ **relatively** ADV relativ, verhältnismäßig

relax [rɪ'læks] **1** VI sich entspannen **2** VT lockern **relaxation** [riːlæk'seɪʃən] S Entspannung *f* **relaxed** ADJ entspannt **relaxing** ADJ erholsam, entspannend

release [rɪ'liːs] **1** S Entlassung *f*; **new/recent ~** (*CD*) Neuerscheinung *f* **2** VT (*Geisel*) freilassen; (*Gefangene*) entlassen; (*Bremse*) lösen; (*Nachricht*) veröffentlichen; (*CD*) herausbringen

relentlessly [rɪ'lentləslɪ] ADV erbarmungslos; unaufhörlich

relevance ['reləvəns] S Relevanz *f* (*to* für) **relevant** ADJ relevant (*to* für)

reliable, **reliably** [rɪ'laɪəbl, -blɪ] ADJ & ADV zuverlässig **reliant** [rɪ'laɪənt] ADJ **~ on** abhängig von

relic ['relɪk] S Relikt *n*

relief [rɪ'liːf] S Erleichterung *f*, Hilfe *f* **relieve** [rɪ'liːv] VT (*Schmerzen etc*) lindern; (*Lange-*

weile) überwinden; *(j-n bei etw)* ablösen; **I'm ~d** ich bin erleichtert
religion [rɪˈlɪdʒən] S Religion *f* **religious** [rɪˈlɪdʒəs] ADJ religiös
relish [ˈrelɪʃ] **1** S *(für Essen)* würzige Soße **2** V/T genießen; Gefallen finden an *+dat*
reluctant [rɪˈlʌktənt] ADJ widerwillig; **be ~ to do sth** etw nur ungern tun **reluctantly** ADV widerwillig
rely on [rɪˈlaɪɑːn] V/T sich verlassen auf *+akk*; *(finanziell)* abhängig sein von
remain [rɪˈmeɪn] V/I bleiben; *(als Rest)* übrig bleiben **remainder** S *a.* MATH Rest *m* **remaining** ADJ übrig **remains** S PL Überreste *pl*
remark [rɪˈmɑːrk] **1** S Bemerkung *f* **2** V/T bemerken **remarkable**, **remarkably** ADJ & ADV bemerkenswert
remedy [ˈremədɪ] S Mittel *n* *(for* gegen)
remember [rɪˈmembər] **1** V/T sich erinnern an *+akk*; denken an *+akk*, nicht vergessen **2** V/I sich erinnern
remind [rɪˈmaɪnd] V/T erinnern *(of, about* an *+akk)* **reminder** S Mahnung *f*
remnant [ˈremnənt] S Rest *m*
remote [rɪˈmoʊt] **1** ADJ abgelegen; *(Chance)* gering **2** S TV Fernbedienung *f* **remote control** S Fernsteuerung *f*, Fernbedienung *f*
removal [rɪˈmuːvəl] S Entfernung *f* **remove** [rɪˈmuːv] V/T entfernen; *(Deckel)* abnehmen; *(Zweifel)* zerstreuen
rename [riːˈneɪm] V/T umbenennen
renew [rɪˈnuː] V/T erneuern; verlängern lassen
renovate [ˈrenəveɪt] V/T renovieren
renowned [rɪˈnaʊnd] ADJ berühmt *(for* für)
rent [rent] **1** S Miete *f*; **for ~** zu vermieten **2** V/T *(als Mieter)* mieten; *(als Eigentümer)* vermieten **rent out** V/T vermieten **rental** **1** S Miete *f*; *(für Auto etc)* Leihgebühr *f* **2** ADJ Miet-
reorganize [riːˈɔːrgənaɪz] V/T umorganisieren
rep [rep] S WIRTSCH Vertreter(in) *m(f)*
Rep *abk* = Republican; Republikaner(in) *m(f)*; republikanisch
repair [rɪˈper] **1** S Reparatur *f* **2** V/T reparieren; wiedergutmachen
repay [rɪˈpeɪ] *irr* V/T zurückzahlen; vergelten
repeat [rɪˈpiːt] **1** S RADIO, TV Wiederholung *f* **2** V/T wiederholen **repetition** [repəˈtɪʃən] S Wiederholung *f*
replace [rɪˈpleɪs] V/T ersetzen *(with* durch); zurückstellen, zurücklegen **replacement** S Ersatz *m*; *(Arbeitsplatz)* Vertre-

tung *f*
replay **1** ['ri:pleɪ] S Wiederholung *f* **2** [ri:'pleɪ] V/T (*Spiel*) wiederholen
replica ['replɪkə] S Kopie *f*
reply [rɪ'plaɪ] **1** S Antwort *f* **2** V/I antworten
report [rɪ'pɔ:rt] **1** S Bericht *m*; (*Schule*) Zeugnis *n* **2** V/T berichten; melden; (*bei der Polizei*) anzeigen **3** V/I sich melden
represent [reprɪ'zent] V/T darstellen; (*seine Firma etc*) vertreten **representation** [reprɪzen'teɪʃən] S Darstellung *f* **representative** [reprɪ'zentətɪv] **1** S Vertreter(in) *m(f)*; POL Abgeordnete(r) *m/f(m)* **2** ADJ repräsentativ (*of* für)
reproduce [ri:prə'du:s] **1** V/T reproduzieren **2** V/I BIOL sich fortpflanzen **reproduction** [ri:prə'dʌkʃən] S Reproduktion *f*; BIOL Fortpflanzung *f*
reptile ['reptaɪl] S Reptil *n*
republic [rɪ'pʌblɪk] S Republik *f* **republican**, **Republican** POL **1** ADJ republikanisch; **the Republican Party** die Republikanische Partei **2** S Republikaner(in) *m(f)*
repulsive [rɪ'pʌlsɪv] ADJ abstoßend
reputation [repjə'teɪʃən] S Ruf *m*
request [rɪ'kwest] **1** S Bitte *f* (*for* um); **on ~** auf Wunsch **2** V/T bitten um
require [rɪ'kwaɪr] V/T brauchen; (*als Anforderung*) verlangen **required** ADJ erforderlich **requirement** S Anforderung *f*; (*Job etc*) Bedingung *f*
rerun ['ri:rʌn] S Wiederholung *f*
rescue ['reskju:] **1** S Rettung *f* **2** V/T retten
research [rɪ'sɜ:rtʃ] **1** S Forschung *f* **2** V/I forschen (*into* über *+akk*) **3** V/T erforschen **researcher** S Forscher(in) *m(f)*
resemblance [rɪ'zembləns] S Ähnlichkeit *f* (*to* mit) **resemble** V/T ähneln *+dat*
resent [rɪ'zent] V/T übel nehmen
reservation [rezər'veɪʃən] S Reservierung *f*; (*Zweifel*) Vorbehalt *m*; (*für Indianer*) Reservat *n* **reserve** [rɪ'zɜ:rv] **1** S Vorrat *m* (*of* an *+dat*); (*Verhalten*) Zurückhaltung *f*; SPORT Reservespieler(in) *m(f)*; (*in Landschaft*) Naturschutzgebiet *n* **2** V/T reservieren **reserved** ADJ reserviert
residence ['rezɪdəns] S Wohnsitz *m*; (*in Land, Stadt*) Aufenthalt *m* **resident** ['rezɪdənt] S Bewohner(in) *m(f)*, Einwohner(in) *m(f)*; Assistenzarzt *m*, Assistenzärztin *f* (*ab zweitem Jahr der Facharztausbildung*)
resign [rɪ'zaɪn] **1** V/T (*Amt, Posten*) zurücktreten von; (*Job*) kündigen **2** V/I (*von Amt*) zurücktreten; (*Job*) kündigen

resignation [rezɪg'neɪʃən] S Rücktritt *m*, Kündigung *f*
resist [rɪ'zɪst] V/T widerstehen *+dat* **resistance** S Widerstand *m* (*to* gegen)
resolution [rezə'lu:ʃən] S Vorsatz *m*; Beschluss *m*
resolve [rɪ'zɑ:lv] V/T lösen
resort [rɪ'zɔ:rt] **1** S Urlaubsort *m*; **as a last ~** als letzter Ausweg **2** V/I **~ to** greifen zu; (*Gewalt*) anwenden
resources [rɪ'sɔ:rsəz] S PL (Geld)mittel *pl*; (*Kohle, Erdöl etc*) Bodenschätze *pl*
respect [rɪ'spekt] **1** S Respekt *m* (*for* vor *+dat*), Rücksicht *f* (*for* auf *+akk*); **with ~ to** in Bezug auf *+akk*; **in this ~** in dieser Hinsicht **2** V/T respektieren **respectable** [rɪ'spektəbl] ADJ (*Person*) angesehen; (*Gegend*) anständig; (*Leistung*) beachtlich **respected** [rɪ'spektəd] ADJ angesehen
respective [rɪ'spektɪv] ADJ jeweilig **respectively** ADV beziehungsweise
respond [rɪ'spɑ:nd] V/I antworten (*to* auf *+akk*), reagieren (*to* auf *+akk*); (*auf Behandlung*) ansprechen (*to* auf *+akk*) **response** [rɪ'spɑ:ns] S Antwort *f*, Reaktion *f*
responsibility [rɪspɑ:nsə'bɪləti] S Verantwortung *f* **responsible** [rɪ'spɑ:nsəbl] ADJ verantwortlich (*for* für); verantwortungsbewusst; (*Arbeit*) verantwortungsvoll
rest [rest] **1** S (*Erholung*) Ruhe *f*; (*Wanderung etc*) Pause *f*; (*Überbleibsel*) Rest *m*; **have** (*od* **take**) **a ~** sich ausruhen; Pause machen **2** V/I sich ausruhen; (*an Baum, Mauer etc*) lehnen (*on, against* an *+dat*, gegen)
rest area S Raststätte *f* (*mit Tankstelle*)
restaurant ['restərɑ:nt] S Restaurant *n*
restless ['restləs] ADJ unruhig
restore [rɪ'stɔ:r] V/T restaurieren; (*Ruhe*) wiederherstellen; (*Gebiet*) zurückgeben
restrain [rɪ'streɪn] V/T zurückhalten; **~ oneself** sich beherrschen
restrict [rɪ'strɪkt] V/T beschränken (*to* auf *+akk*) **restricted** ADJ beschränkt **restriction** [rɪ'strɪkʃən] S Einschränkung *f* (*on +gen*)
rest room ['restru:m] S Toilette *f*
result [rɪ'zʌlt] **1** S Ergebnis *n*, Folge *f*; **as a ~ of** infolge *+gen* **2** V/I **~ in** führen zu; **~ from** sich ergeben aus
resume [rɪ'zu:m] V/T wieder aufnehmen; fortsetzen
résumé ['rezəmeɪ] S Lebenslauf *m*
resuscitate [rɪ'sʌsəteɪt] V/T wiederbeleben
retail ['ri:teɪl] ADV im Einzelhandel **retailer** S Einzelhändler(in) *m(f)*

retain [rɪ'teɪn] V/T behalten; (*Hitze*) halten
retire [rɪ'taɪr] V/I in den Ruhestand treten; sich zurückziehen **retired** ADJ pensioniert **retirement** S Ruhestand *m* **retirement benefits** S PL Rente *f* **retirement plan** S Rentenversicherung *f*
retrain [ri:'treɪn] V/I sich umschulen lassen
retreat [rɪ'tri:t] **1** S Rückzug *m* (*from* aus); Zufluchtsort *m* **2** V/I sich zurückziehen
retrieve [rɪ'tri:v] V/T wiederbekommen; (*die Lage etc*) retten; (*Daten*) abrufen
return [rɪ'tɜ:rn] **1** S Rückkehr *f*; (*von Sache etc*) Rückgabe *f*; (*Profit*) Gewinn *m*; (*Tennis*) Return *m*; **in ~** als Gegenleistung (*for* für) **2** V/I zurückkehren; (*Symptome*) wieder auftreten **3** V/T zurückgeben; **I ~ed his call** ich habe ihn zurückgerufen **returnable** ADJ Pfand- **return key** S IT Eingabetaste *f*
reunification [ri:ju:nɪfɪ'keɪʃən] S Wiedervereinigung *f*
reunion [ri:'ju:njən] S Treffen *n* **reunite** [ri:jʊ'naɪt] V/T wieder vereinigen
reveal [rɪ'vi:l] V/T enthüllen; verraten **revealing** ADJ aufschlussreich; (*Kleid*) freizügig
revenge [rɪ'vendʒ] S Rache *f*, Revanche *f*; **take ~ on sb (for sth)** sich an j-m (für etw) rächen
revenue ['revənu:] S Einnahmen *pl*
reverse [rɪ'vɜ:rs] **1** S Rückseite *f*; Gegenteil *n*; AUTO Rückwärtsgang *m* **2** ADJ umgekehrt **3** V/T umkehren; (*Beschluss*) umstoßen **4** V/I rückwärtsfahren
review [rɪ'vju:] **1** S Rezension *f*, Kritik *f*; Überprüfung *f* **2** V/T (*Buch, Film etc*) rezensieren; (*Lage, Entscheidung*) überprüfen
revise [rɪ'vaɪz] V/T revidieren; (*Text*) überarbeiten **revision** [rɪ'vɪʒən] S (*von Text*) Überarbeitung *f*
revive [rɪ'vaɪv] V/T (*Person*) wiederbeleben; (*Tradition etc*) wieder aufleben lassen
revolt [rɪ'voʊlt] S Aufstand *m* **revolting** ADJ widerlich
revolution [revə'lu:ʃən] S POL *fig* Revolution *f* **revolutionary** **1** ADJ revolutionär **2** S Revolutionär(in) *m(f)*
revolve [rɪ'vɑ:lv] V/I sich drehen (*around* um) **revolver** S Revolver *m* **revolving door** S Drehtür *f*
reward [rɪ'wɔ:rd] **1** S Belohnung *f* **2** V/T belohnen **rewarding** ADJ lohnend
rewind [ri:'waɪnd] *irr* V/T zurückspulen
rheumatism ['ru:mətɪzəm] S Rheuma *n*
rhinoceros [raɪ'nɑ:sərəs] S

Nashorn *n*
rhubarb ['ru:bɑ:rb] S Rhabarber *m*
rhyme [raɪm] **1** S Reim *m* **2** V/I sich reimen (*with* auf *+akk*)
rhythm ['rɪðəm] S Rhythmus *m*
RI *abk* = Rhode Island
rib [rɪb] S Rippe *f*
ribbon ['rɪbən] S Band *n*
rice [raɪs] S Reis *m* **rice pudding** S Milchreis *m*
rich [rɪtʃ] **1** ADJ reich; (*Essen*) schwer **2** S PL **the ~** die Reichen *pl*
rid ⟨rid, rid⟩ [rɪd] V/T **get ~ of sb/sth** j-n/etw loswerden
ridden ['rɪdn] *pperf von* ride
riddle ['rɪdl] S Rätsel *n*
ride ⟨rode, ridden⟩ [raɪd, roʊd, 'rɪdn] **1** V/T reiten; (*Fahrrad*) fahren **2** V/I reiten; (*auf Fahrrad*) fahren **3** S Fahrt *f*; (*auf Pferd*) (Aus)ritt *m*; **go for a ~** spazieren fahren; (*auf Pferd*) reiten gehen; **give sb a ~** j-n im Auto mitnehmen; **take sb for a ~** *umg* j-n verschaukeln, j-n verarschen
ridiculous [rɪ'dɪkjələs] ADJ lächerlich; **don't be ~** red keinen Unsinn!
riding ['raɪdɪŋ] **1** S Reiten *n* **2** ADJ Reit-
right [raɪt] **1** ADJ richtig; (*seitenmäßig*) rechte(r, s); (*Beruf etc*) passend; **be ~** (*Person*) recht haben; (*Uhr*) richtig gehen; **that's ~** das stimmt! **2** S Recht *n* (*to* auf *+akk*); (*Seite*) rechte Seite; **the Right** POL die Rechte; **on/to the ~** rechts (*of* von) **3** ADV rechts; (*Bewegung, Richtung*) nach rechts; (*ohne Umweg*) direkt; (*exakt*) genau; **~ away** sofort; **~ now** im Moment; (*gleich*) sofort
right angle S rechter Winkel
right-handed ADJ rechtshändig **right-hand side** S rechte Seite **rightly** ADV zu Recht **right of way** S AUTO Vorfahrt *f* **right-wing** ADJ Rechts-; rechtsgerichtet
rigid ['rɪdʒəd] ADJ starr; streng
rim [rɪm] S Rand *m*; (*Rad*) Felge *f*
rind [raɪnd] S (*Käse*) Rinde *f*; (*Speck*) Schwarte *f*; (*Obst*) Schale *f*
ring ⟨rang, rung⟩ [rɪŋ, ræŋ, rʌŋ] **1** V/T & V/I (*Glocke*) läuten; (*Telefon*) klingeln **2** S Ring *m*; Kreis *m*; (*Zirkus*) Manege *f* **ring finger** S Ringfinger *m* **ringtone** S Klingelton *m*
rink [rɪŋk] S Eisbahn *f*, Rollschuhbahn *f*
rinse [rɪns] V/T spülen
riot ['raɪət] S Aufruhr *m*
rip [rɪp] **1** S Riss *m* **2** V/T zerreißen **3** V/I reißen **rip off** V/T *umg* (*j-n*) abzocken **rip up** V/T zerreißen
ripe [raɪp] ADJ (*Frucht, Obst*) reif
ripen V/I reifen
rise ⟨rose, risen⟩ [raɪz, roʊz, 'rɪzn] **1** V/I aufstehen; (*Sonne*)

aufgehen; (*Preise, Temperatur*) steigen; (*Gelände*) ansteigen **2** S Anstieg *m* (*in +gen*); (*zur Macht*) Aufstieg *m* (*to* zu); (*in Gelände*) Steigung *f* **risen** [ˈrɪzn] *pperf von* rise

risk [rɪsk] **1** S Risiko *n* **2** V/T riskieren **risky** ADJ riskant

ritual [ˈrɪtʃʊəl] S Ritual *n*

rival [ˈraɪvəl] S Rivale *m*, Rivalin *f* (*for* um); WIRTSCH Konkurrent(in) *m(f)* **rivalry** S Rivalität *f*; WIRTSCH, SPORT Konkurrenz *f*

river [ˈrɪvər] S Fluss *m*; **the Mississippi River** der Mississippi **riverside** **1** S Flussufer *n* **2** ADJ am Flussufer

roach [roʊtʃ] S Schabe *f*

road [roʊd] S Straße *f*; *fig* Weg *m*; **on the ~** unterwegs **roadblock** S Straßensperre *f* **roadmap** S Straßenkarte *f* **roadside** S Straßenrand *m* **roadsign** S Verkehrsschild *n* **roadwork** S (*Straße, Autobahn*) Bauarbeiten *pl* **roadworthy** ADJ fahrtüchtig

roar [rɔːr] **1** S Brüllen *n*, Donnern *n* **2** V/I brüllen (*with* vor *+dat*)

roast [roʊst] **1** S Braten *m* **2** ADJ **~ beef** Rinderbraten *m*; **~ chicken** Brathähnchen *n*; **~ potatoes** *pl im Backofen gebratene Kartoffeln* **3** V/T braten

rob [rɑːb] V/T bestehlen; ausrauben **robbery** S Raub *m*

robe [roʊb] S Morgenrock *m*; Robe *f*, Talar *m*

robot [ˈroʊbɑːt] S Roboter *m*

rock [rɑːk] **1** S (*Material*) Stein *m*; (*größer*) Felsbrocken *m*; MUS Rock *m*; **on the ~s** (*Getränk*) mit Eis; (*Ehe*) gescheitert **2** V/T & V/I schaukeln; (*tanzen*) rocken **rock bottom** S *fig* Tiefpunkt **rock climbing** S Klettern *n*

rocket [ˈrɑːkət] S Rakete *f*; (*Salat*) Rucola *m*

Rockies [ˈrɑːkɪz] S PL **the ~** die Rocky Mountains *pl*

rocking chair [ˈrɑːkɪŋtʃer] S Schaukelstuhl *m*

rocky [ˈrɑːkɪ] ADJ felsig; steinig **Rocky Mountains** S PL Rocky Mountains *pl* (*Gebirge im Westen der USA*)

rod [rɑːd] S (*aus Eisen etc*) Stange *f*; Rute *f*

rode [roʊd] *prät von* ride

role [roʊl] S Rolle *f* **role model** S Vorbild *n*

roll [roʊl] **1** S Rolle *f*; (*aus Brotteig*) Brötchen *n* **2** V/T rollen; (*Zigarette*) drehen **3** V/I rollen **roll out** **1** V/T ausrollen **2** V/I hinausrollen; **~ (to …)** sich (nach …) auf den Weg machen **roll over** V/I sich umdrehen **roll up** **1** V/I *umg* antanzen **2** V/T (*Teppich*) aufrollen; **~ one's sleeves** die Ärmel hochkrempeln **roller** S (Locken)wickler *m* **roller coaster** S Achterbahn *f* **roller**

skates SPL Rollschuhe *pl* **roller-skating** S Rollschuhlaufen *n* **rolling pin** S Nudelholz *n* **roll-on (deodorant)** S Deoroller *m*

ROM [rɑːm] *akr* = read only memory; ROM *m*

Roman Catholic [roʊmən-ˈkæθlɪk] **1** ADJ römisch-katholisch **2** S Katholik(in) *m(f)*

romance [roʊˈmæns] S Romantik *f*, Romanze *f*

Romania [roʊˈmeɪnɪə] S Rumänien *n* **Romanian** **1** ADJ rumänisch **2** S Rumäne *m*, Rumänin *f*; (*Sprache*) Rumänisch *n*

romantic [roʊˈmæntɪk] ADJ romantisch

roof [ruːf] S Dach *n*

rookie [ˈrʊkɪ] S *umg* Grünschnabel *m*

room [ruːm] S Zimmer *n*, Raum *m*; (*größer*) Saal *m*; (*Fläche*) Platz *m*; *fig* Spielraum *m*

roomer S Untermieter(in) *m(f)* **roommate** S Zimmergenosse *m*, Zimmergenossin *f*; (*in Wohnung*) Mitbewohner(in) *m(f)* **room service** S Zimmerservice *m*

rooster [ˈruːstər] S Haushahn *m*

root [ruːt] S Wurzel *f* **root beer** S *Limonade aus Kräuter- und Wurzelextrakten*

rope [roʊp] S Seil *n*

rose [roʊz] **1** *prät von* rise **2** S Rose *f*

rosé [roʊˈzeɪ] S Rosé(wein) *m*

rot [rɑːt] VI verfaulen

rotate [roʊˈteɪt] **1** VT rotieren lassen **2** VI rotieren **rotation** [roʊˈteɪʃən] S Rotation *f*; **in ~** abwechselnd

rotten [ˈrɑːtn] ADJ (*Ei, Obst etc*) faul; (*Person, Verhalten*) gemein; (*Wetter etc*) scheußlich; (*krank*) elend

rough [rʌf] ADJ rau; (*Gelände, Weg*) uneben; (*Person, Schätzung*) grob; (*Überfahrt*) stürmisch; (*Zeit*) hart; (*Vorstellung*) ungefähr **roughly** ADV grob; (*in etwa*) ungefähr

round [raʊnd] **1** ADJ rund **2** ADV herum, umher **3** PRÄP um; (*umgebend*) um (... herum); (*innerhalb von Stadt etc*) in ... herum **4** S Runde *f*; (*Toast*) Scheibe *f* **5** VT (*Ecke*) biegen um **round off** VT abrunden **round up** VT (*Preis*) aufrunden; (*Vieh*) zusammentreiben **round trip** S Rundreise *f* **round-trip ticket** S Rückfahrkarte *f*; (*Flug*) Rückflugticket *n*

route [ruːt, raʊt] S Route *f*; ≈ Bundesstraße *f*; (*Bus etc*) Linie *f*; *fig* Weg *m*

routine [ruːˈtiːn] **1** S Routine *f* **2** ADJ Routine-

row [roʊ] **1** S Reihe *f*; **three times in a ~** dreimal hintereinander **2** VT & VI rudern **rowboat** [ˈroʊboʊt] S Ruderboot *n* **row house** [ˈroʊhaʊs] S

Reihenhaus *n*
R.S.V.P. *abk* = répondez s'il vous plaît; u. A. w. g.
rub [rʌb] V/T reiben **rub in** V/T einmassieren
rubber ['rʌbər] S Gummi *m*; *umg* (*Kondom*) Gummi *m*
rubble ['rʌbl] S Schutt *m*
ruby ['ru:bɪ] S Rubin *m*
rude [ru:d] ADJ unhöflich; (*Witz*) unanständig
rug [rʌg] S Teppich *m*; Bettvorleger *m*
rugged ['rʌgəd] ADJ (*Küste*) zerklüftet; (*Gesichtszüge*) markant
ruin ['ru:ɪn] **1** S Ruine *f*; (*finanziell etc*) Ruin *m* **2** V/T ruinieren
rule [ru:l] **1** S Regel *f*; (*eines Herrschers*) Herrschaft *f* **2** V/T & V/I regieren; (*Richter*) entscheiden **ruler** S Lineal *n*; (*Person*) Herrscher(in) *m(f)*
rum [rʌm] S Rum *m*
rumble ['rʌmbl] V/I (*Magen*) knurren; (*Zug etc*) rumpeln
rummage ['rʌmɪdʒ] V/I herumstöbern
rumor ['ru:mər] S Gerücht *n*
run ⟨ran, run⟩ [rʌn, ræn] **1** V/T laufen; (*Wasser, Programm etc*) laufen lassen; (*als Manager*) leiten, führen; (*ein Auto etc*) unterhalten; **I ran her home** ich habe sie nach Hause gefahren **2** V/I laufen; rennen; (*Bus, Zug*) fahren; (*Weg*) verlaufen; (*Wasser, Programm*) laufen; (*Fluss, Wasser*) fließen; (*Farben*) verlaufen; **~ for President** für die Präsidentschaft kandidieren; **be ~ning low** knapp werden **3** S Lauf *m*; (*Folge, Serie*) Reihe *f*; (*auf Ware*) Ansturm *m* (*on* auf *+akk*); (*in Strumpfhose*) Laufmasche *f*; (*Baseball*) Lauf *m*; **go for a ~** laufen gehen; (*in Auto*) eine Spazierfahrt machen; **on the ~** auf der Flucht (*from* vor *+dat*) **run away** V/I weglaufen **run down** V/T (*Fußgänger etc*) umfahren **run into** V/T (*Bekannte*) zufällig treffen; (*Problem*) stoßen auf *+akk* **run off** V/I weglaufen **run out** V/I hinausrennen; (*Flüssigkeit*) auslaufen; (*Zeit*) ablaufen; (*Geld, Vorräte*) ausgehen; **he ran out of money** ihm ging das Geld aus **run over** V/T (*Fußgänger*) überfahren **run up** V/T (*Rechnung*) machen
rung [rʌŋ] *pperf von* **ring**
runner ['rʌnər] S Läufer(in) *m(f)* **running** ['rʌnɪŋ] **1** S SPORT Laufen *n*; (*Geschäft*) Leitung *f*, Führung *f* **2** ADJ (*Wasser*) fließend; **3 days ~** 3 Tage hintereinander **runny** ['rʌnɪ] ADJ flüssig; (*Nase*) laufend
runway ['rʌnweɪ] S Start- und Landebahn *f*
rural ['rʊrəl] ADJ ländlich
rush [rʌʃ] **1** S Eile *f*; (*auf Karten etc*) Ansturm *m* (*for* auf *+akk*); **be in a ~** es eilig haben;

there's no ~ es eilt nicht **2** VT hastig machen; (*Mahlzeit*) hastig essen; **~ sb to the hospital** j-n auf dem schnellsten Weg ins Krankenhaus bringen **3** VI eilen **rush hour** S Hauptverkehrszeit *f*
rusk [rʌsk] S Zwieback *m*
Russia ['rʌʃə] S Russland *n*
Russian **1** ADJ russisch **2** S Russe *m*, Russin *f*; (*Sprache*) Russisch *n*
rust [rʌst] **1** S Rost *m* **2** VI rosten **rusty** ['rʌstɪ] ADJ rostig
rutabaga [ru:tə'beɪgə] S Steckrübe *f*
RV *abk* = recreational vehicle; Wohnmobil *n*
rye [raɪ] S Roggen *m*

S

sack [sæk] S Sack *m*
sacred ['seɪkrəd] ADJ heilig
sacrifice ['sækrəfaɪs] **1** S Opfer *n* **2** VT opfern
sad [sæd] ADJ traurig
saddle ['sædl] S Sattel *m*
sadly ['sædlɪ] ADV leider
safe [seɪf] **1** ADJ sicher; in Sicherheit; vorsichtig; **have a ~ journey** gute Fahrt! **2** S Safe *m* **safeguard** **1** S Schutz *m* **2** VT schützen (*against* vor *+dat*) **safely** ADV sicher; (*ankommen*) wohlbehalten; (*fahren*) vorsichtig **safety** S Sicherheit *f* **safety belt** S Sicherheitsgurt *m* **safety island** S Verkehrsinsel *f* **safety pin** S Sicherheitsnadel *f*
Sagittarius [sædʒə'terɪəs] S ASTROL Schütze *m*
said [sed] *prät, pperf von* **say**
sail [seɪl] **1** S Segel *n*; **set ~** losfahren (*for* nach) **2** VI segeln; mit dem Schiff fahren; (*Schiff*) auslaufen (*for* nach) **3** VT (*Jacht*) segeln mit; (*Schiff*) steuern **sailboat** S Segelboot *n* **sailing** S **go ~** segeln gehen **sailor** S Seemann *m*; Matrose *m*
saint [seɪnt] S Heilige(r) *m/f(m)*
sake [seɪk] S **for the ~ of** um *+gen* … willen; **for your ~** deinetwegen, dir zuliebe
salad ['sæləd] S Salat *m* **salad dressing** S Salatsoße *f*
salary ['sælərɪ] S Gehalt *n*
sale [seɪl] S Verkauf *m*, Ausverkauf *m*; **for ~** zu verkaufen **sales clerk** S Verkäufer(in) *m(f)* **salesman** ⟨-men *pl*⟩ S Verkäufer *m*; Vertreter *m* **sales tax** S ≈ Umsatzsteuer *f* **saleswoman** ⟨-women *pl*⟩ S Verkäuferin *f*; Vertreterin *f*
salmon ['sæmən] S Lachs *m*
saloon [sə'lu:n] S (*Bar*) Kneipe *f* (*im Westernstil*)
salt [sɔ:lt] **1** S Salz *n* **2** VT salzen **salt shaker** S Salzstreuer *m* **salty** ADJ salzig

same [seɪm] **1** ADJ **the ~** der/die/das gleiche, die gleichen *pl*; der-/die-/dasselbe, dieselben *pl* **2** PRON **the ~** der/die/das Gleiche, die Gleichen *pl*; der-/die-/dasselbe, dieselben *pl*; **the ~ to you** gleichfalls; **it's all the ~ to me** es ist mir egal **3** ADV **the ~** gleich
sample ['sæmpl] **1** S Probe *f*; (*von Stoff*) Muster *n* **2** V/T probieren
sanctuary ['sæŋktʃʊərɪ] S (*Ort*) Zuflucht *f*; (*für Tiere*) Schutzgebiet *n*
sand [sænd] S Sand *m*
sandal ['sændl] S Sandale *f*
sandwich ['sænwɪtʃ] S Sandwich *n*
sandy ['sændɪ] ADJ sandig
sang [sæŋ] *prät von* sing
sanitary ['sænətərɪ] ADJ hygienisch **sanitary napkin** S Damenbinde *f*
sank [sæŋk] *prät von* sink
Santa (Claus) ['sæntə(klɔ:z)] S der Weihnachtsmann
sarcastic [sɑ:r'kæstɪk] ADJ sarkastisch
sardine [sɑ:r'di:n] S Sardine *f*
sassy ['sæsɪ] ADJ frech; forsch
sat [sæt] *prät, pperf von* sit
Sat *abk* = Saturday; Sa.
satellite ['sætəlaɪt] S Satellit *m* **satellite dish** S Satellitenschüssel *f*
satisfaction [sætəs'fækʃən] S Zufriedenheit *f* **satisfactory** [sætəs'fæktərɪ] ADJ zufriedenstellend **satisfied** ['sætəsfaɪd] ADJ zufrieden (*with* mit)
satisfy ['sætəsfaɪ] V/T zufriedenstellen; (*Bedingungen*) erfüllen; (*Bedürfnis, Nachfrage*) befriedigen **satisfying** ADJ befriedigend
Saturday ['sætərdeɪ] S Samstag *m*, Sonnabend *m*; → Tuesday
sauce [sɒ:s] S Soße *f* **saucepan** S Kochtopf *m* **saucer** S Untertasse *f*
Saudi Arabia [saʊdɪə'reɪbɪə] S Saudi-Arabien *n*
sauna ['sɒ:nə] S Sauna *f*
sausage ['sɒ:sɪdʒ] S Wurst *f*
save [seɪv] **1** V/T retten (*from* vor *+dat*); (*Geld, Zeit*) sparen; (*Kräfte*) schonen; IT speichern **2** V/I sparen **saving** S Sparen *n*; **~s** *pl* Ersparnisse *pl*; **~s account** Sparkonto *n*
savory ['seɪvərɪ] ADJ pikant
saw [sɒ:] **1** V/T & V/I sägen **2** S Säge *f* **3** *prät von* see
saxophone ['sæksəfoʊn] S Saxophon *n*
say ⟨said, said⟩ [seɪ, sed] **1** V/T sagen (*to sb* j-m); (*Gebet*) sprechen; **what does the letter ~?** was steht im Brief?; **he's said to be rich** er soll reich sein **2** S **have a ~ in sth** bei etw ein Mitspracherecht haben **3** ADV zum Beispiel **saying** S Sprichwort *n*
SC *abk* = South Carolina
scab [skæb] S Schorf *m*

scaffold(ing) ['skæfəld(ɪŋ)] S (Bau)gerüst *n*
scale [skeɪl] S (*Landkarte*) Maßstab *m*; (*Thermometer*) Skala *f*; (*Gehälter*) Tarifsystem *n*; MUS Tonleiter *f*; (*Fisch*) Schuppe *f*; *fig* Ausmaß *m*; **to ~** maßstab(s)gerecht **scales** S PL Waage *f*
scallion ['skælɪən] S Frühlingszwiebel *f*
scalp [skælp] S Kopfhaut *f*
scam [skæm] **1** S Betrug *m* **2** V/T **~ sb** j-n betrügen
scan [skæn] **1** V/T genau prüfen; (*schnell lesen*) überfliegen; IT scannen **2** S MED Ultraschall *m*
scandal ['skændl] S Skandal *m*
Scandinavia [skændɪ'neɪvɪə] S Skandinavien *n* **Scandinavian** **1** ADJ skandinavisch **2** S Skandinavier(in) *m(f)*
scanner ['skænər] S Scanner *m*
scar [skɑ:r] S Narbe *f*
scarce [skers] ADJ selten; (*Vorräte*) knapp **scarcely** ADV kaum
scare [sker] **1** S Panik *f* **2** V/T erschrecken; **be ~d** Angst haben (*of* vor *+dat*)
scarf ⟨scarves *pl*⟩ [skɑ:rf, skɑ:rvz] S Schal *m*; (*auf Kopf*) Kopftuch *n*
scary ['skerɪ] ADJ gruselig
scatter ['skætər] V/T verstreuen; (*Saatgut etc*) streuen; (*Demonstranten etc*) auseinandertreiben
scene [si:n] S Ort *m*; THEAT Szene *f*; (*für Betrachter*) Anblick *m* **scenery** ['si:nərɪ] S Landschaft *f*; THEAT Kulissen *pl* **scenic** ['si:nɪk] ADJ (*Gegend*) malerisch, landschaftlich schön
scent [sent] S (*Duftstoff*) Parfüm *n*; (*Geruch*) Duft *m*
schedule ['skedʒʊəl] **1** S (*von Veranstaltungen*) Programm *n*; (*bei Arbeit*) Zeitplan *m*; (*Verzeichnis*) Liste *f*; Fahr-, Flugplan *m*; **on ~** planmäßig; **be behind ~ with sth** mit etw in Verzug sein **2** V/T planen; ansetzen **scheduled** ADJ (*Abfahrt etc*) planmäßig; **~ flight** Linienflug *m*
scheme [ski:m] **1** S Plan *m*, Projekt *n*; (*gegen Person*) Intrige *f* **2** V/I intrigieren
scholarship ['skɑ:lərʃɪp] S Stipendium *n*
school [sku:l] S Schule *f*; (*an Universität etc*) Fachbereich *m*; Universität *f* **schoolchild** ⟨schoolchildren⟩ S Schüler(in) *m(f)* **schoolteacher** S Lehrer(in) *m(f)* **schoolwork** S Schularbeiten *pl*
sciatica [saɪ'ætɪkə] S Ischias *m*
science ['saɪəns] S Wissenschaft *f*; (*speziell*) Naturwissenschaft *f* **scientific** [saɪən'tɪfɪk] ADJ wissenschaftlich **sci-**

entist ['saɪəntəst] S Wissenschaftler(in) *m(f)*; (*speziell*) Naturwissenschaftler(in) *m(f)*
scissors ['sɪzərz] S PL Schere *f*
scone [skoʊn, skɒ:n] S *kleines süßes Hefebrötchen, das oft Nüsse oder Preiselbeeren enthält*
scoop [sku:p] **1** S (*für Eis etc*) Portionierer *m*; (*von Eis etc*) Kugel *f*; (*Presse*) Exklusivbericht *m*; Erstmeldung *f* **2** V/T **~ (up)** schaufeln
scooter ['sku:tər] S (Motor)roller *m*; (Tret)roller *m*
scope [skoʊp] S Umfang *m*; (*Spielraum*) Möglichkeit *f*
score [skɔ:r] **1** S SPORT Spielstand *m*, Spielergebnis *n*; (*bei Quiz*) Punktestand *m*; MUS Partitur *f*; **keep (the) ~** mitzählen **2** V/T (*Punkt*) erzielen **3** V/I punkten; (*Punktestand*) mitzählen; **~ with sb** j-n ins Bett kriegen **scoreboard** S Anzeigetafel *f*
scornful ['skɔ:rnfəl] ADJ verächtlich
Scorpio ‹-s *pl*› ['skɔ:rpɪoʊ] S ASTROL Skorpion *m*
scorpion ['skɔ:rpɪən] S Skorpion *m*
Scot [skɑ:t] S Schotte *m*, Schottin *f* **Scotch** [skɑ:tʃ] S schottischer Whisky, Scotch *m* **Scotch tape®** S ≈ Tesafilm® *m* **Scotland** ['skɑ:tlənd] S Schottland *n* **Scotsman** ‹-men *pl*› S Schotte *m* **Scotswoman** ‹-women *pl*› S Schottin *f* **Scottish** ADJ schottisch
scout [skaʊt] S Pfadfinder(in) *m(f)*
scrambled eggs [skræmbld-'egz] S PL Rührei *n*
scrap [skræp] **1** S Stückchen *n*, Fetzen *m*; (*Metall*) Schrott *m* **2** V/T verschrotten; (*Plan*) verwerfen
scrape [skreɪp] **1** S Kratzer *m* **2** V/T (*Auto*) schrammen; (*Mauer*) streifen
scratch [skrætʃ] **1** S Kratzer *m*; **from ~** ganz von vorne; von Grund auf **2** V/T kratzen; (*Lackierung etc*) zerkratzen **scratch card** S Rubbellos *n*
scream [skri:m] **1** S Schrei *m* **2** V/I schreien (*with* vor *+dat*); **~ at sb** j-n anschreien
screen [skri:n] **1** S TV, IT Bildschirm *m*; FILM Leinwand *f* **2** V/T (*Film*) zeigen; (*Bewerber, Gepäck*) überprüfen
screw [skru:] **1** S Schraube *f* **2** V/T schrauben (*to* an *+akk*); *vulg* (*Sex haben mit*) ficken, poppen; **~ off/on** (*Deckel*) ab-/aufschrauben **screw up** V/T (*Papier*) zusammenknüllen; (*Pläne, Urlaub etc*) vermasseln **screwdriver** S Schraubenzieher *m*
scribble ['skrɪbl] V/T & V/I kritzeln
script [skrɪpt] S (*Theaterstück*) Text *m*; (*Film*) Drehbuch *n*;

(*arabische etc*) Schrift *f*
scroll [skroʊl] VI IT scrollen
scrub [skrʌb] VT schrubben
scruffy ['skrʌfɪ] ADJ ungepflegt
scuba-diving ['sku:bədaɪvɪŋ] S Sporttauchen *n*
sculpture ['skʌlptʃər] S KUNST Bildhauerei *f*; Skulptur *f*
SD *abk* = South Dakota
sea [si:] S Meer *n*, See *f* **seaboard** S Küste *f* **seafood** S Meeresfrüchte *pl* **seagull** S Möwe *f*
seal [si:l] 1 S (*Tier*) Robbe *f*; (*Stempel*) Siegel *n*; TECH Verschluss *m*; (*ringförmig*) Dichtung *f* 2 VT versiegeln; (*Briefumschlag*) zukleben
seam [si:m] S Naht *f*
search [sɜ:rtʃ] 1 S Suche *f* (*for* nach) 2 VI suchen (*for* nach) 3 VT durchsuchen **search engine** S IT Suchmaschine *f*
seashell ['si:ʃel] S Muschel *f* **seashore** S Strand *m* **seasick** ADJ seekrank **seaside resort** S Seebad *n*
season ['si:zn] 1 S Jahreszeit *f*; Saison *f*; **high/off-~** Hoch-/Nebensaison *f* 2 VT würzen **seasoning** S Gewürz *n* **season ticket** S BAHN Zeitkarte *f*; THEAT Abonnement *n*; SPORT Dauerkarte *f*
seat [si:t] 1 S (*in Theater etc*) Platz *m*; (*Stuhl*) Sitz *m*; **take a ~** setzen Sie sich 2 VT (*von Saal etc*) Sitzplätze haben für; **remain ~ed** sitzen bleiben **seat belt** S Sicherheitsgurt *m*
seaweed ['si:wi:d] S Seetang *m*
secluded [sɪ'klu:dəd] ADJ abgelegen
second ['sekənd] 1 ADJ zweite(r, s) 2 ADV an zweiter Stelle; (*Aufzählung*) zweitens; (*ankommen, fertig sein*) als Zweite(r, s) 3 S Sekunde *f*; (*Moment*) Augenblick *m* **second-hand** ADJ & ADV gebraucht; (*Info*) aus zweiter Hand **secondly** ADV zweitens
secret ['si:krət] 1 S Geheimnis *n* 2 ADJ geheim; (*Verehrer*) heimlich
secretary ['sekrəterɪ] S Sekretär(in) *m(f)*; (*Regierung*) Minister(in) *m(f)* **Secretary of State** S Außenminister(in) *m(f)*
secretly ['si:krətlɪ] ADV heimlich
section ['sekʃən] S Teil *m*; (*von Dokument*) Abschnitt *m*; (*Firma*) Abteilung *f*
secure [sɪ'kjʊr] 1 ADJ sicher (*from* vor *+dat*); (*sicher montiert*) fest 2 VT befestigen; (*Fenster, Tür*) fest verschließen **securely** ADV fest; (*gesichert*) sicher **security** [sɪ'kjʊrətɪ] S Sicherheit *f* **security guard** S (*auf Parkplatz etc*) Wächter(in) *m(f)*; (*in Museum*) Aufseher(in) *m(f)*
sedative ['sedətɪv] S Beruhi-

gungsmittel *n* **seduce** [sɪ'du:s] VT verführen **see** ⟨saw, seen⟩ [si:, sɒ:, si:n] **1** VT sehen; (*begreifen*) verstehen; (*zur Kontrolle*) nachsehen; (*begleiten*) bringen; (*Verwandte etc*) besuchen; (*zwecks Beratung*) sprechen; **~ the doctor** zum Arzt gehen; **~ you** tschüs!; **~ you on Friday** bis Freitag! **2** VI sehen; (*begreifen*) verstehen; (*zur Kontrolle*) nachsehen **see about** VT sich kümmern um **see off** VT verabschieden **see out** VT zur Tür bringen **see to** VT sich kümmern um **seed** [si:d] S (*Pflanze*) Samen *m*; (*Obst*) Kern *m* **seedy** ['si:dɪ] ADJ (*Lokal etc*) zwielichtig **seeing eye dog** S Blindenhund *m* **seek** ⟨sought, sought⟩ [si:k, sɒ:t] VT suchen **seem** [si:m] VI scheinen **seen** [si:n] *pperf von* **see see-through** ADJ durchsichtig **segment** ['segmənt] S Teil *m* **seize** [si:z] VT packen; (*wegnehmen*) beschlagnahmen; (*Gelegenheit*) ergreifen **seldom** ['seldəm] ADV selten **select** [sə'lekt] **1** ADJ exklusiv **2** VT auswählen **selection** [sə'lekʃən] S Auswahl *f* (*of* an *+dat*) **self** ⟨selves *pl*⟩ [self, selvz] S Selbst *n*, Ich *n* **self-centered** [self'sentərd] ADJ egozentrisch **self-confidence** [self'kɑ:nfədəns] S Selbstbewusstsein *n* **self-confident** [self'kɑ:nfədənt] ADJ selbstbewusst **self-conscious** [self'kɑ:nʃəs] ADJ befangen, verklemmt **self-contained** [selfkən'teɪnd] ADJ (*Wohnung*) separat **self-control** [selfkən'troʊl] S Selbstbeherrschung *f* **self-defense** [selfdɪ'fens] S Selbstverteidigung *f* **self-employed** [selfem'plɔɪd] ADJ selbstständig **selfish** ['selfɪʃ] ADJ egoistisch, selbstsüchtig **self-pity** [self'pɪtɪ] S Selbstmitleid *n* **self-respect** [selfrɪ'spekt] S Selbstachtung *f* **self-service** [self'sɜ:rvəs] **1** S Selbstbedienung *f* **2** ADJ Selbstbedienungs- **sell** ⟨sold, sold⟩ [sel, soʊld] **1** VT verkaufen **2** VI (*Ware*) sich verkaufen **sell out** VT **be sold out** ausverkauft sein **sell-by date** S Haltbarkeitsdatum *n* **seltzer** ['seltsər] S Selterswasser *n* **semester** [sə'mestər] S Semester *n* **semicircle** ['semɪsɜ:rkl] S Halbkreis *m* **semicolon** S Strichpunkt *m*, Semikolon *n* **semi-final** S Halbfinale *n* **senate** ['senət] S Senat *m* **senator** ['senətər] S Senator(in) *m(f)* **send** ⟨sent, sent⟩ [send, sent] VT schicken; **~ her my best**

wishes grüße sie von mir
send for VT (*Arzt etc*) holen lassen; (*Hilfe etc*) anfordern
sender S Absender(in) *m(f)*
senior ['si:njər] 1 ADJ älter; (*Beamter*) höher; (*Schüler*) älter; (*Jahr*) letzte(r, s) 2 S (*Universität, Highschool*) Student(in) *im vierten Jahr* **senior (citizen)** S Senior(in) *m(f)*
sensation [sen'seɪʃən] S Gefühl *n*, Sensation *f* **sensational** ADJ sensationell
sense [sens] 1 S Sinn *m*; (*Empfindung*) Gefühl *n*; (*Vernunft*) Verstand *m*; **~ of smell** Geruchssinn *m*; **have a ~ of humor** Humor haben; **make ~** einen Sinn ergeben; (*Entscheidung*) Sinn machen 2 VT spüren
sensible, **sensibly** ['sensəbl, -blɪ] ADJ & ADV vernünftig
sensitive ['sensətɪv] ADJ empfindlich (*to* gegen); sensibel; (*Thema*) heikel
sent [sent] *prät, pperf von* send
sentence ['sentəns] 1 S LING Satz *m*; JUR Strafe *f* 2 VT verurteilen (*to* zu)
sentimental [sentə'mentl] ADJ sentimental
separate 1 ['seprət] ADJ getrennt, separat; einzeln 2 ['sepəreɪt] VT trennen (*from* von); **they're ~d** (*Ehepaar*) sie leben getrennt 3 ['sepəreɪt] VI sich trennen **separately** ['seprətlɪ] ADV getrennt; (*behandeln*) einzeln
September [sep'tembər] S September *m*; **in ~** im September; **on ~ 2nd** am 2. September; **at the beginning/in the middle/at the end of ~** Anfang/Mitte/Ende September; **last/next ~** letzten/nächsten September
septic ['septɪk] ADJ vereitert
sequel ['si:kwəl] S (*Film*) Fortsetzung *f* (*to* von)
sequence ['si:kwəns] S Reihenfolge *f*
Serbia ['sɜ:rbɪə] S Serbien *n*
sergeant ['sɑ:rdʒənt] S Polizeimeister(in) *m(f)*; MIL Feldwebel(in) *m(f)*
serial ['sɪrɪəl] 1 S TV Serie *f* 2 ADJ Serien-; serienmäßig; IT seriell
series ['sɪri:z] S SG Reihe *f*; TV, RADIO Serie *f*
serious ['sɪrɪəs] ADJ ernst; (*Krankheit, Fehler*) schwer; (*Diskussion*) ernsthaft; **are you ~?** ist das dein Ernst? **seriously** ADV ernsthaft; (*verletzt*) schwer; **~?** im Ernst?
sermon ['sɜ:rmən] S REL Predigt *f*
servant ['sɜ:rvənt] S Diener(in) *m(f)* **serve** [sɜ:rv] 1 VT (*Kunden*) bedienen; (*Essen*) servieren; (*Land etc*) dienen +*dat*; (*Strafe*) verbüßen; **I'm being ~d** ich werde schon bedient; **it ~s him right** es geschieht ihm recht 2 VI dienen

(*as* als); (*Tennis*) aufschlagen **3** S (*Tennis*) Aufschlag *m* **server** S IT Server *m* **service** ['sɜːrvəs] **1** S Bedienung *f*, Dienstleistung *f*; (*Verkehr*) Verbindung *f*; (*Geschirr*) Service *n*; REL Gottesdienst *m*; (*Tennis*) Aufschlag *m*; **in the ~s** beim Militär **2** VT AUTO, TECH warten **service area** S Raststätte *f* (*mit Tankstelle*) **service charge** S Bedienung *f* **service provider** S IT Provider *m* **service station** S Tankstelle *f* (mit Reparaturwerkstatt)

session ['seʃən] S Sitzung *f*

set ⟨set, set⟩ [set] **1** VT (*platzieren*) stellen; (*flach*) legen; (*Dinge*) anordnen; (*Tisch*) decken; (*Falle, Rekord*) aufstellen; (*Zeit, Preis*) festsetzen; (*Uhr*) stellen (*for* auf *+akk*); **~ free** freilassen; **the novel is ~ in Baltimore** der Roman spielt in Baltimore **2** VI (*Sonne*) untergehen; (*Zement*) fest werden **3** S (*gleiche Dinge*) Satz *m*; (*Besteck, Möbel*) Garnitur *f*; (*Gruppe von Menschen*) Kreis *m*; RADIO, TV Apparat *m*; (*Tennis*) Satz *m*; THEAT Bühnenbild *n*; FILM (Film)kulisse *f* **4** ADJ festgelegt; (*in Erwartung etw zu tun*) bereit; **~ meal** Menü *n* **set aside** VT (*Geld*) beiseitelegen; (*Zeit*) einplanen **set off** **1** VI aufbrechen (*for* nach) **2** VT (*Alarm*) auslösen; (*Feuerwerk*) zünden **set out** **1** VI aufbrechen (*for* nach) **2** VT (*Stühle etc*) aufstellen; **~ to do sth** beabsichtigen, etw zu tun **set up** VT (*Firma*) gründen; (*Zelt, Kamera*) aufbauen; (*Treffen*) vereinbaren **setback** S Rückschlag *m* **setting** ['setɪŋ] S (*Roman, Film*) Schauplatz *m*; (*von Haus etc*) Umgebung *f*

settle ['setl] **1** VT (*Rechnung, Schulden*) begleichen; (*Streit*) beilegen; (*Frage*) klären; (*Magen*) beruhigen **2** VI **~ (down)** sich einleben; (*psychisch*) sich beruhigen **settle in** VI sich einleben; (*in neuem Job*) sich eingewöhnen **settlement** S (*Schulden*) Begleichung *f*; (*aus Häusern*) Siedlung *f* **settler** S Siedler(in) *m(f)*

setup ['setʌp] S Organisation *f*; (*Umstände*) Situation *f*

seven ['sevn] **1** NUM sieben **2** S Sieben *f*; → **eight seventeen** [sevn'tiːn] **1** NUM siebzehn **2** S Siebzehn *f*; → **eight seventeenth** ADJ siebzehnte(r, s); → **eighth seventh** ['sevnθ] **1** ADJ siebte(r, s) **2** S Siebtel *n*; → **eighth seventieth** ['sevntɪəθ] ADJ siebzigste(r, s); → **eighth seventy** ['sevntɪ] **1** NUM siebzig **2** S Siebzig *f*; → **eight, eighty**

several ['sevrəl] ADJ & PRON mehrere

severe [sɪ'vɪr] ADJ (*Strafe*) schwer; (*Schmerz*) stark; (*Win-*

ter) hart **severely** ADV (*bestrafen*) hart; (*verletzen*) schwer

sew ⟨sewed, sewn⟩ [soʊ, soʊd, soʊn] V/T & V/I nähen

sewage ['suːɪdʒ] S Abwasser *n* **sewer** ['suːər] S Abwasserkanal *m*

sewing machine ['soʊɪŋməʃiːn] S Nähmaschine *f* **sewn** [soʊn] *pperf von* sew

sex [seks] S Sex *m*; (*männlich oder weiblich*) Geschlecht *n* **sexism** ['seksɪzəm] S Sexismus *m* **sexist** ['seksəst] 1 ADJ sexistisch 2 S Sexist(in) *m(f)* **sexual** ['sekʃʊəl] ADJ sexuell; **~ intercourse** Geschlechtsverkehr *m* **sexuality** [sekʃʊ'ælətɪ] S Sexualität *f* **sexy** ['seksɪ] ADJ sexy, geil

shack [ʃæk] S Hütte *f*

shade [ʃeɪd] 1 S (*von Baum etc*) Schatten *m*; (*von Lampe*) (Lampen)schirm *m*; (*Farbenspektrum*) Farbton *m*; **~s** *pl* Sonnenbrille *f* 2 V/T abschirmen

shadow ['ʃædoʊ] S Schatten *m*

shady ['ʃeɪdɪ] ADJ schattig; *fig* zwielichtig

shake ⟨shook, shaken⟩ [ʃeɪk, ʃʊk, 'ʃeɪkn] 1 V/T schütteln; (*emotional; Druckwelle*) erschüttern; **~ hands with sb** j-m die Hand geben 2 V/I (*Hand, Stimme*) zittern; (*Gebäude*) schwanken **shaken** ['ʃeɪkn] *pperf von* shake **shaky** ['ʃeɪkɪ] ADJ (*Hand, Stimme*) zittrig; (*Stuhl*) wackelig

shall ⟨should⟩ [ʃæl, ʃʊd] V/AUX werden; (*in Fragen*) sollen

shallow ['ʃæloʊ] ADJ seicht; (*Person*) oberflächlich

shame [ʃeɪm] S (*Gefühl*) Scham *f*; (*Tat etc*) Schande *f*; **what a ~** wie schade!

shampoo [ʃæm'puː] 1 S Shampoo *n* 2 V/T (*Haare*) waschen; (*Teppich*) schamponieren

shape [ʃeɪp] 1 S Form *f*, Gestalt *f*; Verfassung *f* 2 V/T formen **-shaped** [ʃeɪpt] *Suffix* -förmig

share [ʃer] 1 S Anteil *+dat* (*in, of* an); FIN Aktie *f* 2 V/T & V/I teilen **shareholder** S Aktionär(in) *m(f)*

shark [ʃɑːrk] S Haifisch *m*

sharp [ʃɑːrp] 1 ADJ scharf; (*Nadel*) spitz; (*Person*) scharfsinnig; (*Schmerz*) heftig; (*Anstieg, Sinken*) abrupt 2 ADV **at 2 o'clock ~** Punkt 2 Uhr

shatter ['ʃætər] 1 V/T zerschmettern; *fig* zerstören 2 V/I zerspringen

shave ⟨shaved, shaved *od* shaven⟩ [ʃeɪv, ʃeɪvd, 'ʃeɪvn] 1 V/T rasieren 2 V/I sich rasieren 3 S Rasur *f* **shaven** ['ʃeɪvn] 1 *pperf von* shave 2 ADJ (*Kopf*) kahl geschoren **shaver** S ELEK Rasierapparat *m* **shaving brush** S Rasierpinsel *m* **shaving foam** S Rasierschaum *m*

shawl [ʃɒːl] S Tuch *n*

she [ʃiː] PRON sie

shed ⟨shed, shed⟩ [ʃed] **1** S Schuppen *m* **2** V/T (*Tränen, Blut*) vergießen; (*Haare, Blätter*) verlieren

she'd [ʃiːd] *kontr von* **she had; she would**

sheep ⟨- *pl*⟩ [ʃiːp] S Schaf *n*

sheer [ʃɪr] ADJ (*Wahnsinn*) rein; (*Klippe*) steil

sheet [ʃiːt] S Betttuch *n*; (*Papier*) Blatt *n*; (*Metall*) Platte *f*; (*Glas*) Scheibe *f*

shelf ⟨shelves *pl*⟩ [ʃelf, ʃelvz] S Bücherbord *n*, Regal *n* **shelf-stable milk** S H-Milch *f*

she'll [ʃiːl] *kontr von* **she will; she shall**

shell [ʃel] **1** S (*von Ei, Nuss etc*) Schale *f*; (*am Strand*) Muschel *f* **2** V/T (*Erbsen, Nüsse*) schälen **shellfish** S (*Essen*) Meeresfrüchte *pl*

shelter [ˈʃeltər] **1** S (*vor Regen*) Schutz *m*; (*Behausung*) Unterkunft *f* **2** V/T schützen (*from* vor *+dat*) **3** V/I sich unterstellen **sheltered** ADJ (*Platz*) geschützt; (*Leben*) behütet

shelves [ʃelvz] *pl* Regal *n*

shepherd [ˈʃepərd] S Schäfer *m*

she's [ʃiːz] *kontr von* **she is; she has**

shield [ʃiːld] **1** S Schild *m*; *fig* Schutz *m* **2** V/T schützen (*from* vor *+dat*)

shift [ʃɪft] **1** S (*Wechsel*) Veränderung *f*; (*Arbeitszeit*) Schicht *f* **2** V/T (*Möbel*) verrücken; **~ gear(s)** AUTO schalten; (*im Gespräch*) das Thema wechseln **3** V/I sich bewegen; rutschen **shift key** S Umschalttaste *f*

shin [ʃɪn] S Schienbein *n*

shine ⟨shone, shone⟩ [ʃaɪn, ʃɑːn] **1** V/I glänzen; (*Sonne*) scheinen; (*Lampe*) leuchten **2** V/T (*Schuhe*) polieren **3** S Glanz *m* **shiny** [ˈʃaɪnɪ] ADJ glänzend

ship [ʃɪp] **1** S Schiff *n* **2** V/T (*Waren*) versenden; (*per Schiff*) verschiffen **shipment** S (*Waren*) Sendung *f*; (*auf Schiff*) Ladung *f*

shirt [ʃɜːrt] S Hemd *n*

shit [ʃɪt] S *vulg* Scheiße *f*; **I don't give a ~** es ist mir scheißegal **shitty** [ˈʃɪtɪ] ADJ *umg* beschissen

shiver [ˈʃɪvər] V/I zittern (*with* vor *+dat*)

shock [ʃɑːk] **1** S Schock *m*; ELEK Schlag *m* **2** V/T schockieren **shock absorber** S Stoßdämpfer *m* **shocked** ADJ schockiert (*by* über *+akk*) **shocking** ADJ schockierend

shoe [ʃuː] S Schuh *m* **shoelace** S Schnürsenkel *m*

shone [ʃɑːn] *prät, pperf von* shine

shook [ʃʊk] *prät von* shake

shoot ⟨shot, shot⟩ [ʃuːt, ʃɑːt] **1** V/T anschießen; erschießen; FILM drehen; *umg* (*Rauschgift*) drücken **2** VI schießen (*at* auf +*akk*) **3** S (*von Pflanze*) Trieb *m* **4** INT **~!** Mist! **shooting** S Schießerei *f*; Erschießung *f*

shop [ʃɑːp] **1** S Geschäft *n*, Laden *m*; Werkstatt *f* **2** VI einkaufen **shopkeeper** S Geschäftsinhaber(in) *m(f)* **shoplifting** S Ladendiebstahl *m* **shopping** S (*Tätigkeit*) Einkaufen *n*; **do the ~** einkaufen; **go ~** einkaufen gehen **shopping cart** S Einkaufswagen *m* **shopping center** S Einkaufszentrum *n* **shopping mall** S Einkaufszentrum *n* **shop window** S Schaufenster *n*

shore [ʃɔːr] S Ufer *n*; **on ~** an Land

short [ʃɔːrt] ADJ kurz; (*Person*) klein; **be ~ of money** knapp bei Kasse sein; **be ~ of time** wenig Zeit haben; **~ of breath** kurzatmig; **cut ~** (*Urlaub*) abbrechen; **we're two ~** wir haben zwei zu wenig **shortage** [ˈʃɔːrtɪdʒ] S Knappheit *f* (*of* an +*dat*) **short circuit** S Kurzschluss *m* **shortcut** S (*Strecke*) Abkürzung *f*; IT Shortcut *m* **shorten** VT kürzen; (*zeitlich*) verkürzen **shortly** ADV bald **shorts** S PL Shorts *pl* **short-sighted** ADJ kurzsichtig **short-sleeved** ADJ kurzärmelig **short-term** ADJ kurzfristig

shot [ʃɑːt] **1** *prät, pperf von* **shoot** **2** S Schuss *m*; FOTO, FILM Aufnahme *f*; (*Injektion*) Spritze *f*; (*Alkohol*) Schuss *m*

should [ʃʊd] **1** *prät von* **shall** **2** V/AUX sollen; müssen

shoulder [ˈʃoʊldər] S Schulter *f*; (*Autobahn*) Seitenstreifen *m*

shouldn't [ˈʃʊdnt] *kontr von* **should not** **should've** [ˈʃʊdəv] *kontr von* **should have**

shout [ʃaʊt] **1** S Schrei *m*, Ruf *m* **2** VT rufen; (*Befehl*) brüllen **3** VI schreien; **~ at sb** j-n anschreien

shove [ʃʌv] **1** VT (*andere Leute*) schubsen; (*Gegenstand*) schieben **2** VI (*in Menschenmenge*) drängeln

shovel [ˈʃʌvl] **1** S Schaufel *f* **2** VT schaufeln

show ⟨showed, shown⟩ [ʃoʊ, ʃoʊd, ʃoʊn] **1** VT zeigen; **~ sb in** j-n hereinführen; **~ sb out** j-n zur Tür bringen **2** S FILM, THEAT Vorstellung *f*; TV Show *f*; (*Kunst*) Ausstellung *f* **show around** VT herumführen; **show sb around the town** j-m die Stadt zeigen **show off** VI *pej* angeben **show up** VI auftauchen

shower [ˈʃaʊər] **1** S Dusche *f*; (*Regen*) Schauer *m*; Party *f* (*für Braut oder junge Mutter*); **take a ~** duschen **2** VI duschen

showing [ˈʃoʊɪŋ] S FILM Vorstellung *f* **shown** [ʃoʊn] *pperf von* **show** **showroom** [ˈʃoʊruːm] S Ausstellungsraum *m*

shrank [ʃræŋk] *prät von* **shrink**

shred [ʃred] **1** S Fetzen *m* **2** VT (*Papier*) (im Reißwolf) zerkleinern
shrimp [ʃrɪmp] S Garnele *f*
shrink [ʃrɪŋk] **1** VI ‹shrank, shrunk› [ʃræŋk, ʃrʌŋk] schrumpfen; (*Kleidung beim Waschen*) eingehen **2** S *umg* Psychiater(in) *m(f)*; Psychoanalytiker(in) *m(f)*
shrivel up [ʃrɪvl'ʌp] VI schrumpfen; runzlig werden
shrug [ʃrʌg] VT & VI ~ **(one's shoulders)** die Achseln zucken
shrunk [ʃrʌŋk] *pperf von* shrink
shudder ['ʃʌdər] VI schaudern; (*Erde*) beben
shuffle ['ʃʌfl] VT & VI (*Karten*) mischen
shut ‹shut, shut› [ʃʌt] **1** VT zumachen, schließen; ~ **your mouth** *umg* halt den Mund! **2** VI schließen **3** ADJ geschlossen **shut down** **1** VT schließen; (*Computer*) ausschalten **2** VI schließen; (*Computer*) sich ausschalten **shut off** VT (*Gas*) abstellen; (*Gerät, Motor*) abschalten, ausschalten **shut up** **1** VT (*Person*) zum Schweigen bringen **2** VI den Mund halten
shutter ['ʃʌtər] S (Fenster)laden *m*; FOTO Verschluss *m*
shuttle bus ['ʃʌtlbʌs] S Shuttlebus *m*, Zubringerbus *m*
shuttle service ['ʃʌtlsɜːrvəs] S Pendelverkehr *m*
shy [ʃaɪ] ADJ schüchtern; (*Tier*) scheu
sick [sɪk] ADJ krank; (*Witz*) makaber; **be out** ~ wegen Krankheit fehlen; **I feel ~ to my stomach** mir ist schlecht; **be ~ of sb/sth** j-n/etw satthaben; **it makes me ~** *fig* es ekelt mich an **sickness** S Krankheit *f*
side [saɪd] **1** S Seite *f*; (*von Straße*) Rand *m*; (*von Berg*) Hang *m*; **by my ~** neben mir; **~ by ~** nebeneinander **2** ADJ (*Eingang etc*) Seiten- **sideburns** S PL Koteletten *pl* **side dish** S Beilage *f* **side effect** S Nebenwirkung *f* **side order** S Beilage *f* **side street** S Seitenstraße *f* **sidewalk** S Bürgersteig *m* **sideways** ADV seitwärts
sieve [sɪv] S Sieb *n*
sigh [saɪ] VI seufzen
sight [saɪt] S Sehvermögen *n*; Anblick *m*; **~s** *pl* Sehenswürdigkeiten *pl*; **lose ~ of** aus den Augen verlieren **sightseeing** S **go ~** Sehenswürdigkeiten besichtigen; **~ tour** Rundfahrt *f*
sign [saɪn] **1** S Zeichen *n*; Schild *n* **2** VT unterschreiben **3** VI unterschreiben; **~ in/out** sich ein-/austragen **sign up** VI sich einschreiben; MIL sich verpflichten
signal ['sɪgnl] **1** S Signal *n* **2** VI (*in Auto*) blinken
signature ['sɪgnətʃər] S Un-

terschrift *f*
significant [sɪg'nɪfəkənt] ADJ bedeutend, wichtig; (*statistisch; Ereignis*) bedeutsam
sign language ['saɪnlæŋgwɪdʒ] S Zeichensprache *f*
signpost S Wegweiser *m*
silence ['saɪləns] 1 S Stille *f*; (*von Person*) Schweigen *n*; **~!** Ruhe! 2 V/T zum Schweigen bringen **silent** ADJ still; (*Person*) schweigsam; **she remained ~** sie schwieg
silk [sɪlk] 1 S Seide *f* 2 ADJ Seiden-
silly ['sɪlɪ] ADJ dumm, albern
silver ['sɪlvər] 1 S Silber *n* 2 ADJ Silber-, silbern **silverware** S Besteck *n*
similar ['sɪmələr] ADJ ähnlich (*to dat*) **similarity** [sɪmə'lærətɪ] S Ähnlichkeit *f* (*to* mit)
simple ['sɪmpl] ADJ einfach; (*Kleid, Zimmer*) schlicht **simplify** ['sɪmpləfaɪ] V/T vereinfachen **simply** ADV einfach; bloß; schlicht
simulate ['sɪmjəleɪt] V/T simulieren
simultaneously [sɪməl'teɪnɪəslɪ] ADV gleichzeitig
sin [sɪn] 1 S Sünde *f* 2 V/I sündigen
since [sɪns] 1 ADV seitdem; inzwischen 2 PRÄP seit *+dat* 3 KONJ (*zeitlich*) seit, seitdem; (*begründend*) da, weil; **it's ages ~ I've seen him** ich habe ihn seit Langem nicht mehr gesehen
sincere [sɪn'sɪr] ADJ aufrichtig **sincerely** ADV aufrichtig; **Sincerely yours** mit freundlichen Grüßen
sing ⟨sang, sung⟩ [sɪŋ, sæŋ, sʌŋ] V/T & V/I singen **singer** ['sɪŋər] S Sänger(in) *m(f)*
single ['sɪŋgl] 1 ADJ (*Fall etc*) einzig; (*nicht doppelt*) einfach; (*Zimmer etc*) Einzel-; (*alleinstehend*) ledig 2 S MUS Single *f* **single-handedly** ADV im Alleingang **single parent** S Alleinerziehende(r) *m/f(m)*
singular ['sɪŋgjələr] S Singular *m*
sinister ['sɪnəstər] ADJ unheimlich, finster
sink ⟨sank, sunk⟩ [sɪŋk, sæŋk, sʌŋk] 1 V/T (*Schiff*) versenken 2 V/I sinken 3 S Spülbecken *n*; (*in Bad*) Waschbecken *n*
sip [sɪp] V/T nippen an *+dat*
sir [sɜːr] S (*als Anrede*) mein Herr (*im Deutschen meist unübersetzt*)
sirloin steak [sɜːrlɔɪn'steɪk] S Lendensteak *n*
sister ['sɪstər] S Schwester *f* **sister-in-law** ⟨sisters-in-law⟩ S Schwägerin *f*
sit ⟨sat, sat⟩ [sɪt, sæt] V/I sitzen; (*Platz nehmen*) sich setzen; (*Komitee, Gericht*) tagen **sit down** V/I sich hinsetzen **sit up** V/I sich aufsetzen
site [saɪt] S Platz *m*; (*bei Umbau, Neubau*) Baustelle *f*; (*im Internet*) Site *f*

sitting ['sɪtɪŋ] S Sitzung *f* **sitting room** S Wohnzimmer *n*
situated ['sɪtʃʊeɪtəd] ADJ **be ~** liegen **situation** [sɪtʃʊ'eɪʃən] S Situation *f*, Lage *f*; (*Arbeit*) Stelle *f*
six [sɪks] **1** NUM sechs **2** S Sechs *f*; → eight **sixpack** S (*Bier etc*) Sechserpack *n*; (*Muskeln*) Waschbrettbauch *m* **sixteen** [sɪks'tiːn] **1** NUM sechzehn **2** S Sechzehn *f*; → eight **sixteenth** ADJ sechzehnte(r, s); → eighth **sixth** [sɪksθ] **1** ADJ sechste(r, s) **2** S Sechstel *n*; → eighth **sixtieth** ['sɪkstɪəθ] ADJ sechzigste(r, s); → eighth **sixty** ['sɪkstɪ] **1** NUM sechzig **2** S Sechzig *f*; → eight, eighty
size [saɪz] S Größe *f*
sizzle ['sɪzl] V/I brutzeln
skate [skeɪt] **1** S Schlittschuh *m*; (*mit Rollen*) Rollschuh *m* **2** V/I Schlittschuh laufen; Rollschuh laufen **skateboard** S Skateboard *n* **skating** S Eislauf *m*; (*auf Straße etc*) Rollschuhlauf *m* **skating rink** S Eisbahn *f*; Rollschuhbahn *f*
skeleton ['skelətn] S Skelett *n*
skeptical ['skeptɪkəl] ADJ skeptisch
sketch [sketʃ] **1** S Skizze *f*; THEAT Sketch *m* **2** V/T skizzieren
ski [skiː] **1** S Ski *m* **2** V/I Ski laufen **ski boot** S Skistiefel *m*
skid [skɪd] V/I AUTO schleudern
skier ['skiːər] S Skiläufer(in) *m(f)* **skiing** ['skiːɪŋ] S Skilaufen *n*; **go ~** Ski laufen gehen
skill [skɪl] S Geschick *n*; (*erlernt*) Fertigkeit *f* **skilled** ADJ geschickt (*at*, *in* in +*dat*); (*Arbeiter*) Fach-; (*Arbeit*) fachmännisch
skillet ['skɪlət] S Bratpfanne *f*
skillful ['skɪlfəl] ADJ geschickt
skim [skɪm] V/T **~ (through)** (*lesend*) überfliegen **skim milk** S Magermilch *f*
skin [skɪn] S Haut *f*; (*Pelztier*) Fell *n*; (*Frucht*) Schale *f* **skinny** ADJ dünn
skip [skɪp] **1** V/I hüpfen **2** V/T (*Text*) überspringen; (*Mahlzeit*) ausfallen lassen; (*Schule*) schwänzen
ski pole ['skiːpoʊl] S Skistock *m* **ski resort** S Skiort *m*
skirt [skɜːrt] S Rock *m*
ski tow ['skiːtoʊ] S Schlepplift *m*
skull [skʌl] S Schädel *m*
skunk [skʌŋk] S Stinktier *n*
sky [skaɪ] S Himmel *m* **skydiving** S Fallschirmspringen *n* **skylight** S Dachfenster *n* **skyscraper** S Wolkenkratzer *m*
slam [slæm] V/T (*Tür*) zuschlagen **slam on** V/T **~ the brakes** voll auf die Bremse treten
slap [slæp] **1** S Klaps *m*; (*auf Backe*) Ohrfeige *f* **2** V/T schlagen; **~ sb's face** j-n ohrfeigen
slash [slæʃ] **1** S Schrägstrich *m* **2** V/T (*Gesicht, Reifen etc*) auf-

schlitzen; (*Preise*) stark herabsetzen
slaughter ['slɒːtər] VT (*Tiere*) schlachten; (*Menschen*) abschlachten
slave [sleɪv] S Sklave *m*, Sklavin *f* **slavery** ['sleɪvərɪ] S Sklaverei *f*
sleazy ['sliːzɪ] ADJ (*Kneipe, Viertel*) schäbig, anrüchig
sled [sled] S **1** S Schlitten *m* **2** VI Schlitten fahren
sleep ⟨slept, slept⟩ [sliːp, slept] **1** VI schlafen **2** S Schlaf *m* **sleep in** VI ausschlafen **sleeper** S BAHN Schlafwagenzug *m*; (*Waggon*) Schlafwagen *m* **sleeping bag** S Schlafsack *m* **sleeping car** S Schlafwagen *m* **sleeping pill** S Schlaftablette *f* **sleepless** ADJ schlaflos **sleepy** ADJ schläfrig; (*Ort*) verschlafen
sleet [sliːt] S Schneeregen *m*
sleeve [sliːv] S Ärmel *m* **sleeveless** ADJ ärmellos
sleigh [sleɪ] S (Pferde)schlitten *m*
slender ['slendər] ADJ schlank; *fig* gering
slept [slept] *prät, pperf von* sleep
slice [slaɪs] **1** S Scheibe *f*; (*Kuchen etc*) Stück *n* **2** VT in Scheiben schneiden
slick [slɪk] ADJ raffiniert, clever; (*Geschäftsmann*) aalglatt
slicker ['slɪkər] S Regenmantel *m*
slid [slɪd] *prät, pperf von* slide
slide ⟨slid, slid⟩ [slaɪd, slɪd] **1** VT gleiten lassen; (*Stuhl*) schieben **2** VI gleiten; rutschen **3** S FOTO Dia *n*; (*Spielplatz*) Rutschbahn *f*; (*in PowerPoint®*) Folie *f*
slight [slaɪt] ADJ leicht; (*Problem, Unterschied*) klein; **not in the ~est** nicht im Geringsten **slightly** ADV etwas; (*verletzt*) leicht
slim [slɪm] **1** ADJ schlank; (*Buch*) dünn; (*Chance etc*) gering **2** VI abnehmen
sling ⟨slung, slung⟩ [slɪŋ, slʌŋ] **1** VT werfen **2** S (*für Arm*) Schlinge *f*
slip [slɪp] **1** S Flüchtigkeitsfehler *m*; **~ of paper** Zettel *m* **2** VT (*legen, schieben*) stecken; **~ on/off** (*Kleidung*) an-/ausziehen; **it ~ped my mind** ich habe es vergessen **3** VI (aus)rutschen **slipper** S Hausschuh *m* **slippery** ADJ (*Straße, Weg*) glatt; (*Fisch, Seife*) glitschig
slit ⟨slit, slit⟩ [slɪt] **1** VT aufschlitzen **2** S Schlitz *m*
slope [sloʊp] **1** S Neigung *f*; (*von Berg*) Hang *m* **2** VI (*Gelände etc*) schräg sein **sloping** ADJ (*Dach etc*) schräg
sloppy ['slɑːpɪ] ADJ (*Arbeit, Person etc*) schlampig **sloppy joe** [slɑːpɪ'dʒoʊ] S *gewürzte, gebratene Hackfleischmasse auf einem Brötchen*
slot [slɑːt] S Schlitz *m*; IT Steck-

platz *m* **slot machine** S Automat *m*, Spielautomat *m*
Slovak ['slouvæk] 1 ADJ slowakisch 2 S (*Person*) Slowake *m*, Slowakin *f*; (*Sprache*) Slowakisch *n* **Slovakia** [slou'vækıə] S Slowakei *f*
Slovene ['slouvi:n] 1 ADJ slowenisch 2 S (*Person*) Slowene *m*, Slowenin *f*; (*Sprache*) Slowenisch *n* **Slovenia** [slou'vi:nıə] S Slowenien *n* **Slovenian** [slou'vi:nıən] 1 ADJ slowenisch 2 S (*Person*) Slowene *m*, Slowenin *f*; (*Sprache*) Slowenisch *n*
slow [slou] ADJ langsam; (*Geschäfte*) flau; **be ~** (*Uhr*) nachgehen; (*Person*) begriffsstutzig sein **slow down** V/I langsamer werden; langsamer fahren/gehen **slowly** ADV langsam **slow motion** S Zeitlupe *f*
slump [slʌmp] 1 S Rückgang *m* (*in* an *+dat*) 2 V/I (*in Sessel etc*) sich fallen lassen; (*Preise*) stürzen
slung [slʌŋ] *prät, pperf von* sling
slurred [slɜ:rd] ADJ undeutlich
slush [slʌʃ] S Schneematsch *m*
slut [slʌt] S *pej* Schlampe *f*
smack [smæk] 1 S Klaps *m* 2 V/T einen Klaps geben 3 ADV *umg* direkt
small [smɒ:l] ADJ klein **small print** S **the ~** das Kleingedruckte
smart [smɑ:rt] ADJ intelligent; (*Aussehen*) schick **smartass** S *umg* Klugscheißer(in) *m(f)* **smart card** S Chipkarte *f* **smartly** ADV (*gekleidet*) schick
smash [smæʃ] 1 V/T zerschlagen; *fig* vernichten 2 V/I zerbrechen; krachen (*into* gegen) **smashed** [smæʃt] ADJ *umg* sturzbesoffen
smear [smır] 1 S (*Tinte, Blut etc*) Fleck *m*; MED Abstrich *m*; *fig* Verleumdung *f* 2 V/T schmieren; (*schmutzig machen*) beschmieren; *fig* verleumden
smell ⟨smelt *od* smelled, smelt *od* smelled⟩ [smel, smelt, smeld] 1 V/T riechen 2 V/I riechen (*of* nach); stinken 3 S Geruch *m*; Gestank *m* **smelly** ADJ übel riechend
smelt [smelt] *prät, pperf von* smell
smile [smaıl] 1 S Lächeln *n* 2 V/I lächeln; **~ at sb** j-n anlächeln
smog [smɑ:g] S Smog *m*
smoke [smouk] 1 S Rauch *m* 2 V/T rauchen; (*Fleisch, Fisch*) räuchern 3 V/I rauchen **smoked** ADJ geräuchert **smoke detector** S Rauchmelder *m* **smoker** S Raucher(in) *m(f)* **smoking** S Rauchen *n*; **'no ~'** „Rauchen verboten"
smooth [smu:ð] 1 ADJ glatt; (*Flug, Schiffsüberfahrt*) ruhig; (*Bewegung*) geschmeidig; (*pro-

blemlos) reibungslos; *pej* *(Person)* aalglatt **2** VT glatt streichen; glätten **smoothly** ADV *(problemlos)* reibungslos
smuggle ['smʌgl] VT schmuggeln
snack [snæk] S Imbiss *m* **snack bar** S Imbissstube *f*
snail [sneɪl] S Schnecke *f*
snake [sneɪk] S Schlange *f*
snap [snæp] **1** S *(Foto)* Schnappschuss *m* **2** ADJ *(Entschluss)* spontan **3** VT zerbrechen; *(Seil)* zerreißen **4** VI brechen; *(Seil)* reißen; *(beißen)* schnappen *(at* nach); *umg* ausrasten **snap fastener** S Druckknopf *m* **snapshot** S Schnappschuss *m*
snatch [snætʃ] VT schnappen
sneak [sni:k] VI schleichen **sneakers** S PL Turnschuhe *pl*
sneeze [sni:z] VI niesen
sniff [snɪf] **1** VI schniefen; *(Hund)* schnüffeln *(at* an *+dat)* **2** VT schnuppern an *+dat*
snobbish ['snɑ:bɪʃ] ADJ versnobt
snooze [snu:z] **1** VI schlummern, dösen **2** S **have a ~** ein Nickerchen machen
snore [snɔ:r] VI schnarchen
snorkel ['snɔ:rkl] S Schnorchel *m* **snorkeling** S Schnorcheln *n*
snow [snoʊ] **1** S Schnee *m* **2** VI schneien **snowball** S Schneeball *m* **snowboard** S Snowboard *n* **snowboarding** S Snowboarding *n* **snowdrift** S Schneewehe *f* **snowflake** S Schneeflocke *f* **snowman** ⟨-men *pl*⟩ S Schneemann *m* **snowplow** S Schneepflug *m* **snowstorm** S Schneesturm *m* **snowy** ADJ schneereich; verschneit
snug [snʌg] ADJ gemütlich
snuggle up [snʌgl'ʌp] VI sich ankuscheln *(to* an *+akk)*
so [soʊ] **1** ADV so; **~ do I** ich auch; **I hope ~** hoffentlich; **30 or ~** etwa 30; **~ what?** na und?; **and ~ on** und so weiter **2** KONJ also, deshalb
soak [soʊk] VT durchnässen; *(Wäsche)* einweichen **soaking** ADJ **~ (wet)** klatschnass
soap [soʊp] S Seife *f* **soap (opera)** S Seifenoper *f*
sob [sɑ:b] VI schluchzen
sober ['soʊbər] ADJ nüchtern **sober up** VI nüchtern werden
so-called ['soʊkɔ:ld] ADJ sogenannt
soccer ['sɑ:kər] S Fußball *m*
sociable ['soʊʃəbl] ADJ gesellig
social ['soʊʃəl] ADJ sozial; *(gerne unter Leuten)* gesellig **socialize** VI unter die Leute gehen **social security** S Sozialversicherung *f*
society [sə'saɪətɪ] S Gesellschaft *f*; Verein *m*
sock [sɑ:k] S Socke *f*
soda ['soʊdə] S *(Sodawasser)*

Soda *f*; Limo *f*
sofa ['soʊfə] S Sofa *n* **sofa bed** S Schlafcouch *f*
soft [sɑːft] ADJ weich; (*Stimme, Musik*) leise; (*Licht*) gedämpft; (*Mensch*) gutmütig; (*Person*) nachgiebig; **~ drink** alkoholfreies Getränk **softly** ADV sanft; (*sprechen*) leise **soft toy** S Plüschtier *n* **software** S IT Software *f*
soil [sɔɪl] S Erde *f*, Boden *m*
solar ['soʊlər] ADJ Sonnen-, Solar-
sold [soʊld] *prät, pperf von* **sell**
soldier ['soʊldʒər] S Soldat(in) *m(f)*
sole [soʊl] **1** S Sohle *f*; (*Fisch*) Seezunge *f* **2** V/T besohlen **3** ADJ einzig; alleinig **solely** ADV nur
solemn ['sɑːləm] ADJ feierlich; (*Mensch*) ernst
solid ['sɑːlɪd] ADJ fest; (*Gold etc*) massiv; (*stabil*) solide; (*Freund*) verlässlich
solitary ['sɑːlətərɪ] ADJ einsam; (*Haus, Mensch etc*) einzeln **solitude** ['sɑːlətuːd] S Einsamkeit *f*
soluble ['sɑːljəbl] ADJ löslich **solution** [sə'luːʃən] S Lösung *f* (*to +gen*) **solve** [sɑːlv] V/T lösen
somber ['sɑːmbər] ADJ düster
some [sʌm] **1** ADJ etwas; einige; **~ woman (or other)** irgendeine Frau; **would you like ~ more (wine)?** möchten Sie noch etwas (Wein)? **2** PRON etwas; einige **3** ADV etwa
somebody PRON (irgend)jemand **someday** ADV irgendwann **somehow** ADV irgendwie **someone** PRON → somebody **someplace** ADV → somewhere **something** ['sʌmθɪŋ] **1** PRON (irgend)etwas **2** ADV **~ like 20** ungefähr 20 **sometime** ADV irgendwann **sometimes** ADV manchmal **somewhere** ADV irgendwo; (*gehen etc*) irgendwohin; **~ else** irgendwo anders; irgendwo anders hin
son [sʌn] S Sohn *m*
song [sɑːŋ] S Lied *n*, Song *m*
son-in-law ⟨sons-in-law⟩ ['sʌnɪnlɒː] S Schwiegersohn *m*
soon [suːn] ADV bald; früh; **as ~ as possible** so bald wie möglich **sooner** ADV (*zeitlich*) früher; (*tun*) lieber
soothe [suːð] V/T beruhigen; (*Schmerzen*) lindern
sophisticated [sə'fɪstəkeɪtəd] ADJ (*Person*) kultiviert; (*Maschine etc*) hoch entwickelt; (*Plan*) ausgeklügelt
sophomore ['sɑːfəmɔːr] S (*Universität, Highschool*) *Student(in) im zweiten Jahr*
sore [sɔːr] **1** ADJ **be ~** wehtun; **have a ~ throat** Halsschmerzen haben **2** S wunde Stelle
sorrow ['sɑːroʊ] S Kummer *m*
sorry ['sɑːrɪ] ADJ (*Anblick*) traurig; **(I'm) ~** Entschuldigung!;

I'm ~ (*bedauernd*) es tut mir leid; **~?** wie bitte?; **I feel ~ for him** er tut mir leid

sort [sɔ:rt] **1** S Art *f*; **what ~ of movie is it?** was für ein Film ist das?; **a ~ of** eine Art *+gen*; **all ~s of things** alles Mögliche **2** ADV **~ of** *umg* irgendwie **3** V/T sortieren; regeln **sort out** V/T sortieren; (*Probleme*) lösen

sought [sɒ:t] *prät, pperf von* seek

soul [soʊl] S Seele *f*; MUS Soul *m*

sound [saʊnd] **1** ADJ (*in guter Verfassung*) gesund; (*Konstruktion etc*) sicher; (*Entscheidung, Rat*) vernünftig; (*Theorie*) stichhaltig; (*Prügel*) tüchtig **2** S Geräusch *n*; MUS Klang *m*; TV Ton *m* **3** V/I (*sich anhören*) klingen (*like* wie) **soundcard** S IT Soundkarte *f*

soup [su:p] S Suppe *f*

sour [saʊr] ADJ sauer; *fig* mürrisch

source [sɔ:rs] S Quelle *f*; *fig* Ursprung *m*

south [saʊθ] **1** S Süden *m*; **to the ~ of** südlich von **2** ADV nach Süden **3** ADJ Süd- **South Africa** S Südafrika *n* **South America** S Südamerika *n* **South American** **1** ADJ südamerikanisch **2** S Südamerikaner(in) *m(f)* **southbound** ADJ (in) Richtung Süden **southern** ['sʌðərn] ADJ Süd-, südlich **southward(s)** ['saʊθwərd(z)] ADV nach Süden

souvenir [su:və'nɪr] S Andenken *n* (*of* an *+akk*)

sow **1** ⟨sowed, sown *od* sowed⟩ [soʊ, soʊd, soʊn] V/T säen; (*Feld*) besäen **2** [saʊ] S (*Schwein*) Sau *f*

soybean ['sɔɪbi:n] S Sojabohne *f* **soy sauce** ['sɔɪsɔ:s] S Sojasoße *f*

spa [spɑ:] S Kurort *m*

space [speɪs] S Platz *m*, Raum *m*; (*All*) Weltraum *m*; (*Lücke*) Zwischenraum *m*; (*zum Parken*) Lücke *f* **space bar** S Leertaste *f* **spacecraft** ⟨- *pl*⟩ S Raumschiff *n* **space shuttle** S Raumfähre *f* **spacious** ['speɪʃəs] ADJ geräumig

spade [speɪd] S Spaten *m*; **~s** *pl* (*Karten*) Pik *n*

spaghetti [spə'getɪ] S SG Spaghetti *pl*

Spain [speɪn] S Spanien *n*

Spaniard ['spænɪərd] S Spanier(in) *m(f)* **Spanish** ['spænɪʃ] **1** ADJ spanisch **2** S (*Sprache*) Spanisch *n*

spare [sper] **1** ADJ Ersatz-; **~ room** Gästezimmer *n*; **~ time** Freizeit *f* **2** S Ersatzteil *n* **3** V/T (*mit Fragen*) verschonen; **could you ~ a moment?** hättest du/hätten Sie einen Moment Zeit?

spark [spɑ:rk] S Funke *m*

sparkle ['spɑ:rkl] V/I funkeln

sparkling water S Mineralwasser *n* mit Kohlensäure

sparkling wine S Schaumwein *m*, Sekt *m* **spark plug** S Zündkerze *f*
sparsely ['spɑːrslɪ] ADV ~ **populated** dünn besiedelt
spasm ['spæzəm] S MED Krampf *m*
speak ⟨spoke, spoken⟩ [spiːk, spoʊk, 'spoʊkən] **1** V/T sprechen **2** V/I sprechen (*to* mit, zu); (*Rede halten*) reden; **~ing** TEL am Apparat **speak up** V/I lauter sprechen **speaker** S Sprecher(in) *m(f)*; (*vor Publikum*) Redner(in) *m(f)*; (*Stereoanlage*) Lautsprecher *m*, Box *f*
special ['speʃəl] **1** ADJ besondere(r, s), speziell **2** S (*Speisekarte*) Tagesgericht *n* **special delivery** S Eilzustellung *f* **specialist** S Spezialist(in) *m(f)*; TECH Fachmann *m*, Fachfrau *f*; MED Facharzt *m*, Fachärztin *f* **specialize** V/I sich spezialisieren (*in* auf *+akk*) **specially** ADV besonders; extra **special offer** S Sonderangebot *n* **specialty** ['speʃəltɪ] S Spezialität *f*
species ['spiːʃiːz] S SG Art *f*
specific [spɪ'sɪfɪk] ADJ spezifisch; (*präzise*) genau **specify** ['spesəfaɪ] V/T genau angeben
specimen ['spesəmən] S Exemplar *n*; (*von Gestein, Urin*) Probe *f*
spectacle ['spektəkl] S Schauspiel *n* **spectacular** [spek'tækjʊlər] ADJ spektakulär
spectator [spek'teɪtər] S Zuschauer(in) *m(f)*
sped [sped] *prät, pperf von* speed
speech [spiːtʃ] S Rede *f*, Sprache *f* **speechless** ADJ sprachlos (*with* vor *+dat*)
speed ⟨sped *od* speeded, sped *od* speeded⟩ [spiːd, sped, 'spiːdəd] **1** V/I rasen; zu schnell fahren **2** S Geschwindigkeit *f*; (*Film*) Lichtempfindlichkeit *f* **speed up** **1** V/T beschleunigen **2** V/I schneller werden/fahren **speedboat** S Rennboot *n* **speed bump** S Bodenschwelle *f* **speed limit** S Geschwindigkeitsbegrenzung *f* **speedometer** [spɪ'dɑːmətər] S Tachometer *m* **speed trap** S Radarfalle *f*
spell [spel] **1** V/T buchstabieren; (richtig) schreiben **2** S Weile *f*; **a cold/hot ~** ein Kälteeinbruch/eine Hitzewelle; (*Magie*) Zauber *m* **spellchecker** S IT Rechtschreibprüfung *f* **spelling** S (Recht)schreibung *f*; **~ mistake** Schreibfehler *m*
spend ⟨spent, spent⟩ [spend, spent] V/T (*Geld*) ausgeben (*on* für); (*Zeit*) verbringen **spent** [spent] *prät, pperf von* spend
sperm [spɜːrm] S Sperma *n*
sphere [sfɪr] S Kugel *f*; *fig* Sphäre *f*
spice [spaɪs] **1** S Gewürz *n*; *fig* Würze *f* **2** V/T würzen **spicy** ['spaɪsɪ] ADJ würzig

spider ['spaɪdər] S Spinne *f* **spike** [spaɪk] S Spitze *f*, Spike *m*

spill ⟨spilt *od* spilled, spilt *od* spilled⟩ [spɪl, spɪlt, spɪld] VT verschütten

spin ⟨spun, spun⟩ [spɪn, spʌn] **1** VI (*Rad etc*) sich drehen **2** VT (*etw*) drehen **3** S Drehung *f*

spinach ['spɪnɪtʃ] S Spinat *m*

spine [spaɪn] S Rückgrat *n*; (*von Tier, Pflanze*) Stachel *m*; (*von Buch*) Rücken *m*

spiral ['spaɪrəl] **1** S Spirale *f* **2** ADJ spiralförmig

spirit ['spɪrət] S Geist *m*, Stimmung *f*; (*Tapferkeit*) Mut *m*; (*Enthusiasmus*) Elan *m*; **~s** *pl* Spirituosen *pl* **spiritual** ['spɪrətʃʊəl] ADJ geistig; REL geistlich

spit ⟨spit, spit⟩ [spɪt] **1** VI spucken **2** S (*zum Grillen*) (Brat)-spieß *m*; (*im Mund*) Spucke *f* **spit out** VT ausspucken

spite [spaɪt] S Boshaftigkeit *f*; **in ~ of** trotz *+gen* **spiteful** ADJ boshaft

splash [splæʃ] **1** VT (*j-n, etw*) bespritzen **2** VI spritzen; planschen **splashguard** S Schutzblech *n*

splinter ['splɪntər] S Splitter *m*

split ⟨split, split⟩ [splɪt] **1** VT (*Holz etc*) spalten; (*Geld, Gruppe etc*) teilen **2** VI (*Felsen etc*) sich spalten **3** S (*in Fels etc*) Spalt *m*; (*in Kleidung*) Riss *m*; *fig* Spaltung *f* **split up** **1** VI (*Partner*) sich trennen **2** VT (*etw*) aufteilen **split ends** SPL (Haar)spliss *m*

spoil [spɔɪl] **1** VT verderben; (*Kind*) verwöhnen **2** VI (*Nahrungsmittel*) verderben

spoke [spoʊk] **1** *prät von* speak **2** S Speiche *f* **spoken** ['spoʊkən] *pperf von* speak

spokesperson ⟨-people *pl*⟩ ['spoʊkspɜːrsən, -piːpl] S Sprecher(in) *m(f)*

sponge [spʌndʒ] S Schwamm *m* **sponge cake** S Biskuitkuchen *m*

sponsor ['spɑːnsər] **1** S Sponsor(in) *m(f)* **2** VT unterstützen; sponsern

spontaneously [spɑːn'teɪnɪəslɪ] ADV spontan

spoon [spuːn] S Löffel *m*

sport [spɔːrt] S Sport *m* **sports car** S Sportwagen *m* **sports center** S Sportzentrum *n* **sportsman** ⟨-men *pl*⟩ S Sportler *m* **sportswoman** ⟨-women *pl*⟩ S Sportlerin *f*

spot [spɑːt] **1** S Punkt *m*; (*Farbe etc*) Fleck *m*; (*Platz*) Stelle *f* **2** VT entdecken; erkennen **spotless** ADJ blitzsauber **spotlight** S Scheinwerfer *m*

spouse [spaʊs] S Gatte *m*, Gattin *f*

spout [spaʊt] S Schnabel *m*

sprain [spreɪn] VT **~ one's ankle** sich den Knöchel verstauchen

sprang [spræŋ] *prät von* spring
spray [spreɪ] **1** S Spray *n od m*, Spraydose *f* **2** V/T besprühen; (*lackieren*) spritzen
spread ⟨spread, spread⟩ [spred] **1** V/T ausbreiten; (*Neuigkeit, Krankheit*) verbreiten; (*Butter etc*) streichen **2** V/I (*Neuigkeit, Krankheit*) sich verbreiten **3** S (*von Krankheit, Religion*) Verbreitung *f*; (*für Brot*) Aufstrich *m*
spring ⟨sprang, sprung⟩ [sprɪŋ, spræŋ, sprʌŋ] **1** V/I (*hüpfen*) springen **2** S Frühling *m*; (*in Matratze, Sofa*) Feder *f*; (*von Wasser*) Quelle *f* **springboard** S Sprungbrett *n*
sprinkle ['sprɪŋkl] V/T (be)streuen; (*Flüssigkeit*) (be)träufeln **sprinkler** S (*für Rasen*) Rasensprenger *m*; (*für Brandfall*) Sprinkler *m*
sprint [sprɪnt] V/I rennen; SPORT sprinten
sprout [spraʊt] **1** S (*Pflanze*) Trieb *m*; (*Saatgut*) Keim *m* **2** V/I sprießen
sprung [sprʌŋ] *pperf von* spring
spun [spʌn] *prät, pperf von* spin
spy [spaɪ] **1** S Spion(in) *m(f)* **2** V/I spionieren; **~ on sb** j-m nachspionieren
squad [skwɑ:d] S SPORT Kader *m*
square [skwer] **1** S Quadrat *n*; (*in Stadt*) Platz *m*; (*Schachbrett etc*) Feld *n* **2** ADJ quadratisch, Quadrat-; *umg* **be ~** quitt sein **3** V/T (*Zahl*) ins Quadrat erheben **square dance** S Squaredance *m* (*amerikanischer Volkstanz*)
squash [skwɑ:ʃ] **1** S SPORT Squash *n*; (*Gemüse*) Kürbis *m* **2** V/T zerquetschen
squeak [skwi:k] V/I quietschen; (*Tier*) quieken
squeal [skwi:l] V/I (*Person*) kreischen (*with* vor *+dat*); *umg* petzen
squeeze [skwi:z] **1** V/T drücken; (*Orange*) auspressen **2** V/I **~ into the car** sich in den Wagen hineinzwängen
squid [skwɪd] S Tintenfisch *m*
squirrel ['skwɪrəl] S Eichhörnchen *n*
Sr *abk* = senior; Senior *m*
St **1** *abk* = saint; St. **2** *abk* = street; Str.
stab [stæb] V/T einstechen auf *+akk*, erstechen **stabbing** ADJ (*Schmerz*) stechend
stabilize ['steɪbəlaɪz] **1** V/T stabilisieren **2** V/I sich stabilisieren
stable ['steɪbl] **1** S Stall *m* **2** ADJ stabil
stack [stæk] **1** S Stapel *m* **2** V/T (auf)stapeln
stadium ['steɪdɪəm] S Stadion *n*
staff [stæf] S Personal *n*
stage [steɪdʒ] **1** S THEAT Bühne *f*; (*Moment*) Zeitpunkt *m*;

(*von Projekt etc*) Stadium *n*; (*einer Reise*) Etappe *f* **2** VT THEAT aufführen, inszenieren; (*Event etc*) veranstalten
stagger ['stægər] **1** VI wanken **2** VT verblüffen
stagnate [stæg'neɪt] VI stagnieren
stain [steɪn] S Fleck *m*
stained-glass window S Buntglasfenster *n* **stainless steel** S rostfreier Stahl
stair [ster] S (Treppen)stufe *f*; **~s** *pl* Treppe *f* **staircase** S Treppe *f*
stake [steɪk] S Pfahl *m*; (*Wette*) Einsatz *m*; FIN Anteil *m* (*in* an *+dat*); **be at ~** auf dem Spiel stehen
stale [steɪl] ADJ (*Brot*) alt; (*Bier*) schal
stalk [stɔːk] **1** S Stiel *m* **2** VT sich anpirschen an *+akk*; (*j-m*) nachstellen *+dat*
stall [stɒːl] **1** S (*auf Markt*) (Verkaufs)stand *m*; (*Stall*) Box *f*; Toilettenzelle *f* **2** VT (*Motor*) abwürgen **3** VI den Motor abwürgen; (*Auto*) stehen bleiben
stamina ['stæmənə] S Durchhaltevermögen *n*
stammer ['stæmər] VI & VT stottern
stamp [stæmp] **1** S Briefmarke *f*; (*auf Dokument*) Stempel *m* **2** VT (*Pass*) stempeln; (*Post*) frankieren
stand ⟨stood, stood⟩ [stænd, stʊd] **1** VI stehen; (*bei Wahl*) kandidieren **2** VT (*irgendwohin*) stellen; (*j-n, etw*) aushalten **3** S (*auf Markt etc*) Stand *m*; (*in Stadion*) Tribüne *f*; (*für Kleider, Fahrräder*) Ständer *m*; (*für kleine Sachen*) Gestell *n* **stand by** **1** VI sich bereithalten; danebenstehen **2** VT halten zu; stehen zu **stand for** VT (*verkörpern*) stehen für; (*tolerieren*) hinnehmen **stand in for** VT einspringen für **stand out** VI auffallen **stand up** **1** VI aufstehen **2** VT versetzen **stand up for** VT sich einsetzen für
standard ['stændərd] **1** S Norm *f*, Standard *m* **2** ADJ Standard-
stand-by ['stændbaɪ] **1** S Reserve *f*; **on ~** in Bereitschaft **2** ADJ (*Flug*) Stand-by- **standpoint** S Standpunkt *m*
standstill S Stillstand *m*
stank [stæŋk] *prät von* stink
star [stɑːr] **1** S Stern *m*; (*Person*) Star *m* **2** VT **the movie ~s George Clooney** der Film zeigt George Clooney in der Hauptrolle **3** VI die Hauptrolle spielen
starch [stɑːrtʃ] S Stärke *f*
stare [ster] VI starren; **~ at** anstarren
starfish ['stɑːrfɪʃ] S Seestern *m*
Stars and Stripes S PL Sternenbanner *n* (*Nationalflagge der USA*)

star sign ['stɑːrsaɪn] S Sternzeichen *n*

start [stɑːrt] **1** S Anfang *m*, Beginn *m*; SPORT Start *m*; (*vor Verfolgern*) Vorsprung *m* **2** V/T anfangen; (*Motor etc*) starten; (*Firma etc*) gründen **3** V/I anfangen; (*Auto etc*) anspringen; (*zu Reise*) aufbrechen; SPORT starten **start off** **1** V/T (*Diskussion etc*) anfangen **2** V/I anfangen, beginnen; (*zu Reise*) aufbrechen

startle ['stɑːrtl] V/T erschrecken; (*vor Schreck*) zusammenfahren **startling** ADJ überraschend; (*negativ*) alarmierend, bestürzend; (*Ähnlichkeit etc*) erstaunlich

starve [stɑːrv] V/I hungern; verhungern; **I'm starving** ich habe einen Riesenhunger

state [steɪt] **1** S Zustand *m*; POL Staat *m*; **the States** *pl* die Staaten *pl* **2** ADJ Staats-; staatlich **3** V/T erklären; (*Namen, Fakten*) angeben **State Department** S Außenministerium *n* **statement** ['steɪtmənt] S Erklärung *f*; (*bei Polizei*) Aussage *f*; (*Bank*) Kontoauszug *m* **stateside** S *umg* **1** ADJ in den Staaten **2** ADV in den Staaten; in die Staaten

station ['steɪʃən] **1** S Bahnhof *m*; (*U-Bahn*) Station *f*; (*Polizei, Feuerwehr*) Wache *f*; TV, RADIO Sender *m* **2** V/T MIL stationieren

stationery ['steɪʃənerɪ] S Schreibwaren *pl*

station wagon ['steɪʃənwægən] S Kombiwagen *m*

statistics [stə'tɪstɪks] S SG OD PL Statistik *f*

statue ['stætʃuː] S Statue *f*

status ['steɪtəs] S Status *m*, Ansehen *n*

stay [steɪ] **1** S Aufenthalt *m* **2** V/I bleiben; (*Hotel etc*) wohnen (*with* bei); **~ the night** übernachten **stay away** V/I wegbleiben; sich fernhalten **stay in** V/I zu Hause bleiben **stay out** V/I (*von zu Hause*) wegbleiben **stay up** V/I aufbleiben

steady ['stedɪ] **1** ADJ gleichmäßig; stetig; (*Einkommen, Freundin etc*) fest; (*Arbeitskraft*) zuverlässig; (*Hand*) ruhig; **they've been going ~ for two years** sie sind seit zwei Jahren fest zusammen **2** V/T (*Nerven*) beruhigen

steak [steɪk] S Steak *n*; (*von Fisch*) Filet *n*

steal ⟨stole, stolen⟩ [stiːl, stoʊl, 'stoʊlən] V/T stehlen

steam [stiːm] **1** S Dampf *m* **2** V/T GASTR dämpfen **steam up** V/I (*Fenster*) beschlagen

steel [stiːl] **1** S Stahl *m* **2** ADJ Stahl-

steep [stiːp] ADJ steil

steeple ['stiːpl] S Kirchturm *m*

steer [stɪr] V/T & V/I steuern; lenken **steering** S AUTO Lenkung *f* **steering wheel** S

Steuer *n*, Lenkrad *n*
stem [stem] S Stiel *m*
step [step] **1** S Schritt *m*; (*von Treppe*) Stufe *f*; (*Handlung*) Maßnahme *f* **2** V/I treten; **~ this way, please** hier entlang, bitte **step down** V/I zurücktreten **stepbrother** S Stiefbruder *m* **stepdaughter** S Stieftochter *f* **stepfather** S Stiefvater *m* **stepmother** S Stiefmutter *f* **stepsister** S Stiefschwester *f* **stepson** S Stiefsohn *m*
stereo ⟨-s *pl*⟩ ['sterıoʊ] S Stereo *n*
sterile ['sterəl] ADJ steril **sterilize** ['sterəlaız] V/T sterilisieren
stew [stu:] S Eintopf *m*
steward ['stu:ərd] S Steward *m* **stewardess** S Stewardess *f*
stick ⟨stuck, stuck⟩ [stık, stʌk] **1** V/T kleben; (*Nadel etc*) stecken; *umg* (*in die Tasche etc*) tun **2** V/I (*Tür etc*) klemmen; (*fest an etw*) haften **3** S Stock *m*; (*Hockey*) Schläger *m*; (*Kreide*) Stück *n*; (*Sellerie*) Stange *f* **stick out** **1** V/T **stick one's tongue out (at sb)** (j-m) die Zunge herausstrecken **2** V/I (*Zahn, Rippen*) vorstehen; (*Ohren*) abstehen; (*hervorstechen*) auffallen **stick to** V/T sich halten an *+akk* **sticker** ['stıkər] S Aufkleber *m* **sticky** ['stıkı] ADJ klebrig; (*Wetter*) schwül
stiff [stıf] ADJ steif
stifling ['staıflıŋ] ADJ drückend
still [stıl] **1** ADJ still **2** ADV (immer) noch; immerhin; (*dasitzen etc*) still
stimulate ['stımjəleıt] V/T anregen, stimulieren
sting ⟨stung, stung⟩ [stıŋ, stʌŋ] **1** V/T (*mit Stachel*) stechen **2** V/I (*Salbe etc*) brennen **3** S (*von Insekt*) Stich *m*
stingy ['stındʒı] ADJ *umg* geizig
stink ⟨stank, stunk⟩ [stıŋk, stæŋk, stʌŋk] **1** V/I stinken (*of* nach) **2** S Gestank *m*
stir [stɜ:r] V/T (um)rühren **stir-fry** V/T (unter Rühren) kurz anbraten
stitch [stıtʃ] **1** S (*Nähen*) Stich *m*; (*Stricken*) Masche *f*; **he had to have ~es** er musste genäht werden **2** V/T nähen
stock [stɑ:k] **1** S Vorrat *m* (*of an +dat*); (*an Waren*) Bestand *m*; (*für Suppe*) Brühe *f*; **~s and shares** *pl* Aktien und Wertpapiere *pl*; **be in/out of ~** vorrätig/nicht vorrätig sein **2** V/T (*Waren*) führen **stockbroker** S Börsenmakler(in) *m(f)* **stock exchange** S Börse *f*
stocking ['stɑ:kıŋ] S Strumpf *m*
stock market ['stɑ:kmɑ:rkət] S Börse *f*
stole [stoʊl] *prät von* **steal** **stolen** ['stoʊlən] *pperf von* **steal**
stomach ['stʌmək] S Magen

m, Bauch m **stomachache** ['stʌməkeɪk] S Magenschmerzen pl
stone [stoʊn] **1** S Stein m; (in Obst) Kern m, Stein m **2** ADJ Stein-, aus Stein **stony** ADJ steinig
stood [stʊd] prät, pperf von stand
stool [stu:l] S Hocker m
stop [stɑ:p] **1** S Halt m; (für Bus, Zug etc) Haltestelle f **2** V/T (Auto etc) anhalten; (einem Missstand) ein Ende machen +dat; (beenden, einstellen) aufhören mit; (etw Geplantes) verhindern; (Blutung) stillen; (Motor etc) abstellen; (Zahlungen) einstellen; **~ doing sth** aufhören, etw zu tun; **~ sb (from) doing sth** j-n daran hindern, etw zu tun; **~ it** hör auf (damit)! **3** V/I (Auto) anhalten; (auf Fahrt) haltmachen; (Person, Uhr, Herz) stehen bleiben; (Regen etc) aufhören **stop by** V/I vorbeischauen **stop over** V/I haltmachen; übernachten **stoplight** S Ampelanlage f; Ampel f **stopover** S (auf Reise) Zwischenstation f **stopper** S Stöpsel m **stop sign** S Stoppschild n
storage ['stɔ:rɪdʒ] S Lagerung f **store** [stɔ:r] **1** S Geschäft n; (großes Geschäft) Kaufhaus n; Vorrat m (of an +dat); (für Vorräte) Lager n **2** V/T lagern; IT speichern **storekeeper** S Ladenbesitzer(in) m(f) **storeroom** S Lagerraum m
storm [stɔ:rm] **1** S Sturm m, Gewitter n **2** V/T & V/I stürmen
stormy ADJ stürmisch
story ['stɔ:rɪ] S Geschichte f; (Roman etc) Handlung f; (in Gebäude) Stock m, Stockwerk n
stove [stoʊv] S Herd m, Ofen m
stow [stoʊ] V/T verstauen
straight [streɪt] **1** ADJ gerade; (Haare) glatt; (Person) ehrlich (with zu); (Whisky etc) pur; umg (sexuell) hetero **2** ADV direkt; sofort; (trinken) pur; (denken) klar; **~ ahead/on** geradeaus **straightaway** ADV sofort **straightforward** ADJ einfach; (Mensch) aufrichtig, unkompliziert
strain [streɪn] **1** S Belastung f **2** V/T (Augen etc) überanstrengen; (Seil, Beziehung) belasten; (Gemüse) abgießen; **~ a muscle** sich einen Muskel zerren **strainer** S Sieb n
strand [strænd] **1** S (aus Wolle) Faden m; (von Haaren) Strähne f **2** V/T **be (left) ~ed** (Person) festsitzen
strange [streɪndʒ] ADJ seltsam; (unbekannt) fremd **strangely** ADV seltsam; seltsamerweise **stranger** S Fremde(r) m/f(m)
strangle ['stræŋgl] V/T erdrosseln
strap [stræp] **1** S Riemen m; (Kleid) Träger m; (Uhr) Band n

2 VT (*befestigen*) festschnallen (*to* an *+dat*)
strategy ['strætədʒɪ] S Strategie *f*
straw [strɒ:] S Stroh *n*; (*für Getränk*) Strohhalm *m* **strawberry** S Erdbeere *f*
stray [streɪ] **1** S streunendes Tier **2** ADJ streunend **3** VI streunen
streak [stri:k] S Streifen *m*; (*im Haar*) Strähne *f*; (*im Charakter*) Zug *m*
stream [stri:m] **1** S Strom *m*, Bach *m* **2** VI strömen
street [stri:t] S Straße *f* **streetcar** S Straßenbahn *f* **street lamp**, **street light** S Straßenlaterne *f* **street map** S Stadtplan *m*
strength [streŋθ] S Kraft *f*, Stärke *f* **strengthen** VT verstärken; *fig* stärken
strenuous ['strenjʊəs] ADJ anstrengend
stress [stres] **1** S Stress *m*; (*von Wort*) Betonung *f* **2** VT betonen; (*belasten*) stressen **stressed (out)** ADJ gestresst
stretch [stretʃ] **1** S (*Land*) Stück *n*; (*Straße, Fluss*) Strecke *f* **2** VT (*Material*) dehnen; (*Seil, Zeltplane*) spannen; (*j-n leistungsmäßig*) fordern; **~ one's legs** sich die Beine vertreten **3** VI (*Person*) sich strecken; (*Gebiet*) sich erstrecken (*to* bis zu) **stretch out** **1** VT ausstrecken **2** VI (*Person, Tier*) sich strecken; (*auf Bett*) sich ausstrecken **stretcher** S Krankentrage *f* **stretch limo** ⟨-s *pl*⟩ S Großraumlimousine *f*
strict, **strictly** [strɪkt, -lɪ] ADJ & ADV (*Lehrer, Eltern*) streng; (*Anweisung*) genau
strike ⟨struck, struck⟩ [straɪk, strʌk] **1** VT (*Streichholz*) anzünden; (*Kopf gegen etw*) schlagen; (*Gold, Erdöl etc*) finden; **it struck me as strange** es kam mir seltsam vor **2** VI streiken; (*Serienmörder*) zuschlagen; (*Uhr*) schlagen **3** S Streik *m*; **be on ~** streiken **striking** ADJ auffallend
string [strɪŋ] S (*für Paket etc*) Schnur *f*; MUS, TENNIS Saite *f*
strip [strɪp] **1** S Streifen *m* **2** VI sich ausziehen, strippen
stripe [straɪp] S Streifen *m* **striped** ADJ gestreift
stroke [strəʊk] **1** S MED, TENNIS ETC Schlag *m*; (*beim Zeichnen, Malen*) Strich *m* **2** VT streicheln
stroll [strəʊl] **1** S Spaziergang *m* **2** VI spazieren **stroller** S (*für Kleinkind*) Buggy *m*
strong [strɑ:ŋ] ADJ stark; (*gesund*) robust; (*Tisch*) stabil; (*Schuhe*) fest; (*Einfluss*) groß **strongly** ADV stark; (*glauben*) fest; (*gebaut*) stabil
struck [strʌk] *prät, pperf von* strike
structural, **structurally** ['strʌktʃərəl, -lɪ] ADJ & ADV

strukturell **structure** ['strʌktʃər] S Struktur *f*; (*Gebäude, Brücke*) Konstruktion *f*, Bau *m*
struggle ['strʌgl] 1 S Kampf *m* (*for* um) 2 V/I kämpfen (*for* um); sich abmühen
stub [stʌb] S (*Zigarette*) Kippe *f*; (*Scheck etc*) Abschnitt *m*
stubble ['stʌbl] S Stoppelbart *m*; (*Feld*) Stoppeln *pl*
stubborn ['stʌbərn] ADJ stur
stuck [stʌk] 1 *prät, pperf von* stick 2 ADJ **be ~** (*Fenster etc*) klemmen; (*bei Arbeit etc*) nicht mehr weiterwissen; **get ~** (*im Schnee etc*) stecken bleiben
student ['stu:dənt] S Student(in) *m(f)*; (*Schule*) Schüler(in) *m(f)*
studio ⟨-s *pl*⟩ ['stu:dɪoʊ] S Studio *n*
study ['stʌdɪ] 1 S Untersuchung *f*; (*Raum*) Arbeitszimmer *n* 2 V/T & V/I studieren
stuff [stʌf] 1 S Zeug *n*; (*Besitztümer*) Sachen *pl* 2 V/T (*in Tasche etc*) stopfen; GASTR füllen
stuffing S GASTR Füllung *f*
stuffy ['stʌfɪ] ADJ (*Luft etc*) stickig; (*Person*) spießig
stumble ['stʌmbl] V/I stolpern
stun [stʌn] V/T fassungslos machen, verblüffen
stung [stʌŋ] *prät, pperf von* sting
stunk [stʌŋk] *pperf von* stink
stunning ['stʌnɪŋ] ADJ fantastisch; atemberaubend; (*völlig unerwartet*) überwältigend; unfassbar
stupid ['stu:pɪd] ADJ dumm
stupidity [stu:'pɪdətɪ] S Dummheit *f*
sturdy ['stɜ:rdɪ] ADJ stabil; robust
stutter ['stʌtər] V/I & V/T stottern
style [staɪl] 1 S Stil *m* 2 V/T (*Haare*) stylen **stylish** ['staɪlɪʃ] ADJ elegant, schick
subconscious [sʌb'kɑ:nʃəs] 1 ADJ unterbewusst 2 S Unterbewusstsein *n*
subject ['sʌbdʒɪkt] 1 S Thema *n*; (*in Schule*) Fach *n*; LING Subjekt *n* 2 ADJ **be ~ to** abhängen von; (*als Opfer etc*) unterworfen sein *+dat*
submarine [sʌbmə'ri:n] S U-Boot *n*
submerge [səb'mɜ:rdʒ] 1 V/T eintauchen 2 V/I tauchen
submit [səb'mɪt] 1 V/T (*Bewerbung*) einreichen 2 V/I (*aufgeben*) sich ergeben
subordinate [sə'bɔ:rdənət] 1 ADJ untergeordnet (*to +dat*) 2 S Untergebene(r) *m/f(m)*
subscription [səb'skrɪpʃən] S (*von Zeitung etc*) Abonnement *n*
subsequently ['sʌbsəkwəntlɪ] ADV später, anschließend
subside [səb'saɪd] V/I (*Hochwasser*) zurückgehen; (*Sturm*) sich legen; (*Gebäude*) sich senken; (*Schmerzen*) nachlassen

substance ['sʌbstəns] S Substanz *f*
substantial [səb'stænʃəl] ADJ beträchtlich; (*Verbesserung*) wesentlich; (*Mahlzeit*) reichhaltig
substitute ['sʌbstətu:t] **1** S Ersatz *m;* SPORT Ersatzspieler(in) *m(f)* **2** V/T ersetzen (*for* durch)
subtitle ['sʌbtaɪtl] S Untertitel *m*
subtle ['sʌtl] ADJ (*Unterschied*) fein; (*Plan*) raffiniert
subtract [səb'trækt] V/T abziehen (*from* von)
suburb ['sʌbɜ:rb] S Vorort *m* **suburban** [sə'bɜ:rbən] ADJ vorstädtisch, Vorstadt-
subway ['sʌbweɪ] S BAHN U-Bahn *f*
succeed [sək'si:d] **1** V/I erfolgreich sein; **he ~ed (in doing it)** es gelang ihm(, es zu tun) **2** V/T nachfolgen *+dat* **success** [sək'ses] S Erfolg *m* **successful**, **successfully** ADJ & ADV erfolgreich **successor** S Nachfolger(in) *m(f)*
such [sʌtʃ] **1** ADJ solche(r, s); **~ a book** so ein Buch, ein solches Buch; **~ as** wie **2** ADV so **3** PRON **as ~** als solche(r, s)
suck [sʌk] V/T lutschen; (*Flüssigkeit*) saugen; **it ~s** *umg* das ist beschissen **sucker** ['sʌkər] S *umg* Trottel *m;* **be a ~ for sth** für etw eine Schwäche haben
sudden ['sʌdn] ADJ plötzlich; **all of a ~** ganz plötzlich **suddenly** ADV plötzlich
sue [su:] V/T verklagen
suede [sweɪd] S Wildleder *n*
suffer ['sʌfər] **1** V/T erleiden **2** V/I leiden (*from* an *+dat*)
sufficient [sə'fɪʃənt] ADJ ausreichend
suffocate ['sʌfəkeɪt] V/T & V/I ersticken
sugar ['ʃʊgər] **1** S Zucker *m* **2** V/T zuckern **sugary** ADJ süß
suggest [sə'dʒest] V/T vorschlagen; andeuten **suggestion** [sə'dʒestʃən] S Vorschlag *m*
suicide ['sʊɪsaɪd] S Selbstmord *m*
suit [su:t] **1** S Anzug *m;* (*für Frau*) Kostüm *n;* (*bei Kartenspiel*) Farbe *f* **2** V/T (*Termin etc*) passen *+dat;* (*Kleidung, Farben*) stehen *+dat;* (*Klima*) bekommen *+dat* **suitable** ['su:təbl] ADJ geeignet (*for* für) **suitcase** S Koffer *m*
suite [swi:t] S (*Zimmerflucht*) Suite *f;* (*Sofa und Sessel*) Sitzgarnitur *f*
sulk [sʌlk] V/I schmollen
sum [sʌm] S Summe *f*, Betrag *m*
summarize ['sʌməraɪz] V/T & V/I zusammenfassen **summary** S Zusammenfassung *f*
summer ['sʌmər] S Sommer *m* **summer camp** S Ferienlager *n* **summertime** S Sommer *m*

summit ['sʌmət] S̲ *a.* POL Gipfel *m*
summon ['sʌmən] V̲/̲T̲ *(Arzt etc)* rufen; *(in sein Büro)* zitieren **summons** ['sʌmənz] S̲ ̲S̲G̲ JUR Vorladung *f*
sun [sʌn] S̲ Sonne *f*
Sun *abk* = Sunday; So.
sunbathe ['sʌnbeɪð] V̲/̲I̲ sich sonnen **sunblock** S̲ Sunblocker *m* **sunburn** S̲ Sonnenbrand *m* **sunburnt** A̲D̲J̲ **be/get ~** einen Sonnenbrand haben/bekommen
sundae ['sʌndeɪ] S̲ Eisbecher *m*
Sunday ['sʌndeɪ] S̲ Sonntag *m*; → Tuesday
sung [sʌŋ] *pperf von* sing
sunglasses ['sʌnglæsəz] S̲ ̲P̲L̲ Sonnenbrille *f*
sunk [sʌŋk] *pperf von* sink
sunlight ['sʌnlaɪt] S̲ Sonnenlicht *n* **sunny** ['sʌnɪ] A̲D̲J̲ sonnig **sunny-side up** A̲D̲J̲ *(Ei)* nur auf einer Seite gebraten **sunrise** S̲ Sonnenaufgang *m* **sunroof** S̲ AUTO Schiebedach *n* **sunscreen** S̲ Sonnenschutzmittel *n* **sunset** S̲ Sonnenuntergang *m* **sunshade** S̲ Sonnenschirm *m* **sunshine** S̲ Sonnenschein *m* **sunstroke** S̲ Sonnenstich *m* **suntan** S̲ (Sonnen)bräune *f*; **~ lotion** *(od* **oil)** Sonnenöl *n*
super ['su:pər] **1** A̲D̲J̲ *umg* toll **2** *abk* = superintendent; Hausmeister(in) *m(f)*
superb [su:'pɜ:rb] A̲D̲J̲ ausgezeichnet
superficial [su:pər'fɪʃəl] A̲D̲J̲ oberflächlich
superintendent [su:pərɪn'tendənt] S̲ Hausmeister(in) *m(f)*
superior [sʊ'pɪrɪər] **1** A̲D̲J̲ besser *(to* als); *(beruflich)* höhergestellt *(to* als), höher **2** S̲ Vorgesetzte(r) *m/f(m)*
supermarket ['su:pərmɑ:rkət] S̲ Supermarkt *m*
superstition [su:pər'stɪʃən] S̲ Aberglaube *m* **superstitious** [su:pər'stɪʃəs] A̲D̲J̲ abergläubisch
supervise ['su:pərvaɪz] V̲/̲T̲ beaufsichtigen **supervisor** ['su:pərvaɪzər] S̲ Aufsicht *f*
supper ['sʌpər] S̲ Abendessen *n*
supplement **1** ['sʌpləmənt] S̲ Zusatz *m*; *(zusätzlicher Betrag)* Zuschlag *m*; *(von Zeitung)* Beilage *f* **2** ['sʌpləment] V̲/̲T̲ ergänzen **supplementary** [sʌplə'mentərɪ] A̲D̲J̲ zusätzlich
supplier [sə'plaɪər] S̲ Lieferant(in) *m(f)* **supply** [sə'plaɪ] **1** V̲/̲T̲ *(als Händler)* liefern; *(jemanden)* versorgen; *(Getränke, Musik etc)* sorgen für **2** S̲ Vorrat *m (of* an *+dat)*
support [sə'pɔ:rt] **1** S̲ Unterstützung *f*; TECH Stütze *f* **2** V̲/̲T̲ tragen, stützen; *(Familie)* ernähren, unterhalten; *(Partei)* unterstützen

suppose [sə'poʊz] V/T annehmen; **you're not ~d to smoke here** du darfst/Sie dürfen hier nicht rauchen
surcharge ['sɜːrtʃɑːrdʒ] S Zuschlag *m*
sure [ʃʊr] 1 ADJ sicher; **make ~ you lock up** vergiss/vergessen Sie nicht abzuschließen 2 ADV **~!** klar! **surely** ADV sicher(lich)
surf [sɜːrf] 1 S Brandung *f* 2 V/I SPORT surfen 3 V/T **~ the Internet** im Internet surfen
surface ['sɜːrfəs] 1 S Oberfläche *f* 2 V/I auftauchen
surfboard ['sɜːrfbɔːrd] S Surfbrett *n* **surfer** S Surfer(in) *m(f)*
surfing S Surfen *n*
surgeon ['sɜːrdʒən] S Chirurg(in) *m(f)* **surgery** ['sɜːrdʒərɪ] S Operation *f*; **have ~** operiert werden
surname ['sɜːrneɪm] S Nachname *m*
surprise [sər'praɪz] 1 S Überraschung *f* 2 V/T überraschen
surprising ADJ überraschend
surprisingly ADV erstaunlich; überraschenderweise, erstaunlicherweise
surrender [sə'rendər] 1 V/I sich ergeben (*to +dat*) 2 V/T (*Waffen, Pass*) abgeben
surround [sə'raʊnd] V/T umgeben; umringen **surrounding** 1 ADJ umliegend 2 S **~s** *pl* Umgebung *f*
survey 1 ['sɜːrveɪ] S Umfrage *f*; (*über Literatur etc*) Überblick *m* (*of* über *+akk*); (*Land*) Vermessung *f* 2 [sər'veɪ] V/T überblicken; (*Land*) vermessen
survive [sər'vaɪv] V/T & V/I überleben
sushi ['suːʃɪ] S Sushi *n*
suspect 1 ['sʌspekt] S Verdächtige(r) *m/f(m)* 2 ['sʌspekt] ADJ verdächtig 3 [sə'spekt] V/T verdächtigen (*of +gen*), vermuten
suspend [sə'spend] V/T (*von Arbeit, Amt*) suspendieren; (*Zahlung*) vorübergehend einstellen; (*Spieler*) sperren; (*befestigen*) aufhängen **suspenders** S PL Hosenträger *pl*
suspense [sə'spens] S Spannung *f*
suspicious [sə'spɪʃəs] ADJ misstrauisch (*of sb/sth* j-m/etw gegenüber); verdächtig
swallow ['swɑːloʊ] V/T & V/I schlucken
swam [swæm] *prät von* swim
swamp [swɑːmp] S Sumpf *m*
swan [swɑːn] S Schwan *m*
swap [swɑːp] V/T & V/I tauschen; **~ sth for sth** etw gegen etw eintauschen
sway [sweɪ] V/I schwanken
swear ⟨swore, sworn⟩ [swer, swɔːr, swɔːrn] V/I schwören; fluchen
sweat [swet] 1 S Schweiß *m*; **no ~** kein Problem 2 V/I schwitzen **sweater** S Pullover *m* **sweaty** ADJ verschwitzt

Swede [swiːd] S Schwede *m*, Schwedin *f* **Sweden** S Schweden *n* **Swedish** 1 ADJ schwedisch 2 S (*Sprache*) Schwedisch *n*

sweep ⟨swept, swept⟩ [swiːp, swept] V/T & V/I kehren, fegen

sweet [swiːt] ADJ süß; lieb **sweet-and-sour** ADJ süßsauer **sweetcorn** S Mais *m* **sweeten** V/T süßen **sweetener** S Süßstoff *m* **sweetheart** S Schatz *m* **sweet potato** S Süßkartoffel *f*

swell ⟨swelled, swollen *od* swelled⟩ [swel, sweld, 'swoʊlən] 1 V/I ~ **(up)** (an)schwellen 2 ADJ *umg*, *meist ironisch* toll **swelling** S MED Schwellung *f*

sweltering ['sweltərɪŋ] ADJ (*Hitze*) drückend

swept [swept] *prät*, *pperf von* sweep

swiftly ['swɪftlɪ] ADV schnell

swim ⟨swam, swum⟩ [swɪm, swæm, swʌm] 1 V/I schwimmen 2 S **go for a ~** schwimmen gehen **swimmer** S Schwimmer(in) *m(f)* **swimming** S Schwimmen *n*; **go ~** schwimmen gehen **swimming pool** S Schwimmbad *n*, Swimmingpool *m* **swimsuit** S Badeanzug *m*

swindle ['swɪndl] V/T betrügen (*out of* um)

swine [swaɪn] S Schwein *n* **swine flu** S Schweinegrippe *f*

swing ⟨swung, swung⟩ [swɪŋ, swʌŋ] 1 V/T & V/I schwingen 2 S Schaukel *f*

swipe [swaɪp] V/T (*Kreditkarte etc*) durchziehen; *umg* (*stehlen*) klauen **swipe card** S Magnetkarte *f*

Swiss [swɪs] 1 ADJ schweizerisch 2 S Schweizer(in) *m(f)*

switch [swɪtʃ] 1 S ELEK Schalter *m* 2 V/I wechseln (*to* zu) **switch off** V/T abschalten, ausschalten **switch on** V/T anschalten, einschalten **switchboard** S TEL Vermittlung *f*

Switzerland ['swɪtsərlænd] S die Schweiz

swivel ['swɪvl] 1 V/I sich drehen 2 V/T drehen, schwenken

swollen ['swoʊlən] 1 *pperf von* swell 2 ADJ MED geschwollen; (*Bauch*) aufgebläht

sword [sɔːrd] S Schwert *n*

swore [swɔːr] *prät von* swear **sworn** [swɔːrn] *pperf von* swear

swum [swʌm] *pperf von* swim

swung [swʌŋ] *prät*, *pperf von* swing

syllable ['sɪləbl] S Silbe *f*

symbol ['sɪmbəl] S Symbol *n* **symbolic** [sɪm'bɑːlɪk] ADJ symbolisch **symbolize** ['sɪmbəlaɪz] V/T symbolisieren

symmetrical [sɪ'metrɪkəl] ADJ symmetrisch

sympathetic [sɪmpə'θetɪk] ADJ mitfühlend; verständnisvoll **sympathize** ['sɪmpəθaɪz] V/I mitfühlen (*with sb* mit j-m) **sympathy** ['sɪmpəθɪ] S Mitleid *n;* (*Todesfall*) Beileid *n;* (*Einfühlungsvermögen*) Verständnis *n*

symphony ['sɪmfənɪ] S Sinfonie *f*

symptom ['sɪmptəm] S Symptom *n*

synagogue ['sɪnəgɑːg] S Synagoge *f*

synopsis [sɪ'nɑːpsɪs] S Zusammenfassung *f;* Abriss *m,* der Handlung

synthetic [sɪn'θetɪk] ADJ synthetisch

Syria ['sɪrɪə] S Syrien *n*

syringe [sə'rɪndʒ] S Spritze *f*

system ['sɪstəm] S System *n* **systematic** [sɪstə'mætɪk] ADJ systematisch

T

tab [tæb] S (*von Kleidung*) Aufhänger *m;* IT Tabulator *m;* **pick up the ~** *umg* die Rechnung übernehmen

table ['teɪbl] S Tisch *m;* (*Liste*) Tabelle *f* **tablecloth** S Tischdecke *f* **tablespoon** S Servierlöffel *m,* Esslöffel *m*

tablet ['tæblət] S Tablette *f*

table tennis ['teɪbltenəs] S Tischtennis *n* **table wine** S Tafelwein *m*

tabloid ['tæblɔɪd] S Boulevardzeitung *f*

taboo [tæ'buː] **1** S Tabu *n* **2** ADJ tabu

tack [tæk] S (*kleiner Nagel*) Stift *m;* Reißzwecke *f*

tackle ['tækl] **1** S SPORT Angriff *m;* (*zum Angeln etc*) Ausrüstung *f* **2** V/T in Angriff nehmen; SPORT angreifen

tacky ['tækɪ] ADJ *umg* kitschig, billig und geschmacklos

taco ⟨-s *pl*⟩ ['tækoʊ] S Taco *m* (*Maisfladen mit scharfer Füllung aus Hackfleisch, Tomaten, Käse, Salat etc*)

tactful ['tæktfəl] ADJ taktvoll

tactic(s) ['tæktɪk(s)] S (PL) Taktik *f*

taffy ['tæfɪ] S Toffee *n;* Sahnebonbon *n*

tag [tæg] S Schild *n,* Etikett *n*

tail [teɪl] S Schwanz *m* **tailgate** ['teɪlgeɪt] AUTO **1** S Heckklappe *f* **2** V/T (*im Verkehr*) drängeln, zu dicht auffahren

taillight S AUTO Rücklicht *n*

tailor ['teɪlər] S Schneider(in) *m(f)*

tailpipe ['teɪlpaɪp] S AUTO Auspuffrohr *n*

take ⟨took, taken⟩ [teɪk, tʊk, 'teɪkn] V/T nehmen; mitnehmen; (*irgendwohin*) bringen; (*subtrahieren*) abziehen (*from* von); (*Preis etc*) bekommen; FIN, WIRTSCH einnehmen; (*Zug, Taxi etc*) nehmen, fahren mit; (*Reise, Spaziergang, Kurs,*

Foto) machen;; (*Telefonat*) entgegennehmen; (*Entscheidung, Vorkehrungen*) treffen; (*Risiko*) eingehen; (*Rat, Arbeit*) annehmen; (*Hitze, Schmerzen*) ertragen; (*Nachricht etc*) aufnehmen; (*vom Volumen*) Platz haben für; **how long does it ~?** wie lange dauert es?; **it ~s 4 hours** man braucht 4 Stunden; **I ~ it that ...** ich nehme an, dass ...; **~ place** stattfinden; **~ part in** teilnehmen an *+dat* **take after** VT nachschlagen *+dat* **take along** VT mitnehmen **take apart** VT auseinandernehmen **take away** VT wegnehmen (*from sb* j-m); (*subtrahieren*) abziehen (*from* von) **take back** VT zurückbringen; zurücknehmen **take down** VT abnehmen; (*Namen, Notizen*) aufschreiben **take in** VT (*Bedeutung etc*) begreifen; (*j-n bei sich*) aufnehmen; (*täuschen*) hereinlegen **take off** **1** VI (*Flugzeug*) starten **2** VT (*Kleider*) ausziehen; (*Hut, Deckel*) abnehmen; (*von Preis*) abziehen; (*Tag*) freinehmen **take on** VT (*Aufgabe, Verantwortung*) übernehmen; (*Personal*) einstellen; SPORT antreten gegen **take out** VT herausnehmen; (*Person, Hund*) ausführen; (*Versicherung*) abschließen; (*Geld vom Konto*) abheben **take over** **1** VT übernehmen **2** VI **he took over (from me)** er hat mich abgelöst **take to** VT (*Person*) mögen; **~ doing sth** anfangen, etw zu tun **take up** VT (*Teppich etc*) hochnehmen; (*Dinge: Platz*) einnehmen; (*Zeit*) in Anspruch nehmen; (*Hobby*) anfangen mit; (*neue Stelle*) antreten; (*Angebot*) annehmen **taken** ['teɪkn] **1** *pperf von* take **2** ADJ (*Sitzplatz*) besetzt **takeoff** ['teɪkɑ:f] S FLUG Start *m* **takeout** ['teɪkaʊt] S Essen *n* zum Mitnehmen; Restaurant *n* mit Straßenverkauf

tale [teɪl] S Geschichte *f*

talent ['tælənt] S Talent *n* **talented** ADJ begabt

talk [tɔ:k] **1** S Gespräch *n*; (*Geschwätz*) Gerede *n*; (*vor Publikum*) Vortrag *m* **2** VI sprechen, reden; sich unterhalten **3** VT sprechen; (*Unsinn*) reden; (*Politik, Geschäfte*) reden über *+akk*; **~ sb into doing/out of doing sth** j-n überreden/j-m ausreden, etw zu tun **talk over** VT besprechen **talkative** ADJ gesprächig **talk show** S Talkshow *f*

tall [tɔ:l] ADJ groß; (*Gebäude, Baum*) hoch

tame [teɪm] **1** ADJ zahm **2** VT (*Tier*) zähmen

tampon ['tæmpɑ:n] S Tampon *m*

tan [tæn] **1** S (Sonnen)bräune *f*; **get/have a ~** braun werden/sein **2** VI braun werden

tangerine [tændʒəˈriːn] S Mandarine *f*
tank [tæŋk] S Tank *m*; (*für Fische*) Aquarium *n*; MIL Panzer *m*
tanker [ˈtæŋkər] S (*Schiff*) Tanker *m*; (*Fahrzeug*) Tankwagen *m*
tanned [tænd] ADJ braun
tap [tæp] **1** S (*für Wasser*) Hahn *m*; leichtes Klopfen **2** V/T & V/I klopfen
tape [teɪp] **1** S (*zum Kleben*) Klebeband *n*; (*für Aufnahmen*) Tonband *n*; (*Audio-, Videokassette*) Kassette *f* **2** V/T aufnehmen **tape up** V/T (*Paket etc*) zukleben **tape measure** S Maßband *n* **tape recorder** S Tonbandgerät *n*
tap water [ˈtæpwɔːtər] S Leitungswasser *n*
target [ˈtɑːrgət] S Ziel *n*, Zielscheibe *f* **target group** S Zielgruppe *f*
tariff [ˈtærəf] S Preisliste *f*; (*Steuer auf Importe*) Zoll *m*
tart [tɑːrt] S (Obst)kuchen *m*; (Obst)törtchen *n*
tartar(e) sauce [tɑːrtərˈsɒːs] S Remouladensoße *f*
task [tæsk] S Aufgabe *f*, Pflicht *f*
taste [teɪst] **1** S Geschmack *m*; Geschmackssinn *m*; (*ein bisschen von etw*) Kostprobe *f* **2** V/T schmecken; probieren **3** V/I (*Essen, Getränk*) schmecken (*of* nach) **tasteful** ADJ geschmackvoll **tasteless** ADJ geschmacklos **tasty** ADJ lecker
taught [tɒːt] *prät, pperf von* teach
Taurus [ˈtɔːrəs] S ASTROL Stier *m*
tax [tæks] **1** S Steuer *f* (*on* auf +*akk*) **2** V/T besteuern **taxation** [tækˈseɪʃən] S Besteuerung *f* **tax-free** ADJ steuerfrei
taxi [ˈtæksɪ] **1** S Taxi *n* **2** V/I (*Flugzeug*) rollen **taxi stand** S Taxistand *m*
T-bone steak [tiːboʊnˈsteɪk] S T-Bone-Steak *n* (*aus dem Rippenstück mit anhängendem Filet*)
tea [tiː] S Tee *m* **teabag** S Teebeutel *m*
teach ⟨taught, taught⟩ [tiːtʃ, tɒːt] **1** V/T unterrichten; beibringen **2** V/I unterrichten
teacher S Lehrer(in) *m(f)*
team [tiːm] S SPORT Mannschaft *f*, Team *n*
teapot [ˈtiːpɑːt] S Teekanne *f*
tear [tɪr] S Träne *f*
tear ⟨tore, torn⟩ [ter, tɔːr, tɔːrn] **1** V/T zerreißen **2** S Riss *m* **tear up** V/T (*Papier*) zerreißen
tease [tiːz] V/T (*j-n*) necken (*about* wegen)
teaspoon [ˈtiːspuːn] S Teelöffel *m*
technical [ˈteknɪkəl] ADJ technisch; Fach- **technically** ADV technisch **technique** [tekˈniːk] S Technik *f* **technology** [tekˈnɑːlədʒɪ] S Technolo-

gie *f*, Technik *f*
teen(age) ['ti:n(eɪdʒ)] ADJ Teenager- **teenager** S Teenager *m* **teens** [ti:nz] S PL **in one's ~** im Teenageralter
teeth [ti:θ] *pl von* tooth
teetotal [ti:'toʊtl] ADJ abstinent
telephone ['teləfoʊn] **1** S Telefon *n* **2** V/I telefonieren **3** V/T anrufen **telephone booth** S Telefonzelle *f* **telephone call** S Telefonanruf *m* **telephone directory** S Telefonbuch *n* **telephone number** S Telefonnummer *f*
telephoto lens [teləfoʊtoʊ'lenz] S Teleobjektiv *n*
telescope ['teləskoʊp] S Teleskop *n*
television ['teləvɪʒən] S Fernsehen *n* **television (set)** S Fernseher *m*
tell ⟨told, told⟩ [tel, toʊld] **1** V/T sagen (*sb sth* j-m etw); erzählen; (*den Unterschied*) erkennen; (*Geheimnis*) verraten; **~ sb about sth** j-m von etw erzählen; **~ sth from sth** etw von etw unterscheiden **2** V/I wissen **tell apart** V/T unterscheiden **tell off** V/T schimpfen
teller ['telər] S Kassierer(in) *m(f)*
temp [temp] **1** S Aushilfskraft *f* **2** V/I als Aushilfskraft arbeiten
temper ['tempər] S Wut *f*, Laune *f*; **lose one's ~** die Beherrschung verlieren **temperamental** [tempərə'mentl] ADJ launisch
temperature ['temprətʃər] S Temperatur *f*; MED Fieber *n*
temple ['templ] S Tempel *m*; ANAT Schläfe *f*
temporarily [tempə'rerəlɪ] ADV vorübergehend **temporary** ['tempərerɪ] ADJ vorübergehend; provisorisch
tempt [tempt] V/T in Versuchung führen **temptation** [temp'teɪʃən] S Versuchung *f* **tempting** ADJ verlockend
ten [ten] **1** NUM zehn **2** S Zehn *f*; → eight
tenant ['tenənt] S Mieter(in) *m(f)*, Pächter(in) *m(f)*
tend [tend] V/I **~ to do sth** dazu neigen, etw zu tun; **~ toward(s)** neigen zu **tendency** ['tendənsɪ] S Tendenz *f*
tender ['tendər] ADJ zärtlich; empfindlich; (*Fleisch*) zart **tenderloin** ['tendərlɔɪn] S Filet *n*
tendon ['tendən] S Sehne *f*
ten-gallon hat [tengælən'hæt] S breitrandiger Cowboyhut
tennis ['tenəs] S Tennis *n* **tennis court** S Tennisplatz *m* **tennis racket** S Tennisschläger *m*
tense [tens] ADJ angespannt; gespannt **tension** ['tenʃən] S Spannung *f*; (*psychisch*) Anspannung *f*
tent [tent] S Zelt *n*

tenth [tenθ] **1** ADJ zehnte(r, s) **2** S Zehntel *n*; → **eighth**

tent peg ['tentpeg] S Hering *m*

term [tɜ:rm] S (*Wort*) Ausdruck *m*; **~s** *pl* Bedingungen *pl*; **in the long/short ~** langfristig/kurzfristig; **in ~s of ...** was ... betrifft

terminal ['tɜ:rmənl] **1** S (*von Bus etc*) Endstation *f*; FLUG Terminal *m*; IT Terminal *n*; ELEK Pol *m* **2** ADJ MED unheilbar

terminate ['tɜ:rməneɪt] V/T (*Vertrag*) lösen; (*Schwangerschaft*) abbrechen

terrace ['terəs] S Terrasse *f*

terrible ['terəbl] ADJ schrecklich

terrific [tə'rɪfɪk] ADJ fantastisch

terrify ['terəfaɪ] V/T erschrecken; **be terrified** schreckliche Angst haben (**of** vor *+dat*)

territory ['terətɔ:rɪ] S Gebiet *n*

terror ['terər] S Schrecken *m*; POL Terror *m* **terrorism** S Terrorismus *m* **terrorist** S Terrorist(in) *m(f)*

test [test] **1** S Test *m*; (*Schule*) Klassenarbeit *f*; (*Führerschein*) Prüfung *f*; **put to the ~** auf die Probe stellen **2** V/T testen; (*Schule*) prüfen

Testament ['testəmənt] S **the Old/New ~** das Alte/Neue Testament

test-drive ['testdraɪv] V/T Probe fahren

testicle ['testəkl] S Hoden *m*

testify ['testəfaɪ] V/I JUR aussagen

tetanus ['tetənəs] S Tetanus *m*

Tex-mex [teks'meks] ADJ *umg* texanisch-mexikanisch

text [tekst] **1** S Text *m*; (*von Brief etc*) Wortlaut *m*; (*übers Handy*) SMS *f* **2** V/T (*SMS-Nachricht*) simsen, SMSen; **~ sb** j-m simsen, j-m eine SMS schicken; **I'll ~ it to you** ich schicke es dir per SMS **textbook** S Lehrbuch *n* **text message** S SMS *f*

texture ['tekstʃər] S Beschaffenheit *f*

Thailand ['taɪlænd] S Thailand *n*

than [ðæn] PRÄP & KONJ als

thank [θæŋk] V/T danken *+dat*; **~ you (very much)** danke (sehr) **thankful** ADJ dankbar **thankfully** ADV zum Glück **thanks** S PL Dank *m*; **~** danke!; **~ to** dank *+gen* **Thanksgiving (Day)** S Erntedankfest *n* (*4. Donnerstag im November*)

that [ðæt, ðət] **1** ADJ der/die/das; jene(r, s); **I like ~ one** ich mag das da **2** PRON das; (*im Relativsatz*) der/die/das, die *pl*; **~ is (to say)** das heißt **3** KONJ dass **4** ADV so **that's** [ðæts] *kontr von* **that is; that has**

thaw [θɒ:] **1** V/I tauen; (*Einge-*

frorenes) auftauen **2** V/T auftauen lassen
the [ðə, ði:] ART der/die/das, die *pl*; **by ~ hour** pro Stunde; **~ … ~ better** je …, desto besser
theater ['θɪətər] S Theater *n*; (*für Vorlesungen etc*) Saal *m*
theft [θeft] S Diebstahl *m*
their [ðer] ADJ ihr; **they brushed ~ teeth** sie putzten sich die Zähne **theirs** PRON ihre(r, s); **it's ~** es gehört ihnen; **a friend of ~** ein Freund von ihnen
them [ðəm, ðem] PRON (*direktes Objekt*) sie; (*indirektes Objekt*) ihnen; **it's ~** sie sind's
theme [θi:m] S Thema *n*; MUS Motiv *n*; Titelmusik *f*
themselves [ðəm'selvz] PRON sich; selbst; **(all) by ~** allein
then [ðen] **1** ADV (*zu jener Zeit*) damals; (*danach*) dann; (*also doch*) also; (*außerdem*) ferner; **from ~ on** von da an; **by ~** bis dahin **2** ADJ damalig
theoretically [θi:ə'retɪkəlɪ] ADV theoretisch **theory** ['θi:ərɪ] S Theorie *f*; **in ~** theoretisch
therapy ['θerəpɪ] S Therapie *f*
there [ðer] ADV dort; dorthin; **~ is/are** es gibt; **it's over ~** es ist da drüben; **~ you are** (*bei Übergabe*) bitte schön **therefore** ADV daher, deshalb
thermometer [θər'mɑ:mətər] S Thermometer *n*
these [ði:z] PRON & ADJ diese; dies, das
they [ðeɪ] PRON *pl* sie; (*die Leute im Allgemeinen*) man; (*in Bezug auf unbestimmte Person*) er/sie
they'd [ðeɪd] *kontr von* **they had; they would they'll** [ðeɪl] *kontr von* **they will; they shall they've** [ðeɪv] *kontr von* **they have**
thick [θɪk] ADJ dick; (*Nebel etc*) dicht; (*Flüssigkeit*) dickflüssig; *umg* (*blöd*) dumm
thief ⟨thieves *pl*⟩ [θi:f, θi:vz] S Dieb(in) *m(f)*
thigh [θaɪ] S Oberschenkel *m*
thin [θɪn] ADJ dünn
thing [θɪŋ] S Ding *n*, Sache *f*; **how are ~s?** wie geht's?
think ⟨thought, thought⟩ [θɪŋk, θɒ:t] V/T & V/I denken; meinen; **I ~ so** ich denke schon; **I don't ~ so** ich glaube nicht **think about** V/T denken an *+akk*, nachdenken über *+akk*; (*meinen*) halten von **think of** V/T denken an *+akk*; (*Idee, Vorschlag etc*) sich ausdenken; (*beurteilen*) halten von; (*an Namen etc*) sich erinnern an *+akk* **think over** V/T überdenken **think up** V/T sich ausdenken
third [θɜ:rd] **1** ADJ dritte(r, s) **2** S Drittel *n*; → **eighth thirdly** ADV drittens **third party insurance** S Haftpflichtversicherung *f*

thirst [θɜːrst] S Durst *m* (*for* nach) **thirsty** ADJ **be ~** Durst haben
thirteen [θɜːr'tiːn] **1** NUM dreizehn **2** S Dreizehn *f*; → eight **thirteenth** ADJ dreizehnte(r, s); → eighth **thirtieth** ['θɜːrtɪəθ] ADJ dreißigste(r, s); → eighth **thirty** ['θɜːrtɪ] **1** NUM dreißig **2** S Dreißig *f*; → eight, eighty
this [ðɪs] **1** ADJ diese(r, s); **~ morning** heute Morgen **2** PRON das, dies; **~ is Mark** (*Telefon*) hier spricht Mark
thong [θɒːŋ] S (*Sandale*) Flip-Flop® *m*; (*Unterwäsche*) String *m*
thorn [θɔːrn] S Dorn *m*, Stachel *m*
thorough ['θɜːroʊ] ADJ gründlich **thoroughly** ['θɜːrəlɪ] ADV gründlich; (*zustimmen etc*) völlig
those [ðoʊz] **1** PRON die da, jene; **~ who** diejenigen, die **2** ADJ die, jene
though [ðoʊ] **1** KONJ obwohl; **as ~** als ob **2** ADV aber
thought [θɒːt] **1** *prät, pperf von* think **2** S Gedanke *m*, Überlegung *f* **thoughtful** ADJ rücksichtsvoll; aufmerksam; (*Blick*) nachdenklich **thoughtless** ADJ rücksichtslos, gedankenlos
thousand ['θaʊzənd] NUM **(one) ~, a ~** tausend; **~s of** Tausende von
thread [θred] **1** S Faden *m* **2** V/T einfädeln; auffädeln
threat [θret] S Drohung *f*, Bedrohung *f* (*to* für) **threaten** V/T bedrohen **threatening** ADJ bedrohlich
three [θriː] **1** NUM drei **2** S Drei *f*; → eight **three-dimensional** ADJ dreidimensional **three-quarters** S PL drei Viertel *pl*
threshold ['θreʃhoʊld] S Schwelle *f*
threw [θruː] *prät von* throw
thrift store ['θrɪftstɔːr] S Secondhandladen *m*
thrilled [θrɪld] ADJ **be ~ (with sth)** sich (über etw *akk*) riesig freuen **thrilling** ADJ aufregend
thrive [θraɪv] V/I gedeihen (*on* bei); *fig* florieren
throat [θroʊt] S Hals *m*, Kehle *f*
throbbing ['θrɑːbɪŋ] ADJ (*Schmerz*) pochend
thrombosis [θrɑːm'boʊsəs] S Thrombose *f*
throne [θroʊn] S Thron *m*
through [θruː] **1** PRÄP durch; (*zeitlich*) während *+gen*; (*aufgrund von*) aus, durch; (*als Zeitspanne*) bis; **Monday ~ Friday** Montag bis einschließlich Freitag **2** ADV durch; **put sb ~** TEL j-n verbinden (*to* mit) **3** ADJ (*Fahrkarte, Zug*) durchgehend; **be ~ with sb/sth** mit j-m/etw fertig sein **throughout**

[θruːˈaʊt] 1 PRÄP (*örtlich*) überall in *+dat*; (*zeitlich*) während *+gen*; ~ **the night** die ganze Nacht hindurch 2 ADV überall; die ganze Zeit

throw ⟨threw, thrown⟩ [θroʊ, θruː, θroʊn] 1 V/T werfen; abwerfen; (*Party*) geben 2 S Wurf *m* **throw away** V/T wegwerfen **throw in** V/T (*gratis*) dazugeben **throw out** V/T wegwerfen; (*Person*) hinauswerfen (*of* aus) **throw up** V/T & V/I *umg* sich übergeben

thrown [θroʊn] *pperf von* throw

thru → through

thrust ⟨thrust, thrust⟩ [θrʌst] V/T & V/I stoßen

thruway [ˈθruːweɪ] S Schnellstraße *f*

thumb [θʌm] 1 S Daumen *m* 2 V/T ~ **a lift** per Anhalter fahren **thumbtack** S Reißzwecke *f*

thunder [ˈθʌndər] 1 S Donner *m* 2 V/I donnern **thunderstorm** S Gewitter *n*

Thur(s) *abk* = Thursday; Do.

Thursday [ˈθɜːrzdeɪ] S Donnerstag *m*; → Tuesday

thyme [taɪm] S Thymian *m*

tick [tɪk] 1 V/I (*Uhr*) ticken 2 S ZOOL Zecke *f*

ticket [ˈtɪkət] S (Fahr)karte *f*; (*für Flug*) Flugschein *m*, Ticket *n*; (*Theater etc*) (Eintritts)karte *f*; (*an Ware*) (Preis)schild *n*; (*Lotterie*) Los *n*; (*Parkplatz*) Parkschein *m*; (*Falschparken etc*) Strafzettel *m* **ticket machine** S Fahrscheinautomat *m*, Parkscheinautomat *m* **ticket office** S BAHN Fahrkartenschalter *m*; THEAT Kasse *f*

tickle [ˈtɪkl] V/T kitzeln

tide [taɪd] S Gezeiten *pl*; **the ~ is in/out** es ist Flut/Ebbe

tidy [ˈtaɪdɪ] 1 ADJ ordentlich 2 V/T aufräumen **tidy up** V/T & V/I aufräumen

tie [taɪ] 1 S Krawatte *f*; SPORT Unentschieden *n*; (*Beziehung*) Bindung *f* 2 V/T (*festmachen*) binden (*to* an *+akk*); (*Hände etc*) zusammenbinden; (*Knoten*) machen **tie up** V/T (*Tier*) anbinden; (*Paket*) verschnüren; (*Schnürsenkel*) binden; (*Boot*) festmachen

tiger [ˈtaɪgər] S Tiger *m*

tight [taɪt] 1 ADJ (*Kleidung*) eng; (*Knoten*) fest; (*Deckel etc*) fest sitzend; (*Kontrolle*) streng; (*zeitlich*) knapp; (*Zeitplan*) eng; *umg* **that's ~** das ist toll/cool 2 ADV (*schließen*) fest; (*ziehen*) stramm; **sleep ~** schlaf gut! **tighten** V/T (*Schraube*) anziehen; (*Gürtel*) enger machen; (*Kontrolle*) verschärfen

tile [taɪl] S Dachziegel *m*; (*Fußboden, Wand*) Fliese *f*

till [tɪl] PRÄP & KONJ → until

tilt [tɪlt] 1 V/T kippen; (*Kopf*) neigen 2 V/I sich neigen

timber [ˈtɪmbər] S (Bau)holz *n*

time [taɪm] 1 S Zeit *f*; (*Gele-*

genheit) Mal *n*; MUS Takt *m*; **what ~ is it?, what's the ~?** wie spät ist es?, wie viel Uhr ist es?; **take one's ~ (with sth)** sich (bei etw) Zeit lassen; **have a good ~** Spaß haben; **in two weeks' ~** in zwei Wochen; **at ~s** manchmal; **at the same ~** gleichzeitig; **all the ~** die ganze Zeit; **by the ~ he ...** bis er ...; *(zurückliegend)* als er ...; **for the ~ being** vorläufig; **in ~** rechtzeitig; **on ~** pünktlich; **this ~** diesmal; **five ~s six** fünf mal sechs; **four ~s a year** viermal im Jahr; **three at a ~** drei auf einmal **2** V/T *(mit Stoppuhr)* stoppen **time difference** S Zeitunterschied *m* **timer** S Timer *m*, Schaltuhr *f* **timetable** S Fahrplan *m* **time zone** S Zeitzone *f*

timid ['tımәd] ADJ ängstlich

tin [tın] S Blech *n* **tinfoil** S Alufolie *f*

tinsel ['tınsәl] S = Lametta *n*

tinted ['tıntәd] ADJ getönt

tiny ['taını] ADJ winzig

tip [tıp] **1** S Trinkgeld *n*; *(Hinweis)* Tipp *m*; *(spitzes Ende)* Spitze *f*; *(Zigarette)* Filter *m* **2** V/T Trinkgeld geben *+dat* **tip over** V/T & V/I umkippen

tipsy ['tıpsı] ADJ beschwipst

tiptoe ['tıptoʊ] S **on ~** auf Zehenspitzen

tire ['taır] **1** S Reifen *m* **2** V/T müde machen **3** V/I müde werden **tired** ADJ müde; **be ~ of doing sth** es satthaben, etw zu tun

tire pressure ['taırpreʃәr] S Reifendruck *m*

tiresome ['taırsәm] ADJ lästig

tiring ADJ ermüdend

tissue ['tıʃu:] S ANAT Gewebe *n*; *(aus Zellstoff)* Papier(taschen)tuch *n*

title ['taıtl] S Titel *m*

TM *abk* = trademark Marke *f*

TN *abk* = Tennessee

to [tu:, tә, tʊ] PRÄP **zu**; *(mit Namen etc)* nach; *(räumlich, zeitlich)* bis; *(mit Verb im Infinitiv)* zu; *(vor Uhrzeit)* vor; **~ Seattle/Iraq** nach Seattle/in den Irak; **I've been ~ Miami** ich war schon mal in Miami; **go ~ the theater** ins Theater gehen; **he came ~ say sorry** er kam, um sich zu entschuldigen

toast [toʊst] **1** S Toast *m*; **propose a ~ to sb** einen Toast auf j-n ausbringen **2** V/T *(Brot)* toasten; *(bei Feier)* trinken auf *+akk* **toaster** S Toaster *m*

tobacco ⟨-es *pl*⟩ [tә'bækoʊ] S Tabak *m*

toboggan [tә'bɑ:gәn] S Schlitten *m*

today [tә'deı] ADV heute; **a week from ~** heute in einer Woche; **~'s newspaper** die Zeitung von heute

toddler ['tɑ:dlәr] S Kleinkind *n*

toe [toʊ] S Zehe *f*, Zeh *m* **toe-**

nail S Zehennagel *m*
tofu ['toʊfu:] S Tofu *m*
together [tə'geðər] ADV zusammen
toilet ['tɔɪlət] S Toilette *f* **toilet paper** S Toilettenpapier *n* **toiletries** ['tɔɪlətrɪz] S PL Toilettenartikel *pl*
token ['toʊkən] S Marke *f*; (*als Geschenk*) Gutschein *m*; (*Gegenstand, der etw ausdrückt*) Zeichen *n*
told [toʊld] *prät, pperf von* **tell**
tolerant ['tɑ:lərənt] ADJ tolerant (*of* gegenüber) **tolerate** ['tɑ:ləreɪt] V/T tolerieren; ertragen
toll [toʊl] S Gebühr *f* **toll-free** ADJ & ADV TEL gebührenfrei **toll road** S gebührenpflichtige Straße
tomato ⟨-es *pl*⟩ [tə'meɪtoʊ] S Tomate *f*
tomb [tu:m] S Grabmal *n* **tombstone** S Grabstein *m*
tomorrow [tə'mɔ:roʊ] ADV morgen; **~ morning/evening** morgen früh/Abend; **the day after ~** übermorgen
ton [tʌn] S Tonne *f* (*907 kg*); **~s of books** *umg* eine Menge Bücher
tongue [tʌŋ] S Zunge *f*
tonic (water) ['tɑ:nɪk(wɔ:tər)] S Tonic *n*
tonight [tə'naɪt] ADV heute Abend; heute Nacht
tonsillitis [tɑ:nsə'laɪtəs] S Mandelentzündung *f* **tonsils** ['tɑ:nslz] S PL Mandeln *pl*
too [tu:] ADV zu; (*ebenfalls*) auch; **~ much/many** zu viel/viele; **me ~** ich auch
took [tʊk] *prät von* **take**
tool [tu:l] S Werkzeug *n* **toolbar** S IT Symbolleiste *f*
tooth ⟨teeth⟩ [tu:θ, ti:θ] S Zahn *m* **toothache** ['tu:θeɪk] S Zahnschmerzen *pl* **toothbrush** S Zahnbürste *f* **toothpaste** S Zahnpasta *f*
top [tɑ:p] **1** S Spitze *f*; (*Berg*) Gipfel *m*; (*Baum*) Krone *f*; (*Straße*) oberes Ende; (*Tube, Schreibstift*) Kappe *f*; (*Kiste etc*) Deckel *m*; (*Bikini*) Oberteil *n*; (*Kleidungsstück*) Top *n*; **at the ~ of the page** oben auf der Seite; **on ~** oben; **on ~ of** auf *+dat*; (*als Dreingabe etc*) zusätzlich zu **2** ADJ (*Stockwerk etc*) oberste(r, s); (*Preis etc*) höchste(r, s); (*beste(r, s)*) Spitzen-; (*Schüler etc*) beste(r, s) **3** V/T übersteigen; übertreffen; (*in Liga*) an erster Stelle liegen in *+dat*; **~ped with cream** mit Sahne obendrauf **top up** V/T auffüllen; (*Handykarte etc*) aufladen
topic ['tɑ:pɪk] S Thema *n* **topical** ADJ aktuell
topless ['tɑ:pləs] ADJ & ADV oben ohne
topping ['tɑ:pɪŋ] S Belag *m*, Garnierung *f*
tore [tɔ:r] *prät von* **tear**
torment [tɔ:r'ment] V/T quälen

torn [tɔ:rn] *pperf von* tear
tornado ⟨-es *pl*⟩ [tɔ:r'neɪdoʊ] S Tornado *m*
torrential [tə'renʃəl] ADJ (*Regen*) sintflutartig
tortoise ['tɔ:rtəs] S Schildkröte *f*
torture ['tɔ:rtʃər] **1** S Folter *f*; *fig* Qual *f* **2** VT foltern
toss [tɒ:s] VT (*Ball etc*) werfen; (*Salat*) anmachen
total ['toʊtl] **1** S Gesamtsumme *f*; **a ~ of 30** insgesamt 30; **in ~** insgesamt **2** ADJ total; Gesamt- **3** VT sich belaufen auf *+akk*; (*Auto*) zu Schrott fahren; **be ~ed** einen Totalschaden haben **totally** ADV total
touch [tʌtʃ] **1** S Berührung *f*; Tastsinn *m*; (*von Ironie, Traurigkeit*) Spur *f*; **be/keep in ~ with sb** mit j-m in Verbindung stehen/bleiben; **get in ~ with sb** sich mit j-m in Verbindung setzen **2** VT berühren; (*emotional*) bewegen **touchdown** S FLUG Landung *f*; (*in Football*) Touchdown *m* **touching** ADJ rührend **touch screen** S Touchscreen *m* **touchy** ADJ empfindlich, zickig
tough [tʌf] ADJ hart; (*Material*) robust; (*Fleisch*) zäh
tour [tʊr] **1** S Tour *f* (*of* durch); Rundgang *m* (*of* durch); (*Popgruppe etc*) Tournee *f* **2** VT eine Tour/einen Rundgang/eine Tournee machen durch **3** VI (*Urlaub etc*) umherreisen **tour guide** S Reiseleiter(in) *m(f)*
tourism ['tʊrɪzəm] S Tourismus *m*, Fremdenverkehr *m*
tourist S Tourist(in) *m(f*
tourist guide S (*Buch*) Reiseführer *m*; (*Person*) Fremdenführer(in) *m(f)* **tourist office** S Fremdenverkehrsamt *n*
tournament ['tʊrnəmənt] S Turnier *n*
tour operator ['tʊrɑ:pəreɪtər] S Reiseveranstalter *m*
tow [toʊ] VT abschleppen; (*Anhänger etc*) ziehen
toward(s) [tə'wɔ:rd(z) twɔ:rd(z)] PRÄP auf … zu; **we walked ~ the station** wir gingen in Richtung Bahnhof; **my feelings ~ him** meine Gefühle ihm gegenüber
tow-away zone ['toʊəweɪzoʊn] S Halteverbotszone *f* (*in der geparkte Wagen von der Polizei abgeschleppt werden*)
towel ['taʊəl] S Handtuch *n*
tower ['taʊər] S Turm *m*
towing service ['toʊɪŋ sɜ:rvəs] S Pannendienst *m*
town [taʊn] S Stadt *f* **town hall** S Rathaus *n*
towrope ['toʊroʊp] S Abschleppseil *n* **tow truck** S Abschleppwagen *m*
toxic ['tɑ:ksɪk] ADJ giftig, Gift-
toy [tɔɪ] S Spielzeug *n*
trace [treɪs] **1** S Spur *f* **2** VT ausfindig machen
track [træk] S (*von Tier, Reifen etc*) Spur *f*; (*Pfad*) Weg *m*,

BAHN Bahnsteig *m*; Gleis *n*; (*auf CD*) Stück *n* **track and field** [trækən'fi:ld] S Leichtathletik *f* **track down** V/T ausfindig machen **tracksuit** S Trainingsanzug *m*

tractor ['træktər] S Traktor *m* **tractor trailer** S Sattelschlepper *m*

trade [treɪd] **1** S Handel *m*; Branche *f*; Geschäft *n*; (*Beruf, Gewerbe*) Handwerk *n* **2** V/I handeln (*in* mit) **3** V/T tauschen (*for* gegen) **trademark** S Marke *f*

tradition [trə'dɪʃən] S Tradition *f* **traditional**, **traditionally** ADJ & ADV traditionell

traffic ['træfɪk] S Verkehr *m*; *pej* (*mit Drogen*) Handel *m* (*in* mit) **traffic circle** S Kreisverkehr *m* **traffic cop** S *umg* Verkehrspolizist(in) *m(f)* **traffic jam** S Stau *m* **traffic light** S Verkehrsampel *f*

tragedy ['trædʒədɪ] S Tragödie *f* **tragic** ['trædʒɪk] ADJ tragisch

trail [treɪl] **1** S Spur *f*; (*Pfad*) Weg *m* **2** V/T (*Verbrecher*) verfolgen; (*Wohnwagen etc*) schleppen; (*Spur etc*) hinter sich herziehen; SPORT zurückliegen hinter *+dat* **3** V/I (*auf dem Boden etc*) schleifen; SPORT weit zurückliegen

trailer S Anhänger *m*; Wohnwagen *m*; FILM Trailer *m* **trailer park** S Wohnwagenpark *m*

train [treɪn] **1** S BAHN Zug *m* **2** V/T (*Mitarbeiter etc*) ausbilden; SPORT trainieren **3** V/I SPORT trainieren; **~ as** (*od* **to be**) **a teacher** eine Ausbildung als Lehrer machen **trained** ADJ ausgebildet **trainee** S Auszubildende(r) *m/f(m)*; Praktikant(in) *m(f)* **trainer** S SPORT Trainer(in) *m(f)* **training** S Ausbildung *f*; SPORT Training *n*

train station S Bahnhof *m*

tranquilizer ['træŋkwəlaɪzər] S Beruhigungsmittel *n*

transaction [træn'zækʃən] S Geschäft *n*

transatlantic [trænzət'læntɪk] ADJ transatlantisch, Transatlantik-

transfer **1** ['trænsfɜ:r] S (*Geld*) Überweisung *f*; Umsteigekarte *f*; (*im Beruf*) Versetzung *f* **2** [træns'fɜ:r] V/T (*Geld*) überweisen (*to sb* an j-n); (*Patient*) verlegen; (*Mitarbeiter*) versetzen; SPORT transferieren **3** [træns'fɜ:r] V/I (*bei Reise*) umsteigen

transferable [træns'fɜ:rəbl] ADJ übertragbar

transform [træns'fɔ:rm] V/T umwandeln **transformation** [trænsfər'meɪʃən] S Umwandlung *f*

transfusion [træns'fju:ʒən] S Transfusion *f*

transition [træn'zɪʃən] S Übergang *m* (*from ... to* von ... zu)

translate [trænz'leɪt, 'trænzleɪt] V/T & V/I übersetzen **translation** [trænz'leɪʃən] S Übersetzung *f* **translator** [trænz'leɪtər, 'trænzleɪtər] S Übersetzer(in) *m(f)*
transparent [træns'pærənt] ADJ durchsichtig
transplant MED **1** [træns'plænt] V/T transplantieren **2** ['trænsplænt] S Transplantation *f*
transport **1** ['trænspɔːrt] S Beförderung *f* **2** [træns'pɔːrt] V/T befördern, transportieren **transportation** [trænspɔːr'teɪʃən] S Beförderung *f*; **public ~** öffentliche Verkehrsmittel *pl*
trap [træp] **1** S Falle *f* **2** V/T **be ~ped** (*im Schnee, in Job etc*) festsitzen
trash [træʃ] S Schund *m*; (*Müll*) Abfall *m* **trash can** S Abfalleimer *m* **trashy** ADJ kitschig, Schund-
traumatic [trɔː'mætɪk] ADJ traumatisch
travel ['trævl] **1** S Reisen *n* **2** V/I reisen **3** V/T (*Entfernung*) zurücklegen; (*Land*) bereisen **travel agency** S Reisebüro *n* **traveler** S Reisende(r) *m/f(m)* **traveler's check** S Reisescheck *m*
tray [treɪ] S Tablett *n*; (*für Post etc*) Ablage *f*
tread [tred] S (*Reifen*) Profil *n* **tread on** ⟨trod, trodden⟩ [tred, trɑːd, 'trɑːdən] V/T treten auf *+akk*
treasure ['treʒər] **1** S Schatz *m* **2** V/T schätzen
treat [triːt] **1** S besondere Freude; **it's my ~** das geht auf meine Kosten **2** V/T behandeln; **~ sb (to sth)** j-n (zu etw) einladen; **~ oneself to sth** sich etw gönnen **treatment** ['triːtmənt] S Behandlung *f*
treaty ['triːtɪ] S Vertrag *m*
tree [triː] S Baum *m*
tremble ['trembl] V/I zittern
tremendous [trə'mendəs] ADJ gewaltig; *umg* toll
trend [trend] S Tendenz *f*, Mode *f*, Trend *m*
trespass ['trespæs] V/I **'no ~ing'** „Betreten verboten"
trial ['traɪəl] S JUR Prozess *m*; (*Test*) Versuch *m*, Probe *f*
triangle ['traɪæŋgl] S Dreieck *n*; MUS Triangel *f* **triangular** [traɪ'æŋgjʊlər] ADJ dreieckig
tribe [traɪb] S Stamm *m*
trick [trɪk] **1** S Trick *m*; Streich *m* **2** V/T hereinlegen **tricky** ['trɪkɪ] ADJ schwierig, heikel; (*Lage*) verzwickt
trigger ['trɪgər] **1** S (*von Gewehr*) Abzug *m* **2** V/T auslösen
trim [trɪm] V/T (*Haare*) nachschneiden; (*Nägel*) schneiden; (*Hecke*) stutzen **trimmings** S PL Verzierungen *pl*; Zubehör *n*; GASTR Beilagen *pl*
trip [trɪp] **1** S Reise *f*; (*kurz*) Ausflug *m* **2** V/I stolpern (*over*

über *+akk)*
triple ['trɪpl] **1** ADJ dreifach **2** ADV dreimal so viel **3** V/I sich verdreifachen
tripod ['traɪpɑ:d] S Stativ *n*
triumph ['traɪəmf] S Triumph *m*
trivial ['trɪvɪəl] ADJ trivial
trod [trɑ:d] *prät von* **tread**
trodden ['trɑ:dn] *pperf von* **tread**
trolley ['trɑ:lɪ] S Straßenbahn *f*
trooper ['tru:pər] S Staatspolizist(in) *m(f)*; berittene(r) Polizist(in) **troops** [tru:ps] S PL MIL Truppen *pl*
trophy ['troʊfɪ] S Trophäe *f*
tropical ['trɑ:pɪkl] ADJ tropisch
trouble ['trʌbl] **1** S Schwierigkeiten *pl*, Sorgen *pl*; *(Anstrengung)* Mühe *f*; *(Aufruhr)* Unruhen *pl*; MED Beschwerden *pl*; **get into ~** Ärger bekommen **2** V/T beunruhigen; stören **troubled** ADJ beunruhigt **trouble-free** ADJ problemlos
trout [traʊt] S Forelle *f*
truck [trʌk] S Lastwagen *m* **trucker** S Lastwagenfahrer(in) *m(f)* **truck farm** S Gemüsegärtnerei *f* **truck lane** S Kriechspur *f* **truck stop** S Fernfahrerraststätte *f*
true [tru:] ADJ wahr; echt
truly ['tru:lɪ] ADV wirklich; **Yours ~** *(am Briefende)* mit freundlichen Grüßen
trumpet ['trʌmpɪt] S Trompete *f*
trunk [trʌŋk] S *(von Baum)* Stamm *m*; AUTO Kofferraum *m*; ANAT Rumpf *m*; *(von Elefant)* Rüssel *m*; *(großer Koffer)* Überseekoffer *m* **trunks** S PL Badehose *f*
trust [trʌst] **1** S Vertrauen *n* *(in zu)* **2** V/T vertrauen *+dat* **trustworthy** ADJ vertrauenswürdig
truth [tru:θ] S Wahrheit *f* **truthful** ADJ ehrlich; *(Aussage)* wahrheitsgemäß
try [traɪ] **1** S Versuch *m* **2** V/T versuchen; ausprobieren; *(Essen etc)* probieren; JUR vor Gericht stellen; *(Geduld etc)* auf die Probe stellen **3** V/I versuchen; sich bemühen **try on** V/T anprobieren **try out** V/T ausprobieren
T-shirt ['ti:ʃɜ:rt] S T-Shirt *n*
tub [tʌb] S Becher *m*; Badewanne *f*
tube [tu:b] S Rohr *n*; *(aus Gummi etc)* Schlauch *m*; *(Zahnpasta)* Tube *f*; *umg* Glotze *f*
tuck [tʌk] V/T *(etw in etw)* stecken
Tue(s) *abk* = Tuesday; Di.
Tuesday ['tu:zdeɪ] S Dienstag *m*; **(on) ~** (am) Dienstag; **(on) ~s** dienstags; **this/last/next/every ~** diesen/letzten/nächsten/jeden Dienstag; **(on) ~ morning/afternoon/evening** (am) Dienstagmorgen/-nach-

mittag/-abend

tug [tʌg] **1** vt ziehen **2** vi ziehen (*at* an *+dat*)

tuition [tuː'ɪʃən] s Studiengebühren *pl*; Unterricht *m*

tulip ['tuːlɪp] s Tulpe *f*

tumble ['tʌmbl] vi fallen

tummy ['tʌmɪ] s *umg* Bauch *m*

tumor ['tuːmər] s Tumor *m*

tuna ['tuːnə] s Thunfisch *m*

tune [tuːn] **1** s Melodie *f*; **be in/out of ~** (*Instrument*) gestimmt/verstimmt sein; (*Sänger*) richtig/falsch singen **2** vt (*Instrument*) stimmen; (*Radio etc*) einstellen (*to* auf *+akk*)

tunnel ['tʌnl] s Tunnel *m*; Unterführung *f*

turbulence ['tɜːrbjələns] s FLUG Turbulenzen *pl*

turkey ['tɜːrkɪ] s Truthahn *m*

Turkey ['tɜːrkɪ] s die Türkei

turmoil ['tɜːrmɔɪl] s Aufruhr *m*

turn [tɜːrn] **1** s Drehung *f*; **make a left ~** nach links abbiegen; **it's your ~** du bist dran/Sie sind dran; **in ~** abwechselnd; **take ~s** sich abwechseln **2** vt drehen; umdrehen; (*um Ecke*) biegen um; (*Seite*) umblättern; (*umändern*) verwandeln (*into* in *+akk*) **3** vi sich drehen; sich umdrehen; (*Fahrer, Auto etc*) abbiegen; (*Zustand verändern*) werden; (*Wetter*) umschlagen; **~ into sth** sich in etw *akk* verwandeln; **~ left/right** links/rechts abbiegen **turn around** **1** vt umdrehen **2** vi sich umdrehen; (*unterwegs*) umkehren **turn away** vt (*j-n, etw*) abweisen **turn back** **1** vt (*j-n, etw*) zurückweisen **2** vi (*auf Wanderung etc*) umkehren **turn down** vt (*Angebot etc*) ablehnen; (*Fernseher etc*) leiser stellen; (*Heizung*) kleiner stellen **turn off** **1** vi abbiegen **2** vt (*Gerät*) ausschalten; (*Hahn*) zudrehen; (*Maschine, den Strom*) abstellen; **turn sb off** j-n abtörnen **turn on** vt (*Gerät*) einschalten; (*Wasserhahn*) aufdrehen; (*Maschine, den Strom*) anstellen; *umg* (*Aussehen etc*) anmachen, antörnen **turn out** **1** vt (*das Licht*) ausmachen; (*seine Taschen*) leeren **2** vi sich entwickeln; **as it turned out** wie sich herausstellte **turn over** **1** vt umdrehen **2** vi sich umdrehen; (*Auto*) sich überschlagen **turn to** vt sich zuwenden *+dat* **turn up** **1** vi auftauchen **2** vt (*Radio etc*) lauter stellen; (*Heizung*) höher stellen **turning point** s Wendepunkt *m*

turnip ['tɜːrnəp] s Rübe *f*

turnout ['tɜːrnaʊt] s Beteiligung *f*; (*für Auto*) Haltebucht *f* **turnpike** ['tɜːrnpaɪk] s gebührenpflichtige Autobahn **turn signal** s AUTO Blinker

m
turquoise ['tɜːrkwɔɪz] ADJ türkis
turtle ['tɜːrtl] S Schildkröte *f*
turtleneck (sweater) S Rollkragenpullover *m*
tutor ['tuːtər] **1** S Privatlehrer(in) *m(f)* **2** V/T **~ sb** j-m Privatunterricht/Nachhilfe geben
tux [tʌks], **tuxedo** ⟨-s *pl*⟩ [tʌk'siːdoʊ] S Smoking *m*
TV [tiː'viː] **1** S Fernsehen *n*; (*Gerät*) Fernseher *m*; **watch ~** fernsehen; **on ~** im Fernsehen **2** ADJ Fernseh-; **~ dinner** Fertiggericht *n*
tweet [twiːt] **1** S eine Nachricht auf Twitter® (*Internetdienst zum Versand von Textnachrichten*) **2** V/I twittern
tweezers ['twiːzərz] S PL Pinzette *f*
twelfth [twelfθ] ADJ zwölfte(r, s); → **eighth twelve** [twelv] **1** NUM zwölf **2** S Zwölf *f*; → eight
twentieth ['twentɪəθ] ADJ zwanzigste(r, s); → eighth
twenty ['twentɪ] **1** NUM zwanzig **2** S Zwanzig *f*; → eight, eighty
twice [twaɪs] ADV zweimal; **~ as much/many** doppelt so viel/viele
twig [twɪg] S Zweig *m*
twilight ['twaɪlaɪt] S Dämmerung *f*
twin [twɪn] **1** S Zwilling *m* **2** ADJ Zwillings-; **~ beds** zwei Einzelbetten
twinkle ['twɪŋkl] V/I funkeln
twist [twɪst] V/T drehen, winden; (*Wahrheit*) verdrehen; **I've ~ed my ankle** ich bin mit dem Fuß umgeknickt
twister S *umg* Wirbelsturm *m*, Tornado *m*
twitter ['twɪtər] V/I & V/T *umg* (*Vogel*) zwitschern; IT twittern
Twitter® ['twɪtər] *Eigenname* Twitter® (*Internetdienst zum Versand von Textnachrichten*)
two [tuː] **1** NUM zwei; **break sth in ~** etw in zwei Teile brechen **2** S Zwei *f*; **the ~ of them** die beiden; → eight
two-way ADJ **~ traffic** Gegenverkehr *m*
TX *abk* = Texas
tycoon [taɪ'kuːn] S Industriemagnat *m*
type [taɪp] S Typ *m*; Art *f*; Schrift(art) *f*
typical ['tɪpɪkəl] ADJ typisch (*of* für)

U

UFO [juːef'oʊ] *abk* = unidentified flying object; Ufo *n*
ugly ['ʌglɪ] ADJ hässlich
ulcer ['ʌlsər] S Geschwür *n*
ultimate ['ʌltəmət] ADJ letzte(r, s); (*Autorität*) höchste(r, s)

ultimately ADV letzten Endes; schließlich **ultrasound** ['ʌltrəsaʊnd] S MED Ultraschall *m* **umbrella** [ʌm'brelə] S Schirm *m* **umpire** ['ʌmpaɪr] S Schiedsrichter(in) *m(f)* **umpteen** ['ʌmpti:n] NUM *umg* zig; **~ times** zigmal **UN** S SG *abk* = United Nations; VN (= *Vereinte Nationen*) **unable** [ʌn'eɪbl] ADJ unfähig; **be ~ to do sth** etw nicht tun können **unacceptable** [ʌnək'septəbl] ADJ inakzeptabel, unannehmbar **unanimous** [ju:'nænəməs] ADJ & ADV einmütig **unattached** [ʌnə'tætʃt] ADJ ungebunden **unattended** [ʌnə'tendəd] ADJ unbeaufsichtigt **unauthorized** [ʌn'ɔ:θəraɪzd] ADJ unbefugt **unavailable** [ʌnə'veɪləbl] ADJ nicht erhältlich; (*Person*) nicht erreichbar **unavoidable** [ʌnə'vɔɪdəbl] ADJ unvermeidlich **unaware** [ʌnə'wer] ADJ **be ~ of sth** sich einer Sache *gen* nicht bewusst sein **unbearable** [ʌn'berəbl] ADJ unerträglich **unbeatable** [ʌn'bi:təbl] ADJ unschlagbar **unbelievable** [ʌnbɪ'li:vəbl] ADJ unglaublich **uncertain** [ʌn'sɜ:rtən] ADJ unsicher **uncle** ['ʌŋkl] S Onkel *m* **Uncle Sam** S die USA; die Regierung der USA; **pay ~ (taxes)** Steuern bezahlen **uncomfortable** [ʌn'kʌmfərtəbl] ADJ unbequem **unconscious** [ʌn'kɑ:nʃəs] ADJ MED bewusstlos **uncover** [ʌn'kʌvər] V/T aufdecken **undecided** [ʌndɪ'saɪdəd] ADJ unschlüssig **under** ['ʌndər] **1** PRÄP unter *+dat*; (*mit Bewegung*) unter *+akk*; (*mit Zeit, Summe*) weniger als **2** ADV unten; darunter; **children aged eight and ~** Kinder bis zu acht Jahren **underage** [ʌndər'eɪdʒ] ADJ minderjährig **undercarriage** ['ʌndərkærɪdʒ] S Fahrgestell *n* **underdone** [ʌndər'dʌn] ADJ GASTR nicht gar/durch **underestimate** [ʌndər'estəmeɪt] V/T unterschätzen **undergo** [ʌndər'goʊ] *irr* V/T (*Erfahrung*) durchmachen; (*einer Operation, einem Test*) sich unterziehen *+dat* **underground** ['ʌndərgraʊnd] ADJ unterirdisch **underline** [ʌndər'laɪn] V/T unterstreichen **underneath** [ʌndər'ni:θ] **1** PRÄP unter *+dat*; (*mit Bewegung, Richtung*) unter *+akk* **2** ADV darunter **underpants** ['ʌndərpænts] S PL Unterhose *f* **undershirt** ['ʌndərʃɜ:rt] S Unterhemd *n* **undershorts** ['ʌndərʃɔ:rts] S PL Unterhose *f* **understand** ⟨understood,

understood› [ʌndər'stænd, ʌndər'stʊd] *irr* V/T & V/I verstehen; **I ~ that …** (*weiß*) ich habe gehört, dass …; (*verstehe*) ich habe Verständnis dafür, dass …; **make oneself understood** sich verständlich machen **understanding** ADJ verständnisvoll

undertake [ʌndər'teɪk] *irr* V/T sich verpflichten; (*Aufgabe*) übernehmen **undertaker** ['ʌndərteɪkər] S Leichenbestatter(in) *m(f)*; Bestattungsinstitut *n* **underwater** 1 [ʌndər'wɔːtər] ADV unter Wasser 2 ['ʌndərwɔːtər] ADJ Unterwasser- **underwear** ['ʌndərwer] S Unterwäsche *f*

undo [ʌn'duː] *irr* V/T (*Schnürsenkel etc*) aufmachen; (*j-s Arbeit*) zunichtemachen; IT rückgängig machen **undoubtedly** [ʌn'daʊtədlɪ] ADV zweifellos **undress** [ʌn'dres] 1 V/T ausziehen 2 V/I sich ausziehen **uneasy** [ʌn'iːzɪ] ADJ unbehaglich **unemployed** [ʌnɪm'plɔɪd] 1 ADJ arbeitslos 2 S PL **the ~** die Arbeitslosen *pl* **unemployment** [ʌnɪm'plɔɪmənt] S Arbeitslosigkeit *f* **unequal** [ʌn'iːkwəl] ADJ ungleich **uneven** [ʌn'iːvən] ADJ uneben; (*Wettkampf*) ungleich **unexpected** [ʌnɪk'spektəd] ADJ unerwartet **unfamiliar** [ʌnfə'mɪljər] ADJ **be ~ with sb/sth** j-n/etw nicht kennen

unfasten [ʌn'fɑːsn] V/T aufmachen **unfit** [ʌn'fɪt] ADJ ungeeignet (*for* für); nicht fit **unforeseen** [ʌnfɔːr'siːn] ADJ unvorhergesehen **unforgettable** [ʌnfər'getəbl] ADJ unvergesslich **unfortunate** [ʌn'fɔːrtʃənət] ADJ unglücklich; bedauerlich **unfortunately** ADV leider **unfounded** [ʌn'faʊndəd] ADJ unbegründet **unhappy** [ʌn'hæpɪ] ADJ unglücklich; unzufrieden **unhealthy** [ʌn'helθɪ] ADJ ungesund **unheard-of** [ʌn'hɜːrdɑːv] ADJ gänzlich unbekannt; (*schockierend*) unerhört **unhurt** [ʌn'hɜːrt] ADJ unverletzt

uniform ['juːnəfɔːrm] 1 S Uniform *f* 2 ADJ einheitlich **unify** ['juːnəfaɪ] V/T vereinigen **unimportant** [ʌnɪm'pɔːrtənt] ADJ unwichtig **uninhabited** [ʌnɪn'hæbətəd] ADJ unbewohnt **uninstall** [ʌnɪn'stɒːl] V/T IT deinstallieren **unintentional** [ʌnɪn'tenʃənl] ADJ unabsichtlich

union ['juːnjən] S Vereinigung *f*; (*politisch*) Union *f*

unique [juː'niːk] ADJ einzigartig

unit ['juːnət] S Einheit *f*; (*von Maschine, System*) Teil *n*; (*in Schule*) Lektion *f*

unite [juː'naɪt] 1 V/T vereinigen; **the United Nations** *sg* die Vereinten Nationen *pl*; **the United States (of America)** *sg*

die Vereinigten Staaten (von Amerika) *pl* **2** VI sich vereinigen
universe ['ju:nɪvɜ:rs] S Universum *n*
university [ju:nɪ'vɜ:rsətɪ] S Universität *f*
unkind [ʌn'kaɪnd] ADJ unfreundlich (*to* zu) **unknown** [ʌn'noʊn] ADJ unbekannt (*to* +*dat*) **unleaded** [ʌn'ledəd] ADJ bleifrei
unless [ən'les] KONJ es sei denn, wenn ... nicht
unlicensed [ʌn'laɪsənst] ADJ (*Kneipe*) ohne Lizenz
unlike [ʌn'laɪk] PRÄP im Gegensatz zu; **it's ~ her to be late** es sieht ihr gar nicht ähnlich, zu spät zu kommen **unlikely** ADJ unwahrscheinlich
unload [ʌn'loʊd] V/T ausladen **unlock** [ʌn'lɑ:k] V/T aufschließen **unlucky** [ʌn'lʌkɪ] ADJ unglücklich; **be ~** Pech haben **unmistakable** [ʌnmə'steɪkəbl] ADJ unverkennbar **unnecessary** [ʌn'nesəserɪ] ADJ unnötig **unoccupied** [ʌn'ɑ:kjəpaɪd] ADJ frei; leer stehend **unpack** [ʌn'pæk] V/T & V/I auspacken **unpleasant** [ʌn'pleznt] ADJ unangenehm **unplug** [ʌn'plʌg] V/T den Stecker herausziehen von **unpredictable** [ʌnprə'dɪktəbl] ADJ unberechenbar **unreasonable** [ʌn'ri:znəbl] ADJ unvernünftig; (*Forderung*) übertrieben **unreliable** [ʌnrɪ'laɪəbl] ADJ unzuverlässig **unsafe** [ʌn'seɪf] ADJ nicht sicher; gefährlich **unscrew** [ʌn'skru:] V/T abschrauben **unsuccessful** [ʌnsək'sesfʊl] ADJ erfolglos **unsuitable** [ʌn'su:təbl] ADJ ungeeignet (*for* für)
until [ən'tɪl] **1** PRÄP bis; **not ~** erst **2** KONJ bis; **she won't come ~ you invite her** sie kommt erst, wenn du sie einlädst/wenn Sie sie einladen
unusual, unusually [ʌn'ju:ʒl, -ɪ] ADJ & ADV ungewöhnlich **unwanted** [ʌn'wɑ:ntəd] ADJ unerwünscht, ungewollt **unwell** [ʌn'wel] ADJ krank **unwilling** [ʌn'wɪlɪŋ] ADJ **be ~ to do sth** nicht bereit sein, etw zu tun **unwind** [ʌn'waɪnd] *irr* **1** V/T abwickeln **2** V/I (*abschalten*) sich entspannen **unwrap** [ʌn'ræp] V/T auspacken **unzip** [ʌn'zɪp] V/T den Reißverschluss aufmachen an +*dat*; IT entzippen
up [ʌp] **1** PRÄP **climb ~ a tree** einen Baum hinaufklettern; **go ~ the street/the stairs** die Straße entlanggehen/die Treppe hinaufgehen; **farther ~ the hill** weiter oben auf dem Berg **2** ADV oben; (*Richtung*) nach oben; (*aus dem Bett*) auf; **~ there** dort oben; **~ and down** (*gehen, hüpfen*) auf und ab; **what's ~?** *umg* was

ist los?; **~ to $100** bis zu 100 Dollar; **what's she ~ to?** was macht sie da?; (*bei Plan*) was hat sie vor?; **it's ~ to you** das liegt bei dir; **I don't feel ~ to it** ich fühle mich dem nicht gewachsen **update** **1** ['ʌpdeɪt] S Aktualisierung *f*, Update *n* **2** [ʌp'deɪt] V/T aktualisieren

upgrade [ʌp'greɪd] V/T (*Computer*) aufrüsten; **we were ~d** (*im Hotel*) das Hotel hat uns ein besseres Zimmer gegeben; (*Flug*) wir haben ein Upgrade bekommen **uphill** [ʌp'hɪl] ADV bergauf

upon [ə'pɑ:n] PRÄP → on

upper ['ʌpər] ADJ obere(r, s); Ober-

upright ['ʌpraɪt] ADJ & ADV aufrecht **uproar** ['ʌprɔ:r] S Aufruhr *m* **upset** [ʌp'set] **1** *irr* V/T umkippen; (*beunruhigen*) aufregen; (*traurig machen*) bestürzen; (*beleidigen*) kränken; (*Pläne*) durcheinanderbringen **2** ADJ (*beunruhigt*) aufgeregt; (*traurig*) bestürzt; (*beleidigt*) gekränkt; **~ stomach** ['ʌpset] Magenverstimmung *f* **upside down** [ʌpsaɪd'daʊn] ADV verkehrt herum; *fig* drunter und drüber **upstairs** [ʌp'sterz] ADV oben; nach oben **upstate** **1** ['ʌpsteɪt] ADJ **~ New York** im Norden des Staates New York **2** [ʌp'steɪt] ADV im Norden (des Bundesstaates); (*Richtung*) in den Norden (des Bundesstaates) **up-to-date** [ʌptə'deɪt] ADJ modern; aktuell; **keep sb ~** j-n auf dem Laufenden halten **uptown** **1** ['ʌptaʊn] ADJ im Norden (der Stadt); im Villenviertel **2** [ʌp'taʊn] ADV im Norden (der Stadt); im Villenviertel; (*Richtung*) in den Norden (der Stadt); ins Villenviertel

upward(s) ['ʌpwərd(z)] ADV nach oben

urban ['ɜr:bən] ADJ städtisch, Stadt-

urge [ɜ:rdʒ] **1** S Drang *m* **2** V/T drängen **urgent**, **urgently** ['ɜ:rdʒənt, -lɪ] ADJ & ADV dringend

urine ['jʊrɪn] S Urin *m*

us [ʌs] PRON uns; **it's ~** wir sind's; **both of ~** wir beide

US, **USA** S SG *abk* = United States (of America) USA *pl*

USB drive, **USB stick** S IT USB-Stick *m*

use **1** [ju:s] S Gebrauch *m*, Benutzung *f*; **it's no ~ (doing that)** es hat keinen Zweck(, das zu tun); **it's (of) no ~ to me** das kann ich nicht brauchen **2** [ju:z] V/T benutzen, gebrauchen; verwenden; (*Methode, Wissen*) anwenden **use up** V/T aufbrauchen **used** **1** [ju:zt] ADJ gebraucht **2** [ju:st] V/AUX **be ~ to sb/sth** an j-n/etw gewöhnt sein; **get ~ to sb/sth** sich an j-n/etw gewöhnen; **she ~ to live here** sie hat früher mal hier gewohnt **useful** ['ju:sfʊl] ADJ nützlich **useless** ['ju:sləs] ADJ nutzlos; unbrauchbar; (*Widerspruch*) zwecklos **user** ['ju:zər] S Benutzer(in) *m(f)* **user-friendly** ADJ benutzerfreundlich

usual ['ju:ʒʊəl] ADJ üblich, gewöhnlich **usually** ADV normalerweise

UT *abk* = Utah

utensil [ju:'tensl] S Gerät *n*

uterus ['ju:tərəs] S Gebärmutter *f*

utilize ['ju:təlaɪz] V/T verwenden

utterly ['ʌtərlɪ] ADV völlig

U-turn ['ju:tɜ:rn] S AUTO Wende *f*; **make a ~** wenden

V

VA *abk* = Virginia

vacancy ['veɪkənsɪ] S offene Stelle; (*Hotel*) freies Zimmer **vacant** ['veɪkənt] ADJ (*Zimmer, Toilette*) frei; (*Stelle*) offen; (*Haus*) leer stehend **vacate** [veɪ'keɪt] V/T räumen; (*Sitz*) frei machen

vacation [veɪ'keɪʃən] **1** S Ferien *pl*, Urlaub *m*; (*Universität*) (Semester)ferien *pl*; **go on ~** in Urlaub fahren **2** V/I Urlaub machen **vacationer** S Urlauber(in) *m(f)*

vaccinate ['væksəneɪt] V/T impfen **vaccination** [væksə'neɪʃən] S Impfung *f*

vacuum ['vækju:m] **1** S Vakuum *n* **2** V/T & V/I (staub)saugen **vacuum (cleaner)** S Staubsauger *m*

vagina [və'dʒaɪnə] S Scheide *f*

vague [veɪg] ADJ vage; (*Ähnlichkeit*) entfernt **vaguely** ADV in etwa, irgendwie

vain [veɪn] ADJ (*Versuch etc*) vergeblich; (*Mensch*) eitel; **in ~** vergeblich, umsonst

valet parking [væleɪ'pɑ:rkɪŋ] S Parkservice *m*

valid ['vælɪd] ADJ gültig; (*Grund etc*) stichhaltig

valley ['vælɪ] S Tal *n*

valuable ['væljʊbl] ADJ wertvoll; (*Zeit*) kostbar **valuables** S PL Wertsachen *pl* **value** ['vælju:] **1** S Wert *m* **2** V/T (*Freundschaft etc*) schätzen

valve [vælv] S Ventil *n*

van [væn] S AUTO Lieferwagen *m*

vanilla [və'nɪlə] S Vanille *f*

vanish ['vænɪʃ] V/I verschwinden

variable ['verɪəbl] ADJ unbeständig; (*Qualität*) unterschiedlich; (*Höhe etc*) regulierbar **varied** ['verɪd] ADJ vielseitig; (*Karriere*) bewegt; (*Arbeit, Ernährung*) abwechslungsreich

variety [və'raɪətɪ] S Abwechslung *f*, Vielfalt *f* (*of* an

+*dat*); (*Pflanzen, Tiere*) Art *f*
various ['veriəs] ADJ verschieden
varnish ['vɑ:rnɪʃ] **1** S Lack *m* **2** V/T lackieren
vary ['verɪ] **1** V/T verändern **2** V/I unterschiedlich sein; sich verändern; (*Preise etc*) schwanken
vase [veɪz] S Vase *f*
vast [væst] ADJ riesig; weit
VCR *abk* = video cassette recorder; Videorekorder *m*
VD *abk* = venereal disease; Geschlechtskrankheit *f*
veal [vi:l] S Kalbfleisch *n*
vegan ['vi:gən] **1** S Veganer(in) *m(f)* **2** ADJ vegan
vegetable ['vedʒtəbl] S Gemüse *n*
vegetarian [vedʒə'terɪən] **1** S Vegetarier(in) *m(f)* **2** ADJ vegetarisch
veggie ['vedʒɪ] *umg* **1** S Vegetarier(in) *m(f)*; Gemüse *n* **2** ADJ vegetarisch **veggieburger** S Veggieburger *m*, Gemüseburger *m*
vehicle ['vi:ɪkl] S Fahrzeug *n*
veil [veɪl] S Schleier *m*
vein [veɪn] S Ader *f*
Velcro® ['velkroʊ] S (*Verschluss*) Klettband *n*
velvet ['velvət] S Samt *m*
vending machine ['vendɪŋməʃi:n] S Automat *m*
venison ['venəsn] S Rehfleisch *n*
vent [vent] S Öffnung *f*
ventilation [ventə'leɪʃən] S Belüftung *f* **ventilator** ['ventəleɪtər] S Ventilator *m*; **be on a ~** künstlich beatmet werden
venture ['ventʃər] **1** S Unternehmung *f*; WIRTSCH Unternehmen *n* **2** V/I (sich) wagen
venue ['venju:] S Veranstaltungsort *m*
verb [vɜ:rb] S Verb *n*
verdict ['vɜ:rdɪkt] S Urteil *n*
verge [vɜ:rdʒ] **1** S Rand *m*; **be on the ~ of doing sth** im Begriff sein, etw zu tun **2** V/I **~ on** grenzen an +*akk*
verify ['verəfaɪ] V/T bestätigen; überprüfen
vermin ['vɜ:rmən] S PL Schädlinge *pl*, Ungeziefer *n*
verruca [ve'ru:kə] S Warze *f*
versatile ['vɜ:rsətəl] ADJ vielseitig
verse [vɜ:rs] S Poesie *f*; (*von Gedicht, Lied*) Strophe *f*
version ['vɜ:rʒən] S Version *f*
versus ['vɜ:rsəs] PRÄP gegen
vertical ['vɜ:rtɪkəl] ADJ senkrecht, vertikal
very ['verɪ] **1** ADV sehr; **~ much** sehr **2** ADJ genau; **at that ~ moment** gerade in dem Augenblick; **at the ~ top** ganz oben; **the ~ best** der/die/das Allerbeste
vest [vest] S Weste *f*
vet [vet] **1** S Tierarzt *m*, Tierärztin *f* **2** *abk* = veteran; Veteran(in) *m(f)*

veteran ['vetərən] **1** S Veteran(in) (m(f) **2** ADJ erfahren; altgedient
veterinarian [vetrə'neriən] S Tierarzt m, Tierärztin f
via ['viːə] PRÄP über +akk
vibe [vaɪb] S Atmosphäre f; (Ahnung) Gefühl n
vibrate [vaɪ'breɪt] V/I vibrieren
vice [vaɪs] **1** S Laster n **2** PRÄF Vize-, stellvertretend
vice versa [vaɪs'vɜːrsə] ADV umgekehrt
vicinity [vɪ'sɪnətɪ] S **in the ~** in der Nähe (of +gen)
vicious ['vɪʃəs] ADJ brutal; gemein **vicious circle** S Teufelskreis m
victim ['vɪktəm] S Opfer n
victory ['vɪktərɪ] S Sieg m
video ⟨-s pl⟩ ['vɪdɪoʊ] **1** ADJ Video- **2** S Video n **video camera** S Videokamera f **video cassette** S Videokassette f **video recorder** S Videorekorder m **videotape** **1** S Videoband n **2** V/T (auf Video) aufnehmen
Vienna [vɪ'enə] S Wien n
Vietnam [viːet'næm] S Vietnam n
view [vjuː] **1** S Blick m (of auf +akk), Aussicht f; (über etw) Meinung f **2** V/T betrachten; (Haus) besichtigen **viewer** S TV Zuschauer(in) m(f) **viewpoint** S fig Standpunkt m
village ['vɪlɪdʒ] S Dorf n
villain ['vɪlən] S Schurke m; (in Film etc) Bösewicht m
vinegar ['vɪnɪgər] S Essig m
vineyard ['vɪnjərd] S Weinberg m
vintage ['vɪntɪdʒ] S (von Wein) Jahrgang m
violate ['vaɪəleɪt] V/T (Abkommen) brechen; (Rechte, Regeln) verletzen
violence ['vaɪləns] S Gewalt f; (von Person) Gewalttätigkeit f
violent ADJ brutal; (Tod) gewaltsam
violin [vaɪə'lɪn] S Geige f, Violine f
virgin ['vɜːrdʒən] S Jungfrau f
Virgo ['vɜːrgoʊ] S ASTROL Jungfrau f
virtual ['vɜːrtʃʊəl] ADJ IT virtuell **virtually** ADV praktisch
virtue ['vɜːrtʃuː] S Tugend f
virus ['vaɪrəs] S MED, IT Virus n
visa ['viːzə] S Visum n
visibility [vɪzə'bɪlətɪ] S METEO Sichtweite f **visible** ['vɪzəbl] ADJ sichtbar; sichtlich **visibly** ADV sichtlich
vision ['vɪʒən] S Sehvermögen n; (Voraussicht) Weitblick m; (Traum, Fantasie) Vision f
visit ['vɪzət] **1** S Besuch m, Aufenthalt m **2** V/T besuchen **visiting hours** S PL Besuchszeiten pl **visitor** S Besucher(in) m(f); **~s' book** Gästebuch n
visual ['vɪʒʊəl] ADJ Seh-; visuell **visualize** V/T sich vorstel-

len **visually** ADV visuell; **~ impaired** sehbehindert
vital ['vaɪtl] ADJ unerlässlich, wesentlich; (*Moment etc*) entscheidend **vitally** ADV äußerst
vitamin ['vaɪtəmən] S Vitamin *n*
vivid ['vɪvəd] ADJ anschaulich; (*Fantasie etc*) lebhaft
V-neck ['vi:nek] S V-Ausschnitt *m*
vocabulary [voʊ'kæbjəlerɪ] S Wortschatz *m*, Vokabular *n*
vocal ['voʊkəl] ADJ Stimm-; Gesangs-; (*Protest*) lautstark
vocation [voʊ'keɪʃən] S Berufung *f* **vocational** ADJ Berufs-; **~ college/school** Berufsschule *f*
vodka ['vɑ:dkə] S Wodka *m*
voice [vɔɪs] **1** S Stimme *f* **2** V/T äußern
void [vɔɪd] **1** S Leere *f* **2** ADJ JUR ungültig
volcano <-es *pl*> [vɑ:l'keɪnoʊ] S Vulkan *m*
volleyball S SPORT Volleyball *m*
volt [voʊlt] S Volt *n* **voltage** S Spannung *f*
volume ['vɑ:ljəm] S Lautstärke *f*; (*Container etc*) Volumen *n*; (*Geschäft etc*) Umfang *m*; (*Buch*) Band *m* **volume control** S Lautstärkeregler *m*
voluntary, **voluntarily** ['vɑ:lənterɪ, -lɪ] ADJ & ADV freiwillig; (*Arbeit*) ehrenamtlich
volunteer [vɑ:lən'tɪr] **1** S Freiwillige(r) *m/f(m)* **2** V/I sich freiwillig melden
vomit ['vɑ:mət] V/I sich übergeben
vote [voʊt] **1** S Stimme *f*; (*Vorgang*) Wahl *f*; (*Ausgang*) Abstimmungsergebnis *n*; (*als Bürgerrecht*) Wahlrecht *n* **2** V/T (*bei Abstimmung*) wählen; **they ~d him chairman** sie wählten ihn zum Vorsitzenden **3** V/I wählen; **~ for/against sth** für/gegen etw stimmen **voter** S Wähler(in) *m(f)*
voucher ['vaʊtʃər] S Gutschein *m*
vow [vaʊ] S Gelöbnis *n*
vowel ['vaʊəl] S Vokal *m*
voyage ['vɔɪɪdʒ] S Reise *f*
vs *abk* = versus; gegen
VT *abk* = Vermont
vulgar ['vʌlgər] ADJ vulgär, ordinär
vulnerable ['vʌlnərəbl] ADJ verwundbar; verletzlich; anfällig
vulture ['vʌltʃər] S Geier *m*

W

WA *abk* = Washington
wade [weɪd] V/I waten **wading pool** S Planschbecken *n*
wafer ['weɪfər] S Waffel *f*; REL Hostie *f*

waffle ['wɑːfl] S Waffel *f* **waffle iron** S Waffeleisen *n*
wag [wæg] VT wedeln mit
wage [weɪdʒ] S Lohn *m*
wagon ['wægən] S Fuhrwerk *n*; AUTO Wagen *m*
waist [weɪst] S Taille *f* **waistline** S Taille *f*
wait [weɪt] **1** S Wartezeit *f* **2** VI warten (*for* auf *+akk*); **~ and see** abwarten; **~ a minute** Moment mal! **waiter** S Kellner *m* **waiting** S **'no ~'** „Halteverbot" **waiting room** S MED Wartezimmer *n*; BAHN Wartesaal *m* **waitress** S Kellnerin *f*
wake ⟨woke *od* waked, woken⟩ [weɪk, woʊk, 'woʊkən] **1** VT wecken **2** VI aufwachen **wake up** **1** VT aufwecken **2** VI aufwachen **wake-up call** S TEL Weckruf *m*
walk [wɔːk] **1** S Spaziergang *m*; (*länger*) Wanderung *f*; (*Strecke*) Weg *m*; **go for a ~** spazieren gehen; **it's only a five-minute ~** es sind nur fünf Minuten zu Fuß **2** VI gehen; spazieren gehen; wandern **3** VT (*Hund*) ausführen **walking** S **go ~** wandern **walking shoes** S PL Wanderschuhe *pl*
wall [wɔːl] S (*in Zimmer*) Wand *f*; (*im Freien*) Mauer *f*
wallet ['wɑːlət] S Brieftasche *f*; Portemonnaie *n*
wallpaper ['wɔːlpeɪpər] **1** S Tapete *f*; IT Bildschirmhintergrund *m* **2** VT tapezieren
walnut ['wɔːlnʌt] S Walnuss *f*
wander ['wɑːndər] VI herumwandern
want [wɑːnt] **1** S Mangel *m* (*of* an *+dat*), Bedürfnis *n* **2** VT wollen; (*benötigen*) brauchen **want ad** S Kleinanzeige *f*
war [wɔːr] S Krieg *m*
ward [wɔːrd] S (*in Klinik*) Station *f*; (*in Stadt*) Bezirk *m*; (*Kind*) Mündel *n*
wardrobe ['wɔːrdroʊb] S Kleiderschrank *m*
warehouse ['werhaʊs] S Lagerhaus *n*
warfare ['wɔːrfer] S Krieg *m*, Kriegsführung *f*
warm [wɔːrm] **1** ADJ warm; herzlich; **I'm ~** mir ist warm **2** VT wärmen; (*Essen*) aufwärmen **warm up** **1** VT (*Essen*) aufwärmen; (*Zimmer*) erwärmen **2** VI (*Essen, Zimmer*) warm werden; SPORT sich aufwärmen **warmly** ADV warm; herzlich **warmth** S Wärme *f*, Herzlichkeit *f*
warn [wɔːrn] VT warnen (*of, against* vor *+dat*); **~ sb not to do sth** j-n davor warnen, etw zu tun **warning** S Warnung *f* **warning light** S Warnlicht *n* **warning triangle** S AUTO Warndreieck *n*
warranty ['wɔːrəntɪ] S Garantie *f*
wart [wɔːrt] S Warze *f*
wary ['werɪ] ADJ vorsichtig;

(*Blick etc*) misstrauisch
was [wʌz, wəz] *prät von* **be**
wash [wɑːʃ] **1** V/T waschen; (*Geschirr*) abwaschen; **~ the dishes** (das Geschirr) abwaschen **2** V/I sich waschen **wash off** V/T abwaschen **wash up** V/I sich waschen **washable** ADJ waschbar **washbag** S Kulturbeutel *m* **washcloth** S Waschlappen *m* **washer** S TECH Dichtungsring *m*; (*Gerät*) Waschmaschine *f* **washing** S Wäsche *f* **washing machine** S Waschmaschine *f* **washing powder** S Waschpulver *n* **washroom** S Toilette *f*
wasn't ['wʌznt] *kontr von* **was not**
wasp [wɑːsp] S Wespe *f*
WASP [wɑːsp] *akr* = White Anglo-Saxon Protestant; *weißer Amerikaner protestantischen Glaubens und angelsächsischer Herkunft*
waste [weɪst] **1** S Abfall *m*, Verschwendung *f* **2** ADJ überschüssig **3** V/T verschwenden (*on* an *+akk*); (*Chance*) vertun **waste basket** S Papierkorb *m*
watch [wɑːtʃ] **1** S (Armband)uhr *f* **2** V/T beobachten; aufpassen auf *+akk*; (*Film etc*) sich ansehen; **~ TV** fernsehen **3** V/I zusehen; Wache halten; **~ for sb/sth** nach j-m/etw Ausschau halten; **~ out** pass auf!
water ['wɔːtər] **1** S Wasser *n* **2** V/T (*Pflanzen*) gießen **3** V/I (*Auge*) tränen; **my mouth is ~ing** mir läuft das Wasser im Mund zusammen **water down** V/T verdünnen **waterbed** S Wasserbett *n* **watercolor** S Aquarell *n*; (*Farbe*) Wasserfarbe *f* **waterfall** S Wasserfall *m* **watering pot** S Gießkanne *f* **water level** S Wasserstand *m* **watermelon** S Wassermelone *f* **waterproof** ADJ wasserdicht **water-skiing** S Wasserskilaufen *n* **water sports** S PL Wassersport *m* **watertight** ADJ wasserdicht **watery** ADJ wässerig
wave [weɪv] **1** S Welle *f* **2** V/T (*Fahne etc*) schwenken; (*Hand, Fahne*) winken mit **3** V/I (*Person*) winken; (*Flagge*) wehen **wavelength** S Wellenlänge *f* **wavy** ['weɪvɪ] ADJ wellig
wax [wæks] S Wachs *n*; (*im Ohr*) Ohrenschmalz *n*
way [weɪ] S Weg *m*, Richtung *f*; (*Benehmen*) Art *f*; **could you tell me the ~ to … ?** wie komme ich (am besten) zu … ?; **we went the wrong ~** wir sind in die falsche Richtung gefahren/gegangen; **lose one's ~** sich verirren; **make ~ for sb/sth** j-m/etw Platz machen; **the other ~ around** andersherum; **one ~ or another** irgendwie; **in a ~** in gewisser Weise; **by the ~** übrigens; **'~ in'** „Ein-

gang"; '**~ out**' „Ausgang"; **no ~** *umg* kommt nicht infrage! **wayside** ['weɪsaɪd] S Rastplatz *m*
we [wiː] PRON wir
weak [wiːk] ADJ schwach **weaken** 1 V/T schwächen 2 V/I schwächer werden
wealth [welθ] S Reichtum *m* **wealthy** ADJ reich
weapon ['wepən] S Waffe *f*
wear ⟨wore, worn⟩ [wer, wɔːr, wɔːrn] 1 V/T (*Kleidung etc*) tragen 2 V/I sich abnutzen 3 S Kleidung *f*; Abnutzung *f* **wear off** V/I (*Gefühl etc*) nachlassen **wear out** 1 V/T abnutzen; (*Person*) erschöpfen 2 V/I sich abnutzen
weather ['weðər] S Wetter *n* **weather forecast** S Wettervorhersage *f*
weave ⟨wove *od* weaved, woven *od* weaved⟩ [wiːv, woʊv, 'woʊvn] V/T (*Stoff*) weben; (*Korb etc*) flechten
web [web] S *a. fig* Netz *n*; **the Web** das Web, das Internet **webcam** ['webkæm] S Webcam *f* **web page** S Webseite *f* **website** S Website *f*
we'd [wiːd] *kontr von* **we had; we would**
Wed *abk* = Wednesday; Mi.
wedding ['wedɪŋ] S Hochzeit *f* **wedding anniversary** S Hochzeitstag *m* **wedding ring** S Ehering *m* **wedding shower** S *Party für die zukünftige Braut*
Wednesday ['wenzdeɪ] S Mittwoch *m*; → Tuesday
weed [wiːd] 1 S Unkraut *n* 2 V/T jäten
week [wiːk] S Woche *f*; **twice a ~** zweimal in der Woche; **a ~ from Friday** Freitag in einer Woche; **in two ~s' time, in two ~s** in zwei Wochen **weekday** S Wochentag *m* **weekend** S Wochenende *n*; **on the ~** am Wochenende **weekly** ADJ & ADV wöchentlich; Wochen-
weenie ['wiːnɪ] S *umg* Wiener Würstchen *n*; (*Person*) Schwächling *m*
weep ⟨wept, wept⟩ [wiːp, wept] V/I weinen
weigh [weɪ] V/T & V/I wiegen **weight** [weɪt] S Gewicht *n*; **lose/put on ~** abnehmen/zunehmen
weird [wɪrd] ADJ seltsam **weirdo** ['wɪrdoʊ] S *umg* Spinner(in) *m(f)*
welcome ['welkəm] 1 S Empfang *m* 2 ADJ willkommen; (*Nachricht, Neuigkeit etc*) angenehm; **~ to Washington** willkommen in Washington! 3 V/T begrüßen **welcoming** ADJ freundlich
welfare ['welfer] S Wohl *n*; Sozialhilfe *f*; **be on ~** Sozialhilfe beziehen
well [wel] 1 S Brunnen *m*; Bohrloch *n* 2 ADJ gesund; **are**

you ~? geht es dir/Ihnen gut?; **feel ~** sich wohlfühlen **3** INT nun **4** ADV gut; **it may ~ be** das kann wohl sein; **as ~** auch; **~ over 60** weit über 60

we'll [wi:l] *kontr von* **we will**

well-behaved [welbɪ'heɪvd] ADJ brav **well-done** ADJ (*Steak*) durchgebraten **well-known** ADJ bekannt **well-off** ADJ wohlhabend **well-paid** ADJ gut bezahlt

went [went] *prät von* **go**

wept [wept] *prät, pperf von* **weep**

were [wɜ:r] *prät von* **be**

we're [wɪr, wi:r] *kontr von* **we are**

weren't [wɜ:rnt] *kontr von* **were not**

west [west] **1** S Westen *m* **2** ADV (*Richtung*) nach Westen **3** ADJ West- **westbound** ADJ (in) Richtung Westen **western** **1** ADJ West-, westlich **2** S FILM Western *m* **Westerner** S Weststaatler(in) *m(f)* **westward(s)** ['westwərdz] ADV nach Westen

wet ⟨wet, wet⟩ [wet] **1** V/T nass machen **2** ADJ nass, feucht; **'~ paint'** „frisch gestrichen" **wetsuit** S Taucheranzug *m*

we've [wi:v] *kontr von* **we have**

whale [weɪl] S Wal *m*

wharf ⟨-s *od* wharves *pl*⟩ [wɔ:rf, wɔ:rvz] S Kai *m*

what [wa:t, wʌt] **1** PRON & INT was; **~'s your name?** wie heißt du?/wie heißen Sie?; **~ are they talking about?** worüber reden sie?; **~ for?** wozu? **2** ADJ welche(r, s) **whatever** [wʌt'evər] PRON was (auch immer); egal, was **what's** *kontr von* **what is; what has**

wheat [wi:t] S Weizen *m*

wheel [wi:l] **1** S Rad *n*; (*im Auto*) Lenkrad *n* **2** V/T (*Fahrrad*) schieben **wheelchair** S Rollstuhl *m*

when [wen] **1** ADV (*in Fragen*) wann **2** KONJ wenn; (*bei Vergangenheit*) als **whenever** [wen'evər] ADV immer wenn; wann immer

where [wer] **1** ADV wo; wohin; **~ are you from?** woher kommst du/kommen Sie? **2** KONJ wo **whereabouts** **1** [werə'baʊts] ADV wo **2** ['werəbaʊts] S PL Aufenthaltsort *m* **whereas** [wer'æz] KONJ während, wohingegen

wherever [wer'evər] KONJ wo immer

whether ['weðər] KONJ ob

which [wɪtʃ] **1** ADJ welche(r, s); **~ one?** welche(r, s)? **2** PRON (*Frage*) welche(r, s); (*Relativsatz*) der/die/das, die *pl*; was **whichever** [wɪtʃ'evər] ADJ & PRON welche(r, s) auch immer

while [waɪl] **1** S Weile *f*; **for a ~** eine Zeit lang; **a short ~ ago** vor Kurzem **2** KONJ während; (*einschränkend*) obwohl

whine [waɪn] VI jammern **whip** [wɪp] **1** S Peitsche *f* **2** V/T peitschen; **~ped cream** Schlagsahne *f*
whirl [wɜːrl] V/T & V/I herumwirbeln **whirlpool** S (*in Fluss etc*) Strudel *m*; (*als Sitzbad*) Whirlpool *m* **whirlwind** S Wirbelwind *m*
whisk [wɪsk] **1** S Schneebesen *m* **2** V/T (*Sahne etc*) schlagen
whisker ['wɪskər] S (*von Tier*) Schnurrhaar *n*
whiskey ['wɪskɪ] S Whisky *m*
whisper ['wɪspər] V/I & V/T flüstern
whistle ['wɪsl] **1** S Pfiff *m*; Pfeife *f* **2** V/T & V/I pfeifen
white [waɪt] **1** S Weiß(e) *n* (*von Ei*) Eiweiß *n* **2** ADJ weiß; (*Fleisch*) hell; (*vor Angst*) blass; **the White House** das Weiße Haus (*Amts- und Wohnsitz des Präsidenten der USA*) **white-water rafting** S Rafting *n*
who [huː] PRON (*in Fragen*) wer; wen; wem; (*im Relativsatz*) der/die/das, die *pl* **whoever** [huː'evər] PRON wer auch immer
whole [hoʊl] **1** ADJ ganz **2** S Ganze(s) *n*; **on the ~** im Großen und Ganzen **wholefood** S Vollwertkost *f* **whole milk** S Vollmilch *f* **wholesale** ADV im Großhandel **wholesaler** S Großhändler(in) *m(f)*
wholesome ADJ gesund
wholewheat ADJ Vollkorn-
wholly ['hoʊlɪ] ADV völlig
whom [huːm] PRON (*in Fragen*) wen; wem; (*im Relativsatz*) den/die/das, die *pl*
whore [hɔːr] S Hure *f*
whose [huːz] **1** ADJ (*in Fragen*) wessen; (*im Relativsatz*) dessen/deren/dessen, deren *pl* **2** PRON wessen; **~ is this?** wem gehört das?
why [waɪ] ADV & KONJ warum; **that's ~** deshalb
WI *abk* = Wisconsin
wicked ['wɪkəd] ADJ böse; schlecht
wide [waɪd] **1** ADJ breit; weit; (*Angebot, Auswahl*) groß **2** ADV weit **wide-awake** ADJ hellwach **widely** ADV weit; allgemein **widen** V/T verbreitern; *fig* erweitern **widescreen TV** S Breitbildfernseher *m* **widespread** ADJ weit verbreitet
widow ['wɪdoʊ] S Witwe *f*
widower S Witwer *m*
width [wɪdθ] S Breite *f*
wiener ['wiːnər] S Wiener Würstchen *n*
wife ⟨wives *pl*⟩ [waɪf, waɪvz] S (Ehe)frau *f*
wig [wɪg] S Perücke *f*
wild [waɪld] **1** ADJ wild; (*Emotion etc*) heftig; (*Plan, Idee*) verrückt **2** S **in the ~** in freier Wildbahn **wilderness** ['wɪldərnəs] S Wildnis *f* **wildlife** S Tier- und Pflanzenwelt *f*
wildly ADV wild; (*begeistert etc*) maßlos
will [wɪl] **1** V/AUX werden; I

won't be back until late ich komme erst spät zurück; **the car won't start** das Auto will nicht anspringen; **~ you have some coffee?** möchtest du/möchten Sie eine Tasse Kaffee? **2** S Wille *m*, Wunsch *m*; (*für Todesfall*) Testament *n*
willing ADJ bereitwillig; bereit **willingly** ADV gern(e)
wimp [wɪmp] S Weichei *n*
win ⟨won, won⟩ [wɪn, wʌn] **1** V/T & V/I gewinnen **2** S Sieg *m*
wind ⟨wound, wound⟩ [waɪnd, waʊnd] V/T (*Seil, Verband*) wickeln **wind up** V/T (*Uhr*) aufziehen; (*Konferenz, Rede*) abschließen
wind [wɪnd] S Wind *m* **windmill** S Windmühle *f*
window ['wɪndoʊ] S Fenster *n*; (*Bank, Post® etc*) Schalter *m*
windowpane S Fensterscheibe *f* **window-shopping** S **go ~** einen Schaufensterbummel machen **windowsill** S Fensterbrett *n*
windpipe ['wɪndpaɪp] S Luftröhre *f* **windshield** S Windschutzscheibe *f* **windshield wiper** S Scheibenwischer *m*
windsurfer S Windsurfer(in) *m(f)*; (*Brett*) Surfbrett *n* **windsurfing** S Windsurfen *n*
windy ['wɪndɪ] ADJ windig
wine [waɪn] S Wein *m* **wine list** S Weinkarte *f* **wine tasting** S Weinprobe *f*
wing [wɪŋ] S Flügel *m*; FLUG Tragfläche *f*
wink [wɪŋk] V/I zwinkern
winner ['wɪnər] S Gewinner(in) *m(f)*; Sieger(in) *m(f)*
winning **1** ADJ siegreich **2** S **~s** *pl* Gewinn *m*
wino ⟨-s *pl*⟩ ['waɪnoʊ] S *umg* Penner *m*; Säufer *m*
winter ['wɪntər] S Winter *m* **wintertime** S Winterzeit *f*
wint(e)ry ['wɪntrɪ] ADJ winterlich
wipe [waɪp] V/T abwischen; **~ one's nose** sich die Nase putzen **wipe off** V/T abwischen **wipe out** V/T vernichten; ausrotten; (*Daten*) löschen
wire [waɪr] **1** S Draht *m*; ELEK Leitung *f* **2** V/T (*Gerät*) anschließen
wisdom ['wɪzdəm] S Weisheit *f* **wisdom tooth** S Weisheitszahn *m*
wise, **wisely** [waɪz, -lɪ] ADJ & ADV weise
wish [wɪʃ] **1** S Wunsch *m* (*for* nach); **best ~es** herzliche Grüße **2** V/T wünschen; wollen
witch [wɪtʃ] S Hexe *f*
with [wɪð] PRÄP mit; bei; (*Ursache*) vor *+dat*
withdraw [wɪð'drɔː] *irr* **1** V/T zurückziehen; (*Geld*) abheben; (*Aussage*) zurücknehmen **2** V/I sich zurückziehen
wither ['wɪðər] V/I verwelken
withhold [wɪð'hoʊld] *irr* V/T vorenthalten (*from sb* j-m)
within [wɪð'ɪn] PRÄP innerhalb

+*gen*; ~ **walking distance** zu Fuß erreichbar **without** [wɪð-'aʊt] PRÄP ohne
withstand [wɪð'stænd] *irr* V/T standhalten +*dat*
witness ['wɪtnəs] **1** S Zeuge *m*, Zeugin *f* **2** V/T Zeuge sein
witty ['wɪtɪ] ADJ geistreich, witzig
wives [waɪvz] *pl von* **wife**
wobble ['wɑ:bl] V/I wackeln **wobbly** ADJ wackelig
woke [woʊk] *prät von* **wake**
woken ['woʊkn] *pperf von* **wake**
wolf ⟨wolves *pl*⟩ [wʊlf, wʊlvz] S Wolf *m*
woman ⟨women⟩ ['wʊmən, 'wɪmɪn] S Frau *f*
womb [wu:m] S Gebärmutter *f*
women ['wɪmɪn] *pl von* **woman**
won [wʌn] *prät, pperf von* **win**
wonder ['wʌndər] **1** S Wunder *n*, Staunen *n* **2** V/T & V/I sich fragen **wonderful, wonderfully** ADJ & ADV wunderbar
won't [woʊnt] *kontr von* **will not**
wood [wʊd] S Holz *n*; **~s** *pl* Wald *m* **wooden** ADJ Holz-; *fig* hölzern **woody** **1** ADJ waldig; holzig **2** S *vulg* (*Erektion*) Latte *f*
wool [wʊl] S Wolle *f* **woolen** ADJ Woll-
word [wɜ:rd] **1** S Wort *n*; (*Versprechen*) Ehrenwort *n*; **~s** *pl* (*Lied, Gedicht*) Text *m*; **have a ~ with sb** mit j-m sprechen; *umg* **~!** einverstanden! **2** V/T formulieren **word processor** S Textverarbeitungsprogramm *n*
wore [wɔ:r] *prät von* **wear**
work [wɜ:rk] **1** S Arbeit *f*; (*künstlerisches etc*) Werk *n*; **he's at ~** er ist in/auf der Arbeit; **out of ~** arbeitslos **2** V/I arbeiten (*at, on* an +*dat*); (*Maschine, Plan etc*) funktionieren; (*Medizin*) wirken; (*Plan etc*) klappen **3** V/T (*Maschine*) bedienen **work out** **1** V/I (*Plan etc*) klappen; (*Summe*) aufgehen; (*in Fitnesscenter etc*) trainieren **2** V/T (*Preis etc*) ausrechnen; (*Plan*) ausarbeiten
worker S Arbeiter(in) *m(f)*
workman ⟨-men *pl*⟩ S Handwerker *m* **workout** S SPORT Fitnesstraining *n*, Konditionstraining *n* **work permit** S Arbeitserlaubnis *f* **workplace** S Arbeitsplatz *m* **workshop** S Werkstatt *f*; (*Treffen*) Workshop *m*
world [wɜ:rld] S Welt *f* **World War** S Weltkrieg *m* **world-wide** ADJ & ADV weltweit
worm [wɜ:rm] S Wurm *m*
worn [wɔ:rn] **1** *pperf von* **wear** **2** ADJ (*Kleidung*) abgetragen; (*Reifen*) abgefahren **worn-out** ADJ abgenutzt; (*Person*) erschöpft
worried ['wɜ:rɪd] ADJ besorgt

worry ['wɜːrɪ] **1** S Sorge *f* **2** V/T Sorgen machen *+dat* **3** V/I sich Sorgen machen (*about* um); **don't ~** keine Sorge! **worrying** ADJ beunruhigend

worse [wɜːrs] **1** ADJ *Komparativ von* bad; schlechter; (*Schmerz, Fehler etc*) schlimmer **2** ADV *Komparativ von* badly; schlechter **worsen** **1** V/T verschlechtern **2** V/I sich verschlechtern

worship ['wɜːrʃəp] V/T anbeten, anhimmeln

worst [wɜːrst] **1** ADJ *Superlativ von* bad; schlechteste(r, s); schlimmste(r, s) **2** ADV *Superlativ von* badly; am schlechtesten **3** S **the ~ is over** das Schlimmste ist vorbei; **at (the) ~** schlimmstenfalls

worth [wɜːrθ] **1** S Wert *m* **2** ADJ **it is ~ $50** es ist 50 Dollar wert; **~ seeing** sehenswert; **it's ~ it** es lohnt sich **worthless** ['wɜːrθləs] ADJ wertlos **worthwhile** [wɜːrθ'waɪl] ADJ lohnend, lohnenswert **worthy** ['wɜːrðɪ] ADJ würdig

would [wʊd] V/AUX **if you asked he ~ come** wenn du ihn fragtest/Sie ihn fragten, würde er kommen; **I ~ have told you, but …** ich hätte es dir gesagt, aber …; **~ you like a drink?** möchtest du/möchten Sie etwas trinken?; **he ~n't help me** er wollte mir nicht helfen **wouldn't** ['wʊdnt] *kontr von* **would not**

would've ['wʊdəv] *kontr von* **would have**

wound **1** [wuːnd] S Wunde *f* **2** [wuːnd] V/T verwunden; verletzen **3** [waʊnd] *prät, pperf von* **wind**

wove [woʊv] *prät von* **weave** **woven** ['woʊvn] *pperf von* **weave**

wrap [ræp] V/T (ein)wickeln **wrap up** V/T einwickeln **wrapping paper** S Packpapier *n*; Geschenkpapier *n*

wreath [riːθ] S Kranz *m*

wreck [rek] **1** S Wrack *n*; **a nervous ~** ein Nervenbündel **2** V/T (*Auto*) zu Schrott fahren; *fig* zerstören **wreckage** ['rekɪdʒ] S Trümmer *pl* **wrecking service** S Abschleppdienst *m*

wrench [rentʃ] S Schraubenschlüssel *m*

wrestling ['reslɪŋ] S Ringen *n*

wring out ⟨wrung, wrung⟩ [rɪŋ'aʊt, rʌŋ] V/T auswringen

wrinkle ['rɪŋkl] S Falte *f*

wrist [rɪst] S Handgelenk *n* **wristwatch** S Armbanduhr *f*

write ⟨wrote, written⟩ [raɪt, roʊt, 'rɪtən] **1** V/T schreiben; (*Scheck*) ausstellen **2** V/I schreiben **write down** V/T aufschreiben **write out** V/T ausschreiben; (*Scheck*) ausstellen **writer** S Verfasser(in) *m(f)*, Schriftsteller(in) *m(f)* **writing** S Schrift *f*, Schreiben *n*; **in ~** schriftlich **writing paper** S Schreibpapier *n* **written** ['rɪt-

ən] *pperf von* **write**
wrong [rɒːŋ] ADJ falsch; (*moralisch*) unrecht; **you're ~** du hast/Sie haben unrecht; **what's ~ with your leg?** was ist mit deinem/Ihrem Bein los?; **I dialed the ~ number** ich habe mich verwählt; **don't get me ~** versteh/verstehen Sie mich nicht falsch; **go ~** schiefgehen **wrongly** ADV falsch; zu Unrecht
wrote [roʊt] *prät von* **write**
wussy ['wʊsɪ] S *umg* Feigling *m*, Waschlappen *m*
WV *abk* = West Virginia
WY *abk* = Wyoming

X-ing ['krɑːsɪŋ] S Übergang *m*
XL *abk* = extra large; XL, übergroß
Xmas ['krɪsməs, 'eksməs] S Weihnachten *n*
X-ray ['eksreɪ] **1** S Röntgenaufnahme *f* **2** V/T röntgen
xylophone ['zaɪləfoʊn] S Xylophon *n*

yacht [jɑːt] S Jacht *f* **yachting** S Segeln *n*
yam [jæm] S Süßkartoffel *f*
Yankee ['jæŋkɪ] S Nordstaatler(in) *m(f)*
yard [jɑːrd] S Hof *m*; Garten *m*; (*Längenmaß*) Yard *n* (*0,91 m*) **yard sale** S *privater Verkauf von gebrauchten Gegenständen*
yawn [jɔːn] V/I gähnen
yd *abk* = yard(s)
year [jɪr] S Jahr *n*; **a five-year-old** ein(e) Fünfjährige(r) **yearly** ADJ & ADV jährlich
yeast [jiːst] S Hefe *f*
yell [jel] V/I & V/T schreien; **~ at sb** j-n anschreien
yellow ['jeloʊ] ADJ gelb; **the Yellow Pages®** *pl* die Gelben Seiten *pl*
yes [jes] **1** ADV ja; (*Antwort auf verneinte Fragen*) doch **2** S Ja *n*
yesterday ['jestərdeɪ] ADV gestern; **the day before ~** vorgestern
yet [jet] **1** ADV noch; bis jetzt; (*Frage*) schon;; **~ again** schon wieder; **as ~** bis jetzt **2** KONJ doch
yield [jiːld] **1** S Ertrag *m* **2** V/T (*Ergebnis, Ernte*) hervorbringen;

(*Profit, Zinsen*) bringen **3** VI nachgeben (*to +dat*); MIL sich ergeben (*to +dat*); **'~'** AUTO „Vorfahrt beachten"

YMCA *abk* = Young Men's Christian Association CVJM *m*

yoga ['joʊgə] S Yoga *n*

yog(h)urt ['joʊgərt] S Jog(h)urt *m*

yolk [joʊk] S Eigelb *n*

you [juː] PRON (*als Subjekt*) du/Sie/ihr; man; (*als direktes Objekt*) dich/Sie/euch; (*als indirektes Objekt*) dir/Ihnen/ihnen **you'd** [juːd] *kontr von* **you had; you would** **you'll** [juːl] *kontr von* **you will; you shall**

young [jʌŋ] ADJ jung **youngster** ['jʌŋstər] S Jugendliche(r) *m/f(m)*

your [jʊr] ADJ dein(e); (*Höflichkeitsform*) Ihr(e); (*pl*) euer(e); (*Höflichkeitsform*) Ihr(e); **did you hurt ~ leg?** hast du dir/haben Sie sich das Bein verletzt? **you're** [jʊr] *kontr von* **you are** **yours** [jʊrz] PRON (*sg*) deine(r, s); (*Höflichkeitsform*) Ihre(r, s); (*pl*) eure(r, s); (*Höflichkeitsform*) Ihre(r, s); **is this ~?** gehört das dir/Ihnen?; **a friend of ~** ein Freund von dir/Ihnen; **Yours ...** (*Briefende*) Dein/Deine ..., Ihr/Ihre ... **yourself** [jʊr'self] PRON *sg* dich; (*Höflichkeitsform*) sich; **did you do it ~?** hast du/haben Sie es selbst gemacht?; **(all) by ~** allein **yourselves** [jʊr'selvz] PRON *pl* euch; (*Höflichkeitsform*) sich

youth [juːθ] S Jugend *f*; Jugendliche(r) *m/f(m)* **youth hostel** S Jugendherberge *f*

you've [juːv] *kontr von* **you have**

yummy ['jʌmɪ] ADJ *umg* lecker

YWCA *abk* = Young Women's Christian Association CVJM *m*

Z

zap [zæp] *umg* **1** VT IT löschen; (*Speise*) in der Mikrowelle erhitzen; (*in Computerspiel*) abknallen **2** VI TV zappen **zapper** S TV *umg* Fernbedienung *f*

zebra ['ziːbrə] S Zebra *n*

zero ⟨-es *pl*⟩ ['ziːroʊ] S Null *f*

zigzag ['zɪgzæg] **1** S Zickzack *m* **2** VI im Zickzack gehen/fahren

zip [zɪp] VT **~ (up)** den Reißverschluss zumachen; IT zippen **zip code** S Postleitzahl *f* **zipper** S Reißverschluss *m*

zodiac ['zoʊdɪæk] S Tierkreis *m*

zone [zoʊn] S Zone *f*, Gebiet *n*; (*in Stadt*) Bezirk *m*

zoo [zuː] S Zoo *m*

zoom [zuːm] **1** VI brausen, sausen **2** S **~ (lens)** Zoomobjektiv *n* **zoom in** VI FOTO heranzoomen (*on* an *+akk*)

zucchini ⟨-(s) *pl*⟩ [zuˈkiːnɪ] S Zucchini *f*

Deutsch - Englisch

A

à PRÄP *+akk* at … each
Aal M eel
ab **1** PRÄP *+dat* from; **von jetzt ~** from now on; **Berlin ~ 16:30 Uhr** departs Berlin 16.30; **~ 18** (*Alter*) from the age of 18 **2** ADV off; **links ~** to the left; **~ und zu** (*od* **an**) now and then (*od* again); **der Knopf ist ~** the button has come off
abbauen V/T (*Zelt*) take down; (*verringern*) reduce
abbeißen V/T bite off
abbestellen V/T cancel
abbiegen V/I turn off; (*Straße*) bend; **nach links/rechts ~** turn left/right
Abbildung F illustration
abblasen V/T *fig* call off
abblenden V/T & V/I AUTO (**die Scheinwerfer**) **~** dim one's headlights **Abblendlicht** N dimmed headlights *pl*
abbrechen V/T break off; (*Gebäude*) pull down; (*aufhören*) stop; (*Computerprogramm*) abort
abbremsen V/I brake, slow down
abbringen V/T **j-n von einer Idee ~** talk sb out of an idea; **j-n vom Thema ~** get sb away from the subject; **davon lasse ich mich nicht ~** nothing will make me change my mind about it
abbuchen V/T to debit (*von* to)
abdanken V/I resign
abdrehen **1** V/T (*Gas, Wasser*) turn off; (*Licht*) switch off **2** V/I (*Schiff, Flugzeug*) change course
Abend M evening; **am ~** in the evening; **zu ~ essen** have dinner; **heute/morgen/gestern ~** this/tomorrow/yesterday evening; **guten ~!** good evening **Abendbrot** N supper **Abendessen** N dinner **Abendgarderobe** F evening dress **Abendkasse** F box office **Abendkleid** N evening dress **Abendmahl** N **das ~** (Holy) Communion
abends ADV in the evening; **montags ~** (on) Monday evenings
Abenteuer N adventure
aber KONJ but; (*jedoch*) however; **oder ~** alternatively; **~ ja!** (but) of course; **das ist ~ nett von Ihnen** that's really nice

of you
abergläubisch ADJ superstitious
abfahren V/I leave (*od* depart) (*nach* for); (*Ski*) ski down **Abfahrt** F departure; (*von Autobahn*) exit; (*Ski*) descent; (*Piste*) run **Abfahrtslauf** M (*Ski*) downhill **Abfahrtszeit** F departure time
Abfall M waste; (*Müll*) garbage **Abfalleimer** M garbage can
abfällig ADJ disparaging
abfertigen V/T (*Pakete*) prepare for dispatch; (*an der Grenze*) clear **Abfertigungsschalter** M (*am Flughafen*) check-in desk
abfinden 1 V/T pay off 2 V/R **sich mit etw ~** come to terms with sth **Abfindung** F (*Entschädigung*) compensation; (*von Angestellten*) severance pay
abfliegen V/I (*Flugzeug*) take off; (*Passagier a.*) fly off **Abflug** M departure; (*Start*) takeoff **Abflughalle** F departure lounge **Abflugzeit** F departure time
Abfluss M drain **Abflussrohr** N waste pipe; (*außen*) drainpipe
abfragen V/T test; IT call up
abführen 1 V/I MED have a laxative effect 2 V/T (*Steuern, Gebühren*) pay; **j-n ~ lassen** take sb into custody **Abführmittel** N laxative
Abgabe F handing in; (*von Ball*) pass; (*Steuer*) tax; (*einer Erklärung*) giving **abgabenfrei** ADJ tax-free **abgabenpflichtig** ADJ liable to tax
Abgase PL AUTO exhaust fumes *pl* **Abgas(sonder)untersuchung** F (exhaust) emissions test
abgeben 1 V/T (*Gepäck, Schlüssel*) leave (*bei* with); (*Schularbeit etc*) hand in; (*Wärme*) give off; (*Erklärung, Urteil*) make 2 V/R **sich mit j-m ~** associate with sb; **sich mit etw ~** bother with sth
abgehen V/I (*Post*) go; (*Knopf etc*) come off; (*abgezogen werden*) be taken off; (*Straße*) branch off; **von der Schule ~** leave school; **sie geht mir ab** I really miss her; **was geht denn hier ab?** *umg* what's going on here?
abgehetzt ADJ exhausted
abgelaufen ADJ (*Pass*) expired; (*Zeit, Frist*) up; **die Milch ist ~** the milk is past its expiration date
abgelegen ADJ remote
abgemacht INT OK, it's a deal
abgeneigt ADJ **einer Sache ~ sein** be averse to sth; **ich wäre nicht ~, das zu tun** I wouldn't mind doing that
Abgeordnete(r) M/F(M) (elected) representative
abgepackt ADJ prepackaged
abgerissen ADJ **der Knopf ist**

~ the button has come off
abgesehen ADJ **es auf j-n/etw ~ haben** be after sb/sth; **~ von** apart from
abgespannt ADJ (*Person*) exhausted, worn out
abgestanden ADJ stale; (*Bier*) flat
abgestorben ADJ (*Pflanze*) dead; (*Finger*) numb
abgestumpft ADJ (*Person*) insensitive
abgetragen ADJ (*Kleidung*) worn
abgewöhnen V/T **j-m etw ~** cure sb of sth; **sich etw ~** give sth up
abhaken V/T check off
abhalten V/T (*Versammlung*) hold; **j-n von etw ~** (*fernhalten*) keep sb away from sth; (*hindern*) keep sb from sth
abhanden ADJ **~ kommen** get lost
Abhang M slope
abhängen **1** V/T (*Bild*) take down; (*Anhänger*) uncouple; (*Verfolger*) shake off **2** V/I **von j-m/etw ~** depend on sb/sth; **das hängt davon ab, ob ...** it depends (on) whether ... **abhängig** ADJ dependent (*von* on)
abhauen **1** V/T (*abschlagen*) cut off **2** V/I *umg* (*verschwinden*) scram; **hau ab!** beat it!
abheben **1** V/T (*Geld*) withdraw; (*Telefonhörer, Spielkarte*) pick up **2** V/I (*Flugzeug*) take off; (*Rakete*) lift off; (*Karten*) cut
abholen V/T collect; (*am Bahnhof etc*) meet; (*mit dem Auto*) pick up
abhorchen V/T MED listen to
abhören V/T (*Vokabeln*) test; (*Telefongespräch*) tap; (*Tonband etc*) listen to
Abitur N *German school-leaving examination*, ≈ High School Diploma
abkaufen V/T **j-m etw ~** buy sth from sb; **das kauf ich dir nicht ab!** *umg* (*glauben*) I don't buy it
abklingen V/I (*Schmerz*) ease; (*Wirkung*) wear off
abkommen V/I get away; **von der Straße ~** leave the road; **von einem Plan ~** give up a plan; **vom Thema ~** get off the point
Abkommen N agreement
abkoppeln V/T (*Anhänger*) unhitch
abkratzen **1** V/T scrape off **2** V/I *umg* (*sterben*) kick the bucket, croak
abkühlen V/I & V/R & V/T cool down
abkürzen V/T (*Wort*) abbreviate; **den Weg ~** take a short cut **Abkürzung** F (*Wort*) abbreviation; (*Weg*) short cut
abladen V/T unload
Ablage F (*für Akten*) tray; (*Aktenordnung*) filing system
Ablauf M (*Abfluss*) drain; (*von Ereignissen*) course; (*einer Frist,*

Zeit) expiry **ablaufen** VI (*abfließen*) drain away; (*Ereignisse*) happen; (*Frist, Zeit, Pass*) expire
ablegen **1** VT put down; (*Kleider*) take off; (*Gewohnheit*) get out of; (*Prüfung*) take, sit; (*Akten*) file away **2** VI (*Schiff*) cast off
ablehnen **1** VT reject; (*Einladung*) decline; (*missbilligen*) disapprove of; (*Bewerber*) turn down **2** VI decline
ablenken VT distract; **vom Thema ~** change the subject
Ablenkung F distraction
ablesen VT (*Text, Rede*) read; **das Gas/den Strom ~** read the gas/electricity meter
abliefern VT deliver
abmachen VT (*entfernen*) take off; (*vereinbaren*) agree **Abmachung** F agreement
abmelden **1** VT (*Zeitung*) cancel; (*Auto*) take off the road **2** VR give notice of one's departure; (*im Hotel*) check out; (*vom Verein*) cancel one's membership
abmessen VT measure
abnehmen **1** VT take off, remove; (*Hörer*) pick up; (*Führerschein*) take away; (*Geld*) get (*j-m* out of sb); (*kaufen*) buy (*j--m* from sb); (*umg: glauben*) buy **2** VI decrease; (*schlanker werden*) lose weight; TEL pick up the phone; **fünf Pfund ~** lose five pounds
Abneigung F dislike (*gegen* of); (*stärker*) aversion (*gegen* to)
abnutzen VT & VR wear out
Abonnement N subscription
abonnieren VT subscribe to
abraten VI **j-m von etw ~** advise sb against sth
abräumen VT **den Tisch ~** clear the table; **das Geschirr ~** clear away the dishes; (*Preis etc*) walk off with
Abrechnung F settlement; (*Rechnung*) bill
abregen VR *umg* calm down, cool it; **reg dich ab!** take it easy
Abreise F departure **abreisen** VI leave (*nach* for) **Abreisetag** M day of departure, departure date
abreißen **1** VT (*Haus*) pull down; (*Blatt*) tear off; **den Kontakt nicht ~ lassen** stay in touch **2** VI (*Knopf etc*) come off
abrunden VT **eine Zahl nach oben/unten ~** round a number up/down
abrupt ADJ abrupt
ABS N *abk* = Antiblockiersystem; AUTO ABS
Abs. *abk* = Absender; from
absagen **1** VT cancel, call off; (*Einladung*) turn down **2** VI (*ablehnen*) decline; **ich muss leider ~** I'm afraid I can't come
Absatz M WIRTSCH sales *pl*; (*neuer Abschnitt*) paragraph; (*Schuh*) heel

abschaffen V/T abolish, do away with
abschalten V/T & V/I *a. fig* switch off
abschätzen V/T estimate; (*Lage*) assess
abscheulich ADJ disgusting
abschicken V/T send off
abschieben V/T (*ausweisen*) deport
Abschied M parting; **~ nehmen** say good-bye (*von j-m* to sb) **Abschiedsfeier** F farewell party
Abschleppdienst M AUTO breakdown service **abschleppen** V/T tow **Abschleppseil** N towrope **Abschleppwagen** M tow truck
abschließen V/T (*Tür*) lock; (*beenden*) conclude, finish; (*Vertrag, Handel*) conclude **Abschluss** M (*Beendigung*) close, conclusion; (*von Vertrag, Handel*) conclusion
abschmecken V/T (*kosten*) taste; (*würzen*) season
abschminken 1 V/R take one's make-up off 2 V/T *umg* **sich etw ~** get sth out of one's mind
abschnallen V/R undo one's seatbelt
abschneiden 1 V/T cut off 2 V/I **gut/schlecht ~** do well/badly
Abschnitt M (*von Buch, Text*) section; (*Kontrollabschnitt*) stub
abschrauben V/T unscrew
abschrecken V/T deter, put off
abschreiben V/T copy (*bei, von* from, off); (*verloren geben*) write off; WIRTSCH (*absetzen*) deduct
abschüssig ADJ steep
abschwächen V/T lessen; (*Behauptung, Kritik*) tone down
abschwellen V/I (*Entzündung*) go down; (*Lärm*) die down
absehbar ADJ foreseeable; **in ~er Zeit** in the foreseeable future **absehen** 1 V/T (*Ende, Folgen*) foresee 2 V/I **von etw ~** refrain from sth
abseits 1 ADV out of the way; SPORT offside 2 PRÄP *+gen* away from
absenden V/T send off; (*Post*) mail **Absender(in)** M(F) sender
absetzen 1 V/T (*Glas, Brille etc*) put down; (*aussteigen lassen*) drop (off); WIRTSCH sell; FIN deduct; (*streichen*) drop 2 V/R (*sich entfernen*) get away; (*sich ablagern*) be deposited
Absicht F intention; **mit ~** on purpose **absichtlich** ADJ intentional, deliberate
absolut ADJ absolute
abspeichern V/T IT save
absperren V/T block (*od* close) off; (*Tür*) lock **Absperrung** F (*Vorgang*) blocking (*od* closing) off; (*Sperre*) barricade
abspielen 1 V/T (*CD etc*) play 2 V/R happen

abspringen VI jump down/off; *(von etw Geplantem)* drop out *(von* of*)*
abspülen VT rinse; *(Geschirr)* wash
Abstand M distance; *(zeitlich)* interval; ~ **halten** keep one's distance
abstauben VT & VI dust; *umg (stehlen)* lift
Abstecher M detour
absteigen VI *(vom Rad etc)* get off, dismount; *(in Gasthof)* stay *(in +dat* at*)*
abstellen VT *(niederstellen)* put down; *(Auto)* park; *(ausschalten)* turn *(od* switch*)* off; *(Missstand, Unsitte)* stop **Abstellraum** M storeroom
Abstieg M *(vom Berg)* descent; SPORT relegation
abstimmen **1** VI vote **2** VT *(Termine, Ziele)* fit in *(auf +akk* with*)*; **Dinge aufeinander** ~ coordinate things **3** VR come to an agreement *(od* arrangement*)*
abstoßend ADJ repulsive
abstrakt ADJ abstract
abstreiten VT deny
Abstrich M MED smear; **~e machen** cut back *(an +dat* on*)*; *(weniger erwarten)* lower one's sights
Absturz M fall; FLUG, IT crash **abstürzen** VI fall; FLUG, IT crash
absurd ADJ absurd
Abszess M abscess
abtauen VT & VI thaw; *(Kühlschrank)* defrost
Abtei F abbey
Abteil N compartment
Abteilung F *(in Firma, Kaufhaus)* department; *(in Krankenhaus)* section
abtreiben **1** VT *(Kind)* abort **2** VI be driven off course; MED *(Abtreibung vornehmen)* carry out an abortion; *(Abtreibung vornehmen lassen)* have an abortion **Abtreibung** F abortion
abtrocknen VT dry
abwarten **1** VT wait for; **das bleibt abzuwarten** that remains to be seen **2** VI wait
abwärts ADV down
abwaschen VT *(Schmutz)* wash off; *(Geschirr)* wash
Abwasser N sewage
abwechseln VR alternate; **sich mit j-m** ~ take turns with sb **abwechselnd** ADV alternately **Abwechslung** F change; **zur** ~ for a change
abweisen VT turn away; *(Antrag)* turn down **abweisend** ADJ unfriendly
abwesend ADJ absent **Abwesenheit** F absence
abwiegen VT weigh (out)
abwischen VT *(Gesicht, Tisch etc)* wipe; *(Schmutz)* wipe off
abzählen VT count; *(Geld)* count out
Abzeichen N badge
abzeichnen **1** VT draw, copy;

(*Dokument*) initial **2** VR stand out; *fig* (*bevorstehen*) loom
abziehen **1** VT take off; (*Bett*) strip; (*Schlüssel*) take out; (*subtrahieren*) take away, subtract **2** VI go away
Abzug M (*Foto*) print; (*Öffnung*) vent; (*Truppen*) withdrawal; (*Betrag*) deduction **abzüglich** PRÄP +*gen* minus
abzweigen **1** VI branch off **2** VT set aside **Abzweigung** F junction
Accessoires PL accessories *pl*
ach INT oh; **~ so!** oh, I see; **~ was!** (*Überraschung*) really?; (*Ärger*) don't talk nonsense
Achse F axis; AUTO axle
Achsel F shoulder; (*Achselhöhle*) armpit
Achsenbruch M AUTO broken axle
acht NUM eight; **heute in ~ Tagen** in a week('s time), a week from today
Acht F **sich in ~ nehmen** be careful (*vor* +*dat* of), watch out (*vor* +*dat* for); **etw außer ~ lassen** disregard sth
achte(r, s) ADJ eighth; → dritte **Achtel** N (*Bruchteil*) eighth; (*Wein etc*) eighth of a liter; (*Glas Wein*) ≈ small glass
achten **1** VT respect **2** VI pay attention (*auf* +*akk* to)
Achterbahn F roller coaster
achtgeben VI take care (*auf* +*akk* of), pay attention (*auf* +*akk* to)
achthundert NUM eight hundred **achtmal** ADV eight times
Achtung **1** F attention; (*Ehrfurcht*) respect **2** INT look out
achtzehn NUM eighteen
achtzehnte(r, s) ADJ eighteenth; → dritte **achtzig** NUM eighty **achtzigste(r, s)** ADJ eightieth
Acker M field
Adapter M adapter
addieren VT add (up)
Ader F vein
Adjektiv N adjective
Adler M eagle
adoptieren VT adopt **Adoption** F adoption **Adoptivkind** N adopted child
Adrenalin N adrenalin
Adressbuch N directory; (*persönliches*) address book **Adresse** F address **adressieren** VT address (*an* +*akk* to)
Advent M Advent
Adverb N adverb
Aerobic N aerobics *sg*
Affäre F affair
Affe M monkey
Afghanistan N Afghanistan
Afrika N Africa **Afrikaner(in)** M(F) African **afrikanisch** ADJ African
After M anus
Aftershave N aftershave
AG F *abk* = Aktiengesellschaft; corp.
Agent(in) M(F) agent **Agentur** F agency

aggressiv ADJ aggressive
ähneln 1 V/I +*dat* be like, resemble 2 V/R be alike (*od* similar)
ahnen V/T suspect; **du ahnst es nicht!** would you believe it?
ähnlich ADJ similar (*dat* to); **j-m ~ sehen** look like sb **Ähnlichkeit** F similarity
Ahnung F idea; (*Vermutung*) suspicion; **keine ~!** no idea **ahnungslos** ADJ unsuspecting
Ahorn M maple
Aids N Aids **Aidstest** M Aids test
Airbag M AUTO airbag
Akademie F academy **Akademiker(in)** M(F) (university) graduate
akklimatisieren V/R acclimatize oneself
Akku M (storage) battery
Akkusativ M accusative (case)
Akne F acne
Akrobat(in) M(F) acrobat
Akt M act; KUNST nude
Akte F file; **etw zu den ~n legen** *a. fig* file sth away **Aktenkoffer** M briefcase
Aktie F stock, share **Aktiengesellschaft** F corporation
Aktion F (*Kampagne*) campaign; (*Einsatz*) operation
Aktionär(in) M(F) shareholder
aktiv ADJ active **aktivieren** V/T activate
aktualisieren V/T update **aktuell** ADJ (*Thema*) topical; (*modern*) up-to-date; (*Problem*) current; **nicht mehr ~** no longer relevant
Akupunktur F acupuncture
Akustik F acoustics *sg*
akut ADJ acute
Akzent M accent; (*Betonung*) stress
akzeptieren V/T accept
Alarm M alarm **Alarmanlage** F alarm system **alarmieren** V/T alarm; **die Polizei ~** call the police
albern ADJ silly
Albtraum M nightmare
Album N album
Algen PL algae *pl*; (*Meeresalgen*) seaweed *sg*
Alibi N alibi
Alimente PL (*für Kind*) child support *sg*; (*für geschiedenen Partner*) alimony *sg*
Alkohol M alcohol **alkoholfrei** ADJ non-alcoholic; **~es Getränk** soft drink **Alkoholiker(in)** M(F) alcoholic **alkoholisch** ADJ alcoholic **Alkoholtest** M breath test
All N universe
alle(r, s) 1 INDEF PR all; **wir ~** all of us; **~ beide** both of us/you/them; **~ vier Jahre** every four years; **~ 100 Meter** every 100 meters; → alles 2 ADV *umg* (*zu Ende*) finished
Allee F avenue
allein ADJ & ADV alone; (*ohne Hilfe*) on one's own, by oneself
alleinerziehend ADJ **~e**

Mutter single mother **Alleinerziehende(r)** M/F(M) single mother/father/parent **alleinstehend** ADJ single, unmarried
allerbeste(r, s) ADJ very best
allerdings ADV (*zwar*) admittedly; (*gewiss*) certainly, sure
allererste(r, s) ADJ very first; **zu allererst** first of all
Allergie F allergy **Allergiker(in)** M(F) allergy sufferer **allergisch** ADJ allergic (*gegen* to)
allerhand ADJ *umg* all sorts of; **das ist doch ~!** (*Vorwurf*) that's the limit!
Allerheiligen N All Saints' Day
allerhöchste(r, s) ADJ very highest **allerhöchstens** ADV at the very most **allerlei** ADJ all sorts of **allerletzte(r, s)** ADJ very last **allerwenigste(r, s)** ADJ very least
alles INDEF PR everything; **~ Gute** all the best; **~ in allem** all in all; → alle
allgemein ADJ general; **im Allgemeinen** in general **Allgemeinarzt** M, **Allgemeinärztin** F family practitioner
Alligator M alligator
alljährlich ADJ annual
allmählich **1** ADJ gradual **2** ADV gradually
Allradantrieb M all-wheel drive
Alltag M everyday life **alltäglich** ADJ everyday; (*gewöhnlich*) ordinary; (*tagtäglich*) daily
allzu ADV all too
Alpen PL **die ~** the Alps *pl*
Alphabet N alphabet **alphabetisch** ADJ alphabetical
Alptraum M → Albtraum
als KONJ (*vergleichend*) than; (*zeitlich*) when; **~ Kind** as a child; **nichts ~ (Ärger)** nothing but (trouble); **anders ~** different from; **erst ~** only when; **~ ob** as if
also **1** KONJ (*folglich*) so, therefore **2** ADV & INT so; **~ gut** (*od* **schön**)! okay then
alt ADJ old; **wie ~ sind Sie?** how old are you?; **28 Jahre ~** 28 years old; **vier Jahre älter** four years older
Altar M altar
Alter N age; (*hohes*) old age; **im ~ von** at the age of; **er ist in meinem ~** he's my age
alternativ ADJ alternative; (*umweltbewusst*) environmentally conscious; (*Landwirtschaft*) organic **Alternative** F alternative
Altersheim N retirement home
Altglas N used glass **Altglascontainer** M glass recycling container **altmodisch** ADJ old-fashioned **Altpapier** N waste paper **Altstadt** F old town
Alufolie F tinfoil
Aluminium N aluminum

Alzheimerkrankheit F Alzheimer's (disease)
am *kontr von* **an dem ~ 2. Januar** on January 2nd; **~ Morgen** in the morning; **~ Strand** on the beach; **~ Bahnhof** at the station; **was gefällt Ihnen ~ besten?** what do you like best?
Amateur(in) M(F) amateur
ambulant ADJ outpatient; **kann ich ~ behandelt werden?** can I have it done as an outpatient? **Ambulanz** F (*Krankenwagen*) ambulance; (*in der Klinik*) outpatients' department
Ameise F ant
amen INT amen
Amerika N America **Amerikaner(in)** M(F) American; **er ist ~** he is American **amerikanisch** ADJ American
Ampel F traffic light
Amsel F blackbird
Amt N (*Dienststelle*) office, department; (*Posten*) post **amtlich** ADJ official **Amtszeichen** N TEL dial tone
amüsant ADJ amusing **amüsieren** 1 V/T amuse 2 V/R enjoy oneself, have a good time
an 1 PRÄP *+dat* **~ der Wand** on the wall; **~ der Mississippi** on the Mississippi; **alles ist ~ seinem Platz** everything is in its place; **~ einem kalten Tag** on a cold day; **~ Ostern** at Easter 2 PRÄP *+akk* **~ die Tür klopfen** knock at the door; **~s Meer fahren** go to the seaside; **~ die 40 Grad** (*fast*) nearly 40 degrees 3 ADV **von ... ~** from ... on; **das Licht/Radio ist ~** the light/radio is on
anal ADJ anal
Analyse F analysis **analysieren** V/T analyse
Ananas F pineapple
anbaggern V/T *umg* come on to
Anbau M AGR cultivation; (*Gebäude*) extension **anbauen** V/T AGR cultivate; (*Gebäudeteil*) build on
anbehalten V/T keep on
anbei ADV enclosed; **~ sende ich ...** please find enclosed ...
anbeten V/T worship
anbieten 1 V/T offer 2 V/R volunteer
anbinden V/T tie up
Anblick M sight
anbraten V/T brown
anbrechen 1 V/T start; (*Vorräte, Ersparnisse*) break into; (*Flasche, Packung*) open 2 V/I start; (*Tag*) break; (*Nacht*) fall
anbrennen V/T & V/I burn; **das Fleisch schmeckt angebrannt** the meat tastes burnt
anbringen V/T (*herbeibringen*) bring; (*befestigen*) fix, attach
Andacht F devotion; (*Gottesdienst*) prayers *pl*
andauern V/I continue, go on **andauernd** ADJ continual
Andenken N memory; (*Gegen-*

stand) souvenir
andere(r, s) ADJ (*weitere*) other; (*verschieden*) different; (*folgend*) next; **am ~n Tag** the next day; **von etw/j-d ~m sprechen** talk about sth/sb else; **unter ~m** among other things **andererseits** ADV on the other hand
ändern **1** V/T alter, change **2** V/R change
andernfalls ADV otherwise
anders ADV differently (*als* from); **jemand/irgendwo ~** someone/somewhere else; **sie ist ~ als ihre Schwester** she's not like her sister; **es geht nicht ~** there's no other way **anders(he)rum** ADV the other way around **anderswo** ADV somewhere else
anderthalb NUM one and a half
Änderung F change, alteration
andeuten V/T indicate; (*Wink geben*) hint at
androhen V/T **j-m etw ~** threaten sb with sth
aneinander ADV at/on/to one another (*od* each other); **~ denken** think of each other; **sich ~ gewöhnen** get used to each other **aneinandergeraten** V/I clash **aneinanderlegen** V/T put together
anerkennen V/T (*Staat, Zeugnis etc*) recognize; (*würdigen*) appreciate **Anerkennung** F recognition; (*Würdigung*) appreciation
anfahren **1** V/T (*fahren gegen*) run into; (*Ort, Hafen*) stop (*od* call) at; (*liefern*) deliver; **j-n ~** *fig* (*schimpfen*) shout at sb **2** V/I start; (*losfahren*) drive off
Anfall M MED attack **anfällig** ADJ delicate; (*Maschine*) temperamental; **~ für** prone to
Anfang M beginning, start; **zu/am ~** to start with; **~ Mai** at the beginning of May; **sie ist ~ 20** she's in her early twenties **anfangen** V/T & V/I begin, start; **damit kann ich nichts ~** that's no use to me
Anfänger(in) M(F) beginner
anfangs ADV at first **Anfangsbuchstabe** M first (*od* initial) letter
anfassen **1** V/T (*berühren*) touch **2** V/I **kannst du mal mit ~?** can you give me a hand?
Anflug M FLUG approach; (*Hauch*) trace
anfordern V/T demand **Anforderung** F request (*von* for); (*Anspruch*) demand
Anfrage F inquiry
anfreunden V/R **sich mit j-m ~** make (*od* become) friends with sb
anfühlen V/R feel; **es fühlt sich gut an** it feels good
Anführungszeichen PL quotation marks *pl*
Angabe F TECH specification;

umg (*Prahlerei*) showing off; (*Tennis*) serve; **~n** *pl* (*Auskunft*) details *pl*; **die ~n waren falsch** (*Info*) the information was wrong **angeben** **1** VT (*Name, Grund*) give; (*zeigen*) indicate; (*bestimmen*) set **2** VI *umg* (*prahlen*) boast; SPORT serve **Angeber(in)** M(F) *umg* show-off **angeblich** ADJ alleged

angeboren ADJ innate; MED congenital

Angebot N offer; WIRTSCH supply (*an +dat* of); **~ und Nachfrage** supply and demand

angebracht ADJ appropriate

angebunden ADJ **kurz ~** curt

angeheitert ADJ tipsy

angehen **1** VT concern; **das geht dich nichts an** that's none of your business; **ein Problem ~** tackle a problem; **was ihn angeht** as far as he's concerned, as for him **2** VI (*Feuer*) catch; (*beginnen*) *umg* begin **angehend** ADJ prospective

Angehörige(r) M/F(M) relative

Angeklagte(r) M/F(M) accused, *defendant*

Angel F fishing rod; (*an der Tür*) hinge

Angelegenheit F affair, matter

angeln **1** VT catch **2** VI fish **Angeln** N angling, fishing **Angelrute** F fishing rod

angemessen ADJ appropriate, suitable

angenehm ADJ pleasant, nice; **~!** (*bei Vorstellung*) pleased to meet you

angenommen **1** ADJ assumed **2** KONJ **~, es regnet, was machen wir dann?** suppose it rains, what do we do then?

angesehen ADJ respected

angesichts PRÄP *+gen* in view of, considering

Angestellte(r) M/F(M) employee

angetan ADJ **von j-m/etw ~ sein** be impressed by (*od* taken with) sb/sth

angewiesen ADJ **auf j-n/etw ~ sein** be dependent on sb/sth

angewöhnen VT **sich etw ~** get used to doing sth **Angewohnheit** F habit

Angina F tonsillitis **Angina Pectoris** F angina

Angler(in) M(F) angler

angreifen VT attack; (*anfassen*) touch; (*beschädigen*) damage **Angriff** M attack; **etw in ~ nehmen** get started on sth

Angst F fear; **~ haben** be afraid (*od* scared) (*vor +dat* of); **j-m ~ machen** scare sb **ängstigen** **1** VT frighten **2** VR worry (*um, wegen +dat* about) **ängstlich** ADJ nervous; (*besorgt*) worried

anhaben VT (*Kleidung*) have on, wear; (*Licht*) have on

anhalten VI stop; (*andauern*) continue **anhaltend** ADJ con-

tinuous **Anhalter(in)** M(F) hitch-hiker; **per ~ fahren** hitch-hike
anhand PRÄP *+gen* with; **~ von** by means of
Anhang M (*Buch*) appendix; IT attachment **anhängen** V/T hang up; BAHN (*Wagen*) couple; (*Zusatz*) add (on); **j-m etw ~** *umg* (*unterschieben*) pin sth on sb **Anhänger** M AUTO trailer; (*am Koffer*) tag; (*Schmuck*) pendant **Anhänger(in)** M(F) supporter **Anhängerkupplung** F towbar
anhänglich ADJ *pej* clingy
Anhieb M **auf ~** straight away; **das kann ich nicht auf ~ sagen** I can't say offhand
anhimmeln V/T worship, idolize
anhören **1** V/T listen to **2** V/R sound; **das hört sich gut an** that sounds good
Animateur(in) M(F) host/hostess
Anis M aniseed
Anker M anchor **ankern** V/T & V/I anchor **Ankerplatz** M anchorage
anklicken V/T IT click on
anklopfen V/I knock (*an +akk* on)
ankommen V/I arrive; **bei j-m gut ~** go down well with sb; **es kommt darauf an** it depends (*ob* on whether); **darauf kommt es nicht an** that doesn't matter
ankotzen V/T *vulg* **es kotzt mich an** it makes me sick
ankreuzen V/T mark with a cross
ankündigen V/T announce
Ankunft F arrival **Ankunftszeit** F arrival time
Anlage F (*Veranlagung*) disposition; (*Begabung*) talent; (*Park*) grounds *pl*; (*zu Brief etc*) enclosure; (*Stereoanlage*) stereo (system); TECH plant; FIN investment
Anlass M cause (*zu* for); (*Ereignis*) occasion; **aus diesem ~** for this reason **anlassen** V/T (*Motor*) start; (*Licht, Kleidung*) leave on **anlässlich** PRÄP *+gen* on the occasion of
Anlauf M run-up **anlaufen** V/I begin; (*Film*) open; (*Fenster*) mist up; (*Metall*) tarnish
anlegen **1** V/T put (*an +akk* against/on); (*Schmuck*) put on; (*Garten*) lay out; (*Geld*) invest; (*Gewehr*) aim (*auf +akk* at); **es auf etw ~** be out for sth **2** V/I (*Schiff*) berth, dock **3** V/R **sich mit j-m ~** *umg* pick a quarrel with sb **Anlegestelle** F moorings *pl*
anlehnen **1** V/T lean (*an +akk* against); (*Tür*) leave ajar **2** V/R lean (*an +akk* against)
Anleitung F instructions *pl*
Anliegen N matter; (*Wunsch*) request
Anlieger(in) M(F) resident
anlügen V/T lie to

anmachen VT (*befestigen*) attach; (*einschalten*) switch on; (*Salat*) dress; *umg* (*aufreizen*) turn on; *umg* (*ansprechen*) come on to; *umg* (*belästigen*) harass

Anmeldeformular N application form; (*bei Amt*) registration form **anmelden** **1** VT (*Besuch etc*) announce **2** VR (*beim Arzt etc*) make an appointment; (*bei Amt, für Kurs etc*) register **Anmeldeschluss** M deadline for applications; registration deadline **Anmeldung** F registration; (*Antrag*) application

annähen VT **einen Knopf (an den Mantel) ~** sew a button on (one's coat)

annähernd ADV roughly; **nicht ~** nowhere near

Annahme F acceptance; (*Vermutung*) assumption **annehmbar** ADJ acceptable **annehmen** VT accept; (*Namen*) take; (*Kind*) adopt; (*vermuten*) suppose, assume

Annonce F advertisement

annullieren VT cancel

anöden VT *umg* bore stiff

anonym ADJ anonymous

Anorak M windbreaker; (*mit Kapuze*) parka

anpacken VT (*Problem, Aufgabe*) tackle; **mit ~** lend a hand

anpassen **1** VT *fig* adapt (*+dat* to) **2** VR adapt (an *+akk* to)

anprobieren VT try on

Anrede F form of address **anreden** VT address

anregen VT stimulate **Anregung** F stimulation; (*Vorschlag*) suggestion

Anreise F journey; **der Tag der ~** the day of arrival **anreisen** VI arrive **Anreisetag** M day of arrival

Anreiz M incentive

anrichten VT (*Speisen*) prepare; (*Schaden*) cause

Anruf M call **Anrufbeantworter** M answering machine **anrufen** VT TEL call

ans *kontr von* **an das**

Ansage F announcement; (*auf Anrufbeantworter*) recorded message **ansagen** VT announce; **angesagt sein** be recommended; (*modisch sein*) be the in thing

anschaffen VT buy

anschauen VT look at

Anschein M appearance; **dem** (*od* **allem**) **~ nach ...** it looks as if ...; **den ~ erwecken, hart zu arbeiten** give the impression of working hard **anscheinend** **1** ADJ apparent **2** ADV apparently

anschieben VT **könnten Sie mich mal ~?** AUTO could you give me a push?

Anschlag M notice; (*Attentat*) attack **anschlagen** **1** VT (*Plakat*) put up; (*beschädigen*) chip **2** VI (*wirken*) take effect; **mit etw an etw ~** bang sth

against sth
anschließen 1 VT ELEK, TECH connect (*an +akk* to); (*mit Stecker*) plug in 2 VI & VR (**sich**) **an etw ~** (*Gebäude etc*) adjoin sth; (*zeitlich*) follow sth 3 VR join (*j-m/einer Gruppe* sb/a group) **anschließend** 1 ADJ adjacent; (*zeitlich*) subsequent 2 ADV afterward(s); **~ an** following **Anschluss** M ELEK, BAHN connection; (*von Wasser, Gas etc*) supply; **im ~ an** following **Anschlussflug** M connecting flight
anschnallen 1 VT (*Skier*) put on 2 VR fasten one's seat belt
Anschrift F address
anschwellen VI swell (up)
ansehen VT look at; (*bei etw zuschauen*) watch; **j-n/etw als etw ~** look on sb/sth as sth; **das sieht man ihm an** he looks it
an sein VI → an
ansetzen 1 VT (*Termin*) fix; (*zubereiten*) prepare 2 VI (*anfangen*) start, begin; **zu etw ~** prepare to do sth
Ansicht F (*Meinung*) view, opinion; (*Anblick*) sight; **meiner ~ nach** in my opinion **Ansichtskarte** F postcard
ansonsten ADV otherwise
Anspielung F allusion (*auf +akk* to)
ansprechen 1 VT speak to; (*gefallen*) appeal to 2 VI **auf etw ~** (*Patient*) respond to sth
ansprechend ADJ attractive
Ansprechpartner(in) M(F) contact
anspringen VI AUTO start
Anspruch M claim; (*Recht*) right (*auf +akk* to); **etw in ~ nehmen** take advantage of sth; **~ auf etw haben** be entitled to sth **anspruchslos** ADJ undemanding; (*bescheiden*) modest **anspruchsvoll** ADJ demanding
Anstalt F institution
Anstand M decency **anständig** ADJ decent; *fig umg* proper; (*groß*) considerable
anstarren VT stare at
anstatt PRÄP *+gen* instead of
anstecken 1 VT pin on; MED infect; **j-n mit einer Erkältung ~** pass one's cold on to sb 2 VR **ich habe mich bei ihm angesteckt** I caught it from him 3 VI *fig* be infectious **ansteckend** ADJ infectious **Ansteckungsgefahr** F danger of infection
anstehen VI (*in Warteschlange*) stand in line; (*erledigt werden müssen*) be on the agenda
anstelle PRÄP *+gen* instead of
anstellen 1 VT (*einschalten*) turn on; (*Arbeit geben*) employ; (*machen*) do; **was hast du wieder angestellt?** what have you been up to now? 2 VR stand in line; *umg* **stell dich nicht so an!** stop making such a fuss
Anstoß M impetus; SPORT

kick-off **anstoßen** **1** VT push; (*mit Fuß*) kick **2** VI knock, bump; (*mit Gläsern*) drink (a toast) (*auf +akk* to) **anstößig** ADJ offensive; (*Kleidung etc*) indecent

anstrengen **1** VT strain **2** VR make an effort **anstrengend** ADJ tiring

Antarktis F Antarctic

Anteil M share (*an +dat* in); **~ nehmen an** (*mitleidig*) sympathize with; (*sich interessieren*) take an interest in

Antenne F antenna

Antibabypille F **die ~** the pill **Antibiotikum** N MED antibiotic

antik ADJ antique

Antiquariat N antiquarian bookshop; (*modernes Antiquariat*) used bookstore

Antiquitäten PL antiques *pl*

antörnen VT *umg* turn on

Antrag M proposal; POL motion; (*Formular*) application form; **einen ~ stellen auf** make an application for

antreffen VT find

antreiben VT TECH drive; (*anschwemmen*) wash up; **j-n zur Arbeit ~** make sb work

antreten VT **eine Reise ~** set off on a journey

Antrieb M TECH drive; (*Motivation*) impetus

antun VT **j-m etwas ~** do sth to sb; **sich etwas ~** (*Selbstmord begehen*) kill oneself

Antwort F answer, reply **antworten** VI answer, reply; **j-m ~** answer sb; **auf etw ~** answer sth

anvertrauen VT **j-m etw ~** entrust sb with sth

Anwalt M, **Anwältin** F lawyer

anweisen VT (*anleiten*) instruct; (*zuteilen*) allocate (*j-m etw* sth to sb) **Anweisung** F instruction; FIN payment; (*Formular*) payment slip; (*Überweisung*) transfer

anwenden VT use; (*Gesetz, Regel*) apply **Anwender(in)** M(F) user **Anwendung** F use; IT application

anwesend ADJ present **Anwesenheit** F presence

anwidern VT disgust

Anwohner(in) M(F) resident

Anzahl F number (*an +dat* of) **anzahlen** VT pay a deposit on; **100 Dollar ~** pay a deposit of 100 dollars **Anzahlung** F deposit

Anzeichen N sign; MED symptom

Anzeige F (*Werbung*) advertisement; (*elektronisch*) display; (*bei Polizei*) report **anzeigen** VT (*Temperatur, Zeit*) indicate, show; (*elektronisch*) display; (*bekannt geben*) announce; **j-n/einen Autodiebstahl bei der Polizei ~** report sb/a stolen car to the police

anziehen **1** VT attract; (*Klei-*

dung) put on; (*Schraube, Seil*) tighten **2** V/R get dressed **anziehend** ADJ attractive
Anzug M suit
anzüglich ADJ suggestive
anzünden V/T light; (*Haus etc*) set fire to
anzweifeln V/T doubt
Aperitif M aperitif
Apfel M apple **Apfelmus** N apple purée **Apfelsine** F orange
Apostroph M apostrophe
Apotheke F pharmacy **apothekenpflichtig** ADJ only available at the pharmacy **Apotheker(in)** M(F) pharmacist
Apparat M (piece of) apparatus; (*Telefon*) (tele)phone; RADIO, TV set; **am ~!** TEL speaking; **am ~ bleiben** TEL hold the line
Appartement N studio apartment
Appetit M appetite; **guten ~!** enjoy your meal! **appetitlich** ADJ appetizing
Applaus M applause
Aprikose F apricot
April M April; → Juni; **~, ~!** April fool! **Aprilscherz** M April fool's joke
apropos ADV by the way; **~ Urlaub ...** while we're on the subject of vacations ...
Aquarell N watercolor
Aquarium N aquarium
Araber(in) M(F) Arab **arabisch** ADJ Arab; (*Ziffer, Sprache*) Arabic; (*Meer, Wüste*) Arabian
Arbeit F work; (*Stelle*) job; (*Erzeugnis*) piece of work **arbeiten** V/I work **Arbeiter(in)** M(F) worker; (*ungelernt*) laborer **Arbeitgeber(in)** M(F) employer **Arbeitnehmer(in)** M(F) employee **Arbeitsagentur** F (un)employment agency **Arbeitsamt** N employment office **Arbeitserlaubnis** F work permit **arbeitslos** ADJ unemployed **Arbeitslose(r)** M/F(M) unemployed person; **die ~n** *pl* the unemployed *pl* **Arbeitslosengeld** N (income-related) unemployment benefit **Arbeitslosenhilfe** F (non-income-related) unemployment benefit **Arbeitslosigkeit** F unemployment **Arbeitsplatz** M job; (*Ort*) workplace **Arbeitsspeicher** M IT main memory **Arbeitszeit** F working hours *pl* **Arbeitszimmer** N study
Architekt(in) M(F) architect **Architektur** F architecture
Archiv N archives *pl*
arg **1** ADJ bad; (*schrecklich*) awful **2** ADV (*sehr*) terribly
Ärger M annoyance; (*stärker*) anger; (*Unannehmlichkeiten*) trouble **ärgerlich** ADJ (*zornig*) angry; (*lästig*) annoying **ärgern** **1** V/T annoy **2** V/R get annoyed

Argument N argument
Arktis F Arctic
arm ADJ poor
Arm M arm; (*Fluss*) branch
Armaturenbrett N instrument panel; AUTO dashboard
Armband N bracelet **Armbanduhr** F (wrist)watch
Armee F army
Ärmel M sleeve
Armut F poverty
Aroma N aroma
arrogant ADJ arrogant
Arsch M *vulg* ass **Arschloch** N *vulg* asshole
Art F (*Weise*) way; (*Sorte*) kind, sort; (*bei Tieren*) species; **auf diese ~ (und Weise)** in this way; **das ist nicht seine ~** that's not like him
Arterie F artery
artig ADJ good, well-behaved
Artikel M (*Ware*) article, item; (*Zeitung*) article
Artischocke F artichoke
Artist(in) M(F) (circus) performer
Arznei F medicine **Arzt** M doctor **Arzthelfer(in)** M(F) doctor's assistant **Ärztin** F (female) doctor **ärztlich** ADJ medical; **sich ~ behandeln lassen** undergo medical treatment
Asche F ashes *pl*; (*von Zigarette*) ash **Aschenbecher** M ashtray
Asiat(in) M(F) Asian **asiatisch** ADJ Asian **Asien** N Asia
Aspekt M aspect
Asphalt M asphalt
Aspirin® N aspirin
Ass N (*Karten, Tennis*) ace
Assistent(in) M(F) assistant
Ast M branch
Asthma N asthma
Astrologie F astrology **Astronaut(in)** M(F) astronaut **Astronomie** F astronomy
Asyl N asylum; (*Heim*) home; (*für Obdachlose*) shelter **Asylant(in)** M(F), **Asylbewerber(in)** M(F) asylum seeker
Atelier N studio
Atem M breath **atemberaubend** ADJ breathtaking **Atembeschwerden** PL breathing difficulties *pl* **atemlos** ADJ breathless **Atempause** F breather
Athlet(in) M(F) athlete
Atlantik M Atlantic (Ocean)
Atlas M atlas
atmen V/T & V/I breathe **Atmung** F breathing
Atom N atom **Atombombe** F atom bomb **Atomkraftwerk** N nuclear power station **Atommüll** M nuclear waste **Atomwaffen** PL nuclear weapons *pl*
Attentat N assassination (*auf +akk* of); (*Versuch*) assassination attempt
Attest N certificate
attraktiv ADJ attractive
ätzend ADJ *umg* revolting; (*schlecht*) lousy

au INT ouch; **~ ja!** yeah
Aubergine F eggplant
auch KONJ also, too; (*selbst, sogar*) even; (*wirklich*) really; **oder ~** or; **ich ~** so do I; **ich ~ nicht** me neither; **wer/was ~ immer** whoever/whatever; **ich gehe jetzt - ich ~** I'm going now - so am I; **das weiß ich ~ nicht** I don't know either
audiovisuell ADJ audiovisual
auf **1** PRÄP +*akk od dat* (*räumlich*) on; **~ der Reise/dem Tisch** on the way/the table; **~ der Post®/der Party** at the post office/the party; **~ Deutsch** in German **2** PRÄP +*akk* (*hinauf*) up; (*in Richtung*) to; (*nach*) after; **~ eine Party gehen** go to a party; **bis ~ ihn** except for him; **~ einmal** suddenly; (*gleichzeitig*) at once **3** ADV (*offen*) open; **~ sein** *umg* be open; (*Mensch*) be up; **~ und ab** up and down; **~!** (*los!*) come on!; **~ dass** so that
aufatmen V/I breathe a sigh of relief
aufbauen V/T (*errichten*) put up; (*schaffen*) build up; (*gestalten*) construct; (*gründen*) found, base (*auf +akk* on)
aufbewahren V/T keep, store
aufbleiben V/I (*Tür, Laden etc*) stay open; (*Mensch*) stay up
aufblenden V/I & V/T (*Scheinwerfer*) put (one's headlights) on high beam
aufbrechen **1** V/T break open **2** V/I burst open; (*gehen*) leave; (*abreisen*) set off
aufdrängen **1** V/T **j-m etw ~** force sth on sb **2** V/R intrude (*j-m* on sb) **aufdringlich** ADJ pushy
aufeinander ADV (*übereinander*) on top of each other; **~ achten** look after each other
aufeinanderfolgen V/I follow one another **aufeinanderprallen** V/I crash into one another
Aufenthalt M stay; (*Zug*) stop **Aufenthaltsgenehmigung** F residence permit **Aufenthaltsraum** M lounge
aufessen V/T eat up
auffahren V/I (*Auto*) run (*od* crash) (*auf +akk* into); (*herankommen*) drive up **Auffahrt** F (*am Haus*) drive; (*Autobahn*) ramp **Auffahrunfall** M rear-end collision; (*mehrere Fahrzeuge*) pile-up
auffallen V/I stand out; **j-m ~** strike sb; **das fällt gar nicht auf** nobody will notice **auffallend** ADJ striking **auffällig** ADJ conspicuous; (*Kleidung, Farbe*) striking
auffangen V/T (*Ball*) catch; (*Stoß*) cushion
auffassen V/T understand **Auffassung** F view; (*Meinung*) opinion; (*Auslegung*) concept; (*Auffassungsgabe*) grasp

auffordern VT (*befehlen*) call upon; (*bitten*) ask
auffrischen VT (*Kenntnisse*) brush up
aufführen 1 VT THEAT perform; (*in einem Verzeichnis*) list; (*Beispiel*) give 2 VR (*sich benehmen*) behave **Aufführung** F THEAT performance
Aufgabe F job, task; (*Schule*) exercise; (*Hausaufgabe*) homework
Aufgang M (*Treppe*) staircase
aufgeben 1 VT (*verzichten auf*) give up; (*Paket*) mail; (*Gepäck*) check in; (*Bestellung*) place; (*Inserat*) insert; (*Rätsel, Problem*) set 2 VI give up
aufgehen VI (*Sonne, Teig*) rise; (*sich öffnen*) open; (*klar werden*) dawn (*j-m* on sb)
aufgelegt ADJ **gut/schlecht ~** in a good/bad mood
aufgeregt ADJ excited
aufgeschlossen ADJ open (-minded)
aufgrund, auf Grund PRÄP *+gen* on the basis of; (*wegen*) because of
aufhaben 1 VT (*Hut etc*) have on; **viel ~** (*Schule*) have a lot of homework to do 2 VI (*Geschäft*) be open
aufhalten 1 VT (*j-n*) detain; (*Entwicklung*) stop; (*Tür, Hand*) hold open; (*Augen*) keep open 2 VR (*wohnen*) live; (*vorübergehend*) stay
aufhängen VT hang up
aufheben VT (*vom Boden etc*) pick up; (*aufbewahren*) keep
aufholen 1 VT (*Zeit*) make up 2 VI catch up
aufhören VI stop; **~, etw zu tun** stop doing sth
aufklären VT (*Missverständnis etc*) clear up; (*Rätsel*) solve; **j-n ~** enlighten sb; (*sexuell*) tell sb the facts of life
Aufkleber M sticker
aufkommen VI (*Wind*) get up; (*Zweifel, Gefühl*) arise; (*Mode etc*) appear on the scene; **für den Schaden ~** pay for the damage
Aufladegerät N charger
aufladen VT load; (*Handy etc*) charge; (*Handykarte etc*) top up
Auflage F edition; (*von Zeitung*) circulation; (*Bedingung*) condition
auflassen VT (*Hut, Brille*) keep on; (*Tür*) leave open
Auflauf M (*Menschen*) crowd; (*Speise*) bake
auflegen 1 VT (*CD, Schminke etc*) put on; (*Hörer*) put down 2 VI TEL hang up
aufleuchten VI light up
auflösen 1 VT (*in Flüssigkeit*) dissolve 2 VR (*in Flüssigkeit*) dissolve; **der Stau hat sich aufgelöst** traffic is back to normal **Auflösung** F (*von Rätsel*) solution; (*von Bildschirm*) resolution
aufmachen 1 VT open; (*Klei-*

dung) undo **2** VR set out (*nach* for)
aufmerksam ADJ attentive; **j-n auf etw ~ machen** draw sb's attention to sth **Aufmerksamkeit** F attention; (*Konzentration*) attentiveness; (*Geschenk*) small token
aufmuntern VT (*ermutigen*) encourage; (*aufheitern*) cheer up
Aufnahme F FOTO photo (-graph); (*einzelne*) shot; (*in Verein, Krankenhaus etc*) admission; (*Beginn*) beginning; (*auf Tonband etc*) recording **aufnehmen** VT (*in Krankenhaus, Verein etc*) admit; (*Musik*) record; (*beginnen*) take up; (*in Liste*) include; (*begreifen*) take in; **mit j-m Kontakt ~** get in touch with sb
aufpassen VI (*aufmerksam sein*) pay attention; (*vorsichtig sein*) take care; **auf j-n/etw ~** keep an eye on sb/sth
Aufprall M impact **aufprallen** VI **auf etw ~** hit sth, crash into sth
Aufpreis M surcharge
aufpumpen VT pump up
Aufputschmittel N stimulant
aufräumen VT & VI (*Dinge*) clear away; (*Zimmer*) tidy up
aufrecht ADJ upright
aufregen **1** VT excite; (*ärgern*) annoy **2** VR get worked up **aufregend** ADJ exciting **Aufregung** F excitement
aufreißen VT (*Tüte*) tear open; (*Tür*) fling open; (*Person*) *umg* pick up
Aufruf M FLUG, IT call; (*öffentlicher*) appeal **aufrufen** VT (*auffordern*) call upon (*zu* for); (*Namen*) call out; FLUG call; IT call up
aufrunden VT (*Summe*) round up
aufs *kontr von* **auf das**
Aufsatz M essay
aufschieben VT (*verschieben*) postpone; (*verzögern*) put off; (*Tür*) slide open
Aufschlag M (*auf Preis*) extra charge; (*Tennis*) serve **aufschlagen** **1** VT (*öffnen*) open; (*verwunden*) cut open; (*Zelt*) pitch, put up; (*Lager*) set up **2** VI (*Tennis*) serve; **auf etw ~** (*aufprallen*) hit sth
aufschließen **1** VT unlock, open up **2** VI (*aufrücken*) close up
aufschneiden **1** VT cut open; (*in Scheiben*) slice **2** VI (*angeben*) boast, show off
Aufschnitt M cold cuts *pl*; (*bei Käse*) (assorted) sliced cheeses *pl*
aufschreiben VT write down
Aufschrift F inscription; (*Etikett*) label
Aufschub M (*Verzögerung*) delay; (*Vertagung*) postponement
Aufsehen N stir; **großes ~ erregen** cause a sensation **Auf-**

seher(in) M/F guard; (*im Betrieb*) supervisor; (*im Museum*) attendant; (*im Park*) keeper
aufsetzen **1** V/T put on; (*Dokument*) draw up **2** V/I (*Flugzeug*) touch down
Aufsicht F supervision; (*bei Prüfung*) invigilation; **die ~ haben** be in charge
aufspannen V/T (*Schirm*) put up
aufsperren V/T (*Mund*) open wide; (*aufschließen*) unlock
aufspringen V/I jump (*auf +akk* onto); (*hochspringen*) jump up; (*sich öffnen*) spring open
aufstehen V/I get up; (*Tür*) be open
aufstellen V/T (*aufrecht stellen*) put up; (*aufreihen*) line up; (*nominieren*) put up; (*Liste, Programm*) draw up; (*Rekord*) set up
Aufstieg M (*auf Berg*) ascent; (*Fortschritt*) rise; (*beruflich, im Sport*) promotion
Aufstrich M spread
auftanken V/T & V/I (*Auto*) tank up; (*Flugzeug*) refuel
auftauchen V/I turn up; (*aus Wasser etc*) surface; (*Frage, Problem*) come up
auftauen **1** V/T (*Speisen*) defrost **2** V/I thaw
Auftrag M WIRTSCH order; (*Arbeit*) job; (*Anweisung*) instructions *pl*; (*Aufgabe*) task; **im ~ von** on behalf of **auftragen** V/T (*Salbe etc*) apply; (*Essen*) serve
auftreten V/I appear; (*Problem*) come up; (*sich verhalten*) behave **Auftritt** M (*des Schauspielers*) entrance; *fig* (*Szene*) scene
aufwachen V/I wake up
aufwachsen V/I grow up
Aufwand M expenditure; (*Kosten a.*) expense; (*Anstrengung*) effort **aufwändig** ADJ costly
aufwärmen V/T & V/R warm up
aufwärts ADV upward(s); **mit etw geht es ~** things are looking up for sth
aufwecken V/T wake up
aufwendig ADJ → aufwändig
aufwischen V/T wipe up; (*Fußboden*) wipe
aufzählen V/T list
aufzeichnen V/T sketch; (*schriftlich*) note down; (*auf Band etc*) record **Aufzeichnung** F (*schriftlich*) note; (*Tonband etc*) recording; (*Film*) record
aufziehen **1** V/T (*öffnen*) pull open; (*Uhr*) wind (up); *umg* (*necken*) tease; (*Kinder*) bring up; (*Tiere*) rear **2** V/I (*Gewitter*) gather
Aufzug M (*Fahrstuhl*) elevator; (*Kleidung*) get-up; THEAT act
Auge N eye; **unter vier ~n** in private; **etw im ~ behalten** keep sth in mind **Augenarzt** M, **Augenärztin** F eye doctor **Augenblick** M moment;

im ~ at the moment **Augenbraue** F eyebrow **Augenlid** N eyelid **Augenoptiker(in)** M(F) optician **Augentropfen** PL eyedrops *pl* **Augenzeuge** M, **Augenzeugin** F eyewitness

August M August; → Juni

Auktion F auction

aus **1** PRÄP +*dat* (*aus dem Innern von*) out of; (*von ... her*) from; (*Material*) made of; **~ Berlin kommen** come from Berlin; **~ Versehen** by mistake; **~ Angst** out of fear **2** ADV out; (*beendet*) finished, over; **ein/~** TECH on/off; **auf etw ~ sein** be after sth; **von mir ~** (*was mich angeht*) as far as I'm concerned; **von mir ~!** (*mir ist es egal*) I don't care **Aus** N SPORT **ins ~ gehen** to go out (of play)

ausatmen V/I breathe out

ausbauen V/T (*Haus, Straße*) extend; (*Motor etc*) remove

ausbessern V/T repair; (*Kleidung*) mend

ausbilden V/T educate; (*Lehrling etc*) train; (*Fähigkeiten*) develop **Ausbildung** F education; (*von Lehrling etc*) training; (*von Fähigkeiten*) development

Ausblick M view; *fig* outlook

ausbrechen V/I break out; **in Tränen ~** burst into tears; **in Gelächter ~** burst out laughing

ausbreiten **1** V/T spread (out); (*Arme*) stretch out **2** V/R spread

Ausbruch M (*Krieg, Seuche etc*) outbreak; (*Vulkan*) eruption; (*Gefühle*) outburst; (*von Gefangenen*) escape

ausbuhen V/T boo

Ausdauer F perseverance; SPORT stamina

ausdehnen V/T stretch; *fig* (*Macht*) extend

ausdenken V/T **sich etw ~** come up with sth

Ausdruck **1** M (Ausdrücke *pl*) expression **2** M (Ausdrucke *pl*) (*Computerausdruck*) printout **ausdrucken** V/T IT print (out)

ausdrücken **1** V/T (*formulieren*) express; (*Zigarette*) put out; (*Zitrone etc*) squeeze **2** V/R express oneself **ausdrücklich** **1** ADJ express **2** ADV expressly

auseinander ADV (*getrennt*) apart; **~ schreiben** write as separate words **auseinandergehen** V/I (*Menschen*) separate; (*Meinungen*) differ; (*Gegenstand*) fall apart **auseinanderhalten** V/T tell apart **auseinandersetzen** **1** V/T (*erklären*) explain **2** V/R **sich ~** (*sich beschäftigen*) look (*mit* at); (*sich streiten*) argue (*mit* with) **Auseinandersetzung** F (*Streit*) argument; (*Diskussion*) debate

Ausfahrt F (*des Zuges etc*) departure; (*Autobahn, Garage*

etc) exit
ausfallen VI (*Haare*) fall out; (*nicht stattfinden*) be canceled; (*nicht funktionieren*) break down; (*Strom*) be cut off; (*Resultat haben*) turn out; **groß/klein ~** (*Kleidung, Schuhe*) be too big/too small
ausfindig machen VT discover
ausflippen VI *umg* freak out
Ausflug M excursion, outing
Ausflugsziel N destination
Ausfluss M MED discharge
ausfragen VT question
Ausfuhr F export
ausführen VT (*verwirklichen*) carry out; (*Person*) take out; WIRTSCH export; (*darlegen*) explain
ausführlich **1** ADJ detailed **2** ADV in detail
ausfüllen VT fill up; (*Fragebogen etc*) fill in (*od* out)
Ausgabe F (*Geld*) expenditure; IT output; (*Buch*) edition; (*Nummer*) issue
Ausgang M way out, exit; (*Flugsteig*) gate; (*Ende*) end; (*Ergebnis*) result
ausgeben **1** VT (*Geld*) spend; (*austeilen*) distribute; **j-m etw ~** (*spendieren*) buy sb sth **2** VR **sich für etw/j-n ~** pass oneself off as sth/sb
ausgebucht ADJ fully booked
ausgefallen ADJ (*ungewöhnlich*) unusual
ausgehen VI (*abends etc*) go out; (*Benzin, Kaffee etc*) run out; (*Haare*) fall out; (*Feuer, Licht etc*) go out; (*Resultat haben*) turn out; **davon ~, dass** assume that; **ihm ging das Geld aus** he ran out of money
ausgelassen ADJ exuberant
ausgeleiert ADJ worn out
ausgenommen KONJ & PRÄP *+gen od dat* except
ausgerechnet ADV **~ du** you of all people; **~ heute** today of all days
ausgeschildert ADJ signposted
ausgeschlafen ADJ **bist du ~?** did you get enough sleep?
ausgeschlossen ADJ (*unmöglich*) impossible, out of the question
ausgesprochen **1** ADJ (*absolut*) out-and-out; (*unverkennbar*) marked **2** ADV extremely
ausgezeichnet ADJ excellent
ausgiebig ADJ (*Gebrauch*) thorough; (*Essen*) substantial
ausgießen VT (*Getränk*) pour out; (*Gefäß*) empty
ausgleichen **1** VT even out **2** VI SPORT equalize
Ausguss M (*Spüle*) sink; (*Abfluss*) outlet
aushalten **1** VT bear, stand; **nicht auszuhalten sein** be unbearable **2** VI hold out
aushändigen VT **j-m etw ~** hand sth over to sb
Aushang M notice
Aushilfe F temporary help;

(*im Büro*) temp
auskennen V/R know a lot (*bei, mit* about); (*an einem Ort*) know one's way around
auskommen V/I **gut/schlecht mit j-m ~** get on well/badly with sb; **mit etw ~** get by with sth
Auskunft F information; (*nähere*) details *pl*; (*Schalter*) information desk; TEL information
auslachen V/T laugh at
ausladen V/T (*Gepäck etc*) unload; **j-n ~** (*Gast*) tell sb not to come
Auslage F display; **~n** *pl* (*Kosten*) expenses
Ausland N foreign countries *pl*; **im/ins ~** abroad **Ausländer(in)** M(F) foreigner **ausländerfeindlich** ADJ hostile to foreigners, xenophobic
ausländisch ADJ foreign
Auslandsgespräch N international call **Auslandskrankenschein** M *health insurance certificate for foreign countries* **Auslandsschutzbrief** M *international* (*motor*) *insurance cover* (*documents pl*)
auslassen **1** V/T leave out; (*Wort etc a.*) omit; (*überspringen*) skip; (*Wut, Ärger*) vent (*an +dat* on) **2** V/R **sich über etw ~** speak one's mind about sth
auslaufen V/I (*Flüssigkeit*) run out; (*Tank etc*) leak; (*Schiff*) leave port; (*Vertrag*) expire
auslegen V/T (*Waren*) display; (*Geld*) lend; (*Text etc*) interpret; (*technisch ausstatten*) design (*für, auf +akk* for)
ausleihen V/T (*verleihen*) lend; **sich etw ~** borrow sth
ausloggen V/I IT log out (*od* off)
auslösen V/T (*Explosion, Alarm*) set off; (*hervorrufen*) cause **Auslöser** M FOTO shutter release
ausmachen V/T (*Licht, Radio*) turn off; (*Feuer*) put out; (*Termin, Preis*) fix; (*vereinbaren*) agree; (*Anteil darstellen, betragen*) represent; (*bedeuten*) matter; **macht es Ihnen etwas aus, wenn ...?** would you mind if ...?; **das macht mir nichts aus** I don't mind
Ausmaß N extent
Ausnahme F exception **ausnahmsweise** ADV as an exception, just this once
ausnutzen V/T (*Zeit, Gelegenheit, Einfluss*) use; (*j-n, Gutmütigkeit*) take advantage of
auspacken V/T unpack
ausprobieren V/T try (out)
Auspuff M TECH exhaust **Auspuffrohr** N exhaust (pipe) **Auspufftopf** M AUTO muffler
ausrauben V/T rob
ausräumen V/T (*Dinge*) clear away; (*Schrank, Zimmer*) empty; (*Bedenken*) put aside
ausrechnen V/T calculate,

work out
Ausrede F excuse
ausreden **1** V/I finish speaking **2** V/T **j-m etw ~** talk sb out of sth
ausreichend ADJ sufficient, satisfactory; (*Schulnote*) ≈ D
Ausreise F departure; **bei der ~** on leaving the country **Ausreiseerlaubnis** F exit visa
ausreisen V/I leave the country
ausreißen **1** V/T tear out **2** V/I come off; *umg* (*davonlaufen*) run away
ausrenken V/T **sich den Arm ~** dislocate one's arm
ausrichten V/T (*Botschaft*) deliver; (*Gruß*) pass on; (*erreichen*) **ich konnte bei ihr nichts ~** I couldn't get anywhere with her; **j-m etw ~** tell sb sth
ausrufen V/T (*über Lautsprecher*) announce; **j-n ~ lassen** page sb **Ausrufezeichen** N exclamation point
ausruhen V/I & V/R rest
Ausrüstung F equipment
ausrutschen V/I slip
ausschalten V/T switch off; *fig* eliminate
Ausschau F **~ halten** look out (*nach* for)
ausscheiden **1** V/T MED give off, secrete **2** V/I leave (*aus etw* sth); SPORT be eliminated
ausschlafen **1** V/I & V/R have a good sleep **2** V/T sleep off
Ausschlag M MED rash; **den ~ geben** *fig* tip the balance
ausschlagen **1** V/T (*Zahn*) knock out; (*Einladung*) turn down **2** V/I (*Pferd*) kick out
ausschlaggebend ADJ decisive
ausschließen V/T lock out; *fig* exclude **ausschließlich** **1** ADV exclusively **2** PRÄP *+gen* excluding
Ausschnitt M (*Teil*) section; (*von Kleid*) neckline; (*aus Zeitung*) cutting
Ausschreitungen PL riots *pl*
ausschütten V/T (*Flüssigkeit*) pour out; (*Gefäß*) empty
aussehen V/I look; **gut ~** (*Person*) be good-looking; (*Sache*) be looking good; **es sieht nach Regen aus** it looks like rain; **es sieht schlecht aus** things look bad
außen ADV outside; **nach ~** outward(s); **von ~** from (the) outside **Außenbordmotor** M outboard motor **Außenminister(in)** M(F) foreign minister **Außenseite** F outside **Außenseiter(in)** M(F) outsider **Außenspiegel** M side mirror
außer **1** PRÄP *+dat* (*abgesehen von*) except (for); **nichts ~** nothing but; **~ Betrieb** out of order; **~ sich sein** be beside oneself (*vor* with); **~ Atem** out of breath **2** KONJ (*ausgenommen*) except; **~ wenn** unless; **~ dass** except **außer-**

dem KONJ besides
äußere(r, s) ADJ outer, external
außergewöhnlich **1** ADJ unusual **2** ADV exceptionally **außerhalb** PRÄP +*gen* outside
äußerlich ADJ external
äußern **1** V/T express; (*zeigen*) show **2** V/R give one's opinion; (*sich zeigen*) show itself
außerordentlich ADJ extraordinary **außerplanmäßig** ADJ unscheduled
äußerst ADV extremely **äußerste(r, s)** ADJ utmost; (*räumlich*) farthest; (*Termin*) last possible
Äußerung F remark
aussetzen **1** V/T (*Kind, Tier*) abandon; (*Belohnung*) offer; **ich habe nichts daran auszusetzen** I have no objection to it **2** V/I (*aufhören*) stop; (*Pause machen*) drop out; (*beim Spiel*) miss a turn
Aussicht F (*Blick*) view; (*Chance*) prospect **aussichtslos** ADJ hopeless **Aussichtsplattform** F observation platform
ausspannen V/I (*erholen*) relax
aussperren **1** V/T lock out **2** V/R lock oneself out
Aussprache F (*von Wörtern*) pronunciation; (*Gespräch*) (frank) discussion **aussprechen** **1** V/T pronounce; (*äußern*) express **2** V/R talk (*über* +*akk* about) **3** V/I (*zu Ende sprechen*) finish speaking
ausspülen V/T rinse (out)
Ausstattung F (*Ausrüstung*) equipment; (*Einrichtung*) furnishings *pl*; (*von Auto*) fittings *pl*
ausstehen **1** V/T endure; **ich kann ihn nicht ~** I can't stand him **2** V/I (*noch nicht da sein*) be outstanding
aussteigen V/I get out (*aus* of); **aus dem Bus/Zug ~** get off the bus/train **Aussteiger(in)** M(F) dropout
ausstellen V/T display; (*auf Messe, in Museum etc*) exhibit; *umg* (*ausschalten*) switch off; (*Scheck etc*) make out; (*Pass etc*) issue **Ausstellung** F exhibition
aussterben V/I die out
ausstrahlen V/T radiate; (*Programm*) broadcast **Ausstrahlung** F RADIO, TV broadcast; *fig* (*von Person*) charisma
ausstrecken **1** V/R stretch out **2** V/T (*Hand*) reach out (*nach* for)
aussuchen V/T choose
Austausch M exchange **austauschen** V/T exchange (*gegen* for)
austeilen V/T distribute; (*aushändigen*) hand out
Auster F oyster
austragen V/T (*Post*) deliver; (*Wettkampf*) hold
Australien N Australia **Australier(in)** M(F) Australian

australisch ADJ Australian
austrinken 1 V/T (*Glas*) drain; (*Getränk*) drink up 2 V/I finish one's drink
austrocknen V/I dry out; (*Fluss*) dry up
ausüben V/T (*Beruf, Sport*) practice; (*Einfluss*) exert
Ausverkauf M sale **ausverkauft** ADJ (*Karten, Artikel*) sold out
Auswahl F selection, choice (*an +dat* of) **auswählen** V/T select, choose
auswandern V/I emigrate
auswärtig ADJ (*nicht am/vom Ort*) not local; (*ausländisch*) foreign **auswärts** ADV (*außerhalb der Stadt*) out of town; SPORT **~ spielen** play away **Auswärtsspiel** N away match
auswechseln V/T replace; SPORT substitute
Ausweg M way out
ausweichen V/I get out of the way; **j-m/einer Sache ~** move aside for sb/sth; *fig* avoid sb/sth
Ausweis M (*Personalausweis*) identity card, ID; (*für Bibliothek etc*) card **ausweisen** 1 V/T expel 2 V/R prove one's identity **Ausweispapiere** PL identification documents *pl*
auswendig ADV by heart
auswuchten V/T AUTO (*Räder*) balance
auszahlen 1 V/T (*Summe*) pay (out); (*Person*) pay off 2 V/R be worth it
auszeichnen 1 V/T (*ehren*) honor; WIRTSCH price 2 V/R distinguish oneself
ausziehen 1 V/T (*Kleidung*) take off 2 V/R undress 3 V/I (*aus Wohnung*) move out
Auszubildende(r) M/F(M) trainee
authentisch ADJ authentic, genuine
Auto N car; **~ fahren** drive **Autoatlas** M road atlas **Autobahn** F freeway **Autobahnauffahrt** F on-ramp **Autobahnausfahrt** F off-ramp **Autobahngebühr** F toll **Autobahnkreuz** N freeway interchange **Autobahnring** M beltway **Autofahrer(in)** M(F) driver, motorist **Autofahrt** F drive
Autogramm N autograph
Automarke F make of car
Automat M vending machine
Automatik F AUTO automatic transmission **Automatikschaltung** F automatic gear shift **Automatikwagen** M automatic
automatisch 1 ADJ automatic 2 ADV automatically
Automechaniker(in) M(F) car mechanic **Autonummer** F license number **Autoradio** N car radio **Autoreifen** M car tire **Autoreisezug** M auto train **Autoschlüssel** M car key **Autotelefon** N car

phone **Autounfall** M car accident **Autoverleih** M, **Autovermietung** F car rental; (*Firma*) car rental company **Autowaschanlage** F car wash **Autowerkstatt** F car repair shop, garage

Avocado F avocado

Axt F ax(e)

Azubi M, F *abk* = Auszubildende; trainee

B

Baby N baby **Babybett** N crib **Babyfläschchen** N baby's bottle **Babynahrung** F baby food **Babysitter(in)** M(F) babysitter **Babysitz** M child seat **Babywickelraum** M baby-changing room

Bach M stream

Backblech N cookie sheet

Backbord N port (side)

Backe F cheek

backen V/T & V/I bake

Backenzahn M molar

Bäcker(in) M(F) baker **Bäckerei** F bakery **Backofen** M oven **Backpulver** N baking powder

Backstein M brick

Backwaren PL bread, cakes and pastries *pl*

Bad N bath; (*Schwimmen*) swim; (*Ort*) spa; **ein ~ nehmen** take a bath **Badeanzug** M swimsuit **Badehose** F swimming trunks *pl* **Badekappe** F swimming cap **Bademantel** M bathrobe **Bademeister(in)** M(F) pool attendant **Bademütze** F swimming cap **baden** **1** V/I take a bath; (*schwimmen*) swim **2** V/T bathe

Badeort M spa **Badesachen** PL swimming things *pl* **Badeschaum** M bubble bath, bath foam **Badetuch** N bath towel **Badewanne** F (bath)tub **Badezeug** N swimming gear **Badezimmer** N bathroom

Bagger M excavator **Baggersee** M *artificial lake in quarry etc, used for bathing*

Bahamas PL **die ~** the Bahamas *pl*

Bahn F (*Eisenbahn*) railroad; (*Rennbahn*) track; (*für Läufer*) lane; ASTRON orbit **Bahnfahrt** F railroad journey **Bahnhof** M station; **am** (*od* **auf dem**) **~** at the station **Bahnlinie** F railroad line **Bahnpolizei** F railroad police **Bahnsteig** M platform **Bahnstrecke** F railroad line **Bahnübergang** M railroad crossing

Bakterien PL bacteria *pl*, germs *pl*

bald ADV (*zeitlich*) soon; (*beinahe*) almost; **bis ~!** see you soon (*od* later) **baldig** ADJ quick,

speedy
Balken M beam
Balkon M balcony
Ball M ball; (*Tanz*) dance, ball
Ballett N ballet
Ballon M balloon
Ballspiel N ball game
Bambus M bamboo
Banane F banana
Band **1** M (*Buch*) volume **2** N (*aus Stoff*) ribbon, tape; (*Fließband*) production line; (*Tonband*) tape; ANAT ligament **3** F (*Musikgruppe*) band
Bandage F bandage **bandagieren** V/T bandage
Bande F (*Gruppe*) gang
Bänderriss M MED torn ligament
Bandscheibe F ANAT disc **Bandwurm** M tapeworm
Bank **1** F (*Sitzbank*) bench **2** F FIN bank
Bankautomat M cash machine, ATM **Bankkarte** F bank card **Bankkonto** N bank account **Bankleitzahl** F bank routing number **Banknote** F banknote, bill **Bankverbindung** F (*Kontonummer etc*) banking (*od* account) details *pl*
bar ADJ **~es Geld** cash; **etw (in) ~ bezahlen** pay sth (in) cash
Bar F bar
Bär M bear
barfuß ADJ barefoot
Bargeld N cash **bargeldlos** ADJ cashless
Barkeeper M, **Barmann** M bartender
barsch ADJ brusque
Barscheck M open check
Bart M beard **bärtig** ADJ bearded
Barzahlung F cash payment
Basar M bazaar
Baseballmütze F baseball cap
Basilikum N basil
Basis F basis
Basketball M basketball
Bass M bass
basteln **1** V/T make **2** V/I make things, do handicrafts
Batterie F battery **batteriebetrieben** ADJ battery-powered
Bau **1** M (*Bauen*) building, construction; (*Aufbau*) structure; (*Baustelle*) building site **2** M (Baue *pl*) (*Tier*) burrow **3** M (Bauten *pl*) (*Gebäude*) building **Bauarbeiten** PL construction work *sg*; (*Straßenbau*) roadwork *sg* **Bauarbeiter(in)** M(F) construction worker
Bauch M stomach **Bauchnabel** M navel **Bauchschmerzen** PL stomachache *sg* **Bauchspeicheldrüse** F pancreas **Bauchweh** N stomachache
bauen V/T & V/I build; TECH construct
Bauer M farmer; (*Schach*) pawn **Bäuerin** F farmer; (*Frau des Bauern*) farmer's wife **Bau-**

ernhof M farm
baufällig ADJ dilapidated
Baujahr N year of construction; **der Wagen ist ~ 2010** the car is a 2010 model, the car was made in 2010
Baum M tree
Baumarkt M home-improvement market, DIY store
Baumwolle F cotton
Bauplatz M building site
Baustein M (*für Haus*) stone; (*Spielzeug*) brick; *fig* element
Baustelle F building site; (*bei Straßenbau*) roadwork
Bauunternehmer(in) M(F) building contractor **Bauwerk** N building
Bayern N Bavaria
beabsichtigen V/T intend
beachten V/T (*Aufmerksamkeit schenken*) pay attention to; (*Vorschrift etc*) observe; **nicht ~** ignore **beachtlich** ADJ considerable
Beachvolleyball N beach volleyball
Beamte(r) M, **Beamtin** F official; (*Staatsbeamter*) civil servant
beanspruchen V/T claim; (*Zeit, Platz*) take up; **j-n ~** keep sb busy
beanstanden V/T complain about **Beanstandung** F complaint
beantragen V/T apply for
beantworten V/T answer
bearbeiten V/T work; (*Material, Daten*) process; CHEM treat; (*Fall etc*) deal with; (*Buch etc*) revise; *umg* (*beeinflussen wollen*) work on **Bearbeitungsgebühr** F handling (*od* service) charge
beatmen V/T **j-n ~** give sb artificial respiration
beaufsichtigen V/T supervise; (*bei Prüfung*) proctor
beauftragen V/T instruct; **j-n mit etw ~** give sb the job of doing sth
Becher M mug; (*ohne Henkel*) tumbler; (*für Jogurt*) pot; (*aus Pappe*) tub
Becken N bowl; (*Spüle*) sink; (*zum Schwimmen*) pool; MUS cymbal; ANAT pelvis
bedanken V/R say thank you; **sich bei j-m für etw ~** thank sb for sth
Bedarf M need (*an* for); WIRTSCH demand (*an* for); **je nach ~** according to demand; **bei ~** if necessary **Bedarfshaltestelle** F flag stop
bedauerlich ADJ regrettable
bedauern V/T regret; (*bemitleiden*) feel sorry for **bedauernswert** ADJ (*Zustände*) regrettable; (*Mensch*) unfortunate
bedeckt ADJ covered; (*Himmel*) overcast
bedenken V/T consider **Bedenken** N (*Überlegen*) consideration; (*Zweifel*) doubt; (*Skrupel*) scruples *pl* **bedenklich**

ADJ dubious; (*Zustand*) serious
bedeuten VT mean; **j-m nichts/viel ~** mean nothing/a lot to sb **bedeutend** ADJ important; (*beträchtlich*) considerable **Bedeutung** F meaning; (*Wichtigkeit*) importance
bedienen **1** VT serve; (*Maschine*) operate **2** VR (*beim Essen*) help oneself **Bedienung** F service; (*Kellner/Kellnerin*) waiter/waitress; (*Verkäufer(in)*) sales clerk; (*Zuschlag*) service charge **Bedienungsanleitung** F operating instructions *pl* **Bedienungshandbuch** N instruction manual
Bedingung F condition; **unter der ~, dass** on condition that; **unter diesen ~en** under these circumstances
bedrohen VT threaten
Bedürfnis N need
beeilen VR hurry
beeindrucken VT impress
beeinflussen VT influence
beeinträchtigen VT affect
beenden VT end; (*fertigstellen*) finish
beerdigen VT bury **Beerdigung** F burial; (*Feier*) funeral
Beere F berry; (*Traubenbeere*) grape
Beet N bed
befahrbar ADJ passable; SCHIFF navigable **befahren** **1** VT (*Straße*) use; (*Pass*) drive over; (*Fluss etc*) navigate **2** ADJ **stark/wenig ~** busy/quiet
Befehl M order; IT command **befehlen** **1** VT order; **j-m ~, etw zu tun** order sb to do sth **2** VI give orders
befestigen VT fix; (*mit Schnur, Seil*) attach; (*mit Klebestoff*) stick
befeuchten VT moisten
befinden VR be
befolgen VT (*Rat etc*) follow
befördern VT (*transportieren*) transport; (*beruflich*) promote **Beförderung** F transportation; (*beruflich*) promotion **Beförderungsbedingungen** PL terms *pl* of transportation
Befragung F questioning; (*Umfrage*) opinion poll
befreundet ADJ friendly; **~ sein** be friends (*mit j-m* with sb)
befriedigen VT satisfy **befriedigend** ADJ satisfactory; (*Schulnote*) ≈ C **Befriedigung** F satisfaction
befristet ADJ limited (*auf +akk* to)
befruchten VT fertilize; *fig* stimulate
Befund M findings *pl*; MED diagnosis
befürchten VT fear
befürworten VT support
begabt ADJ gifted, talented **Begabung** F talent, gift
begegnen VI meet (*j-m* sb), meet with (*einer Sache dat* sth)
begehen VT (*Straftat*) commit; (*Jubiläum etc*) celebrate
begehrt ADJ sought-after; (*Fe-*

rienziel) popular
begeistern **1** VT fill with enthusiasm; *(inspirieren)* inspire **2** VR **sich für etw ~** be/get enthusiastic about sth **begeistert** ADJ enthusiastic
Beginn M beginning; **zu ~** at the beginning **beginnen** VT & VI start, begin
beglaubigen VT certify
begleiten VT accompany **Begleiter(in)** M(F) companion **Begleitung** F company; MUS accompaniment
beglückwünschen VT congratulate *(zu* on)
begraben VT bury **Begräbnis** N burial; *(Feier)* funeral
begreifen VT understand
Begrenzung F boundary; *fig* restriction
Begriff M concept; *(Vorstellung)* idea; **im ~ sein, etw zu tun** be just about to do sth; **schwer von ~ sein** be slow on the uptake
begründen VT *(rechtfertigen)* justify **Begründung** F explanation; *(Rechtfertigung)* justification
begrüßen VT greet; *(willkommen heißen)* welcome **Begrüßung** F greeting; *(Empfang)* welcome
behaart ADJ hairy
behalten VT keep; *(im Gedächtnis)* remember; **etw für sich ~** keep sth to oneself
Behälter M container
behandeln VT treat **Behandlung** F treatment
behaupten **1** VT claim, maintain **2** VR assert oneself **Behauptung** F claim
beheizen VT heat
behelfen VR **sich mit/ohne etw ~** make do with/without sth
beherbergen VT accommodate
beherrschen **1** VT *(Situation, Gefühle)* control; *(Instrument)* master **2** VR control oneself **Beherrschung** F control *(über +akk* of); **die ~ verlieren** lose one's self-control
behilflich ADJ helpful; **j-m ~ sein** help sb *(bei* with)
behindern VT hinder; *(Verkehr, Sicht)* obstruct **Behinderte(r)** M/F(M) disabled person **behindertengerecht** ADJ suitable for disabled people
Behörde F authority; **die ~n** *pl* the authorities *pl*
bei PRÄP *+dat (örtlich: in der Nähe von)* near, by; *(zum Aufenthalt)* at; *(zeitlich)* at, on; *(während)* during; *(Umstand)* in; **~m Friseur** at the hairdresser; **~ uns zuhause** at our place; *(in unserem Land)* in our country; **~ Nacht** at night; **~ Tag** by day; **~ Nebel** in fog; **~ Regen findet die Veranstaltung im Saal statt** if it rains the event will take place in the

hall; **etw ~ sich haben** have sth on one; **~m Fahren** while driving
beibehalten V/T keep
beibringen V/T **j-m etw ~** (*mitteilen*) break sth to sb; (*lehren*) teach sb sth
beide(s) INDEF PR both; **meine ~n Brüder** my two brothers, both my brothers; **wir ~** both (*od* the two) of us; **keiner von ~n** neither of them; **alle ~** both (of them); **~s ist sehr schön** both are very nice
beieinander ADV together
Beifahrer(in) M(F) passenger **Beifahrersitz** M passenger seat
Beifall M applause
beige ADJ beige
Beigeschmack M aftertaste
Beil N ax(e)
Beilage F GASTR side dish; (*Gemüse*) vegetables *pl*; (*zu Buch etc*) supplement
beiläufig **1** ADJ casual **2** ADV casually
Beileid N condolences *pl*; **(mein) herzliches ~** please accept my sincere condolences
beiliegend ADJ enclosed
Bein N leg
beinah(e) ADV almost, nearly
beinhalten V/T contain
beisammen ADV together **Beisammensein** N get-together
beiseite ADV aside **beiseitelegen** V/T **etw ~** (*sparen*) put sth by
Beispiel N example; **sich an j-m/etw ein ~ nehmen** take sb/sth as an example; **zum ~** for example
beißen **1** V/T bite **2** V/I bite; (*stechen: Rauch, Säure*) sting **3** V/R (*Farben*) clash
Beitrag M contribution; (*für Mitgliedschaft*) subscription; (*Versicherung*) premium **beitragen** V/T & V/I contribute (*zu* to)
bekannt ADJ well-known; (*nicht fremd*) familiar; **mit j-m ~ sein** know sb; **~ geben** announce; **j-n mit j-m ~ machen** introduce sb to sb **Bekannte(r)** M/F(M) friend; (*entfernter*) acquaintance **Bekanntschaft** F acquaintance
bekiffen V/R *umg* get stoned
beklagen V/R complain
Bekleidung F clothing
bekommen **1** V/T get; (*erhalten*) receive; (*Kind*) have; (*Zug, Grippe*) catch, get; **wie viel ~ Sie dafür?** how much is that? **2** V/I **j-m ~** (*Essen*) agree with sb; **wir ~ schon** (*bedient werden*) we're being served
beladen V/T load
Belag M coating; (*auf Zähnen*) plaque; (*auf Zunge*) fur
belasten V/T load; (*Körper*) strain; (*Umwelt*) pollute; *fig* (*mit Sorgen etc*) burden; WIRTSCH (*Konto*) debit; JUR incriminate

belästigen V/T bother; (*stärker*) pester; (*sexuell*) harass **Belästigung** F annoyance; **sexuelle ~** sexual harassment
belebt ADJ (*Straße etc*) busy
Beleg M WIRTSCH receipt; (*Beweis*) proof **belegen** V/T (*Brot*) spread; (*Platz*) reserve; (*Kurs, Vorlesung*) register for; (*beweisen*) prove **belegt** ADJ TEL busy; (*Hotel*) full; (*Zunge*) coated; **~es Brötchen** sandwich; **der Platz ist ~** this seat is taken **Belegtzeichen** N TEL busy tone
beleidigen V/T insult; (*kränken*) offend **Beleidigung** F insult; JUR slander; (*schriftliche*) libel
beleuchten V/T light; (*bestrahlen*) illuminate; *fig* examine **Beleuchtung** F lighting; (*Bestrahlung*) illumination
Belgien N Belgium **Belgier(in)** M(F) Belgian **belgisch** ADJ Belgian
Belichtung F exposure
Belieben N **(ganz) nach ~** (just) as you wish **beliebig** **1** ADJ **jedes ~e Muster** any pattern; **jeder ~e** anyone **2** ADV **~ lange** as long as you like; **~ viel** as many (*od* much) as you like **beliebt** ADJ popular
beliefern V/T supply
bellen V/I bark
Belohnung F reward
Belüftung F ventilation
belügen V/T lie to
bemerkbar ADJ noticeable; **sich ~ machen** (*Mensch*) attract attention; (*Zustand*) become noticeable **bemerken** V/T (*wahrnehmen*) notice; (*sagen*) remark **bemerkenswert** ADJ remarkable **Bemerkung** F remark
bemitleiden V/T pity
bemühen V/R try (hard), make an effort **Bemühung** F effort
benachbart ADJ neighboring
benachrichtigen V/T inform **Benachrichtigung** F notification
benachteiligen V/T (put at a) disadvantage; (*wegen Rasse etc*) discriminate against
benehmen V/R behave **Benehmen** N behavior
beneiden V/T envy; **j-n um etw ~** envy sb sth
benommen ADJ dazed
benötigen V/T need
benutzen V/T use **Benutzer(in)** M(F) user **benutzerfreundlich** ADJ user-friendly **Benutzerkennung** F user ID **Benutzeroberfläche** F IT user/system interface **Benutzung** F use **Benutzungsgebühr** F charge
Benzin N AUTO gas **Benzinkanister** M gas can **Benzinpumpe** F gas pump **Benzintank** M gas tank **Benzinuhr** F fuel gauge
beobachten V/T observe **Beobachtung** F observation

bequem ADJ comfortable; (*Ausrede*) convenient; (*faul*) lazy; **machen Sie es sich ~** make yourself at home **Bequemlichkeit** F comfort; (*Faulheit*) laziness

beraten 1 VT advise; (*besprechen*) discuss 2 VR consult **Beratung** F advice; (*bei Arzt etc*) consultation

berauben VT rob

berechnen VT calculate; WIRTSCH charge **berechnend** ADJ (*Mensch*) calculating

berechtigen VT entitle (*zu +dat* to); *fig* justify **berechtigt** ADJ justified; **zu etw ~ sein** be entitled to sth

bereden VT (*besprechen*) discuss

Bereich M area; (*Ressort, Gebiet*) field

bereisen VT travel through

bereit ADJ ready; **zu etw ~ sein** be ready for sth; **sich ~ erklären, etw zu tun** agree to do sth **bereiten** VT prepare; (*Kummer*) cause; (*Freude*) give **bereitlegen** VT lay out **bereitmachen** VR get ready **bereits** ADV already **Bereitschaft** F readiness; **~ haben** (*Arzt*) be on call **bereitstehen** VI be ready

bereuen VT regret

Berg M mountain; (*kleiner*) hill; **in die ~e fahren** go to the mountains **bergab** ADV downhill **bergauf** ADV uphill

bergen VT (*retten*) rescue

bergig ADJ mountainous

Bergschuh M climbing boot

Bergsteigen N mountaineering **Bergsteiger(in)** M(F) mountaineer **Bergtour** F mountain hike

Bergung F (*Rettung*) rescue; (*von Toten, Fahrzeugen*) recovery

Bergwacht F mountain rescue service **Bergwerk** N mine

Bericht M report **berichten** VT & VI report

berichtigen VT correct

Berlin N Berlin

Bermudashorts PL Bermuda shorts *pl*

berüchtigt ADJ notorious, infamous

berücksichtigen VT take into account; (*Antrag, Bewerber*) consider

Beruf M occupation; (*akademischer*) profession; (*Gewerbe*) trade; **was sind Sie von ~?** what do you do (for a living)? **beruflich** ADJ professional **Berufsausbildung** F vocational training **Berufsschule** F vocational college **berufstätig** ADJ employed **Berufsverkehr** M commuter traffic

beruhigen 1 VT calm 2 VR (*Mensch, Situation*) calm down **beruhigend** ADJ reassuring **Beruhigungsmittel** N sedative

berühmt ADJ famous **berühren** 1 VT touch; (*gefühlsmäßig bewegen*) move; (*betreffen*) affect; (*flüchtig erwähnen*) mention, touch on 2 VR touch
besaufen VR *umg* get hammered
beschädigen VT damage
beschäftigen 1 VT occupy; (*beruflich*) employ 2 VR **sich mit etw ~** occupy oneself with sth; (*sich befassen*) deal with sth **beschäftigt** ADJ busy, occupied **Beschäftigung** F (*Beruf*) employment; (*Tätigkeit*) occupation; (*geistige*) preoccupation (*mit* with)
Bescheid M information; **~ wissen** be informed (*od* know) (*über +akk* about); **ich weiß ~** I know; **j-m ~ geben** (*od* sagen) let sb know
bescheiden ADJ modest
bescheinigen VT certify; (*bestätigen*) acknowledge **Bescheinigung** F certificate; (*Quittung*) receipt
beschimpfen VT (*mit Kraftausdrücken*) swear at
beschissen ADJ *vulg* shitty
beschlagnahmen VT confiscate
Beschleunigung F acceleration
beschließen VT decide on; (*beenden*) end **Beschluss** M decision
beschränken 1 VT limit, restrict (*auf +akk* to) 2 VR restrict oneself (*auf +akk* to) **Beschränkung** F limitation, restriction
beschreiben VT describe; (*Papier*) write on **Beschreibung** F description
beschuldigen VT accuse (*gen* of) **Beschuldigung** F accusation
beschützen VT protect (*vor +dat* from)
Beschwerde F complaint; **~n** *pl* (*Leiden*) trouble *sg* **beschweren** 1 VT weight down; *fig* burden 2 VR complain
beschwipst ADJ tipsy
beseitigen VT remove; (*Problem*) get rid of; (*Müll*) dispose of **Beseitigung** F removal; (*von Müll*) disposal
Besen M broom
besetzen VT (*Haus, Land*) occupy; (*Platz*) take; (*Posten*) fill; (*Rolle*) cast **besetzt** ADJ full; TEL busy; (*Platz*) taken; (*WC*) occupied **Besetztzeichen** N busy tone
besichtigen VT (*Museum*) visit; (*Sehenswürdigkeit*) have a look at; (*Stadt*) tour
besiegen VT defeat
Besitz M possession; (*Eigentum*) property **besitzen** VT own; (*Eigenschaft*) have **Besitzer(in)** M(F) owner
besoffen ADJ *umg* hammered
besondere(r, s) ADJ special;

(*bestimmt*) particular; (*eigentümlich*) peculiar; **nichts Besonderes** nothing special **Besonderheit** F special feature; (*besondere Eigenschaft*) peculiarity **besonders** ADV especially, particularly; (*getrennt*) separately

besorgen V/T (*beschaffen*) get (*j-m* for sb); (*kaufen a.*) purchase; (*erledigen: Geschäfte*) deal with

besprechen V/T discuss **Besprechung** F discussion; (*Konferenz*) meeting **Besprechungsraum** M consultation room

besser ADJ better; **es geht ihm ~** he feels better; **~ gesagt** or rather; **~ werden** improve

bessern **1** V/T improve **2** V/R improve; (*Mensch*) mend one's ways **Besserung** F improvement; **gute ~!** get well soon

beständig ADJ constant; (*Wetter*) settled

Bestandteil M component

bestätigen V/T confirm; (*Empfang, Brief*) acknowledge **Bestätigung** F confirmation; (*von Brief*) acknowledgement

beste(r, s) **1** ADJ best; **das ~ wäre, wir ...** it would be best if we ... **2** ADV **sie singt am ~n** she sings best; **so ist es am ~n** it's best that way; **am ~n gehst du gleich** you'd better go at once

bestechen V/T bribe **Bestechung** F bribery

Besteck N cutlery, flatware

bestehen **1** V/I be, exist; (*andauern*) last; **~ auf** insist on; **~ aus** consist of **2** V/T (*Probe, Prüfung*) pass; (*Kampf*) win

bestehlen V/T rob

bestellen V/T order; (*reservieren*) book; (*Grüße, Auftrag*) pass on (*j-m* to sb); (*kommen lassen*) send for **Bestellnummer** F order number **Bestellung** F WIRTSCH order; (*das Bestellen*) ordering

bestens ADV very well

bestimmen V/T determine; (*Regeln*) lay down; (*Tag, Ort*) fix; (*ernennen*) appoint; (*vorsehen*) mean (*für* for) **bestimmt** **1** ADJ definite; (*gewiss*) certain; (*entschlossen*) firm **2** ADV definitely; (*wissen*) for sure **Bestimmung** F (*Verordnung*) regulation; (*Zweck*) purpose

bestrafen V/T punish

bestrahlen V/T illuminate; MED treat with radiotherapy

bestreiten V/T (*leugnen*) deny

bestürzt ADJ dismayed

Besuch M visit; (*Mensch*) visitor; **~ haben** have visitors/a visitor **besuchen** V/T visit; (*Schule, Kino etc*) go to **Besucher(in)** M(F) visitor **Besuchszeit** F visiting hours *pl*

betäuben V/T MED anesthetize **Betäubung** F anesthetic; **örtliche ~** local anesthetic

Bete F **Rote ~** beet **beteiligen** 1 V/R **sich an etw ~** take part in sth, participate in sth 2 V/T **j-n an etw ~** involve sb in sth **Beteiligung** F participation; (*Anteil*) share; (*Besucherzahl*) attendance
beten V/I pray
Beton M concrete
betonen V/T stress; (*hervorheben*) emphasize **Betonung** F stress; *fig* emphasis
Betracht M **in ~ ziehen** take into consideration; **in ~ kommen** be a possibility; **nicht in ~ kommen** be out of the question **betrachten** V/T look at; **~ als** regard as **beträchtlich** ADJ considerable
Betrag M amount, sum **betragen** 1 V/T amount (*od* come) to 2 V/R behave
betreffen V/T concern; (*Regelung etc*) affect; **was mich betrifft** as for me **betreffend** ADJ relevant, in question
betreten V/T enter; (*Bühne etc*) step onto
betreuen V/T look after; (*Reisegruppe, Abteilung*) be in charge of **Betreuer(in)** M(F) (*Pfleger*) carer; (*Kinderbetreuer*) childcare provider; (*von Reisegruppe*) group leader
Betrieb M (*Firma*) firm; (*Anlage*) plant; (*Tätigkeit*) operation; (*Treiben*) bustle; **außer ~ sein** be out of order; **in ~ sein** be in operation **betriebsbereit** ADJ operational **Betriebsrat** M (*Gremium*) employee organization **Betriebssystem** N IT operating system
betrinken V/R get drunk
betroffen ADJ (*bestürzt*) shaken; **von etw ~ werden/sein** be affected by sth
Betrug M deception; JUR fraud **betrügen** V/T deceive; JUR defraud; (*Partner*) cheat on **Betrüger(in)** M(F) cheat
betrunken ADJ drunk
Bett N bed; **ins** (*od* **zu**) **~ gehen** go to bed; **das ~ machen** make the bed **Bettbezug** M comforter cover **Bettdecke** F blanket
betteln V/I beg
Bettlaken N sheet
Bettler(in) M(F) beggar
Bettsofa N sofa bed **Betttuch** N sheet **Bettwäsche** F bed linen **Bettzeug** N bedding
beugen 1 V/T bend 2 V/R bend; (*sich fügen*) submit (*dat* to)
Beule F (*Schwellung*) bump; (*Delle*) dent
beunruhigen V/T & V/R worry
beurteilen V/T judge
Beute F (*von Dieb*) booty, loot; (*von Tier*) prey
Beutel M bag
Bevölkerung F population
bevollmächtigt ADJ authorized (*zu etw* to do sth)
bevor KONJ before **bevorste-**

hen VI (Schwierigkeiten) lie ahead; (Gefahr) be imminent; j-m ~ (Überraschung etc) be in store for sb **bevorstehend** ADJ forthcoming **bevorzugen** VT prefer
bewachen VT guard **bewacht** ADJ guarded
bewegen VT & VR move; **j-n dazu ~, etw zu tun** get sb to do sth; **es bewegt sich etwas** *fig* things are beginning to happen **Bewegung** F movement; PHYS motion; (*innere*) emotion; (*körperlich*) exercise **Bewegungsmelder** M motion sensor
Beweis M proof; (*Zeugnis*) evidence **beweisen** VT prove; (*zeigen*) show
bewerben VR apply (*um* for) **Bewerbung** F application
bewilligen VT allow; (*Geld*) grant
bewirken VT cause, bring about
bewohnen VT live in **Bewohner(in)** M(F) inhabitant; (*von Haus*) resident
bewölkt ADJ cloudy, overcast
bewundern VT admire **bewundernswert** ADJ admirable
bewusst **1** ADJ conscious; (*absichtlich*) deliberate; **sich einer Sache ~ sein** be aware of sth **2** ADV consciously; (*absichtlich*) deliberately **bewusstlos** ADJ unconscious **Bewusstlosigkeit** F unconsciousness **Bewusstsein** N consciousness; **bei ~** conscious
bezahlen VT pay; (*Ware, Leistung*) pay for **Bezahlung** F payment
bezeichnen VT (*kennzeichnen*) mark; (*nennen*) call; (*beschreiben*) describe **Bezeichnung** F (*Name*) name; (*Begriff*) term
beziehen **1** VT (*Bett*) change; (*Haus, Position*) move into; (*erhalten*) receive; (*Zeitung*) take **2** VR refer (*auf +akk* to) **Beziehung** F (*Verbindung*) connection; (*Verhältnis*) relationship; **~en haben** (*vorteilhaft*) have connections (*od* contacts); **in dieser ~** in this respect **beziehungsweise** ADV or; (*genauer gesagt*) or rather
Bezirk M district
Bezug M (*Überzug*) cover; (*von Kopfkissen*) pillowcase; **in ~ auf** with regard to **bezüglich** PRÄP *+gen* concerning
bezweifeln VT doubt
BH M bra
Bibel F Bible
Biber M beaver
Bibliothek F library
biegen **1** VT & VR bend **2** VI turn (*in +akk* into) **Biegung** F bend
Biene F bee
Bier N beer; **helles ~** beer; **dunkles ~** dark beer; **zwei ~, bitte!** two beers, please **Bier-**

garten M beer garden
bieten **1** VT offer; (*bei Versteigerung*) bid; **sich etw ~ lassen** put up with sth **2** VR (*Gelegenheit*) present itself (*dat* to)
Bikini M bikini
Bild N picture; (*gedankliches*) image; (*Foto*) photo
bilden **1** VT form; (*geistig*) educate; (*ausmachen*) constitute **2** VR (*entstehen*) form; (*lernen*) educate oneself
Bilderbuch N picture book
Bildhauer(in) M(F) sculptor
Bildschirm M screen **Bildschirmschoner** M screensaver **Bildschirmtext** M viewdata, videotext
Bildung F formation; (*Wissen, Benehmen*) education **Bildungsurlaub** M educational vacation; (*von Firma*) study leave
billig ADJ cheap; (*gerecht*) fair **Billigflieger** M budget airline **Billigflug** M cheap flight
Binde F bandage; (*Armbinde*) band; (*Damenbinde*) sanitary napkin **Bindehautentzündung** F conjunctivitis **binden** VT tie; (*Buch*) bind; (*Soße*) thicken **Bindestrich** M hyphen **Bindfaden** M string **Bindung** F bond, tie; (*Skibindung*) binding
Biokost F health food **Biologie** F biology **biologisch** ADJ biological; (*Anbau*) organic
Birke F birch
Birne F (*Obst*) pear; ELEK (light) bulb
bis **1** PRÄP +*akk* (*räumlich, bis zu/an*) to, as far as; (*zeitlich*) till, until; (*bis spätestens*) by; **Sie haben ~ Dienstag Zeit** you have until (*od* till) Tuesday; **~ hierher** this far; **~ in die Nacht** into the night; **~ auf Weiteres** until further notice; **~ bald/gleich!** see you later/soon; **~ auf etw** (*einschließlich*) including sth; (*ausgeschlossen*) except sth; **~ zu** up to; **von ... ~ ...** from ... to ... **2** KONJ (*mit Zahlen*) to; (*zeitlich*) until, till
Bischof M bishop
bisher ADV up to now, so far
Biskuit N sponge (cake)
Biss M bite
bisschen **1** ADJ **ein ~ Salz/Liebe** a bit of salt/love; **ich habe kein ~ Hunger** I'm not a bit hungry **2** ADV **ein ~** a bit; **kein ~** not at all
bissig ADJ (*Hund*) vicious; (*Bemerkung*) cutting
Bit N IT bit
bitte INT please; **(wie) ~?** (I beg your) pardon?, excuse me?; **~ (schön)!** (*als Antwort auf danke*) you're welcome, that's alright; **hier, ~** here you are **Bitte** F request **bitten** VT & VI ask (*um* for)
bitter ADJ bitter
Blähungen PL MED wind *sg*
blamieren **1** VR make a fool of oneself **2** VT **j-n ~** make

sb look a fool
Blankoscheck M blank check
Blase F bubble; MED blister; ANAT bladder
blasen V/I blow; **j-m einen ~** *vulg* give sb a blow job
Blasenentzündung F cystitis
blass ADJ pale
Blatt N leaf; (*von Papier*) sheet **blättern** V/I IT scroll; **in etw ~** leaf through sth **Blätterteig** M puff pastry (*od* paste) **Blattsalat** M green salad **Blattspinat** M spinach
blau ADJ blue; *umg* (*betrunken*) hammered; GASTR boiled; **~es Auge** black eye; **~er Fleck** bruise **Blaubeere** F blueberry **Blaulicht** N flashing blue light **blaumachen** V/I skip work; (*in Schule*) play hooky **Blauschimmelkäse** M blue cheese
Blech N sheet metal; (*Backblech*) cookie sheet **Blechschaden** M AUTO damage to the bodywork
Blei N lead
bleiben V/I stay; **lass das ~!** stop it; **das bleibt unter uns** that's (just) between us; **mir bleibt keine andere Wahl** I have no other choice
bleich ADJ pale **bleichen** V/T bleach
bleifrei ADJ (*Benzin*) unleaded **bleihaltig** ADJ (*Benzin*) leaded
Bleistift M pencil
Blende F FOTO aperture
Blick M look; (*kurz*) glance; (*Aussicht*) view; **auf den ersten ~** at first sight; **einen ~ auf etw werfen** have a look at sth **blicken** V/I look; **sich ~ lassen** show up
blind ADJ blind **Blinddarm** M appendix **Blinddarmentzündung** F appendicitis **Blinde(r)** M/F(M) blind person/man/woman; **die ~n** *pl* the blind *pl* **Blindenhund** M seeing-eye dog **Blindenschrift** F braille
blinken V/I (*Stern, Lichter*) twinkle; (*aufleuchten*) flash; AUTO signal **Blinker** M AUTO turn signal
blinzeln V/I blink
Blitz M (flash of) lightning; FOTO flash **blitzen** V/I FOTO use a/the flash; **es blitzte und donnerte** there was thunder and lightning **Blitzlicht** N flash
Block M block; (*von Papier*) pad **Blockhaus** N log cabin **blockieren** 1 V/T block 2 V/I jam; (*Räder*) lock **Blockschrift** F block letters *pl*
blöd ADJ stupid
Blog M *od* N IT blog
blond ADJ blond; (*Frau*) blonde
bloß 1 ADJ (*unbedeckt*) bare; (*alleinig*) mere 2 ADV only; **geh mir ~ aus dem Weg** just get out of my way

blühen VI bloom; *fig* flourish
Blume F flower; (*von Wein*) bouquet **Blumengeschäft** N florist (shop) **Blumenkohl** M cauliflower **Blumenladen** M florist (shop) **Blumenstrauß** M bunch; (*als Geschenk*) bouquet **Blumentopf** M flowerpot
Bluse F blouse
Blut N blood **Blutbild** N blood count **Blutdruck** M blood pressure
Blüte F (*Pflanzenteil*) flower, bloom; (*Baumblüte*) blossom; *fig* prime
bluten VI bleed
Blütenstaub M pollen
Bluter M MED hemophiliac **Bluterguss** M hematoma; (*blauer Fleck*) bruise **Blutgruppe** F blood type **blutig** ADJ bloody **Blutprobe** F blood sample **Bluttransfusion** F blood transfusion **Blutung** F bleeding **Blutvergiftung** F blood poisoning **Blutwurst** F blood sausage
Bock M (*Reh*) buck; (*Schaf*) ram; (*Gestell*) trestle; SPORT vaulting horse; **ich hab keinen ~ (drauf)** *umg* I don't feel like it
Boden M ground; (*Fußboden*) floor; (*von Meer, Fass*) bottom; (*Speicher*) attic **Bodenpersonal** N ground staff **Bodenschätze** PL mineral resources *pl*
Bodensee M **der ~** Lake Constance
Bogen M (*Biegung*) curve; (*in der Architektur*) arch; (*Waffe, Instrument*) bow; (*Papier*) sheet
Bohne F bean; **grüne ~n** *pl* green beans *pl*; **weiße ~n** *pl* navy beans *pl* **Bohnenkaffee** M real coffee **Bohnensprosse** F beansprout
bohren VT drill **Bohrer** M drill
Boiler M water heater
Boje F buoy
Bombe F bomb
Bon M (*Kassenzettel*) receipt; (*Gutschein*) voucher, coupon
Bonbon N candy
Bonus M bonus; (*Punktvorteil*) bonus points *pl*
Boot N boat **Bootsverleih** M boat rental
Bord M **an ~ (eines Schiffes)** on board (a ship); **an ~ gehen** (*Schiff*) go on board; (*Flugzeug*) board; **von ~ gehen** disembark **Bordcomputer** M dashboard computer
Bordell N brothel
Bordkarte F boarding card
Bordstein M curb
borgen VT borrow; **j-m etw ~** lend sb sth; **sich etw ~** borrow sth
Börse F stock exchange
bös ADJ → böse **bösartig** ADJ malicious; MED malignant
Böschung F slope; (*Uferböschung*) embankment

böse ADJ bad; (*stärker*) evil; (*Wunde*) nasty; (*zornig*) angry; **bist du mir ~?** are you angry with me?
boshaft ADJ malicious
Bosnien und Herzegowina N Bosnia and Herzegovina
böswillig ADJ malicious
botanisch ADJ **~er Garten** botanical gardens *pl*
Botschaft F message; POL embassy **Botschafter(in)** M(F) ambassador
Bouillon F stock
Boutique F boutique
Bowle F punch
Box F (*Behälter, Pferdebox*) box; (*Lautsprecher*) speaker; (*bei Autorennen*) pit
boxen V/I box **Boxer** M (*Hund, Sportler*) boxer **Boxershorts** PL boxer shorts *pl* **Boxkampf** M boxing match
Boykott M boycott
Branchenverzeichnis N yellow pages® *pl*
Brand M fire
Brandwunde F burn
Brasilien N Brazil
braten V/T roast; (*auf dem Rost*) grill; (*in der Pfanne*) fry **Braten** M roast; (*roher*) joint **Bratensoße** F gravy **Brathähnchen** N roast chicken **Bratkartoffeln** PL fried potatoes *pl* **Bratpfanne** F frying pan, skillet **Bratwurst** F fried sausage; (*gegrillte*) grilled sausage
Brauch M custom
brauchen V/T (*nötig haben*) need (*für, zu* for); (*erfordern*) require; (*Zeit*) take; (*gebrauchen*) use; **wie lange wird er ~?** how long will it take him?; **du brauchst es nur zu sagen** you only need to say; **das braucht (seine) Zeit** it takes time; **ihr braucht es nicht zu tun** you don't have (*od* need) to do it; **sie hätte nicht zu kommen ~** she needn't have come
brauen V/T brew **Brauerei** F brewery
braun ADJ brown; (*von Sonne*) tanned **Bräune** F brownness; (*von Sonne*) tan
Brause F (*Dusche*) shower; (*Getränk*) soda
Braut F bride **Bräutigam** M bridegroom
brav ADJ (*artig*) good, well-behaved
brechen **1** V/T break; (*erbrechen*) bring up; **sich den Arm ~** break one's arm **2** V/I break; (*erbrechen*) vomit, throw up **Brechreiz** M nausea
Brei M (*Breimasse*) mush; (*Haferbrei*) oatmeal
breit ADJ wide; (*Schultern*) broad; **zwei Meter ~** two meters wide **Breite** F breadth; (*bei Maßangaben*) width; GEO latitude; **der ~ nach** widthways **Breitengrad** M (degree of) latitude
Bremsbelag M brake lining

Bremse F brake; ZOOL horsefly **bremsen** **1** VI brake **2** VT (*Auto*) brake; *fig* slow down **Bremsflüssigkeit** F brake fluid **Bremslicht** N brake light **Bremspedal** N brake pedal **Bremsspur** F tire marks *pl* **Bremsweg** M braking distance

brennen VI burn; (*in Flammen stehen*) be on fire; **es brennt!** fire!; **das Licht ~ lassen** leave the light on **Brennholz** N firewood **Brennnessel** F stinging nettle **Brennstoff** M fuel

Brett N board; (*länger*) plank; (*Regal*) shelf; (*Spielbrett*) board; **Schwarzes ~** bulletin board; **~er** *pl* (*Ski*) skis *pl* **Brettspiel** N board game

Brezel F pretzel

Brief M letter **Brieffreund(in)** M(F) penfriend **Briefkasten** M mailbox **Briefmarke** F stamp **Briefpapier** N writing paper **Brieftasche** F billfold, wallet **Briefträger(in)** M(F) mailman/mailwoman **Briefumschlag** M envelope

Brille F glasses *pl*; (*Schutzbrille*) goggles *pl* **Brillenetui** N glasses case

bringen VT (*herbringen*) bring; (*mitnehmen, vom Sprecher weg*) take; (*holen, herbringen*) get, fetch; FILM, THEAT show; RADIO, TV broadcast; **~ Sie mir bitte noch ein Bier** could you bring me another beer, please?; **j-n nach Hause ~** take sb home; **j-n dazu ~, etw zu tun** make sb do sth; **j-n auf eine Idee ~** give sb an idea

Brise F breeze

Brite M, **Britin** F British person, Briton; **die ~n** the British

britisch ADJ British

Brocken M bit; (*größer*) lump, chunk

Brokkoli M broccoli

Brombeere F blackberry

Bronchitis F bronchitis

Bronze F bronze

Brosche F brooch

Brot N bread; (*Laib*) loaf **Brotaufstrich** M spread **Brötchen** N roll **Brotzeit** F (*Pause*) break; (*Essen*) snack

Browser M IT browser

Bruch M (*Brechen*) breaking; (*Bruchstelle; mit Partei, Tradition etc*) break; MED (*Eingeweidebruch*) rupture, hernia; (*Knochenbruch*) fracture; MATH fraction **brüchig** ADJ brittle

Brücke F bridge

Bruder M brother

Brühe F (*Suppe*) (clear) soup, broth; (*Grundlage*) stock **Brühwürfel** M stock cube

brüllen VI roar; (*Stier*) bellow; (*vor Schmerzen*) scream (with pain)

brummen **1** VI (*Bär, Mensch*) growl; (*brummeln*) mutter; (*Insekt*) buzz; (*Motor, Radio*) drone

2 VT growl
brünett ADJ brunette
Brunnen M fountain; (*tief*) well; (*natürlich*) spring
Brust F breast; (*beim Mann*) chest **Brustschwimmen** N breaststroke **Brustwarze** F nipple
brutal ADJ brutal
brutto ADV gross
Bube M boy; (*Karten*) jack
Buch N book
Buche F beech (tree)
buchen VT book; (*Betrag*) enter
Bücherei F library
Buchhalter(in) M(F) accountant **Buchhandlung** F bookstore
Büchse F can
Buchstabe M letter **buchstabieren** VT spell
Bucht F bay
Buchung F booking; WIRTSCH entry
Buckel M hump
bücken V/R bend down
Bude F (*auf Markt*) stall; *umg* (*Wohnung*) place
Büfett N sideboard; **kaltes ~** cold buffet
Büffel M buffalo
Bügel M (*für Kleider*) hanger; (*Steigbügel*) stirrup; (*von Brille*) sidepiece; (*von Skilift*) T-bar **Bügelbrett** N ironing board **Bügeleisen** N iron **Bügelfalte** F crease **bügelfrei** ADJ non-iron **bügeln** VT & VI iron
Bühne F stage **Bühnenbild** N set
Bulgare M, **Bulgarin** F Bulgarian **Bulgarien** N Bulgaria **bulgarisch** ADJ Bulgarian **Bulgarisch** N Bulgarian
Bulimie F bulimia
Bulle M bull; *umg* (*Polizist*) cop
Bummel M stroll **bummeln** VI stroll; (*trödeln*) dawdle; (*faulenzen*) loaf around **Bummelzug** M slow train
bums INT bang
bumsen VI *vulg* screw
Bund **1** M (*von Hose, Rock*) waistband; (*Freundschaftsbund*) bond; (*Organisation*) association; POL confederation **2** N bunch; (*von Stroh etc*) bundle
Bundes- IN ZSSGN Federal; (*auf Deutschland bezogen auch*) German **Bundeskanzler(in)** M(F) Chancellor **Bundesland** N state, Land **Bundesliga** F **Erste/Zweite ~** First/Second Division **Bundespräsident(in)** M(F) President **Bundesrat** M (*in Deutschland*) Upper House (of the German Parliament); (*in der Schweiz*) Council of Ministers **Bundesregierung** F Federal Government **Bundesrepublik** F Federal Republic; **~ Deutschland** Federal Republic of Germany **Bundesstraße** F ≈ state highway **Bundestag** M Lower House (of the German

Parliament) **Bundeswehr** F (German) armed forces *pl*
Bündnis N alliance
bunt 1 ADJ colorful; (*von Programm etc*) varied; **~e Farben** bright colors 2 ADV (*anstreichen*) in bright colors **Buntstift** M crayon, colored pencil
Burg F castle
Bürger(in) M(F) citizen **bürgerlich** ADJ (*Rechte, Ehe etc*) civil; (*vom Mittelstand*) middle-class; *pej* bourgeois **Bürgermeister(in)** M(F) mayor **Bürgersteig** M sidewalk
Büro N office **Büroklammer** F paper clip
Bürokratie F bureaucracy
Bursche M boy; (*Typ*) guy
Bürste F brush **bürsten** V/T brush
Bus M bus **Busbahnhof** M bus station
Busch M bush; (*Strauch*) shrub
Busen M breasts *pl*
Busfahrer(in) M(F) bus driver **Bushaltestelle** F bus stop
Businessclass F business class
Busreise F bus tour
Bußgeld N fine
Büstenhalter M bra
Busverbindung F bus connection
Butter F butter **Butterbrot** N slice of bread and butter **Buttermilch** F buttermilk
Button M button
Byte N byte

bzw. ADV *abk* = beziehungsweise

C

ca. ADV *abk* = circa; approx
Cabrio N convertible
Café N café **Cafeteria** F cafeteria
Call-Center N call center
campen V/I camp **Camping** N camping **Campingbus** M camper **Campingplatz** M campground
Cappuccino M cappuccino
CD F *abk* = Compact Disc; CD **CD-Brenner** M CD burner, CD writer **CD-Player** M CD player **CD-ROM** F *abk* = Compact Disc Read Only Memory; CD-ROM **CD-ROM-Laufwerk** N CD-ROM drive **CD-Spieler** M CD player
Cello N cello
Celsius N celsius
Cent M (*von Dollar und Euro*) cent
Champagner M champagne
Champignon M mushroom
Chance F chance; **die ~n stehen gut** the prospects are good
Chaos N chaos **chaotisch** ADJ chaotic
Charakter M character **cha-**

rakteristisch ADJ characteristic (*für* of)
Charisma N charisma
charmant ADJ charming
Charterflug M charter flight **chartern** V/T charter
Chat M IT chat **chatten** V/I IT chat
checken V/T (*überprüfen*) check; *umg* (*verstehen*) get
Check-in M check-in **Check--in-Schalter** M check-in desk
Chef(in) M(F) boss **Chefarzt** M, **Chefärztin** F chief physician
Chemie F chemistry **chemisch** ADJ chemical; **~e Reinigung** dry cleaning
Chemotherapie F chemotherapy
Chili M chili
China N China **Chinakohl** M bok choy **Chinarestaurant** N Chinese restaurant **Chinese** M Chinese **Chinesin** F Chinese (woman); **sie ist ~** she's Chinese **chinesisch** ADJ Chinese **Chinesisch** N Chinese
Chip M IT chip **Chipkarte** F smart card
Chips PL (*Kartoffelchips*) chips *pl*
Chirurg(in) M(F) surgeon
Chlor N chlorine
Choke M choke
Cholesterin N cholesterol
Chor M choir; THEAT chorus
Christ(in) M(F) Christian
Christbaum M Christmas tree **Christi Himmelfahrt** F the Ascension (of Christ)
Christkind N baby Jesus; (*das Geschenke bringt*) ≈ Santa Claus **christlich** ADJ Christian
Chrom N chrome; CHEM chromium
chronisch ADJ chronic
chronologisch **1** ADJ chronological **2** ADV in chronological order
circa ADV about, approximately
City F downtown area
Clementine F clementine
clever ADJ clever, smart
Clique F group; *pej* clique
Club M club **Cluburlaub** M club vacation
Cocktail M cocktail **Cocktailtomate** F cherry tomato
Cognac M cognac
Cola F Coke®, cola
Comic M comic strip; (*Heft*) comic
Compact Disc F compact disc
Computer M computer **Computerfreak** M computer nerd **computergesteuert** ADJ computer-controlled
Computergrafik F computer graphics *pl* **computerlesbar** ADJ machine-readable
Computerspiel N computer game
Container M (*zum Transport*) container; (*für Bauschutt etc*) Dumpster®

cool ADJ *umg* cool
Cornflakes PL cornflakes *pl*
Couch F couch **Couchtisch** M coffee table
Coupon M coupon
Cousin M cousin **Cousine** F cousin
Crack N (*Droge*) crack
Creme F cream; GASTR mousse
Croissant N croissant
Curry **1** M curry powder **2** N (*indisches Gericht*) curry
Cursor M IT cursor
Cybercafé N cybercafé **Cyberspace** M cyberspace

D

da **1** ADV (*dort*) there; (*hier*) here; (*dann*) then; **~ oben/drüben** up/over there; **~, wo** where; **~ sein** be there; **ist jemand ~?** is there anybody there?; **ich bin gleich wieder ~** I'll be right back; **ist noch Brot ~?** is there any bread left?; **es ist keine Milch mehr ~** we've run out of milk; **~ kann man nichts machen** there's nothing you can do **2** KONJ as
dabei ADV (*räumlich*) close to it; (*zeitlich*) at the same time; (*obwohl, doch*) though; **~ fällt mir ein …** that reminds me …; **~ kam es zu einem Unfall** this led to an accident; **ich finde nichts ~** I don't see anything wrong with it; **es bleibt ~** that's settled; **~ sein** (*anwesend*) be present; (*beteiligt*) be involved; **ich bin ~!** count me in; **er war gerade ~ zu gehen** he was just (*od* on the point of) leaving **dabeibleiben** V/I stick with it; **ich bleibe dabei** I'm not changing my mind **dabeihaben** V/T **er hat seine Schwester dabei** he's brought his sister; **ich habe kein Geld dabei** I haven't got any money on me
Dach N roof **Dachboden** M attic, loft **Dachgepäckträger** M roofrack **Dachrinne** F gutter
dadurch **1** ADV (*räumlich*) through it; (*durch diesen Umstand*) in that way; (*deshalb*) because of that, for that reason **2** KONJ **~, dass** because; **~, dass er hart arbeitete** (*indem*) by working hard
dafür ADV for it; (*anstatt*) instead; **~ habe ich 50 Dollar bezahlt** I paid 50 dollars for it; **ich bin ~ zu bleiben** I'm for (*od* in favor of) staying; **~ ist er ja da** that's what he's there for; **er kann nichts ~** he can't help it
dagegen ADV against it; (*im Vergleich damit*) in comparison;

(*bei Tausch*) for it; **ich habe nichts ~** I don't mind
daheim ADV at home
daher **1** ADV (*räumlich*) from there; (*Ursache*) that's why **2** KONJ (*deshalb*) that's why
dahin ADV (*räumlich*) there; (*zeitlich*) then; (*vergangen*) gone; **bis ~** (*zeitlich*) till then; (*örtlich*) up to there; **bis ~ muss die Arbeit fertig sein** the work must be finished by then
dahinter ADV behind it **dahinterkommen** V/I find out
damals ADV at that time, then
Dame F lady; (*Karten*) queen; (*Spiel*) checkers *sg* **Damenbinde** F sanitary napkin **Damenkleidung** F ladies' wear **Damentoilette** F ladies' bathroom
damit **1** ADV with it; (*begründend*) by that; **genug ~!** that's enough **2** KONJ so that
Damm M dyke; (*Staudamm*) dam; (*am Hafen*) mole; (*Bahn-, Straßendamm*) embankment
Dämmerung F twilight; (*am Morgen*) dawn; (*am Abend*) dusk
Dampf M steam; (*Dunst*) vapor **Dampfbügeleisen** N steam iron **dampfen** V/I steam
dämpfen V/T GASTR steam; (*Geräusch*) deaden; (*Begeisterung*) dampen
Dampfer M steamer
Dampfkochtopf M pressure cooker
danach ADV after that; (*zeitlich a.*) afterward(s); (*demgemäß*) accordingly; **mir ist nicht ~** I don't feel like it; **~ sieht es aus** that's what it looks like
Däne M Dane
daneben ADV beside it; (*im Vergleich*) in comparison
Dänemark N Denmark **Dänin** F Dane, Danish woman/girl **dänisch** ADJ Danish **Dänisch** N Danish
dank PRÄP *+dat od gen* thanks to **Dank** M thanks *pl*; **vielen ~!** thank you very much; **j-m ~ sagen** thank sb **dankbar** ADJ grateful; (*Aufgabe*) rewarding **danke** INT thank you, thanks; **nein ~!** no, thank you; **~, gerne!** yes, please **danken** V/I **j-m für etw ~** thank sb for sth; **nichts zu ~!** you're welcome
dann ADV then; **bis ~!** see you (later); **~ eben nicht** suit yourself
daran ADV (*räumlich*) on it; (*befestigen*) to it; (*stoßen*) against it; **es liegt ~, dass ...** it's because ...
darauf ADV (*räumlich*) on it; (*zielgerichtet*) toward(s) it; (*danach*) afterward(s); **es kommt ganz ~ an, ob ...** it all depends (on) whether ...; **ich freue mich ~** I'm looking forward to it; **am Tag ~** the next day **darauffolgend** ADJ

(*Tag, Jahr*) next, following
daraus ADV from it; **was ist ~ geworden?** what became of it?
darin ADV in it; **das Problem liegt ~, dass ...** the basic problem is that ...
Darlehen N loan
Darm M intestine; (*Wurstdarm*) skin **Darmgrippe** F gastroenteritis
darstellen V/T represent; THEAT play; (*beschreiben*) describe **Darsteller(in)** M(F) actor/actress **Darstellung** F representation; (*Beschreibung*) description
darüber ADV (*räumlich*) above it, over it; (*fahren*) over it; (*mehr*) more; (*währenddessen*) meanwhile; (*sprechen, streiten, sich freuen*) about it
darum ADV (*deshalb*) that's why; **es geht ~, dass ...** the point (*od* thing) is that ...
darunter ADV (*räumlich*) under it; (*dazwischen*) among them; (*weniger*) less; **was verstehen Sie ~?** what do you understand by that? **darunterfallen** V/I be included
das **1** ART the; **er hat sich ~ Bein gebrochen** he's broken his leg; **vier Dollar ~ Kilo** four dollars a kilo **2** DEM PR that (one), this (one); **~ Auto da** that car; **ich nehme ~ da** I'll take that one; **~ heißt** that is; **~ sind Amerikaner** they're American **3** REL PR (*Sache*) that, which; (*Person*) who, that; **~ Auto, ~ er kaufte** the car (that (*od* which)) he bought; **~ Mädchen, ~ nebenan wohnt** the girl who (*od* that) lives next door
dass KONJ that; **so ~** so that; **es sei denn, ~** unless; **ohne ~ er grüßte** without saying hello
dasselbe DEM PR the same
Datei F IT file **Dateimanager** M file manager
Daten PL data *pl* **Datenbank** F database **Datenschutz** M data protection **Datenträger** M data carrier
datieren V/T date
Dativ M dative (case)
Dattel F date
Datum N date
Dauer F duration; (*Länge*) length; **auf die ~** in the long run; **für die ~ von zwei Jahren** for (a period of) two years **dauerhaft** ADJ lasting; (*Material*) durable **Dauerkarte** F season ticket **dauern** V/I last; (*Zeit benötigen*) take; **es hat sehr lange gedauert, bis er ...** it took him a long time to ...; **wie lange dauert es denn noch?** how much longer will it be?; **das dauert mir zu lange** I can't wait that long **dauernd** **1** ADJ lasting; (*ständig*) constant **2** ADV always, constantly; **er lachte ~** he kept laughing; **unterbrich mich**

nicht ~ stop interrupting me
Dauerwelle F permanent
Daumen M thumb
Daunendecke F comforter
davon ADV of it; (*räumlich*) away; (*weg von*) from it; (*Grund*) because of it; **ich hätte gerne ein Pfund ~** I'd like a pound of that; **~ habe ich gehört** I've heard of it; (*Geschehen*) I've heard about it; **das kommt ~, wenn ...** that's what happens when ...; **was habe ich ~?** what's the point?; **auf und ~** up and away **davonlaufen** V/I run away
davor ADV (*räumlich*) in front of it; (*zeitlich*) before; **ich habe Angst ~** I'm afraid of it
dazu ADV (*zusätzlich*) on top of that, as well; (*zu diesem Zweck*) for it, for that purpose; **ich möchte Reis ~** I'd like rice with it; **und ~ noch** and in addition; **~ fähig sein, etwas zu tun** be capable of doing sth; **wie kam es ~?** how did it happen? **dazugehören** V/I belong to it **dazukommen** V/I (*zu j-m*) join sb; **kommt noch etwas dazu?** anything else?
dazwischen ADV in between; (*Unterschied etc*) between them; (*in einer Gruppe*) among them **dazwischenkommen** V/I **wenn nichts dazwischenkommt** if all goes well; **mir ist etwas dazwischengekommen** something has cropped up
dealen V/I *umg* (*mit Drogen*) deal in drugs **Dealer(in)** M(F) *umg* dealer, pusher
Deck N deck; **an ~** on deck
Decke F cover; (*für Bett*) blanket; (*für Tisch*) tablecloth; (*von Zimmer*) ceiling
Deckel M lid
decken **1** V/T cover; (*Tisch*) set **2** V/R (*Interessen*) coincide; (*Aussagen*) correspond **3** V/I (*den Tisch decken*) set the table
Decoder M decoder
defekt ADJ faulty **Defekt** M fault, defect
definieren V/T define **Definition** F definition
deftig ADJ (*Preise*) steep; **ein ~es Essen** a good solid meal
dehnbar ADJ flexible, elastic
dehnen V/T & V/R stretch
dein POSS PR (*adjektivisch*) your
deine(r, s) POSS PR (*substantivisch*) yours; of you **deinetwegen** ADV (*wegen dir*) because of you; (*dir zuliebe*) for your sake
deinstallieren V/T (*Programm*) uninstall
Dekoration F decoration; (*in Laden*) window dressing **dekorativ** ADJ decorative **dekorieren** V/T decorate; (*Schaufenster*) dress
Delfin M dolphin
delikat ADJ (*lecker*) delicious; (*heikel*) delicate **Delikatesse** F delicacy

Delle F *umg* dent
Delphin M dolphin
dem *dat sg von* **der/das**; **wie ~ auch sein mag** be that as it may
demnächst ADV shortly, soon
Demokratie F democracy **demokratisch** ADJ democratic
demolieren V/T demolish
Demonstration F demonstration **demonstrieren** V/T & V/I demonstrate
den 1 ART *akk sg, dat pl von* der; **sie hat sich ~ Arm gebrochen** she's broken her arm 2 DEM PR him; (*Sache*) that one 3 REL PR (*Person*) who, that, whom; (*Sache*) which, that; **der Typ, auf ~ sie steht** the guy (who) she likes; **der Berg, auf ~ wir geklettert sind** the mountain (that) we climbed
denkbar 1 ADJ **das ist ~** that's possible 2 ADV **~ einfach** extremely simple **denken** 1 V/T & V/I think (*über +akk* about); **an j-n/etw ~** think of sb/sth; (*sich erinnern, berücksichtigen*) remember sb/sth; **woran denkst du?** what are you thinking about?; **denk an den Kaffee!** don't forget the coffee 2 V/R (*sich vorstellen*) imagine; **das kann ich mir ~** I can (well) imagine
Denkmal N monument **Denkmalschutz** M monument preservation; **unter ~** stehen be listed
denn 1 KONJ for, because 2 ADV then; (*nach Komparativ*) than; **was ist ~?** what's wrong?; **ist das ~ so schwierig?** is it really that difficult?
dennoch KONJ still, nevertheless
Deo N, **Deodorant** N deodorant **Deoroller** M roll-on deodorant **Deospray** M *od* N deodorant spray
Deponie F waste disposal site
Depressionen PL **an ~ leiden** suffer from depression *sg* **deprimieren** V/T depress
der 1 ART the; (*dat*) to the; (*gen*) of the; **~ arme Marc** poor Marc; **~ Vater ~ Besitzerin** the owner's father 2 DEM PR that (one), this (one); **~ mit ~ Brille** the one (*od* him) with the glasses 3 REL PR (*Person*) who, that; (*Sache*) which, that; **jeder, ~ ...** anyone who ...; **er war ~ erste, ~ es erfuhr** he was the first to know
derart ADV so; (*solcher Art*) such **derartig** ADJ **ein ~er Fehler** such a mistake, a mistake like that
deren 1 DEM PR (*Person*) her; (*Sache*) its; (*pl*) their 2 REL PR (*Person*) whose; (*Sache*) of which
dergleichen DEM PR **und ~ mehr** and the like, and so on; **nichts ~** no such thing
derjenige DEM PR the one; **~,**

der (*relativ*) the one who (*od* that)
dermaßen ADV so much; (*mit adj*) so
derselbe DEM PR the same (person/thing)
deshalb ADV therefore; **~ frage ich ja** that's why I'm asking
Design N design **Designer(in)** M(F) designer
Desinfektionsmittel N disinfectant **desinfizieren** V/T disinfect
dessen **1** PRON, *gen von* der, das; (*Person*) his; (*Sache*) its; **ich bin mir ~ bewusst** I'm aware of that **2** REL PR (*Person*) whose; (*Sache*) of which
Dessert N dessert; **zum** (*od* **als**) **~** for dessert
destilliert ADJ distilled
desto ADV **je eher, ~ besser** the sooner, the better
deswegen KONJ therefore
Detail N detail; **ins ~ gehen** go into detail
Detektiv(in) M(F) detective
deutlich ADJ clear; (*Unterschied*) distinct
deutsch ADJ German **Deutsch** N German; **auf ~** in German; **ins ~e übersetzen** translate into German **Deutsche(r)** M/F(M) German **Deutschland** N Germany
Devise F motto; **~n** *pl* FIN foreign currency *sg* **Devisenkurs** M exchange rate
Dezember M December; →
Juni
dezent ADJ discreet
d. h. *abk von* **das heißt**; i. e. (*gesprochen: i. e. oder that is*)
Dia N slide
Diabetes M MED diabetes **Diabetiker(in)** M(F) diabetic
Diagnose F diagnosis
diagonal ADJ diagonal
Dialekt M dialect
Dialog M dialog(ue); IT dialog
Dialyse F MED dialysis
Diamant M diamond
Diät F diet; **eine ~ machen** be on a diet; (*anfangen*) go on a diet
dich PERS PR you; **~ (selbst)** (*reflexiv*) yourself; **pass auf ~ auf** look after yourself; **reg ~ nicht auf** don't get upset
dicht **1** ADJ dense; (*Nebel*) thick; (*Gewebe*) close; (*wasserdicht*) watertight; (*Verkehr*) heavy **2** ADV **~ an/bei** close to; **~ bevölkert** densely populated
Dichter(in) M(F) poet; (*Autor*) writer
Dichtung F AUTO gasket; (*Dichtungsring*) washer; (*Gedichte*) poetry **Dichtungsring** M TECH washer
dick ADJ thick; (*Person*) fat **Dickdarm** M colon **Dickkopf** M stubborn (*od* pigheaded) person **Dickmilch** F sour milk
die **1** ART the; **~ arme Sarah** poor Sarah **2** DEM PR (*sg*) that

(one), this (one), (*pl*) those (ones); ~ **mit den langen Haaren** the one (*od* her) with the long hair; **ich nehme ~ da** I'll take that one (*od* those) **3** REL PR (*Person*) who, that; (*Sache*) which, that; **sie war ~ erste, ~ es erfuhr** she was the first to know **4** *pl von* der, die, das

Dieb(in) M(F) thief **Diebstahl** M theft **Diebstahlsicherung** F burglar alarm

diejenige DEM PR the one; **~, die** (*relativ*) the one who (*od* that); **~n** (*pl*) those *pl*, the ones *pl*

Diele F hall

Dienst M service; **außer ~** retired; **~ haben** be on duty

Dienstag M Tuesday; → Mittwoch **dienstags** ADV (on) Tuesdays; → mittwochs

Dienstbereitschaft F **~ haben** (*Arzt*) be on call **diensthabend** ADJ **der ~e Arzt** the doctor on duty **Dienstleistung** F service **dienstlich** ADJ official; **er ist ~ unterwegs** he's away on business **Dienstreise** F business trip **Dienststelle** F department **Dienstwagen** M company car **Dienstzeit** F office hours *pl*; MIL term of service

diesbezüglich ADJ (*formell*) on this matter

diese(r, s) DEM PR this (one); (*pl*) these (ones); **~ Frau** this woman; **~ Leute** these people; **ich nehme diese/diesen/dieses** (*hier*) I'll take this one; (*dort*) I'll take that one; **ich nehme ~** *pl* (*hier*) I'll take these (ones); (*dort*) I'll take those (ones)

Diesel M AUTO diesel

dieselbe DEM PR the same; **es sind immer ~n** it's always the same people

Dieselmotor M diesel engine **Dieselöl** N diesel (oil)

diesig ADJ hazy, misty

diesmal ADV this time

Dietrich M skeleton key

Differenz F difference

digital ADJ digital **Digitalfernsehen** N digital television, digital TV **Digitalkamera** F digital camera

Diktatur F dictatorship

Ding N thing; **vor allen ~en** above all; **der Stand der ~e** the state of affairs; **das ist nicht mein ~** *umg* it's not my sort of thing **Dingsbums** N *umg* thingy, thingamajig

Dinkel M BOT spelt

Dinosaurier M dinosaur

Diplom N diploma

Diplomat(in) M(F) diplomat

dir PERS PR (to) you; **hat er ~ geholfen?** did he help you?; **ich werde es ~ erklären** I'll explain it to you; (*reflexiv*) **wasch ~ die Hände** go and wash your hands; **ein Freund von ~** a friend of yours

direkt **1** ADJ direct; (*Frage*) straight **2** ADV directly; (*sofort*) immediately; **~ am Bahnhof** right next to the station **Direktflug** M direct flight
Direktor(in) M(F) director; (*Schule*) principal
Direktübertragung F live broadcast
Dirigent(in) M(F) conductor **dirigieren** V/T direct; MUS conduct
Diskette F disk, diskette **Diskettenlaufwerk** N disk drive
Diskjockey M disc jockey **Disko** F *umg* disco
diskret ADJ discreet
diskriminieren V/T discriminate against
Diskussion F discussion **diskutieren** V/T & V/I discuss
Display N display
disqualifizieren V/T disqualify
Distanz F distance
Disziplin F discipline
divers ADJ various
dividieren V/T divide (*durch* by); **8 dividiert durch 2 ist 4** 8 divided by 2 is 4
DJ M *abk* = Diskjockey; DJ
doch **1** ADV **das ist nicht wahr!** — **~!** that's not true — yes it is; **nicht ~!** oh no; **er kommt ~?** he will come, won't he?; **er hat es ~ gemacht** he did it after all; **setzen Sie sich ~** do sit down, please **2** KONJ (*aber*) but
Doktor(in) M(F) doctor
Dokument N document **Dokumentarfilm** M documentary **dokumentieren** V/T document
Dollar M dollar
dolmetschen V/T & V/I interpret **Dolmetscher(in)** M(F) interpreter
Dom M cathedral
Domäne F domain, province; IT (*Domain*) domain
Domino N dominoes *sg*
Donau F Danube
Döner M, **Döner Kebab** M doner kebab
Donner M thunder **donnern** V/I **es donnert** it's thundering
Donnerstag M Thursday; → Mittwoch **donnerstags** ADV (on) Thursdays; → mittwochs
doof ADJ *umg* stupid
dopen V/T dope **Doping** N doping **Dopingkontrolle** F drugs test
Doppel N duplicate; SPORT doubles *sg* **Doppelbett** N double bed **Doppelhaushälfte** F duplex **doppelklicken** V/I double-click **Doppelname** M double name **Doppelpunkt** M colon **Doppelstecker** M two-way adaptor **Doppelstunde** F (*Unterrichtsstunde*) double period **doppelt** ADJ double; **in ~er Ausführung** in duplicate **Doppelzimmer** N double

room
Dorf N village
Dorn M BOT thorn
Dörrobst N dried fruit
dort ADV there; **~ drüben** over there **dorther** ADV from there
Dose F box; (*Blechdose*) can
dösen V/I doze
Dosenbier N canned beer **Dosenöffner** M can opener
Dotter M (egg) yolk
downloaden V/T download
Downsyndrom N MED Down's syndrome
Dozent(in) M(F) assistant professor
Dr. *abk* = Doktor
Drache M dragon **Drachen** M (*Spielzeug*) kite; SPORT hang-glider **Drachenfliegen** N hang-gliding
Draht M wire **Drahtseilbahn** F cable railway
Drama N drama **dramatisch** ADJ dramatic
dran ADV *umg kontr von* **daran**; **gut ~ sein** (*reich*) be well-off; (*glücklich*) be fortunate; (*gesundheitlich*) be well; **schlecht ~ sein** be in a bad way; **wer ist ~?** whose turn is it?; **ich bin ~** it's my turn; **bleib ~!** TEL hang on
Drang M (*Trieb*) urge (*nach* for); (*Druck*) pressure
drängeln V/T & V/I push
drängen **1** V/T (*schieben*) push; (*antreiben*) urge **2** V/I (*eilig sein*) be urgent; (*Zeit*) press; **auf etw ~** press for sth
drankommen V/I **wer kommt dran?** who's turn is it?, who's next?
drauf *umg kontr von* **darauf**; **gut/schlecht ~ sein** be in a good/bad mood
Draufgänger(in) M(F) daredevil
draufkommen V/I remember; **ich komme nicht drauf** I can't think of it
draußen ADV outside
Dreck M dirt, filth **dreckig** ADJ dirty, filthy
drehen **1** V/T & V/I turn; (*Zigaretten*) roll; (*Film*) shoot **2** V/R turn; (*um Achse*) rotate; **sich ~ um** (*handeln von*) be about
Drehtür F revolving door **Drehzahlmesser** M tachometer
drei NUM three; **~ viertel voll** three-quarters full; **es ist ~ viertel neun** it's a quarter to nine **Drei** F three; (*Schulnote*) ≈ C **Dreieck** N triangle **dreieckig** ADJ triangular **dreifach** **1** ADJ triple **2** ADV three times **dreihundert** NUM three hundred **Dreikönigstag** M Epiphany **dreimal** ADV three times **Dreirad** N tricycle **dreispurig** ADJ three-lane
dreißig NUM thirty **dreißigste(r, s)** ADJ thirtieth; → dritte
Dreiviertelstunde F **eine ~** three quarters of an hour

dreizehn NUM thirteen **dreizehnte(r, s)** ADJ thirteenth; → dritte
dressieren V/T train
Dressing N (salad) dressing
Dressman M (male) model
drin *umg kontr von* **darin** in it
dringen V/I (*Wasser, Licht, Kälte*) penetrate (*durch* through, *in +akk* into); **auf etw ~** insist on sth **dringend, dringlich** ADJ urgent
drinnen ADV inside
dritt ADV **wir sind zu ~** there are three of us **dritte(r, s)** ADJ third; **die Dritte Welt** the Third World; **3. September** September 3rd (*gesprochen: September third*); **am 3. September** on September 3rd (*gesprochen: on September third*); **München, den 3. September** Munich, September 3rd **Drittel** N (*Bruchteil*) third **drittens** ADV thirdly
Droge F drug **drogenabhängig, drogensüchtig** ADJ addicted to drugs
Drogerie F drugstore
drohen V/I threaten (*j-m* sb); **mit etw ~** threaten to do sth
dröhnen V/I (*Motor*) roar; (*Stimme, Musik*) boom; (*Raum*) resound
Drohung F threat
drüben ADV over there; (*auf der anderen Seite*) on the other side
drüber *umg kontr von* **darüber**
Druck **1** M PHYS pressure; *fig* (*Belastung*) stress; **j-n unter ~ setzen** put sb under pressure **2** M TYPO (*Vorgang*) printing; (*Produkt, Schriftart*) print **Druckbuchstabe** M block letter; **in ~n schreiben** print **drucken** V/T & V/I print
drücken **1** V/T & V/I (*Knopf, Hand*) press; (*zu eng sein*) pinch; *fig* (*Preise*) keep down **2** V/R **sich vor etw ~** get out of sth **drückend** ADJ oppressive
Drucker M IT printer
Druckknopf M snap **Drucksache** F printed matter **Druckschrift** F block letters *pl*
drunten ADV down there
drunter *umg kontr von* **darunter**
Drüse F gland
du PERS PR you; **bist ~ es?** is it you?; **wir sind per ~** we're on first-name terms
ducken V/T & V/R duck
Duett N duet
Duft M scent **duften** V/I smell nice; **es duftet nach …** it smells of …
dulden V/T tolerate
dumm ADJ stupid **Dummheit** F stupidity; (*Tat*) stupid thing **Dummkopf** M idiot
dumpf ADJ (*Ton*) muffled; (*Erinnerung*) vague; (*Schmerz*) dull
Düne F dune
Dünger M fertilizer

dunkel ADJ dark; (*Stimme*) deep; (*Ahnung*) vague; (*rätselhaft*) obscure; (*verdächtig*) dubious; **im Dunkeln tappen** *fig* be in the dark **dunkelblau** ADJ dark blue **dunkelblond** ADJ light brown **dunkelhaarig** ADJ dark-haired **Dunkelheit** F darkness

dünn ADJ thin; (*Kaffee*) weak

Dunst M haze; (*leichter Nebel*) mist; CHEM vapor

dünsten V/T GASTR steam

Duo N duo

Dur N MUS major (key)

durch **1** PRÄP +*akk* through; (*mittels*) by; (*Zeit*) during; **~ Amerika reisen** travel across the USA **2** ADV (*Fleisch*) well done; **das ganze Jahr ~** all through the year, the whole year long; **darf ich bitte ~?** can I get through, please?

durchaus ADV absolutely; **~ nicht** not at all

Durchblick M view **durchblicken** V/I look through; *umg* (*verstehen*) understand (*bei etw* sth); **etw ~ lassen** *fig* hint at sth

Durchblutung F circulation

durchbrennen V/I (*Sicherung*) blow; (*Draht*) burn through; *umg* (*davonlaufen*) run away

durchdacht ADV **gut ~** well thought-out

durchdrehen **1** V/T (*Fleisch*) mince **2** V/I (*Räder*) spin; *umg* (*nervlich*) crack up

durcheinander ADV in a mess; *umg* (*verwirrt*) confused **Durcheinander** N (*Verwirrung*) confusion; (*Unordnung*) mess **durcheinanderbringen** V/T mess up; (*verwirren*) confuse **durcheinanderreden** V/I talk (all) at the same time

Durchfahrt F way through

Durchfall M MED diarrhea

durchfallen V/I fall through; (*in Prüfung*) fail

durchfragen V/R ask one's way

durchführen V/T carry out

Durchgang M passage; SPORT round; (*bei Wahl*) ballot **Durchgangsverkehr** M through traffic

durchgebraten ADJ well done

durchgefroren ADJ frozen to the bone

durchgehen V/I go through (*durch etw* sth); (*ausreißen: Pferd*) break loose; (*Mensch*) run away **durchgehend** ADJ (*Zug*) through; **~ geöffnet** open all day

durchhalten **1** V/I hold out **2** V/T (*Tempo*) keep up; **etw ~** (*bis zum Schluss*) see sth through

durchkommen V/I get through; (*Patient*) pull through

durchlassen V/T (*j-n*) let through; (*Wasser*) let in

durchlesen V/T read through

durchleuchten VT X-ray **durchmachen** VT go through; (*Entwicklung*) undergo; **die Nacht ~** make a night of it
Durchmesser M diameter
Durchreise F journey through; **auf der ~** passing through; (*Güter*) in transit **Durchreisevisum** N transit visa
durchreißen VT & VI tear (in two)
Durchsage F announcement
durchschauen VT (*j-n, Lüge*) see through
durchschlagen VR struggle through
durchschneiden VT cut (in two)
Durchschnitt M (*Mittelwert*) average; **im ~** on average **durchschnittlich** 1 ADJ average 2 ADV (*im Durchschnitt*) on average
durchsetzen 1 VT get through 2 VR (*Erfolg haben*) succeed; (*sich behaupten*) get one's way
durchsichtig ADJ transparent, see-through
durchstellen VT TEL put through
durchstreichen VT cross out
durchsuchen VT search (*nach* for) **Durchsuchung** F search
Durchwahl F direct dialing; (*Nummer*) extension
durchziehen VT (*Plan*) carry through
Durchzug M draft
dürfen VI **etw tun ~** (*Erlaubnis*) be allowed to do sth; **darf ich?** may I?; **das darfst du nicht (tun)!** you mustn't do that; **was darf es sein?** what can I do for you?; **er dürfte schon dort sein** he should be there by now
dürr ADJ (*mager*) skinny
Durst M thirst; **~ haben** be thirsty **durstig** ADJ thirsty
Dusche F shower **duschen** VI & VR take a shower **Duschgel** N shower gel
Düse F nozzle; TECH jet **Düsenflugzeug** N jet (aircraft)
düster ADJ dark; (*Gedanken, Zukunft*) gloomy
duzen 1 VT *address as 'du'* 2 VR **sich ~ (mit j-m)** *address each other as 'du', be on first-name terms*
DVD F *abk* = Digital Versatile Disk; DVD **DVD-Player** M DVD player **DVD-Rekorder** M DVD recorder
dynamisch ADJ dynamic

E

Ebbe F low tide
eben 1 ADJ level; (*glatt*)

smooth **2** ADV just; (*bestätigend*) exactly
ebenfalls ADV also, as well; (*Antwort: gleichfalls!*) you too **ebenso** ADV just as; **~ gut** just as well
Echo N echo
echt ADJ (*Leder, Gold*) real, genuine
EC-Karte F ≈ debit card
Ecke F corner; MATH angle; **an der ~** at the corner; **gleich um die ~** just around the corner **eckig** ADJ rectangular
Economyclass F coach (class), economy class
Effekt M effect
egal ADJ **das ist ~** it doesn't matter; **das ist mir ~** I don't care, it's all the same to me; **~ wie teuer** no matter how expensive
egoistisch ADJ selfish
ehe KONJ before
Ehe F marriage **Ehefrau** F wife
ehemalig ADJ former **ehemals** ADV formerly
Ehemann M husband **Ehepaar** N married couple
eher ADV (*früher*) sooner; (*lieber*) rather; (*mehr*) more; **je ~, desto besser** the sooner the better
Ehering M wedding ring
eheste(r, s) **1** ADJ (*früheste*) first **2** ADV **am ~n** (*am wahrscheinlichsten*) most likely
Ehre F honor **ehren** V/T honor
Ehrenwort N word of honor
ehrgeizig ADJ ambitious
ehrlich ADJ honest
Ei N egg
Eiche F oak (tree)
Eichhörnchen N squirrel
Eid M oath
Eidechse F lizard
Eierbecher M eggcup **Eierstock** M ovary **Eieruhr** F egg timer
Eifersucht F jealousy **eifersüchtig** ADJ jealous (*auf +akk* of)
Eigelb N egg yolk
eigen ADJ own; (*typisch*) characteristic (*j-m* of sb); (*eigenartig*) peculiar **eigenartig** ADJ peculiar **Eigenschaft** F quality; CHEM, PHYS property
eigentlich **1** ADJ actual, real **2** ADV actually, really; **was denken Sie sich ~ dabei?** what on earth do you think you're doing?
Eigentum N property **Eigentümer(in)** M(F) owner **Eigentumswohnung** F condominium
eignen V/R **sich ~ für** be suited for; **er würde sich als Lehrer ~** he'd make a good teacher
Eilbrief M express letter, special-delivery letter **Eile** F hurry **eilen** V/I (*dringend sein*) be urgent; **es eilt nicht** there's no hurry **eilig** ADJ hurried; (*dringlich*) urgent; **es ~ haben** be in a hurry

Eimer M bucket
ein ADV **nicht ~ noch aus wissen** not know what to do; **~ - aus** *(Schalter)* on - off
ein(e) ART a; *(vor gesprochenem Vokal)* an; **~es Tages** one day
einander PRON one another, each other
einarbeiten 1 V/T train 2 V/R get used to the work
einatmen V/T & V/I breathe in
Einbahnstraße F one-way street
einbauen V/T build in; *(Motor etc)* install, fit **Einbauküche** F fitted kitchen
einbiegen V/I turn *(in* into)
einbilden V/T **sich etw ~** imagine sth
einbrechen V/I *(in Haus)* break in; *(Dach etc)* fall in, collapse **Einbrecher(in)** M(F) burglar
einbringen 1 V/T *(Ernte)* bring in; *(Gewinn)* yield; **j-m etw ~** bring *(od* earn) sb sth 2 V/R **sich in etw ~** make a contribution to sth
Einbruch M *(Haus)* break-in, burglary; **bei ~ der Nacht** at nightfall
Einbürgerung F naturalization
einchecken V/T check in
eincremen V/T & V/R put some cream on
eindeutig 1 ADJ clear, obvious 2 ADV clearly
eindringen V/I *(gewaltsam)* force one's way in *(in +akk* -to); *(in Haus)* break in *(in +akk* -to); *(Gas, Wasser)* get in *(in +akk* -to)
Eindruck M impression
eine(r, s) INDEF PR one; *(jemand)* someone; **~r meiner Freunde** one of my friends; **~r nach dem andern** one after the other
eineiig ADJ *(Zwillinge)* identical
eineinhalb NUM one and a half
einerseits ADV on the one hand
einfach 1 ADJ *(nicht kompliziert)* simple; *(Mensch)* ordinary; *(Essen)* plain; *(nicht mehrfach)* single; **~e Fahrkarte** one-way ticket 2 ADV simply; *(nicht mehrfach)* once
Einfahrt F *(Vorgang)* driving in; *(eines Zuges)* arrival; *(Ort)* entrance
Einfall M *(Idee)* idea **einfallen** V/I *(Licht etc)* fall in; *(einstürzen)* collapse; **ihm fiel ein, dass ...** it occurred to him that ...; **ich werde mir etwas ~ lassen** I'll think of something; **was fällt Ihnen ein!** what do you think you're doing?
Einfamilienhaus N detached house
einfarbig ADJ all one color; *(Stoff etc)* self-colored
Einfluss M influence
einfrieren V/T & V/I freeze
einfügen V/T fit in; *(zusätzlich)* add; IT insert

Einfuhr F import **Einfuhrbestimmungen** PL import regulations *pl*
einführen V/T introduce; (*Ware*) import **Einführung** F introduction
Eingabe F (*Dateneingabe*) input **Eingabetaste** F IT return (*od* enter) key
Eingang M entrance **Eingangshalle** F entrance hall, lobby
eingeben V/T (*Daten etc*) enter, key in
eingebildet ADJ imaginary; (*eitel*) arrogant
Eingeborene(r) M/F(M) native
eingehen **1** V/I (*Sendung, Geld*) come in, arrive; (*Tier, Pflanze*) die; (*Stoff*) shrink; **auf etw ~** agree to sth; **auf j-n ~** respond to sb **2** V/T (*Vertrag*) enter into; (*Wette*) make; (*Risiko*) take
eingelegt ADJ (*in Essig*) pickled
eingeschaltet ADJ (switched) on
eingeschlossen ADJ locked in; (*inklusive*) included
eingewöhnen V/R settle in
eingießen V/T pour
eingreifen V/I intervene **Eingriff** M intervention; (*Operation*) operation
einhalten V/T (*Versprechen etc*) keep
einheimisch ADJ (*Produkt, Mannschaft*) local **Einheimische(r)** M/F(M) local
Einheit F (*Geschlossenheit*) unity; (*Maß*) unit **einheitlich** ADJ uniform
einholen V/T (*Vorsprung aufholen*) catch up with; (*Verspätung*) make up for; (*Rat, Erlaubnis*) ask for
einhundert NUM one (*od* a) hundred
einig ADJ (*vereint*) united; **sich ~ sein** agree
einige **1** INDEF PR *pl* some; (*mehrere*) several **2** UNBEST ZAHLWORT some; **~ hundert Dollar** some hundred dollars
einigen V/R agree (*auf +akk* on)
einigermaßen ADV fairly, quite; (*leidlich*) reasonably
einiges INDEF PR something; (*ziemlich viel*) quite a bit; (*mehreres*) a few things
Einkauf M purchase; **Einkäufe (machen)** (to do one's) shopping **einkaufen** **1** V/T buy **2** V/I go shopping **Einkaufsbummel** M shopping trip
Einkaufstasche F, **Einkaufstüte** F shopping bag
Einkaufswagen M shopping cart **Einkaufszentrum** N shopping mall
einklemmen V/T jam
Einkommen N income
einladen V/T (*j-n*) invite; (*Gegenstände*) load; **j-n zum Essen ~** take sb out for a meal; **ich lade dich ein** (*bezahle*) it's my treat **Einladung** F invitation
Einlass M admittance; **~ ab 18**

Uhr doors open at 6 p.m. **einlassen** VR **sich mit j-m/auf etw ~** get involved with sb/sth
einleben VR settle down
einlegen VT (*Film etc*) put in; (*marinieren*) marinate; **eine Pause ~** take a break
einleiten VT start; (*Maßnahmen*) introduce; (*Geburt*) induce **Einleitung** F introduction; (*von Geburt*) induction
einleuchten VI **j-m ~** be (*od* become) clear to sb **einleuchtend** ADJ clear
einloggen VI IT log on (*od* in)
einlösen VT (*Scheck*) cash; (*Gutschein*) redeem; (*Versprechen*) keep
einmal ADV once; (*früher*) before; (*in Zukunft*) some day; (*erstens*) first; **~ im Jahr** once a year; **noch ~** once more, again; **ich war schon ~ hier** I've been here before; **warst du schon ~ in Deutschland?** have you ever been to Germany?; **nicht ~** not even; **auf ~** suddenly; (*gleichzeitig*) at once, in one go **einmalig** ADJ unique; (*einmal geschehend*) single; (*prima*) fantastic
einmischen VR interfere (*in +akk* with)
Einnahme F (*Geld*) revenue; (*von Medizin*) taking **einnehmen** VT (*Medizin*) take; (*Geld*) take in; (*Standpunkt, Raum*) take up; **j-n für sich ~** win sb over
einordnen **1** VT put in order; (*klassifizieren*) classify; (*Akten*) file **2** VR AUTO get in lane; **sich rechts/links ~** get into the right/left lane
einpacken VT pack (up)
einparken VT & VI park
einplanen VT allow for
einprägen VT **sich etw ~** remember sth; (*auswendig lernen*) memorize sth
einräumen VT (*Bücher, Geschirr*) put away; (*Schrank*) put things in
einreden VT **j-m/sich etw ~** talk sb/oneself into (believing) sth
einreiben VT **sich mit etw ~** rub sth into one's skin
einreichen VT hand in; (*Antrag*) submit
Einreise F entry **Einreisebestimmungen** PL entry regulations *pl* **Einreiseerlaubnis** F, **Einreisegenehmigung** F entry permit **einreisen** VI enter (*in ein Land* a country)
Einreisevisum N entry visa
einrichten **1** VT (*Wohnung*) furnish; (*gründen*) establish, set up; (*arrangieren*) arrange **2** VR (*in Haus*) furnish one's home; (*sich vorbereiten*) prepare oneself (*auf +akk* for); (*sich anpassen*) adapt (*auf +akk* to) **Einrichtung** F (*Wohnung*) furnishings *pl*; (*öffentliche Anstalt*) institution; (*Schwimmbad etc*) facility

eins NUM one **Eins** F one; (*Schulnote*) ≈ A
einsam ADJ lonely
einsammeln V/T collect
Einsatz M (*Teil*) insert; (*Verwendung*) use; (*Spieleinsatz*) stake; (*Risiko*) risk; MUS entry
einschalten V/T ELEK switch on
einschätzen V/T assess; (*schätzen*) estimate
einschenken V/T pour
einschiffen V/R embark (*nach* for)
einschlafen V/I fall asleep, doze off; **mir ist der Arm eingeschlafen** my arm's gone to sleep
einschlagen 1 V/T (*Fenster*) smash; (*Zähne, Schädel*) smash in; (*Weg, Richtung*) take 2 V/I hit (*in etw akk* sth, *auf j-n* sb); (*Blitz*) strike; (*Anklang finden*) be a success
einschließen V/T (*j-n*) lock in; (*Gegenstand*) lock away; (*umgeben*) surround; *fig* (*beinhalten*) include **einschließlich** 1 ADV inclusive 2 PRÄP +*gen* including; **von Montag bis ~ Freitag** Monday thru Friday
einschränken 1 V/T limit, restrict; (*verringern*) cut down on 2 V/R cut down (on expenditure)
einschreiben V/R register; (*Schule*) enrol **Einschreiben** N registered letter; **etw per ~ schicken** send sth by special delivery
einschüchtern V/T intimidate
einsehen V/T (*verstehen*) see; (*Fehler*) recognize; (*Akten*) have a look at
einseitig ADJ one-sided
einsenden V/T send in
einsetzen 1 V/T put in; (*in Amt*) appoint; (*Geld*) stake; (*verwenden*) use 2 V/I (*beginnen*) set in; MUS enter, come in 3 V/R work hard; **sich für j-n/etw ~** support sb/sth
Einsicht F insight
einsperren V/T lock up
einspringen V/I (*aushelfen*) step in (*für* for)
Einspruch M objection (*gegen* to)
einspurig ADJ single-lane
einstecken V/T pocket; ELEK (*Stecker*) plug in; (*Brief*) mail; (*mitnehmen*) take; (*hinnehmen*) swallow
einsteigen V/I (*in Auto*) get in; (*in Bus, Zug, Flugzeug*) get on; (*sich beteiligen*) get involved
einstellen 1 V/T (*beenden*) stop; (*Geräte*) adjust; (*Kamera*) focus; (*Sender, Radio*) tune in; (*unterstellen*) put; (*in Firma*) employ, hire 2 V/R **sich auf j-n/etw ~** adapt to sb/prepare oneself for sth **Einstellung** F (*von Gerät*) adjustment; (*von Kamera*) focusing; (*von Arbeitern*) hiring; (*Meinung*) attitude
einstürzen V/I collapse
eintägig ADJ one-day

eintauschen VT exchange (*gegen* for)
eintausend NUM one (*od* a) thousand
einteilen VT (*in Teile*) divide (up) (*in +akk* into); (*Zeit*) organize
eintönig ADJ monotonous
Eintopf M stew
eintragen **1** VT (*in eine Liste*) put down, enter **2** V/R put one's name down, register
eintreffen VI happen; (*ankommen*) arrive
eintreten VI (*hineingehen*) enter (*in etw akk* sth); (*in Klub, Partei*) join (*in etw akk* sth); (*sich ereignen*) occur; **~ für** support
Eintritt M admission **Eintrittskarte** F (entrance) ticket **Eintrittspreis** M admission fee
einverstanden **1** INT okay, all right **2** ADJ **mit etwas ~ sein** agree to sth, accept sth
Einwanderer M, **Einwanderin** F immigrant **einwandern** VI immigrate
einwandfrei ADJ perfect, flawless
Einwegflasche F non-returnable bottle
einweichen VT soak
einweihen VT (*Gebäude*) inaugurate, open; **j-n in etw ~** let sb in on sth **Einweihungsparty** F housewarming party
einwerfen VT (*Ball, Bemerkung etc*) throw in; (*Brief*) mail; (*Geld*) put in, insert; (*Fenster*) smash
einwickeln VT wrap up; *fig* **j-n ~** take sb in
Einwohner(in) M(F) inhabitant
Einwohnermeldeamt N *registration office for residents*
Einwurf M (*Öffnung*) slot; SPORT throw-in
Einzahl F singular
einzahlen VT pay in (*auf ein Konto* -to an account)
Einzelbett N single bed **Einzelfahrschein** M one-way ticket **Einzelgänger(in)** M(F) loner **Einzelhandel** M retail trade **Einzelkind** N only child
einzeln **1** ADJ individual; (*getrennt*) separate; (*einzig*) single; **~e ...** several ..., some ...; **der/die Einzelne** the individual; **im Einzelnen** in detail **2** ADV separately; (*verpacken, aufführen*) individually; **~ angeben** specify; **~ eintreten** enter one by one
Einzelzimmer N single room **Einzelzimmerzuschlag** M single-room supplement
einziehen **1** VT **den Kopf ~** duck **2** VI (*in ein Haus*) move in
einzig **1** ADJ only; (*einzeln*) single; (*einzigartig*) unique; **das Einzige** the only thing; **der/die Einzige** the only person **2** ADV only **einzigartig** ADJ unique

Eis N ice; (*Speiseeis*) ice cream **Eisbahn** F ice(-skating) rink **Eisbär** M polar bear **Eisbecher** M (ice cream) sundae **Eisberg** M iceberg **Eisbergsalat** M iceberg lettuce **Eiscafé** N, **Eisdiele** F ice cream parlor
Eisen N iron **Eisenbahn** F railroad **eisern** ADJ iron
eisgekühlt ADJ chilled **Eishockey** N hockey **Eiskaffee** M iced coffee **eiskalt** ADJ ice-cold; (*Temperatur*) freezing **eislaufen** V/I skate **Eistee** M iced tea **Eiswürfel** M ice cube **Eiszapfen** M icicle
eitel ADJ vain
Eiter M pus
Eiweiß N egg white; CHEM, BIOL protein
ekelhaft, **ek(e)lig** ADJ disgusting, revolting **ekeln** V/R be disgusted (*vor +dat* at)
EKG N *abk* = Elektrokardiogramm; ECG
Ekzem N MED eczema
elastisch ADJ elastic
Elch M elk; (*nordamerikanischer*) moose
Elefant M elephant
elegant ADJ elegant
Elektriker(in) M(F) electrician **elektrisch** ADJ electric **Elektrizität** F electricity **Elektroauto** N electric car **Elektrogerät** N electrical appliance **Elektrogeschäft** N electrical store **Elektroherd** M electric stove **Elektromotor** M electric motor **Elektronik** F electronics *sg* **elektronisch** ADJ electronic **Elektrorasierer** M electric razor
Element N element
elend ADJ miserable **Elend** N misery
elf NUM eleven **Elfmeter** M SPORT penalty (kick) **elfte(r, s)** ADJ eleventh; → dritte
Ell(en)bogen M elbow
Eltern PL parents *pl* **Elternzeit** F parental leave
E-Mail F IT e-mail; **j-m eine ~ schicken** e-mail sb, send sb an e-mail; **j-m etwas per ~ schicken** e-mail sth to sb
E-Mail-Adresse F e-mail address **e-mailen** V/T e-mail
Emoticon N emoticon
emotional ADJ emotional
Empfang M (*Rezeption, Veranstaltung*) reception; (*Erhalten*) receipt; **in ~ nehmen** receive
empfangen V/T receive
Empfänger(in) **1** M(F) recipient; (*Adressat*) addressee **2** M TECH receiver **Empfängnisverhütung** F contraception **Empfangshalle** F reception area
empfehlen V/T recommend **Empfehlung** F recommendation
empfinden V/T feel **empfindlich** ADJ (*Mensch*) sensitive; (*Stelle*) sore; (*reizbar*) touchy; (*Material*) delicate

empört ADJ indignant (*über* at) **Ende** N end; (*Film, Roman*) ending; **am ~** at the end; (*schließlich*) in the end; **~ Mai** at the end of May; **~ der Achtzigerjahre** in the late eighties; **sie ist ~ zwanzig** she's in her late twenties; **zu ~** over, finished **enden** V/I end; **der Zug endet hier** this service (*od* train) terminates here **endgültig** ADJ final; (*Beweis*) conclusive
endlich ADV at last, finally; (*am Ende*) eventually **Endspiel** N final; (*Endrunde*) finals *pl* **Endstation** F terminus **Endung** F ending
Energie F energy; **~ sparend** energy-saving **Energiebedarf** M energy requirement **Energieverbrauch** M energy consumption
energisch ADJ (*entschlossen*) forceful
eng **1** ADJ narrow; (*Kleidung*) tight; *fig* (*Freundschaft, Verhältnis*) close; **das wird ~** *umg* (*zeitlich*) time's running out **2** ADV **~ befreundet sein** be close friends
engagieren **1** V/T engage **2** V/R commit oneself, be committed (*für* to)
Engel M angel
England N England **Engländer(in)** M(F) Englishman/-woman; **die ~** *pl* the English *pl* **englisch** ADJ English; GASTR rare **Englisch** N English; **ins ~e übersetzen** translate into English
Enkel M grandson **Enkelin** F granddaughter
enorm ADJ enormous; *fig* tremendous
Entbindung F MED delivery
entdecken V/T discover **Entdeckung** F discovery
Ente F duck
entfernen **1** V/T remove; IT delete **2** V/R go away **entfernt** ADJ distant; **15 km von X ~** 15 km away from X; **20 km voneinander ~** 20 km apart **Entfernung** F distance; **aus der ~** from a distance
entführen V/T kidnap **Entführer(in)** M(F) kidnapper **Entführung** F kidnapping
entgegen **1** PRÄP *+dat* contrary to **2** ADV toward(s); **dem Wind ~** against the wind **entgegengesetzt** ADJ (*Richtung*) opposite; (*Meinung*) opposing **entgegenkommen** V/I **j-m ~** come to meet sb; *fig* accommodate sb **entgegenkommend** ADJ (*Verkehr*) oncoming; *fig* obliging
entgegnen V/T reply (*auf +akk* to)
entgehen V/I **j-m ~** escape sb's notice; **sich etw ~ lassen** miss sth
entgleisen V/I BAHN be derailed; *fig* (*Mensch*) misbehave

Enthaarungscreme F hair remover
enthalten 1 V/T (*Behälter*) contain; (*Preis*) include 2 V/R abstain (*+gen* from)
entkoffeiniert ADJ decaffeinated
entkommen V/I escape
entkorken V/T uncork
entlang PRÄP *+akk od dat* **~ dem Fluss, den Fluss ~** along the river **entlanggehen** V/I walk along
entlassen V/T (*Patient*) discharge; (*Arbeiter*) dismiss
entlasten V/T **j-n ~** (*Arbeit abnehmen*) relieve sb of some of his/her work
entmutigen V/T discourage
entnehmen V/T take (*+dat* from)
entrahmt ADJ (*Milch*) skim (-med)
entschädigen V/T compensate **Entschädigung** F compensation
entscheiden V/T & V/I & V/R decide; **sich für/gegen etw ~** decide on/against sth **entscheidend** ADJ decisive; (*Frage, Problem*) crucial **Entscheidung** F decision
entschließen V/R decide (*zu, für* on), make up one's mind **Entschluss** M decision
entschuldigen 1 V/T excuse 2 V/R apologize; **sich bei j-m für etw ~** apologize to sb for sth 3 V/I **entschuldige!, ~ Sie!** (*vor einer Frage*) excuse me; (*Verzeihung!*) (I'm) sorry, excuse me **Entschuldigung** F apology; (*Grund*) excuse; **j-n um ~ bitten** apologize to sb; **~!** (*bei Zusammenstoß*) (I'm) sorry, excuse me; (*vor einer Frage*) excuse me; (*wenn man etw nicht verstanden hat*) (I beg your) pardon?, excuse me?
entsetzlich ADJ dreadful, appalling
entsorgen V/T dispose of
entspannen 1 V/T (*Körper*) relax; POL (*Lage*) ease 2 V/R relax; *umg* chill out **Entspannung** F relaxation
entsprechen V/I *+dat* correspond to; (*Anforderungen, Wünschen etc*) comply with **entsprechend** 1 ADJ appropriate 2 ADV accordingly 3 PRÄP *+dat* according to, in accordance with
entstehen V/I (*Schwierigkeiten*) arise; (*gebaut werden*) be built; (*hergestellt werden*) be created
enttäuschen V/T disappoint **Enttäuschung** F disappointment
entweder KONJ **~ … oder …** either … or …; **~ oder!** take it or leave it
entwerfen V/T (*Möbel, Kleider*) design; (*Plan, Vertrag*) draft
entwerten V/T devalue; (*Fahrschein*) validate **Entwerter** M ticket validation machine
entwickeln V/T & V/R *a.* FOTO

develop; (*Mut, Energie*) show, display **Entwicklung** F development; FOTO developing **Entwicklungsland** N developing country

Entwurf M outline; (*Design*) design; (*Vertragsentwurf, Konzept*) draft

entzückend ADJ delightful, charming

Entzug M withdrawal; (*Behandlung*) detox

entzünden V/R catch fire; MED become inflamed **Entzündung** F MED inflammation

Epidemie F epidemic

Epilepsie F epilepsy

er PERS PR (*Person*) he; (*Sache*) it; **~ ist's** it's him

Erbe 1 M heir 2 N inheritance; *fig* heritage **erben** V/T inherit **Erbin** F heiress **erblich** ADJ hereditary

erbrechen V/T & V/R vomit **Erbrechen** N vomiting

Erbschaft F inheritance

Erbse F pea

Erdapfel M *österr* potato **Erdbeben** N earthquake **Erdbeere** F strawberry **Erde** F (*Planet*) earth; (*Boden*) ground; (*Erdreich*) soil **Erdgas** N natural gas **Erdgeschoss** N first floor **Erdkunde** F geography **Erdnuss** F peanut **Erdöl** N (mineral) oil **Erdrutsch** M landslide **Erdteil** M continent

ereignen V/R happen, take place **Ereignis** N event

erfahren 1 V/T learn, find out; (*erleben*) experience 2 ADJ experienced **Erfahrung** F experience

erfinden V/T invent **erfinderisch** ADJ inventive, creative **Erfindung** F invention

Erfolg M success; (*Folge*) result; **viel ~!** good luck **erfolglos** ADJ unsuccessful **erfolgreich** ADJ successful

erforderlich ADJ necessary

erforschen V/T explore; (*untersuchen*) investigate

erfreulich ADJ pleasing, pleasant; (*Nachricht*) good

erfrieren V/I freeze to death; (*Pflanzen*) be killed by frost

Erfrischung F refreshment

erfüllen 1 V/T (*Raum*) fill; (*Bitte, Wunsch etc*) fulfill 2 V/R come true

ergänzen 1 V/T (*hinzufügen*) add; (*vervollständigen*) complete 2 V/R complement one another **Ergänzung** F completion; (*Zusatz*) supplement

ergeben 1 V/T (*Betrag*) come to; (*zum Ergebnis haben*) result in 2 V/R surrender; (*folgen*) result (*aus* from) 3 ADJ devoted; (*demütig*) humble **Ergebnis** N result

ergreifen V/T seize; (*Beruf*) take up; (*Maßnahme, Gelegenheit*) take; (*rühren*) move

erhalten V/T (*bekommen*) receive; (*bewahren*) preserve; **gut ~ sein** be in good condition **erhältlich** ADJ available **erheblich** ADJ considerable **erhitzen** V/T heat (up) **erhöhen** 1 V/T raise; (*verstärken*) increase 2 V/R increase **erholen** V/R recover; (*sich ausruhen*) have a rest **erholsam** ADJ restful **Erholung** F recovery; (*Entspannung*) relaxation, rest

erinnern 1 V/T remind (*an +akk* of) 2 V/R remember (*an etw akk* sth) **Erinnerung** F memory; (*Andenken*) souvenir; (*Mahnung*) reminder

erkälten V/R catch a cold **erkältet** ADJ **(stark) ~ sein** have a (bad) cold **Erkältung** F cold

erkennen V/T recognize; (*sehen, verstehen*) see **erkenntlich** ADJ **sich ~ zeigen** show one's appreciation

erklären V/T explain; (*kundtun*) declare **Erklärung** F explanation; (*Aussage*) declaration

erkundigen V/R inquire (*nach* about)

erlauben V/T allow, permit; **j-m ~, etw zu tun** allow (*od* permit) sb to do sth; **sich etw ~** permit oneself sth; **~ Sie(, dass ich rauche)?** do you mind (if I smoke)?; **was ~ Sie sich?** what do you think you're doing? **Erlaubnis** F permission

Erläuterung F explanation; (*zu Text*) comment

erleben V/T experience; (*schöne Tage etc*) have; (*Schlimmes*) go through; (*miterleben*) witness; (*noch miterleben*) live to see **Erlebnis** N experience

erledigen V/T (*Angelegenheit, Aufgabe*) deal with **erledigt** ADJ (*beendet*) finished; (*gelöst*) dealt with; *umg* (*erschöpft*) pooped

erleichtert ADJ relieved

Erlös M proceeds *pl*

ermahnen V/T (*warnend*) warn

ermäßigt ADJ reduced **Ermäßigung** F reduction

ermitteln 1 V/T find out; (*Täter*) trace 2 V/I JUR investigate

ermöglichen V/T make possible (*dat* for)

ermorden V/T murder

ermüdend ADJ tiring

ermutigen V/T encourage

ernähren 1 V/T feed; (*Familie*) support 2 V/R support oneself; **sich ~ von** live on **Ernährung** F (*Essen*) food

erneuern V/T renew; (*restaurieren*) restore; (*renovieren*) renovate; (*auswechseln*) replace

ernst 1 ADJ serious 2 ADV **j-n/etw ~ nehmen** take sb/sth seriously **Ernst** M seriousness; **das ist mein ~** I'm quite serious; **im ~?** seriously? **ernsthaft** 1 ADJ serious 2 ADV seriously

Ernte F harvest **Erntedankfest** N Thanksgiving (Day) (*4. Donnerstag im November*) **ernten** V/T harvest; (*Lob etc*) earn

erobern V/T conquer

eröffnen VT open **Eröffnung** F opening
erotisch ADJ erotic
erpressen VT *(j-n)* blackmail; *(Geld etc)* extort **Erpressung** F blackmail; *(von Geld)* extortion
erraten VT guess
erregen **1** VT excite; *(sexuell)* arouse; *(ärgern)* annoy; *(hervorrufen)* arouse **2** VR get worked up **Erreger** M MED germ; *(Virus)* virus
erreichbar ADJ **~ sein** be within reach; *(Person)* be available; **zu Fuß/mit dem Wagen leicht ~ sein** be within easy walking/driving distance **erreichen** VT reach; *(Zug etc)* catch
Ersatz M replacement; *(auf Zeit)* substitute; *(Ausgleich)* compensation **Ersatzreifen** M AUTO spare tire **Ersatzteil** N spare (part)
erscheinen VI appear; *(wirken)* seem
erschöpft ADJ exhausted **Erschöpfung** F exhaustion
erschrecken **1** VT frighten **2** VI get a fright **erschreckend** ADJ alarming **erschrocken** ADJ frightened
erschwinglich ADJ affordable
ersetzen VT replace; *(Auslagen)* reimburse
erst ADV first; *(anfangs)* at first; *(nicht früher, nur)* only; *(nicht bis)* not until; **~ recht** all the more; **~ recht nicht** even less
erstatten VT *(Kosten)* refund; **Anzeige gegen j-n ~** report sb to the police
erstaunlich ADJ astonishing
erstaunt ADJ surprised
erstbeste(r, s) ADJ **das ~ Hotel** any old hotel; **der Erstbeste** just anyone **erste(r, s)** ADJ first; → dritte; **zum ~n Mal** for the first time; **er wurde Erster** he came first; **Erste Hilfe leisten** give first aid **erstens** ADV first(ly), in the first place
ersticken VI *(Mensch)* suffocate; **in Arbeit ~** be snowed under with work
erstklassig ADJ first-class
erstmals ADV for the first time
erstrecken VR extend, stretch *(auf, über +akk* to, over)
ertappen VT catch
erteilen VT *(Rat, Erlaubnis)* give
Ertrag M yield; *(Gewinn)* proceeds *pl* **ertragen** VT *(Schmerzen)* bear, stand; *(dulden)* put up with **erträglich** ADJ bearable; *(nicht zu schlecht)* tolerable
ertrinken VI drown
erwachsen ADJ grown-up; **~ werden** grow up **Erwachsene(r)** M/F(M) adult, grown-up
erwähnen VT mention
erwarten VT expect; *(warten auf)* wait for

erwerbstätig ADJ employed **erwidern** V/T reply; (*Gruß, Besuch*) return **erwischen** V/T *umg* catch (*bei etw* doing sth) **erwünscht** ADJ desired; (*willkommen*) welcome **Erz** N ore **erzählen** V/T tell (*j-m etw* sb sth) **Erzählung** F story, tale **erzeugen** V/T produce; (*Strom*) generate **Erzeugnis** N product **erziehen** V/T bring up; (*geistig*) educate; (*Tier*) train **Erzieher(in)** M(F) educator; (*im Kindergarten*) kindergarten teacher **Erziehung** F upbringing; (*Bildung*) education **es** PERS PR (*Sache, im nom und akk*) it; (*Baby, Tier*) he/she; **ich bin ~** it's me; **~ ist kalt** it's cold; **~ gibt ...** there is .../there are ...; **ich hoffe ~** I hope so **Esel** M donkey **Espresso** M espresso **essbar** ADJ edible **essen** V/T & V/I eat; **zu Mittag/Abend ~** have lunch/dinner; **was gibt's zu ~?** what's for lunch/dinner?; **~ gehen** eat out **Essen** N (*Mahlzeit*) meal; (*Nahrung*) food **Essig** M vinegar **Esslöffel** M dessert spoon **Esszimmer** N dining room **Este** M, **Estin** F Estonian **Estland** N Estonia **estnisch** ADJ Estonian **Estnisch** N Estonian **Etage** F floor, story; **in** (*od* **auf**) **der ersten ~** on the second floor **Etagenbett** N bunk bed **Etappe** F stage **ethnisch** ADJ ethnic **E-Ticket** N (*elektronisches Ticket*) e-ticket **Etikett** N label **etliche** INDEF PR *pl* several, quite a few **etliches** INDEF PR quite a lot **etwa** ADV (*ungefähr*) about; (*vielleicht*) perhaps; (*beispielsweise*) for instance **etwas** **1** INDEF PR something; (*verneinend, fragend*) anything; (*ein wenig*) a little; **~ Neues** something/anything new; **~ zu essen** something to eat; **~ Salz** some salt **2** ADV a bit, a little; **~ mehr** a little more **EU** F *abk* = Europäische Union; EU **euch** PERS PR (*dat, akk von ihr*) you, (to) you; **~ (selbst)** (*reflexiv*) yourselves; **wo kann ich ~ treffen?** where can I meet you?; **sie schickt es ~** she'll send it to you; **ein Freund von ~** a friend of yours; **setzt ~ bitte** please sit down; **habt ihr ~ amüsiert?** did you enjoy yourselves? **euer** POSS PR (*adjektivisch*) your; **~ David** (*am Briefende*) Yours, David **euere(r, s)** POSS PR →

eure
Eule F owl
eure(r, s) POSS PR (*substantivisch*) yours; **das ist ~** that's yours **euretwegen** ADV (*wegen euch*) because of you; (*euch zuliebe*) for your sake
Euro M (*Währung*) euro **Europa** N Europe **Europäer(in)** M(F) European **europäisch** ADJ European; **Europäische Union** European Union
evangelisch ADJ Protestant
eventuell 1 ADJ possible 2 ADV possibly, perhaps
ewig ADJ eternal; **er hat ~ gebraucht** it took him ages **Ewigkeit** F eternity
Ex M od F ex **Ex-** IN ZSSGN ex-, former
exakt ADJ precise
Examen N exam
Exemplar N specimen; (*Buch*) copy
Exil N exile
Existenz F existence; (*Unterhalt*) livelihood, living **existieren** V/I exist
exklusiv ADJ exclusive **exklusive** ADV & PRÄP +*gen* excluding
exotisch ADJ exotic
Experte M, **Expertin** F expert
explodieren V/I explode **Explosion** F explosion
Export M export **exportieren** V/T export
Express M, **Expresszug** M express (train)
extra 1 ADJ *umg* (*gesondert*) separate; (*zusätzlich*) extra 2 ADV (*gesondert*) separately; (*speziell*) specially; (*absichtlich*) on purpose **Extra** N extra
extrem 1 ADJ extreme 2 ADV extremely
exzellent ADJ excellent

F

fabelhaft ADJ fabulous, marvelous
Fabrik F factory
Fach N compartment; (*Schulfach, Sachgebiet*) subject **Facharzt** M, **Fachärztin** F specialist **Fachausdruck** M technical term
Fächer M fan
Fachfrau F specialist, expert **Fachmann** M specialist, expert
fad(e) ADJ (*Essen*) bland; (*langweilig*) dull
Faden M thread
fähig ADJ capable (*zu*, +*gen* of) **Fähigkeit** F ability
Fahndung F search
Fahne F flag
Fahrausweis M ticket **Fahrbahn** F road; (*Spur*) lane
Fähre F ferry
fahren 1 V/T drive; (*Rad*) ride; (*befördern*) drive, take; 50

km/h ~ drive at (*od* do) 50 kph **2** VI (*sich bewegen*) go; (*Autofahrer*) drive; (*Schiff*) sail; (*abfahren*) leave; **mit dem Auto/Zug ~** go by car/train; **rechts ~!** keep to the right **Fahrer(in)** M(F) driver **Fahrerflucht** F **~ begehen** fail to stop after an accident **Fahrersitz** M driver's seat

Fahrgast M passenger **Fahrgeld** N fare **Fahrgemeinschaft** F car pool **Fahrkarte** F ticket **Fahrkartenautomat** M ticket machine **Fahrkartenschalter** M ticket office

fahrlässig ADJ negligent

Fahrplan M schedule, timetable **Fahrpreis** M fare

Fahrrad N bicycle **Fahrradweg** M bike path

Fahrschein M ticket **Fahrscheinautomat** M ticket machine **Fahrscheinentwerter** M ticket validation machine **Fahrscheinkontrolle** F ticket inspection

Fahrschule F driving school **Fahrschüler(in)** M(F) student driver

Fahrstuhl M elevator

Fahrt F journey; (*kurz*) trip; AUTO drive; **auf der ~ nach Las Vegas** on the way to Las Vegas; **nach drei Stunden ~** after traveling for three hours; **gute ~!** have a good trip **Fahrtkosten** PL traveling expenses *pl*

fahrtüchtig F (*Person*) fit to drive; (*Auto*) roadworthy

Fahrtunterbrechung F break in the journey, stop

Fahrverbot N **~ erhalten/haben** be banned from driving

Fahrzeug N vehicle **Fahrzeugbrief** M (vehicle) registration document **Fahrzeughalter(in)** M(F) registered owner **Fahrzeugpapiere** PL vehicle documents *pl*

fair ADJ fair

Fakultät F faculty

Fall M (*Sturz*) fall; (*Sachverhalt, juristisch*) case; **auf jeden ~, auf alle Fälle** in any case; (*bestimmt*) definitely; **auf keinen ~** on no account; **für den ~, dass ...** in case ...

Falle F trap

fallen VI fall; **etw ~ lassen** drop sth

fällig ADJ due

falls ADV if; (*für den Fall, dass*) in case

Fallschirm M parachute **Fallschirmspringen** N parachuting, parachute jumping

falsch ADJ (*unrichtig*) wrong; (*unehrlich, unecht*) false; **~ verbunden** sorry, wrong number

fälschen VT forge **Fälschung** F forgery, fake

Faltblatt N leaflet

Falte F (*Knick*) fold; (*Haut*) wrinkle; (*Rock*) pleat **falten** VT fold **faltig** ADJ (*zerknittert*)

creased; (*Haut, Gesicht*) wrinkled
Familie F family **Familienangehörige(r)** M/F(M) family member **Familienname** M surname **Familienstand** M marital status
Fan M fan
fangen 1 V/T catch 2 V/R (*nicht fallen*) steady oneself; *fig* compose oneself
Fantasie F imagination
fantastisch ADJ fantastic
Farbe F color; (*zum Malen etc*) paint; (*für Stoff*) dye **färben** V/T color; (*Stoff, Haar*) dye **farbig** ADJ colored **Farbstoff** M dye; (*für Lebensmittel*) coloring
Fasching M Mardi Gras
Faschismus M fascism
Faser F fiber
Fass N barrel; (*Öl*) drum
fassen 1 V/T (*ergreifen*) grasp; (*enthalten*) hold; (*Entschluss*) take; (*verstehen*) understand; **nicht zu ~!** unbelievable 2 V/R compose oneself **Fassung** F (*Umrahmung*) mount; (*Brille*) frame; (*Lampe*) socket; (*Wortlaut*) version; (*Beherrschung*) composure; **j-n aus der ~ bringen** throw sb; **die ~ verlieren** lose one's cool
fast ADV almost, nearly
fasten V/I fast
Fastnacht F (*Fasching*) Mardi Gras
faul ADJ (*Obst, Gemüse*) rotten; (*Mensch*) lazy; (*Ausrede*) lame
faulen V/I rot **faulenzen** V/I do nothing, hang around
Faulheit F laziness **faulig** ADJ rotten; (*Geruch, Geschmack*) foul
Faust F fist **Fausthandschuh** M mitten
Fax N fax **faxen** V/I & V/T fax **Faxgerät** N fax machine **Faxnummer** F fax number
Februar M February; → Juni
Feder F feather; (*Füllfederhalter*) penpoint; TECH spring **Federung** F suspension
Fee F fairy
fegen V/I & V/T sweep
fehlen V/I (*abwesend sein*) be absent; **etw fehlt j-m** sb lacks sth; **was fehlt ihm?** what's wrong with him?; **du fehlst mir** I miss you; **es fehlt an ...** there's no ...
Fehler M mistake, error; (*Mangel, Schwäche*) fault **Fehlermeldung** F IT error message
Fehlzündung F AUTO misfire
Feier F celebration; (*Party*) party **feierlich** ADJ solemn **feiern** V/T & V/I celebrate, have a party **Feiertag** M holiday; **gesetzlicher ~** public holiday
feig(e) ADJ cowardly
Feige F fig
Feigling M coward
Feile F file
fein ADJ fine; (*vornehm*) refined
Feind(in) M(F) enemy **feindlich** ADJ hostile
Feinkost F delicacies *pl* **Fein-**

kostladen M delicatessen
Feld N field; (*Schach*) square; SPORT pitch
Felge F (wheel) rim
Fell N fur; (*von Schaf*) fleece
Fels M, **Felsen** M rock; (*Klippe*) cliff **felsig** ADJ rocky
feministisch ADJ feminist
Fenchel M fennel
Fenster N window **Fensterbrett** N windowsill **Fensterladen** M shutter **Fensterplatz** M windowseat **Fensterscheibe** F windowpane
Ferien PL vacation *sg*; **~ haben/machen** be/go on vacation **Ferienhaus** N vacation home **Ferienlager** N vacation camp; (*für Kinder im Sommer*) summer camp **Ferienort** M vacation resort **Ferienwohnung** F vacation apartment
fern ADJ distant, far-off; **von ~** from a distance **Fernbedienung** F remote control **Ferne** F distance; **aus der ~** from a distance
ferner ADJ & ADV further; (*außerdem*) besides
Fernflug M long-distance flight **Ferngespräch** N long-distance call **ferngesteuert** ADJ remote-controlled **Fernglas** N binoculars *pl* **Fernlicht** N high beam
fernsehen V/I watch television
Fernsehen N television; **im ~** on television **Fernseher** M TV (set) **Fernsehkanal** M TV channel **Fernsehprogramm** N (*Sendung*) TV program; (*Zeitschrift*) TV guide **Fernsehserie** F TV series *sg*
Fernstraße F major road
Fernverkehr M long-distance traffic
Ferse F heel
fertig ADJ (*bereit*) ready; (*beendet*) finished; **~ machen** (*beenden*) finish; **sich ~ machen** get ready; **mit etw ~ werden** be able to cope with sth; **auf die Plätze, ~, los!** on your marks, get set, go! **Fertiggericht** N TV (*od* frozen) dinner **fertigmachen** V/T **j-n ~** (*kritisieren*) give sb hell; (*zur Verzweiflung bringen*) drive sb mad
fest ADJ firm; (*Nahrung*) solid; (*Gehalt*) regular; (*Schuhe*) sturdy; (*Schlaf*) sound
Fest N party; REL festival
Festbetrag M fixed amount
festbinden V/T tie (*an +dat* to)
festhalten **1** V/T hold onto **2** V/R hold on (*an +dat* to)
Festival N festival
Festland N mainland
festlegen **1** V/T fix **2** V/R commit oneself
festlich ADJ festive
festmachen V/T fasten; (*Termin etc*) fix **festnehmen** V/T arrest
Festnetz N TEL landline **Festplatte** F IT hard disk

festsetzen V/T fix
Festspiele PL festival *sg*
feststehen V/I be fixed
feststellen V/T establish; (*sagen*) remark
Festung F fortress
Festzelt N marquee
Fete F party
fett ADJ (*dick*) fat; (*Essen etc*) greasy; (*Schrift*) bold **Fett** N fat; TECH grease **fettarm** ADJ low-fat **fettig** ADJ fatty; (*schmierig*) greasy
feucht ADJ damp; (*Luft*) humid **Feuchtigkeit** F dampness; (*Luftfeuchtigkeit*) humidity **Feuchtigkeitscreme** F moisturizing cream
Feuer N fire; **haben Sie ~?** have you got a light? **Feueralarm** M fire alarm **feuerfest** ADJ fireproof **Feuerlöscher** M fire extinguisher **Feuermelder** M fire alarm **Feuertreppe** F fire escape **Feuerwehr** F fire service **Feuerwerk** N fireworks *pl* **Feuerzeug** N (cigarette) lighter
ficken V/T & V/I *vulg* fuck
Fieber N temperature, fever; **~ haben** have a high temperature **Fieberthermometer** N thermometer
fies ADJ *umg* nasty
Figur F figure; (*im Schach*) piece
Filet N fil(l)et
Filiale F WIRTSCH branch
Film M movie **filmen** V/T & V/I film
Filter M filter **Filterkaffee** M filter coffee **filtern** V/T filter **Filterpapier** N filter paper
Filz M felt **Filzschreiber** M, **Filzstift** M felt(-tip) pen, felt-tip
Finale N SPORT final
Finanzamt N IRS (*Internal Revenue Service*) **finanziell** ADJ financial **finanzieren** V/T finance
finden V/T find; (*meinen*) think; **ich finde nichts dabei, wenn ...** I don't see what's wrong with ...; **ich finde es gut/schlecht** I like/don't like it
Finger M finger **Fingerabdruck** M fingerprint **Fingernagel** M fingernail
Finne M, **Finnin** F Finn, Finnish man/woman **finnisch** ADJ Finnish **Finnisch** N Finnish **Finnland** N Finland
finster ADJ dark; (*verdächtig*) dubious; (*verdrossen*) grim; (*Gedanke*) dark **Finsternis** F darkness
Firewall F IT firewall
Firma F firm
Fisch M fish; **~e** *pl* ASTROL Pisces *sg* **fischen** V/T & V/I fish **Fischer(in)** M(F) fisherman/-woman **Fischerboot** N fishing boat
Fisole F green bean
fit ADJ fit **Fitness** F fitness **Fitnesscenter** N fitness center,

gym **Fitnesstrainer(in)** M(F) fitness trainer, personal trainer
fix ADJ (*schnell*) quick; **~ und fertig** exhausted
fixen V/I *umg* shoot up **Fixer(in)** M(F) *umg* junkie
FKK F *abk* = Freikörperkultur; nudism **FKK-Strand** M nudist beach
flach ADJ flat; (*Gewässer, Teller*) shallow; **~er Absatz** low heel **Flachbildschirm** M flat screen
Fläche F area; (*Oberfläche*) surface
Flagge F flag
flambiert ADJ flambé(ed)
Flamme F flame
Flasche F bottle; **eine ~ sein** *umg* be useless **Flaschenöffner** M bottle opener **Flaschenpfand** N deposit
flatterhaft ADJ fickle **flattern** V/I flutter
flauschig ADJ fluffy
Flaute F calm; WIRTSCH recession
flechten V/T braid; (*Kranz*) bind
Fleck M, **Flecken** M spot; (*Schmutz*) stain **Fleckentferner** M stain remover **fleckig** ADJ spotted; (*mit Schmutzflecken*) stained
Fledermaus F bat
Fleisch N flesh; (*Essen*) meat **Fleischbrühe** F meat stock **Fleischer(in)** M(F) butcher **Fleischerei** F butcher shop
fleißig ADJ diligent, hard-working
flexibel ADJ flexible
flicken V/T mend **Flickzeug** N repair kit
Fliege F fly; (*Krawatte*) bow tie
fliegen V/T & V/I fly
Fliese F tile
Fließband N conveyor belt; (*als Einrichtung*) production (*od* assembly) line **fließen** V/I flow **fließend** ADJ (*Rede, Deutsch*) fluent; (*Übergänge*) smooth; **~(es) Wasser** running water
flirten V/I flirt
Flitterwochen PL honeymoon *sg*
Flocke F flake
Floh M flea **Flohmarkt** M flea market
Floß N raft
Flosse F fin; (*Schwimmflosse*) flipper
Flöte F flute; (*Blockflöte*) recorder
Fluch M curse **fluchen** V/I swear, curse
Flucht F flight **flüchten** V/I flee (*vor +dat* from) **flüchtig** ADJ **ich kenne ihn nur ~** I don't know him very well at all **Flüchtling** M refugee
Flug M flight **Flugbegleiter(in)** M(F) flight attendant **Flugblatt** N leaflet
Flügel M wing; MUS grand piano
Fluggast M passenger (*on a plane*) **Fluggesellschaft** F

airline **Flughafen** M airport **Fluglotse** M air-traffic controller **Flugnummer** F flight number **Flugplan** M flight schedule **Flugplatz** M airport; (*klein*) airfield **Flugschein** M plane ticket **Flugschreiber** M flight recorder, black box **Flugsteig** M gate **Flugticket** N plane ticket **Flugverbindung** F flight connection **Flugverkehr** M air traffic **Flugzeug** N plane **Flugzeugentführung** F hijacking

Fluorzahnpasta F fluoride toothpaste

Flur M hall; (*Treppenflur*) staircase

Fluss M river; (*Fließen*) flow

flüssig ADJ liquid **Flüssigkeit** F liquid

flüstern V/T & V/I whisper

Flut F flood; (*Gezeiten*) high tide **Flutlicht** N floodlight

Fohlen N foal

Föhn M hairdryer **föhnen** V/T dry; (*beim Friseur*) blow-dry

Folge F (*Reihe, Serie*) series *sg*; (*Aufeinanderfolge*) sequence; (*Fortsetzung eines Romans*) installment; (*Fortsetzung einer Fernsehserie*) episode; (*Auswirkung*) result; **~n haben** have consequences **folgen** V/I follow (*j-m* sb); (*gehorchen*) obey (*j-m* sb) **folgend** ADJ following **folgendermaßen** ADV as follows **folglich** ADV consequently

Folie F foil; (*für Projektor*) transparency; (*in PowerPoint®*) slide

fordern V/T demand

fördern V/T promote; (*unterstützen*) help

Forderung F demand

Forelle F trout

Form F form; (*Gestalt*) shape; (*Gussform*) mold; (*Backform*) baking pan; **in ~ sein** be in good form **Formalität** F formality **Format** N format **formatieren** V/T (*Diskette*) format; (*Text*) edit **formen** V/T form, shape **förmlich** ADJ formal; (*buchstäblich*) real **formlos** ADJ informal **Formular** N form **formulieren** V/T formulate

forschen V/I search (*nach* for); (*wissenschaftlich*) (do) research **Forscher(in)** M(F) researcher **Forschung** F research

Forst M forest

fort ADV away; (*verschwunden*) gone **fortbewegen** **1** V/T move away **2** V/R move **Fortbildung** F further education; (*im Beruf*) further training **fortfahren** V/I go away; (*weitermachen*) continue **fortgehen** V/I go away **fortgeschritten** ADJ advanced **Fortpflanzung** F reproduction

Fortschritt M progress; **~e machen** make progress **fort-**

schrittlich ADJ progressive
fortsetzen V/T continue **Fortsetzung** F continuation; (*folgender Teil*) installment; **~ folgt** to be continued
Foto **1** N photo **2** M (*Fotoapparat*) camera **Fotograf(in)** M(F) photographer **Fotografie** F photography; (*Bild*) photograph **fotografieren** **1** V/T photograph **2** V/I take photographs **Fotohandy** N camera phone **Fotokopie** F photocopy **fotokopieren** V/T photocopy
Foul N foul
Foyer N foyer
Fr. F *abk* = Frau; Mrs.; (*unverheiratet, neutral*) Ms.
Fracht F freight; SCHIFF cargo **Frachter** M freighter
Frack M tails *pl*
Frage F question; **das ist eine ~ der Zeit** it's a matter (*od* question) of time; **das kommt nicht in ~** that's out of the question **Fragebogen** M questionnaire **fragen** V/T & V/I ask **Fragezeichen** N question mark **fragwürdig** ADJ dubious
Franken **1** M (*Schweizer Währung*) Swiss franc **2** N (*Land*) Franconia
frankieren V/T stamp; (*maschinell*) frank
Frankreich N France **Franzose** M, **Französin** F Frenchman/-woman; **die ~n** *pl* the French *pl* **französisch** ADJ French **Französisch** N French
Frau F woman; (*Ehefrau*) wife; (*Anrede*) Mrs.; (*unverheiratet, neutral*) Ms. **Frauenarzt** M, **Frauenärztin** F gynecologist
Fräulein N (*junge Dame*) young lady; (*veraltet als Anrede*) Miss
frech ADJ sassy
frei ADJ free; (*Straße*) clear; (*Mitarbeiter*) freelance; **ein ~er Tag** a day off; **~e Arbeitsstelle** vacancy; **Zimmer ~** room(s) for rent; **im Freien** in the open air **Freibad** N open-air (swimming) pool **freiberuflich** ADJ freelance **freig(i)ebig** ADJ generous **Freiheit** F freedom **freilassen** V/T (set) free **freilich** ADV of course **Freilichtbühne** F open-air theater **freimachen** V/R undress **freinehmen** V/T **sich einen Tag ~** take a day off **Freisprechanlage** F hands-free phone/kit
Freitag M Friday; → Mittwoch **freitags** ADV (on) Fridays; → mittwochs
freiwillig ADJ voluntary
Freizeit F spare (*od* free) time **Freizeithemd** N sports shirt **Freizeitkleidung** F leisure wear **Freizeitpark** M amusement park
fremd ADJ (*nicht vertraut*) strange; (*ausländisch*) foreign;

(*nicht eigen*) someone else's **Fremde(r)** M/F(M) (*Unbekannter*) stranger; (*Ausländer*) foreigner **Fremdenführer(in)** M(F) (tourist) guide **Fremdenverkehr** M tourism **Fremdenverkehrsamt** N tourist office **Fremdsprache** F foreign language **Fremdsprachenkenntnisse** PL knowledge *sg* of foreign languages

Frequenz F RADIO frequency

fressen V/T & V/I (*Tier*) eat; (*Mensch*) guzzle

Freude F joy, delight **freuen** **1** V/T please; **es freut mich, dass ...** I'm pleased that ... **2** V/R be pleased (*über +akk* about); **sich auf etw ~** look forward to sth

Freund M friend; (*in Beziehung*) boyfriend **Freundin** F friend; (*in Beziehung*) girlfriend **freundlich** ADJ friendly; (*liebenswürdig*) kind **freundlicherweise** ADV kindly **Freundschaft** F friendship

Frieden M peace **Friedhof** M cemetery **friedlich** ADJ peaceful

frieren V/T & V/I freeze; **ich friere, es friert mich** I'm freezing

Frikadelle F burger

frisch ADJ fresh; (*lebhaft*) lively; **sich ~ machen** freshen up **Frischhaltefolie** F plastic wrap **Frischkäse** M cream cheese

Friseur(in) M(F) hairdresser **frisieren** **1** V/T **j-n ~** do sb's hair **2** V/R do one's hair

Frist F period; (*Zeitpunkt*) deadline; **eine ~ einhalten** meet a deadline

Frisur F hairdo, hairstyle

frittieren V/T deep-fry

froh ADJ happy; **~e Weihnachten!** Merry Christmas!

fröhlich ADJ happy, cheerful

Frosch M frog

Frost M frost; **bei ~** in frosty weather **Frostschutzmittel** N anti-freeze

Frucht F fruit; (*Getreide*) corn **fruchtig** ADJ fruity **Fruchtsaft** M fruit juice **Fruchtsalat** M fruit salad

früh ADJ & ADV early; **heute ~** this morning; **um fünf Uhr ~** at five (o'clock) in the morning; **~ genug** soon enough **früher** **1** ADJ earlier; (*ehemalig*) former **2** ADV formerly, in the past **frühestens** ADV at the earliest **Frühjahr** N, **Frühling** M spring **Frühlingsrolle** F spring roll **Frühlingszwiebel** F scallion

Frühstück N breakfast **frühstücken** V/I have breakfast **Frühstücksbüfett** N breakfast buffet

frühzeitig ADJ early

Frust M *umg* frustration **frustrieren** V/T frustrate

Fuchs M fox

fühlen V/T & V/I & V/R feel

führen **1** V/T lead; (*Geschäft*)

run; (*Buch*) keep **2** VI lead, be in the lead **3** VR behave **Führerschein** M driver's license **Führung** F leadership; (*eines Unternehmens*) management; MIL command; (*in Museum, Stadt*) guided tour; **in ~ liegen** be in the lead
füllen VT & VR fill; GASTR stuff
Füller M, **Füllfederhalter** M fountain pen
Füllung F filling
Fund M find **Fundbüro** N lost and found **Fundsachen** PL lost property *sg*
fünf NUM five **Fünf** F five; (*Schulnote*) ≈ F **fünfhundert** NUM five hundred **fünfmal** ADV five times **fünfte(r, s)** ADJ fifth; → dritte **Fünftel** N fifth **fünfzehn** NUM fifteen **fünfzehnte(r, s)** ADJ fifteenth; → dritte **fünfzig** NUM fifty **fünfzigste(r, s)** ADJ fiftieth
Funk M radio; **über ~** by radio
Funke M spark **funkeln** VI sparkle
Funkgerät N radio **Funktaxi** N radio taxi, radio cab
Funktion F function **funktionieren** VI work, function
für PRÄP *+akk* for; **was ~ (ein) ...?** what kind (*od* sort) of ...?; **Tag ~ Tag** day after day
Furcht F fear **furchtbar** ADJ terrible **fürchten** **1** VT be afraid of, fear **2** VR be afraid (*vor +dat* of) **fürchterlich** ADJ awful
füreinander ADV for each other
Fürst(in) M(F) prince/princess
Furunkel N boil
Furz M *vulg* fart **furzen** VI *vulg* fart
Fuß M foot; (*von Glas, Säule etc*) base; (*von Möbel*) leg; **zu ~** on foot; **zu ~ gehen** walk **Fußball** M soccer **Fußballspiel** N soccer match **Fußballspieler(in)** M(F) soccer player **Fußboden** M floor **Fußgänger(in)** M(F) pedestrian **Fußgängerüberweg** M crosswalk **Fußgängerzone** F pedestrian zone **Fußgelenk** N ankle **Fußpilz** M athlete's foot **Fußtritt** M kick; **j-m einen ~ geben** give sb a kick, kick sb **Fußweg** M footpath
Futter N feed; (*Heu etc*) fodder; (*Stoff*) lining **füttern** VT feed; (*Kleidung*) line

Gabe F gift
Gabel F fork **Gabelung** F fork
gaffen VI gape
Gage F fee
gähnen VI yawn

Galerie F gallery
Galle F gall; (*Organ*) gall bladder **Gallenstein** M gallstone
galoppieren VI gallop
gammeln VI loaf (*od* hang) around
Gang M walk; (*im Flugzeug*) aisle; (*Essen, Ablauf*) course; (*Flur etc*) corridor; (*Durchgang*) passage; AUTO gear; **den zweiten ~ einlegen** change into second gear; **etw in ~ bringen** get sth going **Gangschaltung** F gears *pl* **Gangway** F FLUG steps *pl*; SCHIFF gangway
Gans F goose **Gänsehaut** F goose bumps *pl*
ganz 1 ADJ whole; (*vollständig*) complete; **~ Amerika** all of America; **sein ~es Geld** all his money; **den ~en Tag** all day; **die ~e Zeit** all the time 2 ADV quite; (*völlig*) completely; **es hat mir ~ gut gefallen** I quite liked it; **~ schön viel** quite a lot **ganztägig** ADJ all-day; (*Arbeit, Stelle*) full-time
gar 1 ADJ done, cooked 2 ADV at all; **~ nicht/nichts/keiner** not/nothing/nobody at all; **~ nicht schlecht** not bad at all
Garage F garage
Garantie F guarantee **garantieren** VT guarantee
Garderobe F (*Kleidung*) wardrobe; (*Abgabe*) checkroom
Gardine F curtain
Garn N thread
Garnele F shrimp
garnieren VT decorate; (*Speisen*) garnish
Garten M garden **Gärtner(in)** M(F) gardener **Gärtnerei** F nursery
Gas N gas; **~ geben** AUTO accelerate; *fig* get a move on
Gasheizung F gas heating
Gasherd M gas stove **Gaskocher** M camping stove
Gaspedal N gas pedal
Gasse F alley
Gast M guest; **Gäste haben** have guests **Gästebett** N spare bed **Gästebuch** N visitors' book **Gästehaus** N guest house **Gästezimmer** N guest room **gastfreundlich** ADJ hospitable **Gastgeber(in)** M(F) host/hostess
Gasthaus N, **Gasthof** M inn **Gastland** N host country
Gastritis F gastritis
Gaststätte F restaurant; (*Trinklokal*) bar **Gastwirt(in)** M(F) restaurant owner; (*Trinklokal*) bar owner
Gaumen M palate
geb. ADJ *abk* = geboren(e) 1 b. 2 née; → geboren
Gebäck N pastries *pl*; (*Kekse*) cookies *pl*
Gebärmutter F womb
Gebäude N building
geben 1 VT & VI give (*j-m etw* sb sth, sth to sb); (*Karten*) deal; **lass dir eine Quittung ~** ask for a receipt 2 VT UNPERS **es gibt** there is/are; (*in Zukunft*)

there will be; **das gibt's nicht** I don't believe it **3** V/R (*sich verhalten*) behave, act; **das gibt sich wieder** it'll sort itself out
Gebet N prayer
Gebiet N area; (*Hoheitsgebiet*) territory; *fig* field
gebildet ADJ educated; (*belesen*) well-read
Gebirge N mountains *pl*
Gebiss N teeth *pl*; (*künstlich*) dentures *pl*
Gebläse N fan, blower
geboren ADJ born; **Andrea Jordan, ~e Christian** Andrea Jordan, née Christian
geborgen ADJ secure, safe
gebrauchen V/T use **Gebrauchsanweisung** F directions *pl* for use **gebraucht** ADJ used; **etw ~ kaufen** buy sth secondhand **Gebrauchtwagen** M secondhand (*od* used) car
Gebühr F charge; (*Maut*) toll; (*Honorar*) fee **gebührenfrei** ADJ free of charge; (*Telefonnummer*) toll-free **gebührenpflichtig** ADJ subject to charges; **~e Straße** toll road
Geburt F birth **gebürtig** ADJ **er ist ~er Schweizer** he is Swiss by birth **Geburtsdatum** N date of birth **Geburtsjahr** N year of birth **Geburtsname** M birth name; (*einer Frau*) maiden name **Geburtsort** M birthplace **Geburtstag** M birthday; **Herzlichen Glückwunsch zum ~!** Happy Birthday! **Geburtsurkunde** F birth certificate
Gebüsch N bushes *pl*
Gedächtnis N memory; **im ~ behalten** remember
Gedanke M thought; **sich über etw ~n machen** think about sth; (*besorgt*) be worried about sth **Gedankenstrich** M dash
Gedeck N place setting; (*Speisenfolge*) set meal
Gedenkstätte F memorial
Gedicht N poem
Gedränge N crush, crowd
Geduld F patience **geduldig** ADJ patient
geehrt ADJ **Sehr ~er Herr Young** Dear Mr. Young
geeignet ADJ suitable
Gefahr F danger; **auf eigene ~** at one's own risk **gefährden** V/T endanger **gefährlich** ADJ dangerous
Gefälle N gradient, slope
gefallen V/I **j-m ~** please sb; **er/es gefällt mir** I like him/it; **sich etw ~ lassen** put up with sth
Gefallen M favor; **j-m einen ~ tun** do sb a favor
Gefängnis N prison
Gefäß N (*Behälter*) container, receptacle; ANAT, BOT vessel
gefasst ADJ composed, calm; **auf etw ~ sein** be prepared (*od* ready) for sth

Geflügel N poultry
gefragt ADJ in demand
Gefrierfach N freezer compartment **Gefrierschrank** M (upright) freezer **Gefriertruhe** F (chest) freezer
Gefühl N feeling
gegebenenfalls ADV if need be
gegen PRÄP +*akk* against; (*im Austausch für*) (in return) for; **~ 8 Uhr** about 8 o'clock; **Deutschland ~ die USA** Germany versus the USA; **etwas ~ Husten** (*Mittel*) something for a cough
Gegend F area; **hier in der ~** around here
gegeneinander ADV against one another **Gegenfahrbahn** F opposite lane **Gegenmittel** N remedy (*gegen* for) **Gegenrichtung** F opposite direction **Gegensatz** M contrast; **im ~ zu** in contrast to **gegensätzlich** ADJ conflicting **gegenseitig** ADJ mutual; **sich ~ helfen** help each other
Gegenstand M object; (*Thema*) subject
Gegenteil N opposite; **im ~** on the contrary **gegenteilig** ADJ opposite, contrary
gegenüber **1** PRÄP +*dat* opposite; (*zu j-m*) to(wards) **2** ADV opposite **gegenüberstehen** V/T face; (*Problemen*) be faced with **gegenüberstellen** V/T confront (+*dat* with); *fig* compare (+*dat* with)
Gegenverkehr M oncoming traffic **Gegenwart** F present (tense)
Gegner(in) M(F) opponent
Gehalt **1** M content **2** N salary
gehässig ADJ spiteful, nasty
gehbehindert ADJ **sie ist ~** she can't walk properly
geheim ADJ secret; **etw ~ halten** keep sth secret **Geheimnis** N secret; (*rätselhaft*) mystery **geheimnisvoll** ADJ mysterious **Geheimnummer** F, **Geheimzahl** F (*von Kreditkarte*) PIN number
gehen **1** V/T & V/I go; (*zu Fuß*) walk; (*funktionieren*) work; **über die Straße ~** cross the street **2** V/I UNPERS **wie geht es (dir)?** how are you (*od* things)?; **mir/ihm geht es gut** I'm/he's (doing) fine; **geht das?** is that possible?; **geht's noch?** can you still manage?; **es geht** not too bad, OK; **es geht um …** it's about …
Gehirn N brain **Gehirnerschütterung** F concussion
Gehör N hearing
gehorchen V/I obey (*j-m* sb)
gehören **1** V/I belong (*j-m* to sb); **wem gehört das Buch?** whose book is this?; **gehört es dir?** is it yours? **2** V/R UNPERS **das gehört sich nicht** it's not done

Gehweg M sidewalk
Geier M vulture
Geige F violin
geil ADJ horny; *umg* (*toll*) fantastic
Geisel F hostage
Geist M spirit; (*Gespenst*) ghost; (*Verstand*) mind
geizig ADJ stingy
gekonnt ADJ skillful
Gel N gel
Gelächter N laughter
geladen ADJ loaded; ELEK live; *fig* furious
gelähmt ADJ paralyzed
Gelände N land, terrain; (*Fabrik, Sportgelände*) grounds *pl*; (*Baugelände*) site
Geländer N railing; (*Treppengeländer*) banister
Geländewagen M off-road vehicle
gelassen ADJ calm, composed
Gelatine F gelatine
gelaunt ADJ **gut/schlecht ~** in a good/bad mood
gelb ADJ yellow **Gelbsucht** F jaundice
Geld N money **Geldautomat** M cash machine, ATM **Geldbeutel** M, **Geldbörse** F wallet **Geldschein** M bill **Geldstrafe** F fine **Geldstück** N coin **Geldwechsel** M exchange of money **Geldwechselautomat** M, **Geldwechsler** M change machine
Gelee N jelly
Gelegenheit F opportunity; (*Anlass*) occasion **gelegentlich** **1** ADJ occasional **2** ADV occasionally
Gelenk N joint
gelernt ADJ skilled
gelingen V/I succeed; **es ist mir gelungen, ihn zu erreichen** I managed to get hold of him
gelten **1** V/T (*wert sein*) be worth; **j-m viel/wenig ~** mean a lot/not mean much to sb **2** V/I (*gültig sein*) be valid; (*erlaubt sein*) be allowed; **etw ~ lassen** accept sth
Gemälde N painting, picture
gemäß **1** PRÄP *+dat* in accordance with **2** ADJ appropriate (*dat* to)
gemein ADJ (*niederträchtig*) mean, nasty
Gemeinde F district, community; (*Pfarrgemeinde*) parish; (*Kirchengemeinde*) congregation
gemeinsam **1** ADJ joint, common **2** ADV together, jointly
Gemeinschaft F community
gemischt ADJ mixed
Gemüse N vegetables *pl* **Gemüsehändler(in)** M(F) produce store owner
gemustert ADJ patterned
gemütlich ADJ comfortable, cozy; (*Mensch*) good-natured, easy-going; **mach es dir ~** make yourself at home
genau **1** ADJ exact, precise **2** ADV exactly, precisely; **~ in**

der **Mitte** right in the middle; ~ **genommen** strictly speaking; **ich weiß es ~** I know for certain (*od* for sure) **genauso** ADV exactly the same (way); ~ **groß/viel/viele Leute** just as big/much/many people (*wie* as)
genehmigen V/T approve; **sich etw ~** indulge in sth **Genehmigung** F approval
Generalkonsulat N consulate general
Generation F generation
genial ADJ brilliant
Genick N (back of the) neck
Genie N genius
genieren V/R feel awkward
genießen V/T enjoy
Genitiv M genitive (case)
genmanipuliert ADJ genetically modified, GM **gentechnisch** ADV ~ **verändert** genetically modified, GM
genug ADV enough
genügen V/I be enough (*j-m* for sb); **danke, das genügt** thanks, that's enough
Genuss M pleasure; (*Zusichnehmen*) consumption
geöffnet ADJ (*Geschäft etc*) open
Geografie F geography
Geologie F geology
Gepäck N baggage, luggage **Gepäckabfertigung** F baggage check-in **Gepäckannahme** F (*zur Beförderung*) baggage office; (*zur Aufbewahrung*) baggage checkroom **Gepäckaufbewahrung** F baggage checkroom **Gepäckausgabe** F baggage office; (*am Flughafen*) baggage reclaim **Gepäckband** N baggage conveyor **Gepäckkontrolle** F baggage check **Gepäckstück** N item of baggage **Gepäckträger** M porter; (*an Fahrrad*) carrier **Gepäckwagen** M baggage car
gepflegt ADJ well-groomed; (*Park*) well looked after
gerade **1** ADJ straight; (*Zahl*) even **2** ADV (*genau*) exactly; (*eben*) just; **warum ~ ich?** why me (of all people)?; ~ **weil** precisely because; ~ **noch** only just; ~ **neben** right next to **geradeaus** ADV straight ahead
Gerät N device, gadget; (*Werkzeug*) tool; (*Radio, Fernseher*) set; (*Zubehör*) equipment
geraten **1** *pperf von* raten **2** V/I turn out; **gut/schlecht ~** turn out well/badly; **an j-n ~** come across sb; **in etw ~** get into sth
geräuchert ADJ smoked
geräumig ADJ roomy
Geräusch N sound; (*unangenehm*) noise
gerecht ADJ fair; (*Strafe, Belohnung*) just
gereizt ADJ irritable
Gericht N JUR court; (*Essen*) dish
gering ADJ small; (*unbedeutend*) slight; (*niedrig*) low; (*Zeit*)

short **geringfügig** **1** ADJ slight, minor **2** ADV slightly **gern(e)** ADV willingly, gladly; **~ mögen** like; **etw ~ tun** like doing sth; **~ geschehen** you're welcome **gernhaben** V/T like
Gerste F barley
Geruch M smell
Gerücht N rumor
Gerümpel N junk
Gerüst N (*auf Bau*) scaffold(-ing); *fig* framework (*zu* of)
gesamt ADJ whole, entire; (*Kosten*) total; (*Werke*) complete **Gesamtschule** F *high school for students of mixed ability*
Gesäß N bottom
Geschäft N business; (*Laden*) store, shop; (*Geschäftsabschluss*) deal **geschäftlich** **1** ADJ commercial **2** ADV on business **Geschäftsführer(in)** M(F) managing director; (*von Laden*) manager **Geschäftsleitung** F executive board **Geschäftsmann** M businessman **Geschäftsreise** F business trip **Geschäftszeiten** PL business (*od* opening) hours *pl*
geschehen V/I happen
Geschenk N present, gift **Geschenkgutschein** M gift voucher **Geschenkpapier** N wrapping paper
Geschichte F story; (*Sache*) affair; HIST history
geschickt ADJ skillful
geschieden ADJ divorced
Geschirr N dishes *pl*; (*zum Kochen*) pots and pans *pl*; (*von Pferd*) harness; **~ spülen** do (*od* wash) the dishes **Geschirrspülmaschine** F dishwasher **Geschirrspülmittel** N dishwashing liquid **Geschirrtuch** N dish towel
Geschlecht N sex; LING gender **Geschlechtskrankheit** F sexually transmitted disease, STD **Geschlechtsverkehr** M sexual intercourse
geschlossen ADJ closed
Geschmack M taste **geschmacklos** ADJ tasteless **Geschmack(s)sache** F **das ist ~** it's a matter of taste **geschmackvoll** ADJ tasteful
Geschoss N (*Stockwerk*) floor
Geschrei N cries *pl*; *fig* fuss
geschützt ADJ protected
Geschwätz N chatter; (*Klatsch*) gossip **geschwätzig** ADJ talkative, gossipy
geschweige ADV **~ (denn)** let alone
Geschwindigkeit F speed; PHYS velocity **Geschwindigkeitsbegrenzung** F speed limit
Geschwister PL brothers and sisters *pl*
geschwollen ADJ (*angeschwollen*) swollen; (*Rede*) bombastic
Geschwulst F growth
Geschwür N ulcer
gesellig ADJ sociable **Gesell-**

schaft F society; (*Begleitung*) company
Gesetz N law **gesetzlich** ADJ legal **gesetzwidrig** ADJ illegal
Gesicht N face; (*Miene*) expression **Gesichtscreme** F face cream **Gesichtswasser** N toner
gespannt ADJ tense; (*begierig*) eager; **ich bin ~, ob ...** I wonder if ...; **auf etw/j-n ~ sein** look forward to sth/to seeing sb
Gespenst N ghost
gesperrt ADJ closed
Gespräch N talk, conversation; (*Diskussion*) discussion; (*Anruf*) call
Gestalt F form, shape; (*Mensch*) figure
Gestank M stench
gestatten V/T permit, allow; **~ Sie?** may I?
Geste F gesture
gestehen V/T confess
gestern ADV yesterday; **~ Abend** last night
gestört ADJ disturbed; (*Rundfunkempfang*) poor
gestreift ADJ striped
gesund ADJ healthy; **wieder ~ werden** get better **Gesundheit** F health; **~!** bless you! **gesundheitsschädlich** ADJ unhealthy
Getränk N drink **Getränkeautomat** M drinks machine **Getränkekarte** F list of drinks
Getreide N cereals *pl*, grain
getrennt ADJ separate; **~ leben** live apart; **~ zahlen** pay separately
Getriebe N AUTO gearbox
Getue N fuss
geübt ADJ experienced
Gewähr F guarantee
Gewalt F (*Macht*) power; (*Kontrolle*) control; (*große Kraft*) force; (*Gewalttaten*) violence **gewaltig** ADJ tremendous; (*Irrtum*) huge
gewandt ADJ (*flink*) nimble; (*geschickt*) skillful; (*erfahren*) experienced
Gewebe N (*Stoff*) fabric; BIOL tissue
Gewehr N rifle, gun
gewellt ADJ (*Haare*) wavy
Gewerbe N trade **Gewerbegebiet** N industrial park **gewerblich** ADJ commercial
Gewerkschaft F labor union
Gewicht N weight; *fig* importance
Gewinn M profit; (*bei Spiel*) winnings *pl* **gewinnen** **1** V/T win; (*erwerben*) gain; (*Kohle, Öl*) extract **2** V/I win; (*profitieren*) gain **Gewinner(in)** M(F) winner
gewiss **1** ADJ certain **2** ADV certainly
Gewissen N conscience; **ein gutes/schlechtes ~ haben** have a clear/bad conscience
Gewitter N thunderstorm

gewöhnen **1** VT **j-n an etw ~** accustom sb to sth **2** VR **sich an j-n/etw ~** get used (*od* accustomed) to sb/sth **Gewohnheit** F habit; (*Brauch*) custom **gewöhnlich** ADJ usual; (*durchschnittlich*) ordinary; *pej* common; **wie ~** as usual **gewohnt** ADJ usual; **etw ~ sein** be used to sth

Gewürz N spice **gewürzt** ADJ seasoned

Gezeiten PL tides *pl*

Giebel M gable

gierig ADJ greedy

gießen VT pour; (*Blumen*) water; (*Metall*) cast **Gießkanne** F watering can

Gift N poison **giftig** ADJ poisonous

Gigabyte N gigabyte

Gin M gin **Gin Tonic** M gin and tonic

Gipfel M summit, peak; POL summit; *fig* (*Höhepunkt*) height

Gips M *a.* MED plaster **Gipsverband** M plaster cast

Giraffe F giraffe

Girokonto N checking account

Gitarre F guitar

Gitter N bars *pl*

glänzen VI *a. fig* shine **glänzend** ADJ shining; *fig* brilliant

Glas N glass; (*Marmelade*) jar **Glascontainer** M glass recycling container **Glasscheibe** F pane (of glass)

Glasur F glaze; GASTR frosting, icing

glatt ADJ smooth; (*rutschig*) slippery; (*Lüge*) downright

Glatteis N (black) ice

Glatze F bald head

glauben VT & VI believe (*an +akk* in); (*meinen*) think; **j-m ~** believe sb

gleich **1** ADJ equal; (*identisch*) same, identical; **es ist mir ~** it's all the same to me **2** ADV equally; (*sofort*) straight away; (*bald*) in a minute; **~ groß/alt** the same size/age; **~ nach/an** right after/at **Gleichberechtigung** F equal rights *pl* **gleichen** **1** VI **j-m/einer Sache ~** be like sb/sth **2** VR be alike **gleichfalls** ADV likewise; **danke ~!** thanks, and the same to you **gleichgültig** ADJ indifferent; (*unbedeutend*) unimportant **gleichmäßig** ADJ regular; (*Verteilung*) even, equal **gleichzeitig** **1** ADJ simultaneous **2** ADV at the same time

Gleis N track, rails *pl*; (*Bahnsteig*) platform

gleiten VI glide; (*rutschen*) slide **Gleitschirmfliegen** N paragliding

Gletscher M glacier

Glied N (*Arm, Bein*) limb; (*Kette*) link; (*Penis*) penis **Gliedmaßen** PL limbs *pl*

glitschig ADJ slippery

glitzern VI glitter; (*Sterne*) twinkle

Glocke F bell
glotzen V/I *umg* stare
Glück N luck; (*Freude*) happiness; **~ haben** be lucky; **viel ~!** good luck!; **zum ~** fortunately **glücklich** ADJ lucky; (*froh*) happy **glücklicherweise** ADJ fortunately **Glückwunsch** M congratulations *pl*; **Herzlichen ~ zum Geburtstag!** Happy Birthday!
Glühbirne F light bulb **glühen** V/I glow
GmbH F *abk* = Gesellschaft mit beschränkter Haftung; ≈ Inc
Gold N gold **golden** ADJ gold; *fig* golden
Golf 1 M gulf 2 N golf **Golfplatz** M golf course **Golfschläger** M golf club
gönnen V/T **ich gönne es ihm** I'm really pleased for him; **sich etw ~** allow oneself sth
Gott M God; (*Gottheit*) god **Gottesdienst** M service **Göttin** F goddess
Grab N grave
graben V/T dig **Graben** M ditch
Grabstein M gravestone
Grad M degree; **wir haben 30 ~ Celsius** it's 30 degrees Celsius; **bis zu einem gewissen ~** (up) to a certain extent
Graffiti PL graffiti *sg*
Grafik F graph; (*Kunstwerk*) graphic; (*Illustration*) diagram **Grafikkarte** F IT graphics card
Gramm N gram
Grammatik F grammar
Grapefruit F grapefruit
Graphik F → Grafik
Gras N grass
grässlich ADJ horrible
Gräte F (fish)bone
gratis ADJ & ADV free (of charge)
gratulieren V/I **j-m (zu etw) ~** congratulate sb (on sth); **(ich) gratuliere!** congratulations!
grau ADJ gray **grauhaarig** ADJ gray-haired
grausam ADJ cruel
gravierend ADJ (*Fehler*) serious
greifen 1 V/T seize; **zu etw ~** *fig* resort to sth 2 V/I (*Regel etc*) have an effect (*bei* on)
grell ADJ harsh
Grenze F boundary; (*Staatsgrenze*) border; (*Schranke*) limit **grenzen** V/I border (*an +akk* on) **Grenzkontrolle** F border control
Grieche M Greek **Griechenland** N Greece **Griechin** F Greek **griechisch** ADJ Greek **Griechisch** N Greek
Grieß M GASTR semolina
Griff M grip; (*Tür etc*) handle **griffbereit** ADJ handy
Grill M grill; (*im Freien*) barbecue
Grille F cricket
grillen 1 V/T grill 2 V/I have a barbecue **Grillfest** N barbe-

cue **Grillkohle** F charcoal
grinsen VI grin; (*höhnisch*) sneer
Grippe F flu
grob ADJ coarse; (*Fehler, Verstoß*) gross; (*Einschätzung*) rough
Grönland N Greenland
groß **1** ADJ big, large; (*hoch*) tall; *fig* great; (*Buchstabe*) capital; (*erwachsen*) grown-up; **im Großen und Ganzen** on the whole **2** ADV greatly **großartig** ADJ wonderful **Großbritannien** N (Great) Britain **Großbuchstabe** M capital letter
Größe F size; (*Länge*) height; *fig* greatness; **welche ~ haben Sie?** what size do you take?
Großeltern PL grandparents *pl* **Großhandel** M wholesale trade **Großmarkt** M supercenter **Großmutter** F grandmother **großschreiben** VT write with a capital letter **Großstadt** F city **Großvater** M grandfather **großzügig** ADJ generous
Grübchen N dimple
Grube F pit
grün ADJ green; **~er Salat** lettuce; **~e Bohnen** green beans
Grund M (*Ursache etc*) reason; (*Erdboden*) ground; (*von See, Gefäß*) bottom; (*Grundbesitz*) land, property; **aus diesem ~** for this reason
gründen VT found **Gründer(in)** M(F) founder
Grundgebühr F basic charge
gründlich ADJ thorough
grundsätzlich ADJ fundamental, basic; **sie kommt ~ zu spät** she's always late **Grundschule** F elementary school **Grundstück** N plot; (*Anwesen*) estate; (*Baugrundstück*) site
Grüne(r) M/F(M) POL Green; **die ~n** the Green Party
Gruppe F group **Gruppenermäßigung** F group discount **Gruppenreise** F group tour
Gruß M greeting; **viele Grüße** best wishes; **Grüße an** regards to; **mit freundlichen Grüßen** Sincerely yours **grüßen** VT greet; **grüß deine Mutter von mir** give my regards to your mother; **Julia lässt (euch) ~** Julia sends (you) her regards
gucken VI look
gültig ADJ valid
Gummi M *od* N rubber **Gummistiefel** M rubber boot
günstig ADJ favorable; (*Preis*) good
gurgeln VI gurgle; (*im Mund*) gargle
Gurke F (*Salatgurke*) cucumber; (*Essiggurke*) pickle
Gurt M belt
Gürtel M belt; GEO zone **Gürtelrose** F shingles *sg*
gut **1** ADJ good; (*Schulnote*) ≈ B; **sehr ~** very good, excellent; (*Schulnote*) ≈ A; **alles Gute!** all

the best **2** ADV well; **~ gehen** (*gut ausgehen*) go well; **es geht ihm ~** he's doing fine; **~ aussehend** good-looking; **~ gelaunt** in a good mood; **~ gemeint** well meant; **schon ~!** it's all right; **mach's ~!** take care, bye

Gutachten N report **Gutachter(in)** M(F) expert

gutartig ADJ MED benign

Güter PL freight **Güterzug** M freight train

gutgläubig ADJ trusting

Guthaben N (credit) balance

gutmütig ADJ good-natured

Gutschein M voucher **Gutschrift** F credit

guttun V/I **j-m ~** do sb good

Gymnasium N *type of high school for students of above-average ability*

Gymnastik F exercises *pl*

Gynäkologe M, **Gynäkologin** F gynecologist

Gyros N doner kebab

H

Haar N hair; **um ein ~** nearly; **sich die ~e schneiden lassen** have one's hair cut **Haarbürste** F hairbrush **Haargel** N hair gel **haarig** ADJ hairy; *fig* nasty **Haarschnitt** M haircut **Haarspange** F barrette **Haarspliss** M split ends *pl* **Haarspray** N hair spray **Haartrockner** M hairdryer **Haarwaschmittel** N shampoo

haben V/T & V/AUX have; **Hunger ~** be hungry; **Ferien ~** be on vacation; **welches Datum ~ wir heute?** what's the date today?; **ich hätte gerne ...** I'd like ...; **hätten Sie etwas dagegen, wenn ...?** would you mind if ...?; **was hast du denn?** what's the matter (with you)?

Haben N WIRTSCH credit

Hacke F (*im Garten*) hoe; (*Ferse*) heel **hacken** V/T chop; (*Loch*) hack; (*Erde*) hoe **Hacker(in)** M(F) IT hacker **Hackfleisch** N ground meat

Hafen M harbor; (*großer*) port **Hafenstadt** F port

Hafer M oats *pl* **Haferflocken** PL oatmeal *sg*

Haft F custody **haftbar** ADJ liable, responsible **haften** V/I stick; **~ für** be liable (*od* responsible) for **Haftnotiz** F Post-it® **Haftpflichtversicherung** F third party insurance **Haftung** F liability

Hagel M hail **hageln** V/I UNPERS hail

Hahn M rooster, cock; (*Wasserhahn*) faucet, tap **Hähnchen** N cockerel; GASTR chicken

Hai(fisch) M shark

Haken M hook; (*Zeichen*) check
halb ADJ half; **~ eins** half past twelve; **eine ~e Stunde** half an hour **Halbfinale** N semi-final **halbieren** V/T halve **Halbinsel** F peninsula **Halbjahr** N half-year **Halbmond** M ASTRON half moon; (*Symbol*) crescent **halbtags** ADV (*arbeiten*) part-time **halbwegs** ADV (*leidlich*) reasonably **Halbzeit** F half; (*Pause*) half-time **Hälfte** F half
Halle F hall **Hallenbad** N indoor (swimming) pool
hallo INT hello, hi
Hals M neck; (*Kehle*) throat **Halsband** N (*für Tiere*) collar **Halsentzündung** F sore throat **Halskette** F necklace **Hals-Nasen-Ohren-Arzt** M, **Hals-Nasen-Ohren-Ärztin** F ear, nose and throat specialist **Halsschmerzen** PL sore throat *sg* **Halstuch** N scarf
halt 1 INT stop 2 ADV **das ist ~ so** that's just the way it is **Halt** M stop; (*fester*) hold; (*innerer*) stability
haltbar ADJ durable; (*Lebensmittel*) non-perishable **Haltbarkeitsdatum** N expiration date
halten 1 V/T keep; (*festhalten*) hold; **~ für** regard as; **~ von** think of; **eine Rede ~** give (*od* make) a speech 2 V/I hold; (*frisch bleiben*) keep; (*stoppen*) stop; **zu j-m ~** stand by sb 3 V/R (*frisch bleiben*) keep **Haltestelle** F stop **Halteverbot** N **hier ist ~** you can't stop here **Haltung** F (*Körper*) posture; *fig* attitude; (*Selbstbeherrschung*) composure
Hammer M hammer; *fig umg* (*Fehler*) howler
Hämorr(ho)iden PL hemorrhoids *pl*, piles *pl*
Hamster M hamster
Hand F hand; **j-m die ~ geben** shake hands with sb; **zu Händen von** for the attention of **Handarbeit** F (*Schulfach*) handicraft; **~ sein** be handmade **Handball** M handball **Handbremse** F parking brake **Handbuch** N handbook, manual
Handel M trade; (*Geschäft*) transaction **handeln** 1 V/I act; WIRTSCH trade; **~ von** be about 2 V/R UNPERS **es handelt sich um ...** it's about ...
Handfeger M brush **Handfläche** F palm **Handgelenk** N wrist **handgemacht** ADJ handmade **Handgepäck** N hand luggage
Händler(in) M(F) dealer
handlich ADJ handy
Handlung F act, action; (*von Roman, Film*) plot
Handschellen PL handcuffs *pl* **Handschrift** F handwriting **Handschuh** M glove **Hand-**

schuhfach N glove compartment **Handtasche** F purse, handbag **Handtuch** N towel **Handwerk** N trade **Handwerker** M workman
Handy N cell, cellphone **Handynummer** F cellphone number
Hang M (*Abhang*) slope; *fig* tendency
Hängematte F hammock
hängen **1** V/I hang; **an der Wand/an der Decke ~** hang on the wall/from the ceiling; **an j-m ~** *fig* be attached to sb; **~ bleiben** get caught (*an +dat* on); *fig* get stuck **2** V/T hang (*an +akk* on)
Hantel F dumbbell
Hardware F IT hardware
harmlos ADJ harmless
harmonisch ADJ harmonious
Harn M urine **Harnblase** F bladder
hart ADJ hard; *fig* harsh; **~ gekocht** (*Ei*) hard-boiled **hartnäckig** ADJ stubborn
Haschisch N hashish
Hase M hare
Haselnuss F hazelnut
Hass M hatred (*auf +akk, gegen* of), hate **hassen** V/T hate
hässlich ADJ ugly; (*gemein*) nasty
Hast F haste, hurry **hastig** ADJ hasty
Haube F a. AUTO hood; (*Mütze*) cap
hauchdünn ADJ (*Schicht, Scheibe*) wafer-thin
hauen V/T hit
Haufen M pile; **ein ~ Geld** (*viel Geld*) a lot of money
häufig **1** ADJ frequent **2** ADV frequently, often
Hauptbahnhof M central (*od* main) station **Haupteingang** M main entrance **Hauptgericht** N main course, entrée
Häuptling M chief
Hauptquartier N headquarters *pl* **Hauptrolle** F leading role **Hauptsache** F main thing **hauptsächlich** ADV mainly, chiefly **Hauptsaison** F high (*od* peak) season **Hauptschule** F ≈ junior high school **Hauptstadt** F capital **Hauptstraße** F main road; (*im Stadtzentrum*) main street **Hauptverkehrszeit** F rush hour
Haus N house; **nach ~e** home; **zu ~e** at home **Hausarbeit** F housework **Hausaufgabe** F (*Schule*) homework; **~n** *pl* homework *sg* **Hausbesitzer(in)** M(F) house owner; (*Vermieter*) landlord/-lady **Hausflur** M hall **Hausfrau** F housewife **hausgemacht** ADJ homemade **Haushalt** M household; POL budget
häuslich ADJ domestic
Hausmann M house-husband
Hausmannskost F *good plain cooking* **Hausmeis-**

ter(in) M(F) janitor **Hausnummer** F house number **Hausschlüssel** M front-door key **Hausschuh** M slipper **Haustier** N pet **Haustür** F front door
Haut F skin **Hautarzt** M, **Hautärztin** F dermatologist **Hautcreme** F skin cream
Hebamme F midwife
Hebel M lever
heben V/T raise, lift
Hebräisch N Hebrew
Heck N (*von Boot*) stern; (*von Auto*) rear **Heckantrieb** M rear-wheel drive
Hecke F hedge
Heckklappe F tailgate **Heckscheibe** F rear window
Hefe F yeast
Heft N notebook, exercise book; (*Ausgabe*) issue
heftig ADJ violent; (*Kritik, Streit*) fierce
Heftklammer F paper clip **Heftpflaster** N Band-Aid®
Heidelbeere F blueberry
heidnisch ADJ (*Brauch*) pagan
heikel ADJ (*Angelegenheit*) awkward; (*wählerisch*) fussy
heil ADJ (*Sache*) in one piece, intact **heilbar** ADJ curable
heilen 1 V/T cure 2 V/I heal
heilig ADJ holy **Heiligabend** M Christmas Eve **Heilige(r)** M/F(M) saint
Heilpraktiker(in) M(F) natural health practitioner
heim ADV home **Heim** N home
Heimat F home (town/country)
heimfahren V/I drive home **Heimfahrt** F journey home **heimisch** ADJ (*Bevölkerung, Brauchtum*) local; (*Tiere, Pflanzen*) native **heimkommen** V/I come (*od* return) home
heimlich ADJ secret
Heimreise F journey home **Heimspiel** N SPORT home game **Heimweg** M way home **Heimweh** N homesickness; **~ haben** be homesick
Heirat F marriage **heiraten** 1 V/I get married 2 V/T marry **Heiratsantrag** M proposal; **er hat ihr einen ~ gemacht** he proposed to her
heiser ADJ hoarse
heiß ADJ hot; (*Diskussion*) heated; **mir ist ~** I'm hot
heißen 1 V/I be called; (*bedeuten*) mean; **ich heiße Tom** my name is Tom; **wie ~ Sie?** what's your name?; **wie heißt sie mit Nachnamen?** what's her last name?; **wie heißt das auf Englisch?** what's that in English? 2 V/I UNPERS **es heißt** (*man sagt*) it is said; **es heißt in dem Brief ...** it says in the letter ...; **das heißt** that is
Heißluftherd M fan-assisted oven
heiter ADJ cheerful; (*Wetter*) bright
heizen V/T heat **Heizkörper**

M radiator **Heizöl** N fuel oil **Heizung** F heating
Hektar N hectare
Hektik F **nur keine ~!** take it easy **hektisch** ADJ hectic
Held M hero **Heldin** F heroine
helfen **1** V/I help (*j-m bei etw* sb with sth); (*nützen*) be of use **2** V/I UNPERS **es hilft nichts, du musst ...** it's no use, you have to ... **Helfer(in)** M(F) helper; (*Mitarbeiter*) assistant
hell ADJ bright; (*Farbe*) light; (*Hautfarbe*) fair **hellblau** ADJ light blue **hellblond** ADJ ash-blond **hellgelb** ADJ pale yellow
Helm M helmet **Helmpflicht** F compulsory wearing of helmets
Hemd N shirt
hemmen V/T check; (*behindern*) hamper; **gehemmt sein** be inhibited **Hemmung** F (*psychisch*) inhibition; (*moralisch*) scruple
Henkel M handle
Henne F hen
Hepatitis F hepatitis
her ADV here; **wo ist sie ~?** where is she from?; **das ist zehn Jahre ~** that was ten years ago
herab ADV down **herablassend** ADJ (*Bemerkung*) condescending **herabsehen** V/I **auf j-n ~** look down on sb **herabsetzen** V/T reduce; *fig* disparage
heran ADV **näher ~!** come closer **herankommen** V/I approach; **~ an** be able to get at; *fig* be able to get hold of **heranwachsen** V/I grow up
herauf ADV up **heraufbeschwören** V/T evoke; (*verursachen*) cause **heraufziehen** **1** V/T pull up **2** V/I approach; (*Sturm*) gather
heraus ADV out **herausbekommen** V/T (*Geheimnis*) find out; (*Rätsel*) solve **herausbringen** V/T bring out **herausfinden** V/T find out **herausfordern** V/T challenge **Herausforderung** F challenge **herausgeben** V/T (*Buch*) edit; (*veröffentlichen*) publish; **j-m zwei Cent ~** give sb two cents change **herausholen** V/T get out (*aus* of) **herauskommen** V/I come out; **dabei kommt nichts heraus** nothing will come of it **herausstellen** V/R turn out (*als* to be) **herausziehen** V/T pull out
Herbst M fall, autumn
Herd M stove
Herde F herd; (*Schafe*) flock
herein ADV in; **~!** come in **hereinfallen** V/I **wir sind auf einen Betrüger hereingefallen** we were taken in by a swindler **hereinlegen** V/T **j-n ~** *fig* take sb for a ride
Herfahrt F journey here; **auf**

der ~ on the way here
Hergang M course (of events)
Hering M herring
herkommen V/I come; **wo kommt sie her?** where does she come from?
Heroin N heroin
Herpes M MED herpes
Herr M (*vor Namen*) Mr.; (*Mann*) gentleman; (*Adliger, Gott*) Lord; **mein ~!** sir; **meine ~en!** gentlemen; **Sehr geehrte Damen und ~en** Dear Sir or Madam **Herrentoilette** F men's bathroom
herrichten V/T prepare
herrlich ADJ marvelous, splendid
Herrschaft F rule; (*Macht*) power **herrschen** V/I rule; (*bestehen*) be
herstellen V/T make; (*industriell*) manufacture **Hersteller(in)** M(F) manufacturer **Herstellung** F production
herüber ADV over
herum ADV around; **um etw ~** around sth; **du hast den Pulli falsch ~ an** you're wearing your sweater inside out; **anders ~** the other way around **herumfahren** V/I drive around **herumkommen** V/I **sie ist viel in der Welt herumgekommen** she's been around the world; **um etw ~** (*vermeiden*) get out of sth **herumkriegen** V/T talk around **herumtreiben** V/R hang around
herunter ADV down **heruntergekommen** ADJ (*Gebäude, Gegend*) run-down; (*Person*) down-at-heel **herunterhandeln** V/T get down **herunterholen** V/T bring down **herunterkommen** V/I come down **herunterladen** V/T IT download
hervor ADV out **hervorbringen** V/T produce; (*Wort*) utter **hervorheben** V/T emphasize, stress **hervorragend** ADJ excellent **hervorrufen** V/T cause, give rise to
Herz N heart; (*Karten*) hearts *pl*; **von ganzem ~en** wholeheartedly; **sich etw zu ~en nehmen** take sth to heart **Herzanfall** M heart attack **Herzbeschwerden** PL heart trouble *sg* **herzhaft** ADJ (*Essen*) substantial; **~ lachen** have a good laugh **Herzinfarkt** M heart attack **Herzklopfen** N MED palpitations *pl* **herzkrank** ADJ **sie ist ~** she's got a heart condition **herzlich** ADJ (*Empfang, Mensch*) warm; **~en Glückwunsch** congratulations **Herzschlag** M heartbeat; (*Herzversagen*) heart failure **Herzschrittmacher** M pacemaker
heterosexuell ADJ heterosexual
Hetze F (*Eile*) rush **hetzen** V/T & V/R rush
Heu N hay

heuer ADV this year **heulen** VI howl; (*weinen*) cry **Heuschnupfen** M hay fever **Heuschrecke** F grasshopper; (*größer*) locust **heute** ADV today; **~ Abend/früh** this evening/morning; **~ Nacht** tonight; (*letzte Nacht*) last night; **~ in acht Tagen** a week from today **heutig** ADJ **die ~e Zeitung** today's paper **heutzutage** ADV nowadays **Hexe** F witch **Hexenschuss** M lumbago **hier** ADV here; **~ entlang** this way **hierbleiben** VI stay here **hierher** ADV here **hiermit** ADV with this **hiesig** ADJ local **Hi-Fi-Anlage** F hi-fi (system) **high** ADJ *umg* high **Highlife** N high life; **~ machen** live it up **Hightech** N high tech **Hilfe** F help; (*für Notleidende, finanziell*) aid; **~!** help!; **um ~ bitten** ask for help **hilflos** ADJ helpless **hilfsbereit** ADJ helpful **Hilfsmittel** N aid **Himbeere** F raspberry **Himmel** M sky; REL heaven **Himmelfahrt** F Ascension **Himmelsrichtung** F direction **himmlisch** ADJ heavenly **hin** ADV there; **~ und her** to and fro; **~ und zurück** there and back; **bis zur Mauer ~** up to the wall; **das ist noch lange ~** (*zeitlich*) that's a long way off **hinab** ADV down **hinabgehen** VI go down **hinauf** ADV up **hinaufgehen** VI & VT go up **hinaufsteigen** VI climb (up) **hinaus** ADV out **hinausgehen** VI go out; **~ über** exceed **hinauslaufen** VI run out; **~ auf** come to, amount to **hinausschieben** VI put off, postpone **hinauswerfen** VT throw out; (*aus Firma*) fire **hinbringen** VT **ich bringe Sie hin** I'll take you there **hindern** VT prevent; **j-n daran ~, etw zu tun** stop (*od* prevent) sb from doing sth **Hindernis** N obstacle **hindurch** ADV through; **das ganze Jahr ~** throughout the year, all year round; **die ganze Nacht ~** all night (long) **hinein** ADV in **hineingehen** VI go in; **~ in** go into, enter **hineinpassen** VI fit in; **~ in** fit into **hinfahren** **1** VI go there **2** VT take there **Hinfahrt** F outward journey **hinfallen** VI fall (down) **Hinflug** M outward flight **hingehen** VI go there; (*Zeit*) pass **hinhalten** VT hold out; (*warten lassen*) put off **hinken** VI limp **hinlegen** **1** VT put down **2** VR lie down **hinnehmen** VT *fig* put up with, take **Hinreise** F outward journey **hinsetzen** VR sit down **hinsichtlich**

PRÄP +*gen* with regard to **hinstellen** 1 V/T put (down) 2 V/R stand
hinten ADV at the (*od* in) back; (*im Auto*) in the back; (*dahinter*) behind
hinter PRÄP +*dat od akk* behind; (*nach*) after; **~ j-m her sein** be after sb; **etw ~ sich bringen** get sth over (and done) with
Hinterachse F rear axle
Hinterbein N hind leg **Hinterbliebene(r)** M/F(M) **die Hinterbliebenen** the bereaved
hintere(r, s) ADJ rear, back
hintereinander ADV (*in einer Reihe*) one behind the other; (*hintereinander her*) one after the other; **drei Tage ~** three days running (*od* in a row)
hintergehen V/T deceive
Hintergrund M background
hinterher ADV (*zeitlich*) afterward(s) **Hinterkopf** M back of the head **hinterlassen** V/T leave; **j-m eine Nachricht ~** leave a message for sb **hinterlegen** V/T leave (*bei* with)
Hintern M *umg* butt
Hinterradantrieb M AUTO rear-wheel drive **Hinterteil** N back (part); *umg* (*Hintern*) butt **Hintertür** F back door
hinüber ADV over; **~ sein** *umg* (*kaputt*) be ruined; (*verdorben*) have gone bad **hinübergehen** V/I go over
hinunter ADV down **hinuntergehen** V/I & V/T go down
hinunterschlucken V/T *a. fig* swallow
Hinweg M outward journey
hinwegsetzen V/R **sich über etw ~** ignore sth
Hinweis M (*Andeutung*) hint; (*Anleitung*) instruction **hinweisen** V/I **j-n auf etw ~** point sth out to sb
hinzu ADV in addition **hinzufügen** V/T add
Hirn N brain; (*Verstand*) brains *pl* **Hirnhautentzündung** F meningitis
Hirsch M deer; (*als Speise*) venison
historisch ADJ historical
Hit M MUS, IT hit **Hitliste** F, **Hitparade** F charts *pl*
Hitze F heat **hitzebeständig** ADJ heat-resistant **Hitzewelle** F heatwave **hitzig** ADJ hot-tempered; (*Debatte*) heated **Hitzschlag** M heatstroke
HIV N *abk* = Human Immunodeficiency Virus; HIV **HIV-negativ** ADJ HIV-negative **HIV-positiv** ADJ HIV-positive
H-Milch F extended shelf life milk, shelf-stable milk
HNO-Arzt M, **HNO-Ärztin** F ENT specialist
Hobby N hobby
hoch ADJ high; (*Baum, Haus*) tall; (*Schnee*) deep; **der Zaun ist drei Meter ~** the fence is three meters high; **~ begabt** extremely gifted; **das ist mir zu ~** that's beyond me; **~ soll**

sie leben!, sie lebe ~! three cheers for her!; **4 ~ 2 ist 16** 4 squared is 16; **4 ~ 5** 4 to the power of 5 **Hoch** N METEO high **hochachtungsvoll** ADV *(in Briefen)* Sincerely yours **Hochbetrieb** M **es herrscht ~** they/we are extremely busy **Hochdeutsch** N High German **Hochgebirge** N high mountains *pl* **Hochhaus** N high rise **hochheben** V/T lift (up) **Hochschule** F college; *(Universität)* university **Hochsitz** M highchair **Hochsommer** M midsummer **Hochsprung** M high jump

höchst ADV highly, extremely **höchste(r, s)** ADJ highest; *(äußerste)* extreme **höchstens** ADV at the most **Höchstgeschwindigkeit** F maximum speed

Hochstuhl M highchair

höchstwahrscheinlich ADV very probably

Hochwasser N high water; *(Überschwemmung)* floods *pl*

Hochzeit F wedding **Hochzeitsreise** F honeymoon **Hochzeitstag** M wedding day; *(Jahrestag)* wedding anniversary

hocken V/I & V/R squat, crouch

Hocker M stool

Hoden M testicle

Hof M *(Hinterhof)* yard; *(Innenhof)* courtyard; *(Bauernhof)* farm; *(Königshof)* court

hoffen V/I hope *(auf +akk* for); **ich hoffe es** I hope so **hoffentlich** ADV hopefully; **~ nicht** I hope not **Hoffnung** F hope **hoffnungslos** ADJ hopeless

höflich ADJ polite **Höflichkeit** F politeness

hohe(r, s) ADJ → hoch

Höhe F height; *(Anhöhe)* hill; *(einer Summe)* amount; *(Flughöhe)* altitude **Höhenangst** F vertigo **Höhepunkt** M *(einer Reise)* high point; *(einer Veranstaltung)* highlight; *(eines Films; sexuell)* climax

höher ADJ & ADV higher

hohl ADJ hollow

Höhle F cave

holen V/T get, fetch; *(abholen)* pick up; *(Atem)* catch; **die Polizei ~** call the police; **j-n/etw ~ lassen** send for sb/sth

Holland N Holland **Holländer(in)** M(F) Dutchman/-woman **holländisch** ADJ Dutch

Hölle F hell

holperig ADJ bumpy

Holz N wood **Holzboden** M wooden floor **hölzern** ADJ wooden **Holzkohle** F charcoal

Homebanking N home banking, online banking **Homepage** F home page **Hometrainer** M exercise machine

homöopathisch ADJ homeopathic

homosexuell ADJ homosexu-

al
Honig M honey **Honigmelone** F honeydew melon
Honorar N fee
Hopfen M BOT hop; (*beim Brauen*) hops *pl*
horchen V/I listen (*auf +akk* to); (*an der Tür*) eavesdrop
hören V/T & V/I (*passiv, mitbekommen*) hear; (*zufällig*) overhear; (*aufmerksam zuhören; Radio, Musik*) listen to; **ich habe schon viel von Ihnen gehört** I've heard a lot about you **Hörer** M TEL receiver **Hörer(in)** M(F) listener **Hörgerät** N hearing aid
Horizont M horizon
Hormon N hormone
Hornhaut F hard skin; (*des Auges*) cornea
Horoskop N horoscope
Hörsaal M lecture hall
Hose F pants *pl*; (*Unterhose*) underpants *pl*; **eine ~** a pair of pants; **kurze ~** (pair of) shorts *pl* **Hosenschlitz** M fly **Hosentasche** F pants pocket **Hosenträger** M suspenders *pl*
Hotel N hotel; **in welchem ~ seid ihr?** which hotel are you staying at? **Hoteldirektor(in)** M(F) hotel manager **Hotelkette** F hotel chain **Hotelzimmer** N hotel room
Hubraum M cubic capacity
hübsch ADJ (*Mädchen, Kind, Kleid*) pretty; (*gut aussehend; Mann, Frau*) good-looking, cute
Hubschrauber M helicopter
Huf M hoof **Hufeisen** N horseshoe
Hüfte F hip
Hügel M hill **hügelig** ADJ hilly
Huhn N hen; GASTR chicken **Hühnchen** N chicken **Hühnerauge** N MED corn
Hülle F cover; (*für Ausweis*) case; (*Zellophan*) wrapping
Hummel F bumblebee
Hummer M lobster **Hummerkrabbe** F king prawn
Humor M humor; **~ haben** have a sense of humor **humorvoll** ADJ humorous
humpeln V/I hobble
Hund M dog **Hundeleine** F dog leash
hundert NUM hundred **hundertprozentig** ADJ & ADV one hundred percent **hundertste(r, s)** ADJ hundredth
Hündin F she-dog, bitch
Hunger M hunger; **~ haben/bekommen** be/get hungry **hungern** V/I go hungry; (*ernsthaft, dauernd*) starve
Hupe F horn **hupen** V/I honk one's horn
hüpfen V/I hop; (*springen*) jump
Hürde F hurdle
Hure F whore
hurra INT hooray
husten V/I cough **Husten** M

cough **Hustenbonbon** N̄ cough drop **Hustensaft** M̄ cough syrup

Hut M̄ hat

hüten **1** V/T look after **2** V/R watch out; **sich ~, etw zu tun** take care not to do sth; **sich ~ vor** beware of

Hütte F̄ hut; (*Holzhütte*) cabin

Hydrant M̄ hydrant

hygienisch ADJ hygienic

Hyperlink M̄ hyperlink

hypnotisieren V/T hypnotize

Hypothek F̄ mortgage

hysterisch ADJ hysterical

I

ich PERS PR I; **~ bin's** it's me; **~ nicht** not me; **hier bin ~!** here I am; **~ Idiot!** stupid me

Icon N̄ IT icon

ideal ADJ ideal **Ideal** N̄ ideal

Idee F̄ idea

identifizieren V/T & V/R identify

identisch ADJ identical

Idiot(in) M(F) idiot **idiotisch** ADJ idiotic

Idol N̄ idol

idyllisch ADJ idyllic

Igel M̄ hedgehog

ignorieren V/T ignore

ihm PERS PR (*dat sg von er/es*) (to) him; (to) it; **wie geht es ~?** how is he?; **ein Freund von ~** a friend of his

ihn PERS PR (*akk sg von er*) (*Person*) him; (*Sache*) it

ihnen PERS PR (*dat pl von sie*) (to) them; **wie geht es ~?** how are they?; **ein Freund von ~** a friend of theirs

Ihnen PERS PR (*dat sg und pl von Sie*) (to) you; **wie geht es ~?** how are you?; **ein Freund von ~** a friend of yours

ihr **1** PERS PR (*2. Person pl*) you; **~ seid's** it's you **2** PERS PR (*dat sg von sie*) (*Person*) (to) her; (*Sache*) (to) it; **er schickte es ~** he sent it to her; **er hat ~ die Haare geschnitten** he cut her hair; **wie geht es ~?** how is she?; **ein Freund von ~** a friend of hers **3** POSS PR (*adjektivisch*) (*sg, Person*) her; (*sg, Sache*) its; (*pl*) their

Ihr POSS PR (*adjektivisch*) your; **~(e) XY** (*am Briefende*) Yours, XY

ihre(r, s) POSS PR (*substantivisch*) (*sg*) hers; (*pl*) theirs

Ihre(r, s) POSS PR (*substantivisch*) yours

ihretwegen **1** ADV (*wegen ihr*) because of her; (*ihr zuliebe*) for her sake **2** ADV (*wegen ihnen*) because of them; (*ihnen zuliebe*) for their sake **Ihretwegen** ADV (*wegen Ihnen*) because of you; (*Ihnen zuliebe*) for your sake

Ikone F̄ icon

illegal ADJ illegal
Illusion F illusion; **sich ~en machen** delude oneself
Illustration F illustration
Illustrierte F (glossy) magazine
im *kontr von* **in dem**; **~ Bett** in bed; **~ Fernsehen** on TV; **~ Radio** on the radio; **~ Bus/Zug** on the bus/train; **~ Januar** in January; **~ Stehen** (while) standing up
Imbiss M snack **Imbissbude** F snack bar
immer ADV always; **~ mehr** more and more; **~ wieder** again and again; **~ noch** still; **~ noch nicht** still not; **für ~** forever; **~ wenn ich ...** every time I ...; **~ schöner/trauriger** more and more beautiful/sadder and sadder; **was/wer/wo/wann (auch) ~** whatever/whoever/wherever/whenever **immerhin** ADV after all **immerzu** ADV all the time
Immigrant(in) M(F) immigrant
Immobilien PL property *sg*, real estate *sg* **Immobilienmakler(in)** M(F) realtor
immun ADJ immune (*gegen* to) **Immunschwäche** F immunodeficiency **Immunsystem** N immune system
impfen V/T vaccinate **Impfpass** M vaccination card **Impfstoff** M vaccine **Impfung** F vaccination
imponieren V/I impress (*j-m* sb)
Import M import **importieren** V/T import
impotent ADJ impotent
imstande ADJ **~ sein** be in a position; (*fähig*) be able
in **1** PRÄP *+akk* in(to); to; **~ die Stadt** into town; **~ die Schule gehen** go to school **2** PRÄP *+dat* in; (*zeitlich*) in; (*während*) during; (*innerhalb*) within; **~ der Stadt** in town; **~ der Schule** at school; **heute ~ acht Tagen** a week from today; **Dienstag ~ einer Woche** a week from Tuesday **3** ADV **~ sein** (*in Mode sein*) be in
inbegriffen ADJ included
indem KONJ **sie gewann, ~ sie mogelte** she won by cheating
Inder(in) M(F) Indian
Indianer(in) M(F) American Indian, Native American **indianisch** ADJ American Indian, Native American
Indien N India
indirekt ADJ indirect
indisch ADJ Indian
individuell ADJ individual
Industrie F industry **Industrie-** IN ZSSGN industrial
ineinander ADV in(to) one another (*od* each other)
Infarkt M (*Herzinfarkt*) heart attack
Infektion F infection **Infektionskrankheit** F infectious disease **infizieren** **1** V/T infect **2** V/R be infected

infolge PRÄP *+gen* as a result of, owing to **infolgedessen** ADV consequently

Informatik F computer science **Informatiker(in)** M(F) computer scientist

Information F information **Informationsschalter** M information desk **informieren** **1** V/T inform; **falsch ~** misinform **2** V/R find out (*über +akk* about)

infrage ADV **das kommt nicht ~** that's out of the question; **etw ~ stellen** question sth

Infrastruktur F infrastructure

Ingenieur(in) M(F) engineer

Ingwer M ginger

Inhaber(in) M(F) owner; (*von Lizenz*) holder

Inhalt M contents *pl*; (*eines Buchs etc*) content; MATH volume; (*Flächeninhalt*) area **Inhaltsangabe** F summary **Inhaltsverzeichnis** N table of contents

Initiative F initiative; **die ~ ergreifen** take the initiative

Injektion F injection

inklusive ADV & PRÄP inclusive (*gen* of)

inkonsequent ADJ inconsistent

Inland N POL, WIRTSCH home; **im ~** at home; GEO inland **Inlandsflug** M domestic flight **Inlandsgespräch** N domestic call

Inliner PL, **Inlineskates** PL SPORT in-line skates *pl*

innen ADV inside **Innenarchitekt(in)** M(F) interior designer **Innenhof** M (inner) courtyard **Innenminister(in)** M(F) minister of the interior **Innenseite** F inside **Innenspiegel** M rearview mirror **Innenstadt** F downtown area

innere(r, s) ADJ inner; (*im Körper, inländisch*) internal **Innere(s)** N inside; (*Mitte*) center; *fig* heart **innerhalb** ADV & PRÄP *+gen* within; (*räumlich*) inside **innerlich** ADJ internal; (*geistig*) inner **innerste(r, s)** ADJ innermost

Innovation F innovation

inoffiziell ADJ unofficial; (*zwanglos*) informal

Insasse M, **Insassin** F AUTO passenger; (*Anstalt*) inmate

insbesondere ADV particularly, in particular

Inschrift F inscription

Insekt N insect, bug **Insektenschutzmittel** N insect repellent **Insektenstich** M (*von Wespe, Biene*) insect sting; (*von Mücke*) insect bite

Insel F island

Inserat N advertisement

insgesamt ADV altogether, all in all

Insider(in) M(F) insider

insofern **1** ADV in that respect; (*deshalb*) (and) so **2** KONJ if; **~ als** in so far as

Installateur(in) M(F) (*Klempner*) plumber; (*Elektroinstallateur*) electrician **installieren** V/T IT install
Instinkt M instinct
Institut N institute
Institution F institution
Instrument N instrument
Insulin N insulin
Inszenierung F production
intakt ADJ intact
intellektuell ADJ intellectual
intelligent ADJ intelligent **Intelligenz** F intelligence
intensiv ADJ (*gründlich*) intensive; (*Gefühl, Schmerz*) intense **Intensivstation** F intensive care unit
interaktiv ADJ interactive
interessant ADJ interesting **Interesse** N interest; **~ haben an** be interested in **interessieren** **1** V/T interest **2** V/R be interested (*für* in)
Interface N IT interface
Internat N boarding school
international ADJ international
Internet N Internet, Net; **im ~** on the Internet; **im ~ surfen** surf the Net **Internetanschluss** M Internet connection **Internetcafé** N Internet café, cybercafé **internetfähig** ADJ Internet-ready **Internetfirma** F dotcom company **Internethandel** M e-commerce **Internetseite** F web page **Internetzugang** M Internet access
Internist(in) M(F) internist
interpretieren V/T interpret (*als* as)
Interpunktion F punctuation
Interview N interview **interviewen** V/T interview
intim ADJ intimate
intolerant ADJ intolerant
investieren V/T invest
inwiefern ADV in what way; (*in welchem Ausmaß*) to what extent **inwieweit** ADV to what extent
inzwischen ADV meanwhile
Irak M **(der) ~** Iraq
Iran M **(der) ~** Iran
Ire M Irishman
irgend ADV **~ so ein Idiot** some idiot; **wenn ~ möglich** if at all possible **irgendein, irgendeine(r, s)** INDEF PR some; (*fragend, im Bedingungssatz; beliebig*) any **irgendetwas** INDEF PR something; (*fragend, im Bedingungssatz*) anything **irgendjemand** INDEF PR somebody, someone; (*fragend, im Bedingungssatz*) anybody, anyone **irgendwann** ADV sometime; (*zu beliebiger Zeit*) any time **irgendwie** ADV somehow **irgendwo** ADV somewhere, someplace; (*fragend, im Bedingungssatz*) anywhere, anyplace
Irin F Irishwoman **irisch** ADJ Irish **Irland** N Ireland
ironisch ADJ ironic

irre ADJ crazy, mad; (*toll*) terrific **Irre(r)** M/F(M) lunatic **irreführen** V/T mislead **irren** V/I & V/R be mistaken **irrsinnig** ADJ mad, crazy **Irrtum** M mistake, error **irrtümlich** 1 ADJ mistaken 2 ADV by mistake

Ischias M sciatica

Islam M Islam **islamisch** ADJ Islamic

Island N Iceland

isolieren V/T isolate; ELEK insulate

Israel N Israel **Israeli** M, F Israeli **israelisch** ADJ Israeli

IT F *abk* = Informationstechnologie; IT

Italien N Italy **Italiener(in)** M(F) Italian **italienisch** ADJ Italian **Italienisch** N Italian

J

ja ADV yes; **aber ~!** yes, of course; **~, wissen Sie ...** well, you know ...; **ich glaube ~** I think so; **sag's ihr ~ nicht!** don't you dare tell her; **das sag ich ~** that's what I'm trying to say

Jacht F yacht **Jachthafen** M marina

Jacke F jacket; (*Wolljacke*) cardigan

Jackett N jacket

Jagd F hunt; (*Jagen*) hunting **jagen** 1 V/I hunt 2 V/T hunt; (*verfolgen*) chase **Jäger(in)** M(F) hunter

Jahr N year; **ein halbes ~** six months *pl*; **in den neunziger ~en** in the nineties; **mit sechzehn ~en** at (the age of) sixteen **Jahrestag** M anniversary **Jahreszahl** F date, year **Jahreszeit** F season **Jahrgang** M (*Wein*) year, vintage; **der ~ 1989** (*Personen*) those born in 1989 **Jahrhundert** N century **jährlich** ADJ yearly, annual **Jahrmarkt** M fair **Jahrtausend** N millennium **Jahrzehnt** N decade

jähzornig ADJ hot-tempered

Jalousie F (venetian) blind

jämmerlich ADJ pathetic

jammern V/I moan

Januar M January; → Juni

Japan N Japan **japanisch** ADJ Japanese **Japanisch** N Japanese

jaulen V/I howl

jawohl ADV yes (of course)

je ADV ever; (*jeweils*) each; **~ nach** depending on; **~ nachdem** it depends; **~ schneller desto besser** the faster the better

Jeans F jeans *pl*

jede(r, s) 1 UNBEST ZAHLWORT (*insgesamt gesehen*) every; (*einzeln gesehen*) each; (*jede(r, s) beliebige*) any; **~s Mal** every time, each time; **~n zweiten**

Tag every other day; **bei ~m Wetter** in any weather **2** INDEF PR everybody; (*jeder Einzelne*) each; **~r von euch/uns** each of you/us **jedenfalls** ADV in any case **jederzeit** ADV at any time **jedesmal** ADV every time
jedoch ADV however
jemals ADV ever
jemand INDEF PR somebody, someone; (*in Frage und Verneinung*) anybody, anyone
Jemen M Yemen
jene(r, s) DEM PR that (one); (*pl*) those (ones)
jenseits **1** ADV on the other side **2** PRÄP *+gen* on the other side of; *fig* beyond
Jetlag M jet lag
jetzig ADJ present
jetzt ADV now; **erst ~** only now; **~ gleich** right now; **bis ~** so far, up to now; **von ~ an** from now on
jeweils ADV **~ zwei zusammen** two at a time; **zu ~ 5 Dollar** at 5 dollars each
Job M job **jobben** V/I *umg* work, have a job
Jod N iodine
Joga N yoga
joggen V/I jog **Jogging** N jogging **Jogginghose** F jogging pants *pl*
Jog(h)urt M *od* N yoghurt
Johannisbeere F **Schwarze ~** blackcurrant; **Rote ~** redcurrant
Joint M *umg* joint
jonglieren V/I juggle
Jordanien N Jordan
Journalist(in) M(F) journalist
Joystick M IT joystick
jubeln V/I cheer
Jubiläum N jubilee; (*Jahrestag*) anniversary
jucken **1** V/I itch **2** V/T **es juckt mich am Arm** my arm is itching **Juckreiz** M itch
Jude M, **Jüdin** F Jew; **sie ist Jüdin** she's Jewish **jüdisch** ADJ Jewish
Judo N judo
Jugend F youth **Jugendgruppe** F youth group **Jugendherberge** F youth hostel **Jugendherbergsausweis** M youth hostel card **jugendlich** ADJ youthful **Jugendliche(r)** M/F(M) young person **Jugendzentrum** N youth center
Juli M July; → Juni
jung ADJ young
Junge M boy
Junge(s) N young animal; **die ~n** *pl* the young *pl*
Jungfrau F virgin; ASTROL Virgo
Junggeselle M bachelor
Juni M June; **im ~** in June; **am 4. ~** on June 4th (*gesprochen: on June fourth*); **Anfang/Mitte/Ende ~** at the beginning/in the middle/at the end of June; **letzten/nächsten ~** last/next June

Junkfood N GASTR junk food **Jura** OHNE ARTIKEL (*Studienfach*) law **Jurist(in)** M(F) lawyer **juristisch** ADJ legal
Justiz F justice
Juwel N jewel **Juwelier(in)** M(F) jeweler

K

Kabel N ELEK wire; (*stark*) cable **Kabelfernsehen** N cable television
Kabeljau M cod
Kabine F cabin; (*im Schwimmbad*) cubicle
Kabrio N convertible
Kachel F tile
Käfer M beetle, bug
Kaff N *umg* dump
Kaffee M coffee; **~ kochen** make some coffee **Kaffeekanne** F coffeepot **Kaffeemaschine** F coffee maker **Kaffeetasse** F coffee cup
Käfig M cage
kahl ADJ (*Mensch, Kopf*) bald; (*Baum, Wand*) bare
Kahn M boat; (*Lastkahn*) barge
Kai M quay
Kaiser M emperor **Kaiserin** F empress **Kaiserschnitt** M MED cesarean (section)
Kajak M *od* N kayak **Kajakfahren** N kayaking
Kajüte F cabin
Kakao M cocoa; (*Getränk*) (hot) chocolate
Kakerlake F cockroach
Kaktee F, **Kaktus** M cactus
Kalb N calf **Kalbfleisch** N veal **Kalbsbraten** M roast veal **Kalbsschnitzel** N veal cutlet, schnitzel
Kalender M calendar; (*Taschenkalender*) planner, datebook
Kalk M lime; (*in Knochen*) calcium
Kalorie F calorie **kalorienarm** ADJ low-calorie
kalt ADJ cold; **mir ist (es) ~** I'm cold **kaltblütig** ADJ cold-blooded **Kälte** F cold; *fig* coldness
Kamel N camel
Kamera F camera
Kamerad(in) M(F) friend; (*als Begleiter*) companion
Kamerafrau F, **Kameramann** M camerawoman/-man
Kamille F camomile
Kamin M (*außen*) chimney; (*innen*) fireplace
Kamm M comb; (*Berg*) ridge; (*Hahn*) crest **kämmen** V/R **sich ~, sich die Haare ~** comb one's hair
Kampf M fight; (*Schlacht*) battle; (*Wettbewerb*) contest; *fig* (*Anstrengung*) struggle **kämpfen** V/I fight (*für, um* for)
Kampfsport M martial art

Kanada N Canada **Kanadier(in)** M(F) Canadian **kanadisch** ADJ Canadian
Kanal M (*Fluss*) canal; (*Rinne, TV*) channel
Kandidat(in) M(F) candidate
Kandis(zucker) M rock candy
Känguru N kangaroo
Kaninchen N rabbit
Kanister M can
Kännchen N pot; **ein ~ Kaffee** a pot of coffee **Kanne** F (*Krug*) jug; (*Kaffeekanne*) pot; (*Milchkanne*) churn; (*Gießkanne*) can
Kante F edge
Kantine F canteen
Kanton M canton
Kanu N canoe
Kanzler(in) M(F) chancellor
Kap N cape
Kapelle F (*Gebäude*) chapel; MUS band
Kaper F caper
kapieren V/T & V/I *umg* understand; **kapiert?** got it?
Kapital N capital
Kapitän M captain
Kapitel N chapter
Kappe F cap
Kapsel F capsule
kaputt ADJ *umg* broken; (*Mensch*) exhausted **kaputtgehen** V/I break; (*Schuhe*) fall apart **kaputtmachen** V/T break; (*j-n*) wear out
Kapuze F hood
Karaffe F carafe; (*mit Stöpsel*) decanter
Karamell M caramel
Karat N carat
Karate N karate
Kardinal M cardinal
Karfreitag M Good Friday
kariert ADJ checkered; (*Papier*) squared
Karies F (tooth) decay
Karikatur F caricature
Karneval M carnival
Karo N square; (*Karten*) diamonds *pl*
Karosserie F AUTO body (-work)
Karotte F carrot
Karriere F career
Karte F card; (*Landkarte*) map; (*Speisekarte*) menu; (*Eintrittskarte, Fahrkarte*) ticket; **mit ~ bezahlen** pay by credit card; **~n spielen** play cards
Kartenspiel N card game
Kartentelefon N cardphone
Kartenvorverkauf M advance booking
Kartoffel F potato **Kartoffelbrei** M mashed potatoes *pl*
Kartoffelchips PL potato chips *pl* **Kartoffelsalat** M potato salad
Karton M cardboard; (*Schachtel*) (cardboard) box
Karussell N carousel, merry-go-round
Käse M cheese **Käsekuchen** M cheesecake **Käseplatte** F cheeseboard
Kasino N (*Spielkasino*) casino
Kasse F (*in Geschäft*) cash re-

gister; (*im Supermarkt*) checkout; (*Geldkasten*) cashbox; (*Theater*) box office; (*Kino*) ticket office; (*Krankenkasse*) health insurance **Kassenbon** M, **Kassenzettel** M receipt

Kassette F (small) box; (*Tonband*) cassette **Kassettenrekorder** M cassette recorder

kassieren 1 V/T take 2 V/I **darf ich ~?** would you like to pay now? **Kassierer(in)** M(F) cashier

Kastanie F chestnut

Kasten M (*Behälter*) box; (*Getränkekasten*) crate

Kat M *abk* = Katalysator

Katalog M catalog

Katalysator M AUTO catalytic converter

Katarr(h) M catarrh

Katastrophe F catastrophe, disaster

Kategorie F category

Kater M tomcat; *umg* (*nach zu viel Alkohol*) hangover

Kathedrale F cathedral

Katholik(in) M(F) Catholic **katholisch** ADJ Catholic

Katze F cat

Kauderwelsch N (*unverständlich*) gibberish

kauen V/T & V/I chew

Kauf M purchase; (*Kaufen*) buying; **ein guter ~** a bargain; **etw in ~ nehmen** put up with sth **kaufen** V/T buy **Käufer(in)** M(F) buyer **Kauffrau** F businesswoman **Kaufhaus** N department store **Kaufmann** M businessman; (*im Einzelhandel*) storekeeper

Kaugummi M chewing gum

kaum ADV hardly, scarcely

Kaution F deposit; JUR bail

KB N, **Kbyte** N *abk* = Kilobyte; KB

Kegel M (*beim Bowling*) pin; MATH cone **Kegelbahn** F bowling alley **kegeln** V/I (*bowlen*) bowl

Kehle F throat **Kehlkopf** M larynx

kehren V/T (*fegen*) sweep

Keilriemen M AUTO fan belt

kein INDEF PR no, not ... any; **ich habe ~ Geld** I have no money, I don't have any money **keine(r, s)** INDEF PR (*Person*) no one, nobody; (*Sache*) not ... any, none; **~r von ihnen** none of them; (*bei zwei Personen/Sachen*) neither of them; **ich will keins von beiden** I don't want either (of them) **keinesfalls** ADV on no account, under no circumstances

Keks M cookie; **j-m auf den ~ gehen** *umg* get on sb's nerves

Keller M cellar; (*Geschoss*) basement

Kellner M waiter **Kellnerin** F waitress

kennen V/T know; **wir ~ uns seit 2007** we've known each other since 2007 **kennenlernen** V/T get to know; **sich ~** get to know each other; (*zum*

ersten Mal) meet
Kenntnis F knowledge; **seine ~se** his knowledge
Kennwort N *a.* IT password
Kennzeichen N mark, sign; AUTO license plate
Kerl M guy
Kern M *(Obst)* seed; *(Pfirsich, Kirsche etc)* stone; *(Nuss)* kernel; *(Atomkern)* nucleus; *fig* heart, core
Kernenergie F nuclear energy **Kernkraft** F nuclear power **Kernkraftwerk** N nuclear power station
Kerze F candle; *(Zündkerze)* plug
Ket(s)chup M *od* N ketchup
Kette F chain; *(Halskette)* necklace
keuchen V/I pant
Keule F club; GASTR leg; *(von Hähnchen a.)* drumstick
Keyboard N MUS keyboard
Kfz N *abk* = Kraftfahrzeug
Kichererbse F chickpea, garbanzo
kichern V/I giggle
Kickboard® N micro scooter
Kicker M *(Spiel)* foosball
kidnappen V/T kidnap
Kidney-Bohne F kidney bean
Kiefer **1** M jaw **2** F pine **Kieferorthopäde** M, **Kieferorthopädin** F orthodontist
Kies M gravel **Kiesel** M, **Kieselstein** M pebble
kiffen V/I *umg* smoke pot
Kilo N kilo **Kilobyte** N kilobyte **Kilogramm** N kilogram
Kilometer M kilometer **Kilometerstand** M ≈ mileage
Kilowatt N kilowatt
Kind N child; **sie bekommt ein ~** she's having a baby **Kinderarzt** M, **Kinderärztin** F pediatrician **Kinderbetreuung** F childcare **Kinderbett** N crib **Kinderfahrkarte** F child's ticket **Kindergarten** M kindergarten **Kindergärtner(in)** M(F) kindergarten teacher **Kindergeld** N child benefit **Kinderkrankheit** F childhood illness **Kinderkrippe** F day-care center **Kindermädchen** N nanny **Kinderportion** F children's portion **kindersicher** ADJ childproof **Kindersicherung** F childproof safety catch; *(an Flasche)* childproof cap **Kindersitz** M child seat **Kinderteller** M *(im Restaurant)* children's portion **Kindertragetasche** F bassinet **Kinderwagen** M baby carriage **Kinderzimmer** N children's (bed)room **Kindheit** F childhood **kindisch** ADJ childish **kindlich** ADJ childlike
Kinn N chin
Kino N movie theater; **ins ~ gehen** go to the movies
Kiosk M kiosk
Kippe F *umg (Zigarettenstummel)* cigarette end
Kirche F church **Kirchturm**

M church tower; (*mit Spitze*) steeple
Kirmes F fair
Kirsche F cherry **Kirschtomate** F cherry tomato
Kissen N cushion; (*Kopfkissen*) pillow
Kiste F box; (*Truhe*) chest
Kita F *abk* = Kindertagesstätte; day-care center
kitschig ADJ kitschy, cheesy
kitzelig ADJ *a. fig* ticklish **kitzeln** V/T & V/I tickle
Kiwi F (*Frucht*) kiwi (fruit)
Klage F complaint; JUR lawsuit
klagen V/I complain (*über +akk* about, *bei* to) **kläglich** ADJ pitiful; (*Niederlage*) pathetic
Klammer F (*in Text*) bracket; (*Büroklammer*) clip; (*Wäscheklammer*) clothespin; (*Zahnklammer*) braces *pl* **klammern** V/R cling (*an +akk* to)
Klang M sound
Klappbett N folding bed
klappen V/I UNPERS (*gelingen*) work; **es hat gut geklappt** it went well
klappern V/I rattle; (*Geschirr*) clatter **Klapperschlange** F rattlesnake
Klappstuhl M folding chair
klar ADJ clear; **sich im Klaren sein** be clear (*über +akk* about); **alles ~?** everything okay?
klären **1** V/T (*Flüssigkeit*) purify; (*Probleme, Frage*) clarify **2** V/R clear itself up
klarkommen V/I **mit etw ~** cope with something; **kommst du klar?** are you managing all right?; **mit j-m ~** get along with sb **klarmachen** V/T **j-m etw ~** make sth clear to sb
klarstellen V/T clarify
Klärung F (*von Frage, Problem*) clarification
klasse ADJ *umg* great, brilliant
Klasse F class; (*Schuljahr*) grade; **erster ~ reisen** travel first class; **in welche ~ gehst du?** which grade are you in?
Klassenarbeit F test **Klassenlehrer(in)** M(F) class teacher **Klassenzimmer** N classroom
Klassik F (*Zeit*) classical period; (*Musik*) classical music
Klatsch M (*Gerede*) gossip
klatschen V/I (*schlagen*) smack; (*Beifall*) applaud, clap; (*reden*) gossip **klatschnass** ADJ soaking (wet)
Klaue F claw; *umg* (*Schrift*) scrawl
klauen V/T *umg* swipe
Klavier N piano
Klebeband N adhesive tape
kleben **1** V/T stick (*an +akk* to) **2** V/I (*klebrig sein*) be sticky
klebrig ADJ sticky **Klebstoff** M glue **Klebstreifen** M adhesive tape
Klecks M blob; (*Tinte*) blot
Kleid N dress; **~er** *pl* (*Kleidung*) clothes *pl* **Kleiderbügel** M coat hanger **Kleiderschrank**

M closet **Kleidung** F clothing

klein ADJ small, little; (*Finger*) little; **mein ~er Bruder** my little (*od* younger) brother; **als ich noch ~ war** when I was a little boy/girl; **etw ~ schneiden** chop sth up **Kleinanzeige** F classified ad **Kleinbuchstabe** M lowercase letter **Kleinbus** M minibus **Kleingeld** N change **Kleinigkeit** F trifle; (*Zwischenmahlzeit*) snack **Kleinkind** N toddler **kleinschreiben** V/T **etw ~** (*mit kleinem Anfangsbuchstaben*) lowercase sth **Kleinstadt** F small town

Klempner(in) M(F) plumber

Kletterhalle F SPORT indoor climbing center, indoor climbing gym **klettern** V/I climb

Klettverschluss M Velcro® fastening

klicken V/I *a.* IT click

Klient(in) M(F) client

Klima N climate **Klimaanlage** F air conditioning **klimatisiert** ADJ air-conditioned

Klinge F blade

Klingel F bell **klingeln** V/I ring **Klingelton** M ringtone

klingen V/I sound

Klinik F clinic; (*Krankenhaus*) hospital

Klinke F handle

Klippe F cliff; (*im Meer*) reef; *fig* hurdle

Klischee N *fig* cliché

Klo N *umg* john **Klobrille** F toilet seat **Klopapier** N toilet paper

klopfen V/T & V/I knock; (*Herz*) thump

Kloß M (*im Hals*) lump; GASTR dumpling

Kloster N (*für Männer*) monastery; (*für Frauen*) convent

Klub M club

klug ADJ clever

knabbern V/T & V/I nibble

Knäckebrot N crispbread

knacken V/T & V/I crack

Knall M bang **knallen** V/I bang

knapp ADJ (*kaum ausreichend*) scarce; (*Sieg*) narrow; **~ bei Kasse sein** be short of money; **~ zwei Stunden** just under two hours

kneifen V/T & V/I pinch; (*sich drücken*) back out (*vor +dat* of)

Kneipe F *umg* bar

kneten V/T knead; (*formen*) mold

knicken V/T & V/I (*brechen*) break; (*Papier*) fold

Knie N knee; **in die ~ gehen** bend one's knees **Kniegelenk** N knee joint **Kniekehle** F back of the knee **knien** V/I kneel **Kniescheibe** F kneecap

knipsen 1 V/T punch; FOTO snap 2 V/I FOTO take snaps

knirschen V/I crunch; **mit den Zähnen ~** grind one's teeth

knitterfrei ADJ non-crease

knittern VI crease
Knoblauch M garlic **Knoblauchzehe** F clove of garlic
Knöchel M (*Finger*) knuckle; (*Fuß*) ankle
Knochen M bone **Knochenbruch** M fracture **Knochenmark** N marrow
Knödel M dumpling
Knopf M button **Knopfdruck** M **auf ~** at the touch of a button **Knopfloch** N buttonhole
knoten VT knot **Knoten** M knot; MED lump
knurren VI (*Hund*) growl; (*Magen*) rumble; (*Mensch*) grumble
knusprig ADJ crisp; (*Keks*) crunchy
knutschen VI *umg* smooch
k. o. ADJ SPORT knocked out; *fig* wiped out
Koalition F coalition
Koch M cook; (*im Restaurant*) chef **Kochbuch** N cookbook
kochen VT & VI cook; (*Wasser*) boil; (*Kaffee, Tee*) make **Köchin** F cook; (*im Restaurant*) chef **Kochlöffel** M wooden spoon **Kochnische** F kitchenette **Kochplatte** F hotplate **Kochrezept** N recipe **Kochtopf** M saucepan
Kode M code
Köder M bait
Koffein N caffeine **koffeinfrei** ADJ decaffeinated
Koffer M (suit)case **Kofferraum** M AUTO trunk
Kognak M brandy
Kohl M cabbage
Kohle F coal; (*Holzkohle*) charcoal; *umg* (*Geld*) cash, dough **Kohlehydrat** N carbohydrate **Kohlendioxid** N carbon dioxide **Kohlensäure** F (*in Getränken*) fizz; **ohne ~** still, non-carbonated; **mit ~** sparkling, carbonated
Koje F cabin; (*Bett*) bunk
Kokain N cocaine
Kokosnuss F coconut
Kolben M TECH piston
Kolik F colic
Kollaps M collapse
Kollege M, **Kollegin** F colleague
Köln N Cologne
Kolonne F convoy
Koma N coma
Kombi M station wagon **Kombination** F combination; (*Folgerung*) deduction
kombinieren **1** VT combine **2** VI reason; (*vermuten*) guess
Komfort M conveniences *pl*; (*Bequemlichkeit*) comfort
Komiker(in) M(F) comedian, comic **komisch** ADJ funny
Komma N comma
kommen VI come; (*näher kommen*) approach; (*passieren*) happen; (*gelangen, geraten*) get; (*erscheinen*) appear; (*in die Schule, das Gefängnis etc*) go; **zu sich ~** come around (*od* to); **zu etw ~** (*bekommen*) acquire sth; (*Zeit dazu finden*)

get around to sth **kommend** ADJ coming; **~e Woche** next week; **in den ~en Jahren** in the years to come
Kommentar M commentary; **kein ~** no comment
Kommissar(in) M(F) inspector
Kommode F chest of drawers
Kommunikation F communication
Kommunion F REL communion
Kommunismus M communism
Komödie F comedy
kompakt ADJ compact
Kompass M compass
kompatibel ADJ compatible
kompetent ADJ competent
komplett ADJ complete
Kompliment N compliment; **j-m ein ~ machen** pay sb a compliment; **~!** congratulations!
kompliziert ADJ complicated
Komponist(in) M(F) composer
Kompost M compost
Kompromiss M compromise
Kondition F (*Leistungsfähigkeit*) condition; **sie hat eine gute ~** she's in good shape
Konditorei F cake shop; (*mit Café*) café
Kondom N condom
Konfektionsgröße F size
Konferenz F conference
Konfession F religion; (*christlich*) denomination
Konfetti N confetti
Konfirmation F REL confirmation
Konflikt M conflict
konfrontieren V/T confront
Kongress M conference; **der ~** (*Parlament der USA*) Congress
König M king **Königin** F queen **königlich** ADJ royal **Königreich** N kingdom
Konkurrenz F competition
können V/T & V/I be able to, can; (*wissen*) know; **~ Sie Deutsch?** can (*od* do) you speak German?; **ich kann nicht kommen** I can't come; **das kann sein** that's possible; **ich kann nichts dafür** it's not my fault
konsequent ADJ consistent
konservativ ADJ conservative
Konserven PL canned food **Konservendose** F can
konservieren V/T preserve **Konservierungsmittel** N preservative
Konsonant M consonant
Konsul(in) M(F) consul **Konsulat** N consulate
Kontakt M contact **kontaktfreudig** ADJ sociable **Kontaktlinsen** PL contact lenses *pl*
Kontinent M continent
Konto N account **Kontoauszug** M (bank) statement **Kontoinhaber(in)** M(F) account holder **Kontonummer** F account number **Kontostand** M balance

Kontrast M contrast
Kontrolle F control; (*Aufsicht*) supervision; (*Passkontrolle*) passport control **kontrollieren** V/T control; (*nachprüfen*) check
Konzentration F concentration **Konzentrationslager** N HIST concentration camp **konzentrieren** V/T & V/R concentrate
Konzept N rough draft
Konzern M firm
Konzert N concert; (*Stück*) concerto **Konzertsaal** M concert hall
koordinieren V/T coordinate
Kopf M head **Kopfhörer** M headphones *pl* **Kopfkissen** N pillow **Kopfsalat** M lettuce **Kopfschmerzen** PL headache *sg* **Kopfstütze** F headrest **Kopftuch** N headscarf
Kopie F copy **kopieren** V/T *a.* IT copy **Kopierer** M, **Kopiergerät** N copier
Kopilot(in) M(F) co-pilot
Korb M basket; **j-m einen ~ geben** *fig* turn sb down
Kord M corduroy
Kordel F cord
Kork, **Korken** M cork **Korkenzieher** M corkscrew
Korn N grain
Körper M body **Körperbau** M build **Körpergeruch** M body odor **körperlich** ADJ physical **Körperverletzung** F physical injury
korrekt ADJ correct
Korrespondent(in) M(F) correspondent **Korrespondenz** F correspondence
korrigieren V/T correct
Kosmetik F cosmetics *pl* **Kosmetiksalon** M beauty parlor
Kost F (*Nahrung*) food; (*Verpflegung*) board
kostbar ADJ precious; (*teuer*) costly, expensive
kosten **1** V/T cost **2** V/T & V/I (*versuchen*) taste **Kosten** PL costs *pl*, cost; (*Ausgaben*) expenses *pl*; **auf ~ von** at the expense of **kostenlos** ADJ free (of charge) **Kostenvoranschlag** M estimate
köstlich ADJ (*Essen*) delicious; **sich ~ amüsieren** have a marvelous time
Kostprobe F taster; *fig* sample
Kostüm N costume; (*Damenkostüm*) suit
Kot M excrement
Kotelett N chop, cutlet
Koteletten PL sideburns *pl*
Kotflügel M AUTO wing
kotzen V/I *vulg* puke, throw up
Krabbe F shrimp; (*größer*) prawn; (*Krebs*) crab
krabbeln V/I crawl
Krach M crash; (*andauernd*) noise; *umg* (*Streit*) quarrel
Kraft F strength; POL, PHYS force; (*Fähigkeit*) power; **in ~ treten** come into effect **Kraftausdruck** M swearword

Kraftfahrzeug N motor vehicle **Kraftfahrzeugbrief**, **Kraftfahrzeugschein** M vehicle registration document **Kraftfahrzeugsteuer** F vehicle tax **Kraftfahrzeugversicherung** F car insurance **kräftig** ADJ strong; (*gesund*) healthy; (*Farben*) intense, strong **Kraftstoff** M fuel **Kraftwerk** N power station
Kragen M collar
Krähe F crow
Kralle F claw; (*Parkkralle*) (Denver) boot
Kram M stuff
Krampf M cramp; (*zuckend*) spasm **Krampfader** F varicose vein
Kran M crane
krank ADJ ill, sick
kränken V/T hurt
Krankengymnastik F physiotherapy **Krankenhaus** N hospital **Krankenkasse** F health insurance **Krankenpfleger** M (male) nurse **Krankenschein** M *health insurance certificate* **Krankenschwester** F nurse **Krankenversicherung** F health insurance **Krankenwagen** M ambulance **Krankheit** F illness; (*durch Infektion hervorgerufen*) disease
Kränkung F insult
Kranz M wreath
kratzen V/T & V/I scratch **Kratzer** M scratch
kraulen **1** V/I (*schwimmen*) do the crawl **2** V/T (*streicheln*) pet
Kraut N (*Kohl*) cabbage **Kräuter** PL herbs *pl* **Kräutertee** M herbal tea **Krautsalat** M coleslaw
Krawatte F tie
kreativ ADJ creative
Krebs M ZOOL crab; MED cancer; ASTROL Cancer
Kredit M credit; **auf ~** on credit; **einen ~ aufnehmen** take out a loan **Kreditkarte** F credit card
Kreide F chalk
Kreis M circle; (*Bezirk*) district
Kreislauf M MED circulation; *fig* (*der Natur etc*) cycle **Kreislaufstörungen** PL MED **ich habe ~** I've got problems with my circulation **Kreisverkehr** M traffic circle
Kresse F cress
Kreuz N cross; ANAT small of the back; (*Karten*) clubs *pl*; **mir tut das ~ weh** I've got backache **Kreuzfahrt** F cruise **Kreuzschlüssel** M AUTO wheel brace **Kreuzschmerzen** PL backache *sg* **Kreuzung** F (*Verkehrskreuzung*) intersection; (*Züchtung*) cross **Kreuzworträtsel** N crossword (puzzle)
kriechen V/I crawl; (*unauffällig*) creep
Krieg M war
kriegen V/T *umg* get; (*erwischen*) catch; **sie kriegt ein**

Kind she's having a baby; **ich kriege noch Geld von dir** you still owe me some money
Krimi M *umg* thriller **Kriminalität** F criminality **Kriminalpolizei** F detective force, ≈ FBI **Kriminalroman** M detective novel **kriminell** ADJ criminal
Krippe F (*Futterkrippe*) manger; (*Weihnachtskrippe*) crèche; (*Kinderkrippe*) daycare center
Krise F crisis
Kristall **1** M crystal **2** N (*Glas*) crystal
Kritik F criticism; (*Rezension*) review **Kritiker(in)** M(F) critic **kritisch** ADJ critical
kritzeln V/T & V/I scribble, scrawl
Kroatien N Croatia
Krokodil N crocodile
Krone F crown
Krücke F crutch
Krug M jug; (*Bierkrug*) mug
Krümel M crumb
krumm ADJ crooked
Kruste F crust
Kruzifix N crucifix
Kuba N Cuba
Kübel M tub; (*Eimer*) bucket
Kubikmeter M cubic meter
Küche F kitchen; (*Kochen*) cooking
Kuchen M cake
Küchenmaschine F food processor **Küchenpapier** N kitchen paper **Küchenschrank** M (kitchen) cupboard
Kuckuck M cuckoo
Kugel F ball; MATH sphere; MIL bullet; (*Weihnachtskugel*) bauble; (*Eis*) scoop **Kugellager** N ball bearing **Kugelschreiber** M (ballpoint) pen
Kuh F cow
kühl ADJ cool **Kühlbox** F cool box **kühlen** V/T cool **Kühler** M AUTO radiator **Kühlerhaube** F AUTO hood **Kühlschrank** M fridge, refrigerator **Kühltasche** F cool bag **Kühltruhe** F freezer
Kuli M *umg* (*Kugelschreiber*) pen
Kulisse F scenery
Kult M cult
Kultur F culture; (*Lebensform*) civilization **Kulturbeutel** M toiletries bag **kulturell** ADJ cultural
Kümmel M caraway seeds *pl*
Kummer M grief, sorrow
kümmern **1** V/R **sich um j-n ~** look after sb; **sich um etw ~** see to sth **2** V/T concern
Kumpel M *umg* buddy
Kunde M customer **Kundendienst** M customer service **Kunden(kredit)karte** F chargecard **Kundennummer** F customer number
kündigen **1** V/I hand in one's notice; (*Mieter*) give notice that one is moving out; **j-m ~** give sb his/her notice; (*Vermieter*) give sb notice to quit **2** V/T

cancel; (*Vertrag*) terminate; **j-m die Stellung ~** give sb his/her notice **Kündigung** F (*Arbeitsverhältnis*) dismissal; (*Vertrag*) termination; (*Abonnement*) cancellation; (*Frist*) notice

Kundin F customer **Kundschaft** F customers *pl*

künftig ADJ future

Kunst F art; (*Können*) skill **Kunstgewerbe** N arts and crafts *pl* **Künstler(in)** M(F) artist **künstlerisch** ADJ artistic

künstlich ADJ artificial

Kunststoff M synthetic material **Kunststück** N trick **Kunstwerk** N work of art

Kupfer N copper

Kuppel F dome

kuppeln V/I AUTO operate the clutch **Kupplung** F coupling; AUTO clutch

Kur F course of treatment; (*am Kurort*) cure

Kurbel F winder

Kürbis M pumpkin

Kurierdienst M courier service

Kurort M health resort

Kurs M course; FIN rate; (*Wechselkurs*) exchange rate

kursiv **1** ADJ italic **2** ADV in italics

Kurve F curve; (*Straßenkurve*) bend **kurvenreich** ADJ (*Straße*) winding

kurz ADJ short; (*zeitlich a.*) brief; **~ vorher/darauf** shortly before/after; **kannst du ~ kommen?** could you come here for a minute?; **~ gesagt** in short **kurzärmelig** ADJ short-sleeved **kürzen** V/T cut short; (*in der Länge*) shorten; (*Gehalt*) reduce **kurzerhand** ADV on the spot **kurzfristig** ADJ short-term; **~ abgesagt werden** be called off at short notice **Kurzgeschichte** F short story **kürzlich** ADV recently **Kurzschluss** M ELEK short circuit **kurzsichtig** ADJ short-sighted **Kurzurlaub** M short vacation

Kusine F cousin

Kuss M kiss **küssen** V/T & V/R kiss

Küste F coast; (*Ufer*) shore **Küstenwache** F coastguard

Kutsche F carriage; (*geschlossene*) coach

Kuvert N envelope

Kuvertüre F coating

Kuwait N Kuwait

L

Labor N lab

Labyrinth N maze

lächeln V/I smile **Lächeln** N smile **lachen** V/I laugh **lächerlich** ADJ ridiculous

Lachs M salmon

Lack M varnish; (*Farblack*) lacquer; (*an Auto*) paint **lackieren** VT varnish; (*Auto*) spray **Lackschaden** M scratch (on the paintwork)

Ladegerät N (battery) charger **laden** VT *a.* IT load; (*einladen*) invite; (*Handy etc*) charge

Laden M store, shop; (*Fensterladen*) shutter **Ladendieb(in)** M(F) shoplifter **Ladendiebstahl** M shoplifting

Ladung F load; SCHIFF, FLUG cargo

Lage F position, situation

Lager N camp; WIRTSCH warehouse; TECH bearing **Lagerfeuer** N campfire **lagern** VT store

Lagune F lagoon

lahm ADJ lame; (*langweilig*) dull **lähmen** VT paralyze **Lähmung** F paralysis

Laib M loaf

Laie M layman, layperson

Laken N sheet

Lakritze F licorice

Lamm N (*a. Lammfleisch*) lamb

Lampe F lamp; (*Glühbirne*) bulb **Lampenschirm** M lampshade

Land N (*Gelände*) land; (*Nation*) country; (*Bundesland*) state, Land; **auf dem ~(e)** in the country

Landebahn F runway **landen** VT & VI land

Länderspiel N international (match)

Landesgrenze F national border, frontier **Landeswährung** F national currency **landesweit** ADJ nationwide

Landhaus N country house

Landkarte F map **Landkreis** M *administrative region*, ≈ district

ländlich ADJ rural

Landschaft F countryside; (*schöne*) scenery; KUNST landscape **Landstraße** F country road

Landung F landing **Landungsbrücke** F, **Landungssteg** M gangway

Landwirtschaft F agriculture, farming **landwirtschaftlich** ADJ agricultural

lang ADJ long; (*Mensch*) tall; **ein zwei Meter ~er Tisch** a table two meters long; **den ganzen Tag ~** all day long **langärmelig** ADJ long-sleeved **lange** ADV (for) a long time; **ich bleibe nicht ~** I won't stay long; **es ist ~ her, dass wir uns gesehen haben** it's a long time since we saw each other

Länge F length; GEO longitude

langen VI *umg* (*ausreichen*) be enough; *umg* (*fassen*) reach (*nach* for); **mir langt's** I've had enough

Langeweile F boredom

langfristig **1** ADJ long-term **2** ADV in the long term

Langlauf M cross-country skiing

langsam **1** ADJ slow **2** ADV slowly

Langschläfer(in) M(F) late riser

längst ADV **sie sollte ~ da sein** she should have been here long ago (*od* a long time ago); **als sie kam, waren wir ~ weg** when she arrived we had long since left

Langstreckenflug M long-haul flight

Languste F crayfish, crawfish

langweilen V/T bore; **ich langweile mich** I'm bored **langweilig** ADJ boring

Lappen M cloth, rag; (*Staublappen*) duster

Laptop M laptop

Lärm M noise

Lasche F flap

Laser M laser **Laserdrucker** M laser printer

lassen V/I & V/T (*erlauben*) let; (*an einem Ort, in einem Zustand*) leave; (*aufhören mit*) stop; **etw machen ~** have sth done; **sich die Haare schneiden ~** have one's hair cut; **j-n etw machen ~** make sb do sth; **lass das!** stop it

lässig ADJ casual

Last F load; (*Bürde*) burden

Laster N vice; *umg* truck

lästern V/I **über j-n/etw ~** make nasty remarks about sb/sth

lästig ADJ annoying; (*Person*) tiresome

Last-Minute-Flug M last-minute flight

Lastwagen M truck

Latein N Latin

Laterne F lantern; (*Straßenlaterne*) streetlight

Latte F slat; SPORT bar

Latz M bib **Lätzchen** N bib

Latzhose F overalls *pl*

lau ADJ (*Wind, Luft*) mild

Laub N foliage

Lauch M leeks *pl*; **eine Stange ~** a leek **Lauchzwiebel** F scallion

Lauf M run; (*Wettlauf*) race; (*Entwicklung*) course **Laufbahn** F career **laufen** V/I & V/T run; (*gehen*) walk; (*funktionieren*) work; **mir läuft die Nase** my nose is running; **was läuft im Kino?** what's playing at the movies? **laufend** ADJ running; (*Monat, Ausgaben*) current; **auf dem Laufenden sein/halten** be/keep up-to-date **Läufer** M (*Teppich*) rug; (*Schach*) bishop **Läufer(in)** M(F) SPORT runner **Laufmasche** F run **Laufwerk** N IT drive

Laune F mood; **gute/schlechte ~ haben** be in a good/bad mood **launisch** ADJ moody

Laus F louse

lauschen V/I listen; (*heimlich*) eavesdrop

laut **1** ADJ loud **2** ADV loudly; (*lesen*) aloud **3** PRÄP *+gen od dat* according to

läuten VT & VI ring
lauter ADV *umg* (*nichts als*) nothing but
Lautsprecher M loudspeaker
Lautstärke F loudness; RADIO, TV volume
lauwarm ADJ lukewarm
Lavendel M lavender
Lawine F avalanche
leasen VT lease **Leasing** N leasing
leben VT & VI live; (*am Leben sein*) be alive; **wie lange ~ Sie schon hier?** how long have you been living here?; **von … ~** (*Nahrungsmittel etc*) live on …; (*Beruf, Beschäftigung*) make one's living from … **Leben** N life **lebend** ADJ living **lebendig** ADJ alive; (*lebhaft*) lively **lebensgefährlich** ADJ very dangerous; (*Verletzung*) critical **Lebensgefährte** M, **Lebensgefährtin** F partner **Lebenshaltungskosten** PL cost *sg* of living **lebenslänglich** ADJ for life; **~ bekommen** get life **Lebenslauf** M resumé **Lebensmittel** PL food *sg* **Lebensmittelgeschäft** N grocery store **Lebensmittelvergiftung** F food poisoning **lebensnotwendig** ADJ vital **Lebensstandard** M standard of living **Lebenszeichen** N sign of life
Leber F liver **Leberfleck** M mole
Lebewesen N living being
lebhaft ADJ lively; (*Erinnerung, Eindruck*) vivid
Lebkuchen M gingerbread
leblos ADJ lifeless
Leck N leak **lecken** **1** VI (*Loch haben*) leak **2** VT & VI (*schlecken*) lick
lecker ADJ delicious, tasty
Leder N leather
ledig ADJ single
leer ADJ empty; (*Seite*) blank; (*Batterie*) dead **leeren** VT & VR empty **Leerlauf** M (*Gang*) neutral **Leerung** F emptying; (*Briefkasten*) collection
legal ADJ legal, lawful
legen **1** VT put, place; (*Eier*) lay **2** VR lie down; (*Sturm, Begeisterung*) die down; (*Schmerz, Gefühl*) wear off
leger ADJ casual
Lehm M loam; (*Ton*) clay
Lehne F arm(rest); (*Rückenlehne*) back(rest) **lehnen** VT & VR lean
Lehrbuch N textbook **Lehre** F teaching; (*beruflich*) apprenticeship; (*moralisch*) lesson **lehren** VT teach **Lehrer(in)** M(F) teacher **Lehrgang** M course **Lehrling** M apprentice **lehrreich** ADJ instructive
Leibwächter(in) M(F) bodyguard
Leiche F corpse **Leichenwagen** M hearse
leicht **1** ADJ light; (*einfach*) easy, simple; (*Erkrankung*) slight **2** ADV (*mühelos, schnell*)

easily; (*geringfügig*) slightly **Leichtathletik** F track and field **leichtfallen** V/T **j-m ~** be easy for sb **leichtsinnig** ADJ careless; (*stärker*) reckless

leid ADJ **j-n/etw ~ sein** be tired of sb/sth **Leid** N grief, sorrow **leiden** V/I & V/T suffer (*an, unter +dat* from); **ich kann ihn/es nicht ~** I can't stand him/it **Leiden** N suffering; (*Krankheit*) illness

Leidenschaft F passion **leidenschaftlich** ADJ passionate

leider ADV unfortunately; **~ ja/nein** I'm afraid so/not

leidtun V/I **es tut mir/ihm leid** I'm/he's sorry; **er tut mir leid** I'm sorry for him

leihen V/T **j-m etw ~** lend sb sth; **sich etw von j-m ~** borrow sth from sb **Leihwagen** M rental car

Leim M glue

Leine F cord; (*für Wäsche*) line; (*Hundeleine*) leash

Leinen N linen **Leinwand** F KUNST canvas; FILM screen

leise **1** ADJ quiet; (*sanft*) soft **2** ADV quietly

Leiste F ledge; (*Zierleiste*) strip; ANAT groin

leisten V/T (*Arbeit*) do; (*vollbringen*) achieve; **j-m Gesellschaft ~** keep sb company; **sich etw ~** (*gönnen*) treat oneself to sth; **ich kann es mir nicht ~** I can't afford it

Leistenbruch M hernia

Leistung F performance; (*gute*) achievement

leiten V/T lead; (*Firma*) run; (*in eine Richtung*) direct; ELEK conduct

Leiter F ladder

Leiter(in) M(F) (*von Geschäft*) manager

Leitplanke F crash barrier

Leitung F (*Führung*) direction; TEL line; (*von Firma*) management; (*Wasserleitung*) pipe; (*Kabel*) cable **Leitungswasser** N tap water

Lektion F lesson

Lektüre F (*Lesen*) reading; (*Lesestoff*) reading matter

Lende F (*Speise*) loin; (*vom Rind*) sirloin

lenken V/T steer; (*Blick*) direct (*auf +akk* toward(s)); **j-s Aufmerksamkeit auf etw ~** draw sb's attention to sth **Lenker** M (*von Fahrrad, Motorrad*) handlebars *pl* **Lenkrad** N steering wheel **Lenkradschloss** N steering lock **Lenkstange** F handlebars *pl*

lernen V/T & V/I learn; (*für eine Prüfung*) study

lesbisch ADJ lesbian

Lesebuch N reader **lesen** V/I & V/T read; (*ernten*) pick **Leser(in)** M(F) reader **leserlich** ADJ legible **Lesezeichen** N bookmark

Lette M, **Lettin** F Lett, Latvian **lettisch** ADJ Lettish, Latvian **Lettisch** N Latvian **Lettland** N Latvia

letzte(r, s) ADJ last; (*neueste*) latest; (*endgültig*) final; **zum ~n Mal** for the last time; **am ~n Montag** last Monday; **in ~r Zeit** lately, recently **letztens** ADV (*vor kurzem*) recently

Leuchte F lamp, light **leuchten** V/I shine; (*Feuer, Zifferblatt*) glow **Leuchtreklame** F neon sign **Leuchtturm** M lighthouse

leugnen **1** V/T deny **2** V/I deny everything

Leukämie F leukemia

Leukoplast® N Band-Aid®

Leute PL people *pl*

Lexikon N encyclopedia

Libanon M **der ~** Lebanon

Libelle F dragonfly

liberal ADJ liberal

Licht N light **lichtempfindlich** ADJ sensitive to light **Lichtempfindlichkeit** F light sensitivity **Lichthupe** F **die ~ betätigen** flash one's lights **Lichtjahr** N light year **Lichtschalter** M light switch **Lichtschutzfaktor** M sun protection factor, SPF

Lichtung F clearing

Lid N eyelid **Lidschatten** M eyeshadow

lieb ADJ (*nett*) nice; (*teuer, geliebt*) dear; (*liebenswert*) sweet; **das ist ~ von dir** that's nice of you; **Lieber Herr X** Dear Mr. X **Liebe** F love **lieben** V/T love; (*sexuell*) make love to **liebenswürdig** ADJ kind **lieber** ADV rather; **ich möchte ~ nicht** I'd rather not; **welches ist dir ~?** which one do you prefer?; → gern, lieb **Liebesbrief** M love letter **Liebespaar** N lovers *pl* **liebevoll** ADJ loving **Liebhaber(in)** M(F) lover **lieblich** ADJ lovely; (*Wein*) sweet **Liebling** M darling **Lieblings-** IN ZSSGN favorite **liebste(r, s)** ADJ favorite **liebsten** ADV **am ~ esse ich ...** my favorite food is ...; **am ~ würde ich bleiben** I'd really like to stay

Liechtenstein N Liechtenstein

Lied N song; REL hymn

liefern V/T deliver; (*beschaffen*) supply **Lieferung** F delivery

Liege F (*beim Arzt*) couch; (*Notbett*) cot; (*Gartenliege*) lounger **liegen** V/I lie; (*sich befinden*) be; **mir liegt nichts/viel daran** it doesn't matter to me/it matters a lot to me; **woran liegt es nur, dass ...?** why is it that ...?; **~ bleiben** (*Mensch*) stay lying down; (*im Bett*) stay in bed; (*Ding*) be left (behind); **~ lassen** (*vergessen*) leave behind **Liegestuhl** M deckchair **Liegestütz** M push-up

Lift M elevator

Liga F league, division

light ADJ (*Cola*) diet; (*fettarm*) low-fat; (*kalorienarm*) low-calo-

rie; (*Zigaretten*) mild
Likör M liqueur
lila ADJ purple
Lilie F lily
Limette F lime
Limo F *umg* soda **Limonade** F soda; (*mit Zitronengeschmack*) lemonade
Limone F lime
Limousine F sedan; (*mit Trennwand*) limousine
lindern V/T relieve, soothe
Lineal N ruler
Linie F line **Linienflug** M scheduled flight **liniert** ADJ ruled, lined
Link M IT link
Linke F left-hand side; (*Hand*) left hand; POL left (wing) **linke(r, s)** ADJ left; **auf der ~n Seite** on the left, on the left-hand side **links** ADV on the left; **~ abbiegen** turn left; **~ von** to the left of; **~ oben** at the top left **Linkshänder(in)** M(F) left-handed person, lefty **linksherum** ADV to the left, counterclockwise
Linse F lentil; (*optisch*) lens
Lippe F lip **Lippenstift** M lipstick
lispeln V/I lisp
List F cunning; (*Trick*) trick
Liste F list
Litauen N Lithuania **Litauer(in)** M(F) Lithuanian **litauisch** ADJ Lithuanian **Litauisch** N Lithuanian
Liter M *od* N liter
literarisch ADJ literary **Literatur** F literature
Litschi F lychee, litchi
Lizenz F license
Lkw M *abk* = Lastkraftwagen; truck
Lob N praise **loben** V/T praise
Loch N hole **lochen** V/T punch **Locher** M hole puncher
Locke F curl **locken** V/T (*anlocken*) lure; (*Haare*) curl **Lockenstab** M curling irons *pl*
Lockenwickler M curler
locker ADJ (*Schraube, Zahn*) loose; (*Haltung*) relaxed; (*Person*) easy-going **lockern** V/T & V/R loosen
lockig ADJ curly
Löffel M spoon; **ein ~ Mehl** a spoonful of flour
Loge F THEAT box
logisch ADJ logical
Lohn M reward; (*Arbeitslohn*) pay, wages *pl*
lohnen V/R be worth it; **es lohnt sich nicht zu warten** it's no use waiting
Lohnerhöhung F pay raise
Lohnsteuer F income tax
Lokal N (*Gaststätte*) restaurant; (*Kneipe*) bar
Lokomotive F locomotive
Lorbeerblatt N GASTR bay leaf
los ADJ loose; **~!** go on!; **j-n/etw ~ sein** be rid of sb/sth; **was ist ~?** what's the matter?, what's up?; **dort ist**

nichts/viel ~ there's nothing/a lot going on there
Los N (*Schicksal*) lot, fate; (*Lotterie etc*) ticket
löschen V/T (*Feuer, Licht*) put out, extinguish; (*Durst*) quench; (*Tonband*) erase; (*Daten, Zeile*) delete
lose ADJ loose
Lösegeld N ransom
losen V/I draw lots
lösen **1** V/T (*lockern*) loosen; (*Rätsel*) solve; CHEM dissolve; (*Fahrkarte*) buy **2** V/R (*abgehen*) come off; (*Zucker etc*) dissolve; (*Problem, Schwierigkeit*) (re)-solve itself
losfahren V/I leave **losgehen** V/I set out; (*anfangen*) start
loslassen V/T let go
löslich ADJ soluble
Lösung F (*eines Rätsels, Problems, Flüssigkeit*) solution
loswerden V/T get rid of
Lotterie F lottery **Lotto** N national lottery; **~ spielen** play the lottery
Löwe M ZOOL lion; ASTROL Leo
Lücke F gap
Luft F air; (*Atem*) breath **Luftballon** M balloon **luftdicht** ADJ airtight **Luftdruck** M METEO atmospheric pressure; (*in Reifen*) air pressure
lüften V/T air; (*Geheimnis*) reveal
Luftfahrt F aviation **Luftfeuchtigkeit** F humidity **Luftfilter** M air filter **Luftfracht** F air freight **Luftmatratze** F air mattress **Luftpost** F airmail **Luftpumpe** F (bicycle) pump **Luftröhre** F windpipe
Lüftung F ventilation
Luftverschmutzung F air pollution **Luftwaffe** F air force **Luftzug** M draft
Lüge F lie **lügen** V/I lie **Lügner(in)** M(F) liar
Luke F hatch
Lumpen M rag
Lunchpaket N packed lunch
Lunge F lungs *pl* **Lungenentzündung** F pneumonia
Lupe F magnifying glass; **etw unter die ~ nehmen** *fig* have a close look at sth
Lust F joy, delight; (*Neigung*) desire; **~ auf etw haben** feel like sth; **~ haben, etw zu tun** feel like doing sth
lustig ADJ (*komisch*) amusing, funny; (*fröhlich*) cheerful
lutschen **1** V/T suck **2** V/I **~ an** suck **Lutscher** M lollipop
Luxemburg N Luxembourg
Luxemburger(in) M(F) Luxembourger; **er ist Luxemburger** he's from Luxembourg **luxemburgisch** ADJ Luxembourgian, from Luxembourg
luxuriös ADJ luxurious **Luxus** M luxury
Lymphdrüse F lymph gland
Lyrik F poetry

M

machbar ADJ feasible
machen **1** V/T (*herstellen, verursachen*) make; (*tun, erledigen*) do; (*kosten*) be; **das Essen/einen Fehler ~** make dinner/a mistake; **ein Foto ~** take a photo; **was machst du?** what are you doing?; (*beruflich*) what do you do (for a living)?; **das Bett ~** make the bed; **was macht das?** (*kostet*) how much is that?; **das macht zwanzig Dollar** that's twenty dollars; **einen Spaziergang ~** go for a walk; **Urlaub ~** go on vacation; **eine Pause ~** take a break; **einen Kurs ~** take a course; **das macht nichts** it doesn't matter **2** V/R **sich an die Arbeit ~** get down to work
Macht F power **mächtig** ADJ powerful; *umg* (*ungeheuer*) enormous **machtlos** ADJ powerless
Mädchen N girl **Mädchenname** M maiden name
Made F maggot
Magazin N magazine
Magen M stomach **Magenbeschwerden** PL stomach trouble *sg* **Magen-Darm-Infektion** F gastroenteritis **Magengeschwür** N stomach ulcer **Magenschmerzen** PL stomachache *sg*
mager ADJ (*Fleisch, Wurst*) lean; (*Person*) thin; (*Käse, Joghurt*) low-fat **Magermilch** F skim milk **Magersucht** F anorexia **magersüchtig** ADJ anorexic
magisch ADJ magical
Magnet M magnet
mähen V/T & V/I mow
mahlen V/T grind
Mahlzeit **1** F meal; (*für Baby*) feed **2** INT (*guten Appetit*) enjoy your meal
mahnen V/T urge; **j-n schriftlich ~** send sb a reminder **Mahngebühr** F fine **Mahnung** F warning; (*schriftlich*) reminder
Mai M May; → **Juni** **Maifeiertag** M May Day
Mail F e-mail; **j-m eine ~ schicken** mail sb, e-mail sb **Mailbox** F IT mailbox **mailen** V/I & V/T e-mail
Mais M corn **Maiskolben** M corn cob; GASTR corn on the cob
Majonäse F mayonnaise
Majoran M marjoram
Make-up N make-up
Makler(in) M(F) broker; (*Immobilienmakler*) realtor
Makrele F mackerel
mal ADV (*beim Rechnen*) times, multiplied by; (*beim Messen*) by; *umg* (*einmal = früher*) once; (*einmal = zukünftig*) some day; **4 ~ 3 ist 12** 4 times 3 is (*od*

equals) twelve; **da habe ich ~ gewohnt** I used to live there
Mal N (*Zeitpunkt*) time; (*Markierung*) mark; **jedes ~** every time; **ein paar ~** a few times
Malaria F malaria
Malaysia N Malaysia
Malediven PL Maldives *pl*
malen VT & VI paint **Maler(in)** M(F) painter **Malerei** F painting **malerisch** ADJ picturesque
malnehmen VT multiply (*mit* by)
Malta N Malta **Maltese** M, **Maltesin** F Maltese **maltesisch** ADJ Maltese **Maltesisch** N Maltese
Malz N malt
Mama F mom(my)
man INDEF PR you; (*förmlich*) one; (*jemand*) someone, somebody; (*die Leute*) they, people *pl*; **wie schreibt ~ das?** how do you spell that?; **~ sagt, dass ...** they (*od* people) say that ...
managen VT *umg* manage **Manager(in)** M(F) manager
manche(r, s) INDEF PR (*einige*) some; (*viele*) many **manchmal** ADV sometimes
Mandant(in) M(F) client
Mandarine F mandarin, tangerine
Mandel F almond; **~n** ANAT tonsils *pl* **Mandelentzündung** F tonsillitis
Mangel M (*Fehlen*) lack; (*Knappheit*) shortage (*an +dat* of); (*Fehler*) defect, fault **mangelhaft** ADJ (*Ware*) faulty; (*Schulnote*) ≈ F
Mango F mango
Manieren PL manners *pl*
Maniküre F manicure
manipulieren VT manipulate
Manko N deficiency
Mann M man; (*Ehemann*) husband **Männchen** N **es ist ein ~** (*Tier*) it's a he **männlich** ADJ masculine; BIOL male
Mannschaft F SPORT *fig* team; SCHIFF, FLUG crew
Mansarde F attic
Manschettenknopf M cufflink
Mantel M coat
Mappe F briefcase; (*Aktenmappe*) folder
Maracuja F passion fruit
Marathon M marathon
Märchen N fairy tale
Margarine F margarine
Marienkäfer M ladybug
Marille F apricot
Marine F navy
marinieren VT marinate
Marionette F puppet
Mark N (*Knochenmark*) marrow; (*Fruchtmark*) pulp
Marke F (*Warensorte*) brand; (*Fabrikat*) make; JUR trademark; (*Briefmarke*) stamp; (*Essenmarke*) voucher, ticket; (*aus Metall etc*) disc; (*Messpunkt*) mark
markieren VT mark **Markie-**

rung F marking; (*Zeichen*) mark
Markise F awning
Markt M market; **auf den ~ bringen** launch **Markthalle** F covered market **Marktlücke** F gap in the market **Marktplatz** M market place **Marktwirtschaft** F market economy
Marmelade F jelly, jam; (*Orangenmarmelade*) marmalade
Marmor M marble
Marone F chestnut
Marsch M march
Märtyrer(in) M(F) martyr
März M March; → **Juni**
Marzipan N marzipan
Maschine F machine; (*Motor*) engine **Maschinenbau** M mechanical engineering
Masern PL MED measles *sg*
Maske F mask **Maskenball** M masquerade ball
Maskottchen N mascot
Mass F (*Bier*) liter of beer
Maß N measure; (*Mäßigung*) moderation; (*Grad*) degree, extent; **~e** (*Person*) measurements; (*Raum*) dimensions; **in gewissem/hohem ~e** to a certain/high degree
Massage F massage
Masse F mass; (*von Menschen*) crowd; (*Großteil*) majority **massenhaft** ADV masses (*od* loads) of **Massenkarambolage** F pile-up **Massenmedien** PL mass media *pl*
Masseur(in) M(F) masseur/masseuse
maßgeschneidert ADJ (*Kleidung*) made-to-measure
massieren V/T massage
mäßig ADJ moderate
massiv ADJ solid; *fig* massive
maßlos ADJ extreme
Maßnahme F measure, step
Maßstab M rule, measure; *fig* standard; **im ~ von 1:5** on a scale of 1:5
Mast M mast; ELEK pylon
Material N material; (*Arbeitsmaterial*) materials *pl* **materialistisch** ADJ materialistic
Materie F matter
Mathematik F mathematics *sg*
Matratze F mattress
Matrose M sailor
Matsch M mud; (*Schnee*) slush **matschig** ADJ (*Boden*) muddy; (*Schnee*) slushy; (*Obst*) mushy
matt ADJ weak; (*glanzlos*) dull; FOTO matt; (*Schach*) mate
Matte F mat
Matura F *Austrian school-leaving examination*, ≈ High School Diploma
Mauer F wall
Maul N mouth; *umg* trap; **halt's ~!** shut your face (*od* trap)! **Maulesel** M mule **Maulkorb** M muzzle **Maulwurf** M mole
Maurer(in) M(F) bricklayer
Maus F mouse **Mausefalle** F

mousetrap **Mausklick** M mouse click **Mauspad** N mouse pad **Maustaste** F mouse button
Maut F toll **Mautgebühr** F toll **mautpflichtig** ADJ **~e Straße** toll road, turnpike **Mautstelle** F tollbooth, tollgate **Mautstraße** F toll road, turnpike
maximal ADV **ihr habt ~ zwei Stunden Zeit** you've got two hours at (the) most; **~ vier Leute** a maximum of four people
Mayonnaise F mayonnaise
MB N, **Mbyte** N *abk* = Megabyte; MB
Mechanik F mechanics *sg*; (*Getriebe*) mechanics *pl* **Mechaniker(in)** M(F) mechanic **mechanisch** ADJ mechanical **Mechanismus** M mechanism
meckern V/I (*Ziege*) bleat; *umg* (*schimpfen*) moan
Medaille F medal
Medien PL media *pl*
Medikament N medicine
meditieren V/I meditate
medium ADJ (*Steak*) medium
Medizin F medicine (*gegen* for) **medizinisch** ADJ medical
Meer N sea; **am ~** by the sea **Meeresfrüchte** PL seafood *sg* **Meeresspiegel** M sea level **Meerrettich** M horseradish **Meerschweinchen** N guinea pig
Megabyte N megabyte
Mehl N flour
mehr **1** INDEF PR more; **~ will ich nicht ausgeben** I don't want to spend any more; **was willst du ~?** what more do you want? **2** ADV **immer ~ (Leute)** more and more (people); **~ als fünf Minuten** more than five minutes; **es ist kein Brot ~ da** there's no bread left; **nie ~** never again **mehrdeutig** ADJ ambiguous **mehrere** INDEF PR several **mehreres** INDEF PR several things **mehrfach** ADJ multiple; (*wiederholt*) repeated **Mehrfachstecker** M multiple plug **Mehrheit** F majority **mehrmals** ADV repeatedly **mehrsprachig** ADJ multilingual **Mehrwertsteuer** F sales tax **Mehrzahl** F majority; (*Plural*) plural
meiden V/T avoid
Meile F mile
mein POSS PR (*adjektivisch*) my **meine(r, s)** POSS PR (*substantivisch*) mine
meinen V/T & V/I (*glauben, der Ansicht sein*) think; (*sagen*) say; (*sagen wollen, beabsichtigen*) mean; **das war nicht so gemeint** I didn't mean it like that
meinetwegen ADV (*wegen mir*) because of me; (*mir zuliebe*) for my sake; (*von mir aus*) as far as I'm concerned

Meinung F opinion; **meiner ~ nach** in my opinion **Meinungsumfrage** F opinion poll **Meinungsverschiedenheit** F disagreement (*über* about)

meist ADV mostly **meiste(r, s)** INDEF PR most; **die ~n (Leute)** most people; **die ~ Zeit** most of the time; **das ~ (davon)** most of it; **die ~n von ihnen** most of them **meistens** ADV mostly; (*zum größten Teil*) for the most part

Meister(in) M(F) master; SPORT champion **Meisterschaft** F championship **Meisterwerk** N masterpiece

melden **1** V/T report **2** V/R report (*bei* to); (*Schule*) raise one's hand; (*freiwillig*) volunteer; (*auf etw, am Telefon*) answer **Meldung** F announcement; (*Bericht*) report; IT message

Melodie F tune, melody

Melone F melon

Menge F quantity; (*Menschen*) crowd; **eine ~** (*große Anzahl*) a lot (*+gen* of)

Mensa F cafeteria

Mensch M human being, man; (*Person*) person; **kein ~** nobody; **~!** (*bewundernd*) wow!; (*verärgert*) goddamn it! **Menschenmenge** F crowd **Menschenrechte** PL human rights *pl* **Menschenverstand** M **gesunder ~** common sense **Menschheit** F humanity, mankind **menschlich** ADJ human; (*human*) humane

Menstruation F menstruation

Mentalität F mentality, mindset

Menthol N menthol

Menü N set meal; IT menu **Menüleiste** F IT menu bar

Merkblatt N leaflet **merken** V/T (*bemerken*) notice; **sich etw ~** remember sth **Merkmal** N feature **merkwürdig** ADJ odd

Messbecher M measuring jug

Messe F fair; REL mass

messen **1** V/T measure; (*Temperatur, Puls*) take **2** V/R compete

Messer N knife

Messing N brass

Metall N metal

Meter M *od* N meter **Metermaß** N tape measure

Methode F method

Metzger(in) M(F) butcher **Metzgerei** F butcher shop

Mexiko N Mexico

MEZ F *abk* = mitteleuropäische Zeit; Central European Time

mich PERS PR me; **~ (selbst)** (*reflexiv*) myself; **ich fühle ~ wohl** I feel fine

Miene F look, expression

mies ADJ *umg* lousy

Miesmuschel F mussel

Mietauto N → **Mietwagen**
Miete F rent **mieten** V/T rent
Mieter(in) M(F) tenant **Mietshaus** N apartment house
Mietvertrag M rental agreement **Mietwagen** M rental car; **sich einen ~ nehmen** rent a car
Migräne F migraine
Migrant(in) M(F) migrant
Mikrofon N microphone
Mikrowelle F, **Mikrowellenherd** M microwave (oven)
Milch F milk **Milchkaffee** M milky coffee **Milchpulver** N powdered milk **Milchreis** M rice pudding **Milchshake** M milk shake
mild ADJ mild; (*Richter*) lenient; (*freundlich*) kind
Militär N military, army
Milliarde F billion **Milligramm** N milligram **Milliliter** M milliliter **Millimeter** M millimeter **Million** F million **Millionär(in)** M(F) millionaire
Milz F spleen
Minderheit F minority
minderjährig ADJ underage
minderwertig ADJ inferior
Mindest- IN ZSSGN minimum **mindeste(r, s)** ADJ least **mindestens** ADV at least
Mine F mine; (*Bleistift*) lead; (*Kugelschreiber*) refill
Mineralwasser N mineral water
Minibar F minibar **Minigolf** N miniature golf
minimal ADJ minimal
Minimum N minimum
Minirock M miniskirt
Minister(in) M(F) minister **Ministerium** N ministry **Ministerpräsident(in)** M(F) (*von Bundesland*) prime minister (*of a Bundesland*)
minus ADV minus **Minus** N deficit; **im ~ sein** be in the red; (*Konto*) be overdrawn
Minute F minute
Minze F mint
mir PERS PR (to) me; **kannst du ~ helfen?** can you help me?; **kannst du es ~ erklären?** can you explain it to me?; **ich habe ~ einen neuen Rechner gekauft** I bought (myself) a new computer; **ein Freund von ~** a friend of mine
mischen V/T mix; (*Karten*) shuffle **Mischung** F mixture (*aus* of)
missachten V/T ignore **Missbrauch** M abuse; (*falscher Gebrauch*) misuse **missbrauchen** V/T misuse (*zu* for); (*sexuell*) abuse **Misserfolg** M failure **Missgeschick** N (*Panne*) mishap **misshandeln** V/T ill-treat
Mission F mission
misslingen V/I fail **misstrauen** V/T *+dat* distrust **Misstrauen** N mistrust, suspicion (*gegenüber* of) **misstrauisch** ADJ distrustful; (*argwöhnisch*)

suspicious **Missverständnis** N misunderstanding **missverstehen** V/T misunderstand
Mist M *umg* nonsense; (*von Kühen*) dung; (*als Dünger*) manure
Mistel F mistletoe
mit **1** PRÄP +*dat* with; (*mittels*) by; **~ der Bahn** by train; **~ der Kreditkarte bezahlen** pay by credit card; **~ 10 Jahren** at the age of 10; **wie wär's ~ ...?** how about ...? **2** ADV along, too; **wollen Sie ~?** do you want to come along?
Mitarbeiter(in) M(F) (*Angestellter*) employee
mitbekommen V/T *umg* (*aufschnappen*) catch; (*hören*) hear; (*verstehen*) get
mitbenutzen V/T share
Mitbewohner(in) M(F) (*in Wohnung*) roommate
mitbringen V/T bring along **Mitbringsel** N small present
miteinander ADV with one another; (*gemeinsam*) together
miterleben V/T see (with one's own eyes)
Mitesser M blackhead
Mitfahrgelegenheit F ride
mitgeben V/T **j-m etw ~** give sb sth (to take along)
Mitgefühl N sympathy
mitgehen V/I go/come along
mitgenommen ADJ worn out, exhausted
Mitglied N member
mithilfe PRÄP +*gen* **~ von** with the help of
mitkommen V/I come along; (*verstehen*) follow
Mitleid N pity; **~ haben mit** feel sorry for
mitmachen **1** V/T take part in **2** V/I take part
mitnehmen V/T take along; (*anstrengen*) wear out, exhaust
mitschreiben **1** V/I take notes **2** V/T take down
Mitschüler(in) M(F) schoolfriend; (*Klassenkamerad*) classmate
mitspielen V/I (*in Mannschaft*) play; (*bei Spiel*) join in; **in einem Stück ~** act in a play
Mittag M midday; **gestern ~** at midday yesterday, yesterday lunchtime; **zu ~ essen** have lunch **Mittagessen** N lunch **mittags** ADV at lunchtime, at midday **Mittagspause** F lunch break
Mitte F middle; **~ Juni** in the middle of June; **sie ist ~ zwanzig** she's in her mid-twenties
mitteilen V/T **j-m etw ~** inform sb of sth **Mitteilung** F notification
Mittel N means *sg*; (*Maßnahme, Methode*) method; MED remedy (*gegen* for)
mittelalterlich ADJ medieval **Mittelamerika** N Central America **Mitteleuropa** N Central Europe **Mittelfinger** M middle finger **mittelmäßig** ADJ mediocre **Mittelmeer** N Mediterranean (Sea)

Mittelpunkt M center; **im ~ stehen** be the center of attention
mittels PRÄP *+gen* by means of
mitten ADV in the middle; **~ auf der Straße/in der Nacht** in the middle of the street/night
Mitternacht F midnight
mittlere(r, s) ADJ middle; (*durchschnittlich*) average
mittlerweile ADV meanwhile
Mittwoch M Wednesday; **(am) ~** (on) Wednesday; **(am) ~ Morgen/Nachmittag/Abend** (on) Wednesday morning/afternoon/evening; **diesen/letzten/nächsten ~** this/last/next Wednesday; **jeden ~** every Wednesday; **~ in einer Woche** a week from Wednesday **mittwochs** ADV (on) Wednesdays; **~ abends** (*jeden Mittwochabend*) (on) Wednesday evenings
mixen V/T mix **Mixer** M (*Küchengerät*) blender
mobben V/T harass (*od* bully) (at work)
Möbel N piece of furniture; **die ~** *pl* the furniture *sg* **Möbelwagen** M moving truck
mobil ADJ mobile; (*mitnehmbar*) portable **Mobiltelefon** N cell, cellphone
möblieren V/T furnish
Mode F fashion
Model N model
Modell N model
Modem N IT modem
Mode(n)schau F fashion show
Moderator(in) M(F) (*Diskussion*) moderator; (*Nachrichtensendung*) anchor; (*Unterhaltungssendung*) host
modern ADJ modern; (*modisch*) fashionable **modisch** ADJ fashionable
Modus M IT mode; *fig* way
Mofa N moped
mogeln V/I cheat
mögen V/T & V/I like; **ich möchte ...** I would like ...; **ich möchte lieber bleiben** I'd rather stay; **möchtest du lieber Tee oder Kaffee?** would you prefer tea or coffee?
möglich ADJ possible; **so bald wie ~** as soon as possible
möglicherweise ADV possibly **Möglichkeit** F possibility
möglichst ADV as ... as possible
Mohn M (*Blume*) poppy; (*Samen*) poppy seed
Möhre F, **Mohrrübe** F carrot
Mokka M mocha
Molkerei F dairy
Moll N minor (key)
mollig ADJ cozy; (*dicklich*) plump
Moment M moment; **im ~** at the moment; **einen ~ bitte!** just a minute **momentan** 1 ADJ momentary 2 ADV at the moment

Monat M month; **sie ist im dritten ~** (*schwanger*) she's two months pregnant **monatlich** ADJ & ADV monthly; **~ 100 Euro zahlen** pay 100 euros a month (*od* every month) **Monatskarte** F monthly season ticket
Mönch M monk
Mond M moon
Monitor M IT monitor
monoton ADJ monotonous
Montag M Monday; → Mittwoch **montags** ADV (on) Mondays; → mittwochs
Monteur(in) M(F) fitter **montieren** V/T assemble, set up
Monument N monument
Moos N moss
Moped N moped
Moral F (*Werte*) morals *pl* **moralisch** ADJ moral
Mord M murder **Mörder(in)** M(F) murderer/murderess
morgen ADV tomorrow; **~ früh** tomorrow morning **Morgen** M morning; **am ~** in the morning **Morgenmantel** M dressing gown **morgens** ADV in the morning; **um 3 Uhr ~** at 3 (o'clock) in the morning, at 3 a.m.
Morphium N morphine
morsch ADJ rotten
Mosaik N mosaic
Moschee F mosque
Moskito M mosquito
Moslem M, **Moslime** F Muslim
Motel N motel
motivieren V/T motivate
Motor M engine; ELEK motor **Motorboot** N motorboat **Motorenöl** N engine oil **Motorrad** N motorcycle **Motorradfahrer(in)** M(F) motorcyclist **Motorroller** M (motor) scooter **Motorschaden** M engine trouble
Motte F moth
Motto N motto
Mountainbike N mountain bike
Möwe F (sea)gull
MP3-Player M MP3 player
Mücke F gnat; (*tropische*) mosquito **Mückenstich** M mosquito bite
müde ADJ tired
muffig ADJ (*Geruch*) musty; (*Gesicht, Mensch*) grumpy
Mühe F trouble, pains *pl*; **sich große ~ geben** go to a lot of trouble
Mühle F mill; (*Kaffeemühle*) grinder
Müll M garbage **Müllabfuhr** F garbage disposal
Mullbinde F gauze bandage
Müllcontainer M waste container **Mülleimer** M, **Mülltonne** F garbage can **Müllwagen** M garbage truck
multikulturell ADJ multicultural
Multimedia- IN ZSSGN multimedia
multiple Sklerose F multiple

sclerosis
Multiplexkino N multiplex (movie theater)
multiplizieren V/T multiply (*mit* by)
Mumps M mumps *sg*
München N Munich
Mund M mouth; **halt den ~!** shut up! **Mundart** F dialect
münden V/I flow (*in +akk* into)
Mundgeruch M bad breath **Mundharmonika** F mouth organ
mündlich ADJ oral
Mundschutz M mask **Mundwasser** N mouthwash
Munition F ammunition
Münster N cathedral
munter ADJ lively
Münzautomat M vending machine **Münze** F coin **Münzeinwurf** M slot **Münzrückgabe** F coin return **Münztelefon** N pay phone **Münzwechsler** M change machine
murmeln V/T & V/I murmur, mutter
mürrisch ADJ sullen, grumpy
Muschel F mussel; (*Muschelschale*) shell
Museum N museum
Musical N musical
Musik F music **musikalisch** ADJ musical **Musiker(in)** M(F) musician **Musikinstrument** N musical instrument **musizieren** V/I play music
Muskat M nutmeg
Muskel M muscle **Muskelkater** M **~ haben** be stiff **Muskelriss** M torn muscle **Muskelzerrung** F pulled muscle
muskulös ADJ muscular
Müsli N muesli
Muslim(in) M(F) Muslim
Muss N must
müssen V/I must, have to; **er hat gehen ~** he (has) had to go; **sie müsste schon längst hier sein** she should have arrived a long time ago; **du musst es nicht tun** you don't have to do it, you needn't do it; **ich muss mal** I have to go to the bathroom
Muster N (*Dessin*) pattern, design; (*Probe*) sample
Mut M courage; **j-m ~ machen** encourage sb **mutig** ADJ brave, courageous
Mutter **1** F mother **2** F (*Schraubenmutter*) nut **Muttersprache** F mother tongue
Muttertag M Mother's Day
Mutti F mom(my)
mutwillig ADJ deliberate
Mütze F cap

N

na INT **~ also!**, **~ bitte!** see?, what did I tell you?; **~ ja** well; **~ und?** so what?

Nabel M navel
nach PRÄP *+dat* (*zeitlich*) after; (*in Richtung*) to; (*gemäß*) according to; **~ zwei Stunden** after two hours, two hours later; **es ist fünf ~ sechs** it's five after (*od* past) six; **der Zug ~ Detroit** the train for (*od* to) Detroit; **~ rechts/links** to the right/left; **~ Hause** home; **~ oben/hinten/unten** up/back/down; **~ und ~** gradually
nachahmen V/T imitate
Nachbar(in) M(F) neighbor
 Nachbarschaft F neighborhood
nachdem KONJ after; (*weil*) since; **je ~ (ob/wie)** depending on (whether/how)
nachdenken V/I think (*über +akk* about) **nachdenklich** ADJ thoughtful
nacheinander ADV one after another (*od* the other)
Nachfolger(in) M(F) successor
nachforschen V/T investigate
nachgeben V/I give in (*j-m* to sb)
nachgehen V/I follow (*j-m* sb); (*erforschen*) inquire (*einer Sache dat* into sth); **die Uhr geht (zehn Minuten) nach** this watch is (ten minutes) slow
nachher ADV afterward(s)
Nachhilfe F (private) tutoring
nachholen V/T catch up with; (*Versäumtes*) make up for
nachkommen V/I follow; **einer Verpflichtung ~** fulfill an obligation
nachlassen **1** V/T (*Summe*) take off **2** V/I decrease, ease off; (*schlechter werden*) deteriorate **nachlässig** ADJ negligent, careless
nachlaufen V/I run after, chase (*j-m* sb)
nachmachen V/T imitate, copy (*j-m etw* sth from sb); (*fälschen*) counterfeit
Nachmittag M afternoon; **heute ~** this afternoon; **am ~** in the afternoon **nachmittags** ADV in the afternoon; **um 3 Uhr ~** at 3 (o'clock) in the afternoon, at 3 p.m.
Nachnahme F cash on delivery; **per ~** COD
Nachname M last name
nachprüfen V/T check
nachrechnen V/T check
Nachricht F (piece of) news *sg*; (*Mitteilung*) message
 Nachrichten PL news *sg*
Nachsaison F off-season
nachschauen **1** V/I **j-m ~** gaze after sb **2** V/T (*prüfen*) check
nachschicken V/T forward
nachschlagen V/T look up
nachsehen V/T (*prüfen*) check
Nachspeise F dessert
nächste(r, s) ADJ next; (*nächstgelegen*) nearest
Nacht F night; **in der ~** during the night; (*bei Nacht*) at night
 Nachtdienst M night duty; **~ haben** (*Apotheke*) be open

all night **Nachtklub** M nightclub
Nachteil M disadvantage
Nachtflug M night flight **Nachthemd** N (*für Damen*) nightdress; (*für Herren*) nightshirt
Nachtisch M dessert
Nachtleben N nightlife
nachträglich ADV **~ alles Gute zum Geburtstag!** Happy belated birthday!
nachts ADV at night; **um 11 Uhr ~** at 11 (o'clock) at night, at 11 p.m.; **um 2 Uhr ~** at 2 (o'clock) in the morning, at 2 a.m. **Nachtschicht** F night shift **Nachttisch** M bedside table **Nachtzug** M night train
Nachweis M proof
Nachwirkung F after-effect
nachzahlen **1** VI pay extra **2** VT **20 Dollar ~** pay 20 dollars extra
nachzählen VT check
Nacken M (nape of the) neck
nackt ADJ naked; (*Tatsachen*) plain, bare **Nacktbadestrand** M nudist beach
Nadel F needle; (*Stecknadel*) pin
Nagel M nail **Nagelbürste** F nail brush **Nagelfeile** F nail file **Nagellack** M nail polish **Nagellackentferner** M nail polish remover **Nagelschere** F nail scissors *pl*
nah(e) **1** ADJ & ADV (*räumlich*) near(by); (*zeitlich*) near; (*Verwandte, Freunde*) close **2** PRÄP +*dat* near (to), close to **Nähe** F (*Umgebung*) vicinity; **in der ~** nearby; **in der ~ von** near to **nahegehen** VI **j-m ~** upset sb **naheliegen** VI be obvious
nähen VT & VI sew
nähere(r, s) ADJ (*Erklärung, Erkundigung*) more detailed; **die ~ Umgebung** the immediate area **Nähere(s)** N details *pl*
nähern VR approach
nahezu ADV virtually, almost
Nähmaschine F sewing machine
nahrhaft ADJ nourishing, nutritious **Nahrung** F food **Nahrungsmittel** N food
Naht F seam; MED stitches *pl*, suture; TECH join
Nahverkehr M local traffic
Nähzeug N sewing kit
naiv ADJ naive
Name M name
nämlich ADV that is to say, namely; (*denn*) since
Napf M bowl, dish
Narbe F scar
Narkose F anesthetic
naschen VT & VI nibble
Nase F nose **Nasenbluten** N nosebleed; **~ haben** have a nosebleed **Nasenloch** N nostril **Nasentropfen** PL nose drops *pl*
Nashorn N rhinoceros
nass ADJ wet **Nässe** F wetness

Nation F nation **national** ADJ national **Nationalfeiertag** M national holiday **Nationalhymne** F national anthem **Nationalität** F nationality **Nationalmannschaft** F national team **Nationalpark** M National Park **Nationalspieler(in)** M(F) international (player)

NATO F *abk* = North Atlantic Treaty Organization; NATO, Nato

Natur F nature **Naturkost** F health food **natürlich** **1** ADJ natural **2** ADV naturally; (*selbstverständlich*) of course **Naturpark** M nature reserve **Naturschutz** M conservation **Naturschutzgebiet** N nature reserve **Naturwissenschaft** F (natural) science **Naturwissenschaftler(in)** M(F) scientist

Navi N *abk* = Navigationssystem *umg* AUTO GPS **Navigationssystem** N AUTO navigation system

n. Chr. *abk* = nach Christus; A.D.

Nebel M fog, mist **nebelig** ADJ foggy, misty **Nebelscheinwerfer** M fog light **Nebelschlussleuchte** F AUTO rear fog light

neben PRÄP +*akk od dat* next to; (*außer*) apart from, besides **nebenan** ADV next door **nebenbei** ADV at the same time; (*außerdem*) additionally; (*beiläufig*) incidentally **nebeneinander** ADV side by side **Nebenfach** N minor

nebenher ADV (*zusätzlich*) besides; (*gleichzeitig*) at the same time; (*daneben*) alongside

Nebenkosten PL extra charges *pl*, extras *pl* **nebensächlich** ADJ minor **Nebensaison** F off-season **Nebenstraße** F side street **Nebenwirkung** F side effect

neblig ADJ foggy, misty

necken V/T tease

Neffe M nephew

negativ ADJ negative **Negativ** N FOTO negative

nehmen V/T take; **den Bus ~** take the bus; **j-n/etw ernst ~** take sb/sth seriously

neidisch ADJ envious

neigen V/I **zu etw ~** tend toward(s) sth **Neigung** F (*des Geländes*) slope; (*Tendenz*) inclination; (*Vorliebe*) liking

nein ADV no

Nektarine F nectarine

Nelke F carnation; (*Gewürz*) clove

nennen V/T name; (*mit Namen*) call

Nerv M nerve; **j-m auf die ~en gehen** get on sb's nerves **nerven** V/T **j-n ~** *umg* get on sb's nerves **Nervenzusammenbruch** M nervous breakdown **nervös** ADJ nervous

Nest N nest; *pej* (*Ort*) dump

nett ADJ nice; (*freundlich*) kind; **sei so ~ und ...** do me a favor and ...
netto ADV net
Netz N net; (*System*) network; (*Stromnetz*) power supply **Netzanschluss** M power supply connection **Netzwerk** N IT network
neu ADJ new; (*Sprache, Geschichte*) modern; **die ~esten Nachrichten** the latest news **Neubau** M new building **neuerdings** ADV recently **Neuerung** F innovation; (*Reform*) reform
Neugier F curiosity **neugierig** ADJ curious (*auf +akk* about); **ich bin ~, ob ...** I wonder whether (*od* if) ...
Neuheit F novelty **Neuigkeit** F news *sg* **Neujahr** N New Year; **Prosit ~!** Happy New Year! **neulich** ADV recently, the other day
neun NUM nine **neunhundert** NUM nine hundred **neunmal** ADV nine times **neunte(r, s)** ADJ ninth; → dritte **Neuntel** N ninth **neunzehn** NUM nineteen **neunzehnte(r, s)** ADJ nineteenth; → dritte **neunzig** NUM ninety **Neunzigerjahre** PL nineties *pl* **neunzigste(r, s)** ADJ ninetieth
Neurologe M, **Neurologin** F neurologist **neurotisch** ADJ neurotic
Neuseeland N New Zealand
Neustart M IT restart, reboot
neutral ADJ neutral
neuwertig ADJ nearly new
nicht **1** ADV not; **er kommt ~** (*überhaupt nicht*) he doesn't come; (*diesmal*) he isn't coming; **sie wohnt ~ mehr hier** she doesn't live here any more; **gar ~** not at all; **ich kenne ihn auch ~** I don't know him either; **noch ~** not yet; **~ berühren!** do not touch **2** PRÄF non-
Nichte F niece
Nichtraucher(in) M(F) non-smoker **Nichtraucherzone** F non-smoking area
nichts INDEF PR nothing; **ich habe ~ gesagt** I didn't say anything; **macht ~** never mind
Nichtschwimmer(in) M(F) non-swimmer
nichtssagend ADJ meaningless
nicken V/I nod
Nickerchen N nap
nie ADV never; **~ wieder** (*od* **mehr**) never again; **fast ~** hardly ever
nieder **1** ADJ (*niedrig*) low; (*gering*) inferior **2** ADV down **niedergeschlagen** ADJ depressed **Niederlage** F defeat
Niederlande PL Netherlands *pl* **Niederländer(in)** M(F) Dutchman/Dutchwoman **niederländisch** ADJ Dutch **Niederländisch** N Dutch

Niederlassung F branch **Niederschlag** M METEO precipitation; (*Regen*) rainfall **niedlich** ADJ sweet, cute **niedrig** ADJ low **niemals** ADV never **niemand** INDEF PR nobody, no one; **ich habe ~en gesehen** I haven't seen anyone; **~ von ihnen** none of them **Niere** F kidney **Nierensteine** PL kidney stones *pl* **nieseln** V/I UNPERS drizzle **Nieselregen** M drizzle **niesen** V/I sneeze **Niete** F (*Los*) blank; *pej* (*Mensch*) failure; TECH rivet **Nikotin** N nicotine **Nilpferd** N hippopotamus **nippen** V/I sip; **an etw ~** sip sth **nirgends** ADV nowhere **Nische** F niche **Niveau** N level; **sie hat ~** she's got class **nobel** ADJ (*großzügig*) generous; *umg* (*luxuriös*) classy **noch** 1 ADV still; (*außerdem*) else; **wer kommt ~?** who else is coming?; **~ nie** never; **~ nicht** not yet; **immer ~** still; **~ einmal** (once) again; **~ am selben Tag** that (very) same day; **~ besser/mehr/jetzt** even better/more/now; **wie heißt sie ~?** what's her name again?; **~ ein Bier, bitte** another beer, please 2 KONJ nor **nochmal(s)** ADV again, once more

Nominativ M nominative (case) **Nonne** F nun **Nonstop-Flug** M nonstop flight, direct flight **Nord** M north **Nordamerika** N North America **Norddeutschland** N Northern Germany **Norden** M north **Nordeuropa** N Northern Europe **Nordic Walking** N SPORT Nordic Walking **nördlich** ADJ northern; (*Kurs, Richtung*) northerly **Nordost(en)** M northeast **Nordpol** M North Pole **nordwärts** ADV north, northward(s) **Nordwest(en)** M northwest **Nordwind** M north wind **nörgeln** V/I grumble **Norm** F norm; (*Größenvorschrift*) standard **normal** ADJ normal **normalerweise** ADV normally **Norwegen** N Norway **Not** F need; (*Armut*) poverty; (*Elend*) hardship; (*Bedrängnis*) trouble; **zur ~** if necessary; (*gerade noch*) just about **Notar(in)** M(F) notary public **Notarzt** M, **Notärztin** F emergency doctor **Notarztwagen** M emergency doctor's car **Notaufnahme** F ER, emergency room **Notausgang** M emergency exit **Notbremse** F emergency brake **Notdienst** M after-hours service **notdürftig** ADJ scanty;

(*behelfsmäßig*) makeshift
Note F (*in Schule*) grade; MUS note
Notebook N IT notebook
Notfall M emergency **notfalls** ADV if necessary
notieren V/T note down
nötig ADJ necessary; **etw ~ haben** need sth
Notiz F note **Notizblock** M notepad **Notizbuch** N notebook
notlanden V/I make a forced (*od* emergency) landing **Notlandung** F emergency landing **Notruf** M emergency call **Notrufnummer** F emergency number **Notrufsäule** F emergency (tele)phone
notwendig ADJ necessary
Nougat M *od* N nougat
November M November; → Juni
Nr. *abk* = Nummer; No., no.
Nu M **im ~** in no time
nüchtern ADJ sober; (*Magen*) empty
Nudel F noodle; **~n** *pl* (*italienische*) pasta *sg*
null NUM zero; **~ Uhr** midnight **Null** F zero; *pej* (*Mensch*) dead loss **Nulltarif** M **zum ~** free of charge
Nummer F number **nummerieren** V/T number **Nummernschild** N AUTO license plate
nun 1 ADV now; **von ~ an** from now on 2 INT well; **~ gut!** all right then; **es ist ~ mal so** that's the way it is
nur ADV only; **nicht ~ ..., sondern auch ...** not only ..., but also ...
Nürnberg N Nuremberg
Nuss F nut **Nussknacker** M nutcracker
Nutte F *umg* hooker
nutzen, nützen 1 V/T use (*zu etw* for sth); **was nützt es?** what use is it? 2 V/I be of use; **das nützt nicht viel** that doesn't help much **Nutzen** M usefulness; (*Gewinn*) profit **nützlich** ADJ useful
Nylon N nylon

Oase F oasis
ob KONJ if, whether; **so als ~** as if; **und ~!** you bet
obdachlos ADJ homeless
oben ADV (*am oberen Ende*) at the top; (*obenauf*) on (the) top; (*im Haus*) upstairs; (*in einem Text*) above; **da ~** up there; **von ~ bis unten** from top to bottom; **siehe ~** see above
Ober M waiter
obere(r, s) ADJ upper, top
Oberfläche F surface **oberflächlich** ADJ superficial

Obergeschoss N upper floor
oberhalb ADV & PRÄP *+gen* above
Oberkörper M upper body
Oberlippe F upper lip
Oberschenkel M thigh
oberste(r, s) ADJ very top, topmost
Oberteil N top **Oberweite** F bust/chest measurement
Objekt N object
objektiv ADJ objective
Objektiv N lens
obligatorisch ADJ compulsory, obligatory
Observatorium N observatory
Obst N fruit **Obstkuchen** M fruit tart **Obstsalat** M fruit salad
obwohl KONJ although
öd(e) ADJ waste; *fig* dull
oder KONJ or; **~ aber** or else; **er kommt doch, ~?** he's coming, isn't he?
Ofen M oven; (*Heizofen*) heater; (*Kohleofen, Herd*) stove
offen 1 ADJ open; (*aufrichtig*) frank; (*Stelle*) vacant 2 ADV frankly; **~ gesagt** to be honest
offenbar ADJ obvious **offensichtlich** ADJ evident, obvious
öffentlich ADJ public **Öffentlichkeit** F (*Leute*) public
offiziell ADJ official
offline ADV IT offline
öffnen V/T & V/R open **Öffner** M opener **Öffnung** F opening **Öffnungszeiten** PL opening times *pl*
oft ADV often; **schon ~** many times **öfter** ADV more often (*od* frequently) **öfters** ADV often, frequently
ohne KONJ & PRÄP *+akk* without; **~ weiteres** without a second thought; (*sofort*) immediately; **~ mich** count me out
Ohnmacht F PL unconsciousness; **in ~ fallen** faint **ohnmächtig** ADJ unconscious; **sie ist ~** she has fainted
Ohr N ear; (*Gehör*) hearing
Öhr N eye
Ohrenschmerzen PL earache *sg* **Ohrfeige** F slap (in the face) **Ohrläppchen** N earlobe **Ohrringe** PL earrings *pl*
oje INT oh dear
okay INT OK, okay
Ökoladen M health food store **ökologisch** ADJ ecological; **~e Landwirtschaft** organic farming
ökonomisch ADJ economic; (*sparsam*) economical
Ökosystem N ecosystem
Oktober M October; → **Juni**
Öl N oil **ölen** V/T oil; TECH lubricate **Ölfilter** M oil filter **Ölgemälde** N oil painting **Ölheizung** F oil-fired central heating **ölig** ADJ oily
oliv ADJ olive-green **Olive** F olive **Olivenöl** N olive oil
Ölteppich M oil slick **Öl-**

wechsel M oil change
Olympiade F Olympic Games *pl* **olympisch** ADJ Olympic
Oma F, **Omi** F grandma
Omelett N, **Omelette** F omelette
Omnibus M bus
Onkel M uncle
online ADV IT online **Onlineshop** M online store
OP M *abk* = Operationssaal; operating room, OR
Opa M, **Opi** M grandpa
Oper F opera; (*Gebäude*) opera house
Operation F operation
operieren 1 V/I operate 2 V/T operate on
Opernhaus N opera house, opera **Opernsänger(in)** M(F) opera singer
Opfer N sacrifice; (*Mensch*) victim; **ein ~ bringen** make a sacrifice
Opposition F opposition
Optiker(in) M(F) optician
optimal ADJ optimal, optimum
optimistisch ADJ optimistic
oral ADJ oral **Oralverkehr** M oral sex
orange ADJ orange **Orange** F orange **Orangenmarmelade** F marmalade **Orangensaft** M orange juice
Orchester N orchestra
Orden M REL order; MIL decoration
ordentlich 1 ADJ (*anständig*) respectable; (*geordnet*) tidy, neat 2 ADV properly
ordinär ADJ common, vulgar; (*Witz*) dirty
ordnen V/T sort out **Ordner** M (*bei Veranstaltung*) steward; (*Aktenordner*) file; IT folder
Ordnung F order; (*Geordnetsein*) tidiness; **(geht) in ~!** (that's) all right
Oregano M oregano
Organ N organ; (*Stimme*) voice
Organisation F organization
organisieren 1 V/T organize; *umg* (*beschaffen*) get hold of 2 V/R organize
Organismus M organism
Orgasmus M orgasm
Orgel F organ
orientalisch ADJ oriental
orientieren V/R get one's bearings **Orientierung** F orientation **Orientierungssinn** M sense of direction
original ADJ original; (*echt*) genuine **Original** N original
originell ADJ original; (*komisch*) witty
Orkan M hurricane
Ort M place; (*Dorf*) village
Orthopäde M, **Orthopädin** F orthopedist
örtlich ADJ local **Ortschaft** F village, small town **Ortsgespräch** N local call **Ortstarif** M local rate **Ortszeit** F local time
Ost M east **Ostdeutschland** N Eastern Germany **Osten** M east

Osterei N Easter egg **Osterhase** M Easter bunny **Ostermontag** M Easter Monday **Ostern** N Easter; **an** (*od* **zu**) ~ at Easter; **frohe** ~ Happy Easter
Österreich N Austria **Österreicher(in)** M(F) Austrian **österreichisch** ADJ Austrian
Ostersonntag M Easter Sunday
Osteuropa N Eastern Europe **Ostküste** F east coast **östlich** ADJ eastern; (*Kurs, Richtung*) easterly **Ostsee** F **die** ~ the Baltic (Sea) **Ostwind** M east(erly) wind
outen V/T out
oval ADJ oval
Ozean M ocean; **der Stille** ~ the Pacific (Ocean)
Ozon N ozone **Ozonschicht** F ozone layer

P

paar ADJ **ein** ~ a few; **ein** ~ **Mal** a few times; **ein** ~ **Äpfel** some apples
Paar N pair; (*Ehepaar*) couple
pachten V/T lease
Päckchen N package; (*Zigaretten*) pack; (*zum Verschicken*) small parcel, package **packen** V/T pack; (*fassen*) grasp, seize; *umg* (*schaffen*) manage; *fig* (*fesseln*) grip **Packpapier** N brown paper **Packung** F package; (*Zigaretten*) pack **Packungsbeilage** F package insert
Pädagoge M, **Pädagogin** F teacher **pädagogisch** ADJ educational
Paddel N paddle **Paddelboot** N canoe **paddeln** V/I paddle
Paket N package; (*Postpaket*) parcel; IT package **Paketbombe** F parcel bomb
Pakistan N Pakistan
Palast M palace
Palästina N Palestine **Palästinenser(in)** M(F) Palestinian
Palme F palm (tree) **Palmsonntag** M Palm Sunday
Pampelmuse F grapefruit
Panda(bär) M panda
Pandemie F pandemic
paniert ADJ GASTR breaded
Panik F panic
Panne F AUTO breakdown; (*Missgeschick*) slip **Pannendienst** M towing service
Panzer M MIL tank
Papa M dad(dy), pa
Papagei M parrot
Papaya F papaya
Papier N paper; **~e** *pl* (*Ausweispapiere*) papers *pl*; (*Dokumente, Urkunden*) papers *pl*, documents *pl* **Papierkorb** M waste basket; IT recycle bin **Papiertaschentuch** N (pa-

per) tissue **Papiertonne** F paper recycling container
Pappbecher M paper cup **Pappe** F cardboard **Pappkarton** M cardboard box
Paprika M (*Gewürz*) paprika; (*Schote*) (bell) pepper
Papst M pope
Paradeiser M *österr* tomato
Paradies N paradise
Paragliding N paragliding
Paragraph M paragraph; JUR section
parallel ADJ parallel
Paranuss F Brazil nut
Parasit M parasite
parat ADJ ready; **etw ~ haben** have sth ready
Pärchen N couple
Parfüm N perfume
Park M park **Parkbank** F park bench
Parkdeck N parking level
parken V/T & V/I park
Parkett N parquet flooring; THEAT parquet
Parkhaus N parking garage
parkinsonsche Krankheit F Parkinson's disease
Parkkralle F AUTO (Denver) boot **Parklicht** N parking light **Parklücke** F parking space **Parkplatz** M (*für ein Auto*) parking space; (*für mehrere Autos*) parking lot **Parkscheibe** F parking disc **Parkscheinautomat** M pay point; (*Parkscheinausgabegerät*) ticket machine **Parkuhr** F parking meter **Parkverbot** N (*Stelle*) no-parking zone; **hier ist ~** you can't park here
Parlament N parliament
Partei F party
Parterre N first floor
Partitur F MUS score
Partizip N participle
Partner(in) M(F) partner **Partnerschaft** F partnership; **eingetragene ~** civil union **Partnerstadt** F twin town
Party F party **Partyservice** M catering service
Pass M pass; (*Ausweis*) passport
passabel ADJ reasonable
Passagier M passenger
Passamt N passport office **Passbild** N passport photo
passen V/I (*Größe*) fit; (*Farbe, Stil*) go (*zu* with); (*auf Frage*) pass; **passt (es) dir morgen?** does tomorrow suit you?; **das passt mir gut** that suits me fine **passend** ADJ suitable; (*zusammenpassend*) matching; (*angebracht*) fitting; (*Zeit*) convenient
passieren V/I happen
passiv ADJ passive
Passkontrolle F passport control
Passwort N password
Paste F paste
Pastete F (*warmes Gericht*) pie; (*ohne Teig*) pâté
Pastor(in) M(F) minister
Pate M godfather **Patenkind** N godchild

Patient(in) M(F) patient
Patin F godmother
Patrone F cartridge
patschnass ADJ soaking wet
pauschal ADJ (*Kosten*) inclusive; (*Urteil*) sweeping **Pauschale** F, **Pauschalgebühr** F flat rate (charge) **Pauschalpreis** M flat rate; (*für Hotel, Reise*) all-inclusive price **Pauschalreise** F package tour
Pause F break; THEAT interval; (*Kino etc*) intermission; (*Innehalten*) pause
Pavillon M pavilion
Pazifik M Pacific (Ocean)
PC M *abk* = Personal Computer, PC
PDF N *abk* = Portable Document Format; IT PDF, pdf **PDF-Datei** F IT PDF file, pdf file
Pech N *fig* bad luck; **~ haben** be unlucky; **~ gehabt!** tough (luck)
Pedal N pedal
Pediküre F pedicure
Peeling N (facial/body) scrub
peinlich ADJ (*unangenehm*) embarrassing, awkward; (*genau*) painstaking; **es war mir sehr ~** I was totally embarrassed
Peitsche F whip
Pelikan M pelican
Pellkartoffeln PL potatoes *pl* boiled in their skins
Pelz M fur
pendeln V/I (*Zug, Bus*) shuttle; (*Mensch*) commute **Pendelverkehr** M shuttle traffic; (*für Pendler*) commuter traffic **Pendler(in)** M(F) commuter
Penis M penis
Pension F (*Geld*) pension; (*Ruhestand*) retirement; (*für Gäste*) guesthouse, B&B **pensioniert** ADJ retired
Peperoni F chili
per PRÄP +*akk* by, per; (*pro*) per; (*bis*) by
perfekt ADJ perfect
Periode F period
Perle F *a. fig* pearl
perplex ADJ dumbfounded
Person F person; **ein Tisch für drei ~en** a table for three **Personal** N staff, personnel **Personalausweis** M identity card **Personalien** PL particulars *pl* **Personenschaden** M injury to persons **persönlich** **1** ADJ personal; (*auf Briefen*) private **2** ADV personally; (*selbst*) in person **Persönlichkeit** F personality
Perücke F wig
pervers ADJ perverted
pessimistisch ADJ pessimistic
Pest F plague
Pesto N *od* M GASTR pesto
Petersilie F parsley
Petroleum N kerosene
Pfad M path **Pfadfinder** M boy scout **Pfadfinderin** F girl scout
Pfahl M post, stake
Pfand N security; (*Flaschen-*

pfand) deposit; (*im Spiel*) forfeit **Pfandflasche** F returnable bottle
Pfanne F (frying) pan, skillet
Pfannkuchen M pancake
Pfarrei F parish **Pfarrer(in)** M(F) priest
Pfau M peacock
Pfeffer M pepper **Pfefferkuchen** M gingerbread **Pfefferminze** F peppermint **Pfeffermühle** F pepper mill **Pfefferstreuer** M pepperbox
Pfeife F whistle; (*für Tabak, von Orgel*) pipe **pfeifen** VT & VI whistle
Pfeil M arrow
Pferd N horse **Pferdeschwanz** M (*Frisur*) ponytail **Pferdestall** M stable
Pfifferling M chanterelle
Pfingsten N Pentecost
Pfirsich M peach
Pflanze F plant **pflanzen** VT plant **Pflanzenfett** N vegetable fat
Pflaster N (*für Wunde*) Band Aid®; (*Straßenpflaster*) pavement
Pflaume F plum
Pflege F care; (*Krankenpflege*) nursing; (*von Autos, Maschinen*) maintenance **pflegebedürftig** ADJ in need of care **pflegeleicht** ADJ easy-care; *fig* easy to handle **pflegen** VT look after; (*Kranke*) nurse; (*Beziehungen*) foster; (*Fingernägel, Gesicht*) take care of; (*Daten*) maintain **Pflegepersonal** N nursing staff **Pflegeversicherung** F long-term care insurance
Pflicht F duty **pflichtbewusst** ADJ conscientious **Pflichtfach** N (*Schule*) compulsory subject
pflücken VT pick
Pforte F gate **Pförtner(in)** M(F) porter
Pfosten M post
Pfote F paw
pfui INT ugh
Pfund N pound
Pfütze F puddle
Phantasie F → Fantasie
phantastisch ADJ → fantastisch
Phase F phase
Philippinen PL Philippines *pl*
Philosophie F philosophy
pH-neutral ADJ pH-balanced
Photo N → Foto
pH-Wert M pH-value
Physik F physics *sg*
physisch ADJ physical
Pianist(in) M(F) pianist
Pickel M pimple; (*Werkzeug*) pickax(e)
Picknick N picnic; **ein ~ machen** have a picnic
piepsen VI chirp
piercen VT **sich die Nase ~ lassen** have one's nose pierced **Piercing** N (body) piercing
Pik N (*Karten*) spades *pl*

pikant ADJ spicy
Pilates N SPORT Pilates
Pilger(in) M(F) pilgrim **Pilgerfahrt** F pilgrimage
Pille F (*Antibabypille*) pill; **sie nimmt die ~** she's on the pill
Pilot(in) M(F) pilot
Pilz M (*essbar*) mushroom; (*giftig*) toadstool; MED fungus
PIN F PIN (number)
pingelig ADJ *umg* fussy
Pinguin M penguin
Pinie F pine **Pinienkern** M pine nut
pink ADJ shocking pink
pinkeln V/I *umg* pee
Pinsel M (paint)brush
Pinzette F tweezers *pl*
Pirat(in) M(F) pirate
Pistazie F pistachio
Piste F (*Ski*) piste; FLUG runway
Pistole F pistol
Pixel N IT pixel
Pizza F pizza **Pizzaservice** M pizza delivery service **Pizzeria** F pizzeria
Pkw M *abk* = Personenkraftwagen; car
Plakat N poster
Plan M plan; (*Karte*) map **planen** V/T plan
Planet M planet
planmäßig ADJ scheduled
Plan(t)schbecken N wading pool **plan(t)schen** V/I splash around
Planung F planning
Plastik **1** F sculpture **2** N (*Kunststoff*) plastic **Plastikfolie** F plastic film; (*Frischhaltefolie*) plastic wrap **Plastiktüte** F plastic bag
Platin N platinum
platt ADJ flat; *umg* (*überrascht*) flabbergasted; *fig* (*geistlos*) flat, boring
Platte F FOTO, TECH, GASTR plate; (*Steinplatte*) flag; (*Schallplatte*) record **Plattenspieler** M record player
Plattform F platform **Plattfuß** M flat foot; (*Reifen*) flat (tire)
Platz M place; (*Sitzplatz*) seat; (*freier Raum*) space, room; (*in Stadt*) square; (*Sportplatz*) playing field; **nehmen Sie ~** please sit down, take a seat; **ist dieser ~ frei?** is this seat taken?
Plätzchen N spot; (*Gebäck*) cookie
platzen V/I burst; (*Bombe*) explode
Platzkarte F seat reservation **Platzreservierung** F seat reservation **Platzverweis** M SPORT **er erhielt einen ~** he was ejected **Platzwunde** F laceration, cut
plaudern V/I chat, talk
pleite ADJ *umg* broke **Pleite** F (*Bankrott*) bankruptcy; *umg* (*Reinfall*) flop
Plombe F lead seal; (*Zahnplombe*) filling **plombieren** V/T (*Zahn*) fill
plötzlich **1** ADJ sudden **2** ADV suddenly, all at once

Plural M plural
plus ADV plus; **fünf ~ sieben ist zwölf** five plus seven is twelve; **zehn Grad ~** ten degrees above zero **Plus** N plus; FIN profit; *(Vorteil)* advantage
Po M *umg* butt
Podcast M IT podcast
poetisch ADJ poetic
Pointe F punch line
Pokal M goblet; SPORT cup
pökeln V/T pickle
Pol M pole
Pole M Pole **Polen** N Poland
Police F (insurance) policy
polieren V/T polish
Polin F Pole, Polish woman
Politik F politics *sg*; *(eine bestimmte)* policy **Politiker(in)** M(F) politician **politisch** ADJ political
Politur F polish
Polizei F police *pl* **Polizeibeamte(r)** M, **Polizeibeamtin** F police officer **Polizeirevier** N, **Polizeiwache** F police station **Polizist(in)** M(F) policeman/-woman
Pollen M pollen **Pollenflug** M pollen count
polnisch ADJ Polish **Polnisch** N Polish
Polterabend M *party prior to a wedding at which old cups, plates etc. are smashed to bring good luck*
Polyester M polyester
Polypen PL MED adenoids *pl*
Pommes frites PL French fries *pl*
Pony **1** M *(Frisur)* bangs *pl* **2** N *(Pferd)* pony
Popmusik F pop (music)
poppen *umg* **1** V/I *(Sex haben)* do it **2** V/T screw
populär ADJ popular
Pornografie F pornography
Porree M leeks *pl*; **eine Stange ~** a leek
Portemonnaie N wallet
Portion F portion, helping
Porto N postage
Portrait, **Porträt** N portrait
Portugal N Portugal **Portugiese** M Portuguese **Portugiesin** F Portuguese **portugiesisch** ADJ Portuguese **Portugiesisch** N Portuguese
Porzellan N china
Position F position
positiv ADJ positive
Post® F post office; *(Briefe)* mail **Postamt** N post office **Postbote** M, **Postbotin** F mailman/-woman
Posten M post, position
Poster N poster
Postfach N post-office box, PO box **Postkarte** F postcard
Postleitzahl F zip code
Poststempel M postmark
Potenz F MATH power; *(eines Mannes)* potency
PR F *abk* = Public Relations; PR
prächtig ADJ splendid
prahlen V/I boast, brag
Praktikant(in) M(F) trainee
Praktikum N practical train-

ing **praktisch** ADJ practical; **~er Arzt** general (*od* family) practitioner
Praline F chocolate
Prämie F (*bei Versicherung*) premium; (*Belohnung*) reward; (*von Arbeitgeber*) bonus
Präservativ N condom
Präsident(in) M(F) president
Praxis F practice; (*Behandlungsraum*) doctor's office; (*von Anwalt*) office
präzise ADJ precise, exact
predigen V/T & V/I preach **Predigt** F sermon
Preis M (*zu zahlen*) price; (*bei Sieg*) prize **Preisausschreiben** N competition
Preiselbeere F cranberry
preisgünstig ADJ inexpensive **Preisliste** F price list **Preisschild** N price tag **Preisträger(in)** M(F) prizewinner **preiswert** ADJ inexpensive
Prellung F bruise
Premiere F premiere, first night
Prepaidhandy N prepaid cellphone **Prepaidkarte** F prepaid card
Presse F press
pressen V/T press
prickeln V/I tingle
Priester(in) M(F) priest/(woman) priest
primitiv ADJ primitive
Prinz M prince **Prinzessin** F princess
Prinzip N principle; **im ~** basically; **aus ~** on principle
privat ADJ private **Privatfernsehen** N commercial television **Privatgrundstück** N private property **privatisieren** V/T privatize
pro PRÄP *+akk* per; **5 Euro ~ Stück/Person** 5 euros each/per person **Pro** N pro
Probe F test; (*Teststück*) sample; THEAT rehearsal **Probefahrt** F test drive; **eine ~ machen** go for a test drive **Probezeit** F trial period **probieren** V/T & V/I try; (*Wein, Speise*) taste, sample
Problem N problem
Produkt N product **Produktion** F production; (*produzierte Menge*) output **produzieren** V/T produce
Professor(in) M(F) professor
Profi M pro
Profil N profile; (*von Reifen, Schuhsohle*) tread
Profit M profit **profitieren** V/I profit (*von* from)
Prognose F prediction; (*Wetter*) forecast
Programm N program; TV channel **Programmheft** N program **programmieren** V/T program **Programmierer(in)** M(F) programmer
Projekt N project
Projektor M projector
Promille N (blood) alcohol level; **0,8 ~** 0.08 percent **Promillegrenze** F legal alcohol

limit
prominent ADJ prominent **Prominenz** F VIPs *pl*, prominent figures *pl*; *umg* (*Stars*) the glitterati *pl*
Propeller M propeller
prosit INT cheers
Prospekt M leaflet, brochure
prost INT cheers
Prostituierte(r) M/F(M) prostitute
Protest M protest
Protestant(in) M(F) Protestant **protestantisch** ADJ Protestant
protestieren V/I protest (*gegen* against)
Prothese F artificial arm/leg; (*Gebiss*) dentures *pl*
Protokoll N (*bei Sitzung*) minutes *pl*; IT protocol; (*bei Polizei*) statement
protzen V/I show off **protzig** ADJ flashy
Proviant M provisions *pl*
Provider M IT (service) provider
Provinz F province
Provision F WIRTSCH commission
provisorisch ADJ provisional
provozieren V/T provoke
Prozent N percent
Prozess M (*Vorgang*) process; JUR trial; (*Rechtsfall*) (court) case **prozessieren** V/I go to court (*mit* against)
Prozession F procession
Prozessor M IT processor
prüde ADJ prudish
prüfen V/T test; (*nachprüfen*) check **Prüfung** F (*Schule*) exam; (*Überprüfung*) check; **eine ~ machen** (*Schule*) take an exam
Prügelei F fight **prügeln** **1** V/T beat **2** V/R fight
PS **1** *abk* = Pferdestärke; hp **2** *abk* = Postskript(um); PS
Pseudonym N pseudonym
Psychiater(in) M(F) psychiatrist **psychisch** ADJ psychological; (*Krankheit*) mental **Psychologe** M, **Psychologin** F psychologist **Psychologie** F psychology **psychosomatisch** ADJ psychosomatic **Psychotherapie** F psychotherapy
Pubertät F puberty
Publikum N audience; SPORT crowd
Pudding M pudding
Puder M powder **Puderzucker** M powdered sugar
Pulli M, **Pullover** M sweater, pullover
Puls M pulse
Pulver N powder **Pulverkaffee** M instant coffee **Pulverschnee** M powder snow
Pumpe F pump **pumpen** V/T pump; *umg* (*verleihen*) lend; *umg* (*sich ausleihen*) borrow
Punkt M point; (*bei Muster*) dot; (*Satzzeichen*) period; **~ zwei Uhr** at two o'clock sharp
pünktlich ADJ punctual, on

time **Pünktlichkeit** F punctuality
Punsch M punch
Pupille F pupil
Puppe F doll
pur ADJ pure; (*völlig*) sheer; (*Whisky*) straight
Püree N puree; (*Kartoffelpüree*) mashed potatoes *pl*
Puste F *umg* breath; **außer ~ sein** be out of breath **pusten** V/I blow; (*keuchen*) puff
Pute F turkey
Putz M (*Mörtel*) plaster
putzen V/T clean; **sich die Nase ~** blow one's nose; **sich die Zähne ~** brush one's teeth **Putzfrau** F cleaner **Putzlappen** M cloth **Putzmittel** N cleanser, cleaner
Puzzle N jigsaw (puzzle)
Pyjama M pajamas *pl*
Pyramide F pyramid

Quadrat N square **quadratisch** ADJ square **Quadratmeter** M square meter
quaken V/I (*Frosch*) croak; (*Ente*) quack
Qual F pain, agony; (*seelisch*) anguish **quälen** **1** V/T torment **2** V/R struggle; (*geistig*) torment oneself **Quälerei** F torture, torment
qualifizieren V/T & V/R qualify; (*einstufen*) label
Qualität F quality
Qualle F jellyfish
Qualm M thick smoke **qualmen** V/T & V/I smoke
Quantität F quantity
Quarantäne F quarantine
Quark M quark (cheese)
Quartett N quartet
Quartier N accommodation, accommodations *pl*
quasi ADV more or less
Quatsch M *umg* nonsense
quatschen V/I *umg* chat
Quecksilber N mercury
Quelle F spring; (*eines Flusses*) source
quer ADV crossways, diagonally; (*rechtwinklig*) at right angles **Querschnitt** M cross section **querschnittsgelähmt** ADJ paraplegic **Querstraße** F side street
quetschen V/T squash, crush; MED bruise **Quetschung** F bruise
quietschen V/I squeal; (*Tür, Bett*) squeak; (*Bremsen*) screech
quitt ADJ square, even
Quittung F receipt
Quiz N quiz
Quote F rate; WIRTSCH quota

R

Rabatt M discount
Rabbi M, **Rabbiner** M rabbi
Rache F revenge, vengeance
Rachen M throat
rächen 1 V/T avenge 2 V/R take (one's) revenge (*an +dat* on)
Rad N wheel; (*Fahrrad*) bike; ~ **fahren** cycle; **mit dem ~ fahren** go by bike
Radar M *od* N radar **Radarfalle** F speed trap **Radarkontrolle** F radar speed check
radeln V/I *umg* cycle **Radfahrer(in)** M(F) cyclist **Radfahrweg** M bike path, bikeway
radieren V/T erase **Radiergummi** M eraser
Radieschen N radish
radikal ADJ radical
Radio N radio; **im ~** on the radio
radioaktiv ADJ radioactive
Radiologe M, **Radiologin** F radiologist
Radiowecker M radio alarm (clock)
Radkappe F AUTO hub cap
Radler(in) M(F) cyclist **Radlerhose** F cycling shorts *pl*
Radtour F cycling tour **Radweg** M bike path, bikeway
raffiniert ADJ crafty, cunning; (*Zucker*) refined
Rafting N white-water rafting
Rahm M cream
rahmen V/T frame **Rahmen** M frame
Rakete F rocket
rammen V/T ram
Rampe F ramp
Ramsch M junk
ran *umg kontr von* **heran**
Rand M edge; (*von Brille, Tasse etc*) rim; (*auf Papier*) margin; (*Schmutzrand, unter Augen*) ring; *fig* verge, brink
randalieren V/I (go on the) rampage
Rang M rank; (*in Wettbewerb*) place; THEAT balcony
ranzig ADJ rancid
rar ADJ rare, scarce
rasant ADJ quick, rapid
rasch ADJ quick
rascheln V/I rustle
rasen V/I (*sich schnell bewegen*) race; (*toben*) rave; **gegen einen Baum ~** crash into a tree
Rasen M lawn
rasend ADJ (*vor Wut*) furious
Rasenmäher M lawnmower
Rasierapparat M razor; (*elektrischer*) shaver **Rasiercreme** F shaving cream **rasieren** V/T & V/R shave **Rasierer** M shaver **Rasierklinge** F razor blade **Rasierpinsel** M shaving brush **Rasierschaum** M shaving foam **Rasierzeug** N shaving gear

Rasse F race; (*Tiere*) breed **Rassismus** M racism **Rassist(in)** M(F) racist **rassistisch** ADJ racist
Rast F rest, break; **~ machen** have a rest (*od* break) **Raststätte** F AUTO rest area
Rasur F shave
Rat M (piece of) advice; **um ~ fragen** ask for advice
Rate F installment; **etw auf ~n kaufen** buy sth on the installment plan
raten V/T & V/I guess; (*empfehlen*) advise (*j-m* sb)
Rathaus N town hall; (*in Großstadt*) city hall
Ration F ration
ratlos ADJ at a loss, helpless **ratsam** ADJ advisable
Rätsel N puzzle; (*Worträtsel*) riddle; **das ist mir ein ~** it's a mystery to me **rätselhaft** ADJ mysterious
Ratte F rat
rau ADJ rough, coarse; (*Wetter*) harsh
Raub M robbery; (*Beute*) loot **rauben** V/T steal; **j-m etw ~** rob sb of sth **Räuber(in)** M(F) robber **Raubkopie** F pirated copy **Raubtier** N predator **Raubüberfall** M mugging **Raubvogel** M bird of prey
Rauch M smoke; (*Abgase*) fumes *pl* **rauchen** V/T & V/I smoke **Raucher(in)** M(F) smoker
Räucherlachs M smoked salmon **räuchern** V/T smoke
rauchig ADJ smoky **Rauchmelder** M smoke detector **Rauchverbot** N smoking ban; **hier ist ~** it's no smoking here
rauf *umg kontr von* **herauf**
rauh ADJ → **rau**
Raum M space; (*Zimmer, Platz*) room; (*Gebiet*) area
räumen V/T clear; (*Wohnung, Platz*) vacate; (*wegbringen*) shift, move; (*in Schrank etc*) put away
Raumfähre F space shuttle **Raumfahrt** F space travel **Raumschiff** N spacecraft, spaceship **Raumstation** F space station
Raupe F caterpillar
raus *umg kontr von* **heraus, hinaus**; **~!** (get) out!
Rausch M intoxication; **einen ~ haben/kriegen** be/get drunk **Rauschgift** N drug **Rauschgiftsüchtige(r)** M/F(M) drug addict
rausfliegen V/I *umg* be kicked out
raushalten V/R *umg* **halt du dich da raus!** you (just) keep out of it
räuspern V/R clear one's throat
rausschmeißen V/T *umg* throw out
Razzia F raid
reagieren V/I react (*auf +akk* to) **Reaktion** F reaction

real ADJ real **realisieren** V/T (*merken*) realize; (*verwirklichen*) implement **realistisch** ADJ realistic **Realität** F reality
Realschule F ≈ junior high school
rebellieren V/I rebel
Rebhuhn N partridge
rechnen 1 V/T & V/I calculate; **~ mit** expect; (*bauen auf*) count on 2 V/R pay off, turn out to be profitable **Rechner** M calculator; (*Computer*) computer **Rechnung** F calculation(s); WIRTSCH check; **die ~, bitte!** can I have the check, please?; **das geht auf meine ~** this is on me
recht 1 ADJ (*richtig, passend*) right; **mir soll's ~ sein** it's alright by me; **mir ist es ~** I don't mind; **~ haben** be right; **j-m ~ geben** take sb's point, agree with sb 2 ADV really, quite; (*richtig*) right(ly); **ich weiß nicht ~** I don't really know; **es geschieht ihm ~** it serves him right
Recht N right; JUR law
Rechte F right-hand side; (*Hand*) right hand; POL right (wing) **rechte(r, s)** ADJ right; **auf der ~n Seite** on the right, on the right-hand side
Rechteck N rectangle **rechteckig** ADJ rectangular
rechtfertigen 1 V/T justify 2 V/R justify oneself
rechtlich ADJ legal **rechtmäßig** ADJ legal, lawful
rechts ADV on the right; **~ abbiegen** turn right; **~ von** to the right of; **~ oben** at the top right
Rechtsanwalt M, **Rechtsanwältin** F lawyer
Rechtschreibung F spelling
Rechtshänder(in) M(F) right-handed person, righty **rechtsherum** ADV to the right, clockwise **rechtsradikal** ADJ POL extreme right-wing **Rechtsverkehr** M driving on the right
rechtswidrig ADJ illegal
rechtwinklig ADJ right-angled
rechtzeitig 1 ADJ timely 2 ADV in time
recyceln V/T recycle **Recycling** N recycling
Redakteur(in) M(F) editor **Redaktion** F editing; (*Leute*) editorial staff; (*Büro*) editorial office(s)
Rede F speech; (*Gespräch*) talk; **eine ~ halten** make a speech **reden** 1 V/I talk, speak 2 V/T say; (*Unsinn etc*) talk **Redewendung** F idiom **Redner(in)** M(F) speaker
reduzieren V/T reduce
Referat N paper; **ein ~ halten** present a paper (*über +akk* on)
reflektieren V/T reflect
Reform F reform **Reformhaus** N health food store **reformieren** V/T reform
Regal N shelf; (*Möbelstück*)

shelves *pl*
Regel F rule; MED period **regelmäßig** ADJ regular **regeln** V/T regulate, control; (*Angelegenheit*) settle **Regelung** F regulation
Regen M rain **Regenbogen** M rainbow **Regenmantel** M raincoat **Regenschirm** M umbrella **Regenwald** M rain forest **Regenwurm** M earthworm
Regie F direction
regieren V/T & V/I govern, rule **Regierung** F government
Region F region **regional** ADJ regional
Regisseur(in) M(F) director
regnen V/I UNPERS rain **regnerisch** ADJ rainy
regulär ADJ regular **regulieren** V/T regulate, adjust
Reh N deer; (*Fleisch*) venison
Reibe F, **Reibeisen** N grater **reiben** V/T rub; GASTR grate **reibungslos** ADJ smooth
reich ADJ rich
Reich N empire; (*eines Königs*) kingdom
reichen **1** V/I reach; (*genügen*) be enough, be sufficient (*j-m* for sb) **2** V/T hold out; (*geben*) pass, hand; (*anbieten*) offer
reichhaltig ADJ ample, rich
reichlich ADJ (*Trinkgeld*) generous; (*Essen*) ample; **~ Zeit** plenty of time **Reichtum** M wealth
reif ADJ ripe; (*Mensch, Urteil*) mature **reifen** V/I mature; (*Obst*) ripen
Reifen M ring, hoop; (*von Auto*) tire **Reifendruck** M tire pressure **Reifenpanne** M puncture **Reifenwechsel** M tire change
Reihe F row; (*von Tagen etc*) *umg* (*Anzahl*) series *sg*; **der ~ nach** one after the other; **er ist an der ~** it's his turn **Reihenfolge** F order, sequence **Reihenhaus** N row house
rein **1** *umg kontr von* **herein, hinein** **2** ADJ pure; (*sauber*) clean
reinigen V/T clean **Reinigung** F cleaning; (*Geschäft*) (dry) cleaner **Reinigungsmittel** N cleanser, cleaner
reinlegen V/T **j-n ~** take sb for a ride
Reis M rice
Reise F journey; (*auf Schiff*) voyage **Reiseapotheke** F first-aid kit **Reisebüro** N travel agency **Reisebus** M bus **Reiseführer(in)** M(F) (*Mensch*) tour guide; (*Buch*) guide(book) **Reisegepäck** N baggage, luggage **Reisegesellschaft** F (*Veranstalter*) tour operator **Reisegruppe** F tourist party, group of tourists **Reiseleiter(in)** M(F) tour guide **reisen** V/I travel; **~ nach** go to **Reisende(r)** M/F(M) traveler **Reisepass** M passport **Reisescheck** M

traveler's check **Reisetasche** F carryall **Reiseveranstalter** M tour operator **Reiseversicherung** F travel insurance **Reiseziel** N destination
reißen V/T & V/I tear; (*ziehen*) pull, drag
Reißnagel M thumbtack **Reißverschluss** M zipper **Reißzwecke** F thumbtack
reiten V/T & V/I ride
Reiz M stimulus; (*angenehm*) charm; (*Verlockung*) attraction **reizen** V/T stimulate; (*unangenehm*) annoy; (*verlocken*) appeal to, attract **reizend** ADJ charming **Reizung** F irritation
Reklamation F complaint
Reklame F advertising; (*im Fernsehen*) commercial
reklamieren V/I complain (*wegen* about)
Rekord M record
relativ 1 ADJ relative 2 ADV relatively
relaxen V/I relax
Religion F religion **religiös** ADJ religious
rennen V/T & V/I run **Rennen** N running; (*Wettbewerb*) race **Rennrad** N racing bike
renommiert ADJ famous, noted (*wegen, für* for)
renovieren V/T renovate **Renovierung** F renovation
rentabel ADJ profitable
Rente F pension **Rentenversicherung** F pension (*od* retirement) plan
Rentier N reindeer
rentieren V/R pay, be profitable
Rentner(in) M(F) pensioner, senior (citizen)
Reparatur F repair **Reparaturwerkstatt** F repair shop; AUTO garage **reparieren** V/T repair
Reportage F report **Reporter(in)** M(F) reporter
Republik F republic
Reservat N nature reserve **Reserve** F reserve **Reservekanister** M spare can **Reserverad** N AUTO spare wheel
reservieren V/T reserve **Reservierung** F reservation
resignieren V/I give up **resigniert** ADJ resigned
Respekt M respect **respektieren** V/T respect
Rest M rest, remainder; (*Überreste*) remains *pl*
Restaurant N restaurant
restaurieren V/T restore
restlich ADJ remaining
Resultat N result
retten V/T save, rescue
Rettich M radish (*large white or red variety*)
Rettung F rescue; (*Hilfe*) help; (*Rettungsdienst*) ambulance service **Rettungsboot** N lifeboat **Rettungshubschrauber** M rescue helicopter **Rettungsring** M life preserver **Rettungswagen** M

ambulance
Reue F remorse; (*Bedauern*) regret
revanchieren V/R (*für Hilfe etc*) return the favor
Revolution F revolution
Rezept N GASTR recipe; MED prescription **rezeptfrei** ADJ non-prescription
Rezeption F (*im Hotel*) reception
rezeptpflichtig ADJ available only on prescription
Rhabarber M rhubarb
Rhein M Rhine
Rheuma N rheumatism
Rhythmus M rhythm
richten **1** V/T (*lenken*) direct (*auf +akk* to); (*Waffe, Kamera*) point (*auf +akk* at); (*Brief, Anfrage*) address (*an +akk* to) **2** V/R **sich ~ nach** (*Regel etc*) keep to; (*Mode, Beispiel*) follow; (*abhängen von*) depend on
Richter(in) M(F) judge
richtig **1** ADJ right, correct; (*echt*) proper **2** ADV *umg* (*sehr*) really **richtigstellen** V/T **etw ~** (*berichtigen*) correct sth
Richtlinie F guideline
Richtung F direction; (*Tendenz*) tendency
riechen V/T & V/I smell; **nach etw ~** smell of sth
Riegel M bolt; GASTR bar
Riese M giant **Riesengarnele** F king prawn **riesengroß** ADJ gigantic, huge **Riesenrad** N Ferris wheel **riesig** ADJ enormous, huge
Riff N reef
Rind N cow; (*Bulle*) bull; GASTR beef; **~er** *pl* cattle *pl*
Rinde F (*Baum*) bark; (*Käse*) rind; (*Brot*) crust
Rinderbraten M roast beef **Rindfleisch** N beef
Ring M ring; (*Straße*) beltway **Ringfinger** M ring finger **ringsherum** ADV all around
Rippe F rib
Risiko N risk; **auf eigenes ~** at one's own risk **riskant** ADJ risky **riskieren** V/T risk
Riss M tear; (*in Mauer, Tasse etc*) crack **rissig** ADJ cracked; (*Haut*) chapped
Ritter M knight
Rivale M, **Rivalin** F rival
Robbe F seal
Roboter M robot
robust ADJ robust
Rock M skirt
Rockmusik F rock (music)
rodeln V/I toboggan
Roggen M rye **Roggenbrot** N rye bread
roh ADJ raw; (*Mensch*) coarse, crude **Rohkost** F raw fruit and vegetables *pl*
Rohr N pipe **Röhre** F tube; (*Backröhre*) oven **Rohrzucker** M cane sugar
Rohstoff M raw material
Rolle F roll; THEAT role
rollen V/T & V/I roll
Roller M scooter
Rollkragenpullover M tur-

tleneck sweater **Rollladen** M, **Rollo** M (roller) shutters *pl* **Rollstuhl** M wheelchair **rollstuhlgerecht** ADJ suitable for wheelchairs **Rolltreppe** F escalator

Roman M novel

Romantik F romance **romantisch** ADJ romantic

römisch-katholisch ADJ Roman Catholic

röntgen V/T X-ray **Röntgenaufnahme** F, **Röntgenbild** N X-ray

rosa ADJ pink

Rose F rose

Rosenkohl M (Brussels) sprouts *pl*

Rosé(wein) M rosé (wine)

rosig ADJ rosy

Rosine F raisin

Rosmarin M rosemary

Rost M rust; (*zum Braten*) grill **Rostbratwurst** F grilled sausage **rosten** V/I rust **rösten** V/T roast, grill; (*Brot*) toast **rostfrei** ADJ rustproof; (*Stahl*) stainless **rostig** ADJ rusty

rot ADJ red; **~ werden** blush; **Rote Bete** beet; **bei Rot über die Ampel fahren** run a red light; **das Rote Kreuz** the Red Cross

Röteln PL German measles *sg*

rothaarig ADJ red-haired

rotieren V/I rotate

Rotkehlchen N robin **Rotkohl** M, **Rotkraut** N red cabbage **Rotlichtviertel** N red-light district **Rotwein** M red wine

Rouge N rouge

Route F route

Routine F experience; (*Trott*) routine

Rubbellos N scratch-off ticket **rubbeln** V/T rub

Rübe F turnip; **Gelbe ~** carrot; **Rote ~** beet

rüber *umg kontr von* **herüber, hinüber**

rückbestätigen V/T (*Flug etc*) reconfirm

rücken V/T & V/I move; **könntest du ein bisschen ~?** could you move over a bit?

Rücken M back **Rückenlehne** F back(rest) **Rückenmark** N spinal cord **Rückenschmerzen** PL backache *sg* **Rückenschwimmen** N backstroke **Rückenwind** M tailwind

Rückerstattung F refund **Rückfahrkarte** F round-trip ticket **Rückfahrt** F return journey **Rückfall** M relapse **Rückflug** M return flight **Rückgabe** F return **rückgängig** ADJ **etw ~ machen** cancel sth **Rückgrat** N spine, backbone **Rückkehr** F return **Rücklicht** N rear light **Rückreise** F return journey; **auf der ~** on the way back

Rucksack M backpack **Rucksacktourist(in)** M(F) backpacker

Rückschritt M step back **Rückseite** F back; **siehe ~** see overleaf
Rücksicht F consideration; **~ nehmen auf** show consideration for **rücksichtslos** ADJ inconsiderate; (*Fahren*) reckless **rücksichtsvoll** ADJ considerate
Rücksitz M back seat **Rückspiegel** M AUTO rear-view mirror **Rückvergütung** F refund **rückwärts** ADV backward(s), back **Rückwärtsgang** M AUTO reverse (gear) **Rückweg** M return journey, way back **Rückzahlung** F repayment
Ruder N oar; (*Steuer*) rudder **Ruderboot** N rowboat **rudern** V/T & V/I row
Ruf M call, cry; (*Ansehen*) reputation **rufen** V/T & V/I call; (*schreien*) cry **Rufnummer** F (tele)phone number
Ruhe F rest; (*Ungestörtheit*) peace, quiet; (*Gelassenheit, Stille*) calm; (*Schweigen*) silence; **lass mich in ~!** leave me alone! **ruhen** V/I rest **Ruhestand** M retirement; **im ~ sein** be retired **Ruhetag** M closing day; **montags ~ haben** be closed (on) Mondays
ruhig ADJ quiet; (*bewegungslos*) still; (*Hand*) steady; (*gelassen*) calm
Ruhm M fame, glory
Rührei N scrambled egg(s)
rühren **1** V/T move; (*umrühren*) stir **2** V/R move; (*sich bemerkbar machen*) say something **rührend** ADJ touching, moving
Ruine F ruin **ruinieren** V/T ruin
rülpsen V/I burp, belch
rum *umg kontr von* **herum**
Rum M rum
Rumäne M, **Rumänin** F Romanian **Rumänien** N Romania **rumänisch** ADJ Romanian **Rumänisch** N Romanian
Rummel M (*Trubel*) hustle and bustle; (*Jahrmarkt*) fair; (*Medienrummel*) hype **Rummelplatz** M fairground
rumoren V/I **es rumort in meinem Bauch/Kopf** my stomach is rumbling/my head is spinning
Rumpf M ANAT trunk; FLUG fuselage; SCHIFF hull
Rumpsteak N rump steak
rund **1** ADJ round **2** ADV (*etwa*) around; **~ um etw** around sth **Runde** F round; (*in Rennen*) lap **Rundfahrt** F tour (*durch* of) **Rundfunk** M (*Rundfunkanstalt*) broadcasting service; **im ~** on the radio **Rundgang** M tour (*durch* of); (*von Wächter*) round **Rundreise** F tour (*durch* of)
runter *umg kontr von* **herunter, hinunter** **runterscrollen** V/T IT scroll down
runzelig ADJ wrinkled **run-**

zeln V/T **die Stirn ~** frown
Russe M Russian
Rüssel M (*Elefant*) trunk; (*Schwein*) snout
Russin F Russian **russisch** ADJ Russian **Russisch** N Russian **Russland** N Russia
Rüstung F (*Ritterrüstung*) armor; (*Waffen*) armaments *pl*
Rutsch M **guten ~ (ins neue Jahr)!** Happy New Year! **Rutschbahn** F, **Rutsche** F slide **rutschen** V/I slide; (*ausrutschen*) slip **rutschig** ADJ slippery
rütteln V/T & V/I shake

S

s. *abk* = siehe; see **S.** *abk* = Seite; p.
Saal M hall; (*für Sitzungen*) room
sabotieren V/T sabotage
Sache F thing; (*Angelegenheit*) affair, business; (*Frage*) matter; **bei der ~ bleiben** keep to the point **sachkundig** ADJ competent **Sachlage** F situation **sachlich** ADJ (*objektiv*) objective; (*nüchtern*) matter-of-fact; (*inhaltlich*) factual **sächlich** ADJ LING neuter **Sachschaden** M material damage
sacht(e) ADV softly, gently
Sachverständige(r) M/F(M) expert
Sack M sack; *pej* (*Mensch*) bastard **Sackgasse** F dead end, cul-de-sac
Safe M safe
Safer Sex M safe sex
Saft M juice **saftig** ADJ juicy
Sage F legend
Säge F saw
sagen V/T & V/I say (*j-m* to sb), tell (*j-m* sb); **wie sagt man ... auf Englisch?** what's ... in English?
sägen V/T & V/I saw
Sahne F cream
Saison F season
Saite F string
Sakko N jacket
Salami F salami
Salat M salad; (*Kopfsalat*) lettuce **Salatbar** F salad bar **Salatschüssel** F salad bowl **Salatsoße** F salad dressing
Salbe F ointment
Salbei M sage
Salmonellenvergiftung F salmonella (poisoning)
Salto M somersault
Salz N salt **salzarm** ADJ low-salt **salzen** V/T salt **salzig** ADJ salty **Salzkartoffeln** PL boiled potatoes *pl* **Salzstreuer** M salt shaker **Salzwasser** N salt water
Samen M seed; (*Sperma*) sperm
sammeln V/T collect **Sammlung** F collection

Samstag M Saturday; → Mittwoch **samstags** ADV (on) Saturdays; → mittwochs
samt PRÄP *+dat* (along) with, together with
Samt M velvet
sämtliche(r, s) ADJ all (the)
Sand M sand
Sandale F sandal
sandig ADJ sandy **Sandkasten** M sandbox **Sandstrand** M sandy beach
sanft ADJ soft, gentle
Sänger(in) M(F) singer
sanieren V/T redevelop; (*Gebäude*) renovate; (*Betrieb*) restore to profitability
sanitär ADJ sanitary; **~e Anlagen** *pl* sanitation *sg*
Sanitäter(in) M(F) paramedic
Sardelle F anchovy
Sarg M coffin
Satellit M satellite **Satellitenfernsehen** N satellite TV **Satellitenschüssel** F *umg* satellite dish
satt ADJ full; (*Farbe*) rich, deep; **~ machen** be filling; **~ sein** (*gesättigt*) be full; **j-n/etw ~ sein** be fed up with sb/sth
Sattel M saddle
satthaben V/T **j-n/etw ~** (*nicht mehr mögen*) be fed up with sb/sth
Satz M LING sentence; MUS movement; (*Tennis*) set; (*Kaffee*) grounds *pl*; (*Sprung*) jump; WIRTSCH rate
Sau F sow; *pej* (*Mensch*) bastard
sauber ADJ clean; (*ironisch*) fine; **~ machen** clean **Sauberkeit** F cleanness; (*von Person*) cleanliness **säubern** V/T clean
saublöd ADJ *umg* really stupid, dumb
Sauce F sauce; (*zu Braten*) gravy
Saudi-Arabien N Saudi Arabia
sauer ADJ sour; CHEM acid; *umg* (*verärgert*) mad **Sauerkirsche** F sour cherry **Sauerrahm** M sour cream **Sauerstoff** M oxygen
saufen **1** V/T drink; *umg* (*Mensch*) knock back **2** V/I drink
saugen V/T & V/I suck; (*mit Staubsauger*) vacuum **Säugetier** N mammal **Säugling** M infant, baby
saugut ADJ *umg* awesome, wicked
Säule F column, pillar
Saum M hem; (*Naht*) seam
Sauna F sauna
Säure F acid
Saustall M pigsty **Sauwetter** N **was für ein ~** *umg* what lousy weather
Saxophon N saxophone
S-Bahn F commuter railroad
scannen V/T scan **Scanner** M scanner
schäbig ADJ shabby
Schach N chess; (*Stellung*) check **Schachbrett** N chess-

board **Schachfigur** F chess piece **schachmatt** ADJ checkmate
Schacht M shaft
Schachtel F box; (*von Zigaretten*) pack
schade INT what a pity
Schädel M skull **Schädelbruch** M fractured skull
schaden V/I damage, harm (*j-m* sb); **das schadet nichts** it won't do any harm **Schaden** M damage; (*Verletzung*) injury; (*Nachteil*) disadvantage; **einen ~ verursachen** cause damage **Schadenersatz** M compensation, damages *pl* **schadhaft** ADJ faulty; (*beschädigt*) damaged **schädigen** V/T damage; (*j-n*) do harm to, harm **schädlich** ADJ harmful (*für* to) **Schadstoff** M harmful substance **schadstoffarm** ADJ low-emission
Schaf N sheep
schaffen **1** V/T create; (*Platz*) make **2** V/T (*erreichen*) manage, do; (*erledigen*) finish; (*Prüfung*) pass; **j-m zu ~ machen** cause sb trouble
Schaffner(in) M(F) conductor
Schafskäse M sheep's (milk) cheese
schal ADJ (*Getränk*) flat
Schal M scarf
Schale F skin; (*abgeschält*) peel; (*Nuss, Muschel, Ei*) shell; (*Geschirr*) bowl, dish
schälen **1** V/T peel; (*Tomate, Mandel*) skin; (*Erbsen, Eier, Nüsse*) shell; (*Getreide*) husk **2** V/R peel
Schall M sound **Schalldämpfer** M AUTO muffler **Schallplatte** F record
schalten **1** V/T switch **2** V/I AUTO shift gear **Schalter** M (*auf Post®, Bank*) counter; (*an Gerät*) switch **Schalterhalle** F main hall **Schalthebel** M gear shift **Schaltjahr** N leap year **Schaltknüppel** M gear shift **Schaltung** F gear shift
Scham F shame; (*Schamgefühl*) modesty **schämen** V/R be ashamed
Schande F disgrace
Schar F (*von Vögeln*) flock; (*Menge*) crowd; **in ~en** in droves
scharf ADJ (*Messer, Kritik*) sharp; (*Essen*) hot; **auf etw ~ sein** *umg* be keen on sth
Schärfe F sharpness; (*Strenge*) rigor; FOTO focus
Scharlach M MED scarlet fever
Scharnier N hinge
Schaschlik M *od* N (shish) kebab
Schatten M shadow; **30 Grad im ~** 30 degrees in the shade **schattig** ADJ shady
Schatz M treasure; (*Mensch*) love
schätzen V/T (*abschätzen*) estimate; (*Gegenstand*) value; (*würdigen*) value, esteem; (*vermu-*

ten) reckon **Schätzung** F estimate; (*das Schätzen*) estimation; (*von Wertgegenstand*) valuation **schätzungsweise** ADV roughly, approximately

schauen V/I look; **ich schau mal, ob …** I'll go and have a look whether …; **schau, dass …** see (to it) that …

Schauer M (*Regen*) shower; (*Schreck*) shudder

Schaufel F shovel; **~ und Besen** dustpan and brush **schaufeln** V/T shovel

Schaufenster N store window

Schaukel F swing **schaukeln** V/I rock; (*mit Schaukel*) swing

Schaum M foam; (*Seifenschaum*) lather; (*Bierschaum*) froth **Schaumbad** N bubble bath **schäumen** V/I foam **Schaumfestiger** M styling mousse **Schaumgummi** M foam (rubber) **Schaumwein** M sparkling wine

Schauplatz M scene

Schauspiel N spectacle; THEAT play **Schauspieler(in)** M(F) actor/actress

Scheck M check **Scheckheft** N checkbook **Scheckkarte** F check card

Scheibe F disc; (*von Brot, Käse etc*) slice; (*Glasscheibe*) pane **Scheibenwischer** M AUTO windshield wiper

Scheide F ANAT vagina

scheiden V/T (*trennen*) separate; **sich ~ lassen** get a divorce; **sie hat sich von ihm ~ lassen** she divorced him **Scheidung** F divorce

Schein M light; (*Anschein*) appearance; (*Geld*) bill **scheinbar** ADJ apparent **scheinen** V/I (*Sonne*) shine; (*den Anschein haben*) seem **Scheinwerfer** M floodlight; THEAT spotlight; AUTO headlight

Scheiß- IN ZSSGN *vulg* damned **Scheiße** F *vulg* shit, crap **scheißegal** ADJ *vulg* **das ist mir ~** I don't give a damn **scheißen** V/I *vulg* shit

Scheitel M part

scheitern V/I fail (*an +dat* because of)

Schema N scheme, plan; (*Darstellung*) diagram

Schenkel M thigh

schenken V/T give; **er hat es mir geschenkt** he gave it to me (as a present)

Scherbe F broken piece, fragment

Schere F scissors *pl*; (*groß*) shears *pl*; **eine ~** a pair of scissors/shears

Scherz M joke

scheu ADJ shy **scheuen** **1** V/R **sich ~ vor** be afraid of, shrink from **2** V/T shun **3** V/I (*Pferd*) shy

scheuern V/T scrub

Scheune F barn

scheußlich ADJ dreadful

Schi M → **Ski**

Schicht F layer; (*in Gesellschaft*) class; (*in Fabrik etc*) shift **schick** ADJ stylish **schicken** 1 V/T send 2 V/R (*sich beeilen*) hurry up **Schicksal** N fate **Schiebedach** N AUTO sunroof **schieben** V/T & V/I push; **die Schuld auf j-n ~** put the blame on sb **Schiebetür** F sliding door **Schiedsrichter(in)** M(F) referee; (*Tennis, Baseball etc*) umpire **schief** 1 ADJ crooked 2 ADV crooked(ly) **schiefgehen** V/I *umg* (*misslingen*) go wrong **schielen** V/I squint **Schienbein** N shin **Schiene** F rail; MED splint **schießen** 1 V/T shoot; (*Ball*) kick; (*Tor*) score; (*Foto*) take 2 V/I shoot (*auf +akk* at) **Schiff** N ship; (*in Kirche*) nave **Schifffahrt** F shipping **Schiffsreise** F voyage **schikanieren** V/T harass; (*Schule*) bully **Schild** 1 M (*Schutz*) shield 2 N sign; **was steht auf dem ~?** what does the sign say? **Schilddrüse** F thyroid gland **schildern** V/T describe **Schildkröte** F tortoise; (*Wasserschildkröte*) turtle **Schimmel** M mold; (*Pferd*) white horse **schimmeln** V/I go moldy **schimpfen** 1 V/T tell off 2 V/I (*sich beklagen*) complain; **mit j-m ~** tell sb off **Schimpfwort** N swearword **Schinken** M ham **Schirm** M (*Regenschirm*) umbrella; (*Sonnenschirm*) sunshade **Schlacht** F battle **schlachten** V/T slaughter **Schlachter(in)** M(F) butcher **Schlaf** M sleep **Schlafanzug** M pajamas *pl* **Schlafcouch** F sofa bed **Schläfe** F temple **schlafen** V/I sleep; **schlaf gut!** sleep well; **hast du gut geschlafen?** did you sleep all right?; **er schläft noch** he's still asleep; **~ gehen** go to bed **schlaff** ADJ slack; (*kraftlos*) limp; (*erschöpft*) exhausted **Schlafgelegenheit** F place to sleep **Schlaflosigkeit** F sleeplessness **schläfrig** ADJ sleepy **Schlafsack** M sleeping bag **Schlaftablette** F sleeping pill **Schlafwagen** M sleeping car, sleeper **Schlafzimmer** N bedroom **Schlag** M blow; ELEK shock **Schlagader** F artery **Schlaganfall** M MED stroke **schlagartig** ADJ sudden **schlagen** 1 V/T hit; (*besiegen*) beat; (*Sahne*) whip 2 V/I (*Herz*) beat; (*Uhr*) strike; **mit dem Kopf gegen etw ~** bang one's head against sth 3 V/R fight **Schläger** M SPORT bat; (*Tennis*) racket; (*Golf*) (golf)

club; (*Hockey*) hockey stick; (*Mensch*) brawler **Schlägerei** F fight, brawl
schlagfertig ADJ quick-witted **Schlagloch** N pothole **Schlagsahne** F whipping cream; (*bereits geschlagen*) whipped cream **Schlagzeile** F headline **Schlagzeug** N drums *pl*; (*in Orchester*) percussion
Schlamm M mud
schlampig ADJ *umg* sloppy
Schlange F snake; (*von Menschen*) line; **~ stehen** line up, stand in line
schlank ADJ slim
schlapp ADJ limp
schlau ADJ clever, smart; (*raffiniert*) crafty, cunning
Schlauch M hose; (*in Reifen*) inner tube **Schlauchboot** N rubber dinghy
schlecht **1** ADJ bad; **mir ist ~** I feel sick; **die Milch ist ~** the milk has gone bad **2** ADV badly; **es geht ihm ~** he's having a hard time; (*gesundheitlich*) he's not feeling well; (*finanziell*) he's pretty hard up **schlechtmachen** V/T **j-n ~** (*herabsetzen*) run sb down
schleichen V/I creep
Schleier M veil
Schleife F IT, FLUG, ELEK loop; (*Band*) bow
Schleim M slime; MED mucus
schlendern V/I stroll
schleppen V/T drag; (*Auto, Schiff*) tow; (*tragen*) lug **Schlepplift** M ski tow
schleudern **1** V/T hurl; (*Wäsche*) spin **2** V/I AUTO skid
schlicht ADJ simple, plain
schlichten V/T (*Streit*) settle
schließen V/T & V/I & V/R close, shut; (*beenden*) close; (*Freundschaft, Ehe*) enter into; (*folgern*) infer (*aus* from) **Schließfach** N locker
schließlich ADV finally; (*schließlich doch*) after all
schlimm ADJ bad **schlimmer** ADJ worse **schlimmste(r, s)** ADJ worst **schlimmstenfalls** ADV at (the) worst
Schlips M tie
Schlitten M sled, toboggan; (*mit Pferden*) sleigh **Schlittenfahren** N tobogganing **Schlittschuh** M ice skate; **~ laufen** ice-skate
Schlitz M slit; (*für Münze*) slot; (*an Hose*) fly
Schloss N lock; (*Burg*) castle **Schlosser(in)** M(F) (*für Schlösser*) locksmith
Schlucht F gorge, ravine
schluchzen V/I sob
Schluckauf M hiccups *pl* **schlucken** V/T & V/I swallow
schlürfen V/T & V/I slurp
Schluss M end; (*Schlussfolgerung*) conclusion; **am ~** at the end; **mit j-m ~ machen** finish (*od* split up) with sb
Schlüssel M *a. fig* key **Schlüsselbein** N collarbone

Schlüsselbund M bunch of keys **Schlüsselloch** N keyhole
Schlussfolgerung F conclusion **Schlusslicht** N taillight **Schlussverkauf** M closeout sale
schmal ADJ narrow; (*Mensch, Buch etc*) slim
Schmalz N (*Schweineschmalz*) lard
schmecken V/T & V/I taste (*nach* of); **es schmeckt ihm** he likes it; **lass es dir ~!** enjoy your meal
Schmeichelei F flattery **schmeichelhaft** ADJ flattering **schmeicheln** V/I **j-m ~** flatter sb
schmeißen V/T *umg* chuck, throw
schmelzen V/T & V/I melt
Schmerz M pain; (*Trauer*) grief; **~en haben** be in pain; **~en im Rücken haben** have a pain in one's back **schmerzen** V/T & V/I hurt **Schmerzensgeld** N compensation **schmerzhaft, schmerzlich** ADJ painful **Schmerzmittel** N painkiller **schmerzstillend** ADJ painkilling **Schmerztablette** F painkiller
Schmetterling M butterfly
schmieden V/T forge; (*pläne*) make
schmieren 1 V/T smear; (*ölen*) lubricate, grease; (*bestechen*) bribe 2 V/T & V/I (*unsauber schreiben*) scrawl **Schmiergeld** N *umg* bribe **schmierig** ADJ greasy
Schminke F make-up
schminken V/R put one's make-up on
schmollen V/I sulk
Schmuck M jewelry; (*Verzierung*) decoration **schmücken** V/T decorate
schmuggeln V/T & V/I smuggle
schmunzeln V/I smile
schmusen V/I (kiss and) cuddle
Schmutz M dirt, filth
schmutzig ADJ dirty
Schnabel M beak, bill; (*Ausguss*) spout
Schnake F (*Stechmücke*) mosquito
Schnäppchen N *umg* bargain
schnappen 1 V/T (*fangen*) catch 2 V/I **nach Luft ~** gasp for breath **Schnappschuss** M FOTO snap(shot)
Schnaps M schnapps
schnarchen V/I snore
schnaufen V/I puff, pant
Schnauzbart M mustache
Schnauze F snout, muzzle; (*Ausguss*) spout; *umg* (*Mund*) trap; **die ~ voll haben** have had enough
schnäuzen V/R blow one's nose
Schnecke F snail
Schnee M snow **Schneeball** M snowball **Schneebrille** F snow goggles *pl* **Schneeflo-**

cke F snowflake **Schneegrenze** F snowline **Schneekette** F AUTO snow chain **Schneemann** M snowman **Schneepflug** M snowplow **Schneeregen** M sleet **Schneesturm** M snowstorm, blizzard **Schneetreiben** N driving snow **Schneewehe** F snowdrift

Schneide F edge; (*Klinge*) blade **schneiden** 1 V/T cut; **sich die Haare ~ lassen** have one's hair cut 2 V/R cut oneself **Schneider(in)** M(F) tailor; (*für Damenmode*) dressmaker **Schneidezahn** M incisor

schneien V/I UNPERS snow

schnell 1 ADJ quick, fast 2 ADV quickly, fast; **mach ~!** hurry up! **Schnelldienst** M express service **Schnellimbiss** M snack bar **Schnellstraße** F expressway

schneuzen V/R → schnäuzen

Schnitt M cut; (*Schnittpunkt*) intersection; (*Querschnitt*) (cross) section; (*Durchschnitt*) average **Schnitte** F slice; (*belegt*) sandwich **Schnittlauch** M chives *pl* **Schnittstelle** F IT *fig* interface **Schnittwunde** F cut, gash

Schnitzel N (*Papier*) scrap; GASTR cutlet, schnitzel

schnitzen V/T carve

Schnorchel M snorkel **schnorcheln** V/I go snorkeling, snorkel

schnüffeln V/I sniff

Schnuller M pacifier

Schnulze F (*Film, Roman*) tearjerker

Schnupfen M cold

schnuppern V/I sniff

Schnur F string, cord; ELEK cord **schnurlos** ADJ (*Telefon*) cordless

Schnurrbart M mustache

Schnürsenkel M shoelace

Schock M shock; **unter ~ stehen** be in (a state of) shock **schockieren** V/T shock

Schokolade F chocolate **Schokoriegel** M candy bar

schon ADV already; **ist er ~ da?** is he here yet?; **warst du ~ einmal da?** have you ever been there?; **ich war ~ einmal da** I've been there before; **~ damals** even then; **~ 1999** as early (*od* as long ago) as 1999

schön ADJ beautiful; (*nett*) nice; (*Frau*) beautiful, pretty; (*Mann*) handsome; (*Wetter*) fine; **~e Grüße** best wishes; **~es Wochenende** have a nice weekend

schonen 1 V/T (*pfleglich behandeln*) look after 2 V/R take it easy

Schönheit F beauty

Schonkost F light food

Schöpfung F creation

Schorf M scab

Schornstein M chimney **Schornsteinfeger(in)** M(F) chimney sweep

Schoß M lap
schottisch ADJ Scottish, Scots **Schottland** N Scotland
schräg ADJ slanting; (*Dach*) sloping; (*Linie*) diagonal; *umg* (*unkonventionell*) wacky
Schrank M cupboard; (*Kleiderschrank*) closet
Schranke F barrier
Schrankwand F wall unit
Schraube F screw **schrauben** V/T screw **Schraubenschlüssel** M wrench **Schraubenzieher** M screwdriver **Schraubverschluss** M screw top, screw cap
Schreck M, **Schrecken** M terror; (*Angst*) fright; **j-m einen ~ einjagen** give sb a fright **schreckhaft** ADJ jumpy **schrecklich** ADJ terrible, dreadful
Schrei M scream; (*Ruf*) shout
Schreibblock M writing pad **schreiben** V/T & V/I write; (*buchstabieren*) spell; **wie schreibt man ...?** how do you spell ...? **Schreiben** N writing; (*Brief*) letter **Schreibfehler** M spelling mistake **schreibgeschützt** ADJ (*Diskette*) write-protected **Schreibtisch** M desk **Schreibwaren** PL stationery *sg* **Schreibwarenladen** M stationery store
schreien V/T & V/I scream; (*rufen*) shout
Schreiner(in) M(F) carpenter
Schrift F (*Handschrift*) handwriting; (*Schriftart*) typeface; (*Schrifttyp*) font **schriftlich** **1** ADJ written **2** ADV in writing **Schriftsteller(in)** M(F) writer
Schritt M step; **~ für ~** step by step **Schrittmacher** M MED pacemaker
Schrott M scrap metal; *fig* nonsense
schrubben V/I & V/T scrub **Schrubber** M scrubbing brush
schrumpfen V/I shrink
Schubkarren M wheelbarrow **Schublade** F drawer
schubsen V/T shove, push
schüchtern ADJ shy
Schuh M shoe **Schuhcreme** F shoe polish **Schuhgeschäft** N shoe store **Schuhgröße** F shoe size **Schuhlöffel** M shoehorn
Schulabschluss M school-leaving qualification
schuld ADJ **wer ist ~ daran?** whose fault is it?; **er ist ~** it's his fault, he's to blame **Schuld** F guilt; (*Verschulden*) fault; **~ haben** be to blame (*an +dat* for); **er hat ~** it's his fault **schulden** V/T owe (*j-m etw* sb sth) **Schulden** PL debts *pl*; **~ haben** be in debt; **~ machen** run up debts **schuldig** ADJ guilty (*an +dat* of); (*gebührend*) due; **j-m etw ~ sein** owe sb sth
Schule F school; **in der ~** at

school; **in die ~ gehen** go to school **Schüler(in)** M(F) student **Schüleraustausch** M school exchange **Schulfach** N subject **Schulferien** PL school vacation *sg* **schulfrei** ADJ **morgen ist ~** there's no school tomorrow **Schulfreund(in)** M(F) schoolfriend **Schuljahr** N school year **Schulkenntnisse** PL **~ in Französisch** school(-level) French **Schulklasse** F class **Schulleiter(in)** M(F) principal

Schulter F shoulder

Schulung F training; (*Veranstaltung*) training course

Schuppen PL (*im Haar*) dandruff *sg*

Schürfwunde F graze

Schürze F apron

Schuss M shot; **mit einem ~ Wodka** with a dash of vodka

Schüssel F bowl

Schuster(in) M(F) shoemaker

Schutt M rubble

Schüttelfrost M shivering fit **schütteln** V/T & V/R shake

schütten **1** V/T pour; (*Zucker, Kies etc*) tip **2** V/I UNPERS pour (down)

Schutz M protection (*gegen, vor* against, from); (*Unterschlupf*) shelter; **j-n in ~ nehmen** stand up for sb **Schutzblech** N fender

Schütze M (*beim Fußball*) scorer; ASTROL Sagittarius

schützen V/T **j-n gegen/vor etw ~** protect sb against/from sth **Schutzimpfung** F inoculation, vaccination

schwach ADJ weak; **~e Augen** poor eyesight *sg* **Schwäche** F weakness **Schwachstelle** F weak point

Schwager M brother-in-law **Schwägerin** F sister-in-law

Schwamm M sponge

Schwan M swan

schwanger ADJ pregnant; **in der dreizehnten Woche/im dritten Monat ~ sein** be twelve weeks/two months pregnant **Schwangerschaft** F pregnancy **Schwangerschaftsabbruch** M abortion **Schwangerschaftstest** M pregnancy test

schwanken V/I sway; (*Preise, Zahlen*) fluctuate; (*zögern*) hesitate; (*taumeln*) stagger

Schwanz M tail; *vulg* (*Penis*) cock

Schwarm M swarm; *umg* (*angehimmelte Person*) heartthrob **schwärmen** V/I swarm; **~ für** be crazy about

schwarz ADJ black; **mir wurde ~ vor Augen** everything went black **Schwarzarbeit** F illicit work **Schwarzbrot** N black bread **schwarzfahren** V/I travel without a ticket **schwarzsehen** V/I *umg* (*pessimistisch sein*) be pessimistic (*für* about) **Schwarzwald** M Black Forest **schwarz-weiß**

ADJ black and white
schwatzen V/I chatter **Schwätzer(in)** M(F) chatterbox; (*Schwafler*) gasbag; (*Klatschmaul*) gossip
schweben V/I float; (*hoch*) soar
Schwede M Swede **Schweden** N Sweden **Schwedin** F Swede **schwedisch** ADJ Swedish **Schwedisch** N Swedish
Schwefel M sulphur
schweigen V/I be silent; (*nicht mehr reden*) stop talking **Schweigen** N silence
Schwein N pig; *umg* (*Glück*) luck; *umg* (*gemeiner Mensch*) swine **Schweinebraten** M roast pork **Schweinefleisch** N pork **Schweinegrippe** F swine flu **Schweinerei** F mess; (*Gemeinheit*) dirty trick
Schweiß M sweat
schweißen V/T & V/I weld
Schweiz F **die ~** Switzerland **Schweizer(in)** M(F) Swiss **Schweizerdeutsch** N Swiss German **schweizerisch** ADJ Swiss
Schwelle F doorstep; *a. fig* threshold
schwellen V/I swell (up) **Schwellung** F swelling
schwer **1** ADJ heavy; (*schwierig*) difficult, hard; (*schlimm*) serious, bad **2** ADV (*sehr*) really; (*verletzt etc*) seriously, badly **Schwerbehinderte(r)** M/F(M) severely disabled person **schwerfallen** V/I **j-m ~** (*Schwierigkeiten bereiten*) be difficult for sb **schwerhörig** ADJ hard of hearing
Schwert N sword
Schwester F sister; MED nurse
Schwiegereltern PL parents-in-law *pl* **Schwiegermutter** F mother-in-law **Schwiegersohn** M son-in-law **Schwiegertochter** F daughter-in-law **Schwiegervater** M father-in-law
schwierig ADJ difficult, hard **Schwierigkeit** F difficulty; **in ~en kommen** get into trouble; **j-m ~en machen** make things difficult for sb
Schwimmbad N swimming pool **Schwimmbecken** N swimming pool **schwimmen** V/I swim; (*treiben*) float **Schwimmer(in)** M(F) swimmer **Schwimmflosse** F flipper **Schwimmflügel** M water wing **Schwimmreifen** M swim ring **Schwimmweste** F life jacket
Schwindel M dizziness; (*Anfall*) dizzy spell; (*Betrug*) swindle **schwindelfrei** ADJ **nicht ~ sein** suffer from vertigo; **~ sein** have a head for heights **schwindlig** ADJ dizzy; **mir ist ~** I feel dizzy
Schwips M **einen ~ haben** be tipsy
schwitzen V/I sweat
schwören V/T & V/I swear; **einen Eid ~** take an oath

schwul ADJ gay
schwül ADJ muggy
Schwung M swing; (*Triebkraft*) momentum; *fig* (*Energie*) energy; **in ~ kommen** get going
Schwur M oath
scrollen V/I IT scroll
sechs NUM six **Sechs** F six; (*Schulnote*) ≈ F **sechshundert** NUM six hundred **sechsmal** ADV six times **sechste**(r, s) ADJ sixth; → **dritte Sechstel** N sixth **sechzehn** NUM sixteen **sechzehnte**(r, s) ADJ sixteenth; → **dritte sechzig** NUM sixty **sechzigste**(r, s) ADJ sixtieth
Secondhandladen M thrift store
See **1** F sea; **an der ~** by the sea **2** M lake; **am ~** by the lake **Seehund** M seal **Seeigel** M sea urchin **seekrank** ADJ seasick
Seele F soul
Seeleute PL seamen *pl*, sailors *pl*
seelisch ADJ mental, psychological
Seelöwe M sea lion **Seemann** M sailor, seaman **Seemeile** F nautical mile **Seemöwe** F seagull **Seepferdchen** N sea horse **Seerose** F water lily **Seestern** M starfish
Segel N sail **Segelboot** N yacht **Segelfliegen** N gliding **segeln** V/T & V/I sail **Segelschiff** N sailing ship
sehbehindert ADJ partially sighted
sehen V/T & V/I see; (*in bestimmte Richtung*) look; **gut/schlecht ~** have good/bad eyesight; **kann ich das mal ~?** can I have a look at it?; **wir ~ uns morgen!** see you tomorrow
Sehenswürdigkeiten PL sights *pl*
Sehne F tendon; (*an Bogen*) string
sehnen V/R long (*nach* for) **Sehnsucht** F longing **sehnsüchtig** ADJ longing
sehr ADV very; (*mit Verben*) a lot, very much; **zu ~** too much
seicht ADJ shallow
Seide F silk
Seife F soap **Seifenoper** F soap (opera)
Seil N rope; (*Kabel*) cable **Seilbahn** F cableway, aerial tramway
sein V/I & V/AUX be; **lass das ~!** leave that!; (*hör auf*) stop that!; **das kann ~** that's possible
sein POSS PR (*adjektivisch*) (*männlich*) his, (*weiblich*) her, (*sächlich*) its; **jeder hat ~e Sorgen** everyone has their problems **seine**(r, s) POSS PR (*substantivisch*) (*männlich*) his, (*weiblich*) hers **seinetwegen** ADV (*wegen ihm*) because of him; (*ihm zuliebe*) for his sake
seit KONJ (*bei Zeitpunkt*) since;

(*bei Zeitraum*) for; **er ist ~ Montag hier** he's been here since Monday; **er ist ~ einer Woche hier** he's been here for a week; **~ langem** for a long time **seitdem** ADV & KONJ since

Seite F side; (*in Buch*) page; **zur ~ gehen** step aside **Seitensprung** M affair **Seitenstechen** N (a) stitch **Seitenstraße** F side street **Seitenstreifen** M shoulder **Seitenwind** M crosswind

seither ADV since (then)

seitlich ADJ side

Sekretär(in) M(F) secretary **Sekretariat** N secretary's office

Sekt M sparkling wine

Sekte F sect

Sekunde F second

selbst 1 PRON **ich ~** I ... myself; **du/Sie ~** you ... yourself; **er ~** he ... himself; **sie ~** she ... herself; **wir haben es ~ gemacht** we did it ourselves; **mach es ~** do it yourself; **von ~** by itself; **das versteht sich ja von ~** that goes without saying 2 ADV even

selbständig ADJ → selbstständig

Selbstauslöser M FOTO self-timer **Selbstbedienung** F self-service **Selbstbeherrschung** F self-control **Selbstbeteiligung** F (*einer Versicherung*) deductible **selbstbewusst** ADJ (self-)confident **selbstklebend** ADJ self-adhesive **Selbstmord** M suicide **Selbstmordattentäter(in)** M(F) suicide bomber **selbstsicher** ADJ self-assured **selbstständig** ADJ independent; (*arbeitend*) self-employed **selbstverständlich** 1 ADJ obvious; **ich halte das für ~** I take that for granted 2 ADV naturally **Selbstvertrauen** N self-confidence

Sellerie M *od* F (*Knollensellerie*) celeriac; (*Stangensellerie*) celery

selten 1 ADJ rare 2 ADV seldom, rarely

seltsam ADJ strange

Semester N semester **Semesterferien** PL vacation *sg*

Seminar N seminar

Semmel F roll **Semmelbrösel** PL breadcrumbs *pl*

Senat M senate

senden 1 V/T send 2 V/T & V/I RADIO, TV broadcast **Sender** M (*TV*) channel; (*Radio*) station; (*Anlage*) transmitter **Sendung** F RADIO, TV broadcasting; (*Programm*) program

Senf M mustard

Senior(in) M(F) senior (citizen)

senken 1 V/T lower 2 V/R sink

senkrecht ADJ vertical

Sensation F sensation

sensibel ADJ sensitive

sentimental ADJ sentimental

separat ADJ separate

September M September; →

Juni
Serbien N Serbia
Serie F series *sg*
seriös ADJ (*ernsthaft*) serious; (*anständig*) respectable
Serpentine F hairpin (bend)
Serum N serum
Server M IT server
Service 1 N (*Geschirr*) service 2 M service
servieren V/T & V/I serve
Serviette F napkin
Servolenkung F AUTO power steering
Sesam M sesame seeds *pl*
Sessel M armchair **Sessellift** M chairlift
Set M *od* N set; (*Tischset*) tablemat
setzen 1 V/T put; (*Segel*) set 2 V/R settle; (*hinsetzen*) sit down; **~ Sie sich doch** please sit down
Seuche F epidemic
seufzen V/T & V/I sigh
Sex M sex **sexistisch** ADJ sexist **Sexualität** F sexuality **sexuell** ADJ sexual
Shampoo N shampoo
Shorts PL shorts *pl*
Shuttlebus M shuttle bus
sich REFL PR (*sg männlich*) himself; (*sg weiblich*) herself; (*sg sächlich*) itself; (*pl*) themselves; (*nach Sie*) yourself; (*nach Sie im pl*) yourselves; (*unbest, nach man*) oneself; **er hat ~ verletzt** he hurt himself; **sie kennen ~** they know each other; **sie hat ~ sehr gefreut** she was very pleased; **er hat ~ das Bein gebrochen** he's broken his leg
sicher ADJ safe (*vor +dat* from); (*gewiss*) certain (*gen* of); (*zuverlässig*) reliable; (*selbstsicher*) confident; **aber ~!** of course, sure **Sicherheit** F safety; (*Aufgabe von Sicherheitsbeamten*) FIN security; (*Gewissheit*) certainty; (*Selbstsicherheit*) confidence; **mit ~** definitely **Sicherheitsgurt** M seat belt **sicherheitshalber** ADV just to be on the safe side **Sicherheitskontrolle** F FLUG security check **Sicherheitsnadel** F safety pin **Sicherheitsvorkehrung** F safety precaution **sicherlich** ADV certainly; (*wahrscheinlich*) probably
sichern V/T secure (*gegen* against); (*schützen*) IT protect; (*Daten*) back up **Sicherung** F (*Sichern*) securing; (*Vorrichtung*) safety device; (*an Waffen*) safety catch; ELEK fuze; IT backup
Sicht F sight; (*Aussicht*) view **sichtbar** ADJ visible **sichtlich** ADJ evident, obvious **Sichtverhältnisse** PL visibility *sg* **Sichtweite** F **in/außer ~** within/out of sight
sie PERS PR (*3. Person sg*) she; (*3. Person pl*) they; (*akk von sg*) her; (*akk von pl*) them; (*für eine Sache*) it; **da ist ~ ja** there she

is; **da sind ~ ja** there they are; **ich kenne ~** (*Frau*) I know her; (*mehrere Personen*) I know them
Sie PERS PR (*Höflichkeitsform, nom und akk*) you
Sieb N sieve; (*Teesieb*) strainer
sieben NUM seven **siebenhundert** NUM seven hundred **siebenmal** ADV seven times **siebte(r, s)** ADJ seventh; → dritte **Siebtel** N seventh **siebzehn** NUM seventeen **siebzehnte(r, s)** ADJ seventeenth; → dritte **siebzig** NUM seventy **siebzigste(r, s)** ADJ seventieth
Siedlung F (*Wohngebiet*) housing development
Sieg M victory **siegen** V/I win **Sieger(in)** M(F) winner
siezen V/T address as 'Sie'
Signal N signal
Silbe F syllable
Silber N silver **Silberhochzeit** F silver wedding **Silbermedaille** F silver medal
Silikon N silicone
Silvester N, **Silvesterabend** M New Year's Eve
simpel ADJ simple
simsen V/T & V/I *umg* text
simultan ADJ simultaneous
Sinfonie F symphony
singen V/T & V/I sing; **richtig/falsch ~** sing in tune/out of tune
Single **1** F (*CD*) single **2** M (*Mensch*) single
Singular M singular
sinken V/I sink; (*Preise etc*) fall, go down
Sinn M (*Bedeutung*) sense, meaning; **~ machen** make sense; **das hat keinen ~** it's no use **sinnlich** ADJ sensuous; (*erotisch*) sensual; (*Wahrnehmung*) sensory **sinnlos** ADJ (*unsinnig*) stupid; (*Verhalten*) senseless; (*zwecklos*) pointless; (*bedeutungslos*) meaningless **sinnvoll** ADJ meaningful; (*vernünftig*) sensible
Sirup M syrup
Sitte F custom
Situation F situation
Sitz M seat **sitzen** V/I sit; (*Bemerkung, Schlag*) strike home; (*Gelerntes*) have sunk in; **der Rock sitzt gut** the skirt is a good fit **Sitzgelegenheit** F place to sit down **Sitzplatz** M seat **Sitzung** F meeting; IT session
Skandal M scandal
Skandinavien N Scandinavia
Skateboard N skateboard
Skelett N skeleton
skeptisch ADJ sceptical
Ski M ski; **~ laufen** (*od* **fahren**) ski **Skianzug** M ski suit **Skibrille** F ski goggles *pl* **Skifahren** N skiing **Skigebiet** N skiing area **Skihose** F ski pants *pl* **Skikurs** M skiing course **Skiläufer(in)** M(F) skier **Skilehrer(in)** M(F) ski instructor **Skilift** M ski-lift **Skischuh** M ski boot **Skisprin-**

gen N ski jumping **Skistiefel** M ski boot **Skistock** M ski pole **Skiurlaub** M ski(ing) vacation

Skizze F sketch

Skonto M *od* N discount

Skorpion M ZOOL scorpion; ASTROL Scorpio

Skulptur F sculpture

S-Kurve F double bend

Slip M (pair of) briefs *pl*; (*Damenslip*) (pair of) panties *pl* **Slipeinlage** F panty liner

Slowake M, **Slowakin** F Slovak **Slowakei** F Slovakia **slowakisch** ADJ Slovakian **Slowakisch** N Slovakian

Slowene M, **Slowenin** F Slovene **Slowenien** N Slovenia **slowenisch** ADJ Slovenian **Slowenisch** N Slovenian

Smog M smog

Smoking M tuxedo

SMS F *abk* = Short Message Service; (*Nachricht*) text message; **ich schicke dir eine ~** I'll text you, I'll send you a text (message)

Snowboard N snowboard **Snowboardfahren** N snowboarding

so 1 ADV so; (*auf diese Weise*) like this; (*ungefähr*) about; **fünf Euro oder ~** five euros or so; **~ ein** such a; **~ ... wie ...** as ... as ...; **und ~ weiter** and so on; **~ viel** as much (*wie* as); **~ weit sein** be ready; **~ weit wie** (*od* **als**) **möglich** as far as possible 2 KONJ so; (*vor Adjektiv*) as

sobald KONJ as soon as

Socke F sock

Sodbrennen N heartburn

Sofa N sofa

sofern KONJ if, provided (that)

sofort ADV immediately, at once

Software F software

sogar ADV even; **kalt, ~ sehr kalt** cold, in fact very cold

sogenannt ADJ so-called

Sohle F sole

Sohn M son

Soja F soy **Sojasprossen** PL beansprouts *pl*

solang(e) KONJ as long as

Solarium N tanning studio

Solarzelle F solar cell

solche(r, s) DEM PR such; **eine ~ Frau, solch eine Frau** such a woman, a woman like that; **~ Sachen** things like that, such things; **ich habe ~ Kopfschmerzen** I've got such a headache; **ich habe ~n Hunger** I'm so hungry

Soldat(in) M(F) soldier

solid(e) ADJ solid; (*Leben, Mensch*) respectable

Soll N FIN debit; (*Arbeitsmenge*) quota, target

sollen V/I be supposed to; (*Verpflichtung*) shall, ought to; **soll ich?** shall I?; **du solltest besser nach Hause gehen** you'd better go home; **sie soll sehr reich sein** she's said to be very rich; **was soll das?** what's all that about?

Solo N solo

Sommer M summer **Sommerfahrplan** M summer timetable **Sommerferien** PL summer vacation *sg* **sommerlich** ADJ summery; (*Sommer-*) summer **Sommerreifen** M normal tire **Sommersprossen** PL freckles *pl* **Sommerzeit** F summertime; (*Uhrzeit*) daylight saving time

Sonderangebot N special offer **sonderbar** ADJ strange, odd **Sondermüll** M hazardous waste

sondern KONJ but; **nicht nur …, ~ auch** not only …, but also

Sonderpreis M special price **Sonderschule** F special school **Sonderzeichen** N IT special character

Sonnabend M Saturday; → Mittwoch **sonnabends** ADV (on) Saturdays; → mittwochs

Sonne F sun **sonnen** V/R sunbathe **Sonnenaufgang** M sunrise **Sonnenbrand** M sunburn **Sonnenbrille** F sunglasses *pl*, shades *pl* **Sonnencreme** F sun cream **Sonnendach** N (*Auto*) sunroof **Sonnendeck** N sun deck **Sonnenmilch** F suntan lotion **Sonnenöl** N suntan oil **Sonnenschein** M sunshine **Sonnenschirm** M sunshade **Sonnenstich** M sunstroke **Sonnenstudio** N tanning studio **Sonnenuhr** F sundial **Sonnenuntergang** M sunset **sonnig** ADJ sunny

Sonntag M Sunday; → Mittwoch **sonntags** ADV (on) Sundays; → mittwochs

sonst ADV (*außerdem*) else; (*andernfalls*) otherwise, (or) else; (*normalerweise*) normally, usually; **~ noch etwas?** anything else?; **~ nichts** nothing else

sooft KONJ whenever

Sorge F worry; (*Fürsorge*) care; **sich um j-n ~n machen** be worried about sb **sorgen** **1** V/I **für j-n ~** look after sb; **für etw ~** take care of sth, see to sth **2** V/R worry (*um* about) **sorgfältig** ADJ careful

sortieren V/T sort (out)

sosehr KONJ however much

Soße F sauce; (*zu Braten*) gravy

Soundkarte F IT sound card

Souvenir N souvenir

soviel KONJ as far as

soweit KONJ as far as

sowie KONJ (*wie auch*) as well as; (*sobald*) as soon as

sowohl KONJ **~ … als** (*od* **wie**) **auch** both … and

sozial ADJ social **Sozialhilfe** F welfare **Sozialismus** M socialism **Sozialversicherung** F social security **Sozialwohnung** F subsidized apartment

sozusagen ADV so to speak

Spachtel M spatula

Spaghetti PL spaghetti *sg* **Spalte** F crack; (*Gletscher*) crevasse; (*in Text*) column **spalten** V/T & V/R split **Spange** F clasp; (*Haarspange*) barrette **Spanien** N Spain **Spanier(in)** M(F) Spaniard **spanisch** ADJ Spanish **Spanisch** N Spanish **spannen** 1 V/T (*straffen*) tighten 2 V/I be tight **spannend** ADJ exciting, gripping **Spannung** F tension; ELEK voltage; *fig* suspense **Sparbuch** N savings book; (*Konto*) savings account **sparen** V/T & V/I save **Spargel** M asparagus **Sparkasse** F savings bank **Sparkonto** N savings account **spärlich** ADJ meager; (*Bekleidung*) scanty **sparsam** ADJ economical **Spaß** M joke; (*Freude*) fun; **es macht mir ~** I enjoy it, it's (great) fun; **viel ~!** have fun! **spät** ADJ & ADV late; **zu ~ kommen** be late **Spaten** M spade **später** ADJ & ADV later **spätestens** ADV at the latest **Spätvorstellung** F late-night performance **spazieren** V/I stroll, walk; **~ gehen** go for a walk **Spaziergang** M walk **Speck** M bacon fat; (*durchwachsen*) bacon **Spedition** F (*für Umzug*) (house) moving firm **Speiche** F spoke **Speichel** M saliva **Speicher** M (*Dachboden*) attic; IT memory **speichern** V/T IT store; (*sichern*) save **Speise** F food; (*Gericht*) dish **Speisekarte** F menu **Speiseröhre** F gullet, esophagus **Speisesaal** M dining hall **Speisewagen** M dining car **Spende** F donation **spenden** V/T donate, give **spendieren** V/T **j-m etw ~** treat sb to sth **Sperre** F barrier; (*Verbot*) ban **sperren** V/T block; SPORT suspend; (*verbieten*) ban **Sperrstunde** F closing time **Sperrung** F closing **Spesen** PL expenses *pl* **spezialisieren** V/R specialize (*auf +akk* in) **Spezialist(in)** M(F) specialist **Spezialität** F specialty **speziell** 1 ADJ special 2 ADV especially **Spiegel** M mirror **Spiegelei** N fried egg **Spiel** N game; (*Tätigkeit*) play(-ing); (*Karten*) pack, deck **Spielautomat** M (*ohne Geldgewinn*) gaming machine; (*mit Geldgewinn*) slot machine **spielen** V/T & V/I play; (*um Geld*) gamble; THEAT perform, act; **Klavier ~** play the piano **spielend** ADV easily **Spieler(in)** M(F) player; (*um Geld*) gambler **Spielfeld** N (*für Fußball, Hockey*) field; (*für Basketball*) court **Spielplatz** M playground **Spielraum** M room to maneuver **Spielsachen** PL toys *pl* **Spielverderber(in)** M(F) spoilsport **Spielzeug** N toys *pl*; (*einzelnes*) toy

spießig ADJ square, uncool

Spikes PL SPORT spikes *pl*; AUTO studs *pl*

Spinat M spinach

Spinne F spider **spinnen** V/T & V/I spin; *umg* (*Unsinn reden*) talk nonsense; (*verrückt sein*) be crazy; **du spinnst!** you must be crazy **Spinnwebe** F cobweb

Spion(in) M(F) spy **spionieren** V/I spy; *fig* snoop around

Spirale F spiral; MED coil

Spirituosen PL spirits *pl*, liquor *sg*

Spiritus M spirit

spitz ADJ (*Nase, Kinn*) pointed; (*Bleistift, Messer*) sharp; (*Winkel*) acute **Spitze** F point; (*von Finger, Nase*) tip; (*Bemerkung*) taunt, dig; (*erster Platz*) lead; (*Gewebe*) lace **Spitzer** M pencil sharpener **Spitzname** M nickname

Spliss M split ends *pl*

sponsern V/T sponsor **Sponsor(in)** M(F) sponsor

spontan ADJ spontaneous

Sport M sport; **~ treiben** do sport **Sportanlage** F sports complex **Sportart** F sport **Sportbekleidung** F sportswear **Sportgeschäft** N sports store **Sporthalle** F gymnasium, gym **Sportlehrer(in)** M(F) sports instructor; (*Schule*) gym teacher **Sportler(in)** M(F) sportsman/-woman **sportlich** ADJ sporting; (*Mensch*) sporty **Sportplatz** M sports (*od* playing) field **Sportverein** M sports club **Sportwagen** M sports car

Sprache F language; (*Sprechen*) speech **Sprachenschule** F language school **Sprachkurs** M language course

Spray M *od* N spray

Sprechanlage F intercom **sprechen** V/T & V/I speak (*j-n, mit j-m* to sb); (*sich unterhalten*) talk (*mit* to, *über, von* about); **~ Sie Deutsch?** do you speak German?; **kann ich bitte mit David ~?** (*am Telefon*) can I speak to David, please? **Sprecher(in)** M(F) speaker; (*Ansager*) announcer **Sprechstunde** F consultation; (*Arzt, Anwalt etc*) office hours *pl* **Sprechzimmer** N consulting room

Sprichwort N proverb

Springbrunnen M fountain

springen V/I jump; (*Glas*) crack; (*mit Kopfsprung*) dive

Sprit M *umg* (*Benzin*) gas

Spritze F (*Gegenstand*) syringe; (*Injektion*) injection, shot; (*an*

Schlauch) nozzle **spritzen** **1** VT spray; MED inject **2** VI splash; MED give injections
Spruch M saying
Sprudel M sparkling mineral water; (*süßer*) soda **sprudeln** VI bubble
Sprühdose F aerosol (can) **sprühen** VT & VI spray; *fig* sparkle **Sprühregen** M drizzle
Sprung M jump; (*Riss*) crack **Sprungbrett** N springboard **Sprungturm** M diving platforms *pl*
Spucke F spit **spucken** VT & VI spit
spuken VI (*Geist*) walk; **hier spukt es** this place is haunted
Spülbecken N sink
Spule F spool; ELEK coil
Spüle F sink **spülen** VT & VI rinse; (*Geschirr*) wash the dishes; (*Toilette*) flush **Spülmaschine** F dishwasher **Spülmittel** N dishwashing liquid **Spültuch** N dishcloth **Spülung** F (*von WC*) flush
Spur F trace; (*Fußspur, Radspur*) track; (*Fährte*) trail; (*Fahrspur*) lane; **die ~ wechseln** change lanes *pl*
spüren VT feel; (*merken*) notice
Squash N squash
Staat M state **staatlich** ADJ state(-); (*vom Staat betrieben*) state-run **Staatsangehörigkeit** F nationality **Staatsanwalt** M, **Staatsanwältin** F district attorney **Staatsbürger(in)** M(F) citizen **Staatsbürgerschaft** F nationality
Stab M rod; (*Gitter*) bar **Stäbchen** N (*Essstäbchen*) chopstick **Stabhochsprung** M pole vault
stabil ADJ stable; (*Möbel*) sturdy
Stachel M spike; (*von Tier*) spine; (*von Insekten*) sting **Stachelbeere** F gooseberry **Stacheldraht** M barbed wire **stachelig** ADJ prickly
Stadion N stadium
Stadt F town; (*groß*) city; **in der ~** in town **Stadtautobahn** F urban expressway **Stadtführer** M (*Heft*) city guide **Stadtführung** F city sightseeing tour **Stadthalle** F municipal hall **städtisch** ADJ municipal **Stadtmitte** F downtown area **Stadtplan** M (street) map **Stadtrand** M outskirts *pl* **Stadtrundfahrt** F city tour
Stahl M steel
Stall M stable; (*Kaninchen*) hutch; (*Schweine*) pigsty; (*Hühner*) henhouse
Stamm M (*Baum*) trunk; (*von Menschen*) tribe **stammen** VI **~ aus** come from **Stammgast** M regular (guest) **Stammkunde** M, **Stammkundin** F regular (customer)
Stammtisch M *table re-*

served for regulars
Stand M (*Wasser, Benzin*) level; (*Stehen*) standing position; (*Zustand*) state; (*Spielstand*) score; (*auf Messe etc*) stand
Ständer M (*Gestell*) stand; *umg* (*Erektion*) hard-on
Standesamt N *official building in which civil weddings are conducted*
ständig ADJ permanent; (*ununterbrochen*) constant, continual
Standlicht N parking lights *pl*
Standort M position **Standpunkt** M standpoint **Standspur** F AUTO shoulder
Stange F stick; (*Stab*) pole; (*Metall*) bar; (*Zigaretten*) carton
Stapel M pile
Star 1 M MED cataract 2 M (*in Film etc*) star
stark ADJ strong; (*heftig, groß*) heavy; (*Maßangabe*) thick **Stärke** F strength; (*Dicke*) thickness; (*Wäschestärke, Speisestärke*) starch **stärken** V/T strengthen; (*Wäsche*) starch
starr ADJ stiff; (*unnachgiebig*) rigid; (*Blick*) staring
starren V/I stare
Start M start; FLUG takeoff **Startbahn** F runway **starten** V/T & V/I start; FLUG take off **Startmenü** N IT start menu
Station F (*Haltestelle*) stop; (*Bahnhof*) station; (*im Krankenhaus*) ward **stationär** ADJ stationary; **~e Behandlung** in-patient treatment; **j-n ~ behandeln** treat sb as an in-patient
Statistik F statistics *pl*
Stativ N tripod
statt KONJ & PRÄP +*gen od dat* instead of; **~ zu arbeiten** instead of working
stattfinden V/I take place
Statue F statue
Statusleiste F, **Statuszeile** F IT status bar
Stau M (*im Verkehr*) (traffic) jam; **im ~ stehen** be stuck in a traffic jam
Staub M dust; **~ wischen** dust **staubig** ADJ dusty **staubsaugen** V/T & V/I vacuum **Staubsauger** M vacuum cleaner **Staubtuch** N duster
Staudamm M dam
staunen V/I be astonished (*über +akk* at)
Stausee M reservoir **Stauung** F (*von Wasser*) damming-up; (*von Blut, Verkehr*) congestion
Stauwarnung F traffic report
Steak N steak
stechen V/T & V/I (*mit Nadel etc*) prick; (*mit Messer*) stab; (*mit Finger*) poke; (*Biene*) sting; (*Mücke*) bite; (*Sonne*) burn; (*Kartenspiel*) trump **Stechen** N sharp pain, stabbing pain **Stechmücke** F mosquito
Steckdose F outlet **stecken** 1 V/T put; (*Nadel*) stick; (*beim Nähen*) pin 2 V/I (*festsitzen*) be stuck; (*Nadeln*) be (sticking);

der Schlüssel steckt the key is in the door **Stecker** M plug
Steg M bridge
stehen 1 V/I stand (*zu* by); (*sich befinden*) be; (*stillstehen*) have stopped; **was steht im Brief?** what does it say in the letter?; **j-m (gut) ~** suit sb; **~ bleiben** (*Uhr*) stop; **~ lassen** leave 2 V/I UNPERS **wie steht's?** SPORT what's the score?
stehlen V/T steal
steif ADJ stiff
steigen V/I (*Preise, Temperatur*) rise; (*klettern*) climb
steigern V/T & V/R increase
Steigung F incline, gradient
steil ADJ steep **Steilhang** M steep slope
Stein M stone **Steinbock** M ZOOL ibex; ASTROL Capricorn **steinig** ADJ stony **Steinschlag** M falling rocks *pl*
Stelle F place, spot; (*Arbeit*) post, job; (*Amt*) office; **ich an deiner ~** if I were you **stellen** 1 V/T put; (*Uhr etc*) set (*auf +akk* to); (*zur Verfügung stellen*) provide 2 V/R (*bei Polizei*) give oneself up; **sich schlafend ~** pretend to be asleep **Stellenangebot** N job offer, vacancy **stellenweise** ADV in places **Stellplatz** M parking space **Stellung** F position; **zu etw ~ nehmen** comment on sth **Stellvertreter(in)** M(F) representative; (*amtlich*) deputy
Stempel M stamp **stempeln** V/T stamp; (*Briefmarke*) cancel
sterben V/I die
Stereoanlage F stereo (system)
steril ADJ sterile **sterilisieren** V/T sterilize
Stern M star **Sternschnuppe** F shooting star **Sternzeichen** N star sign, sign of the zodiac; **welches ~ bist du?** what's your star sign?
stets ADV always
Steuer 1 N AUTO steering wheel 2 F tax **Steuerberater(in)** M(F) tax adviser **Steuerbord** N starboard **Steuererklärung** F tax declaration **steuerfrei** ADJ tax-free; (*Waren*) duty-free **Steuerknüppel** M control column; FLUG, IT joystick **steuern** V/T & V/I steer; (*Flugzeug*) pilot; (*Entwicklung, Tonstärke*) IT control **steuerpflichtig** ADJ taxable **Steuerung** F AUTO steering; (*Vorrichtung*) controls *pl*; FLUG piloting; *fig* control
Stich M (*von Insekt*) sting; (*von Mücke*) bite; (*durch Messer*) stab; (*beim Nähen*) stitch; (*Färbung*) tinge; (*Kartenspiel*) trick; KUNST engraving
Stickerei F embroidery
stickig ADJ stuffy, close
Stiefbruder M stepbrother
Stiefel M boot
Stiefmutter F stepmother
Stiefschwester F stepsister

Stiefsohn M stepson **Stieftochter** F stepdaughter **Stiefvater** M stepfather
Stiege F *österr* steps *pl*
Stiel M handle; BOT stalk; **ein Eis am ~** a Popsicle®
Stier M ZOOL bull; ASTROL Taurus
Stift M (*aus Holz*) peg; (*Nagel*) tack; (*zum Schreiben*) pen; (*Farbstift*) crayon; (*Bleistift*) pencil
Stil M style
still ADJ quiet; (*unbewegt*) still
stillen V/T (*Säugling*) breast-feed
stillhalten V/I keep still **stillstehen** V/I stand still
Stimme F voice; (*bei Wahl*) vote
stimmen V/I be right; **stimmt!** that's right; **hier stimmt was nicht** there's something wrong here; **stimmt so!** (*beim Bezahlen*) keep the change
Stimmung F mood; (*Atmosphäre*) atmosphere
stinken V/I stink (*nach* of)
Stipendium N scholarship; (*als Unterstützung*) grant
Stirn F forehead **Stirnhöhle** F sinus
Stock 1 M (Stöcke *pl*) stick 2 M (Stockwerke *pl*) floor, story **Stockbett** N bunk bed **Stöckelschuhe** PL high-heels *pl* **Stockwerk** N floor; **im ersten ~** on the second floor
Stoff M (*Gewebe*) material; (*Materie*) matter; (*von Buch etc*) subject (matter)
stöhnen V/I groan (*vor* with)
stolpern V/I stumble, trip
stolz ADJ proud
stoppen V/T & V/I stop; (*mit Uhr*) time **Stoppschild** N stop sign **Stoppuhr** F stopwatch
Stöpsel M plug; (*für Flaschen*) stopper
Storch M stork
stören V/T disturb; (*behindern*) interfere with; **darf ich dich kurz ~?** can I trouble you for a minute?; **stört es dich, wenn ...?** do you mind if ...?
stornieren V/T cancel
Störung F disturbance; (*in der Leitung*) fault
Stoß M (*Schub*) push; (*Schlag*) blow; (*mit Fuß*) kick; (*Haufen*) pile **Stoßdämpfer** M shock absorber
stoßen 1 V/T (*mit Druck*) shove, push; (*mit Schlag*) knock; (*mit Fuß*) kick; (*anstoßen*) bump 2 V/R bang oneself
Stoßstange F AUTO bumper
stottern V/T & V/I stutter
Strafe F punishment; SPORT penalty; (*Gefängnisstrafe*) sentence; (*Geldstrafe*) fine **strafen** V/T punish **Strafstoß** M penalty kick **Straftat** F (criminal) offense **Strafzettel** M ticket
Strahl M ray, beam; (*Wasser*) jet **strahlen** V/I radiate; *fig* beam

Strähne F strand; (*weiß, gefärbt*) streak
Strand M beach; **am ~** on the beach
strapazieren V/T (*Material*) be hard on; (*Mensch, Kräfte*) be a strain on
Straße F road; (*in der Stadt*) street **Straßenarbeiten** PL roadwork *sg*, road repairs *pl* **Straßenbahn** F streetcar **Straßencafé** N sidewalk café **Straßenglätte** F slippery roads *pl* **Straßenrand** M **am ~** at the roadside **Straßenschild** N street sign **Straßensperre** F roadblock **Straßenverhältnisse** PL road conditions *pl* **Straßenverzeichnis** N street index
Strategie F strategy
Strauch M bush, shrub
Strauß M bunch; (*als Geschenk*) bouquet
Strecke F route; (*Entfernung*) distance; BAHN line
strecken V/T & V/R stretch
streckenweise ADV (*teilweise*) in parts; (*zeitweise*) at times
Streich M trick, prank
streicheln V/T stroke
streichen V/T (*anmalen*) paint; (*durchstreichen*) delete; (*nicht genehmigen*) cancel
Streichholz N match
Streichholzschachtel F matchbox
Streifen M (*Linie*) stripe; (*Stück*) strip; (*Film*) film **Streifenwagen** M patrol car
Streik M strike **streiken** V/I be on strike
Streit M argument (*um, wegen* about, over) **streiten** V/I & V/R argue (*um, wegen* about, over)
streng ADJ (*Blick*) severe; (*Lehrer*) strict; (*Geruch*) sharp
Stress M stress **stressen** V/T stress (out) **stressig** ADJ *umg* stressful
streuen V/T scatter
Strich M (*Linie*) line **Strichjunge** M male prostitute **Strichkode** M bar code **Strichmädchen** N hooker **Strichpunkt** M semicolon
Strick M rope
stricken V/T & V/I knit **Strickjacke** F cardigan **Stricknadel** F knitting needle
String M, **Stringtanga** M G-string, thong
Stripper(in) M(F) stripper
Stroh N straw **Strohhalm** M (drinking) straw
Strom M river; *fig* stream; ELEK current **Stromanschluss** M connection **Stromausfall** M power outage
strömen V/I stream, pour
Strömung F current
Stromzähler M electricity meter
Strophe F verse
Strudel M (*in Fluss*) whirlpool; (*Gebäck*) strudel
Struktur F structure; (*von Material*) texture

Strumpf M (*Damenstrumpf*) stocking; (*Socke*) sock **Strumpfhose** F (pair of) pantyhose *pl*
Stück N piece; (*etwas*) bit; (*Zucker*) lump; THEAT play
Student(in) M(F) student **Studentenausweis** M student card **Studentenwohnheim** N dormitory **Studienabschluss** M qualification (*at the end of college education*) **Studienplatz** M university/college place **studieren** V/T & V/I study **Studium** N studies *pl*; **während seines ~s** while he is/was studying
Stufe F step; (*Entwicklungsstufe*) stage
Stuhl M chair
stumm ADJ silent; MED dumb
stumpf ADJ blunt; (*teilnahmslos, glanzlos*) dull **stumpfsinnig** ADJ dull
Stunde F hour; (*Unterrichtsstunde*) class; **in welcher ~ habt ihr Mathe?** what period do you have math?; **eine halbe ~** half an hour **Stundenkilometer** M **80 ~** 80 kilometers an hour **stundenlang** ADV for hours **Stundenplan** M schedule **stündlich** ADJ hourly
stur ADJ stubborn; (*stärker*) pigheaded
Sturm M storm **stürmen** V/I (*Wind*) blow hard; (*rennen*) storm **Stürmer(in)** M(F) striker, forward **stürmisch** ADJ stormy; *fig* tempestuous; (*Zeit*) turbulent; (*Liebhaber*) passionate; (*Beifall, Begrüßung*) tumultuous **Sturmwarnung** F gale warning
Sturz M fall; POL overthrow
stürzen **1** V/T (*werfen*) hurl; POL overthrow; (*umkehren*) overturn **2** V/I fall; (*rennen*) dash **Sturzhelm** M crash helmet
Stute F mare
Stütze F support; (*Hilfe*) help; *umg* (*Arbeitslosenunterstützung*) welfare
stutzig ADJ perplexed, puzzled; (*misstrauisch*) suspicious
Styropor® N Styrofoam®
subjektiv ADJ subjective
Substanz F substance
subtrahieren V/T subtract
Subvention F subsidy **subventionieren** V/T subsidize
Suche F search (*nach* for); **auf der ~ nach etw sein** be looking for sth **suchen** **1** V/T look for; IT search **2** V/I look, search (*nach* for) **Suchmaschine** F IT search engine
Sucht F mania; MED addiction
süchtig ADJ addicted **Süchtige(r)** M/F(M) addict
Süd M south **Südafrika** N South Africa **Südamerika** N South America **Süddeutschland** N Southern Germany **Süden** M south; **im ~ Deutschlands** in the south of

Germany **Südeuropa** N Southern Europe **südlich** ADJ southern; (*Kurs, Richtung*) southerly **Südost(en)** M southeast **Südpol** M South Pole **Südstaaten** PL (*der USA*) the Southern States *pl*, the South *sg* **südwärts** ADV south, southward(s) **Südwest(en)** M southwest **Südwind** M south wind

Summe F sum; (*Gesamtsumme*) total

summen V/I & V/T hum; (*Insekt*) buzz

Sumpf M marsh; (*subtropischer*) swamp **sumpfig** ADJ marshy

Sünde F sin

super ADJ *umg* super, great **Super** N (*Benzin*) premium (gas) **Supermarkt** M supermarket

Suppe F soup **Suppenwürfel** M stock cube

Surfbrett N surfboard **surfen** V/I surf; **im Internet ~** surf the Internet **Surfer(in)** M(F) surfer

Sushi N sushi

süß ADJ sweet **süßen** V/T sweeten **Süßigkeit** F (*Bonbon etc*) candy **Süßkartoffel** F yam, sweet potato **süßsauer** ADJ sweet-and-sour **Süßspeise** F dessert **Süßstoff** M sweetener **Süßwasser** N fresh water

Sweatshirt N sweatshirt

Swimmingpool M (swimming) pool

Sylvester N → Silvester

Symbol N symbol **Symbolleiste** F IT toolbar

Symmetrie F symmetry **symmetrisch** ADJ symmetrical

sympathisch ADJ nice; **j-n ~ finden** like sb

Symphonie F symphony

Symptom N symptom (*für* of)

Synagoge F synagogue

synchronisiert ADJ (*Film*) dubbed

Synthetik F synthetic (fiber) **synthetisch** ADJ synthetic

Syrien N Syria

System N system **systematisch** ADJ systematic **Systemsteuerung** F IT control panel

Szene F scene

T

Tabak M tobacco **Tabakladen** M cigar store, smoke shop

Tabelle F table

Tablett N tray

Tablette F tablet, pill

Tabulator M tabulator, tab

Tacho(meter) M AUTO speedometer

Tafel F *a.* MATH table; (*Anschlagtafel, Wandtafel*) board; (*Gedenktafel*) plaque; **eine ~**

Schokolade a candy bar
Tag M day; (*Tageslicht*) daylight; **guten ~!** good morning/afternoon; **am ~** during the day; **sie hat ihre ~e** she's got her period; **eines ~es** one day **Tagebuch** N diary **tagelang** ADJ for days (on end) **Tagesanbruch** M daybreak **Tagesausflug** M day trip **Tagesgericht** N dish of the day **Tageskarte** F (*Fahrkarte*) day ticket; **die ~** (*Speisekarte*) today's menu **Tageslicht** N daylight **Tagesordnung** F agenda **Tagestour** F day trip **Tageszeitung** F daily newspaper **täglich** ADJ & ADV daily **tags(über)** ADV during the day **Tagung** F conference
Tai Chi N tai chi
Taille F waist
Takt M (*Taktgefühl*) tact; MUS time **Taktik** F tactics *pl*
Tal N valley
Talent N talent **talentiert** ADJ talented
Talkmaster(in) M(F) talk show host **Talkshow** F talk show
Tampon M tampon
Tang M seaweed
Tanga M G-string, thong
Tank M tank **Tankanzeige** F fuel gauge **Tankdeckel** M fuel cap **tanken** V/I get some gas; FLUG refuel **Tanker** M (oil) tanker **Tankstelle** F gas station
Tanne F fir **Tannenzapfen** M fir cone
Tante F aunt **Tante-Emma--Laden** M grocery store
Tanz M dance **tanzen** V/T & V/I dance **Tänzer(in)** M(F) dancer
Tapete F wallpaper **tapezieren** V/T & V/I wallpaper
Tarif M tariff, (scale of) fares/charges *pl*
Tasche F bag; (*Hosentasche*) pocket; (*Handtasche*) purse **Taschen-** IN ZSSGN pocket **Taschenbuch** N paperback **Taschendieb(in)** M(F) pickpocket **Taschengeld** N allowance **Taschenlampe** F flashlight **Taschenmesser** N pocket knife **Taschenrechner** M pocket calculator **Taschentuch** N handkerchief
Tasse F cup; **eine ~ Kaffee** a cup of coffee
Tastatur F keyboard **Taste** F button; (*von Klavier, Computer*) key **Tastenkombination** F IT shortcut
Tat F action
Täter(in) M(F) culprit
Tätigkeit F activity; (*Beruf*) occupation
tätowieren V/T tattoo **Tätowierung** F tattoo (*an +dat* on)
Tatsache F fact **tatsächlich** 1 ADJ actual 2 ADV really
Tau 1 N (*Seil*) rope 2 M dew
taub ADJ deaf
Taube F pigeon; (*Friedenssymbol*) dove

taubstumm ADJ deaf-and--dumb **Taubstumme(r)** M/F(M) deaf-mute
tauchen **1** V/T dip **2** V/I dive; SCHIFF submerge **Tauchen** N diving **Taucher(in)** M(F) diver **Taucheranzug** M diving (*od* wet) suit **Taucherbrille** F diving goggles *pl* **Tauchermaske** F diving mask
tauen V/I UNPERS thaw
Taufe F baptism **taufen** V/T baptize; (*nennen*) christen
taugen V/I be suitable (*für* for); **nichts ~** be no good
Tausch M exchange **tauschen** V/T exchange, swap
täuschen **1** V/T deceive **2** V/I be deceptive **3** V/R be wrong **täuschend** ADJ deceptive **Täuschung** F deception; (*optisch*) illusion
tausend NUM a thousand; **vier~** four thousand; **~ Dank!** thanks a lot **tausendmal** ADV a thousand times **tausendste(r, s)** ADJ thousandth **Tausendstel** N (*Bruchteil*) thousandth
Taxi N taxi **Taxifahrer(in)** M(F) taxi driver **Taxistand** M taxi stand
Team N team **Teamarbeit** F teamwork
Technik F technology; (*angewandte*) engineering; (*Methode*) technique **Techniker(in)** M(F) engineer; SPORT, MUS technician **technisch** ADJ technical
Teddybär M teddy bear
Tee M tea **Teebeutel** M teabag **Teekanne** F teapot **Teelöffel** M teaspoon
Teer M tar
Teesieb N tea strainer **Teetasse** F teacup
Teich M pond
Teig M dough **Teigwaren** PL pasta *sg*
Teil **1** M part; (*Anteil*) share; **zum ~** partly **2** N part; (*Bestandteil*) component **teilen** V/T & V/R divide; (*mit j-m*) share (*mit* with); **20 durch 4 ~** divide 20 by 4
Teilnahme F participation (*an +dat* in) **teilnehmen** V/I take part (*an +dat* in) **Teilnehmer(in)** M(F) participant
teils ADV partly **teilweise** ADV partially, in part **Teilzeit** F **~ arbeiten** work part-time
Teint M complexion
Telefon N (tele)phone **Telefonanruf** M, **Telefonat** N (tele)phone call **Telefonanschluss** M (tele)phone connection **Telefonauskunft** F directory assistance **Telefonbuch** N (tele)phone directory **Telefongebühren** PL (tele)-phone charges *pl* **Telefongespräch** N (tele)phone conversation **telefonieren** V/I **ich telefoniere gerade (mit ...)** I'm on the phone (to ...) **telefonisch** ADJ (tele)phone; (*Be-*

nachrichtigung) by (tele)phone **Telefonkarte** F phonecard **Telefonnummer** F (tele)-phone number **Telefonrechnung** F (tele)phone bill **Telefonverbindung** F (tele)-phone connection **Telefonzelle** F phone booth

Teleobjektiv N telephoto lens **Teleskop** N telescope

Teller M plate

Tempel M temple

Temperament N temperament; *(Schwung)* liveliness **temperamentvoll** ADJ lively

Temperatur F temperature; **bei ~en von 30 Grad** at temperatures of 30 degrees

Tempo N *(Geschwindigkeit)* speed **Tempolimit** N speed limit

Tempotaschentuch® N *(Papiertaschentuch)* (paper) tissue, ≈ Kleenex®

Tendenz F tendency; *(Absicht)* intention

Tennis N tennis **Tennisball** M tennis ball **Tennisplatz** M tennis court **Tennisschläger** M tennis racket **Tennisspieler(in)** M(F) tennis player

Tenor M tenor

Teppich M carpet **Teppichboden** M (wall-to-wall) carpeting

Termin M *(Zeitpunkt)* date; *(Frist)* deadline; *(Arzttermin etc)* appointment

Terminal N IT, FLUG terminal

Terminkalender M planner, datebook **Terminplaner** M *(in Buchform)* personal organizer, Filofax®; *(Taschencomputer)* personal digital assistant, PDA

Terrasse F terrace; *(hinter einem Haus)* patio

Terror M terror **Terroranschlag** M terrorist attack **terrorisieren** V/T terrorize **Terrorismus** M terrorism **Terrorist(in)** M(F) terrorist

Tesafilm® M Scotch tape®

Test M test

Testament N will; **das Alte/Neue ~** the Old/New Testament

testen V/T test **Testergebnis** N test results *pl*

Tetanus M tetanus **Tetanusimpfung** F tetanus vaccination

teuer ADJ expensive

Teufel M devil **Teufelskreis** M vicious circle

Text M text; *(Liedertext)* words *pl*, lyrics *pl* **Textmarker** M highlighter **Textverarbeitung** F word processing

Thailand N Thailand

Theater N theater; *umg* fuss; **ins ~ gehen** go to the theater **Theaterkasse** F box office **Theaterstück** N (stage) play

Theke F *(Schanktisch)* bar; *(Ladentisch)* counter

Thema N subject, topic; **kein ~!** no problem

Theologie F theology

theoretisch ADJ theoretical; **~ stimmt das** that's right in theory **Theorie** F theory
Therapeut(in) M(F) therapist **Therapie** F therapy; **eine ~ machen** undergo therapy
Thermometer N thermometer **Thermoskanne®** F Thermos® (flask) **Thermostat** M thermostat
These F theory
Thron M throne
Thunfisch M tuna
Thymian M thyme
Tick M tic; (*Eigenart*) quirk; (*Fimmel*) craze **ticken** V/I tick; **er tickt nicht ganz richtig** he's crazy
Ticket N (plane) ticket
tief ADJ deep; (*Ausschnitt, Ton, Sonne*) low; **2 Meter ~** 2 meters deep **Tief** N METEO low; (*seelisch*) depression **Tiefdruck** M METEO low pressure **Tiefe** F depth **Tiefgarage** F underground parking garage **tiefgekühlt** ADJ frozen **Tiefkühlfach** N freezer compartment **Tiefkühlkost** F frozen food **Tiefkühltruhe** F freezer **Tiefpunkt** M low
Tier N animal **Tierarzt** M, **Tierärztin** F vet(erinarian) **Tiergarten** M zoo **Tierhandlung** F pet store **Tierheim** N animal shelter **tierisch** **1** ADJ animal **2** ADV *umg* totally, really **Tierpark** M zoo **Tierquälerei** F cruelty to animals **Tierschützer(in)** M(F) animal rights campaigner
Tiger M tiger
timen V/T time **Timing** N timing
Tinte F ink **Tintenfisch** M cuttlefish; (*klein*) squid; (*achtarmig*) octopus **Tintenfischringe** PL calamari *pl*
Tipp M tip **tippen** V/T & V/I tap; *umg* (*schreiben*) type; *umg* (*raten*) guess
Tisch M table **Tischdecke** F tablecloth **Tischtennis** N table tennis **Tischtennisschläger** M paddle
Titel M title **Titelbild** N cover picture **Titelverteidiger(in)** M(F) defending champion
Toast M toast **toasten** V/T toast **Toaster** M toaster
Tochter F daughter
Tod M death **Todesopfer** N casualty **Todesstrafe** F death penalty **todkrank** ADJ terminally ill; (*sehr krank*) seriously ill **tödlich** ADJ deadly, fatal; **er ist ~ verunglückt** he was killed in an accident **todmüde** ADJ *umg* dead tired **todsicher** ADJ *umg* dead certain
Tofu M tofu, bean curd
Toilette F bathroom, restroom **Toilettenpapier** N toilet paper
tolerant ADJ tolerant (*gegen* of)
toll ADJ mad; (*Treiben*) wild;

umg (*großartig*) great **Tollwut** F rabies *sg*
Tomate F tomato **Tomatenmark** N tomato paste **Tomatensaft** M tomato juice
Tombola F raffle
Ton **1** M (*Erde*) clay **2** M (*Töne pl*) (*Laut*) sound; MUS note; (*Redeweise*) tone; (*Farbton, Nuance*) shade
tönen **1** V/I sound **2** V/T shade; (*Haare*) tint
Toner M toner **Tonerkassette** F toner cartridge
Tonne F (*Fass*) barrel; (*Gewicht*) tonne, metric ton
Tönung F hue; (*für Haar*) tint
Top N top
Topf M pot **Töpfer(in)** M(F) potter **Töpferei** F pottery; (*Gegenstand*) piece of pottery
Tor N gate; SPORT goal; **ein ~ schießen** score a goal **Torhüter(in)** M(F) goalkeeper
torkeln V/I stagger
Tornado M tornado
Torte F cake; (*Obsttorte*) flan
Torwart(in) M(F) goalkeeper
tot ADJ dead; **~er Winkel** blind spot
total ADJ total, complete **Totalschaden** M total loss
Tote(r) M/F(M) dead man/woman; (*Leiche*) corpse **töten** V/T & V/I kill **Totenkopf** M skull
totlachen V/R kill oneself laughing
Toto N *od* M *lottery based on the results of soccer matches*
totschlagen V/T beat to death; **die Zeit ~** kill time
Touchscreen M touch screen
Tour F trip; (*Rundfahrt*) tour
Tourismus M tourism **Tourist(in)** M(F) tourist **touristisch** ADJ tourist; *pej* touristy
Tournee F tour
traben V/I trot
Tracht F (*Kleidung*) traditional costume
Tradition F tradition **traditionell** ADJ traditional
Trafik F *österr* cigar store, smoke shop
tragbar ADJ portable
träge ADJ sluggish, slow
tragen V/T carry; (*Kleidung, Brille, Haare*) wear; (*Namen, Früchte*) bear **Träger** M (*an Kleidung*) strap
tragisch ADJ tragic **Tragödie** F tragedy
Trainer(in) M(F) trainer, coach
trainieren V/T & V/I train; (*j-n a.*) coach; (*Übung*) practice
Training N training **Trainingsanzug** M tracksuit
Traktor M tractor
Trambahn F streetcar
trampen V/I hitchhike **Tramper(in)** M(F) hitchhiker
Träne F tear **tränen** V/I water
Transfusion F transfusion
Transitverkehr M transit traffic **Transitvisum** N transit visa
Transplantation F transplant; (*Hauttransplantation*)

graft
Transport M transport(ation) **transportieren** V/T transport
Transvestit M transvestite
Traube F (*einzelne Beere*) grape; (*ganze Frucht*) bunch of grapes **Traubenzucker** M glucose
trauen 1 V/I **j-m/einer Sache ~** trust sb/sth 2 V/R dare 3 V/T marry; **sich ~ lassen** get married
Trauer F sorrow; (*für Verstorbenen*) mourning
Traum M dream **träumen** V/T & V/I dream (*von* of, about) **traumhaft** ADJ dreamlike; *fig* wonderful
traurig ADJ sad (*über +akk* about)
Trauschein M marriage certificate **Trauung** F wedding ceremony **Trauzeuge** M, **Trauzeugin** F witness (*at wedding ceremony*), ≈ best man/maid of honor
Travellerscheck M traveler's check
treffen 1 V/R meet 2 V/T & V/I hit; (*Bemerkung*) hurt; (*begegnen*) meet; (*Entscheidung*) make; (*Maßnahmen*) take **Treffen** N meeting **Treffpunkt** M meeting place
treiben 1 V/T drive; (*Sport*) do 2 V/I (*im Wasser*) drift; (*Pflanzen*) sprout **Treiber** M IT driver **Treibhaus** N greenhouse **Treibstoff** M fuel
trennen 1 V/T separate; (*teilen*) divide 2 V/R separate; **sich von j-m ~** leave sb; **sich von etw ~** part with sth **Trennung** F separation
Treppe F stairs *pl*; (*im Freien*) steps *pl*
Tresen M (*in Kneipe*) bar; (*in Laden*) counter
Tresor M safe
Tretboot N pedal boat **treten** 1 V/I step 2 V/T kick
treu ADJ (*gegenüber Partner*) faithful; (*Kunde, Fan*) loyal **Treue** F (*eheliche*) faithfulness; (*von Kunde, Fan*) loyalty
Tribüne F stands *pl*; (*Rednertribüne*) platform
Trick M trick **Trickfilm** M cartoon
Trieb M urge; (*Instinkt*) drive; (*an Baum etc*) shoot **Triebwerk** N engine
Trikot N shirt, jersey
trinkbar ADJ drinkable **trinken** V/T & V/I drink; **einen ~ gehen** go out for a drink **Trinkgeld** N tip **Trinkhalm** M (drinking) straw **Trinkwasser** N drinking water
Trio N trio
Tritt M (*Schritt*) step; (*Fußtritt*) kick
Triumph M triumph **triumphieren** V/I triumph (*über +akk* over)
trivial ADJ trivial
trocken ADJ dry **Trockenheit** F dryness **trockenlegen** V/T

(*Baby*) change **trocknen** V/T & VI dry **Trockner** M dryer
Trödel M *umg* junk **Trödelmarkt** M flea market
trödeln VI *umg* dawdle
Trommel F drum **Trommelfell** N eardrum **trommeln** VT & VI drum
Trompete F trumpet
Tropf M MED drip; **am ~ hängen** be on a drip **tröpfeln** VI drip; **es tröpfelt** it's drizzling **tropfen** VT & VI drip **Tropfen** M drop **tropfenweise** ADV drop by drop **tropfnass** ADJ dripping wet
tropisch ADJ tropical
Trost M consolation, comfort **trösten** VT console, comfort **trostlos** ADJ bleak; (*Verhältnisse*) grim **Trostpreis** M consolation prize
trotz PRÄP *+gen od dat* in spite of **Trotz** M defiance **trotzdem** 1 ADV nevertheless 2 KONJ although **trotzig** ADJ defiant
trüb ADJ dull; (*Flüssigkeit, Glas*) cloudy; *fig* gloomy
trügerisch ADJ deceptive
Truhe F chest
Trumpf M trump
Trunkenheit F intoxication; **~ am Steuer** drunk driving
Truthahn M turkey
Tscheche M, **Tschechin** F Czech **Tschechien** N Czech Republic **tschechisch** ADJ Czech **Tschechisch** N Czech
tschüs(s) INT bye
T-Shirt N T-shirt
Tube F tube
Tuberkulose F tuberculosis, TB
Tuch N cloth; (*Halstuch*) scarf; (*Kopftuch*) headscarf
tüchtig ADJ competent; (*fleißig*) efficient
Tugend F virtue **tugendhaft** ADJ virtuous
Tulpe F tulip
Tumor M tumor
tun 1 VT (*machen*) do; (*legen*) put; **was tust du da?** what are you doing?; **das tut man nicht** you shouldn't do that; **j-m etw ~** (*antun*) do sth to sb 2 VI act; **so ~, als ob** act as if 3 V/R UNPERS **es tut sich etwas** something is happening
Tuner M tuner
Tunfisch M tuna
Tunnel M tunnel
tupfen VT & VI dab; (*mit Farbe*) dot **Tupfen** M dot
Tür F door; **vor/an der ~** at the door; **an die ~ gehen** answer the door
Türkei F **die ~** Turkey
Türkis M turquoise
Turm M tower; (*spitzer Kirchturm*) steeple; (*Schach*) rook, castle
turnen VI do gymnastics **Turnen** N gymnastics *sg*; (*Schule*) physical education, PE **Turnhalle** F gym(nasium)
Turnier N tournament

Turnschuh M sneaker
Türschild N doorplate **Türschloss** N lock
tuscheln V/T & V/I whisper
Tüte F bag
TÜV M *akr* = Technischer Überwachungsverein; vehicle inspection
Typ M type; (*Auto*) model; (*Mann*) guy
Typhus M typhoid
typisch ADJ typical (*für* of); **~ Marcus!** that's just like Marcus; **~ amerikanisch!** that's so American

U

u. a. *abk* = und andere(s); unter anderem, unter anderen; and others; among other things
U-Bahn F subway
übel ADJ bad; (*moralisch*) wicked; **mir ist ~** I feel sick to my stomach; **diese Bemerkung hat er mir ~ genommen** he took offense at my remark
Übelkeit F nausea
üben V/T & V/I practice
über PRÄP +*dat od akk* (*werfen, springen*) over; (*hoch über*) above; (*quer über*) across; (*oberhalb von*) above; (*Route*) via; (*betreffend*) about; (*mehr als*) over, more than; **~ das Wochenende** over the weekend
überall ADV everywhere
überbacken ADJ **(mit Käse) ~** au gratin
überbelichten V/T FOTO overexpose
überbieten V/T outbid; (*übertreffen*) surpass; (*Rekord*) break
Überbleibsel N remnant
Überblick M overview; *fig* (*in Darstellung*) survey; (*Fähigkeit zu verstehen*) grasp (*über +akk* of)
überbuchen V/T overbook **Überbuchung** F overbooking
übereinander ADV on top of each other; (*sprechen etc*) about each other
übereinstimmen V/I agree (*mit* with)
überfahren V/T AUTO run over **Überfahrt** F crossing
Überfall M (*Banküberfall*) robbery; MIL raid; (*auf j-n*) assault **überfallen** V/T attack; (*Bank*) raid
überfällig ADJ overdue
überfliegen V/T fly over; (*Buch*) skim through
überflüssig ADJ superfluous
überfordern V/T demand too much of; (*Kräfte*) overtax; **da bin ich überfordert** (*bei Antwort*) you've got me there
Überführung F (*Brücke*) overpass

überfüllt ADJ overcrowded
Übergabe F handover
Übergang M crossing; (*Wandel, Überleitung*) transition **Übergangslösung** F temporary solution, stopgap
übergeben 1 V/T hand over 2 V/R be sick, vomit
Übergepäck N excess baggage **Übergewicht** N excess weight; **(10 Kilo) ~ haben** be (10 kilos) overweight
überglücklich ADJ overjoyed
überhaupt ADV at all; (*im Allgemeinen*) in general
überheblich ADJ arrogant
überholen V/T overtake; TECH overhaul **Überholspur** F passing lane **überholt** ADJ outdated
überhören V/T miss, not catch; (*absichtlich*) ignore
überladen 1 V/T overload 2 ADJ *fig* cluttered
überlassen V/T **j-m etw ~** leave sth to sb
überlaufen V/I (*Flüssigkeit*) overflow
überleben V/T & V/I survive **Überlebende(r)** M/F(M) survivor
überlegen 1 V/T consider; **sich etw ~** think about sth; **er hat es sich anders überlegt** he's changed his mind 2 ADJ superior (*dat* to) **Überlegung** F consideration
übermäßig ADJ excessive
übermorgen ADV the day after tomorrow
übernächste(r, s) ADJ **~ Woche** the week after next
übernachten V/I spend the night (*bei j-m* at sb's place) **Übernachtung** F overnight stay; **~ mit Frühstück** bed and breakfast
übernehmen 1 V/T take on; (*Amt, Geschäft*) take over 2 V/R take on too much
überprüfen V/T check **Überprüfung** F check; (*Überprüfen*) checking
überqueren V/T cross
überraschen V/T surprise **Überraschung** F surprise
überreden V/T persuade; **er hat mich überredet** he talked me into it
überreichen V/T hand over
überschätzen V/T overestimate
überschlagen 1 V/T (*berechnen*) estimate 2 V/R somersault; (*Auto*) overturn; (*Stimme*) crack
überschneiden V/R (*Linien etc*) intersect; (*Termine*) clash
Überschrift F heading
Überschwemmung F flood
übersehen V/T (*Gelände*) look (out) over; (*nicht beachten*) overlook
übersetzen V/T translate (*aus* from, *in +akk* into) **Übersetzer(in)** M(F) translator **Übersetzung** F translation
Übersicht F overall view;

(*Darstellung*) survey **übersichtlich** ADJ clear
überstehen V/T (*durchstehen*) get over
Überstunden PL overtime *sg*
überstürzt ADJ hasty
übertragbar ADJ transferable; MED infectious **übertragen** **1** V/T transfer (*auf +akk* to); RADIO broadcast; (*Krankheit*) transmit **2** V/R spread (*auf +akk* to) **3** ADJ figurative **Übertragung** F RADIO broadcast; (*von Daten*) transmission
übertreffen V/T surpass
übertreiben V/T & V/I exaggerate **Übertreibung** F exaggeration **übertrieben** ADJ exaggerated
überwachen V/T supervise; (*Verdächtigen*) keep under surveillance
überweisen V/T transfer; (*Patienten*) refer (*an +akk* to) **Überweisung** F transfer; (*von Patienten*) referral
überwiegend ADV mainly
überwinden **1** V/T overcome **2** V/R make an effort, force oneself
überzeugen V/T convince **Überzeugung** F conviction
überziehen V/T (*bedecken*) cover; (*Jacke etc*) put on; (*Konto*) overdraw; **die Betten frisch ~** change the sheets
üblich ADJ usual
übrig ADJ remaining; **ist noch Saft ~?** is there any juice left?; **die Übrigen** *pl* the rest *pl*; **im Übrigen** besides; **~ bleiben** be left (over) **übrigens** ADV besides; (*nebenbei bemerkt*) by the way **übrighaben** V/T **für j-n etwas ~** *umg* (*j-n mögen*) have a soft spot for sb
Übung F practice; (*im Sport, Aufgabe etc*) exercise
Ufer N (*Fluss*) bank; (*Meer, See*) shore; **am ~** on the bank/shore
Uhr F clock; (*am Arm*) watch; **wie viel ~ ist es?** what time is it?; **1 ~** 1 o'clock; **20 ~** 8 o'clock, 8 p.m. **Uhrzeit** F time (of day)
UKW *abk* = Ultrakurzwelle; VHF
Ultrakurzwelle F very high frequency **Ultraschallaufnahme** F MED (ultrasound) scan
um **1** PRÄP *+akk* (*räumlich*) around; (*zeitlich*) at; **~ etw kämpfen** fight for sth **2** KONJ (*damit*) (in order) to; **zu klug, ~ zu ...** too clever to ... **3** ADV (*ungefähr*) about; **die Ferien sind ~** the vacation is over; **die Zeit ist ~** time's up; → umso
umarmen V/T embrace
Umbau M rebuilding; (*zu etwas*) conversion (*zu* into) **umbauen** V/T rebuild; (*zu etwas*) convert (*zu* into)
umblättern V/T & V/I turn over
umbringen V/T kill
umbuchen V/I change one's

reservation/flight
umdrehen V/T & V/R turn (around); (*umkehren*) turn back **Umdrehung** F turn; PHYS, AUTO revolution
umfahren V/T knock down
umfallen V/I fall over
Umfang M (*Ausmaß*) extent; (*von Buch*) size; (*Reichweite*) range; MATH circumference **umfangreich** ADJ extensive
Umfrage F survey
Umgang M company; (*mit j-m*) dealings *pl* **umgänglich** ADJ sociable **Umgangssprache** F colloquial language, slang
Umgebung F surroundings *pl*; (*Milieu*) environment; **meine ~** (*Personen*) the people around me
umgehen **1** V/I (*Gerücht*) go around; **~ (können) mit** (know how to) handle **2** V/T avoid; (*Schwierigkeit, Verbot*) get around **Umgehungsstraße** F bypass
umgekehrt **1** ADJ reverse; (*gegenteilig*) opposite **2** ADV the other way around; **und ~** and vice versa
umhören V/R ask around
umkehren **1** V/I turn back **2** V/T reverse
umkippen **1** V/T tip over **2** V/I overturn; *fig* change one's mind; *umg* (*ohnmächtig werden*) pass out
Umkleidekabine F changing-room cubicle **Umkleideraum** M changing room
umleiten V/T divert **Umleitung** F detour
umrechnen V/T convert (*in +akk* into) **Umrechnung** F conversion **Umrechnungskurs** M rate of exchange
Umriss M outline
umrühren V/I & V/T stir
Umsatz M turnover
umschalten V/I turn over
Umschlag M cover; (*Buch*) jacket; MED compress; (*Brief*) envelope
Umschulung F retraining
umsehen V/R look around; (*suchen*) look out (*nach* for)
umso ADV all the; **~ mehr** all the more; **~ besser** so much the better
umsonst ADV (*vergeblich*) in vain; (*gratis*) for nothing
Umstand M circumstance; **Umstände** *pl fig* fuss; **j-m Umstände machen** cause sb a lot of trouble; **unter diesen/keinen Umständen** under these/no circumstances; **unter Umständen** possibly **umständlich** ADJ (*Methode*) complicated; (*Ausdrucksweise*) long-winded; (*Mensch*) tedious
umsteigen V/I change (trains/buses)
umstellen **1** V/T (*an anderen Ort*) change around **2** V/R adapt (*auf +akk* to) **Umstellung** F change; (*Umgewöh-

nung) adjustment
Umtausch M exchange **umtauschen** V/T exchange; *(Währung)* change
Umweg M detour
Umwelt F environment **Umweltbelastung** F environmental pollution **Umweltschutz** M environmental protection **Umweltschützer(in)** M(F) environmentalist **Umweltverschmutzung** F pollution **umweltverträglich** ADJ environmentally-friendly
umwerfen V/T knock over; *fig (ändern)* upset; *fig umg (j-n)* stun
umziehen 1 V/T & V/R change 2 V/I move (house) **Umzug** M *(Straßenumzug)* procession; *(Wohnungsumzug)* move
unabhängig ADJ independent **Unabhängigkeitstag** M Independence Day, Fourth of July
unabsichtlich ADV unintentionally
unangenehm ADJ unpleasant **Unannehmlichkeit** F inconvenience; **~en** *pl* trouble *sg*
unanständig ADJ indecent **unappetitlich** ADJ *(Essen)* unappetizing; *(abstoßend)* off-putting **unbeabsichtigt** ADJ unintentional **unbedeutend** ADJ insignificant, unimportant; *(Fehler)* slight
unbedingt 1 ADJ unconditional 2 ADV absolutely
unbefriedigend ADJ unsatisfactory **unbegrenzt** ADJ unlimited **unbekannt** ADJ unknown **unbeliebt** ADJ unpopular **unbemerkt** ADJ unnoticed **unbequem** ADJ *(Stuhl, Mensch)* uncomfortable **unbeständig** ADJ *(Wetter)* unsettled; *(Lage)* unstable; *(Mensch)* unreliable **unbestimmt** ADJ indefinite **unbewusst** ADJ unconscious **unbezahlt** ADJ unpaid **unbrauchbar** ADJ useless
und KONJ and; **~ so weiter** and so on; **na ~?** so what?
undankbar ADJ *(Person)* ungrateful; *(Aufgabe)* thankless **undenkbar** ADJ inconceivable **undeutlich** ADJ indistinct **undicht** ADJ leaky **uneben** ADJ uneven **unecht** ADJ *(Schmuck etc)* fake **unehelich** ADJ *(Kind)* illegitimate **unendlich** ADJ endless; MATH infinite **unentbehrlich** ADJ indispensable **unentgeltlich** ADJ free (of charge) **unentschieden** ADJ undecided; **~ enden** SPORT end in a draw **unerfreulich** ADJ unpleasant **unerlässlich** ADJ indispensable **unerträglich** ADJ unbearable **unerwartet** ADJ unexpected **unfähig** ADJ incompetent; **~ sein, etw zu tun** be incapable of doing sth **unfair** ADJ unfair
Unfall M accident **Unfallsta-**

tion F emergency room **Unfallstelle** F scene of an/the accident **Unfallversicherung** F accident insurance
unfreundlich ADJ unfriendly
Ungar(in) M(F) Hungarian **ungarisch** ADJ Hungarian **Ungarisch** N Hungarian **Ungarn** N Hungary
Ungeduld F impatience **ungeduldig** ADJ impatient
ungeeignet ADJ unsuitable
ungefähr 1 ADJ approximate 2 ADV approximately; **~ 10 Kilometer** about 10 kilometers; **wann ~?** about what time?; **wo ~?** whereabouts?
ungefährlich ADJ harmless; (*sicher*) safe
ungeheuer 1 ADJ huge 2 ADV *umg* enormously **Ungeheuer** N monster
ungehorsam ADJ disobedient (*gegenüber* to) **ungenießbar** ADJ inedible; (*Getränk*) undrinkable **ungenügend** ADJ unsatisfactory; (*Schulnote*) ≈ F **ungepflegt** ADJ (*Garten*) untended; (*Aussehen*) unkempt; (*Hände*) neglected **ungerade** ADJ odd
ungerecht ADJ unjust **ungerechtfertigt** ADJ unjustified **Ungerechtigkeit** F injustice, unfairness
ungern ADV reluctantly **ungeschickt** ADJ clumsy **ungeschminkt** ADJ without make-up **ungesund** ADJ unhealthy
ungewiss ADJ uncertain **ungewöhnlich** ADJ unusual
Ungeziefer N vermin *pl*
ungezwungen ADJ relaxed
unglaublich ADJ incredible
Unglück N (*Unheil*) misfortune; (*Pech*) bad luck; (*Unglücksfall*) disaster **unglücklich** ADJ unhappy; (*erfolglos*) unlucky; (*unerfreulich*) unfortunate **unglücklicherweise** ADV unfortunately
ungültig ADJ invalid **ungünstig** ADJ inconvenient **unheilbar** ADJ incurable; **~ krank sein** be terminally ill
unheimlich 1 ADJ eerie 2 ADV *umg* incredibly
unhöflich ADJ impolite
Uni F college
Uniform F uniform
Universität F university
Unkenntnis F ignorance
unklar ADJ unclear
Unkosten PL expenses *pl*
Unkraut N weeds *pl*
unlogisch ADJ illogical **unmissverständlich** ADJ unambiguous
unmittelbar ADJ immediate; **~ darauf** immediately afterward(s)
unmöbliert ADJ unfurnished
unmöglich ADJ impossible
unnötig ADJ unnecessary
UNO F *akr* = United Nations Organization; UN
unordentlich ADJ untidy **Unordnung** F disorder

unpassend ADJ inappropriate; (*Zeit*) inconvenient **unpersönlich** ADJ impersonal **unpraktisch** ADJ impractical
unrecht ADJ **~ haben** be wrong **Unrecht** N wrong; **zu ~** wrongly; **im ~ sein** be wrong
unregelmäßig ADJ irregular **unreif** ADJ unripe **unruhig** ADJ restless; **~ schlafen** have a bad night's sleep
uns PERS PR (*akk, dat von wir*) us, (to) us; **~ (selbst)** (*reflexiv*) ourselves; **sehen Sie ~?** can you see us?; **er schickte es ~** he sent it to us; **ein Freund von ~** a friend of ours; **wir haben ~ hingesetzt** we sat down; **wir haben ~ amüsiert** we enjoyed ourselves; **wir mögen ~** we like each other
unscharf ADJ FOTO blurred, out of focus **unschlüssig** ADJ undecided **unschuldig** ADJ innocent
unser POSS PR (*adjektivisch*) our **unsere(r, s)** POSS PR (*substantivisch*) ours **unseretwegen** ADV (*wegen uns*) because of us; (*uns zuliebe*) for our sake
unseriös ADJ dubious **unsicher** ADJ (*ungewiss*) uncertain; (*Person, Job*) insecure
Unsinn M nonsense
unsterblich ADJ immortal **unsympathisch** ADJ unpleasant; **er ist mir ~** I don't like him
unten ADV below; (*im Haus*) downstairs; (*an der Treppe etc*) at the bottom; **nach ~** down
unter PRÄP *+akk od dat* under, below; (*bei Menschen*) among; (*während*) during
Unterarm M forearm
Unterbewusstsein N subconscious
unterbrechen V/T interrupt **Unterbrechung** F interruption; **ohne ~** nonstop
unterdrücken V/T suppress; (*Leute*) oppress
untere(r, s) ADJ lower
untereinander ADV (*räumlich*) one below the other; (*gegenseitig*) each other; (*miteinander*) among themselves/yourselves/ourselves
Unterführung F underpass
untergehen V/I go down; (*Sonne a.*) set; (*Volk*) perish; (*Welt*) come to an end; (*im Lärm*) be drowned out
Untergeschoss N basement **Untergewicht** N **(3 Kilo) ~ haben** be (3 kilos) underweight **Untergrund** M foundation; POL underground **Untergrundbahn** F subway
unterhalb ADV & PRÄP *+gen* below; **~ von** below
Unterhalt M maintenance **unterhalten** **1** V/T maintain; (*belustigen*) entertain **2** V/R talk; (*sich belustigen*) enjoy oneself **Unterhaltung** F (*Belustigung*) entertainment; (*Gespräch*) talk, conversation

Unterhemd N undershirt **Unterhose** F underpants *pl*; (*für Damen*) panties *pl*
unterirdisch ADJ underground
Unterkunft F accommodation, accommodations *pl* **Unterlage** F (*Beleg*) document; (*Schreibunterlage*) pad
unterlassen V/T **es ~, etw zu tun** (*versäumen*) fail to do sth; (*bleiben lassen*) refrain from doing sth **unterlegen** ADJ inferior (*dat* to); (*besiegt*) defeated
Unterleib M abdomen
Untermiete F **zur ~ wohnen** be a subtenant **Untermieter(in)** M(F) subtenant
unternehmen V/T (*Reise*) go on; (*Versuch*) make; **etwas ~** do something (*gegen* about) **Unternehmen** N undertaking; WIRTSCH company **Unternehmer(in)** M(F) entrepreneur
Unterricht M classes *pl* **unterrichten** V/T teach
unterschätzen V/T underestimate
unterscheiden **1** V/T distinguish (*von* from, *zwischen* between) **2** V/R differ (*von* from)
Unterschenkel M lower leg
Unterschied M difference; **im ~ zu dir** unlike you **unterschiedlich** ADJ different
unterschreiben V/T sign **Unterschrift** F signature
Untersetzer M tablemat; (*für Gläser*) coaster
unterste(r, s) ADJ lowest, bottom
unterstellen V/R take shelter **unterstreichen** V/T *a. fig* underline
unterstützen V/T support **Unterstützung** F support
untersuchen V/T MED examine; (*Polizei*) investigate **Untersuchung** F examination; (*polizeiliche*) investigation
Untertasse F saucer **Unterteil** N lower part, bottom **Untertitel** M subtitle
untervermieten V/T sublet
Unterwäsche F underwear
unterwegs ADV on the way
unterzeichnen V/T sign
untreu ADJ unfaithful **unüberlegt** **1** ADJ ill-considered **2** ADV without thinking **unüblich** ADJ unusual **unverantwortlich** ADJ irresponsible **unverbindlich** **1** ADJ not binding; (*Antwort*) noncommittal **2** ADV WIRTSCH without obligation **unverbleit** ADJ unleaded **unverheiratet** ADJ unmarried, single **unvermeidlich** ADJ unavoidable **unvernünftig** ADJ silly **unverschämt** ADJ impudent **unverständlich** ADJ incomprehensible **unverträglich** ADJ (*Essen*) indigestible **unverzüglich** ADJ immediate **unvollständig** ADJ incomplete **unvorsichtig** ADJ

careless **unwahrscheinlich** **1** ADJ improbable, unlikely **2** ADV *umg* incredibly

Unwetter N thunderstorm

unwichtig ADJ unimportant **unwiderstehlich** ADJ irresistible **unwillkürlich** **1** ADJ involuntary **2** ADV instinctively **unwohl** ADJ unwell, ill **unzählig** ADJ innumerable, countless **unzerbrechlich** ADJ unbreakable **unzertrennlich** ADJ inseparable **unzufrieden** ADJ dissatisfied **unzugänglich** ADJ inaccessible **unzumutbar** ADJ unacceptable **unzutreffend** ADJ inapplicable; (*unwahr*) incorrect **unzuverlässig** ADJ unreliable

üppig ADJ (*Essen*) lavish; (*Vegetation*) lush

uralt ADJ ancient, very old

Uraufführung F premiere

Urenkel M great-grandson **Urenkelin** F great-granddaughter **Urgroßeltern** PL great-grandparents *pl* **Urgroßmutter** F great-grandmother **Urgroßvater** M great-grandfather

Urheber(in) M(F) originator; (*Autor*) author

Urin M urine **Urinprobe** F urine specimen

Urkunde F document

Urlaub M vacation; **im ~** on vacation; **in ~ fahren** go on vacation **Urlauber(in)** M(F) vacationer **Urlaubsort** M vacation resort **urlaubsreif** ADJ ready for a vacation **Urlaubszeit** F vacation period

Urologe M, **Urologin** F urologist

Ursache F cause (*für* of); **keine ~!** not at all; (*bei Entschuldigung*) that's all right

Ursprung M origin **ursprünglich** **1** ADJ original **2** ADV originally

Urteil N (*Meinung*) opinion; JUR verdict; (*Strafmaß*) sentence **urteilen** V/I judge

Urwald M jungle

USA PL USA *sg*

USB-Stick M IT USB stick, USB key

User(in) M(F) IT user

usw. *abk* = und so weiter; etc

V

vage ADJ vague

Vagina F vagina

Valentinstag M St Valentine's Day

Vandalismus M vandalism

Vanille F vanilla

variieren V/T & V/I vary

Vase F vase

Vater M father **väterlich** ADJ paternal **Vaterschaft** F fatherhood; JUR paternity **Va-**

terschaftstest M paternity test **Vatertag** M Father's Day **Vaterunser** N **das ~ (beten)** (to say) the Lord's Prayer
V-Ausschnitt M V-neck
v. Chr. *abk* = vor Christus; B.C.
Veganer(in) M(F) vegan **Vegetarier(in)** M(F) vegetarian **vegetarisch** ADJ vegetarian
Vene F vein
Ventil N valve
Ventilator M ventilator
verabreden 1 V/T arrange 2 V/R arrange to meet (*mit j-m* sb); **ich bin schon verabredet** I'm already meeting someone **Verabredung** F arrangement; (*Termin*) appointment; (*zum Ausgehen*) date
verabschieden 1 V/T say goodbye to; (*Gesetz*) pass 2 V/R say goodbye
verachten V/T despise **verächtlich** ADJ contemptuous; (*verachtenswert*) contemptible **Verachtung** F contempt
verallgemeinern V/T generalize
Veranda F porch
veränderlich ADJ changeable **verändern** V/T & V/R change **Veränderung** F change
veranlassen V/T cause
veranstalten V/T organize **Veranstalter(in)** M(F) organizer **Veranstaltung** F event **Veranstaltungsort** M venue
verantworten 1 V/T take responsibility for 2 V/R **sich für etw ~** answer for sth **verantwortlich** ADJ responsible (*für* for) **Verantwortung** F responsibility (*für* for)
verärgern V/T annoy
verarschen V/T *umg* make a sucker out of
Verb N verb
Verband M MED bandage; (*Bund*) association **Verband(s)kasten** M first aid box
verbergen V/T & V/R hide (*vor +dat* from)
verbessern 1 V/T improve; (*berichtigen*) correct 2 V/R improve; (*berichtigen*) correct oneself **Verbesserung** F improvement; (*Berichtigung*) correction
verbiegen V/I & V/R bend
verbieten V/T forbid; **j-m ~, etw zu tun** forbid sb to do sth
verbinden 1 V/T connect; (*kombinieren*) combine; MED bandage; **können Sie mich mit ... ~?** TEL can you put me through to ...? 2 V/R CHEM combine **Verbindung** F connection
verbleit ADJ leaded
Verbot N ban (*für, von* on) **verboten** ADJ forbidden; **es ist ~** it's not allowed; **es ist ~, hier zu parken** you're not allowed to park here; **Rauchen ~** no smoking

verbrannt ADJ burnt
Verbrauch M consumption **verbrauchen** V/T use up **Verbraucher(in)** M(F) consumer
Verbrechen N crime **Verbrecher(in)** M(F) criminal
verbreiten V/T & V/R spread
verbrennen V/T burn **Verbrennung** F burning; (*in Motor*) combustion
verbringen V/T spend
verbunden ADJ **falsch ~** sorry, wrong number
Verdacht M suspicion **verdächtig** ADJ suspicious **verdächtigen** V/T suspect
verdammt INT *umg* damn
verdanken V/T **j-m etw ~** owe sth to sb
verdauen V/T *a. fig* digest **Verdauung** F digestion
Verdeck N top
verderben **1** V/T spoil; (*schädigen*) ruin; (*moralisch*) corrupt; **ich habe mir den Magen verdorben** I've got an upset stomach **2** V/I (*Lebensmittel*) go off
verdienen V/T earn; (*moralisch*) deserve **Verdienst** **1** M earnings *pl* **2** N merit; (*Leistung*) service (*um* to)
verdoppeln V/T double
verdorben ADJ spoilt; (*geschädigt*) ruined; (*moralisch*) corrupt
verdrehen V/T twist; (*Augen*) roll
verdünnen V/T dilute
verdunsten V/I evaporate
verdursten V/I die of thirst
verehren V/T admire; REL worship **Verehrer(in)** M(F) admirer
Verein M association; (*Klub*) club
vereinbaren V/T arrange **Vereinbarung** F agreement, arrangement
vereinigen V/T & V/R unite **Vereinigte Staaten (von Amerika)** PL United States *sg* (of America) **Vereinigung** F union; (*Verein*) association **Vereinte Nationen** PL United Nations *sg*
vereisen **1** V/I (*Straße*) freeze over; (*Fenster*) ice up **2** V/T MED freeze
verfahren **1** V/I proceed **2** V/R get lost **Verfahren** N procedure; TECH method; JUR proceedings *pl*
verfallen V/I decline; (*Fahrkarte etc*) expire; **~ in** lapse into **Verfallsdatum** N expiration date
verfärben V/R change color; (*Wäsche*) discolor
Verfasser(in) M(F) author, writer **Verfassung** F condition; POL constitution
verfaulen V/I rot
verfehlen V/T miss
Verfilmung F screen version
verfluchen V/T curse
verfolgen V/T pursue; POL per-

secute
verfügbar ADJ available **verfügen** V/I **über etw ~** have sth at one's disposal **Verfügung** F order; **j-m zur ~ stehen** be at sb's disposal
verführen V/T tempt; (*sexuell*) seduce **verführerisch** ADJ seductive
vergangen ADJ past; **~e Woche** last week **Vergangenheit** F past
Vergaser M AUTO carburetor
vergeben V/T forgive (*j-m etw* sb for sth) **vergebens** ADV in vain **vergeblich** 1 ADV in vain 2 ADJ vain, futile
vergehen 1 V/I pass 2 V/R **sich an j-m ~** indecently assault sb **Vergehen** N offense
vergessen V/T forget **vergesslich** ADJ forgetful
vergeuden V/T squander, waste
vergewaltigen V/T rape **Vergewaltigung** F rape
vergewissern V/R make sure
vergiften V/T poison **Vergiftung** F poisoning
Vergleich M comparison; JUR settlement; **im ~ zu** compared to (*od* with) **vergleichen** V/T compare (*mit* to, with)
Vergnügen N pleasure; **viel ~!** enjoy yourself/yourselves **vergnügt** ADJ cheerful **Vergnügungspark** M amusement park
vergriffen ADJ (*Buch*) out of print; (*Ware*) out of stock
vergrößern V/T enlarge; (*Menge*) increase; (*mit Lupe*) magnify **Vergrößerung** F enlargement; (*Menge*) increase; (*mit Lupe*) magnification **Vergrößerungsglas** N magnifying glass
verhaften V/T arrest
verhalten V/R behave **Verhalten** N behavior
Verhältnis N relationship (*zu* with); MATH ratio; **~se** *pl* circumstances *pl*, conditions *pl*; **im ~ von 1 zu 2** in a ratio of 1 to 2 **verhältnismäßig** 1 ADJ relative 2 ADV relatively
verhandeln V/I negotiate (*über etw akk* sth) **Verhandlung** F negotiation
verheimlichen V/T keep secret (*j-m* from sb)
verheiratet ADJ married
verhindern V/T prevent; **sie ist verhindert** she can't make it
Verhör N interrogation; (*gerichtlich*) examination **verhören** 1 V/T interrogate; (*bei Gericht*) examine 2 V/R mishear
verhungern V/I starve to death
verhüten V/T prevent **Verhütung** F prevention; (*mit Pille, Kondom etc*) contraception **Verhütungsmittel** N contraceptive
verirren V/R get lost
Verkauf M sale **verkaufen**

VT sell; **zu ~** for sale **Verkäufer(in)** M(F) seller; (*beruflich*) salesperson; (*in Laden*) sales clerk **verkäuflich** ADJ for sale

Verkehr M traffic; (*Sex*) intercourse; (*Umlauf*) circulation **verkehren** VI (*Bus etc*) run; **~ mit** associate (*od* mix) with **Verkehrsampel** F traffic light **Verkehrsamt** N tourist office **Verkehrsinsel** F traffic island **Verkehrsmeldung** F traffic report **Verkehrsmittel** N means *sg* of transportation; **öffentliche ~** *pl* public transportation *sg* **Verkehrsschild** N traffic sign **Verkehrsunfall** M road accident **Verkehrszeichen** N traffic sign

verkehrt ADJ wrong; (*verkehrt herum*) the wrong way around; (*Pullover etc*) inside out

verklagen VT take to court

verkleiden **1** VT & VR dress up (*als* as) **2** VR dress up (*als* as); (*um unerkannt zu bleiben*) disguise oneself **Verkleidung** F (*Karneval*) costume

verkleinern VT reduce; (*Zimmer, Gebiet etc*) make smaller

verkommen **1** VI deteriorate; (*Mensch*) go downhill **2** ADJ (*Haus*) dilapidated; (*moralisch*) depraved

verkraften VT cope with

verkratzt ADJ scratched

verkühlen VR get a chill

verkürzen VT shorten

Verlag M publishing company

verlangen **1** VT (*fordern*) demand; (*wollen*) want; (*Preis*) ask; (*erwarten*) ask (*von* of); (*fragen nach*) ask for; (*Pass etc*) ask to see; **~ Sie Herrn X** ask for Mr. X **2** VI **~ nach** ask for

verlängern VT extend; (*Pass, Erlaubnis*) renew **Verlängerung** F extension; SPORT overtime; (*von Pass, Erlaubnis*) renewal **Verlängerungsschnur** F extension cable **Verlängerungswoche** F extra week

verlassen **1** VT leave **2** VR rely (*auf +akk* on) **3** ADJ desolate; (*Mensch*) abandoned **verlässlich** ADJ reliable

Verlauf M course **verlaufen** **1** VI (*Weg, Grenze*) run (*entlang* along); (*zeitlich*) pass; (*Farben*) run **2** VR get lost; (*Menschenmenge*) disperse

verlegen **1** VT move; (*verlieren*) mislay; (*Buch*) publish **2** ADJ embarrassed **Verlegenheit** F embarrassment; (*Situation*) difficulty

Verleih M (*Firma*) rental company **verleihen** VT lend; (*vermieten*) rent (out); (*Preis, Medaille*) award

verleiten VT **j-n dazu ~, etw zu tun** induce sb to do sth

verlernen VT forget

verletzen VT injure; *fig* hurt **Verletzte(r)** M/F(M) injured

person **Verletzung** F injury; (*Verstoß*) violation
verlieben V/R fall in love (*in j-n* with sb) **verliebt** ADJ in love
verlieren V/T & V/I lose
verloben V/R get engaged (*mit* to) **Verlobte(r)** M/F(M) fiancé/fiancée **Verlobung** F engagement
verlosen V/T raffle **Verlosung** F raffle
Verlust M loss
vermehren V/T & V/R multiply; (*Menge*) increase
vermeiden V/T avoid
vermeintlich ADJ supposed
vermieten V/T rent (out) **Vermieter(in)** M(F) landlord/-lady
vermischen V/T & V/R mix
vermissen V/T miss **vermisst** ADJ missing; **j-n als ~ melden** report sb missing
Vermögen N fortune
vermuten V/T suppose; (*argwöhnen*) suspect **vermutlich** **1** ADJ probable **2** ADV probably **Vermutung** F supposition; (*Verdacht*) suspicion
vernachlässigen V/T neglect
vernichten V/T destroy **vernichtend** ADJ *fig* crushing; (*Blick*) withering; (*Kritik*) scathing
Vernunft F reason **vernünftig** ADJ sensible; (*Preis*) reasonable
veröffentlichen V/T publish
verordnen V/T MED prescribe **Verordnung** F order; MED prescription
verpachten V/T lease (out) (*an +akk* to)
verpacken V/T pack; (*einwickeln*) wrap up **Verpackung** F packaging
verpassen V/T miss
verpflegen V/T feed **Verpflegung** F feeding; (*Kost*) food; (*in Hotel*) board
verpflichten **1** V/T oblige; (*anstellen*) engage **2** V/R commit oneself (*etw zu tun* to doing sth)
verprügeln V/T beat up
verraten **1** V/T betray; (*Geheimnis*) divulge; **aber nicht ~!** but don't tell anyone **2** V/R give oneself away
verrechnen **1** V/T **~ mit** set off against **2** V/R miscalculate
Verrechnungsscheck M check for deposit only
verregnet ADJ rainy
verreisen V/I go away (*nach* to); **sie ist (geschäftlich) verreist** she's away (on business)
verrenken V/T contort; MED dislocate; **sich den Knöchel ~** sprain (*od* twist) one's ankle
verringern V/T reduce
verrostet ADJ rusty
verrückt ADJ mad, crazy; **es macht mich ~** it's driving me crazy
versagen V/I fail **Versagen** N failure **Versager(in)** M(F) failure
versammeln V/T & V/R assem-

ble, gather **Versammlung** F meeting
Versand M dispatch; (*Abteilung*) dispatch department **Versandhaus** N mail-order company
versäumen V/T miss; (*unterlassen*) neglect; **~, etw zu tun** fail to do sth
verschätzen V/R miscalculate
verschenken V/T give away; (*Chance*) waste
verschicken V/T send off
verschieben V/T (*auf später*) postpone, put off; (*an anderen Ort*) move
verschieden ADJ different; (*mehrere*) various; **sie sind ~ groß** they are of different sizes; **Verschiedene** *pl* various people/things *pl*; **Verschiedenes** various things *pl*
verschimmelt ADJ moldy
verschlafen **1** V/T sleep through; *fig* miss **2** V/I & V/R oversleep
verschlechtern V/R deteriorate, get worse **Verschlechterung** F deterioration
verschließbar ADJ lockable **verschließen** V/T close; (*mit Schlüssel*) lock
verschlimmern **1** V/T make worse **2** V/R get worse
verschlossen ADJ locked; *fig* reserved
verschlucken **1** V/T swallow **2** V/R choke (*an +dat* on)
Verschluss M lock; (*von Kleid*) fastener; FOTO shutter; (*Stöpsel*) stopper
verschmutzen V/T get dirty; (*Umwelt*) pollute
verschneit ADJ snow-covered
verschnupft ADJ **~ sein** have a cold
verschonen V/T spare (*j-n mit etw* sb sth)
verschreiben V/T MED prescribe **verschreibungspflichtig** ADJ available only on prescription
verschweigen V/T keep secret; **j-m etw ~** keep sth from sb
verschwenden V/T waste **Verschwendung** F waste
verschwiegen ADJ discreet; (*Ort*) secluded
verschwinden V/I disappear, vanish; **verschwinde!** get lost!
Versehen N **aus ~** by mistake **versehentlich** ADV by mistake
versenden V/T send off
versetzen **1** V/T transfer; (*verpfänden*) pawn; *umg* (*bei Verabredung*) stand up **2** V/R **sich in j-n** (*od* **j-s Lage**) **~** put oneself in sb's place
verseuchen V/T contaminate
versichern V/T insure; (*bestätigen*) assure; **versichert sein** be insured **Versichertenkarte** F health-insurance card **Versicherung** F insurance **Versicherungskarte** F **grüne ~** *insurance document for*

driving abroad **Versicherungspolice** F insurance policy
versinken V/I sink
versöhnen 1 V/T reconcile 2 V/R become reconciled
versorgen 1 V/T provide, supply (*mit* with); (*Familie*) look after 2 V/R look after oneself **Versorgung** F provision; (*Unterhalt*) maintenance; (*für Alter etc*) benefit
verspäten V/R be late **verspätet** ADJ late **Verspätung** F delay; **(eine Stunde) ~ haben** be (an hour) late
versprechen 1 V/T promise 2 V/R **ich habe mich versprochen** I didn't mean to say that
Verstand M mind; (*Vernunft*) (common) sense; **den ~ verlieren** lose one's mind **verständigen** 1 V/T inform 2 V/R communicate; (*sich einigen*) come to an understanding **Verständigung** F communication **verständlich** ADJ understandable **Verständnis** N understanding (*für* of); (*Mitgefühl*) sympathy **verständnisvoll** ADJ understanding
Verstärker M amplifier
verstauchen V/T sprain **verstaucht** *pperf von* verstauchen sprained
Versteck N hiding place **verstecken** V/T & V/R hide (*vor +dat* from)
verstehen 1 V/T understand; **falsch ~** misunderstand 2 V/R get on (*mit* with)
verstellbar ADJ adjustable
verstellen 1 V/T move; (*Uhr*) adjust; (*versperren*) block; (*Stimme, Handschrift*) disguise 2 V/R pretend, put on an act
verstopfen V/T block up; MED constipate **Verstopfung** F obstruction; MED constipation
Verstoß M infringement, violation (*gegen* of)
Versuch M attempt; (*wissenschaftlich*) experiment **versuchen** V/T try
vertauschen V/T exchange; (*versehentlich*) mix up
verteidigen V/T defend
verteilen V/T distribute
Vertrag M contract; POL treaty
vertragen 1 V/T stand, bear 2 V/R get along (with each other); (*sich aussöhnen*) make it up
vertrauen V/I **j-m/einer Sache ~** trust sb/sth **Vertrauen** N trust (*zu, in* in); **ich habe kein ~ zu ihm** I don't trust him; **ich hab's ihm im ~ gesagt** I told him in confidence **vertraulich** ADJ (*geheim*) confidential **vertraut** ADJ **sich mit etw ~ machen** familiarize oneself with sth
vertreten V/T represent; (*Ansicht*) hold **Vertreter(in)** M(F) representative
Vertrieb M (*Abteilung*) sales

department
verunglücken VI have an accident; **tödlich ~** be killed in an accident
verursachen VT cause
verurteilen VT condemn
verwählen VR dial the wrong number
verwalten VT manage; (*behördlich*) administer **Verwalter(in)** M(F) manager **Verwaltung** F management; (*amtlich*) administration
verwandt ADJ related (*mit* to) **Verwandte(r)** M/F(M) relative, relation **Verwandtschaft** F relationship; (*Menschen*) relatives *pl*
verwarnen VT warn; SPORT caution
verwechseln VT confuse (*mit* with); (*halten für*) mistake (*mit* for)
verweigern VT refuse
verwenden VT use **Verwendung** F use
verwirklichen VT realize; **sich selbst ~** fulfill oneself
verwirren VT confuse **Verwirrung** F confusion
verwöhnen VT spoil
verwunderlich ADJ surprising **Verwunderung** F astonishment
verwüsten VT devastate
verzählen VR miscount
verzehren VT consume
Verzeichnis N (*Liste*) list; (*Katalog*) catalog; (*in Buch*) index; IT directory
verzeihen VT & VI forgive (*j-m etw* sb for sth); **~ Sie bitte, …** (*vor Frage etc*) excuse me, …; **~ Sie die Störung** sorry to disturb you **Verzeihung** F **~!** sorry; **~, …** (*vor Frage etc*) excuse me, …; **(j-n) um ~ bitten** apologize (to sb)
verzichten VI **auf etw ~** do without sth; (*aufgeben*) give sth up
verziehen **1** VT (*Kind*) spoil; **das Gesicht ~** pull a face **2** VR go out of shape; (*verschwinden*) disappear
verzieren VT decorate
verzögern **1** VT delay **2** VR be delayed **Verzögerung** F delay
verzweifeln VI despair (*an* of) **verzweifelt** ADJ desperate **Verzweiflung** F despair
Vetter M cousin
vgl. *abk* = vergleiche cf
vibrieren VI vibrate
Video N video; **auf ~ aufnehmen** video **Videokamera** F video camera **Videokassette** F video (cassette) **Videorekorder** M video recorder **Videospiel** N video game
Vieh N cattle
viel **1** INDEF PR a lot (of), lots of; **~ Arbeit** a lot of work, lots of work; **~e Leute** a lot of people, lots of people, many people; **zu ~** too much; **zu ~e** too

many; **sehr ~** a great deal of; **sehr ~e** a great many; **ziemlich ~/~e** quite a lot of; **nicht ~** not much, not a lot of; **nicht ~e** not many, not a lot of; **sie sagt nicht ~** she doesn't say a lot; **gibt es ~?** is there much?, is there a lot?; **gibt es ~e?** are there many?, are there a lot? **2** ADV a lot; **sehr ~** a great deal; **ziemlich ~** quite a lot; **~ besser** much better; **~ teurer** much more expensive; **~ zu ~** far too much

vielleicht ADV perhaps; **~ ist sie krank** perhaps she's ill, she might be ill; **weißt du ~, wo er ist?** do you know where he is (by any chance)?

vielmal(s) ADV many times; **danke ~s** many thanks **vielmehr** ADV rather **vielseitig** ADJ many-sided; (*Interessen*) varied; (*Mensch, Gerät*) versatile

vier NUM four; **auf allen ~en** on all fours; **unter ~ Augen** in private, privately **Vier** F four; (*Schulnote*) ≈ D **viereckig** ADJ four-sided; (*quadratisch*) square **vierfach** ADJ **die ~e Menge** four times the amount **vierhundert** NUM four hundred **viermal** ADV four times **vierspurig** ADJ four-lane

viert ADV **wir sind zu ~** there are four of us **vierte(r, s)** ADJ fourth; → dritte

Viertel N (*Stadtviertel*) quarter, district; (*Bruchteil*) quarter; (*Viertelliter*) quarter-liter; **~ vor drei, drei viertel drei** a quarter to three; **~ nach drei** a quarter after (*od* past) three; **viertel drei** a quarter after (*od* past) two **Viertelfinale** N quarter-final **vierteljährlich** ADJ quarterly **Viertelstunde** F quarter of an hour

vierzehn NUM fourteen; **in ~ Tagen** in two weeks **vierzehntägig** ADJ two-week **vierzehnte(r, s)** ADJ fourteenth; → dritte **vierzig** NUM forty **vierzigste(r, s)** ADJ fortieth

Vietnam N Vietnam

Vignette F freeway permit

Villa F villa

violett ADJ purple

Violine F violin

Virus M *od* N virus

Visitenkarte F calling card

Visum N visa

Vitamin N vitamin

Vitrine F (glass) cabinet; (*Schaukasten*) display case

Vogel M bird **Vogelgrippe** F bird flu, avian flu **vögeln** VI & VT *vulg* screw

Voicemail F voice mail

Vokal M vowel

Volk N people *pl*; (*Nation*) nation **Volksfest** N festival; (*Jahrmarkt*) fair **Volkshochschule** F adult education center **Volkslied** N folksong **Volksmusik** F folk music

volkstümlich ADJ popular; (*herkömmlich*) traditional; (*Kunst*) folk
voll ADJ full (*von* of) **Vollbremsung** F **eine ~ machen** slam on the brakes **vollends** ADV completely
Volleyball M volleyball
Vollgas N **mit ~** at full throttle; **~ geben** step on it
völlig **1** ADJ complete **2** ADV completely
volljährig ADJ of age **Vollkaskoversicherung** F fully comprehensive insurance **vollklimatisiert** ADJ fully air-conditioned **vollkommen** **1** ADJ complete **2** ADV completely **Vollkornbrot** N whole-wheat bread **vollmachen** V/T fill (up) **Vollmacht** F authority; (*Urkunde*) power of attorney **Vollmilch** F whole milk **Vollmilchschokolade** F milk chocolate **Vollmond** M full moon **Vollnarkose** F general anesthetic **vollständig** ADJ complete **volltanken** V/I fill up **Vollwertkost** F wholefood **vollzählig** ADJ complete
Volt N volt
Volumen N volume
vom *kontr von* **von dem**; (*räumlich, zeitlich, Ursache*) from; **ich kenne sie nur ~ Sehen** I only know her by sight
von PRÄP *+dat* (*räumlich, zeitlich*) from; (*statt gen, bestehend aus*) of; (*im Passiv*) by; **ein Freund ~ mir** a friend of mine; **~ mir aus** *umg* if you like; **~ wegen!** no way
voneinander ADV from each other
vor PRÄP *+dat od akk* (*zeitlich*) before; (*räumlich*) in front of; **fünf ~ drei** five to three; **~ 2 Tagen** 2 days ago; **~ Wut/Liebe** with rage/love; **~ allem** above all
vorangehen V/I go ahead; **einer Sache ~** precede sth **vorankommen** V/I make progress
voraus ADV **j-m ~ sein** be ahead of sb; **im Voraus** in advance **vorausfahren** V/I drive on ahead **vorausgesetzt** KONJ provided (that) **Voraussage** F prediction; (*Wetter*) forecast **voraussagen** V/T predict **voraussehen** V/T foresee **voraussetzen** V/T assume **Voraussetzung** F requirement, prerequisite **voraussichtlich** **1** ADJ expected **2** ADV probably **vorauszahlen** V/T pay in advance
vorbei ADV past, over, finished **vorbeibringen** V/T drop by (*od* in) **vorbeifahren** V/I drive past **vorbeigehen** V/I pass by, go past; (*verstreichen, aufhören*) pass **vorbeikommen** V/I drop by **vorbeilassen** V/T **kannst du die Leute ~?** would you let these people pass?;

lässt du mich bitte mal vorbei? can I get past, please?
vorbereiten 1 VT prepare 2 VR get ready (*auf, für* for) **Vorbereitung** F preparation
vorbestellen VT book in advance; (*Essen*) order in advance **Vorbestellung** F booking, reservation
vorbeugen VI prevent (*dat* sth) **vorbeugend** ADJ preventive **Vorbeugung** F prevention
Vorbild N (role) model **vorbildlich** ADJ model, ideal
Vorderachse F front axle **vordere(r, s)** ADJ front **Vordergrund** M foreground **Vorderradantrieb** M AUTO front-wheel drive **Vorderseite** F front **Vordersitz** M front seat **Vorderteil** M *od* N front (part)
voreilig ADJ hasty, rash; **~e Schlüsse ziehen** jump to conclusions
voreingenommen ADJ biased
vorenthalten VT **j-m etw ~** withhold sth from sb
vorerst ADV for the moment
vorfahren VI (*vorausfahren*) drive on ahead; **vor das Haus ~** drive up to the house; **fahren Sie bis zur Ampel vor** drive as far as the traffic light
Vorfahrt F AUTO right of way; **~ achten** yield **Vorfahrtsschild** N yield sign **Vorfahrtsstraße** F major road
Vorfall M incident
vorführen VT demonstrate; (*Film*) show; THEAT perform
Vorgänger(in) M(F) predecessor
vorgehen VI (*vorausgehen*) go on ahead; (*nach vorn*) go forward; (*handeln*) act, proceed; (*Uhr*) be fast; (*Vorrang haben*) take precedence; (*passieren*) go on **Vorgehen** N procedure
Vorgesetzte(r) M/F(M) superior
vorgestern ADV the day before yesterday
vorhaben VT plan; **hast du schon was vor?** have you got anything on?; **ich habe vor, nach Los Angeles zu fahren** I'm planning to go to Los Angeles
vorhalten VT **j-m etw ~** accuse sb of sth
vorhanden ADJ existing; (*erhältlich*) available
Vorhang M curtain
Vorhaut F foreskin
vorher ADV before; **zwei Tage ~** two days before; **~ essen wir** we'll eat first **Vorhersage** F forecast **vorhersehen** VT foresee
vorhin ADV just now, a moment ago
vorkommen VI (*nach vorne kommen*) come forward; (*geschehen*) happen; (*scheinen*) seem (to be); **sich dumm ~**

feel stupid
Vorlage F model
vorlassen V/T **j-n ~** let sb go first
vorläufig ADJ temporary
vorlesen V/T read out
vorletzte(r, s) ADJ last but one; **am ~n Samstag** (on) the Saturday before last
Vorliebe F preference
vormachen V/T **kannst du es mir ~?** can you show me how to do it?; **j-m etwas ~** *fig* (*täuschen*) fool sb
Vormittag M morning; **am ~** in the morning; **heute ~** this morning **vormittags** ADV in the morning; **um 9 Uhr ~** at 9 (o'clock) in the morning, at 9 a.m.
vorn(e) ADV in front; **von ~ anfangen** start at the beginning; **nach ~** to the front; **weiter ~** further up; **von ~ bis hinten** from beginning to end
Vorname M first name; **wie heißt du mit ~** what's your first name?
vornehm ADJ distinguished; (*Benehmen*) refined; (*fein, elegant*) elegant
vornehmen V/T **sich etw ~** start on sth; **sich ~, etw zu tun** (*beschließen*) decide to do sth
vornherein ADV **von ~** from the start
Vorort M suburb
vorrangig ADJ priority
Vorrat M stock, supply **vorrätig** ADJ in stock
Vorrecht N privilege
Vorruhestand M early retirement **Vorsaison** F early season
Vorsatz M intention; JUR intent **vorsätzlich** ADJ intentional; JUR premeditated
Vorschau F preview; (*Film*) trailer
Vorschlag M suggestion, proposal **vorschlagen** V/T suggest, propose; **ich schlage vor, dass wir gehen** I suggest we go
vorschreiben V/T stipulate; **j-m etw ~** dictate sth to sb
Vorschrift F regulation, rule; (*Anweisung*) instruction **vorschriftsmäßig** ADJ correct
Vorsicht F care; **~!** look out!; (*Schild*) caution; **~ Stufe!** mind the step **vorsichtig** ADJ careful **vorsichtshalber** ADV just in case
Vorsorge F precaution; (*Vorbeugung*) prevention **Vorsorgeuntersuchung** F checkup **vorsorglich** ADV as a precaution
Vorspeise F appetizer
vorstellen V/T (*bekannt machen*) introduce, put forward; (*vor etw*) put in front; **sich etw ~** imagine sth **Vorstellung** F (*Bekanntmachen*) introduction; THEAT performance; (*Gedanke*) idea **Vorstellungs-**

gespräch N interview
vortäuschen V/T feign
Vorteil M advantage (*gegenüber* over) **vorteilhaft** ADJ advantageous
Vortrag M talk (*über +akk* on); (*akademisch*) lecture; **einen ~ halten** give a talk
vorüber ADV over **vorübergehen** V/I pass **vorübergehend** **1** ADJ temporary **2** ADV temporarily, for the time being
Vorurteil N prejudice
Vorverkauf M advance booking
vorverlegen V/T bring forward
Vorwahl F TEL area code
Vorwand M pretext, excuse; **unter dem ~, dass** with the excuse that
vorwärts ADV forward **vorwärtsgehen** V/I *fig* make progress
vorweg ADV in advance **vorwegnehmen** V/T anticipate
vorwerfen V/T **j-m etw ~** accuse sb of sth
vorwiegend ADV mainly
Vorwort N preface
Vorwurf M reproach; **sich Vorwürfe machen** reproach oneself; **j-m Vorwürfe machen** accuse sb **vorwurfsvoll** ADJ reproachful
vorzeigen V/T show
vorzeitig ADJ premature, early
vorziehen V/T (*lieber haben*) prefer
vorzüglich ADJ excellent
vulgär ADJ vulgar
Vulkan M volcano

W

Waage F scales *pl*; ASTROL Libra **waagerecht** ADJ horizontal
wach ADJ awake; **~ werden** wake up **Wache** F guard
Wachs N wax
wachsen V/I **1** V/I grow **2** V/T (*Skier*) wax **Wachstum** N growth
Wächter(in) M(F) guard; (*auf Parkplatz*) security guard
wackelig ADJ wobbly; *fig* shaky **Wackelkontakt** M loose connection **wackeln** V/I (*Stuhl*) be wobbly; (*Zahn, Schraube*) be loose; **mit dem Kopf ~** waggle one's head
Wade F ANAT calf
Waffe F weapon
Waffel F waffle; (*Keks, Eiswaffel*) wafer
wagen V/T risk; **es ~, etw zu tun** dare to do sth
Wagen M AUTO, BAHN car **Wagenheber** M jack **Wagentyp** M model, make
Wahl F choice; POL election
wählen **1** V/T choose; TEL di-

al; POL vote for; (*durch Wahl ermitteln*) elect **2** V/I choose; TEL dial; POL vote **Wähler(in)** M(F) voter **wählerisch** ADJ choosy **Wahlkampf** M election campaign **wahllos** ADV at random **Wahlwiederholung** F redial

Wahnsinn M madness; **~!** amazing! **wahnsinnig** **1** ADJ insane, mad **2** ADV *umg* incredibly

wahr ADJ true; **das darf doch nicht ~ sein!** I don't believe it; **nicht ~?** that's right, isn't it?

während **1** PRÄP *+gen* during **2** KONJ while **währenddessen** ADV meanwhile, in the meantime

Wahrheit F truth

wahrnehmbar ADJ noticeable, perceptible **wahrnehmen** V/T perceive

wahrscheinlich **1** ADJ probable, likely **2** ADV probably **Wahrscheinlichkeit** F probability

Währung F currency

Wahrzeichen N symbol

Waise F orphan

Wal M whale

Wald M wood; (*groß*) forest **Waldbrand** M forest fire **Waldsterben** N forest dieback

Wales N Wales

Walkman® M walkman®, personal stereo

Wallfahrt F pilgrimage

Walnuss F walnut

wälzen **1** V/T roll; (*Bücher*) pore over; (*Probleme*) deliberate on **2** V/R wallow; (*vor Schmerzen*) roll around; (*im Bett*) toss and turn

Walzer M waltz

Wand F wall

Wandel M change **wandeln** V/T & V/R change

Wanderer M, **Wanderin** F hiker **Wanderkarte** F hiking map **wandern** V/I hike; (*Blick*) wander; (*Gedanken*) stray **Wanderschuh** M walking shoe **Wanderstiefel** M hiking boot **Wanderung** F hike; **eine ~ machen** go on a hike **Wanderweg** M hiking trail

Wandschrank M built-in closet

Wange F cheek

wann ADV when; **seit ~ ist sie da?** how long has she been here?; **bis ~ bleibt ihr?** how long are you staying?

Wanne F (bath)tub

Wappen N coat of arms

Ware F product; **~n** goods *pl* **Warenhaus** N department store

warm ADJ warm; (*Essen*) hot; **~ laufen** warm up; **mir ist es zu ~** I'm too warm **Wärme** F warmth **wärmen** **1** V/T warm; (*Essen*) warm (*od* heat) up **2** V/I (*Kleidung, Sonne*) be warm **3** V/R warm up; (*gegenseitig*) keep

each other warm **Wärmflasche** F hot-water bottle
Warnblinkanlage F AUTO hazard lights *pl* **Warndreieck** N AUTO warning triangle **warnen** V/T warn (*vor dat* about, of) **Warnung** F warning
Warteliste F waiting list **warten** 1 V/I wait (*auf +akk* for); **warte mal!** wait (*od* hang on) a minute 2 V/T TECH service
Wärter(in) M(F) attendant
Wartesaal M, **Wartezimmer** N waiting room
Wartung F service; (*das Warten*) servicing
warum ADV why
Warze F wart
was 1 INT PR what; **~ kostet das?** what does it cost?, how much is it?; **~ für ein Auto ist das?** what kind of car is that?; **~ für eine Farbe?** what color?; **~ ist/gibt's?** what is it?, what's up? 2 REL PR **du weißt, ~ ich meine** you know what I mean; **~ (auch) immer** whatever 3 INDEF PR *umg* (*etwas*) something; **soll ich dir ~ mitbringen?** do you want me to bring you anything?
Waschanlage F AUTO car wash **waschbar** ADJ washable **Waschbecken** N sink
Wäsche F washing; (*schmutzig*) laundry; **in der ~** in the wash **Wäscheklammer** F clothes pin **Wäscheleine** F clothesline
waschen 1 V/T & V/I wash 2 V/R wash up; **sich die Haare ~** wash one's hair
Wäscherei F laundry **Wäscheständer** M drying rack **Wäschetrockner** M (clothes) dryer
Waschgelegenheit F washing facilities *pl* **Waschlappen** M washcloth; *umg* (*Mensch*) wuss **Waschmaschine** F washing machine **Waschmittel** N, **Waschpulver** N soap powder **Waschraum** M washroom **Waschsalon** M laundromat **Waschstraße** F car wash
Wasser N water; **fließendes ~** running water **wasserdicht** ADJ watertight; (*Uhr etc*) waterproof **Wasserfall** M waterfall **Wasserfarbe** F watercolor **wasserfest** ADJ watertight, waterproof **Wasserhahn** M faucet, tap **wässerig** ADJ watery **Wasserkessel** M kettle **Wasserkocher** M electric kettle **Wasserleitung** F water pipe **wasserlöslich** ADJ water-soluble **Wassermann** M ASTROL Aquarius **Wassermelone** F water melon **Wasserschaden** M water damage **wasserscheu** ADJ scared of water **Wasserski** N water--skiing **Wassersport** M water sports *pl* **wasserundurchlässig** ADJ watertight, water-

proof **Wasserversorgung** F water supply **Wasserwerk** N waterworks *pl*
waten V/I wade
Watt 1 N GEO mud flats *pl* 2 N ELEK watt
Watte F cotton **Wattestäbchen** N Q-tip®
WC N restroom **WC-Reiniger** M toilet cleaner
Web N IT Web **Webseite** F IT web page
Wechsel M change; SPORT substitution **Wechselgeld** N change **wechselhaft** ADJ (*Wetter*) changeable **Wechseljahre** PL menopause *sg* **Wechselkurs** M exchange rate **wechseln** 1 V/T change; (*Blicke*) exchange; **Geld ~** change some money; (*in Kleingeld*) get some change; **Euro in Dollar ~** change euros into dollars 2 V/I change; **kannst du ~?** can you change this? **Wechselstrom** M alternating current, AC **Wechselstube** F currency exchange office
Weckdienst M wake-up call service **wecken** V/T wake (up) **Wecker** M alarm clock **Weckruf** M wake-up call
wedeln V/I (*Ski*) wedel; **der Hund wedelte mit dem Schwanz** the dog wagged its tail
weder KONJ **~ ... noch ...** neither ... nor ...
weg ADV away; (*los, ab*) off; **er war schon ~** he had already left (*od* gone); **Hände ~!** hands off; **weit ~** a long way away (*od* off)
Weg M way; (*Pfad*) path; (*Route*) route; **j-n nach dem ~ fragen** ask sb the way; **auf dem ~ sein** be on the way
wegbleiben V/I stay away **wegbringen** V/T take away
wegen PRÄP *+gen od dat* because of
wegfahren V/I drive away; (*abfahren*) leave; (*in Urlaub*) go away **Wegfahrsperre** F AUTO (engine) immobilizer **weggehen** V/I go away **wegkommen** V/I get away; *fig* **gut/schlecht ~** come off well/badly **weglassen** V/T leave out **weglaufen** V/I run away **weglegen** V/T put aside **wegmüssen** V/I **ich muss weg** I've got to go **wegnehmen** V/T take away **wegräumen** V/T clear away **wegrennen** V/I run away **wegschicken** V/T send away **wegschmeißen** V/T throw away **wegsehen** V/I look away **wegtun** V/T put away
Wegweiser M signpost
wegwerfen V/T throw away **wegwischen** V/T wipe off **wegziehen** V/I move (away)
weh ADJ sore; → wehtun
wehen V/T & V/I blow; (*Fahne*) flutter
Wehen PL labor pains *pl*

Wehrdienst M military service
wehren V/R defend oneself
wehtun V/I hurt; **j-m/sich ~** hurt sb/oneself
Weibchen N **es ist ein ~** (*Tier*) it's a she **weiblich** ADJ feminine; BIOL female
weich ADJ soft; **~ gekocht** (*Ei*) soft-boiled **Weichspüler** M (*für Wäsche*) fabric softener
Weide F (*Baum*) willow; (*Grasfläche*) meadow
weigern V/R refuse **Weigerung** F refusal
Weiher M pond
Weihnachten N Christmas **Weihnachtsabend** M Christmas Eve **Weihnachtsbaum** M Christmas tree **Weihnachtsfeier** F Christmas party **Weihnachtsferien** PL Christmas vacation *sg* **Weihnachtsgeld** N Christmas bonus **Weihnachtsgeschenk** N Christmas present **Weihnachtskarte** F Christmas card **Weihnachtslied** N Christmas carol **Weihnachtsmann** M Santa (Claus) **Weihnachtstag** M **erster ~** Christmas Day; **zweiter ~** day after Christmas **Weihnachtszeit** F Christmas season
weil KONJ because
Weile F while, short time; **es kann noch eine ~ dauern** it could take some time
Wein M wine; (*Pflanze*) vine **Weinbrand** M brandy
weinen V/T & V/I cry
Weinglas N wine glass **Weinkarte** F wine list **Weinkeller** M wine cellar **Weinprobe** F wine tasting **Weintraube** F grape
weise ADJ wise
Weise F manner, way; **auf diese (Art und) ~** this way
weisen V/T show
Weisheit F wisdom **Weisheitszahn** M wisdom tooth
weiß ADJ white **Weißbier** N ≈ wheat beer **Weißbrot** N white bread **Weißkohl** M, **Weißkraut** N (white) cabbage **Weißwein** M white wine
weit **1** ADJ wide; (*Begriff*) broad; (*Reise, Wurf*) long; (*Kleid*) loose; **wie ~ ist es ...?** how far is it ...?; **so ~ sein** be ready **2** ADV far; **~ verbreitet** widespread; **~ gereist** widely traveled; **~ offen** wide open; **das geht zu ~** that's going too far
weiter **1** ADJ (*weiter weg*) farther (*od* further) (away); (*zusätzlich*) further; **~e Informationen** further information *sg* **2** ADV further; **~!** go on; (*weitergehen!*) keep moving; **~ nichts/niemand** nothing/nobody else; **und so ~** and so on **Weiterbildung** F further training **weiterempfehlen** V/T recommend **weitererzählen** V/T **nicht ~!** don't tell

anyone **weiterfahren** V/I go on (*nach* to, *bis* as far as) **weitergeben** V/T pass on **weitergehen** V/I go on **weiterhelfen** V/I **j-m ~** help sb **weiterhin** ADV **etw ~ tun** go on doing sth

weitermachen V/T & V/I continue **weiterreisen** V/I continue one's journey

weitgehend **1** ADJ considerable **2** ADV largely **weitsichtig** ADJ (*Sehkraft, auch fig*) farsighted **Weitsprung** M long jump **Weitwinkelobjektiv** N FOTO wide-angle lens

Weizen M wheat **Weizenbier** N ≈ wheat beer

welche(r, s) **1** INT PR what; (*auswählend*) which (one); **~ Geschmacksrichtung willst du?** which flavor do you want?; **~r ist es?** which (one) is it? **2** REL PR (*Person*) who; (*Sache*) which, that; **zeig mir, ~r es war** show me which one of them it was **3** INDEF PR *umg* some; **hast du Kleingeld? - ja, ich hab' ~s** have you got any change? - yes, I've got some

welken V/I wither

Welle F wave **Wellenlänge** F wavelength **Wellensittich** M budgerigar, budgie

Wellness F wellness

Welpe M puppy

Welt F world; **auf der ~** in the world; **auf die ~ kommen** be born **Weltall** N universe **weltbekannt** ADJ, **weltberühmt** ADJ world-famous **Weltkrieg** M world war **Weltmacht** F world power **Weltmeister(in)** M(F) world champion **Weltmeisterschaft** F world championship; (*im Fußball*) World Cup **Weltraum** M space **Weltreise** F trip around the world **Weltrekord** M world record **Weltstadt** F metropolis **weltweit** ADJ worldwide, global

wem PRON, *dat von* wer; who ... to, (to) whom; **~ hast du's gegeben?** who did you give it to?; **~ gehört es?** who does it belong to?, whose is it?; **~ auch immer es gehört** whoever it belongs to

wen PRON, *akk von* wer; who, whom; **~ hast du besucht?** who did you visit?; **~ möchten Sie sprechen?** who would you like to speak to?

Wende F turning point; (*Veränderung*) change; **die ~** HIST the fall of the Berlin Wall **Wendekreis** M AUTO turning circle

wenden V/T & V/I & V/R turn (around); (*um 180°*) make a U-turn; **sich an j-n ~** turn to sb; **bitte ~!** please turn over, PTO

wenig **1** INDEF PR little; **~(e)** (*pl*) few; **(nur) ein (klein) ~** (just) a little (bit); **ein ~ Zucker**

a little bit of sugar, a little sugar; **wir haben ~ Zeit** we haven't got much time; **zu ~** too little; (*pl*) too few; **nur ~e wissen** only a few know **2** ADV **er spricht ~** he doesn't talk much; **~ bekannt** little known **wenigstens** ADV at least

wenn KONJ (*falls*) if; (*zeitlich*) when **wennschon** ADV **na ~** so what?

wer 1 INT PR who; **~ von euch?** which (one) of you? **2** REL PR anybody/anyone who; **~ das glaubt, ist dumm** anyone who believes that is stupid; **~ auch immer** whoever **3** INDEF PR somebody/someone; (*in Fragen*) anybody/anyone; **ist da ~?** is (there) anybody there?

Werbefernsehen N TV commercials *pl* **werben 1** V/T win; (*Mitglied*) recruit **2** V/I advertise **Werbespot** M commercial **Werbung** F advertising

werden 1 V/I get, become; **alt/müde/reich ~** get old/tired/rich; **was willst du ~?** what do you want to be? **2** V/AUX (*Futur*) will; (*Entschluss*) be going to; (*Passiv*) be; **er wird uns (schon) fahren** he'll drive us; **er wird uns abholen** he's going to pick us up; **es wird gerade diskutiert** it's being discussed

werfen V/T throw

Werft F shipyard, dockyard

Werk N (*Kunstwerk, Buch etc*) work; (*Fabrik*) factory; (*Mechanismus*) works *pl* **Werkstatt** F workshop; AUTO garage **Werktag** M working day **werktags** ADV (on) weekdays, during the week **Werkzeug** N tool **Werkzeugkasten** M toolbox

wert ADJ worth; **es ist etwa 50 Dollar ~** it's worth about 50 dollars; **das ist nichts ~** it's worthless **Wert** M worth; FIN value; **~ legen auf** attach importance to **Wertangabe** F declaration of value **Wertbrief** M insured letter **Wertgegenstand** M valuable object **wertlos** ADJ worthless **Wertmarke** F token **Wertpapiere** PL securities *pl* **Wertsachen** PL valuables *pl* **Wertstoff** M recyclable waste **wertvoll** ADJ valuable

Wesen N being; (*Natur, Charakter*) nature

wesentlich 1 ADJ significant; (*beträchtlich*) considerable **2** ADV considerably

weshalb ADV why

Wespe F wasp

wessen PRON, *gen von* **wer**; whose

West M west **Westdeutschland** N Western Germany

Weste F vest; (*Wollweste*) cardigan

Westen M west; **im ~ Deutschlands** in the western

part of Germany **Westeuropa** N Western Europe **Westküste** F west coast **westlich** ADJ western; (*Kurs, Richtung*) westerly **Westwind** M west (-erly) wind

weswegen ADV why

Wettbewerb M competition

Wettbüro N betting office

Wette F bet; **eine ~ abschließen** make a bet **wetten** V/T & V/I bet (*auf +akk* on); **ich habe mit ihm gewettet, dass …** I bet him that …; **ich wette mit dir um 50 Dollar** I'll bet you 50 dollars; **~, dass?** wanna bet?

Wetter N weather **Wetterbericht** M, **Wettervorhersage** F weather forecast

Wettkampf M contest **Wettlauf** M, **Wettrennen** N race

Whirlpool® M jacuzzi®

Whisky M (*schottischer*) whisky; (*irischer, amerikanischer*) whiskey

wichtig ADJ important

wickeln V/T (*Schnur*) wind (*um* around); (*Schal, Decke*) wrap (*um* around); **ein Baby ~** change a baby's diaper **Wickelraum** M baby changing room **Wickeltisch** M baby changing table

Widder M ZOOL ram; ASTROL Aries *sg*

wider PRÄP *+akk* against

widerlich ADJ disgusting

widerrufen V/T withdraw; (*Auftrag, Befehl etc*) cancel

widersprechen V/I contradict (*j-m* sb) **Widerspruch** M contradiction

Widerstand M resistance **widerstandsfähig** ADJ resistant (*gegen* to)

widerwärtig ADJ disgusting

widerwillig ADJ unwilling, reluctant

widmen **1** V/T dedicate **2** V/R **sich j-m/etw ~** devote oneself to sb/sth **Widmung** F dedication

wie **1** ADV how; **~ viel** how much; **~ viele Menschen?** how many people?; **~ geht's?** how are you?; **~ das?** how come?; **~ bitte?** excuse me? **2** KONJ **(so) schön ~ …** as beautiful as …; **~ du weißt** as you know; **~ ich das hörte** when I heard that; **ich sah, ~ er rauskam** I saw him coming out

wieder ADV again; **~ ein(e) …** another …; **~ erkennen** recognize; **etw ~ gutmachen** make up for sth; **~ verwerten** recycle

wiederbekommen V/T get back

wiederholen V/T repeat **Wiederholung** F repetition

Wiederhören N TEL **auf ~** goodbye

wiederkommen V/I come back

wiedersehen V/T see again;

(*wieder treffen*) meet again **Wiedersehen** N reunion; **auf ~!** goodbye
Wiedervereinigung F reunification
Wiege F cradle **wiegen** V/T & V/I (*Gewicht*) weigh
Wien N Vienna
Wiese F meadow
wieso ADV why
wievielte(r, s) ADJ **zum ~n Mal?** how many times?; **den Wievielten haben wir heute?** what's the date today?; **am Wievielten hast du Geburtstag?** what date is your birthday?
wieweit KONJ to what extent
wild ADJ wild
Wild N game
wildfremd ADJ *umg* **ein ~er Mensch** a complete (*od* total) stranger **Wildleder** N suede **Wildschwein** N (wild) boar **Wildwasserfahren** N white-water rafting
Wille M will
willen PRÄP *+gen* **um ... ~** for the sake of ...; **um Himmels ~!** for heaven's sake; (*betroffen*) goodness me
willkommen ADJ welcome
Wimper F eyelash **Wimperntusche** F mascara
Wind M wind
Windel F diaper
windig ADJ windy; *fig* dubious **Windmühle** F windmill **Windpocken** PL chickenpox *sg* **Windschutzscheibe** F AUTO windshield **Windsurfen** N windsurfing **Windsurfer(in)** M(F) windsurfer
Winkel M MATH angle; (*in Raum*) corner
winken V/T & V/I wave
Winter M winter **Winterfahrplan** M winter timetable **winterlich** ADJ wintry **Winterreifen** M winter tire **Winterschlussverkauf** M winter sales *pl* **Wintersport** M winter sports *pl* **Winterzeit** F (*Uhrzeit*) standard time
winzig ADJ tiny
wir PERS PR we; **~ alle** all of us; **~ drei** the three of us; **~ sind's** it's us; **~ nicht** not us
Wirbel M whirl; (*Trubel*) hurly-burly; (*Aufsehen*) fuss; ANAT vertebra **Wirbelsäule** F spine
wirken V/I be effective; (*erfolgreich sein*) work; (*scheinen*) seem
wirklich ADJ real **Wirklichkeit** F reality
wirksam ADJ effective **Wirkung** F effect
wirr ADJ confused **Wirrwarr** M confusion
Wirt M (*Vermieter*) landlord; (*von Speiselokal*) restaurant owner; (*von Trinklokal*) bar owner **Wirtin** F (*Vermieterin*) landlady; (*von Speiselokal*) restaurant owner; (*von Trinklokal*) bar owner

Wirtschaft F economy; (*Speiselokal*) restaurant; (*Trinklokal*) bar **wirtschaftlich** ADJ economic; (*sparsam*) economical
Wirtshaus N (*Speiselokal*) restaurant; (*Trinklokal*) bar
wischen V/T & V/I wipe **Wischer** M wiper
wissen V/T know; **weißt du schon, …?** did you know …?; **woher weißt du das?** how do you know?; **das musst du selbst ~** that's up to you **Wissen** N knowledge
Wissenschaft F science **Wissenschaftler(in)** M(F) scientist; (*Geisteswissenschaftler*) academic **wissenschaftlich** ADJ scientific; (*geisteswissenschaftlich*) academic
Witwe F widow **Witwer** M widower
Witz M joke; **mach keine ~e!** you're kidding; **das soll wohl ein ~ sein** you've got to be joking **witzig** ADJ funny
WLAN N *abk* = wireless local area network; IT WiFi, wireless network, wireless LAN
wo **1** ADV where; **überall, ~ ich hingehe** wherever I go **2** KONJ **jetzt, ~ du da bist** now that you're here; **~ ich dich gerade spreche** while I'm talking to you **woanders** ADV somewhere else **wobei** ADV **~ mir einfällt …** which reminds me …
Woche F week; **während** (*od* **unter**) **der ~** during the week; **einmal die ~** once a week **Wochenende** N weekend; **am ~** on the weekend; **wir fahren übers ~ weg** we're going away for the weekend **Wochenendurlaub** M weekend break **Wochenkarte** F weekly (season) ticket **wochenlang** ADV for weeks (on end) **Wochenmarkt** M weekly market **Wochentag** M weekday **wöchentlich** ADJ & ADV weekly
Wodka M vodka
wodurch ADV **~ unterscheiden sie sich?** what's the difference between them?; **~ hast du es gemerkt?** how did you notice? **wofür** ADV (*relativ*) for which; (*Frage*) what … for; **~ brauchst du das?** what do you need that for? **woher** ADV where … from **wohin** ADV where … to
wohl ADV well; (*behaglich*) at ease, comfortable; (*vermutlich*) probably; (*gewiss*) certainly **Wohl** N **zum ~!** cheers! **wohlbehalten** ADV safe and sound **Wohlstand** M prosperity, affluence
Wohnblock M apartment house **wohnen** V/I live **Wohngemeinschaft** F shared apartment **wohnhaft** ADJ resident **Wohnküche** F combined kitchen and living room **Wohnmobil** N camp-

er, RV **Wohnort**, **Wohnsitz** M place of residence **Wohnung** F apartment **Wohnungstür** F front door **Wohnwagen** M trailer **Wohnzimmer** N living room

Wolf M wolf

Wolke F cloud **Wolkenkratzer** M skyscraper **wolkenlos** ADJ cloudless **wolkig** ADJ cloudy

Wolldecke F (woolen) blanket **Wolle** F wool

wollen 1 V/AUX want; **sie wollte ihn nicht sehen** she didn't want to see him; **~ wir gehen?** shall we go?; **~ Sie bitte …** will (*od* would) you please … 2 V/T want; **ich will lieber bleiben** I'd prefer to stay; **er will, dass ich aufhöre** he wants me to stop; **ich wollte, ich wäre/hätte …** I wish I were/had … 3 V/I want to; **ich will nicht** I don't want to; **was du willst** whatever you like; **wo willst du hin?** where do you want to go?; (*wohin gehst du?*) where are you going?

Wolljacke F cardigan

womit ADV what … with; **~ habe ich das verdient?** what have I done to deserve that?

womöglich ADV possibly

woran ADV **~ denkst du?** what are you thinking of?; **~ ist er gestorben?** what did he die of?; **~ sieht man das?** how can you tell? **worauf** ADV **~ wartest du?** what are you waiting for? **woraus** ADV **~ ist das gemacht?** what is it made of?

Wort 1 N (*Vokabel*) word 2 N (*Äußerung*) word; **mit anderen ~en** in other words; **j-n beim ~ nehmen** take sb at his/her word **Wörterbuch** N dictionary **wörtlich** ADJ literal

worüber ADV **~ redet sie?** what is she talking about? **worum** ADV **~ geht's?** what is it about? **worunter** ADV **~ leidet er?** what is he suffering from? **wovon** ADV (*relativ*) from which; **~ redest du?** what are you talking about? **wozu** ADV (*relativ*) to/for which; (*interrogativ*) what … for/to; (*warum*) why; **~?** what for?; **~ brauchst du das?** what do you need it for?; **~ soll das gut sein?** what's it for?

Wrack N wreck

wühlen V/I rummage; (*Tier*) root

wund ADJ sore **Wunde** F wound

Wunder N miracle; **es ist kein ~** it's no wonder **wunderbar** ADJ wonderful, marvelous **Wunderkerze** F sparkler **wundern** 1 V/R be surprised (*über +akk* at) 2 V/T surprise **wunderschön** ADJ beautiful **wundervoll** ADJ wonderful

Wundstarrkrampf M teta-

nus
Wunsch M wish (*nach* for) **wünschen** V/T wish; **sich etw ~** want sth; **ich wünsche dir alles Gute** I wish you all the best **wünschenswert** ADJ desirable
Wurf M throw; ZOOL litter
Würfel M dice; MATH cube **würfeln** 1 V/I throw (the dice); (*Würfel spielen*) play dice 2 V/T (*Zahl*) throw; GASTR dice
Wurm M worm
Wurst F sausage; **das ist mir ~** *umg* I could care less
Würstchen N frankfurter
Würze F seasoning, spice
Wurzel F root
würzen V/T season, spice **würzig** ADJ spicy
wüst ADJ (*unordentlich*) chaotic; (*ausschweifend*) wild; (*öde*) desolate; *umg* (*heftig*) terrible
Wüste F desert
Wut F rage, fury; **ich habe eine ~ auf ihn** I'm really mad at him **wütend** ADJ furious
WWW N *abk* = World Wide Web; WWW

X

x-beinig ADJ knock-kneed
x-beliebig ADJ **ein ~es Buch** any book (you like)
x-mal ADV umpteen times
Xylophon N xylophone

Y

Yacht F yacht
Yoga N *od* M yoga

Z

zackig ADJ (*Linie etc*) jagged; *umg* (*Tempo*) brisk
zaghaft ADJ timid
zäh ADJ tough
Zahl F number **zahlbar** ADJ payable **zahlen** V/T & V/I pay; **~ bitte!** could I have the check, please?; **bar ~** pay cash **zählen** V/T & V/I count (*auf +akk* on); **~ zu** be one of **Zahlenschloss** N combination lock **Zähler** M counter; (*für Strom, Wasser*) meter **zahlreich** ADJ numerous **Zahlung** F payment
zahm ADJ tame **zähmen** V/T tame
Zahn M tooth **Zahnarzt** M, **Zahnärztin** F dentist **Zahnbürste** F toothbrush **Zahncreme** F toothpaste **Zahn-**

ersatz M dentures *pl* **Zahnfleisch** N gums *pl* **Zahnfüllung** F filling **Zahnklammer** F braces *pl* **Zahnpasta** F, **Zahnpaste** F toothpaste **Zahnschmerzen** PL toothache *sg* **Zahnseide** F dental floss **Zahnspange** F braces *pl* **Zahnstocher** M toothpick

Zange F pliers *pl*; (*Zuckerzange*) tongs *pl*; ZOOL pincers *pl*

zanken V/I & V/R quarrel

Zäpfchen N ANAT uvula; MED suppository

zapfen V/T (*Bier*) pull **Zapfsäule** F gas pump

zappeln V/I wriggle; (*unruhig sein*) fidget

zappen V/I zap, channel surf

zart ADJ soft; (*Braten etc*) tender; (*fein, schwächlich*) delicate **zartbitter** ADJ (*Schokolade*) dark

zärtlich ADJ tender, affectionate **Zärtlichkeit** F tenderness; **~en** *pl* hugs and kisses *pl*

Zauber M magic; (*Bann*) spell **Zauberei** F magic **Zauberer** M magician **zauberhaft** ADJ enchanting **Zauberin** F magician **Zauberkünstler(in)** M(F) magician, conjuror **zaubern** V/I do magic **Zauberspruch** M (magic) spell

Zaun M fence

z. B. *abk* = zum Beispiel; e.g., eg

Zebra N zebra **Zebrastreifen** M crosswalk

Zecke F tick

Zehe F toe; (*Knoblauch*) clove **Zehennagel** M toenail **Zehenspitze** F tip of one's toes

zehn NUM ten **zehnmal** ADV ten times **zehntausend** NUM ten thousand **zehnte(r, s)** ADJ tenth; → dritte **Zehntel** N tenth

Zeichen N sign; (*Schriftzeichen*) character **Zeichenblock** M sketch pad **Zeichensetzung** F punctuation **Zeichensprache** F sign language **Zeichentrickfilm** M cartoon

zeichnen V/T & V/I draw **Zeichnung** F drawing

Zeigefinger M index finger

zeigen **1** V/T show; **sie zeigte uns die Stadt** she showed us around the town; **zeig mal!** let me see **2** V/I point (*auf +akk* to, at) **3** V/R show oneself; **es wird sich ~** time will tell **Zeiger** M pointer; (*Uhr*) hand

Zeile F line

Zeit F time; **ich habe keine ~** I haven't got time; **lass dir ~** take your time; **von ~ zu ~** from time to time **Zeitarbeit** F temporary work **zeitgenössisch** ADJ contemporary, modern **zeitgleich** **1** ADJ simultaneous **2** ADV at exactly the same time **zeitig** ADJ early **Zeitkarte** F season ticket **Zeitlupe** F slow motion

Zeitplan M schedule **Zeitpunkt** M point in time **Zeitraum** M period (of time)
Zeitschrift F magazine; (*wissenschaftliche*) periodical
Zeitung F newspaper **Zeitungsartikel** M newspaper article **Zeitungskiosk** M, **Zeitungsstand** M newsstand
Zeitunterschied M time difference **Zeitverschiebung** F time lag **Zeitvertreib** M **zum ~** to pass the time **Zeitzone** F time zone
Zelle F cell
Zellophan® N cellophane®
Zelt N tent **zelten** V/I camp, go camping **Zeltplatz** M campground
Zement M cement
Zentimeter M *od* N centimeter
Zentner M (metric) hundredweight; (*in Deutschland*) fifty kilos; (*in Österreich und der Schweiz*) one hundred kilos
zentral ADJ central **Zentrale** F central office; TEL exchange **Zentralheizung** F central heating **Zentralverriegelung** F AUTO central locking **Zentrum** N center
zerbrechen V/T & V/I break **zerbrechlich** ADJ fragile
Zeremonie F ceremony
zerkleinern V/T cut up; (*zerhacken*) chop (up) **zerkratzen** V/T scratch **zerlegen** V/T take to pieces; (*Fleisch*) carve; (*Gerät, Maschine*) dismantle **zerquetschen** V/T squash **zerreißen** 1 V/T tear to pieces 2 V/I tear
zerren 1 V/T drag; **sich einen Muskel ~** pull a muscle 2 V/I tug (*an +dat* at) **Zerrung** F MED pulled muscle
zerschlagen 1 V/T smash 2 V/R come to nothing
zerschneiden V/T cut up
zerstören V/T destroy **Zerstörung** F destruction
zerstreuen 1 V/T scatter; (*Menge*) disperse; (*Zweifel etc*) dispel 2 V/R (*Menge*) disperse **zerstreut** ADJ scattered; (*Mensch*) absent-minded; (*kurzfristig*) distracted
zerteilen V/T split up
Zertifikat N certificate
Zettel M piece of paper; (*Notizzettel*) note
Zeug N *umg* stuff; (*Ausrüstung*) gear; **dummes ~** nonsense
Zeuge M, **Zeugin** F witness
Zeugnis N certificate; (*Schule*) report; (*Referenz*) reference
zickig ADJ *umg* bitchy
Zickzack M **im ~ fahren** zigzag (across the road)
Ziege F goat
Ziegel M brick; (*Dach*) tile
Ziegenkäse M goat's cheese
ziehen 1 V/T draw; (*zerren*) pull; (*Spielfigur*) move; (*züchten*) rear 2 V/I (*zerren*) pull; (*sich bewegen*) move; (*Rauch,*

Wolke etc) drift; **den Tee ~ lassen** let the tea stand **3** VI UNPERS **es zieht** there's a draft **4** V/R *(Treffen, Rede)* drag on
Ziel N *(Reise)* destination; SPORT finish; *(Absicht)* goal, aim **zielen** V/I aim *(auf +akk* at) **Zielgruppe** F target group **ziellos** ADJ aimless **Zielscheibe** F target
ziemlich **1** ADJ considerable; **ein ~es Durcheinander** quite a mess; **mit ~er Sicherheit** with some certainty **2** ADV rather, quite; **~ viel** quite a lot
zierlich ADJ dainty; *(Frau)* petite
Ziffer F figure; **römische ~n** *pl* Roman numerals *pl* **Zifferblatt** N dial, face
zig ADJ *umg* umpteen
Zigarette F cigarette **Zigarettenautomat** M cigarette machine **Zigarettenschachtel** F cigarette pack **Zigarettenstummel** M cigarette end **Zigarillo** M cigarillo **Zigarre** F cigar
Zimmer N room; **haben Sie ein ~ für zwei Personen?** do you have a room for two people? **Zimmermädchen** N chambermaid **Zimmermann** M carpenter **Zimmerpflanze** F house plant **Zimmerschlüssel** M room key **Zimmerservice** M room service **Zimmervermittlung** F accommodation agency
Zimt M cinnamon
Zinn N tin; *(legiertes)* pewter
Zinsen PL interest *sg*
Zipfel M corner; *(spitz)* tip; *(Hemd)* tail; *(Wurst)* end
zirka ADV about, approximately
Zirkel M MATH (pair of) compasses *pl*
Zirkus M circus
zischen V/I hiss
Zitat N quotation *(aus* from) **zitieren** V/T quote
Zitrone F lemon **Zitronenlimonade** F lemonade **Zitronensaft** M lemon juice
zittern V/I tremble *(vor +dat* with)
zivil ADJ civilian; *(Preis)* reasonable **Zivil** N plain clothes *pl*; MIL civilian clothes *pl* **Zivildienst** M community service *(for conscientious objectors)*
zögerlich ADJ hesitant **zögern** V/I hesitate
Zoll M customs *pl*; *(Abgabe)* duty **Zollabfertigung** F customs clearance **Zollamt** N customs office **Zollbeamte(r)** M, **Zollbeamtin** F customs official **Zollerklärung** F customs declaration **zollfrei** ADJ duty-free **Zollgebühren** PL customs duties *pl* **Zollkontrolle** F customs check **Zöllner(in)** M(F) customs officer **zollpflichtig** ADJ liable to duty
Zone F zone

Zoo M zoo
Zoom N zoom (shot); (*Objektiv*) zoom (lens)
Zopf M braid
Zorn M anger **zornig** ADJ angry (*über etw* about sth, *auf j-n* with sb)
zu 1 KONJ (*mit Infinitiv*) to 2 PRÄP +*dat* (*bei Richtung, Vorgang*) to; (*bei Orts-, Zeit-, Preisangabe*) at; (*Zweck*) for; **~r Post® gehen** go to the post office; **~ Hause** at home; **~ Weihnachten** at Christmas; **fünf Bücher ~ 20 Euro** five books at 20 euros each; **~m Fenster herein** through the window; **~ meiner Zeit** in my time 3 ADV (*zu sehr*) too; **~ viel** too much; **~ wenig** not enough 4 ADJ *umg* shut; **Tür ~!** shut the door
zuallererst ADV first of all **zuallerletzt** ADV last of all
Zubehör N accessories *pl*
zubereiten V/T prepare **Zubereitung** F preparation
zubinden V/T do (*od* tie) up
Zucchini PL zucchini *pl*
züchten V/T (*Tiere*) breed; (*Pflanzen*) grow
zucken V/I jerk; (*krampfhaft*) twitch; **mit den Schultern ~** shrug (one's shoulders)
Zucker M sugar; MED diabetes *sg* **Zuckerdose** F sugar bowl **zuckerkrank** ADJ diabetic **Zuckerwatte** F cotton candy
zudecken V/T cover up
zudrehen V/T turn off
zueinander ADV to one another; (*mit Verb*) together **zueinanderhalten** V/I stick together
zuerst ADV first; (*zu Anfang*) at first; **~ einmal** first of all
Zufahrt F access; (*Einfahrt*) drive(way) **Zufahrtsstraße** F access road; (*Autobahn*) ramp
Zufall M chance; (*Ereignis*) coincidence; **durch ~** by accident; **so ein ~!** what a coincidence **zufällig** 1 ADJ chance 2 ADV by chance; **weißt du ~, ob ...?** do you happen to know whether ...?
zufrieden ADJ content(ed); (*befriedigt*) satisfied; **lass sie ~** leave her alone (*od* in peace) **zufriedengeben** V/R **sich mit etw ~** settle for sth **Zufriedenheit** F contentment; (*Befriedigtsein*) satisfaction
zufügen V/T add (*dat* to); **j-m Schaden/Schmerzen ~** cause sb harm/pain
Zug M BAHN train; (*Luft*) draft; (*Ziehen*) pull; (*Schach*) move; (*Charakterzug*) trait; (*an Zigarette*) puff, drag; (*Schluck*) gulp
Zugabe F extra; (*in Konzert etc*) encore
Zugabteil N train compartment
Zugang M access; **„kein ~!"** 'no entry'

Zugauskunft F train information office/desk **Zugbegleiter(in)** M(F) conductor
zugeben V/T (*zugestehen*) admit **zugegeben** ADV admittedly
zugehen 1 V/I (*schließen*) shut; **auf j-n/etw ~** walk toward(s) sb/sth; **dem Ende ~** be coming to a close 2 V/I UNPERS (*sich ereignen*) happen; **es ging lustig zu** we/they had a lot of fun
Zügel M rein
Zugführer(in) M(F) conductor
zugig ADJ drafty
zügig ADJ speedy
Zugluft F draft
Zugpersonal N train staff
zugreifen V/I *fig* seize the opportunity; (*beim Essen*) help oneself; **~ auf** IT access
Zugrestauraunt N dining car, diner
Zugriffsberechtigung F IT access right
zugrunde ADV **~ gehen** perish; **~ gehen an** (*sterben*) die of
Zugschaffner(in) M(F) conductor **Zugunglück** N train crash
zugunsten PRÄP *+gen od dat* in favor of
Zugverbindung F train connection
zuhaben V/I be closed
zuhalten V/T **sich die Nase ~** hold one's nose; **sich die Ohren ~** hold one's hands over one's ears; **die Tür ~** hold the door shut
Zuhause N home
zuhören V/I listen (*dat* to) **Zuhörer(in)** M(F) listener
zukleben V/T seal
zukommen V/I come up (*auf +akk* to); **j-m etw ~ lassen** give (*od* send) sb sth; **etw auf sich ~ lassen** take sth as it comes
Zukunft F future **zukünftig** 1 ADJ future 2 ADV in future
zulassen V/T (*hereinlassen*) admit; (*erlauben*) permit; (*Auto*) license; *umg* (*nicht öffnen*) keep shut **zulässig** ADJ permissible, permitted
zuletzt ADV finally, at last
zuliebe ADV **j-m ~** for sb's sake
zum *kontr von* **zu dem**; **~ dritten Mal** for the third time; **~ Trinken** for drinking
zumachen 1 V/T shut; (*Kleidung*) do up 2 V/I shut
zumindest ADV at least
zumuten 1 V/T **j-m etw ~** expect sth of sb 2 V/R **sich zu viel ~** overdo things
zunächst ADV first of all; **~ einmal** to start with
Zunahme F increase
Zuname M surname, last name
zünden V/T & V/I AUTO fire **Zündkerze** F AUTO spark plug **Zündschloss** N ignition lock **Zündschlüssel** M ignition key **Zündung** F ignition
zunehmen 1 V/I increase;

(*Mensch*) put on weight **2** VT **5 Kilo ~** put on 5 kilos
Zunge F tongue **Zungenkuss** M French kiss
zunichtemachen VT (*zerstören*) ruin
zunutze ADV **sich etw ~ machen** make use of sth
zurechtfinden VR find one's way around **zurechtkommen** VI cope (*mit etw* with sth) **zurechtmachen** **1** VT prepare **2** VR get ready
zurück ADV back
zurückbekommen VT get back **zurückblicken** VI look back (*auf +akk* at) **zurückbringen** VT (*hierhin*) bring back; (*woandershin*) take back **zurückerstatten** VT refund **zurückfahren** VI go back **zurückgeben** VT give back **zurückgehen** VI go back; (*zeitlich*) date back (*auf +akk* to)
zurückhalten **1** VT hold back; (*hindern*) prevent **2** VR hold back **zurückhaltend** ADJ reserved
zurückholen VT fetch back **zurückkommen** VI come back; **auf etw ~** return (*od* get back) to sth **zurücklassen** VT leave behind **zurücklegen** VT put back; (*Geld*) put by; (*reservieren*) keep back; (*Strecke*) cover **zurücknehmen** VT take back **zurückrufen** VT call back **zurückschicken** VT send back **zurückstellen** VT put back **zurücktreten** VI step back; (*von Amt*) retire **zurückverlangen** VT **etw ~** ask for sth back **zurückzahlen** VT pay back
zurzeit ADV at present
Zusage F promise; (*Annahme*) acceptance **zusagen** **1** VT promise **2** VI accept; **j-m ~** (*gefallen*) appeal to sb
zusammen ADV together
Zusammenarbeit F collaboration **zusammenarbeiten** VI work together
zusammenbrechen VI collapse; (*psychisch*) break down **Zusammenbruch** M collapse; (*psychischer*) breakdown
zusammenfassen VT summarize; (*vereinigen*) unite **Zusammenfassung** F summary
zusammengehören VI belong together **zusammenhalten** VI stick together
Zusammenhang M connection; **im/aus dem ~** in/out of context **zusammenhängen** VI be connected **zusammenhängend** ADJ coherent **zusammenhang(s)los** ADJ incoherent
zusammenklappen VI & VT fold up **zusammenlegen** **1** VT fold up **2** VI (*Geld sammeln*) club together **zusammennehmen** **1** VT summon up; **alles zusammengenommen** all in all **2** VR pull oneself to-

gether **zusammenpassen** VI go together; (*Personen*) be suited **zusammenrechnen** VT add up
Zusammensein N get-together
zusammensetzen 1 VT put together 2 VR **sich ~ aus** be composed of **Zusammensetzung** F composition
Zusammenstoß M crash, collision **zusammenstoßen** VI crash (*mit* into)
zusammenzählen VT add up
zusammenziehen VI (*in Wohnung etc*) move in together
Zusatz M addition **zusätzlich** 1 ADJ additional 2 ADV in addition
zuschauen VI watch **Zuschauer(in)** M(F) spectator; **die ~** *pl* THEAT the audience *sg*
zuschicken VT send
Zuschlag M extra charge; (*Fahrkarte*) supplement **zuschlagpflichtig** ADJ subject to an extra charge; BAHN subject to a supplement
zuschließen VT lock up
zusehen VI watch (*j-m* sb); (*dafür sorgen*) make sure
zusichern VT **j-m etw ~** assure sb of sth
Zustand M state, condition
zustande ADV **~ bringen** bring about; **~ kommen** come about **zuständig** ADJ (*Behörde*) relevant; **~ für** responsible for
Zustellung F delivery
zustimmen VI agree (*Sache dat* to sth, *j-m* with sb) **Zustimmung** F approval
zustoßen VI *fig* happen (*j-m* to sb)
Zutaten PL ingredients *pl*
zutrauen VT **j-m etw ~** think sb is capable of sth; **ich würde es ihr ~** (*etw Negatives*) I wouldn't put it past her **Zutrauen** N confidence (*zu* in) **zutraulich** ADJ trusting; (*Tier*) friendly
zutreffen VI be correct; **~ auf** apply to; **Zutreffendes bitte streichen** please delete as applicable
Zutritt M entry; (*Zugang*) access; **~ verboten!** no entry
zuverlässig ADJ reliable **Zuverlässigkeit** F reliability
Zuversicht F confidence **zuversichtlich** ADJ confident
zuvor ADV before; (*zunächst*) first **zuvorkommen** VI **j-m ~** beat sb to it
Zuwachs M increase, growth; *umg* (*Baby*) addition to the family
zuwider ADV **es ist mir ~** I hate (*od* detest) it
zuzüglich PRÄP *+gen* plus
Zwang M (*innerer*) compulsion; (*Gewalt*) force **zwängen** VT & VR squeeze (*in +akk* into)
zwanglos ADJ informal
zwanzig NUM twenty **zwanzigste(r, s)** ADJ twentieth; →

dritte

zwar ADV **und ~ …** (*genauer*) …, to be precise; **das ist ~ schön, aber …** it is nice, but …

Zweck M purpose **zwecklos** ADJ pointless

zwei NUM two **Zwei** F two; (*Schulnote*) ≈ B **Zweibettzimmer** N double room (*with two beds*) **zweideutig** ADJ ambiguous; (*unanständig*) suggestive **zweifach** ADJ & ADV double

Zweifel M doubt **zweifellos** ADV undoubtedly **zweifeln** V/I doubt (*an etw dat* sth) **Zweifelsfall** M **im ~** if in doubt

Zweig M branch **Zweigstelle** F branch

zweihundert NUM two hundred **zweimal** ADV twice **zweisprachig** ADJ bilingual **zweispurig** ADJ AUTO two-lane **zweit** ADV **wir sind zu ~** there are two of us **zweite(r, s)** ADJ second; → dritte **zweitens** ADV secondly; (*bei Aufzählungen*) second **zweitgrößte(r, s)** ADJ second largest **Zweitschlüssel** M spare key

Zwerg(in) M(F) dwarf

Zwetschge F plum

zwicken V/T pinch

Zwieback M rusk

Zwiebel F onion; (*von Blume*) bulb

Zwilling M twin; **~e** *pl* ASTROL Gemini *sg*

zwingen V/T force

zwinkern V/I blink; (*absichtlich*) wink

zwischen PRÄP *+akk od dat* between **Zwischenablage** F IT clipboard **zwischendurch** ADV in between **Zwischenlandung** F stopover **Zwischenraum** M space **Zwischenstopp** M stopover **Zwischenzeit** F **in der ~** in the meantime

zwitschern V/T & V/I twitter, chirp

zwölf NUM twelve **zwölfte(r, s)** ADJ twelfth; → dritte

Zylinder M cylinder; (*Hut*) top hat

zynisch ADJ cynical

Zypern N Cyprus **Zypriot(in)** M(F) Cypriot **zyprisch** ADJ Cypriot

Anhang

Zahlen

Grundzahlen

0 *null* zero
1 *eins* one
2 *zwei* two
3 *drei* three
4 *vier* four
5 *fünf* five
6 *sechs* six
7 *sieben* seven
8 *acht* eight
9 *neun* nine
10 *zehn* ten
11 *elf* eleven
12 *zwölf* twelve
13 *dreizehn* thirteen
14 *vierzehn* fourteen
15 *fünfzehn* fifteen
16 *sechzehn* sixteen
17 *siebzehn* seventeen
18 *achtzehn* eighteen
19 *neunzehn* nineteen
20 *zwanzig* twenty
21 *einundzwanzig* twenty-one
22 *zweiundzwanzig* twenty-two
30 *dreißig* thirty
31 *einunddreißig* thirty-one
40 *vierzig* forty
41 *einundvierzig* forty-one
50 *fünfzig* fifty
51 *einundfünfzig* fifty-one
60 *sechzig* sixty
61 *einundsechzig* sixty-one
70 *siebzig* seventy
80 *achtzig* eighty
90 *neunzig* ninety
100 *(ein)hundert* a *od* one hundred
101 *hundert(und)eins* one hundred (and) one
200 *zweihundert* two hundred
572 *fünfhundert(und)zweiundsiebzig* five hundred (and) seventy-two
1000 *(ein)tausend* a *od* one thousand
1998 *als Jahreszahl: neunzehnhundertachtundneunzig* nineteen (hundred and) ninety-eight
2000 *zweitausend* two thousand
2010 *als Jahreszahl: zweitausendzehn* two thousand (and) ten
5044 *fünfzig vierundvierzig am Telefon:* five 0 [oʊ] (*od* zero) double four
1,000,000 *eine Million* a *od* one million
2,000,000 *zwei Millionen* two million
1,000,000,000 *eine Milliarde* a *od* one billion

Ordnungszahlen

1st *erste* first
2nd *zweite* second
3rd *dritte* third
4th *vierte* fourth
5th *fünfte* fifth
6th *sechste* sixth
7th *sieb(en)te* seventh
8th *achte* eighth
9th *neunte* ninth
10th *zehnte* tenth
11th *elfte* eleventh
12th *zwölfte* twelfth
13th *dreizehnte* thirteenth
14th *vierzehnte* fourteenth
15th *fünfzehnte* fifteenth
16th *sechzehnte* sixteenth
17th *siebzehnte* seventeenth
18th *achtzehnte* eighteenth
19th *neunzehnte* nineteenth
20th *zwanzigste* twentieth
21st *einundzwanzigste* twenty-first
22nd *zweiundzwanzigste* twenty-second
23rd *dreiundzwanzigste* twenty-third
30th *dreißigste* thirtieth
31st *einunddreißigste* thirty-first
40th *vierzigste* fortieth
41st *einundvierzigste* forty-first
50th *fünfzigste* fiftieth
51st *einundfünfzigste* fifty-first
60th *sechzigste* sixtieth
61st *einundsechzigste* sixty-first
70th *siebzigste* seventieth
80th *achtzigste* eightieth
90th *neunzigste* ninetieth
100th *hundertste* (one) hundredth
101st *hundert(und)erste* hundred (and) first
200th *zweihundertste* two hundredth
300th *dreihundertste* three hundredth
572nd *fünfhundert(und)zweiundsiebzigste* five hundred (and) seventy-second
1000th *tausendste* (one) thousandth
1,000,000th *millionste* (one) millionth

Bruchzahlen und Rechenvorgänge

½	*ein halb* one half / a half
1½	*eineinhalb* one and a half
2½	*zweieinhalb* two and a half
⅓	*ein Drittel* one third / a third
⅔	*zwei Drittel* two thirds
¼	*ein Viertel* one quarter / a quarter, one fourth
¾	*drei Viertel* three quarters, three fourths
⅕	*ein Fünftel* one fifth / a fifth
3⅘	*drei vier Fünftel* three and four fifths
⅝	*fünf Achtel* five eighths
75%	*fünfundsiebzig Prozent* seventy-five percent
0.45	*null Komma vier fünf* (zero [ˈzɪroʊ]) point four five
2.5	*zwei Komma fünf* two point five
7 + 8 = 15	*sieben und/plus acht ist fünfzehn* seven and/plus eight is/equals fifteen
9 − 4 = 5	*neun minus/weniger vier ist fünf* nine minus four is/equals five
2 × 3 = 6	*zwei mal drei ist sechs* two times three is/equals six
20 : 5 = 4	*zwanzig dividiert/geteilt durch fünf ist vier* twenty divided by five is/equals four

Maße und Gewichte

Längenmaße

1 inch	2,54 cm
1 foot	30,48 cm
1 yard	91,439 cm
1 mile	1,609 km

Hohlmaße

1 pint	0,473 l
1 quart	0,946 l
1 gallon	3,785 l
1 barrel	119,228 l

Handelsgewichte

1 grain	0,065 g
1 ounce	28,35 g
1 pound	453,592 g
1 stone	14 pounds = 6,35kg
1 quarter	12,701 kg
1 hundredweight	100 pounds = 45,359 kg
1 ton	907,185 kg

Temperaturumrechnung

Fahrenheit | Celsius

°F	°C	
212°	100°	Siedepunkt
176°	80°	
140°	60°	
122°	50°	
104°	40°	
86°	30°	
68°	20°	
50°	10°	
32°	0°	Gefrierpunkt
14°	−10°	
0°	−17.8°	

°Fahrenheit $= (\frac{9}{5}\ °C) + 32$

°Celsius $= (°F - 32) \cdot \frac{5}{9}$

Amerikanische Währung

1 $ = 100 cents

Münzen

1 ¢ (one *od* a cent, a penny)
5 ¢ (five cents, a nickel)
10 ¢ (ten cents, a dime)
25 ¢ (twenty-five cents, a quarter)
50 ¢ (fifty cents, a half-dollar)

Banknoten

$ 1 (one *od* a dollar, a buck)
$ 5 (five dollars *od* bucks)
$ 10 (ten dollars *od* bucks)
$ 20 (twenty dollars *od* bucks)
$ 50 (fifty dollars *od* bucks)
$ 100 (one *od* a hundred dollars *od* bucks)

Feiertage in den USA

(nicht alle sind arbeitsfreie Tage)

New Year's Day	1. Januar	Neujahrstag
Martin Luther King Day	dritter Montag im Januar	zum Gedenken an Martin Luther King und die Bürgerrechtsbewegung
Washington's Birthday/Presidents' Day	dritter Montag im Februar	zum Gedenken an George Washington und alle nachfolgenden Präsidenten
Good Friday		Karfreitag
Easter Monday		Ostermontag
Memorial Day	letzter Montag im Mai	zum Gedenken an alle im Krieg Gefallenen
Independence Day	4. Juli	Unabhängigkeitstag
Labor Day	erster Montag im September	Tag der Arbeit
Columbus Day	12. Oktober	zum Gedenken an die Landung von Kolumbus auf den Westindischen Inseln
Halloween [hæloʊ'iːn]	31. Oktober	Tag vor Allerheiligen
Veterans Day	11. November	Tag der Kriegsveteranen

…abama [ælə'bæmə]	AL	The Cotton State
Alaska [ə'læskə]	AK	The Last Frontier
…a [ærɪ'zoʊnə]	AZ	The Grand Canyon State
… ['ɑːrkənsɒː]	AR	The Land of Opportunity
… …lə'fɔːrnjə]	CA	The Golden State
… …ædoʊ]	CO	The Centennial State
… …kət]	CT	The Constitution State
	DE	The First State
	FL	The Sunshine State
	GA	The Empire State of the South
		The Aloha State

Thanksgiving Day	Donnerstag vor dem letzten Sonntag im November	zum Gedenken a… Erntedankfest 16…
Christmas Day	25. Dezember	1. Weihnachtstag
New Year's Eve	31. Dezember	Silvester

Nebraska [nə'bræskə]	NE	The Cornhusker State
Nevada [nɪ'vædə]	NV	The Silver State
New Hampshire [nu: 'hæmpʃər]	NH	The Granite State
New Jersey [nu: 'dʒɜ:rzɪ]	NJ	The Garden State
New Mexico [nu: 'meksɪkoʊ]	NM	The Land of Enchantment
New York [nu: 'jɔ:rk]	NY	The Empire State
North Carolina [nɔ:rθ kerə'laɪnə]	NC	The Tar Heel State
North Dakota [nɔ:rθ də'koʊtə]	ND	The Sioux State
Ohio [oʊ'haɪoʊ]	OH	The Buckeye Sta
Oklahoma [oʊklə'hoʊmə]	OK	The Sooner St
Oregon ['ɔ:rɪgən]	OR	The Beaver S
Pennsylvania [pensl'veɪnjə]	PA	The Keysto
Rhode Island [roʊd 'aɪlənd]	RI	Little Rho
South Carolina [saʊθ kerə'laɪnə]	SC	The Pal
South Dakota [saʊθ də'koʊtə]	SD	The
Tennessee [tenə'si:]	TN	Th
Texas ['teksəs]	TX	T
Utah ['ju:tɒ:]	UT	
Vermont [vər'mɑ:nt]	VT	
Virginia [vər'dʒɪnjə]	VA	
Washington ['wɑ:ʃɪŋtən]	WA	
West Virginia [west vər'dʒɪnjə]	W	
Wisconsin [wɪ'skɑ:nsɪn]		
Wyoming [waɪ'oʊmɪŋ]		

Für Autofahrer in den USA

... ahead – Achtung ... voraus (z. B. **construction ahead** = Ankündigung einer Baustelle)
bumpy road – schlechte Straße
business loop – Innenstadtroute
call box – Notrufsäule
caution – Vorsicht
center lane – mittlere Fahrbahn/Spur
chains – Schneeketten
closed to traffic – gesperrt
construction – Baustelle
crossroads – Kreuzung
danger – Gefahrenstelle
dead end – Sackgasse
deer crossing – Achtung Wildwechsel
detour – Umleitung
dip – Bodensenke
do not enter – Einfahrt verboten
do not tailgate – Abstand halten
downtown – Innenstadt
emergency parking/stopping only – Parken/Halten nur in Notfällen
falling rocks – Steinschlag
flash flood area – Überschwemmungsgebiet
food & lodging – Raststätte, Hotel, Motel
freeway – breiter, kreuzungsfreier Highway
fuel – Benzin
full service – (Zapfsäule mit) Bedienung
game crossing – Wildwechsel
garage – Reparaturwerkstatt
gas (leaded, unleaded) – (verbleites, bleifreies) Benzin
gas station – Tankstelle
grade – Gefälle, Steigung
high beam – Fernlicht
intersection – Kreuzung
keep off median – Mittelstreifen nicht befahren
lane – Fahrstreifen, Spur
lane ends – Fahrstreifen/Spur endet
maximum speed – Höchstgeschwindigkeit
men at work – Baustelle
merge – Einmündung, einfädeln
merge left/right – links/rechts

einordnen
merging traffic – einfädelnder Verkehr
miles per hour (mph) – Meilen pro Stunde
mudslide – Bergrutsch
narrow bridge – enge Brücke
next exit – nächste Ausfahrt
no entry – kein Eingang, gesperrt
no facilities – keine Toiletten, Restaurants oder Tankstellen
no left/right turn – Linksabbiegen/Rechtsabbiegen verboten
no parking/stopping anytime – absolutes Parkverbot/ Halteverbot
no passing – Überholverbot
no through street – Sackgasse
no U-turn – Wenden verboten
one way street – Einbahnstraße
pass – überholen
pass with care – vorsichtig überholen
pedestrians – Fußgänger
pothole – Schlagloch
premium (gas) – Super(benzin)
prohibited – verboten
radiator water – Kühlwasser
railroad crossing – Bahnübergang
recreational vehicle (RV) – Wohnmobil
reduced speed – verringerte Geschwindigkeit
regular (gas) – Normal(benzin)
rental car – Mietwagen
rental car return – Mietwagenrückgabe
repair shop – Reparaturwerkstatt
residential area – Wohngebiet
rest area – Rastplatz
rest rooms – Toiletten
right of way – Vorfahrt
road under construction – Baustelle
rockslide – Bergrutsch
rough road – unebene Straße
school bus – Schulbus
school crossing – Achtung Schulkinder
school zone – Schule
self service – Selbstbedienung
service station – Tankstelle
signal – Ampel
skid marks – Bremsspuren
slippery when wet – Schleudergefahr bei Nässe

speed limit – Geschwindigkeitsbegrenzung
speed zone – Zone mit Geschwindigkeitsbegrenzung
stay in lane – Fahrspur nicht wechseln
steep grade – starkes Gefälle, starke Steigung
straight ahead – geradeaus
thru traffic – Durchgangsverkehr
traffic light(s) – Ampel
truck lane – Lkw-Spur
turn left/right – nach links/rechts (abbiegen)
turn on headlights – Licht einschalten
two way traffic – Gegenverkehr
U-turn – wenden
watch for – Achtung, aufpassen auf
winding road – kurvenreiche Straße
work/workers/roadwork – Straßenbauarbeiten
wrong way – Einfahrt verboten
X-ing/crossing – (z. B. Tiere) kreuzen
yield – Vorfahrt beachten

Amerikanische Verkehrsschilder

Vorfahrt beachten

Höchstgeschwindigkeit 55 Meilen

Halteverbot

Parkverbot

Kreuzung

Einmündung

Wenden verboten

Gefälle

Scharfe Kurve

Kurve: vorgeschriebene Geschwindigkeit 35 Meilen

Kreuzung US-Highway mit State Highway

Bahnübergang

Speisekarte

breakfast | Frühstück

bacon ['beɪkn]	Frühstücksspeck
bagel ['beɪgl]	Bagel (ringförmiges Brotteiggebäck)
eggs over easy [egz oʊvər 'iːzɪ]	von beiden Seiten gebratene Eier
English muffin [ɪŋglɪʃ 'mʌfɪn]	flaches Milchbrötchen, das meist getoastet gegessen wird
French toast [frentʃ 'toʊst]	armer Ritter
fried eggs sunny-side up [fraɪd egz sʌnɪsaɪd 'ʌp]	Spiegeleier
grits [grɪts]	Hafergrütze
maple syrup/sirup [meɪpl 'sɪrəp]	Ahornsirup
pancakes ['pænkeɪks]	Pfannkuchen
western omelette [westərn 'ɑːmlət]	Omelett mit Käse, Paprika, Schinken und Zwiebeln

starters, hors d'œuvres | Vorspeisen

Caesar salad [siːzər 'sæləd]	Cäsarsalat (Blattsalat mit Croûtons, meist mit Knoblauchdressing)
Caesar salad with chicken [siːzər sæləd wɪθ 'tʃɪkən]	Cäsarsalat mit Hühnchenbrust
Caesar salad with shrimp [siːzər sæləd wɪθ 'ʃrɪmp]	Cäsarsalat mit Garnelen

chef salad [ʃef 'sæləd]	gemischter Salat mit Käse und Schinken
chicken (noodle) soup [tʃıkən (nu:dl) 'su:p]	Hühnersuppe (mit Nudeln)
cobb salad [kɑ:b 'sæləd]	klassischer gemischter Salat mit stark gewürzter Vinaigrette
eggrolls ['egroʊlz]	Frühlingsrollen
shrimp cocktail [ʃrımp 'kɑ:kteıl]	Krabbencocktail
smoked salmon and cream cheese [smoʊkt sæmən ənd kri:m 'tʃi:z]	geräucherter Lachs mit Frischkäse
soup du jour [su:p dy 'ʒu:r]	Tagessuppe

snacks and sandwiches | Snacks und Sandwiches

BLT (bacon, lettuce and tomato) [bi:el'ti:]	Sandwich mit Frühstücksspeck, Salat und Tomaten
cheeseburger ['tʃi:zbɜ:rgər]	Cheeseburger
cheesesteak ['tʃi:zsteık]	mit Käse überbackenes Fleisch in einem Sandwich
club sandwich [klʌb 'sænwıdʒ]	mit kaltem Truthahn oder Huhn, Frühstücksspeck, Salat, Mayonnaise und Tomate belegtes „Doppeldecker"-Sandwich
corn dog ['kɔ:rn dɒ:g]	Hotdog im frittierten Teigmantel am Stiel

crabcake ['kræbkeɪk]	Krabbenfleischfrikadelle
fish fillet sandwich [fɪʃ fɪleɪ 'sænwɪdʒ]	Sandwich mit frittiertem Fischfilet
grilled cheese sandwich [grɪld tʃi:z 'sænwɪdʒ]	gegrilltes Käsesandwich
hamburger ['hæmbɜ:rgər]	Hamburger
hero ['hɪroʊ]	längliches Sandwich gefüllt mit Fleisch, Käse und Salat
hoagie ['hoʊgɪ]	längliches Sandwich gefüllt mit Fleisch, Käse und Salat
pastrami sandwich [pəstrɑ:mɪ 'sænwɪdʒ]	Sandwich mit geräuchertem Rindfleisch
peanut butter and jelly sandwich [pi:nət bʌtər ənd dʒelɪ 'sænwɪdʒ]	Sandwich mit Erdnussbutter und Marmelade
popcorn shrimp [pɑ:pkɔ:rn 'ʃrɪmp]	Mini-Krabben
Reuben sandwich [ru:bən 'sænwɪdʒ]	Sandwich mit gepökeltem Rindfleisch, Schweizer Käse und Sauerkraut
roast/smoked turkey breast sandwich [roʊst/smoʊkt tɜ:rkɪ brest 'sænwɪdʒ]	Sandwich mit gebratener/geräucherter Truthahnbrust
taco ['tɑ:koʊ]	Taco (beliebig gefüllte Tortilla)
tuna melt sandwich [tu:nə melt 'sænwɪdʒ]	gegrilltes Sandwich mit Thunfisch und Käse
veggie burger ['vedʒɪ bɜ:rgər]	Gemüseburger
wrap [ræp]	dünnes, zu Rollen gewickeltes Fladenbrot mit beliebiger Füllung

meat dishes | Fleischgerichte

baked chicken [beɪkt 'tʃɪkən]	gebackenes Hähnchen
barbecued/BBQ'd ['bɑːrbɪkjuːd]	gegrillt
barbecued chicken [bɑːrbɪkjuːd 'tʃɪkən]	mit Barbecuesoße gegrilltes Hähnchen
broiled [brɔɪld]	(auf dem Rost) gebraten
buffalo wings ['bʌfəloʊ wɪŋz]	Hähnchenflügel
chicken fingers [tʃɪkən 'fɪŋgərz]	frittierte Hähnchenbruststreifen in länglicher Form
chicken pot pie [tʃɪkən pɑːt 'paɪ]	mit Teig überbackenes Huhn mit Gemüse
chicken wings ['tʃɪkən wɪŋz]	Hähnchenflügel
chili ['tʃɪlɪ]	Chili con Carne
fried [fraɪd]	(in der Pfanne) gebraten
fried chicken [fraɪd 'tʃɪkən]	(in der Pfanne) gebratenes Huhn
meatloaf ['miːtloʊf]	Art Hackbraten
New York strip steak [nuː jɔːrk 'strɪp steɪk]	Beefsteak
pork chop [pɔːrk 'tʃɑːp]	Schweinekotelett
pot roast [pɑːt 'roʊst]	Schmorbraten
roast chicken [roʊst 'tʃɪkən]	Brathähnchen
roasted ['roʊstɪd]	gebraten
stuffed bell pepper [stʌft 'bel pepər]	gefüllte Paprikaschote
stuffed lamb chop [stʌft læm 'tʃɑːp]	gefülltes Lammkotelett
stuffed pork chop [stʌft pɔːrk 'tʃɑːp]	gefülltes Schweinekotelett

tenderloin steak [tendərlɔɪn 'steɪk]	Lendensteak

fish and seafood | Fisch und Meeresfrüchte

catch of the day [kætʃ əv ðə 'deɪ]	Tagesfisch
catfish ['kætfɪʃ]	Wels
clam chowder [klæm 'tʃaʊdər]	dicke Muschelsuppe mit Sellerie, Zwiebeln etc.
od [kɑ:d]	Kabeljau
ed clams [fraɪd 'klæmz]	panierte Muscheln
ackerel ['mækrəl]	Makrele
ysters on the half-shell stərz ɑ:n ðə 'hæf ʃel]	Austern in der Schale
llock ['pɑ:lək]	Seelachs
lmon ['sæmən]	Lachs
scallops ['skæləps]	Jakobsmuscheln
shrimp(s) ['ʃrɪmp(s)]	Garnelen
steamed clams [sti:md 'klæmz]	gedünstete Venusmuscheln
steamed mussels [sti:md 'mʌslz]	gedünstete Miesmuscheln
stuffed flounder [stʌft 'flaʊndər]	gefüllte Flunder
swordfish ['sɔ:rdfɪʃ]	Schwertfisch
tuna ['tu:nə]	Thunfisch

extras | Beilagen

baked beans [beɪkt 'bi:nz]	gekochte Bohnen in Tomatensoße
baked potato [beɪkt pə'teɪtoʊ]	Ofenkartoffel
boiled potatoes [bɔɪld pə'teɪtoʊz]	Salzkartoffeln
French fries ['frentʃ fraɪz]	Pommes frites
guacamole [gwɑ:kə'moʊlɪ]	Avokadosoße
hash browned potatoes/ hash browns [hæʃ braʊnd pə'teɪtoʊz/hæʃ 'braʊnz]	Bratkartoffeln
mashed potatoes [mæʃt pə'teɪtoʊz]	Kartoffelpüree
onion rings ['ʌnjən rɪŋz]	frittierte Zwiebelringe
potatoes au gratin [pəteɪtoʊz oʊ 'grætn]	Kartoffelgratin
salsa ['sælsə]	scharfe rote Chilisoße
sweet potatoes [swi:t pə'teɪtoʊz]	Süßkartoffeln
tortilla [tɔ:r'ti:ə]	Tortilla (Maismehlfladen)

vegetables | Gemüse und Salat

bell pepper ['bel pepər]	(grüne) Paprikaschote
chickpeas ['tʃɪkpi:z]	Kichererbsen
chili peppers ['tʃɪlɪ pepərz]	Peperoni
coleslaw ['koʊlslɒ:]	Krautsalat

corn [kɔːrn]	Mais
corn on the cob [kɔːrn ɑːn ðə 'kɑːb]	Maiskolben
eggplant ['egplænt]	Aubergine
green pepper [griːn 'pepər]	(grüne) Paprikaschote
iceberg lettuce [aɪsbɜːrg 'letəs]	Eisbergsalat
jalapeños [hɑːlə'peɪnjoʊz]	Peperoni
stir-fried ['stɜːrfraɪd]	im Wok gebraten

…heese | Käse

… **cheese** [bluː 'tʃiːz]	Blauschimmelkäse
…**e cheese** [kɑːtɪdʒ 'tʃiːz]	Hüttenkäse
…**heese** [kriːm 'tʃiːz]	Frischkäse

… and sweets | Nachspeisen

… 'paɪ]	Apfelkuchen
… luːberɪ 'paɪ]	Heidelbeerkuchen
… [bɒːstən	Vanillecremekuchen mit Schokoladenguss
…	Brownie (Schokoladenkuchen mit Nüssen)
… zkeɪk]	Käsekuchen
… erɪ 'paɪ]	Kirschkuchen
… ɪm 'paɪ]	Limettenkuchen mit Baiserhaube
… n 'paɪ]	Kürbiskuchen

shortcake [ˈʃɔːrtkeɪk]	Biskuittörtchen mit Früchten und Sahne
waffles [ˈwɑːflz]	Waffeln

alcoholic drinks | Alkoholische Getränke

beer [bɪr]	Bier
blush [blʌʃ]	Rosé(wein)
house wine [ˈhaʊs waɪn]	Hauswein
red wine [red ˈwaɪn]	Rotwein
rosé [roʊˈzeɪ]	Rosé(wein)
white wine [waɪt ˈwaɪn]	Weißwein
wine by the glass [waɪn baɪ ðə ˈglæs]	offener Wein

non-alcoholic drinks | Alkoholfreie Getränke

chocolate milk [tʃɑːklɪt ˈmɪlk]	Kakao
club soda [klʌb ˈsoʊdə]	Soda, Sodawasser
cola [ˈkoʊlə]	Cola
diet cola [daɪət ˈkoʊlə]	Cola light®
ginger ale [dʒɪndʒər ˈeɪl]	Gingerale (Ingwerlimon
iced tea [aɪst ˈtiː]	Eistee
juice [dʒuːs]	Saft
milk [mɪlk]	Milch
milkshake [ˈmɪlkʃeɪk]	Milchshake

sparkling water [spɑːrklɪŋ	Mineralwasser
… wɒːtər]	Leitungswasser

Getränke

coffe…

de…

c…

che…

key lime pie [kiː la…

pumpkin pie [pʌmpk…

…bled

blow – blew – blown

break – broke – broken

breed – bred – bred

bring – brought – brought

build – built – built

burn – burnt/burned – burned

burst – burst – burst

buy – bought – bought

can – could – (been able)

cast – cast – cast

…med/dreamt –

dreamed/dreamt

drink – drank – drunk

drive – drove – driven

eat – ate – eaten

fall – fell – fallen

feed – fed – fed

feel – felt – felt

fight – fought – fought

find – found – found

flee – fled – fled

fling – flung…

fly – fle…

Unregelmäßige englische Verben

Die an erster Stelle stehende Form bezeichnet das **present tense** (Präsens), nach dem ersten Gedankenstrich steht das **past tense** (Präteritum), nach dem zweiten das **past participle** (Partizip Perfekt).

arise – arose – arisen
awake – awoke/awaked – awoken
be – was, were – been
bear – bore – borne
beat – beat – beaten/beat
become – became – become
begin – began – begun
bend – bent – bent
bet – bet/betted – bet/betted
bid – bid – bid
bind – bound – bound
bite – bit – bitten
bleed – bled

catch – caught – caught
choose – chose – chosen
cling – clung – clung
come – came – come
cost – cost – cost
creep – crept – crept/creeped
cut – cut – cut
deal – dealt – dealt
dig – dug – dug
do – did – done
draw – drew – drawn
dream – dreamed/

forbid – forbade – forbidden
forget – forgot – forgotten
forgive – forgave – forgiven
freeze – froze – frozen
get – got – got/gotten
give – gave – given
go – went – gone
grind – ground – ground
grow – grew – grown
hang – hung – hung
have – had – had
hear – heard – heard
hide – hid – hidden
hit – hit – hit
hold – held – held
hurt – hurt – hurt
keep – kept – kept
kneel – knelt/kneeled – knelt/kneeled
know – knew – known
lay – laid – laid
lead – led – led
leap – leapt/leaped – leapt/leaped
leave – left – left
lend – lent – lent
let – let – let
lie – lay – lain
light – lit/lighted – lit/lighted
lose – lost – lost
make – made – made
may – might
mean – meant – meant
meet – met – met
mistake – mistook – mistaken
mow – mowed – mown/mowed
must – (had to) – (had to)
pay – paid – paid
put – put – put
quit – quit – quit
read – read – read
rid – rid – rid
ride – rode – ridden
ring – rang – rung
rise – rose – risen
run – ran – run
say – said – said
see – saw – seen
seek – sought – sought
sell – sold – sold
send – sent – sent
set – set – set
sew – sewed – sewn
shake – shook – shaken
shall – should
shave – shaved – shaved/shaven
shed – shed – shed
shine – shone – shone
shoot – shot – shot

show – showed – shown
shrink – shrank – shrunk
shut – shut – shut
sing – sang – sung
sink – sank – sunk
sit – sat – sat
sleep – slept – slept
slide – slid – slid
sling – slung – slung
slit – slit – slit
smell – smelt/smelled – smelt/smelled
sow – sowed – sown/sowed
speak – spoke – spoken
speed – sped/speeded – sped/speeded
spend – spent – spent
spill – spilt/spilled – spilt/spilled
spin – spun – spun
spit – spit – spit
split – split – split
spread – spread – spread
spring – sprang – sprung
stand – stood – stood
steal – stole – stolen
stick – stuck – stuck
sting – stung – stung
stink – stank – stunk
strike – struck – struck
swear – swore – sworn
sweep – swept – swept
swell – swelled – swollen/swelled
swim – swam – swum
swing – swung – swung
take – took – taken
teach – taught – taught
tear – tore – torn
tell – told – told
think – thought – thought
throw – threw – thrown
thrust – thrust – thrust
tread – trod – trodden
wake – woke/waked – woken
wear – wore – worn
weave – wove/weaved – woven/weaved
weep – wept – wept
wet – wet – wet
win – won – won
wind – wound – wound
wring – wrung – wrung
write – wrote – written

trempé; *boat* plein d'eau; **watermelon** pastèque *f*; **waterproof** imperméable; **waterside** bord *m* de l'eau; **waterskiing** ski *m* nautique; **watertight** *compartment* étanche; *fig*: *alibi* parfait; **waterway** voie *f* d'eau; **watery** *soup* trop clair; *coffee* trop léger

watt [wɑːt] watt *m*

wave[1] [weɪv] *n in sea* vague *f*

wave[2] [weɪv] **1** *n of hand* signe *m* **2** *v/i with hand* saluer; *of flag* flotter **3** *v/t flag etc* agiter

'wavelength RAD longueur *f* d'onde; ***be on the same ~*** *fig* être sur la même longueur d'onde

waver ['weɪvər] hésiter

wavy ['weɪvɪ] ondulé

wax [wæks] cire *f*

way [weɪ] (*method, manner*) façon *f*; (*route*) chemin *m* (***to*** de); ***this ~*** (*like this*) comme ça; (*in this direction*) par ici; ***by the ~*** (*incidentally*) au fait; ***in a ~*** (*in certain respects*) d'une certaine façon; ***lose one's ~*** se perdre; ***be in the ~*** (*be an obstruction*) gêner le passage; *disturb*) gêner; ***no ~!*** pas question!; **way in** entrée *f*; **way of life** mode *m* de vie; **way out** sortie *f*; *fig* issue *f*

we [wiː] nous

weak [wiːk] faible; *tea, coffee* léger; **weaken 1** *v/t* affaiblir **2** *v/i* s'affaiblir; *in negotiation etc* faiblir; **weakness** faiblesse *f*

wealth [welθ] richesse *f*; **wealthy** riche

weapon ['wepən] arme *f*

wear [wer] **1** *n*: **~ *(and tear)*** usure *f* **2** *v/t* (*have on*) porter; (*damage*) user **3** *v/i* (*wear out*) s'user; **~ *well*** (*last*) faire bon usage

◆ **wear down** user

◆ **wear off** *of effect* se dissiper

◆ **wear out 1** *v/t* (*tire*) épuiser; *shoes, carpet* user **2** *v/i of shoes, carpet* s'user

wearily ['wɪrɪlɪ] avec lassitude; **weary** las

weather ['weðər] **1** *n* temps *m* **2** *v/t crisis* survivre à; **weather-beaten** hâlé; **weather forecast** prévisions météorologiques *fpl*, météo *f*; **weatherman** présentateur *m* météo

weave [wiːv] **1** *v/t cloth* tisser **2** *v/i of cyclist* se faufiler

web [web] *of spider* toile *f*: ***the ~*** COMPUT le Web; **web page** page *f* de Web; **web site** site *m* Web

wedding ['wedɪŋ] mariage *m*; **wedding anniversary** anniversaire *m* de mariage; **wedding day** jour *m* de mariage; **wedding dress** robe *f* de mariée; **wedding ring** alliance *f*

wedge [wedʒ] *to hold sth in*

place cale *f*; *of cheese etc* morceau *m*

Wednesday ['wenzdeɪ] mercredi *m*

weed [wi:d] **1** *n* mauvaise herbe *f* **2** *v/t* désherber; **weedkiller** herbicide *f*; **weedy** F chétif

week [wi:k] semaine *f*; ***a ~ tomorrow*** demain en huit; **weekday** jour *m* de la semaine; **weekend** week-end *m*; ***on the ~*** *this one* ce week-end; *every one* le week-end; **weekly 1** *adj* hebdomadaire **2** *n magazine* hebdomadaire *m* **3** *adv be published* toutes les semaines; *be paid* à la semaine

weep [wi:p] pleurer

wee-wee ['wi:wi:] F pipi *m* F; ***do a ~*** faire pipi

weigh [weɪ] peser

◆ **weigh up** (*assess*) juger

weight [weɪt] poids *m*; **weightlessness** apesanteur *f*; **weightlifter** haltérophile *m/f*; **weightlifting** haltérophilie *f*; **weighty** *fig* (*important*) sérieux

weir [wɪr] barrage *m*

weird [wɪrd] bizarre; **weirdo** F cinglé(e) *m(f)* F

welcome ['welkəm] **1** *adj* bienvenu; ***you're ~!*** je vous en prie! **2** *n* accueil *m* **3** *v/t* accueillir; *fig*: *news, announcement* se réjouir de; *opportunity* saisir

weld [weld] souder

welfare ['welfer] bien-être *m*; *financial assistance* sécurité *f* sociale; ***be on ~*** toucher les allocations; **welfare check** chèque *m* d'allocations; **welfare state** État *m* providence; **welfare worker** assistant social *m*, assistante sociale *f*

well[1] [wel] *n for water, oil* puits *m*

well[2] [wel] **1** *adv* bien; ***~ done!*** bien!; ***as ~*** (*too*) aussi; ***as ~ as*** (*in addition to*) en plus de; ***very ~*** *acknowledging order* entendu; *reluctantly agreeing* très bien; ***~, ~!*** *surprise* tiens, tiens!; ***~ …*** *uncertainty, thinking* eh bien … **2** *adj*: ***be ~*** aller bien; **well-balanced** équilibré; **well-behaved** bien élevé; **well-being** bien-être *m*; **well-done** *meat* bien cuit; **well-dressed** bien habillé; **well-earned** bien mérité; **well-heeled** F cossu; **well-informed** bien informé; **well-known** connu; **well-meaning** plein de bonnes intentions; **well-off** riche; **well-timed** bien calculé; **well-wisher** personne *f* apportant son soutien

west [west] **1** *n* ouest *m* **2** *adj* ouest *inv*; *wind* d'ouest **3** *adv travel* vers l'ouest; **westerly** *wind* d'ouest; *direction* vers l'ouest; **western 1** *adj* de l'Ouest **2** *n movie* western *m*; **Westerner** occidental(e); **westernized** occidentalisé;

West Indian 1 *adj* antillais **2** *n* Antillais(e) *m(f)*; **West Indies**: ***the ~*** les Antilles *fpl*; **westward** vers l'ouest
wet [wet] mouillé; (*rainy*) humide; **wet suit** *for diving* combinaison *f* de plongée
whack [wæk] F (*blow*) coup *m*
whale [weɪl] baleine *f*
what [wɑːt] **1** *pron* ◇: ***~?*** quoi?; ***~ for?*** (*why?*) pourquoi?; ***so ~?*** et alors?
◇ *as object*: ***~ did he say?*** qu'est-ce qu'il a dit?, qu'a-t-il dit?; ***~ is that?*** qu'est-ce que c'est?; ***~ is it?*** (*what do you want?*) qu'est-ce qu'il y a?
◇ *as subject* qu'est-ce qui; ***~ just fell off?*** qu'est-ce qui vient de tomber?
◇ *relative as object* ce que; ***I did ~ I could*** j'ai fait ce que j'ai pu
◇ *relative as subject* ce qui; ***I didn't see ~ happened*** je n'ai pas vu ce qui s'est passé
◇ *suggestions*: ***~ about heading home?*** et si nous rentrions? **2** *adj* quel, quelle; *pl* quels, quelles; ***~ color is the car?*** de quelle couleur est la voiture?
whatever [wɑːt'evər]: ***~ the season*** quelle que soit la saison; ***~ you do*** quoi que tu fasses; ***ok, ~*** F ok, si vous le dites
wheat [wiːt] blé *m*
wheel [wiːl] roue *f*; (*steering ~*) volant *m*; **wheelchair** fauteuil *m* roulant; **wheel clamp** *Br* sabot *m* de Denver
wheeze [wiːz] respirer péniblement
when [wen] quand; ***on the day ~*** le jour où; **whenever** *each time* chaque fois que; *regardless of when* n'importe quand
where [wer] où; ***~ from?*** d'où?; ***~ to?*** où?; ***this is ~ I used to live*** c'est là que j'habitais; **whereas** tandis que; **wherever 1** *conj* partout où; ***sit ~ you like*** assieds-toi où tu veux **2** *adv* où (donc); ***~ can it be?*** où peut-il bien être?
whet [wet] *appetite* aiguiser
whether ['weðər] (*if*) si; ***~ you approve or not*** que tu sois (*subj*) d'accord ou pas
which [wɪʧ] **1** *adj* quel, quelle; *pl* quels, quelles **2** *pron* ◇ *interrogative* lequel, laquelle; *pl* lesquels, lesquelles; ***~ are your favorites?*** lesquels préférez-vous?
◇ *relative*: *subject* qui; *object* que; *after prep* lequel, laquelle; *pl* lesquels, lesquelles
whiff [wɪf]: ***catch a ~ of*** sentir
while [waɪl] **1** *conj* pendant que; (*although*) bien que (*+subj*) **2** *n*: ***a long ~*** longtemps; ***for a ~*** pendant un moment
whim [wɪm] caprice *m*
whimper ['wɪmpər] pleurnicher; *of animal* geindre

whine [waɪn] *of dog etc* gémir; F (*complain*) pleurnicher
whip [wɪp] **1** *n* fouet *m* **2** *v/t* (*beat*) fouetter; *cream* battre; F (*defeat*) battre à plates coutures
whirlpool ['wɜːrlpuːl] *in river* tourbillon *m*; *for relaxation* bain *m* à remous
whisk [wɪsk] **1** *n* fouet *m* **2** *v/t eggs* battre
whiskey ['wɪskɪ] whisky *m*
whisper ['wɪspər] chuchoter
whistle ['wɪsl] **1** *n sound* sifflement *m*; *device* sifflet *m* **2** *v/t & v/i* siffler
white [waɪt] **1** *n color, of egg* blanc *m*; *person* Blanc *m*, Blanche *f* **2** *adj* blanc; **white-collar worker** col *m* blanc; **White House** Maison *f* Blanche; **white lie** pieux mensonge *m*; **whitewash 1** *n* blanc *m* de chaux; *fig* maquillage *m* de la vérité **2** *v/t* blanchir à la chaux; **white wine** vin *m* blanc
whittle ['wɪtl] *wood* tailler au couteau
◆ **whittle down** réduire
whizzkid ['wɪzkɪd] F prodige *m*
who [huː] *interrogative* qui; *relative*: *subject* qui; *object* que; ***the woman ~ you saw*** la femme que tu as vue; **whoever** qui que ce soit; ***~ gets the right answer*** celui/celle qui trouve la bonne réponse
whole [hoʊl] **1** *adj* entier; ***the ~ town*** toute la ville **2** *n* tout *m*, ensemble *m*; ***on the ~*** dans l'ensemble; **whole-hearted** inconditionnel; **wholesale** de gros; *fig* en masse; **wholesaler** grossiste *m/f*; **wholesome** sain; **wholly** totalement
whom [huːm] *fml* qui
whore [hɔːr] putain *f*
whose [huːz] *interrogative* à qui; *relative* dont; ***~ is this?*** à qui c'est?; ***a country ~ economy is boomimg*** un pays dont l'économie prospère
why [waɪ] pourquoi
wicked ['wɪkɪd] méchant
wicker ['wɪkər] osier *m*
wicket ['wɪkɪt] *in station, bank etc* guichet *m*
wide [waɪd] *street, field* large; *experience* vaste; ***be 12 foot ~*** faire 3 mètres et demi de large; **widely** largement; ***~ known*** très connu; **widen 1** *v/t* élargir **2** *v/i* s'élargir; **wide-open** grand ouvert; **wide-ranging** de vaste portée; **widespread** répandu
widow ['wɪdoʊ] veuve *f*; **widower** veuf *m*
width [wɪdθ] largeur *f*
wield [wiːld] *weapon* manier; *power* exercer
wife [waɪf] femme *f*
wig [wɪg] perruque *f*
wiggle ['wɪgl] *tooth etc* remuer; *hips* tortiller

wild [waɪld] **1** *adj animal, flowers* sauvage; *teenager* rebelle; *party* fou; *scheme* délirant; *applause* frénétique
wilderness ['wɪldərnɪs] désert *m*
'wildlife faune *f* et flore *f*
wilful *Br* → **willful**
will[1] [wɪl] *n* LAW testament *m*
will[2] [wɪl] *n* (*willpower*) volonté *f*
will[3] [wɪl] *v/aux*: ***I ~ let you know tomorrow*** je vous le dirai demain; ***the car won't start*** la voiture ne veut pas démarrer; ***~ you tell her that …?*** est-ce que tu pourrais lui dire que …?; ***~ you stop that!*** veux-tu arrêter!
willful ['wɪlfl] *person, refusal* volontaire; **willing** *helper* de bonne volonté; ***be ~ to do sth*** être prêt à faire qch; **willingly** (*with pleasure*) volontiers; **willingness** empressement *m*; **willpower** volonté *f*
willy-nilly [wɪlɪ'nɪlɪ] (*at random*) au petit bonheur la chance
wilt [wɪlt] *of plant* se faner
wily ['waɪlɪ] rusé
wimp [wɪmp] F poule *f* mouillée
win [wɪn] **1** *n* victoire *f* **2** *v/t & v/i* gagner; *prize* remporter
wince [wɪns] tressaillir
wind[1] [wɪnd] *n* vent *m*; (*flatulence*) gaz *m*
wind[2] [waɪnd] **1** *v/i of path, river* serpenter **2** *v/t* enrouler
◆ **wind up 1** *v/t clock, car window* remonter; *speech* terminer; *affairs* conclure; *company* liquider **2** *v/i* (*finish*) finir
'wind-bag F moulin *m* à paroles F; **windfall** *fig* aubaine *f*
winding ['waɪndɪŋ] *path* qui serpente
window ['wɪndoʊ] *also* COMPUT fenêtre *f*; *of airplane, boat* hublot *m*; *of store* vitrine *f*; ***in the ~*** *of store* dans la vitrine; **window seat** *on train* place *f* côté fenêtre; *on airplane* place côté hublot; **window-shop**: ***go ~ping*** faire du lèche-vitrines; **windowsill** rebord *m* de fenêtre; **windshield**, *Br* **windscreen** pare-brise *m*; **windshield wiper** essuie-glace *m*; **windsurfer** véliplanchiste *m/f*; **windsurfing** planche *f* à voile; **windy** venteux; ***it's so ~*** il y a tellement de vent
wine [waɪn] vin *m*; **wine cellar** cave *f* (à vin); **wine list** carte *f* des vins; **winery** établissement *m* viticole
wing [wɪŋ] *of bird, airplane*, SP aile *f*; **wingspan** envergure *f*
wink [wɪŋk] *of person* cligner des yeux
winner ['wɪnər] gagnant(e) *m*(*f*); **winning** gagnant; **winning post** poteau *m* d'arrivée; **winnings** gains *mpl*
winter ['wɪntər] hiver *m*; **win-**

ter sports sports *mpl* d'hiver; **wintry** d'hiver
wipe [waɪp] essuyer; *tape* effacer; **wiper** ['waɪpər] → ***windshield wiper***
wire ['waɪr] fil *m* de fer; *electrical* fil *m* électrique; **wireless phone** téléphone *m* sans fil; **wiring** ELEC installation *f* électrique; **wiry** *person* nerveux
wisdom ['wɪzdəm] sagesse *f*
wise [waɪz] sage; **wisecrack** F vanne *f* F; **wisely** *act* sagement
wish [wɪʃ] **1** *n* vœu *m*; ***best ~es*** cordialement; *for birthday, Christmas* meilleurs vœux **2** *v/t* souhaiter
◆ **wish for** vouloir
wisp [wɪsp] *of hair* mèche *m*; *of smoke* traînée *f*
wistful ['wɪstfl] nostalgique; **wistfully** avec nostalgie
wit [wɪt] (*humor*) esprit *m*; *person* homme *m*/femme *f* d'esprit
witch [wɪʧ] sorcière *f*; **witch-hunt** *fig* chasse *f* aux sorcières
with [wɪð] avec; ***~ no money*** sans argent; ***tired ~ waiting*** fatigué d'attendre; ***the woman ~ blue eyes*** la femme aux yeux bleus; ***I live ~ my aunt*** je vis chez ma tante; ***are you ~ me?*** (*do you understand?*) est-ce que vous me suivez?
withdraw [wɪð'drɒː] **1** *v/t* retirer **2** *v/i* se retire; **withdrawal** retrait *m*; **withdrawal symptoms** (symptômes *mpl* de) manque *m*; **withdrawn** *person* renfermé
wither ['wɪðər] se faner
with'hold *information, name, payment* retenir; *consent* refuser
with'in (*inside*) dans; *in expressions of time* en moins de; *in expressions of distance* à moins de
with'out sans
with'stand résister à
witness ['wɪtnɪs] **1** *n* témoin *m* **2** *v/t* être témoin de
witticism ['wɪtɪsɪzm] mot *m* d'esprit; **witty** plein d'esprit
wobble ['wɑːbl] osciller; **wobbly** bancal
wolf [wʊlf] **1** *n* loup *m* **2** *v/t*: ~ **(*down*)** engloutir
woman ['wʊmən] femme *f*; **womanizer** coureur *m* de femmes; **womanly** féminin
womb [wuːm] utérus *m*
women ['wɪmɪn] *pl* → ***woman***; **women's lib** libération *f* des femmes
wonder ['wʌndər] **1** *n* (*amazement*) émerveillement *m*; ***no ~!*** pas étonnant! **2** *v/i* se poser des questions; ***I ~ if you could help*** je me demandais si vous pouviez m'aider; **wonderful** merveilleux; **wonderfully** (*extremely*) merveilleusement
won't [woʊnt] → ***will not***

wood [wʊd] bois *m*; **wooded** boisé; **wooden** (*made of wood*) en bois; **woodpecker** pic *m*; **woodwork** *parts made of wood* charpente *f*; *activity* menuiserie *f*

wool [wʊl] laine *f*; **woolen**, *Br* **woollen 1** *adj* en laine **2** *n* lainage *m*

word [wɜːrd] **1** *n* mot *m*; *of song*, (*promise*) parole *f* **2** *v/t article*, *letter* formuler; **word processor** traitement *m* de texte

work [wɜːrk] **1** *n* travail *m*; ***out of ~*** au chômage **2** *v/i of person* travailler; *of machine*, (*succeed*) marcher

◆ **work out 1** *v/t solution*, (*find out*) trouver; *problem* résoudre **2** *v/i at gym* s'entraîner; *of relationship etc* bien marcher

workable ['wɜːrkəbl] *solution* possible; **workaholic** F bourreau *m* de travail; **workday** (*hours of work*) journée *f* de travail; (*not weekend*) jour *m* de travail; **worker** travailleur(-euse) *m*(*f*); **workforce** main-d'œuvre; **work hours** heures *fpl* de travail; **working class** classe *f* ouvrière; **working-class** ouvrier; **working hours** → ***work hours***; **workload** quantité *f* de travail; **workman** ouvrier *m*; **workmanlike** de professionnel; **workmanship** fabrication *f*; **work of art** œuvre *f* d'art; **workout** séance *f* d'entraînement; **work permit** permis *m* de travail; **workshop** *also seminar* atelier *m*

world [wɜːrld] monde *m*; **world-class** de niveau mondial; **World Cup** *in soccer* Coupe *f* du monde; **world-famous** mondialement connu; **worldly** du monde; *person* qui a l'expérience du monde; **world record** record *m* mondial; **world war** guerre *f* mondiale; **worldwide 1** *adj* mondial **2** *adv* dans le monde entier

worn-'out *shoes*, *carpet* trop usé; *person* éreinté

worried ['wʌrɪd] inquiet; **worry 1** *n* souci *m* **2** *v/t* inquiéter **3** *v/i* s'inquiéter; **worrying** inquiétant

worse [wɜːrs] **1** *adj* pire **2** *adv play*, *perform*, *feel* plus mal; **worsen** empirer

worship ['wɜːrʃɪp] **1** *n* culte *m* **2** *v/t God* honorer; *fig*: *person*, *money* vénérer

worst [wɜːrst] **1** *adj* pire **2** *adv*: ***the areas ~ affected*** les régions les plus (gravement) touchées

worth [wɜːrθ]: ***be ~ …*** valoir; ***be ~ it*** valoir la peine; **worthwhile**: ***it's not ~ waiting*** cela ne vaut pas la peine d'attendre

worthy ['wɜːrðɪ] *person*, *cause* digne

would [wʊd]: ***I ~ help if I could*** je vous aiderais si je pouvais; ***~ you like to go to the movies?*** est-ce que tu voudrais aller au cinéma?; ***~ you tell her …?*** pourriez-vous lui dire que …?

wound [wu:nd] **1** *n* blessure *f* **2** *v/t with weapon, words* blesser

wow [waʊ] *int* oh là là!

wrap [ræp] *gift* envelopper; *scarf etc* enrouler; **wrapping** emballage *m*; **wrapping paper** papier *m* d'emballage

wrath [ræθ] colère *f*

wreath [ri:θ] couronne *f*

wreck [rek] **1** *n of ship* navire *m* naufragé; *of car* épave *f* **2** *v/t* détruire; **wreckage** *of ship* épave *m*; *of airplane* débris *mpl*; *of marriage, career* restes *mpl*; **wrecker** *truck* dépanneuse *f*

wrench [rentʃ] **1** *n tool* clef *f* **2** *v/t (pull)* arracher

wrestle ['resl] lutter; **wrestler** lutteur(-euse) *m(f)*; **wrestling** lutte *f*

wriggle ['rɪgl] *(squirm)* se tortiller

wrinkle ['rɪŋkl] *in skin* ride *f*; *in clothes* pli *m*

wrist [rɪst] poignet *m*; **wristwatch** montre *f*

write [raɪt] écrire; *check* faire ◆ **write off** *debt* amortir; *car* bousiller F

writer ['raɪtər] *of letter, book, song* auteur *m/f*; *of book* écrivain *m/f*; **write-up** critique *f*

writhe [raɪð] se tordre

writing ['raɪtɪŋ] *(handwriting, script)* écriture *f*; *(words)* inscription *f*; ***in ~*** par écrit; **writing paper** papier *m* à lettres

wrong [rɒ:ŋ] **1** *adj information, decision, side, number* mauvais; *answer also* faux; ***be ~*** *of person* avoir tort; *of answer* être mauvais; *morally* être mal; ***get the ~ train*** se tromper de train; ***what's ~?*** qu'est-ce qu'il y a? **2** *adv* mal; ***go ~*** *of person* se tromper; *of marriage, plan etc* mal tourner **3** *n* mal *m*; *injustice* injustice *f*; **wrongful** injuste; **wrongly** à tort

wry [raɪ] ironique

X, Y

xenophobia [zenoʊ'foʊbɪə] xénophobie *f*

X-ray ['eksreɪ] **1** *n* radio *f* **2** *v/t* radiographier

yacht [jɑ:t] yacht *m*; **yachting** voile *f*

Yank [jæŋk] F Ricain(e) *m(f)* F

yank [jæŋk] *v/t* tirer violemment

yard[1] [jɑːrd] *of prison etc* cour *f*; *behind house* jardin *m*; *for storage* dépôt *m*
yard[2] [jɑːrd] *measurement* yard *m*
'yardstick point *m* de référence
yarn [jɑːrn] (*thread*) fil *m*; F (*story*) (longue) histoire *f*
yawn [jɒːn] **1** *n* bâillement *m* **2** *v/i* bâiller
year [jɪr] année; ***be six ~s old*** avoir six ans; **yearly 1** *adj* annuel **2** *adv* tous les ans
yeast [jiːst] levure *f*
yell [jel] **1** *n* hurlement *m* **2** *v/t & v/i* hurler
yellow ['jeloʊ] jaune
yelp [jelp] **1** *n of animal* jappement *m*; *of person* glapissement *m* **2** *v/i of animal* japper; *of person* glapir
yes [jes] oui; *after negative question* si; **yes man** *pej* béni-oui-oui *m* F
yesterday ['jestərdeɪ] hier; ***the day before ~*** avant-hier
yet [jet] **1** *adv*: ***the best ~*** le meilleur jusqu'ici; ***as ~*** pour le moment; ***have you finished ~?*** as-tu (déjà) fini?; ***he hasn't arrived ~*** il n'est pas encore arrivé; ***~ bigger*** encore plus grand **2** *conj* (*however*) néanmoins
yield [jiːld] **1** *n from crops, investment etc* rendement *m* **2** *v/t fruit, good harvest* produire; *interest* rapporter **3** *v/i* (*give way*) céder; AUT céder la priorité
yoga ['joʊgə] yoga *m*
yoghurt ['joʊgərt] yaourt *m*
yolk [joʊk] jaune *m* (d'œuf)
you [juː] ◇ *familiar singular*: *subject* tu; *object* te; *before vowel* t'; *after prep* toi; ***he knows ~*** il te connaît; ***for ~*** pour toi
◇ *polite singular, familiar plural and polite plural, all uses* vous
◇ *indefinite* on; ***~ never know*** on ne sait jamais
young [jʌŋ] jeune; **youngster** jeune *m/f*; *child* petit(e) *m(f)*
your [jʊr] *familiar* ton, ta; *pl* tes; *polite* votre; *pl familiar and polite* vos
yours [jʊrz] *familiar* le tien, la tienne; *pl* les tiens, les tiennes; *polite* le/la vôtre; *pl* les vôtres; ***a friend of ~*** un(e) de tes ami(e)s; un(e) de vos ami(e)s; ***~*** *at end of letter* bien amicalement
your'self *familiar* toi-même; *polite* vous-même; *reflexive* te; *polite* se; *after prep* toi; *polite* vous; ***did you hurt ~?*** est-ce que tu t'es fait mal/est-ce que vous vous êtes fait mal?
your'selves vous-mêmes; *reflexive* vous; *after prep* vous; ***did you hurt ~?*** est-ce que vous vous êtes fait mal?
youth [juːθ] jeunesse *f*; (*young man*) jeune homme *m*; (*young people*) jeunes

mpl; **youth club** centre *m* pour les jeunes; **youthful** juvénile

yuppie ['jʌpɪ] F yuppie *m/f*

Z

zap [zæp] F COMPUT (*delete*) effacer; (*kill*) éliminer; (*hit*) donner un coup à; (*send*) envoyer vite fait

zeal [zi:l] zèle *m*

zero ['zɪroʊ] zéro *m*

zest [zest] *enjoyment* enthousiasme *m*

zigzag ['zɪgzæg] **1** *n* zigzag *m* **2** *v/i* zigzaguer

zilch [zɪltʃ] F que dalle F

zip ['zɪp] *Br* fermeture *f* éclair

◆ **zip up** *dress, jacket* remonter la fermeture éclair de; COMPUT compresser

'zip code code *m* postal; **zipper** fermeture *f* éclair

zit [zɪt] F *on face* bouton *m*

zone [zoʊn] zone *f*

zonked [zɑ:ŋkt] P (*exhausted*) crevé F

zoo [zu:] jardin *m* zoologique

zoology [zu:'ɑ:lədʒɪ] zoologie *f*

'zoom lens zoom *m*

zucchini [zu:'ki:nɪ] courgette *f*

Verbes irréguliers anglais

Vous trouverez ci-après les trois formes principales de chaque verbe : l'infinitif, le prétérit et le participe passé.

arise - arose - arisen
awake - awoke - awoken, awaked
be (am, is, are) - was (were) - been
bear - bore - borne
beat - beat - beaten
become - became - become
begin - began - begun
bend - bent - bent
bet - bet, betted - bet, betted
bid - bid - bid
bind - bound - bound
bite - bit - bitten
bleed - bled - bled
blow - blew - blown
break - broke - broken
breed - bred - bred
bring - brought - brought
broadcast - broadcast - broadcast
build - built - built
burn - burnt, burned - burnt, burned
burst - burst - burst
buy - bought - bought
cast - cast - cast
catch - caught - caught
choose - chose - chosen
cling - clung - clung
come - came - come
cost (*v/i*) - cost - cost
creep - crept - crept
cut - cut - cut
deal - dealt - dealt
dig - dug - dug
dive - dived, dove [douv] (1) - dived
do - did - done
draw - drew - drawn
dream - dreamt, dreamed - dreamt, dreamed
drink - drank - drunk
drive - drove - driven
eat - ate - eaten
fall - fell - fallen
feed - fed - fed
feel - felt - felt
fight - fought - fought
find - found - found
flee - fled - fled
fling - flung - flung
fly - flew - flown
forbid - forbad(e) - forbidden
forecast - forecast(ed) - forecast(ed)
forget - forgot - forgotten
forgive - forgave - forgiven
freeze - froze - frozen
get - got - got, gotten (2)
give - gave - given

go - went - gone
grind - ground - ground
grow - grew - grown
hang - hung, hanged - hung, hanged (3)
have - had - had
hear - heard - heard
hide - hid - hidden
hit - hit - hit
hold - held - held
hurt - hurt - hurt
keep - kept - kept
kneel - knelt, kneeled - knelt, kneeled
know - knew - known
lay - laid - laid
lead - led - led
lean - leaned, leant - leaned, leant (4)
leap - leaped, leapt - leaped, leapt (4)
learn - learned, learnt - learned, learnt (4)
leave - left - left
lend - lent - lent
let - let - let
lie - lay - lain
light - lighted, lit - lighted, lit
lose - lost - lost
make - made - made
mean - meant - meant
meet - met - met
mow - mowed - mowed, mown
pay - paid - paid
plead - pleaded, pled - pleaded, pled (5)
prove - proved - proved, proven
put - put - put
quit - quit(ted) - quit(ted)
read - read [red] - read [red]
ride - rode - ridden
ring - rang - rung
rise - rose - risen
run - ran - run
saw - sawed - sawn, sawed
say - said - said
see - saw - seen
seek - sought - sought
sell - sold - sold
send - sent - sent
set - set - set
sew - sewed - sewed, sewn
shake - shook - shaken
shed - shed - shed
shine - shone - shone
shit - shit(ted), shat - shit(ted), shat
shoot - shot - shot
show - showed - shown
shrink - shrank - shrunk
shut - shut - shut
sing - sang - sung
sink - sank - sunk
sit - sat - sat
slay - slew - slain
sleep - slept - slept
slide - slid - slid

sling - slung - slung
slit - slit - slit
smell - smelt, smelled - smelt, smelled
sow - sowed - sown, sowed
speak - spoke - spoken
speed - sped, speeded - sped, speeded
spell - spelt, spelled - spelt, spelled (4)
spend - spent - spent
spill - spilt, spilled - spilt, spilled
spin - spun - spun
spit - spat - spat
split - split - split
spoil - spoiled, spoilt - spoiled, spoilt
spread - spread - spread
spring - sprang, sprung - sprung
stand - stood - stood
steal - stole - stolen
stick - stuck - stuck
sting - stung - stung
stink - stunk, stank - stunk
stride - strode - stridden
strike - struck - struck
swear - swore - sworn
sweep - swept - swept
swell - swelled - swollen
swim - swam - swum
swing - swung - swung
take - took - taken
teach - taught - taught
tear - tore - torn
tell - told - told
think - thought - thought
thrive - throve - thriven, thrived (6)
throw - threw - thrown
thrust - thrust - thrust
tread - trod - trodden
wake - woke, waked - woken, waked
wear - wore - worn
weave - wove - woven (7)
weep - wept - wept
win - won - won
wind - wound - wound
write - wrote - written

(1) **dove** n'est pas utilisé en anglais britannique
(2) **gotten** n'est pas utilisé en anglais britannique
(3) **hung** pour les tableaux mais **hanged** pour les meurtriers
(4) l'anglais américain n'emploie normalement que la forme en **-ed**
(5) **pled** s'emploie en anglais américain ou écossais
(6) la forme **thrived** est plus courante
(7) mais **weaved** au sens de *se faufiler*

Numbers / Les nombres

Cardinal Numbers / Les nombres cardinaux

0 zero, *Br aussi* nought *zéro*
1 one *un*
2 two *deux*
3 three *trois*
4 four *quatre*
5 five *cinq*
6 six *six*
7 seven *sept*
8 eight *huit*
9 nine *neuf*
10 ten *dix*
11 eleven *onze*
12 twelve *douze*
13 thirteen *treize*
14 fourteen *quatorze*
15 fifteen *quinze*
16 sixteen *seize*
17 seventeen *dix-sept*
18 eighteen *dix-huit*
19 nineteen *dix-neuf*
20 twenty *vingt*
21 twenty-one *vingt et un*
22 twenty-two *vingt-deux*
30 thirty *trente*
31 thirty-one *trente et un*
40 forty *quarante*
50 fifty *cinquante*
60 sixty *soixante*
70 seventy *soixante-dix*
71 seventy-one *soixante et onze*
72 seventy-two *soixante-douze*
79 seventy-nine *soixante-dix-neuf*
80 eighty *quatre-vingts*
81 eighty-one *quatre-vingt-un*
90 ninety *quatre-vingt-dix*
91 ninety-one *quatre-vingt-onze*
100 a hundred, one hundred *cent*
101 a hundred and one *cent un*
200 two hundred *deux cents*
300 three hundred *trois cents*
324 three hundred and twenty-four *trois cent vingt-quatre*
1000 a thousand, one thousand *mille*
2000 two thousand *deux mille*

1959	one thousand nine hundred and fifty-nine *mille neuf cent cinquante-neuf*
2000	two thousand *deux mille*
1 000 000	a million, one million *un million*
2 000 000	two million *deux millions*
1 000 000 000	a billion, one billion *un milliard*

Notes / Remarques:

i) **vingt** and **cent** take an -s when preceded by another number, except if there is another number following.
ii) If **un** is used with a following noun, then it is the only number to agree
(one man **un homme**; one woman **une femme**).
iii) 1.25 (one point two five) = 1,25 (un virgule vingt-cinq)
iv) 1,000,000 (en anglais) = 1 000 000 ou 1.000.000 (in French)

Ordinal Numbers / Les nombres ordinaux

1st	first	$1^{er}/1^{ère}$	*premier / première*
2nd	second	2^{e}	*deuxième*
3rd	third	3^{e}	*troisième*
4th	fourth	4^{e}	*quatrième*
5th	fifth	5^{e}	*cinquième*
6th	sixth	6^{e}	*sixième*
7th	seventh	7^{e}	*septième*
8th	eighth	8^{e}	*huitième*
9th	ninth	9^{e}	*neuvième*
10th	tenth	10^{e}	*dixième*
11th	eleventh	11^{e}	*onzième*
12th	twelfth	12^{e}	*douzième*
13th	thirteenth	13^{e}	*treizième*
14th	fourteenth	14^{e}	*quatorzième*
15th	fifteenth	15^{e}	*quinzième*

16th	sixteenth	16ᵉ	*seizième*
17th	seventeenth	17ᵉ	*dix-septième*
18th	eighteenth	18ᵉ	*dix-huitième*
19th	nineteenth	19ᵉ	*dix-neuvième*
20th	twentieth	20ᵉ	*vingtième*
21st	twenty-first	21ᵉ	*vingt et unième*
22nd	twenty-second	22ᵉ	*vingt-deuxième*
30th	thirtieth	30ᵉ	*trentième*
31st	thirty-first	31ᵉ	*trente et unième*
40th	fortieth	40ᵉ	*quarantième*
50th	fiftieth	50ᵉ	*cinquantième*
60th	sixtieth	60ᵉ	*soixantième*
70th	seventieth	70ᵉ	*soixante-dixième*
71st	seventy-first	71ᵉ	*soixante et onzième*
80th	eightieth	80ᵉ	*quatre-vingtième*
90th	ninetieth	90ᵉ	*quatre-vingt-dixième*
100th	hundredth	100ᵉ	*centième*
101st	hundred and first	101ᵉ	*cent unième*
1000th	thousandth	1000ᵉ	*millième*
2000th	two thousandth	2000ᵉ	*deux millième*
1,000,000th	millionth	1 000 000ᵉ	*millionième*

Dates / Les dates

1996	nineteen ninety-six	*mille neuf cent quatre-vingt-seize*
2005	two thousand (and) five	*deux mille cinq*

November 10/11 (ten, eleven), *Br* **the 10th/11th of November**
le dix/onze novembre

March 1 (first), *Br* **the 1st of March**
le premier mars

MUS	Musik
N, *n*	Neutrum
nom	Nominativ
NUM	Zahlwort, Numerale
od	oder
österr	österreichische Variante
pej	pejorativ, abwertend
PERS PR	Personalpronomen
PHYS	Physik
PL, *pl*	Plural
POL	Politik
POSS PR	Possessivpronomen
PPERF, *pperf*	past participle – *Partizip Perfekt*
PRÄF	Präfix
PRÄP	Präposition
prät	past tense – *Präteritum*
PRON	Pronomen
®	eingetragene Marke
RADIO	Radio
REFL PR	Reflexivpronomen
REL	Religion
REL PR	Relativpronomen
S	Substantiv
sb	somebody – *jemand/jemandem/jemanden*
SCHIFF	Schifffahrt
schweiz	schweizerische Variante
SG, *sg*	Singular
S PL	Substantiv, das nur im Plural vorkommt
SPORT	Sport
S SG	Pluralsubstantiv, das oft mit Singular gebraucht wird
sth	something – *etwas*
TECH	Technik
TEL	Telefon
THEAT	Theater
TV	Fernsehen
TYPO	Typografie, Buchdruck
umg	umgangssprachlich
UNBEST, *unbest*	unbestimmt
UNPERS, *unpers*	unpersönlich
V/AUX	Hilfsverb
V/I	intransitives Verb
V/R	reflexives Verb
V/T	transitives Verb

Abkürzungen und Symbole

a.	auch
abk	Abkürzung
ADJ	Adjektiv
ADV	Adverb
AGR	Landwirtschaft
akk	Akkusativ
akr	Akronym
ANAT	Anatomie
ART	Artikel
ASTROL	Astrologie
ASTRON	Astronomie
AUTO	Auto, Verkehr
BAHN	Bahn
BIOL	Biologie
BOT	Botanik
CHEM	Chemie
dat	Dativ
DEM PR	Demonstrativpronomen
ELEK	Elektrotechnik, Elektronik
etw	etwas
F, *f*	Femininum
fig	figurativ, übertragen
FILM	Film, Kino
FIN	Finanzen
FLUG	Luftfahrt
FOTO	Fotografie
GASTR	Kochkunst und Gastronomie
gen	Genitiv
HIST	Geschichte
INDEF PR	Indefinitpronomen
INT	Interjektion
INT PR	Interrogativpronomen
irr	unregelmäßig
IT	Informationstechnologie
j-d	jemand
j-m	jemandem
j-n	jemanden
j-s	jemandes
JUR	Jura, Rechtswesen
KONJ	Konjunktion
kontr	Kontraktion
KUNST	Kunst
LING	Linguistik, Sprachwissenschaft
M, *m*	Maskulinum
MATH	Mathematik
MED	Medizin
METEO	Meteorologie
MIL	Militär